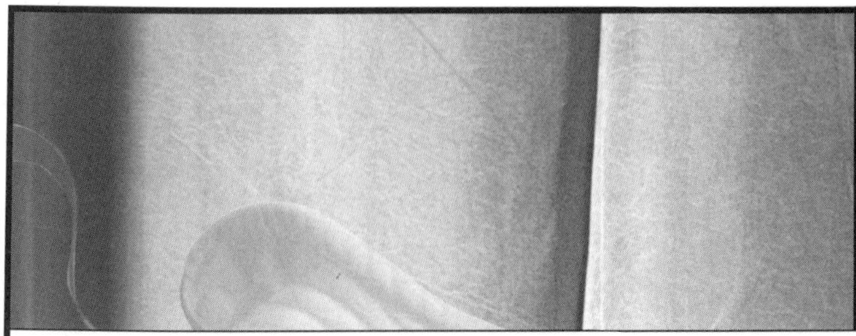

Show Time

A Chronology of Broadway and the Theatre from Its Beginnings to the Present

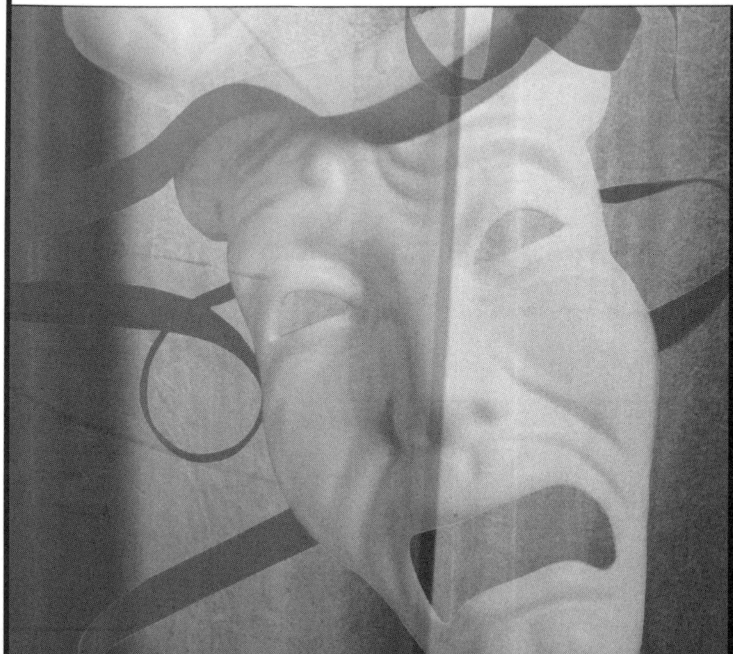

GENE BROWN

MACMILLAN•USA

This book is dedicated to my mother, Estelle Brown,
and to the memory of Molly Picon, "our Molly."

MACMILLAN
A Simon & Schuster Macmillan Company
1633 Broadway
New York, NY 10019

Macmillan Publishing books may be purchased for business or sales promotional use.
For information please write:
Special Markets Department, Macmillan Publishing USA, 1633 Broadway, New York, NY 10019.

Brown, Gene.
Show Time / Gene Brown.
p. cm.
Includes bibliographical references and index.
ISBN 0-02-860830-5 (hc). —ISBN 0-02-862072-0
1. Theater—New York (State)—New York—20th century—Chronology.
2. Theater—New York (State)—New York—19th century—Chronology.
I. Title
PN2277.N5B69 1997
792'.09747'1—DC21 97-16529
CIP

10 9 8 7 6 5 4 3 2 1

Printed in the United States of America

Design by Nick Anderson

Acknowledgments

The following people generously supplied research material for *Show Time*: Marilyn Annan, Mary Magdalena Hernandez, Sandy Izhakoff, Mary Ellen Kelly, Margaret Rose, David Rousso, Harilyn Rousso, and Richard Watts.

Marilyn Annan, of the *New York Times* Reference Library, as usual, was there with helpful suggestions and good cheer. One of my closest friends, she also offered some extra, backstage support that was greatly appreciated at a crucial turning point.

Margaret Rose and the staff of the Raymond Fogelman Library at the New School were helpful, as they have been on previous books. It's always great to know they are there. Margaret was an especially good guide through the thicket of recent productions, so many of which she has seen and remembered.

My colleague Mary Ellen Kelly took valuable time out from her important research on David Belasco to supply me with theatrical gems she had uncovered and often pointed me in the right direction so that I might mine the archives myself for material I might otherwise have missed. Her fine, constructively critical intelligence and her deliciously wicked wit—not to mention her trove of show business trivia!—added a good deal of pleasure to my research. And she also introduced me to the terrific bleu-cheese burgers at Barrymore's.

Storm Harrigan kept me refueled and flying with banana bread, chocolate brownies, and other assorted goodies, fresh from the oven. Thanks, neighbor!

The staff of the Billy Rose Theatre Collection at the Library for the Performing Arts at Lincoln Center really deserves a separate page of acknowledgments: no Billy Rose, no book. For anyone who truly loves the theatre, this research library's unique collection of scrapbooks, clippings, scripts, letters, photographs, posters, and *Playbills* is a dream come true. And the people who run it make sure that everyone, from college students to published authors, receives the help needed to explore its riches. I am especially grateful to Dr. Roderick Bladel and Christine Karatnytsky for their help, advice, support, and friendship throughout the long months of research.

My publisher, Natalie Chapman, takes the "producer's" credit for *Show Time*. As much as any Flo Ziegfeld, Jed Harris, Harold Prince, or Garth Drabinsky, she got the show going. To call Mary Ann Lynch, my editor, the equivalent of a director would be to shortchange her. The spirit of Maxwell Perkins has not entirely left publishing, as many fear, as long as there are people like Mary Ann still around. Friend, advisor, cheerleader, and, of course, critic when I needed it, she has been all this and more. Thanks, too, to her hardworking assistant Michelle Tupper, an understudy who got to go on. She deserves and receives my applause.

Tracey Moore, no stranger to the stage, did a great job on these boards, too. Thanks, Tracey! I would also like to thank Mart Hulswit of the Episcopal Actors' Guild and Nils Hanson of the Ziegfeld Club for their invaluable last-minute help with photographs.

Sheree Bykofsky, my agent, offered support and encouragement within and beyond the script.

Finally, there must have been times during my research on *Show Time* when life seemed like a revolving stage door for Harilyn Rousso. But just as in any great production, it all comes together at showtime—still. There's romance, melodrama, lots of comedy, and just enough mystery. We continue to light the lights, and the curtain keeps going up. Gonna be a long run, I'd say.

Contents

Introduction vii

The Birth of Broadway 1
1826–1914

Broadway Comes of Age 21
1914–1942

Broadway in Transition 153
1942–1967

Inhibitions and Censorship Break Down 283
1967–1982

The Age of the Mega-Musical 365
1982–1997

Bibliography 429

Index 433

Introduction

On February 9, 1913, the *Pittsburgh Dispatch*, in an article on David Belasco's Broadway production of *A Good Little Devil*, referred to its star Mary Pickford as "The Maude Adams of the Movies." But the theatre's days as the standard against which film, that upstart art form, might be measured were already numbered. Even as it was about to enter its golden era, the Broadway stage was beginning to take second place to the screen in American popular culture.

The movies not only made new memories, they also obliterated earlier ones. It is not Douglas Fairbanks's films of the 1920s that brought him into the public eye. He was a "matinée idol" on Broadway as early as the first decade of the century. Fred Astaire was a great musical comedy star on Broadway for 15 years, dancing mainly with his sister Adele, before he ever sashayed up to Ginger Rogers in *Flying Down to Rio*. Astaire first put on a top hat and tails not for RKO but on Broadway in the 1927 Gershwin musical *Funny Face*.

I grew up devouring movies at Saturday matinées. The theatre was something my parents went to on Saturday nights. But in the summer of 1961, at the end of my freshman year in college, I took a date to see Zero Mostel, Eli Wallach, and Anne Jackson on Broadway in Eugene Ionesco's *Rhinoceros*. As they say, you always remember your first time. Before our eyes, Mostel magically transformed himself into a raging, herd-obsessed beast—and did it without makeup or special effects. The image of that performance remains vividly with me to this day.

I was hooked; and with previews, balcony seats, and off-Broadway still pegged to a student's budget, I began to indulge. But I soon realized that there seemed to be a dimension missing from my theatregoing—a dimension that was omnipresent when it came to the movies: the past. On television and in repertory houses (and later, on tape), the movies from before my time were accessible. I viewed the early careers of stars I knew in their prime and was able to enjoy performances of screen luminaries whose lights had long since gone out.

But it's not so in the theatre, where a final curtain has almost always drawn a permanent veil over the temporary excitement of a performance. The sparks and the lightning crackle and then are gone for good. Yet for those who care about the theatre, on Broadway and elsewhere, the past still colors the present.

Lou Diamond Phillips in *The King and I* performs in the shadow of Yul Brynner. When did Brynner originate the role that he so often revived, and how was *he* received? Christopher Plummer re-creates the great Barrymore in a virtual one-man show. When did John Barrymore make his mark on Broadway? How did the original, legendary production of *Show Boat* differ from the recent revival? (For one thing, the top ticket price was $5.50.)

When did Broadway itself become the Great White Way? When did the decline of Forty-second Street—now so gaudily renovated and relit—set in? What did it cost to see a show in the 1940s (and what did the check come to for pre-theatre dinner for two)?

What was it like when Jeanne Eagels, not Joan Crawford, was Sadie Thompson in *Rain*? What kind of an actor was the young Humphrey Bogart in his decade on Broadway? Who played the boogie man—portrayed so deliciously on the screen by Raymond Massey—in the Broadway performance of *Arsenic and Old Lace*? (It was Boris Karloff, eventually replaced by Erich von Stroheim.) Has Hollywood been accurate in its frequent depictions of Broadway? Was Fanny Brice's Nicky Arnstein anything like Omar Sharif?

Show Time answers these and thousands of other questions that theatre-lovers are likely to have, or would have if they thought they could easily and entertainingly find the answers. It does so in a season-by-season chronology format that permits the reader to relive each theatrical year as it happened. The beauty of a chronology, aside from its obvious reference value in telling you what happened when, is in its ability to bring back a time past. In these pages, you can relive the season, see it unfold and develop, opening night by opening night, just as it happened then.

To enhance that experience, I have taken as much material as was possible and appropriate from original sources, such as *Variety*, *The New York Times*, and *Playbill*. There are quotes from the critics, producers, actors and actresses, and from others in the theatre. They express attitudes contemporary then, and many come with headlines that make us cringe now with their racism and homophobia. Before she becomes the lovable, rascally "Last of the Red Hot Mamas," Sophie Tucker first makes her mark as "The Great Coon Shouter." In the 1926–27 season, the estimable *New York Times* critic Brooks Atkinson, writing of *The Captive*, finds "loathsome" the very thought of a lesbian relationship in the play. And *Variety* is still referring to "Homos" right up through the late 1960s. It is, after all, the past.

The reader will also find a wealth of tantalizing "might-have-beens," the turns that theatre history might have taken but didn't. For example, in October 1951, *Variety* reports that Rodgers and Hammerstein may write a musical based on Shaw's *Pygmalion*, starring Mary Martin, but it was Lerner and Loewe who eventually wrote *My Fair Lady*.

Show Time also covers vaudeville, the widely popular art form that supplied comedians and musical comedy stars to the Broadway stage. Vaudeville also provided an alternate venue for Broadway stars, allowing them to offer excerpts from their most famous roles in a popular format, as well as providing a training ground for future Broadway stars—Fred and Adele Astaire, for instance.

Show Time organizes time as it is structured on Broadway. (The stage may reflect life in some ways but not when it comes to the calendar.) Critic Peter Filichia once suggested that a true theatre buff would be someone who sent "Season's Greetings" cards on June 1. The theatre season has to begin sometime, and although it's October before the boards are truly active with new shows, the commonly accepted season-ending date of May 31 makes June 1 the opening of the theatrical year, and so it is in this chronology.

Coverage starts with the early nineteenth century and begins in detail, with a season-by-season chronology, in the 1914–1915 season. As Europe goes to war, the modern musical is being born at the Princess Theatre in New York. The year-old Palace Theatre, although off to a shaky start, is already becoming the Mecca of vaudeville. And a young playwright named Eugene O'Neill has decided to become "an artist or nothing."

Curtain up.

HOW TO USE THIS BOOK

The following should be helpful as a guide to using this book.

YEARLY OVERVIEW Each year begins with a paragraph highlighting the outstanding events and trends of the season and suggesting the flavor and spirit of the time. The assemblage of theatre facts that follow have been collected not only to put the season in numerical perspective but also to present the oddities and bits of trivia that further define the feel and tone of the time.

Any compilation of annual theatre awards could stretch into a book by itself, so I have confined this section to what seems the most important: the Pulitzer Prize, The New York Drama Critics Circle Awards and, of course, the Tonys.

The Timeline that completes the overview does not necessarily list everything of importance that happened that season. Rather, it is meant to give some sense of how the season unfolded—what was happening at any given time between June and May—and its chronological relationship to other theatre events and trends.

PERSONALITIES Anyone who cares about the theatre, even casually, cares about the personalities who strut its stages, write its hits and flops, and make it all happen. The lives, words, and often the antics as well as the art of people such as Jeanne Eagels, John Barrymore, Marilyn Miller, Flo Ziegfeld, Tallulah Bankhead, Tennessee Williams, Ethel Merman, David Merrick, Zero Mostel, Andrew Lloyd Webber, and Patti LuPone color our memories and enrich the experience of what we call "theatre." This section chronicles their doings and undoings, preserving their indiscretions and eccentricities as well as personal triumphs and tragedies.

PLAYS AND MUSICALS There are so many productions that belong in this book and so little space for them in one volume. I therefore had to make some often painful choices. Besides chronicling the obvious productions of lasting value—John Barrymore's *Hamlet*, the original *Show Boat*, *A Chorus Line*, *Angels in America*—and certain notable productions in regional theatres, I have tried to represent the average season on and off-Broadway, with its panoply of good to very good, if not always great, shows. And I have not neglected those memorable, even treasured (at least in hindsight) turkeys, for which we all give a silent, if guilty, thanks. What, after all, would Broadway be without the occasional *Carrie*, *Nick and Nora*, or *Moose Murders*?

For each production, I have noted the theatre at which it played and have indicated the number of performances in parenthesis. I have used the most reliable sources I could find to arrive at this number. Occasionally, the total varied slightly from source to source, with benefits and special performances—for the armed forces, for example—presumably causing the discrepancy. The number does not include previews or off-Broadway performances of shows that have moved to Broadway, unless noted.

Major Broadway theatres that appear often in this book, with the year they opened and their former names, if any, include the Neil Simon (1927, Alvin); Ambassador (1921); Brooks Atkinson (1921, Mansfield); Barrymore (1921); Vivian Beaumont (1965); Martin Beck (1924); Belasco (1907, Stuyvesant); Biltmore (1925); Booth (1913); Broadhurst (1917); Broadway (1930, Colony); Circle in the Square (1972); Cort (1912); Forty-sixth Street (1924); Gershwin (1972, Uris); John Golden (1927, Masque); Helen Hayes (1912, the Little Theatre); Imperial (1923); Longacre (1913); Lunt-Fontanne (1910, Globe); Lyceum (1903); Majestic (1927); Marquis (1986); Minskoff (1973); Music Box (1921); Eugene O'Neill (1925, Forrest, Coronet); Nederlander (1921, National, Billy Rose, Trafalger); Palace (1913, as a vaudeville house, reopened in 1966 as a legitimate theatre); Plymouth (1917); Royale (1927, Golden); Shubert (1913); St. James (1927, Erlanger); Walter Kerr (1921, Ritz); and the Winter Garden (1911).

Once prominent theatres that have been demolished include the Bijou, Casino, Century, Earl Carroll's, Empire, Forty-eighth Street, Forty-fourth Street, George M. Cohan, the original Helen Hayes, Hippodrome, Maxine Elliott's, Morosco, Playhouse, Princess, Vanderbilt, and the Ziegfeld. Some houses, such as Henry Miller's Theatre and the Mark Hellinger are used today for other purposes. (The Mark Hellinger is now a church.) Legitimate theatres that once lined Forty-second Street and then became movie houses include the Eltinge, Gaiety, Sam H. Harris, Liberty, Lyric, New Amsterdam, and the Republic. At the end of 1996, the Republic reopened as the New Victory, and the Disney-renovated New Amsterdam opened its doors as a legitimate theatre once again in 1997. The new Ford Center of the Performing Arts encloses the facades of the old Lyric and Apollo Theatres.

Among the important regional theatres are the Arena Stage in Washington, D.C., the Mark Taper Forum in Los Angeles, and Minneapolis's Tyrone Guthrie Theatre.

BUSINESS AND SOCIETY Broadway means business—for New York City and for the whole country—because it now attracts a sizable foreign tourist audience, comprising 10–15 percent of tickets sold overall, and a higher percentage for musical spectaculars such as *Cats* and *The Phantom of the Opera*. As much as any other business, the business of Broadway involves marketing and labor-management relations. The most important organizations involved in these activities are the following:

Actors Equity: Founded in 1912 and beginning operations the next year, Equity came into its own when it successfully confronted producers in the great strike of 1919. Over the years, in addition to serving as an actors' union, negotiating and administering contracts, it has dealt with racism and, in the 1940s and 1950s, the issue of communism in its ranks.

The Dramatists Guild: Evolving out of several previous organizations that sought to speak for writers, The Dramatists Guild became a force in 1925 over the issue of movie rights to plays and other matters affecting royalties. It negotiated its first contract with producers the next year.

The League of American Theatres and Producers: Originally the League of New York Theatres when it was founded in 1930 and then The League of New York Theatres and Producers, it took its present name in 1985. It is the voice of management in labor negotiations and sets general business policy for the Broadway theatre as a whole.

BIRTHS, DEATHS, AND MARRIAGES I have used the following abbreviations: b. = "is born"; d. = "dies"; m. = "marries." The name in parenthesis after a birth is the actor or actress's real name. I have tried to choose figures representative of each era, so a few names, especially from the early period, may not be familiar. When I thought this might be the case, I identified them.

PHOTOGRAPHS AND ILLUSTRATIONS Sources for the photographs and illustrations are cited throughout.

PHOTO CREDITS

Archive Photo	*ARCH*
Author's Collection	*BROWN*
Lynch Collection	*LYNCH*
Movie Star News	*MSN*
Photofest	*PF*
Playbill	*PB*
Ziegfeld Club Incorporated	*ZCI*

Photo opposite: George M. Cohan *ARCH*

The Birth of Broadway

1826–1914

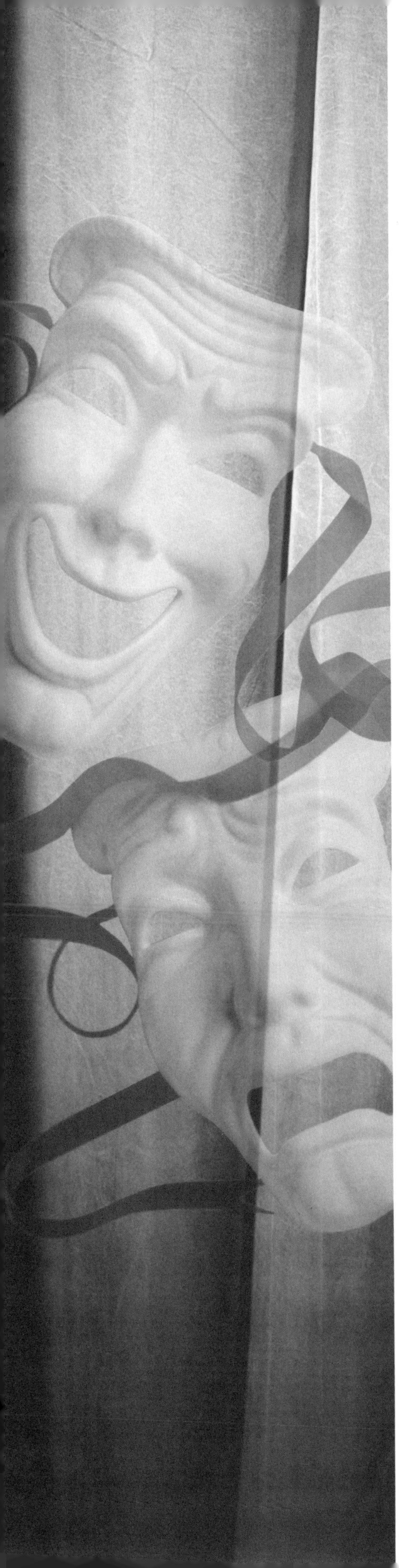

1826–1914

1826

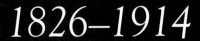

MARCH • James H. Hackett debuts at the Park Theatre in *Love in a Village*.

JUNE 23 Edwin Forrest, who with James H. Hackett will become America's first popular, native-born actors, makes his New York debut at the Park Theatre in *Othello*.

OCTOBER • The 3,000-seat Bowery Theatre opens in New York. It is the first to have a press agent, and its glass-shaded gas-jet lighting is also new. It will become famous for its sometimes rowdy working-class audience.

1828

MARCH 20 Playwright Hendrik Ibsen b.

1829

FEBRUARY 20 Joseph Jefferson b.

1831

JULY • William Chapman and his theatrical company cast off from Pittsburgh to float down the Ohio and Mississippi on the first show boat to reach the South.

1833

NOVEMBER 13 Edwin Booth b.

1834

JUNE 7 Fanny Kemble marries southern planter Pierce Butler, becoming the first major actress in America to marry a wealthy man.

1836

JULY 15 Critic William Winter b.

1837

MAY 28 Vaudeville producer Tony Pastor b.

1839

FEBRUARY 1 Playwright James Herne (James Aherne) b.

DECEMBER • William Mitchell begins a decade of producing burlesques and musical entertainments at the Olympic Theatre on Broadway. Weber and Fields's Music Hall, *The Ziegfeld Follies*, and other revues evolve from Mitchell's shows.

1840

OCTOBER 12 Helena Modjeska b.

1844

OCTOBER 23 Sarah Bernhardt b.

Sarah Bernhardt *PF*

1845

MARCH 24 Playwright Anna Cora Mowatt's *Fashion* opens at the Park Theatre for a record run of 20 performances. She will later become a prominent actress.

1847

MAY 8 Producer Oscar Hammerstein, grandfather of Oscar Hammerstein II, b.

SEPTEMBER 21 Maurice Barrymore (Herbert Blythe), father of Ethel, Lionel, and John, b.

OCTOBER 14 James O'Neill, father of Eugene O'Neill, b. (The year is also given as 1849.)

1848

FEBRUARY 27 Ellen Terry b.

1849

MAY 10 British actor William Macready, who has been feuding with American star Edwin Forrest, is appearing in *Macbeth* at the Astor Place Opera House. Macready's American tour has incited anti-British feeling, compounded by working-class resentment at the support that Macready has drawn from New York's upper crust. Tonight, a crowd of 1,000 lays siege to the theatre, and in the ensuing riot, 22 are killed.

1851

• Vaudeville producer and theatre magnate Frederick F. Proctor b.

AUGUST 22 Producer Daniel Frohman, brother of Charles Frohman, b.

1853

• The *New York Clipper*, covering theatre, begins weekly publication.

JULY 18 George L. Aiken's *Uncle Tom's Cabin* (325)—the first production to perform Wednesday and Saturday matinées—opens at the National Theatre, with Cordelia Howard as Eva. It is thought to be the first Broadway play unaccompanied by any afterpiece or other work. **25** Producer-director-playwright David Belasco b.

OCTOBER 13 Lillie Langtry (Emilie Le Breton) b.

NOVEMBER 13 John Drew b.

1854

FEBRUARY 7 Francis Wilson b.

OCTOBER 16 Playwright Oscar Wilde b.

1855

• Jacob Adler b.

JULY 24 William Gillette b.

1856

• Minstrel show producer Lew Dockstadter b.

MARCH 9 Eddie Foy b.

JULY 26 Playwright George Bernard Shaw b.

1857

JANUARY 8 Playwright Thomas Augustus b.

MAY 24 Richard Mansfield b. **28** Robert C. Hilliard b.

JULY 25 Nat Goodwin b.

David Belasco, known as the "Bishop of Broadway" for his clerical-like collar—those who worked with him called him the "Guv'nor" *PF*

DECEMBER 9 Playwright-librettist Edgar Smith b.

1858

MARCH 30 De Wolfe Hopper b.

MAY 29 Producer Marc Klaw b.

JUNE 28 Otis Skinner b.

1859

JANUARY 31 Critic James Gibbons Huneker b.

FEBRUARY 1 Composer Victor Herbert b.

DECEMBER 6 E.(Edward) H.(Hugh) Sothern b.

1860

FEBRUARY 1 Henry Miller, actor, producer, director, and father of producer Gilbert Miller, b.

APRIL 22 Ada Rehan (Bridget Crehan) b.

MAY 4 Producer Abraham L. Erlanger b.

JUNE 17 Producer Charles Frohman, brother of Daniel Frohman, b.

AUGUST 25 George Fawcett b.

DECEMBER 28 Lyricist Harry B. Smith b.

1861

MAY 14 Critic Alan Dale b.

JULY 30 Producer-playwright-publisher Harrison Grey Fiske b.

DECEMBER 4 Lillian Russell (Nellie Leonard) b.

1862

JUNE • May Irwin (Ada Campbell) b. **10** Mrs. Leslie Carter (Caroline Louise Dudley) b.

JULY 29 Playwright Booth Tarkington (Newton Booth Tarkington) b.

1863

JUNE 19 Producer William A. Brady b.

JULY 21 C. (Charles) Aubrey Smith b.

1864

• Theatre executive Alexander Pantages b.

JANUARY 17 Edna Wallace Hopper b. (The year is also given as 1874.)

NOVEMBER 26 Edwin Booth opens at the Winter Garden for 100 performances of *Hamlet*, a record in New York that will stand until John Barrymore's 1923 production.

1865

FEBRUARY 9 Mrs. Patrick Campbell (Beatrice Tanner) b.

APRIL 14 John Wilkes Booth shoots President Lincoln at Ford's Theatre in Washington, D.C., during a performance of *Our American Cousin*, starring Laura Keene. The assassin's brother, Edwin, refrains from acting for the next two years.

MAY 2 Playwright Clyde Fitch (William Clyde Fitch) b.

OCTOBER 22 Raymond Hitchcock b. (The year is sometimes given as 1871.)

DECEMBER 19 Minnie Maddern Fiske (Minnie Maddern)—billed as "Mrs. Fiske"—b. **25** Fay Templeton b.

1866

APRIL 4 Drama teacher George Pierce Baker b.

AUGUST 17 Julia Marlowe (Sarah Frost) b.

SEPTEMBER 3 Joseph Jefferson opens at the Olympic Theatre in *Rip Van Winkle*, the play with which he will become identified. **12** *The Black Crook* (475), a musical extravaganza with scantily dressed chorus girls, the first Broadway show to run for at least a year, opens at Niblo's Garden. Tickets range from $.05 to $1.50. The 1954 musical, *The Girl in Pink Tights*, starring Zizi Jeanmaire, is about this show.

NOVEMBER 28 David Warfield b.

1867

JANUARY 1 Performer-producer Lew Fields (Lewis Schanfield), father of Dorothy, Herbert, and Joseph Fields, b. **16** Playwright George V. Hobart b.

APRIL 13 Producer George C. Tyler b.

MAY 13 Effie Shannon b.

JUNE 28 Playwright Luigi Pirandello b.

JULY 3 Producer Martin Beck b.

AUGUST 11 Actor-producer Joseph Weber, of Weber & Fields, b. **14** Playwright John Galsworthy b.

1868

FEBRUARY 5 Maxine Elliott (Jessie McDermot) b. **12** William Faversham b.

APRIL 10 George Arliss (George Andrews) b.

MAY 12 Al Shean (Alfred Schoenberg), uncle of the Marx Brothers and half of the vaudeville team of Gallagher and Shean, and Yiddish Theatre actor-producer-playwright Boris Tomashevsky, b. **30** Producer Charles Dillingham b.

1869

JANUARY 2 Playwright Bayard Veiller b.

MARCH 21 Producer Flo Ziegfeld b.

MAY 2 Tyrone Power, Sr. (Frederick Tyrone Power), father of Tyrone Power, b.

NOVEMBER 9 Marie Dressler b.

1870

JANUARY 3 Producer A. (Albert) H. (Herman) Woods b.

AUGUST 4 Vaudevillian Harry Lauder b.

DECEMBER 21 *Saratoga* (101), a comedy starring Fanny Davenport and the first popular play by Bronson Howard, America's first professional playwright, opens at the Fifth Avenue Theatre. Its producer, Augustin Daly, only last year established a company at the theatre that will ultimately include John Drew, Ada Rehan, and Otis Skinner.

1871

APRIL 24 Blanche Ring b. (The year is also given as 1877.)

AUGUST 17 Playwright Jesse Lynch Williams, winner of the first Pulitzer Prize for Drama, b.

1872

• Producer-director Jesse Bonstelle (Laura Justine Bonstelle) b.

FEBRUARY 3 Producer Sam H. Harris b.

MARCH 15 Lee Shubert b.

MAY 26 Set designer Joseph Urban b.

NOVEMBER 11 Maude Adams (Maude Kiskadden) b.

1873

• Playwright Clare Kummer (Clare Beecher), niece of William Gillette, b.

MARCH 7 Critic Percy Hammond b. **18** Anna Held b.

MAY 1 Agent William Morris b. **19** Sime Silverman, founder of *Variety*, b. **21** Richard Bennett, father of Joan, Constance, and Barbara Bennett, b.

AUGUST 12 Producer-director Augustin Duncan b. **18** Lyricist-librettist Otto Harbach (Otto Hauerbach) b. **19** Fred Stone b.

DECEMBER 23 Critic Burns Mantle b.

1874

JANUARY 25 Playwright W. Somerset Maugham b.

MARCH 24 Harry Houdini (Eric Weisz) b.

MAY 17 Bertha Kalich b. **27** Dustin Farnum, brother of William Farnum, b. **28** John Emerson b.

JUNE 2 Lulu Glaser b. **27** Producer John Golden b.

NOVEMBER 27 Playwright Eugene Walter b.

DECEMBER 23 Charles Waldron b.

1875

• Frank Craven b. • Sam Shubert b. • Bert Williams (Egbert Williams) b.

FEBRUARY 28 Actress-lyricist Rida Johnson Young b.

MARCH 28 Helen Westley (Henrietta Maney) b.

JUNE 20 Producer Oliver Morosco (Oliver Morosco Mitchell) b.

OCTOBER 20 Producer-playwright Edgar Selwyn b.

1876

• Producer Arthur Hammerstein, son of Oscar Hammerstein and uncle of Arthur Hammerstein II, b.

FEBRUARY 24 Victor Moore b.

JUNE 12 Irene Franklin b.

JULY 4 William Farnum, brother of Dustin Farnum, b.

OCTOBER 22 Cissie Loftus (Marie Cecilia Loftus Brown) b.

NOVEMBER 2 Playwright Jules Goodman b.

1877

• Producer Arch Selwyn, brother of Edgar Selwyn, b.

MAY 7 Playwright Richard Tully b.

AUGUST 16 Composer Karl Hoschna b.

OCTOBER 15 Actor-producer-director Hassard Short (Hubert Hassard-Short) b.

DECEMBER 22 Helena Modjeska makes her New York debut at the Fifth Avenue Theatre in *Adrienne Lecouvreur*.

1878

• Playwright Rachel Crothers b.

JANUARY 27 Constance Collier b.

MARCH 29 Frank Tinney (Aloysius Tinney) b.

APRIL 28 Lionel Barrymore, son of Maurice Barrymore, brother of Ethel and John, b.

MAY 25 Bill "Bojangles" Robinson (Luther Robinson) b.

JUNE 4 Alla Nazimova (Alla Leventon) b. (The year is also given as 1879.)

JULY 3 Actor-producer-composer-director George M. Cohan b.

AUGUST 1 Eva Tanguay b.

OCTOBER 4 Producer-director Arthur Hopkins b.

NOVEMBER 12 Charles Gilpin b.

1879

• Dudley Digges b.

JANUARY 4 The *New York Dramatic Mirror* begins publication.

MARCH 18 Emma Carus b. **30** Walter Hampden (Walter Hampden Dougherty) b.

APRIL 9 W.C. Fields (William Claude Dukenfield) b.

AUGUST 15 Ethel Barrymore, daughter of Maurice Barrymore and sister of John and Lionel, b. **18** Vaudeville producer-songwriter Gus Edwards b.

SEPTEMBER 17 Daly's Theatre opens at Broadway and Thirtieth Street. **17** O.P. Heggie b.

NOVEMBER 4 Will Rogers b.

DECEMBER 7 Composer Rudolph Friml b. **25** Grace George b.

1880

• Broadway has become a generic term for American theatre, with shows premiering in New York and then brought to other cities and towns by road companies. In New York, the theatre district is centered at Union Square and Fourteenth Street. • Nora Bayes b. • Laura Hope Crews b. • Eugene Howard (Isidore Levkowitz) b.

MARCH 4 Playwright Channing Pollock b. **29** David Belasco and James A. Herne's *Hearts of Oak*, the New York debut for each, opens at the Fifth Avenue Theatre. It features stage realism to the point where the audience can smell the baked beans and buckwheat cakes in a dinner scene.

JUNE 29 Producer Harry Frazee b.

AUGUST 15 Jacob J. (J.J.) Shubert b. **6** Playwright-producer Philip Moeller b.

SEPTEMBER 14 John Halliday b.

NOVEMBER • Ballad singer Lillian Russell debuts at Tony Pastor's Music Hall. **8** Sarah Bernhardt, opening in *Adrienne Lecouvreur* at the Booth Theatre in her American debut (the first of nine U.S. tours extending through 1916), has been guaranteed $1,000 a performance and a private railroad car for touring.

1881

• Percy Waram b.

JANUARY 17 Producer Morris Gest b.

JULY 3 Leon Errol b. **23** Margaret Illington (Maude Light), an actress who will marry producer Daniel Frohman, b.

AUGUST 6 Leo Carillo b.

OCTOBER 11 Translator-critic-playwright Stark Young b. **15** Lyricist P. (Pelham) G. (Grenville) Wodehouse b. **24** Tony Pastor begins the modern age of vaudeville when he offers shows for the "family" trade at his Fourteenth Street theatre in New York City. He's competing with Harrigan and Hart, playing a few blocks away. **26** Margaret Wycherly (Margaret De Wolfe) b.

NOVEMBER 28 Composer Louis Hirsch b.

1882

JANUARY 4 Wallack's Theatre opens at Broadway and Thirtieth Street, near the current site of Macy's in Herald Square, with *The School for Scandal.*

Herald Square—the theatre district of the 1880s BROWN

FEBRUARY 14 Critic George Jean Nathan b. **15** John Barrymore, son of Maurice Barrymore and brother of Ethel and Lionel, b.

MAY 10 Thurston Hall b. **28** Playwright Avery Hopwood b.

JUNE 8 The Actors Fund of America is organized to hold benefit performances for old, ill, and indigent actors. The Board of Trustees includes Edwin Booth, Joseph Jefferson, and P.T. Barnum. **12** Playwright Roi Cooper Megrue b.

JULY 1 Playwright Susan Glaspell b.

OCTOBER 29 Playwright Jean Giraudoux b.

NOVEMBER 6 Lillie Langtry makes her American debut at Wallack's Theatre in *The Unequal Match*. **23** Librettist and playwright Guy Bolton b.

1883

• Playwright Hatcher Hughes b.

JANUARY 10 Florence Reed b. **24** Estelle Winwood (Estelle Goodwin) b.

MAY 14 Female impersonator Julian Eltinge (William Dalton) b. **23** Douglas Fairbanks, one of the great Broadway matinée idols of the early years of the century before moving to Beverly Hills, b.

JUNE 16 Crystal Herne (Katherine Chrystal Herne) b.

JULY 6 B.F. Keith begins a policy of continuous vaudeville, upstairs from his ground floor freak show in Boston.

OCTOBER • British actor Henry Irving, on the first of his six American tours, plays four weeks in repertory at the Star Theatre (formerly Wallack's). In his 100-person company is Ellen Terry, also making her American debut.

1884

• Gaby Deslys (Gabrielle Deslys) b.

JANUARY 13 Sophie Tucker (Sophie Kalish) b.

FEBRUARY 16 Joe Smith, of the vaudeville team of Smith and Dale, and lyricist-composer Bert Kalmar b.

MARCH 23 Clarence Derwent b. **31** Playwright Sean O'Casey (Sean O'Cathasaigh) b.

APRIL 1 Laurette Taylor (Loretta Cooney) b. **6** Walter Huston, father of John and Angelica, b.

MAY 26 Charles Winninger (Karl Winninger) b.

JULY 3 Producer Gilbert Miller, son of Henry Miller, b.

SEPTEMBER 4 The musical/revue *Adonis* (603) opens at the Bijou Opera House. The star, Henry E. Dixey, collaborated on the writing of the show with William Gill and E.E. Rice.

AUGUST 20 Julia Sanderson (Julia Sackett) b. (The year is also given as 1887.)

OCTOBER 3 The Lyceum School of Acting, which will become the American Academy of Dramatic Arts, is founded in New York City. **4** Columnist-playwright-author Damon Runyon b.

DECEMBER 14 Jane Cowl b.

1885

JANUARY 27 Composer Jerome Kern b. **28** Mary Boland b.

MARCH 1 Lionel Atwill b.

AUGUST 19 Elsie Ferguson b. **31** Playwright Dubose Heyward b.

SEPTEMBER 6 Otto Kruger b.

DECEMBER 14 Producer Brock Pemberton b.

1886

JANUARY 3 Josephine Hull (Josephine Sherwood) b.

FEBRUARY 4 Playwright Edward Sheldon b.

APRIL 13 Willie Howard (Wilhelm Levkowitz) b.

MAY 23 Actor-playwright James Gleason b. **26** Al Jolson (Asa Joelson) b.

JUNE 6 Frances Starr b. **12** Producer-songwriter Ray Goetz b.

AUGUST 6 Billie Burke b.

SEPTEMBER 20 Producer John Murray Anderson b.

NOVEMBER 2 Philip Merivale b. **9** Ed Wynn (Isaiah Edwin Leopold) b. **23** Librettist-playwright Guy Bolton b.

1887

JANUARY 12 Producer Theresa Helburn b. **19** Critic Alexander Woollcott b.

JUNE 19 Blanche Yurka (Blanche Jurka) b. **25** Producer-director-actor-playwright George Abbott b. **30** The Orpheum Theatre, anchor of what will become the Orpheum circuit of vaudeville houses, opens in San Francisco.

JULY 29 Composer Sigmund Romberg b.

AUGUST 15 Novelist and playwright Edna Ferber b.

OCTOBER 20 Julia Marlowe makes her New York debut in *Ingomar* at the Bijou.

NOVEMBER 11 Roland Young b.

DECEMBER 6 Lynn Fontanne (Lillie Louise Fontanne) b. **12** Set designer Robert E. Jones b.

1888

JANUARY 7 The Players club is incorporated, bringing together luminaries from many professions along with theatre people. Edwin Booth donates the Grammercy Park building in which it is housed.

FEBRUARY 8 Edith Evans b.

MAY 11 Composer Irving Berlin (Israel Baline) b. **13** De Wolfe Hopper, at Wallack's Theatre, gives his first reading of "Casey at the Bat," which becomes his signature routine.

JUNE 16 Bobby Clark b. **26** Set designer Lee Simonson b. **27** Antoinette Perry, after whom the Tony Awards will be named, mother of Margaret Perry, b.

AUGUST 17 Monty Woolley (Edgar Montillon) b.

OCTOBER 16 Playwright Eugene O'Neill is born in the Barrett House, a hotel in what will become Times Square. His father is actor James O'Neill, who will play the lead in *The Count of Monte Cristo* more than 6,000 times.

NOVEMBER 23 Harpo Marx (Adolph Arthur Marx) b. (Several other years are also sometimes given.) **24** Cathleen Nesbitt b.

DECEMBER 7 Critic Heywood Broun b. **15** Playwright Maxwell Anderson b.

1889

• George M. Cohan joins his family's vaudeville act. • Oscar Shaw b. (1891 is also given as the year.)

FEBRUARY 4 Actor-director Richard Boleslavski b.

MARCH 16 Elsie Janis b. **29** Playwright-director Howard Lindsay b.

JULY 15 Marjorie Rambeau b.

SEPTEMBER 1 Glenn Anders b. **9** Bronson Howard's *Shenandoah* (250), producer Charles Frohman's first success, starring Henry Miller and Viola Allen, opens at the Star Theatre. **15** Critic, actor, and humorist Robert Benchley b. **19** Ernest Truex b.

NOVEMBER 16 Playwright-director George S. Kaufman b. **19** Clifton Webb (Clifton Webb Parmalee Hollenbeck), b. (Other years in the '90s are sometimes listed.)

1890

• Joe Cook b. • Producer George White b.

MARCH 19 Minnie Maddern marries Harrison Grey Fiske, editor and publisher of the *New York Dramatic Mirror*. She will be known professionally as "Mrs. Fiske."

MAY 19 Clyde Fitch's *Beau Brummell* (150), starring Richard Mansfield, opens at the Madison Square Theatre. Fitch is the first American playwright with an international reputation. **21** Composer Harry Tierney b. **30** Producer Lawrence Langner b.

JUNE 26 Jeanne Eagels b. (The year is also given as 1884.)

JULY 7 Tom Powers b.

OCTOBER 2 Groucho Marx (Julius Marx) b. **3** Henry Hull b.

NOVEMBER 1 James Barton b. **23** Jacob Ben-Ami (Jacob Shtchirin) b.

DECEMBER 13 Playwright Marc Connelly b.

1891

• Producer Alexander Aarons b. • Helen Broderick, mother of Broderick Crawford, b. • Joe Schenck of the vaudeville team of Van and Schenck b.

MARCH 5 Chic Johnson (Harold Johnson), of Olsen and Johnson, b. **22** Chico Marx (Leonard Marx) b.

JUNE 9 Composer Cole Porter b. **11** Press agent Richard Maney b. **26** Playwright Sidney Howard b.

JULY 16 Blossom Seeley b.

OCTOBER 29 Fanny Brice (Fannie Borach) b.

NOVEMBER 5 Producer Vinton Freedly b. **9** *A Trip to Chinatown* (657), a musical set in San Francisco but having nothing to do with Chinatown, opens at the Madison Square Theatre. The best remembered of the Charles Hoyt–Percy Gaunt songs is "The Bowery."

DECEMBER 7 Fay Bainter b. **9** James A. Herne's *Margaret Fleming*, brings an Ibsen-influenced realism to the American stage at Palmer's Theatre. *The New York Times* complains that it focuses on the lives of "everyday nonentities." There are "many unpleasant expressions not often heard on the stage," and "[t]he life it portrays is sordid and mean, and its effect upon a sensitive mind is depressing."

1892

• Leo G. Carroll b.

JANUARY 23 Producer Earl Carroll b. **31** Eddie Cantor (Edward Israel Itzkowitz) b.

FEBRUARY 9 Peggy Wood (Margaret Wood) b. **17** Hendrik Ibsen's *Hedda Gabler* has its American premiere at the Amberg Theater. *The New York Times* calls it "a finely written prose drama" and remarks on how it contrasts with the usual stage fare in New York: "One does not want to look at cartoons all the time."

MAY 16 Osgood Perkins (James Ridley Osgood Perkins), father of Anthony Perkins, b.

JUNE 13 Basil Rathbone b. **28** Producer Max Gordon (Mechel Salpeter) b.

JULY 21 Lenore Ulric (Lenore Ulrich) b.

AUGUST 17 Mae West b. **19** Alfred Lunt b.

SEPTEMBER 28 Playwright Elmer Rice (Elmer Reizenstein) b.

OCTOBER 15 Ina Claire (Ina Fagan) b. **25** Jennie Dolly (Jancsi Deutsch) and Rosie Dolly (Roszicka Deutsch), twins—the Dolly Sisters—b.

NOVEMBER 6 Ole Olsen (John Sigvard Olsen), of Olsen and Johnson, b.

DECEMBER 21 Edith Taliaferro, sister of Mabel Taliaferro, b. **23** Ann Pennington b. (Other years in this decade are also given.) **31** Jason Robards, Sr., father of Jason Robards, Jr., b.

1893

JANUARY 23 "The stranger from Italy is a forcible and interesting actress," *The New York Times* will say of Eleanora Duse's American debut in *Camille* at the Fifth Avenue Theatre. When a reporter tries to interview her, she turns him away: "Away from the stage I do not exist. I wish to be left alone." **25** Charles Frohman opens his Empire Theatre with *The Girl I Left Behind Me*, by David Belasco and Franklyn Fyles. The theatre, at Broadway and Fortieth, faces the Metropolitan Opera House, pushing the northern edge of the Rialto to the southern border of what will become Times Square.

FEBRUARY 10 Jimmy Durante b. **16** Katharine Cornell b. For many years she will give 1898 as her birth year. **20** Playwright Russel Crouse b.

APRIL 3 Leslie Howard (Leslie Stainer) b. **11** Lou Holtz and Robert Halliday b. **6** Playwright Anita Loos (Anita Beers—Loos is her mother's maiden name) b. **27** Stage designer Norman Bel Geddes, father of Barbara Bel Geddes, b.

MAY 22 The American Theater opens, on previously residential Forty-second Street, with *The Prodigal Daughter*. It's the first major move of the theatre district into what will become Times Square.

JUNE 7 Edwin Booth d. **9** Playwright S. (Samuel) N. (Nathaniel) Behrman b. **5** Charlotte Greenwood b.

JULY 5 De Wolfe Hopper m. Edna Wallace.

AUGUST 5 The *New York Dramatic Mirror* reports that "the descendant of the late Pat Rooney, known as young Pat Rooney [he's 14 years old] will head the Pat Rooney company . . . young Rooney is possessed of undoubted talent and his versatility is remarkable." The paper also reports in this issue that Victor Herbert "is regarded by many as the coming man in American opera composition." **22** Critic and playwright Dorothy Parker (Dorothy Rothschild) b.

SEPTEMBER • B.F. Keith and E.F. Albee take over the Union Square Theatre, bringing to New York City their growing chain of variety theatres, begun with the Bijou in Boston in 1885.

DECEMBER 2 William Gaxton (Arturo Gaxiola) b. **10** Songwriter Lew Brown b. **17** Director Erwin Piscator b. **24** Ruth Chatterton b. **25** Belle Baker b.

1894

• The average yearly salary for an actor is about $875, slightly less than what a post office employee makes. *Billboard* is founded.

JANUARY 25 Ethel Barrymore makes her debut at the Empire Theatre in *The Rivals*.

FEBRUARY 14 Jack Benny (Benjamin Kubelsky) b. **28** Playwright Ben Hecht b.

MARCH 17 Playwright Paul Green, whose *The House of Connelly* will be the Group Theatre's first production, b.

MAY 22 The headline over *The New York Times* review of a "variety performance" at Koster & Bial's Concert Hall states that ". . . What They Now Call 'Vaudeville' May Be Seen at Its Best." **29** Beatrice Lillie b. **31** Fred Allen b.

SEPTEMBER 17 Richard Mansfield opens at the Herald Square Theatre in what he will describe as "a little satirical comedy, of no great weight." It is *Arms and the Man*—the first American production of any George Bernard Shaw play. While acknowledging that the audience enjoyed it, the *New York Dramatic Mirror* cautions: "The dialogue, however, is too ironical to obtain any great degree of popularity with the average theatregoer." **20** Patricia Collinge b.

NOVEMBER 25 Playwright Laurence Stallings b. **28** Critic Brooks Atkinson (Justin Brooks Atkinson) b.

1895

• Jimmy Savo b.

JANUARY 16 Irene Bordoni b. **25** Florence Mills (Florence Winfrey) b.

FEBRUARY 21 Librettist Joseph Fields, son of Lew Fields and brother of Dorothy and Herbert Fields, b.

MARCH 22 Joseph Schildkraut b.

APRIL 15 Paul M. Potter's *Trilby* (208), starring Virginia Harned and William Lackaye, opens at the Garden Theatre. **21** Otis Skinner m. his leading lady, Maude Durbin. **22** The first American production of Oscar Wilde's *The Importance of Being Earnest*, starring Henry Miller, William Faversham, and Viola Allen, is at the Empire. Calling it a "burlesque comedy," *The New York Times*, compares it unfavorably to the work of W.S. Gilbert (of Gilbert and Sullivan), complaining that "Almost every line is avowedly and laboriously witty."

MAY 2 Lyricist Lorenz Hart b.

JUNE 1 The *New York Dramatic Mirror* celebrates Queen Victoria's knighting of Henry Irving, the first actor to attain this honor, as a deed that "has broken down the traditions that for centuries placed actors outside the social pale." **29** The *New York Dramatic Mirror* begins a separate section for "The Vaudeville Stage," noting that "it is steadily coming into nearer relations with the regular stage, so many of whose shining lights have had beginning upon it."

JULY 4 Lyricist Irving Caesar—"Swanee," "Tea for Two"—b. **6** Attacking recent plays that have dwelt on social problems and social pathology, the *New York Dramatic Mirror* maintains that audiences want "pictures of life in its nobler and happier aspects, as they relate to normal existence." **12** Oscar Hammerstein II, grandson of Oscar Hammerstein, b. **13** Sidney Blackmer b.

AUGUST • Appearing at Keith's Union Square Theatre are the Four Cohans, "one of the neatest and cleverest acts ever seen at this house," according to the *Dramatic Mirror*. **13** Bert Lahr (Irving Larheim) b.

OCTOBER 20 Playwright Morrie Ryskind b.

NOVEMBER 5 Playwright Charles MacArthur b. **25** Oscar Hammerstein's Olympia Theatre opens in Longacre Square (shortly to become Times Square). It seats several thousand for a variety of musical entertainments.

Weber and Fields PF

1896

• Clare Eames b. The actress will marry playwright Sidney Howard. • Glenn Hunter b.

JANUARY 20 George Burns (Nathan Birnbaum) b. **27** Lyricist-producer Buddy De Sylva (George Gard De Sylva) b. (The year is also given as 1895.)

APRIL 4 Playwright Robert E. Sherwood b. **10** Edith Day b.

MAY • The Actors Society of America is formed to foster the professionalization of acting and deal with the problems of actors.

JUNE 18 Playwright Philip Barry b.

AUGUST 30 Raymond Massey b. **31** Members of the Theatre Syndicate, led by producers Marc Klaw and Abraham Erlanger, sign an agreement pooling their theatres for the purpose of controlling bookings.

SEPTEMBER 5 Vaudeville comedians Joe Weber and Lew Fields open their Weber and Fields's Music Hall in the 665-seat theatre, previously called the Imperial, with "The Art of Maryland," a parody of *The Heart of Maryland*, starring Mrs. Leslie Carter. Weber and Fields are famous for the routine, with German accents: "Who vass dat lady I saw you with last night? That vass no lady. She vass my wife." **8** Lyricist Howard Dietz b. **21** With the opening of *The Parlor Match* at the Herald Square Theatre, Flo Ziegfeld debuts as a Broadway producer. He's having an affair with the star, Anna Held, who, he leads the press to believe, takes milk baths.

OCTOBER 30 Ruth Gordon b.

DECEMBER 1 Composer Ray Henderson b. **6** Lyricist Ira Gershwin (Israel Gershvin) b.

1897

MARCH 26 Louise Groody b.

APRIL 7 Columnist-critic Walter Winchell (Walter Winschel) b. **17** Playwright Thornton Wilder b. **19** Vivienne Segal b.

MAY 31 Margalo Gillmore b.

JULY 26 Librettist Herbert Fields, son of Lew Fields and brother of Dorothy and Joseph, b.

AUGUST 31 Fredric March (Ernest Frederick McIntyre Bickel) b.

SEPTEMBER 5 Morris Carnovsky b. **30** James Barrie's *The Little Minister* (300) opens at the Empire Theatre, with Maude Adams in her first starring role.

NOVEMBER 2 Dennis King b. **17** Frank Fay b.

DECEMBER 1 Cyril Ritchard (Cyril Trimnel-Ritchard) b.

1898

FEBRUARY 10 Judith Anderson (Frances Margaret Anderson) b. (The year is also given as 1899.) **10** Playwright Bertolt Brecht (Eugen Bertholt Brecht) b. **28** Molly Picon b.

MARCH 26 The *New York Dramatic Mirror* prints the text of the agreement that created the Theatre Syndicate two years ago.

APRIL 3 George Jessel b. **8** Lyricist-librettist E. (Edgar) Y. "Yip" Harburg (Isidore Hochberg) b. **9** Paul Robeson b. **14** Lee Tracy (William Lee Tracy) b.

JUNE 15 Menasha Skulnik b.

JULY 4 Gertrude Lawrence (Gertrude Klasen—her father's middle name is Lawrence) b.

AUGUST 10 Jack Haley b.

SEPTEMBER 1 Marilyn Miller (Mary Ellen Reynolds; original stage name: Marilynn Miller) b. **8** David Warfield makes his Broadway debut in *Hurly Burly*, starring Fay Templeton, at the Weber and Fields's Music Hall. **26** George Gershwin (Jacob Gershvin) b. **28** Composer Vincent Youmans b.

NOVEMBER 24 Critic Ward Morehouse b.

DECEMBER 6 Producer-director Herman Shumlin b. **28** Playwright Rose Franken b. **29** Jules Bledsoe b.

1899

• The theatre district lies between Twentieth and Fortieth streets. Orchestra seats at legitimate theatres cost $2.00, and balcony admission is $.50. Vaudeville tickets at Tony Pastor's on Fourteenth Street run from $.20 to $.30. • Vaudeville has become family entertainment. In one theatre, a backstage "Notice to Performers" warns: "Such words as [l]iar, [s]lob, [s]on-of-a-[g]un, [d]evil, [s]ucker, [d]amn, and all other words unfit for the ears of ladies and children, . . . and any references to questionable streets, resorts, localities and barrooms are prohibited under fine of instant discharge."

JANUARY 11 Eva Le Gallienne is born. Her father is British poet Richard Le Gallienne, and her mother is a Danish writer.

MARCH 25 Playwright Bella Spewack (Bella Cohen) b.

JULY 1 Charles Laughton b.

SEPTEMBER 5 Luella Gear b. **6** Producer Billy Rose (William Rosenberg) b. **16** Playwright Samuel Spewack b. **20** Actor-director-producer-playwright Elliott Nugent b.

OCTOBER 14 Lillian Gish, sister of Dorothy Gish b.

NOVEMBER 6 William Gillette stars in his own play, *Sherlock Holmes* (256), at the Garrick. **29** William Young's *Ben Hur* (194), based on the Lew Wallace novel—the General is at the Broadway Theatre tonight—opens, with Edward Morgan and William S. Hart.

DECEMBER 16 Noel Coward b. **26** The Hebrew Actors Union, the first union of theatrical performers in New York, is formed.

1900

• "Coon" songs permeate the American musical stage, including "I Never Liked a Nigger With a Beard" and "All Coons Look Alike to Me."

JANUARY 19 Mady Christians (Marguerita Christians) b. **25** Mildred Dunnock b.

FEBRUARY 5 Olga Nethersole opens at Wallack's Theatre in *Sapho*, the story of a seductress who reforms. The leading man carries her upstairs to a bedroom, scandalizing the audience. **23** New York

Olga Nethersole

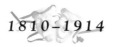

City police arrest Olga Nethersole, starring in *Sapho*, and several other members of the company. **25** Producer-director Jed Harris (Jacob Hirsch Horowitz) b. **26** Helena Modjeska begins a repertory season at the Fifth Avenue Theatre.

MARCH 2 Composer Kurt Weill b. **5** *Madame Butterfly* (24), by David Belasco (from a story by John Luther Long), starring Blanche Bates, opens at the Herald Square Theatre. It will be immortalized in the Puccini opera based on it. **5** *Sapho* is closed by the police after 29 performances.

APRIL 7 Following the acquittal of Olga Nethersole, *Sapho* reopens at Wallack's, where it will run for another 55 performances.

MAY • B.F. Keith begins to organize vaudeville bookings along monopolistic lines similar to those of the Theatre Syndicate. His booking operation will become the United Booking Office and will be fought by an independent, William Morris. **5** Sam, Lee, and J.J. Shubert, "The Boys from Syracuse," move into the New York City theatre scene when they lease the Herald Square Theatre. They put Richard Mansfield under contract and have reached an agreement with Abe Erlanger, later their enemy, to book the Syndicate's shows into their house.

JUNE 1 The White Rats vaudeville union is organized. Founders include David Montgomery and Fred Stone. **3** Abel Green, editor of *Variety* from 1933 to 1973, b. **21** Dorothy Stickney b.

JULY 2 Director Tyrone Guthrie (William Tyrone Guthrie) b. **3** Critic John Mason Brown b.

AUGUST 2 Helen Morgan b.

SEPTEMBER 17 E.H. Sothern, soon to become one of the era's foremost Shakespeareans, opens in *Hamlet* opposite his wife, Virginia Harned, as Ophelia, at the Garden Theatre. **27** James A. Herne wrote and stars in *Sag Harbor*, the premiere production at Oscar Hammerstein's Republic Theatre on Forty-second Street. Lionel Barrymore also stars in this drama of two brothers vying for one woman.

OCTOBER • Helen Morgan b. **1** *David Harum* (148) by R. and M.W. Hitchcock, starring William H. Crane, opens at the Garrick. **10** Helen Hayes (Helen Hayes Brown) b. **18** Lotte Lenya (Karoline Blamauer) b. **31** Ethel Waters b.

NOVEMBER 12 *Florodora* (505)—often misspelled "Floradora"—opens at the Casino Theatre. In the audience are Diamond Jim Brady and William Randolph Hearst. A sextet in the chorus sings Leslie Stuart's "Tell Me, Pretty Maiden," one of the earliest hit songs from a Broadway musical, and the first sung only by a chorus. Several of the show's chorus girls, making $25 a week, marry millionaires. **25** Helen Gahagan and Composer Arthur Schwartz b. **30** Oscar Wilde d.

1901

• *Theatre Magazine* founded. Its theatre critic will be Arthur Hornblow.

FEBRUARY 4 With the opening of Clyde Fitch's *Captain Jinks of the Horse Marines* (168) at the Garrick, 21-year-old Ethel Barrymore triumphs and tells her landlady that she will be taking larger quarters in her rooming house. *The New York Times* says that Barrymore is "entirely too young and undeveloped to be put forward as a star," although she "will bear a good deal of watching." **25** George M. Cohan makes his Broadway debut in *The Governor's Son*, which he also wrote, at the Savoy.

MARCH 19 Stage designer Joe Mielziner b. **25** Ed Begley b.

APRIL 5 Melvyn Douglas (Melvin Hesselberg) b.

MAY 20 *Brixton Burglary* (48), the first play produced by the Shuberts in their New York City house, the Herald Square Theatre, opens with Lionel Barrymore in the cast. **30** Cornelia Otis Skinner b.

JUNE 1 Playwright John Van Druten b. **2** James A. Herne d. **3** Maurice Evans b. **10** Composer Frederick Loewe b. His father, tenor Edmund Loewe, will be the first Prince Danilo in *The Merry Widow* in 1906. **22** Jack Whiting b.

SEPTEMBER 5 Florence Eldridge (Florence McKechnie) b. **18** Harold Clurman b. **23** David Warfield attains recognition as a dramatic star with the opening at the Bijou of *The Auctioneer* (105), written and produced by David Belasco, with whom Warfield will often work. **26** Donald Cook b. **28** Broadway columnist Ed Sullivan b.

OCTOBER 14 E.H. Sothern secures recognition as a Broadway star with the opening at the Garden Theatre of *If I Were King* (56). Co-star Cecilia Loftus is the former wife of the playwright, Justin H. McCarthy. **15** Claire Luce b.

NOVEMBER 2 Paul Ford (Paul Ford Weaver) b. **17** Lee Strasberg (Israel Strassberg) b.

DECEMBER 12 Helen Menken b.

1902

• Rosetta Duncan b. • Critic Wolcott Gibbs b.

JANUARY 13 British actors, Mrs. Patrick Campbell and George Arliss, make their Broadway debuts in repertory at the Republic. **27** Lulu Glaser has her biggest hit in *Dolly Varden* (154) at the Herald Square Theatre.

FEBRUARY 10 Stella Adler, daughter of Jacob Adler and sister of Luther Adler, b. **19** John W. Bubbles (John W. Sublett), half of the vaudeville team of Buck and Bubbles, b.

MARCH 9 Will Geer b.

APRIL 20 Donald Wolfit b.

JUNE 2 *A Chinese Honeymoon*, the Shubert's second New York production and their first hit, opens at the Casino Theatre. **28** Richard Rodgers b.

SEPTEMBER 8 Queenie Smith b. **13** Producer-agent Leland Hayward b. **22** John Houseman (Jacques Haussman) b. **24** Producer Cheryl Crawford b.

DECEMBER 3 Blanche Bates and George Arliss star in David Belasco and John Luther Long's *Darling of the Gods* (182) at the Belasco Theatre. **19** Ralph Richardson b. **29** *Sultan of Sulu* (192), a musical by George Ade and Alfred G. Wathall and starring Frank Moulan, opens at Wallack's Theatre. It begins a vogue of shows placing Americans in exotic locales.

1903

• Sophie Kalish marries Louis Tuck, to whose name she adds "er" to produce the stage name Sophie Tucker.

JANUARY 20 The first production of *The Wizard of Oz* (293), adapted for Broadway by author Frank Baum, opens at William Randolph Hearst's new Majestic Theatre on Columbus Circle. Anna Laughlin is Dorothy, Fred Stone, the Scarecrow, and David Montgomery, the Tin Man (Montgomery and Stone have been performing as a vaudeville act since 1894). **31** Tallulah Bankhead, daughter of a Congressman, granddaughter of a U.S. Senator from Alabama, and niece of another Senator, is born.

FEBRUARY 18 *In Dahomey* (53), the first American musical written and played by African-Americans and produced on Broadway in a legitimate theatre, opens at the New York Theatre. Will Marion Cook wrote the music, poet Paul Laurence Dunbar the lyrics, and it stars Bert Williams and George Walker.

APRIL 10 Playwright Clare Boothe (Anne Clare Boothe, later Clare Boothe Luce) b.

MAY 4 Luther Adler, son of Jacob Adler and brother of Stella Adler, b. **17** Critic Elliot Norton b.

JUNE 21 Theatrical illustrator Al Hirschfeld b.

SEPTEMBER 13 Claudette Colbert (Lily Chachoin) b.

OCTOBER 12 The New Amsterdam Theatre, future home of *The Ziegfeld Follies*, opens on Forty-second Street with a production of *A Midsummer Night's Dream*. And the Lyric opens on the same street with *Old Heidelberg*, starring Richard Mansfield. **13** Victor Herbert's *Babes in Toyland* (192), with lyrics by Glen MacDonough, follows *The Wizard of Oz* into the Majestic Theatre. Starring William Norris, Bessie Wynn, and Mabel Barrison, it introduces "March of the Toys" and "Toyland." **19** Ethel Barrymore opens in *Cousin Kate*, inaugurating the Hudson Theatre on Forty-fourth Street.

NOVEMBER 2 Laurette Taylor makes her New York debut in *From Rags to Riches* at the New Star Theatre. **2** The Lyceum Theatre debuts with *The Proud Prince*.

DECEMBER 9 David Belasco's *Sweet Kitty Bellairs* (206), a costume drama at the Belasco, features Henrietta Crossman and the debut of Jane Cowl. **28** John Barrymore makes his New York stage debut in Clyde Fitch's *Glad of It*. It also stars Lucile Watson and Thomas Meighan. **30** A fire in Chicago's fireproof Iroquois Theatre, which opened a month ago, kills 602. Eddie Foy is performing in *Mr. Bluebeard* when the blaze erupts.

1904

JANUARY 4 George Bernard Shaw's *Candida* (133) has its New York premiere at the Madison Square Theatre, with Arnold Daly as Marchbanks. *The New York Times* finds it "brilliantly original and dramatic." **5** William Farnum opens in *The Virginian* (138) at the Manhattan Theatre. Owen Wister and Kirke La Shelle have adapted Wister's novel for the stage. **10** Ray Bolger b.

FEBRUARY 11 Playwright S. (Sidney) J. (Joseph) Perelman b.

The former Longacre Square has become Times Square BROWN

APRIL 4 John Gielgud, grandnephew of Ellen Terry, b. **9** New York's Longacre Square, which runs from Forty-second to Forty-seventh streets, is renamed Times Square, in honor of *The New York Times* building under construction at its southern tip.

MAY 23 In *The Southerners* (36), a musical by Will Marion Cook at the Criterion, the otherwise white cast is joined by what *The New York Times* calls a "chorus of real live coons," probably the first such interracial mixture on the New York stage. **3** Libby Holman (Elizabeth Holzman) b.

JUNE 14 June Walker, mother of actor John Kerr, b. **17** Ralph Bellamy b.

AUGUST 4 Helen Kane (Helen Schroeder), the "Boop-Boop-a-Doop girl," b.

SEPTEMBER 6 David Warfield stars in *The Music Master* (627), by Charles Klein, at the Belasco. **19** *Mr. Wix of Wickham*, an unsuccessful musical at the Bijou, is the Broadway debut of female impersonator Julian Eltinge and of 19-year-old Jerome Kern, who has written several of the songs. **19** Julia Marlowe and E.H. Sothern appear together for the first time—in Chicago, at the Illinois Theatre, in *Romeo and Juliet*. **20** George Ade's comedy, *The College Widow* (278), on which the 1917 Jerome Kern musical, *Leave It to Jane* is based, opens at the Garden Theatre.

OCTOBER 24 Playwright Moss Hart b.

NOVEMBER 6 Selena Royle b. **7** George M. Cohan has written, directed and, says the *New York Herald*, makes "his debut as a star" in *Little Johnny Jones* (52), at the Liberty on Forty-second Street. It is also Cohan's first collaboration with coproducer Sam Harris. The *Herald* likes Cohan's songs, even though they are "not burdened with startling originality." They include "Give My Regards to Broadway" and "The Yankee Doodle Boy" ("I'm a Yankee Doodle Dandy"), a showstopper. **15** Ethel Barrymore, opening in Thomas Raceward's *Sunday* at the Hudson, has one memorable line in this soon forgotten play: "That's all there is. There isn't anymore."

DECEMBER 12 *Leah Kleschna* (131), a play by C.M.S. McLellan, with Minnie Maddern Fiske and George Arliss, opens at the Manhattan Theatre. Mrs. Fiske plays a thief who discovers that she has stolen from a man who once saved her life.

1905

• Choreographer Agnes DeMille, niece of Cecil B. DeMille b.

FEBRUARY 15 Harold Arlen (Hyman Arluck), a cantor's son, b. **28** Agent Audrey Wood b.

MARCH 2 Composer Marc Blitzstein b. **15** Actress-director Margaret Webster, daughter of May Whitty, b. **26** Maurice Barrymore d.

APRIL 12 The Hippodrome, at Sixth Avenue and Forty-third Street, opens for two shows a day with *A Yankee Circus on Mars*, with famous French clown Marceline. Seating 5,200, it is the world's largest legitimate theatre. **23** Joseph Jefferson d.

MAY 12 Sam Shubert d. in a train accident near Pittsburgh. **16** Henry Fonda b. **22** Yiddish Theatre star Bertha Kalich makes her Broadway debut in Sardou's *Fedora* at the American Theatre.

JUNE • The Shuberts, David Belasco, and the Fiskes join forces to combat the

Syndicate, headed by Klaw and Erlanger. **12** Will Rogers begins his vaudeville career with a performance of trick lassoing at Keith's Union Square in New York. He is starting to work humor into his act. **19** Mildred Natwick and George Voskovec b. **20** Playwright Lillian Hellman b.

JULY 15 Librettist Dorothy Fields, daughter of Lew Fields and sister of Joseph and Herbert, b.

AUGUST 28 Sam Levene b. **31** Actor-teacher Sanford Meisner b.

OCTOBER 20 Anthony Comstock, Secretary of the Society for the Suppression of Vice, writes to Arnold Daly, who is about to stage the American premiere of Shaw's *Mrs. Warren's Profession*, a play about prostitution, calling Daly's attention to recent adverse court decisions regarding "[George] Bernard Shaw's filthy products." **23** Edwin Milton Royle's *The Squaw Man* (222), starring William Faversham and William S. Hart, opens at Wallack's. **31** New York City Police Commissioner McAdoo, who attended a performance last night, calls George Bernard Shaw's *Mrs. Warren's Profession* "revolting, indecent, and nauseating where it is not boring," shuts it down and arrests the house manager at the Garrick Theatre, where scalpers were briefly getting $25 a ticket.

NOVEMBER • Sarah Bernhardt arrives in the U.S. for what the Shuberts are billing as her "farewell tour." When the Syndicate blocks her appearance in many of the country's better legitimate theatres, the Shuberts have her appear in a circus tent to gain sympathy and publicity. The tour will gross $1 million. **6** Thirty-two-year-old Maude Adams stars in the premiere of James Barrie's *Peter Pan*, written for her, opening at the Empire Theatre. **14** David Belasco's *The Girl of the Golden West* (224) opens at the Belasco. Blanche Bates, Robert Hilliard, and Frank Keenan star in this melodrama, in which the heroine wins a poker game in which the life of her beloved is at stake. Bat Masterson, whose Western "exploits" were largely myth, reviews it in the *New York Telegraph* (December 27). "It is a tale well told without exaggeration," writes the man who knows of such things, "without any of the flamboyant creations of the dime novelist." It will become a Puccini opera in 1910. **20** Charles Klein's *The Lion and the Mouse* (586), starring Richard Bennett, opens at the Lyceum. The leading characters are based on muckraking journalist Ida Tarbell and John D. Rockefeller. **26** Playwright-actor Emlyn Williams b.

DECEMBER 16 *Variety*, charging $.05 a copy, begins publication. **26** Lynn Fontanne debuts in the chorus of *Cinderella* at the Drury Lane in London. **31** Composer Jule Styne b.

1906

• George Pierce Baker begins his playwriting course at Harvard—English 47—whose attendees will include Edward Sheldon, Eugene O'Neill, George Abbott, John Mason Brown, Sidney Howard, Philip Barry, and S.N. Behrman. • Bettina Hall b.

JANUARY 1 Victor Moore, Fay Templeton, and Donald Brian are in George M. Cohan's musical, *Forty-five Minutes from Broadway* (90), opening at the New Amsterdam. One of the show's five songs is "Mary's A Grand Old Name." Moore, playing Kid Burns, becomes a major Broadway star.

FEBRUARY 27 Franchot Tone b.

MARCH • Flo Ziegfeld quarrels with the Shuberts over a coproducing deal he made with them a year ago. It will grow into a feud of several decades' duration and Ziegfeld will cast his lot with Klaw and Erlanger of the rival Syndicate. **15** Veree Teasdale b.

MAY 13 Playwright Samuel Beckett b. **23** Henrik Ibsen d.

JUNE 4 Actor-director Richard Whorf b. **19** Jane Cowl m. Adolph Klauber, drama critic for *The New York Times*, and later a producer. **25** Harry K. Thaw, millionaire husband of chorus girl Evelyn Nesbit, shoots to death architect Stanford White at the Roof Garden Theatre atop Madison Square Garden during the opening night performance of *Mamzelle Champagne*. Thaw has been obsessed with White's seduction of his wife before their marriage.

JULY 18 Playwright Clifford Odets b. **26** Gracie Allen b.

SEPTEMBER • Broadway columnist Leonard Lyons b. **24** *The Red Mill* (274), Victor Herbert and Henry Blossom's musical, starring Fred Stone and David Montgomery, who play characters named Kid Conner and Con Kidder, introduces the song "Because You're You."

OCTOBER 17 Carlotta Nillson stars at the Madison Square Theatre in *The Three of Us* (227), Rachel Crothers's first successful play, about the owners of a gold mine. **22** Playwright Sidney Kingsley b.

NOVEMBER 13 Hermione Baddley (Hermione Clinton-Baddley), whose ancestor, Sir Henry Clinton, captured New York in the American Revolution, b. **19** In *The New York Idea* (66), at the Lyric, Minnie Maddern Fiske and John Mason star in a comedy about marriage and divorce, by Langdon Mitchell. **27** *Rose of the Rancho* (327), by David Belasco and Richard W. Tully, opens at the Belasco Theatre. Frances Starr is the heroine in this drama of old California.

DECEMBER 4 George Broadhurst's *The Man of the Hour* (479) opens at the Savoy, with George Fawcett in the cast. Love, politics, and the corruption of Tammany Hall are the themes. **9** Long before she will become "The Last of the Red-Hot Mamas," Sophie Tucker, in black face, debuts professionally at the One Hundred Sixteenth Street Music Hall in New York. Tucker will be billed for several years as "The World Renowned Coon Shouter."

1907

JANUARY • Marc Klaw and Abraham Erlanger of the Syndicate are indicted for violating the antitrust laws through the practice of monopolizing theatrical bookings, but a judge will throw the case out.

MARCH 23 Richard Mansfield closes in *A Parisian Romance*, his last stage performance.

APRIL 28 The Shuberts make their peace with Klaw and Erlanger, and together they form the United States Amusement Company to produce vaudeville, challenging the Keith circuit's United Booking Office. By November, Keith and Albee will buy them off, leaving only William Morris, independent booker, to counter the U.B.O.

MAY • The sheet music for "Marie From Sunny Italy" is published, bearing the

Victor Herbert PF

name of coauthor I. Berlin—the first time Israel Baline has used the name Irving Berlin. **22** Laurence Olivier b.

JUNE • Princeton University drops Eugene O'Neill "for poor academic standing." **22** Producer Mike Todd (Michael Goldbogen) b.

JULY 8 *The Follies of 1907*, the first of Flo Ziegfeld's annual extravaganzas, which won't bear his name until 1911, opens at the New York Theater Roof, renamed the Jardin de Paris. Lyricist Harry B. Smith has probably named the show from his newspaper column, "Follies of the Day." Emulating a Parisian review, this $13,000 production has "girls and girls, and then girls," as the *New York Telegraph* puts it—a chorus of 50 or so "Anna Held Girls." (Held is Ziegfeld's wife.)

AUGUST 30 Richard Mansfield d. and Shirley Booth (Thelma Booth Ford) b. **31** John Drew stars, and Billie Burke makes her Broadway debut, in My *Wife* (129), at the Empire.

SEPTEMBER 22 Shepperd Strudwick b.

OCTOBER 17 David Belasco opens his Stuyvesant Theatre—he will rename it the Belasco—with *A Grand Army Man*, starring William Warfield and Antoinette Perry. **21** Franz Lehar's *The Merry Widow* (416) opens at the New Amsterdam, making "The Merry Widow Waltz" ubiquitous throughout the country. Donald Brian plays Prince Danilo, with Ethel Jackson as the first of several Sonias.

NOVEMBER 16 The Friars Club is incorporated. Wells Hawks is the first Abbot. **18** *The Witching Hour* (212), by Augustus Thomas, opens at the Hackett Theatre. John Mason stars in a play about hypnosis and mental telepathy. **23** Ruth Etting b. **27** Phoebe Brand b.

DECEMBER 3 William C. DeMille's *The Warrens of Virginia* (190), a Civil War melodrama at the Belasco, stars Frank Keenan and Emma Dunn. Also in the cast are Cecil B. DeMille and Gladys Smith (Mary Pickford). **22** Peggy Ashcroft (Edith Margaret Emily Ashcroft) b.

1908

JANUARY 16 Ethel Merman (Ethel Zimmerman) b. (She will also give 1909 and 1912 as her year of birth.)

FEBRUARY 3 George M. Cohan, whose *Fifty Miles From Boston* opens tonight at the Garrick, has invited vaudeville old-timer Ned Harrigan to be present. When the curtain goes up, he discovers that one of the characters is called Harrigan and that the show's big number is "H-A Double R-I-G-A-N." **25** Eugene Walter's *Paid in Full* (167) opens at the Astor. Lillian Albertson is the wife who will do almost anything for her worthless husband until she finally sees the light.

MARCH 5 Rex Harrison b. **20** Michael Redgrave b.

MAY 9 Producer Leonard Sillman b. **26** Robert Morley b. **27** Composer-lyricist Harold Rome b. **30** An ad in *The Dramatic Mirror* urges: "Turn Your Opera House Into a Moving Picture Nickelodeon This Summer."

JUNE 15 Flo Ziegfeld's *Follies of 1908* (120) opens at the Jardin de Paris. It is most notable for Nora Bayes's introduction of a song she and her husband, Jack Norworth, have written: "Shine on Harvest Moon." **19** Mildred Natwick b.

JULY • The *New York Telegraph*, under the Headline "Find New Comedian," reports: "The Pacific Coast has been talking for three months about a singing comedian named Al Jolson. . . . Almost a month ago stories of the big success of Jolson reached the ears of Lew Dockstadter, who journeyed to Fort Worth to hear the new comedian. Jolson made a big hit with Dockstadter and was immediately engaged." Jolson will join Dockstadter's Minstrels, the biggest minstrel show in America, in August. **12** Milton Berle (Milton Berlinger) b. **25** Jack Gilford (Jacob Gellman) b.

AUGUST 10 *The Traveling Salesman* (280), James Forbes's comedy at the Liberty, in which an attempted swindle is the problem and marriage is the solution, stars Gertrude Coghlan and Frank McIntyre. **17** In *The Man From Home* (496), by Booth Tarkington and Harry L. Wilson, at the Astor, a Hoosier, played by William Hodge, proves more stalwart

Flo Ziegfeld ZCI

than several members of Britain's nobility. **26** Tony Pastor d. **30** Fanny Borach, appearing in Birmingham, Alabama, in *The Girls from Happyland*, for the first time uses the professional name Fanny Brice. **31** Playwright William Saroyan b.

SEPTEMBER 22 Blanche Bates stars at the Stuyvesant in *The Fighting Hope* (231), by William J. Hurlbut, in which she plays a wife, seeking to exonerate her convicted husband, only to find evidence of his guilt. **29** *A Gentleman From Mississippi* (407) opens at the Bijou. Douglas Fairbanks stars in this tale of political corruption and romance, written by Harrison Rhodes and Thomas A. Wise, who is also in the cast.

OCTOBER 5 Director Joshua Logan b.

NOVEMBER 16 Burgess Meredith b. **17** *Salvation Nell* (71), by Edward Sheldon, opens at the Hackett Theatre. A landmark in American theatrical realism, it stars Minnie Maddern Fiske in a drama that sympathetically portrays bar patrons and prostitutes.

DECEMBER 30 Maxine Elliott stars in *The Chaperone* at the opening of Maxine Elliott's Theatre, said to have been financed by J.P. Morgan.

1909

JANUARY 19 Eugene Walter's *The Easiest Way* (157), with Frances Starr in the lead role, opens at the Stuyvesant-Belasco. This story of a kept woman is notable for Starr's final lines, to her maid: "Dress up my body and paint my face. I'm going to Rector's to make a hit, and to hell with the rest." *The New York Times* comments: "With so few economic options for women, the blame is more society's, the play suggests, than that of the women's weak morals."

MARCH 24 In *A Fool There Was* (93), a play by Porter Emerson Browne, at the Liberty, Robert Hilliard plays a man destroyed by the wiles of "The Woman," played by Katherine Kaelred. Theda Bara plays her in the 1915 film that will make her the "Vamp."

APRIL 8 Helena Modjeska d. **23** Martin Beck's 2,500-seat Orpheum Theatre, replacing the house destroyed by the 1906 earthquake, opens in San Francisco. **29** Tom Ewell b.

MAY 4 Howard Da Silva (Howard Silverblatt) b.

JUNE • Producer Morris Gest m. Reina Belasco, daughter of producer David Belasco. **7** Jessica Tandy b. **14** Flo Ziegfeld's *Follies of 1909* (64) opens at the Jardin de Paris. Nora Bayes, Sophie Tucker, Mae Murray, Lillian Lorraine and later in the run, Eva Tanguay, star. Tucker, who leaves after five weeks, will call herself "the girl Ziegfeld forgot to glorify." A highlight of the show is an airplane, flying over the audience on a monorail.

AUGUST 15 The *Pittsburgh Dispatch* headline, "The Gay White Way On Old Broadway Is All A-Dazzle Now," suggests the image of the Times Square theatre district that America is coming to accept. With theatres reopening after their summer hiatus, "it will be the White Way in reality, for there has been added to the electric display quite a number of attractive signs, and with the theatres in full swing the sight will surely dazzle the visitor."

SEPTEMBER • In a move aimed at independent vaudeville producer William Morris, Martin Beck says that acts playing in houses other than his Orpheum circuit in the West will have no chance of being booked into an Orpheum theatre. Next year Beck will also feud with the United Booking Office and William Hammerstein over bookings. **4** Winchell Smith's comedy, *The Fortune Hunter* (345), John Barrymore's first major success, is the opening attraction at the Gaiety Theatre. Barrymore "is now lost to musical comedy forever," *The New York Times* hopes. The paper says that "there is no reason to doubt his possibilities." **4** Playwright Clyde Fitch d. **7** Director Elia Kazan (Elia Kazanjoglous) b. **13** Actor-director Herbert Berghof b.

OCTOBER 2 Eugene O'Neill marries the pregnant Kathleen Jenkins and leaves immediately, alone, for a mining expedition to Honduras. He will never see her again, and they will divorce in 1912. **30** The *New York Dramatic Mirror*, reviewing the Three Keatons at the Victoria, says that 16-year-old Buster ought to be allowed to do more singing. In fact, he could "develop into an excellent comedian, singer and possibly a monologist. That he has a future upon the stage goes without saying."

NOVEMBER 6 The New Theatre, wih Winthrop Ames as artistic director and Lee Shubert as business manager, inaugurates its maiden season of repertory with *Antony and Cleopatra*, starring Julia Marlowe and E.H. Sothern. Funded by New York's upper crust, the project seeks to raise the level of theatre in the city. **8** Katharine Hepburn b. **9** The New Theatre's only American play in its maiden season, Edward Sheldon's *The Nigger*, opens in repertory. With a theme of Southern race relations, it does well, despite the admonition of agent Alice Kauser to playwright Sheldon that "[t]he nigger problem is not one the American people wish to see on the boards." **10** *Seven Days* (397), a comedy by Mary Roberts Rinehart and Avery Hopwood, opens at the Astor. It stars Herbert Corthell, Lucille La Verne and Hope Latham. **22** Nine-year-old Helen Hayes—her name shortened from Helen Hayes Brown by producer Lew Fields—makes her Broadway debut in Victor Herbert's *Old Dutch* at the Herald Square Theatre. According to *The Evening World*, "The kiddie knows a thing or two." Also in the cast are John Bunny and Vernon Castle. Victor Herbert is conducting, and in the audience are Diamond Jim Brady and Lillian Russell.

DECEMBER 21 Clyde Fitch's last play, *The City* (190), starring Walter Hampden and Lucille Watson in a drama that combines politics, drugs, and incest, creates a sensation at the Lyceum with its line: "You're a goddamn liar!" Two women fainted when it opened in New Haven on November 15. **30** Antoinette Perry m. wealthy executive Frank Frueauff.

1910

• Eugene O'Neill goes to sea on a four-rigger, bound for Argentina.

JANUARY 10 *The Old Town* (171), a musical by George Ade and Gustav Luders, is the first presentation at the new Globe Theatre (later the Lunt-Fontanne), co-owned by producer Charles Dillingham. Fred Stone and Dave Montgomery star, and Peggy Wood makes her Broadway debut. **12** Patsy Kelly (Bridget Kelly) b.

FEBRUARY 4 Eddie Foy, Jr. b.

MARCH 12 Producer Roger L. Stevens b. **20** Writing in the *Chicago Tribune*, critic Percy Hammond notes that Eugene Walter is a "maker of sturdy, exciting, cinematographic plays." It is probably one of the first serious pieces in which the stage is seen in terms of the screen, rather than the reverse.

MAY 15 Constance Cummings (Constance Halverstadt) b. **21** Nancy Walker, (Anna Swoyer), daughter of vaudevillian Dewey Barto, b.

JUNE 10 Juveniles Walter Winchell and George Jessel are part of Gus Edward's *Song Revue*, opening at the Hudson Theatre in Union Hill, New Jersey. **10** Julie Haydon (Donella Lightfoot Donaldson) b. **18** E. (Everett) G. Marshall b. **20** Bert Williams, Fanny

Brice, and Lillian Lorraine star in Flo Ziegfeld's *Follies of 1910* (88), opening at the Jardin de Paris. Williams is the first black artist to appear in a major white show, and newspapers report some dissension in the company about his starring role. At his request, his contract specifies that he will not appear together with any female performers and that the show will not tour in the South. **23** Playwright Jean Anouilh b. **29** Lyricist-composer Frank Loesser b.

AUGUST 12 Eddie Foy debuts with his new act, "The Seven Little Foys," at a Lambs Club picnic. **30** *Madame Sherry* (231), by Otto Harbach and Karl Hoschna—one of their six collaborations—opens at the New Amsterdam. "Every Little Movement" is the hit song ("Put Your Arms Around Me, Honey" is interpolated), and the stars are Jack Gardner, Ralph Herz, and Lina Abarbanell.

SEPTEMBER 1 John Barrymore m. Katherine Harris. **3** The Stuyvesant Theatre, which opened in 1907, is renamed the Belasco. **19** *Get-Rich-Quick Wallingford* (424), George M. Cohan's comedy, his first nonmusical triumph, opens at the Gaiety. Frances Ring and Hale Hamilton star.

OCTOBER 4 Ed Wynn makes his Broadway debut in Alfred E. Aaron's musical, *The Deacon and the Lady*, at the New York Theatre. **20** Adelaide Hall b.

NOVEMBER 5 Sophie Tucker is arrested in Portland, Oregon for singing "The Angle Worm Wiggle" at the Pantages Theatre. The charges will be dismissed. In January, *Variety* reported that her "Soul Kiss" song had left a New York audience "stunned by its clever daring." **7** Victor Herbert's *Naughty Marietta* (136), with book and lyrics by Rida Johnson Young, opens at the New York Theatre. It stars Emma Trentini and Orville Harrold, from producer Oscar Hammerstein's opera company. **7** Lynn Fontanne makes her Broadway debut in *Mr. Preedy and the Countess* (24) at Nazimova's Thirty-ninth Street Theatre. **7** The American Federation of Labor charters the White Rats vaudeville union., led by Harry Mountford.

DECEMBER 13 Lillian Roth (Lillian Rutstein) b. **18** Playwright and librettist Abe Burrows (Abram Borowitz) b. **19** Playwright Jean Genet b.

1911

• Benay Venuata b.

JANUARY 15 Producer-director Cy Feuer b.

The Winter Garden Theatre will become the Shuberts' flagship house and the home of many of Al Jolson's shows LYNCH

MARCH 13 Hazel Dawn makes her Broadway debut in *The Pink Lady* (312), a musical by Ivan Caryl and C.M.S. McLellan, at the New Amsterdam. **20** The Winter Garden, a 1600-seat Shubert showcase opens with *La Belle Paree* (104), a revue with music by Jerome Kern. Ending the evening, a blackfaced Al Jolson, in his Broadway debut, sings "Paris Is A Paradise for Coons." **26** Playwright Tennessee Williams (Thomas Lanier Williams) b.

MAY 11 Phil Silvers b. **27** Vincent Price b.

JUNE 10 Playwright Terrence Rattigan b. **26** *The Ziegfeld Follies of 1911* (80), for the first time bearing the producer's name, opens at the Jardin de Paris. The stars include Fanny Brice, Bert Williams, the Dolly Sisters, George White, Bessie McCoy, Lillian Lorraine and, appearing for the first time, Leon Errol. The score includes numbers by Irving Berlin and Jerome Kern.

JULY • Fanny Brice gets into a backstage fistfight at *The Ziegfeld Follies* with Ziegfeld's mistress and cast member Lillian Lorraine. **16** Ginger Rogers (Virginia McMath) b. **18** Hume Cronyn b.

SEPTEMBER 18 George Arliss scores a stage triumph in *Disraeli* (280), opening at Wallack's Theatre. He will repeat the role in the 1929 film. **26** George Broadhurst's *Bought and Paid For* (431), opening at producer William Brady's Playhouse, elevates Frank Craven to stardom. **27** French entertainer Gaby Deslys makes her American debut in the otherwise unremarkable *The Revue of Revues* (55), at the Winter Garden.

OCTOBER • Eugene O'Neill has one line in his father's touring production of *The Count of Monte Cristo*, abbreviated for vaudeville. O'Neill says, "Is he . . ." over the body of a character who has just died. Like his brother, Jamie, also in the show, Eugene often goes on drunk while their mother watches from the wings in a drug-induced stupor. **17** David Belasco's *The Return of Peter Grimm* (231) stars David Warfield, at the Belasco Theatre, in the story of a man who returns from the dead to right a wrong. **20** The Fulton Theatre (later the Helen Hayes) opens with *The Cave Man*.

NOVEMBER 20 Players from Ireland's Abbey Theatre, among them Arthur Sinclair, Sara Allgood, J.M. Kerrigan, Cathleen Nesbitt, and Una O'Connor, open a repertory season at Maxine Elliott's Theatre. The season of a several weeks is a failure and is marked by a disturbance at a performance of *The Playboy of the Western World* when potatoes come flying out of the audience toward the stage. **27** Producer David Merrick (David Margulois) b.

DECEMBER 8 Lee J. Cobb b. **23** Karl Hoschna d. **25** Edward Knoblauch's play, *Kismet* (184), starring Otis Skinner as the beggar poet of Baghdad, opens at the Knickerbocker.

1912

• Laurette Taylor m. playwright J. Hartley Manners.

JANUARY 8 Opening at Daly's Theatre, Laurette Taylor makes her first important mark on Broadway in a drama of passion and sacrifice on a Hawaiian island. Walton Tully's play,*The Bird of Paradise* (112), Oliver Morosco's first major production, will become the operetta *Luana* in 1930 and a film in 1932 and 1951. **8** José Ferrer (José Vincente Ferrer de Otero y Cintron) b.

FEBRUARY • Irving Berlin m. singer Dorothy Goetz. She d. of typhoid fever on July 17. **2** Composer Burton Lane b.

MARCH 5 *Whirl of Society* (136), a revue opening at the Winter Garden, stars Al Jolson, who has become a Shubert meal ticket. Blossom Seeley is also in the cast.

APRIL 5 *The Wall Street Girl* (56), opening at the Cohan, is Karl Hoschna's last musical. In the cast are Charles Winninger, Blanche Ring singing "I Want a Regular Man," and Will Rogers twirling a rope and making comic patter. **9** August Strindberg's *The Father* (31) opens at the Lyceum. Coproducer Warner Oland stars. **22** Ed Gallagher and Al Shean (uncle of the Marx Brothers) debut in *The Rose Maid* (176), an operetta by Bruno Granichstaedten and Robert B. Smith, at the Globe. **30** Eve Arden (Eunice Quedens) b.

MAY • Eugene O'Neill attempts suicide by a drug overdose. **25** Reviewing Mae West, who is doing a solo act for the first time, *Variety* editor Sime Silverman notes: "She is of the eccentric type. She sings rag melodies and dresses oddly, but still lacks that touch of class that is becoming requisite nowadays in the first class houses."

JUNE 4 Rosalind Russell b.

JULY 22 The Shuberts stage the *Passing Show of 1912* (136), the first of 12 annual revues, with Charlotte Greenwood, Trixie Friganza and Eugene and Willie Howard, who are moving from vaudeville to Broadway.

AUGUST • Eugene O'Neill becomes a reporter for the New London *Telegraph*. **15** Wendy Hiller b.

SEPTEMBER 11 Jane Cowl achieves stardom as a woman wrongfully accused of theft in *Within the Law* (541), by Bayard Veiller, opening as the premiere production at the new Eltinge Theatre on Forty-second Street.

OCTOBER 11 Eugene O'Neill and Kathleen Jenkins are divorced. **21** *The Ziegfeld Follies of 1912* (88) opens in the fall for the first time at the Moulin Rouge. It features Lillian Lorraine, Bert Williams, and Leon Errol.

NOVEMBER • Eugene O'Neill develops tuberculosis. He will spend five months in a sanitarium, where he will begin to write plays. • Fanny Brice meets gambler Nicky Arnstein while performing in Baltimore in the show *The Whirl of Society*. **13** *The Red Petticoat*, a musical at Daly's Theatre, has the first complete Broadway score composed by Jerome Kern. **21** Weber and Fields make their last Broadway appearance together at the new Weber and Fields's Music Hall (later the Forty-fourth Street Theatre) with a vaudeville/revue called *Roly Poly* (60), starring Nora Bayes and Marie Dressler. **24** Playwright Garson Kanin, brother of playwright Michael Kanin and brother-in-law of playwright Fay Kanin, b. **28** Blanche Bates m. journalist George Creel, causing a rift with her mentor, producer David Belasco, who did not want her to marry at all.

Lillian Lorraine *ZCI*

DECEMBER 2 Rudolph Friml's first operetta, *The Firefly* (120), with book and lyrics by Otto Hauerbach, opens at the Lyric. It stars Emma Trentini. **2** The comedy team of Clark and McCullough—Bobby Clark and Paul McCullough—previously a circus act, make their vaudeville debut at the Opera House in New Brunswick, New Jersey. **20** *Peg o' My Heart* (603), starring Laurette Taylor as an appealing orphan in a play by her husband, J. Hartley Manners, inaugurates the Cort Theatre on Forty-eighth Street. On the cover of the program is the quote: "Oh, there's nothing half so sweet as life's young dream." It will have the longest run thus far for any straight play and will become Taylor's signature role. **22** Actors Equity is founded.

1913

JANUARY 8 Austin Strong's *A Good Little Devil* (131), starring Mary Pickford, Lillian Gish (in her Broadway debut) and Ernest Truex, opens at the Republic. **9** Anna Held divorces Flo Ziegfeld, her common law husband. **18** Danny Kaye (David Daniel Kominski) b.

FEBRUARY • The Shuberts and Klaw and Erlanger reach an agreement not to compete in booking and controlling theatres in Boston, Chicago, St.Louis, and Philadelphia. • Vaudevillians Nora Bayes and Jack Norwith, "The Happiest Married Couple of the Stage," are divorced. **3** Paul Reuben's musical, *The Sunshine Girl* (160), starring Julia Sanderson, opens at the Knickerbocker but draws much of its business from the public's new obsession with ballroom dancing and the presence in the cast of Vernon and Irene Castle. **6** Al Jolson opens in *The Honeymoon Express* (158) at the Winter Garden, with Gaby Deslys and Fanny Brice, in a musical farce.

Laurette Taylor in *Peg O' My Heart* PF

MARCH 6 Ella Logan b. **14** *Damaged Goods* (66) stars Richard Bennett in play by Eugene Brieux about syphilis. This is a special matinée at the Fulton Theatre that leads to another on March 17 and then regular performances next month. The show's press agent, Edward Bernays, is the founder of modern public relations and the nephew of Sigmund Freud. It will be filmed by Mutual in 1915. **14** John Garfield (Jules Garfinkel) b. **21** Sophie Tucker is divorced from Louis Tuck. **22** Karl Malden (Malden Sekulovich) b. **24** Built by Martin Beck, the $1,000,000, 1,736-seat Palace Theatre in Times Square, the first $2 house and soon to become the Mecca of vaudeville, opens with a Monday matinée. The first two-shows-a-day bill includes a Spanish violinist, dancers, a pantomimist, a cartoonist, a high wire act, an operetta excerpt with a cast of 30, and comedian Ed Wynn. *Variety*'s headline, "Palace $2 Vaudeville a Joke," exemplifies the negative critical reaction that greets the new showplace. The paper calls the show "the worst exhibition of showmanship New York has known." *Billboard* will report of Ed Wynn that his work "will in no way tend to increase his reputation as a funmaker." But after the first few months, stars such as Ethel Barrymore and Sarah Bernhardt will begin to fill the house.

MAY 1 The Longacre Theatre opens its doors for the first time with *Are You a Crook?* (11), a farce by William J. Hurlbut and Frances Whitehouse. **3** Playwright William Inge b. **26** The Actors Equity, founded in 1912, formally comes into being as an active theatre union. **31** *Variety* notes that actors De Wolfe Hopper and Nat Goodwin have married again. Each is on his fifth wife.

JUNE • Show business-connected enterprises are having trouble renting office space in Times Square because landlords fear that they will keep other tenants away. **16** *The Ziegfeld Follies of 1913* (96) debuts at the New Amsterdam, where it will play for 13 of the next 16 years. Leon Errol is the star of this year's edition. Comic Frank Tinney and dancer Ann Pennington are making their first appearances in the show.

JULY 8 Critic Walter Kerr b.

AUGUST 16 *Potash and Perlmutter* (441), by Montague Glass and Charles Klein, opens at the Cohan Theatre. Based on stories that appeared in *The Saturday Evening Post*, this "indescribably enjoyable" comedy, according to *The Times*, stars Barney Bernard and Alexander Carr as garment manufacturers with money problems. *Variety* reports that preference for first-night seats has gone to "applicants that come from the vicinity of Canal Street and Broadway," meaning Jewish businessmen who look like they could be in the play. **28** Ethel Barrymore makes her Palace debut in the Richard Harding Davis play, *Civilization*.

SEPTEMBER 8 Victor Herbert's *Sweethearts* (136) opens at the New Amsterdam, where star Christie MacDonald sings the title tune. **22** George M. Cohan's *Seven Keys to Baldpate* (320), a comedy/mystery starring Wallace Eddinger, based on Earl Derr Bigger's novel, is at the Astor. The drama opens at the Baldpate Inn on a dark and stormy night with the caretakers preparing for a visitor. "Mebbe the feller's committed some crime and is comin' here to hide," says one.

OCTOBER 2 The Shubert Theatre opens with a production of *Hamlet*. *The New York Times* reports that "[o]utside the congestion of vehicles of all sorts was greatly relieved by the private roadway connecting Forty-fourth and Forty-fifth Streets." This space, between the Shubert and Booth Theatres (the Booth will open shortly) and the Astor Hotel, is Shubert Alley. **16** The Booth Theatre opens on Forty-fifth Street with *The Great Adventure* (52), a play by Arnold Bennett. In the cast is young Guthrie McClintic. **27** The Palace Theatre, nominally controlled by producer Martin Beck, is taken over by B.F. Keith and the United Booking Office and will be officially known as B.F. Keith's Palace Theatre. The takeover stems from a complicated financial deal in which the theatre's need to use the United Booking Office to secure talent and the UBO's need to pay off Oscar Hammerstein, who had exclusive rights to use that talent in his own theatre in Times Square, led to Keith's gaining a controlling stake in the Palace.

NOVEMBER • The on-again, off-again truce between the Shuberts and the Theatre Syndicate is on again. **5** Vivian Leigh (Vivien Hartley) b. **23** The Chorus People's Alliance, a union for chorus girls, is formed under the auspices of the American Federation of Labor. **25** With the opening of *The Misleading Lady* (183) at the Fulton, George Abbott makes his stage debut, beginning a 76-year career on Broadway. Lewis Stone is the star in the drama directed by Holbrook Blinn.

DECEMBER 1 Mary Martin b. **12** Producer Margo Jones b. **16** British teenager Eva Le Gallienne, who aspires to a career in the theatre, is taken to a performance of Sarah Bernhardt in *Jeanne Doré* and afterward goes backstage to meet the great actress. The youngster is awestruck.

1914

JANUARY 10 Sigmund Romberg's first musical production *The Whirl of the World* (161), an unexceptional revue, opens at the Winter Garden. It stars "Jew comedian" (*Variety*) Willie Howard. Also in the cast are his brother, Eugene, and Lillian Lorraine. **30** David Wayne (Wayne McMeekan) b.

FEBRUARY 17 Arthur Kennedy (John Arthur Kennedy) b. **20** According to *Variety*, President Wilson attends vaudeville shows regularly.

MARCH • The dance craze has started to diminish nightly theatre attendance, and some producers are thinking of countering it with daily matinées so that people can go out dancing at night and still see a show. **24** George Bernard Shaw's new play, *Pygmalion*, has its American premiere at the Irving Place Theater—in German! Its world premiere last fall, in Vienna, was also in German. *The New York Times* calls it "a comedy of phonetics," in which a Professor Higgins plays to the Galatea represented by one Liza Doolittle. The performance, according to *The Times*, was "well-received." **26** B.F. Keith d.

APRIL 11 Producer Flo Ziegfeld marries Billie Burke in between the matinée and evening performances of *Jerry*, in which Burke is starring at the Lyceum. Ziegfeld's first name, Florenz, is spelled "Florence" on their marriage certificate. When reporters ask Anna Held, Ziegfeld's first wife, how she feels about the marriage, she says, "[T]hat is a matter of perfect indifference to me . . . one wants a husband who can talk something besides business to his wife." She goes on: "Remarriage is like eating something that has been cooked before, something that if you wish to enjoy, you must heat up. And even then it is not the same." **17** Playwright Edward Chodorov, brother of Jerome Chodorov, b.

MAY • For the first time in large numbers, stage actors at liberty are beginning to accept summer work in the movies. • Emulating a custom begun in the Yiddish theatre, Broadway houses are stirring up end-of-the-season business with half-price tickets. **24** Lilli Palmer (Lillie Peiser) b. **27** Laurette Taylor breaks the record tonight for continuous performances by an actress when she plays in *Peg O' My Heart* for the 600th time. Women in the audience receive free perfume to commemorate the event.

Show Boat—a memorable, landmark musical. BROWN

Broadway Comes of Age

1914–1942

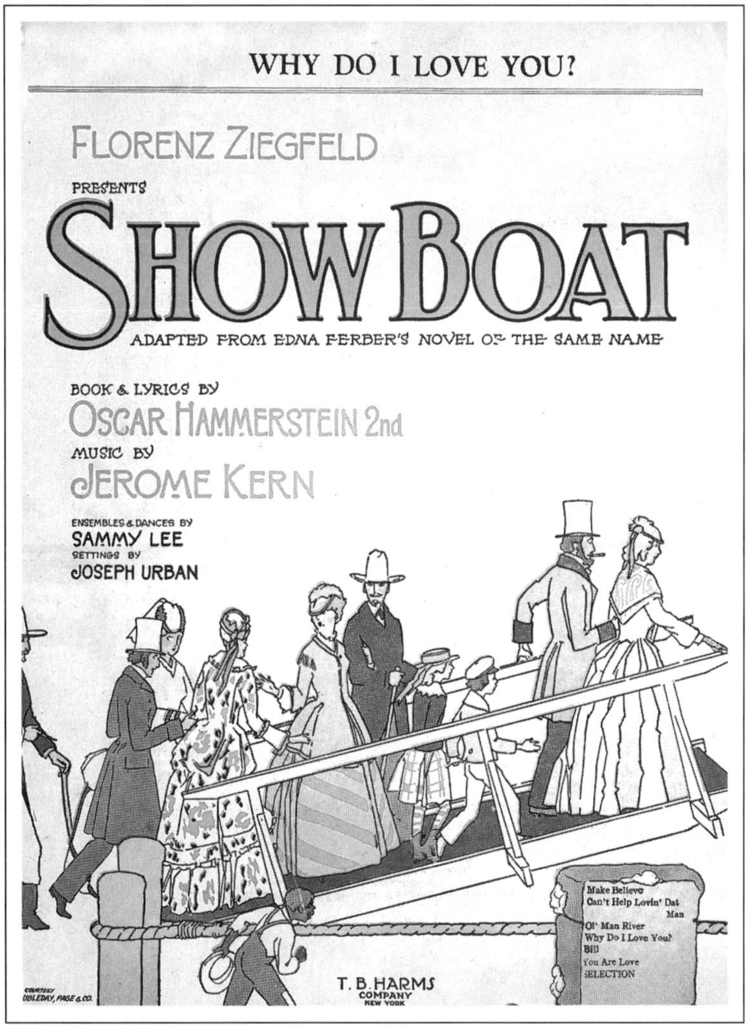

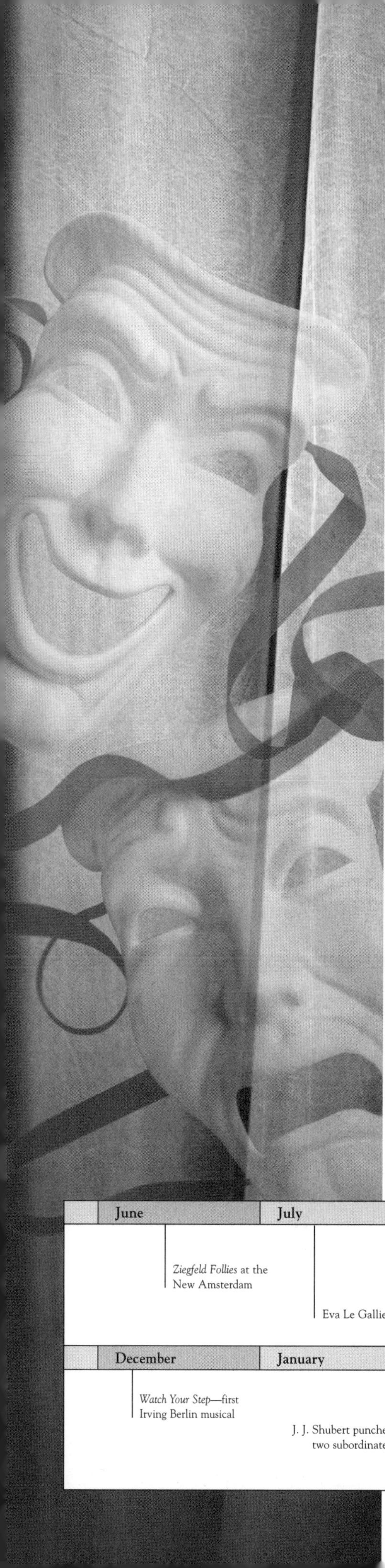

1914–15

New sounds fill the air. Jerome Kern's innovative "They Wouldn't Believe Me," in 4/4 time, is a sign that the Broadway musical is about to segue away from the waltz. At the Princess Theatre, a new series of musicals also foreshadows the modern era. Broadway revues are raiding vaudeville for talent, and Shaw's *Pygmalion*, first heard in New York in German(!), debuts in English. Eugene O'Neill decides to be "an artist or nothing," Actors Equity is already having problems with the importing of British actors, Marilyn Miller is an ingenue, Alexander Woollcott is *critic non-grata* at Shubert shows, and producer Charles Frohman goes down with the ship—the *Lusitania*.

- Popular spots for after the show: Murray's, the Claridge, the New York Roof, Rector's, Churchill's, Reisenweber's, the 400 Club, and then breakfast at Jack's or Ciro's
- New type of entertainment: the midnight revue, at restaurants and Broadway rooftops
- What Sophie Tucker is not allowed to sing on the Keith circuit: "Who Paid the Rent for Mrs. Rip Van Winkle?"
- Vaudeville impresario Martin Beck's nickname among professionals: "Two-Beers Beck"
- What 15-year-old pianist George Gershwin is told at Remick's, the Tin Pan Alley song publisher where he's begun to work, when he submits a song he's written: "You're here as a pianist, not a writer."
- Average weekly gross at the Palace: $21,000, from which $6–8,000 is net
- First Irving Berlin musical: *Watch Your Step*
- What President Woodrow Wilson says about vaudeville and theatre (quoted in the *New York Dramatic Mirror*): "If there is a bad act at a vaudeville show, you can rest reasonably secure that the next one may not be so bad; but from a bad play, there is no escape."
- Number of New York theatres controlled by producer Charles Frohman: 5
- How Nora Bayes is billed: "The Greatest Single Woman Singing Comedienne in the World"
- Why chorus girls aren't what they used to be: they're thinner, are beginning to appear with completely bare legs, and are doing more dancing and less parading en masse

Productions on Broadway: 133

June	July	August	September	October	November
Ziegfeld Follies at the New Amsterdam	Eva Le Gallienne stage debut	War disrupts vaudeville	No war jokes in Orpheum theatres	Alfred Drake born	Chorines must wear "knee panties" in Boston

December	January	February	March	April	May
Watch Your Step—first Irving Berlin musical	J. J. Shubert punches two subordinates	Washington Square Players debut	First Princess Theatre musical	Shuberts ban critic Alexander Woollcott	Producer Charles Frohman goes down with *Lusitania*

Personalities

JUNE • George M. Cohan becomes abbot of the Friars Club. **21** Sixteen-year-old Marilyn Miller, who opened June 10 in *The Passing Show of 1914*, is described by *The New York Times* as "[o]ne of the most fascinating ingenues to have her name flashed across Broadway this season."

JULY 16 Twenty-five-year-old Eugene O'Neill writes to Harvard Professor George Pierce Baker, asking to enroll in Baker's famed drama classes. O'Neill, whose first one-act plays are about to be published, declares that rather than settling for being "a mediocre journeyman playwright," he has decided to become "an artist or nothing." Baker admits him. **21** Eva Le Gallienne makes her stage debut in *Monna Vanna* at the Queens Theatre in London. **27** Keith circuit manager Edward F. Albee orders Sophie Tucker to drop from her act the song, "Who Paid the Rent for Mrs. Rip Van Winkle," which she sang at today's Palace Theatre matinée.

Marilyn Miller ZCI

SEPTEMBER 26 *Variety* reviews the Four Marx Bros. and Co., performing in Chicago. Leonard [Chico] does Italian dialect and plays the piano, and Arthur [Harpo], while using makeup that is "not pleasant," is a fine harpist. The reviewer merely mentions the presence of Julius [Groucho] and notes that Milton [Gummo] is the handsome one. "It looks

Plays and Musicals

JUNE 1 *The Ziegfeld Follies of 1914* (112) is at the New Amsterdam. Bert Williams, Leon Errol, Ann Pennington, and Ed Wynn, in his first *Follies* and first stage appearance outside vaudeville, are the stars.

AUGUST 14 *Twin Beds* (411), a farce by Salisbury Field and Margaret Mayo, starring Madge Kennedy, opens at the Fulton Theatre. The outbreak of war today in Europe is distracting potential audiences, so advertising signs are placed on trucks and wagons, with the drivers told to "break down" at busy intersections. **19** *On Trial* (365), by Elmer Reizenstein (not yet Elmer Rice), opens at the Candler Theatre. Starring Frederick Perry and Mary Ryan, it adopts the cinematic flashback technique and is an early instance of a drama encompassing a whole trial. **24** *The Girl From Utah* (120), a British musical by Paul Reubens and Sidney Jones, starring Julia Sanderson, Donald Brian, and Joseph Cawthorn, opens at the Knickerbocker. Several Jerome Kern songs are interpolated, including his first hit, "They Didn't Believe Me," an innovative number in 4/4 time rather than the waltz tempo more typical of musicals, foreshadowing the future direction of show tunes. **26** Roi Cooper Megrue's mystery *Under Cover* (349) opens at the Cort. William Courtenay, De Witt C. Jennings, Lucille Watson, Lily Cahill, and Rae Selwyn, wife of the show's producer, are in the cast.

SEPTEMBER 8 *It Pays to Advertise* (399), a farce about selling soap, by Roi Cooper Megrue and Walter Hackett, opens at the Cohan Theatre. The cast includes Grant Mitchell and Ruth Shepley. **28** *Daddy Long Legs* (264), starring Ruth Chatterton in a comedy by Jean Webster, in which an orphan falls in love with her benefactor, opens at the Gaiety. It catapults Chatterton—"[S]he is all grace," says *Theatre* magazine—to stardom. **30** George Broadhurst's *The Law of the Land* (221), starring Julia Dean as a woman who deserves to get away with murder, opens at the Forty-eighth Street Theatre. Hearst's *American* sends a replacement for its critic, Alan Dale, because the playwright had been complaining about Dale. Dale, who has been with the paper for 19 years, will resign.

Business and Society

JULY • Equity denies producers' charges that they discriminate against British actors working in America.

AUGUST 7 *Variety*'s second page headline is "Europe's Wild Dream War Stopping Show Business." Some vaudeville performers are stranded abroad, while others have trouble converting money paid to them in foreign currencies. Elsie Janis, playing the Palace in New York, demands to be paid in gold. Producers are worried about foreign acts they've booked, while American actors are concerned with a possible influx of British performers.

SEPTEMBER • The Orpheum circuit is keeping war jokes off its stages to support President Wilson's neutrality policy.

OCTOBER 26 Theatre attendance is down around the country, and there is talk of cutting salaries for legitimate players similar to the 15 percent cuts made last week by the United Booking Office on its circuit of vaudeville theatres.

NOVEMBER 4 After the exposed flesh in *The Passing Show of 1914* disturbs Mayor Curley, Boston's "Purity Squad" threatens producers who allow bare legs in their

Births, Deaths, and Marriages

JUNE 6 Robert Benchley m. Gertrude Darling.

JULY 3 Leueen MacGrath b. (She sometimes gave the year as 1919.)

OCTOBER 4 Critic Brendan Gill b. **7** Alfred Drake (Alfred Capurro) b.

NOVEMBER 13 Playwright William Gibson b.

FEBRUARY 28 Zero Mostel (Samuel Mostel), son of a rabbi, b.

APRIL 27 Bert and Betty Wheeler, vaudeville partners, m.

MAY 3 Betty Comden b. **6** Orson Welles (George Orson Welles) b. **7** Broadway's

like a good piece of property" is the verdict.

OCTOBER 21 Producer Charles Frohman signs a new, five-year contract with Billie Burke, scotching rumors that he would drop her because she has married and has, thus, in Frohman's view, surrendered her allure.

NOVEMBER 3 The *Columbus [Ohio] Dispatch*, reviewing Gus Edwards's kiddie act at the Keith's, praises Little Georgie (16-year-old George Jessel), "who excels in a Yiddish song and an imitation of Eddie Foy." The paper also reports that "Eddie Cantor [a senior member of the troupe at 22] is one of the most refreshing blackfaces seen here in a long while. . . . When he has restrained the ultrafeminine, slap-me-on-the-wrist imitation just a trifle there will be hardly anything in his act that will not deserve the highest praise." **17** Irving Berlin creates his own music publishing company, Irving Berlin, Inc.

DECEMBER 28 Eva Tanguay, billed as "The Girl Who Made Vaudeville Famous," makes her Palace debut. **30** Producer Harrison Grey Fiske, husband of actress Minnie Maddern Fiske and former editor and publisher of the *Dramatic Mirror*, files for bankruptcy.

JANUARY 1 *Variety* notes that revues, rapidly gaining in popularity, are leaning heavily on vaudeville talent, such as Joe and Buster Keaton, W. C. Fields, Leo Carrillo, and Cantor (Eddie) and Lee for their casts. **6** An Ohio judge dismisses charges against vaudeville star Eddie Foy for violating the state's child labor law by having three of his children below the age of 14 perform with him. He's running into similar problems in other states. **23** J. J. Shubert, incensed that the managers of the Shubert-controlled Hippodrome will not send over to the Winter Garden the trumpets and drums he says are needed there for an upcoming show, goes to the Hippodrome himself to retrieve them. He argues with and then punches two of the managers and fires them. **24** Alla Nazimova is so popular in the one-act play *War Brides* at the Palace that she will be held over, playing a total of three weeks.

OCTOBER 6 Ferenc Molnar's *The Phantom Rival* (127), which *The New York Times's* Alexander Woollcott calls "one of the few really fine comedies of recent years," opens at the Belasco. It stars Leo Ditrichstein and Laura Hope Crews. **12** George Bernard Shaw's *Pygmalion* receives its initial U.S. performance in English at the Park Theatre, with Mrs. Patrick Campbell, who also starred in it on the London stage, in this production. **20** David Montgomery and Fred Stone open at the Globe in *Chin-Chin* (295), a musical by Ivan Caryll and Anne Caldwell, based on the story of Aladdin, in which "[e]v'ry chink goes just as dippy as a coon from Mis-si-si-pi."

NOVEMBER 10 The 299-seat Punch and Judy Theatre opens on Forty-ninth Street with Harold Chapin's *The Marriage of Columbine*, a British import that will not make it to Christmas.

DECEMBER 8 The first of Irving Berlin's 21 musicals, *Watch Your Step* (175), at the Amsterdam, features the final appearance of the team of Irene and Vernon Castle. It capitalizes on the new craze for dancing and ragtime and introduces "Play A Simple Melody." The show is virtually plotless, almost a revue, and Harry B. Smith is credited with the "[b]ook (if any)." The *Times* refers to Berlin as "the young master of syncopation." **25** George M. Cohan's revue, *Hello, Broadway* (123), opens at the Astor. Cohan has dropped the plot, letting his sketches stand on their own, and he has the performers, including Peggy Wood and Louise Dresser, help change the scenery as they enter and exit, quickening the pace to something reminiscent of the Weber and Fields burlesques.

JANUARY 5 Flo Ziegfeld's *Midnight Frolic*, the first of a series of annual shows that resembles a night club performance—the audience is seated at tables—opens on the New Amsterdam Theatre roof. A dance orchestra plays during intermission and after the show. Set designer Joseph Urban, working with Ziegfeld for the first time, will be with him through 1931. **7** Owen Davis's *Sinners* (220), about a small-town girl who goes wrong in the big city, opens at the Playhouse. The cast includes Alice Brady, Emma Dunn and

---

shows. They agree to have their chorines wear tights and "knee panties."

FEBRUARY • The United Booking Office warns vaudeville acts that they may have trouble getting stage bookings if they take picture work, considered to be a rival ("opposition") business. Producers are also worried that alternative offers of employment may make performers feel more independent.

APRIL • The Justice Department is investigating several major producers, including Edgar Selwyn and Charles Dillingham, for possible antitrust violations, just as the Department recently launched a similar inquiry into professional baseball.

---

most prominent producer, Charles Frohman, and librettist Charles Klein are among the more than 1,000 passengers killed when a German torpedo hits the *Lusitania*.

Personalities

FEBRUARY 2 Billie Burke, performing in Boston at the Hollis Theatre, pricks her finger on a bouquet of roses before her performance. During the show, she collapses and almost dies of blood poisoning. **27** The Marx Brothers play the Palace, with a 45-minute musical comedy, *Home Again.*

APRIL 1 The Shuberts, annoyed by *New York Times* critic Alexander Woollcott's review of their last show, *Taking Chances*—"vulgar," wrote the critic—bar him from tonight's opening of their play, *The Revolt,* at Maxine Elliott's Theatre. In return, the *Times* says it will not review any Shubert shows and won't accept their ads. **3** It took a court order to get *The New York Times* critic Alexander Woollcott into the Shubert Theatre to review *Trilby* tonight. Woollcott will write that the play "is well worth going to see—even if you have to get in by the aid of an injunction."

MAY 1 Producer Charles Frohman boards the *Lusitania* for the Atlantic crossing. One of his associates, concerned that he will be traveling in a war zone, is reported to have asked him, "Aren't you afraid of the U-Boats, C.F.?" Frohman replies with bravado: "Only of the IOU's." **10** Billie Burke is performing in *Jerry* in Stillwater, Minnesota when she is informed of the death of her producer, Charles Frohman, three days ago in the sinking of the *Lusitania.* She becomes hysterical and collapses in the wings, forcing the manager to bring down the curtain. **31** Laurette Taylor is in London, in her 1,000th performance of *Peg O' My Heart,* when the show is interrupted by the first German Zeppelin raid on the city. Cast and audience have to go down into the basement until the danger has passed.

Plays and Musicals

future film director, John Cromwell.

FEBRUARY 12 The Neighborhood Playhouse, run by the Henry Street Settlement House and largely subsidized by Alice and Irene Lewisohn, opens on Grand Street on the Lower East Side with a biblical piece called *Jephthah's Daughter.* **19** "Art Colonists Act Plays" is *The New York Times* headline describing The Washington Square Players' inauguration tonight of their first season of repertory at the Bandbox Theatre. They are at the heart of the "little theatre" movement. Of the evening's program of one-act plays, the *Times* especially likes Edward Goodman's *Eugenically Speaking,* about "a girl suffering from a rush of Shaw to the head."

APRIL 20 The opening of *Nobody Home* (135) at the 299-seat Princess Theatre marks a major step in the evolution of American musical comedy. This is the first show to integrate fully book, music, and lyrics in a two-act format. It's also the first in a series of small-scale shows known as the Princess Theatre Musicals. Most of the music is by Jerome Kern, and the book is by Guy Bolton. George Anderson and Alice Dovey star, and in the chorus is Marion Davis, soon to change her last name to Davies.

MAY 29 *The Passing Show of 1915* (145) opens at the Winter Garden. Marilyn Miller, who made her Broadway debut in last year's edition, achieves stardom in the show. Willie and Eugene Howard are also in the cast.

Business and Society

Births, Deaths, and Marriages

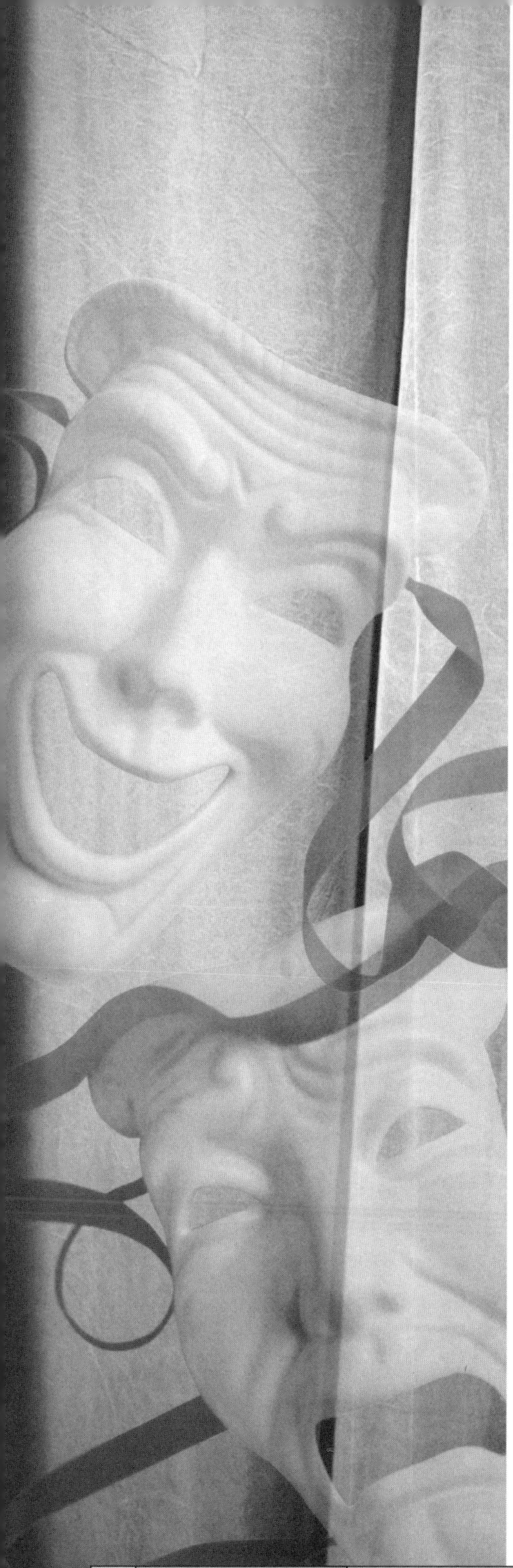

1915–16

The new medium of film is creating artistic and commercial soul-searching on Broadway. With D. W. Griffith's *Birth of a Nation* having opened on Forty-second Street recently, the Shuberts and David Belasco will be looking into film's possibilities. Producer William Brady says that stemming the competition from the screen would be like trying "to hold Niagara in leash." David Warfield, Maude Adams, and John Drew will have nothing to do with it, although Drew's Barrymore niece and nephews will take a different tack. Mrs. Leslie Carter and Mrs. Fiske flop as movie stars. Meanwhile, the meteor that is Jeanne Eagels begins to light up Broadway.

- Retail price of musical comedy sheet music: $.10–$.30
- Amount paid to the Weber and Fields vaudeville team at the Palace: $3,800 a week
- What Al Jolson sings in *Robinson Crusoe, Jr.*: "Yaka Hula Hickey Dula"
- Gross receipts of *Chin Chin*, closing after 64 weeks on Broadway: $1,850,000
- Net profit from *Chin Chin*: $320,000
- George Gershwin's first published song: "When You Want 'Em, You Can't Get 'Em, When You've Got 'Em, You Don't Want 'Em"
- How much Gershwin earns for his first song: $5
- Price per share of initial stock offering from the 10-year-old *Variety*: $25
- What Fanny Brice performs at the Palace when she follows Ruth St. Denis on the bill: "Becky Back in Ballet"
- First Cole Porter song on Broadway: "Esmerelda"
- Among the songs left out of *See America First*, Cole Porter's first Broadway musical: "Bichloride of Mercury"
- What it costs to sit in a Broadway balcony: $1.25
- Price of a movie: $.25
- What *The New York Times* says about the new Shaw play, *Major Barbara*: "It should appeal immensely to all those who enjoy Shaw and to all those who wish it thought [that] they enjoy Shaw."
- Number of *Ziegfeld Follies* Joseph Urban will design: 12
- One of Marion Davies' benefits from employment in Irving Berlin's *Stop! Look! Listen!*: meeting William Randolph Hearst
- What they're now calling Sophie Tucker, formerly known as "The Great Coon Shouter": "The Mary Garden of Ragtime"

Productions on Broadway: 115

June — Joseph Urban designs his first *Follies*

July — Cole Porter's Broadway debut

August — Vivienne Segal introduces "Auf Wiedersehn"

September — Leon Errol has nervous breakdown

October — Arthur Miller born

November — Houdini clashes with boxing champ

December — Ruth Gordon's Broadway debut—as a boy

January — Keith Theatre in New York gives Green Stamps

February — Court rules Shuberts can bar critic

March — George Gershwin works in Tin Pan Alley

April — John Barrymore success in *Justice*

May — William Morris reopens agency

Personalities

JUNE 8 "Yale Man, Song Writer, Has a Fine Future," is the *New Haven Evening Register's* headline above a story quoting agent-producer Elizabeth Marbury, who says of Cole Porter that he "is the one man of the many who can measure up to the standard set by the late Sir Arthur Sullivan. This looks like a boast, but watch him."

JULY • The management of the Keith's Theatre in Washington, D.C. cancels an appearance of Victor Moore and his wife, Emma Littlefield, because he is currently appearing in a film playing in town. **13** Billie Burke leaves the Frohman organization, signing to make a movie, *Peggy*, for Thomas Ince. She is one of the first major Broadway stars to make this move. **13** Playing the Palace tonight are Bert & Bettie Wheeler. Bert Wheeler, who does a Charlie Chaplin imitation, is the future stage and screen partner of Robert Woolsey—of Wheeler and Woolsey.

AUGUST 9 Weber and Fields are reunited at the Palace, which is sold out. Also on the bill is Harry Houdini.

SEPTEMBER • An overworked Leon Errol, a star of *The Ziegfeld Follies of 1915*, as well as its stage manager, has a nervous breakdown. **10** Reviewing Fanny Brice at the Palace, *Variety* says that when she "learns to refrain from starting to disrobe before she is out of sight of the audience her new act will be a step—several of them, in fact—in the right direction."

NOVEMBER 19 Vaudevillian and future musical comedy star William Gaxton, in a letter in *Variety*, replies to performer Billy Gaston's charge that Gaxton is "trading on his name." Gaxton points out that he's used the name for "six or seven years" and that he derived it from his real name, William Gaxiola. **30** Harry Houdini, at the Orpheum in Los Angeles, spots boxing champion Jess Willard in the audience and asks him to come to the stage. Willard resists, and when Houdini insists, the boxer, angry that he's being urged to make a free appearance, calls Houdini a "faker" and "four-flusher." The

Plays and Musicals

JUNE 21 *The Ziegfeld Follies of 1915* (104) opens at the New Amsterdam, featuring Joseph Urban's striking set designs and the *Follies* debut of W. C. Fields, whom the *Times* describes as "an expert juggler with a sense of humor, who comes from the halls of the two-a-day." Fields plays pool with himself. Bert Williams, Ed Wynn, Mae Murray, George White, Olive Thomas, Leon Errol, and Ina Claire are also in the cast.

JULY 22 *Hands Up* (52), opening at the Forty-fourth Street Theatre, has Cole Porter's first Broadway show tune, the interpolated "Esmerelda."

AUGUST 5 *The Blue Paradise* (356) opens at the Casino Theatre. Vivienne Segal, in her debut, steals the show with a new Sigmund Romberg melody, his first hit, "*Auf Wiedersehn.*" **10** *The Boomerang* (522), a comedy by Winchell Smith and Victor Mapes, starring Arthur Byron and Martha Hedman, opens at the Belasco. **26** *Common Clay* (316), by Cleves Kinkead, a student in George Pierce Baker's playwriting class at Harvard, opens at the Republic. Jane Cowl and John Mason star in this drama about a seduced maid who sues for support for her illegitimate child, only to find that she is herself the illegitimate daughter of the judge who is trying her suit. Kinkead won a competition for Harvard students with this work.

SEPTEMBER 13 *Hit-the-Trail-Holiday* (336), George M. Cohan's farce poking fun at preacher Billy Sunday, opens at the Astor. The show has been tailored for the talents of Cohan's brother-in-law and star, Fred Niblo (future silent film director).

OCTOBER 9 Emily Stevens, a cousin of Minnie Maddern Fiske, plays the totally immoral, self-absorbed title character in Louis Kaufman Anspacher's *The Unchastened Woman* (193), opening at the Thirty-ninth Street Theatre. **21** Roi Cooper Megrue and Montague Glass's *Abe and Mawruss* (196), retitled in January *Potash and Perlmutter in Society* to take advantage of audience recognition of the popular characters, opens at the Lyric. The cast includes Barney Bernard, Julius

Business and Society

AUGUST • Producers are complaining that chorus girls are in short supply because they're getting more lucrative work as movie extras. **20** *Variety* reports that the increasing number of movie theatres in Times Square is worrying stage producers. The January issue of *Atlantic Monthly* carried an article observing that the working class audience that used to fill theatre galleries at $1.25 is now to be found in the $.25 seats at the movies—when they are not at the local vaudeville house.

OCTOBER • The Metropolitan Opera is reported to have forbidden its stars from performing in vaudeville, where they have been tempted by large fees. **26** Federal Court Judge Learned Hand dismisses an antitrust suit against vaudeville's United Booking Office.

NOVEMBER 16 An agreement among producers not to sell tickets at a discount to agencies unravels when it is learned that Klaw and Erlanger have gone back to making such sales.

JANUARY • Keith's Royal, a vaudeville house in the Bronx, becomes the first theatre in

Births, Deaths, and Marriages

JUNE • Eddie Cantor m. Ida Tobias.

JULY 11 Yul Brynner b. (Other dates are also given.)

SEPTEMBER 3 Kitty Carlisle (Catherine Conn) b.

OCTOBER 17 Playwright Arthur Miller b.

DECEMBER 2 Adolph Green b. **7** Eli Wallach b.

JANUARY 8 Ada Rehan d.

MARCH 3 Producer Robert Whitehead b.

audience greets this with loud booing, and Willard leaves.

DECEMBER 21 Playing one of the boys at the Empire Theatre in the revival of *Peter Pan* with Maude Adams is Ruth Gordon in her Broadway debut.

JANUARY 17 The *New York Telegraph* says of 22-year-old ingenue Jeanne Eagels, appearing in *The Outcast*, that she "has youth, beauty and great personal charm. She also possesses a subtlety in the detail of her portrayal that is remarkable in one who is playing her first big part on Broadway."

FEBRUARY • Fanny Brice, at the Palace, follows dancer Ruth St. Denis on the bill

Fanny Brice ZCI

Tannen, and Louise Dresser. **23** Eva Le Gallienne makes her Broadway debut in *Mrs. Boltay's Daughters* (17), a comedy directed and coproduced by Harrison Grey Fiske at the Comedy Theatre.

NOVEMBER 6 Avery Hopwood's farce, *Fair and Warmer* (377), starring Madge Kennedy, Ralph Morgan, John Cumberland, and Janet Beecher, opens at the Eltinge Theatre. **10** *The Great Lover* (245) opens at the Longacre. In this play by Leo Ditrichstein and Fanny and Frederic Hatton, Ditrichstein stars as an opera singer who very closely resembles Victor Maurel of the Metropolitan Opera.

DECEMBER 23 Rudolph Friml and Otto Harbach's operetta, *Katinka* (220), starring May Naudain, opens at the Forty-fourth Street Theatre. **23** Jerome Kern's *Very Good Eddie* (341), with lyrics by Schuyler Greene and book by Guy Bolton and Philip Bartholomae, stars Ernest Truex and opens at the Princess Theatre. The most prominent of the songs is "Babes in the Wood." **25** *Stop! Look! Listen!* (105), at the Globe, adds "I Love a Piano" and "The Girl on the Magazine

New York to give S & H trading stamps to women at each matinée performance.

FEBRUARY 4 *Variety*, declaring that "[t]he curse of vaudeville is theft of material," announces a "Protected Material" Department, in which performers may file a sealed description of their act, to be opened and publicized if they feel it is being stolen. **22** Holding that producers may prevent a critic from attending their plays, the New York State Court of Appeals rules against Alexander Woollcott in his suit against the Shuberts, who have barred him from their theatres because of his negative reviews. **29** The Managers Protective Association, lately inactive, is revived to counter the White Rats, the vaudeville union that's becoming more militant under leader Harry Mounteford. The managers say that they "have always been willing to meet the actor in a social organization," but not in a union.

APRIL • The Vaudeville Benevolent & Protective Association, a pro-management group opposed to the White Rats, is chartered.

MAY 29 Members of Actors Equity vote to seek affiliation with the American Federation of Labor.

Personalities

with a parody of classical dance called "Becky Back in Ballet." When the audience calls for an encore, "the funniest woman in vaudeville," as she's billed, tells them, "I ain't got no more material. What do you want from my young Jewish life?" **5** In a story headlined "Why Sophie Tucker Dropped 'Coon Shouting,'" the *Cincinnati Tribune* reports that too many people were imitating what she was doing. She also didn't like it. "It was pretty rough stuff," she says, "and I guess all my stuff was rough." Now she's being billed as "The Mary Garden of Ragtime," an allusion to the popular opera singer.

MARCH 1 On the recommendation of Sophie Tucker, song plugger George Gershwin is hired by Tin Pan Alley titan Harry von Tilzer. **13** Belle Baker spots Al Jolson in an orchestra seat at a Palace matinée and asks him to join her onstage in "Where Did Robinson Crusoe Go With Friday on Saturday Night?" Jolson objects to her singing this song from his current show, *Robinson Crusoe, Jr.*, thinking that he had exclusive rights to it. Rather than join her, he walks up the aisle and out of the theatre.

MAY 15 George Gershwin's first song, "When You Want 'Em, You Can't Get 'Em; When You Got 'Em, You Don't Want 'Em," is copyrighted.

Plays and Musicals

Cover" to the Irving Berlin pantheon. The cast includes Marion Sunshine, Gaby Deslys, and Marion Davies, who will meet publisher William Randolph Hearst during the show's run.

FEBRUARY 17 Al Jolson opens at the Winter Garden in *Robinson Crusoe, Jr.* (139), with music by Sigmund Romberg.

MARCH 28 *See America First* (15), a musical at Maxine Elliott's Theatre starring Clifton Webb, has the first Broadway score by Cole Porter.

APRIL 3 John Barrymore opens in *Justice* (104) at the Candler Theatre. John Galsworthy's drama of the degradation of a law clerk to the point of suicide and the decline into prostitution of the woman he loves costars Cathleen Nesbitt and O. P. Heggie. *The New York Times* says that the audience can watch Barrymore "step forward into a new position on the American stage." Now, the paper proclaims, "he comes into his own."

Business and Society

Births, Deaths, and Marriages

1916–17

Broadway goes to war, to the tune of George M. Cohan's "Over There." The Provincetown Players need to qualify as a private club because their modest house in Greenwich Village does not meet New York's safety standards for theatres. But they do bring to its humble boards the first staging in the city of a Eugene O'Neill play. Will Rogers makes his *Follies* debut, the first Gershwin tune is heard in a Broadway show, and while Alfred Lunt dallies with Lillie Langtry, Lynn Fontanne is making an impression with the critics. Vaudeville managers crush the White Rats, and vaudevillian Harry Houdini escapes from the "Chinese Water Torture Cell." About the only thing he hasn't gotten out of yet is an ironclad contract.

- Cost of dinner at Rector's, the famous theatre district restaurant at Broadway and Forty-eighth Street: $1.50
- George Gershwin's first Broadway tune: "The Making of a Girl"
- Largest electric sign on the Great White Way: Wrigley's Chewing Gum
- Why singer Blossom Seeley cancels her vaudeville bookings in October: her husband, Rube Marquard, is pitching in the World Series
- How serious John Barrymore is about becoming an accomplished actor: he's given up drinking—temporarily
- Technological breakthrough: the Minsky brothers invent the burlesque house runway at their Lower East Side theatre
- What Eddie Cantor sings in Flo Ziegfeld's *Midnight Frolic*: "Oh, How She Could Yacki, Hacki, Wicki, Wacki, Woo"
- Number of performances that makes a show a hit: more than 100
- How J. J. Shubert, locked in an ugly divorce battle with his wife, Catherine, characterizes their son: "not his"
- Happy Holidays: Keith circuit contracts call for three performances a day rather than two on Thanksgiving and New Year's Day
- Rent paid by the Provincetown Players for their Playwrights Theatre at 139 MacDougal Street: $100 a month
- Number of subscribers for Provincetown Players: 550
- Dimensions of their first theatre on MacDougal Street in Greenwich Village:
  stage: 10 1/2 feet by 14 feet
  auditorium: 15 feet by 30 feet
  seating capacity: 150
- What Columbia University student Lorenz Hart writes in the student newspaper about Oscar Hammerstein II, who appears in the 1916 Varsity show, *The Peace Pirates*: "He proved to be thoroughly original and distinctly funny, and demonstrated his ability to 'put over' a song. He also wrote the Shakespeare burlesque in Act II and contributed humor far above the level of horseplay in his impersonation of Nijinsky."
- What Lorenz Hart's role is in the same show: he's playing Mary Pickford
- Person whom Oscar Hammerstein II is introduced to backstage at the varsity show: 14-year-old Richard Rodgers, whose brother is one of Oscar's fraternity brothers
- Katharine Cornell's only line in *Bushido*: "My son, my son."
- Ed Wynn's first line in *The Passing Show of 1916*: "This show is terrible."
- Where Ira Gershwin is writing song lyrics: at the St. Nicholas Russian and Turkish Bath in Harlem, in which his father has invested
- Singer introducing George M. Cohan's "Over There": Nora Bayes

Productions on Broadway: 126

June	July	August	September	October	November
George Gershwin's Broadway debut	Will Rogers's *Follies* debut	Polio outbreak cancels vaudeville child acts	Provincetown Players manifesto	Eddie Cantor billed as "New Nut"	Eugene O'Neill's New York debut

December	January	February	March	April	May
Variety says "too much Yiddish" in show business	John Raitt born	Morosco Theatre opens	Eugene O'Neill arrested as spy	White Rats vaudeville union crushed	George M. Cohan writes "Over There"

Personalities

AUGUST • Alfred Lunt, 24 and unemployed, uses his ability to learn a part overnight to snare a role opposite the popular Laura Hope Crews in the touring production of the one-act play, *Her Husband's Wife*. For the two weeks he shares the stage with Crews, he will also share her bed. In his next job, he will repeat that kind of dual role with the 64-year-old Lillie Langtry, with whom he will star in *Ashes*. (Crews recommended Lunt to Langtry, presumably for his acting prowess.) • An outbreak of infantile paralysis (polio) brings the cancellation of engagements for many acts involving children, including Eddie Foy and His Seven Foys. • Eugene O'Neill and writer Louise Bryant, who remains involved with writer and political activist John Reed, become lovers and will continue the relationship after Bryant's marriage to Reed.

OCTOBER • Singer Blossom Seeley is released from her vaudeville bookings for two weeks to watch her husband, Rube Marquard, pitch in the World Series. **20** *Variety* reviews Flo Ziegfeld's *Midnight Frolic*, a cabaret performance on the Amsterdam Roof, where front tables go for $3. A Ziegfeld newcomer, Eddie Cantor, billed as a "New Nut," "left the impression of a hybrid Al Jolson–Will Rogers. He did fairly well. . . ." He sings, "Oh, How She Could Yacki, Hacki, Wicki, Wacki, Woo."

Eddie Cantor

Plays and Musicals

JUNE 12 *The Ziegfeld Follies of 1916* (112) opens at the New Amsterdam. Will Rogers, not in the cast on opening night, will make his *Follies* debut on July 23. In the cast: Fanny Brice, Theda Bara, Ina Claire, W. C. Fields, and Bert Williams. **22** *The Passing Show of 1916* (140), at the Winter Garden, stars Ed Wynn. The *Times* reports the show's composers as Victor Herbert, Sigmund Romberg, and "others." One of the others is 17-year-old George Gershwin, making his first mark on Broadway with "The Making of a Girl," for which Romberg takes joint credit.

Will Rogers MSN

JULY 28 The Provincetown Players give Eugene O'Neill his first production, staging his *Bound East for Cardiff*, a drama of a dying sailor, at their Wharf Theatre.

AUGUST 9 Marjorie Rambeau is a crook—or is she?—in Max Marcin's *Cheating Cheaters* (286), a comedy at the Eltinge in which everyone is pretending to be someone else. **18** Producer John Golden has his first hit in *Turn to the Right* (435), a comedy by Winchell Smith and John E. Hazzard, opening at the Gaiety Theatre.

SEPTEMBER 2 Jules Eckert Goodman's *The Man Who Came Back* (457) is at the Playhouse. Henry Hull plays a man whose downward spiral has taken him to a Chinese opium den, where he makes a

Business and Society

JULY • William Morris has formed an organization of 52 theatres across the country under the banner of William Morris Associated Variety to fight the United Booking Office's talent monopoly.

SEPTEMBER 5 In a formal manifesto, the Provincetown Players declare it their intention "to encourage the writing of American plays of artistic, literary and dramatic—as opposed to Broadway—merit." They pledge in each production to remain faithful to the playwright's intentions.

OCTOBER 21 "Many Plays but Slim Audiences" is today's *Dramatic Mirror* concerned headline.

NOVEMBER • *Theatre Arts* magazine begins publication as a quarterly. **21** The American Federation of Labor designates the vaudeville White Rats as the primary labor group representing theatrical workers, stymieing Actors Equity's bid to speak independently for legitimate stage performers.

DECEMBER 1 A *Variety* editorial complains: "There is too much 'Yiddish' just at pre-

Births, Deaths, and Marriages

JUNE 23 Irene Worth b.

SEPTEMBER 14 Playwright-critic-translator Eric Bentley b.

OCTOBER 14 Actress Carlotta Monterey (future wife of Eugene O'Neill) m. Canfield Chapman. **25** Earl Carroll m. film actress Marcelle Hontobot.

NOVEMBER 8 June Havoc (June Hovick), sister of Gypsy Rose Lee, b.

DECEMBER • Texas Guinan, vaudeville and night club performer, m. Julian Johnson, movie magazine editor.

JANUARY 29 John Raitt b.

NOVEMBER 13 Katharine Cornell flubbed her first audition for the Washington Square Players but has since caught on and tonight debuts in a Noh play, *Bushido*, in which she has one line of dialogue: "My son, my son." **27** During rehearsals for *The Harp of Life*, opening tonight, Lynn Fontanne receives word that her fiancé, Edmund Byrne, had been killed in action in France.

DECEMBER 25 Harry Houdini performs his "Chinese Water Torture Cell" escape at the Palace. Also on the bill are Blossom Seeley and Emma Carus.

FEBRUARY • J. J. Shubert and his wife, Catherine, are divorced after a long and messy court battle during which J. J. vociferously insisted that their son, John, was "not his." The final proceedings, in Buffalo, New York, are held in a locked courtroom, on Saturday and under guard, to keep them as secret as possible.

MARCH 10 A critic in the *New York Mirror* comments on the current season: "I am always happy to hail a newcomer to the ranks of young actresses, and Miss [Fay] Bainter, Jeanne Eagels, and Lynne Fontaine *[sic]*, who have contributed hits to the present season, are certainly a trio one may be glad to watch with a fine certainty that when their wings are fledged for higher flights, we shall be able to say: 'I told you so.'" **28** Eugene O'Neill, known in Provincetown, Massachusetts ,for his pacifist beliefs, is arrested briefly on the false report that he is spying for the Germans. **28** The *New York Herald-Tribune* headline over a review reads: "Oscar Hammerstein 2d, Comedian in Columbia Show, 'Home James!'"

APRIL • America's entry into the World War is reflected on the stage. Vaudeville audiences are standing for any song that even slightly suggests patriotism. Irving Berlin has written the official Navy recruiting song, "For Your Country and My Country," and is singing it in New York theatres. And the Mayor of Oakland, California threatens to arrest former minstrel show producer Lew Dockstadter, now a vaudeville single act, for joking about Army life, which might hurt recruiting. **14** *The Review*, commenting on the recent per-

---

fateful decision that will turn things around for himself and his girlfriend, played by Mary Nash. **14** Can a stock broker win a $10,000 bet by going 24 hours without telling even one lie? William Collier manages it in James Montgomery's comedy, *Nothing But the Truth* (332), at the Longacre. **25** A comedy by Frederic and Fanny Hatton, *Upstairs and Down* (320), in which the poor are found to be no more pleasant than the rich, opens at the Cort. Christine Norman stars with Leo Carillo.

OCTOBER 23 Ruth Chatterton is a Virginia blueblood turned servant, whose good looks save the day—and the plantation—in *Come Out of the Kitchen* (224), a comedy by A. E. Thomas. It opens at the Cohan Theatre. **31** Playwright Clare Kummer comes into her own with the opening of her comedy, *Good Gracious, Annabelle* (111), at the Republic. It stars Walter Hampden, Lola Fisher, Edwin Nicander, and Roland Young.

NOVEMBER 3 The Provincetown Players open their first New York season at their Playwrights Theatre on MacDougal Street in Greenwich Village. On tonight's bill of one-act plays is Eugene O'Neill's *Bound East for Cardiff*, described by the *Evening Sun* as "real" and "subtly tense," with the author appearing in the cast. The Players presented it at their Wharf Theatre in July. **6** *The Century Girl* (200), a revue with music by Victor Herbert and Irving Berlin, produced by Flo Ziegfeld and Charles Dillingham, opens at the Century. It stars Leon Errol, Elsie Janis, and Hazel Dawn and has a grand staircase designed by Joseph Urban, which becomes a hallmark of Ziegfeld shows. **20** Bayard Veiller's mystery, *The Thirteenth Chair* (328), features his wife, Margaret Wycherly, as a medium who solves a murder by means of a séance. **27** Philip Merivale and Laurette Taylor open in *The Harp of Life* (136), by Taylor's husband, J. Hartley Manners. On December 10, The *Sun* will say of a secondary cast member that "one of the successes made this season by players hitherto unknown to Broadway was registered . . . by a young English girl, Lynn Fontanne." The Globe, where this play opens, will become the Lunt-Fontanne Theatre.

---

sent in all show entertainments as a matter of fact. Some comedians couldn't be funny without it, either because it fits their face or they know of nothing else." The paper says that Yiddish should be confined to plays or sketches in which the characters would naturally speak in that tongue and to audiences that can be expected to understand it.

JANUARY • Worried about several plays that have been quick flops, several producers are engaged in a round of ticket price cutting.

MARCH • In response to agitation for a closed shop and an increasing number of local strikes and walkouts throughout the country by the White Rats labor union, vaudeville managers state that only members of the National Vaudeville Artists, a company union, will be booked in their houses. *Variety* is backing the managers in the increasingly bitter struggle.

APRIL 10 The White Rats call off their wildcat strikes, trying to soften their admission of failure by suggesting that they are cooperating with the war effort. The organization faces bankruptcy and is through as a factor in labor management relations.

FEBRUARY 14 J. J. Shubert and his wife, Katherine, are divorced.

MARCH 15 George S. Kaufman m. Beatrice Bakrow.

APRIL 12 Frank Fay m. fellow vaudevillian Frances White—a match that will last only a few months. **20** David Montgomery d.

Personalities

formances of the Washington Square Players, notes that "there is a new face that stands out—clear out. Katharine Cornell—in 'Plots and Playwrights' [which opened March 21]. A dead white young American Duse has dropped from the skies." "Watch her," the publication advises. **17** John Barrymore's success in *Peter Ibbetson*, opening tonight, has him taking himself so seriously as an actor that he will teetotal for the next two years.

MAY 12 George M. Cohan, who wrote "You're a Grand Old Flag," has been under pressure to write something for America's entry into World War I. This afternoon, Nora Bayes introduces it at the Thirty-ninth Street Theatre to a rousing reception. It's called "Over There."

Plays and Musicals

FEBRUARY 5 Earl Carroll's musical, *Canary Cottage* (112), starring Trixie Friganza and Charles Ruggles, is the premiere attraction at the 905-seat Morosco Theater, another Shubert house, on Forty-fifth Street. **20** *Oh, Boy!* (463) (retitled *Oh, Joy!* in London), by Jerome Kern, Guy Bolton, and P. G. Wodehouse, opens at the Princess Theatre—the peak of that house's famed series of musicals. The cast includes Edna May Oliver and Tom Powers.

MARCH 12 W. Somerset Maugham's comedy, *Our Betters* (112), starring Crystal Herne, is at the Hudson. It will be revived in 1928 and filmed, with Constance Bennett, in 1933.

APRIL 17 *Peter Ibbetson* (71), by John N. Raphael, is at the Republic, where an opening night mishap involving falling scenery exposes stagehands at work. The play stars Lionel and John Barrymore, Madge Evans, Constance Collier, and Laura Hope Crews.

Business and Society

Births, Deaths, and Marriages

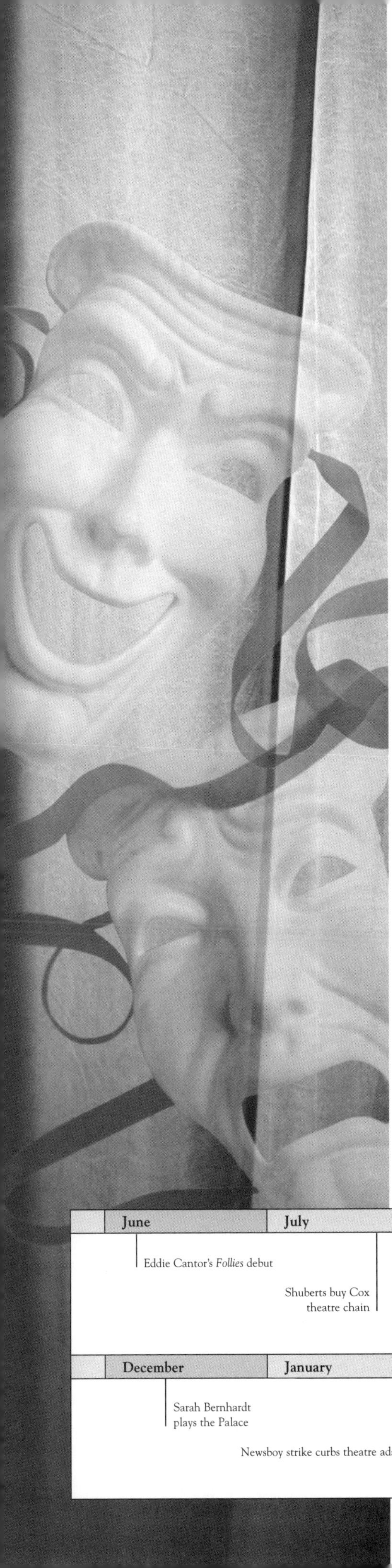

1917–18

Eddie Cantor, debuting in *The Ziegfeld Follies*, is in transition from the blackface, swishing comic who told dirty jokes to America's premiere family entertainer. George Jessel's voice is deepening, Will Rogers is getting political, Oscar Hammerstein II decides not to be a lawyer, and the Shuberts are now a national power. Anything German is *verboten*, so Sigmund Romberg's *Maytime* is a "musical play," not an "operetta," thank you, and it's Mr. Harbach, please, not "Hauerbach." The Plymouth and Broadhurst theatres open, Helen Hayes is a "find," the first Pulitzer Prize for Drama is awarded, Fred Astaire delights in his Broadway debut, but dancer Mata Hari makes a fatal misstep.

- Headline on a *New York Times* article: "Who Is Eugene O'Neill?"
- Average cost of producing a musical: $25,000
- Cost of producing *The Ziegfeld Follies*: about $90,000
- New average top ticket price for shows: $3.00
- Cost of the room at the Hotel Algonquin occupied by 16-year-old Tallulah Bankhead: $21 a week
- What John says to Ethel Barrymore, upon seeing Tallulah Bankhead and being impressed by her profile: "Did father ever play Alabama?"
- What Tallulah Bankhead says in her Broadway debut: not a thing
- Song Jerome Kern keeps out of *Oh, Lady! Lady!*: "Bill," which will end up in *Show Boat*
- Price George M. Cohan gets for "Over There": $25,000
- How much George S. Kaufman is making at *The New York Times*: $36 a week
- New on Broadway: the Brooks Costume Company, which, with its purchase of the stock of costumes left by producer Charles Frohman, has evolved from a company formed in 1906 to sell uniforms to the Rialto's biggest costumer
- Al Jolson's workload from December 30 through January 3: 10 performances of *Robinson Crusoe, Jr.*, in two cities
- What the Shuberts are paying Al Jolson: $2,500 a week plus 25 percent of the profits
- Cost of Jolson's private railroad car for the tour of *Robinson Crusoe, Jr.*: $55 a day, with porter, cook, and waiter
- What *Variety* offers the men of show business who enlist in the armed forces: a free subscription
- Number of pages in *Variety*'s annual anniversary issue: 264, the most until 1929
- Why *In the Zone* is significant for Eugene O'Neill: it's his first play that makes money
- What cast members have to do to get their name up in lights at the Winter Garden: pay the Shuberts $25
- What the new Pulitzer Prize for Drama is awarded for: ". . . for the original American play, performed in New York, which shall best represent the educational value and power of the stage in raising the standards of good morals, good taste and good manners."

Productions on Broadway: 156

First Pulitzer Prize for Drama: *Why Marry* (Jesse Lynch Williams)

June	July	August	September	October	November
Eddie Cantor's *Follies* debut	Shuberts buy Cox theatre chain	Peggy Wood becomes a Broadway star	Broadhurst Theatre opens	Alfred Lunt's Broadway debut	Fred Astaire's Broadway debut

December	January	February	March	April	May
Sarah Bernhardt plays the Palace	Newsboy strike curbs theatre ads	Irving Berlin becomes an American citizen	Tallulah Bankhead's silent Broadway debut	John Barrymore sells war bonds	Washington Square Players disband

Personalities

JUNE 27 According to *Variety*, "Oscar Hammerstein 2d, grandson of the famous Oscar and son of the late William Hammerstein, has deserted the law and will assist his uncle Arthur in the producing field."

JULY 6 *Variety* reports that the increasing popularity of revues has producers raiding vaudeville for performers, including Frank Fay, Eddie Cantor, Leo Carillo, Charlotte Greenwood, Trixie Friganza, Fanny Brice, George White, and the Dolly Sisters. **16** Gus Edwards's kiddie act, the "Bandbox Revue," playing the Palace, features "Cuddles" and Georgie (Jessel). According to *Variety*'s review, "Georgie's voice is now very deep."

AUGUST • Oscar Hammerstein II is hired by his uncle Arthur as his production stage manager. The understanding is that he won't waste his time writing for the theatre. **3** *Variety* reports: "Marguerite Zell, known on the variety stage as Mata Hart, a Japanese dancer, has been sentenced to death by a Paris court-martial for espionage." Actually, she performs as a Javanese dancer and calls herself Mata Hari.

SEPTEMBER • Vaudevillian Nora Bayes is entertaining at Army training camps. **17** George S. Kaufman joins *The New York Times* drama department at $36 a week. **21** "Tyler's 17-Year-Old 'Find'" headlines *Variety* over a brief item describing producer George Tyler's exciting discovery of the teenager he has cast in the lead of his production of *Pollyanna* in Rochester, New York: Helen Hayes. According to the paper, "[H]er present manager proclaims her as one of the stars within a very few seasons."

OCTOBER • Eugene O'Neill begins to make a literary impact with the publication of his play *The Long Voyage Home* in H.L. Mencken and George Jean Nathan's *The Smart Set.*

NOVEMBER • The Dolly Sisters lose their Keith theatres vaudeville bookings when they agree to an engagement at a hotel cabaret. The United Booking Office is

Plays and Musicals

JUNE 12 Eddie Cantor, in blackface, makes his *Ziegfeld Follies* (111) debut at the New Amsterdam, singing "Just You and Me" with Fanny Brice. Also in the show are W.C. Fields, Bert Williams, and Will Rogers.

AUGUST 15 Potash and Perlmutter are back and in the film business in *Business Before Pleasure* (357), a comedy at the Eltinge by Jules Goodman and Montague Glass, starring Barney Bernard and Alexander Carr. **16** *Maytime* (492), by Sigmund Romberg and Rida Johnson Young, opens at the Shubert. Peggy Wood becomes a star in this "musical play," so designated by the Shuberts so as not to suggest—as with "operetta"—images of Germany, now the enemy. **22** In the *Eyes of Youth* (414), by Charles Guernon and Max Marcin, Marjorie Rambeau is a woman who must choose between the future she knows and the one that's unknown. It opens at Maxine Elliott's Theatre. **27** Clothes make the man, for a while, at least, in the comedy *A Tailor-Made Man* (398), opening at the Cohan and Harris Theatre. The author is Harry James Smith and the stars are Grant Mitchell and Helen MacKellar. **28** *Leave It to Jane* (167), a Jerome Kern–Guy Bolton–P.G. Wodehouse musical, based on the 1904 play *The College Widow*, opens at the Longacre. The stars are Edith Hallor, Robert Pitkin, and Oscar Shaw.

SEPTEMBER 6 George Middleton and Guy Bolton's *Polly With a Past* (315), produced and directed by David Belasco at his theatre, stars Ina Claire. **24** *Lombardi, Ltd.* (296), a comedy at the Morosco by Frederic and Fanny Hatton; Leo Carillo stars. **27** The Broadhurst Theatre opens with a performance of Shaw's *Misalliance* (52), with Maclyn Arbuckle.

OCTOBER 3 In *Tiger Rose* (384), at the Lyceum, three men, including a Canadian Mountie and the murderer he's tracking, love the title character, played by Lenore Ulric. The playwright, Willard Mack, Pedro De Cordoba and Calvin Thomas also star. **10** The Plymouth Theatre, on Forty-fifth Street opens its doors with Clare Kummer's comedy *A*

Business and Society

JUNE 8 *Variety* offers a free subscription to any theatrical man who enlists in the armed forces. In the same issue, the Theatrical Liberty Loan Committee appeals to professionals to buy U.S. Liberty Bonds.

JULY • The Shuberts buy the large theatre chain assembled by George Cox of Cincinnati, who died last year. They now have an interest in at least one theatre in most major U.S. cities.

AUGUST • The vaudeville managers, who had blacklisted performers participating in the White Rats strike, begin to rebook some of them, except for the union's hard core, whom they refer to as "the anarchists."

NOVEMBER • The Shuberts are offering to put up in lights outside the Winter Garden the name of any performer willing to pay $25 a week for the "honor." One minor performer in the current production has taken them up on it. **1** With box office business off, theatres must also cope with a 10 percent war tax on tickets. A few managers are cutting salaries to make up for the business downturn.

DECEMBER 16 The Shuberts announce

Births, Deaths, and Marriages

JUNE 6 *New York Tribune* drama critic Heywood Broun m. feminist Ruth Hale. They will become part of the lively literary set identified with the Hotel Algonquin. **30** Lena Horne b., and Critic William Winter d.

AUGUST 13 Claudia McNeil b. **21** Oscar Hammerstein II m. Myra Finn.

SEPTEMBER 24 Pauline Frederick m. actor-playwright Willard Mack. She was named corespondent in Marjorie Rambeau's recent divorce suit against Mack.

OCTOBER 5 Donald Pleasance b. **13** Sophie Tucker m. her accompanist, Frank Westphal, in Chicago. Afterward, they go to a restaurant for dinner, where they are welcomed by the house pianist playing a

The Dolly Sisters, one of vaudeville's most famous acts LYNCH

trying to maintain exclusive control over acts it books into vaudeville houses. • George M. Cohan sells all the rights to his song "Over There" to Leo Feist for $25,000. The sheet music has already sold 440,000 at $.10 each. **4** Spotting the beginning of a possibly important career, a *New York Times* article poses the question: "Who Is Eugene O'Neill?" **5** Promoting a show at the Hippodrome, Harry Houdini escapes from a straitjacket while hanging by his feet from a crane in Times Square. **7** The program of *Kitty Darlin'*, opening tonight at the Casino, reveals that lyricist Otto Hauerbach has become Otto Harbach, a concession to anti-German sentiment.

DECEMBER 10 Comedian George Rockwell,

Successful Calamity. Transferring from the Booth, where it premiered on February 5, it stars William Gillette and Estelle Winwood. **16** *Jack o' Lantern* (265), an Ivan Caryll musical, opens at the Globe.

It stars Fred Stone and features Joseph Urban's striking sets. **17** *Romance and Arabella* (29), a comedy by William Hurlbut at the Harris Theatre, marks the Broadway debut of 25-year-old Alfred

Lunt. **31** The Washington Square Players perform Eugene O'Neill's *In the Zone* on a bill of one-act plays at the Comedy Theatre.

NOVEMBER 2 The Provincetown Players open their season with Eugene O'Neill's *The Long Voyage Home*, directed by Nina Moise, at the Playwrights' Theatre. **5** *Miss 1917* (48), with music by Victor Herbert and Jerome Kern, gives $35-a-week rehearsal pianist George Gershwin his first Broadway work. The book and lyrics of this Charles Dillingham–Flo Ziegfeld production at the Century are by Guy Bolton and P.G. Wodehouse. **28** Fred and Adele Astaire debut on Broadway in *Over the Top* (78), a revue at the Forty-fourth Street Roof.

---

that their working relationship on theatre bookings with producers Klaw and Erlanger, who dominated the old Theatre Syndicate, has broken down after several years of cooperation.

JANUARY • Theatre reviews and ads are hard to come by in New York as newsboys and newsdealers strike because they are not receiving enough of the recent increase in the price of the papers from $.01 to $.02. **19** To conserve fuel, theatres are ordered by the federal government to close on 10 successive Tuesdays. *Variety*, criticizing the plan, calculates that for every 1,800 people going to the theatre, 600 homes do not use fuel.

MARCH • Vaudeville's United Booking Office warns theatre managers to censor all songs about "peace," fearing that they may be German propaganda.

MAY • In a bylined article in *Theatre* magazine, Al Jolson discusses blackface performers: "In other days, the audience liked to think that they were actually seeing a [N]egro, but the modern audience likes to know that the fellow who is getting the laughs is white—and in some small towns, especially through the South, I have felt the unfriendliness of an audience disappear at once when I remove my gloves and show my white

---

jazzed-up version of the wedding march, disturbing another diner, Polish pianist Ignace Paderweski.

NOVEMBER 2 Ray Walston b.

DECEMBER 2 Actor-director-producer Ezra Stone b. **4** John Barrymore and Katherine Harris divorce. **12** Director Alan Schneider (Abram Schneider) b. **18** Ossie Davis b.

FEBRUARY 13 Set designer Oliver Smith b. **15** Vernon Castle d. in a plane crash. **18** Producer Arnold Saint-Suber b.

APRIL 12 Eugene O'Neill m. Agnes Boulton.

Personalities

father of future American Nazi Party leader George Lincoln Rockwell, is playing the Palace, doing female impersonations. **19** Sarah Bernhardt is playing the Palace for three weeks in a series of playlets, forcing singer Belle Baker, held over for a second week, to take second billing. The French star is on the last of her nine U.S. tours. **29** The Akron Club, a group of student athletes, stages a benefit show, *One Minute, Please*, at the Plaza Hotel in New York City, with music by 15-year-old Richard Rodgers.

JANUARY 7 After several years away from vaudeville, female impersonator Julian Eltinge opens at the Palace, drawing standing room crowds. **25** In a letter in *Variety*, Sophie Tucker complains that taxes designed to cut down on rail travel to help the war effort hurt vaudevillians, who must ride the rails.

FEBRUARY 6 Irving Berlin becomes an American citizen.

MARCH 8 Vaudeville hoofer Walter Winchell, the future gossip columnist, and his wife, Rita Green, are doing a song and dance act at the American Roof. According to *Variety*, their performance "isn't one to bring forth any volume of applause, but it's pleasant."

APRIL • John Barrymore is active in the Liberty Loan drive in Chicago, where one of Mary Pickford's curls is auctioned off for $15,000. **23** At the Palace Theatre, the America's Over There League, George M. Cohan presiding, is encouraging volunteers to entertain U.S. troops in Europe. The Y.M.C.A. will transport and house the entertainers "over there."

MAY • Marilyn Miller leaves the Shuberts, with whom she's been since 1914, when the contract she signed last year is ruled invalid on a technicality. She will now sign with Flo Ziegfeld and appear in his *Follies*.

Plays and Musicals

DECEMBER 24 *Parlor, Bedroom and Bath* (232), C.W. Bell and Mark Swan's farce at the Republic, stars John Cumberland and Sydney Shield. **25** The first Pulitzer Prize for Drama will go to *Why Marry?* (120), a comedy by Jesse Lynch Williams, opening at the Astor. Starring Estelle Winwood, Shelly Hull, Edward Breese, and Nat Goodwin (much-married offstage), the play contrasts marriage with cohabitation. The *Times* calls it "perhaps the most intelligent and searching satire on social institutions ever written by an American." **25** The subject is aviation in *Going Up* (351), opening at the Liberty. Louis Hirsch wrote the music, Otto Harbach wrote the words, and Frank Craven and Edith Day star.

JANUARY 22 Ruth Gordon has her first major role in Hugh Stanislaus Stange and Stannard Mears's stage adaptation of Booth Tarkington's novel, *Seventeen* (225), at the Booth.

FEBRUARY 1 *Oh, Lady! Lady!* (219) is the last of the Princess Theatre musicals by Jerome Kern, Guy Bolton and P.G. Wodehouse. The cast includes Vivienne Segal, Carl Randall, and Edward Abeles. Kern keeps one song out of the show because it does not seem to fit in, and it won't be heard until the 1927 *Show Boat*: "Bill." **14** Al Jolson stars in *Sinbad* (388) at the Winter Garden. The score is by Sigmund Romberg, but Jolson also interpolates, down on one knee, George Gershwin's "Swanee" and "Mammy" and Jean Schwartz's "Rock-A-Bye Your Baby with a Dixie Melody." **18** *The Copperhead* (120), by Augustus Thomas, at the Shubert, stars Lionel Barrymore.

MARCH 13 Tallulah Bankhead has a bit part at the Bijou in *Squab Farm* (45), by Frederic and Fanny Hatton, a play about Hollywood. But she has no lines in her first Broadway show.

APRIL 1 Henry Miller stars in *The Fountain of Youth* (32), by Louis Evan Shipman, the first production at Henry Miller's Theatre.

Business and Society

hands." This is especially true if the minstrel makes jokes at the expense of a white female cast member. **14** The Federal Trade Commission files a complaint charging violation of the antitrust laws by the Vaudeville Managers Protective Association, the United Booking Office, E.F. Albee, A. Paul Keith, and Sime Silverman, editor of *Variety*. They're charged with trying to blackball members of the White Rats performers union. **18** The Washington Square Players declare bankruptcy. With many of its members having gone off to war, the group disbands.

Births, Deaths, and Marriages

Al Jolson

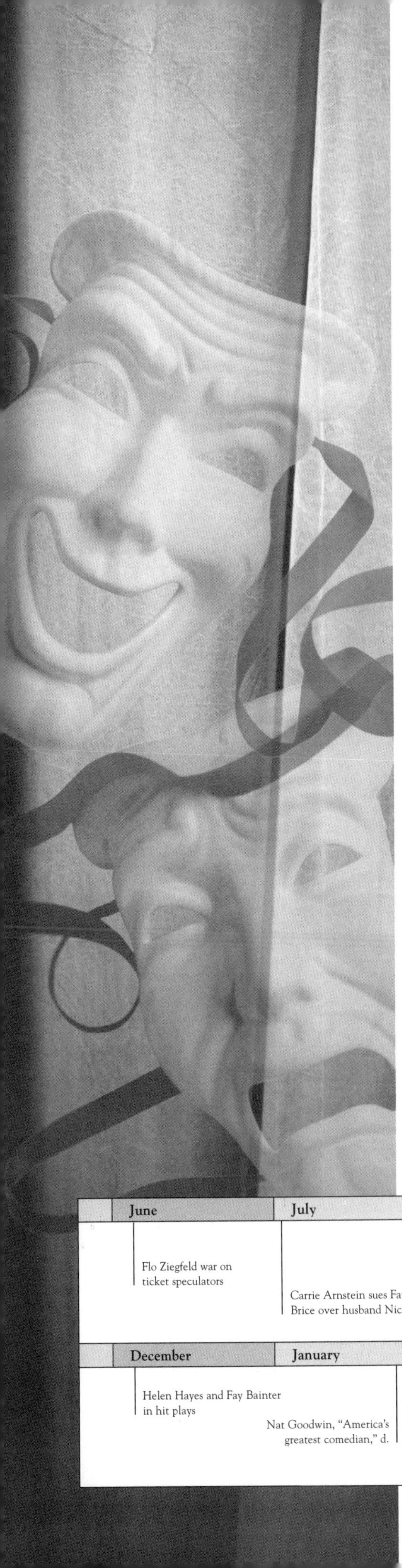

1918–19

"Oh, how I hate to get up in the morning," sings Sergeant Irving Berlin, in *Yip, Yip, Yaphank*! But "God Bless America," which had been destined for that show, will remain in the trunk for the next 20 years. The flu, more than war losses, is decimating the ranks of stage performers. E.F. Albee gains total control of the Keith circuit, the government tries to curb ticket scalping, and the Theatre Guild stages its first production. J.J. Shubert gets physical with the wrong person and gets punched. Funny lady Fanny Brice marries Nicky Arnstein, proving that she's no lucky lady. With the war over, Americans want to be entertained and have fun, while Broadway producers, in deciding to confront Actors Equity, head-on, prove that they do not.

- Number of soldiers in the cast of Irving Berlin's *Yip, Yip, Yaphank!*: 350
- Example of corny humor from *Yip, Yip, Yaphank!*:
  First soldier: "Why are the legitimate theatres losing money to the picture houses?"
  Second soldier: "Because it is easier to fil-um."
- Why *The New York Times* likes *Yip, Yip, Yaphank!*: it will persuade the parents of draftees that "the soldier's life is after all a happy one."
- Cost of staging *John Ferguson*, the Theatre Guild's first hit: $984
- Amount that the Theatre Guild has left in the bank before the success of *John Ferguson*: $19.50
- Salary paid Theatre Guild actors: $25 a week
- Fanny Brice's vaudeville income: $1,000 a week
- Cost of staging *The Ziegfeld Follies*: $100,000
- *The Ziegfeld Follies*' weekly payroll: $20,000
- Number of chorus girls in *The Ziegfeld Follies* (June 1918): 74
- Average salary of a chorus girl in the *Follies*: $40 a week
- Highest paid chorus girl in the 1918 *Follies*: Jessica Reed, who is getting $125 a week
- Flo Ziegfeld's ideal *Follies* "girl": 36-26-38
- Weekly gross of the *Follies*: $24,000
- Net weekly profit from the *Follies*: $10,000
- What Will Rogers quips in *The Ziegfeld Follies of 1918*: "England should give Ireland home rule, but reserve the motion picture rights."
- Duration of theatrical partnership of producers Marc Klaw and Abraham Erlanger—Klaw & Erlanger—now breaking up: 30 years
- New limit on ticket price premiums: $.50
- How vaudeville performers should never address audiences, according to *Variety*: "Folks"

Productions on Broadway: 149

June	July	August	September	October	November
Flo Ziegfeld war on ticket speculators	Carrie Arnstein sues Fanny Brice over husband Nick	Alan Jay Lerner born	George S. Kaufman's Broadway debut	Flu epidemic hits show business	The War ends, but ticket tax stays

December	January	February	March	April	May
Helen Hayes and Fay Bainter in hit plays	Nat Goodwin, "America's greatest comedian," d.	Antitrust investigation of vaudeville	State-Lake Theatre opens in Chicago	Fanny Brice m. Nicky Arnstein	George Gershwin's first Broadway musical

Personalities

JUNE 2 The first Pulitzer Prize for Drama, which includes a check for $1,000, is awarded to Jesse Lynch Williams for last year's *Why Marry?*

JULY • Carrie Arnstein files an alienation of affection suit against Fanny Brice, charging that the entertainer has been intimate with her husband Nick for years.

SEPTEMBER 11 A *New York Times* editorial commends Irving Berlin for his *Yip, Yip, Yaphank!* because it should convince prospective draftees that military life isn't so bad and will persuade the parents of these young men that "the soldier's life is

Lillian Lorraine ZCI

Plays and Musicals

JUNE 18 *The Ziegfeld Follies of 1918* (151) opens at the New Amsterdam. W.C. Fields has given up billiards for a golf routine. Will Rogers, Eddie Cantor, Ann Pennington, Lillian Lorraine, and Marilyn Miller, in her *Follies* debut, also star. *The New York Times* says that Eddie Cantor's "blackface bit before the curtain was funny here and there, but suffered a trifle from the need of a pencil, blue or otherwise."

JULY 22 In *Friendly Enemies* (440), by Samuel Shipmen and Aaron Hoffman, at the Hudson Theatre, two German-Americans, old friends, whose loyalties in the Great War lie on different sides, are reunited by a tragedy. Sam Bernard and Louis Mann star.

AUGUST 19 *Yip, Yip, Yaphank!* (32), an army camp musical by Sergeant Irving Berlin, opens at the Century Theatre. Soldiers—350 of them—from Camp Upton play all parts. Berlin himself sings "Oh, How I Hate to Get Up in the Morning." "Mandy" is sung by soldiers in drag wearing blackface. "God Bless America," written by Berlin for the show but dropped because he thinks it may be too "sticky," will not surface until 1938, when Kate Smith introduces it on radio. **26** Frank Bacon stars in *Lightnin'* (1,291), at the Gaiety. Bacon and Winchell Smith coauthored

Business and Society

JUNE • Vaudeville managers begin to remove acts whose members were born in Germany. They are particularly suspicious of performers claiming to be "Dutch" and of acts that seem overzealous in displaying American flags. The Chief of Military Intelligence in Washington has warned managers that German propaganda could be spouted from the stage through jokes. He gives as an example: First person: "I am in the Home Guard now." Second Person: "You protect the homes?" First Person: "Yes! I take care of the soldier's wives while the soldiers are in France." **12** Flo Ziegfeld declares war on ticket speculators and unscrupulous brokers, who have been especially active with seats for his shows. He will sell *Follies* tickets only at the box office and offer none to brokers.

JULY 3 The federal government says there will be no special railroad rates for show business people.

OCTOBER 10 The flu epidemic is closing theatres across the country. *Variety*'s weekly list of show business people killed by the outbreak is longer than its tally of those who have fallen in the War. Today, the New York City Health Commissioner meets with Broadway producers, who

Births, Deaths, and Marriages

JUNE 8 Robert Preston (Robert Preston Meservy) b.

JULY 14 Playwright-producer Arthur Laurents b.

AUGUST 2 Beatrice Straight b. **13** Anna Held d. **31** Lyricist Alan Jay Lerner, son of the founder of the Lerner stores, b.

OCTOBER 11 Choreographer-director Jerome Robbins (Jerome Rabinowitz) b. **27** Teresa Wright b.

NOVEMBER • Irene Bordoni m. songwriter E. Ray Goetz.

JANUARY 31 Nat Goodwin, described by *Variety* as "America's greatest comedian," d.

after all a happy one." The draftee is also helped to understand "that the American soldier should always appear cheerful, no matter what happens." **22** The *New York Sun*, noting Jeanne Eagels's success as a new David Belasco star in the play *Daddies*, classifies her as the fourth of Belasco's "little girls," young female stars he has built up. The others are Frances Starr, Lenore Ulric, and Ina Claire.

OCTOBER • During a rehearsal for *Little Simplicity*, J.J. Shubert, accustomed to intimidating and even roughing up associates when he strongly disagrees with them, makes the mistake of pushing star Walter Catlett, who promptly knocks J.J. into the orchestra pit.

NOVEMBER 5 Several acts at the Palace Theatre, including Blossom Seeley, Benny Fields, and the dancing Cansinos, find themselves sliding on talcum powder that some prankster has sprinkled on the stage.

DECEMBER 6 Actor James O'Neill, father of Eugene O'Neill, is hit by an automobile after getting off a streetcar on Broadway.

JANUARY 2 Six performances of *Sinbad* in three days is too much even for Al Jolson, who collapses backstage at the Winter Garden.

FEBRUARY 28 *Variety* complains that Georgie Price and other Palace Theatre acts have been addressing the audience as "Folks." "Even admitting an artist should address the audience at all, it should never be other than 'Ladies and Gentlemen' at the Palace. That 'Folks' thing sounds ruralitic." On the bill with Price this week are dancers Ruth St. Denis and Ted Shawn and George White, who recently introduced the 'Shimmy' to Broadway.

MARCH 16 Marie Dressler, at a benefit at the Hippodrome, attacks Ed Wynn, who has not shown up to emcee, as he promised. "I can only wish for the old school of actors who kept their word," she tells the audience. Producer Arthur Hammerstein, in whose show, *Sometime*, Wynn is appearing, says Wynn had not

---

this story of the West, with last-minute help from George Abbott. It's the first Broadway play to give more than 1,000 performances. **30** Maurice Schwartz's production of Z. Libin's *Man and His Shadow*, at the Irving Place Theatre, marks the birth of the Yiddish Art Theatre

SEPTEMBER 5 John L. Hobble's *Daddies* (340), at the Belasco, is a comedy in which bachelors adopt war orphans, one of whom turns out to be a teenager played by Jeanne Eagels. George Abbott costars. **9** *Someone in the House*, starring Lynn Fontanne, is the first George S. Kaufman play to open on Broadway. But the flu epidemic is in full force, and audiences are hard to come by. Kaufman suggests changing the title to *No One in the House*.

OCTOBER 3 John Barrymore appears at the Plymouth in Tolstoy's *Redemption* (204). *Variety* says that the transformation from the "lover of booze and Gypsies to the forlorn spectacle of an emaciated unkempt wreck is a piece of Barrymore work that will live long in the memory of those who see it." Helen Westley and Thomas Mitchell costar. **19** *The Better 'Ole* (353), a musical based on a cartoon character, "Old Bill," opening at the Greenwich Village Theatre, will move to the Cort on Broadway after a month. Charles Coburn stars, the music is by Herman Darewski and Percival Knight (but with many interpolations), and the story is about a German spy in France. It's filmed in 1926. **31** *Three Wise Fools* (316), by Austin Strong and Winchell Smith, who also produced, opens at the Criterion. Harry Davenport is in the cast of this story of three old friends, an old crime, and an old romance that won't go away. **24** With the opening of *Ladies First* (164) at the Broadhurst, starring Nora Bayes, the team of George and Ira Gershwin have their first song in a Broadway show: "The Real American Folk Song." But it does not survive in the score much beyond opening night. **31** The Provincetown Players' staging of Eugene O'Neill's *The Dreaming Kind*, about black gangsters, is notable for the casting of blacks, rather than whites in blackface.

NOVEMBER 27 The last of the Princess Theatre musicals, *Oh, My Dear!* (189), opens with music by Louis Hirsch rather than Jerome Kern. Guy Bolton and P.G.

---

convince him not to close their theatres. **11** The price of *Variety* rises from $.10 to $.15. War Department orders to conserve paper ends the publication's free subscriptions to professionals in the armed forces. **31** The death of A. Paul Keith (son of B.F. Keith), half owner of the Keith circuit of theatres, leaves E.F. Albee in complete control of the Keith circuit.

NOVEMBER • The end of the War and the abating of the flu epidemic leads to a burst of business on Broadway. **11** A standard Actors Equity contract goes into effect. **22** With peace breaking out, *Variety* headlines: "Weary Nation Wants Happiness and Gaiety." But producers are not so happy that the 10 percent war tax will remain. **22** The Provincetown Playhouse opens.

DECEMBER 17 New York City passes a law regulating the sale of theatre tickets and limiting the premium that brokers can charge to $.50 a ticket.

FEBRUARY 3 The Federal Trade Commission opens hearings into antitrust violations in vaudeville.

APRIL 25 Martin Beck orders performers on the Orpheum circuit of vaudeville houses to make no reference to Prohibition in their acts.

MARCH 29 Eileen Heckart b.

APRIL 5 Fanny Brice m. gambler Nicky Arnstein. **29** Celeste Holm b.

MAY 3 Lyricist Betty Comden b. **20** Alice Brady m. actor James Crane, a match that will last less than three years. **24** Marilyn Miller m. actor Frank Carter, who will d. next year in an auto accident.

Personalities

committed himself to appear and calls Dressler's remarks "unfair and uncalled for." **17** Martin Beck's $2,600,000, 3,000-seat State-Lake Theatre in Chicago's Loop opens. On the bill today are Trixie Friganza and Lou Holtz. Nine acts have been booked for the seven-act program so that the theatre can give four shows a day with no act playing more than three shows.

APRIL • Lee and J.J. Shubert are speaking to each other again after a six-month snit.

MAY 9 Eugene O'Neill writes to Professor George Pierce Baker, whose famed English 47 playwriting class O'Neill attended, enclosing a copy of his one-act plays. O'Neill says he's waited until now to contact Baker, "confident that the night would come when I could approach you with that digesting-canary grin, and, pointing to the fiery writing on the wall of some New York theatre, chortle triumphantly: 'Look, Teacher! See what I done!'" **19** *The Light*, the first play by a young dramatist, opens in Springfield, Massachusetts. The local paper headlines its review: "'The Light' Is Not Destined To Shine Very Brilliantly: Crude Production of a Modern Drama By Oscar Hammerstein 2d, Fails to Interest." Hammerstein will always call it "[t]he light that failed."

Plays and Musicals

Wodehouse still provide the book and lyrics. It's set at a health farm.

DECEMBER 20 The Provincetown Players stage Eugene O'Neill's *The Moon of the Caribbees*, directed by Thomas Mitchell (the future movie star). Heywood Broun calls it "pointless." **23** Helen Hayes is in her first hit in J.M. Barrie's comedy *Dear Brutus* (184), at the Empire Theatre. William Gillette heads the cast. **25** Fay Bainter achieves her greatest stage prominence, as a Chinese woman, in the ethnic comedy *East Is West* (680), by Samuel Shipman and John B. Hymer, opening at the Astor.

JANUARY 15 *Up in Mabel's Room* (229), which is where most everyone ends up in this farce by Wilson Collison and Otto Harbach, opens at the Eltinge. John Cumberland and Hazel Dawn are the stars.

APRIL 9 John Barrymore stars at the Plymouth with his brother Lionel in *The Jest* (77), an adaptation of an Italian play by Sem Benelli. **19** *The Bonds of Interest*, a play by Jacinto Benavente, opens at the Garrick. It's the first production by the Theatre Guild, "which is the latest of the semi-amateur societies that bring to the local stage so much that is novel and interesting," according to the *Sun*. With a cast that includes Edna St. Vincent Millay and Dudley Digges, it runs for three weeks.

MAY 12 St. John Ervine's somber drama about Ireland, *John Ferguson* (177), at the Garrick, is the Theatre Guild's first hit. *Variety* says that "while not strictly catering to those of the elevated forehead, it draws an exceedingly 'smart' house." Dudley Digges, Augustin Duncan, and Helen Westley star. In the program, the Guild refutes the "misconception" that it aims to be "non-commercial." **26** George Gershwin's first Broadway musical, *La, La, Lucille* (104), at Henry Miller's Theatre, fails to move the critics—although they recognize its "jazz" element. Alexander Aarons also makes his debut as a Broadway producer.

Business and Society

MAY 2 The split between producers Klaw and Erlanger and the demise of the old Theatre Syndicate spurs New York producers to reorganize to protect their interests, with Sam Harris heading the new Producing Managers Association. The first order of business will be dealing with a newly militant Actors Equity.

Births, Deaths, and Marriages

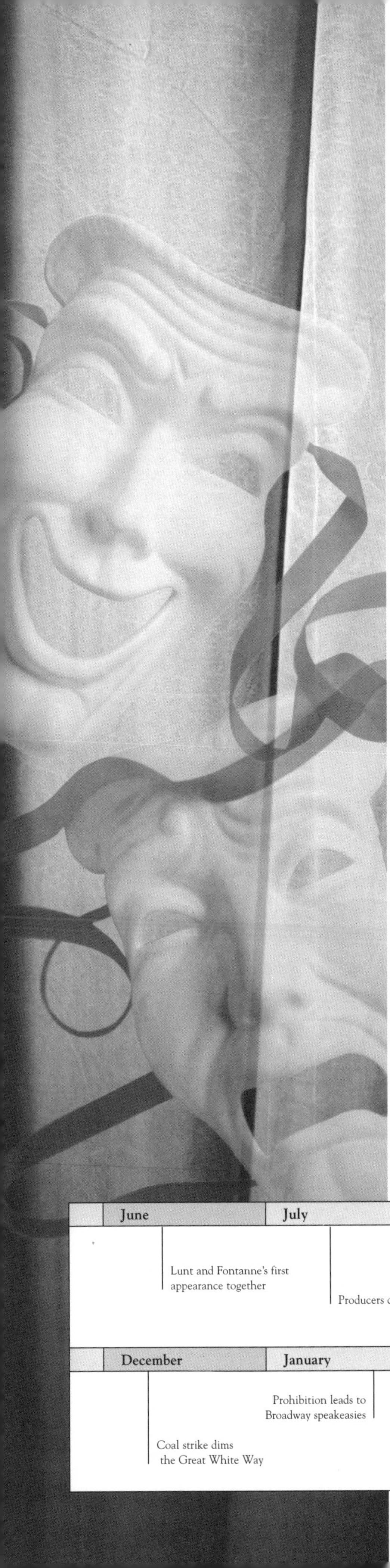

1919–20

Actors Equity becomes a force in the American theatre with its Great Strike. John Barrymore tries Shakespeare, Laurette Taylor gives a riotous performance, and Prohibition makes Broadway nightlife wetter than ever. Two Broadway plays deal with the theme of a woman who forgoes accomplishment outside the home for the sake of her family. *Irene* is enormously successful, the first of George White's *Scandals* is on the boards, and Rodgers and Hart, and Lunt and Fontanne, begin to work together as teams. Bea Lillie's new husband is noble (but not very), and Al Jolson's newly ex-wife says all he had on his mind was "wine, racehorses and women." Sidney Blackmer describes Tallulah Bankhead as "very naughty," and for Irving Berlin, "A Pretty Girl Is Like a Melody."

- Number of cities involved in the Equity strike: 8
- Number of plays closed by the strike: 37
- Number of openings delayed by the strike: 16
- Total cost of the strike: about $3 million
- David Belasco's reaction to the strike: "Starve the actors out."
- Eddie Cantor's reaction to the strike: "I am with the Equity Association and will go back to the cloak and suit trade if they lose their fight against the managers."
- Equity membership before the strike: 2,700
- Equity membership after the strike: 14,000
- Working as a *gaucho* in Argentina: 17-year-old John Houseman
- Percentage of American women who are beautiful, according to Flo Ziegfeld: 5 percent
- Off to a premature start: Richard Rodgers and Oscar Hammerstein II, who collaborate, briefly, on two songs for an amateur show: "Can It" and "Weakness"
- Banned in Boston: bare female legs on the stage without special permission
- Why Broadway producer Harry Frazee may be banned in Boston: he also owns the Boston Red Sox and has sold pitcher-outfielder Babe Ruth to the Yankees
- What Eddie Cantor is paid to record for Brunswick: $225,000 over 5 years (flat fee)
- Percentage of all vaudeville theatres controlled by the Vaudeville Managers Protective Association: 48 percent
- Number of vaudeville performers in the U.S.: 20,000
- Number of vaudeville acts employed each week: 6,000
- At the Palace Theatre: Helen Keller, with her companion, Annie Sullivan
- Cast replacements in *Irene*: Irene Dunne and Jeanette MacDonald; Busby Berkeley plays in the road company
- Will Rogers's comment on the cover of his book, *Rogers-isms: The Cowboy Philosopher on Prohibition*: "You won't find the Country any drier than this Book."
- Number of Broadway plays with more than 300 performances: 6

Number of Broadway productions: 144

Pulitzer Prize for Drama: *Beyond the Horizon* (Eugene O'Neill)

June	July	August	September	October	November
Lunt and Fontanne's first appearance together	Producers decide to crush Actors Equity	Equity strike	*The Gold Diggers*	Playwright Eugene Walter arrested	*Irene*

December	January	February	March	April	May
Coal strike dims the Great White Way	Prohibition leads to Broadway speakeasies	First full-length Eugene O'Neill play	Rodgers and Hart begin collaboration	Riot at Laurette Taylor performance	Fred Stone injured

Personalities

JUNE 9 Alfred Lunt and Lynn Fontanne appear together for the first time in *Made of Money*, opening at the National Theater in Washington, D.C., for a one-week run. They meet during rehearsals and are already in love. (When introduced, Lunt bowed to kiss her hand, tripped, and fell down a flight of stairs.)

JULY 9 George Arliss tells an interviewer: "The end of road touring in America is only a matter of time unless the younger generation reverses its present attitude and turns from blind adoration of film stars to at least equal appreciation of spoken drama."

AUGUST 4 Tallulah Bankhead has her first lead role on Broadway when she takes over for Constance Binney, the star of *39 East*, for six performances. The *Telegram* reports that audiences at Maxine Elliott's Theatre are seeing "probably the youngest leading woman in this city, and certainly the most charming." Sidney Blackmer, in the cast, will remember her as "incorrigible. She wouldn't be trained and she was very naughty." She plays practical jokes on the other players, moving the props around. **16** Tonight, Rodgers and Hart make their professional debut as a team with the interpolated "Any Place With You," in *A Lonely Romeo*, which opened on June 10. It's sung by Eve Lynn and Alan Hale. The show has been exempted from the actor's strike because producer Lew Fields does not belong to the Producing Managers Association, but when it is discovered on August 23 that his silent partners are the Shuberts, the production is shut down. **30** Noel Coward makes his stage debut in England in *The Knight of the Burning Pestle*, with the Birmingham Repertory Company.

SEPTEMBER • In a bylined *Theatre Magazine* article, Flo Ziegfeld writes that only five percent of American women are beautiful. When choosing showgirls, he looks for large, soulful eyes, a straight nose, teeth like pearls, natural hair, small feet, and "a buoyant walk." How does he choose?: "On days of inspection, the girls pass through my office in long lines. As they pass I say 'Yes' or 'No.' That is all."

Plays and Musicals

JUNE 2 *The Scandals of 1919* (128) opens at the Liberty. George White, the creator of this first of a series of 13 revues, will lend his name to them—*George White's Scandals*—beginning in 1922. White and Ann Pennington provide the dancing talent tonight. The revues appear annually through 1926 and feature George Gershwin's music in the early years. **16** Irving Berlin's "A Pretty Girl Is Like A Melody" debuts in *The Ziegfeld Follies of 1919* (171), at the New Amsterdam. Eddie Cantor returns, along with Bert Williams and Marilyn Miller. In the lobby are watercolor poster portraits of the stars by Alberto Vargas, later famous for his *Esquire* magazine pinups.

JULY 15 John Murray Anderson directs the first of eight *Greenwich Village Follies* (232), in the Ziegfeld manner but toned down, at the Greenwich Village Theatre, where its popularity will soon push it uptown to the Nora Bayes Theatre. The hit song of this "revusical" is interpolated by Ted Lewis: "When My Baby Smiles at Me."

SEPTEMBER 13 *Adam and Eva* (312), a comedy by Guy Bolton and George Middleton, opening at the Longacre, has a rich family duped into thinking they are poor so that they might learn how to make a living. Otto Kruger and Ruth Shepley star. **20** "Helen Hayes, the child prodigy, is delicious all the way" in Booth Tarkington's *Clarence* (300), declares *Variety*. It opens at the Hudson Theatre. This comedy about a family in which calm and competence are in short supply also stars Alfred Lunt and Mary Boland. **25** *Roly-Boly Eyes* (100), a musical at the Knickerbocker, is distinguished for Eddie Leonard's singing (in blackface) of his tune, "Ida, Sweet as Apple Cider," later identified with Eddie Cantor. Queenie Smith also stars. **30** *The Gold Diggers* (700), Avery Hopwood's comedy about rich men and chorus girls, starring Ina Claire, is the basis for several 1930s Warner Brothers musicals and the source of a new expression: It's at the Lyceum. Pauline Hall, playing an age-faded chorine, was, in fact, a star in years past.

Business and Society

OCTOBER • The Boston license commissioner, John M. Casey, is trying to convince his counterparts in other cities to set up a national censorship board for theatre similar to the movies' Board of Review.

NOVEMBER 14 *Variety* reports that the lure of movie money is so strong that many producers are staging plays with short runs just to have a chance to sell the film rights. Theatre people are also greatly concerned that movie interests are buying up legitimate houses across the country.

DECEMBER • The Orpheum circuit of vaudeville theatres is reorganized, with Martin Beck as president and director general. And bookings for the entire Keith circuit are consolidated for the first time. • A coal strike causes the temporary dimming of the Great White Way. **26** "There's no denying moving pictures are leaving every other form of amusement in the rear on the business side," says a *Variety* editorial.

JANUARY • A New York City judge declares unconstitutional the city's limit of $.50 on the premium that agencies may add to the price of a ticket. The law

Births, Deaths, and Marriages

JUNE 12 Uta Hagen b. **15** Anita Loos m. John Emerson. **29** Molly Picon m. producer and writer Jacob Kalich, who will take her on a tour of Europe, where she will perfect her Philadelphia-tinged Yiddish.

JULY • Al Jolson and Henrietta Keller are divorced. She says that success has spoiled him. He could think only of "wine, racehorses and women" and called her "a smalltown kid." **9** Ina Claire m. music critic James Whittaker.

AUGUST 1 Oscar Hammerstein d. He and his grandson, Oscar Hammerstein II, were barely acquainted. **12** Choreographer-director Michael Kidd (Milton Greenwald) b. **28** Producer Ernest Martin b.

SEPTEMBER 12 George Jessel m. Florence Courtney, who in a bit more than a year will be suing him for divorce, naming as

OCTOBER 10 Playwright Eugene Walter is arrested for slapping around former *Ziegfeld Follies* chorus girl and movie starlet Nina Whitmore in a Los Angeles hotel room. Walter, now working as a screenwriter, has been having an affair with her. **13** Irving Berlin, playing the Palace, "spots" Eddie Cantor sitting in a box and prevails upon the entertainer to join him on stage.

NOVEMBER • Playwright Wilson Mizner, who has dealt with gambling in his stage works, is given a one-year suspended sentence of hard labor at Sing Sing and fined $1,000 for a gambling conviction.

JANUARY • Leon Errol, doing his comic drunk act, is held over for three weeks at the Palace. **5** Oscar Hammerstein II has his first Broadway credit as a lyricist when *Always You*, with music by Herbert Stothart, opens at the Central Theatre. Heywood Broun finds it "charming." **12** Told that she will no longer review plays for *Vanity Fair*, Dorothy Parker resigns. Managing editor Robert Benchley also resigns in sympathy with Parker. The magazine has been pressured by producers, unhappy with Parker's caustic reviews, to get rid of her.

FEBRUARY • Ignoring Flo Ziegfeld's objections, Eddie Cantor signs a recording contract with Brunswick that pays him $225,000 over five years—flat fee, no royalties—a record for a musical comedy and vaudeville star. • After two rehearsals, Tallulah Bankhead is dismissed from the cast of *The Hottentot* because her voice isn't "strong enough." **1** The Bartholdi Inn, the last theatrical boardinghouse on Broadway in the theatre district, closes. The building is being torn down to make way for Loew's State. Residents have included Eva Tanguay, Charlie Chaplin, Conway Tearle, and Mack Sennett. **16** Helen Keller, who can neither hear nor speak, begins her vaudeville career at Proctor's Theatre in Newark, New Jersey, where she demonstrates how she communicates and sings. Later in the month, she plays the Palace, sharing the bill for a week with Sophie Tucker. *Variety*, reviewing Keller at the Palace, comments: "Miss Keller's turn is uplifting but a bit grisly, especially when

---

OCTOBER 6 Even Dorothy Parker likes Ethel Barrymore in *Déclasées* (257), Zoe Akins's play about an English blueblood with real class. It opens at the Empire. **7** Fritz Kreisler has written most of the music for *Apple Blossoms* (256), at the Globe. The reviewer (or the typesetter) for *The New York Times*, fingers dancing on the keys, praises the "two Adaires," especially Fred (Astaire). **23** *The Passing Show of 1919* (280), at the Winter Garden, has a song interpolation that clicks: "I'm Forever Blowing Bubbles." The cast includes Charles Winninger, Olga Cook, Reginald Denny, Mary Eaton, and Blanche Ring.

NOVEMBER 18 *Irene* (670), at the Vanderbilt and starring Edith Day, establishes a record run for Broadway musicals. The most notable song in this story of a sweet young store clerk, which leads to other shows with Cinderella-like plots, is Harry Tierney and Joseph McCarthy's "Alice Blue Gown"—a tribute to the color and fashion tastes of Alice Roosevelt Longworth. Filmed in 1926 and 1940, it will be revived on Broadway in 1973 with Debbie Reynolds.

DECEMBER 15 John Drinkwater's *Abraham Lincoln* (193), a British import starring Frank McGlynn, opens at the Cort. **22** In James Forbes's *The Famous Mrs. Fair* (343), Blanche Bates plays a woman whose war heroism opens up the possibility of accomplishment in civilian life as well, but she forgoes it for the sake of her family. It's at Henry Miller's Theatre, where Henry Miller is playing her husband, and its theme resurfaces later this season in Rachel Crother's *He and She*.

JANUARY 5 *Always You*, opening at the Central Theatre, the first Broadway musical with lyrics by Oscar Hammerstein II, will run less than three months.

FEBRUARY 2 Eugene O'Neill's first produced full-length play, *Beyond the Horizon* (111), starring Richard Bennett, Edward Arnold, and Helen McKellar, opens for a series of special matineé performances at the Morosco Theater, using cast members of Elmer Rice's *For the Defense*, which is already playing there. New York *Tribune* critic Heywood Broun calls it "a significant and interesting play by a young

---

has been in effect since last spring. **16** Prohibition goes into effect, hurting late-night shows such as *The Midnight Frolic*, which depend on the sale of drinks to bolster the box office. **19** Producer Morris Gest charges that as a result of Wall Street's huge investment in the movies, fueling the conversion of theatres to film and the luring of actors and producers to Hollywood, "the American theatre is going to hell."

FEBRUARY • A flu epidemic puts a dent in Broadway business. **6** Under the weight of snow and sleet, the canopy outside the Playhouse Theatre collapses, killing a pedestrian.

MARCH 31 The F.T.C. dismisses the May 7, 1918, complaint of the vaudeville performers group, the White Rats, which had contended that the managers were violating the antitrust laws. The Commission says that the entertainment business is not covered by these laws. E.F. Albee states that the vaudeville managers try to make their business "an ideal family institution, as far as the managers and artists are concerned, with principles of co-operation and liberality which will set an example for other business interests to emulate."

APRIL • A railroad strike hurts many vaudeville acts and touring theatrical compa-

---

corespondent a member of his vaudeville act.

OCTOBER 17 Henry Irving d.

NOVEMBER • The marriage of Willard Mack and Pauline Frederick is in the divorce courts. **4** Martin Balsam b.

DECEMBER 30 Jo Van Fleet b.

JANUARY • Beatrice Lillie m. Sir Robert Peel, great-grandson of one of Queen Victoria's prime ministers. She will wear her new title, Lady Peel, lightly and will call her autobiography *Every Other Inch a Lady*. Her husband is not very wealthy, and he gambles. **23** Peggy Hopkins m. Stanley Joyce.

FEBRUARY 11 Gaby Deslys d. **19** George Rose b. **24** Nora Bayes m. fourth husband, actor Arthur Gordon. **26** Tony Randall (Leonard Rosenberg) b.

Personalities

she speaks." **21** *The New York Times* reports that Nick Arnstein, Fanny Brice's husband, is "head of a plot to steal $5 million in a Wall Street Bond deal." He will be indicted and imprisoned on the charge, which his wife never believes. Several years ago, she paid his bail by pawning her jewelry when he was arrested for another crime.

MARCH 6 Richard Rodgers and Lorenz Hart are working together for the first time, composing the words and music for the amateur show *You'd Be Surprised.* Later this month, they will also collaborate on the Columbia University varsity show, *Fly With Me*, opening March 24. Rodgers has been cautioned by his brother's friend, Bennett "Beans" Cerf, (future publisher of Random House), that Hart is lazy and unreliable. **31** John Barrymore, performing in *Richard III* at the Plymouth, is in a state of near-collapse from overwork—he's been filming *Dr. Jekyll and Mr. Hyde*, beginning at 8 a.m., while strutting the boards at night. He has a "nervous breakdown" and will spend time at a rest farm, where his therapy includes milking cows.

APRIL29 Laurette Taylor is appearing in *One Night in Rome* at London's Garrick Theatre. Gallery patrons with poor sight lines throw coins at the stage, which boils over into a small riot, stopping the performance. Taylor shouts up to them: "You shouldn't treat a scrubwoman this way."

MAY • Fred Stone, starring in *Tip Top*, has to drop out of the show when he breaks a bone in his foot during a dance number. **28** Lew Fields, impressed by the work of Rodgers and Hart in amateur shows, has hired them to do the score for *Poor Little Ritz Girl*, opening tonight in Boston for a pre-Broadway tryout. The reviews are good, but by the time it reaches the Central Theatre on Broadway on July 27, much of their work will have been revised and replaced, and their contribution to the show will be slighted by reviewers.

Plays and Musicals

author who does not as yet know all the tricks." *The New York Times's* Alexander Woollcott says that with this tragedy of a farm boy trapped by life's circumstances, O'Neill has become "one of our foremost playwrights." Says *Vanity Fair*, in the headline over its review: "At Last An American Tragedy." It will move to the Criterion and then to the Little Theater. **12** In Rachel Crother's *He and She* (28), opening at the Little Theatre, a woman, played by Crothers, glimpses the possibility of worldly accomplishment, only to pull back for the sake of her marriage. The play flopped as *The Herfords* in 1911, as it does now, despite good reviews.

Eugene O'Neill

MARCH 6 In his first Shakespearean role, John Barrymore plays Richard III (27), at the Plymouth. It is acclaimed by the critics, with the *Times's* Alexander Woollcott writing, "It ranks with Ada Rehan's Katherine and Forbes Robertson's Hamlet in this playgoers Shakespearian experience." **8** The *Ziegfeld Nine O'Clock Revue* (78)—also called "The Ziegfeld Girls of 1920"—opens at the New Amsterdam Theatre Roof and stars Fanny Brice, W.C. Fields, and Lillian Lorraine.

APRIL 5 Ed Wynn's activism in last year's Actors Equity Strike has made him a pariah among producers, so he mounts *The Ed Wynn Carnival* (150) himself at the New Amsterdam Theatre. Marion Davies is in the supporting cast.

Business and Society

nies. • Boston prohibits women from appearing on stage in bare legs without special permission of the mayor or license commissioner.

Births, Deaths, and Marriages

MARCH 8 Eileen Herlie b.

The Great Strike of 1919

JULY 1 The Actors Equity contract with the producers expires. Equity demands recognition from management, better pay for rehearsal time, and an eight-performance work week, with extra pay for holiday or Sunday work. The producers resist Equity's push for arbitration. Equity is affiliating with the American Federation of Labor, and Equity and the producers are reaching out to groups in other branches of the entertainment industry to build strength for a coming collision. **22** The Producing Managers Association moves toward a decision to directly contest and crush Actors Equity, hoping to emulate the vaudeville managers' success against the White Rats.

AUGUST 7 Frank Bacon (father of film director Lloyd Bacon), starring in *Lightnin'*, refuses to go on, beginning the Actors Equity Strike. The casts of 11 other shows, two-thirds of major Broadway productions, follow suit tonight. Management has not taken the strike threat seriously and is able to put on only one of these shows—*The Better 'Ole*, at the Booth—with understudies. At the Equity meeting at the Hotel Astor this afternoon, 1,000 players sign the strike resolution. E.H. Sothern offers to mediate, is booed, and will resign from Equity. Audiences crowd the plays and musicals still on the boards. At the Cohan and Harris Theatre, at least, management does not take the Equity action passively. Producer Sam H. Harris is President of the Producing Managers Association. At his theatre, where *The Royal Vagabond* is playing, the stage manager has the curtain raised to show the audience the chorus boys and girls in street clothes and has them voice their opposition to the strike. **10** At Equity strike headquarters, John Drew announces that his nephews, Jack and Lionel, and niece, Ethel Barrymore, support the strike. **11** Flo Ziegfeld joins the Producing Managers Association and obtains an injunction preventing his *Follies* players from striking. The Shuberts sue Actors Equity for $500,000. George M. Cohan, a staunch supporter of management, resigns from the Lambs and the Friars, where strike fever is high, because their members "insult me and my family." He explains that "[t]he stage is my life, but I value my manhood above everything else." **12** The strike spreads to Chicago, closing two shows. Having obtained his injunction preventing his players from walking out, Flo Ziegfeld, who had maintained that he was not a member of the Producing Managers Association, now acknowledges that he is a member. His chorus girls respond by helping to set up Chorus Equity, which will receive support from Ethel Barrymore and Marie Dressler and a donation of $100,000 from Lillian Russell. Meanwhile, management takes out a full-page ad in *The New York Times* attacking Equity and warning its members to consult their lawyers because they "are personally liable for all damages and losses to the Managers caused by the strike." Signers include David Belasco, Lee Shubert, Arthur Hammerstein, George M. Cohan, John Golden, Flo Ziegfeld, Walter Wanger, Sam Harris, and Charles Coburn. **12** Ed Wynn, who has decided to join the Actors Equity Strike as a matter of principle, receives a telegram from his father-in-law, actor Frank Keenan: "At last I am proud of my Jewish son-in-law." **13** Eddie Cantor and other performers refuse to go on at the New Amsterdam, closing down *The Ziegfeld Follies*. Marilyn Miller is the only cast member willing to cross a picket line. **18** Members of Actors Equity, including Ethel and Lionel Barrymore, Eddie Cantor, Marie Dressler and W.C. Fields, begin a series of benefit performances to raise money for the strike. This afternoon, Dressler and Eddie Foy are among union members who stage a parade down Broadway in the rain. **21** Playwrights, remaining neutral in the strike, organize The Stage Writers Protection Association with Otto Harbach as president. **22** A *Variety* editorial, supporting Actors Equity, says that the producers "brought upon themselves" the strike. **24** George M. Cohan accepts the presidency of the antistrike Actors Fidelity League (known as "Fido"). **25** Striking Equity members will ignore the injunction against their action obtained in court today by the Producing Managers Association. The judge says that actors trying to interfere with the reopening of theatres is "just as illegal as if the torch was applied to them." **26** The Teamsters Union walks out in support of Actors Equity, closing down the Hippodrome. Samuel Gompers pledges the support of the American Federation of Labor. Equity members are talking about organizing a cooperative organization with the playwrights to stage productions without the producers. The antistrike Actors Fidelity League now claims 1,630 members, including Adelaide Wilson, daughter of Equity head Francis Wilson. **30** Producing Managers Association unity is breached when the Hippodrome management recognizes Actors Equity and Chorus Equity.

SEPTEMBER 5 Shubert theatres across the country close when stagehands and musicians join the Actors Equity Strike. **6** The Actors Equity Strike is settled at 3:00 a.m. and later today—Saturday night—some shows will reopen. Equity is triumphant, securing recognition from management and better conditions for its members.

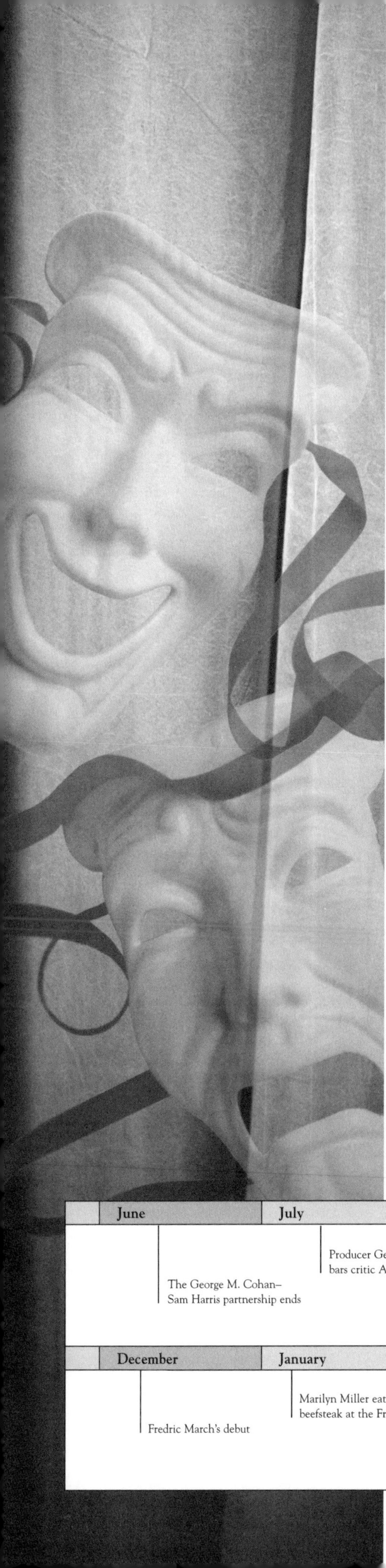

1920–21

For the Drama League, it's "guess who's coming to dinner?" Charles Gilpin, who is black, is headed for their awards ceremony—making some members very uncomfortable—and making theatre history in *The Emperor Jones*, in which he actually plays a black man. The New York Society for the Suppression of Vice has one word for many current productions—"orgies"—while *The New York Times* worries about films bidding up stage actors' salaries. Flo Ziegfeld celebrates "The Leg of Nations" but denounces Eddie Cantor. Marilyn Miller, starring in *Sally* and about to become Mary Pickford's sister-in-law, eats beefsteak at the Friars, where women rarely tread, and calls Flo Ziegfeld "a lousy son of a bitch."

- What Marilyn Miller is making in *Sally*: a percentage of the gross—said to be 10 percent—which brings her $3,000 a week, more than any other musical comedy star is earning
- What Robert Benchley (affectionately) calls Nora Bayes: "a vaudevillianess"
- Number of big-time, two-a-day vaudeville houses in the United States: 71
- Number of two-a-day houses in New York City: 9
- Gross receipts after one year from the musical *Irene*: $940,000
- Cost of staging *Irene*: $40,000
- Fanny Brice's reaction to charges that her husband, Nick Arnstein, has masterminded a Wall Street bond theft: "He couldn't mastermind an electric bulb into a socket."
- Number of plays by Avery Hopwood on Broadway: 4—*The Gold Diggers*, *Ladies Night*, *The Bat*, and *Spanish Love*—a current record, according to *Variety*
- Royalties earned by Avery Hopwood this season: about $500,000
- Number of musicals staged by Leon Errol: 4
- Number of vaudeville acts produced by Errol: 6
- Number of nervous breakdowns recently suffered by Leon Errol: only 1
- Number of Theatre Guild subscribers: 1,500
- Number of Broadway shows produced by the Shuberts: 19
- Salary paid Charles Gilpin, starring in *The Emperor Jones*: $50 a week
- Price of a complete luncheon, with music, at Shanley's, on Broadway at Forty-third Street: $1.00
- Title of the Republican campaign song, credited to Al Jolson: "Harding, You're the Man for Us"
- Number of new plays on Broadway in August: 21—producers are taking advantage of the curtailment of travel to Europe because of the aftereffects of the war

Productions on Broadway: 152

Pulitzer Prize for Drama: *Miss Lulu Bett* (Zona Gale)

June	July	August	September	October	November
The George M. Cohan–Sam Harris partnership ends	Producer George Broadhurst bars critic Alan Dale	*Variety* warns entertainers away from politics	*The Bat*	The Eddie Cantor–Flo Ziegfeld split gets ugly	*The Emperor Jones*

December	January	February	March	April	May
Fredric March's debut	Marilyn Miller eats beefsteak at the Friars	Drama League worries about Charles Gilpin	Equity members vote for a closed shop	*Irene* breaks long-run record	"I'm Just Wild About Harry"

Personalities

JUNE 20 Eugene O'Neill writes to critic George Jean Nathan: "I rate myself as a beginner—with prospects."

JULY 19 Producer George Broadhurst has again banned New York *American* critic Alan Dale from his theatre for writing an overly critical review of one of Broadhurst's productions.

AUGUST 20 Al Jolson's active role in the presidential campaign as president of the Harding and Coolidge Theatrical League causes *Variety* to warn entertainers who get involved in partisan politics that they could lose the "good will" of their audience.

SEPTEMBER • Jacob Adler begins his farewell tour as Shylock in *The Merchant of Venice*. He performs in Yiddish, while the rest of the cast speaks in English. **1** Eddie Cantor leaves Flo Ziegfeld to go with the Shuberts. The entertainer says he's switching producers because Ziegfeld has not provided him with the show promised in the contract he signed last October 7. The Shuberts are paying him $1,450 a week on a two-year contract. **13** George Jessel is at the Palace in a one-hour revue called *Troubles of 1920*, featuring Jessel in a Jewish mother-and-son bit.

OCTOBER 18 Alexander Woollcott writes in the *Times* about Helen Hayes in today's new play, *Bab*: "Probably we will all go comparing her to Marie Tempest until the day comes when suddenly we find ourselves speaking of some newcomer as a young Helen Hayes." **29** Flo Ziegfeld has challenged Eddie Cantor's use of a skit about an osteopath in the Shubert's *Broadway Brevities*, claiming Cantor lifted it from the 1919 *Follies*. Cantor says that he wrote it, but in a letter today in *Variety*, Ziegfeld says that someone else penned it and that Cantor's only contribution was that while in the *Follies*, he "started kidding in the scene and adding lines of his own that were vulgar."

NOVEMBER • Former child actress Lillian Roth enters vaudeville. **20** Small-time vaudevillian Walter Winchell writes to a fellow performer about Winchell's accepting the position of assistant editor

Plays and Musicals

JUNE 22 *The Ziegfeld Follies* (120), starring W.C. Fields and Fanny Brice, who sings "I'm an Indian"—with Eddie Cantor a last-minute addition—opens at the New Amsterdam. There is still bitterness between Cantor and Ziegfeld over last year's strike, and Cantor will drop out after a week. *Variety* finds the show disappointing. Even the "Leg of Nations" number "meant little after so much nakedness of late years."

AUGUST 9 Can a man hide in a Turkish bath on *Ladies Night* (375)? This comedy, by Avery Hopwood and Charlton Andrews, starring John Cumberland, is at the Eltinge. According to tomorrow's *World*, "the only clean thing about last night's performance was the water." **16** Gilda Varesi plays the singer whose opera career comes between her and her husband in Dolly Burn's comedy *Enter Madame* (350), at the Garrick. **23** *The Bat* (867), a mystery in a haunted house by Mary Roberts Rinehart and Avery Hopwood, collaborating on their second play in as many weeks, opens at the Morosco. Effie Ellser and Mary Voke star. **30** Holbrook Blinn stars at the Comedy Theatre in *The Bad Man* (342), Porter Brown's western satire.

SEPTEMBER 13 George Sidney plays a businessman who overcomes anti-Semitism in *Welcome Stranger* (309), a comedy by Aaron Hoffman, at the Cohan and Harris Theatre. **27** The denizens of *The Tavern* (252) are not drunk; they're crazy escapees from a mental hospital. Arnold Daly stars in this play by Cora Gantt, revised by George M. Cohan, at the George M. Cohan Theatre.

OCTOBER 5 Fred Stone dances and jokes his way through *Tip Top* (246), an Ivan Caryll musical, also featuring the Duncan Sisters, at the Globe. **18** In *Mary* (220), a musical by Louis Hirsch, Otto Harbach and Frank Mandel, opening at the Knickerbocker, a young man has to strike it rich before he realizes that he's in love. It stars Jack McGowan and Janet Velie. **20** Frank Craven wrote and stars in *The First Year* (725), a comedy at the Little

Business and Society

JUNE • John Emerson is elected president of Actors Equity. **27** According to *The New York Times*, the going rate for screen rights to successful plays has risen to about $100,000, double the price of a year ago. Picture companies are now financing plays to get the inside track on these rights. **30** George M. Cohan and Sam Harris dissolve their producing partnership.

NOVEMBER • Sam Harris, the Selwyns, and Arthur Hopkins set up their own booking combination.

JANUARY 24 The Shuberts announce that they are setting up a circuit of at least 20 vaudeville theatres to compete with the Keith circuit. The venture will fail.

MARCH • Members of Actors Equity vote for a closed shop. Beginning with the 1921–1922 season, all actors on the legitimate stage will have to hold an Equity card.

MAY • The railroads report an unusually high failure rate among road shows. As many as 3,000 chorus girls are unemployed in New York. **5** The New York Society for the Suppression of Vice, in its

Births, Deaths, and Marriages

JULY 24 Producer Alexander Cohen b.

AUGUST 5 John Barrymore m. Blanche Thomas (poet "Michael Strange"). **10** James O'Neill, father of playwright Eugene O'Neill, who toured the country for years in *The Count of Monte Cristo*, d. **14** Walter Connolly m. Nedda Harrigan, daughter of Edward Harrigan of Harrigan and Hart.

SEPTEMBER 14 Kay Medford (Kathleen Regan) b.

OCTOBER • Sophie Tucker sues Frank Westphal for divorce. • Blossom Seeley divorces baseball pitcher Rube Marquard. **17** Montgomery Clift (Edward Montgomery Clift) b. **27** Nanette Fabray (Nanette Fabares) b.

of the Keith circuit's "Vaudeville News." The new journalist has taken the job, "believing that the future of such a position holds remarkable things for me (if I show 'em what I am made of) and has unlimited possibilities."

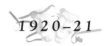

DECEMBER 21 Marilyn Miller, growing less and less fond of Flo Ziegfeld, acknowledges the producer's backstage visit on *Sally*'s opening night with "Hello, you lousy son of a bitch." **23** Frederick Bickel, making his Broadway debut in a minor role in *Deburau*, at the Belasco, is also the understudy for the play's star, Lionel Atwill, whom he will replace for one week during the play's run. Bickel has not yet changed his name to Fredric March.

JANUARY 23 The Friars honor Leon Errol and Marilyn Miller with a beefsteak dinner for their triumph in *Sally*. Miller is the first woman accorded this kind of honor by the club.

FEBRUARY 18 The Drama League, voting for outstanding stage personalities of the past year, points to the inclusion of Charles Gilpin, starring in the *Emperor Jones*. But the awards are given out at a dinner, and Gilpin is black. What to do? Some members suggest he be sent a "nice letter" instead of a dinner invitation. But when he's a winner with the final vote on February 20, and other winners denounce his possible exclusion, he will be invited. **26** At the musical *Sally* tonight, sitting in a box and drawing a good deal of attention are Mary Pickford and Douglas Fairbanks, brought by Mary's brother, Jack, to see the object of his affections, Marilyn Miller, perform.

MARCH 4 Al Jolson, who organized the Harding Theatrical League to back the candidacy of Warren G. Harding, has a prominent place in the inaugural parade today. **6** At the Drama League's award dinner, Charles Gilpin, almost excluded because he is black, receives an ovation. **14** What is probably the first radio variety show, featuring the Duncan Sisters, now performing in Fred Stone's *Tip Top*, is broadcast from Ossining, New York, and is heard hundreds of miles away.

APRIL • Producer Oliver Morosco is arrest-

Theatre, about the beginning of a marriage.

NOVEMBER 1 Eugene O'Neill's *The Emperor Jones* (204), starring Charles Gilpin, opens at the Neighborhood Playhouse. *The New York Times* says Gilpin's "is an uncommonly powerful and imaginative performance. . . . Mr. Gilpin is a negro." The *New York Clipper* says the casting is appropriate, "by reason of his natural color." The *Clipper* sees O'Neill as a different American playwright, "[w]hich doesn't mean that we consider him a greater or better dramatic writer than George M. Cohan or Eugene Walter," it hastens to add. The play moves to the Selwyn Theatre on Broadway on December 27 and to the Princess Theatre on January 29. Paul Robeson stars in the London production and in the 1933 film. **10** The Theatre Guild gives the American premiere of George Bernard Shaw's antiwar *Heartbreak House* (125) at the Garrick. In the cast are Helen Westley, Albert Perry, Effie Shannon, and Dudley Digges. **17** Yiddish Theatre star Jacob Ben-Ami makes his English-speaking debut at the Greenwich Village Theatre in *Samson and Delilah* (143), by Sven Lange. **17** The Apollo Theatre opens on Forty-second Street with a Herbert Stothart musical, *Jimmie* (71), starring Frances White. **23** Roland Young plays a man who can afford his own production of *Hamlet* in Clare Kummer's comedy, *Rollo's Wild Oat* (228), opening at the Punch and Judy Theatre.

DECEMBER 21 Marilyn Miller opens in Jerome Kern and Guy Bolton's *Sally* (570) at the New Amsterdam, with Leon Errol and Walter Catlett. Heywood Broun writes that Kern "seems to have set his heart on popularizing a tinkling tune called 'Look For the Silver Lining' which is ingratiating enough in its own mushy way. . . ." Helen Morgan is in the chorus. Miller also stars in the 1929 film. **27** Zona Gale's comedy, *Miss Lulu Bett* (201), destined for a Pulitzer Prize, opens at the Belmont. Carroll McComas plays the spinster sister who is married off as a joke—and experiences the happy consequences that result.

JANUARY 18 George Arliss and Ronald Colman star in *The Green Goddess* (440),

---

annual report, likens some farces and musicals to "orgies." **27** A *New York Times* editorial warns Broadway producers who have been touting their shows with risqué ads that they "are next in line" after the movies to suffer demands for censorship.

DECEMBER 29 Viveca Lindfors b.

JANUARY 31 Carol Channing b.

FEBRUARY 9 Critic James Gibbons Huneker d.

Times Square in the 1920s BROWN

Personalities

ed for violating the Volstead Act (Prohibition). • The original Sardi's opens on West Forty-forth Street on the site of the future St. James Theatre. Vincent Sardi waits on tables while his wife cooks. **22** *Billboard* reports that Flo Ziegfeld "will not stand for any of the artists under him exercising their talents through radio." Ziegfeld and Eddie Cantor have already parted ways over the comedian-singer's desire to make records, a technology that the showman is only now finally coming to accept.

MAY • In an affectionate portrait of Nora Bayes in *Everybody's Magazine*, Robert Benchley refers to her as "essentially a vaudevillianess." One thing that endears her to him, besides her singing—she introduced George M. Cohan's "Over There"—is her eccentric habit of signing communications, "Your Loving Son, Nora Bayes."

Plays and Musicals

by William Archer, who was the first to translate Ibsen into English. This exotic drama, at the Booth, involves a plane that crashes in mysterious, exotic Central Asia.

FEBRUARY 11 *The Rose Girl* (110), a musical, is the premiere attraction at The Ambassador Theatre, opening on West Forty-ninth Street. The music is by Anselm Goetzel, with lyrics by William Carey. It stars Mabel Withee and Charles Purcell.

MARCH 2 Katharine Cornell, Tallulah Bankhead, and Francine Larrimore are flappers in Rachel Crothers's comedy, *Nice People* (247), at the Klaw Theatre.

APRIL 18 Ethel and John Barrymore are the attractions in *Clair de Lune* (64), by Michael Strange (*nom de plume* of Blanche Thomas, who is married to John), opening at the Empire. Its top price of $5 for an orchestra seat at all performances, not just on opening night or other special occasions, is the highest ever for a straight dramatic play. **18** With its 604th performance, *Irene* breaks the New York stage record for musicals set 40 years ago by *Evangeline*. **20** The Theatre Guild production of *Liliom* (300), the Ferenc Molnár play on which Rodgers and Hammerstein's *Carousel* will be based, opens at the Garrick. Eva Le Gallienne and Joseph Schildkraut have the leads.

MAY 23 *Shuffle Along* (504), a musical by Eubie Blake and Noble Sissel, with an all-black cast, opens at the Sixty-third Street Theatre. This musical, says *The New York Times*, is infused with "the melody popularly supposed to be inherent in the Negro." Florence Mills sings, "I'm Just Wild About Harry." "Love Will Find a Way" also debuts. Paul Robeson will join the show during the run, and Josephine Baker will sing in the touring company's chorus.

Business and Society

Births, Deaths, and Marriages

MARCH 3 Diana Barrymore, daughter of John Barrymore, b. **8** Ethel Barrymore's lawyer confirms reports that she has separated from her husband, Russel Colt, but will not seek a divorce for religious reasons and to protect their children.

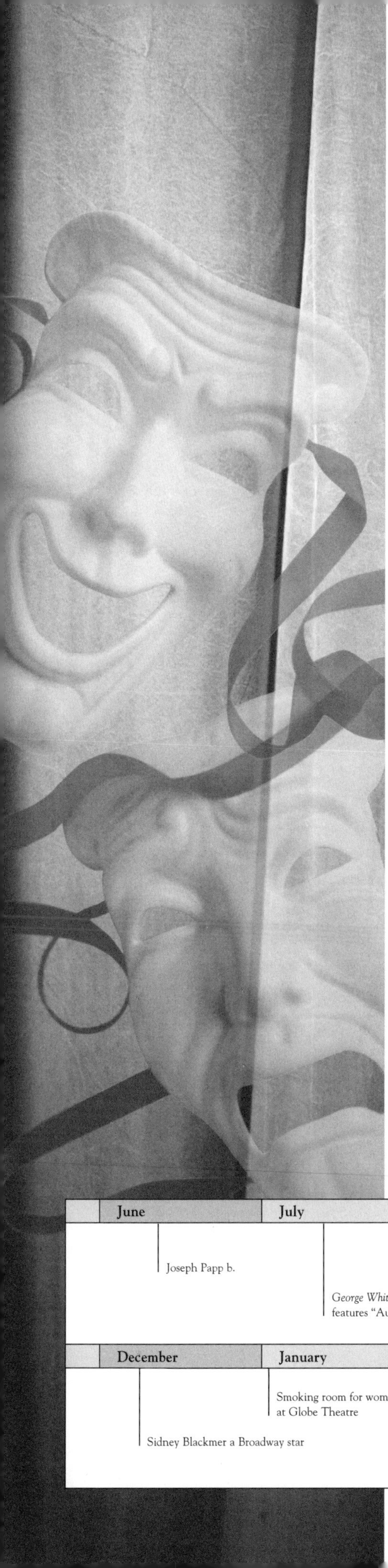

1921–22

Now it's radio, not only films, that stage producers have to worry about. Stagelighting begins to take on an artistic as well as utilitarian function. Marilyn Miller defends bobbed hair, and Fanny Brice sings "My Man," while her man is unavailable. Katharine Cornell marries Guthrie McClintic, Al Jolson gets his name on a theatre, Irving Berlin owns his own theatre, and 20-year-old Harold Clurman, studying at the Sorbonne, is sharing an apartment with young composer Aaron Copland, to whom he is distantly related by marriage. The Shuberts outbid Keith's for Will Rogers, and Eugene O'Neill criticizes people who have criticized *Anna Christie*. For the first time, there's a classic choice for that after-the-show bite: Lindy's or Sardi's?

- How *Variety* misspells Tallulah Bankhead's name: "Talulla Bunkhead"
- Cost of a shore dinner at Feltman's: $2.75
- Cost of staging *The Music Box Revue*: $187,613, a new record for revues
- Top ticket price for *The Music Box Revue*: $5.50
- How long it takes Anne Nichols to write *Abie's Irish Rose*: 3 days.
- How long it takes Anne Nichols to get *Abie's Irish Rose* produced: 3 years.
- Who plays financial angel to the beloved and sentimental *Abie's Irish Rose*: notorious gambler Arnold Rothstein.
- Winner of Robert Benchley's contest for best comment on *Abie's Irish Rose*: Harpo Marx, who calls it "[n]o worse than a common cold."
- Amount lost by the Theatre Guild on its production of George Bernard Shaw's *Back to Methuselah*: about $15,000
- Number of fares collected at Times Square subway stations (1921): 46,608,899
- Name changed: Vaudeville fiddler-comedian Ben Benny, who has already had to change his name once, from Benjamin Kubelsky, because of its similarity to another performer's name, faces the problem again. Now entertainer Ben Bernie is threatening to sue. The result is one final variation—Jack Benny
- New social phenomenon: women smoking in theatre lobbies
- What the producers of *The Demi-Virgin* put in their ad in *The New York Times* when the paper won't print the name of their play: "Are you one of the 168,423 persons who have already seen the most famous play in America at the Eltinge Theatre?"

Productions on Broadway: 194

Pulitzer Prize for Drama: *Anna Christie* (Eugene O'Neill)

June	July	August	September	October	November
Joseph Papp b.	*George White's Scandals* features "Aunt Jemima"	Lindy's opens	Katharine Cornell m. Guthrie McClintic	Shuberts and Keith circuit vie for Will Rogers	*Anna Christie*

December	January	February	March	April	May
Sidney Blackmer a Broadway star	Smoking room for women at Globe Theatre	*The Cat and the Canary*	Play jury system set up	Producers cut salaries during box office slump	*Abie's Irish Rose*

Personalities

AUGUST • Marilyn Miller, whose bobbed hair has made news, tells an interviewer about the reluctance of businesses to hire a girl with bobbed hair: "I think it's a grievous instance of transgression upon the rights of women." • The young actress modeling what seem to be masculine sporting clothes in the Abercrombie and Fitch ad in *Theatre Magazine* is Eva Le Gallienne. **1** Ethel Barrymore makes her Palace Theatre debut. **20** Leo and Clara Lindemann open Lindy's restaurant—immortalized by Damon Runyon as "Mindy's" in one of his Broadway stories—on Broadway near Fiftieth Street. They host Broadway personalities and serve the world's most famous cheesecake. **29** Loew's State Theatre, featuring vaudeville, opens a block south of the Palace in Times Square, with appearances by David Warfield, W.C. Fields, Ted Lewis, Frank Fay, Fanny Brice, Jack Dempsey, and other luminaries.

SEPTEMBER • Heywood Broun, writing about *The Ziegfeld Follies* in *Vanity Fair*, reflects on its joining of bare flesh to social significance and patriotic solemnity. Broun feels "a little like a Peeping Tom in the presence of Godiva and generally I cover my eyes in order that they may be preserved for the final processional in which one girl will be Coal, another Aviation, and a third the Monroe Doctrine." **19** Gallagher and Shean are at the Palace, singing "Mr. Gallagher and Mr. Shean."

OCTOBER • J.J. Shubert writes to Al Jolson that "your association with a lot of race track touts is not what Mr. Al Jolson should be coupled with." **31** A bidding war between the Shubert and Keith circuits and his new fame in Hollywood nets Will Rogers what the Shuberts claim is the highest vaudeville salary ever. They pay him $8,600 for two weeks at the Winter Garden in New York, beginning tonight.

DECEMBER 18 Eugene O'Neill, in a letter in *The New York Times*, replies to people who have criticized "the compromise happy ending" in *Anna Christie*. Calling

Plays and Musicals

JUNE 21 With *Sally* still filling the New Amsterdam, its usual home, *The Ziegfeld Follies* (119) opens at the Globe. This edition, "Best of Them All," according to *The New York Times*, has Fanny Brice singing "Second-Hand Rose" and "My Man," which the audience associates with her star-crossed marriage to gambler Nicky Arnstein. W.C. Fields also stars in this year's *Follies*.

JULY 11 *George White's Scandals* (97), at the Liberty Theatre, features the music of George Gershwin and a cast that includes White, Ann Pennington, Lou Holtz, and "Aunt Jemima."

AUGUST 1 Hazel Dawn stars in *Getting Gertie's Garters* (120), a farce about the problems involved in returning an intimate present to a former sweetie who has married someone else. It opens at the Republic. **13** *Dulcy* (246), a satire on advertising and the movies, opening at the Frazee Theatre, is by George S. Kaufman and Marc Connelly. It stars Lynn Fontanne as the heroine whose greatest desire is to be helpful. **25** Donald Meek (playing a character named "Richard Burton"), Ernest Truex, June Walker, and Hedda Hopper star in *Six-Cylinder Love* (430), a comedy at the Sam H. Harris Theatre. **27** *Lightnin'*, starring Frank Bacon, closes after 1,291 performances, currently a record for Broadway plays.

SEPTEMBER 1 The National Theatre opens on West Forty-first Street with Sidney Howard's *Swords*. **5** Gilbert Emery's *The Hero* (80), at the Belmont, is about a veteran who is everything but what the title says—until the last thing he ever does. The cast includes Richard Bennett, Fania Marinoff, and Blanche Friderici. **22** Irving Berlin's Music Box Theatre opens on Forty-fifth Street with Berlin's *Music Box Revue of 1921* (440). The first of four editions, it's the only series of shows designed as a vehicle for one composer. This edition features "Say It With Music." Berlin himself appears, and one of the "Eight Little Notes" is Miriam Hopkins. **29** Sigmund Romberg's *Blossom Time* (592), with lyrics by Dorothy Donnelly, about the composer Franz

Business and Society

SEPTEMBER 19 The Shubert's new vaudeville circuit begins operations.

OCTOBER 18 *The New York Times*, offended by the title, won't run ads for *The Demi-Virgin*.

NOVEMBER • The Keith office instructs the Palace Theatre management to curb the boisterous applause of song pluggers at matinées, who break into an ovation every time their songs appear in an act.

DECEMBER 2 "What is vaudeville coming to?" asks *Variety*, noting the policy of the State-Lake Theatre in Chicago, which has been staging vaudeville acts and a movie in continuous performances at popular prices. It is a model for what will become the first-run, downtown movie theatres of the 1930s and 1940s, which will supplant the vaudeville houses. **9** *Variety* notes of the seating at *Shuffle Along*, the Noble Sissle–Eubie Blake black musical: "Colored patrons are allowed in the orchestra, but are so seated they have one side or one-third of the house as a rule given over to them, with the whites taking the other two-thirds." **23** Actors Equity and the Authors

Births, Deaths, and Marriages

JUNE 22 Producer Joseph Papp (Yossel Papirofsky) and choreographer-director Gower Champion b.

JULY 14 Willie Howard m. Emily Miles. Both are in *The Passing Show of 1921*.

AUGUST 3 Composer Richard Adler b.

SEPTEMBER 8 Katharine Cornell m. director Guthrie McClintic.

OCTOBER • Vaudevillian Bee Palmer is sued for divorce by her husband Al Siegel, Sophie Tucker's accompanist, who names Jack Dempsey as a corespondent. She and Dempsey have been appearing on the stage together. Palmer says that Siegel beat her: "I picked him out of the gutter. I married him at midnight on the impulse of the moment."

them "hard of hearing," he writes, "I wanted to have the audience leave with a deep feeling of life flowing on, of the past which is never the past—but always the birth of the future—of a problem solved for the moment but by the very nature of its solution involving new problems."

JANUARY 9 *The New York Times* reports that "Charles Dillingham has installed in the Globe Theatre what he calls 'the first exclusive smoking room for women in a New York theatre.'" Women who have forgotten their cigarettes at home will be given some. The room will be designated the "smoking lounge." **20** *Variety*, in its "Legit Items" column, states that "Talulla Bunkhead" [sic] will step into the lead role in *Danger* as a cast replacement.

In the ornate Keith theatres, films will accompany and then replace vaudeville acts LYNCH

Shubert opens at the Ambassador.

OCTOBER 3 Harry Davenport and Edith King star in *Thank You* (257), a comedy by Tom Cushing and Winchell Smith, at the Longacre. **6** Al Jolson is in *Bombo* (219), at Jolson's Fifty-ninth Street Theatre, singing "April Showers," "Toot, Toot, Tootsie," and "My Mammy." "California Here I Come" is added to the show on the road. The Shuberts have just renamed the Imperial Theatre for their star. **10** *A Bill of Divorcement* (173) opens at the George M. Cohan Theatre. Katharine Cornell is the daughter of a mentally ill man deserted by his wife. Alexander Woollcott, in the *Times*, says that Cornell, in the star-making part, "was little short of fascinating. . . ." **18** *The Demi-Virgin* (268), a comedy by Avery Hopwood, is at the Times Square Theatre. Hazel Dawn and Glenn Anders are movie stars having a hard time with married life. The strip poker scene is a cause célèbre.

NOVEMBER 2 Eugene O'Neill's *Anna Christie* (177), starring Pauline Lord and George Marion, opens at the Vanderbilt. Critics qualify their high praise with reservations about the play's "happy" ending, intimating that O'Neill is beginning to make concessions to the commercial theatre. O'Neill feels it's a "failure," but it will win for him his second Pulitzer Prize. **7** Ed Wynn is *The Perfect Fool* (256) at the George M. Cohan Theatre. The comedian has also written this show, a hodgepodge of skits and musical production numbers. **29** Lenore Ulric stars, at the Belasco Theatre, in David Belasco's hit comedy *Kiki* (580).

DECEMBER 12 Sidney Blackmer achieves Broadway fame with his performance in Clare Kummer's comedy *The Mountain Man* (163), at Maxine Elliott's Theatre.

JANUARY 9 The Theatre Guild's production of Leonid Andreyev's *He Who Gets Slapped* (308), opening at the Garrick, stars Richard Bennett and Margalo Gillmore.

FEBRUARY 4 Nikita Balieff's *Chauve-Souris* (544), a Russian revue, opens at the Forty-ninth Street Theatre. **7** John

League of America join to fight censorship by dealing with any play that might raise the call for censorship. **23** A Grand Jury refuses to indict producer A.H. Woods for *The Demi-Virgin*.

JANUARY • *The Emperor Jones*, with Charles Gilpin in the lead role, is the first play starring an African-American to play in the South—in Norfolk, where it's successful. • George M. Cohan resumes producing in the U.S.

FEBRUARY 3 According to *Variety*, "'Gold Diggers' is now a 'legitimate' term in the musical comedy circles. . . . [D]ramatic agents in submitting lists to producers have one group tabbed as 'gold diggers,' the term now classifying the show girl type of choristor."

MARCH • Boston censor John Casey rules that Ann Pennington must keep her legs covered when she dances in *George White's Scandals*. • The Shuberts and Abraham Erlanger agree to restrict competition between themselves and to avoid booking conflicts in the approximately 500 theatres they control across the country. **3** Under the first page headline, "Vaudeville and Musicians Declare Against Radiophone [radio]," *Variety* reports that "[t]he vaudeville people take

NOVEMBER • Peggy Hopkins Joyce is divorced by Stanley Joyce. She gets to keep her $1 million dollars' worth of jewelry.

JANUARY 7 Vincent Gardenia (Vincent Scognamiglio) b. **21** Paul Scofield b.

FEBRUARY 4 Pauline Frederick m. Dr. Charles Rutherford. **26** Margaret Leighton b.

MARCH 4 Bert Williams d. Critic Heywood Broun writes of him: "There was only one restriction which limited him. Since he was a Negro he must be a funny man. . . . Somehow or other laughing at Bert Williams came to be tied up in people's minds with liberalism, charity and the Thirteenth Amendment." **22** Blossom Seeley m. Benny Fields. The 1952 film *Somebody Loves Me* is about them. **31** Richard Kiley and Executive James M. Nederlander b.

Personalities

FEBRUARY 19 Laurette Taylor recently opened in *The National Anthem*, a play on the evils of drinking and jazz—Taylor is an alcoholic—by her husband, J. Hartley Manners. Today she tells a church audience: "My objection to jazz is that one can't sit still when it is played. You must get up and wear yourself out dancing." **28** Bert Williams collapses onstage in Detroit while performing in *Under the Bamboo Tree*.

MARCH 9 Eugene O'Neill's excitement over the premiere of *The Hairy Ape* in Greenwich Village tonight is dulled by the arrival of his mother's body by train from California, where she died three weeks ago.

APRIL • *Variety* gossips: "Helen Menken and Humphrey Bogart have taken out a license to wed. Mr. Bogart is at present playing in *Up the Ladder*, and Miss Menken was one of the stars in *Drifting*." **15** In a tribute to Bert Williams, Eddie Cantor quotes approvingly the evaluation of the great black comedian made by J.J. Shubert: "Bert Williams was one of the whitest actors I have ever known." **28** An ad in *Variety* touts the talent and appeal "of the attractive, petite, adorable Ruth Etting, who is making an envious name with her pleasant, voluminous voice" in a Chicago revue.

MAY 29 Marilyn Miller announces her engagement to movie actor Jack Pickford, Mary Pickford's brother. Each had a spouse who died violently within the past few years. Flo Ziegfeld, to whom Miller is under contract, is vehemently opposed to the match and tells her that Pickford was dishonorably discharged from the Navy during the war for helping wealthy young men avoid combat.

Plays and Musicals

Willard's *The Cat and the Canary* (349), opening at the National Theatre, becomes a haunted house classic and will be filmed several times. Florence Eldridge and Henry Hull star. **20** *To The Ladies* (128), a comedy by George S. Kaufman and Marc Connelly, opening at the Liberty, stars Otto Kruger as the businessman who gets ahead thanks to his wife, played by Helen Hayes. **27** Americans get their first look at George Bernard Shaw's *Back to Methuselah* (25), as the Theatre Guild opens the first of three parts of the drama at the Garrick.

MARCH 9 Eugene O'Neill's *The Hairy Ape* (120), starring Louis Wolheim and Mary Blair, opens at the Playwrights' Theatre. It will move to the Plymouth on April 17, with Carlotta Monterey replacing Blair (O'Neill does not initially get along with Monterey, who will become his third wife). It's about a primitive-looking man who fits in nowhere and appeals to no one.

APRIL 13 Eddie Cantor stars in *Make It Snappy* (96), a revue at the Winter Garden. Burns Mantle writes of the singer-comedian, appearing mostly in whiteface for the first time, that "Eddie Cantor as a star is a cleaner comedian than was Eddie Cantor as a bad little Jewish boy from the Bronx singing dirty songs in support of some other star. He has washed his face and at least rinsed his humor."

MAY 15 Elliott Nugent coauthored with his father, John Charles Nugent, the comedy *Kempy* (212), opening at the Belmont. **23** Anne Nichols's *Abie's Irish Rose* (2,327) which, according to *Variety*, is about "a Jewish boy, son of an old-fashioned clothing dealer of the 'kike' type, who secretly marries a girl, daughter of an Irishman of the 'flannel-mouth Mick' sort," opens at the Fulton. The reviewer says that the play "may waver while the public decides whether it is to bloom or wilt." Critics hate it; audiences love it. It stars Robert B. Williams and Marie Carroll.

Business and Society

the position that the new fad serves to keep people at home and away from the theatre and may develop into a serious box office menace." An editorial notes that some entertainers have been making free appearances on radio in the hopes of getting publicity but that they should be paid. Next week, the paper will run a banner headline: "Radio Sweeping Country." **10** Trying to hold off government censorship, producers, playwrights, and actors organize a "play jury" system in which panels of representative citizens will view and pass judgment on new productions, with all participants in the shows pledged contractually to abide by any objections the juries raise. **22** A New York City judge stops the police department's attempt to censor *The Hairy Ape*.

APRIL • Producers cut salaries to keep shows going as the box office downturn continues. **12** New York State Governor Miller signs a bill reinstating the $.50 limit on ticket premiums.

MAY 5 "Little Theatres A Craze" says *Variety*'s front-page banner headline. The paper has begun to cover them regularly.

Births, Deaths, and Marriages

APRIL 7 Joseph Schildkraut m. Elsie Porter.

MAY 10 Nancy Walker (Anna Myrtle Swoyer) b. Her father is acrobat Dewey Barto and her grandfather, a circus clown. **24** Siobhan McKenna b. Alfred Lunt and Lynn Fontanne m.

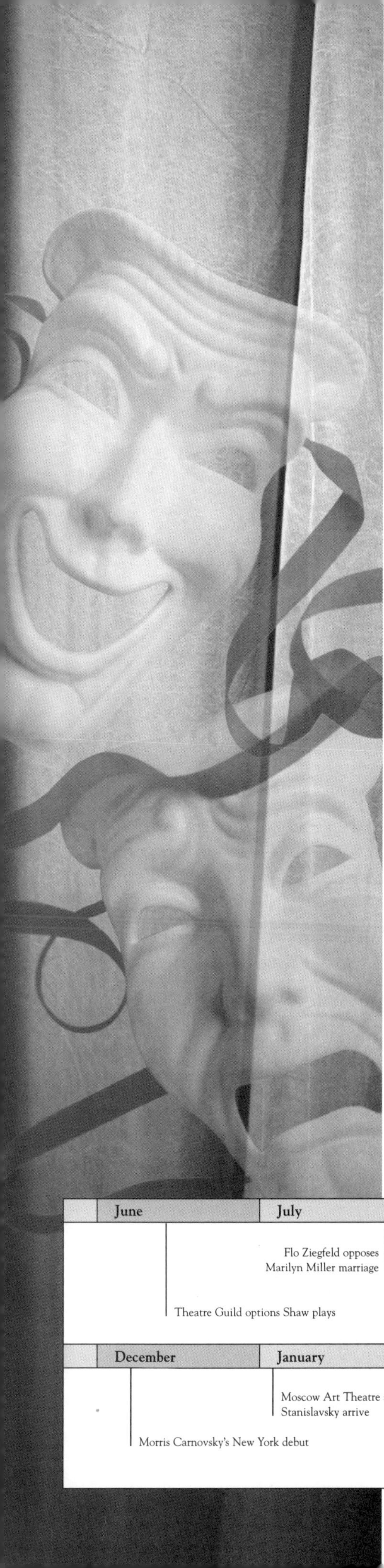

1922–23

The Moscow Art Theatre and Stanislavsky visit Broadway, leaving an indelible impression on American theatre. Jeanne Eagels is a resounding success as Sadie Thompson in *Rain*, but there's already more than one cloud on her horizon. Jane Cowl triumphs in *Romeo and Juliet*, and John Barrymore reaches the pinnacle of Broadway stardom with his *Hamlet* but already hears the siren song of Hollywood. Karel Čapek's *R.U.R.* brings a new word: "robot." Vaudeville has just peaked, but the end is near. Flo Ziegfeld is "Glorifying the American Girl," except when she's his big star Marilyn Miller and wants to marry. And *Variety* says it's even money that *Abie's Irish Rose* won't last out the season.

- Billie Burke's reaction to gossip that her husband, Flo Ziegfeld, is enamored of Marilyn Miller: "Pish tosh"
- How *The New York Times* refers to the "robots" in *R.U.R*: "ape mannikens"
- Number of vaudeville acts at theatres also showing a film: 4–6
- Total cost of salaries for these acts: $60 to $100 a day
- Newest fad in vaudeville acts: dance bands, typified by Paul Whiteman, Vincent Lopez, and Ben Bernie
- Split between George Burns and Gracie Allen in their new vaudeville act: 60–40, which will reach 50–50 as her importance to the act becomes clear
- Students at Professional Children's School in New York City: Ruby Keeler, Lillian Roth, and Milton Berle
- Increase of ticket sales to *The Hairy Ape*, caused by the attempts of the New York City Police to censor it: about one-third, mostly lower priced seats
- Rental cost of electric sign in Times Square advertising *The Ziegfeld Follies*: $1,000 a week
- Most popular playwright on Broadway: Shakespeare, with 2 productions of *Romeo and Juliet* (Ethel Barrymore and Jane Cowl), John Barrymore's *Hamlet*, and David Warfield's Shylock in *The Merchant of Venice*
- Number of performances given by John Barrymore in his record-breaking run in *Hamlet*: 101
- What one of the cast members removing Ophelia's body in *Hamlet* is reported to have said to John Barrymore when he told them that they were supposed to be virgins: "My dear Mr. Barrymore, we are extras, not character actors."
- Amount lost by Theatre Guild: $15,104.23

Productions on Broadway: 174

Pulitzer Prize for Drama: *Icebound* (Owen Davis)

June	July	August	September	October	November
Theatre Guild options Shaw plays	Flo Ziegfeld opposes Marilyn Miller marriage	Prohibition jokes out at Keith theatres	Victor Herbert's last show	Stella Adler's Broadway debut	Jeanne Eagels's *Rain* and Barrymore's *Hamlet*

December	January	February	March	April	May
Morris Carnovsky's New York debut	Moscow Art Theatre and Stanislavsky arrive	Philip Barry's Broadway debut	Sarah Bernhardt d.	Cantor back with Ziegfeld	Lunt and Fontanne's Broadway debut

Personalities

JUNE 12 Fanny Brice opens a four-week engagement at the Palace. Also on this week's bill is actor Lionel Atwill, in his vaudeville debut. **14** Flo Ziegfeld is quoted in the *New York Daily News* on the pending marriage of Marilyn Miller, who, he reminds the public, he made into a star: "The marriage of any female star lowers her drawing capacity, so, naturally, I do not want Miss Miller to marry at just the height of a tremendous success." **16** Billie Burke, Flo Ziegfeld's wife, says that she's heard that Marilyn Miller has been saying that Burke's husband is jealous of Jack Pickford and that Miller has received unwanted romantic overtures from Ziegfeld. Burke's reaction to the gossip: "Pish tosh."

JULY 20 Marilyn Miller says, "I don't want to quarrel with Flo Ziegfeld's wife, but if Billie Burke wants to fight, I'll give her a real one. I've got lots of ammunition and Broadway will understand what I mean." Miller says Ziegfeld tried to bribe her with jewels not to marry Jack Pickford. She reminds Burke that Burke's manager/producer, Charles Frohman, was also unhappy when she married Ziegfeld. "Why, then," Miller says about Billie Burke, "isn't she generous enough to give me a chance?"

AUGUST 5 Georgie Price will miss several performances of the *Spice of 1922* at the Winter Garden after he has a fistfight with the theatre manager.

SEPTEMBER 25 An annual $500 prize to a present or former member of Professor George P. Baker's playwriting course at Harvard this year goes to Philip Barry, for *The Jilts* (later renamed *You and I*). Barry's first produced play, *A Punch for Judy*, premieres this year.

OCTOBER 9 Alexander Woollcott, formerly the drama critic at *The New York Times*, begins his new job, at a higher salary, reviewing plays at the *Herald*. John Corbin has replaced him at the *Times*, where Woollcott's last piece concluded: "Exit the First Grave-Digger. Curtain."

Plays and Musicals

JUNE 5 *The Ziegfeld Follies* (541), at the New Amsterdam, is the first to use the slogan "Glorifying the American Girl." Will Rogers stars, and Gallagher and Shean sing their "Mr. Gallagher and Mr. Shean."

AUGUST 22 *The Old Soak* (423), a comedy about a drunkard and his family, at the Plymouth, is by newspaper columnist Don Marquis (creator of *archy and mehitabel*). Harry Beresford and Minnie Dupree star. **28** *George White's Scandals of 1922* (88) opens at the Globe. In the cast are W.C. Fields and Dolores Costello. The score includes George Gershwin's "I'll Build a Stairway to Paradise." His one-act opera, *Blue Monday*, falls flat with the critics and is removed from the revue.

SEPTEMBER 18 Ina Claire copes with a previous and a future husband in Arthur Richman's comedy *The Awful Truth* (144), at Henry Miller's Theatre. **19** *Orange Blossom* (95), opening at the Fulton, is Victor Herbert's last show.

OCTOBER 2 The Equity Players flop with their first production, *Malvaloca* (48), at the Forty-eighth Street Theatre. **9** At the Garrick, the Theatre Guild presents Karel Čapek's play *R.U.R.* (Rossum's Universal Robots) (182), the futuristic drama which introduces the word "robot." Basil Sydney, Louis Calvert, and Helen Westley star. **23** *The Music Box Revue of 1922* (330) opens at the Music Box Theatre, introducing Irving Berlin's "Pack Up Your Sins and Go to the Devil," sung by Charlotte Greenwood, and "Dance Your Troubles Away." **23** In Channing Pollock's *The Fool* (360), opening at the Times Square Theatre, a Christ-like church rector, played by James Kirkwood, runs into nothing but trouble when he tries to live a true Christian life. **30** *Seventh Heaven* (704), a romantic melodrama by Austin Strong, opens at the Booth. Helen Menken, finding happiness in marriage to a sewer worker, and George Gaul star. **30** Luigi Pirandello's reality-questioning drama, *Six Characters in Search of an Author* (137), is at The Princess Theatre. In the

Business and Society

JUNE • The Theatre Guild receives from George Bernard Shaw the first U.S. option on all his plays—of which the Guild will produce eleven in its first decade of existence. • The Shubert vaudeville organization begins to use radio to publicize its shows, with Shubert performers appearing on the air.

JULY 28 "Big Time Vaudeville Fading Slowly, Say Mgrs," is *Variety*'s headline describing the move toward mixing films with several vaudeville acts at popular prices.

AUGUST • E.F. Albee orders that there be no jokes about Prohibition in Keith vaudeville houses, a policy Orpheum theatres have already adopted. Albee says that the jokes are banned because they've become boring, not because of management's social attitudes.

OCTOBER 31 A U.S. District Court judge, applying the precedent set in the Supreme Court decision a year ago concerning baseball, rules that vaudeville is not part of interstate commerce.

NOVEMBER 6 Keith's $4 million, 3,400-seat Palace Theatre in Cleveland, featuring a

Births, Deaths, and Marriages

JUNE 5 Lillian Russell d. **21** Judy Holliday (Judith Tuvim) b.

JULY 15 Philip Barry m. Ellen Semple. **17** Ruth Etting m. her manager, Martin ("Moe the Gimp") Snyder. **26** Jason Robards, Jr., son of actor Jason Robards, b.

AUGUST 1 Arthur Hill b. **18** Al Jolson m. Alma Osborn (stage name: Ethel Delmar).

OCTOBER • Blanche Yurka m. actor Ian Keith. Nora Bayes and Arthur Gordon are divorced. **29** Playwright Robert E. Sherwood m. Mary Brandon. **31** Barbara Bel Geddes, daughter of stage designer Norman Bel Geddes, b.

NOVEMBER 12 Kim Hunter (Janet Cole) b.

NOVEMBER 10 In a letter in *Variety*, actor Henry Hull says that the cheaper theatre seats in the gallery are no longer filled because of a new, more restrained style of acting has replaced the older histrionics. The "good old gallery gods" are "utterly unable to hear the mutterings and whisperings down on the stage."

DECEMBER 15 Nora Bayes, injured in a St. Louis auto accident in which she is hurled through the windshield, nevertheless will go on with her stage appearance at the Empress Theatre tomorrow night.

JANUARY • Richard Bennett, touring in *He Who Gets Slapped*, makes curtain speeches, criticizing other shows and even his audience if they have not demonstrated sufficient appreciation of his work. • Producer John Golden pronounces of the Moscow Art Theatre: "Most Americans lead a decent, clean, and happy life; they do not have any contact with the degraded individuals, morbid, neurotic, and vicious seen in so many Russian dramas." **4** The Norwalk, Connecticut, *Sentinel* notes of performers in a vaudeville act called "Broadway Bound" that they may well be headed for "a prominent place in the theatrical hall of fame." One of them is 13-year-old Milton Berle. **6** Tallulah Bankhead sails for London, where she will become a presence on the British stage through 1931. **28** The new *Times* critic, John Corbin, wonders about the adulation heaped on the visiting Moscow Art Theatre for its production of "Tchekhoff's" *The Cherry Orchard* and whether that play really is greater than *Rain*.

FEBRUARY • Appearing in *Sally* in Chicago, Leon Errol is hospitalized after he collapses from overwork. **1** "11-Year-Old-Child Censored By Judge," says *Variety*'s headline about a Rochester, New York, magistrate who permits Rose Hovick to maintain custody of daughter, June, whose act was halted by the Society for the Prevention of Cruelty to Children. Rose agrees to tone down June's songs and hire a tutor for her. (The child is June Havoc, and Mama is the *raison d'etre* of the 1959 *Gypsy*.)

MARCH • The Shuberts cancel their five-year contract with Georgie Price, who

---

cast of this "rather slender and technical satire," according to the *Times*, are Florence Eldridge, Moffat Johnson, and Margaret Wycherly. **31** Using the name Lola Adler, Stella Adler, daughter of Yiddish theatre star Jacob Adler and sister of Luther Adler, makes her Broadway debut in *The World We Live In* (112), by Josef and Karel Čapek.

NOVEMBER 7 Jeanne Eagels is loose woman Sadie Thompson in *Rain* (648), by John Colton and Clemence Randolph, at Maxine Elliott's Theatre. Robert Kelly is her puritanical minister nemesis. *The New York Times* says that Eagels displays "an emotional power as fiery and unbridled in effect as it is artistically restrained." **13** George M. Cohan's mystery parody, *Little Nelly Kelly* (276), starring Elizabeth Hines, opens at the Liberty. **13** Glenn Hunter is the accidental movie star in the George S. Kaufman and Marc Connelly satirical look at Hollywood *Merton of the Movies* (398), at the Cort. **16** "In all likelihood, we have a new and lasting Hamlet," says the *Times* about John Barrymore's performance at the Sam Harris Theatre. It will set a new record for the play, with 101 performances. Tyrone Power, Sr. plays Claudius, and Blanche Yurka is Gertrude.

Jeanne Eagels *PF*

DECEMBER 20 Morris Carnovsky makes his New York stage debut in Sholem Asch's *The God of Vengeance* (133), at the Provincetown Playhouse. Also in the cast are Rudolf Schildkraut and Sam Jaffe.

---

lobby rug worth $125,000 and $1 million in art works, opens on Euclid Avenue as a vaudeville house.

DECEMBER 29 *Variety* prints a list of odds on the likelihood of plays having long runs. The paper says of *Abie's Irish Rose*, in its 33 week: "Even money it lasts out season at Republic [Theatre] and 3/1 it doesn't run beyond June."

FEBRUARY • With bowing getting out of hand and shows running too long, the Palace sets a two–curtain- call limit on all acts. • Piqued by *Variety*'s negative view of the Shubert's efforts to become a power in vaudeville, Lee Shubert withdraws his company's ads from the paper.

MARCH • The dance hall craze as an alternative form of entertainment is worrying Broadway producers, especially with the announcement this month that a huge, new one will be built at Broadway and Fifty-third—Roseland. **6** The New York City police shut down *The God of Vengeance*—in its third week on Broadway after moving uptown from Greenwich Village—for obscenity and indecency and arrest Joseph Schildkraut and other members of the company. They will be convicted but win on an appeal. *Variety* says *The God of Vengeance* "is

---

JANUARY 19 Jean Stapleton (Jeanne Murray) b. **29** Paddy Chayefsky (Sidney Chayefsky) b.

MARCH 26 Sarah Bernhardt d.

Personalities

refused to go on at the Central Theatre two weeks ago when he did not get star billing.

APRIL • Eddie Cantor leaves the Shuberts to sign again with Flo Ziegfeld. **12** *Variety* reviews the year-old team of George Burns and Gracie Allen: "He has a good delivery for this style of talk and the girl is an excellent foil. They have more than average personalities. The act lets down in spots, due to the dialogue, and can be strengthened in this respect." Burns is also described as the "lounge lizard type." **25** At the Globe, Ann Pennington is singing in *Jack and Jill*, accompanied on the banjo by her leading man, Brooke Johns. When one of his strings breaks, he walks off into the wings to get another, stranding her in mid-lyric. Eyewitnesses say she follows him offstage and punches him.

John Barrymore

MAY • **17** Reviewing Bert Lahr's act at the Jefferson Theatre downtown, *Variety* finds the "former burlesque comedian" a "scream" and declares that "the big time can use this act in any spot."

Plays and Musicals

The play's subject, prostitution, will cause the police to shut it down. **21** David Warfield is Shylock in *The Merchant of Venice* (92), David Belasco's only production of a classic, at the Belasco Theatre.

JANUARY 8 Constantin Stanislavsky's Moscow Art Theatre begins a two-month repertory season at the Fifty-ninth Street Theatre with a production of Alexei Tolstoy's *Tsar Fyodor Ivanovitch*. **24** Shakespeare's *Romeo and Juliet* (157), with Jane Cowl and Rollo Peters in the title roles, is at Henry Miller's Theatre.

FEBRUARY 7 "Bambalina" is the hit song in *Wildflower* (477), a musical by Herbert Stothart, Vincent Youmans, Otto Harbach, and Oscar Hammerstein II, at the Casino. Edith Day is the star. **10** The Pulitzer Prize will go to Owen Davis's play *Icebound* (170), about a family full of disappointed heirs. It stars Robert Ames, Phyllis Povah, and Edna May Oliver and opens at the Sam H. Harris Theatre. **19** *You and I* (174), Philip Barry's first Broadway play, opens at the Belmont. Lucille Watson, Ferdinand Gottschalk, and H.B. Warner are in the story of a man who regrets the compromises he's made in life.

MARCH 19 Elmer Rice's expressionistic play *The Adding Machine* (72) is at the Garrick. Dudley Digges plays Mr. Zero, and Helen Westley, Margaret Wycherly, and Edward G. Robinson ("Edgar G. Robinson" in the cast box of *Variety*'s review) are also in the cast.

MAY 18 Laurette Taylor stars in *Sweet Nell of Old Drury* (51), at the Forty-eighth Street Theatre. It's the first performance on Broadway for the team of Alfred Lunt and Lynn Fontanne. **24** Lula Vollmer's *Sun-Up* (356) opens at the Provincetown Playhouse.

Business and Society

considered the most disgusting play ever presented on Broadway" and only in Greenwich Village could it be considered a "work of art." The play will reopen in a month but close for good when audiences lose interest.

APRIL 15 Producer Morris Gest's warehouse in Manhattan burns, with the loss of 500 trunks of costumes belonging to the Moscow Art Theatre.

Births, Deaths, and Marriages

1923–24

The American stage is enriched by the Broadway debuts of Gertrude Lawrence and Beatrice Lillie, together in one revue. *Runnin' Wild* introduces the Charleston, and W.C. Fields, as Professor Eustace McGargle in *Poppy*, creates the curmudgeonly con-man persona he will take to sound films. *All God's Chillun Got Wings*, with Paul Robeson in love with a white woman, is a racial hot potato. Walter Hampden's *Cyrano* will stand as the best until he's nosed out by José Ferrer, while Fanny Brice's nose also makes news. Ticket agencies report stiff business from older men, who want to see the naked women in *Artists and Models*. Earl Carroll's *Vanities* begin, and the new act at the Palace is Jack Benny.

- Number of hit plays featuring Judith Anderson: 3—*Peter Weston, The Crooked Square*, and *Cobra*
- Greatest single night loss in a Times Square floating crap game by vaudevillian Lou Clayton (later of Clayton, Jackson, and [Jimmy] Durante): a reported $20,000
- Number of benefits played by Eddie Cantor in the calendar year 1924: 54, according to Cantor
- Amount of income taxes paid by prominent entertainment figures (leaked to the papers by government officials):
  Eddie Cantor: $18,678
  Marilyn Miller: $4,962
  George S. Kaufman: $4,220
  Robert Benchley: $679
- Royalties collected by George S. Kaufman and Marc Connelly for *Beggar on Horseback*: 15 percent on the gross above $10,000, characterized by *Variety* as "[o]ne of the smartest contracts obtained by playwrights for a non-musical show. . . ."
- Why Fanny Brice had a nose job, according to Dorothy Parker: to "cut off her nose to spite her race"
- Biggest problem of small vaudeville houses: comedians who rebuke the audience when they fail to laugh at the performer's jokes (the Keith organization is cracking down on this practice)
- Biggest flop: the Shubert vaudeville circuit
- Number of times Will Rogers performed before President Woodrow Wilson, a big fan of vaudeville: 5
- What Jimmy Durante says, at the Club Durant, about his nose: "Here it is, folks! Yes, it's real! It ain't gonna bite you, and it ain't gonna fall off."
- Percentage of Broadway casts that will have to be Equity members under the new contract: 80 percent, with the rest paying dues
- Show that introduces nudity to Broadway: *Artists and Models*

Productions Broadway: 186

Pulitzer Prize for Drama: *Hell-Bent for Heaven* (Hatcher Hughes)

June	July	August	September	October	November
Jane Cowl ends Broadway run as Juliet	First Earl Carroll *Vanities*	Fanny Brice nose job	W.C. Fields is a con man in *Poppy*	*Runnin' Wild* introduces the Charleston	Walter Hampden's *Cyrano*

December	January	February	March	April	May
Imperial Theatre opens	Beatrice Lillie and Gertrude Lawrence's Broadway debut	*Beggar on Horseback*	Racial controversy over *All God's Chillun Got Wings*	Newcomer Jack Benny at the Palace	Another Equity strike

Personalities

JUNE • George White, bending to pressure from the Shuberts, removes song lyrics in his current *Scandals* that refer to "Jake and Lee." **9** An estimated 3,000 people crowd the block outside Henry Miller's Theatre at this afternoon's matinée to glimpse Jane Cowl, ending her run in *Romeo and Juliet*. And 1,000 are turned away at the box office tonight. **30** Flo Ziegfeld drops the current *Follies* parody of David Belasco, who has been concerned that actor Brandon Tynan is so good that some people will think that it's really Belasco on the stage.

JULY 23 Al Jolson, back from a European trip, tells reporters that "they hate us over there and never miss an opportunity to show their ill will."

AUGUST • John Barrymore is filming *Beau Brummell* in Hollywood. Off the screen, he is seducing 17-year-old Mary Astor, but the greater seduction is that which Hollywood is performing on one of Broadway's greatest stars. He will not appear in a Broadway play again until 1940. **15** "Everything about me has stopped growing except my nose," says Fanny Brice, explaining why she is having a nose job today. She says that it should help her move into more serious dramatic roles. Dorothy Parker writes that Brice has "cut off her nose to spite her race." **20** Lillian Roth, signed for the Broadway production of *Artists and Models*, opening tonight, has been transferred to the less risqué Chicago edition when it's discovered that she is only 15 years old. **25** Critic George Jean Nathan, writing on the current edition of *The Ziegfeld Follies*, refers to blackface comedian Eddie Cantor as a "Jewish Negro."

OCTOBER 17 Fire destroys the Orpheum Theatre in Memphis 30 minutes after the conclusion of a vaudeville show headed by Blossom Seeley.

NOVEMBER 8 The Provincetown Players are reconstituted, with Kenneth Macgowan in charge of production. They have changed the name of their Greenwich Village theatre from the Playwrights

Plays and Musicals

JULY 5 The Earl Carroll Theatre opens on Fifteenth Street with *Vanities of 1923* (204), the first of nine editions of this revue Carroll will produce through 1940. Starting next year, each will be called *Earl Carroll's Vanities*.

AUGUST 15 *Little Jesse James* (385), a musical opening at the Longacre, has the song "I Love You" and the Broadway debuts of future screen star Miriam Hopkins and of Nan Halperin and John Boles. **20** *Artists and Models* (312), at the Shubert, is said to be the first American "leg" show with naked women in other than a tableaux vivant setting: these nudes move. Next month, to compete, Earl Carroll's *Vanities* will also add nudity. **20** Anita Loos and John Emerson's *The Whole Town's Talking* (173), about a clerk mistaken for a gangster, opens at the Bijou. Grant Mitchell and June Bradley star. The film comes out in 1935.

SEPTEMBER 3 Yiddish theatre stalwart Boris Tomashevsky, renaming the Nora Bayes Theatre Tomashevsky's Broadway Theatre, produces *Three Little Businessmen* (44), with Rudolf Schildkraut. **3** The orphan turns out to be an heiress in *Poppy* (328), at the Apollo, with Madge Kennedy in her Broadway debut and W.C. Fields as carnival con man Professor Eustace McGargle, the persona he will use in sound films. Stephen Jones and Arthur

W.C. Fields, professional curmudgeon

Business and Society

JULY • *The Clipper*, the theatrical paper founded in 1853, is taken over by *Variety* and will now cover the outdoor amusement field exclusively.

AUGUST • Performers on the Keith circuit of vaudeville houses are being discouraged from doing "mammy songs," as the public begins to tire of Al Jolson knockoffs.

OCTOBER • *Variety* begins regular coverage of the Yiddish theatre.

JANUARY • *Theatre Arts* magazine becomes a monthly.

FEBRUARY 19 The New York State Court of Appeals upholds the state law limiting agency premiums on theatre tickets to $.50.

MARCH • The Producing Managers Association, soon to be replaced by the Managers Protective Association, complains that Equity is trying to force a closed shop on Broadway. "The theatre is not a shop," David Belasco melodramatically declares. "It represents an art. No manager worthy of the name goes into it for money. We all die poor. But the theatre goes on."

Births, Deaths, and Marriages

JULY • Ethel Barrymore is divorced from Russell G. Colt.

JULY 10 Playwright Jean Kerr (Bridget Jean Collins) b.

AUGUST 10 Clare Boothe m. socialite George Brokaw. There is no dancing at the reception because the country is mourning the death of President Harding.

OCTOBER 30 Herschel Bernardi b.

NOVEMBER 21 Vivian Blaine (Vivian Stapleton) b.

APRIL 3 Marlon Brando b. **21** Eleanora Duse d. in Pittsburgh while on her farewell tour. **22** Producer Arthur Hammerstein m. actress Dorothy Dalton, who was formerly married to actor Lew Cody. **30** Lyricist-composer Sheldon Harnick b.

Theatre to the Provincetown Playhouse. **18** The Club Durant, in which Jimmy Durante has a 25 percent stake, opens on West Fifty-eighth Street. Patrons include Legs Diamond and Mad Dog Coll. **20** Playing in *Cyrano* at the National Theatre, Walter Hampden injures his leg in a balcony scene and will miss several weeks of performances.

DECEMBER 13 Marilyn Miller and Flo Ziegfeld both send telegrams to the newspapers confirming that they have severed their professional ties. Tomorrow, Ziegfeld will claim that she's jealous of his new star, Mary Eaton, about to open in *Kid Boots* with Eddie Cantor.

JANUARY • Beatrice Lillie, opening in *Charlot's Revue* will comment of her stay in Prohibition era New York: "I never saw so much liquor in my life." • John Barrymore, playing in *Hamlet* in Philadelphia, has begun to make funny curtain speeches. One night, he imitates his black valet, doing what one publication refers to as "darky dialect." **12** Gus Edwards, whose vaudeville "kiddie" act nurtured the early careers of Eddie Cantor and Georgie Jessel, files for bankruptcy after flopping as a producer.

FEBRUARY 14 *Variety* reports that Helen MacKellar has turned down a role in Eugene O'Neill's *All God's Chillun Got Wings* because the part involves a white woman marrying a black man. She objects to what the paper terms "radical casting": the black man is going to be played by a black man.

MARCH • Laurette Taylor announces that she and her husband, playwright J. Hartley Manners, in whose plays she has appeared exclusively for a decade, have had a "professional divorce." • In its comments on the preopening controversy over Eugene O'Neill's *All God's Chillun Got Wings*, *The New York Times*, notes that it's about an affair between a black man, played by Paul Robeson, and a white woman, played by the white actress Mary Blair. "[S]ince the actress will be required to kiss the [N]egro's hand at one point, no little concern has been expressed over the manner in which the play will be received." **18** In a statement

---

Samuels wrote the music. **22** *The Music Box Revue* (273), at the Music Box Theatre, features Irving Berlin's "What'll I Do?" sung by Grace Moore, and "Yes, We Have No Bananas" is interpolated. Robert Benchley makes his stage debut in the skit "The Treasurer's Report and Other Aspects of Community Singing."

OCTOBER 1 *Tarnish* (255) is what Ann Harding finds when she looks closely at her fiancé, played by Tom Powers. This play by Gilbert Emery opens at the Belmont. **9** Otto Kruger, Edward Arnold, and June Walker star in the Owen Davis comedy *The Nervous Wreck* (279), opening at the Sam H. Harris Theatre. It will become the 1928 Eddie Cantor musical *Whoopee*. **16** In Lula Vollmer's *The Shame Woman* (276), at the Greenwich Village Theatre, Florence Rittenhouse plays a seduced and abandoned woman who unwittingly creates a tragedy when she describes her ordeal to her adopted daughter. **20** *The Ziegfeld Follies of 1923* (233), at the New Amsterdam, stars Fanny Brice, Bert and Betty Wheeler, and the Paul Whiteman Orchestra. **23** Ferenc Molnár's *The Swan* (253) opens at the Cort. Eva Le Gallienne, Basil Rathbone, Alison Skipworth, and Philip Merivale star in this comedy about a royal romance. **29** In *Runnin' Wild* (213), a black musical opening at the Colonial, Elizabeth Welch sings a song composed by James P. Johnson and Cecil Mack that will spark the biggest dance craze of the decade: "Charleston."

NOVEMBER 1 Walter Hampden scores a critical success in a revival of Rostand's *Cyrano de Bergerac* (250), with Carroll McComas as Roxanne. *The New York Times* call's Hampden's Cyrano "an interpretation of great physical vigor, deep truth and intensity of passion. . . ." It's at the National Theatre. **5** *White Cargo* (864), Leon Gordon's play about the English in Africa, is at the Greenwich Village Theatre. Richard Stevenson and Annette Margules, as Tondeleyo, star.

DECEMBER 25 The Imperial Theatre opens on West Forty-sixth Street with the musical *Mary Jane McKane* (151), with music by Herbert Stothart and Vincent Youmans and lyrics by William Carey Duncan and Oscar Hammerstein II. It stars Mary Hays.

APRIL • The Jewish Theatrical Alliance—later the Jewish Theatre Guild—involving participants in all entertainment fields, is organized. William Morris is president, and Eddie Cantor is another officer.

MAY 14 "Speakeasies are springing up all over the Times square district and invading the domain of the supper and night clubs," reports *Variety*. On May 28, the paper will report: "New Crusade on Broadway Dope Peddlers." **31** Actors Equity goes on strike, closing eight Broadway shows, including *Rain* and *Seventh Heaven*. The issue is the expiration of the contract that came out of the 1919 strike and Equity's demand for a union shop. Many producers have come over, but several, including John Golden, Sam Harris, and Charles Dillingham, hold out. They will soon give in, with the agreement being that 80 percent of casts will have to be union members, and the rest will pay dues.

MAY • Vaudevillians Ole Olsen (of Olsen and Johnson) and Laura Weber m. in a lighthouse in San Francisco, where they are both appearing at the Orpheum. **13** Producer-director Theodore Mann b., and Louis Hirsch d. **26** Victor Herbert d.

Personalities

to the press about public reaction to the theme of miscegenation in *All God's Chillun Got Wings*, Eugene O'Neill says that the play's "intention is confined to portraying the special lives of individual human beings" and that it's not a "race problem" drama. The play, which hasn't yet opened, was published last month in the second issue of *The American Mercury*.

APRIL • *No, No Nanette*, opening for tryouts in Detroit, is lagging at the box office. Worried producer H.H. Frazee pressures Vincent Youmans and Irving Caesar to give the show a musical lift with new

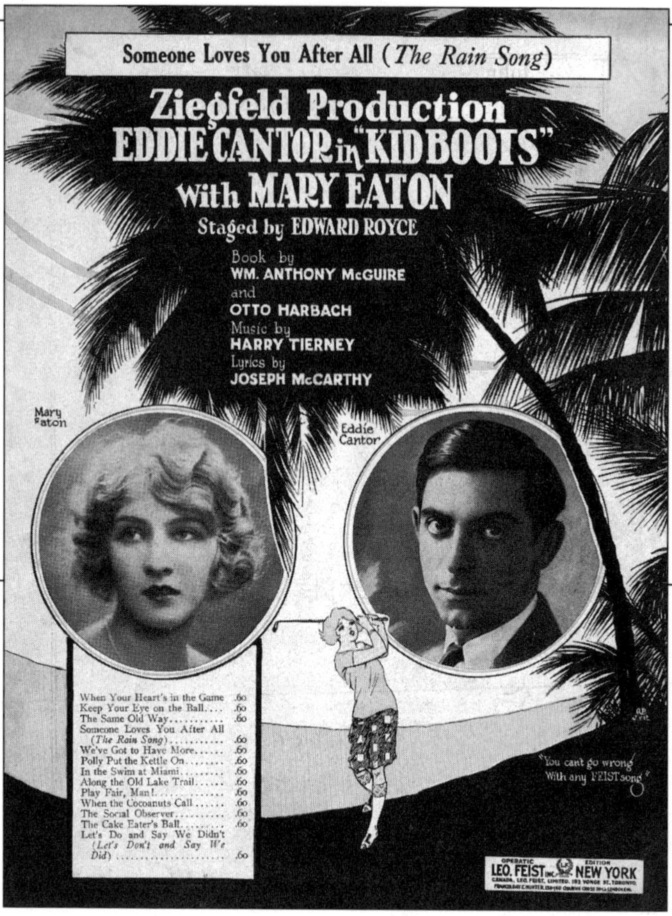

Eddie Cantor stars in *Kid Boots* BROWN

Plays and Musicals

28 George Bernard Shaw's *St. Joan* (214) has its American premiere at the Garrick in a Theatre Guild production. Winifred Lenihan is Joan. **31** Eddie Cantor plays a Palm Beach caddie-bootlegger and sings "Dinah" in *Kid Boots* (479), with a Harry Tierney–Joseph McCarthy score, costarring Mary Eaton, at the Earl Carroll Theatre.

JANUARY 4 *Hell-Bent for Heaven* (122), a play by Hatcher Hughes that will win a Pulitzer Prize when the jury is overruled, opens at the Klaw Theatre. George Abbott, Glenn Anders, and Clara Blandick star in this story of romance, a rural feud, and religious fanaticism. **9** *Charlot's Revue* (298), opening at the Times Square Theatre, introduces American audiences to Beatrice Lillie, Gertrude Lawrence, singing "Limehouse Blues," and Jack Buchanan. Writes critic Percy Hammond of Gertrude Lawrence, "Every man in town is, or will be, in love with her."

FEBRUARY 5 George Kelly's *The Show-Off*

Business and Society

Births, Deaths, and Marriages

material. The result: "Tea for Two" and "I Want to Be Happy." **9** Reviewing this week's show at the Palace, *Variety* notes that newcomer Jack Benny "is a big time asset. He has repose, material and delivery. He relegates his fiddling as incidental although a proficient instrumentalist."

MAY 11 With his play *All God's Chillun Got Wings* about to open, reporters push Eugene O'Neill to say whether he believes in white superiority. He replies: "Spiritually speaking, there is no superiority between the races. We're just a little ahead mentally as a race, though not as individuals." **12** Fanny Brice visits husband Nicky Arnstein in a Washington, D.C., jail just before he is shipped off to prison to serve time for buying stolen bonds. **16** The Pulitzer Prize Advisory Board acknowledges that it overruled the jury's selection of *The Show-Off* by George Kelly for the drama prize and chose instead Hatcher Hughes's *Hell-Bent for Heaven*—announced May 12—after Columbia drama professor Brander Matthews lobbied them to switch. Matthews and Hughes are colleagues on the Columbia faculty, and it is that university that awards the prizes. **29** Comedian Frank Tinney is arrested for assaulting *Ziegfeld Follies* showgirl Imogene Wilson, with whom the married Tinney was having an affair.

(571), at the Playhouse, is a fleshed-out vaudeville sketch that won't win the Pulitzer Prize because the jury's choice is rejected by Columbia University. Regina Wallace and Louis John Bartels star, with Lee Tracy. **12** Roland Young is a struggling composer who decides not to sell out for a marriage that will make him financially comfortable in *Beggar on Horseback* (224), at the Broadhurst. George S. Kaufman and Marc Connelly's play features an expressionistic dream sequence. *The New York Times* says it "bristles with sly and caustic satire, brims with novel and richly colored theatric inventions, and overflows with inconsequent humor and the motley spirit of youth."

APRIL 16 Rachel Crothers's comedy, *Expressing Willie* (293), opens at the Forty-eighth Street Theatre. Richard Sterling is the playboy who must learn to find a woman who will love him for himself and not his inheritance. She's played by Crystal Herne.

MAY 15 Eugene O'Neill's drama of miscegenation, *All God's Chillun Got Wings* (43), starring Paul Robeson, opens at the Provincetown Playhouse. The *Times* says that Robeson gives a performance "that grips attention and tingles in the nerves." This afternoon, without explanation, the city refuses to grant a license to use child actors in the first scene, which is read instead of played. **19** The Marx Brothers make their musical revue debut at the Casino in *I'll Say She Is* (313).

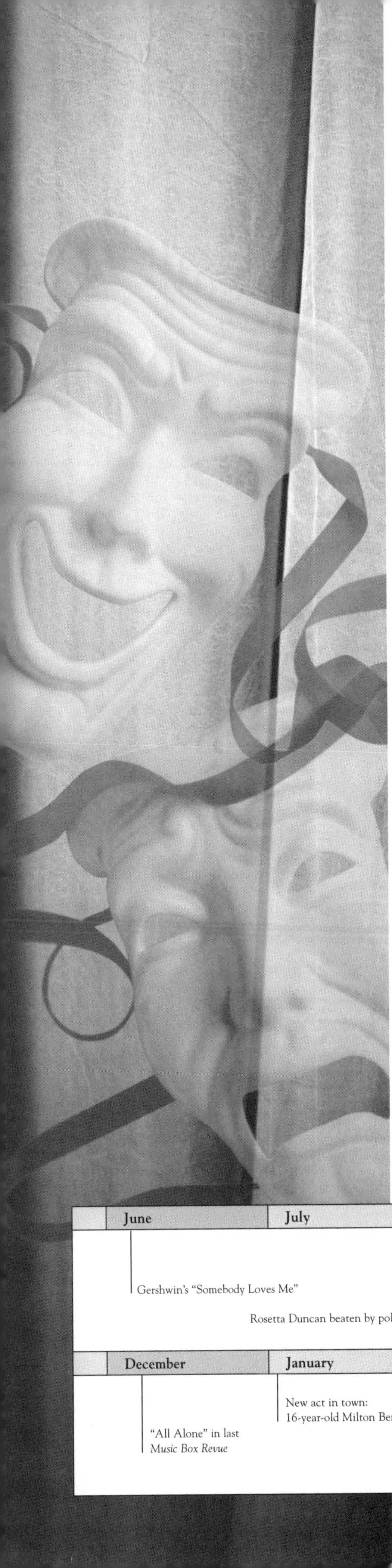

1924–25

Last year it was nudity. Now *What Price Glory* introduces "certain expletives," as the producers put it, to Broadway. In the air is the question of censorship. Lunt and Fontanne are forever paired in the Broadway pantheon after *The Guardsman*. George White's *Scandals of 1924* has a song about Mah-Jongg, the latest craze. It also has George Gershwin's "Somebody Loves Me." Rodgers and Hart will take "Manhattan," Libby Holman takes a torch to Broadway, and the new vaudeville act in town is 16-year-old Milton Berle. George Raft is a dancer at the El Fey Club, a new Broadway hangout. Jack "Legs" Diamond likes to dance there, too. And "Mrs. Winchell's little boy," Walter, invents the Broadway newspaper column.

- Original title of Gershwin musical *Tell Me More*, discarded for its lack of commercial appeal: *My Fair Lady*
- Cut from Gershwin's *Lady, Be Good*, which is running long: "The Man I Love"
- How Morris Gershwin, George and Ira's Yiddish-speaking father, pronounces "Fascinating Rhythm, from *Lady, Be Good*: "Fashion on the River."
- British import, opening in July: *Sweeny Todd*
- Price of a case of the best bootleg Scotch: $54
- Price of Scotch right off the boat: $30
- Phrases censored from vaudeville acts on the Keith-Albee circuit: "wiggling her tra la la," "a sock in the puss," and "Ladies of the Evening" (from Jack Benny's act)
- Phrases forbidden on the Columbia burlesque circuit: "hell," "damn," "God," "cock-eyed liar," "son-of-a-gun," and "son-of-a-Pollack"
- New top ticket price for straight plays on Broadway: $3.00
- Number of wounded veterans in the cast of *What Price Glory?*: 7
- Number of plays among the "Ten Best" in this season's annual *Ten Best Plays* volume, edited by critic Burns Mantle, that were written by American playwrights: all 10, for the first time in the 5-year-old series

Productions on Broadway: 228

Pulitzer Prize for Drama: *They Knew What They Wanted* (Sidney Howard)

June	July	August	September	October	November
Gershwin's "Somebody Loves Me"	Rosetta Duncan beaten by police	New Sophie Tucker title is "Madame"	Walter Winchell becomes daily columnist	Lunt and Fontanne in *The Guardsman*	"The Man I Love" dropped from *Lady, Be Good*

December	January	February	March	April	May
"All Alone" in last *Music Box Revue*	New act in town: 16-year-old Milton Berle	N.Y.P.D. goes after "obscene" plays	Jolson throat trouble closes show	Libby Holman's Broadway debut	Rodgers and Hart's "Manhattan"

Personalities

JUNE • Libby Holman, boarding a train in Cincinnati for New York and a career on Broadway, hears from her father: "Leave your college diploma behind and we'll frame it. It won't interest Flo Ziegfeld, and neither, I fear, will you." **27** After hearing testimony from both Frank Tinney and Imogene Wilson on the charge that Tinney beat her, a grand jury refuses to indict him.

JULY 4 Rosetta Duncan of the Duncan Sisters, who are appearing at Chicago's Selwyn Theatre in *Topsy and Eva*, is beaten by the police in Cicero, Illinois, as a result of a mysterious "misunderstanding" after an auto accident.

AUGUST 5 Flo Ziegfeld fires Imogene "Bubbles" Wilson from his *Follies* because she's seen again with the married comedian Frank Tinney after Ziegfeld warned her to stay away from him. Today, Tinney sails for Europe, just ahead of the process server with notice of his wife's suit for desertion. **11** "Madame" Sophie Tucker, as she now calls herself, opens at the Palace. Also on the bill is Jay C. Flippen, future film character actor, who works in blackface.

SEPTEMBER 20 Walter Winchell debuts as a daily Broadway columnist—"Your Broadway and Mine"—in the five-day-old *New York Evening Graphic*. He reports that Sophie Tucker has left Earl Carroll's *Vanities* in a dispute over stage time. Winchell's base of operations is the El Fey nightclub, where the hostess is Texas Guinan, the champagne is 30 dollars a bottle, and the show business clientele rub elbows with Jack "Legs" Diamond and Arnold Rothstein. Dancer George Raft heads the floor show, and among the chorus girls is Ruby Stevens, soon to become Barbara Stanwyck.

OCTOBER 7 To publicize the nudity in his *Vanities* show, Earl Carroll gets himself arrested and spends a night in jail by hanging paintings of nudes in the lobby of his theatre and then having someone file a complaint.

NOVEMBER • Billy Rose opens his Back Stage Club on West Fifty-sixth Street.

Plays and Musicals

JUNE 30 George White's *Scandals of 1924* (196), opening at the Apollo, introduces Gershwin's "Somebody Loves Me."

AUGUST 11 In *Dancing Mothers* (311), by Edgar Selwyn, Mary Young, Helen Hayes, and John Halliday star in a play about a mother who, upset with her flapper daughter and roaming husband, decides to live it up. In the end, her lark becomes a lifestyle, and she leaves her family. It's at the Booth.

SEPTEMBER 2 Set in Canada, *Rose-Marie* (557), a musical with a murder in its plot, opens at the Imperial. Rudolph Friml and Herbert Sothart have written the music, Oscar Hammerstein II and Otto Harbach, the lyrics, and the stars are Dennis King and Mary Ellis. Nelson Eddie and Jeanette MacDonald sing "Indian Love Call" in the 1936 screen version. **5** *What Price Glory* (435), by Maxwell Anderson and Laurence Stallings, opens at the Plymouth. Louis Wolheim, William Boyd, Leyla Georgie, George Tobias, and Brian Donlevy star in a World War I drama that, according to the *Times*, is "virile, fertile, poetic and Rabelaisian all at once." Its frank language causes a sensation. It will be filmed in 1926 and 1952.

OCTOBER 13 Alfred Lunt and Lynn Fontanne open in *The Guardsman* (274), at the Garrick Theatre. Alexander Woollcott thinks we may be "seeing the first chapter in a partnership destined to be as distinguished as that of Henry Irving and Ellen Terry. Our respective grandchildren will be able to tell." The Lunts, in 1931, make this their only film. **15** Edwin Justus Mayer's comedy *The Firebrand* (287) opens at the Morosco. The subject is the boldly presented love life of the Renaissance artist Benevenuto Cellini, portrayed by Joseph Schildkraut.

NOVEMBER 11 Eugene O'Neill's *Desire Under the Elms* (208), with Walter Huston in his first major role, opens at the Greenwich Village Theatre. Many critics do not like this New England tragedy, in which a son has an affair with and father's a baby by his father's third

Business and Society

SEPTEMBER 5 The program for *What Price Glory* states: "The audience is asked to bear with certain expletives which, under other circumstances, might be used for melodramatic effect, but herein are employed because the mood and truth of the play demand their employment."

NOVEMBER 11 The Martin Beck Theatre opens.

JANUARY • The New York State Court of Appeals reverses the convictions of the producers and cast of *God of Vengeance* for violating the obscenity laws in 1923.

FEBRUARY 9 The Cherry Lane Theatre opens in Greenwich Village. **13** New York City Police Commissioner Enright sends "qualified" officers with stenographers to several theatres tonight to check on salaciousness on the city's stages. **14** Heywood Broun, criticizing his own paper's call four days ago for the censorship of *Ladies of the Evening* and *A Good Bad Woman*, writes in the *World* that such regulation is bound to "touch and flaw *What Price Glory* and *They Knew What They Wanted*." As for obscenity, "[T]he richness of existence depends upon the huge

Births, Deaths, and Marriages

JUNE 3 Colleen Dewhurst b.

JULY 19 Pat Hingle (Martin Patterson Hingle) b.

SEPTEMBER 18 Producer-director Zelda Fichandler (Zelda Diamond) b.

OCTOBER 15 Director José Quintero b. **27** Ruby Dee (Ruby Wallace) b.

NOVEMBER 22 Geraldine Page b.

DECEMBER 20 Ruth Chatterton m. actor Ralph Forbes.

JANUARY 1 Barbara Baxley b.

FEBRUARY 2 Elaine Stritch b. **11** Kim Stanley (Patricia Kimberly Reid) b. **17** Hal Holbrook b.

MARCH 21 Director Peter Brook b.

APRIL 11 Composer Buddy De Sylva m. actress Marie Wallace.

During its seven-month run, patrons will include Al Jolson, Walter Winchell, Mark Hellinger, and gangsters Arnold Rothstein and Waxey Gordon. Singer Helen Morgan entertains, and it is here that she will first climb on the piano, a perch she will make famous as a torch singer. It is also at this club that Rose will meet Fanny Brice, his future wife.

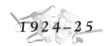

JANUARY • Sophie Tucker files for bankruptcy following the failure of her Cleveland cabaret. **7** *Variety* reviews 16-year-old Milton Berle at Loew's State. On for 12 minutes in the number three spot, Berle sings, dances, and imitates Eddie Cantor. It "should keep him traveling within his present confines without trouble," observes the critic.

Walter Winchell, the first Broadway columnist *MSN*

wife. It will move to Broadway. **24** Sidney Howard's *They Knew What They Wanted* (192), at the Garrick, stars Pauline Lord, Richard Bennett and Glenn Anders in a comedy, set in California's Napa Valley, about a mail order romance. Lines, such as "Tony's a white guy even if he *is* a wop," will not make it into the 1956 musical version, *The Most Happy Fella*.

DECEMBER 1 The first of George and Ira Gershwin's 14 Broadway collaborations, *Lady, Be Good* (330), is at the Liberty. Fred and Adele Astaire are the stars, and the show features "Fascinating Rhythm." The show's title song is sung by Walter Catlett. Cliff Edwards plays Ukelele Ike, a stage name he will keep. It's filmed in 1941. **1** The final edition of *The Music Box Revue* (184), at the theatre of the same name, has Grace Moore and Oscar Shaw singing Irving Berlin's "All Alone." Fanny Brice and Clark and McCullough are also in this production. **2** Sigmund Romberg's *The Student Prince* (608), with lyrics by Dorothy Donnelly, is at the Jolson Theatre. The songs include "Drink, Drink, Drink," "Serenade," and "Golden Days." Howard Marsh, Ilse

gap between the farthest reaches of the mind and the dull ballast of the body." **20** Several producers are summoned to the Manhattan District Attorney's office to discuss obscenity in their plays. David Belasco agrees to revise *The Harem*, but the producers of Eugene O'Neill's *Desire Under the Elms* are refusing to make changes. A group of actors, playwrights, and producers have formed "The Joint Committee Opposed to Censorship." Worried that the state will step in with legislation regulating the theatre, they support the revival of the play jury system, in which panels made up of playgoers will be chosen to evaluate the decency of plays. **21** The New York City Police Department accepts the idea of play juries.

MARCH 3 The first 12-person play jury is chosen in New York.

APRIL 10 Police raid the Minsky brothers' National Winter Garden Theatre on the Lower East Side, a move immortalized in the 1968 film *The Night They Raided Minsky's*.

MAY 12 Critic John Simon b. **26** Alec McCowen (Alexander McCowen) b. **31** Director Julian Beck b.

Personalities

FEBRUARY • The warden of the Leavenworth federal penitentiary calls it a "coincidence" that inmate Nicky Arnstein, husband of Fanny Brice, has been transferred from the coal pile to an easier job at the same time that the daughter of the prison's chief officer has been added to the chorus of *The Music Box Revue*, in which Brice stars. The girl, who has no Broadway experience, was added at Brice's request. **2** Harry Richman, former accompanist for Mae West, is the first entertainer to play the Palace after making his reputation on radio. Richman broadcasts "A Night at the Club Richman" from his cabaret. He

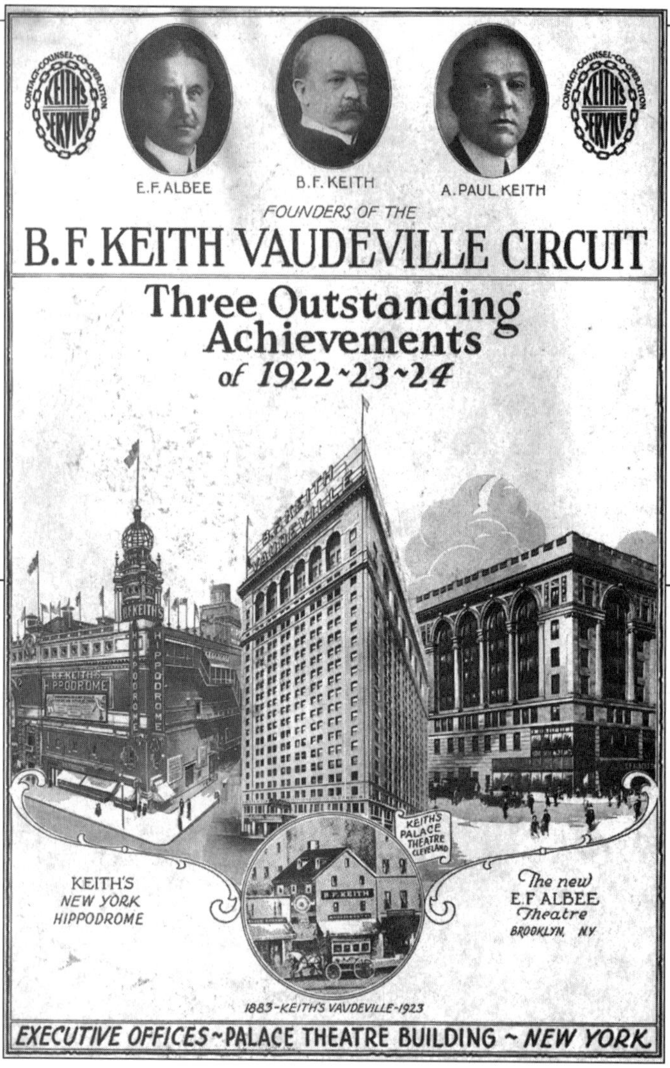

The Keith Circuit dominates vaudeville LYNCH

Plays and Musicals

Marvenga, and Roberta Beatty are featured. It's filmed in 1927 and 1954. **2** Lenore Ulric opens in *The Harem* (183), a comedy by Ernest Vajda, adapted by Avery Hopwood, at the Belasco. **12** Katharine Cornell opens in Shaw's *Candida* (148), at the Forty-eighth Street Theatre. **23** *Topsy and Eva* (165) is at the Sam H. Harris Theatre. The Duncan Sisters wrote and star in this musical version of *Uncle Tom's Cabin*.

JANUARY 5 *Is Zat So* (634), a boxing comedy, coauthored by James Gleason and Richard Taber and starring Gleason, Robert Armstrong, and Sidney Riggs,

Business and Society

Births, Deaths, and Marriages

will stay off the air during his Palace engagement because the Keith-Albee circuit bans radio appearances by its stage artists. **19** John Barrymore opens in *Hamlet* in London. Twenty-year-old John Gielgud notes on his program: "Barrymore is romantic in appearance and naturally gifted with grace, looks, and a capacity to wear period clothes, which makes his brilliantly intellectual performance classical without being duly severe and he has tenderness, remoteness and neurosis all placed with great delicacy and used with immense effectiveness and admirable judgement."

MARCH 8 John Barrymore makes his first radio appearance, in London, in Act II, Scene 2 from *Hamlet*. **14** *Big Boy*, which was taking in a healthy $42,000 a week at the box office, is forced into an early closing at the Winter Garden by star Al Jolson's throat trouble.

APRIL • Vaudevillian Cissie Loftus, appearing at the Orpheum in Kansas City, is garnering newspaper publicity by her public discussion of how she overcame a drug addiction. **13** Now it's "Dame" Sophie Tucker at the Palace, singing "My Yiddisher Momma" in English and Yiddish. Also on the bill are Jack Haley, Jack Benny, and a trained baboon act. **22** Jeanne Eagels, performing in *Rain* in her hometown of Kansas City, walks off the stage in the second act when someone in the overheated house insists on opening the balcony door to the fire escape.

MAY • Lenore Ulric, David Belasco's biggest star, quits *The Harem* and is rumored not to be speaking to the producer. Shoring up his lineup of stars, Belasco signs Fanny Brice to play in a non-comedy role. She will get $2,500 a week and 15 percent of the gross. **11** Vaudevillian Frank Fay does not show up for his scheduled performance at the Riverside Theatre in New York. The comedian has a problem with alcoholism. **17** The Theatre Guild's bulletin for *The Garrick Gaieties* states that "[t]he music for the Gaieties has been written by Mr. Lawrence Hart and the lyrics by Mr. Richard Rodgers"—misspelling Hart's first name and getting their collaboration backwards.

opens at the Thirty-ninth Street Theatre. **26** *Hell's Bells* (139), opening at Wallack's Theatre, is a light comedy. Says The *Daily Mirror*: "Shirley Booth and Humphrey Bogart were a sprightly pair of lovers." It's her Broadway debut. The *World* observes that Bogart should part his hair on the side rather than down the middle.

MAY 17 *The Garrick Gaieties* (211) originates as a one-day showcase for the Theatre Guild's young talent. Its popularity leads to a regular run on June 8. In it are "Manhattan," the first Rodgers and Hart hit, and Sterling Holloway, Libby Holman, Philip Loeb, Sanford Meisner, and 24-year-old Lee Strasberg. The stage manager is Harold Clurman, also 24.

1925–26

The Marx Brothers are a big hit in *The Cocoanuts* (with Chico as "Willie the Wop"), Lenore Ulric plays a black prostitute in *Lulu Belle*, Brooks Atkinson is the new theatre critic at *The New York Times*, and *Variety* calls Noel Coward, new to Broadway, "the English George M. Cohan." The Dramatists Guild secures the interests of playwrights. Joyce Hawley's champagne bath will give Earl Carroll a terrible hangover. George Jessel, a hit on Broadway in *The Jazz Singer*, declines a role in the film but takes every speaking engagement he can get. And Irving Berlin's marriage to socialite Ellin Mackay is celebrated in newspaper stories and Broadway songs, but not by her anti-Semitic father.

- Price of a Theatre Guild subscription (6 plays): $9–$18
- New high price for second balcony seats to a straight play: $2.00, for *Abie's Irish Rose* on a Saturday night and on holidays
- Most profitable vaudeville house in the country: the State-Lake in Chicago, where acts must perform 3 times a day, shows are continuous and salaries low, and the net for 1925 is $676,000
- Cost of producing *The Cocoanuts*: $250,000
- Street price of drugs in Times Square:
  Opium: $75 a can
  Morphine: $45 an ounce
  Heroin and Cocaine: $30 an ounce
- Approximate annual income of Otto Harbach, highest paid lyricist so far and composer of the words for *No, No Nanette*, *Rose-Marie*, and *Sunny*: $500,000
- Irving Berlin's annual income: about $300,000
- What the caustic George S. Kaufman suggests as a title for Irving Berlin's "I'll Be Loving You Always," removed by the composer from the score for *Cocoanuts*: "I'll Be Loving You Thursday." (Berlin's feelings are hurt)
- Amount said to have been won by vaudeville comedian Lou Holtz in one night in a crap game: $71,000
- How Fanny Brice characterizes herself: "a cartoonist working in the flesh"
- Number of straight plays running 100 or more performances and thus qualifying as hits, according to critic Burns Mantle: 33 out of a total of 170 productions
- First show ever seen by future critic Walter Kerr: *No, No Nanette*
- Number of musicals giving at least 100 performances: 20 of 42 productions

Productions on Broadway: 255

Pulitzer Prize for Drama: *Craig's Wife* (George Kelly)

June	July	August	September	October	November
Desire Under the Elms banned in London	Gallagher and Shean split up	Jeanne Eagels m. former football star	Noel Coward's Broadway debut	Angela Lansbury and Gore Vidal b.	Broadway's first modern-dress *Hamlet*; Richard Burton b.

December	January	February	March	April	May
Marx Brothers in *The Cocoanuts*	Irving Berlin m. Ellin Mackay	Joyce Hawley's nude champagne bath	George Jessel begins speaking engagements	Mae West in *Sex*	Helen Menken m. Humphrey Bogart

Personalities

JUNE • The Theatre Guild fires Richard Bennett from *They Knew What They Wanted* when he takes an unauthorized three-day leave and replaces him with Leo Carillo. Bennett says he was ill. **8** Fay Templeton ends a 20-year performing hiatus with an appearance at the Palace with Joe Weber and Lew Fields. She has everyone in tears when she launches into her signature tune, "Ma' Blushin' Rose." Also on the bill: Cissie Loftus, Bill "Bojangles" Robinson, Marie Cahill, and Emma Trentini. A few blocks away, Houdini is at the Hippodrome. **12** In *The Jewish Tribune*, Fanny Brice writes that her fans will be surprised to learn that she did not grow up speaking Yiddish and that "all of the jargon I do know I acquired from association with Jews on the stage. . . ." One of her parents is Hungarian, the other French, and they spoke German at home. **22** With singer Florence Mills headlining, the Palace Theatre management anticipates African-Americans in the audience. *Variety* reports (July 1) that "the week passed through without an untoward incident. The colored patrons purchased the $.85 or less tickets, all upstairs."

JULY • The Gallagher and Shean partnership breaks up. **20** In a curtain speech, Richard Bennett, opening a run at the Palace, attacks Sinclair Lewis and other "intellectuals," including "that bunch at the Hotel Algonquin" for denigrating the average American. **20** George Gershwin is on the cover of *Time*.

AUGUST • Alexander Woollcott joins the *World*, succeeding Heywood Broun as that paper's drama critic. George S. Kaufman returns to the *Times* after working with Irving Berlin on a new show for the Marx Brothers called *Cocoanuts*. Stark Young leaves the *Times*'s drama department, reportedly because publisher Adolph Ochs found his reviews too "highbrow." His replacement is Brooks Atkinson. **1** Producer George White, of "Scandals" fame, has a (victorious) fistfight with producer Rufus LeMaire at Reuben's Restaurant.

Plays and Musicals

SEPTEMBER 7 In *Cradle Snatchers* (485), Russell Medcraft and Norman Mitchell's new comedy at the Music Box Theatre, three wives, played by Mary Boland, Edna May Oliver, and Margaret Dale, carouse with some college boys, one of whom is played by 26-year-old Humphrey Bogart. **14** *The Jazz Singer* (303), by Samson Raphaelson, on which the movies' first talkie will be based, opens at the Fulton. George Jessel—who will turn down an offer to appear in the film—plays Jackie Rabinowitz, the cantor's son. **15** Katharine Cornell stars as Iris March, a character Alexander Woollcott describes as a "shameful, shameless lady," in *The Green Hat* (237), opening at the Broadhurst. Cornell's costar in this romantic drama by Michael Arlen, is Leslie Howard. **16** "Neurasthenia, stimulated by tea, cigarettes and drugs in an 'arty' atmosphere" is how the *Telegram* describes Noel Coward's *The Vortex* (157), at Henry Miller's Theatre, starring Coward, Lillian Braithwaite, and Leo G. Carroll as the effeminate Pauncefort Quentin. The *Times* describes the plot: "A silly mother loses her lover to her son's fiancée. And the boy confesses to taking drugs." Just before the curtain, the boy tells his mother, "You're an awfully rotten woman, really." *Variety* calls the 26-year-old Coward "the English George M. Cohan." **16** *No, No Nanette* (321), opens at the Globe, with Vincent

With *No, No Nanette* struggling in tryouts, Vincent Youmans and Irving Caesar write "Tea for Two" and "I Want to Be Happy"
BROWN

Business and Society

JUNE • Eugene O'Neill's *Desire Under the Elms* is banned from the London stage.

AUGUST • New York radio station WHN informs producers that it will begin reviewing plays right after they conclude on opening night and that Bland Johanson, formerly of *Theatre Magazine*, will do the reviews.

SEPTEMBER • The Keith-Albee theatre circuit, involved for the first time in partisan politics, urges support for State Senator Jimmy Walker, known to favor the entertainment industry, in his campaign for mayor of New York City. • In a harbinger of the deterioration of Forty-second Street, Hubert's Museum, a Coney Island–style emporium, opens. There is already a shooting gallery on the street.

OCTOBER 20 The Goodman Theatre Company begins producing in Chicago with one-act plays by its namesake, William O. Goodman, who died in the flu epidemic of 1918.

DECEMBER 7 The Dramatists Guild, an offshoot of the Author's League, meets to

Births, Deaths, and Marriages

JUNE 21 Maureen Stapleton (Lois Maureen Stapleton) b.

JULY 3 Ziegfeld Follies girl and film actress Lina Basquette m. Sam Warner of the movies' Warner Brothers.

AUGUST 26 Jeanne Eagels m. former college football star Edward H. Coy.

OCTOBER 3 Playwright Gore Vidal b. **13** Playwright Frank Gilroy b. **16** Angela Lansbury b.

NOVEMBER 10 Richard Burton (Richard Jenkins) b.

DECEMBER 2 Julie Harris b. **11** Producer Jed Harris m. actress Anita Green. **30** Lillian Hellman m. writer Arthur Kober. It will last five years.

JANUARY 4 Irving Berlin m. socialite, sil-

OCTOBER 19 For the first time in their careers, Joe Weber and Lew Fields refuse to go on, citing "illness." In fact, it's the second billing to Marie Dressler at the Palace that makes them sick. May Irwin replaces them. In her act today, the hefty Dressler does the new dance craze, the Charleston.

NOVEMBER • Ed Gallagher, formerly of the vaudeville team of Gallagher and Shean, is hospitalized for a nervous breakdown. **4** *Variety* notes the blossoming of a New York stage career: "Jimmy Cagney, the 'little Red' of 'Outside Looking In,' is a former New York scholastic swimming champion. Cagney was a hoofer doing small speaking parts, this being his first straight talking part."

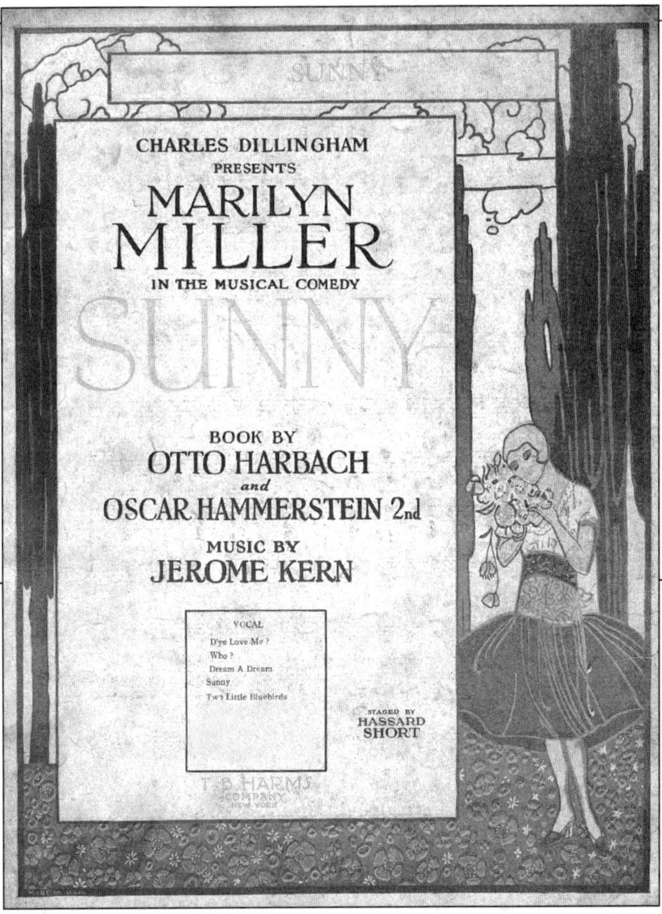

Sunny is the first collaboration between Jerome Kern and Oscar Hammerstein II BROWN

Youman's "Tea for Two" (with lyrics that Irving Caesar considered "temporary") and "I Want to Be Happy." Otto Harbach coauthored the lyrics, and Louise Groody stars as the headstrong young woman who meets a rakish Bible salesman, played by Charles Winninger. **18** Rodgers and Hart's first book show and first hit musical comedy, *Dearest Enemy* (286), opens at the Knickerbocker. The book is by Herbert Fields, their collaborator on several productions. Helen Ford and Charles Purcell star in the story of an American girl who falls in love with a British soldier during the American Revolution. Songs include "Here in My Arms" and "By and Bye." **21** *The Vagabond King* (511), a Rudolph Friml operetta with Brian Hooker's lyrics, opens at the Casino Theatre. Dennis King stars as the roguish poet Francoise Villon. **22** *Sunny* (507), the first of several Jerome Kern-Oscar Hammerstein II shows, is at the New Amsterdam. Marilyn Miller is an American in England without the money to reach her sweetheart in America. Also in the cast are Clifton Webb, Jack Donahue, Mary Hay, Cliff Edwards ("Ukelele Ike"), Joseph Cawthorn, Esther

insure minimum standards with respect to royalties, advances, movie rights, and creative control over their work. Among producers, the Shuberts most avidly oppose the Guild.

MARCH 22 Producers and the Dramatists Guild reach what will be called the Minimum Basic Agreement between them, establishing a sliding royalty scale and securing for playwrights copyright ownership of their works. The issue of the sale of movie rights to plays will go to arbitration, which will bring authors 50 percent of those rights, eventually rising to a 60–40 split in the playwrights' favor in 1935. The agreement will be signed on April 27.

ver mining heiress, and *New Yorker* writer Ellin Mackay, whose anti-Semitic father will disinherit her. (In the 1929 stock market crash, Clarence Mackay loses $36 million in 30 minutes and is rescued from poverty by the son-in-law he despises). Tin Pan Alley songsmiths Al Dubin and Jimmy McHugh celebrate the marriage with "When a Kid Who Came from the East Side (Found a Sweet Society Rose)," and the match will be the basis for the 1928 play *The Song Writer* and the 1930 film *Children of Pleasure*. Berlin's gift to his bride is the copyright to "Always." **7** George Burns m. Gracie Allen. **13** Gwen Verdon (Gwenyth Evelyn Verdon) b. Pigeon-toed and knocked-kneed, she will *need* dancing and corrective shoes as physical rehabilitation. **19** Fritz Weaver b. **31** Playwright George V. Hobart d.

FEBRUARY • Kurt Weill m. Lotte Lenya.

MARCH 30 Sydney Chaplin, son of Charlie Chaplin and Lita Grey, b.

APRIL 9 Henry Miller d.

Personalities

DECEMBER 2 Noting the success of George Jessel in the play *The Jazz Singer*, *Variety* says that the show "has been drawing nothing but Jewish clientele, but there appears to be no limit to them. . . ." Jessel will complain in next week's issue about this ethnic remark.

JANUARY • Ethel Waters walks out of the *Plantation Revue*, a show intended to play on the "colored" theatre circuit, when the producers fail to provide enough playing dates. • Louis Calhern and Walter Catlett have a fistfight at the Lambs Club, from which they are each suspended for a year. **5** Evelyn Nesbit, the showgirl over whom architect Stanford White was murdered in 1906 and who has since appeared widely on the vaudeville stage, unsuccessfully attempts suicide by swallowing Lysol.

FEBRUARY • Producer Oliver Morosco files for bankruptcy. **10** *Variety*, reviewing Kate Smith at the Earl Theatre in Washington, D.C., says, "[G]ive her six months experience and she will blossom out as a blues singer who will grace any man's bill." She "does a dance handling about 200 pounds plus with such good grace as to take her away to a great finish." **15** Lindy's cancels its open-all-night policy after a shooting in the early morning hours in the famous Broadway eatery. **23** At a backstage party given by showman Earl Carroll, model Joyce Hawley is nude in a bathtub full of champagne, from which a number of men drink. When later called before a grand jury investigating this incident, Carroll will deny there was anything alcoholic served, leading to his conviction for perjury and a four-month imprisonment.

MARCH • George Jessel, starring on Broadway in *The Jazz Singer*, is promoting his show by taking paid engagements as master of ceremonies at various functions, a role that will make him the "toastmaster general of the United States."

APRIL 5 Sophie Tucker opens at the Palace while continuing to perform at a New York cabaret, something that the management

Plays and Musicals

Howard, and Pert Kelton. **23** George S. Kaufman's *The Butter and Egg Man* (243), directed by James Gleason, opens at the Longacre. This satire on the business of producing plays, Kaufman's only solo effort on Broadway, stars Robert Middlemass, Lucille Webster, Sylvia Field, and Gregory Kelly. "Mary Martin," the name of one character, will be changed to "Mary Marvin" for the 1966 revival.

OCTOBER 12 *Craig's Wife* (360), George Kelly's Pulitzer Prize-winning drama about a selfish woman who makes a fetish of her worldly goods opens at the Morosco. Crystal Herne and Charles Trowbridge star. The 1936 film stars Rosalind Russell. **20** Channing Pollock's *The Enemy* (203), an idealistic plea for peace, opens at the Times Square Theatre. It stars Fay Bainter and Walter Abel. **21** John Cromwell, who also coproduced, stars in Sidney Howard's *Lucky Sam McCarver* (29), a sardonic look at the career of a man driven to succeed in the America of the Twenties, whether as a bootlegger or stockbroker. It's at the Playhouse.

NOVEMBER 9 Basil Sydney, at the Booth, is Broadway's first modern-dress Hamlet (88), a sartorially Dane-about-Elsinore who puffs his pipe while he ponders his next move. The ghost scenes in this *Hamlet*, according to critic Burns Mantle, are "being played on what appeared to be a terrace at Newport."

DECEMBER 8 *The Cocoanuts* (375), at the Lyric, has music by Irving Berlin and dialogue by George S. Kaufman and Morrie Ryskind, but it's the Marx Brothers ad-libbing that gives the show its character. Margaret Dumont is Groucho's foil in this satire on the current Florida land boom. Harpo improvises what will become his signature routine, chasing a fetching young woman across the stage, while Groucho and Chico turn "viaduct" into "Why a duck?"

JANUARY 23 Eugene O'Neill's tragedy *The Great God Brown* (271), using masks in the style of the ancient Greeks, opens at

Business and Society

Births, Deaths, and Marriages

MAY 3 Director Tom O'Horgan b. **8** Rida Johnson Young d. **13** Beatrice Arthur (Bernice Frankel) b. **15** Playwright Peter Shaffer b. **20** Helen Menken m. Humphrey Bogart.

of this Keith-Albee theatre never permitted in the past. But two-a-day vaudeville is desperate for class acts, which now takes priority over exclusive rights to a performer's services. Nora Bayes was supposed to headline the show but withdrew when told she will share top billing with Tucker. **19** Leon Errol falls and breaks his ankle during a performance of *Louis the 14th* at the Illinois Theatre in Chicago.

the Greenwich Village Theatre. The complicated plot involves the contrast between who people are and how they are presented to the world. The cast includes Robert Keith, William Harrigan, and Eleanor Wesselhoeft.

FEBRUARY 1 In John Colton's *The Shanghai Gesture* (331), at the Martin Beck, Florence Reed is Mother Goddam, madam of a Shanghai whorehouse, who takes revenge on the Englishman who years ago left her with a false promise that he would marry her—and also left her with a child. **9** Edward Sheldon and Charles MacArthur's *Lulu Belle* (461) is at the Belasco. Lenore Ulric, in blackface, is a prostitute who leads several white men astray until she is murdered. Henry Hull also has a starring role. **15** Thomas Mitchell and Mary Philips star in *The Wisdom Tooth* (160), Marc Connelly's comedy at the Little Theatre.

MARCH 15 Sean O'Casey's *Juno and the Paycock* (72) opens at the Mayfair. Augustin Daly stars and directs in this "comedy of Irish character and tragedy of Irish political life," as the *Times* describes it. **17** Rodgers and Hart's *The Girl Friend* (301), at the Vanderbilt, stars Sammy White and Eva Puck.

APRIL 26 Mae West is the star of *Sex* (375), opening at Daly's Theatre. Authorship of the play is credited to "Jane Mast," understood to be the star's pseudonym. *Variety* says it's "a nasty red-light district show." In it, West is a Montreal prostitute. West will be arrested for her ribaldry and serve 10 days in jail.

1926–27

Theatres with both stage and picture shows begin to bill the film on top, and vaudeville stars make sound film shorts. The *Times's* Brooks Atkinson finds the very thought of a lesbian relationship in *The Captive* "loathsome," while Mae West has a problem with *Sex*. A Pulitzer Prize saves *In Abraham's Bosom*. Producer Jed Harris, on the other hand, with four hits, *Broadway*, *Coquette*, *The Front Page*, and *The Royal Family*, doesn't need a prize. Noel Coward calls him "destiny's tot." In the dark of night, Irving Berlin writes "Blue Skies," and the end of George White's *Scandals* series brings forth "The Birth of the Blues."

- Character played by Kate Smith in her Broadway debut: "Tiny Little"
- Number of theatres—stage and film—in the U.S.: about 20,000
- Number that show no films at all: 500
- Number of two-a-day vaudeville houses left when the season begins: 15–10 on the Keith–Albee circuit, 5 on the Orpheum
- Cost of adding "refrigeration" (air conditioning) to a theatre: $100,000 to $200,000. Major vaudeville houses are now installing it
- Cover charge at the Dover Club, where owners Lou Clayton, Eddie Jackson, and Jimmy Durante also perform: $2
- Cover charge at Texas Guinan's 300 Club: $3
- Cover charge at the Black Bottom Club: none, but you "must be known to get in," according to *Variety*
- On the wagon: Eugene O'Neill, after a six-week psychoanalysis
- Five of Laurette Taylor's 10 rules for success for actresses: "Keep your figure"
- The nine "dirtiest" plays on Broadway, according to *Variety*: *Sex*, *Virgin Man*, *The Captive*, *New York Exchange*, *American Tragedy*, *Praying Curve*, *Lulu Belle*, *The Squall*, and *The Night Hawk*
- Gains that are not gotten, ill or otherwise: the boost at the box office that never comes to plays under censorship pressure; the raids, court cases and jailings do not stimulate expected ticket sales
- Big flop: the play jury system
- Bigger flop: attempts to stop ticket speculation and scalping
- Longest-running flop in Broadway history: *The Ladder*, opening October 22 for 794 performances, subsidized by a wealthy patron attracted to its theme of reincarnation
- Amount lost each week by *The Ladder*: $6,500
- Number of people in the audience at the final performance of *The Ladder*: 54
- What George Gershwin says about his brother Ira's feel for sound when writing lyrics: ". . . [D]on't ever let Ira hear you say 'It's Wonderful.' Just 'S wonderful, 'S marvelous."
- Motto of Eva Le Gallienne's Civic Repertory Company: "The theatre should be an instrument for giving, not a machinery for getting."
- Number of subscribers to Le Gallienne's Civic Repertory Company: 8,000
- Showgirl to whom Lee Shubert begins making secret paternity payments: Frederica Bond

Productions on Broadway: 263

Pulitzer Prize for Drama: *In Abraham's Bosom* (Paul Green)

June	July	August	September	October	November
Ann Pennington dances the "Black Bottom"	Three-card monte con men plague theatre district	Smith and Dale in *Earl Carroll Vanities*	Jed Harris's *Broadway*	Eva Le Gallienne's Civic Repertory Theatre	Gershwin's *Oh, Kay!* and Romberg's *The Desert Song*

December	January	February	March	April	May
Jeanne Eagels replaced in *Chicago*	Robert E. Sherwood's first Broadway play	Marilyn Miller back with Ziegfeld	Burns and Allen play the Palace	Mae West goes to jail for *Sex*	Fredric March m. Florence Eldridge

Personalities

JUNE 7 Judith Anderson makes her vaudeville debut at the Palace in *Thieves*, a one-act play.

JULY • Showgirl Joyce Hawley, immortalized by Earl Carroll in a bathtub full of champagne, is broke and hospitalized for observation in Chicago after an overdose of sleeping pills.

AUGUST • Mrs. Leslie Carter is forced into bankruptcy. **4** "Turning summer into winter is growing more common in the present era of show business," notes *Variety*. "It's done by refrigeration." But it's not done at the Martin Beck, where *The Shanghai Gesture* took a one-month hiatus a few days ago after star Florence Reed fainted twice from the heat. **23** George Burns and Gracie Allen make their Palace debut with their 17-minute "Lamb Chops" routine.

SEPTEMBER 20 Making her Broadway debut as "Tiny Little" in *Honeymoon Lane* is Kate Smith.

OCTOBER • Vaudeville comedian Georgie Price is accused of beating up showgirl Kathryn Ray, "the most beautiful girl in the world," at a party. He does not admit guilt but pays her $15,000 to settle the matter. • Longtime vaudeville star Emma Carus has a breakdown and is hospitalized in a California sanitarium after being found legally incompetent. • Jeanne Eagels misses several performances of *Rain*. She is reported to have had a temper tantrum following a party at her home and ordered everyone out, including her husband. • The "Vitaphone Vaudeville" program of sound film shorts released to theatres this month features Al Jolson, George Jessel, Elsie Janis, and Eugene and Willie Howard. **24** Harry Houdini, at the Garrick Theatre in Detroit, goes on despite a ruptured appendix. He will be dead in a week, on Halloween.

NOVEMBER 3 "Yiddish Shows [a]t High Tide; Mollie Picon Tops, $15,000 Week," headlines *Variety*. Picon is in *The Little Devil* at the Second Avenue Theatre. Some of Second Avenue's stars have

Plays and Musicals

JUNE 14 *George White's Scandals* (424) is at the Apollo. The "Black Bottom," danced by Ann Pennington, sets off a new dance craze. Ray Henderson, Buddy De Sylva, and Lew Brown's "The Birth of the Blues" are also in this show.

SEPTEMBER 16 *Broadway* (603), by Philip Dunning and George Abbott, opens at the Broadhurst. Lee Tracy (understudied by James Cagney), stars in the drama about mobsters, murder, romance, and nightclubs. **21** Fanny Brice's foray into drama flounders when *Fanny* (63), in which she's a Yiddish vamp, produced by David Belasco and coauthored by him and Willard Mack, flops at the Lyceum. **28** *Gentlemen Prefer Blondes* (199) opens at the Times Square Theatre. Anita Loos and her husband John Emerson have adapted this comedy from her novel, with June Walker as Lorelei Lee, who aspires to own rocks that sparkle. **29** Opening at the Empire, *The Captive* (160), adapted by Arthur Hornblow from Edouard Bourdet's *La Prisonnière*, is "the tragedy of a young woman, well-bred and of good family, who falls into a twisted relationship with another woman," writes the *Times*'s Brooks Atkinson. In the play, the euphemism "shadows" refers to lesbians, whose relationship Atkinson terms a "loathsome possibility." Helen Menken and Basil Rathbone star.

OCTOBER 22 J. Frank Davis's *Ladder* (794), opening at the Mansfield and starring Antoinette Perry, is a tribute to obsession and cash. The wealthy Edgar B. Davis, to whom this play's theme of reincarnation is a private passion, subsidizes the production, oblivious to the dismal figures posted at the box office. **25** Eva Le Gallienne's Civic Repertory Theatre begins its first season at the Fourteenth Street Theatre with a top price of $1.50. She directs and acts Jacinto Benevente's *Saturday Night*, which is poorly received. But tomorrow night her company will give the first professional, acclaimed production of a Chekhov play in English, *The Three Sisters* (36)—"drenched in humanity," says the *Times*.

Business and Society

JUNE • New York City police close the show *Bunk of 1926* in response to complaints from one of that city's play juries.

JULY 21 The theatre district is plagued by the three-card monte game, in which suckers have to follow one card and pick it out after it's been moved around face-down with sleight-of-hand.

AUGUST • The State-Lake Theatre in Chicago, which has pioneered in combining films with vaudeville at continuous showings, begins to bill the picture over the stage show.

DECEMBER • *Broadway*, at the Broadhurst, sets a new record for gross receipts by a straight play in one week during the final week of the month: $42,040.

JANUARY 1 The Music Corporation of America (MCA) begins to book vaudeville and cabaret acts. **11** The Royale Theatre opens. **19** *Variety* headlines: "'Hi Yaller' Girls No Longer Wanted: Demand Now for 'Dark Brown' Negresses in Shows and Cabarets."

FEBRUARY 28 The U.S. Supreme Court

Births, Deaths, and Marriages

JUNE • Ilka Chase m. Louis Calhern. **4** Director Judith Malina b.

SEPTEMBER 3 Anne Jackson b. **14** Ira Gershwin m. Leonore Strunsky.

OCTOBER 21 Ann Harding m. actor Harry C. Bannister. **31** Harry Houdini d. It is said that producer Charles Dillingham says to Flo Ziegfeld, both pallbearers at the funeral, "I'll bet you a hundred bucks he ain't in there."

NOVEMBER • Bert and Betty Wheeler are divorced, ending their stint as a vaudeville team. **25** Playwright Murray Schisgal b.

DECEMBER • Bill and Louise Frawley divorce, ending their vaudeville act as well as their marriage.

already migrated to Broadway, including Muni Weisenfreund, who is not yet calling himself Paul Muni. **18** Comedian Bobby Clark, starring with his partner Paul McCullough in *The Ramblers* at the Lyric, is assaulted by three drunks at the stage door. McCullough and two stagehands come to his assistance.

DECEMBER • Francine Larrimore replaces Jeanne Eagels in the cast of *Chicago*, now in rehearsals. Eagels is reported to have quarreled with producer Sam Harris over the staging of the play. As a result, George Abbott has replaced Sam Forrest as director. Eagels has left the play to "rest," on her doctor's orders. **11** Flo Ziegfeld announces that he has signed Jerome Kern and Oscar Hammerstein II

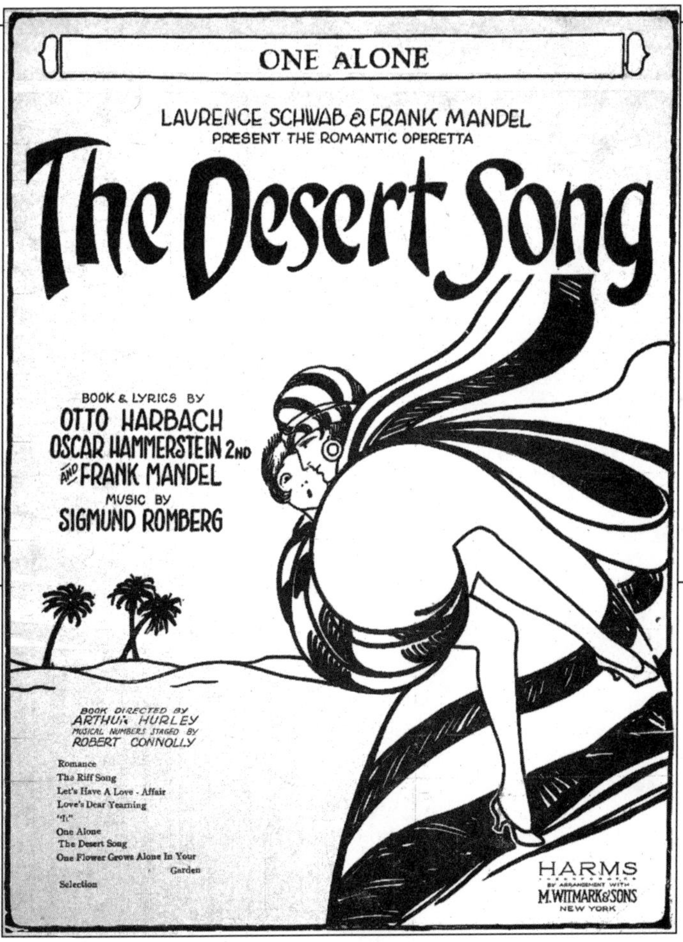

The Desert Song will be filmed three times BROWN

NOVEMBER 8 George and Ira Gershwin's *Oh, Kay!* (256), at the Imperial, stars Gertrude Lawrence, Victor Moore, and Oscar Shaw. Walter Winchell writes that "'Someone to Watch Over Me' has its comforting minor chords." Also in the score are "Clap Yo' Hands" and "Do, Do, Do." The book is by Guy Bolton and P.G. Wodehouse. **11** Jean Bart's *Squall* (444) opens at the Forty-eighth Street Theatre. It's about a gypsy woman who leaves her people to satisfy her lusts with an outsider. The dialogue includes the line: "Me Nubi. Nubi good girl. Nubi stay." Robert Benchley's review riposte is: "Me Benchley. Benchley bad boy. Benchley go." **29** Alfred Lunt and Clare Eames star in Sidney Howard's *Ned McCobb's Daughter* (132), at the John Golden. **29** Ethel Barrymore stars in W. Somerset Maugham's *The Constant Wife* (295), a "deft and sparkling comedy" (the *Times*) about the way that a woman deals with her husband's affair. Also in the cast at Maxine Elliott's Theatre are Frank Conroy, Cora Witherspoon, Veree Teasdale, and C. Aubrey Smith. **30** *The Desert Song* (465), at the Casino Theatre,

strikes down the New York State law regulating the premium that brokers may add to the face value of a ticket. The Court says that the sale of tickets is a "private" enterprise that government can't justify regulating.

MARCH • With the Keith–Albee circuit prohibiting performers from appearing in talking pictures, Warner Brothers threatens to pursue vaudevillians actively. **5** Sardi's Restaurant moves down a few doors to its present location at 234 West Forty-fourth Street. The St. James Theatre is being built at its old site. **28** The Theatre Guild announces that it will expand to Chicago next season, offering a full slate of six plays at the Studebaker Theatre. Next week, the Guild, in its first foray out of New York, will produce Shaw's *Pygmalion* in Philadelphia.

APRIL • The Lewisohns give up trying to subsidize the Neighborhood Playhouse, which will cease producing plays and become a theatre school. **7** New York State Governor Al Smith signs the Wales Theatrical Padlock Bill, which allows local authorities to padlock theatres judged to be staging dirty plays. The Shuberts' lawyer complains that it is "unconstitutional."

JANUARY • Eva Tanguay, 47, m. her accompanist, Alan Parado, 22.

FEBRUARY 27 Playwright Roi Cooper Megrue d.

MARCH 18 Composer John Kander b.

APRIL 2 Critic Kenneth Tynan b. **6** Abe Lastfogel of the William Morris Agency m. vaudevillian Frances Arms. **21** Critic Robert Brustein b.

MAY 13 Critic Clive Barnes b. **23** Gerald Hiken b. **30** Fredric March m. Florence Eldridge.

Personalities

to do a musical version of Edna Ferber's *Show Boat*. **13** Paul Robeson signs to play Joe in the upcoming musical *Show Boat*. However, when the show is delayed, he will be released from his contract and will not assume the role until the 1932 revival. **27** Belle Baker, opening in Rodgers and Hart's *Betsy* tomorrow, asks Irving Berlin for a last-minute song she can add. Berlin works through the night and by morning has composed "Blue Skies." When she flubs the lyrics tomorrow night, Berlin, seated up front, jumps up and sings it with her.

JANUARY • Laurette Taylor is at the Palace for two weeks, playing in a short version of her husband, J. Hartley Manners's play, *The Comedienne*. **1** Producer David Belasco is almost killed in an auto accident. **10** Will Mahoney, one of vaudeville's most popular comedians, opens at the Palace. Ken Murray is also on the bill. **24** Helen Morgan makes her vaudeville debut at the Palace.

FEBRUARY 11 When Basil Rathbone forgets his lines in *The Captive*, the curtain has to be brought down and the act restarted because the prompter's script has been seized for examination by the police, who want to check for obscenity. **21** Marilyn Miller, who gained fame in *The Ziegfeld Follies* and then quarreled with Ziegfeld and left to sign with producer Charles Dillingham, returns to the Ziegfeld fold, signing a five-year contract. Ziegfeld says that she "is unquestionably the outstanding musical comedy star of the world. It was only through a misunderstanding that she left my management."

MARCH • The nightclub act of Clayton, Jackson, and Durante—Lou Clayton, Eddie Jackson, and Jimmy Durante—debuts as a vaudeville team, at Loew's State. • *Variety* notes the long hours being worked by "Rubye [sic] Keeler, little buck dancer of the Silver Slipper," who is also rehearsing the show *Lucky*. Flo Ziegfeld has warned his chorus girls that this kind of "doubling" is unacceptable. • Actress Ann Harding and vaudevillian Ken Murray have nervous breakdowns.

Plays and Musicals

has lyrics by Otto Harbach and Oscar Hammerstein II set to Sigmund Romberg's music. Robert Halliday plays a mild-mannered French soldier in Morocco, secretly "The Red Shadow," leader of the Riffs. Vivienne Segal is the girl who falls in love with his dashing self.

DECEMBER 20 Laura Hope Crews, Earle Larimore, and Margalo Gillmore are the stars of Sidney Howard's *The Silver Cord* (112), at the John Golden Theatre. **30** Francine Larrimore kills her married lover and then basks in the publicity created by her sensational trial in *Chicago* (172). Also in the cast is Charles Bickford. Maurine Watkins's play, which opens at the Music Box Theatre, will be revived as a musical in 1975 and 1996. **30** Opening at the Provincetown Theatre is Paul Green's tragedy, *In Abraham's Bosom* (277), with Jules Bledsoe. *In Abraham's Bosom* will be saved from an early closing by a Pulitzer Prize.

JANUARY 26 Love finds a way to save a floundering marriage in Maxwell Anderson's *Saturday's Children* (310), a comedy. It opens at the Booth and stars Ruth Gordon and Roger Pryor. **31** Mae West's "homosexual comedy drama," *The Drag*, opens for a tryout in Bridgeport. The advance comment about it has increased demands for censorship, and a representative of the New York City Police Department is in the audience. *Variety* describes the heart of the play as "a wired party given by a rich pervert to his group of painted and bedizened men friends." **31** Robert E. Sherwood's first play, *The Road to Rome* (392), starring Jane Cowl and Philip Merivale, opens at the Playhouse.

FEBRUARY 2 The Ziegfeld Theatre opens with *Rio Rita* (494), starring J. Harold Murray, Ethelind Terry, and a new comedy team, Bert Wheeler and Robert Woolsey. Also in the cast is Paulette Goddard. The score is by Harry Tierney and Joseph McCarthy. In December, the show moves to the Lyric to make way for *Show Boat*.

Business and Society

MAY 19 The Shuberts end their holdout and announce that they will abide by the Basic Agreement between playwrights and producers. **28** A federal inquiry into tax evasion by ticket brokers hears testimony about the kinds of trick accounting used to cover it up.

Births, Deaths, and Marriages

19 With much of the company facing a trial, Mae West's *Sex*, raided a month ago, closes. The producer says that the playwright-actress is tired and "was particularly unnerved by the developments of the past month, and is in need of a rest." **28** George Burns and Gracie Allen are at the Palace. Says *Variety*: "The girl has developed into one of the cleverest character comediennes in vaudeville and Burns has smoothed out into an excellent feeder. They have gained assurance and finesse and are ready for the fastest company."

APRIL 12 Producer Earl Carroll, on his way to an Atlanta prison to begin his term for perjury in the 1926 champagne bath incident involving model Joyce Hawley, collapses on the train in Greenville, South Carolina. He will be held at a local hospital until June 7, when he will be taken to Atlanta to begin serving his sentence of a year and a day. **19** Mae West and two others convicted in the *Sex* case receive 10-day jail terms. West will serve her time in the Women's Work House on Welfare Island, where she's assigned "light housework" and finds the uniform "uncomfortable."

MAY 30 Moran and Mack, the most popular blackface comedians in vaudeville today, open at the Palace.

MARCH 21 *Her Cardboard Lover* (152), adapted by Valerie Wyngate and P.G. Wodehouse from a French play by Jacques Deval, opens at the Empire. Jeanne Eagels hires a man to help her forget her ex-husband, only to fall for him. Percy Hammond in the *Tribune* writes that "[a]lthough Miss Eagels excelled as the heroine of the event, Mr. Leslie Howard, in one of the richest roles of the season, rather kidnapped the comedy from its rightful proprietor." **28** The Majestic Theatre opens with *Rufus LeMaire's Affairs*.

APRIL 11 The Lunts star in S.N. Behrman's comedy *The Second Man* (178), at the Guild Theatre, with Margalo Gillmore and Earle Larimore. **25** "Sometimes I'm Happy" and "Hallelujah" are in Vincent Youmans's *Hit the Deck!* (352), with lyrics by Leo Robbin, Clifford Grey, and Irving Caesar, opening at the Belasco. The cast includes Louise Groody, Charles King, and Brian Donlevy.

1927–28

This is Broadway's busiest season of the century, with 264 shows opening, and one of them is extraordinarily special. It may be only "Make Believe," but the people in *Show Boat* seem much more real than characters usually are in musicals, and the music is glorious. Meanwhile, the Keith-Albee and Orpheum theatre circuits merge, on their way from vaudeville, which is dying, to RKO. *Abie's Irish Rose* is still growing, and they're doing "The Varsity Drag" in *Good News*. Jeanne Eagels spirals downward, while Ruby Stevens becomes Barbara Stanwyck, who becomes a Broadway star. Although he prefers Shakespeare, Bela Lugosi settles for *Dracula*. With Fred Astaire and Edward G. Robinson also starring on the Main Stem, Broadway is starting to look and sound like a rehearsal for Hollywood's golden age. And Al Jolson makes a movie that will rock show business to its roots.

- Salary paid to Alfred Lunt and Lynn Fontanne by the Theatre Guild: $400 each per week, plus 5 percent of the box office after a specified amount
- Average weekly salary of top stars in a Broadway play: about $5,000 a week
- Total number of potential weeks of bookings for acts playing two-a-day vaudeville: 14
- Comparable number of weeks in the 1923–1924 season: 52 weeks plus
- Assessed real estate value of the Palace Theatre (1928): $1,620,000
- Palace Theatre average weekly gross: $20,000
- Palace Theatre weekly profit: $6,000, according to Edward F. Albee; $2,000–$3,000, according to *Variety*
- Number of theatres controlled by the new Keith–Albee–Orpheum circuit: 211
- Cost of a Reno divorce: about $1,000
- Cost of a copy of *Variety*: $.25
- Cost of mounting this year's *Ziegfeld Follies*: $300,000
- How the new Alvin Theatre was named: after producers Alexander Aarons and Vinton Freedly

Productions on Broadway: 264—the peak figure for this century

Pulitzer Prize for Drama: *Strange Interlude* (Eugene O'Neill)

June	July	August	September	October	November
Professor Monty Woolley leaves Yale	Neil Simon b.	*Abie's Irish Rose* breaks long-run record	Fanny Brice divorces Nick Arnstein	Bela Lugosi in *Dracula*	Alvin Theatre opens with Fred Astaire in *Funny Face*

December	January	February	March	April	May
Show Boat	Shuberts ban Winchell; Harold Prince b.	Group Theatre forms	Edward Albee b.	Equity suspends Jeanne Eagels	"I Can't Give You Anything But Love" in *Blackbirds of 1928*

Personalities

JUNE • Monty Woolley, Professor of English and coach of the Drama Association at Yale, who has taught Cole Porter and George Abbott, among others, is not reappointed.

JULY 11 Jeanne Eagels can't go on tonight in *Her Cardboard Lover* after an incident of what is being described as "temperament." **11** Ethel Waters makes her Broadway debut, dancing as well as singing in the revue *Africana*, at the Daly. *The New York Times* terms her a "dusky Charlotte Greenwood."

AUGUST 29 *Strike Up the Band*, an anti-war musical by George Gershwin and George S. Kaufman, flops in tryouts. The show's tone is too serious and the wit too caustic for these times. Morrie Ryskind will do a rewrite, and Gershwin will delete "The Man I Love," originally written for *Lady, Be Good* but pulled from there as well, because it's too downbeat. And even then, it will be three years before it reaches Broadway.

SEPTEMBER • Jeanne Eagle's attempt to launch a film career at MGM in *Fires of Youth* with John Gilbert ends when she's fired at the behest of director Monte Belle, who finds her unreliable and difficult to work with. **12** Fanny Brice files for divorce from the twice-imprisoned gambler and swindler Nick Arnstein. Brice says in her suit that her nose job of a few years ago drove Nick away because he couldn't cope with her new "beauty." (She may even believe it.) **29** Sixteen-year-old David Merrick is playing hooky at the movies when a tornado hits his St. Louis high school. Five of his classmates are killed, and 16 others are injured.

OCTOBER 12 *Variety* says that Al Jolson has turned down an offer from the Capitol Theatre in New York City to appear onstage for $20,000 a week because he would be competing with himself. He can be seen and *heard* across the street at the Warner's Theatre, where the film *The Jazz Singer*, the first feature-length talkie, opened six days ago.

NOVEMBER 2 More than 10,000 people

Plays and Musicals

AUGUST 9 With its 2,239 performance at the Republic Theatre, *Abie's Irish Rose* breaks the long run record previously held by *Chu Chin Chow*. **16** *The Ziegfeld Follies* (167), at the New Amsterdam, for the first time has only one star, Eddie Cantor, and one composer, Irving Berlin. But Cantor's big number will be his interpolation of Walter Donaldson's "My Blue Heaven." Ruth Etting sings "Shaking the Blues Away."

SEPTEMBER 1 "Young Barbara Stanwyck, who used to be Ruby Stevens of the cabarets . . . is a fine ingenue," declares *Variety*. "She can emote to tears" in *Burlesque* (372), by George M. Watters and Arthur Hopkins, at the Plymouth. **6** "The Best Things in Life are Free" and "The Varsity Drag" are in *Good News* (557), opening at the Forty-sixth Street Theatre. The lyrics to this show about a football hero and the girl who gets him are by Buddy De Sylva and Lew Brown, with music by Ray Henderson. It stars John Price Jones and Mary Lawlor. **19** Bayard Veiller's *The Trial of Mary Dugan* (437) opens at the National. Ann Harding, in the title role, has a lawyer with a conflict of interest—he committed the murder for which she is being tried.

OCTOBER 5 Hamilton Dean and John Balderston's version of Bram Stoker's *Dracula* (265) opens at the Fulton. Brooks Atkinson finds Bela Lugosi, in the role of the Count, "a little too deliberate and confident." **10** Dubose and Dorothy Heyward's adaptation of his novel *Porgy* (367) opens at the Guild Theatre. Frank Wilson and Evelyn Ellis have the title roles.

NOVEMBER 3 Rodgers and Hart's *A Connecticut Yankee* (418), based on the Mark Twain novel, is at the Vanderbilt. William Gaxton and Contance Carpenter star, the choreography is by Busby Berkeley, and the score features "Thou Swell" and "My Heart Stood Still." **8** Helen Hayes plays a flapper in *Coquette* (366), opening at Maxine Elliott's Theater. *Herald Tribune* critic Percy Hammond writes that "we shall have to enlarge the

Business and Society

JULY 13 *Variety* notes the growing sales of published plays, which people are reading like novels. **25** Ads for today's show at the Palace have billed the film of the Dempsey-Sharkey heavyweight fight over the stage acts.

AUGUST • Dinty Moore's, the famed theatre district restaurant, is padlocked for violating Prohibition. • The William Morris Agency begins to handle talent for legitimate stage productions.

OCTOBER • The Keith-Albee and Orpheum vaudeville theatre circuits agree to merge. Next year, they will form a basic component of the new RKO film company. The Mutual and Columbia burlesque theatre circuits are also merging. • *The American Mercury*'s article, "The Passing of Vaudeville," declares the two-a-day presentation all but dead. **5** The price of *Variety* rises a nickel, to $.25. **12** "Colored Show Folks' Best Season for White Stage Jobs," headlines *Variety*. Opportunities include *Porgy*, which opened two days ago, and the upcoming *Show Boat*.

MARCH 19 Broadway and Hollywood face serious competition from the airwaves

Births, Deaths, and Marriages

JUNE 6 Robert C. Hilliard d. **8** Jerry Stiller b. **27** Choreographer-director Bob Fosse b.

JULY 4 Neil Simon (Marvin Neil Simon) b. **9** John Drew d.

AUGUST 13 Playwright Howard Lindsay m. actress Dorothy Stickney.

SEPTEMBER • It's rained on her parade after all. Fanny Brice divorces Nicky Arnstein. **5** Marcus Loew d.

OCTOBER 1 Tom Bosley b. **25** Barbara Cook b. **18** George C. Scott b.

NOVEMBER 1 Florence Mills d. **18** Emma Carus d. **20** Estelle Parsons b.

DECEMBER 21 Victor Jory m. actress Jean Inness. **28** Ralph Bellamy m Alice Delbridge, an actress in the theatrical company he heads.

file past the coffin of Florence Mills in a Harlem funeral parlor. **21** Fanny Brice, recently divorced from Nicky Arnstein, opens at the Palace. She declines persistent requests from the audience to sing "My Man," but she will do it next week. **23** A *Variety* columnist reports that Broadway's newest star, Barbara Stanwyck, would "rather work a week on the stage than one day in pictures." She "hates the movies."

JANUARY 9 *Her Cardboard Lover* cannot open in Boston this evening as scheduled because Jeanne Eagels is "sick." But she has been seen at clubs and parties during the last few days. **11** The Shuberts, angered by Walter Winchell's snippy comments about their productions, ban the columnist from their theatres. "If I can't go to their openings," Winchell quips, "I'll wait three days and go to the closings." **19** Twenty-four-year-old John Gielgud makes his Broadway debut at the Majestic as the Grand Duke in *The Patriot.* **29** At an American Shakespeare Foundation benefit at the Metropolitan Opera house, Jane Cowl, making her entrance in a scene from *Romeo and Juliet,* walks off without uttering a word when the spotlight fails to pick her up. **30** *The World* assigns Dudley Nichols rather than regular critic Alexander Woollcott to review Eugene O'Neill's *Strange Interlude* because Woollcott has already expressed an opinion about the play in *Vanity Fair,* which Woollcott did not realize would be on sale by the show's opening. In response,

Fred Astaire

already long list of First Actresses, and so far as this season goes, put Miss Hayes at the top." (He will repeat this evaluation in the first issue of *Life* magazine in 1936, following Hayes's triumph in *Victoria Regina,* helping to build her reputation as "The First Lady of the American Theater.") **22** George and Ira Gershwin's *Smarty,* which stumbled in tryouts, has become *Funny Face* (244), with Victor Moore added to the cast. It's at the new Alvin Theatre. Fred and Adele Astaire are the leads. The songs include "'S Wonderful" and the title tune. **22** Edward G. Robinson is a Chicago gangster, Nick Scarsi, in Bartlett Cormack's *The Racket* (119), at the Ambassador. It will become a silent film starring Thomas Meighan. **28** The Irish Players bring Sean O'Casey's *The Plough and the Stars* (48) to the Hudson Theatre. Arthur Sinclair and Sara Allgood star in this controversial play about the Easter Rebellion of 1916.

DECEMBER 26 A record eleven shows open tonight on Broadway. *Excess Baggage* (216), a new comedy at the Ritz by John McGowan, offers Miriam Hopkins as a young woman who rises from vaudeville to the silver screen, only to return to the stage to help the man who got her started. **27** Most of the major critics have gone to see Philip Barry's *Paris Bound,* leaving second-stringers to cover the new musical by Jerome Kern and Oscar Hammerstein II at the Ziegfeld Theatre: *Show Boat* (575). Norma Terris plays Magnolia, Charles Winninger is Cap'n Andy, Edna May Oliver is Parthy, Howard Marsh is Gaylord Ravenal, and Helen Morgan is Julie. While Jules Bledsoe, a black man, plays Joe, Queenie, Joe's wife, is portrayed by Tess Gardella, vaudeville's "Aunt Jemima," a white woman in blackface. Producer Flo Ziegfeld takes the audience's silence to mean "the show's a flop." He needn't worry. "Potential song hits were as common last night as top hats," says the *Times.* They include "Ol' Man River," "Make Believe," "Bill," and "Can't Help Lovin' Dat Man." *Show Boat* films appear in 1929, 1936, and 1951. **28** *The Royal Family* (343), a caricature of the Barrymores, by George S. Kaufman and Edna Ferber, opens at the Selwyn. In the cast are Haidee Wright, Otto Kruger, Sylvia Field, and Ann Andrews.

with the radio debut of "Amos 'n Andy."

MAY 1 The Manhattan District Attorney says he has rejected a complaint from the Shuberts that Eugene O'Neill's *Strange Interlude* is indecent. **15** E.F. Albee sells his holdings in the Keith–Albee–Orpheum circuit for $4,500,000 to Joseph P. Kennedy, who is assembling the components of what will become RKO.

JANUARY • Edna May Oliver m. stockbroker David Pratt. **30** Producer-director Harold Prince b.

FEBRUARY 16 Eddie Foy d. in a hotel in Kansas City, where he's playing at the Orpheum. **17** Lyricist Tom Jones b.

MARCH 12 Playwright Edward Albee, adopted son of Reed Albee, whose father is E.F. Albee, b. **19** Nora Bayes d.

APRIL 1 George Grizzard b.

MAY 21 Critic Alan Dale d.

Personalities

Woollcott resigns. **30** *The Ziegfeld Follies*, scheduled to open in Philadelphia, is canceled because star Eddie Cantor is ill with pleurisy.

FEBRUARY • His marriage to Agnes Boulton breaking up, Eugene O'Neill sails for Europe with Carlotta Monterey. They will remain abroad for more than two years. • Jules Bledsoe, Joe in *Show Boat*, files for bankruptcy. • Marilyn Miller breaks her engagement to screen star Ben Lyon. • Harold Clurman and Lee Strasberg gather a group of actors for some experimental theatre work, out of which will evolve the Group Theatre. • Flo Ziegfeld announces that there will be no Follies this year, attributing his decision to the high cost of top rate talent.

MARCH 4 Critic Richard Watts, in the *Herald Tribune*, discloses that Eugene O'Neill has turned *The Hairy Ape* and *Desire Under the Elms* into screenplays (neither will sell). **19** Producers Gilbert Miller and A.H. Woods file charges with Actors Equity against Jeanne Eagels because their show, *Her Cardboard Lover*, has folded in the Midwest when she was not able to go on. She says that she has been ill; they say she's been drinking.

APRIL 4 *Variety* reports that "Humphrey De Forest Bogard" [sic] will marry actress Mary Philips. **6** Equity suspends Jeanne Eagels for 18 months—until September 1, 1929—for "unethical conduct" in causing the closing of *Her Cardboard Lover*. She responds: "A handful of actors, for whom, with a few exceptions, I have no respect, cannot keep me away from my public, which I know is a big one."

MAY 15 William Kent, one of the stars of the Gershwin musical *Funny Face*, is fired for performing while intoxicated.

Plays and Musicals

JANUARY 9 Eugene O'Neill's *Marco Millions* (92), ostensibly about Marco Polo but also an attack on American business and "Babbitry," opens at the Guild Theatre. Directed by Rouben Mamoulian, it stars Alfred Lunt as Marco, who cannot recognize love while there is wealth to be accumulated, and Margalo Gillmore, Albert Dekker, Morris Carnovsky, and Henry Travers. **10** With only half efforts by George Gershwin and Sigmund Romberg, *Rosalie* (335), at the New Amsterdam, is still a hit. Marilyn Miller, Jack Donahue, and Frank Morgan star, the lyrics are by Ira Gershwin and P.G. Wodehouse, and the most prominent song is Gershwin's "How Long Has This Been Going On?" **30** Eugene O'Neill's nine-act play *Strange Interlude* (426) is at the John Golden. It stars Lynn Fontanne in her last Broadway role without Alfred Lunt, who has reportedly said that if the play had gone on for two more acts, he would have sued for desertion. It was director Philip Moeller's idea to reveal the character's inner thoughts as asides while all other action stops.

MARCH 13 Rudolph Friml's final operetta, *The Three Musketeers* (319), opens at the Lyric. The show, given an elaborate production by Flo Ziegfeld, stars Dennis King and Vivienne Segal.

APRIL 9 Mae West is *Diamond Lil* (171), at the Royale. Mae, who also wrote the play, is on the Bowery, where one of her men is a detective masquerading as a member of the Salvation Army. *She Done Him Wrong* is the 1933 screen version.

MAY 9 Bill "Bojangles" Robinson, Adelaide Hall, Aida Ward, and Elizabeth Welch are among the stars in *Blackbirds of 1928* (518), at the Liberty. Songs include Jimmy McHugh and Dorothy Fields's "Diga Diga Doo," "Doin' the New Low-Down," and "I Can't Give You Anything But Love."

Business and Society

Births, Deaths, and Marriages

1928–29

In Hollywood, money talks as much as pictures, and it's siphoning off a good deal of top Broadway talent. *New York Times* publisher Adolph Ochs is not happy with *The Front Page*'s description of a reporter as "a cross between a bellboy and a whore." Sophie Tucker, who was "The Great Coon Shouter," is now "The Last of the Hot Mammas," and thanks to the Shuberts, Walter Winchell is "the Barred of Broadway." As if gambling on shows wasn't high risk enough—business is turning disturbingly downward at the box office—many producers are betting on stocks as well. Finally, it's a sure thing that gambler-play investor Arnold Rothstein will not return to his favorite table at Lindy's. He should have ordered the cheesecake.

- Number of Broadway houses with stage productions exclusively that are air-cooled: just 2—the Times Square Theatre and the Palace
- First Palace headliner to have her name in lights on the theatre's marquee: Fanny Brice
- Number of Broadway actors, playwrights, and directors placed under contract by movie studios: about 200
- Trend in theatres with films accompanied by stage shows: many are dropping the stage shows as they convert to sound
- What gambler and show investor Arnold Rothstein is eating at Lindy's when summoned to the meeting at which he will be killed: an apple, not the eatery's fabled, fat-laden cheesecake
- Ethnic terms used by *Variety*: "chink," "wop," "hebe" and "yid"
- World's richest actor, after selling his Loew's stock: David Warfield, said to be worth at least $10,000,000—about twice what Eddie Cantor is worth
- What Dorothy Stickney does 8 times a week in *The Front Page*: commits suicide by jumping out of a window, falling through a hole onto a mattress in the basement
- Charles MacArthur's marital promise to Helen Hayes: "With me you may never be rich, but you'll never be bored."
- *Show Boat* salaries, per week (week ending January 26, 1929):

Charles Winninger (Cap'n Andy)	$1,500
Helen Morgan (Julie)	700
Jules Bledsoe (Joe)	400

Productions on Broadway: 225

Pulitzer Prize for Drama: *Street Scene* (Elmer Rice)

June	July	August	September	October	November
Flo Ziegfeld feuds with Earl Carroll	Ellen Terry d.	Helen Hays m. Charles MacArthur	Helen Kane "Boop, Boop-a-Doop" in *Good Boy*	Mae West's *Pleasure Man* raided	Jeanne Eagels says doctor prescribes champagne

December	January	February	March	April	May
Eddie Cantor in *Whoopee*	Jed Harris feuds with George S. Kaufman	Fanny Brice m. Billy Rose	The Palace goes to three shows a day on Sunday	Libby Holman is "Moanin' Low" in *The Little Show*	Broadway's first *Uncle Vanya*

Personalities

JUNE • Flo Ziegfeld is feuding with Earl Carroll over the latter's attempts to hire away some of Ziegfeld's chorines. **6** In a letter in *Variety* in which he mentions being banned from Shubert theatres, columnist and critic Walter Winchell calls himself "the Barred of Broadway." In the same issue, Bill "Bojangles" Robinson takes out an ad in which he complains about imitators of his act, in which he tap dances up and down a flight of stairs, warning "anyone, white or dark, to keep away from it after this day and date." **10** Jeanne Eagels, suspended from Equity productions, opens a vaudeville act in Chicago.

AUGUST • Actor Fred Stone will be hospitalized for several weeks for injuries he suffers when the plane he is piloting crashes. **29** *Variety*, reviewing Ethel Waters at the Palace, is amazed at how she can deliver a hot song such as "Handy Man" with such a cool demeanor. "How that girl can control her cooch should be rewarded somehow." Her reward is the theatre's management telling her to drop the suggestive song.

SEPTEMBER 6 Actors Equity temporarily suspends Paul Robeson, now appearing in the London production of *Show Boat*, because he had promised to appear in a "colored" revue that had been set to open in New York and has folded because he has reneged. Robeson will settle out of court with the producer next year. **12** Flo Ziegfeld, crossing into the U.S. from Canada in a private Pullman car, is arrested and fined when 106 bottles of liquor are found in the car. **17** Buck and Bubbles (Buck Washington and John Bubbles), dancer-singers, make their Palace debut. **28** Producer Jed Harris is on the cover of *Time*.

OCTOBER 7 Opening at the Palace this Sunday is Sophie Tucker, now calling herself "the last of the hot mammas."

NOVEMBER 2 Fanny Brice is the first headliner to have her name in lights on the Palace marquee, where the electric apparatus has just been installed and the words "Keith Albee Vaudeville" removed.

Plays and Musicals

AUGUST 14 Ben Hecht and Charles MacArthur's *The Front Page* (276), the quintessential newspaper drama, directed by George S. Kaufman and starring Lee Tracy as Hildy Johnson, opens at the Times Square Theatre. The *Times* says the authors "have packed an evening with loud, rapid, coarse and unfailing entertainment." Adolph Ochs, the *Times*'s publisher, is less happy, especially about the description of a reporter as "a cross between a bellboy and a whore." Also in the cast are Osgood Perkins, Dorothy Stickney, and Allen Jenkins. It's filmed in 1931, in 1941 as *His Girl Friday*, and in 1974.

SEPTEMBER 5 Jesse Bonstelle has turned her famed stock company into the Detroit Civic Theatre, to be operated on a nonprofit, subscription basis. It opens tonight with Robert E. Sherwood's new play, *The Queen's Husband*. **7** At the Plymouth is Sophie Treadwell's *Machinal* (91), starring Zita Johann in a play about a woman whose unhappiness leads to tragedy. **19** Sigmund Romberg's *New Moon* (509), with lyrics by Oscar Hammerstein II, opens at the Imperial. Set in the time of the French Revolution, with a plot involving the hero's flight to New Orleans, it stars Robert Halliday and Evelyn Herbert, who introduces "Lover, Come Back to Me," and also features "Softly, as in a Morning Sunrise" and "Stouthearted Men." The 1940 film stars Jeanette MacDonald and Nelson Eddy. **25** *Good Boy* (253), opening at the Hammerstein Theatre, with a Harry Ruby–Herbert Stothart–Bert Kalmar score, is notable for Helen Kane (the "Boop, Boop-a-Doop" girl) singing "I Want to Be Loved By You."

OCTOBER 8 In Tom Barry's comedy *Courage* (280), at the Ritz Theatre, the themes are illegitimacy, family ostracism, and the power of an inheritance to turn the tables in life. Janet Beecher, Helen Strikland, and Junior Durkin star. **9** Thomas Mitchell stars in, and coauthors with Floyd Dell, *The Little Accident* (304), a comedy opening at the Morosco. **10** *Hold Everything!* (413), a musical about boxing, by Ray Henderson, Buddy De Sylva and Lew

Business and Society

JUNE 6 According to *Variety*, Wall Street is proving to be a greater draw than Broadway for many, and "[a] lot of showmen have turned to the ticker lately as an occupation." **29** The premium that ticket brokers can charge rises from \$.50 to \$.75.

JULY 6 The first all-talking picture, *The Lights of New York*, opening at the Strand, has a cast made up almost entirely of former vaudevillians. **18** "Talkers Hot After Legit Talent," headlines *Variety*. Paramount has corralled Helen Menken, Fay Bainter, Florence Reed, the Marx Brothers, and Jeanne Eagels. Fox has secured the services of Yiddish Theatre star Muni Wiesenfreund, whose name they will change to Paul Muni.

AUGUST 17 In a letter to Keith–Orpheum managers, Joseph P. Kennedy calls on them to "rejuvenate" vaudeville.

OCTOBER • "Chinks May Take Over Nite Life," says *Variety*'s headline about Chinese restaurants and clubs—"chowmeineries"—in the theatre district, a veritable "Yellow Peril." **3** Police raid Mae West's *Pleasure Man* for the second time in several days, closing it and arresting 52 cast members,

Births, Deaths, and Marriages

JUNE 7 Composer Charles Strouse b. **14** Jeanne Eagels divorces Edward H. Coy.

JULY 1 Playwright Avery Hopwood d. **1** Ellen Terry d.

AUGUST 17 Helen Hayes m. playwright Charles MacArthur in secret because his ex-wife, Carol Frink, is claiming that their divorce is not final and has threatened to stop the wedding. (For advice on contraception, about which the innocent Hayes knows little, she went to Tallulah Bankhead, who is at the other end of the sexual experience spectrum.) **23** Marian Seldes b. **26** Barbara Stanwyck m. vaudevillian Frank Fay.

SEPTEMBER 21 Al Jolson m. Ruby Keeler.

NOVEMBER 23 Composer Jerry Bock b.

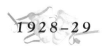

4 At 10:30 P.M., Arnold Rothstein, gambler and show investor, is called away from his usual table near the cashier at Lindy's to a meeting at which he will be shot to death. Rothstein's poker debts may have played a role in his demise. He's eating an apple when summoned, not the establishment's legendary cheesecake. **7** Jeanne Eagels tells reporters that in regard to her suspension by Equity, "The matter of drink has nothing to do with the present case. . . . I do not touch spirits, but . . . my doctor has allowed me a little champagne mainly because he thinks it will help me." **20** Tallulah Bankhead announces in London, where she's performing in *Her Cardboard Lover* at the Lyric, her engagement to Count Anthony de Bosdavi. **20** Equity suspends William Kent a second time for being drunk on the job.

DECEMBER • Although Laurette Taylor's marriage to playwright J. Hartley Manners had been shaky—she fell in love with screen actor John Gilbert a few years ago—Manners's death inaugurates a period of more than 15 years in which Taylor will do more drinking than acting. • Frank Gillmore succeeds John Emerson as head of Actors Equity. **20** Ethel Barrymore inaugurates the theatre named for her by the Shuberts, starring in a play called The *Kingdom of God.*

JANUARY • Jed Harris, who has produced several of George S. Kaufman's shows, is feuding with the playwright. Kaufman,

Ethyl Barrymore

Brown, is at the Broadhurst. Ona Munson, Betty Compton, Jack Whiting, Bert Lahr—achieving musical comedy stardom—and Victor Moore are featured, and the songs include "You're the Cream in My Coffee." It's filmed in 1930.

NOVEMBER 26 Philip Barry's *Holiday* (230) opens at the Plymouth. Ben Smith, Hope Williams, and Dorothy Tree star in this play about a newly rich young man who simply wants to enjoy his hard-earned wealth while he's still young and the fiancée who can't quite accept this notion. It's filmed in 1930 and 1938.

DECEMBER 4 Flo Ziegfeld's *Whoopee* (407) opens at the New Amsterdam. With music by Walter Donaldson and lyrics by Gus Kahn, it stars Eddie Cantor, singing "Makin' Whoopee," and Ruth Etting, whose "Love Me Or Leave Me" will become a signature song for her and will be the title of the 1955 film biography of Etting, starring Doris Day. Cantor is in the 1930 film. **25** A doctor experiments on twins to observe the effect of nature versus nurture in *Brothers* (255), by Herbert Ashton, Jr., at the Forty-eighth Street Theatre. Bert Lytell plays both brothers.

JANUARY 9 Buddy De Sylva, Lew Brown and Ray Henderson's *Follow Thru* (403), a musical about golf and country clubs, which includes "Button Up Your Overcoat," is at the Forty-sixth Street Theatre. Jack Haley and Eleanor Powell are in the cast. The film is released in 1930. **10** Elmer Rice's *Street Scene* (601), with Robert Kelly, Mary Servoss, Erin O'Brien-Moore, Horace Braham, and Beulah Bondi, opens at the Playhouse. Jealousy leads to murder, blighting a young woman's attempts to find happiness. It becomes a 1931 film and a Kurt Weill opera in 1947, with a libretto by Langston Hughes. **14** Maxwell Anderson's *Gypsy* (64) is at the Klaw. Thinking that the unhappy ending—the lead character's pregnancy, abortion, and suicide—is keeping people away despite good reviews, Anderson will substitute a sunnier one but to no avail. Claiborne Foster stars.

FEBRUARY 11 Eugene O'Neill's *Dynamo* (66), opening at the Martin Beck, is not well-received—"A Womb With a View,"

some of them men in drag.

NOVEMBER 6 The electric sign that delivers the news via a ribbon of light bulbs around the Times Tower in Times Square is turned on for the first time, reporting that Herbert Hoover has been elected President.

DECEMBER • Business is way off on Broadway, with 25 legitimate houses dark. Unemployment among New York City actors is said to be the worst in a decade. • The Keith–Orpheum vaudeville circuit becomes part of an entertainment empire that also includes the NBC radio network and RKO pictures. All Keith houses in the New York City area are being wired for sound films by RCA Photophone.

JANUARY • The Authors League calls for a clause covering television in the sale of rights to plays—a precaution in case the technology is perfected any time soon. **21** The new traffic system getting a trial in the theatre district prohibits parking on any of the side streets—15 cars are towed away tonight—cracks down on jaywalking, and bans cabs from cruising in the area, a feature protested by the management of nearby hotels. Some garage owners take advantage of the sudden lack of parking, jacking up their

DECEMBER 14 Sophie Tucker m. Abe Lackerman, who is in the garment business. Anticipating movie work, she's also had a recent face lift.

JANUARY 9 Playwright Brian Friel b.

FEBRUARY • Fanny Brice and showman Billy Rose are married by Mayor Jimmy Walker at New York's City Hall. **12** Lillie Langtry d.

MARCH 21 James Coco b.

MAY 9 After a three-week acquaintance, Ina Claire marries film star John Gilbert. When asked by a reporter how it feels to be married to a big star, Claire replies, "I don't know. Why don't you ask Mr. Gilbert." **16** Oscar Hammerstein II m. Dorothy Blanchard Jacobson.

Personalities

who still heads *The New York Times*'s drama desk, presided over the paper's reprint of an uncomplimentary comment about the Philadelphia tryout of *Serena Blandish*, a new Harris production. The quarrelsome producer is also feuding with Ina Claire. • Irene Bordoni, who last year introduced Cole Porter's "Let's Do It" in *Paris*, is headed for an ugly divorce case with her songwriter-producer-husband E. Ray Goetz, from whom she is separated. He is reported to have raided her apartment and found her there with her business manager, and she has accused him of carrying on with Peggy Hopkins Joyce. • Producer John Golden, in Palm Beach for a golf tournament, is saved from drowning when Rube Goldberg spots him in distress and calls for the lifeguard. **5** The Dainty June dance revue has run into trouble in Topeka, Kansas. "Dainty June"—17-year-old June Hovick—secretly married Weldon Hyde, her dance partner, two months ago. Tonight, her domineering stage mother, Rose Hovick (played by Ethel Merman in *Gypsy*), finds out and has an altercation with her son-in-law, who, according to some reports, punches her in the jaw.

FEBRUARY 3 Frank Fay opens at the Palace, accompanied by his new wife, Barbara Stanwyck. *Variety* will comment (February 13) that she "looks very cute in three-piece black and white pajamas with flared coat, and looks better than she acts, dramatically." It is Fay, at the peak of his career, who seems to be the better bet for the talkies.

MAY • Tallulah Bankhead breaks her engagement to Count Anthony de Bosdavi, who appears not to have been the ideal groom. She discovered that he had not divorced his first wife and had neglected to complete the payments on the Rolls Royce he had given Bankhead.

Plays and Musicals

Noel Coward will call it. There is, however, praise for the attractive legs of the actress who plays the flapper: Claudette Colbert. **21** Rachel Crothers has one of her most popular comedy hits in *Let Us Be Gay* (363), opening at the Little Theatre. Francine Larrimore and Warren William are the husband and wife who separate, then reunite.

APRIL 4 Jill Esmond Moore stars in *Bird in Hand* (500), John Drinkwater's comedy, at the Booth. **30** *The Little Show* (321), a revue written mostly by Arthur Schwartz and Howard Dietz in their first Broadway collaboration, is at the Music Box. Libby Holman sings "Moanin' Low" to Clifton Webb, who dances with her and then chokes her. Also in the cast are Fred Allen, Portland Hoffa, and Constance Cummings.

MAY 24 Broadway gets its first *Uncle Vanya* (2), in a limited run, at the Morosco. "Morris Carnovsky, in a make-up that unhappily suggests Shylock, is an actor to be reckoned with as Uncle Vanya," says the *Times*. Also in the cast is Franchot Tone.

Business and Society

prices to as much as a profiteering $1.25 for the whole evening.

MARCH 10 The Palace, seeking to recoup the increase in salaries for hard-to-get talent—jumping from the recent $8,500 a week to the current top of as much as $12,000—goes to three shows a day on Sundays.

MAY • The loss of Broadway personnel to Hollywood is creating more opportunities for black shows to make it to the Main Stem. There are now several playing—termed a "dark epidemic" by *Variety*. • Margaret Anglin, who has been a member of the Actors Fidelity League since it was formed in opposition to Actors Equity in the great strike of 1919, is one of the last prominent holdouts to give in and finally join Equity.

Births, Deaths, and Marriages

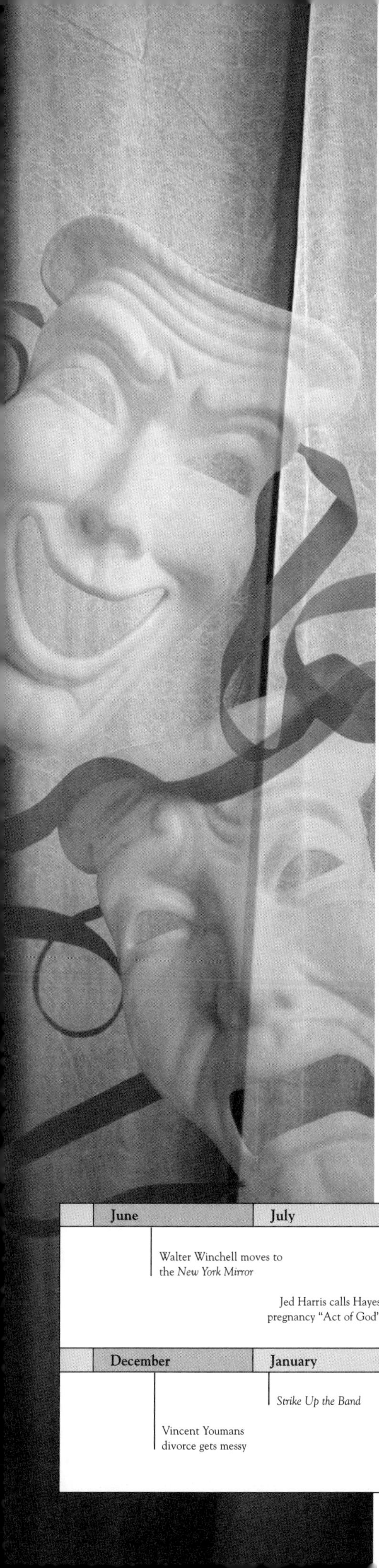

1929–30

The stock market deflates egos and reputations as well as portfolios on Broadway. Flo Ziegfeld, a show business colossus, is left scrambling to keep from completely falling off the cliff. Symbolic of Broadway's problems, he folds *Whoopie* prematurely so he can turn it into a movie. While Jed Harris directs a "luminous" *Uncle Vanya,* college freshman Tennessee Williams learns about critics. New faces on the scene include Jessica Tandy and Burgess Meredith. Stephen Sondheim is born, and Jeanne Eagels dies. The old guard in the legitimate theatre and in vaudeville is passing, with the deaths, within four days of each other, of producer Abraham L. Erlanger and manager E.F. Albee.

- Total number of Theatre Guild subscribers in New York and 13 other cities: 69,000, a figure it will not reach again for almost a decade
- Number of legitimate stage shows at the beginning of the season in theatres actually located on Broadway in the theatre district: none—for the first time, the movies have entirely taken over Broadway, and plays and musicals are confined to the side streets and other avenues
- Number of theatres in the approximately 700-theatre Keith–Orpheum circuit continuing with a vaudeville-only policy: 5, the rest splitting the bill with movies
- Number of vaudeville houses left in the country: 300, down from the 1,500 of five years ago
- Careful with that knife!: 18-year-old Ethel Merman has a tonsillectomy
- Ruined by trading in the grain markets: John Houseman
- Comedian Willie Howard's stock market experience: he "went in a Friar and came out a Lamb"
- What Antoinette Perry is doing the night the stock market crashes, taking much of her wealth with it: she's staying at the Savoy Plaza while her Park Avenue apartment is painted
- Beatrice Lillie's fee for her Palace appearance: $6,500 a week, the same drawn by former heavyweight champion Jack Dempsey for his appearance as a "freak" act
- Tennessee Williams's grades in R.O.T.C. in his freshman year at the University of Missouri: D and F
- Amount that RKO pays vaudeville performers for obligatory radio appearances: 0
- "Eau de greasepaint": the failure of his perfume business launches Joseph Fields, son of Lew Fields, of Weber and Fields, into a writing career. He will coauthor *My Sister Eileen*, *Junior Miss*, and *Wonderful Town*
- Born on the same day as Stephen Sondheim (March 22, 1930): evangelist Pat Robertson
- Gags censored from acts on the Keith-Orpheum circuit:
  "Honeymoon salad is 'let us alone with very little dressing.'"
  "Panama pants completely cover the Canal Zone."
  "She thinks 'lettuce' is a proposition."
  "I'm from New York." "You don't look Jewish."
  "The dog had rabbis."

Productions on Broadway: 233

Pulitzer Prize for Drama: *The Green Pastures* (Marc Connelly)

June	July	August	September	October	November
Walter Winchell moves to the *New York Mirror*	Jed Harris calls Hayes pregnancy "Act of God"	Buck and Bubbles arrested	Ed Wynn feuds with George White	Stock Market crash ruins Flo Ziegfeld	Cole Porter's "You Do Something to Me"

December	January	February	March	April	May
Vincent Youmans divorce gets messy	*Strike Up the Band*	Ruth Etting sings "Ten Cents a Dance" in *Simple Simon*	Jessica Tandy's Broadway debut; Stephen Sondheim b.	Jed Harris's *Uncle Vanya*	Playwright Lorraine Hansberry b.

Personalities

JUNE 10 Walter Winchell's first column appears in the *New York Mirror*, with gossip about dancer Irene Castle expecting a child. Winchell has been replaced at the *Graphic* by Louis Sobol, who, in turn, will be followed by Ed Sullivan. **23** Sophie Tucker headlines the show at the Palace, but this is also the uptown debut of Molly Picon, star of the Yiddish Theatre. Her post-Palace reaction: "Broadway's just like Second Avenue. Except it is wider and has more lights."

JULY • "Romance in the Roaring Forties," the first of Damon Runyon's Broadway stories, appears in *Cosmopolitan*. The character "Waldo Winchester," modeled after columnist Walter Winchell, chronicles "who is running around with who [sic], including guys and dolls." **8** During tryouts of *Show Girl*, opening tonight, in a famous incident later depicted in the film *The Al Jolson Story*, Ruby Keeler freezes. Her husband Al Jolson, sitting in the audience, jumps up and begins to sing "Liza," her next number, putting her back on track. He repeats that performance tonight. **20** With star Helen Hayes pregnant, *Coquette* closes its West Coast engagement early. Producer Jed Harris claims he doesn't have to pay cast members who have run-of-the-play contracts because the pregnancy is an "act of God." The problem will be debated by theologians in the papers, although some on Broadway smell a publicity stunt. He loses in arbitration, which grants the cast two weeks' pay.

AUGUST • Buck and Bubbles, the vaudeville team, are jailed in Chicago, where they are appearing at Keith's Palace, on charges related to a financial dispute with their former manager.

SEPTEMBER • Ed Wynn is feuding with producer George White, claiming the latter stole one of his gags for an edition of his *Scandals*. White says the joke came from Eddie Cantor. **21** Bea Lillie makes her U.S. vaudeville debut at the Palace. And Howard Da Silva makes his stage debut with Eva Le Gallienne's Civic Repertory Company, as a slave in

Plays and Musicals

JUNE 20 *Hot Chocolates* (228), a revue with an all-black cast, opens at the Hudson. Emerging from the pit band to play a new song by Fats Waller, "Ain't Misbehavin'," is Louis Armstrong.

JULY 1 Eddie Cantor has written much of *The Sketch Book* (400), a revue at the Earl Carroll Theatre. Cantor appears in a film sequence, and on the stage are Will Mahoney, Patsy Kelly, and William Demarest.

AUGUST 6 Mildred McCoy stars in Laurence E. Johnson's comedy *It's a Wise Child* (378), at the Belasco, in which she marries not Humphrey Bogart or Harlan Briggs, but rather Minor Watson.

SEPTEMBER 3 Jerome Kern and Oscar Hammerstein team up again for *Sweet Adeline* (234), at the Hammerstein Theatre. Helen Morgan, hard on the heels of her *Show Boat* triumph, is featured. Songs include "Don't Ever Leave Me" and "Why Was I Born?" **18** Preston Sturges's *Strictly Dishonorable* (557) is at the Avon. Muriel Kirkland stars as a young woman who proves resourceful when her date walks out on her at a night spot. It will be filmed in 1931 and 1951.

OCTOBER 2 In *Criminal Code* (174), by Martin Flavin, the letter of the law and the unwritten law among prisoners reduces a man to helplessness. Russell Hardie, Arthur Byron, and Anita Kerry star in this tragedy, at the National Theatre. **9** *June Moon* (273), by George S. Kaufman and Ring Lardner, at the Broadhurst, is based on Lardner's satirical story about Tin Pan Alley, "Some Like Them Cold." The cast includes Norman Foster and Jeanne Dixon.

NOVEMBER 4 *Berkeley Square* (229), by John Lloyd Balderston, opens at the Lyceum. Leslie Howard, who coproduced with Gilbert Miller, stars as a man who travels 150 years into the past to become one of his own ancestors. **5** In Noel Coward's operetta *Bitter Sweet* (157), at the Ziegfeld, Evelyn Lane ponders whether she should marry for love. "I'll

Business and Society

JULY • The Shuberts take over the Masque, Majestic, and Royale Theatres, in which they already had a 50 percent interest, from the Chanins. And the Keith–Orpheum circuit begins to take over some of the Pantages theatres in the West. **1** Eddie Cantor succeeds Fred Stone as president of the National Vaudeville Artists.

AUGUST 8 The historic Miner's Theatre on the Bowery, which had a serious fire six months ago, today burns down for good. **17** Actors Equity abandons its three-month campaign to gain a foothold among Hollywood screen actors, many of whom have migrated to the talkies from Broadway.

OCTOBER 30 *Variety*'s headline reviewing the stock market crash, "Wall Street Lays an Egg," is written by Claude Binyon, who will write and direct in Hollywood.

NOVEMBER • The unexpected failure of several Broadway musicals on the road, including *Follow Thru* and *Good News*, is being ascribed to the new and stiff competition from the talkies. **6** "Broadway, kicked, heeled, punched and gouged by Wall Street, came within an inch of its night-life last week, shattering all records

Births, Deaths, and Marriages

JUNE 4 Producer Harry H. Frazee d. **14** Composer Cy Coleman (Seymour Kaufman) b.

JULY 2 Eugene O'Neill and Agnes Boulton are divorced. **3** Dustin Farnum d. **15** Ray Bolger m. screenwriter Gwen Rickard. **22** Eugene O'Neill m. Carlotta Monterey. **27** Bela Lugosi m. Beatrice Weeks.

AUGUST 29 Bert Lahr m. Mercedes Delpino, his onetime vaudeville partner.

SEPTEMBER 4 Theatre executive Frederick F. Proctor d. **12** Composer Harvey Schmidt b. **14** Playwright Jesse Lynch Williams d. **20** Ann Meara b.

OCTOBER 3 Jeanne Eagels d. of an overdose of drugs and alcohol. She is wearing several thousand dollars' worth of jewelry when her body is discovered. **28** Joan

The Would-Be Gentleman.

OCTOBER • The stock market crash wipes out much of producer Jed Harris's $5 million fortune. He's also beginning to lose his hearing, which will not be fully restored until a 1946 operation. **29** Edward Hutton, of E.F. Hutton, tries all day to reach Flo Ziegfeld to tell him that he's being ruined in the stock market crash. But Ziegfeld's testifying in a suit, disputing a $1,600 bill. His staff is with him, and the office telephone operator is out sick. Tonight, after the loss of several million dollars, he tells his wife, Billie Burke, "I'm through. Nothing can save me."

NOVEMBER 23 Flo Ziegfeld, beset by huge

Flo Ziegfeld, his wife, Billie Burke, and their daughter—a show business family buffeted by the stock market crash *ZCI*

See You Again" is one of the songs. It's filmed in 1933 and 1940. **27** Cole Porter's *Fifty Million Frenchmen* (257), backed by Warner Brothers, opens at the Lyric. William Gaxton gets Genevieve Tobin to marry him for himself, not his money. It introduces "You Do Something to Me" and "Find Me a Primitive Man." The 1931 film has no music.

JANUARY 14 George and Ira Gershwin's *Strike Up the Band* (191), a revised version of the George S. Kaufman–Morrie Ryskind show that flopped in tryouts three years ago, opens at the Times Square Theatre. The title tune and "I've Got a Crush on You" are in this score. The plot is about a threatened war over Swiss chocolate. The cast includes Dudley Clements, Jeff Goff, and Clark and McCullough, who have been written into the new version to lighten it. The 1940 Busby Berkeley film, starring Mickey Rooney and Judy Garland, retains little more than the title song.

FEBRUARY 13 Spencer Tracy is "Killer Mears" in John Wexley's death row drama *The Last Mile* (285), opening at the Sam H. Harris Theatre. Wexley is the nephew of Yiddish Theatre great Maurice Schwartz. It's filmed in 1932. **18** *Simple Simon* (135), a musical comedy by Rodgers and Hart, opening at the Ziegfeld, stars comedian Ed Wynn. Ruth Etting, hired three days ago, introduces "Ten Cents A Dance," originally written for Lee Morse, who couldn't stay sober and was fired during rehearsals. **26** Marc Connelly's *The Green Pastures* (640), a Biblical fantasy with an all-black cast, opens at the Mansfield. The players include Richard B. Harrison as "de Lawd" (he will die during the run of the 1935 revival), Charles H. Moore, and Wesley

for gloom in the country through the Big Break," says *Variety* on its front page. Among those most prominently taking it on the chin and in the wallet are Eddie Cantor, Al Jolson, Jed Harris, Flo Ziegfeld, and George Jessel. **19** Equity turns down the producers' proposal for Sunday shows and a seven-day week.

MARCH • The Hebrew Actors Union forbids its members from appearing in Yiddish-language films for fear they will destroy the Yiddish stage if they do.

Plowright b.

NOVEMBER 23 Shirley Booth m. actor Ed Gardiner. **24** Raymond Hitchcock d.

DECEMBER 12 Playwright John Osborne b. **13** Christopher Plummer (Arthur Christopher Orme Plummer) b. (father of Amanda Plummer)

JANUARY 13 Frances Sternhagen b. Her father is a federal tax court judge and friend of Dean Acheson, future Secretary of State, who is her godfather.

MARCH 2 John Cullum b. **5** Richard Rodgers m. Dorothy Feiner. **7** Producer Abraham L. Erlanger d. "Little Napoleon"'s relationships with various women had often brought him into court. At his death, it is revealed that he apparently had a common-law wife, Charlotte Leslie, a former showgirl. **11** E.F. Albee, former manager of the Keith–Orpheum circuit, d. **22** Lyricist-composer Stephen Sondheim b.

MAY • Eddie Foy, Jr. m. showgirl Barbara

Personalities

stock market losses, closes *Whoopee*, which had been going strong, in order to hasten his coproduction of the film version with Samuel Goldwyn. **25** Eva Le Gallienne is on the cover of *Time*.

DECEMBER • In the Vincent Youmans divorce case, the composer's lawyer pleads his client's poverty in the face of charges from his estranged wife that her husband gave his mother a Rolls Royce last year, had royalties from *Hit the Deck* that totaled $188,000, and signed recent movie contracts that will pay him $120,000.

JANUARY • *Boom Boom*, an inconsequential musical at the Casino, has in its cast Jeanette McDonald, who dances a fandango with Archie Leach, soon to become the movies' Cary Grant.

MARCH • In dismissing plagiarism charges against Richard Tully for *Bird of Paradise*, the New York State Court of Appeals ends a case that has dragged on for 12 years. • Producer Morris Gest is forced into bankruptcy. **18** Jessica Tandy makes her Broadway debut in *The Matriarch* at the Longacre. **26** Mae West's attorney, questioning a witness in the obscenity trial of her play *Pleasure Man*, which includes female impersonators, begins to ask a policeman on the witness stand how he can tell men in drag from women. The judge is so intent on keeping the question from the record that he breaks his gavel ruling it out of order. Newspapers are using asterisks to avoid printing some testimony.

APRIL • Eva Tanguay, once one of vaudeville's highest-paid performers, is playing a half-week at the RKO Bushwick in Brooklyn for $150. **12** The University of Missouri student newspaper praises freshman Tennessee Williams's play *Beauty Is the Word*, but it also adds that "the handling is too didactic and the dialogue often moralistic."

Plays and Musicals

Hill. It's "a play of surpassing beauty," says Brooks Atkinson, "the divine comedy of the modern theatre." It's filmed in 1936.

MARCH 3 *Flying High* (357), at the Apollo, is the last musical by the team of Ray Henderson, Buddy De Sylva, and Lew Brown. It stars Bert Lahr, Kate Smith, Oscar Shaw, and Grace Brinkley. Lahr will also appear in the film version next year.

APRIL 15 Producer Jed Harris debuts as a director at the Cort with an acclaimed revival of Chekhov's *Uncle Vanya*, which the *Times* calls "luminously beautiful." It stars Lillian Gish, resuming her stage career after 17 years in film, Walter Connolly, Osgood Perkins, and Eduardo Ciannelli. It is only a few years since Chekhov's plays began to be produced in English, and the *Times* notes that "[t]o many theatregoers, Chekhov is still an enigma and a bore."

Business and Society

Births, Deaths, and Marriages

Newberry. They met in Ziegfeld's *Show Girl*. **5** Director-actor-playwright Douglas Turner Ward b. **6** Charles Gilpin d. **19** Playwright Lorraine Hansberry b.

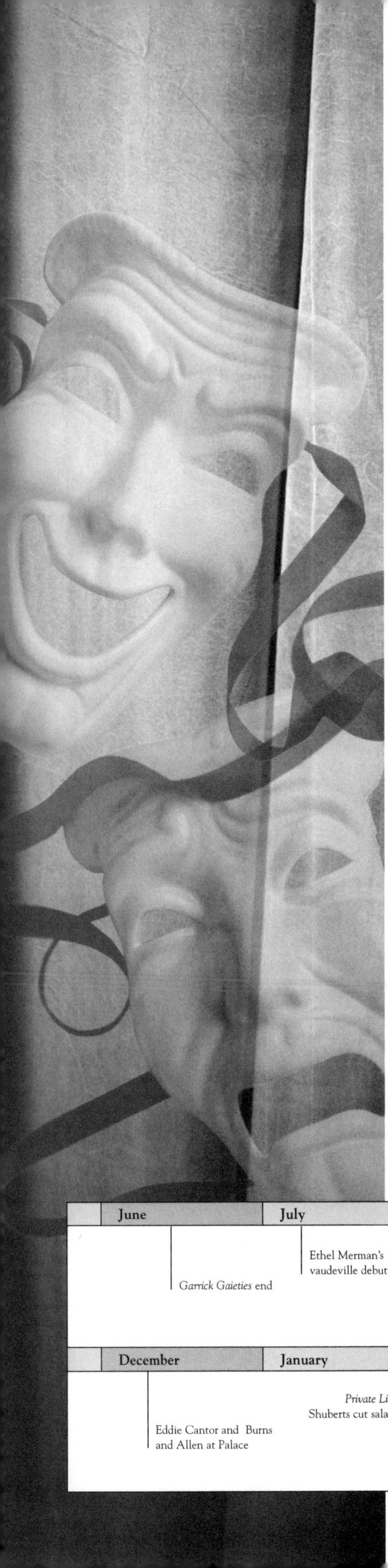

1930–31

With two bread lines in Times Square and half the theatres dark, Broadway does not have to imagine the drama of the Depression. Nevertheless, the George S. Kaufman–Moss Hart collaboration begins, Noel Coward's *Private Lives* arrives, and there's the phenomenon that is Ethel Merman. Joshua Logan, who recently wrote the class show at Princeton and sang in it with classmate James Stewart, is in the Soviet Union, studying with Stanislavsky at the Moscow Art Theatre. Critic George Jean Nathan, apparently obsessed with Eva Le Gallienne's lesbianism, begins a lifelong feud with her, writing about her latest production that "this is the first Camille I have ever seen die of catarrh."

- Price of a Theatre Guild subscription for 6 plays: $10–$16.50. The season will include Maxwell Anderson's *Elizabeth the Queen* and Lynn Rigg's *Green Grow the Lilacs*, and the acting of Lunt and Fontanne, Claude Rains, Dudley Digges, and Morris Carnovsky
- George S. Kaufman's income from the stage: about $7,000 a week
- Kaufman's salary as an actor in *Once In A Life Time*: $400 a week
- Not just another dance band: José Ferrer and his Pied Pipers are touring Europe (Summer of 1930). Ferrer plays the sax, clarinet, and piano, and his fellow Princeton undergraduate Jimmy Stewart plays the accordion
- Pleased to meet you: Lillian Hellman and Dashiell Hammett are introduced
- Among producer-director David Belasco's possessions when he dies: a large library of pornography
- Number of vaudeville acts at the start of the season playing full weeks: about 700, down by about two-thirds from 5 years ago
- Job for vaudevillians no longer able to find bookings: theatre stage doorman
- Percentage of new talking picture talent drawn from the Broadway stage in the past 2 years: close to 75 percent
- Number of years between engagements at the Palace for Ed Wynn: 18
- Number of Broadway plays using revolving stages and other special effects: 5 (*Five Star Final*, *Grand Hotel*, *Roar China*, *House Beautiful*, and *Miracle at Verdun*)
- Words that acts on the Radio–Keith–Orpheum circuit are forbidden to use: "pansy" and "fairy" (because they refer to homosexuality, not because they are bigoted)
- Number of vacant stores on Broadway in the theatre district: more than 50, an average of three per block
- Number of bread lines in Times Square: 2, sponsored by Hearst's *American*
- What you get to eat from the bread line: a hot dog or egg and a cup of coffee
- What George Gershwin tells Ethel Merman after the opening night of *Girl Crazy*: "*Never*, but never go near a singing teacher."

Productions on Broadway: 187

Pulitzer Prize for Drama: *Alison's House* (Susan Glaspell)

June	July	August	September	October	November
Garrick Gaieties end	Ethel Merman's vaudeville debut	Cardinal Hayes attacks "obscene plays"	First George S. Kaufman–Moss Hart play	*Girl Crazy*	Lillian Hellman and Dashiell Hammett

December	January	February	March	April	May
Eddie Cantor and Burns and Allen at Palace	*Private Lives*; Shuberts cut salaries	Bob Hope's Palace debut	Several casts don't get paid	Helen Gahagan m. Melvyn Douglas	David Belasco d.; Eugene O'Neill back in U.S.

Personalities

JULY 8 Reporting on the divorce case of actress Josephine Hutchinson, the *New York Daily News* says that her husband complained that she was with Eva Le Gallienne "morning, noon and night." The story refers to Hutchinson as Le Gallienne's "protegé," and the headline, "Le Gallienne Shadow," uses a euphemism for lesbian. Le Gallienne has had affairs with actress Alla Nazimova and with Mercedes de Acosta, also Greta Garbo's lover. **8** Muriel Kirkland suddenly withdraws from *Strictly Dishonorable* after tonight's performance. Her long-standing feud with her leading man, Tulio Carminati, has come to a head, and there are reports that she slapped him. **9** *Earl Carroll's Vanities* is raided. Carroll and several performers, including fan dancer Faith Bacon, are arrested on obscenity charges. The Catholic Theatre Movement, a group that has attacked "immoral" shows, has come down especially hard on Carroll. The grand jury, however, declines to indict. **9** *Variety* reviews a vaudeville newcomer at the Eighty-sixth Street Theatre—Ethel Merman: "She is a good looking girl with a fair enough voice that might carry much further with special stuff. This is her first stage appearance. She's out of cabaret, so probably has plenty to learn." **29** Who hit whom at the rehearsal of *Luana* tonight? According to reports, choreographer Jack Haskell first berated dancer Sally Rand, whose brother,

Eva Le Gallienne in *Romeo and Juliet* PF

Plays and Musicals

JUNE 4 The last of the *Garrick Gaieties* (155) opens at the Guild Theatre, featuring the Broadway debuts of Imogene Coca and Ray Heatherton.

SEPTEMBER 24 *Once In a Lifetime* (401), the first of eight collaborations between George S. Kaufman and Moss Hart, opens at the Music Box. The cast of this comedy about show business includes Jean Dixon, Grant Mills, and Hugh O'Connell. Kaufman directs, is also in the cast, and, in a curtain speech tonight, credits Hart with most of the writing.

OCTOBER 14 George and Ira Gershwin's *Girl Crazy* (272) opens at the Alvin. Twenty-one-year-old Ethel Merman, in her Broadway debut, sings "Sam and Delilah" and then stops the show with "I've Got Rhythm," holding the "I" for 16 measures. The feat will engender the quip that she can hold a note longer than Chase Manhattan. Ingenue Ginger Rogers, in her second Broadway musical, sings "Embraceable You." Other numbers include "But Not For Me" and "Bidin' My Time." In the show's pit band are Benny Goodman, Glenn Miller, Jimmy Dorsey, and Gene Krupa. The 1943 film stars Mickey Rooney and Judy Garland. **15** Libby Holman, dressed in black, introduces "Body and Soul," by Howard Dietz and Arthur Schwartz, in the revue *Three's A Crowd* (272), at the Selwyn. Clifton Webb and Fred Allen are also in the cast, and Hassard Short's expressive lighting is notable.

NOVEMBER 3 The Theatre Guild presents Maxwell Anderson's *Elizabeth The Queen* (147), starring Alfred Lunt and Lynn Fontanne, at the Guild Theatre. In the *Sun*, Richard Lockridge describes this blank verse drama as "a fine poetic tragedy, ringing and clear." It's filmed in 1939. **13** Viki Baum's *Grand Hotel* (444) is at the National. The Herman Shumlin production stars Sig Ruman, Henry Hull, Sam Jaffe, and Eugenie Leontovich and will become the 1932 MGM film.

DECEMBER 1 Susan Glaspell's *Alison's House* (41), inspired by the life of poet

Business and Society

JULY • The League of New York Theatres begins to regulate the allocation of tickets to ticket agencies, enforcing the $.75 per ticket limit on premiums they can charge.

AUGUST • Equity's president Frank Gillmore attacks "salacious" shows, concerned that they will strengthen sentiment for official censorship.

AUGUST 10 The Catholic Theatre Movement, led by Cardinal Hayes, attacks "obscene plays" in New York City, singling out *Lysistrata* and *Earl Carroll's Vanities* for "animalism."

SEPTEMBER 10 *Variety* is concerned that, like the Paris and Berlin establishments that attract "queers," some Broadway night spots will be trying to bring in the "pansy" trade.

OCTOBER • The number of unemployed actors (legitimate and vaudeville) in New York City is estimated at about 15,000.

DECEMBER • The casts of several shows are being forced to accept salary cuts to compensate for poor business. **7** New

Births, Deaths, and Marriages

JUNE 7 Lionel Atwill m. Louise Cromwell MacArthur, former wife of Major General Douglas MacArthur. **20** Ellis Rabb b. **28** Joe Schenck, of the vaudeville team of Van and Schenck, d.

AUGUST 1 Playwright Julie Bovasso b. **28** Ben Gazzara (Biagio Gazzara) b.

SEPTEMBER 19 Rosemary Harris b. **26** Philip Bosco b.

OCTOBER 10 Playwright Harold Pinter b.

NOVEMBER 1 Playwright A. (Albert) R. (Ramsdell) Gurney b. **3** Mary Martin m. Ben Hagman. Lasting five years, the marriage will produce a son, Larry ("J.R. Ewing" on television's "Dallas"). **8** Clare Eames d. **22** Director Peter Hall b.

in the chorus, punched Haskell. Haskell fires brother and sister. Producer Arthur Hammerstein then fires Haskell, and when he thinks that Haskell is menacing him, he punches the choreographer, who hits back. Haskell presses charges and says that Hammerstein had "orgies" in his office. The charges are dismissed in October.

AUGUST 16 George S. Kaufman leaves *The New York Times*, where he has remained in the drama department for 13 years despite achieving great success as a Broadway playwright.

SEPTEMBER • Weary of performers making grand exits, the Palace management posts a notice back stage: "Please do not make any speeches or thank the audience for their very kind applause or tell them how happy you are to be back. When you finish simply take two bows and if you have anything more to do—do it—do not stall." • Ken Murray is the first major vaudeville personality to appear on television, in an experimental broadcast while playing the Palace Theatre in Chicago. **13** Ethel Merman debuts at the Palace, with Al Siegal accompanying her on the piano. "When her singing some day is as genius-like as Siegal's piano playing and arranging," writes *Variety*'s reviewer, "she will be set by herself." Also on the bill is Ted Healy and his Stooges. **30** A hung jury frees Mae West of obscenity charges for her play *Pleasure Man*.

OCTOBER 5 Bill "Bojangles" Robinson is shot and wounded in Pittsburgh. He's chasing a purse snatcher, firing at him with a gun given to Robinson as a gift by the New York City Police Department. Local officers take Robinson for the criminal and shoot him. **12** Sunday night is guest night at the Palace, where stars in the audience are asked to take a bow or perform. Last week, Al Jolson, who will never officially "play" the Palace, sang two songs. Tonight Jimmy Durante and Ted Lewis come onstage to banter with the emcee, and Jack Benny takes a bow. In the audience, the buzz is about gangster Jack "Legs" Diamond, murdered today in a Times Square hotel.

NOVEMBER • Ed Wynn, appearing in *Simple Simon* at the Shubert Theatre in

Lynn Fontanne LYNCH

Emily Dickinson, opens at Eva Le Gallienne's Civic Repertory Theatre and will move to Broadway after winning the Pulitzer. Le Gallienne, Alma Kruger, and Donald Cameron are in the cast. **30** In Louis Weitzenkorn's *Five Star Final* (175), at the Cort, a hot newspaper story causes a double suicide. It stars Arthur Byron, Merle Maddern, Malcolm Duncan, and Frances Fuller. A film version appears next year.

JANUARY 13 Philip Barry's *Tomorrow and Tomorrow* (206), in which a wife's affair with a psychologist, a guest in her house, has reverberations in years to come, stars Zita Johann, Herbert Marshall, Harvey Stephens, and Osgood Perkins. It's at Henry Miller's Theatre. **26** *Green Grow the Lilacs* (64), Lynn Riggs's play about Oklahoma, on which the 1943 musical, *Oklahoma!* will be based, opens at the Guild Theatre. Franchot Tone is Curley, and June Walker is Laurey. Also in the cast are Helen Westley and, in a minor role, Lee Strasberg. Herbert J. Biberman directs, and there *is* music—cowboy songs—between the scenes. **26** Eva Le Gallienne's Civic Repertory Company scores its biggest success with *Camille* (57). **27** Noel Coward's comedy *Private Lives* (248), which he wrote in four days, opens at the Times Square Theatre. According to Brooks Atkinson, Coward "has nothing to say and manages to say it with complete agility for three acts." Coward and Gertrude Lawrence, who have played it in London, are the ex-

York's Yiddish theatres are closed by the unwillingness of stagehands and musicians to take the salary cut demanded by management to offset poor box office business. **8** The American Theatre on Forty-second Street, which opened as a legitimate house in 1893 and lately has hosted burlesque, is destroyed in a fire.

JANUARY • Moving companies that specialize in shipping props and scenery are offering vaudeville acts free storage, a reflection of the drop-off in bookings. • Lee Shubert, reportedly under pressure from his bankers, orders a 25 percent salary cut throughout the Shubert organization, which for the first time has no new show in rehearsal. • Half the theatres on Broadway are empty. There are 35 shows running now, compared with 45 this time last year, and *Variety* is beginning to use the word "Depression" to describe conditions. **12** Motivated by unemployment in their ranks, Equity members vote to impose a five per cent "tax" on the salaries of all foreign actors on Broadway.

FEBRUARY • The Republic Theatre on Forty-second Street, where *Abie's Irish Rose* played, becomes a Minsky burlesque house.

JANUARY 17 James Earl Jones b.

FEBRUARY 6 Rip Torn (Elmore Torn, Jr.), cousin of screen actress Sissy Spacek, b. **15** Claire Bloom b.

MARCH 20 Hal Linden (Harold Lipshitz) b. He will say that he changed his name at the age of 17. He was returning from a musical engagement in New Jersey, where he played the saxophone, and he passed a huge gas tank with the name of the town on its side: "Linden."

APRIL • Lillian Roth, whose previous fiancé d. three months ago, m. William C. Scott. This match will last a year. **5** Helen Gahagan m. Melvyn Douglas.

MAY 3 Choreographer-director Joe Layton b. **14** David Belasco, the "Bishop of Broadway," whom Katharine Cornell describes as "the most picturesque and authentic theatrical figure this country

Personalities

Philadelphia, refuses to go on until the theatre removes the lobby photos advertising the house's next attraction, Earl Carroll's *Sketch Book*. Wynn is afraid that the pictures, which contain nudes, will offend the family trade. **18** George Jean Nathan's reaction to the play *Tonight Or Never*, opening tonight: "Very well, then: I say, Never." **25** Lillian Hellman begins a relationship with Dashiell Hammett.

DECEMBER 27 Eddie Cantor is at the Palace, where he's drawing $7,700 a week, half the total payroll for the bill, which also includes George Burns and Gracie Allen. At today's opening, Eddie sings to his wife, Ida, who is sitting in a stage box.

FEBRUARY 10 *Time* will write of Harriette Lake, in her Broadway debut tonight in *America's Sweetheart*, that she's "a lovely synthesis, one part Ginger Rogers, one part Ethel Merman." By the time she hits Hollywood, she will be 100 percent Ann Sothern. **28** *Billboard* reviews Bob Hope's February 21 Palace Theatre debut, in which Bea Lillie is the headliner, praising his "youth, ability and natural cleverness." *Variety* (February 25) likes him too but cautions, "That he needs experience and development is apparent all over his manner and act. . . . "

MARCH 17 The Shuberts end their four-year-old feud with Walter Winchell, inviting him to tonight's opening of Al Jolson in *Wonder Bar*. **21** Opening at the Palace on a bill that spans two generations of comedy are Smith and Dale and Burns and Allen. (George Burns and Walter Matthau will star in the film *The Sunshine Boys*, as characters modeled after Smith and Dale).

MAY 2 Eighteen years after he opened the house, Ed Wynn is again playing the Palace. The musical comedy star has not played any vaudeville during that time. **17** Eugene O'Neill returns to the U.S. after more than two years abroad.

Plays and Musicals

mates, remarried to others, who remeet. Supporting them are Laurence Olivier and his wife, Jill Esmond. It's filmed this year and revived on Broadway in 1948 with Tallulah Bankhead, in 1969 with Tammy Grimes, and in 1983 with Elizabeth Taylor and Richard Burton, ex-spouses themselves at the time.

FEBRUARY 9 Katharine Cornell opens in an acclaimed production of *The Barretts of Wimpole Street* (372), beginning her career as an actress-manager. Costarring Brian Aherne and Charles Waldron, it's at the Empire Theatre. It's filmed in 1934 and 1957.

MARCH 5 Rachel Crothers's latest play *As Husbands Go* (148), starring Lily Cahill, about an Iowa housewife wanting an English lover, is at the John Golden.

Business and Society

MARCH • Casts of several shows, including *The Gang's All Here*, complain to Equity that they're not being paid. **4** The price of Variety drops from $.25 to $.15.

APRIL 23 New York State Governor Franklin D. Roosevelt signs a bill amending the Wales Padlock Law, which will now punish only playwrights and producers of shows judged immoral, not the cast and crew.

MAY • The National Variety Artists, the successor organization to vaudeville's White Rats, gives up its New York City clubhouse.

Births, Deaths, and Marriages

has ever known," d. A *New York Times* article about the producer in 1929 said of his importance in set and lighting innovation that "[e]ven Reinhardt would not be Reinhardt if Belasco had not first grasped the wand of the magician of lights." **18** Robert Morse b.

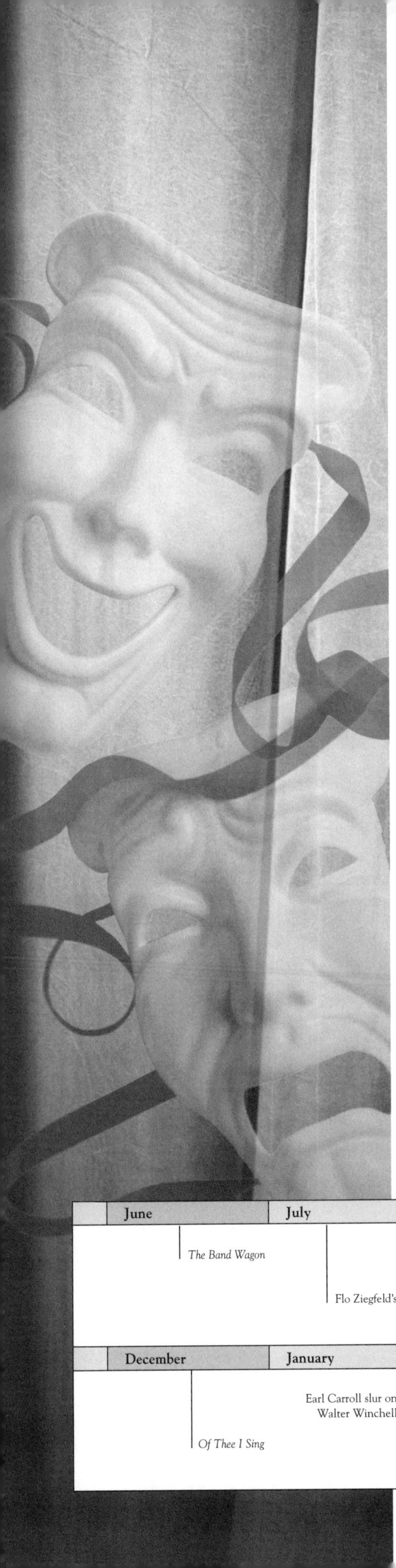

1931–32

The Shuberts are in the hands of the receivers, and Broadway tickets are being discounted, even at New Year's. In many ways, the Main Stem will never be the same again. With the Group Theatre a harbinger of change in acting style, and Orson Welles making his stage debut, Ziegfeld produces his last *Follies*, and the Palace Theatre drops its two-a-day policy and lets the movies in the doors. The Gershwin's *Of Thee I Sing* is the first musical to win the Pulitzer. But coauthor George S. Kaufman would not give even a booby prize to one of its stars, William Gaxton, whose ad-libbing riles the playwright. Kaufman wires Gaxton: "I am watching your performance from the rear of the house. Wish you were here."

- Actors Equity annual dues: $18
- Probably the lowest vaudeville salaries ever in a major house: an average of $1.10 per performance paid to acts at the Lyric Theatre on Forty-second Street in November, 1931
- Line spoken by an actress in S.N. Behrman's comedy *Brief Moment* to critic Alexander Woollcott, making his stage debut: "If you were a woman what a bitch you would have made."
- How one performer at an RKO theatre in New York City responds to management's demand that all acts accept a 25 percent salary cut: "Nuts." (According to *Variety*, May 31, 1932)
- Migrating between Broadway and Hollywood: Eddie Cantor, the Marx brothers, Lee Tracy, Reuben Mamoulian, and Helen Hayes
- George S. Kaufman's cure for the Depression: place the receivers in receivership, do the same to their receivers, and so on . . .
- Number of legitimate Broadway houses: 60
- Number controlled by the Shuberts: 18
- Number of shows at the Winter Garden since Al Jolson opened there in *The Singing Fool* in 1928: none, it's been showing movies
- Number of burlesque theatres on Forty-second Street: two—the Republic and the Eltinge

Productions on Broadway: 207

Pulitzer Prize for Drama, awarded to a musical for the first time: *Of Thee I Sing* (book by George S. Kaufman and Morrie Ryskind; lyrics by Ira Gershwin)

June	July	August	September	October	November
The Band Wagon	Flo Ziegfeld's last *Follies*	Ina Claire divorces John Gilbert	Group Theatre debuts	Mae West is "shy"; Orson Welles debuts	Mike Nichols b.

December	January	February	March	April	May
Of Thee I Sing	Earl Carroll slur on Walter Winchell	Mrs. Fiske d.	Gershwin wants to set *Porgy* to music	Laurette Taylor can't go on	Palace ends two a day

Personalities

JUNE 1 Former sports reporter Ed Sullivan takes over the Broadway column in the *New York Graphic* from Louis Sobel. **1** *Wonder Bar*, in which Al Jolson has been starring, closes suddenly when Jolson, who has battled laryngitis and the heat, decides he's had enough. **8** A group of actors led by Cheryl Crawford, Lee Strasberg, and Harold Clurman leaves New York for Brookfield Centre, Connecticut, to spend the summer rehearsing several plays. By August, they will have chosen a name for themselves: the Group Theatre. **12** Eva Le Gallienne is seriously injured when a propane gas stove explodes at her home.

JULY 26 Harry Richman is about to take fellow cast members of *The Ziegfeld Follies* out on his boat when it blows up on Long Island Sound. *Follies* girl Helen Walsh is killed, and Richman and columnist Mark Hellinger are injured.

AUGUST 1 Kate Smith opens an 11-week run at the Palace, a house record.

OCTOBER • Mae West issues a statement denying that her current play, *The Constant Sinner*, reflects anything about her personal life. She doesn't drink or smoke, and she dresses in black, she insists. "I am, in fact, retiring by nature, in my private life, to the point of shyness." **7** Three days before he is to headline the show at the Palace, Frank Fay pulls out, saying that he must go to Hollywood, where his wife, Barbara Stanwyck, fell off a horse. Stanwyck, however, appears not to have been injured in the mishap. Morton Downey will take Fay's place at the Palace on a bill that also features the Boswell Sisters. **13** Orson Welles makes his professional stage debut at Dublin's Gate Theatre in Leon Feuchtwanger's *Jew Suss*. One paper notes that Welles "held the audience tense." **21** "Conditions are such in the theatre that this voluntary move on my part was unavoidable," says producer A.H. Woods when he files for bankruptcy. The Shuberts, one of his creditors—to the tune of $150,000—were put into receivership yesterday. **31** Eddie Cantor, George Jessel, and Burns and Allen open at the Palace.

Plays and Musicals

JUNE 1 Noel Coward's *The Third Little Show* (136) opens at the Music Box, with Beatrice Lillie sitting in a rickshaw, singing "Mad Dogs and Englishmen." **3** George S. Kaufman, Arthur Schwartz, and Howard Dietz's *The Band Wagon* (260) opens at the New Amsterdam. Fred and Adele Astaire are in their final show together, with a score that includes "Dancing in the Dark." Balcony lighting substitutes for footlights, and set designer Albert Johnson integrates a revolving stage into the flow of the plot. Astaire will also star in the 1953 MGM Vincente Minnelli musical.

JULY 1 *The Ziegfeld Follies* (164), the last produced by the showman himself, opens at the Ziegfeld Theatre. It stars Helen Morgan, Harry Richman, Jack Pearl, Ruth Etting, and Buck and Bubbles.

SEPTEMBER 14 *George White's Scandals* (202), at the Apollo, has a Ray Henderson–Lew Brown score that includes "Life Is Just a Bowl of Cherries" and "The Thrill Is Gone." It also has "That's Why Darkies Were Born." Ethel Merman, Willie and Eugene Howard, Ray Bolger, and Rudy Vallee star, Eleanor Powell has her first Broadway dance role, and in the chorus is young Alice Faye. **28** The Group Theatre's first production, *The House of Connelly* (72), opens at the Martin Beck. This Paul Green play about the end of the Old South is directed by Lee Strasberg and Cheryl Crawford, with a cast that includes Franchot Tone, Stella Adler, Morris Carnovsky, and Clifford Odets. Walter Winchell complains of the actors that "[t]heir mumblings [a]re irritating." **30** Charles Laughton makes his Broadway debut in Jeffrey Dell's tale of murder, *Payment Deferred* (70), with Elsa Lanchester, at the Lyceum. "Mr. Laughton is, in more than one respect, immense," says *The New York Times*, and he "cast[s] a black magic spell." Laughton stars in the 1932 film.

OCTOBER 5 Elmer Rice's play about two American expatriate couples, *The Left Bank* (241), opens at the Little Theatre.

Business and Society

JUNE 15 The Shuberts default on the interest on their bonds.

OCTOBER • The Erlanger organization is in default on the interest on its bonds. **20** The Shubert organization is placed in receivership.

DECEMBER 7 Erlanger's Theatre becomes the St. James. **21** The Shubert Company, already in receivership, is dealt another blow when Lee Shubert is hospitalized for surgery, from which he will need several weeks to recover.

JANUARY • The Palace is losing money at an average of $5,000 a week. It is being pressed by competition from high-budget movie house stage shows, such as the ones at the nearby Warners Hollywood Theatre. • Vaudevillians in the Los Angeles area, who last month organized themselves into the California Artists Protective Association, have to drop their demand for a minimum of $7.50 a day when too many acts are desperate enough to work for less. **1** Of the 18 Broadway shows giving matinées on this New Year's Day at the Depression's peak, 10 have to sell discounted tickets through the "cut-rate" agencies.

Births, Deaths, and Marriages

AUGUST 4 Ina Claire divorces John Gilbert.

SEPTEMBER 17 Anne Bancroft (Anna Maria Italiano) b. **24** Anthony Newley b.

NOVEMBER 6 Director Mike Nichols (Michael Peschkowsky) b. His grandmother wrote the libretto for Richard Strauss's opera, *Salome*, and his grandfather, Gustav Landauer, was head of the German Social Democratic Party. **16** Libby Holman m. tobacco heir Smith Reynolds.

DECEMBER 30 Tyrone Power, Sr. d.

FEBRUARY 15 Minnie Maddern Fiske—"Mrs. Fiske"—d. **16** Gretchen Wyler (Gretchen Wienecke) b.

MARCH 30 *New York Evening Sun* critic

Cantor is getting $8,800 a week, the most ever for any performer in straight vaudeville. The payroll for the entire bill is $16,000. The first week's gross of $37,000 seems to justify the expense.

NOVEMBER 11 Blossom Seeley and Benny Fields, in the road company of *Girl Crazy* in Chicago, are dropped from the production by producer Gregory Ratoff when they insist that a bond be posted to protect their pay against a possible sudden closing. **20** Patsy Kelly, reported to have been quarreling with fellow cast members of *Wonder Bar*, now in Washington, D.C., in which she's featured opposite Al Jolson, faints in her dressing room. The Shuberts try to remove her from the cast, but she will be back in three days when Equity intervenes.

DECEMBER 6 Eddie Foy, Jr. collapses on stage at the Globe during a Sunday night benefit performance of *The Cat and the Fiddle*, reportedly because he has just read in the papers that his wife, showgirl Barbara Newberry, is filing for divorce. **8** *Of Thee I Sing* opens in Boston for a pre-Broadway tryout. The perennially pessimistic George S. Kaufman, who has written the book with Morrie Ryskind, is not convinced by the good reception accorded it by Boston audiences, and on the train to New York after this run, he will ask the Gershwins if they would like to buy part of his interest in the show. They immediately reach for their checkbooks. **14** The government of Hungary

"The Night Was Made for Love" debuts in *The Cat and the Fiddle* BROWN

Franchot Tone

In the cast are Katherine Alexander, Horace Braham, Merle Maddern, and Donald MacDonald. **15** A boy who writes classical music and a girl who writes popular music make beautiful music together. That's *The Cat and the Fiddle* (395), the Jerome Kern–Otto Harbach musical at the Globe. Songs include "The Night Was Made for Love" and "She Didn't Say 'Yes.'" In the cast are Bettina Hall, George Meader, George Metaxa, and Eddie Foy, Jr. **26** Eugene O'Neill's modern retelling of the *Oresteia*, *Mourning Becomes Electra* (157), opens at the Guild Theatre. It stars Alla Nazimova, Earle Larimore, and Alice Brady. Performances of this 14-act trilogy, originally intended to be played on three nights, begin at five and end near midnight. A film version will appear in 1947.

NOVEMBER 6 In Elmer Rice's *Counsellor-at-Law* (397), at the Plymouth, Paul Muni is a Jewish lawyer who attempts to reach the upper echelon of the legal profession through a marriage of convenience but still finds himself confronting anti-Semitism. John Barrymore stars in the 1933 film. **9** Critic Alexander Woollcott makes his stage debut at the Belasco in S.N. Behrman's comedy *Brief Moment* (129). Francine Larrimore, who rises from cabaret chanteuse to society wife, Robert Douglas, and Louis Calherne star. **16** Alfred Lunt and Lynn Fontanne star, with Minor Watson, in Robert Sherwood's *Reunion in Vienna* (264), a comedy about a woman, married to a psy-

MARCH • The Theatre Guild and the Shubert organization pool their subscription lists for out-of-town productions in the new American Theatre Society, enabling theatregoers outside of New York to buy tickets to Guild and Shubert productions with one subscription.

APRIL • RKO is slashing salaries for small-time acts on its theatre circuit, while headliners such as Kate Smith and Jack Haley are demanding and getting higher fees.

MAY 14 The Palace, no longer the "Mecca" of American show business, switches from its two-a-day vaudeville policy, begun with its 1913 opening, to four shows a day plus several movie shorts, becoming a "grind" house. Its $3 top has been dropped to $1, and there are no longer reserved seats. Phil Baker heads the bill this week. But despite the new policy, the house will continue to lose money.

Ward Morehouse m. Jean Dalrymple, producer John Golden's press agent.

APRIL 4 Anthony Perkins, son of actor Osgood Perkins, b. **8** Lyricist Fred Ebb b. **11** Joel Grey (Joel Katz), son of comedian Mickey Katz and father of actress Jennifer Grey, b.

MAY 31 Selena Royle m. Earle Larimore.

Personalities

bars Molly Picon from entering the country because, they, say, her performance in Yiddish during the Christmas season would be "undesirable."

JANUARY 30 Speaking at a dinner in New York, showman Earl Carroll, who mistakenly thinks that Walter Winchell helped send him to prison for perjury a few years ago, tells the columnist in front of the audience: "I don't think you are fit to be with decent people." Carroll is booed off the floor by the other show business luminaries.

FEBRUARY • The Group Theatre cuts its ties to the Theatre Guild to produce independently. Cheryl Crawford, one of the directors, has resigned from the Board of Managers of the Theatre Guild. **26** Composer Vincent Youmans, facing bankruptcy because of his activities as a producer, convinces creditors not to push him over the brink and allow him a year to make good on his debts.

MARCH • Dorothy Parker is recuperating from an overdose of a sleeping medication. • Russel Crouse becomes the press agent for the Theatre Guild. **28** Richard Maney becomes press agent for the Palace Theatre. **29** George Gershwin writes to novelist and playwright Dubose Heyward that "in thinking of ideas for new compositions, I came back to one that I had several years ago—namely, Porgy—and the thought of setting it to music. It is still the most outstanding play that I know, about the colored people."

APRIL 1 *A Night With Barrie,* in which Laurette Taylor is playing in two of James

Plays and Musicals

choanalyst, who can't forget an old love. It's at the Martin Beck.

DECEMBER 26 The Gershwin's *Of Thee I Sing* (441) is at the Music Box. It's "Wintergreen for President" in this parody of American politics. William Gaxton heads the ticket, with Victor Moore as Alexander Throttlebottom, the vice president no one knows. "Who Cares?" and "Love Is Sweeping the Country" are in the score. George S. Kaufman and Moss Hart wrote the book. The first musical to win the Pulitzer Prize, it will also be the first published in book form.

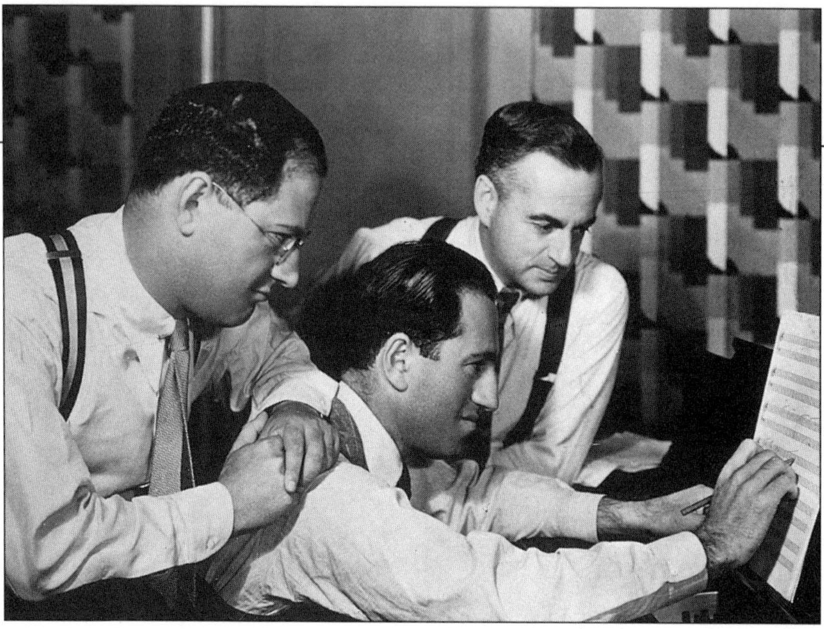

Ira and George Gershwin with Guy Bolton ARCH

Business and Society

Births, Deaths, and Marriages

M. Barrie's short plays, closes after a few performances. The producer says it's because of her "illness," which has caused her to miss a number of performances. Taylor attributes it to "financial matters" but later acknowledges that she just couldn't go on. **9** *Variety*, reviewing Milton Berle at the Palace, says that "he conducted himself like a vet who knows everything worth knowing, including gags—everybody's." (Walter Winchell calls him "The Thief of Bad Gags.") **17** A backstage fire at the Palace injures six people but could have been worse. Sophie Tucker walks to the footlights when she sees the fire curtain drop, and as the people in front start to get up and run toward the exits, she begins to belt out "Some of These Days" to calm the audience.

MAY 2 *Of Thee I Sing* is announced as the winner of the Pulitzer Prize for Drama, beating out the favored *Mourning Becomes Electra*. It's the first musical to take the award. The prize goes to George S. Kaufman, Morrie Ryskind, and Ira Gershwin, who wrote the book and lyrics, leaving the composer, George Gershwin, out in the cold. **7** The Palace Theater opens its final two-a-day straight vaudeville bill, featuring William Demarest.

JANUARY 12 Philip Barry's comedy *The Animal Kingdom* (183) opens at the Broadhurst. Leslie Howard coproduced and stars, with Ilka Chase, Frances Fuller, and William Gargan.

FEBRUARY 17 Irving Berlin's *Face The Music* (165), a satire on Broadway and City Hall, opens at the New Amsterdam. Berlin's first Broadway show in five years features "Let's Have Another Cup of Coffee" sung in an automat, stars Mary Boland, and is directed by George S. Kaufman, with a book by Moss Hart.

APRIL 25 Rose Franken's surprise hit, *Another Language* (348), opens at the Booth. Dorothy Stickney is a wife who has to take drastic measures to make her husband see how domineering his mother is. Glenn Anders and Margaret Wycherly also star. The film appears next year.

MAY 19 *Show Boat* (181) is revived at the new Casino Theatre (formerly the Earl Carroll), where Paul Robeson finally plays the part of Joe. Dennis King, as Gaylord Ravenal, has also been added to the original cast, most of whom are back for this production.

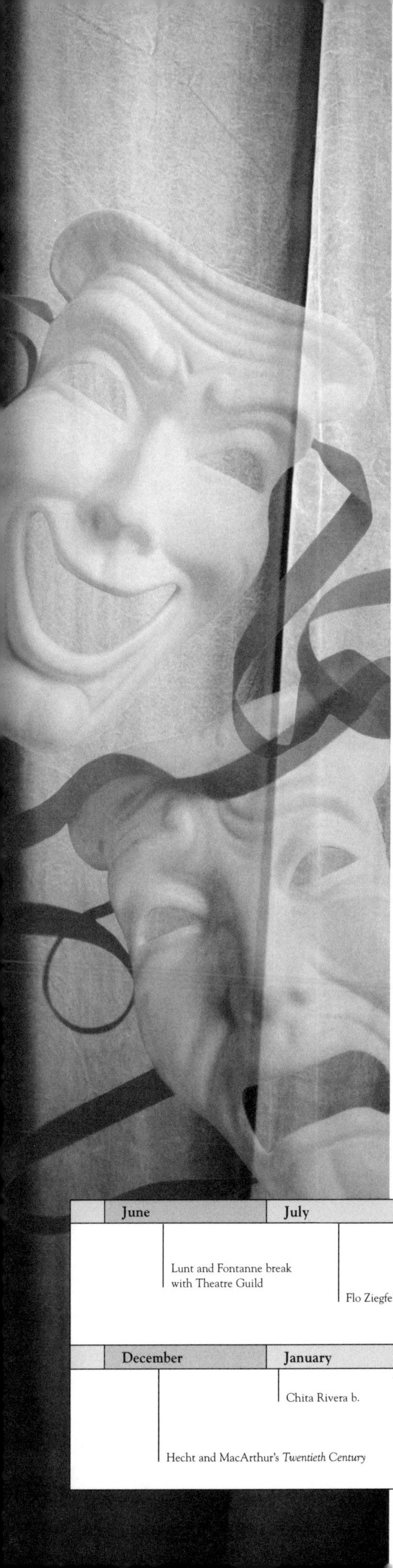

1932–33

"Brother Can You Spare a Dime?" could be Broadway's anthem. The disparity between top stars and the thousands who flesh out the casts of Broadway and other stage shows widens, as there seems to be no bottom to the Depression. Box offices are even accepting checks on the night of the performance, opting for the risk of a bounce over the sure thing of empty seats. Equity appeals to the Federal Reserve to help Broadway producers. Meanwhile, Libby Holman dodges a bullet (her tobacco-heir husband didn't), Ed Sullivan takes his Broadway column to The *Daily News*, Dubose Hayward wants to know if George Gershwin is serious about setting *Porgy* to music, the great Ziegfeld is gone, and *Variety* laments that Broadway "Ain't the Old Street Any More."

- Weekly salaries of top stage entertainers at the height of the Depression:
  Al Jolson: $15,000
  Eddie Cantor: $10,000
  Ed Wynn: $7,500
  Beatrice Lillie: $4,500
  Bert Lahr: $4,500
  Ethel Merman: $2,500
  Jack Benny: $2,000
- Amount of productions that are revivals: about one-third
- Popular ticket price: $1
- Number of reviewers receiving complimentary tickets to Broadway opening nights: about 45 (90 tickets)
- Number of scripts sold to Hollywood for at least $50,000: 2—*Dinner at Eight* and *Design For Living*
- Friars Club dues: reduced from $82.50 a year to $66
- Dues paid to Actors Equity by Noel Coward: almost $300 a week—he has to pay the 5 percent "tax" on foreign actors' earnings, which applies to his percentage of the gross from the successful *Design For Living*
- Number of dance halls in the Broadway theatre district: 17
- Price of a dance with a hostess in the "ten-cents-a-dance halls": as little as $.01

Productions on Broadway: 174

Pulitzer Prize for Drama: *Both Your Houses* (Maxwell Anderson)

June	July	August	September	October	November
Lunt and Fontanne break with Theatre Guild	Flo Ziegfeld d.	Equity asks Federal Reserve to help Broadway	Milton Berle in *Earl Carroll's Vanities*	"Brother Can You Spare a Dime" in *Americana*	Murder charges against Libby Holman dropped

December	January	February	March	April	May
Hecht and MacArthur's *Twentieth Century*	Chita Rivera b.	Aarons-Freedly producing partnership ends	Box offices willing to accept checks	Shuberts buy back theatres at auction	Ina Claire misses first performance for illness

Personalities

JUNE • Alfred Lunt and Lynn Fontanne leave the Theatre Guild over a number of issues, including money. They will return in 1935, when Lunt himself is added to the board, and the couple is given a bigger share of the profits from the plays in which they appear. • Playwright Charles MacArthur's first wife, Carol Frink, sues Helen Hayes for alienation of affection—six years after she and MacArthur divorce.

JULY • George White is evicted from the Apollo Theatre on Forty-second Street for nonpayment of rent. **6** Libby Holman's husband, tobacco heir Smith Reynolds, d. of a gunshot wound, apparently a suicide after quarreling with his wife earlier in the evening. **12** Ed Sullivan moves his Broadway column from the defunct *Graphic* to the *New York Daily News*, where he joins columnists Sidney Skolsky and John Chapman. **21** Flo Ziegfeld loses a suit over unpaid taxes, and one of his associates intimates that the great showman is on the verge of bankruptcy. In fact, when he dies—tomorrow—he will be at least $1 million in debt.

AUGUST • Leland Hayward leaves the American Play Company to start his own talent agency. **4** Libby Holman and her recently deceased husband's best friend are indicted for murder in North Carolina for her husband's death by gunshot on July 6.

SEPTEMBER • Dubose Heyward, trying to fathom George Gershwin's intentions about a musical version of *Porgy*, lets the composer know that Al Jolson is making inquiries about the rights to the work.

OCTOBER • Helen Menken, who says that her creditors have been hounding her rehearsals, files for bankruptcy. **13** In a New York *World-Telegram* interview, Rachel Crothers, America's foremost female playwright, says, "It's still a man's world. He made all the rules. When women juggle them and go in for this so-called freedom they still must lie and cheat and deceive. They can't yet be frank and open and impersonally free as men." **21** George Jean Nathan's negative review of *Dinner at Eight*, based on

Plays and Musicals

SEPTEMBER 27 *Earl Carroll's Vanities* (87), at the Broadway Theatre, includes Harold Arlen's "I Got a Right to Sing the Blues" and is the big Broadway break for vaudevillian Milton Berle.

OCTOBER 2 Maurice Schwartz stars in his own adaptation of I.J. Singer's novel *Yoshe Kalb* at the Yiddish Art Theatre. This episodic tale of a Chassidic rabbi draws the favorable attention of the uptown critics. It will be produced on Broadway next year in English. **5** *Americana* (76), at the Shubert, is memorable for Charles Weidman and Doris Humphries' choreography and the Yip Harburg–Jay Gorney song "Brother Can You Spare a Dime?" sung by ventriloquist Rex Weber on a bread line. **6** Rachel Crothers's *When Ladies Meet* (187), her 26th play in the past 26 years, opens at the Royale. Spring Byington, Walter Abel, and Selena Royle star. It becomes a film in 1933. **22** *Dinner at Eight* (243), by Edna Ferber and George S. Kaufman, opens at the Music Box. The production, using a revolving stage, is likened by many to *Grand Hotel*. The cast includes Judith Wood, Malcolm Duncan, Constance Collier, Conway Tearle, Marguerite Churchill, Eda Heinmann, Sam Levene, and Cesar Romero. MGM's screen version will come out next year.

NOVEMBER 8 Jerome Kern and Oscar Hammerstein's *Music in the Air* (342)

Kern and Hammerstein's *Music in the Air* features "I've Told Every Little Star" BROWN

Business and Society

JULY • The cast of the revival of *Show Boat* takes its second salary cut as business slackens at the box office. **19** With the Palace no longer offering straight vaudeville, Minsky temporarily turning the famous Gaiety Theatre into a burlesque house, and Forty-second Street bereft of legitimate stage shows, *Variety* headlines: "Broadway, Just a Road Now; It Just Ain't the Old Street Any More."

AUGUST • The current issue of Actors Equity's magazine, *Equity*, asks the Federal Reserve to extend credit to established producers. **11** RKO drops big time vaudeville from its West Coast theatres.

SEPTEMBER 24 The Broadway Association announces a campaign to clean up the garishness of Times Square.

NOVEMBER 29 *Variety* moves its radio section ahead of its vaudeville and legitimate departments, placing it right behind pictures.

DECEMBER 10 For the first time, the Loew's chain of theatres surpasses the RKO circuit in playing time available for vaude-

Births, Deaths, and Marriages

JUNE 11 Playwright Athol Fugard b.

JULY 8 Damon Runyon m. dancer Patrice Amati Del Grande. **22** Flo Ziegfeld d. Will Rogers, who refers to the showman as our "benefactor," will make the funeral arrangements.

AUGUST 13 Ruth Chatterton, having recently divorced stage actor Ralph Forbes, m. screen actor George Brent.

SEPTEMBER 9 Sylvia Miles b.

OCTOBER 14 Director-producer Jesse Bonstelle d. **18** Their lawyer announces that Lenore Ulric and Sidney Blackmer have separated.

NOVEMBER 1 William Morris d. while playing pinochle at the Friars Club.

his reading of the script, appears in *Vanity Fair* a day before the play opens. In his review, he refers to some lines that have already been dropped from the production. A similar incident occurred with Alexander Woollcott's review of *Strange Interlude*. **27** Writer and playwright Don Marquis (creator of "archie and mahitabel"), under stress from overwork on his play *The Dark Hours*, becomes temporarily blind while at the Players Club.

NOVEMBER • John Casey, Boston's longtime censor, retires. **14** At the behest of the Reynolds family, murder charges against Libby Holman and her husband's best friend are dropped. The family feels that there is insufficient evidence to fit the "circumstances." The story of Smith Reynolds's apparent suicide and the possibility of his wife's involvement in his death will be portrayed in the 1935 film *Reckless*, starring Jean Harlow. **28** United Theatre Relief is founded by playwright Rachel Crothers to assist unemployed theatre people.

DECEMBER • Producer and actor Charles Coburn, with liabilities of $35,984 and assets of $4, files for bankruptcy. **9** Marilyn Miller announces her engagement to movie actor Don Alvarado. Three days ago, they arrived together in Cherbourg, France, on the liner *Bremen* without money or passports. They were at a Bon Voyage party in New York and missed the last call to go ashore. The French didn't let them in, and they have been allowed to wait in London for the trip back. **26** Katharine Cornell is on the cover of *Time*. **27** Ray Bolger heads the stage show at the opening of the Radio City Music Hall. **28** A U.S. District Court judge dismisses a suit by poet Walter Lowenfels charging that George S. Kaufman, Morrie Ryskind, the Gershwins, and producer Sam Harris plagiarized from Lowenfels' "U.S.A. With Music" for *Of Thee I Sing*.

JANUARY • The desire of top stage personalities to offset the financial uncertainties of the theatre with more reliable airtime is reflected in Ed Wynn's contractual specification in *The Laugh Parade* for one night off per week for a radio broadcast and by similar terms for Jack Pearl, star-

---

opens at the Alvin. Walter Slezak stars in this operetta, with songs "I've Told Ev'ry Little Star," "The Song Is You," and "Spring Is in the Air." **28** Cole Porter's *Gay Divorce* (248), at the Barrymore, introduces "Night and Day." In Fred Astaire's last Broadway show, he's dancing on Broadway for the only time without Adele, his sister. Also in this musical about diverting divorce are Claire Luce, Erik Rhodes, and Luella Gear. The 1934 film is *The Gay Divorcee*.

DECEMBER 12 Critic Brooks Atkinson praises Ina Claire's "radiant, heady acting" in S.N. Behrman's comedy *Biography* (210), costarring Earle Larimore, at the Guild Theatre. **20** Katharine Cornell's production of *Lucrece* (31), translated by Thornton Wilder in his first Broadway venture, sets a new high ticket price for a straight play—$6.50, at the Belasco. **28** *Goodbye Again* (212), a comedy by Allan Scott and George Haight about a writer's romantic life, opens at the Masque, with Osgood Perkins, Sally Bates, Katherine Squire, and Leslie Adams. It will be filmed in 1933. The 1961 movie with the same title, in which Osgood Perkins's son Anthony appears, has no relationship to this play. **29** Ben Hecht and Charles MacArthur's *Twentieth Century* (152) opens at the Broadhurst. They've adapted Charles B. Millholland's unproduced play, replacing the sentimentality with delicious cynicism. George Abbott directs Moffat Johnstone, Eugenie Leontovich, and William Frawley. The character of the producer, Oscar Jaffe, who needs to put his ex-lover under contract to salvage his career, is said to be modeled on Jed Harris, an investor in the play. A 1934 film, it will become the 1978 stage musical *On the Twentieth Century*.

JANUARY 24 Noel Coward's *Design For Living* (135), starring the playwright and Alfred Lunt and Lynn Fontanne, opens at the Barrymore. Says John Mason Brown in the *Post*, "It's topsy-turvy tale of love among the artists is giddier than all the mad dogs and Englishmen who, as Mr. Coward has observed, go out in the midday sun." Half of the proceeds tonight will go toward aiding unemployed actors. The movie is released in 1933.

---

ville acts. The Palace is now using an all-film policy.

JANUARY • The collapse of the vaudeville policy at the new Radio City Music Hall, which will now show films, leaves RKO with $30,000 worth of booking commitments it must redistribute to other theatres.

FEBRUARY • Alexander Aarons and Vinton Freedly dissolve their production partnership after the flop last month of George Gershwin's *Pardon My English*.

MARCH • Many Broadway productions are barely doing enough business to stay open. Some theatres are now accepting checks at the box office, not worrying about their bouncing because the seats will not otherwise be sold. • Representatives of the major vaudeville circuits meet and decide on a concerted effort to slash performer salaries.

APRIL 7 The property of the Shubert organization, which is in receivership, is put up for auction. But the only bidder at the sale is the organization itself, under the new name "Select Theatres," paying the $400,000 minimum set by the court for the property with a paper valuation of $24,000,000.

DECEMBER 2 Elia Kazan m. Mollie Day Thatcher, a play reader for the Group Theatre. **7** Ellen Burstyn (Edna Rae Gilooley) b.

JANUARY 23 Chita Rivera (Conchita del Rivero) b. **29** Lillian Roth m. Judge Benjamin Shalleck. **31** Playwright John Galsworthy d.

FEBRUARY 1 Helen Kane m. Max Hoffman, the actor son of dancer-vaudevillian Gertrude Hoffman.

APRIL 20 Louis Calhern m. actress Natalie Schafer. **26** Carol Burnett b.

MAY 7 Director Gordon Davidson b. **15** Helen Morgan m. Bud Maschke, Jr., a law student.

Personalities

ring in *Pardon My English.* **1** Thornton Wilder, who translated *Lucrece*, which Katharine Cornell is presenting on Broadway, tells the *Herald-Tribune*, "Some day I hope I shall be able to write a play." **24** *Variety*, mentioning that Elmer Rice has had four plays staged in the past two seasons, notes that the playwright "is a radical and success as a showman has not damaged his Communistic beliefs." His 21-scene *We, The People* opened three days ago. **30** Noel Coward is on the cover of *Time*.

FEBRUARY 22 George Burns and Gracie Allen make their radio debut, on Guy Lombardo's show. The move to the airwaves is typical for top vaudeville talent.

MARCH • Vincent Youmans, who had to ask his creditors for more time to pay his debts a year ago, is in the same circumstances now. • Composer Kurt Weill, warned that the Nazis plan to arrest him, flees Germany for Paris.

APRIL 18 The marquee of the Plymouth Theatre announces Laurette Taylor in *Enchantment*, scheduled to open tonight. But she is just not up to it, and the show folds. **21** At a nationally broadcast tribute to the late Flo Ziegfeld at the Ziegfeld Theatre (about to become a movie house), former Follies star Lillian Lorraine is called up from the audience to sing "By the Light of the Silvery Moon." Its composer, Gus Edwards, is about to accompany her on the piano when she is overcome by emotion and has to be assisted back to her seat.

MAY • John Corbin, onetime theatre critic for *The New York Times*, complains in *Scribner's* Magazine that Jewish playwrights "have repeatedly attempted . . . the indictment of the American people entire." He decries their "acrid intelligence." **2** The performance in *Biography* missed by Ina Claire tonight because of a toothache is the first time in her career that illness has forced her out of a show.

Plays and Musicals

FEBRUARY 15 In *One Sunday Afternoon* (338), a star-making vehicle for Lloyd Nolan, a dentist tempted by revenge is contemplating murder, until he learns that life has extracted its own vengeance from his intended victim. James S. Hagan's drama is at the Little Theatre.

MARCH 6 Maxwell Anderson's *Both Your Houses* (120), dealing with corruption in Congress, opens at the Royale. It stars Shepperd Strudwick, Morris Carnovsky, Mary Phillips, J. Edward Bromberg, Jerome Cowan, and Jane Seymour.

APRIL 13 The Bertolt Brecht–Kurt Weill *Threepenny Opera* (12), a hit in Berlin in 1928 and already filmed in Germany, opens at the Empire but will have to await its 1955 off-Broadway revival to be appreciated here. It's a "torpid affectation," says Percy Hammond in the *Herald-Tribune*. Burgess Meredith has a minor role.

Business and Society

Births, Deaths, and Marriages

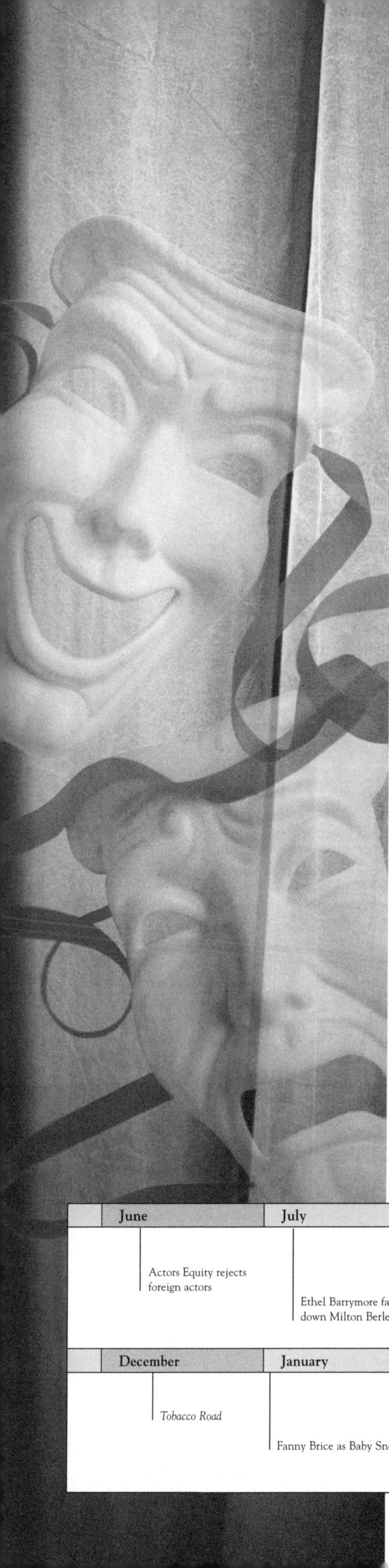

1933–34

The New Deal's NRA comes to Broadway, government money aids unemployed actors, and Actors Equity, sensitive to job loss, is evolving a stronger policy of restricting foreign players. But not all is social significance. In fact, Eugene O'Neill has written a comedy. *Tobacco Road* turns dross into gold, Katharine Cornell takes to the road with 18-year-old Orson Welles in tow, and Ethel Barrymore handles a ticklish situation with Milton Berle. And Broadway is learning to live with disappearing stars. Jimmy Durante has to leave *Strike Me Pink* for Hollywood to fulfill a movie commitment, and the *Gay Divorce* closes when Fred Astaire must go *Flying Down to Rio*.

- Elia Kazan's only line in *Men in White*: "Hello, sweetheart."
- Only member of the Group Theatre who does not appear in *Men in White*: Stella Adler
- What the Republic Theatre, a Minsky burlesque house across the street from Earl Carroll's *Murder at the Vanities*, will put on its marquee: "Slaughter at Minsky's"
- Number of acts in *Four Saints in Three Acts*: 4
- Length of Sally Rand's fan dance at the Chicago Theatre: 7 minutes
- Miles covered by Katharine Cornell's tour: 16,853
- Number of cities and towns in which she plays: 75
- Number of performances on the Cornell tour: 225
- Total audience on the Cornell tour: about 500,000
- What the Friars and Lambs Clubs have in common: they're both in receivership
- Number of permanent stock companies in the 1927–28 season: 165
- Number this season: 30

Productions on Broadway: 151

Pulitzer Prize for Drama: *Men in White* (Sidney Kingsley)

June	July	August	September	October	November
Actors Equity rejects foreign actors	Ethel Barrymore faces down Milton Berle	NRA Blue Eagle lands on Broadway	Irving Berlin's "Easter Parade" finally clicks	Eugene O'Neill comedy	Katharine Cornell takes the show on the road

December	January	February	March	April	May
Tobacco Road	Fanny Brice as Baby Snooks	*Four Saints in Three Acts*—count'em	*New Faces*, with Henry Fonda	George Jessel m. Norma Talmadge	Harold Clurman in the U.S.S.R.

Personalities

JULY 8 Producer Charles Dillingham is forced into bankruptcy.

AUGUST • Ethel Barrymore, appearing at Chicago's Palace Theatre with emcee Milton Berle, avoids the comedian's attempts to clown with her and to see if she is "ticklish." In fact, she appears to have intimidated the brash Berle with her "drop dead" iciness. **26** The abdominal ailment that strikes Tallulah Bankhead today will force her to withdraw from *Jezebel*, now in rehearsals. Miriam Hopkins will replace her.

OCTOBER • Frank Fay's engagement at the

Later known for his films, Broadway song and dance man Clifton Webb introduced Irving Berlin's "Easter Parade"

Plays and Musicals

SEPTEMBER 12 Earl Carroll's *Murder at the Vanities* (280) is "part Minsky, part morgue," says one critic. The cast—including Bela Lugosi—had to rehearse the mystery-musical all through last night to cope with last-minute technical difficulties involving the scenery. A screen version comes out next year. **26** Sidney Kingsley's *Men in White* (351), the Group Theatre's first major success—it has doctors, abortion, and romance—opens at the Broadhurst. Lee Strasberg directs Alexander Kirkland, Margaret Barker, Phoebe Brand, Luther Adler, J. Edward Bromberg, Robert Lewis, Morris Carnovsky, Clifford Odets, and Elia Kazan, who has one line, spoken to a nurse: "Hello, sweetheart." **28** In *Sailor, Beware!* (500), a comedy by Kenyon Nicholson and Charles Robinson, the battle is between the sexes when a U.S. warship docks in the Canal Zone. Brice McFarlane and Audrey Christie star at the Lyceum. **30** Irving Berlin and Moss Hart's revue *As Thousands Cheer* (390) opens at the Music Box. A satire on tabloid newspapers, it features Ethel Waters singing "Heat Wave," "Harlem on My Mind," and "Supper Time" (while a huge tabloid headline behind her proclaims: "Unknown Negro Lynched by Frenzied Mob"). Marilyn Miller and Clifton Webb sing "Easter Parade," a song that failed to click in Berlin's 1917 *Smile and Show Your Dimple*. "Not for All the Rice in China" also debuts.

Business and Society

JUNE 9 Actors Equity declares that foreign actors will no longer be eligible for membership in the organization, although they can still work on the American stage. **20** *Variety* moves its music section ahead of the paper's vaudeville and legitimate departments.

JULY 11 The Stage Relief Fund begins distributing food to needy actors from backstage at the Royale Theatre.

AUGUST 16 President Roosevelt signs the Legitimate Theatre Code for the National Industrial Recovery Act. The code, negotiated on July 21 by producers and performers, stipulates a minimum wage of $40 to $50 a week, depending on the top ticket price. Actors with less than two years of experience will make $25 a week, and chorus boys and girls will get $30. **24** The Dramatists Guild names George S. Kaufman to speak for it in the group that will administer the NRA Theatre Code.

OCTOBER 23 *Vanity Fair* editor Claire (Boothe) Brokaw is appointed to help oversee the legitimate theatre code of the National Recovery Act.

Births, Deaths, and Marriages

JULY 10 Composer-lyricist Jerry Herman b., and set designer Joseph Urban d.

SEPTEMBER • Lenore Ulric divorces Sidney Blackmer. **12** John Houseman and Zita Johann are divorced. **14** Zoe Caldwell b. Pickle packer is among her pre-stage occupations. **17** Dorothy Loudon b. **22** Sime Silverman, founding publisher of *Variety*, d. **25** Sophie Tucker divorces Abe Lackerman. **25** Ring Lardner d.

OCTOBER 28 E.H. Sothern d.

NOVEMBER 5 Texas Guinan d. **26** Robert Goulet b. **28** Heywood Broun and Ruth Hale are divorced.

JANUARY 11 Charles Mack, of the vaudeville team of Moran and Mack, is killed in an auto accident in Arizona. Also in

Michigan Theatre in Detroit is canceled when he fails to show up. • Its finances precarious, Eva Le Gallienne takes her Civic Repertory Company on the road for a season, subletting its Fourteenth Street Theatre to the Theatre Union, a leftist group. But the company's problems are terminal, and this will be its last season.

NOVEMBER 3 According to today's *New York Post*, the Theatre Guild will produce a musical based on the play *Porgy*, and the composer will be George Gershwin. (Gershwin and Heyward signed with the Guild on October 26.) The *Post* reports that Jerome Kern and Oscar Hammerstein II also had the idea of setting the drama to music and intended to star Al Jolson but dropped it when they learned that the Guild had someone else in mind to do the composing. It has not yet been decided if a black cast will perform in the new work or if it will feature "a white mammy singer such as Mr. Jolson." **29** In Buffalo, Katharine Cornell's repertory company, performing *The Barretts of Wimpole Street*, *Candida*, and *Romeo and Juliet*, begins a tour of America—traveling in two special Pullman cars—that will take them 16,853 miles through 75 towns in seven months, playing 225 performances, mostly one-night stands, in front of 500,000 people. Company members include Basil Rathbone and 18-year-old Orson Welles.

DECEMBER • Jerome Kern is annoyed with the fancy arrangements bands are giving his "Smoke Gets in Your Eyes," from *Roberta*, and he threatens to withhold recording rights. **1** Ethel Barrymore, accompanying Eva Le Gallienne to a talk she's giving to society club women in Philadelphia, is enraged at what she perceives to be the disrespectful reception given her friend. Barrymore tells them, "You don't understand anything" and, according to one report, calls them "morons."

FEBRUARY • According to newspaper reports, Eva Le Gallienne, unhappy at the response of the crowd in Minneapolis where she's officiating at a charity auction, calls them "lousy Americans." She later says that she was kidding. **20** *Variety*, reviewing Tallulah Bankhead's guest appearance—

OCTOBER 2 Eugene O'Neill's comedy *Ah, Wilderness!* (289) is at the Guild. Elisha Cooke, Jr. plays a teenager, about to go away to college, who is interested in a young woman played by Ruth Gilbert. George M. Cohan plays his father. Filmed in 1935, it will become the 1959 musical *Take Me Along*. **20** Mordaunt Shairp's *The Green Bay Tree* (163) is a relatively daring treatment of homosexuality for Broadway. The Jed Harris import is at the Cort, with a cast consisting of Leo G. Carroll, Laurence Olivier, Jill Esmond, O.P. Heggie, and James Dale. **21** The much awaited sequel to *Of Thee I Sing*, *Let Them Eat Cake* (90), at the Imperial, with a book by George S. Kaufman and Morrie Ryskind and music by the Gershwins, is a disappointment. William Gaxton, Victor Moore, and Louise Moran reprise their roles from *Of Thee I Sing*. **23** Roland Young, son-in-law of playwright Clare Kummer, stars in her comedy *Her Master's Voice* (224), at the Plymouth. Frances Fuller, also in the cast, is married to the director, Worthington Miner.

NOVEMBER 18 *Roberta* (295), with Jerome Kern's music and Otto Harbach's lyrics, opens at the New Amsterdam. Richard Lockridge, in the *Sun*, writes that Bob Hope "spends what must be a faintly tedious evening lifting up anemic quips and watching them collapse at his feet." Brooks Atkinson thinks he "would be more amusing if he were Fred Allen." "Smoke Gets in Your Eyes" is sung by Tamara. The cast also includes Sidney Greenstreet, Fay Templeton, George Murphy, Lyda Roberti, and, playing the saxophone with the California Collegians, Fred MacMurray. **20** Howard Lindsay's slapstick comedy *She Loves Me Not* (360) is at the Forty-sixth Street Theatre, with Polly Waters, John Beal, and Burgess Meredith. Raymond Sovey's stage design has melded four locations into one set, allowing for rapid-fire scene shifting as well as lines. **27** "Spirited as the season has been for several weeks," the *Times* will report tomorrow, "it was innocent of magnificence until Maxwell Anderson's *Mary of Scotland* (236) arrived at the Alvin last evening." Helen Hayes is Mary Stuart, and Helen Menken is Queen Elizabeth. **29** The nonprofit Theatre Union,

NOVEMBER 20 Both parts of the NBC radio network—the "Red" and the "Blue" network—begin broadcasting a series of programs featuring excerpts from Broadway shows. Broadcasters and movie producers are becoming more conscious of their dependence on Broadway, which is not in great shape, for a supply of new talent.

JANUARY • *New Theater*, an influential magazine with a left wing slant, begins publication. **15** "For the first time in the history of the American stage, the government will aid the unemployed actor," begins *The New York Times*'s account of the $28,000 Civil Works Administration grant to Actors Equity to create free productions to be given in New York City schools.

FEBRUARY 26 *New York Times* critic Brooks Atkinson and playwright Marc Connelly testify before the House Immigration Committee, opposing restrictions on the influx of foreign actors, which Actors Equity head Frank Gillmore supports.

MARCH 11 The *Herald-Tribune* reports that "[i]n the last few years the theater has halted its uptown march and begun to concentrate, shrinking on itself and solidifying, finding a geographical, commer-

the car but not seriously injured are his partner George Moran and film director Mack Sennett. **30** Tammy Grimes b.

FEBRUARY 17 Alan Bates b.

MARCH 11 Margaret Illington d. **16** Lee Strasberg m. Paula Miller.

APRIL 23 George Jessel m. screen actress Norma Talmadge.

Personalities

and U.S. radio debut—on Rudy Vallee's program, says that she "displayed a voice and a manner not susceptible to radio use. It's hard, unfeminine and lacking in nuance."

MARCH 19 Appearing at the Capitol Theatre, Jimmy Durante makes a curtain speech, criticizing Walter Winchell for his false report about backstage conflict between the comedian and vaudeville funny man Lou Holtz.

APRIL • Producer Sam Harris acknowledges that he, the Marx Brothers, and Irving Berlin have lost a substantial amount of money in a gold mine that did not pan out.

MAY 7 Maxwell Anderson's *Mary of Scotland*, recommended unanimously by the three-man Pulitzer Prize jury for this year's prize, is passed over for Sidney Kingsley's *Men in White*. **14** Leonard Lyons begins a column in the *New York Post* that will cover stage personalities as well as other entertainment world luminaries. "The Lyons Den" will be syndicated in about 100 papers, and he will write it for the next 40 years. **19** Harold Clurman, director of the Group Theatre, leaves for the Soviet Union to study Russian theatre. **28** Irving Berlin is on the cover of *Time*.

Plays and Musicals

formed recently to present plays with a social vision at popular prices, mounts its first production at the Civic Repertory Theatre, George Sklar and Albert Maltz's antiwar drama *Peace on Earth* (144), with Jules [John] Garfield.

DECEMBER 4 *Tobacco Road* (3,182), opening at the Masque, will set a new long run record for a straight play. Jack Kirkland's melodrama about the low-life Lester family, based on the best-selling, sensational Erskine Caldwell novel, stars Henry Hull, Margaret Wycherly, Dean Jagger, Ruth Hunter, and Sam Byrd. A cleaned-up version reaches the screen in 1941.

JANUARY 4 *The Ziegfeld Follies* (182), opening at the Winter Garden, is staged by the Shuberts. Fanny Brice, in her sixth *Follies*, for the first time portrays the character 'Baby Snooks,' whom she will popularize on the radio. The cast's other Brice—Brice Hutchins, whose number is "I Like the Look of You"—is the future Robert Cummings. **8** Eugene O'Neill's *Days Without End* (57), the story of a man divided—literally—against himself, opens at the Henry Miller Theatre. It stars Earle Larimore and Stanley Ridges as the two sides of the lead character, with Selena Royle and Robert Loraine. It is O'Neill's last Broadway effort until *The Iceman Cometh* in 1946.

FEBRUARY 20 Gertrude Stein and composer Virgil Thomson's *Four Saints in Three Acts* (48), a comic "opera" that's actually in four acts, with many more saints than four and a libretto that no one seems to understand, opens at the Forty-fourth Street Theatre. **24** Sidney Howard's *Dodsworth* (317), based on the Sinclair Lewis novel and starring Walter Huston and Fay Bainter, with Maria Ouspenskaya, opens at the Shubert. The movie comes out in 1936.

MARCH 15 The first of seven revues called *New Faces* (148), produced by Leonard Sillman, opens at the Fulton. Sillman himself performs in it, as does Imogene Coca and a newcomer named Henry Fonda.

Business and Society

cial and artistic center in the middle '40s."

MAY • The Friars and the Lambs Clubs return to a firmer financial footing.

Births, Deaths, and Marriages

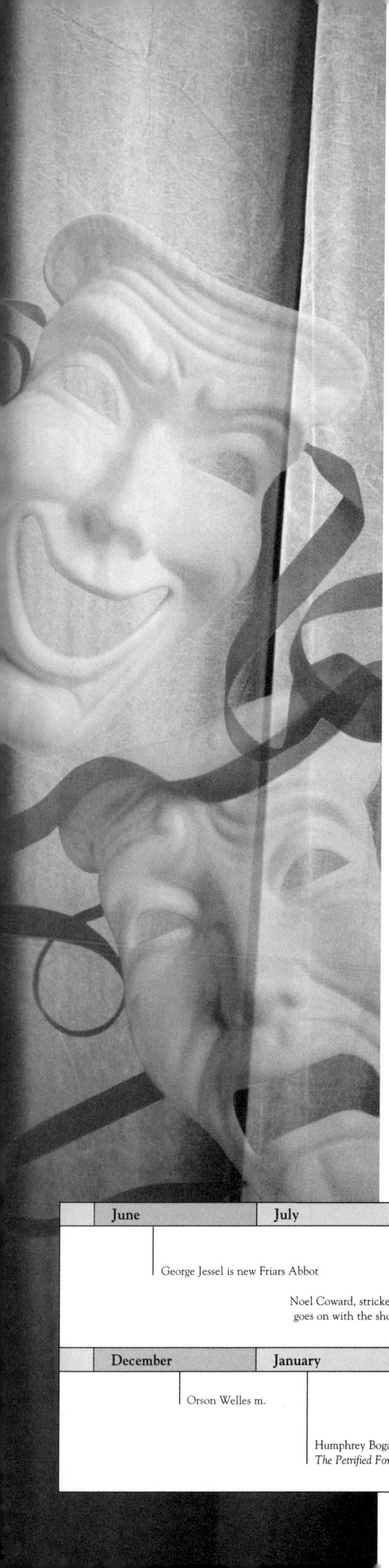

1934–35

The federal government begins to bring plays to the people, Stella Adler thinks some of her Group Theatre colleagues are misinterpreting Stanislavsky, and Elia Kazan joins the Communist Party, a move that will have repercussions decades later. Producer Vinton Freedly brings Howard Lindsay and Russel Crouse together, Hume Cronyn and Joshua Logan make their Broadway debuts, and Miss Lillian Gish plays an unmentionable in Sean O'Casey's *Within the Gates*. Elmer Rice, on the other hand, freely mentions what he thinks of theatre critics: "stupid, jaded, illiterate, drunkards." With *Anything Goes*, Ethel Merman is on her way to becoming an institution, and Lillian Hellman bursts on the scene with *The Children's Hour*.

- Dominant owner of Broadway theatres: the banks
- Amount of *The Petrified Forest* owned by Leslie Howard: 50 percent
- How producer Arthur Hopkins perceives Humphrey Bogart when he hires him, mainly on the sound of his voice, to play the gangster Duke Mantee in *The Petrified Forest*: "He is an antiquated juvenile who has spent most of his stage life in white pants, swinging a tennis racket."
- Cost of new costumes for the cast of *Tobacco Road*: $12.80
- Number of costumes in *The Great Waltz*: 500
- Cost of mounting *The Great Waltz*: $246,000
- Number of stagehands working in *The Great Waltz*: 90
- Number of weeks it takes for *Anything Goes* to earn back its cost: 9 1/2, thought to be a record for a musical
- Reaction of Arturo Toscanini to Ethel Merman in *Anything Goes*: "Castrati! Castrati!," a reference to the Italian singers who were emasculated to cut off the deepening of their voices.
- Ethel Merman's current romantic interest: Winthrop Rockefeller.
- What Ethel Merman says when advised by a friend that Winthrop Rockefeller would not be impressed by her salty language: "Oh, bullshit. I'll bring him down to my level."
- The real love of Ethel Merman's life: Sherman Billingsley, proprietor of the Stork Club. Later in the decade, she will wear a necklace with "Merm" on one side and "Sherm" on the other

Productions on Broadway: 149

Pulitzer Prize for Drama: *The Old Maid* (Zoe Akins)

June	July	August	September	October	November
George Jessel is new Friars Abbot	Noel Coward, stricken, goes on with the show	Helen Morgan cleared of charges by Equity	*Bon Voyage* evolving into *Anything Goes*	Miss Lillian Gish is a w_ _ _e	*The Children's Hour*

December	January	February	March	April	May
Orson Welles m.	Humphrey Bogart in *The Petrified Forest*	Clifford Odets makes his mark	Revolt in Actors Equity	Joshua Logan's Broadway debut	Pulitzer provokes protest

Personalities

JUNE 15 Producer Arch Selwyn files for bankruptcy. **24** Tennessee Williams begins a job in the warehouse of the International Shoe Company, where one of his coworkers, with whom he becomes friendly, is a man named Stanley Kowalski—the name Williams will give the leading male character in *A Streetcar Named Desire*.

JULY • Noel Coward is stricken with an attack of appendicitis while performing at a London theatre in his *Conversation Piece*. He manages to finish the performance and then goes to a hospital for an operation. • A surrogate court judge, deciding that Laurette Taylor is not capable of administering the estate of her late husband, playwright J. Hartley Manners, sets up a trusteeship to dispense the funds.

AUGUST • Back from Paris, where she studied with Stanislavsky, Stella Adler tries to convey to her Group Theatre colleagues the need to get into the emotional life of their characters, rather than reach into their own life histories for motivation. **23** Actors Equity clears Helen Morgan of charges that her drinking and insubordination led to the closing of the show *Memory* in Los Angeles in May. Among the character witnesses testifying in her behalf was Oscar Hammerstein II, who said he never once saw her drunk during the run of *Show Boat*.

SEPTEMBER 1 Noel Coward is stranded onshore in Corsica when the yacht he chartered is smashed on the rocks, sending to the bottom his clothes, papers, and money. He has to walk 20 miles to find a village from which he can cable friends in London for help. **1** Vaudevillian Georgie Price, as George E. Price, a stockbroker trading through Bache & Co., buys a seat on the New York Stock Exchange for $95,000. **5** Sophie Tucker receives a black eye when she steps between two women fighting over her autograph outside the Empire Theatre in London. **8** Two months away from Broadway, the Cole Porter musical *Bon*

Plays and Musicals

SEPTEMBER 22 *The Great Waltz* (297) opens at the 3,822-seat Center Theatre in the new Rockefeller Center and is heavily promoted on NBC radio. This operetta about Johann Strauss, senior and junior, stars Guy Robertson. The film is released in 1938. **29** *Merrily We Roll Along* (155), by George S. Kaufman and Moss Hart, opening at the Music Box Theatre, "is the rebuking story of how proud youth debases itself into shoddy middle age," according to Brooks Atkinson. It stars Kenneth MacKenna, Mary Philips, and Walter Abel. Stephen Sondheim's 1981 musical version will flop.

OCTOBER 17 Gladys George is in *Personal Appearance* (501), a comedy in which she plays a movie star who falls in love with an auto mechanic. Lawrence Riley's play, on which Mae West's 1936 film *Go West, Young Man* is based, is at Henry Miller's Theatre. **18** The role is only that of "A Janitor" in *Hipper's Holiday* (4), and the show flops at Maxine Elliott's Theatre, but it is Hume Cronyn's Broadway debut. **22** For every newspaper except the *Times* and the *Post*, which call her by her rightful name, Lillian Gish is playing an unmentionable or a "harlot" in Sean O'Casey's *Within the Gates* (141), at the National. The program calls her a "whore." Directed by Melvyn Douglas, it's banned in Boston. **30** *The Farmer Takes a Wife* (104), Frank B. Elser and Marc Connelly's comedy about life on the Erie Canal, is at the Forty-sixth Street Theatre. *The New York Times* says that "Henry Fonda, who has his first big opportunity here, gives a manly, modest performance, in a style of captivating simplicity."

NOVEMBER 12 The Abbey Theatre, which includes in its company Arthur Sinclair and Barry Fitzgerald, begins a five-week season at the John Golden Theatre with Sean O'Casey's *The Plough and the Stars*. **20** Lillian Hellman's *The Children's Hour* (691), with its lesbian theme, is the talk of the town when it opens at Maxine Elliott's Theatre. This "venomously tragic" play—Atkinson, in the *Times*—is Hellman's debut as a playwright and stars

Business and Society

AUGUST • Free legitimate stage shows given in New York City's parks this summer have drawn thousands, many of whom have never seen a play.

SEPTEMBER • Actors Equity specifies the procedures for cutting salaries when box office conditions warrant it, with more say for Equity in how it's done. **5** Rehearsals begin on 20 shows, financed by the federal government under the New Deal, that will tour Civilian Conservation Corps sites, entertaining young people employed at them and giving jobs to 300 unemployed actors, each paid $25 a week.

OCTOBER 3 The three members of the Pulitzer Prize Jury, whose choice for the award in May was rejected by Columbia University, which gives out the prize, say they will not serve another year. A Columbia spokesperson counters: "There is nothing to resign from. They are appointed for only one year." (It has been customary to automatically offer to reappoint jurors.) **22** The amended NRA Theatre Code sets a $.75 limit on ticket sale premiums and specifies no more than eight consecutive hours of rehearsal except in the week before opening night.

Births, Deaths, and Marriages

JUNE • Playwright Robert E. Sherwood and Mary Brandon are divorced. **18** George Hearn b.

JULY 2 Playwright Ed Bullins b. **28** Marie Dressler d.

AUGUST 12 Playwright Augustus Thomas d. **30** Producer Charles Dillingham d. His 1930 will, still in effect, leaves $50,000 to his ex-wife and includes bequests of $1,000 each to his barber and chauffeur. But the estate of the bankrupt producer is worth only $4,000.

OCTOBER 1 Marilyn Miller m. chorus boy Chester O'Brien. **4** Ruth Chatterton and George Brent are divorced. **7** Playwright LeRoi Jones (later Imamu Amiri Baraka) b. **24** Set designer Tony Walton b.

DECEMBER 5 Larry Kert (Frederick Lawrence

Voyage, about a shipboard fire, suddenly looks like a bad bet after today's fire on the *Morro Castle*, off Asbury Park, New Jersey, sinks it and takes 125 lives. Authors Guy Bolton and P.G. Wodehouse are unavailable for the rewrite, so producer Vinton Freedly asks director Howard Lindsay, also a writer, to do it. Lindsay asks for help, and Freedly gets him Russel Crouse. The new team also has a new title: *Anything Goes*.

OCTOBER 31 In a speech at Columbia University, playwright Elmer Rice denounces theatre critics as "stupid, jaded illiterate, drunkards." His most recent works, including *We the People*, have not been well received.

NOVEMBER 21 Producer Lew Brown, at the opening of *Calling All Stars* in Boston, tries to smuggle in critic George Holland, banned from the Shubert theatre because of his negative reviews of the brothers' productions. When the doorman tries to stop Holland, Brown shoves the doorman and is then clubbed by a security guard.

DECEMBER 6 At Elsa Maxwell's party for Cole Porter at the Waldorf's Starlight Roof, Ethel Merman is singing "I Get a Kick Out of You." The hostess, playing cupid, brings *Time* publisher Henry Luce and playwright Clare Boothe together. By the end of the evening, Luce tells Boothe: "You are the one woman in my life." **21** Tallulah Bankhead collapses in her dressing room at the Plymouth, reportedly

Ethel Merman

Ann Revere, Katherine Emery, and Florence McGee, in the story of a child's terrible revenge for being disciplined by her teacher. Hellman's screenplay for the 1936 film *These Three* changes the relationship from homo- to heterosexual, but the lesbian theme is restored in the 1962 remake. **21** Walter Winchell says that "[t]he fooling and fun was fervently fondled by the first fans" of Cole Porter's *Anything Goes* (415) tonight, although critic Percy Hammond cautions that some of the dialogue "is not suitable to the ears of bashful theatre-lovers." According to Brooks Atkinson, "'You're the Top' is one of the most congenial songs Mr. Porter has written. . . . If Ethel Merman did not write 'I Get a Kick Out of You' and also the title song of the show she has made them hers now by the swinging gusto of her platform style." "Blow, Gabriel, Blow" and "All Through the Night" are also in the show, at the Alvin, William Gaxton, Bettina Hall, and Victor Moore round out the cast, and the book is by Guy Bolton and P.G. Wodehouse. Merman and Bing Crosby are in the 1936 film.

DECEMBER 20 Katharine Cornell opens in Shakespeare's *Romeo and Juliet* (78), directed by her husband, Guthrie McClintic, at the Martin Beck. The production "is on the high plane of modern magnificence," according to Brooks Atkinson. The cast includes Basil Rathbone as Romeo, George Macready, Moroni Olsen, Brian Aherne, Edith Evans, and Orson Welles, whose Tybalt, writes Percy Hammond in the *Herald-Tribune*, is "sardonic in a fine, unusual fashion."

JANUARY 7 Humphrey Bogart, whose stage career has consisted mostly of playing society types, makes an indelible impression as the gangster Duke Mantee in Robert E. Sherwood's *The Petrified Forest* (194), at the Broadhurst. Leslie Howard is the world-weary intellectual, and Peggy Conklin is the young woman dreaming of a better life. It's on the screen in 1936. **7** Judith Anderson and Helen Menken star in *The Old Maid* (298), Zoe Akins's play about a young woman who doesn't know that her "aunt" is really her mother, opening at the Empire Theatre. The 1939 film version

There's also a small wage increase.

JANUARY 22 *Variety* notes that playing time for engagements in cafés, night clubs, and hotels now exceeds that available in what's left of vaudeville.

MARCH 1 At the Actors Equity quarterly meeting, younger, more left leaning members such as Philip Loeb and Albert Van Dekker (Albert Dekker), calling themselves the Actors Forum, clash with the old guard. The Actors Forum wants closer ties to organized labor.

APRIL • *Waiting for Lefty*, which has just won first prize in a drama tournament in New Haven, is banned as "blasphemous and obscene" by that city's police chief. The New Haven *Sunday Herald* responds by printing the script in its entirety. **6** Two members of the cast of *Waiting for Lefty* are arrested in Boston for using profanity onstage. **23** New York State legalizes Sunday performances of legitimate plays, as long as the performers have at least one other day off. But enabling such performances is left up to local governments.

Kert) b. **24** "Virginia Nicholson Becomes a Bride," says *The New York Times* headline about yesterday's nuptials. Only in the final paragraph does the piece get to the groom. "Mr. [Orson] Welles is a member of Katharine Cornell's *Romeo and Juliet* company. Before that he was with the Irish Players in Ireland. Katharine Cornell, Guthrie McClintic and Thornton Wilder were among the guests."

JANUARY 6 Drama teacher George Pierce Baker d. **9** Heywood Broun m. Constance Fruscello, who as Connie Madison has danced in *The Ziegfeld Follies* and *George White's Scandals*.

FEBRUARY 16 Brian Bedford b. He will make his stage debut, in a school nativity play, as the Virgin Mary.

MARCH 15 Judd Hirsch b.

APRIL 11 Ann Revere m. director Samuel Rosen.

Personalities

from a throat condition, and *Dark Victory* will go dark for several evenings.

JANUARY 18 Ray Bolger, performing in *Life Begins at 8:40* at the Winter Garden, helps to calm an audience that begins to rush to the exits when it smells smoke. Bolger goes into an impromptu tap dance, quipping, "You can't walk out on me!" The fire, a small one on the roof, does not hurt anyone.

MARCH 20 Under the headline "Snubs Films," *Variety* reports that newly successful playwright Clifford Odets "doesn't want to go to Hollywood." He has already turned down five screenwriting offers.

APRIL 1 Laurette Taylor is hospitalized and almost dies from severe anemia. **2** According to the *Herald-Tribune*, Eugene O'Neill has begun working on a seven-play cycle covering five generations of a New England family. **4** Gertrude Lawrence tells a London bankruptcy court that she is in dire financial straits because "while I was in America and engaged I expended a good deal on my trousseau," and she also spent a good deal entertaining her fiancé's friends before the engagement was broken. **26** Producer Jed Harris is arrested and sentenced to three days in jail in Pasadena for ignoring a speeding ticket. **29** Joshua Logan debuts as a Broadway director in the short-lived *To See Ourselves*.

MAY 27 Fire destroys playwright Philip Barry's home in Mt. Kisco, New York.

Plays and Musicals

stars Bette Davis and Miriam Hopkins. **30** John Cecil Holm and George Abbott's *Three Men on a Horse* (812) opens at the Playhouse. This farce about betting on the races features Sam Levene and will bring Shirley Booth her first star billing. The musicals *Banjo Eyes* (1941) and *Let It Ride* (1961) are based on it, and a film is made in 1938.

FEBRUARY 19 Clifford Odets's *Awake and Sing* (184), a production of the Group Theatre, opens at the Belasco. Harold Clurman is directing Stella Adler, Morris Carnovsky, Phoebe Brand, Jules [John] Garfield, Luther Adler, and Sanford Meisner. "Chekhov in the Bronx," John Mason Brown calls this drama of a Jewish family in New York. But Burns Mantle, in the *News*, says it left him cold, "and emotional melodrama should not do that even to a goy."

Humphrey Bogart as Duke Mantee in *The Petrified Forest*

MARCH 26 The Group Theatre's production of Clifford Odets's *Waiting for Lefty*, which had a brief run at the Civic Repertory Theater on Fourteenth Street in January, opens at the Longacre (135) with another Odets play, *Till the Day I Die*. *Waiting for Lefty* is about a taxi drivers' strike. At the end, the audience, whipped into a frenzy, joins in the call for the drivers to "[s]trike!" The cast includes Odets, Elia Kazan, and Lee J. Cobb, and tickets range from $.40 to $1.65.

Business and Society

Births, Deaths, and Marriages

1935–36

The Federal Theatre Project creates jobs and controversy, as the grand experiment in government-subsidized theatre brings charges of "communism," on the one hand, and "censorship," on the other. *Winterset* and *Dead End* typify the political cast of some Broadway plays in mid decade and their concern with the gap between rich and poor. In just a two-night span in October, the world receives the musical cornucopia that is Gershwin's *Porgy and Bess* and Cole Porter's "Begin the Beguine" and "It Was Just One of Those Things." "What elephant?" is Jimmy Durante's perfectly logical query to the cop in *Jumbo*. "What's going on here?" asks José Ferrer, in his first Broadway outing. And Noel Coward denies that he's having a romance with Greta Garbo.

- Starting price of entrees at Jack Dempsey's Times Square restaurant: $.90
- Sign on the luggage store in the Hippodrome building, where *Jumbo*, the circus musical about an elephant, is playing: Trunks
- Amount that investment group headed by Jock Whitney loses on *Jumbo*: $160,000
- How *Jumbo* producer Billy Rose defines an angel: "A guy who likes to wear a black hat and meet blondes"
- Number of stock companies left in the U.S.: 2
- Author-producer split on movie rights to stage plays: 60–40
- Amount that Samuel Goldwyn pays for the screen rights to *Dodsworth*: about $150,000
- Fee for the use of the "Ziegfeld Follies" name in this season's production: 7 percent of the gross, divided between Billie Burke, Ziegfeld's widow, and the estate of producer A.L. Erlanger
- What Charles Laughton sends Helen Hayes in honor of her role in *Victoria Regina*: an actual pair of Victoria's embroidered panties
- Percentage of the Federal Theatre Project budget allocated to wages: 90 percent
- Percentage of Federal Theatre Project personnel who must be drawn from the relief roles: 90 percent
- What critic Percy Hammond writes about a revue he found wanting: "I find that I have knocked everything but the chorus girl's knees, and there God anticipated me."
- Location of opening night party for *Porgy and Bess*: Condé Nast's penthouse

Productions on Broadway: 135

Pulitzer Prize for Drama: *Idiot's Delight* (Robert E Sherwood)

New York Drama Critics Circle Award:
Best Play: *Winterset* (Maxwell Anderson)

June
- Helen Morgan says "ex" threatened to kill her

July
- Hallie Flanagan heads Federal Theatre Project

August
- Will Rogers d. in plane crash

September
- Kurt Weill arrives in New York

October
- *Porgy and Bess* and *Dead End*

November
- O'Neill wins Nobel Prize

December
- Helen Hayes as Queen Victoria

January
- Noel Coward denies romance with Garbo

February
- Fanny Brice illness closes *Follies*

March
- *Idiot's Delight*

April
- Orson Welles's "Voodoo" *Macbeth*

May
- Van Johnson's Broadway debut

Personalities

JUNE 26 *Variety* relates the views of the composer of the musical version of *Porgy*: "Ambitiousness of the cast is made economically possible, says Gershwin, through the fact that colored singers dominate. White voices comparable to them would have made it financially prohibitive in salary costs."

JULY 3 Clifford Odets, who has traveled to Cuba with the League of American Writers to investigate social and economic conditions there, is arrested and deported.

SEPTEMBER • Composer Kurt Weill comes to New York from London to work in the American theatre. **2** Lenore Ulric is playing a scene opposite Frank Allworth at the Broad Street Theatre in Philadelphia in *Portuguese Gal*. They're supposed to be going into a hot dance number, but as he tightly grabs her hand, he slumps to the floor, dead of a heart attack. **11** "What's going on here?" is the only line spoken by José Ferrer, making his Broadway debut as the Second Policeman in *A Slight Case of Murder*. **11** Showgirl Evelyn Hoey, who was in the 1929 *50 Million Frenchmen* and later popularized the Cole Porter song "What Is This Thing Called Love?" is either shot by Henry H. Rogers, Jr., heir to an oil fortune, or commits suicide. On September 24, a coroner's jury will deliver an open verdict—no decision. **23** Lynn Fontanne tears cartilage in her knee when she slips while playing *The Taming of the Shrew* in Philadelphia. She will continue the run with her leg in a cast and use a wheelchair offstage.

NOVEMBER 12 Eugene O'Neill is the second American and the first American playwright to win the Nobel Prize for Literature. Sinclair Lewis won it in 1930. O'Neill says that he will use the money—$40,000—to pay his taxes. **23** Playwright Clare Boothe marries *Time* publisher Henry Luce just two days after her first play *Abide with Me* opened and was savaged by the critics. Yesterday, Boothe, Luce, and a *Time* theatre critic consulted on how the magazine's review should handle her disaster. She suggested "lousy"

Plays and Musicals

SEPTEMBER 26 *Winterset* (195), Maxwell Anderson's blank verse rendering of the aftermath of the Sacco-Vanzetti case, opens at the Martin Beck. Burgess Meredith, the actress known as Margo (in her Broadway debut), Richard Bennett, and Eduardo Ciannelli star. The bleak urban sets were designed by Jo Mielziner.

OCTOBER 10 George and Ira Gershwin's *Porgy and Bess* (124)—"socko folk opera," *Variety* calls it—opens at the Alvin. *The New York Times* music critic, Olin Downs, who refers in passing to the well known "instinct of Negroes to dance," is sure that "many of the songs in the score . . . will reap a quick popularity." The paper's drama critic also reviews the production, based on DuBose and Dorothy Heyward's 1927 play. It stars Todd Duncan and Anne Brown, with John Bubbles and Warren Coleman. **12** Cole Porter's "Begin the Beguine" and "It Was Just One of Those Things" debut at the Imperial in *Jubilee* (169), with a book by Moss Hart. Melville Cooper and Mary Boland play a king and queen who would like a rest from being royal—and get it. The young prince is 14-year-old Montgomery Clift. **24** Langston Hughes's *Mulatto* (373), a drama of miscegenation in the Old South starring Rose McClendon, opens at the Vanderbilt. **28** Producer Norman Bel Geddes's vividly realistic set is a promi-

Burgess Meredith MSN

Business and Society

JUNE • New York City enacts a law permitting legitimate theatre performances on Sundays. • With the NRA and its industrial codes invalidated by the Supreme Court, Actors Equity formally codifies the minimum wages that the theatre code had set up.

JULY • The Actors Equity Council rules that, beginning September 1, the principals in all shows must be paid $20 a week for rehearsals. **5** President Roosevelt signs the American National Theatre and Academy bill, providing for a self-supporting national theatre. Little will come of it until ANTA becomes an ongoing concern in 1950. **26** Hallie Flanagan, who heads the experimental theatre program at Vassar, becomes head of the Federal Theatre Project of the WPA.

AUGUST • The $3 million just allocated to the WPA's Federal Theatre Project triples its budget and will result in a widely expanded program. **6** Actors Equity announces that its membership has approved Sunday legitimate theatre performances but only if performers receive a quarter of their weekly salaries for the

Births, Deaths, and Marriages

JUNE 15 Robert E. Sherwood m. Madeleine Connelly, former wife of playwright Marc Connelly. **19** Helen Morgan divorces Bud Maschke, Jr., accusing him of threatening to kill her after they separated.

JULY 17 Diahann Carroll b.

AUGUST 15 Will Rogers d. in an Alaskan plane crash. W.C. Fields will write of him: "I was with him for years in the Follies and he did an entirely different monologue every night, a thing I have never known in my 37 years of trouping." He also says that "Rogers was the nearest thing to Lincoln that I have ever known." **15** Jim Dale (Jim Smith) b.

SEPTEMBER 16 Director-actor Joseph Chaiken b. **18** Gladys George m. actor Leonard Penn. **23** De Wolfe Hopper,

and "stinking," but Luce just has the piece refer to the show's "tedious psychiatry."

DECEMBER 12 Alla Nazimova, opening in Ibsen's *Ghosts* at the Empire in a six-week engagement, receives 21 curtain calls. **17** Broadway columnist and critic Walter Winchell is attacked by two men outside a theatre district barber shop. Their motive is not clear, although many people hate Winchell.

JANUARY • Broadway columnist Mark Hellinger becomes a producer. **13** According to an Associated Press dispatch, Noel Coward "is very annoyed at reports linking him in a romance in Sweden with Greta Garbo." The playwright's spokesperson states: "Mr. Coward is only interested in art."

FEBRUARY • Alfred Lunt is taking dancing lessons for the hoofing he will do in the upcoming *Idiot's Delight*. The *New York Post* is also claiming that he's taking singing lessons—from Sophie Tucker. **3** Fanny Brice's laryngitis closes down *The Ziegfeld Follies* for several days, which can't go on without her.

MARCH • Ethel Barrymore breaks her shoulder in a fall. • Benny Fields and Blossom Seeley file for bankruptcy. **3** Katharine Cornell, not known to miss performances due to illness, can't open in *Saint Joan* at the Martin Beck because she has lost her voice. **17** Rudy Vallee has

Helen Hayes MSN

nent feature of Sidney Kingsley's *Dead End* (684), at the Belasco. Rich and poor live across the street from one another in this drama. In the cast are Theodore Newton, Elspeth Eric, Joseph Downing, Marjorie Main, and the "Dead End kids"—Leo Gorcey, Billy Halop, Huntz Hall, Bobby Jordan, and Gabriel Dell. Dan Duryea has his first Broadway role, and two of the street kids are Sidney Lumet and Bernard Zanville (later the movies' Dane Clark). It's filmed in 1937.

NOVEMBER 16 *Jumbo* (233), Billy Rose's circus musical, at the Hippodrome, stars Jimmy Durante. Rodgers and Hart's music includes "The Most Beautiful Girl in the World" and "The Circus Is On Parade." The book is by Ben Hecht and Charles MacArthur, and George Abbott is directing his first musical.

> **Sheriff to Durante, who is trying to sneak an elephant past him:** "Where are you going with that elephant?"
> **Durante:** "What elephant?"

27 Bella and Sam Spewack's send-up of Hollywood, *Boy Meets Girl* (669), at the Cort, is directed by George Abbott and stars Jerome Cowan and Allyn Joslyn. It's on the screen in 1938.

DECEMBER 26 Helen Hayes has her most famous role, the queen in Lawrence Housman's *Victoria Regina* (517), at the Broadhurst. Vincent Price plays Prince Albert, a role he originated in the London production. Onstage, Hayes ages from 18 to 80 and plays Queen Victoria with a slight German accent. It is after this play that Hayes will begin to be called "The First Lady of the American Theatre."

JANUARY 21 Owen and Donald Davis's dramatization of Edith Wharton's *Ethan Frome* (119) is at the National, where, *Times* critic Brooks Atkinson writes, the acting of Raymond Massey, Pauline Lord, and Ruth Gordon will "make your heart stand still." Tom Ewell is also in the cast. **30** *The Ziegfeld Follies of 1936* (115), at the Winter Garden, will be suspended in May when star Fanny Brice has to drop out with severe neuritis and will then give an additional 112 perfor-

day, thus effectively killing the idea.

OCTOBER • Elmer Rice is appointed New York Regional Director of the WPA Federal Theatre Project. **22** Perennially dissatisfied with the selection of the jury that awards the Pulitzer Prize for Drama, New York theatre critics form the New York Drama Critics Circle to give out their own award. **27** Elmer Rice, head of the New York area Federal Theatre Project, announces the approval of several production units, including the "Living Newspaper" and the Negro Theatre of Harlem, sponsored by the Urban League and directed by John Houseman. Eva Le Gallienne and producer John Golden will not participate, believing that productions won't be up to par.

DECEMBER • The League of New York Theatres protests as unfair competition plans by the Federal Theatre Projects to produce plays on Broadway. **20** A heated discussion at the Actors Equity meeting at the Hotel Astor on the issue of wages to actors in the Federal Theatre Project leads to a fistfight.

JANUARY 23 Playwright Elmer Rice quits as New York Regional Director of the Federal Theatre Project over the issue of censorship. The "Living Newspaper" is

who was on the stage for 57 years, d.

OCTOBER 1 Julie Andrews (Julia Wells) b. **7** Francis Wilson, first president of Actors Equity, d. **17** Gretchen Cryer (Gretchen Kiger) b. **20** Jerry Orbach b.

JANUARY 2 Lyricist Harry B. Smith d. **10** Burgess Meredith m. actress Margaret Perry (Margaret Frueauff), daughter of Antoinette Perry Freuauff, after whom the Tony Awards will be named. The match lasts two years.

FEBRUARY 7 O.P. Heggie d. **17** Alexander Pantages d.

MARCH 23 Paul McCullough, who teamed with Bobby Clark for 31 years in the comedy team of Clark and McCullough, commits suicide.

APRIL 7 Marilyn Miller d. **11** Musical comedy star George Metaxa m. Byrnece McFadden Muckerman, daughter of mag-

Personalities

words with producer George White, who wants to cut his and everyone else's salary in the current edition of the *Scandals*. They exchange punches, and Vallee will leave the show on March 20. **18** A flood in Pittsburgh forces some members of the *Idiot's Delight* company, in town for a pre-Broadway run, to row to the theatre on opening night. After two evenings and a matinée, the play will shut down, with the Lunts barely able to make their way back to New York.

APRIL 6 Receiving the first Drama Critics Circle award, for *Winterset*, Maxwell Anderson lashes out at the Pulitzer Prize for Drama, which he won two years ago, "because the final authority of its presentation rests with a committee that is aware only dimly and at second hand of what occurs in the theatres of Broadway."

MAY 8 Fanny Brice leaves *The Ziegfeld Follies* because of painful neuritis in her arm.

Plays and Musicals

mances, beginning September 14. Bob Hope sings the new Vernon Duke–Ira Gershwin song, "I Can't get Started," to Eve Arden, and also in the cast are Josephine Baker and Judy Canova. When the show reopens, Bobby Clark replaces Hope, and Gypsy Rose Lee joins the cast.

MARCH 14 The first "Living Newspaper" playlet *Triple A Plowed Under* (85), running slightly more than a half hour, opens at the Biltmore. A scene depicting Communist party leader Earl Browder brings charges of "Communism" against the WPA Federal Theatre Project. The show was produced in conjunction with the Newspaper Guild. **20** The Federal Theatre Project presents T.S. Eliot's verse play *Murder in the Cathedral* (38)—"severely beautiful," says the *Times*—at the Manhattan Theatre. This drama about the martyrdom of St. Thomas à Becket premiered in London last year and has been presented at Yale. Henry Irvine plays Becket. **24** *Idiot's Delight* (299), by Robert E. Sherwood, opens at the Shubert. Alfred Lunt and Lynn Fontanne star in this antifascist, Pulitzer Prize-winning comedy set in an Italian hotel.

APRIL 9 The Negro Theater unit of the Federal Theatre Project performs *Macbeth* (56), Orson Welles's first directing job, at the Lafayette Theatre in Harlem, with a cast that includes Jack Carter and Edna Thomas. Welles has placed the action in nineteenth-century Haiti, leading some to call this the "voodoo" *Macbeth.* **11** Rodgers and Hart's *On Your Toes* (315) opens at the Imperial. Ray Bolger and Tamara Geva star, with Monty Woolley and Luella Gear. Bolger dances George Balanchine's "Slaughter on Tenth Avenue" ballet. "There's a Small Hotel" comes from this show.

MAY 19 The second edition of Leonard Sillman's *New Faces* (192) features the Broadway debut of dancer and future movie star Van Johnson. It's at the Vanderbilt.

Business and Society

not to portray any top foreign government officials. The first production, now postponed, was to have depicted Mussolini and Ethiopian Emperor Halle Selassie.

APRIL 26 Senator Davis of Pennsylvania attacks the WPA Theatre Project for what he calls "alleged Communistic activities within it." He also goes after Hallie Flanagan for her praise of Russia. **29** "B'Way Losing Its Lure: Kids Now Prefer H'Wood Instead," is *Variety*'s page one headline.

MAY 3 Seven Hollywood film studios set up the Bureau of New Plays, headed by Theresa Helbrun of the Theatre Guild. The organization offers scholarships to young playwrights, who will submit their work in a play contest. The studios get first crack at their plays. **11** The Dramatists Guild and the producers reach agreement on a new contract that will give writers 60 percent of the sale price of plays sold to Hollywood and will allow them to retain the rights to their work.

Births, Deaths, and Marriages

azine publisher Bernarr McFadden. *Herald-Tribune* theatre critic Percy Hammond d.

MAY 9 Albert Finney b. Louis Gossett b.

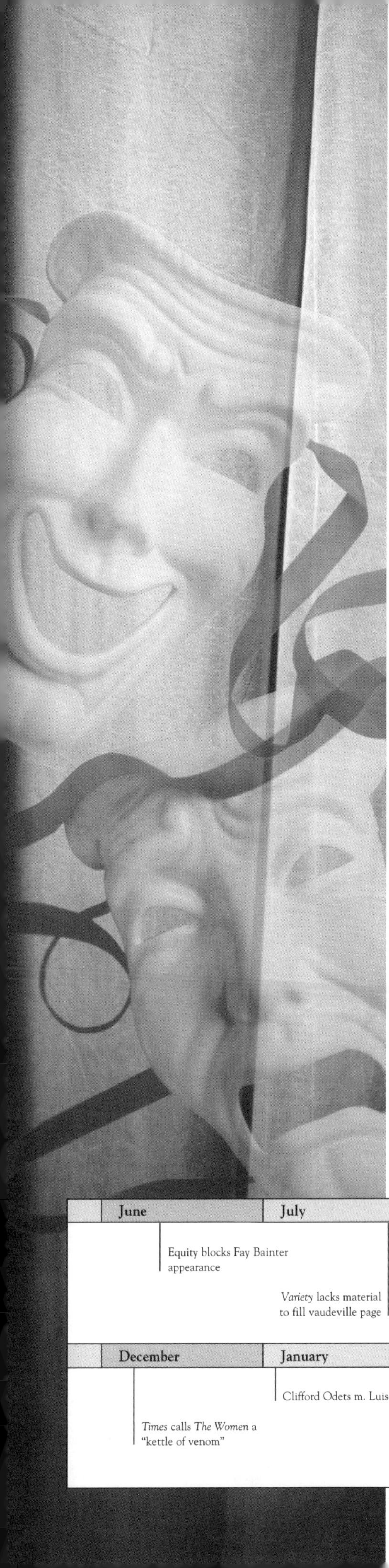

1936–37

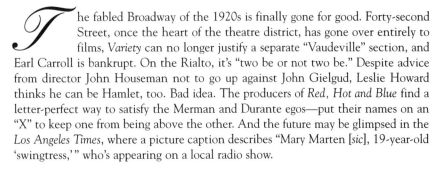

The fabled Broadway of the 1920s is finally gone for good. Forty-second Street, once the heart of the theatre district, has gone over entirely to films, *Variety* can no longer justify a separate "Vaudeville" section, and Earl Carroll is bankrupt. On the Rialto, it's "two be or not two be." Despite advice from director John Houseman not to go up against John Gielgud, Leslie Howard thinks he can be Hamlet, too. Bad idea. The producers of *Red, Hot and Blue* find a letter-perfect way to satisfy the Merman and Durante egos—put their names on an "X" to keep one from being above the other. And the future may be glimpsed in the *Los Angeles Times*, where a picture caption describes "Mary Marten [*sic*], 19-year-old 'swingtress,'" who's appearing on a local radio show.

- What one paper suggests for the new title of *Idiot's Delight* when it plays in Omaha, where the mayor has asked that it be censored: "Idiot's Delete"
- Size of national weekly audience for Federal Theatre Project productions: 500,000, according to the WPA
- Top ticket price for Federal Theatre Project production of Sinclair Lewis's *It Can't Happen Here*: $.55
- Bankrupt Earl Carroll's listed liabilities: $983,892
- Bankrupt Earl Carroll's listed assets: $410,646
- Fear expressed in the will of actor William Gillette, who dies April 29, 1937: that his estate will fall into the hands of some "blithering saphead"
- Length of John Gielgud's *Hamlet* (2 acts): 3 hours and 14 minutes
- Length of John Barrymore's 1922 *Hamlet* (3 acts): 3 hours and 25 minutes
- What Blossom Seeley says about retiring from show business, now that husband Benny Fields is a big hit: "You don't have to be in show business to know that a husband must be the headliner. Second billing is good enough for the wife."
- Whom Cole Porter escorts to the opening of *Red, Hot and Blue!*: Mary Pickford and Merle Oberon
- Cost of staging Rodgers and Hart's *Babes in Arms*: $55,000
- *Babes in Arms* box office gross: $474,000
- Number of Theatre Guild performances given by Dudley Digges: 3,000
- Number of Theatre Guild plays in which Dudley Digges has appeared: 23
- *Variety*, on Gypsy Rose Lee, making her Broadway debut in *The Ziegfeld Follies*: "Her strip tease specialty is rather decorous but it rings the bell."
- College student winning Bureau of New Plays scholarship for promising young playwrights: Arthur Miller

Productions on Broadway: 118

Pulitzer Prize for Drama: *You Can't Take It With You* (George S. Kaufman and Moss Hart)

New York Drama Critics Circle Award:
Best American Play: *High Tor* (Maxwell Anderson)

June	July	August	September	October	November
Equity blocks Fay Bainter appearance	*Variety* lacks material to fill vaudeville page	George S. Kaufman plagued by Mary Astor diary	*Hamlet* swordplay cuts John Gielgud	"X" marks the spot for Merman and Durante	Shirley Booth a star

December	January	February	March	April	May
Times calls *The Women* a "kettle of venom"	Clifford Odets m. Luise Rainer	College student Arthur Miller wins prize	Noel Coward suffers "nervous exhaustion"	Rodgers and Hart's *Babes in Arms*	Forty-second Street falls to films

Personalities

JUNE 22 Fay Bainter, who joined the Actors Fidelity League in 1919 when it opposed Actors Equity in the great strike of that year, is denied permission by Equity to open in a summer stock production of *Caprice*. She has never joined Equity.

JULY 19 Under a photograph of an attractive young woman, the *Los Angeles Times* caption reads: "Dial KHJ at 7 P.M. today and you'll hear Mary Marten [*sic*], 19-year-old 'swingtress' in a program of song novelties. The auburn-haired, brown-eyed miss hails from Wetherford, Tex, where she began her professional career as a dancer." **31** Actress and director Margaret Webster fractures her collarbone in an auto accident in England.

AUGUST • *New York Times* theatre critic Brooks Atkinson begins a two-month tour of theatres in the Soviet Union. **10** Eugene O'Neill informs the Theatre Guild that he has completed two dramas of the six-play cycle he has worked on for several years. **16** George S. Kaufman calls a press conference to respond to the gossip created by the publication of excerpts from film star Mary Astor's diary, including accounts of her torrid affair with the playwright. Kaufman's wife Beatrice, herself a playwright and fiction editor of *Harper's Bazaar*, is traveling in Europe with Irving Berlin and his wife.

SEPTEMBER 7 Vaudevillian Elsie Janis begins to auction the contents of her Tarrytown, New York, estate. She claims it's to raise money for charity, but her friends say that she needs the money. **24** John Gielgud's rehearsal of the swordplay in *Hamlet* is too real, sending him to the hospital with a wrist wound.

OCTOBER 7 Maurice Evans's name is up in lights on Broadway the day after opening to acclaim as Napoleon in *St. Helena.* **8** Showman Earl Carroll files for bankruptcy.

NOVEMBER • After playing in *Three Men on a Horse* on Broadway for two years, Shirley Booth is finally given star billing. • Lawyer Joseph S. Robinson charges

Plays and Musicals

OCTOBER 8 The first of the season's two *Hamlets* is at the Empire, starring John Gielgud in an acclaimed performance, directed by Guthrie McClintic. Judith Anderson is Gertrude, and Lillian Gish is Ophelia. Gielgud's 132 performances break the record set by John Barrymore. **22** *Stage Door* (169), George S. Kaufman and Edna Ferber's backstage comedy-drama, set in a theatrical boarding house, opens at the Music Box. Margaret Sullavan, offstage a former Broadway star now in the movies, plays a stage actress determined not to be tempted by Hollywood. A film version is released in 1937. **27** The WPA Federal Theatre Project's first production by a name author, Sinclair Lewis's *It Can't Happen Here* (95), opens simultaneously in 21 theatres in 18 cities, including at the Adelphi in New York. *Variety* says that "if viewed as a show selling at $.55 top and for the purpose of keeping unemployed actors from going hungry, it's very good; if viewed as the newest play of a Nobel prize winning writer, it's very bad." **29** Cole Porter's *Red, Hot and Blue* (183) is at the Alvin. For its two stars, "X" marks the spot—neither Ethel Merman nor Jimmy Durante will grant the other top billing, so their names are arranged in print on an "X." Costar Bob Hope is not yet big enough to insist on a "Y." Vivian Vance is also in the cast. Songs include "It's De-Lovely" and "Ridin' High." The book, by Howard Lindsay and Russel Crouse, has a running gag about the search for a former sweetheart who has a scar on her cheek, and they don't mean her face.

NOVEMBER 10 Leslie Howard is, indeed, a melancholy Dane, competing with John Gielgud's bravura performance in *Hamlet.* Howard's version (39), at the Imperial, choreographed by Agnes DeMille, with incidental music by Virgil Thompson, costs $75,000, almost twice what Gielgud's did. Howard begins his curtain speech tonight with a diffident, "Well, here we are. . . ." **19** The Group Theatre's production of Paul Green's *Johnny Johnson* (68), a pacifist political satire with Kurt Weill's first Broadway score ("Johnny's Song"), opens at the Forty-fourth Street Theatre. Lee

Business and Society

JULY 15 *Variety* merges its "[v]audeville" and "[n]ite-[c]lubs" sections, explaining that "the vaudeville department has lately been particularly difficult to fill up."

JANUARY • Actors Equity begins to require all applicants for membership to have a name different from anyone who is already a member.

APRIL • More than a decade after the large movie houses in Times Square were air-cooled, several legitimate theatres with hit shows are rushing to become "air-conditioned" by this summer, so they won't have to give up playing dates to the heat. Among them are the Booth (*You Can't Take it With You*), the Plymouth (*Tovarich*), and the Barrymore (*The Women*).

MAY • The Dry Dock Savings Bank, which controls the New Amsterdam Theatre, former home of *The Ziegfeld Follies* and the last legitimate theatre on Forty-second street, sells it to picture interests. • The contract signed by the Dramatists Guild last year, giving playwrights 60 percent of the sale of picture rights, is being blamed by authors who are not at the top of the heap for the decrease in Hollywood involvement in backing new shows. The

Births, Deaths, and Marriages

JUNE 14 Producer Marc Klaw d. **20** Playwright S.N. Behrman m. Elza Heifitz Stone, sister of violinist Jascha Heifitz. Her 10-year-old daughter Barbara, by a previous marriage, will marry *New York Times* reporter and editor Arthur Gelb, with whom she will coauthor a major biography of Eugene O'Neill.

NOVEMBER 15 Agent-producer Leland Hayward m. film star Margaret Sullavan.

DECEMBER 10 Playwright Luigi Pirandello d.

JANUARY 8 Clifford Odets m. film star Luise Rainer. **13** Director Richard Boleslavski d. **30** Vanessa Redgrave b.

APRIL 13 Playwright Lanford Wilson b. **27** Sandy Dennis b. **29** William Gillette,

that Bert Lahr is trying to steal his wife, showgirl Mildred Schroeder. Lahr had been romancing her, they quarreled, and she married Robinson on the rebound. Schroeder separated from her husband shortly after the marriage.

DECEMBER • Some members of the Group Theatre warn that the failure of *Johnny Johnson* shows that "the original opiate and dream of the group is wearing off, habits are forming, people are growing older and more firmly rooted, etc. etc. The hour of crisis impends." Specifically, they note that "perhaps in an attempt to get the spontaneous quality that *Waiting for Lefty* had in its first few performances, Lee [Strasberg] has taken to leaving the actors more and more to seek their own problems and find their own solutions." **11** At an Actors Fund benefit performance, Noel Coward and Gertrude Lawrence are wearing red Harpo Marx wigs. Spotting critic Alexander Woollcott down front in the audience sporting the same wig as a gag to throw them off, they acknowledge him with a smile but don't skip a beat.

JANUARY • Stella Adler leaves the group Theatre to work in Hollywood. • Russel Crouse resigns as the Theatre Guild press agent to devote himself full-time to playwriting. **7** Lotte Lenya makes her New York debut in *The Eternal Road*, directed by Max Reinhardt.

FEBRUARY • Clare Boothe Luce, wife of *Time* magazine publisher Henry Luce, donates all the royalties from her play *The Women* to the Authors League Fund and other causes. **1** The Bureau of New Plays, established last year to award scholarships to promising young playwrights, today announces its first winners. Among them, in the "social relations" category of plays, is Arthur Miller, a student at the University of Michigan, whose work is called *They, Too Arise*. **8** In a *New York Herald-Tribune* interview, Theresa Helburn, Executive Director of the Theatre Guild, says that the Guild's audience, predominantly female, wants plays about romance, not ideas. She offers as an example *Strange Interlude*. "It showed the dream lover, the husband, the romantic lover and the

---

Strasberg directs a cast that includes Russell Collins, Robert Lewis, Sanford Meisner, Lee J. Cobb, Elia Kazan, Albert Van Dekker (he drops the "Van" in films), Luther Adler, Paula Miller, and Jules [John] Garfield. One backer of this left-wing drama is millionaire Jock Whitney.

DECEMBER 14 George S. Kaufman and Moss Hart's hymn to eccentricity, *You Can't Take It With You* (837), is at the Booth. The oddball Vanderhoff clan is headed by Henry Travers, with Josephine Hull, Frank Wilcox, George Heller, Margo Stevenson, George Tobias, and Oscar Polk. Frank Capra's film comes in 1938. **16** With George Abbott's direction and a youthful cast headed by Eddie Albert, José Ferrer, and Frank Albertson, *Brother Rat* (575), by John Monks, Jr. and Fred Finklehoffe, is a comedy hit at the Biltmore. The 1938 film stars Ronald Reagan. **23** Katharine Cornell produces and stars in Maxwell Anderson's *The Wingless Victory* (110), opening at the Empire. She's the dark-skinned, Asian bride of a New England sea captain who kills herself and their children when his family cannot accept her. **26** Clare Booth's *The Women* (657)—"The Girls" and "The Ladies" were earlier titles—an acerbic comedy with an all-female cast, in which a virgin refers to herself as "a frozen asset," opens at the Barrymore. Ilka Chase, Margalo Gillmore, Phyllis Povah, Arlene Francis, Marjorie Main, and Audrey Christie are among the women. Atkinson, in the *Times*, calls it a "kettle of venom." The film is released in 1939.

JANUARY 8 Orson Welles and John Houseman stage Christopher Marlowe's *Dr. Faustus* (128) for Project 891 of the Federal Theatre, at Maxine Elliott's Theatre. Welles directs. **9** Maxwell Anderson's *High Tor* (171) opens at the Martin Beck. Burgess Meredith stars, and Peggy Ashcroft makes her Broadway debut. Hume Cronyn is also in the cast of this play that mixes fantasy and reality and drama and comedy, in a story set in the Hudson River Valley.

FEBRUARY 5 Maurice Evans stars in Shakespeare's *Richard II* (132), directed by Margaret Webster, at the St. James.

---

studios resent the split. **16** A rally at the New Amsterdam Theatre protests the Dunnigan Bill, just passed by the New York State Legislature, which would give license commissioners sole discretion in censoring plays. Helen Hayes, addressing the group, effects the regal style of Queen Victoria, whom she is playing on Broadway, and says of the bill: "We are not amused." Governor Lehman, in fact, will veto it. **18** The Mayor of Omaha demands that the *Idiot's Delight* company censor some of the language and one reference to his city before the play goes on tonight. He backs off only when a prominent churchman says he's being silly. One New York paper says of the tempest that the show should be called "Idiot's Delete."

---

famous for his portrayal of Sherlock Holmes, d. His will exhorts his executors to keep his estate from falling into the hands of some "blithering saphead." **30** Philip Merivale m. actress Gladys Cooper. They are in the cast of *Close Quarters*, now playing in Chicago.

MAY 10 Playwright Arthur Kopit b. **18** Judith Anderson m. Benjamin Lehman.

Personalities

father-friend—and a woman wants all four." She also bemoans the lack of women playwrights. **18** Too ill from his recent appendectomy to travel to Stockholm to accept the Nobel Prize, Eugene O'Neill receives the medal and the check in his Oakland, California, hospital room. **28** James Barton of the cast of *Tobacco Road* has to ad-lib when Maude Odell does not make her entrance. She just dropped dead in her dressing room.

MARCH 7 Noel Coward cancels the remaining performances of *Tonight at Eight-Thirty* because he's suffering from

Gertrude Lawrence and Noel Coward MSN

Plays and Musicals

Evans, whose performance receives an ovation tonight, has gone on despite an abscessed tooth. **9** In Mark Reed's comedy *Yes, My Darling Daughter* (404), at the Playhouse, marriage solves everything. Peggy Conklin, Lucile Watson, and Boyd Crawford star. There's a film version in 1939. **20** Arthur Kober's *Having Wonderful Time* (310) opens at the Lyceum. Jules [John] Garfield, Katherine Locke, and Sheldon Leonard star in this comedy about romance at a mountain resort, which becomes the 1952 musical *Wish You Were Here*.

APRIL 14 Rodgers and Hart's *Babes in Arms* (289) opens at the Shubert. Songs include "The Lady Is a Tramp," "I Wish I Were in Love Again," "Where or When," "My Funny Valentine," and "Johnny One Note." Mitzi Green, Wynn Murray, the Nicholas Brothers, and Ray Heatherton star, Alfred Drake and Dan Dailey are two of the chorus boys, and George

Business and Society

Births, Deaths, and Marriages

"nervous exhaustion." **13** The resumption of the producing partnership between George M. Cohan and Sam Harris, after a gap of 15 years, is short-lived when their *Fulton of Oak Falls*, starring Cohan, flops, losing $35,000. **29** Dudley Digges, in *The Masque of Kings*, gives his 3000th Theatre Guild performance. He's playing the Emperor Franz Josef in his 23rd Guild play. "What the hell do I know about Franz Josef?" the modest Digges says. "Very little. I do the best I can."

APRIL • Cheryl Crawford leaves the Group Theatre, many of whose members have gone to Hollywood. **3** Katharine Hepburn ends a three-month pre-Broadway tour of the Theatre Guild's production of *Jane Eyre*. Attendance has been good because of its star, but the Guild is not happy with Helen Jerome's adaptation, and she refuses to make any more changes in the script.

MAY • The Gramaphone Shop in New York City advertises: "Private Recordings of Four Rabelaisian Songs Exclusively for Gramophone by Beatrice Lillie." They include: "He Was a Gentleman," "I'm a Campfire Girl," "Snoops, the Lawyer," and "There are Fairies at the Bottom of My Garden." **5** According to *Variety*, "Statements in the dailies that Vincent Price, leading man of *Victoria Regina*, has been signed for pix are 'premature.'"

Balanchine stages Broadway's first "dream" ballet. The 1939 Mickey Rooney–Judy Garland film dispenses with most of the music.

MAY 19 *Room Service* (496), by John Murray and Alan Boretz, the rapid-fire comedy directed by George Abbott, on which next year's Marx Brothers film will be based, opens at the Cort. Sam Levene stars, with Philip Loeb and Eddie Albert.

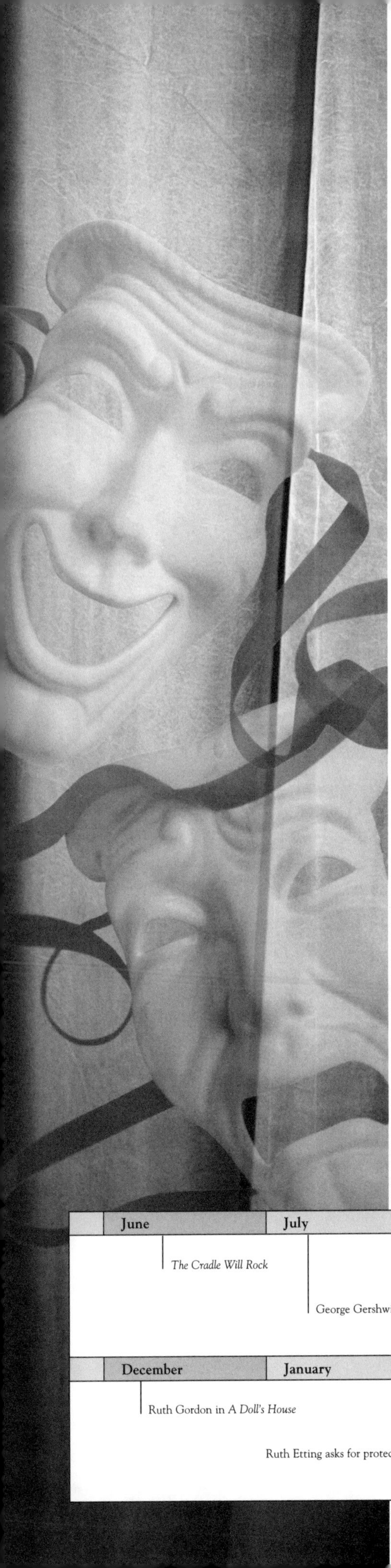

1937–38

With charges of "communism" causing cutbacks in the Federal Theatre Program, cast and audience at *The Cradle Will Rock*'s opening have to take a walk to a backup theatre. In *I'd Rather Be Right*, George M. Cohan plays President Roosevelt, a man he hates; Eva Le Gallienne plays Hamlet, which the critics hate; and Tallulah Bankhead's attempt to play Cleopatra is snakebit. *Our Town* survives a shaky start, The Mercury Theatre and Uta Hagen debut, while Rachel Crothers's long and productive career as a Broadway playwright ends with *Susan and God*. Cole Porter sustains injuries that will plague him for the rest of his life, and George Gershwin is dead at age 38.

- Total Theatre Guild subscriptions in all cities: 100,000
- Number of plays by Rachel Crothers, "the Neil Simon of her day," as the *Times* will later characterize her, that have been produced on Broadway since 1906: 28
- Titles considered and rejected by Clifford Odets for *Golden Boy*: "A Cockeyed Wonder," "Golden Gloves," and "The Manly Art"
- Actors Equity status of *Pins and Needles*, the musical about garment workers: it's non-Equity when it opens because it's nonprofit, with a top of $1.50
- Cost of renting the Venice Theatre when *The Cradle Will Rock* is denied Maxine Elliott's Theatre on opening night: $100
- Number of people in the audience who walk with the cast of *The Cradle Will Rock* from Maxine Elliott's Theatre to the Venice: about 100
- Statistics for Helen Hayes's tour in *Victoria Regina*, September 16 to June 25: plays in 47 cities, 25 states and two Canadian provinces, travels 10,000-plus miles, and grosses about $1,200,000
- Minimum Broadway wage for chorus girls and boys: $35 a week

Productions on Broadway: 111

Pulitzer Prize for Drama: *Our Town* (Thornton Wilder)

New York Drama Critics Circle:
Best American Play: *Of Mice and Men* (John Steinbeck)
Best Foreign Play: *Shadow and Substance* (Paul Vincent Carroll)

June	July	August	September	October	November
The Cradle Will Rock	George Gershwin d.	Eva Le Gallienne plays Hamlet	Someone bombs at the Cleveland Play House	Cole Porter thrown from horse	*Golden Boy* and the Mercury Theatre

December	January	February	March	April	May
Ruth Gordon in *A Doll's House*	Ruth Etting asks for protection	*Our Town*	Uta Hagen's Broadway debut	Eleanor Roosevelt as theatre critic	"Spring Is Here" in *I Married An Angel*

Personalities

AUGUST 23 Eva Le Gallienne plays the lead in *Hamlet*—Sarah Bernhardt once essayed it—in summer stock at the Cape Playhouse in Dennis, Massachusetts. *The New York Times* finds her Danish prince "shrill and unmanly of voice, and pathetically ineffectual in those moments which call for vigorous assault." Also in the cast is Uta Hagen, "a decidedly Nordic young actress making her first professional appearance, as Ophelia. . . ."

OCTOBER 13 Noting that the widow of actor Osgood Perkins, who died last month, has planned a memorial service for him, *Variety* adds that "[a] five-year-old son also survives and emphasized a desire to be present." The child is Anthony Perkins, future film star. **24** Cole Porter is thrown from his horse while riding at a Glen Cove, Long Island, country club and sustains compound fractures in both legs when the animal falls on him. He will be in constant pain for the rest of his life, undergo more than 20 operations, and have a leg amputated in 1958.

NOVEMBER 1 Alfred Lunt is on the cover of *Life* in a scene from *Amphytrion 38*. **5** Jules Garfield, upset that Luther Adler and not he has been chosen for the lead role in the Group Theatre's *Golden Boy*, opening tonight, will go to Hollywood to begin a screen career as John Garfield. In 1952, he will play the boxer in *Golden Boy* on the stage in a successful revival. **10** Tallulah Bankhead's performance in *Antony and Cleopatra* tonight is less interesting than her reviews. John Mason Brown will report that she "barged down the aisle last night as Cleopatra—and sank," while George Jean Nathan crowns her "Queen of the Nil." **23** Robert E. Sherwood, Elmer Rice, and Maxwell Anderson decide to form a group of writers who will produce their own plays. Sherwood, who has just sent *Abe Lincoln in Illinois* to the typist, volunteers his work for the first production of what will become the Playwrights Company.

DECEMBER 26 Frederic March is hospitalized with blood poisoning in his leg, delaying the December 29 opening of *Yr.*

Plays and Musicals

JUNE 16 With an advance sale of 14,000 tickets, The Federal Theatre Project's first musical, Marc Blitzstein's *The Cradle Will Rock*, an anticapitalist satire about unionism in the steel industry, starring Howard Da Silva and Will Geer, is set to open at Maxine Elliott's Theatre. But a cut in the Project's funds—Congress is especially unhappy about subsidizing *this* show—cancels it. Director Orson Welles hastily arranges for an instant, 20-block transfer of cast and audience to the Venice theatre, where the cast will perform from the audience—to cope with union rules—accompanied by Blitzstein's piano from the stage. Welles and John Houseman will take the production into their new Mercury Theatre, reopening it on January 3 (104).

SEPTEMBER 29 Maxwell Anderson's fantasy *The Star Wagon* (223) opens at the Empire. Burgess Meredith is the inventor whose time machine allows him to relive his courtship of his wife, played by Lillian Gish, confirming that he made the right choice.

OCTOBER 7 Rachel Crothers's last Broadway play, *Susan and God* (288), probably the first Broadway show from which scenes will be televised—over the RCA-NBC station—opens at the Plymouth. Gertrude Lawrence stars—"her most incandescent performance," says the *Times*—as a superficial woman whose latest hobby is religion. The 1940 film stars Joan Crawford.

NOVEMBER 1 Alfred Lunt stars in *Amphytrion 38* (152), Jean Giradoux's comedy drawn from Greek legend about Jupiter's love for an earthly woman, at the Shubert. Lynn Fontanne, Sydney Greenstreet and George Meader costar. **2** Rodgers and Hart's *I'd Rather Be Right* (289), starring George M. Cohan—his leg in a cast because of an accident—opens at the Alvin. The book is by George S. Kaufman and Moss Hart. Cohan plays a man he actually hates, Franklin Delano Roosevelt. In the score is "Have You Met Miss Jones?" **4** The Group Theatre's most successful play, *Golden Boy* (250), Clifford Odets's boxing

Business and Society

JUNE • The WPA Federal Theatre Project, its budget cut by Congress, lays off 3,000 of its 11,700 employees nationwide. **26** A *Saturday Evening Post* editorial says "the Reds have taken over" the Federal Theatre Project. The magazine also charges that the agency's childrens' play, *The Revolt of the Beavers*, preaches class warfare.

SEPTEMBER 24 A bomb destroys part of the roof of the Cleveland Play House, where the stagehands union has recently protested the use of nonprofessionals to handle scenery.

NOVEMBER 9 Robert E. Sherwood is elected president of the Dramatists Guild.

DECEMBER 7 Frank Gillmore, who now heads the Associated Actors and Artists of America, the umbrella group for all performers' unions, resigns as president of Actors Equity. Burgess Meredith fills in as acting president.

JANUARY • Theatre people are complaining that U.S. Army Colonel Donald H. Connolly, who administers the WPA in Southern California, is censoring Federal Theatre Project plays that are pro-labor. **31** The United Scenic Artists voice

Births, Deaths, and Marriages

JUNE 29 Director JoAnne Akalaitas b.

JULY 3 Playwright Tom Stoppard (Thomas Straussler—his mother's maiden name is Stoppard) b. **11** George Gershwin, age 38, d. at Cedars of Lebanon Hospital in Los Angeles. Coincidentally, Jerome Kern is also there, recovering from a heart attack brought on by damage to his beloved Bluthner piano by moving men. Only when he hears Gershwin referred to on the radio in the past tense will Kern's family tell him about his friend's death.

AUGUST 8 Dustin Hoffman b. **13** Louise Hovick, a.k.a. Gypsy Rose Lee, m. Robert Mizzy. **31** Tallulah Bankhead m. actor John Emery. One New York paper headlines, "Broadway Agoggier Than Usual Over Tallulah's Wedding."

Obedient Husband, in which he stars with his wife, Florence Eldridge.

JANUARY 5 Ruth Etting asks the Los Angeles District Attorney to protect her against death threats from ex-husband Martin ("Moe the Gimp") Snyder. The New York City District Attorney, Thomas Dewey, asked by reporters if he will comply with requests from Los Angeles to look into Snyder's whereabouts, says: "I never comment on publicity stunts." **6** Phyllis Povah faints onstage during a performance of *The Women*, necessitating the ringing down of the curtain at the Barrymore. **12** Emulating the custom that originated with Grauman's Chinese Theater in Hollywood, the leads in *Between the Devil*, Jack Buchanan, Evelyn Lane and Adele Dixon, leave their footprints in wet cement outside Broadway's Imperial Theatre. **13** Playwright Jack Kirkland, unhappy with Richard Watts, Jr.'s panning of Kirkland's *Tortilla Flat*, which opened last night, seeks out the critic—his classmate at Columbia University—in a bar and punches him. Kirkland, in turn, is knocked down by the bar's owner. **14** The *New York Post* refers to Jessica Tandy, who opened on January 10 in J.B. Priestly's *Time and the Conways*, as "the newest little British stage star." **24** With *Our Town* tryouts going on in Princeton, New Jersey, Rosamond Pinchot, a production assistant and lover of the play's producer Jed Harris, commits suicide when Harris spurns her. She and Harris have both recently been high on Benzedrine.

FEBRUARY 2 *Our Town* has flopped in its Boston tryout, reports *Variety*: "It was to have remained two weeks in the Hub, but after a slimly attended debut performance there, business was reported so weak that the manager sought cancellation of the booking. . . ."

MARCH 3 Cole Porter's *You Never Know* opens for tryouts in New Haven. Libby Holman and Lupe Velez, the screen actress known as "the Mexican spitfire," do not get along, and during a curtain call at one performance, Velez punches Holman, blackening her eye. Their constant friction will cause the director to quit on August 30. **10** Orson Welles, as Brutus, begins his "I love Rome more" speech in the Mercury Theatre's produc-

drama, starring Luther Adler, opens at the Belasco. Harold Clurman directs a cast that also includes Morris Carnovsky, Frances Farmer, Karl Malden in his Broadway debut, Lee J. Cobb, Howard Da Silva, Phoebe Brand, Robert Lewis, and Martin Ritt. It's a 1939 film. **11** "The first really exciting event of the dramatic season turns out to be, of all things, a production of *Julius Caesar*," Richard Watts, Jr. writes in the *Herald-Tribune* of the Mercury Theatre's initial offering. Twenty-two-year-old Orson Welles, playing Brutus "in a blue-serge suit" (*Time*), stars at the Mercury Theatre (157), formerly the Comedy Theatre. Joseph Holland plays Caesar and Martin Gabel, Cassius. The actors play in street clothes against a mostly bare brick backdrop. **23** George S. Kaufman's stage adaptation of John Steinbeck's *Of Mice and Men* (207), starring Wallace Ford as George and Broderick Crawford as Lenny, opens at the Music Box. The film is released in 1939. **27** *Pins and Needles* (1,108), a production of the International Ladies Garment Workers Union, with Harold Rome's score, is at the former Princess Theatre, now the Labor Stage. The actors are ILGWU members. In the show, which keeps changing to advance the union cause, is "Sing Me a Song With Social Significance."

DECEMBER 27 Producer Jed Harris's revival of *A Doll's House* (142), at the Morosco, stars Ruth Gordon, with whom Harris has been romantically linked.

JANUARY 26 Julie Haydon and Cedric Hardwicke star in *Shadow And Substance* (206), a play by Paul Vincent Carroll that, says the *Times*, "glows like a cathedral window." This character study of a young woman and a priest was produced by the Abbey Theatre, from which the rights were secured by producer Eddie Dowling. It's at the John Golden.

FEBRUARY 3 Dudley Digges is a grandfather who holds off the angel of death by forcing him up a tree in Paul Osborne's *On Borrowed Time* (321), at the Longacre. It becomes a film in 1939. **4** Thornton Wilder's *Our Town* (336), produced and directed by Jed Harris, opens at Henry Miller's Theatre, switching next week to the Morosco. Frank Craven is the Stage

Tallulah Bankhead

their concern over the recent spate of bare-stage productions, typified by several Mercury Theatre offerings.

FEBRUARY 4 Despite its bare sets, the stagehands union has insisted on a full complement of workers when *Our Town* opens tonight. Producer Jed Harris, in turn, has hired them but insists that they don't touch anything.

MARCH 14 George Arliss calls for "crushing the [c]ommunists" in Actors Equity.

MAY • The Shubert and Longacre Theatres are being air-conditioned. • The WPA puts a limit of $1,000 a year on the amount that anyone in the Federal Theatre Project can earn. **27** Actor Arthur Bryon is elected president of Actors Equity.

SEPTEMBER 21 Osgood Perkins d. after the Washington, D.C., opening of the pre-Broadway tryout of *Susan and God*, in which he is costarring with Gertrude Lawrence. **29** Stage actors Cornel Wilde and Patricia Knight m.

OCTOBER 6 Lyricist Richard Maltby b. **11** Ron Leibman b. **16** Margo and Francis Lederer, who appear on stage and screen, m.

NOVEMBER 13 Mrs. Leslie Carter d. **21** Playwright Tina Howe, daughter of broadcaster Quincy Howe, b. **30** Ruth Etting divorces Martin ("Moe the Gimp") Snyder.

JANUARY 16 David Merrick, just out of

Personalities

tion of *Julius Caesar* when, suddenly, the rains come. Someone has turned on the theatre's sprinkler system, stopping the action until the ensuing flood can be stemmed. **22** Critic Brooks Atkinson, disappointed by Guido Nadzo's performance in *Spring Thaw*, evokes George S. Kaufman's put-down of the actor: "Nadzo Guido." **28** The *New York World-Telegram* speculates this afternoon, "Anyone would take your wager that the Lunts will triumph tonight in *The Sea Gull*, but a host of playgoers wonder what the show will do for Uta Hagen, who is portraying 'Nina.'" The role has been a star maker in the past. Hagen makes her Broadway debut tonight at the Shubert.

APRIL • First Lady and newspaper columnist Eleanor Roosevelt draws Alexander Woollcott's ire for calling *Our Town* "depressing" and is taken to task by *Times* critic Brooks Atkinson, who feels that a broadside she fired at reviewers of *Save Me the Waltz*—he called it "hackneyed hokum"—was aimed mostly at him. **6** Joseph Holland, playing the title role in the Mercury Theatre's production of *Julius Caesar*, receives the unkindest cut of all in the death scene when he is accidentally stabbed in the arm. When he says, "Et tu, Brute! Then fall, Caesar!" he drops to the floor bleeding. No one notices the wound for almost 10 minutes, until the end of Act III. Then, he's taken to the hospital, where he will recover.

MAY 9 Under the gray whiskers on the cover of *Time* is George Orson Welles, who turned 23 a few days ago, made up for his role as the 88-year-old Captain in Shaw's *Heartbreak House*, the latest Mercury Theatre production. **19** Dudley Digges, usually a character actor, has his name raised above the title at the Longacre, where he's playing in the 126th performance of *On Borrowed Time*. It's his first time in lights on a Broadway marquee.

Plays and Musicals

Manager, Martha Scott is Emily, and John Craven, Franks's son, is George, in this drama of Grover's Corner, New Hampshire. Brooks Atkinson says it's "hauntingly beautiful," but Richard Watts, Jr. finds its "occasional outbursts of cosmic brooding," pretentious. It's on the screen in 1940.

MARCH 28 It's a triumph for the Lunts tonight in Chekhov's *The Sea Gull* (40), newly translated by Stark Young, at the Shubert for a limited run. Making their very successful Broadway debuts are Uta Hagen and, in an acting, not a directing, capacity, Margaret Webster.

APRIL 13 Ezra Stone, as the teenager "Henry Aldrich," whom he will popularize on the radio, opens in Clifford Goldsmith's comedy *What a Life* (538), at the Biltmore. Jackie Cooper is in the 1939 film.

MAY 11 "Spring Is Here" in Rodgers and Hart's *I Married an Angel* (338), at the Shubert. Dennis King plays a banker who gets his wish, embodied in the title. Vera Zorina, in her Broadway debut, is the angel, and Vivienne Segal plays King's sister. Josh Logan is directing his first musical. Zorina's dancing is choreographed by Georges Balanchine, later her offstage husband. The 1942 film is the last pairing of Nelson Eddy and Jeanette MacDonald.

Business and Society

Births, Deaths, and Marriages

law school, m. Leonore Beck, who has just come into an inheritance. Her money launches his producing career.

FEBRUARY 5 Playwright John Guare b.

MARCH 8 Playwright Edgar Smith d. **24** Agents Audrey Wood and William Liebling m.

1938–39

The Playwrights Company is in business, while the Federal Theatre Project is under siege. Play financing continues to evolve, with producers increasingly likely to put together syndicates of backers, or "angels," rather than come up with money themselves. Mary Martin arrives, a poll of theatre notables picks Helen Hayes as the greatest player, Katharine Hepburn owns a hot property in *The Philadelphia Story*, Orson Welles holds a hot potato in his radio production of *The War of the Worlds*, Raymond Massey is Abe Lincoln, Sardi's caters to *Hamlet*, Olsen and Johnson run amok in *Hellzapoppin*, and this season, it's Jane Cowl as Dolly Levi.

- Number of drinks consumed by 182 people at Dorothy Parker's party at the Hotel Algonquin in honor of the opening of Philip Barry's *Here Come the Clowns*: 732, and Parker neglects to pay the bill
- Back taxes owed by Ed Wynn: $174,166
- Whom Libby Holman hires to entertain at her 6-year-old's birthday party: Benny Goodman, Lionel Hampton, Teddy Wilson, Gene Krupa, and Billie Holliday
- Actresses who turned down *No Time for Comedy* before it was offered to Katharine Cornell: Gertrude Lawrence, Ina Claire, and Lynn Fontanne. Katharine Hepburn was also considered but rejected because she is too young
- Earn-back period for *The Little Foxes*: 5 weeks
- Composer of the music for "Never Too Weary to Pray," used in *The Little Foxes*: Meredith Willson
- Profit from the Broadway run of *Knickerbocker Holiday*: none—the black ink will come from road revenues
- Tennessee Williams's college grade in "Modern Drama": D
- Total assessed value of the 40 Broadway legitimate theatres: $30,000,000
- Singer for whom Cole Porter wrote "My Heart Belong's to Daddy": June Knight
- Amount that the government has spent on the Federal Theatre Project: $46,000,000
- Amount that the Federal Theatre Project has taken in at the box office: $2,000,000
- What Heywood Broun calls New York theatre critics: "so much suet pudding"

Productions on Broadway: 98, the first time this has dipped under 100 since the 1902–03 season

Pulitzer Prize for Drama: *Abe Lincoln in Illinois* (Robert E. Sherwood)

New York Drama Critics Circle Award:
Best American Play: none
Best Foreign Play: *The White Steed* (Paul Vincent Carroll)

June	July	August	September	October	November
Gertrude Lawrence on cover of *Life*	Playwrights Company incorporated	Tallulah Bankhead plays sex expert	Olsen and Johnson in *Hellzapoppin*	Walter Huston sings "September Song"	Mary Martin's Broadway debut

December	January	February	March	April	May
José Ferrer m. Uta Hagen	Brooks Atkinson backtracks on Ethel Waters	*The Little Foxes*	Tennessee Williams is runner-up in playwriting contest	*No Time for Comedy*	Ian McKellen b.

Personalities

JUNE 13 Gertrude Lawrence is on the cover of *Life*.

JULY 1 The Playwrights Company is incorporated. The artist-producers are Maxwell Anderson, S.N. Behrman, Sidney Howard, Elmer Rice, and Robert E. Sherwood. Also a member is lawyer John F. Wharton. **23** The *New York Sun* has polled 150 notables, most of them theatre people, to determine the stage's greatest players. Helen Hayes tops the list, followed by, in descending order, Katharine Cornell, the team of Alfred Lunt and Lynn Fontanne, Jeanne Eagels, John Barrymore, Maude Adams, Mrs. Fiske, John Gielgud, David Warfield, and Richard Mansfield.

AUGUST 5 Twenty-seven-year-old Tennessee Williams gets his B.A. in English. His average was pulled down by several D's, including one in Modern Drama. **18** Tallulah Bankhead is playing an author who is an authority on sex in *I Am Different*, opening at the Savoy Theatre in San Diego. Says *Variety*: "La Bankhead was never more Bankhead."

SEPTEMBER 15 Thornton Wilder replaces the vacationing Frank Craven in the role of the Stage Manager in the playwright's *Our Town* on Broadway, taking advantage of the opportunity to put back in some lines that producer Jed Harris had removed. This summer, Sinclair Lewis appeared in the dramatization of his novel *It Can't Happen Here*. Critic John Mason Brown prefers Wilder's acting to Lewis's. **21** For Ethel Barrymore, appearing in *Whiteoaks* at the Plymouth in Boston, the show must go on, despite the great New England hurricane. She needs 45 minutes to go seven blocks from her hotel to the theatre, and the curtain rises an hour late because the gap on the roof where the skylight blew off has to be covered. **26** Richard Rodgers and Lorenz Hart are on the cover of *Time*, celebrating their upcoming show, *The Boys from Syracuse*. **28** *Variety* reports that "Mary Martin, radio and nitery performer, is set for one of the leads in *I'm an American* [retitled *Leave It To Me!*]." She's

Plays and Musicals

SEPTEMBER 22 Ole Olsen and Chic Johnson star in *Hellzapoppin* (1,404), a raucous, nutty, landmark revue, opening at the Forty-sixth Street Theatre. With most of the critics ambivalent, Walter Winchell is the show's chief cheerleader. Ole and Chic are also in the 1941 film. **28** *Kiss the Boys Goodbye* (286), Clare Boothe's satire on the current search for an actress to play Scarlett O'Hara in *Gone With The Wind*, opens at the Henry Miller Theatre. It stars Helen Claire. Mary Martin is in a 1941 film version, a musical, in which the story is generalized into a typical backstage tale.

OCTOBER 10 Robert Morley is the star of *Oscar Wilde* (247), Leslie and Sewell Stokes's play about the author, at the Fulton. **12** Maurice Evans stars in Broadway's first uncut *Hamlet* (96), at the St. James (there had been a single unabridged presentation in the city at the turn of the century). Sardi's, just down the street, has a special buffet for the 30-minute dinner break during the four-and-a-half-hour-show. **15** Robert E. Sherwood's *Abe Lincoln in Illinois* (472), the Playwright Company's first production, opens at the Plymouth. Brooks Atkinson writes that Raymond Massey, as Lincoln, acts "with an artless honesty that is completely overwhelming at the end." He's also in the 1940 film. **19** *Knickerbocker Holiday* (168), directed by Joshua Logan, with book and lyrics by Maxwell Anderson and music by Kurt Weill, is at the Barrymore. Walter Huston, in his musical comedy debut, plays Peter Stuyvesant—Anderson's dictatorial governor of New Amsterdam resembles Franklin D. Roosevelt—singing Weill's "September Song."

NOVEMBER 9 Cole Porter's *Leave It To Me!* (291) opens at the Imperial. It stars William Gaxton, Victor Moore, Sophie Tucker, Tamara (the actress Tamara Drasin, who uses only her first name), and, say the ads, "a [l]arge [s]upporting [c]ast." One of the supporting cast members, says Walter Winchell, is "a delightful newcomer," Mary Martin, who sings "My Heart Belongs to Daddy." Even the

Business and Society

AUGUST • The House Un-American Activities Committee hears charges that the WPA Federal Theatre Project is pro-Communist.

SEPTEMBER • WPA Federal Theatre Project head Hallie Flanagan attacks the House Un-American Activities Committee for permitting wild charges linking the FTP to communism without inviting her agency to defend itself.

JANUARY 13 A parade of 5,000 in lower Manhattan protests cuts in the WPA arts programs and employee dismissals.

FEBRUARY 20 The Shuberts, concerned with the trend for audiences to light matches to read their *Playbill* once the house lights are dimmed, request in the programs that they do not do this.

APRIL • Business is off at Broadway box offices, with out-of-town visitors thought to be postponing trips until after the April 30 opening of the World's Fair. • With a Congressional appropriations bill under consideration, the Federal Theatre Project is coming under attack for unfair competition with commercial productions. **5** Reacting to what he

Births, Deaths, and Marriages

JULY 19 Burgess Meredith and Margaret Perry are divorced. **20** Diana Rigg b.

AUGUST 13 Luther Adler m. screen actress Sylvia Sidney. It will last nine years. **23** Judith Anderson and Benjamin Lehman are divorced.

SEPTEMBER 3 Playwright Caryl Churchill b. Her father is a political cartoonist. **14** Nicol Williamson b.

OCTOBER 22 Derek Jacobi b., and May Irwin d. **27** Fanny Brice divorces showman Billy Rose.

DECEMBER 8 José Ferrer m. Uta Hagen. **14** Ruth Etting m. Myrl Alderman, her pianist, who was shot two months ago by her previous husband, Martin ("Moe the Gimp") Snyder. **24** Vera Zorina m.

replaced June Knight, who has left the show after a week of rehearsals to get married. Cole Porter had written a song for Knight called "My Heart Belongs to Daddy."

OCTOBER 12 A former drama critic himself, Heywood Broun writes in his "It Seems to Me" column in the *World-Telegram* that "taken as a group the drama critics of New York are so much suet pudding." He longs for the days of Alexander Woollcott and William Winter. **16** Consumed by jealousy, Martin ("Moe the Gimp") Snyder, ex-husband of Ruth Etting, shoots her pianist, Myrl Alderman, at Etting's Los Angeles home. Snyder will go to prison, and Alderman will recover and marry Etting. **30** Orson Welles scares thousands of people, who mistake his Halloween broadcast of H.G. Welles's *War of the Worlds* on the "Mercury Theatre of the Air" for a real martian invasion. Most of the radio audience, however, is tuned to the competition on NBC: Edgar Bergen and Charlie McCarthy.

NOVEMBER • Yiddish stage actor and producer Boris Tomashevsky files for bankruptcy. Recently, he's been playing nightclubs. **18** Critic John Mason Brown, in a Town Hall lecture on the theatre, says that Eva Le Gallienne playing Marie Antoinette looks "like she ha[s] just finished her first day on a dude ranch." He also quips that "Libby Holman sings Negro songs as if they came from the banks of the Volga."

DECEMBER • The Shuberts have banned Broadway columnist Leonard Lyons from their theatres for his critical remarks about their productions. **5** *Time's* cover story is about Clifford Odets. *Awake and Sing* and *Waiting for Lefty*, writes the magazine, brought him sudden, overwhelming fame, and "when 28-year-old Odets was not being hailed as the Boy Wonder of the U.S. [t]heatre, he was being acclaimed as its White Hope." **19** *Life's* cover story is "Mary Martin: Texas to Broadway." **20** At the Imperial Theatre, where Mary Martin has been singing "My Heart Belongs to Daddy" in *Leave It To Me!* a telegram arrives announcing the death of her father. Sophie Tucker, also in the cast, tells Martin's assistant to "[g]ive the kid a break" and withhold the news

Communist Party *Daily Worker* likes her, predicting that "her name is surely destined for lights. . . ." Also debuting is the Cole Porter song "Get Out of Town" and chorus boy Gene Kelly. **23** Directed by George Abbott, who has adapted it from Shakespeare's *Comedy of Errors*, the first musical based on the Bard's work, Rodgers and Hart's *The Boys from Syracuse* (235), with the choreography of George Balanchine, opens at the Alvin. The score contains "Falling in Love With Love" and "This Can't be Love." It stars Jimmy Savo, Teddy Hart, and Wynn Murray, with Burl Ives, Eddie Albert, and Betty Bruce.

DECEMBER 22 Laurette Taylor's performance in the revival of *Outward Bound* (255), directed by Otto Preminger and opening tonight at the Playhouse, is her first Broadway success in a decade. Richard Lockridge, in *The Sun*, calls her "superlative." **28** Jane Cowl plays Dolly Levi in Thornton Wilder's *The Merchant of Yonkers* (39), at the Guild Theatre. Percy Waram and Tom Ewell are also in the cast. It will do much better as *The Matchmaker* in 1955 and better yet in 1964, with music, as *Hello Dolly!*

JANUARY 3 Ethel Waters plays a self-sacrificing mother in Dorothy and DuBose Heyward's *Mamba's Daughters* (162), at the Empire. The *Times's* Brooks Atkinson criticizes "her limp, plodding style," saying "she does not go very deep inside her part." Also in the cast are José Ferrer, Canada Lee, and Alberta Hunter. **10** *The White Steed* (136), Paul Vincent Carroll's comedy set in an Irish village, is at the Cort. It stars Barry Fitzgerald, Jessica Tandy, and George Colouris.

FEBRUARY 15 *The Little Foxes* (410), Lillian Hellman's "deliberate exercise in malice" (Brooks Atkinson), opens at the National. Directed by Herman Shumlin, it stars Tallulah Bankhead as Regina, Frank Conroy, Dan Duryea, Patricia Collinge, and Charles Dingle. Bankhead, who is having an affair with Shumlin, quarreled with Hellman in rehearsals. It's a Bette Davis star turn in the 1941 film and a Marc Blitzstein opera, *Regina*, in 1949.

regards as objectionable language in *Idiot's Delight*, Memphis censor Lloyd T. Binford says that in the future, the Lunts will have to submit scripts for approval before they will be allowed to perform. They have been watering down the dialogue for matinées but playing the original in the evening.

MAY • The opening of the World's Fair brings a decline in Broadway ticket sales, not the increase anticipated by producers, who respond with salary cuts.

Georges Balanchine. **31** Rosalind Cash b.

FEBRUARY 28 Choreographer-dancer-director Tommy Tune b.

MARCH 16 Ina Claire m. lawyer William Wallace. **19** Producer Sam Harris, 68, m. Peggy Watson, 38. She's the sister of screen actor George Brent. **27** Libby Holman m. actor Ralph Holmes.

APRIL 18 Yiddish theatre star Bertha Kalich d.

MAY 25 Ian McKellen b.

Personalities

until after tonight's performance. **22** Ed Wynn agrees to pay $174,166 in back income taxes.

JANUARY 6 In response to Brooks Atkinson's negative review of Ethel Waters in *Mamba's Daughters*, which opened at the Empire three days ago, an ad appears in *The New York Times* extolling Waters's performance. Signers include Tallulah Bankhead, Oscar Hammerstein II, Judith Anderson, Carl Van Vechten, and Norman Bel Geddes. **15** Brooks Atkinson, in a Sunday *New York Times* piece, takes a second look at *Mamba's Daughters*, noting that he was under the weather when he first saw it. Now, he says that Ethel Waters gave a fine performance in her first dramatic role. **21** Actress Erin O'Brien-Moore sustains third-degree burns when her dress ignites from a discarded match at Lyon's Chophouse. She's just come from the opening of Kaufman and Hart's *The American Way*. *Variety*'s Jack Pulaski puts out the flames with his bare hands.

FEBRUARY • James Barton is fired as "Jeeter Lester," the lead role in *Tobacco Road*, after run-ins with several cast members. **26** On their first date, Mary Martin and Winthrop Rockefeller, onetime beau of Ethel Merman, are chosen Handsomest Couple at a gathering of New York socialites at El Morocco.

MARCH 6 Tallulah Bankhead is on the cover of *Life*. **21** *The New York Times* reports that the runner-up in the Group Theatre's playwriting contest is Tennessee Williams, "24 years old, of New Orleans, for *American Blues*, a group of three sketches which constitute a full-length play."

APRIL 19 *Variety* notes of 12-year-old Sidney Lumet, now appearing in *My Heart's in the Highlands*, that "his parents visioned Hollywood for their prodigy, but sought too much coin. Lad, however, should make a career on the stage."

Plays and Musicals

MARCH 28 Katharine Hepburn, for whom the part was written, is Tracy Lord in Philip Barry's society comedy *The Philadelphia Story* (417), at the Shubert. Her costars are Shirley Booth, Frank Fenton, Van Heflin and Joseph Cotten. Burns Mantle finds Hepburn "a little overanxious to do her best" on opening night. It's also Hepburn's film, in 1940.

APRIL 13 "What is the [g]od damn meaning of all this stuff?" Burns Mantle, quoting William Saroyan's writing on another matter, will write about *My Heart's in the High Lands* (44), at the Guild Theatre. Saroyan's first play is an impressionistic

Katherine Hepburn

one-act play about poverty, poetry, and any number of other things. Philip Loeb and Art Smith star, with a child actor named Sidney Lumet. **17** S.N. Behrman's *No Time for Comedy* (185), a comedy about a playwright who writes a comedy, starring Katharine Cornell and Laurence Olivier, opens at the Barrymore. It's filmed next year.

Business and Society

Births, Deaths, and Marriages

1939–40

European refugees from the Nazis are enriching American theatre, as they are all the arts. In New York, Erwin Piscator establishes his Dramatic Workshop at the New School, where young Marlon Brando will study and perform. Rachel Crothers, Antoinette Perry, Robert E. Sherwood, Gertrude Lawrence and many others contribute time and money to war relief, while William Saroyan turns down the Pulitzer Prize. When last on Broadway, John Barrymore played Hamlet; now he plays himself. Boston's censor gets taken by—and for—a dummy. The Shuberts manage to contain Bobby Clark, Abbott and Costello, and Carmen Miranda on one stage, and between Ethel Merman and Bert Lahr, there is Cole Porter's "Friendship."

- Cost of dinner and a show at Leon & Eddie's on 52nd Street—from $2.50
- Cost of dinner at the Stork Club—from $2.45, with a $2.00 cover charge after 10 P.M.
- Number of people who will see *Life With Father* on Broadway during its almost 8-year run: 2,810,000
- Speechwriter for Postmaster General and Democratic political operative James Farley: 22-year-old future avant-garde director Alan Schneider
- Actress for whom *DuBarry Was a Lady*, starring Ethel Merman, was originally intended: Mae West
- Ethel Merman's cast replacement in *Du Barry Was a Lady*: Gypsy Rose Lee, the daughter of the woman Merman will play in *Gypsy*
- Government dignitaries played to date by Victor Moore: vice president (twice), ambassador, and senator
- Rejected titles for William Saroyan's *The Time of Your Life*: *The Light Fantastic* and *Sunset Sonata*
- *New York Times* critic Brooks Atkinson's reaction to *Beverly Hills*, a play about Hollywood: "A nice idea sometime would be for someone to write a tender play about kind people."
- The Lunts' annual combined income, estimated by *Variety*: $100,000
- Where veteran actor David Warfied drapes his coat when he plays cards at the Lambs Club: over the shoulders of the club's bust of himself
- Moving to New York: David Merrick, only recently David Margulois—who will stay out of the draft because he has ulcers, even though he has yet to produce a Broadway show
- Return on David Merrick's $5,000 investment in James Thurber's *The Male Animal*: $20,000
- Actors who will study at Erwin Piscator's Dramatic Workshop at the New School: Marlon Brando, Elaine Stritch, Walter Matthau, Tony Curtis, Judith Malina, Bea Arthur, Harry Belafonte, and Rod Steiger
- John Barrymore's attitude toward *My Dear Children*, in which he stars: "What kind of play is it? I'm damned if I know."

Productions on Broadway: 91

Pulitzer Prize for Drama: *The Time of Your Life* (William Saroyan)

New York Drama Critics Circle Award:
Best American Play: *The Time of Your Life* (William Saroyan)

June
- Broadway discovers Carmen Miranda

July
- Bucks County Playhouse opens

August
- Elizabeth Ashley born

September
- Danny Kaye's Broadway debut

October
- *The Man Who Came to Dinner*

November
- *Life With Father*

December
- *DuBarry Was a Lady*

January
- John Barrymore back on Broadway
- Tennessee Williams produced in New York

February

March
- Robert E. Sherwood donates royalties to war relief

April
- Billie Burke auctions off Ziegfeld home

May
- William Saroyan rejects Pulitzer

Personalities

JUNE 5 James Barton, fired from *Tobacco Road* in February after quarreling with other cast members, is back in the show, which slumped at the box office after his departure.

AUGUST • The Revuers, a talented group of young performers playing at the Village Vanguard, include 22-year-old Betty Comden and Adolph Green, 22. Also, 18-year-old Judith Tuvim, not yet blonde and not yet "Judy Holliday."

SEPTEMBER • Newspapers have gotten wind of a possible feud between Katharine Cornell and Francis Lederer, who has taken over Laurence Olivier's part in *No Time for Comedy*. It is said that he accidentally stepped on the hem of her gown during a performance, ripping it and almost pulling it off. The producers of the show are making light of it. **29** Richard Watts, Jr., in the *Herald-Tribune*, will write about a Broadway debut tonight in *The Straw Hat Revue*: "Danny Kaye seems to me what I hope will not sound too patronizing to call a comedian of promise."

OCTOBER 18 The cast of *Too Many Girls* awaits the reviews at La Conga, the club where Desi Arnaz is performing while also in the show. The early papers are brought in by the city's most prominent madam, Polly Adler—Arnaz is one of her

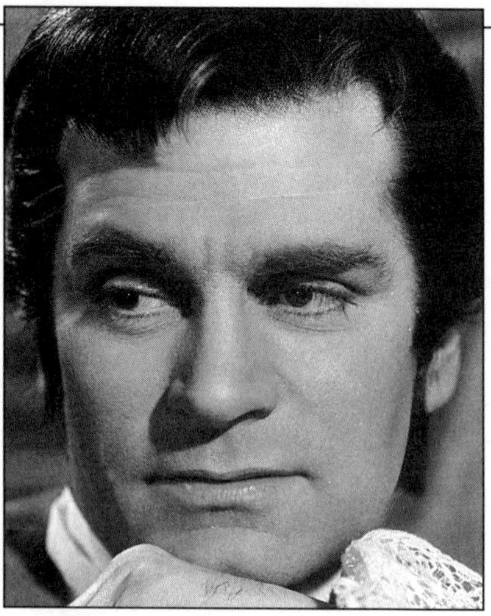

Laurence Olivier

Plays and Musicals

JUNE 19 *The Streets of Paris* (274), a revue at the Broadhurst, features Bobby Clark, Abbott and Costello, and Carmen Miranda. It is, says one reviewer, "about as French as Canarsie." According to the *Times*, Carmen Miranda, whom Lee Shubert has discovered in Brazil, "radiates heat that will tax the Broadhurst's air-conditioning plant this [s]ummer."

JULY 1 A rebuilt mill in New Hope, Pennsylvania, becomes a major summer stock venue with the opening of the Bucks County Playhouse. *Springtime for Henry*, starring Edward Everett Horton and Julie Haydon, is its first production.

OCTOBER 16 George S. Kaufman and Moss Hart's *The Man Who Came to Dinner* (739) opens at the Music Box. Monty Woolley stars in this comedy, a thinly disguised portrait of critic Alexander Woollcott. The role of "Banjo," modeled after Harpo Marx, will be played by him in summer stock. Woolley also stars in the 1941 film. **18** Rodgers and Hart's *Too Many Girls* (249) is at the Imperial, produced and directed by George Abbott and starring Eddie Bracken, Desi Arnaz, Richard Kollmar, and Marcy Wescott, with Van Johnson in the chorus. It introduces "I Didn't Know What Time It Is." **25** William Saroyan's *The Time of Your Life* (185), at the Booth, the first play to take both a Pulitzer Prize and the New York Drama Critic's Award, stars Eddie Dowling, Julie Haydon, Gene Kelly, Celeste Holm, and William Bendix. This "cosmic vaudeville show," as Richard Watts, Jr. calls it, looks at the lives of the denizens of a San Francisco waterfront saloon. The film is released in 1948.

NOVEMBER 3 Sam Levene is a Jewish cop guarding the Nazi consul, played by Otto Preminger, who directs as well and makes his Broadway stage debut, in Clare Boothe's comedy-drama *Margin for Error* (264), at the Booth. Preminger is also in the 1943 film, with Milton Berle. **8** Playwright Howard Lindsay is hoping for a run of six months when *Life With Father* (3,224), the family comedy based on Clarence Day's stories that Lindsay has coauthored with Russel Crouse,

Business and Society

JUNE • Ticket sales on Broadway are picking up. **20** The second-night curtain of *The Streets of Paris* drops at 11:29, before the last act has concluded, with no explanation to the audience. The Shuberts want to avoid paying overtime to the stagehands, which would begin at 11:30. Cuts will be made in the show. **30** Funding ends for The Federal Theatre Project, which begins to shut down.

JULY 31 In an attempt by the stagehands union to seize control of labor organizing throughout the entertainment industry, The International Alliance of Theatrical Stage Employees (IATSE) grants a charter to the American Federation of Actors, led by Sophie Tucker.

AUGUST • Boston censor John Spencer orders dancer Ann Miller to take out the "bumps" in the tryout run of *George White's Scandals*. The show features Willie Howard and The Three Stooges. **6** Helen Hayes and Katharine Cornell publicly criticize Sophie Tucker's willingness to hand over the unionizing of actors to IATSE. **15** The American Federation of Labor orders IATSE to cancel the charter it granted on July 31 to the American

Births, Deaths, and Marriages

JUNE 6 George Fawcett d.

JULY • Playwright Sidney Kingsley m. actress Madge Evans. **9** Yiddish stage star and producer Boris Tomashevsky d. He helped to advance the early careers of Sophie Tucker, Rudolf and Joseph Schildkraut, Morris Gest, Belle Baker, Bertha Kalich, and Jacob Ben-Ami.

AUGUST 23 Pulitzer Prizewinning playwright Sidney Howard d. in a tractor accident. He recently finished the screenplay for *Gone With the Wind*. **30** Elizabeth Ashley (Elizabeth Cole) b.

SEPTEMBER 25 Eddie Bracken m. ingenue Constance Nickerson. **30** Len Cariou b.

OCTOBER 3 Fay Templeton d. **28** Jane Alexander b.

better customers—who announces to all before they get to read them: "Cuban, you are the biggest fucking hit in town!"

NOVEMBER • Cole Porter's "Friendship," sung by Ethel Merman and Bert Lahr in *DuBarry Was a Lady*, now in tryouts, is so popular that the composer is augmenting it with new stanzas tacked on at the end. • The Shuberts are reported to be deeply unhappy about A.J. Liebling's three-part piece on them in the *New Yorker*, in which he calls them "the boys from Syracuse." **2** Milton Berle is the new abbot of the Friars. **27** The *Playbill* for Maxwell Anderson's *Key Largo*, at the Barrymore Theatre, says Uta Hagen "has made one of the most rapid ascents to the theatrical peaks in recent years. She seems to have sprung full-panoplied from the head of Thespis, and has had to do little more than give readings in order to win enviable roles."

DECEMBER • Butterfly McQueen, now in *Swingin' the Dream*, becomes the first black lifetime member of Actors Equity, paying the required 10 years of dues in advance. Equity did not make membership mandatory for black players until after *Green Pastures* in 1930. **10** Critic John Chapman, who spent time with John Barrymore, now playing in *My Dear Children* in Chicago, writes in the *New York Daily News* that the star is drinking sparingly. Barrymore's ad-libs in the performance, thought by many to be alcohol-inspired, are apparently carefully scripted. **23** Critic John Mason Brown upbraids his colleagues for their "well-meant fickleness" in recent years, in which they have alternately anointed Helen Hayes and Katharine Cornell as "the first lady of the American theatre." Brown admits indulging in this himself.

JANUARY • Erwin Piscator, formerly head of the State Theatre in Berlin, launches his Dramatic Workshop at the New School for Social Research in New York City, as a training ground for American stage actors. The faculty includes Stella Adler, John Gassner, Brooks Atkinson, and Erich Leinsdorf. **16** Playwright Rachel Crothers, who during World War I founded Stage Womens War Relief, organizes the American Theatre Wing of

---

opens at the Empire. Alfred Lunt, Walter Huston, Roland Young, and John Halliday have rejected the lead role, which Lindsay has taken himself, costarring with his offstage wife, Dorothy Stickney. It runs for almost eight years, setting a new record for a nonmusical play. **27** Maxwell Anderson's *Key Largo* (105) is at the Barrymore. Guthrie McClintic is directing Paul Muni, Uta Hagen, José Ferrer, and "Carl" Malden, as *The New York Times* cast box lists him. It's filmed in 1948.

DECEMBER 6 Cole Porter's *DuBarry Was a Lady* (408) opens at the Forty-sixth Street Theatre. Ethel Merman and Bert Lahr, according to the *Times*, "make vulgarity honestly exuberant"—although Brooks Atkinson is a bit disturbed by the show's "obscenities." Memorable songs are "Friendship" and "Do I Love You?" Also included is "Well, Did You Evah?" sung by Betty Grable. A film version appears in 1943.

JANUARY 9 Elliott Nugent is a college professor with romantic and political problems in *The Male Animal* (243), a comedy he coauthored with James Thurber. It's at the Cort. Henry Fonda stars in the 1942 film. **31** John Barrymore is back on Broadway for the first time since his celebrated *Hamlet* 18 years ago in a somewhat slighter vehicle, *My Dear Children* (117), a comedy by Catherine Turney and Jerry Horwin, at the Belasco.

MARCH 6 Ernest Hemingway and Benjamin Glazer's Spanish Civil War play *The Fifth Column* (87) is at the Alvin. It stars Franchot Tone, Lee J. Cobb, and Lenore Ulric, with Katherine Locke, who stepped in during rehearsals when Frances Farmer walked out. It's directed by Lee Strasberg. **23** *Separate Rooms* (613), a racy comedy, is at Maxine Elliott's Theatre. The authors are Joseph Carole, Alex Gottlieb, Edmund Joseph, and Alan Dinehart, who also appears in it with Glenda Farrell and Lyle Talbot.

APRIL 29 Robert Sherwood's *There Shall Be No Night* (181), a Pulitzer Prize winner, opens at the Alvin. Alfred Lunt and Lynn Fontanne star, with Sidney Greenstreet and Montgomery Clift, in a story about the Russian invasion of Finland.

Federation of Actors. But the Associated Actors and Artists of America also wants the IATSE-sponsored group dissolved. The impasse threatens a strike that could close down both Broadway and Hollywood. **24** Actors Equity suspends Sophie Tucker for "treason" in trying to lead actors under the banner of IATSE.

SEPTEMBER 3 With war breaking out in Europe, IATSE and the Associated Actors and Artists sign a truce. The American Federation of Actors losses its AFL charter and will be replaced by the American Guild of Variety Artists. Equity reinstates Sophie Tucker, and the danger of an industry-wide strike passes.

OCTOBER 1 The Shuberts buy the Belasco Theatre.

JANUARY • The addition of George Abbott and the Playwrights Company to the League of New York Theatres leaves only a few major producers, among them John Golden, outside the fold.

MARCH • Boston censor John Spencer is conned into insisting that two women in a scene from *Night at Folies Bergères* cover up. They are, in fact, wax dummies.

APRIL • A Broadway slump is being blamed

NOVEMBER 3 Playwright Terrence McNally b. **14** Billy Rose m. Eleanor Holm.

DECEMBER 12 Douglas Fairbanks, Sr. d. **18** Heywood Broun d.

JANUARY 3 Danny Kaye m. composer Sylvia Fine. **14** Director Trevor Nunn b.

FEBRUARY • Lee J. Cobb m. actress Helen Beverly. **11** Bert Lahr, after securing an annulment from his first wife a few days ago on the grounds that she has been clinically insane for at least five years, marries showgirl Mildred Schroeder.

MARCH 3 Maxine Elliott d. **9** Raul Julia b. **10** Playwright David Rabe b. **27** Actor-director Austin Pendleton b.

APRIL 7 William Faversham d. **9** Mrs. Patrick Campbell d. **25** Al Pacino b.

MAY 5 Mary Martin m. film story editor Richard Halliday. **14** Clifford Odets and Luise Rainer divorce. **28** Walter Connolly d.

Personalities

the French and British Relief Fund. Also active are Lucile Watson, Theresa Helburn, Antoinette Perry, Katharine Hepburn, and Gertrude Lawrence.

FEBRUARY 7 John Barrymore is hospitalized for "vitamin deficiency," and performances of *My Dear Children* will be suspended for five days. **10** The Communist party's newspaper, the *Daily Worker*, reports: "The young Southern winner of a $1,000 Rockefeller Playwriting Award, Tennessee Williams, will have the first New York showing of his play *The Long Goodbye*, in a student production at New Theatre School this evening."

MARCH 9 Helen Morgan tells a reporter that she's tired of singing torch songs in clubs and wants to return to the stage as a serious actress. "I guess I'd have to play tragedy," she says. "I guess everything I've done fits me for tragedy." **29** With the opening in Providence, Rhode Island of tryouts for *There Shall Be No Night*, playwright Robert E. Sherwood begins to donate his weekly royalty check—about $2,200—to the American Red Cross and Finnish War Relief.

APRIL 29 Billie Burke auctions off the home, and its contents, that she shared with Flo Ziegfeld. The lot, which includes the cages that housed Ziegfeld's monkeys, brings a total of $42,000.

MAY • Frances Farmer reaches a financial settlement with the Theatre Guild for her walkout from *Fifth Column* while it was in rehearsals. Farmer, who had a run-of-the-play contract, has been having problems with her marriage to actor Leif Erikson, who is now in the musical *Higher and Higher*. **7** William Saroyan, yesterday named winner of this year's Pulitzer Prize for Drama for *The Time of Your Life*, says he won't accept the prize and the check for $1,000 that goes with it because, among other things, such awards represent "wealth patronizing art."

Plays and Musicals

MAY 28 Irving Berlin's *Louisiana Purchase* (444), with a book by Morrie Ryskind and Buddy De Sylva, opens at the Imperial. Berlin's first Broadway show since 1933, a satire on Senator Huey Long, stars Victor Moore, Vera Zorina, Irene Bordoni, and Berlin's discovery, Carol Bruce, who recently received a spread in *Life*. Songs include "It's a Lovely Day Tomorrow." It's the longest-running musical since *Show Boat* and reaches the screen in 1941.

Business and Society

partly on war news, which keeps theatregoers at their radios. • Producers begin a campaign to entice out-of-town theatregoers with the theme that Broadway is "the main entrance to the 1940 World's Fair." The Fair opens its second season on May 11, and they recall last year's dip at the box office when the Fair debuted.

MAY 1 A *Variety* editorial calls for the return of the $2 legitimate show. Six current Broadway shows top out at $2.

Births, Deaths, and Marriages

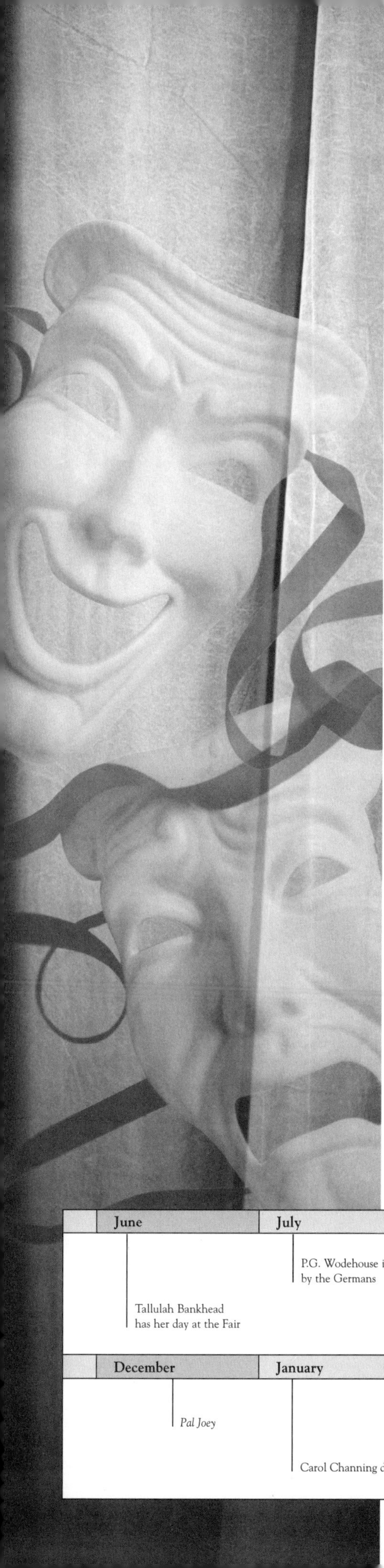

1940–41

Panama Hattie chorus girl June Allyson gets her big break when Betty Hutton can't go on—just like in the movies. The left-wing faction in Equity is being red-baited, and P.G. Wodehouse is in big political trouble. Tennessee Williams has growing pains in Boston, George S. Kaufman and Moss Hart conclude a fruitful partnership, and *Tobacco Road* comes to the end of the road. Al Jolson is back on Broadway, but it's changed, and so has he. (According to Ruby Keeler, he hasn't changed enough.) Eighteen-year-old Carol Channing gets a little exposure, Gertrude Lawrence is a lady in the dark (and in the money), Gene Kelly is a heel in *Pal Joey*, Boris Karloff plays a boogey man, and on the wine menu in *Arsenic and Old Lace* is a nice elderberry.

- Fee that Gertrude Lawrence's character, a magazine editor, pays for each session with her psychoanalyst in *Lady in the Dark*: $10
- Total weekly compensation for Gertrude Lawrence from *Lady in the Dark* (salary plus a percentage of the gross): about $4,300, thought to be the most for an actress in a Broadway show since the days of Marilyn Miller
- Number of husbands 30-year-old actress Lillian Roth has had: 5
- Number of times Ethel Merman marries during the run of *Panama Hattie*: twice (the cast throws rice at her during her curtain call the day she marries William Smith)
- Shows this season based on *New Yorker* stories: 4—*Life With Father*, *Pal Joey*, *My Sister Eileen*, and *Mr. and Mrs. North*
- Players coming into their own or debuting this season: Gene Kelly, Van Johnson, Barbara Bel Geddes, Alfred Drake, Dorothy McGuire, and Danny Kaye
- What *Pal Joey* means to Gene Kelly, according to critic Burns Mantle: ". . . probably make a star of him before long"
- Top price for musicals: $4.40
- Why the road companies of *Life With Father* and *Watch on the Rhine* cannot play in Washington, D.C.: the District has a law against children under 18 appearing on the stage
- Number of actors who have played Jeeter Lester in *Tobacco Road*, closing this season: 5—Henry Hull, James Barton, James Bell, Eddie Garr, and Will Geer
- Number of theatres *Tobacco Road* has played in on Broadway since it opened on December 4, 1932: 3—the Masque, the Forty-eighth Street, and the Forrest
- Number of performances given by *Tobacco Road* in its record-breaking run: 3,180
- Amount grossed by *Tobacco Road*: about $1,500,000
- What John Barrymore says about his divorce from Elaine Barrie: "Women expect you to be the great lover 24 hours a day. They don't realize that you are only showing off when you're up on stage, and that when you come home you want to find a real home. Have someone to talk to—the 'easy slippers' kind of companionship. That's what men really want."

Productions on Broadway: 69

Pulitzer Prize for Drama: *There Shall Be No Night* (Robert E. Sherwood)

New York Drama Critics Award:
Best American Play: *Watch on the Rhine* (Lillian Hellman)
Best Foreign Play: *The Corn Is Green* (Emlyn Williams)

June	July	August	September	October	November
Tallulah Bankhead has her day at the Fair	P.G. Wodehouse is arrested by the Germans	Vivian Leigh m. Laurence Olivier	Al Jolson is back on Broadway	Last Kaufman–Hart play	Donna McKechnie b.

December	January	February	March	April	May
Pal Joey	Carol Channing debuts	Barbara Bel Geddes's Broadway debut	Theatre Guild apologizes for Tennessee Williams flop	*Watch on the Rhine*	Broadway has the measles

Personalities

JUNE 15 It's "Tallulah Bankhead Day" at the World's Fair in New York.

JULY • Beatrice Lillie and John Gielgud tour British military installations, performing in Noel Coward's *Tonight at 8:30.* **21** Lyricist P.G. Wodehouse, a British subject, is arrested in France by the invading Germans. Wodehouse's subsequent radio broadcasts from France, in which he makes light of the conditions of his internment, will be interpreted by many Britons as collaboration with the Nazis. **27** The *New Yorker* reports that Irving Berlin's "God Bless America," which he took out of *Yip, Yip, Yaphank!* and replaced with "We're On Our Way to France," is "rapidly becoming a national institution." When it's played, "school children now stand at attention and elderly gentlemen hold their hats over their hearts." Berlin is "flabbergasted."

AUGUST 13 In a summer stock production of *The Royal Family* at the Maplewood Theatre in Maplewood, New Jersey, coauthor Edna Ferber is playing Fanny Cavendish. Maybe she shouldn't have. Louis Calhern lifts her on opening night and drops her. The *Times* cast box has her as "Enda Ferber," and Brooks Atkinson rates her histrionic talents "halfway between Sinclair Lewis and Alexander Woollcott."

SEPTEMBER 16 Tallulah Bankhead goes on in *The Little Foxes* in Hershey, Pennsylvania, even though she attended her father's funeral this morning in Washington, D.C., where he was Speaker of the House.

OCTOBER 13 In a *New York Times* article, Robert E. Sherwood answers critics who say that he has now seen the error of his earlier pacifism. He says that he's responding to what has happened in his life and in the world. "'There Shall Be No Night' is not a denial of *Idiot's Delight*," he insists. "[I]t is a sequel." **17** John Barrymore begins to appear regularly on Rudy Vallee's "Sealtest Show" on radio. **28** Ethel Merman is on the cover of *Time* magazine.

Plays and Musicals

SEPTEMBER 11 Al Jolson is back on Broadway for the first time in a decade in Burton Lane and Yip Harburg's *Hold On to Your Hats* (158), at the Shubert. Martha Raye costars. **18** Helen Craig is a deaf woman who kills her rapist in Elmer Harris's *Johnny Belinda* (321), opening at the Belasco. Jane Wyman will win an Oscar for the title role in the 1948 screen version.

OCTOBER 17 José Ferrer is in drag, playing in *Charley's Aunt* (233), at the Court. Joshua Logan directs this successful revival. **18** The final George S. Kaufman and Moss Hart collaboration, *George Washington Slept Here* (173), opens at the Lyceum. Ernest Truex, Jean Dixon, and Dudley Digges draw mixed reviews in this comedy about the trials and tribulations of buying a country house where, it turns out, Benedict Arnold, not George Washington, spent the night. **25** *Cabin in the Sky* (156), a musical by Vernon Duke and John Latouche, with an all-black cast and choreography by George Balanchine, opens at the Martin Beck. Ethel Waters, Todd Duncan, Dooley Wilson, Rex Ingram, and Katherine Dunham head the cast, and "Taking a Chance On Love," sung by Waters, is the most prominent song. The film appears in 1944. **30** Cole Porter's *Panama Hattie* (501), in which Ethel Merman dominates a theatre marquee for the first time, opens at the Forty-sixth Street Theatre. In the supporting cast are James Dunn, Arthur Treacher, Betty Hutton, June Allyson, Rags Ragland, Pat Harrington, Lucille Bremer, Betsy Blair, and Vera Ellen. The score includes "Let's Be Buddies." Ann Sothern stars in the 1942 film.

NOVEMBER 26 Ethel Barrymore, "at the peak of her talents," according to *The New York Times*, stars as the teacher, Miss Moffat, in Emlyn Williams's autobiographical *The Corn Is Green* (477), at the National. Bette Davis stars in the 1945 film.

DECEMBER 14 The Studio Theatre, the production arm of the Dramatic Workshop

Business and Society

JUNE 11 The American Negro Theatre is founded in Harlem.

JULY 4 Kansas Congressman William P. Lambertson tells the House: "Seven [c]ommunists are now on the governing council of Equity: Sam Jaffe, Philip Loeb, Emily Marsh, Hiram S. Sherman, Leroy MacLean, Edith L. van Cleve and Alan Hewitt." His remarks are made in a debate on Communist influence in the WPA Theatre Project.

AUGUST • The Provincetown Playhouse in Greenwich Village is placed in receivership.

SEPTEMBER 27 Actors Equity, under pressure from Congressional attacks, goes on record at its quarterly meeting that it opposes communism and is not Communist-influenced.

NOVEMBER 12 The Dramatists Guild endorses the right of first refusal on the movie rights to a play for studios that back a production. Studios have been upset at putting up stage production money, only to see other companies outbid them for the film rights. **24** Sunday night performances come to Broadway in

Births, Deaths, and Marriages

JUNE 16 Playwright Dubose Hyward d. **18** Joshua Logan m. film actress Barbara O'Neil.

JULY 4 Gertrude Lawrence, on her fortieth birthday, m. Richard Aldrich. Actress Constance Collier remarks: "poor Richard Aldrich. He thinks he has married Miss Gertrude Lawrence. He'll soon find out it's Myth Lawrence." **13** Patrick Stewart b.

AUGUST 3 Martin Sheen (Ramon Estevez) b. **30** Vivian Leigh m. Laurence Olivier.

NOVEMBER • Donna McKechnie b. **15** Ethel Merman m. producer William J. Smith, whom she will leave after two months. **16** Producer Martin Beck d. **28** Frank Tinney d.

NOVEMBER • Director Joshua Logan enters a Philadelphia sanitarium for six weeks to treat his first major episode of manic depression. **9** At the Davidson Theatre in Milwaukee, where Tallulah Bankhead is performing in *The Little Foxes*, someone in the audience yells "fire." Without skipping a beat, Bankhead inserts into her lines a comment about the smoke being part of the play and manages to halt an incipient panic and dash for the doors. The culprit proves to be a smoldering cigarette.

DECEMBER • With *Arsenic and Old Lace* holding tryouts in Baltimore, press agent Richard Maney draws attention to one of the show's stars, Boris Karloff, by casting him against type—as Santa Claus, giving away presents to orphans. **10** Speaking at

Boris Karloff is in *Arsenic and Old Lace*

at the New School for Social Research, mounts its first play, *King Lear* (5), starring Sam Jaffe. **25** "If it is possible to make an entertaining comedy out of an odious story, *Pal Joey* [374] is it," Brooks Atkinson will write of the show opening at the Barrymore. John O'Hara has based this tale of a heel—the first Broadway musical antihero—on his own *New Yorker* stories. Rodgers and Hart's score includes "Bewitched, Bothered and Bewildered" and "I Could Write a Book." Gene Kelly, Vivienne Segal, and June Havoc are the stars, with Van Johnson. Successfully revived in 1952, it becomes a film in 1957. **26** *My Sister Eileen* (866) opens at the Biltmore, without an out-of-town tryout. Joseph Fields and Jerome Chodorov have based their play on the short stories of Ruth McKenney, and George S. Kaufman is directing Shirley Booth, Jo Ann Sayers, and Morris Carnovsky in this comedy about sisters who left Ohio for Greenwich Village. It will become the musical *Wonderful Town* in 1953 and will be filmed in 1942 and 1955. **29** Leonard Sillman's revue *All In*

quantity, with 10 shows tonight, including *Hellzapoppin*, *George Washington Slept Here*, *Tobacco Road*, and *The Man Who Came to Dinner*.

DECEMBER 1 Actors Equity doubles its initiation fee to $100 and sets a new weekly minimum salary for all actors at $50.

JANUARY • About half the shows on Broadway have either been sold to Hollywood or have promising screen possibilities. But not *Pal Joey*, according to *Variety*, which is "too censorable," or *Johnny Belinda*, in which there is only "flickering interest." **1** New York State's Mitchell law takes effect, reinforcing the cap of $.75 on the premium that agencies can charge for theatre tickets. All agencies will now be licensed, their employees fingerprinted, and they will be regulated by New York City's Commissioner of Licenses.

FEBRUARY 10 The $283,000 that Paramount pays for the film rights to *Lady in the Dark* is said to be a record for a Broadway show.

MARCH 26 The *New York Mirror* and the *Journal-American*, review *Native Son* two days after it opened. Neither mentions coproducer and director Orson Welles, whose film *Citizen Kane*, William Randolph Hearst has been trying to suppress, believing it to be about himself.

DECEMBER 26 Producer Daniel Frohman d. **28** Ruby Keeler divorces Al Jolson.

MARCH 7 Female impersonator Julian Eltinge (William Dalton) d. W.C. Fields says, "Women went into ecstasies over him. Men went into the smoking room."

Personalities

a New Haven rally of the Committee to Defend America by Aiding the Allies, playwright Robert E. Sherwood attacks isolationist Charles Lindbergh as "a Nazi with a Nazi's Olympian contempt for all democratic processes. . . ." **30** The Theatre Guild program at the Wilbur Theatre in Boston, where *Battle of Angels*, starring Miriam Hopkins, is having its pre-Broadway tryout, says of the young playwright whose first major production this is: "Tennessee Williams . . . is the discovery of Theresa Helburn and Lawrence Langner, coadministrators of the Guild. Born in Columbus, Mississippi, he is thoroughly familiar with the characters and environment of which he writes. *Battle of Angels* is a powerful drama, written with consummate skill and profound sincerity." But not according to *Variety*, which calls it "sordid, with little comic relief, and the final curtain is as amateurish a bit of melodrama as the Guild has ever attempted."

JANUARY 11 The Theatre Guild folds Tennessee Williams's *Battle of Angels* after its two-week Boston tryout. The play will be revived by the Circle Repertory Company off Broadway in the 1974–75 season. **16** *Lady in the Dark*, scheduled to open tonight at the Alvin, will remain in the dark for another week because star Gertrude Lawrence has the flu.

FEBRUARY • Al Jolson coproduced *Hold On To Your Hats*, which opened September 11, so that he can return to Broadway and jump-start his faltering career. Despite continuing strong demand for tickets, the entertainer, who has been ill this winter and wants to leave New York, chooses to suddenly close it and take the show on the road. It flops, marking the end of Jolson as a Broadway star. **3** *Time*'s cover story features Gertrude Lawrence, "the greatest feminine performer in the theatre," appearing in *Lady in the Dark*. The play also has Danny Kaye "as a pansy fashion photographer" and "swarthy Victor Mature, latest in Hollywood's series of almost outrageously beautiful young men, who appears in every costume the feminine audience could wish, from breech clout to dress suit." **11** On

Plays and Musicals

Fun, which will close after two days with a loss of about $130,000, is the first Broadway show in which an African-American, Bill "Bojangles" Robinson, heads a predominantly white cast. **30** Elmer Rice's *Flight to the West* (136), about passengers on a transatlantic flight, at the Guild Theatre, is "the most absorbing American drama of the season," according to Brooks Atkinson. Paul Henreid, Kevin McCarthy, Betty Field, Hugh Marlowe, and Karl Malden are in the cast.

JANUARY 5 Marc Blitzstein's experimental opera *No For an Answer* (3) opens at the Mecca Temple (later the City Center). The *New York Post* notes that "Carol Channing, in the role of a night club singer, shared with the composer a round of applause for her singing of 'I'm Simply Fraught With You,' a burlesque of a sophisticated popular song." The 18-year-old is in her first professional show, along with Martin Ritt. **10** *Arsenic and Old Lace* (1,444), a comedy by Joseph Kesselring about two elderly sisters who use poisoned elderberry wine to practice euthanasia on elderly men, opens at the Fulton. Josephine Hull and Jean Adair are the sisters, Allyn Joslyn plays the good nephew, and Jonathan, the menacing nephew is . . . Boris Karloff. It's a 1944 film. **23** *Lady in the Dark* (467), with music by Kurt Weill, lyrics by Ira Gershwin, and book by Moss Hart, opens at the Alvin. Gertrude Lawrence—a "goddess" says Brooks Atkinson—is a fashion editor whose dreams, recounted in her psychoanalysis, provide the plot line. Supporting are MacDonald Carey and Victor Mature, who plays a witless movie star. Songs include "The Saga of Jenny" and a novelty number, the "Tschaikowsky" song, sung by Danny Kaye, in which he rattles off the names of 50 Russian composers in 43 seconds. The 1944 film stars Ginger Rogers and Ray Milland.

FEBRUARY 12 Rose Franken's comedy *Claudia* (453), starring Dorothy McGuire, is at the Booth. In 1943, McGuire will make her screen debut in the film.

Business and Society

The reviews are no worse than those of the other newspapers.

APRIL • The St. James Theatre begins to distribute programs for *Native Son* after the show rather than before. Each of the 10 scenes ends with a blackout, during which scenery is changed, and there is no intermission. Patrons had been striking matches during this time to read the program, causing the management to worry about a fire. • Hotel rooms in Washington, D.C., are already in short supply because of the defense buildup, and actors playing in that city must often sleep in Pullman cars.

MAY 1 A new New York State law prevents theatres from barring critics and columnists who have displeased the management. **7** The American Negro Theatre begins.

Births, Deaths, and Marriages

opening night of the comedy *Out of the Frying Pan*, 18-year-old Barbara Bel Geddes, in her Broadway debut, comes onstage still trying to zip up her dress and in the midst of her struggle starts to cry, the tears running her mascara into her eye. Someone slips her a towel and she manages to hold the dress together until the scene ends. Brooks Atkinson writes: "Norman Bel Geddes' plump and blonde daughter is still in the apprentice stage of histrionics."

MARCH • The Theatre Guild apologizes to its Boston subscribers for the Tennessee Williams *Battle of Angels* flop of two months ago, acknowledging that it "turned out badly, but who knows whether the next one by the same author may not prove a success?" • Tallulah Bankhead announces her separation from actor John Emery, attributing it to that "ole debbil career, which through force of circumstances has separated us for the better part of our marriage." **1** Shirley Booth is an original member of the cast of the radio show "Duffy's Tavern," premiering tonight. She's married to the star, Ed Gardiner. **2** Moss Hart says in *The New York Times* that he began to write *Lady in the Dark* with Katharine Cornell in mind for the lead role. But the way the play evolved suggested Irene Dunne or Gertrude Lawrence. Lawrence did not come cheap, he says. She wanted "my farm, the Music Box Theatre, Sam Harris's house in Palm Beach, half of Metro-Goldwyn-Mayer, a couple of race horses and five thousand dollars a week."

MAY • Measles hits Broadway, striking especially hard at younger players. Betty Hutton's four-day absence from *Panama Hattie*, beginning May 19, creates an opportunity for June Allyson, described afterward by *Variety* as "a chorine whose performance was rated 'sensational.'" **5** With the capture of his third Pulitzer Prize for drama for *There Shall Be No Night*, announced today, Robert E. Sherwood ties Eugene O'Neill for most awards in this category. Sherwood has won the prize on three of his last four plays, and the fourth was an adaptation and therefore ineligible.

MARCH 24 *Native Son* (114), a play that Richard Wright and Paul Green have fashioned from Wright's novel, is at the St. James. Produced by Orson Welles and John Houseman and directed by Welles, it stars Canada Lee.

APRIL 1 In Lillian Hellman's *Watch on the Rhine* (378), an exiled antifascist German confronts the enemy, who is a guest at a genteel Washington, D.C., household. Paul Lukas, Mady Christians, Lucile Watson, George Colouris, and Ann Blythe star at the Martin Beck. In 1943, it's on the screen. **8** The Experimental Theatre, begun in 1940, gives a single performance of *The Trojan Women* at the Cort. Margaret Webster, who also appears in the play, is directing Dame May Whitty (Webster's mother, offstage), Tamara Geva, and Walter Slezak. **21** William Saroyan's comedy about an eccentric family, *The Beautiful People* (120), which he has produced and directed himself, opens at the Lyceum. Betsy Blair, Eugene Loring, and Curtis Cooksy are in the cast.

MAY 31 *Tobacco Road* closes after a record 3,180 performances.

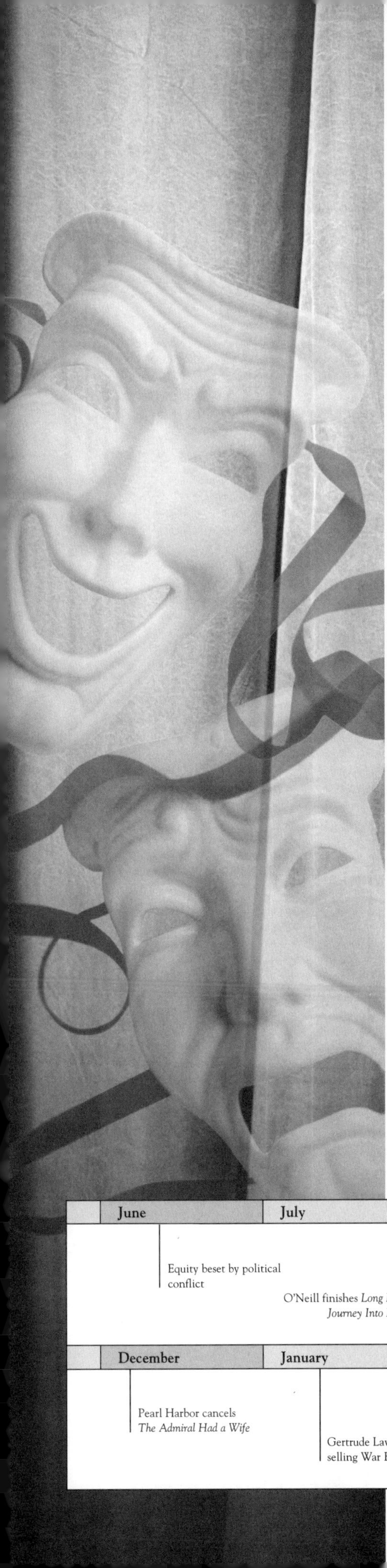

1941–42

The war dims the Great White Way, and Broadway answers the call to arms with the American Theatre Wing, the sale of War Bonds, and The Stage Door Canteen, a model for Hollywood's similar resting spot for people in uniform. Much of the theatre's creative energy has been redirected. Gertrude Lawrence says that Noel Coward has "no time for light and airy flippancies that were once part and parcel of his life." Equity is preoccupied with the issue of communism in its ranks. *New York Times* critic Brooks Atkinson calls this "the worst season for at least 20 years." But it has its points. Nancy Walker debuts, and "New Comedian Welcomed" is the headline that greets a night club appearance by young Zero Mostel, who also makes his Broadway debut. One of the season's points, unfortunately, is a period: John Barrymore is dead.

- Anticipated attendance at The Stage Door Canteen (opens March 1, 1942): 500 a night
- Actual attendance at Stage Door Canteen: 3,000–4,000 a night
- Danny Kaye's starting salary last season for *Lady in the Dark*: $250 a week
- Kaye's weekly compensation for *Let's Face It* this season (salary plus percentage): close to $3,000 a week
- Amount 14-year-old Barbara Cook wins at amateur night at the Roxy Theatre in Atlanta, where she sings "My Devotion": $10—in *cash*
- Comparison that José Quintero, arriving from Panama as a 17-year-old to attend college, will make between his native country and the U.S.: It is like "going straight from a corner grocery store into Bloomingdales."
- Number of plays in the black by the end of the season: 12, the fewest since *Variety* began to keep track in the 1923–1924 season
- Which young actors are hawking copies of *Actors Cues*, Leo Shul's publication carrying casting news, which will become the newspaper *Show Business*: Kirk Douglas, Lauren Bacall, and Shelly Winters
- How John Barrymore viewed moviemaking: "Hollywood in Latrina"
- What John Barrymore said to an actress with whom he was feuding when she walked off the stage in a huff, telling him, "Please remember I am a lady.": "Madam, I will respect your secret."
- What Harpo Marx will say of the late John Barrymore: "The passing of an ordinary man is sad. The passing of a great man is tragic, and doubly tragic when the greatness passes before the man does."
- What's inscribed on John Barrymore's crypt: "Good night, sweet prince."

Productions on Broadway: 83

Pulitzer Prize for Drama: none awarded

New York Drama Critics Circle Award:
Best Foreign Play: *Blithe Spirit* (Noel Coward)

June	July	August	September	October	November
Equity beset by political conflict	O'Neill finishes *Long Day's Journey Into Night*	Saroyan offers film rights to play for free	Nanette Fabares becomes Nanette Fabray	Nancy Walker debuts, and Helen Morgan d.	*Blithe Spirit* and *Junior Miss*

December	January	February	March	April	May
Pearl Harbor cancels *The Admiral Had a Wife*	Gertrude Lawrence selling War Bonds	"New Comedian Welcomed": Zero Mostel	Stage Door Canteen opens	Beatrice Lillie gets terrible news	John Barrymore d.

Personalities

JULY • Eugene O'Neill finishes *Long Day's Journey Into Night*, but it will not be produced until 1956. **31** Tallulah Bankhead is at the Bronx Zoo to donate her lion cub, "Winston Churchill," which she received from the Lions Club of Reno when she went there for a divorce. While posing for a publicity photo, Bankhead is bitten by a monkey.

AUGUST 6 William Saroyan takes a full-page ad in Variety, offering the film rights to *The Time of Your Life* for free to any studio that will produce it without compensation for anyone involved, all revenue to go toward "National Defense."

SEPTEMBER • Nanette Fabares changes her last name to Fabray because it is being mispronounced.

OCTOBER • Carol Channing becomes Eve Arden's understudy in Cole Porter's *Let's Face It* but will go on only once in nine months. • Maurice Evans becomes an American citizen. **24** Following tonight's performance of *Watch on the Rhine*, at the Martin Beck, scenes from Lillian Hellman's anti-Nazi drama are broadcast by shortwave, in German, to Germany. Radio actors, joined by Mady Christians from the play's cast, perform the excerpts, with the audience invited to stay for it.

NOVEMBER 17 Tallulah Bankhead collapses backstage with pneumonia at the end of a performance of *Clash By Night,* in Philadelphia. She's rushed to a hospital, where she will remain until December 3, delaying the play. **26** Irving Larheim legally changes his name to the one he's been using professionally for years, "Bert Lahr."

DECEMBER 2 The former circus acrobat and clown "Youl Bryner," making his New York stage debut tonight in *Twelfth Night,* is Yul Brynner. **7** In a breathtaking example of bad timing, *The Admiral Had a Wife*, a comedy about American naval officers in Hawaii and their spouses, starring Uta Hagen, Alfred Drake, and Red Buttons, is due to open this week. But in view of Japan's attack on Pearl Harbor this morning, it is announced that the

Plays and Musicals

OCTOBER 1 Nineteen-year-old Nancy Walker makes her Broadway debut in *Best Foot Forward* (326), at the Barrymore. Walker auditioned for the show under her real name, Myrtle Swoyer, but George Abbott and Richard Rodgers mistook her for another singer named Walker. She plays "Blind Date," a coed at a school called Winsocki, which lends its name to the show's most famous song, "Buckle Down, Winsocki." Also in the cast is June Allyson. A film version appears in 1943. **29** Danny Kaye's first starring role on Broadway is in Cole Porter's *Let's Face It!* (547), opening at the Imperial. Kaye, who will give way to José Ferrer during the run, is joined by a cast that includes Eve Arden, Vivian Vance, and Nanette Fabray. It's filmed in 1943.

Danny Kaye

NOVEMBER 5 Noel Coward's *Blithe Spirit* (682), at the Morosco, offers audiences high spirits—two, in fact. Atkinson, in the *Times*, says it "is a completely insane farce that is also uproarious." The cast includes Peggy Wood, Clifton Webb, and Mildred Natwick. The film version is out in 1945. **11** John Mason Brown will write of the performance of *Macbeth* (131) he sees tonight: "Not until last night at the National when Maurice Evans and Judith Anderson appeared in it, and the script was given the benefit of Margaret Webster's quickening direction,

Business and Society

JUNE 6 Actors Equity vice presidents, Florence Reed and Peggy Wood, along with several council members, resign when today's election to the council brings victory to several people they regard as radicals with a labor union agenda. Among the winners are Alan Hewitt, accused by one Congressman of being a Communist sympathizer, Myron McCormick, and Mady Christians. Ethel Waters becomes the first black elected to the council. Cornelia Otis Skinner and Dudley Digges will replace Reed and Wood.

SEPTEMBER 26 At a contentious meeting, members of Actors Equity vote for a referendum on the issue of amending its rules to keep out Communists and fascists. Equity president Bert Lytell has threatened to resign if the organization doesn't do something to ward off Congressional criticism on this issue.

OCTOBER • The Yiddish Art Theatre, which has played continuously for 23 years, suspends operations. • The first press agent to reach the new limit of representing six shows, set by the Theatrical Managers and Agents Union, is Richard Maney.

Births, Deaths, and Marriages

JUNE 1 Jennie Dolly of the Dolly Sisters d. **13** Tallulah Bankhead divorces John Emery. **16** Irene Franklin d. **19** Maria Tucci b. **20** Adolph Green m. Elizabeth Reitell.

JULY 2 Producer Sam Harris d. **21** With his longtime partner Joe Weber at his bedside, Lew Fields d. **27** Helen Morgan m. auto dealer Lloyd Johnson.

AUGUST 14 Playwright Tom Eyen b.

SEPTEMBER 17 Morris Carnovsky m. Phoebe Brand. **22** Betsy Blair m. Gene Kelly.

SEPTEMBER 26 Playwright Eugene Walter d.

OCTOBER 1 Ethel Merman and William J. Smith are divorced. **8** Helen Morgan d. at 41 as she started out in show business: broke. Polly Bergen, who will later por-

play is being withdrawn for "rewriting." **13** With air raid sirens wailing and the streets plunged into darkness by a blackout, Katharine Cornell walks a half mile from her Nob Hill hotel to the Curran Theatre in San Francisco to perform in *The Doctor's Dilemma* for the 350 members of the audience who have managed to get there, too. **15** Life's cover story is on Broadway's *Junior Miss*. **18** The Playwrights Company withdraws Robert Sherwood's *There Shall Be No Night*, starring Alfred Lunt and Lynn Fontanne, which is now in Rochester, Minnesota. This drama, which celebrated Finnish resistance to Russian invasion just a few years ago, suddenly seems besides the point. Finland is now allied with Germany, and the U.S.S.R. has become America's ally.

JANUARY • Tallulah Bankhead, star of *Clash By Night*, which is produced by Billy Rose, with whom she's at odds, blurts out to an interviewer from the *World-Telegram* that she wishes the show would close. She will apologize to the cast, saying that she didn't mean it. **1** Joshua Logan gets the approval of his doctors to go back to work after last year's nervous breakdown. **2** Gertrude Lawrence, star of *Lady in the Dark*, is selling defense bonds in the lobby of the Alvin Theatre. **6** Eleanor Roosevelt, arriving with her friend, Joseph P. Lash, at the Mansfield to see *In Time to Come*, a play about President Wilson, sees a picket line in front. Director Otto Preminger is resisting demands by the musicians union that he employ four of their members for the play's incidental music. Mrs. Roosevelt won't cross the line, and her money ($3.30 per ticket) is refunded. **27** Pat Hitchcock, the 12-year-old star of John Van Druten's *Solitaire*, opening at the Plymouth, is the daughter of screen director Alfred Hitchcock.

FEBRUARY 1 Ben Hecht, in a *New York Times* article, characterizes the critical reaction to his *Lily of the Valley*, which opened and closed in less than a week, as "shockingly illiterate and flapdoodle type of bad reporting" and "cruel heigh-de-ho inattentiveness." **23** In a *Chicago Sun* interview, Gertrude Lawrence says that she hasn't heard for a while from Noel

---

have the excitements of the tragedy proven contagious in the contemporary theatre." **18** In *Junior Miss* (710), an adolescent with an overactive imagination causes temporary havoc in the lives of those around her. Patricia Peardon stars at the Lyceum. Jerome Chodorov and Joseph Fields's play will reach the screen in 1945.

DECEMBER 1 Olsen and Johnson are loose again, this time in the revue *Sons O' Fun* (742), at the Winter Garden, with Carmen Miranda, Ella Logan, and Joe Besser. **5** *Angel Street* (1,293), Patrick Hamilton's melodrama that has played in London under the title *Gaslight* (the title of the 1944 Hollywood version), is at the John Golden. Vincent Price is trying to drive his wife, played by Judith Evelyn, crazy. The detective who aids her is Leo G. Carroll. **25** Eddie Cantor is at the Hollywood Theatre, back on Broadway after thirteen years—and back in blackface—in *Banjo Eyes* (126), a musical based on *Three Men on a Horse*. The music is by Vernon Duke, with lyrics by John LaTouche. **28** *In Time to Come* (40), a play by John Huston and Howard Koch about Woodrow Wilson and the League of Nations, is at the Mansfield. It's produced by Otto Preminger and stars Richard Gaines.

JANUARY 22 Cheryl Crawford produces a revival of *Porgy and Bess* (286), at the Majestic, with leads Todd Duncan and Anne Brown from the original cast and Avon Long as Sportin' Life.

Vincent Price

NOVEMBER 1 Minimum pay for chorus girls and boys rises from $35 to $40 a week.

DECEMBER • The weeks before Christmas are often slow at the box office, but this year the war has business down by as much as 25 to 40 percent. **12** Theatre managers meeting with police and fire officials at the Ziegfeld can't seem to get a clear idea of what to do if the war literally does come close to home. They are told to go on with the show in the event of an air raid, not to tell the audience, if possible, but also to keep the house lights on if it happens. **15** The American Theatre Wing, which has been operating as a branch of British War Relief, becomes the American Theatre Wing War Service, an American agency, Rachel Crothers president. Also active are Helen Hayes, Burgess Meredith, Clare Boothe, Ilka Chase, Clifton Webb, Ray Bolger, Gertrude Lawrence, and Cornelia Otis Skinner. **17** *Variety* editorializes: "America is in the war, and show business, ever alert to interpret the American spirit, is pledged to play its inimitable role. Let it be said that Americans will be proud of its performance."

FEBRUARY • Eddie Cantor and Olsen and Johnson, concerned with increasing

---

tray her on TV, will be criticized for saying that Morgan "wasn't such a name. . . . I don't believe that people would accept her today." **20** Producer Jed Harris m. actress Louise Platt.

DECEMBER • Ethel Merman announces that she has m. newspaper executive Robert D. Levitt but won't say when. **4** Milton Berle m. showgirl Joyce Matthews. **25** Blanche Bates d. **29** Lillian Roth m. Edward Goldman.

JANUARY 4 Betty Comden m. designer Steven Kyle. Otis Skinner d. **16** Playwright Elmer Rice m. actress Betty Field. **19** Michael Crawford b.

APRIL 24 Barbra Streisand b.

MAY 10 Joe Weber d. **16** Producer Morris Gest d. **29** John Barrymore d., and Kevin Conway b.

Personalities

Coward. "Of course, it's the war that's responsible. He is, I understand, so completely immersed in propaganda work that he has no time for light and airy flippancies that were once part and parcel of his life. The war has changed the outlook of all of us, and no one more than Noel." **28** Under the headline "New Comedian Welcomed," the *New York Herald-Tribune* reviews the appearance of Zero Mostel at the Café Society Downtown. The critic finds him "immensely funny." **28** Burgess Meredith is drafted.

MARCH 2 The Stage Door Canteen, sponsored by the American Theatre Wing, opens this afternoon in what was formerly The Little Club, under the Forty-fourth Street Theatre, in a space donated by Lee Shubert. Men and women in the service—black or white, despite some sentiment in the planning stages to separate the races—can dance and eat for free and mingle with Broadway stars. Today, Gertrude Lawrence is present with cast members of *Lady in the Dark* to sing "Jenny." Tallulah Bankhead and Walter Pidgeon drop by, and Jane Cowl and Selena Royle are working in the kitchen. The Hollywood Canteen will be modeled after this one. **3** Equity suspends Mary Boland for her sudden exit because of illness from *The Rivals*, playing in Chicago, after she refuses to see one of its doctors, and the Theatre Guild files charges against her. Margaret Anglin comes out of retirement to replace Boland.

APRIL 10 Beatrice Lillie, touring with a show in Manchester, England, is informed that her son has been lost at sea with the sinking of the aircraft carrier *Hermes*. **14** The Theatre Guild, satisfied that Mary Boland was indeed ill when she left *The Rivals* in Chicago on March 3, withdraws the charges it filed against her with Equity. That organization fines her $500 for refusing to see one of its doctors, and she apologizes.

MAY 16 Irked at a photographer who snapped her picture outside the Nixon Theatre in Pittsburgh after he said he wouldn't, Katharine Hepburn breaks his

Plays and Musicals

APRIL 7 *The Moon Is Down* (71), at the Martin Beck, adapted from a John Steinbeck novel about the Nazi invasion of Norway, with a cast that includes Otto Kruger and Lyle Bettger, displeases many critics. But Twentieth Century-Fox will buy it for $300,000 and bring it to the screen next year. **3** European character actor Herbert Berghof makes his Broadway debut at the Belasco in *Nathan the Wise* (28). **24** Two-a-day vaudeville is revived at the Forty-fourth Street Theatre in a show called *Keep 'Em Laughing* (77). Starring are Victor Moore, William Gaxton and night club comedian Zero Mostel. *Variety* editor Abel Green writes that in Mostel, the audience "witnessed another new star being born."

MAY 20 Thomas Job's *Uncle Harry* (430), in which a brother's revenge on his sisters for undermining his romance leads to murder, opens at the Broadhurst. Joseph Schildkraut and Eva Le Gallienne are the stars. It will reach the screen in 1945.

Business and Society

attacks on the loyalty of American entertainers, write to the heads of the major labor organizations, asking them to stand up for those being singled out. • John Golden is the last major producer to join The League of New York Theatres, founded in 1930. He has avoided concerted action with his fellow producers since his disillusionment with such activity in the 1919 Actors Equity Strike.

MARCH • A *Variety* headline describes a new production of *The Mikado*, opening in Cleveland, as "De-Japped." • An unsuccessful campaign to stop the closing of Times Square's last burlesque house, the Gaiety, is supported by Fanny Brice, Al Jolson, and other Broadway luminaries. **21** Actors Equity, by a vote of 552 to 228, approves an amendment to its laws barring fascists and Communists from the organization. The vote is a response to Congressional criticism of leftists in Equity.

MAY 18 The dimout of Broadway's lights as an air raid precaution is intensified, substantially subduing the Great White Way.

Births, Deaths, and Marriages

camera. She's appearing in the play *Without Love*. **19** John Barrymore is rehearsing *Romeo and Juliet* for a performance on Rudy Vallee's "Sealtest" program when he collapses in the studio. He d. 10 days later. **21** Ethel Barrymore sprains her ankle during a performance of *The Corn Is Green*, in Boston. She finishes the show but will be hospitalized and out for four days.

Photo opposite: Alfred Drake and Joan Roberts as Curly and Laurey, in Rodgers and Hammerstein's *Oklahoma!* PF

Broadway in Transition

1942–1967

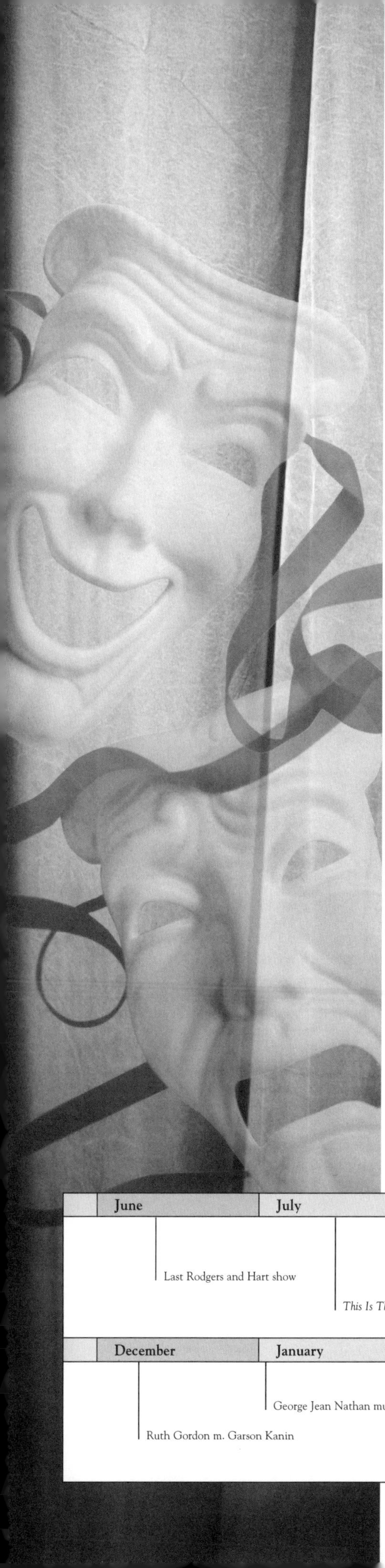

1942–43

The American musical hits a gusher with the first of nine shows by Rodgers and Hammerstein. Scalpers are getting as much as an outrageous $12 for $4.40 orchestra seats for *Oklahoma!*—and that's *Oklahoma!* with an exclamation mark! The American Theatre Wing stages its first *Lunchtime Follies* at a Brooklyn shipyard, and theatre audiences are asked to share their *Playbill* to conserve paper. The often vitriolic critic George Jean Nathan is mugged and—surprise—it's not by an actor. Scholars are asking if Thornton Wilder, in *The Skin of Our Teeth*, cribbed from *Finnegans Wake*. And is that young blonde in *Rosalinda* really Shelley Winters? Katharine Hepburn plays in *Without Love*, without heat; Carmen Miranda, with fruit basket, has left Broadway for Hollywood; and Lorenz Hart winds down toward a sad end.

- Percentage of male members of Actors Equity in the Service: about a third
- What the press agent for *Away We Go* initially feels about changing the title to *Oklahoma*: it's about as good as calling it "New Jersey"
- How the exclamation mark in the title of *Oklahoma!* is added to the show's press release, thousands of which have already been printed and most go out the next day: by hand, with several people working through the night
- Number of musicals in which *Oklahoma!* star Celeste Holm has appeared: none
- Capital needed to produce *Oklahoma!*: $100,000
- Nice story: Producer Mike Todd (or a ticket broker, depending on who is telling it), is said to walk out on a tryout of *Oklahoma!* remarking, "No legs, no jokes, no chance." Winchell attributes it to Todd in his column
- How far in advance you have to buy tickets to get in to see *Oklahoma!*: you can buy them the afternoon of opening night for that night's performance because it's not sold out—after the reviews, good luck!
- What a gracious Lorenz Hart says at Sardi's to his former partner Richard Rodgers after the opening night performance of *Oklahoma!*: "You have at least another *Blossom Time*. This show of yours will run forever."
- First and foremost: Away from the professional stage, *Oklahoma!* will be Rodgers and Hammerstein's most popular musical, with 632 amateur productions through mid 1996
- Longest-running *Ziegfeld Follies*: this season's, with 553 performances
- Number of showgirls in *The Ziegfeld Follies*: 10
- Number of ponies in *The Ziegfeld Follies*: 16
- Cost per week of filling the fruit bowl with fresh fruit for each performance of *The Doughgirls*: $14
- Weekly cost of ice used in air-conditioning systems of Broadway theatres: $250–$350
- Almost certainly the only gentile, non-Yiddish-speaking actress with a lead role in a Yiddish theatre play: Jean Platt, playing the deaf mute in a Yiddish version of *Johnny Belinda*
- Statistics, so far, for Ethel Barrymore's tour in *The Corn Is Green*: 78 one-night stands, 23,000 miles, and 37 states
- What Blythe Danner's German-speaking grandmother, who can't pronounce "th," says about her granddaughter's being named "Blythe": "Vot? You call her Blight? It's a disease of the trees."

Productions on Broadway: 80

Pulitzer Prize for Drama: *The Skin of Our Teeth* (Thornton Wilder)

New York Drama Critics Circle Award:
Best American Play: *The Patriots* (Sidney Kingsley)

June
- Last Rodgers and Hart show

July
- *This Is The Army*

August
- Carmen Miranda buys out contract

September
- Jessica Tandy m. Hume Cronyn

October
- Air raid drills crimp matineés

November
- George M. Cohan d.

December
- Ruth Gordon m. Garson Kanin

January
- George Jean Nathan mugged

February
- Actor's minimum pay rises to $57.50

March
- *Oklahoma!*

April
- Skip Homeier in *Tomorrow the World*

May
- Basement dressing rooms closed

Personalities

JUNE • Erich von Stroheim replaces Boris Karloff in *Arsenic and Old Lace*. **22** The American Theatre Wing stages its first *Lunchtime Follies* at a Brooklyn shipyard. These variety shows will be aimed at boosting morale and increasing productivity, playing to each shift in plants visited. Participants will include Rodgers and Hart, Arlene Francis, Jack Albertson, Sam Jaffe, Zero Mostel, Frederic March, and Shirley Booth.

JULY • Gertrude Lawrence is very much a lady in the dark when a blackout is declared during a show she's giving at a Massachusetts Army base. Lawrence, of course, goes right on singing even when the lights go out. **23** *The New York Times* headline is "Lynn Riggs Play [t]o Be [a] Musical." It reports that the Theatre Guild will produce a musical version, not yet titled, of *Green Grow the Lilacs*. Oscar Hammerstein II will write the book and, according to the paper, the music and lyrics will come from Rodgers and Hart. But Lorenz Hart's drinking and mental deterioration make it impossible for him to work on the show that will become *Oklahoma!* **30** Bill "Bojangles" Robinson, who two nights ago refused to appear at the Philadelphia Stage Door Canteen because of a rumor that black servicemen were not welcome there, relents when reassured that the story is untrue.

AUGUST • Carmen Miranda, now a hit in films, buys her way out of her contract with the Shuberts for $60,000. • Conservative columnist George Sokolsky attacks Zero Mostel for his burlesques of U.S. Congressmen. **10** Paul Robeson, starring in *Othello* at the Brattle Hall summer theatre in Cambridge, Massachusetts, is the first black actor to play the Moor in a U.S. production with an otherwise white cast. *Variety* says that he gives a performance such "that no white man should ever dare presume to play it again, especially since it is to be strongly questioned that any member of the audience, no matter how delicate of sensitivities, [i]s offended by a single moment of the action."

SEPTEMBER • In what is said to be a New

Plays and Musicals

JUNE 3 Rodgers and Hart's longest-running Broadway musical and last collaboration, *By Jupiter* (421), opens at the Shubert. Ray Bolger, in his Broadway breakthrough role, Constance Moore, Benay Venuta, and Vera Ellen are in it. **24** Ken Murray's *Blackouts of 1942*, featuring Marie Wilson, opens at the El Capitan Theatre in Los Angeles, where it will run through World War II.

JUNE 24 Onstage in *Star and Garter* (605), stripper Gypsy Rose Lee is taking it off. Offstage, she has been emptying her pockets to help finance this show that almost didn't survive a disastrous one-performance preview. With burlesque houses outlawed in New York, producer Mike Todd, calling it a "revue," is presenting the bumps and grinds unalloyed and undressed at the Music Box. Georgia Sothern and Bobby Clark are also in the cast. **4** Irving Berlin's *This Is the Army* (113) revue, in which he reprises "Oh, How I Hate to Get Up in the Morning," opens at the Broadway Theatre, with proceeds for the entire run going to the Army Emergency Relief Fund. The 359-man cast—including Burl Ives, Ezra Stone, and Gary Merrill—makes up the only racially integrated unit in the Army, integrated at Berlin's insistence, although he has to be talked out of using the black soldiers in a minstrel number. The show introduces "This Is the Army, Mr. Jones" and follows its Broadway run with a war front tour extending to October 22, 1945. A film version will appear next year.

SEPTEMBER 10 *Janie* (642), a comedy by Josephine Bentham and Herschel Williams, is at Henry Miller's Theatre. In the cast are Gwen Anderson, Frank Amy, and Herbert Evers. A film version appears in 1944.

OCTOBER 7 Maxwell Anderson's *The Eve of St. Mark* (306), the bittersweet story of a romance that ends with a soldier's death, opens at the Cort. In the cast are William Prince, Aline McMahon, and Mary Rolfe. **12** Molly Picon is at the Molly Picon Theatre (formerly the Al Jolson) in *Oy, Is Dus a Leben!* (139), the

Business and Society

JUNE • Stage unions, concerned about the incorporation of the nonprofit production *This Is the Army*, are reassured that this is a precaution to protect composer Irving Berlin's rights to the music after the show ends. • Gas and tire rationing will cut summer stock productions by as much as 50 percent this season. The Bucks County Playhouse moves its shows out of the countryside and into the ballroom of a Philadelphia hotel.

OCTOBER • Touring productions are beginning to encounter difficulties because the railroads are giving priority to the movement of troops and war material. • New York City theatre managers are complaining that the 2:30 starting time for air raid practice alerts is disrupting the beginning of matinées.

NOVEMBER 2 New York City License Commissioner Paul Moss issues summons to three management employees at the Ambassador Theatre, where *Wine, Women and Song*, a thinly disguised burlesque show, is playing. They will be convicted on obscenity charges, and the show will be closed, next month. Pressure is growing to squelch shows like this one and

Births, Deaths, and Marriages

JUNE 13 Sidney Blackmer m. actress Suzanne Kaaren. **13** Frances Farmer and Leif Erikson are divorced, and he m. actress Margaret Hayes.

AUGUST 20 Director Gilbert Moses b. **31** Gypsy Rose Lee m. Alexander Kirkland, currently appearing in *Junior Miss*.

SEPTEMBER 3 Publisher Harrison Grey Fiske d. **23** Ella Logan m. Fred Finklehoffe, producer of *Show Time*, in which she is now appearing. **27** Jessica Tandy m. Hume Cronyn. **27** Stella Adler m. Harold Clurman.

NOVEMBER 5 George M. Cohan d. **9** Edna May Oliver d. **13** Laura Hope Crews d.

DECEMBER 4 Ruth Gordon m. Garson Kanin. **12** Helen Westley d.

York first, the *Herald-Tribune* assigns its new theatre critic, Howard Barnes, who has replaced Richard Watts, Jr., now with the Office of War Information, to cover films as well as stage shows.

OCTOBER • Al Jolson settles for an undisclosed sum with the producer of *Hold On to Your Hats*, the show he quit suddenly last February 1. **6** In a pictorial essay on Zero Mostel, *Look* magazine declares that "[i]n eight short months, this waggish ex-artist has bounced from obscurity to the front line of American funnymen." **8** In a special performance of *This Is the Army*, at the National Theatre in Washington, D.C., Irving Berlin is furious, on making his entrance, to see soldiers in the cast presenting arms toward the box where

Irving Berlin in *This Is the Army*

story of her stage life, by her husband Jacob Kalich. **28** *Rosalinda* (521), an adaptation of *Die Fledermaus*, by Gottfried Reinhardt and John Meehan, Jr., is at the Forty-forth Street Theatre. Dorothy Sarnoff and Oscar Karlweiss star, and also in the cast are Gene Barry and "Shelly Winter," later Shelley Winters.

NOVEMBER 10 Katharine Hepburn is at the St. James in Philip Barry's new comedy *Without Love* (110), costarring Elliott Nugent. Hepburn stars in the 1945 film with Spencer Tracy. **18** Thornton Wilder's allegorical *The Skin of Our Teeth* (355), in which one family encompasses human history, opens at the Plymouth. Directed by Elia Kazan, it stars Tallulah Bankhead, E. G. Marshall, Frederic March, Florence Eldridge, "Dickie" Van Patten, and Montgomery Clift. **25** Alfred Lunt and Lynn Fontanne star in S. N. Behrman's comedy *The Pirate* (176), opening at the Martin Beck. Fontanne is the impressionable wife of the governor of a town in the West Indies, who fantasizes that Lunt is a corsair. The 1948 film musical stars Judy Garland, Gene Kelly, and Walter Slezak.

DECEMBER 21 Katharine Cornell's production of Chekhov's *The Three Sisters* (123)

Star and Garter and *Strip for Action*.

FEBRUARY • The minimum weekly pay for actors rises to $57.50. **8** The *Playbill* distributed in all legitimate theatres today notes that in order to conserve paper for the war effort, patrons are asked to share programs.

MAY • Some patrons are complaining that ticket scalpers are getting as much as $12 for the top-price $4.40 orchestra seats for *Oklahoma!* • New York City orders theatres with basement dressing rooms—commonly assigned to members of the chorus in musicals and used to store costumes—to close them because they are fire hazards. Last November's fatal fire at Boston's Cocoanut Grove is thought to have inspired this move.

JANUARY 23 Critic Alexander Woollcott d. **25** Rex Harrison m. Lilli Palmer.

FEBRUARY 22 Tamara, who sang "Smoke Gets in Your Eyes" in Jerome Kern's *Roberta*, is killed in a plane crash in Portugal while on a U.S.O. tour to entertain troops. Severely disabled in the crash is singer Jane Froman (whose story will be told in the 1952 film *With a Song in My Heart*).

MARCH 8 Lynn Redgrave b. **14** Producer Alexander Aarons d. **29** Frank Gillmore, former president of Actors Equity, d. **31** Christopher Walken b.

APRIL 8 Choreographer-director Michael Bennett (Michael Bennett DiFiglia) b. **12** Actor-director Charles Ludlam b.

MAY 14 Clifford Odets m. actress Betty Grayson. **18** Theatrical artist Al Hirschfeld m. actress Dolly Haas, a match that will produce a daughter Nina, whose name Hirschfeld will work into his drawings.

Personalities

President Roosevelt is sitting, rather than to the composer, as called for in the script. Director Ezra Stone had arranged the change without telling Berlin.

NOVEMBER • Brooks Atkinson leaves *The New York Times* drama desk to serve as a war correspondent in the Far East. Taking his place at the *Times* is Lewis Nichols. • Playwright Clare Boothe Luce is elected to Congress from Connecticut. **25** *Variety* reports that MGM is interested in doing a film biography of Marie Dressler and that Metro has in mind Judy Garland to play the young Dressler in her Weber and Fields Music Hall days. **25** Gentile actress Jean Platt does the seemingly impossible, holding down the lead role in a Yiddish theatre production. She's reprising the title role that she played at the end of the run of *Johnny Belinda* as the deaf mute, in a Yiddish version opening at the Parkway Theatre in Brooklyn.

DECEMBER 7 Bowing to pressure from theatre people, Lee Shubert retracts the closing notice he put up at the Majestic two days ago for the revival of *Native Son*. Shubert claims to be worried that the play could result in legal action over the issue of obscenities, given the present crackdown in New York City. In fact, with the show losing money, he's seeking an excuse to fold it. **10** David Merrick has his first Broadway credit, "Associate Producer," when *The Willow and I* opens at the Windsor. **21** The audience at the St. James is bundled up in their overcoats, with the temperature around zero outside and the temperature inside the theatre not being terribly warm, either. It's reported that Katharine Hepburn, starring in *Without Love*, does not want the radiators going while the curtain is up because they make too much noise. **25** Carol Channing is "Steve," a suspected lesbian nurse, in *Proof Through the Night*.

JANUARY 1 Critic George Jean Nathan is the victim of a late-night New Year's Eve mugging in midtown Manhattan. He's quoted as saying, "I know it couldn't be actors; they aren't as brave or as strong as those yeggs were."

Plays and Musicals

opens at the Barrymore. It costars Judith Anderson, Alexander Knox, Edmund Gwenn and as "An Orderly," 26-year-old Kirk Douglas. **30** *The Doughgirls* (671), a comedy at the Lyceum, by Joseph Fields, stars Doris Nolan, Virginia Field, Arleen Whelan, and Arlene Francis.

JANUARY 7 *Something For the Boys* (422), the third Broadway joining of Ethel Merman with Cole Porter's music—they've done *DuBarry Was a Lady* and *Panama Hattie*—is at the Alvin. A few servicemen, their inheritance, and a woman who receives radio signals in her teeth, make for the plot. Merman sings "Hey, Good Lookin'." **29** With America fighting for democracy, Sidney Kingsley has written *The Patriots* (172), about Washington, Jefferson, and Hamilton, starring Cecil Humphreys, Raymond Edward Johnson, and House Jameson. It's at the National Theatre.

MARCH 3 Helen Hayes plays Harriet Beecher Stowe, and Rhys Williams plays her husband in *Harriet* (377), by Florence Ryerson and Colin Clements. It opens at Henry Miller's Theatre. **17** Joan Caulfield plays teenager Corliss Archer in F. Hugh Herbert's comedy *Kiss and Tell* (962), at the Biltmore. Broadway unknown Richard Widmark is also in the cast. The play is the basis for the 1943 radio program "Meet Corliss Archer." **17** *Variety*'s review of the New Haven tryout (opened March 11) of *Away We Go!*—not yet renamed *Oklahoma!*—says it "should stretch into a sizeable stay on Broadway. Film possibilities are bright." **31** Oh, what a beautiful evenin'! *Oklahoma!* (2,212) at the St. James Theatre, is the first of nine Richard Rodgers and Oscar Hammerstein II musicals. The choreographer Agnes DeMille, in her Broadway debut, innovatively integrates dance, music, and plot with elements of ballet. The director is Rouben Mamoulian. In the cast are Alfred Drake, Joan Roberts, Celeste Holm, Howard Da Silva, and Bambi Linn. The classic score includes the title tune "Oh What a Beautiful Mornin'," "The Surrey With the Fringe on Top," "Kansas City," and "People Will Say

Business and Society

Births, Deaths, and Marriages

FEBRUARY • Director Guthrie McClintic takes over for Edmund Gwenn for 28 performances in *The Three Sisters*, when the British actor is out with pneumonia. • Several scholars are carrying on a running discussion in various periodicals about the extent to which Thornton Wilder borrowed from Joyce's *Finnegans Wake* for *The Skin of Our Teeth*.

MARCH 1 Rumanian-born John Houseman becomes a U.S. citizen. **11** *Away We Go!* opens in New Haven for a tryout. Backers for this musical version of *Green Grow the Lilacs* have been hard to come by, even when treated to Oscar Hammerstein II singing "Oh, What a Beautiful Morning" and "Surrey With the Fringe on Top," from the show, backed by Richard Rodgers at the piano. Finally, Harry Cohn of Columbia Pictures bites for $15,000, and others follow. It is in New Haven that the composer and lyricist convince the Theatre Guild to change the title to *Oklahoma!* (the Guild insists on the exclamation mark).

MAY 23 Writing in *The New York Times* about *Oklahoma!* lyricist Oscar Hammerstein says, "We realized that an actual killing is something the average musical playgoer doesn't bargain for when he buys his ticket. And yet the only honest way to grant Curley and Laurey a future of real fulfillment is to wipe out Jud."

We're in Love." The 1955 film stars Gordon MacRae, Shirley Jones, and Rod Steiger. The original cast recording of this show is a first for U.S. musicals—London productions have been recorded for years.

APRIL 1 The longest-running *Ziegfeld Follies* (553) of all opens at the Winter Garden. This edition stars Milton Berle, Ilona Massey, and Arthur Treacher. **14** Twelve-year-old Skip Homeier, in a role he will repeat in the 1944 screen version, makes his Broadway debut in *Tomorrow the World* (499) as the boy whose anti-Nazi father is killed by the Nazis, who then make the son one of them. Also starring in this play by James Gow and Arnaud d'Usseau, at the Barrymore, are Ralph Bellamy, Dorothy Sands, and Shirley Booth.

MAY 5 Phoebe and Henry Ephron's comedy *Three's a Family* (497), in which adult children return to live with their parents during the wartime housing shortage, opens at the Longacre.

1943–44

The Equity Library Theatre begins modestly in New York, but it will pay extravagant dividends in the young talent it nurtures. Paul Robeson is Othello in a landmark production, with José Ferrer and Uta Hagen. Tennessee Williams, working for MGM, can't get anyone interested in his screenplay "A Gentleman Caller," based on his short story, "Portrait of a Girl in Glass." With the return of prosperity, *Mexican Hayride* revives the $5.50 orchestra seat, not seen on Broadway in years. Mary Martin is a more appropriate Venus than Marlene Dietrich, Jackie Gleason is in drag as "Goofy Gale," Noel Coward says "bloody" on the BBC, and Ray Bolger, entertaining the GI's in the Pacific, is prepared not to dance but to jump—for his life.

- Serving as a camouflage officer with the Army: famed set designer Joe Mielziner
- In the Office of Strategic Services (OSS), outwitting the Nazis: Captain Garson Kanin
- Total number of Theatre Guild subscribers: 80,000
- Minimum capital required to stage a Broadway musical: about $100,000
- Last time a Broadway musical charged a top price of $5.50 at every performance before this season's *Mexican Hayride*: 1932, for *Of Thee I Sing*
- Amount that *This Is the Army* will earn for Army Emergency Relief: about $10,000,000
- George Jean Nathan's approach to criticism: "The drama critic who is without prejudice is on the plane with the general who does not believe in taking human life."
- Broadway's largest theatre, not counting the City Center: the Broadway, seating 1,900
- Reward offered by the St. James Theatre to anyone who can prove that they have paid more than the legal premium for tickets to *Oklahoma!*: $100
- Cast replacements in *Oklahoma!*: Howard Keel and Shelley Winters. The touring company will feature John Raitt, Florence Henderson, Barbara Cook, and Pamela Britton
- Margaret Sullavan and Elliott Nugent, starring in *The Voice of the Turtle*, are the first to use the new dressing rooms at the Morosco—two-room suites with kitchenettes.
- Where Lillian Hellman got the title *The Searching Wind*, according to critic Burns Mantle: "Miss Hellman thinks she got it from a colored maid who once worked for her."

Productions on Broadway: 97

Pulitzer Prize for Drama: none awarded

New York Drama Critics Circle Award:
Best Foreign Play: *Jacobowsky and the Colonel* (Franz Werfel)

June	July	August	September	October	November
Baltimore and D.C. won't get *Othello*	Noel Coward creates a bloody uproar	Irene Worth's Broadway debut	Lunt and Fontanne in Britain	*One Touch of Venus* and *Othello*	Lorenz Hart d.

December	January	February	March	April	May
Ray Bolger prepared to ditch	*Mexican Hayride*	Equity Library Theatre started	Raymond Massey becomes a U.S. citizen	Jackie Gleason in drag	Marlon Brando in *Twelfth Night*

Personalities

JUNE • Eugene O'Neill's daughter, Oona, marries Charlie Chaplin, many years her senior. Never close to her, the appalled playwright will never see or speak to her again. • The Theatre Guild grants Paul Robeson's request that Washington, D.C., and Baltimore be excluded from the tour of *Othello* because their theatres segregate audiences. **19** Noel Coward scandalizes many in Britain when he sings his song "Let's Not Be Beastly to the Germans" with the word "bloody" over the BBC.

JULY 28 Critic Burton Rascoe, in the *New York World-Telegram*, defends Ray Bolger against suggestions that in withdrawing from *By Jupiter*, he was callously putting many people out of a job. Rascoe points out that the singer-dancer has been suffering from exhaustion and needs to rest before traveling to the Pacific to entertain the troops. Rascoe says that one of those carping is the show's composer (Richard Rodgers).

AUGUST • Theresa Helburn and Lawrence Langner of the Theatre Guild are reported to be angry with director Rouben Mamoulian, who is trying to hog most of the credit for the success of *Oklahoma!* • Burns Mantle, who has been the *New York Daily News* theatre critic since 1922, has moved up to critic emeritus, with John Chapman officially taking over the daily reviewing chores. **9** Tennessee Williams, unable to write a screenplay for Lana Turner called *Marriage Is a Private Affair*, is suspended by MGM. Instead, he has written the outline for another screenplay called "A Gentleman Caller,"

Mary Martin LYNCH

Plays and Musicals

AUGUST 3 Irene Worth makes her Broadway debut at the Booth in Martin Vale's crime drama *The Two Mrs. Carrolls* (585). The playwright is actually Marguerite Vale Veiller, whose husband, playwright Bayard Veiller, d. this year. The film version is released in 1947.

OCTOBER 7 *One Touch of Venus* (567), written by S.J. Perelman and Ogden Nash, with music by Kurt Weill, including "Speak Low," opens at the Imperial. Mary Martin has her first Broadway starring role as the statue that comes to life. The film version appears in 1948. **19** *Othello* (295) opens at the Shubert, with

Business and Society

JUNE • The month begins with 24 shows on Broadway, compared with 16 a year ago at this time. War work has fueled prosperity, and limitations on travel have made plays and films more important sources of entertainment than before the war.

OCTOBER 5 Special matinées of *Life With Father, Something for the Boys, Oklahoma!* and *Tomorrow the World*, for which tickets come with the purchase of a War Bond, sell $8,200,000 worth of bonds at a top of $10,000 per bond.

JANUARY 5 New York City License Commissioner Paul Moss, who played in vaudeville in blackface, writes in *Variety*: "Public officials must be on the lookout for those performances which by plain import of language are no more than an appeal to the salaciously disposed. Such shows have a tendency to deprave and corrupt minds, and people who knowingly and for profit present a production for that purpose are a menace to the theatre."

FEBRUARY • New York City newspapers are limiting theatrical advertising to conserve newsprint.

Births, Deaths, and Marriages

JUNE 1 Leslie Howard d. in a plane crash. **14** Choreographer Agnes DeMille m. Walter Prude. **16** Playwright Bayard Veiller d. **21** Director Andre Serban b.

JULY • Victor Moore, whose wife and former vaudeville partner, Emma Littlefield, d. in 1934, announces that he has m. chorus girl Shirley Paige, who appeared in *Pal Joey*. **12** Cissie Loftus d. **14** Jules Bledsoe d.

AUGUST 16 Walter Kerr, director of the Drama Department at Catholic University in Washington, D.C. and future drama critic of the *New York Herald-Tribune* and *The New York Times*, m. Jean Collins, future playwright.

SEPTEMBER 24 Shirley Booth m. William H. Baker, Jr.

based on his short story, "Portrait of a Girl in Glass." But the studio has no interest in what will become *The Glass Menagerie*.

AUGUST 27 Kurt Weill becomes an American citizen. Also taking the oath of citizenship at the Naturalization Bureau, coincidentally, is screen director and Broadway producer Otto Preminger.

SEPTEMBER • Alfred Lunt and Lynn Fontanne leave for Great Britain, where they will remain for most of the next two years. • Helen Hayes's operation for bursitis causes the suspension of *Harriet*, in which she's currently starring at Henry Miller's Theatre.

OCTOBER • George Jean Nathan, Wolcott Gibbs, Stark Young, and Burton Rascoe quit the New York Drama Critics Circle, part of the fallout from last season's controversial award to *The Patriots* for best play. **13** *Variety* reports that Cole Porter has sent Irving Berlin a gold cigarette case to thank him for suggesting to Hal Wallis that Warner Bros. do a film biography of Porter, for which Berlin has also suggested the title, *Night and Day* (1946, with Cary Grant as Porter). On October 27, nevertheless, a *Variety* gossip columnist relates that Porter has qualms about the film, what with recent and scheduled pictures from the studio on George M. Cohan, George Gershwin, Nora Bayes, Marilyn Miller, and Helen Morgan. Porter is said to have told Wallis: "I don't want my epitaph to read 'See Warner Bros. and Die!'" **25** Mary Martin is on the cover of *Life*.

NOVEMBER • Burgess Meredith becomes a captain in the Army Air Corps. **17** At the revival of Rodgers and Hart's *A Connecticut Yankee*, Lorenz Hart has to be rushed out of the Martin Beck's auditorium into the lobby after he gets drunk during intermission and begins to mimic the lyrics out loud. He will be dead in less than a week.

DECEMBER 7 Ray Bolger tells reporters that on his just completed 27,000-mile U.S.O. tour, the plane he was on, 'Pistol Packin' Mama,' got lost between Australia and New Guinea, landing finally with only 20 minutes of fuel to spare, after Bolger had

---

Paul Robeson in the title role and José Ferrer as Iago. It "is one of the most memorable events in the history of the [t]heatre," says Burton Rascoe in the *World-Telegram*. Uta Hagen, married offstage to Ferrer, plays Desdemona. *Variety* notes of the pairing of the black Robeson and white Hagen "that the theatre—and its patrons—are increasingly assuming a tolerance that ha[s] too long been lacking."

NOVEMBER 20 The U.S. Army Air Force produces Moss Hart's *Winged Victory* (212), at the Forty-fourth Street Theatre, as a benefit for the Army Emergency Relief Fund. It follows three ordinary men, played by Don Taylor, Edmond O'Brien, and Mark Daniels, through training and into combat. They are supplemented by a cast of 350, including Lee J. Cobb, Red Buttons, and Barry Nelson. On the production staff is James Nederlander. It's a film in 1944.

DECEMBER 2 Updating Bizet's opera *Carmen* and placing it in the American South with an all-black cast, Oscar Hammerstein II has written *Carmen Jones* (502), opening at the Broadway Theatre. Muriel Smith, Inez Matthews, and Luther Saxon star. The 1954 film stars Dorothy Dandridge and Harry Belafonte. **8** John Van Druten's three-character comedy *The Voice of the Turtle* (1,557), at the Morosco, stars Margaret Sullavan, Elliott Nugent, and Audrey Christie. Sullavan's character, at first stuck with Nugent on a date to do her friend a favor, ends up sticking with him. One of the understudies is Eileen Heckart. The film appears in 1947. **13** Gertrude Lawrence and Conrad Nagel inaugurate the City Center, formerly the Mecca Temple, dedicated two days ago, with a revival of *Susan and God*.

JANUARY 3 Ruth Gordon wrote and stars in *Over 21* (221), directed by George S. Kaufman and opening at the Music Box. Gordon based this farce about a soldier and his writer-wife partly on her own life with her husband, Garson Kanin, and partly on the life of Dorothy Parker. **28** Bobby Clark, Cole Porter's music, and Mike Todd's extravagant production make for a *Mexican Hayride* (479), at the

---

MARCH • New York City is carrying out one of its periodic campaigns against ticket scalping, with several agencies suspended.

APRIL 1 The federal tax on theatre tickets rises from 10 to 20 percent. **21** The government wartime ban on new air-conditioning construction is lifted for the Forty-fourth Street Theatre, where *Winged Victory* is playing.

MAY • The wartime Entertainment Industry Emergency Committee adopts a set of principles calling, in the name of national unity, "for the treatment of blacks as equals in all presentations." Among the authors of the statement are Maxwell Anderson and Lillian Hellman. **17** *Variety* begins a television page.

OCTOBER 31 Producer and director Max Reinhardt d.

NOVEMBER 5 Playwright Sam Shepard (Samuel Shepard Rogers) b. **22** Lorenz Hart d. from alcoholism, malnutrition, and pneumonia. At the behest of Eleanor Roosevelt, Hart was given penicillin, a new medication still in short supply and reserved primarily for the military. A nurse is reported to have related his last words: "What have I lived for?" His attitude toward sunny song lyrics was: "Every silver lining still delineates a great big, dark cloud that, at any moment, can piss down on your head."

JANUARY 24 Barbara Bel Geddes m. Carl Schreuer. **27** Bill "Bojangles" Robinson m. dancer Sue Dash. **31** Playwright Jean Giraudoux d.

FEBRUARY 13 Producer Edgar Selwyn d., and Stockard Channing (Susan Stockard) b.

Personalities

been ordered to don a parachute.

JANUARY • Marlene Dietrich tells reporters that "in spite of all the rumors to the contrary, I am not going around kicking any part of my anatomy for turning down *One Touch of Venus* because it turned out to be such a success and Mary Martin's performance the toast of the town." Although the Spewacks had Dietrich in mind when they wrote it, the rewrites toned down the lead role to the point where she felt it was no longer for her. • Barbara Bennett and her husband, Addison Randall, are fired from the cast of *Victory Belles*, now at the Ambassador, for "horseplay."

FEBRUARY • George Jean Nathan announces that he has provided in his will for an annual monetary prize for drama criticism.

MARCH 2 David Merrick coproduces his first Broadway show, *Bright Boy* (16), opening at the Playhouse. **21** Canadian-born Raymond Massey becomes a U.S. citizen.

APRIL 25 The *New York Daily News* asks six major critics to name the "First Lady of the Broadway Stage." Ethel Barrymore wins with three votes.

MAY • Sidney Blackmer plays two lead roles on Broadway in one week. He opens in *Pretty Little Parlor*, which closes within the week and then, with only two rehearsals, steps in to replace Rys Williams in *Chicken Every Sunday*. **5** Filling out a questionnaire for the Ted Bates Advertising Agency in conjunction with a radio appearance, stage and screen actress Patsy Kelly answers the question "What Living Person Do You Most Admire?" by penciling in "Tallulah." It is said that she and Bankhead are lovers. **26** In *The Morning Telegraph*, critic George Freedly reviews a student production of *Twelfth Night* at the New School for Social Research in New York City. He notes that Marlon Brando handled the role of Sebastian "satisfactorily" and would like to see the young actor in meatier parts.

Plays and Musicals

Winter Garden. Porter's pre-opening assessment of the show, the first Broadway musical in 12 years with a top ticket price of $5.50 every night, is that it "stinks." June Havoc costars. The 1948 film, without music, stars Abbott and Costello.

FEBRUARY 20 The Equity Library Theatre, a showcase for new talent, giving free performances of public domain works at New York Public Libraries, is launched at the Hudson Park branch in Greenwich Village with productions of *Shadow of the Glen* and *Fumed Oak*. A $1,000 contribution from producer John Golden gets it started. Alumni will include Ossie Davis, Lee Grant, Richard Kiley, Ann Meara, Tony Randall, Jason Robards, Jr., Kim Stanley, Elaine Stritch, and Eli Wallach.

APRIL 8 *Follow the Girls* (882), a musical by Phil Charig, Dan Shapiro, and Milton Pascal, with the last book for a musical by Guy Bolton, opens at the New Century Theatre (formerly Jolson's Fifty-ninth Street Theatre). Gertrude Niesen is burlesque performer Bubbles La Marr, with 28-year-old Jackie Gleason in drag as "Goofy Gale." Frequent flashes of feminine flesh makes the show popular with men in uniform. **12** Lillian Hellman's *The Searching Wind* (326), called in the *Sun* by Ward Morehouse "an acrid and powerful drama of anti-appeasement," opens at the Fulton. In the cast are Dudley Digges, Montgomery Clift, Cornelia Otis Skinner, and Dennis King.

Business and Society

Births, Deaths, and Marriages

MARCH 1 Set designer John Napier b.

MAY 21 Burgess Meredith m. film actress Paulette Goddard. It will last six years.

1944–45

On April 19, in an event akin to a rare and splendid astronomical occurrence, in which certain heavenly bodies move near each other for the only time in a lifetime, *Carousel* opens across the street from *Oklahoma!* And that's in a season that has already "seen" an oversized, invisible rabbit. With Marlon Brando, Julie Harris, and Arthur Miller also debuting and Tennessee Williams and Laurette Taylor hailed for *The Glass Menagerie*, it is a good time to be around Broadway. To top it off, business is booming, with an actual theatre shortage for the first time since before the Depression. And World War II is drawing to a close, the big party in Times Square for V-E Day a warm-up for the bigger bash to come when it's all over in August.

- Number of tickets for standees sold each night for *Oklahoma!*: 28
- Top ticket price for *Carousel*: $6.00, $1.20 more than for *Oklahoma!*
- Number of Actors Equity members in the Armed Forces: about 800
- The newspaper *P.M.*'s headline on its review of *Catherine Was Great*: "Mae West Slips on the Steppes"
- What Mae West ad-libs to a character whose sword has come between him and her on opening night of *Catherine Was Great*: "Is that your sword or are you just glad to see me?"
- Number of boys who have played children in *Life With Father* who are now serving in the Armed Forces: 19, including Richard Ney, who also played Greer Garson's son in the film *Mrs. Minniver*
- Number of U.S.O. shows playing abroad: 200
- Staging Army Special Services variety shows in Hawaii: Major Maurice Evans, known for his "GI *Hamlet*"
- What the *New York Journal-American* critic says of one of the players, making his Broadway debut, in *I Remember Mama*: "The Nels of Marlon Brando is, if he doesn't mind me saying so, charming."
- Number of bodies in *Ten Little Indians*: 8
- Number of working telephones retrieved from Broadway shows and theatrical warehouses by New York Telephone: about 80—needed because the Armed Forces have monopolized the supply of new phones

Productions on Broadway: 92

Pulitzer Prize for Drama: *Harvey* (Mary Chase)

New York Drama Critics Circle Award:
Best American Play: *The Glass Menagerie* (Tennessee Williams)

June	July	August	September	October	November
Lindsay and Stickney leave *Life With Father*	Director Alan Schneider makes Broadway acting debut	Margo Jones grant for rep theatre	Ethel Merman out of *Sadie*	Marlon Brando in *I Remember Mama*	*Harvey* and Arthur Miller debut

December	January	February	March	April	May
Noel Coward apologizes to Brooklyn	Ella Logan banned from *N.Y. Daily News*	*Trio* closed down for lesbian theme	*The Glass Menagerie* and Julie Harris debut	*Carousel*	Playwrights complain of drunken critics on opening night

Personalities

JUNE • Howard Lindsay and Dorothy Stickney leave *Life With Father* after some 1,600 performances. • Theatre managers on the touring route of *Othello* next season are told to set aside good orchestra seats for Paul Robeson, who wants to insure that black theatregoers will have access to preferred locations. The seats must be spread throughout the orchestra to avoid segregation. Should Robeson notice a pattern of segregation, he reserves the right to walk off the stage. **29** June Havoc trips over a prop in *Mexican Hayride*, fracturing her knee.

JULY 11 Making his acting debut in a minor part in Maxwell Anderson's *Storm Operation*, at the Belasco, is director Alan Schneider.

AUGUST • Mary Martin is out of *One Touch of Venus* for nine days after collapsing from the heat. The hot weather and the manpower shortage have cut the delivery of ice to some theatres, which need it for their cooling systems. **22** The Dallas *Morning News* reports that producer Margo Jones has received a Rockefeller Foundation grant to look into the possibility of establishing a permanent repertory theatre in Dallas. It will become Theatre '47 in three years.

SEPTEMBER • Clarence Derwent, an actor said to have made a substantial amount of money through his investments, establishes annual cash prizes for the best supporting players on Broadway. **18** Gertrude Lawrence, crossing the Seine to entertain troops in France, has to be rescued from the boat she's on when its motor dies, and it begins to sink. **25** Playwright Robert E. Sherwood resigns as Director of the Overseas Branch of the Office of War Information, a post he has held for several years, to work on President Roosevelt's re-election campaign. **29** Less than two weeks after rehearsals began, Ethel Merman backs out of the lead role in *Sadie*, a musical version of *Rain*, because she is dissatisfied with the lyrics. She's replaced by June Havoc in this show that will flop.

OCTOBER 19 The *Playbill* "Who's Who In

Plays and Musicals

JUNE 27 Agatha Christie's *Ten Little Indians* (425), of whom eight will be dispatched before the final curtain, is at the Broadhurst. Estelle Winwood stars. *And Then There Were None*, in 1945, is the first of four film versions.

AUGUST 21 Edvard Grieg is the subject, and his music is used in Robert Wright and George Forrest's *Song of Norway* (860), at the Imperial. Lawrence Brooks stars, and it's filmed in 1970. **30** Philip Yordan's *Anna Lucasta* (957), about a waterfront prostitute, with echoes of *Anna Christie*, is an American Negro Theatre production at the Mansfield. It stars Hilda Simms and Earle Hyman. Eartha Kitt and Sammy Davis, Jr. are in the 1958 film.

OCTOBER 5 *Bloomer Girl* (657), at the Shubert, Harold Arlen and Yip Harburg's Civil War–era musical, starring Celeste Holm in her breakthrough role, is about women's rights and other progressive movements. Agnes DeMille choreographed, and the score includes "The Eagle and Me." **19** John Van Druten's *I Remember Mama* (714), Rodgers and Hammerstein's producing debut, opens at the Music Box. The comedy stars Mady Christians and Oscar Homolka, with Marlon Brando as Nils, in his Broadway debut. Irene Dunne and Homolka star in the 1948 film, and it becomes one of tele-

Marlon Brando, right, makes his Broadway debut in *I Remember Mama*

Business and Society

JUNE • Producer John Golden gives $100,000 to New York City for projects that advance the cause of the legitimate theatre.

JULY • New York City License Commissioner Paul Moss suspends the Leblang Theatre Ticket Agency for overcharging. It's the first of the major agencies to be suspended.

AUGUST • The U.S.O. Camp Shows, at the request of the government, expands its production of legitimate plays abroad. Meanwhile, officials of the American Theatre Wing are reported to be miffed that their organization hasn't been properly credited for its role in the tour of Katharine Cornell's production of *The Barretts of Wimpole Street*, now playing the Italian war front.

SEPTEMBER 1 Billy Rose takes possession of the Ziegfeld Theatre, which most recently has shown films and will now be reclaimed for the legitimate stage.

OCTOBER • For the first time in a long time, Broadway prosperity has caused a theatre shortage.

Births, Deaths, and Marriages

JUNE 2 Composer Marvin Hamlisch b.

SEPTEMBER 6 Swoosie Kurtz b. She's the daughter of Colonel Frank Kurtz, America's most decorated bomber pilot. Her first name is derived from the nickname of his B-17 Flying Fortress, the "Swoose"—half swan, half goose. **8** Musical comedy star Betty Garret m. film actor Larry Parks.

OCTOBER 22 Richard Bennett d.

NOVEMBER 10 Lyricist Tim Rice b.

JANUARY 10 Vivian Blaine m. agent Manuel Frank. **31** Playwright Richard Tully d.

APRIL 27 Playwright August Wilson b.

The Cast" for the opening of *I Remember Mama* notes: "Marlon Brando (Nels) makes his first professional appearance . . . having served his apprenticeship at the New School, where he studied dramatics with Erwin Piscator and Stella and Luther Adler. Born in Calcutta, India, he came to this country when he was six months old." (Brando was born in Omaha.)

NOVEMBER 6 *Life*'s cover story is "Broadway Hit: 'Bloomer Girl.'" **27** Gertrude Lawrence is on the cover of *Life* in a military uniform.

DECEMBER 4 Noel Coward, whose disparaging remarks about soldiers from Brooklyn in his book *Middle East Diary* has caused a furor in the borough across the river—his friend Beatrice Lillie is "shocked" by what he wrote—apologizes through Walter Winchell's column in the *New York Daily Mirror*. Coward had written of his visit to a hospital of the "mournful little Brooklyn boys lying there in tears amidst alien corn with nothing worse than a bullet wound in the leg or a fractured arm." **9** While visiting Moscow, Lillian Hellman begins an affair with U.S. foreign service officer John Melby. **12** Columnist Earl Wilson confirms that Tallulah Bankhead has broken her pledge, made after the fall of Dunkirk, not to drink until Germany has been defeated. When he asked her about Lillian Hellman's recent comment on actors having little effect on a play, Bankhead replied: "She writes like an angel, but she's a dreary bore, as spinach is a dreary bore. I say she's spinach and I say to hell with her." **18** Frederic March is on the cover of *Life* magazine, in costume for *A Bell for Adano*, which opened 12 days ago. **27** After the small turnout last night for the first Chicago tryout of Tennessee Williams's *The Glass Menagerie*, and virtually no advance sale, the producers draw up a closing notice. But Audrey Wood, Williams's agent, argues passionately and successfully for more time, citing the good reviews. Laurette Taylor, in the pivotal role of Amanda Wingfield, will soon rise above her drinking problem and begin to deliver a memorable performance.

---

vision's first popular programs, starring Peggy Wood, on July 1, 1949.

NOVEMBER 1 Harold Lloyd, Robert Benchley, Edward Everett Horton, and Jack Haley turned down the role of Elwood Dowd in *Harvey* (1,775). Frank Fay, the former vaudevillian who took it, is an alcoholic playing a teetotaler in the Mary Chase comedy about the only person who can see a certain large rabbit. Josephine Hull plays his sister. It's at the Forty-eighth Street Theatre. James Stewart and Hull are in the 1950 film. **21** *The Late George Apley* (384) opens at the Lyceum. Leo G. Carroll has the title role in this John P. Marquand-George S. Kaufman comedy, based on Marquand's novel. It's a film in 1948. **23** Arthur Miller's first play *The Man Who Had All the Luck* (4), about the relationship between success, work, and good fortune, opens at the Forrest Theatre. The *Times* sees in it "a certain amount of merit," and John Chapman in the *Daily News* says, "I hope Mr. Miller will go right back to work writing another piece, for he has a sense of theatre and a real if undeveloped way of making stage characters talk and act human."

DECEMBER 6 *A Bell for Adano* (296), Paul Osburn's adaptation of John Hersey's novel about an American in Sicily, whose efforts on behalf of the people of a small town are finally rewarded, opens at the Cort. It stars Frederic March. **13** *Dear Ruth* (683), a comedy about a teenage girl who writes her way into trouble when she becomes a soldier's pen pal, opens at Henry Miller's Theatre. It stars Lenore Lonergan, Virginia Gilmore, and John Dall. **28** *On the Town* (462) opens at the Adelphi. It's based on the Jerome Robbins-Leonard Bernstein ballet *Fancy Free*, about sailors on shore leave, which premiered at the Metropolitan Opera house on April 18. In this musical, Nancy Walker plays cab driver Brunnhilde Esterhazy. Betty Comden and Adolph Green supply the story and lyrics and are in the cast as well. Among the songs are "New York, New York" and "Lucky to Be Me." The film debuts in 1949.

JANUARY 27 Political corruption, romance, and the Central Park of the 1870s are the

---

NOVEMBER 5 Lee Shubert balks at allowing *Trio*, which deals with lesbianism, to play in the Cort Theatre.

FEBRUARY • With box office business booming, shows to which the ticket agencies have no tickets include: *Harvey*, *I Remember Mama*, *A Bell for Adano*, *The Late George Apley*, *Song of Norway*, *On the Town*, *Dear Ruth*, *Bloomer Girl*, *Up in the Park*, and, naturally, *Oklahoma!* **23** New York City License Commissioner Paul Moss closes down the play *Trio* at the Belasco. At issue is the accusation by a number of clergymen, only one of whom has seen the play, that it's about lesbianism, which the producers deny.

MARCH 1 The new wartime midnight curfew takes the spirit out of Times Square night life.

APRIL 14 Saturday's matineés for all shows have been canceled because of President Roosevelt's funeral.

MAY 1 At a Dramatists Guild meeting, some members charge that critics have been showing up intoxicated on opening nights. **7** News of the German surrender turns the theatre district into a stage for a two-day party.

Personalities

JANUARY • The *New York Daily News* has banned the mention of Ella Logan's name after the singer, returning from a U.S.O. tour, characterized the paper's editorial stance as "fascist." • J.J. Shubert and his nephew, Lawrence Shubert Lawrence, who manages the Shubert theatres in Philadelphia, reportedly come close to blows over the elder Shubert's belief that Lawrence has not sufficiently promoted the show *A Lady Says Yes*. **8** *Life* Magazine has an article and photo essay on Frank Fay, starring in *Harvey*.

MARCH 12 On leave from the Yale School of Drama and playing the role of the daughter in *It's a Gift*, opening tonight is nineteen-year-old Julie Harris, whom the *Playbill* describes as "new to the Broadway stage." Ward Morehouse, in the *Sun*, says that she plays the role "pleasantly," and Louis Kronenberger, in *P.M.*, writes that she's "pretty." **31** George Jean Nathan is reported to have sent a bottle of Scotch to Laurette Taylor, opening in *The Glass Menagerie* tonight. The alcohol-afflicted actress replies: "Thanks for the note of confidence."

APRIL 12 In many Broadway theatres tonight, there are tributes to President Franklin D. Roosevelt, who died earlier today. Tallulah Bankhead, speaking to the audience at the Martin Beck, where she's appearing in Philip Barry's *Foolish Notion*, brings many to tears in a tribute to the fallen leader. **17** The Clarence Derwent Award for the best supporting actress goes to Judy Holliday for her role as the floozy in *Kiss Them for Me*.

Plays and Musicals

basis for Sigmund Romberg's *Up in Central Park* (504), with lyrics by Dorothy Fields, at the Century. Stars include Wilbur Evans, Maureen Cannon, Noah Beery, and Maurice Burke, and among the songs is "Close as Pages in a Book." It's filmed in 1948.

MARCH 14 *Dark of the Moon* (318), a fantasy by Howard Richardson and William Berney set in the Smokey Mountains, is a surprise hit at the Forty-sixth Street Theatre. It stars Richard Hart, Carol Stone, and Georgia Simmons. **31** *The Glass Menagerie* (561) opens at the Playhouse, and Tennessee Williams vaults to the front ranks of American playwrights. Laurette Taylor, as Amanda, makes a fabled comeback from alcoholic oblivion. Julie Haydon is Laura, and Anthony Ross is the gentleman caller in this drama of dreams and memories. It is, says Ward Morehouse, "enchanting." Eddie Dowling produced and plays the part of Tom Wingfield. *Variety*'s review mentions the playwright only in the credits, although a gossip column on the same page sums up his career to date in two paragraphs.

APRIL 19 Rodgers and Hammerstein's *Carousel* (890), directed by Rouben Mamoulian and choreographed by Agnes DeMille, opens at the Majestic, across Forty-fourth Street from the St. James, where *Oklahoma!* is still playing. Ward Morehouse, in the *Sun*, says it has "a fragile beauty and an enchanting score" and that it is "something memorable in the theatre." He especially likes "June Is Bustin' Out All Over," "This Was a Real Nice Clambake," "When I Marry Mr. Snow," "If I Loved You," and "You'll Never Walk Alone." John Raitt as Billy Bigelow and Jan Clayton, debuting on Broadway as Julie Jordan, star in this musical adaptation of Ferenc Molnár's *Liliom*. Bambi Linn is also in the cast. *Carousel* will come to the screen in 1956, with Gordon MacRae and Shirley Jones.

Business and Society

Births, Deaths, and Marriages

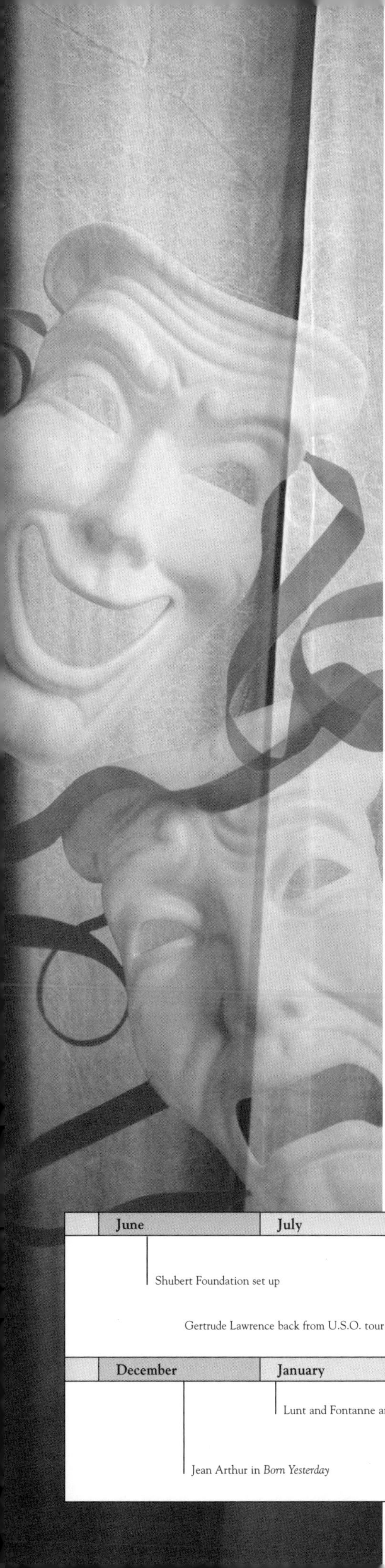

1945–46

"There's No Business Like Show Business," Ethel Merman sings in *Annie Get Your Gun*. But it *is* like everything else in America when it comes to race. Several dramas this season, such as *Deep Are the Roots*, touch on the issue, and black players such as Paul Robeson, Ossie Davis and Ruby Dee, will insist that it be faced. Judy Holliday gets her big break—and very good reviews—when Jean Arthur bows out of *Born Yesterday*. In Tennessee Williams and Donald Windham's *You Touched Me*, another young player draws complaints about mumbling and being too intense. He is Montgomery Clift. The Stage Door Canteen closes, and Jerome Kern is taken to Welfare Island when he collapses on a Manhattan street and is not readily identified. And Lee Shubert had better stop shaking his finger in Milton Berle's face. Berle doesn't think it's funny.

- Number of Stage Door Canteens active during the War: 9, in 9 cities, in 3 countries
- Number of people in uniform served by the Stage Door Canteens: 20,250,000-plus
- Estimated value of the talent appearing at the Stage Door Canteens: $16,000,000
- Number of entertainers and ensembles who appeared at the Stage Door Canteens: 108,950
- Number served by the original Stage Door Canteen in New York (March 2, 1942 to October 28, 1945): 3,250,000
- Estimated number of miles danced by hostesses at the original Stage Door Canteen, according to *Variety*: 10,000,000
- Last song played at the original Stage Door Canteen when it closes on October 28: "Goodnight Sweetheart"
- Miles covered by Gertrude Lawrence's U.S.O. tour: 25,000
- Number of service personnel Gertrude Lawrence played to on her tour: 400,000
- Ethel Merman's compensation for *Annie Get Your Gun*: $3,000 a week plus 10 percent of the gross
- Vincent Youman's middle name: Millie
- Amount deposited with Actors Equity by Rodgers and Hammerstein as salary guarantees for *Annie Get Your Gun*, *I Remember Mama*, the revival of *Show Boat*, and their new show *Happy Birthday*: about $65,000, total
- Profit from the 6-week engagement of The Old Vic at the Century Theatre: $10,000–$15,000 on a gross of $300,000
- Number of tryouts that never reached Broadway this year: more than 25—thought to be a record
- Number of shows with racially mixed casts: at least 6, also probably a record

Productions on Broadway: 76

Pulitzer Prize for Drama: *State of the Union* (Russel Crouse and Howard Lindsay)

New York Drama Critics Award:
Best Musical: *Carousel* (Rodgers and Hammerstein)

June	July	August	September	October	November
Shubert Foundation set up	Gertrude Lawrence back from U.S.O. tour	Producer Oliver Morosco d. broke	Frank Fay creates Equity controversy	Al Hirschfeld's daughter Nina b.	Jerome Kern d.

December	January	February	March	April	May
Jean Arthur in *Born Yesterday*	Lunt and Fontanne are back	Judy Holliday in *Born Yesterday*	Liza Minnelli b.	Hammerstein connected to six hits	*Annie Get Your Gun*

Personalities

JULY 27 Gertrude Lawrence is back in New York after a U.S.O. tour that began in April, covering 25,000 miles in the Pacific, playing to 400,000 servicemen. At some stops, the men demanded "Jenny" from *Lady in the Dark*, even though chaplains often objected to its lyrics.

AUGUST • Wartime newsprint limitations are easing, just in time for Laurette Taylor to receive the star billing in *The Glass Menagerie* called for in her contract—and about which she complained when at first she did not get it.

SEPTEMBER • Performances of *A Bell for Adano* are suspended while Frederic March recuperates from an elbow infection for which he received the new wonder drug penicillin. **9** "The Theatre Guild of the Air" debuts on the radio with *Wings Over Europe*, starring Burgess Meredith. The Guild originally produced it at the Martin Beck on December 10, 1928. **24** Harold Keel takes over the part of Curly in *Oklahoma!* He previously substituted for John Raitt in *Carousel* and achieved his musical breakthrough only last year when he won a music contest while employed by Douglas Aircraft at a war plant. As Howard Keel, he will have a prominent movie career at MGM.

OCTOBER • There's turmoil over the musical *Spring in Brazil*, the Shubert production that appears to need doctoring after a rough Boston tryout. At one point, Lee Shubert angrily shakes his finger in the face of star Milton Berle, who warns him to back off. **20** Theatrical caricaturist Al Hirschfeld and actress Dolly Haas are the parents of a baby girl. "The child has been named Nina," *The New York Times* will report. Her name will be immortalized when her father works it into thousands of his theatrical drawings.

NOVEMBER • Producer Brock Pemberton loses a law suit to Mike Todd, who has a lease on the Forty-eighth Street Theatre, where Pemberton's *Harvey* is playing. Todd wants to bring his own show into the theatre and won't permit tickets to

Plays and Musicals

SEPTEMBER 25 *You Touched Me* (109), a play by Tennessee Williams and Donald Windham, opens at the Booth. This minor work draws tepid reviews at best, and George Freedly, in the *Morning Telegraph*, says that what strengths it has are done in by the production, especially the acting. He singles out Montgomery Clift, who "[i]s wholly inaudible in addition to being miscast as Hadrian. This mumbling of lines; this failure to project beyond the sixth row in the orchestra may come from his feeling his role too intensely." **26** *Deep Are the Roots* (477), a play directed by Elia Kazan about a Southern white woman who loves a black

Montgomery Clift

soldier, is at the Fulton. Arnaud d'Usseau and James Gow have written "a strong and bitter drama," according to Ward Morehouse in the *Sun*. He calls the star, Barbara Bel Geddes, "positively brilliant . . . a completely charming ingenue." *Commonweal* compares her to "an early Helen Hayes."

OCTOBER 16 A revival of Victor Herbert's 1906 *The Red Mill* (531), starring Eddie Foy, Jr. and Michael O' Shea, opens at the Ziegfeld.

NOVEMBER 10 Spencer Tracy is a man looking at the war from up close in Robert E. Sherwood's *The Rugged Path* (81), at the Plymouth. Tracy left the show briefly in Boston, fearing that it wouldn't

Business and Society

JUNE 25 There are special War Loan matinées on this Monday afternoon. **28** Lee and J.J. Shubert set up the Sam Shubert Foundation, with initial assets of $500,000. In 1963, with the death of J.J., the bulk of the Shubert theatre empire will come under the Foundation's control.

JULY 1 Philip Loeb, under attack for his radical political views, is nevertheless reelected to Actors Equity's council, as is Sam Jaffe, Louis Calhern, Leo G. Carroll, Jane Seymour, and Frank Fay.

SEPTEMBER • The minimum pay for actors is raised to $60 a week and to $50 for chorus boys and girls. **28** At an Actors Equity meeting, Frank Fay calls for an investigation of five members who, he says, were at a recent Communist-supported political rally at which the Catholic Church was reviled. In fact, Sono Osato, David Brooks, Luba Malina, the actress known as Margo, and Jean Darling had left the September 24 benefit for Spanish Civil War refugees, at Madison Square Garden, by the time the disputed remarks were made.

OCTOBER 20 Actors Equity censors Frank

Births, Deaths, and Marriages

JULY 13 Alla Nazimova d.

AUGUST 21 Patty McCormick (Patricia Russo) b. The mother of this future "bad seed" is a professional roller skater. **25** Producer Oliver Morosco is killed when hit by a trolley on Hollywood Boulevard. He d. broke.

SEPTEMBER 1 Frank Craven d.. Brooks Atkinson once called Craven, who played the stage manager in *Our Town*, "[t]he best pipe and pants-pocket actor in the business."

OCTOBER 18 Playwright Hatcher Hughes d. **19** John Lithgow b.

NOVEMBER 7 Gus Edwards, whose "kiddie" act in vaudeville helped start the careers of George Jessel and Eddie Cantor, d.

performances of *Harvey* beyond November 30 to be sold at the box office. Pemberton sets up a box office in a nearby barbershop. **8** There is little that the Belasco Theatre *Playbill* can yet say of Eli Wallach, opening tonight in *Skydrift*: "He is a graduate of the U. of Texas, '36, and the Neighborhood Playhouse '40. No previous Broadway record." **11** Jerome Kern, who dies today, had agreed to write the score for a musical based on the life of sharpshooter Annie Oakley. Richard Rodgers and Oscar Hammerstein II, who are producing the show, will now turn to their second choice, Irving Berlin, who will come up with *Annie Get Your Gun*.

DECEMBER 14 Tallulah Bankhead denies today's reports in Chicago papers that she's asked for police protection from gamblers who are trying to extort money from her beyond what she already owes. Bankhead, who is in town to appear in *Foolish Notion*, says that "bodyguards went out with old-time melodramas." **22** Helen Hayes is forced by CBS to drop from her radio program a planned production of *A Family Portrait*, in which Judith Anderson once played on the stage. The network is worried that people might be offended by a Christmas season portrayal of Jesus as only the oldest of several of Joseph and Mary's sons. **26** Reviewing the December 20 New Haven opening of *Born Yesterday* in its pre-Broadway tryout, *Variety* notes that the comedy, starring Jean Arthur, "allows leeway for her special mannerisms, which she capitalizes to the peak." It is, however, a summit she will grace only briefly because illness is about to take her out of the production, providing Judy Holliday with her big break.

JANUARY 9 José Ferrer, in an article in *Variety*, "The Negro in the American Theatre," says that black actors have virtually no chance of landing major roles in the American theatre, but he's optimistic about coming change. Ferrer, for his own part, promises never again to appear before a segregated audience and calls on other actors to do the same. He's currently rehearsing *Strange Fruit*. **28** *Life* Magazine celebrates *Show Boat* with a cover photo of Jan Clayton, who stars in the current revival.

---

work. He was right, although *he* is well-received. **14** *State of the Union* (765), Howard Lindsay and Russel Crouse's comedy about a presidential candidate and his wife, opens at the Hudson. Ralph Bellamy and Ruth Hussey star in the roles that Spencer Tracy and Katharine Hepburn take in the 1948 film.

DECEMBER 14 Betty Field is a young woman who beats the doldrums with daydreams in her husband Elmer Rice's comedy *Dream Girl* (348), at the Coronet. Wendell Corey costars. The 1965 musical *Skyscraper* will be based on it. **26** Gertrude Lawrence is Eliza Doolittle to Raymond Massey's Henry Higgins in a revival of Shaw's *Pygmalion* (179), at the Barrymore.

JANUARY 5 The revival of Jerome Kern's 1927 *Show Boat* (418), opening at the Ziegfeld, stars Jan Clayton, Carol Bruce, and Buddy Ebsen. **23** Alfred Lunt and Lynn Fontanne are in *O Mistress Mine* (452), a Terrence Rattigan domestic comedy. It opens at the Empire.

FEBRUARY 4 Judy Holliday, a replacement for Jean Arthur, who left in tryouts, Paul Douglas, and Gary Merrill shine in Garson Kanin's comedy *Born Yesterday* (1,642), at the Lyceum. Holliday's performance as the not-so-dumb blonde who finally tells Douglas to "drop dead" raises her to stardom. She will also win an Oscar for the 1950 film version. **6** Mary Martin stars in the Raymond Scott musical *Lute Song* (142), at the Plymouth, adapted by Sidney Howard and Will Irwin from an ancient Chinese play, *Pi-Pa-Ki*. Louis Kronenberger, in *P.M.*, writes of Yul Brynner, making his Broadway debut, that "he has looks and grace, but he's not much of an actor. . . ." **18** Katharine Cornell and Cedric Hardwicke open at the Cort in a limited run of Jean Anouilh's *Antigone* (63).

MARCH 30 Harold Arlen and Johnny Mercer collaborate on *St. Louis Woman* (113), with an all-black cast featuring the Nicholas Brothers, Pearl Bailey in her Broadway debut, Rex Ingram, Ruby Hill, and Juanita Hall. In the score is "Come Rain or Come Shine." The show is at the Martin Beck.

Fay for accusing other members of attending a pro-Communist rally at which Catholicism was denounced. The five have been threatened since he made the remarks. **28** The Stage Door Canteen in New York closes.

JANUARY 29 A new agreement between theatre managers and stagehands heads off a threatened strike and nets the workers a 15 percent raise.

FEBRUARY 6 A coal strike brings a voluntary brownout on Broadway, reminiscent of similar darkenings during World War II. **10** Producers Richard Rodgers and Oscar Hammerstein announce that there will be no benefit performances during the run of *Annie Get Your Gun*. They feel that theatre parties encourage ticket speculation, and people who pay top dollar plus for tickets "are the cruelest audience an artist can encounter." They come late and are noisy. **25** The producers of *Follow the Girls*, at the Broadhurst, hire 24 new chorus boys and girls to replace the ones quitting when their demand for a $10-a-week raise, from the $50 they've been getting, is denied.

MARCH • Several shows are adding Sunday performances to put them over the top at the box office. • Clarence Derwent's nomination as the new president of

---

broke. Bing Crosby played him in a 1939 film biography, *The Star Maker*. **11** Jerome Kern collapsed from a stroke a few days ago on Park Avenue and was taken to a municipal hospital on Welfare Island, where he was briefly unidentified until the number on his American Society of Composers, Authors, and Publishers (ASCAP) card was traced. Today, he d. in Doctor's Hospital in Manhattan, where Vincent Youmans lies dying of tuberculosis. **21** Robert Benchley d. His friend Tallulah Bankhead calls him "as gay and thirsty a gentleman as I ever encountered."

DECEMBER 5 Margo m. Eddie Albert. **22** Conrad Nagel m. film actress Lynn Merrick. Glenn Hunter d.

FEBRUARY 5 George Arliss d. Gregory Hines b. Zelda Diamond m. Thomas Fichandler, forming the team that will launch the Arena Stage in Washington, D.C.

Personalities

FEBRUARY 13 *Variety*, assessing the Philadelphia tryout of Robert Ardrey's *Jeb*, about a black soldier back from the war, says: "Ossie Davis, a practical unknown, himself just out of the service after four years in uniform with the Army-Medical Corps, does a crackerjack job as Jeb. . . . Ruby Dee as his sweetheart does exceptionally well with one of the play's most difficult roles." Davis will be making his Broadway debut when *Jeb* (9) opens at the Martin Beck on February 21. Dee has been with the American Negro Theatre and had a walk-on in the 1943 Broadway play *South Pacific* (not the musical). **14** Irene Worth makes her London debut at the Lyric in *The Time of Your Life*. The American-born actress will spend much of her career working in Britain.

MARCH • Rehearsals for *St. Louis Woman*, an all-black musical, have been rocky, with some cast members complaining of demeaning stereotypes in the script. Director Rouben Mamoulian and cast member Pearl Bailey try to calm the protests. • Maxwell Anderson denounces the critics—"the Jukes family of journalism"—who have savaged his *Truckline Cafe* (13). The play, a kind of formica Grand Hotel, which opened on February 27, was produced by Elia Kazan, directed by Harold Clurman, and included in its large cast Karl Malden and Marlon Brando.

MAY 6 "Margaret Leighton of the 'Old Vic'" is the subject of the cover story in this week's *Life*. She's here with the company, making her American debut. **7** Orson Welles's Mercury Theatre production of the musical version of *Around the World in 80 Days* is a bit ragged, and the producer-actor experiences some of it firsthand when it opens in New Haven. In a saloon scene, the bewhiskered Welles loses his beard while imbibing. He ad-libs: "Mighty powerful stuff, that liquor. Burns the whiskers right off a man's face." The show will be jokingly referred to as "Wellesapoppin'."

Plays and Musicals

APRIL 18 *Call Me Mister* (734), at the National Theatre, is Harold Rome's musical portrait of the demobilized serviceman. Featured in the cast are Betty Garrett, who sings "South America, Take It Away," Jules Munshin, and Lawrence Winters. It's a film in 1951.

MAY 16 Ethel Merman is Annie Oakley in Irving Berlin's *Annie Get Your Gun* (1,147), opening after its original debut date was postponed by a structural defect at the Imperial. The score includes "There's No Business Like Show Business," "Anything You Can Do" (much of which Berlin wrote in a taxi), "Doing What Comes Naturally," "The Girl That I Marry," "I Got the Sun in the Morning," "They Say It's Wonderful," and "You Can't Get a Man With a Gun." Mary Martin stars on tour, and it's Merman again in the 1966 revival, to which Berlin adds "Old Fashioned Wedding." The 1950 film version stars Betty Hutton and Howard Keel. **20** The Old Vic's acclaimed production of *Oedipus Rex* (8), starring Laurence Olivier, opens for a limited run at the Century on a double bill with Sheridan's *The Critic*.

Business and Society

Actors Equity, with no opposition, is tantamount to election.

MAY 1 Commenting on Broadway plays not yet sold to Hollywood, *Variety* notes that "*Anna Lucasta, Deep Are the Roots, St. Louis Woman*, and *Carmen Jones* all present race problems for the studios."

Births, Deaths, and Marriages

MARCH 4 Charles Waldron d. **12** Liza Minnelli, daughter of Vincent Minnelli and Judy Garland, half-sister of Lorna Luft, b. **13** Philip Merivale and producer George C. Tyler d. **18** Tom Ewell m. actress Judith Abbott, daughter of producer-director George Abbott. Ewell is now appearing on Broadway in *Apple of His Eye*. The marriage will be over in a year. **27** George Abbott m. actress-dress designer Mary Sinclair.

APRIL 1 Playwright Edward B. Sheldon d. **3** Vera Zorina m. record producer Goddard Lieberson. **5** Vincent Youmans d. **8** Jan Clayton m. Robert Lerner. **22** Lionel Atwill d.

MAY 4 Arlene Francis m. Martin Gabel. **19** Playwright Booth Tarkington d.

1946–47

The Tonys begin without the significance later attached to them. In fact, one of the first awards goes to a dentist and his wife. In this season of *The Iceman Cometh* and *All My Sons*, there is no Pulitzer Prize for Drama awarded. José Ferrer brings forth a memorable *Cyrano*, Orson Welles threatens his critics with a voodoo curse, George White produces one "scandal" too many, Maureen Stapleton debuts, Ingrid Bergman is back on Broadway, and Irving Berlin and Eugene O'Neill are just two guys at a piano, singing in the wee hours. The American Repertory Theatre makes a brave try and then folds, and 22-year-old Colleen Dewhurst, a dental receptionist in Gary, Indiana, last year, is studying to be an actress in New York.

- Irving Berlin's earnings from *Annie Get Your Gun*:
  $2,500 a week from the box office
  $100,000 from the original cast album
  $500,000 from sheet music
  $650,000 from the movie rights
- Cost of tickets to first Tony Awards dinner: $7.50
- What first Tony Award-winners receive: silver compacts for women and gold money clips for men
- First actor to win a Tony and an Oscar in the same year: Frederic March, whose Tony is for *Years Ago*, and Oscar for *The Best Years of Our Lives*
- Why one of the first Tony Awards goes to a dentist: Dr. Ira Katzenberg and his wife receive their award because they attend almost every Broadway opening
- What appeals to the John Gielgud and Donald Wolfit British Theatre troupes touring the U.S.: the food, which is in short supply in war-ravaged Britain
- Biggest problem for those seeing *The Iceman Cometh* at the Martin Beck: finding a place to eat during the intermission
- Number of waiters who have been working at Sardi's since the 1920s: 2
- Number of investors in the American Repertory Theatre: 140
- Plays used by the U.S. Army to help "de-Nazify" Germany: *Our Town*, *The Skin of Our Teeth*, *Awake and Sing*, and *The Adding Machine*

Productions on Broadway: 79

Pulitzer Prize for Drama: None awarded

New York Drama Critics Circle Awards:
Best American Play: *All My Sons* (Arthur Miller)
Best Foreign Play: *No Exit* (Jean-Paul Sartre)
Best Musical: *Brigadoon* (Lerner and Loewe)

The first Tony Awards:
Actor in a Play: José Ferrer (*Cyrano de Bergerac*) and Frederic March (*Years Ago*)
Actress in a Play: Ingrid Bergman (*Joan of Lorraine*) and Helen Hayes (*Happy Birthday*)

June	July	August	September	October	November
Antoinette Perry d.	*Oklahoma!* Broadway's longest-running musical	Moss Hart m. Kitty Carlisle	Brooks Atkinson returns to *The New York Times*	José Ferrer's *Cyrano* and *The Iceman Cometh*	Irving Berlin meets Eugene O'Neill

December	January	February	March	April	May
Beggar's Holiday fiasco	*Finian's Rainbow* and *All My Sons*	O'Neill to Boston censor: no cuts	*Brigadoon*	First Tony Awards	Ella Logan quits *Finian's Rainbow*

Personalities

JUNE 2 Orson Welles, on his radio show, threatens to put a voodoo curse on critics disparaging his production of *Around the World*, which just opened.

JULY 8 The American Theatre Wing begins a professional training program for veterans. Students in it will include Tony Randall, Charleton Heston, Pat Hingle, and James Whitmore. On the faculty: Alfred Lunt, Eva Le Gallienne, José Ferrer, Martha Graham, Richard Rodgers, and Oscar Hammerstein II. **15** Helen Hayes's baby—whose birth Jed Harris once called an "act of God" when he wanted an excuse not to pay the cast of *Coquette*, which was closed by Hayes's pregnancy—has grown up. Tonight, at the Bucks County Playhouse, Mary MacArthur debuts opposite her mother in J. M. Barrie's *Alice Sit-By-the-Fire*, directed by Joshua Logan.

AUGUST • Back in New York for the first time in 12 years, Eugene O'Neill, observing how the landmarks have changed, tells reporters at the Theatre Guild's office, "I don't know Broadway anymore." He appears frail. **23** George White, the producer whose *Scandals* competed with *The Ziegfeld Follies* and *Earl Carroll's Vanities* in the twenties, is sentenced to a year in jail for the July 20 hit-and-run death in California of a newlywed couple. White, who declared bankruptcy in 1942, when he still owned a Rolls Royce but owed $100,000, now has $180 in the bank.

SEPTEMBER • Brooks Atkinson, after stints as a war correspondent and as his newspaper's man in Moscow, returns to the post of *New York Times* drama critic. **11** Vaudevillian Jimmy Savo, who starred in Rodgers and Hart's *The Boys from Syracuse*, has his leg amputated.

OCTOBER 29 In the touring cast of *Call Me Mister*, beginning rehearsals today, are unknowns Bob Fosse, Carl Reiner, Buddy Hackett, and Howard Morris. **15** A year ago, she was a dental receptionist in Gary, Indiana. Tonight, Colleen Dewhurst, age 22, is playing Julie Cavendish in an

Plays and Musicals

JULY 1 *Oklahoma!* with its 1,404th performance, passes *Hellzapoppin* to become Broadway's longest-running musical.

SEPTEMBER 5 Ben Hecht's pageant-drama about the Jews in Palestine *A Flag Is Born* (120), opens at the Alvin. The benefit performances will be extended beyond the originally intended run of a month. The opening cast includes Marlon Brando and Paul Muni and is directed by Luther Adler, with music by Kurt Weill.

OCTOBER 8 José Ferrer is the star in a landmark production of *Cyrano de Bergerac* (193), at the Alvin. Richard Watts, Jr., in the *New York Post*, comparing him to the great Walter Hampden, says of tonight's Cyrano that "he has established a new and higher standard." **9** Eugene O'Neill's *The Iceman Cometh* (136) opens. James Barton is "Hickey," and Dudley Digges makes his final Broadway appearance as "Harry." E. G. Marshall is also in the cast. Brooks Atkinson calls the O'Neill work "one of his best," but Howard Barnes in the *Herald-Tribune* says that the playwright "has peopled the stage of the Martin Beck with fascinating characters, has involved them in a magnificent riddle of life and death, and then has left them and an audience singularly untouched." **14** Cornelia Otis Skinner stars in a revival of Oscar Wilde's *Lady Windermere's Fan* (228), at the Cort. **26** Maureen Stapleton makes her Broadway debut in *Playboy of the Western World* (81), at the Booth, in a minor role, which is also what Julie Harris has this evening. The stars are Burgess Meredith, Irish actress Eithne Dunne, and Mildred Natwick. **31** Helen Hayes is a milquetoast mouse who finally roars—thanks to a few drinks—in *Happy Birthday* (564), an Anita Loos comedy at the Broadhurst.

NOVEMBER 6 The American Repertory Theatre, founded by Eva Le Gallienne, Cheryl Crawford, and Margaret Webster, debuts at the International Theatre with Shakespeare's not terribly popular or familiar *Henry VIII*, starring Victor Jory, Eli Wallach and Efrem Zimbalist, Jr. The repertory idea will not survive the winter. **17** The curtain for *The Iceman Cometh*—

Business and Society

JUNE • At an American Veterans Committee meeting early in the month, black actor Canada Lee decries the whites-only policy of the stagehands union, Local One. Robert E. Sherwood and Marc Blitzstein also attack segregation in the theatre at the session.

AUGUST • Chafing at what he regards as the undue influence that the Dramatists Guild has achieved over how plays are produced, Lee Shubert accuses the organization of violating the antitrust laws.

SEPTEMBER • Actors Equity steps up its pressure on theatres in Baltimore and Washington, D.C., to desegregate. **23** The New York Drama Critics Circle votes to award a "best play" citation every year, without regard to whether or not a certain level of achievement has been reached.

OCTOBER • Vera Allen succeeds the late Antoinette Perry as chairperson of the American Theatre Wing. Other officials include Rachel Crothers, Helen Hayes, and Lee Shubert. • Broadway ticket sales are boosted by foreigners arriving in town for the opening of the new United Nations.

Births, Deaths, and Marriages

JUNE 28 Antoinette Perry d., never knowing that the theatre's most famous award—the Tonys—will be named for her. Newspapers will often mistakenly print a photo of her daughter Margaret, also in the theatre, when they mean to use an image of her mother. "I'm the one who looks like Clara Bow," Margaret will tell the papers. "Mother looked like Ellen Terry."

JULY 2 Ron Silver b. **7** Siobhan McKenna m. actor Dennis O'Dea. **11** Judith Anderson m. producer Luther Greene. Newspapers will report their separation after four months.

AUGUST • Julie Harris m. producer Jay Julien. **10** Kitty Carlisle's beaus have included Sinclair Lewis, Bennett Cerf, George Abbott, George Gershwin, and

American Academy of Dramatic Arts production of *The Royal Family* at the Carnegie Lyceum Theatre in New York. Also in the cast is fellow Academy student James Vickery, whom she will marry next year. **21** Eugene O'Neill is on the cover of *Time* on the occasion of the opening of *The Iceman Cometh*, his first new play since 1934.

NOVEMBER 23 Irving Berlin meets Eugene O'Neill at a small dinner party. Berlin has been "worried about what I [Berlin] was going to say to him." They sit at the piano and until three o'clock in the morning sing songs by Berlin and other composers. O'Neill is so excited by the encounter that later he can't get to sleep.

DECEMBER 2 Ingrid Bergman is on the cover of *Life* Magazine, in costume for *Joan of Lorraine*. **26** *Beggar's Holiday*, a musical updating of John Gay's *Beggar's Opera*, begins its pre-Broadway tryouts. Codirected by John Houseman and Nicholas Ray, with music by Duke Ellington, it stars Libby Holman as Jenny Diver, Alfred Drake as Mack the Knife, and Zero Mostel, about to make his Broadway debut, as Mr. Peachum. It is also star-crossed. Houseman will quit in Boston. George Abbott is brought in and he has Ray, who has been Libby Holman's lover, fire her. Then, Abbott gets rid of Ray. The show does reach Broadway, where it flops.

FEBRUARY • About 5,000 of the 50,000 questionnaires handed out at performances of *Street Scene* and *Joan of Lorraine* have been returned, indicating that theatregoers overwhelmingly think of Brooks Atkinson, of *The New York Times*, as the most important theatre critic. **4** Ella Logan, at loggerheads with producers over the type size accorded her featured billing in *Finian's Rainbow*, will be out for five days with what is being called a throat problem.

MARCH 22 In a pre-Broadway run of *Bathsheba* at Princeton, James Mason is either the victim of a heckler or part of a publicity stunt when a member of the audience climbs on the stage during the play and tells him, "Mr. Mason, sir, I think you stink." The show, which the

---

a four-and-quarter-hour play—has been moved from 5:30 to 7:30 because grabbing a meal at the intermission was too difficult, even though Sardi's had set aside an area on its second floor to accommodate patrons of the Martin Beck. **18** Ingrid Bergman is back on Broadway in Maxwell Anderson's *Joan of Lorraine* (199)—"a magnificent performance," says Brooks Atkinson—directed by Margo Jones, at the Alvin. Bergman takes it to the screen in 1948. **20** Lillian Hellman's prequel to her 1939 *The Little Foxes*, *Another Part of the Forrest* (182), opens at the Fulton. Patricia Neal, Percy Waram, and Leo Genn star, with the support of Mildred Dunnock and Jean Hagen. A film version is out in 1948. **26** Jean-Paul Sartre, described by critic Burns Mantle as "the leader of a new group classified in Paris as [e]xistentialists," is the author of *No Exit* (31), at the Biltmore. Claude Dauphin is the pacifist and Annabella the lesbian.

DECEMBER 3 *Years Ago* (206), a comedy by Ruth Gordon about her own adolescence, at the Mansfield, stars Patricia Kirkland as the girl and Frederic March and Florence Eldridge as her parents. March will win a Tony for his performance—and an Oscar for the film *The Best Years of Our Lives*, which premiered two weeks ago.

JANUARY 9 *Street Scene* (148), Kurt Weill's musical version of the 1929 Elmer Rice play, with a libretto by poet Langston

Ingrid Bergman

---

29 Maxwell Anderson's *Joan of Lorraine*, starring Ingrid Bergman, is picketed when it opens in a Washington, D.C., theatre that does not sell tickets to blacks. **30** *Variety*, noting Equity's fight against racial discrimination, reports that being considered is a proposal "whereby no manager may use a white actor in a part intended for a Negro player by the author, such as butlers, waiters and maids."

---

even Thomas Dewey ("like someone from another planet," she says). She's told her mother, "I'm going to end up like Sophie Tucker singing 'Some of these Days' in a café in Montana." But today, she m. playwright Moss Hart. The ceremony is delayed while he repairs numerous cuts he made while shaving. Still nervous when the photographers go to work, he accidentally trips his bride. **17** Playwright Channing Pollock d.

SEPTEMBER 7 Director Jerry Zaks b.

OCTOBER 10 Ben Vereen b. **17** Producer Cameron Mackintosh b.

NOVEMBER 12 Producer Lynne Meadow b. **18** Donald Meek d.

DECEMBER 7 Laurette Taylor d. **8** John Rubinstein, son of pianist Artur Rubinstein, b. **10** Damon Runyon d. **25** W. C. Fields d.

Personalities

author sees as a tragedy and the star a comedy, has not been doing well with critics or audiences. **30** Alan Jay Lerner, responding to a letter in the *Times* pointing out that a story by a nineteenth-century German writer sounds uncomfortably close to the plot of *Brigadoon*, says it's a coincidence he discovered after writing the first draft of the musical. He says there are many legends involving disappearing towns.

APRIL 2 *Variety*, under the headline "'Tonys' [a]s Awards [f]or Broadway Legit," reports that producer Brock Pemberton has been calling the new theatre awards, named for Antoinette Perry, the "Tonys." **6** The first Tony Awards are handed out at a $7.50 a ticket dinner at the Waldorf Astoria, attended by more than 1,000, including members of the public, who are serenaded by the Meyer Davis Orchestra. The theme is "outstanding contributions," not the "best." Among the winners of the 20 awards are Ingrid Bergman, José Ferrer, Agnes DeMille, Helen Hayes, Elia Kazan, Frederic March, Arthur Miller, Patricia Neal, David Wayne, Kurt Weill, and Burns Mantle.

MAY 31 With her contact expiring and angered over a dispute over the way she was billed, Ella Logan leaves *Finian's Rainbow*, replaced by Dorothy Claire.

José Ferrer as Cyrano

Plays and Musicals

Hughes, opens at the Adelphi. The stars are Ann Jeffreys, Brian Sullivan, Polyna Stoska, Norman Condon, and Don Saxon. **10** Burton Lane and Yip Harburg's *Finian's Rainbow* (725) opens at the Forty-sixth Street Theatre. It features "How Are Things in Glocca Morra?" "If This Isn't Love," "Old Devil Moon," "When I'm Not Near the Girl I Love," and "That Great Come-and-Get-It Day." Ella Logan stars, with Albert Sharpe, Donald Richards, and David Wayne. It's a 1968 film. **29** Arthur Miller's *All My Sons* (328) opens at the Coronet. Ed Begley plays a man with an ugly secret: during World War II, he sold defective plane parts to the military. As a consequence, he loses one son, a pilot, clashes with another son, played by Arthur Kennedy, and ultimately takes his own life. It's made into a movie next year.

FEBRUARY 4 *John Loves Mary* (423), a comedy by Norman Krasna about the consequences of the lies spun around a marriage of convenience, is at the Booth. William Prince and Nina Foch star. The film is released in 1949.

MARCH 13 Lerner and Loewe's *Brigadoon* (581) opens at the Ziegfeld. From this musical about a Scottish town that sleeps but for one day in each century comes "Almost Like Being In Love," "I'll Go Home With Bonnie Jean," and "The Heather on the Hill." Agnes DeMille choreographed, and the cast includes Marion Bell, David Brooks, Pamela Britton, George Keane, Lee Sullivan, Helen Gallagher, and Lidija Franklin. MGM's movie version appears in 1954.

MAY 1 "Are They Drama [o]r Are They Opera," asks the *Journal-American* headline of Gian-Carlo Menotti's *The Telephone* and *The Medium* (36). They're at the Barrymore, where the composer has asked that they be reviewed as dramas.

Business and Society

NOVEMBER 25 A coal strike dims Broadway's bright lights.

JANUARY • In one of the first significant uses of the American National Theatre and Academy (ANTA) since it was formed 12 years ago, the organization becomes the conduit for raising money for the American Repertory Theatre and for the Experimental Theatre.

FEBRUARY • Eugene O'Neill declines to make any of the cuts in *The Iceman Cometh* demanded by the Boston censor, and it will not play there on its upcoming tour. **22** Members of Maurice Evans's touring production of *Hamlet* picket the National Theatre in St. Louis over its segregated seating policy and then go inside to perform.

MARCH 5 Employees of a bar and grill in Philadelphia are arrested when they refuse to serve black cast members of *Anna Lucasta*, including Rex Ingram. **11** Calling it "a slander on American motherhood," the Detroit police censor closes down Eugene O'Neill's *A Moon for the Misbegotten*. It will reopen with a few words deleted, but the production is unsuccessful and does not reach New York.

Births, Deaths, and Marriages

JANUARY 11 Vaudevillian Eva Tanguay d.

MARCH 19 Glenn Close b.

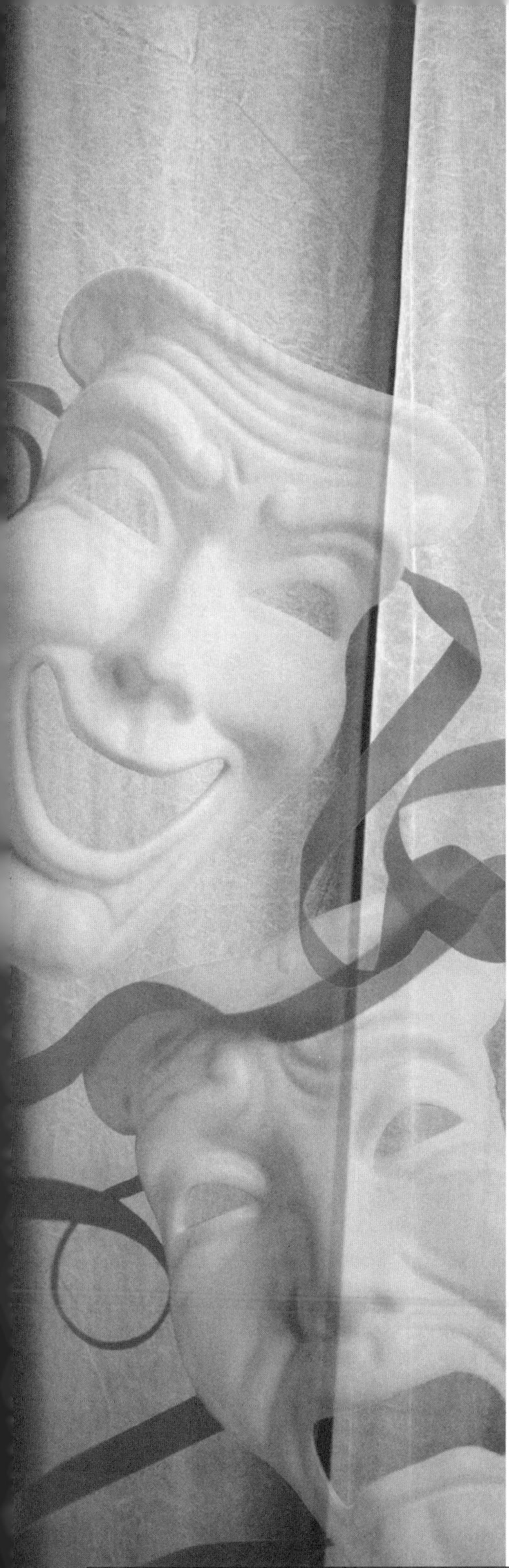

1947–48

"Stellllaaaaa!" the man says, in the most electrifying play of the year, in which a woman depends upon "the kindness of strangers." In Texas, the debut of Margo Jones's Theatre 47 and Nina Vance's Alley Theatre signal the beginning of the rise of a strong regional theatre in America, in which often very small houses, some of them theatres-in-the-round, will eventually originate plays and feed them to Broadway. In Greenwich Village, the New Stages Theatre is the first of many important postwar off-Broadway houses. The Actors Studio begins, Judith Anderson is a stunning *Medea*, Rodgers and Hammerstein's *Allegro* is a less than completely happy experience, and Jason Robards, Jr., not yet doing O'Neill, is playing the rear half of a cow. And who thought that *Life With Father* and *Oklahoma!* would ever actually close?

- Number of creditors named in the involuntary bankruptcy petition filed against producer Mike Todd: 115
- Original title of *A Streetcar Named Desire*: "The Poker Night"
- Elia Kazan's share of the profits from *A Streetcar Named Desire*: 20 percent
- Producer Irene Mayer Selnick's telegram to her office confirming that she has snared *A Streetcar Named Desire*, her first big production: "Blanche has come to live with us."
- Last holdout from old Actors Fidelity League to join Equity: Fay Bainter, who needs an Equity card to do summer stock
- Number of Yiddish Theatres still operating in New York: 4
- Number of George Bernard Shaw plays on Broadway: 3—*Man and Superman*, *John Bull's Other Island*, and *You Never Can Tell*
- Number of investors losing money in the demise of the American Repertory Theatre, which was never intended to be nonprofit: 293
- Number of people employed in the theatre this season as a result of the composing and producing activities of Rodgers and Hammerstein: 1,600

Productions on Broadway: 76

Pulitzer Prize for Drama: *A Streetcar Named Desire* (Tennessee Williams)

New York Drama Critics Circle Awards:
Best American Play: *A Streetcar Named Desire* (Tennessee Williams)
Best Foreign Play: *The Winslow Boy* (Terrence Rattigan)

Tony Awards:
Play: *Mister Roberts* (Thomas Heggen and Joshua Logan)
Actor in a Play: Henry Fonda (*Mister Roberts*), Paul Kelly (*Command Decision*), and Basil Rathbone (*The Heiress*)
Actress in a Play: Judith Anderson (*Medea*), Katharine Cornell (*Antony and Cleopatra*), and Jessica Tandy (*A Streetcar Named Desire*)
Actor in a Musical: Paul Hartman (*Angel in the Wings*)
Actress in a Musical: Grace Hartman (*Angel in the Wings*)

June	July	August	September	October	November
Theatre '47 debuts	*Life With Father* closes	*Variety* says Garfield to star in 'Streetcar'	Actors Studio formed	Judith Anderson in *Medea*	Alley Theatre debuts in Houston

December	January	February	March	April	May
A Streetcar Named Desire	Nancy Walker a star	*Mr. Roberts*	Andrew Lloyd Webber b.	*London Times* attacks O'Neill	*Oklahoma!* closes

Personalities

JULY 14 Film actor James Stewart returns to the stage, temporarily taking over Frank Fay's role as Elwood P. Dowd in *Harvey*, while Fay takes a busman's holiday, doing the show out of town. Two policeman have to be stationed in front of the theatre to control crowds who want to see a movie star. **21** Bea Arthur makes her professional debut, off Broadway, at the Cherry Lane Theatre, in the chorus of *The Dog Beneath the Skin*. **30** Charles Laughton is back on the legitimate stage for the first time in 15 years when he opens at the Coronet Theatre in Los Angeles in Bertolt Brecht's new play *Galileo*.

AUGUST 6 *Variety* reports that John Garfield will have the male lead in Tennessee Williams's new play *A Streetcar Named Desire*. But Garfield's contractual demands will rule him out. Williams's agent, Audrey Wood, and producer Irene Selnick have suggested Edmund O'Brien or Gregory Peck. But Williams likes the reading that Marlon Brando has just given him at the playwright's Provincetown home. Brando even repaired Williams's plumbing. Director Elia Kazan needs coaxing to accept the young actor, however, having heard that he can be difficult and eccentric.

SEPTEMBER 7 Brooks Atkinson, in *The New York Times*, defends Arthur Miller and his play *All My Sons*, productions of which anti-Communist groups have pressured the Army not to allow in occupied Europe. Atkinson says the drama is not Communistic and calls the playwright "a young man of genuine talent for the stage." **12** Under the headline "New Drama School Formed," *The New York Times* reports: "The formation of The Studio, a novel drama school designed especially for young Broadway actors to study and improve themselves at no cost, was announced yesterday. It will be conducted by Elia Kazan, Robert Lewis and Martin Ritt, well-known directors, and Cheryl Crawford, sponsor of *Brigadoon*, who will be in charge of the administration." It is the beginning of the Actors Studio.

Plays and Musicals

JUNE 3 The first modern professional repertory theatre in America, Theatre '47—the name will be updated every New Year's Eve—created by Margo Jones, opens in Dallas. Its 200-seat playhouse is also said to be the first professional theatre-in-the-round in the country. It debuts with William Inge's first play, *Farther Off from Heaven*, an early version of the 1957 *The Dark at the Top of the Stairs*.

JULY 12 *Life With Father* closes on Broadway after 3,213 performances in seven and one-half years. Between the Broadway and touring productions, it has already grossed about $10 million.

SEPTEMBER 29 The happy ending demanded by the producers of *The Heiress* (410) didn't work out of town, so playwrights Ruth and Augustus Goetz have gone back to the plot of the Henry James story. Wendy Hiller, Peter Cookson, and Basil Rathbone star, at the Biltmore. It's on the screen in 1949 and revived on the stage in 1995 with Cherry Jones.

OCTOBER 1 In *Command Decision* (409), Paul Kelly is an officer driven to the brink of suicide by the need to order his bomber pilots on missions that are themselves almost suicidal. William Wister Haines's drama is at the Fulton and in the movies next year. **9** Jule Styne and Sammy Cahn's *High Button Shoes* (727) opens at the Century. It stars Phil Silvers and Nanette Fabray, who sings "Papa, Won't You Dance With Me?" Mack Sennett will win a lawsuit against the show for using his name and the "Keystone Kops" in a Jerome Robbins ballet sequence without permission. **10** Rodgers and Hammerstein's *Allegro*, directed by Agnes DeMille, opens at the Majestic, which has already sold 250,000 tickets and has $750,000 in the box office. *Allegro* (315) has abstract sets, a Greek chorus, and a story about a disillusioned doctor. The cast includes Lisa Kirk, singing "The Gentleman Is a Dope" in her Broadway debut, John Battles, and Roberta Jonay. **20** Robinson Jeffer's adaptation of Euripedes' *Medea* (214), directed by John Gielgud, who is also in the cast as Jason, opens at the National. Star Judith Anderson, according to the

Business and Society

JUNE • Producer Brock Pemberton praises the new Taft-Hartley legislation, which "should discourage the more aggressive unions from continuing to heap ridiculous rules and rates on an industry economically unable to bear them, and should shear them of the arrogance with which they handed out their edicts." **27** Producer Herman Shumlin is convicted of contempt of Congress for refusing to testify about his political activities to the House Un-American Activities Committee. Shumlin, for whom Frederic March and his wife, Florence Eldridge, testified as character witnesses two days ago, will receive a fine and suspended sentence after purging himself of the contempt charge.

AUGUST 14 The League of New York Theatres votes to support Actors Equity's threatened boycott of the National Theatre in Washington, D.C., if it doesn't stop segregating audiences, although the producers have reservations about giving Equity power to say how management should sell tickets.

SEPTEMBER 9 The Actors Equity council reiterates its stand against [C]ommunism,

Births, Deaths, and Marriages

JUNE 5 Playwright David Hare b. **17** Earl Carroll d. in a plane crash.

JULY 3 Betty Buckley b. **4** Producer Mike Todd m. film actress Joan Blondell.

SEPTEMBER 17 Lyricist-composer Bert Kalmar d. **21** Playwright Marsha Norman (Marsha Lee) b.

OCTOBER 5 Gower Champion m. Marjorie Belcher, forming the dance team of Marge and Gower Champion. The marriage will last until 1973. **17** John Halliday d. **24** Dudley Digges d. and Kevin Kline b. **26** Nanette Fabray m. press agent David Teber.

NOVEMBER 30 Playwright David Mamet b.

DECEMBER 21 Producer and former Broadway

OCTOBER • Audiences attending the radio broadcasts of "Scotland Yard" on Monday nights see star Basil Rathbone in costume and makeup for his role as the father in *The Heiress*, the performance of which he rushes to once the program is over. • Bringing up the rear half of a cow in *Jack and the Bean Stalk*, at the Children's World Theatre, is 25-year-old Jason Robards, Jr., in his New York debut. **13** With expectations that Rodgers and Hammerstein have another *Oklahoma!* or *Carousel*, *Life* Magazine devotes its October 13 cover story to *Allegro*. **20** Oscar Hammerstein II is on the cover of *Time*, coinciding with the opening of *Allegro*.

NOVEMBER 19 Gertrude Lawrence, performing *Tonight at 8:30* in Boston, tells a reporter that the city's censor has suggested that she wear a negligee under her nightgown and she will comply.

DECEMBER • The London production of *Finian's Rainbow* closes after only seven weeks. Michael Kidd, the show's dance director, suggests that the British are just not getting the jokes about Sears Roebuck, the TVA, and missing references to aspects of Southern culture. **26** Despite the historic 25½ inch snowfall in New York, only two of eight scheduled Friday matinées are canceled. At the Broadhurst, *Happy Birthday* is closed by a skylight brought down by the weight of the snow. At the Barrymore tonight, which has people standing for *A Streetcar*

Times's Brooks Atkinson, gives "a burning performance in a savage part." She "understands the character more thoroughly than Medea, Euripedes or the scholars, and it would be useless now for anyone else to attempt the part." Debuting on Broadway in a nonspeaking role is Marian Seldes, and literally carrying a spear is Richard Boone. **29** A father is determined to return his son, played by Michael Newell, to the school from which he's been expelled in Terrence Rattigan's *The Winslow Boy* (215), at the Empire.

NOVEMBER 18 Houston's Alley Theatre offers its first play, *A Sound of Hunting*, at a 90-seat converted dance studio, accessible through an alley. Nina Vance is the founding artistic director of this civic, nonprofit theatre.

Tennessee Williams

DECEMBER 3 Tennessee Williams's *A Streetcar Named Desire* (855), with Marlon Brando as Stanley Kowalski, opens at the Barrymore. Elia Kazan directs, Jessica Tandy plays Blanche Du Bois, Kim Hunter is Stella, and Karl Malden is Mitch in this steamy drama of sexual tension, set in New Orleans. Brooks Atkinson calls it

requiring its officers to sign non-Communist oaths, an action that will create tension and dissension at Equity's next membership meeting, on the 19th.

OCTOBER 5 The Actors Studio begins its first session.

NOVEMBER • Moss Hart follows Richard Rodgers as president of the Dramatists Guild. Also this month, Raymond Massey succeeds the late Dudley Digges as a vice president of Actors Equity.

DECEMBER 8 A kitchen fire closes Sardi's restaurant for several days. **21** The 299-seat New Stages Theatre, opening on Bleecker Street in Greenwich Village, is the opening act in the postwar boom in off-Broadway theatre in New York. The house will eventually be the home of Circle in the Square. In the cast of the first play, Barrie Stavis's *The Lamp at Midnight*, about Galileo, is Martin Balsam.

JANUARY • The Shuberts, after trying unsuccessfully for several weeks to evict *Oklahoma!* from the St. James Theatre because attendance is flagging and Lee and J.J. would like to bring in a new musical, give up.

columnist Mark Hellinger d.

JANUARY 4 Judy Holliday m. musician David Oppenheim. **25** June Havoc m. radio producer William Spier.

FEBRUARY 9 Critic Burns Mantle d. **28** Bernadette Peters (Bernadette Lazarra) b. She will choose her stage name from her father Peter's first name.

MARCH 5 Eli Wallach m. Anne Jackson. **22** Composer Andrew Lloyd Webber b.

MAY 5 Tom Ewell m. Marjorie Sanborn. **9** Viola Allen d.

Personalities

Named Desire, Jessica Tandy makes a curtain speech thanking the audience, and the cast applauds the playgoers who braved the blizzard.

JANUARY 18 ANTA stages its first "ANTA Album," a benefit at the Ziegfeld, with Walter Huston singing "September Song," Helen Hayes appearing as Queen Victoria, Dorothy Stickney revisiting *The Front Page*, and John Gielgud as Hamlet. Libby Holman sings "Body and Soul," Cliff Edwards sings "Fascinatin' Rhythm," Buck and Bubbles do "It Ain't Necessarily So," and the show concludes with the chorus from *Oklahoma!* singing the show's title tune. **19** Katharine Cornell is on the cover of *Newsweek*.

FEBRUARY 18 At the curtain tonight of the opening performance of *Mr. Roberts*, Henry Fonda responds to the endless applause—Marlene Dietrich is standing on her seat cheering—"That's all that Josh Logan wrote for us, but if you really want us to, we'll do it all over again. . . ."

MARCH 15 Harold Clurman succeeds Irwin Shaw as theatre critic for *The New Republic*.

APRIL 10 The *London Times Literary Supplement* bitterly attacks Eugene O'Neill's *The Iceman Cometh* for its despair, complaining that the playwright's "whole belief about life contradicts his country's."

MAY • Milton Berle and producer Mike Todd are said to be preparing a new revue called "The Roaring Twenties," to costar Todd's wife, Joan Blondell. But Berle is about to become involved in another project. On May 26, *Variety* runs a story headlined, "Vaude's 'Comeback' Via Vaudio," which begins, "The 'comeback' of vaudeville is television's hottest development." The emphasis will be on variety when the Texaco Star Theatre debuts on NBC on June 8, and when CBS airs the tentatively titled "You're the Top," emceed by Broadway columnist Ed Sullivan, on June 20.

Plays and Musicals

"one of the most perfect marriages of acting and playwriting," writing mostly about Williams and Tandy, with one clause of one sentence on Brando. The Communist Party *Daily Worker* likes the production but says that the play is "empty." It appears as a film in 1951.

JANUARY 29 *Look Ma, I'm Dancin'* (188) was conceived by Jerome Robbins, is directed by George Abbott, has a score by Hugh Martin, and makes its lead player Nancy Walker a Broadway comedy star. It's at the Adelphi.

FEBRUARY 18 *Mr. Roberts* (1,157), adapted by Josh Logan and Thomas Heggen from Heggen's novel, is at the Alvin. Henry Fonda has the title role, David Wayne is Ensign Pulver, and William Harrigan plays the captain. Fonda stars in the 1955 film, with James Cagney, Jack Lemmon, and William Powell.

Henry Fonda

APRIL 30 *Inside U.S.A.* (399), the contents of which have nothing to do with the John Gunther book of the same title, is at the New Century Theatre. The revue stars Beatrice Lillie and Jack Haley, with soon-to-be television personalities Carl Reiner and Herb Shriner. The score is by Arthur Schwartz and Howard Dietz.

MAY 29 *Oklahoma!* closes on Broadway after five years and 2,248 performances.

Business and Society

FEBRUARY • *Theatre Arts*, a combination of *Theatre Arts Magazine* and *Stage Magazine*, begins publication.

APRIL • Producers, for the first time, are taking extra ad space to boast of Tony award winners.

Births, Deaths, and Marriages

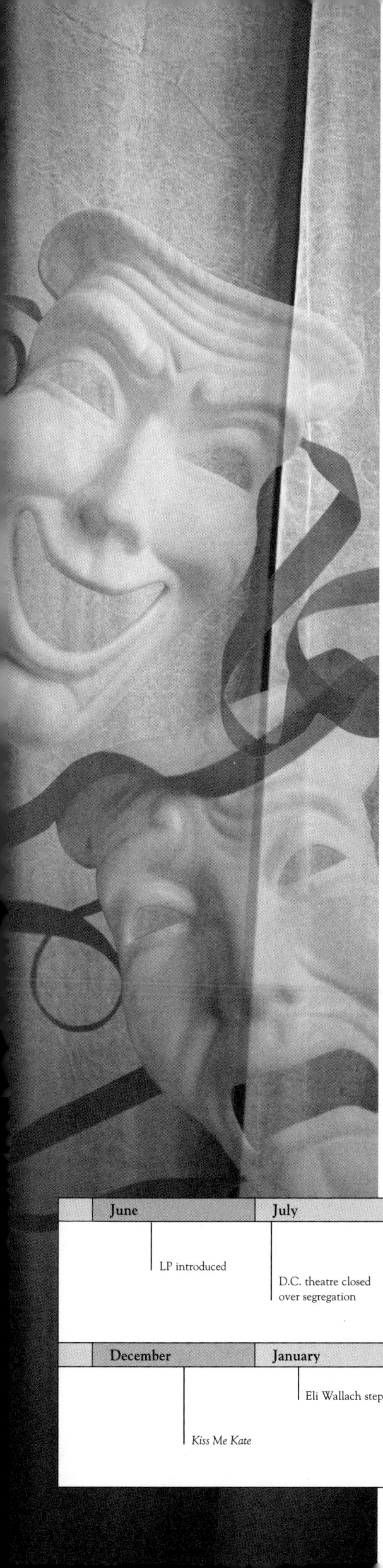

1948–49

The introduction of the long-playing record—the "LP"—leads to the golden age of original cast recordings. Unable to get Frederic March for *Death of A Salesman*, the producers settle for Lee J. Cobb. They also fail to induce Arthur Miller to give his work a more upbeat title. April 7 is truly "some enchanted evening," thanks to Rodgers and Hammerstein, and Rex Harrison makes his Broadway debut. *Lend An Ear*, a revue, "has no big names in it," says one reviewer. But it does have one that will grow bigger: Carol Channing. Tallulah Bankhead will not lend a thing, especially her name, to a shampoo jingle. And Ray Bolger discovers how to put across "Once in Love With Amy": enlist the audience.

- What producer Cheryl Crawford says to Elia Kazan when shown the latest work by Arthur Miller: "Who would want to see a play about an unhappy traveling salesman?"
- Occupation of the father of Elia Kazan, who is directing *Death of a Salesman*: salesman
- Number of copies of *Death of a Salesman* sold in the next year by The Book of the Month Club: 200,000
- How long it took Richard Rodgers to write the music to "Bali Ha'i" in *South Pacific*, once given the lyrics by Oscar Hammerstein II: 5 minutes, and he writes it on the sheet containing Hammerstein's words
- Number of people who will see *South Pacific* at the Majestic before it closes in 1954: 3,500,000
- How *South Pacific* changes Mary Martin: the formerly longhaired singer has a new, shorter hair cut, because onstage she literally does wash that man right out of her hair, and she will keep it short
- Most successful show: *Private Lives*, which costs $25,000 and earns $125,000
- Tag line from *Where's Charley?*: Charley's aunt "comes from Brazil, where the nuts come from."
- Average guarantee received by a Broadway theatre during the run of a production: $3,500–$4,000 a week
- Average running expenses for a Broadway theatre: $4,500 a week
- Take your pick: the original cast album of *Kiss Me Kate* is available on both six 78 rpm records and on one disk in the LP format, introduced in June
- Tennessee Williams's current royalty earnings: about $7,500 a week
- Average pay of dancers in a Broadway show: $82 a week
- Actor unemployment: 80%
- Price of a complete dinner at Schraffts: $2.00

Productions on Broadway: 70

Pulitzer Prize for Drama: *Death of a Salesman* (Arthur Miller)

Drama Critics Circle Award:
Best American Play: *Death of a Salesman* (Arthur Miller)
Best Foreign Play: *The Madwoman of Chaillot* (Jean Giraudoux)
Best Musical: *South Pacific* (Rodgers and Hammerstein)

Tony Awards:
Play: *Death of a Salesman* (Arthur Miller)
Actor in a Play: Rex Harrison (*Anne of the Thousand Days*)
Actress in a Play: Martita Hunt (*The Madwoman of Chaillot*)
Musical: *Kiss Me Kate* (Cole Porter)
Actor in a Musical: Ray Bolger (*Where's Charley?*)
Actress in a Musical: Nanette Fabray (*Love Life*)

June	July	August	September	October	November
LP introduced	D.C. theatre closed over segregation; Nancy Walker m.—briefly		Bankhead says "no benefits"	*Where's Charley?*	Chicago censors Sartre

December	January	February	March	April	May
Kiss Me Kate	Eli Wallach steps in	*Death of a Salesman*	Cobb gets star billing	*South Pacific*	Vaudeville back at Palace

Personalities

JUNE 9 Oscar Hammerstein II, in a letter in *Variety*, chastises the paper for characterizing the work of choreographer Agnes DeMille as passé in its recent headline: "Over-de-Mille-to-Storehouse."

SEPTEMBER • Studying at the Actors Studio: Tom Ewell, David Wayne, Karl Malden, Marlon Brando, Mildred Dunnock, Montgomery Clift, E.G. Marshall, and Kevin McCarthy. • Tallulah Bankhead, about to open in a revival of *Private Lives*, says there will be no benefit performances because, as she puts it, "[T]he audiences that attend them are colder than the polar ice cap. You couldn't thaw them out with a flame thrower or an acetylene torch. I'll have no truck with them." **16** A mistaken cry of "fire" at the Nixon Theatre in Pittsburgh halts the road show of *A Streetcar Named Desire* in mid-scene. When the play resumes, Uta Hagen, playing Blanche Du Bois, draws laughs at a moment intended to be tragic when, following the script, she yells "fire, fire."

OCTOBER • The curtain at the Hudson Theatre, where *Detective Story* is playing, is going up late on Fridays, when star Ralph Bellamy also appears in the live weekly TV drama, "Man Against Crime." **11** During the run of *Where's Charley?* opening tonight, Ray Bolger will convince a junior member of the cast, Gretchen Wienecke, to change her last name to the more theatrical "Wyler." **21** Tallulah Bankhead, live on the radio from her dressing room during an intermission of *Private Lives*, introduces a presidential campaign speech by Harry Truman. **27** Unable to sign Frederic March and Florence Eldridge for *Death of a Salesman*, producers Kermit Bloomgarden and Walter Fried announce the hiring of Lee J. Cobb and Ann Revere for the leads. (A movie commitment forces Revere to give way to Mildred Dunnock.)

NOVEMBER 22 Tallulah Bankhead is on the cover of *Time*, with the caption, "The curtain is always up." **22** Jean-Paul Sartre, in Paris, sues to halt the Broadway opening of *Red Gloves*, an adaptation of his *Les Mains Sales*. The author claims

Plays and Musicals

SEPTEMBER 30 *Edward, My Son* (260), about a father's dishonest pursuit of wealth for the sake of his son (who never appears on stage), opens at the Martin Beck. It stars Robert Morley—coauthor with Noel Langley—and Peggy Ashcroft. A film appears next year.

OCTOBER 4 Tallulah Bankhead and Donald Cook star in a revival of Noel Coward's 1931 *Private Lives* (248), at the Plymouth. Critic John Mason Brown calls Bankhead "a volcano in a hurricane. . . ." **6** Tennessee Williams's *Summer and Smoke* (100), starring Margaret Phillips, opens at the Music Box. *Variety* calls it "a pale, disappointing facsimile" of *The Glass Menagerie* and *A Streetcar Named Desire*. A 1952 revival will begin a critical reevaluation of the work. It's filmed in 1961. **11** Ray Bolger opens at the St. James in Frank Loesser's *Where's Charley?* directed by George Abbott and choreographed by George Balanchine. "Once in Love With Amy," intended to stop the show, doesn't for several weeks until Bolger begins to urge the audience to sing along. "My Darling, My Darling" is also in the score. There is no original cast album because of a musician's strike. Bolger stars in the 1952 screen version.

NOVEMBER 13 Overhauled after it was savaged in Boston, Mike Todd's *As The Girls Go* (414), with a score by Jimmy McHugh and Harold Adamson, is at the Winter Garden. What started as a satire about the first woman president has become a leg show—"the sockiest beauts seen in a Broadway musical in years," says *Variety*—featuring Bobby Clark in his last Broadway appearance. **17** Fay Kanin's comedy *Goodbye, My Fancy* (446) opens at the Morosco. Madeleine Carroll stars, but Shirley Booth—"a worldly secretary with a two-edged weariness that is hilarious," says Brooks Atkinson—almost steals it. **18** Moss Hart's *Light Up the Sky* (216), a satire about the theatre, starring Virginia Field, Sam Levene, and Barry Nelson, opens at the Royale.

DECEMBER 8 Rex Harrison makes his Broadway debut, as Henry VIII, in Maxwell

Business and Society

JUNE 21 Columbia Records introduces the LP, which will help usher in the golden age of original cast recordings.

JULY • Pressured by the New York City Police Department, the producers of *Mr. Roberts* delete some of the play's racy language. They do not publicize the censorship, New York's first in several years, fearing it will hurt ticket sales. **14** After at least one fistfight during negotiations, Actors Equity and the League of New York Theaters have a new contract, increasing minimum salaries to $75 from $65 a week and adding a new cost-of-living provision. **31** Washington, D.C.'s National Theater closes (and will convert to a movie house on October 15) when Actors Equity forbids its members to appear because the theatre segregates audiences by race. The city is now the only major world capital with no legitimate theatre.

AUGUST 25 In a story headlined "1-Act Plays Held Good Possibility [f]or Comeback as Video Material," *Variety* sees lucrative opportunities for playwrights in the new entertainment medium of television.

Births, Deaths, and Marriages

along with his companion and *Vanities* star, Beryl Wallace. **19** José Ferrer and Uta Hagen were divorced a few days ago, and today Ferrer m. actress Phyllis Hill.

JULY 27 Playwright Susan Glaspell d.

AUGUST 1 Nancy Walker m. actor Gar Moore, a match that will last for only 10 months.

OCTOBER 10 Mary Eaton d.

SEPTEMBER 13 Nell Carter b. **26** Mary Beth Hurt (Mary Beth Suppinger) b.

OCTOBER 30 Julian Beck m. Judith Malina.

DECEMBER 9 Ossie Davis m. Ruby Dee. **20** C. Aubrey Smith d.

JANUARY 2 Playwright Christopher Durang b.

that friends of his have seen the tryout in New Haven and say that his work has been turned into an anti-Communist tract.

DECEMBER • Playwright Maxwell Anderson has directed that newspaper ads for his *Anne of the Thousand Days* are to contain no critics' quotes. *The New York Times*'s Brooks Atkinson, playing a practical joke, seeks to pay his own paper to let him insert praise from his review into the show's ad. Anderson, getting wind of the scheme, lets it go through, stating that other critics can do it, too, on "the same pay-as-you-go basis." • Arthur Miller refuses to change the title of his upcoming play *Death of a Salesman*. The producers, who fear it might be box office

Arthur Miller *MSN*

poison, have been pushing for something sunnier. **16** The *New York Sun* says of *Lend An Ear*, a revue opening tonight, "There are no big names in it, but it contains plenty of talent, and several of its members won't remain unknown for long." One of them is 27-year-old Carol Channing.

JANUARY • Tallulah Bankhead threatens to sue *The New York Times*, which reported that she had "crashed" the reviewing stand for diplomats at President Truman's inauguration and fought with a policeman. She says she was arguing with the officer about access for an early departure, so she could get back to New York in time to go on in *Private Lives*. The *Times* retracts its story. **31** Cole Porter is on

Anderson's *Anne of the Thousand Days* (288), at the Shubert. Joyce Redman plays Anne Boleyn because the producer's first choice, Deborah Kerr, could not get clearance to appear from MGM. It's a 1969 film. **27** Jean Giraudoux's *The Madwoman of Chaillot* (368), adapted by Maurice Valency, about eccentrics at a Parisian café, opens at the Belasco. Stars include Martita Hunt, Estelle Winwood, Vladimir Sokoloff, Leora Dana, and John Carradine. **30** Cole Porter's *Kiss Me Kate* (1,077) opens at the New Century. About an acting company performing *The Taming of the Shrew*, with a book by Sam and Bella Spewack—supposedly based on Lunt and Fontanne—it stars Alfred Drake, Patricia Morison, and Lisa Kirk. Songs include "Wunderbar," "Another Opening, Another Show," "So In Love With You Am I," "Why Can't You Behave?" "Too Darn Hot," "Brush Up Your Shakespeare," and "Always True to You (in My Fashion)." The film is released in 1953.

FEBRUARY 10 Arthur Miller's *Death of a Salesman* (742) opens at the Morosco. Elia Kazan directs Lee J. Cobb as Willy Loman, Mildred Dunnock, Arthur Kennedy, and Cameron Mitchell in a tragedy about the struggles of an ordinary man, to whom "attention must be paid." The *Times* calls it "superb," "rich and memorable," a "suburban epic," and "poetry." But *Time* judges it merely "credible," complaining that Miller's writing—"inadequate artistry"—is not up to the play's concept. Notable revivals star

Lee J. Cobb

OCTOBER • The Show of the Month Club is formed by ticket agent Sylvia Siegler. It will cost $15 per year for a pair of orchestra seats each month and $10 to sit in the balcony. Within a year, it will have almost 3,000 members. **29** The Shuberts pay $3,500,000–4,000,000 for the sites of four theatres they have operated for several years: the Booth, Broadhurst, Plymouth, and Shubert theatres. The properties include Shubert Alley.

NOVEMBER 4 Chicago's Police Commissioner notifies the producers of *The Respectful Prostitute*, Jean-Paul Sartre's 1946 work, slated for a December 27 opening, that he will shut it down after the first performance. At issue in this play about prostitution, rape, and lynching is race as well as sex. **21** Frank Fay charges that "at least 80% of all Communists who come into this country come here through theatrical channels."

DECEMBER • The Justice Department begins an inquiry into possible violation of antitrust laws with regard to control of theatres and actor appearances. **30** *Kiss Me Kate*, opening tonight, is the first Broadway musical to have its choreography copyrighted in a written form using Labanotation.

JANUARY 22 The Warner Brothers Theatre becomes the Mark Hellinger.

10 Director-playwright James Lapine b. **12** Willie Howard d., $78,000 in debt. **15** Director Gregory Mosher b.

FEBRUARY 5 Richard Burton m. Sybil Williams.

MARCH 16 Victor Garber b.

APRIL 21 Patti LuPone b. She's the great-great niece of opera diva Adelina Patti.

MAY 26 George S. Kaufman m. Leueen MacGrath, who appeared this season in *Edward, My Son*.

Personalities

the cover of *Time*, with the caption, "A trip to the moon on gossamer wings."

FEBRUARY • Mae West, who has revived her 1928 *Diamond Lil*, is reported to have auditioned men for the show by having them feel her breasts and is said to be carrying on affairs with an actor and a musician in the company. The show's run will be disrupted by her sprained ankle.

MARCH • Tallulah Bankhead sues Proctor & Gamble, NBC, CBS, and the Benton & Bowles advertising agency for appropriating her unique first name in a jingle for Prell Shampoo. According to her papers filed in New York State Supreme Court, the jingle goes: "I'm Tallulah the tube of Prell/And I've got a little something to tell/Your hair can be radiant oh so easy/All you've got to do is take me home and squeeze me." (Bankhead will settle out of court for $5,000.) **3** Lee J. Cobb is raised to star billing in *Death of a Salesman*. **5** A competitive Tennessee Williams writes from Italy to his friend Maria St. Just, hoping "that you will not let the entire season pass without seeing something besides *Death of a Salesman*. Do you know I got five complete sets of notices of that play, sent me by various well-meaning friends in New York? More than I ever got for any play of my own, including the *Menagerie* in London. . . ."

APRIL • José Ferrer, responding to fears of what TV might do to the theatre, writes in *Theatre Arts* about television: "It will immediately create a whole new galaxy of stars and popular favorites, performers and actors, whom the public will fight to see in person." **18** Mary Martin, in a sailor suit, is on the cover of *Life*.

Richard Rodgers and Oscar Hammerstein II

Plays and Musicals

George C. Scott and Dustin Hoffman, and Frederic March is in the 1951 film.

MARCH 23 *Detective Story* (581), Sidney Kingsley's play set in a police station squad room, opens at the Hudson Theatre. It stars Ralph Bellamy, Warren Stevens, Maureen Stapleton, Joseph Wiseman, and Meg Mundy. According to *The Morning Telegraph*, Lee Grant, playing a shoplifter in her Broadway debut, is like "a young Fannie Brice," whose work is acknowledged by a "thunder of applause." Kirk Douglas stars in the 1951 film.

APRIL 7 Rodgers and Hammerstein's *South*

Business and Society

APRIL 19 Chicago lifts its ban on *The Respectful Prostitute* after the producers agree to alter the text.

JUNE 2 Playwright Albert Innaurato b. **17** Producer Earl Carroll d. in a plane crash,

Births, Deaths, and Marriages

Pacific (1,925), directed by Joshua Logan, opens at the Majestic. Mary Martin and the Metropolitan Opera's Ezio Pinza star, with Juanita Hall, Myron McCormick, and William Tabbert. "Some Enchanted Evening," "I'm in Love With a Wonderful Guy," "There is Nothing Like a Dame," "Bali Ha'i," "I'm Gonna Wash That Man Right Out of My Hair," are among the songs. *Time* calls it "a shrewd mixture of tear-jerking and rib-tickling, of sugar and spice and everything twice." It's "magnificent," says *The New York Times*, "as lively, warm, fresh and beautiful as we had all hoped it would be." There's a film in 1958.

MAY 19 After 17 years, vaudeville is revived at the Palace Theatre—eight acts accompanying a movie. Song-and-dance-man Pat Rooney and former vaudevillian Milton Berle are on hand to wish the venture well, but the revival registers as little more than mediocre with the critics.

1949–50

Carol Channing becomes a big Broadway star, the government says the Shuberts have gotten too big, William Inge is on the boards, and Ole Olsen really does break a leg. Stella Adler sets up the Stella Adler Theatre Studio, a training ground for actors. She and Lee Strasberg of the Actors Studio will feud over who has turned out more quality stage artists. Off-Broadway is just beginning to be a factor in New York theatre, and David Merrick sets up shop. Alfred Drake puts his hand and foot prints in wet cement in Shubert Alley, Grauman's Chinese Theatre-style. Bojangles is gone, and a premature curtain falls on an "act of God."

- 25 years of the Lunts: 8,000 performances to an audience of 1,250,000, by their own estimate
- How Stella Adler will describe Lee Strasberg: "not a pleasant man. It's insanity that this personally ugly little man should become the leader of the American theatre."
- What Lee Strasberg will say about Stella Adler: "I haven't wanted to call attention to reviews she got after she left me. She once was a leading lady and she thought, well, sure, on her own she could go places. So, where did Miss Adler go? Is she still working as an actress?"
- Amount taken out of Ezio Pinza's salary for the his more than 50 absences from *South Pacific*: over $25,000
- Pay of leads in successful off-Broadway plays: about $30 a week
- Net operating profit of Broadway theatres: $2,000,000
- Number of performances given by production of *Tobacco Road* with an all-black cast: 7, a disaster
- Where to find Broadway directors, set designers, choreographers, and actors acting as coaches: at the Metropolitan Opera, where new general manager Rudolph Bing will bring in the likes of Alfred Lunt and Joe Mielziner to change the tenor of productions
- Working as a cleaning woman at Saks Fifth Avenue: Ellen Stewart, future founder of La Mama Experimental Theatre

Productions on Broadway: 57

Pulitzer Prize for Drama: *South Pacific* (book by Joshua Logan, music by Richard Rodgers, and lyrics by Oscar Hammerstein II)

New York Theatre Critics Circle Awards:
Best American Play: *The Member of the Wedding* (Carson McCullers)
Best Foreign Play: *The Cocktail Party* (T.S. Eliot)
Best Musical: *The Consul* (Gian-Carlo Menotti)

Tony Awards:
Play: *The Cocktail Party* (T.S. Eliot)
Actor in a Play: Sidney Blackmer (*Come Back, Little Sheba*)
Actress in a Play: Shirley Booth (*Come Back, Little Sheba*)
Musical: *South Pacific* (opened April 1949)
Actor in a Musical: Ezio Pinza (*South Pacific*)
Actress in a Musical: Mary Martin (*South Pacific*)

June	July	August	September	October	November
Hagen for Tandy in *Streetcar*	Nanette Fabray bugged	David Merrick on his own	Off-Broadway pact with Equity	Rodgers and Hammerstein turn down *Moby Dick*	"Bojangles" d.

December	January	February	March	April	May
Gentlemen Prefer Blondes	*The Member of the Wedding*	Antitrust suit against Shuberts	Nonsegregated D.C. theatre	Kurt Weill d.	Pinza leaves *South Pacific*

Personalities

JUNE 1 Uta Hagen, who has been touring in the national company, replaces Jessica Tandy as Blanche in *A Streetcar Named Desire* in the 627th performance. The critics will acclaim Hagen tomorrow, but she will say: "It was a desperate performance. Nothing meshed."

JULY 9 Mike Todd's *As the Girls Go*, playing at the Winter Garden, is forced to suspend performances until September 14 because star Bobby Clark, who sports painted-on spectacles, has developed eye problems. **24** Nanette Fabray, performing in *Bloomer Girl* at an amphitheater in Dallas, becomes hysterical onstage when an insect lodges in her costume. The curtain is rung down, and she requires medical assistance. Fabray had been attacked by a swarm of locusts when she was a child, leaving her with a fear of insects.

AUGUST 24 The *New York Herald-Tribune* reports that David Merrick, who has been working in producer Herman Shumlin's organization, is leaving to produce on his own.

SEPTEMBER 22 Mary MacArthur, the daughter of Helen Hayes and Charles MacArthur, d. of polio. Her birth had been termed an "act of God" by producer Jed Harris, who did not want to pay the cast of the show Hayes had to leave at the time of her pregnancy. And only recently, MacArthur debuted herself, playing opposite her mother, and a promising career was predicted for her.

OCTOBER • Alfred Drake, starring in *Kismet*, and Moira Shearer, the star of the film *The Red Shoes*, which is playing at the Bijou, place their hand and footprints into wet cement in Shubert Alley, which is being enlarged. • Oscar Hammerstein says that he and Richard Rodgers have been asked by the Metropolitan Opera to write a work based on Melville's *Moby Dick*, but they have declined.

NOVEMBER 7 The Lunts, celebrating their 25th anniversary as a team, are on the cover of *Life*. **23** *Variety* notes that Rodgers and Hammerstein have optioned

Plays and Musicals

JULY 15 Irving Berlin and Robert E. Sherwood's *Miss Liberty* (308), starring Allyn Ann McLerie and Eddie Albert, with Dody Goodman, opens at the Imperial, where the $400,000 already in the box office helps it to survive poor reviews. The show, which the *Times* calls "disappointing . . . without sparkle or originality," includes "Let's Take an Old-Fashioned Walk."

OCTOBER 13 Peggy Cass and Louis Nye are in *Touch and Go* (176), a revue by Walter and Jean Kerr, who teach at Catholic University in Washington, D.C. It's at the Broadhurst. **30** The Kurt Weill-Maxwell Anderson musical *Lost in the Stars* (281), directed by Rouben Mamoulian, opens at the Music Box. Based on the Alan Paton novel *Cry, the Beloved Country*, it's about race relations in South Africa, which only recently strengthened its apartheid system. Todd Duncan, Julian Mayfield, Inez Matthews, Warren Coleman and Leslie Banks star. A film version appears in 1974.

NOVEMBER 2 Alfred Lunt and Lynn Fontanne exchange silver for gold at the Shubert. Offstage, celebrating their 25th anniversary as a team, they are, in S.N. Behrman's comedy *I Know, My Love* (246), a couple looking back on 50 years of marriage.

DECEMBER 8 *Gentlemen Prefer Blondes* (740), a musical version of the 1926 play by Anita Loos, with a Jule Styne–Leo Robin score, opens at the Ziegfeld Theatre. Carol Channing, playing Lorelei Lee, does not have star billing on opening night. The supporting cast includes Howard Morris and Charles "Honi" Coles. Among the songs are "Diamonds Are a Girl's Best Friend," "Bye, Bye, Baby," and "A Little Girl from Little Rock." Marilyn Monroe and Jane Russell are in Howard Hawks's 1953 screen version, and an updated stage version, *Lorelei*, also starring Carol Channing, will be mounted in 1973.

JANUARY 5 Carson McCullers's *The Member of the Wedding* (501), starring

Business and Society

JULY • Macy's in New York City is giving away a pair of tickets to *South Pacific* to purchasers of a Westinghouse television. **17** Returning from Europe with a company that has mounted a production of *Hamlet*, Clarence Derwent is detained for several hours and questioned at the airport by the Immigration Service. It is reported that someone has anonymously charged him with leftist activity.

AUGUST 3 A *Variety* article headlined "Off-B'dway Groups Winning Wider Pro Recognition" refers to the just-founded off-Broadway Theatre League, made up of the Interplayers, People's Drama, Studio 7, Off-Broadway, Inc., and We Present.

SEPTEMBER • The Off-Broadway Theatre League reaches a tentative agreement with Equity that will permit those with union cards to work as long as they make up less than half of the cast. Off-Broadway theatre is still being referred to as "experimental." • Signers of a letter in *The Nation*, protesting the recent riot in Peekskill, New York aimed at stopping an open-air concert by Paul Robeson, whose politics some local residents consider to be Communistic, include Arthur Miller,

Births, Deaths, and Marriages

JUNE 6 Burgess Meredith and Paulette Goddard are divorced. **8** Nancy Walker reveals that she has divorced actor Gar Moore. Conflicting career commitments kept them apart for all but six weeks of the 10 months they were married.

JULY 22 Maureen Stapleton m. Max Allentuck, company manager of *Death of a Salesman*.

AUGUST 1 George Moran, of the blackface vaudeville team of Mack and Moran, d. **12** Al Shean, of Gallagher and Shean, d.

NOVEMBER 10 Ann Reinking b. **25** Bill "Bojangles" Robinson d. **27** Ralph Bellamy m. Alice Murphy.

DECEMBER 3 Playwright Philip Barry d.

JANUARY 6 Producer William Brady d.

Tevye's Daughters, a drama based on the short stories of Sholem Aleichem—eventually the source for the 1964 *Fiddler on the Roof*. They are thinking of using unpublished music by Jerome Kern in the show.

DECEMBER • Among the recipients of *Mademoiselle*'s merit awards is 23-year-old Julie Harris, who is building a growing reputation based on her fine performances in unsuccessful plays. **8** The cast of *Gentlemen Prefer Blondes* begins a theatrical tradition—passing on the gypsy robe, a gown to which a patch or emblem is added by the chorus in each musical before giving it to the chorus of the next show. The filled-in robes are retired about every 15 shows. **16** To help out in New York City's water shortage crisis, Mary Martin switches to club soda for her "I'm Going to Wash That Man Right Out of My Hair" shower in *South Pacific* tonight. She actually shampoos her hair at each show and will need upwards of 30 permanents during its run.

JANUARY • The rumor mill has Rex Harrison starring in Rodgers and Hammerstein's musical next season based on *Anna and the King of Siam*. He played the king in the nonmusical screen version, opposite Irene Dunne, in 1946. **9** Carol Channing is on the cover of *Time*. The magazine writes that "on Broadway, an authentic new star is almost as rare a phenomenon as it is in the heavens. Perhaps once in a decade a nova explodes above the Great White Way with enough brilliance to reillumine the whole gaudy legend of show business." They compare her to Ethel Merman, Mary Martin, Fanny Brice, and Marilyn Miller. **17** Told that Maine Senator Margaret Chase Smith may run for vice president on the Republican ticket, Tallulah Bankhead threatens to do the same as a Democrat under the slogan, "Tallulah for Vice!" **17** Gwen Verdon makes her Broadway debut in the revue *Alive and Kicking*. **20** Bob Fosse makes his Broadway debut in *Dance Me A Song*.

MARCH • Edward Johnson, retiring as general manager of the Metropolitan Opera, tells reporters that one of the most notable trends in recent years has been

Carol Channing MSN

Ethel Waters, Brandon De Wilde, and Julie Harris as 12-year-old Frankie, who wants to go on her brother's honeymoon, opens at the Empire. The same cast stars in the 1952 film. **21** T.S. Eliot's *The Cocktail Party* (409), starring Alec Guinness, Irene Worth, Cathleen Nesbitt, and Robert Flemyng, opens at Henry Miller's Theatre. Atkinson, in the *Times*, finds it "verbose and elusive;" Richard Watts, Jr., in the *Post*, calls it "an authentic modern masterpiece." **24** *The Happy Time*, Anita Loos's comedy about a French-Canadian family, opens at the Plymouth (614). Claude Dauphin, Leora Dana, and Johnny Stewart star. It will become a musical in 1968. **26** Katharine Hepburn, with Cloris Leachman and Jay Robinson, open at the Cort in Shakespeare's *As You Like It* (144).

FEBRUARY 15 William Inge's first Broadway play, *Come Back, Little Sheba* (190), opens at the Booth. "Most of it is squandered on dramatic triviality," says Howard Barnes in the *Herald-Tribune*. Sidney Blackmer and Shirley Booth have the leading roles as Doc, a drunkard, and his wife, Lola. Barnes says that "they come close to creating the illusion that William Inge was writing about something of import in this Theatre Guild production." The film version is released in 1952.

MARCH 15 Gian-Carlo Menotti's opera *The Consul* (269), chosen best musical by the New York Drama Critics Circle, opens at the Barrymore. The *Times* sends music critic Olin Downes to review it, but drama critic Brooks Atkinson will

Garson Kanin, Oscar Hammerstein, Juanita Hall, Lee J. Cobb, Moss Hart, Judy Holliday, and Henry Fonda.

DECEMBER • Despite a declining box office since World War II, several shows have been pushing upward the top ticket price, which now reaches as high as $6.60 on weekends.

FEBRUARY 2 Northwestern State College in Louisiana cancels a visit by Margaret Webster's touring production of *The Taming of the Shrew* when she refuses to replace two black actors in minor parts. The head of the college music department has informed her that the school "is for young ladies and young gentlemen of the white race." **21** The federal government files an antitrust suit against the United Booking Office and the Shuberts, charging that their combination of producing and booking shows is a restraint of trade.

MARCH 6 The production of *The Barretts of Wimpole Street*, starring Susan Peters and opening at Gayety Theatre in Washington, D.C., a former burlesque house, is notable for playing to a nonsegregated audience. **10** Sid Silverman, publisher of *Variety* and son of the publication's founder, Sime Silverman, d. Control of the paper passes to Sid's 18-year-old son, Syd.

FEBRUARY 26 Vaudeville music hall star Harry Lauder d.

MARCH 11 Producer Brock Pemberton d. **19** Alan Jay Lerner m. actress Nancy Olson. **22** Producer-director Arthur Hopkins d.

APRIL 2 Bambi Linn and Rod Alexander, both appearing in the musical *Glad to Be Alive*, m. **3** Composer Kurt Weill d. He had been working on a musical version of *Huckleberry Finn*. **7** Walter Huston d.

MAY 28 Bea Arthur m. director Gene Saks.

Personalities

the conjunction of opera with the Broadway musical in the work of Kurt Weill, Gian-Carlo Menotti, and Rodgers and Hammerstein.

APRIL 2 Sidney Blackmer, who has been playing Doc, the drunk, in *Come Back Little Sheba*, tells *The New York Times*, "They say there's a special [p]rovidence that looks out for fools and drunkards, but who takes care of those who impersonate the sots?" In the less than two months that the play has been running, Blackmer, who onstage is really quaffing Coke, tea, or colored water, has been reeling around so realistically that he has broken two ribs, sprained an ankle, and bloodied his nose. **3** *Life's* cover story is on *The Innocents*, depicting Iris Mann and David Cole from the play's cast. **13** Taking an old show business expression too far, Ole Olsen, of Olsen and Johnson, breaks his leg in an auto accident and will not be able to go on when *Tsk, Tsk, Tsk Paree* (retitled *Pardon Our French* when it reaches Broadway in the fall) opens in San Diego in four days.

MAY • Margo Jones's book *Theatre-in-the-Round* is published, spreading the word about the practicality of professional arena theatre, which she has been directing in Dallas since 1947. • Ellen Stewart, future founder of La Mama Experimental Theatre, arrives in New York, where she gets a job as a cleaning woman at Saks Fifth Avenue, but within months she will be working as a dress designer at the store. **31** Ezio Pinza gives his final performance in *South Pacific*. At the curtain, the cast surrounds him and sings "I'm in Love With a Wonderful Guy." He will be succeeded by Ray Middleton.

Plays and Musicals

also write about the show in his Sunday column. **29** Helen Hayes stars in *The Wisteria Trees* (165), Joshua Logan's play based on Chekhov's *The Cherry Tree*, coproduced by Logan with Leland Hayward, at the Martin Beck. Logan has set his play on a Louisiana plantation. The cast includes Peggy Conklin, Kent Smith, Walter Abel, and Ossie Davis.

APRIL 24 *Peter Pan* (321) is revived at the Imperial, with Jean Arthur as the title character and Boris Karloff as Captain Hook.

Business and Society

APRIL 24 Decca recently released a full-length recording of *The Cocktail Party*. Such a recording of a dramatic play is an innovation, and today, with Thomas Mitchell playing Willy Loman, the company records *Death of a Salesman*.

Births, Deaths, and Marriages

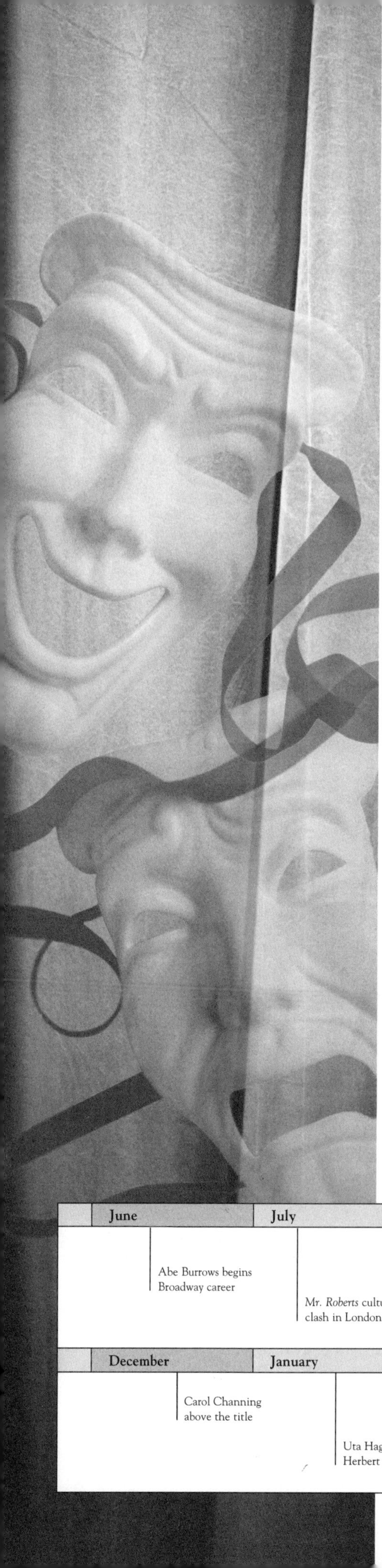

1950–51

With the deaths of Al Jolson and Fanny Brice, each of whom had remained active on radio in recent years, even the echoes of Broadway's golden age of musical comedy and vaudeville are beginning to fade. But there's always a new face. With the help of a regal Yul Brynner in *The King and I*, "the boys have done it again." Abe Burrows begins an illustrious Broadway career, and Frank Loesser brings forth a musical masterpiece in *Guys and Dolls*. Maureen Stapleton gets her truck driver, the Circle in the Square gets going, and critic Brooks Atkinson finds young Richard Burton "sobering."

- Percentage of U.S. population that attends legitimate theatre performances: less than 2 percent
- Cost of staging *Dark of the Moon*, the first production at the Circle in the Square: $2,500
- Jerome Robbins's salary as choreographer of *The King and I* and *Call Me Madam*: about $700 a week
- Robbins's pay for dancing with the New York City Ballet: no more than $100 a week
- RCA's substitute for Ethel Merman on the "original cast" recording of *Call Me Madam* (Merman, under contract to Decca, can't do it): Dinah Shore
- How most of the critics initially got it wrong about *Guys and Dolls*, typified by Howard Barnes in the *Herald-Tribune*: "Loesser's words and music may not rise to the top stratum of Tin Pan Alley creations, but they never trip up the general gusto of the carnival."
- Number of women in the cast of *Stalag 17*: none
- Where Tallulah Bankhead has played in the revival of *Private Lives*, according to her: "Everywhere but underwater."
- What Tallulah Bankhead says on her radio program about Bette Davis, whose "Margo Channing" in the film *All About Eve* is said to be modeled after Bankhead: "I'll pull every hair out of her moustache."
- Number of members of new Arena Stage company in Washington, D.C.: 8
- Salary of Arena Stage company members: $50 a week
- Working capital of Arena Stage: $15,000
- Arena Stage ticket prices: $1.50–$1.90
- Number of Arena Stage subscribers in its first season: 2,300
- How actors at the Arena Stage enter from stage right after they exit from stage left: they have to go outside and walk around the building

Productions on Broadway: 81

Pulitzer Prize for Drama: None awarded

New York Drama Critics Circle Awards:
Best American Play: *Darkness at Noon* (Sidney Kingsley)
Best Foreign Play: *The Lady's Not for Burning* (Chistopher Fry)
Best Musical: *Guys and Dolls* (Frank Loesser)

Tony Awards:
Play: *The Rose Tattoo* (Tennessee Williams)
Actress in a Play: Uta Hagen (*The Country Girl*)
Actor in a Play: Claude Rains (*Darkness at Noon*)
Musical: *Guys and Dolls* (Frank Loesser)
Actress in a Musical: Ethel Merman (*Call Me Madam*)
Actor in a Musical: Robert Alda (*Guys and Dolls*)

June	July	August	September	October	November
Abe Burrows begins Broadway career	*Mr. Roberts* culture clash in London	Arena Stage begins in D.C.	"You're Just In Love" added to *Call Me Madam*	Al Jolson d.	*Guys and Dolls*

December	January	February	March	April	May
Carol Channing above the title	Uta Hagen m. Herbert Berghof	*The Rose Tattoo*	*The King and I*	Ferrer and Holliday at HUAC	Barbara Cook's debut

Personalities

JUNE • Jo Swerling, who had begun the book for a musical called *Guys and Dolls*, has to abandon it for a Hollywood commitment. The producers replace him with Peter Lyon and radio and TV writer Abe Burrows, who has never written for the Broadway stage.

AUGUST • Now it's producer Mike Todd who has optioned "Tevye's Daughters." **11** Jean Arthur, out the Broadway revival of *Peter Pan* with laryngitis, says that she needs a few weeks of rest. Understudy Barbara Baxley takes over, and the producers want to sign Betty Field as a permanent replacement for Arthur (and some rumors have it that Shirley Temple will end up as Peter). But Arthur's run-of-the-play contract is an obstacle, and she returns after two weeks.

SEPTEMBER • Irving Berlin replaces the song "Monotony" in the pre-Broadway, Boston tryout of *Call Me Madam* with a duet for Ethel Merman and Russell Nype: "You're Just In Love." **25** Eugene O'Neill, Jr., the playwright's son by his first marriage, commits suicide, an option his father has been considering. Shane O'Neill, from Eugene's second marriage, was recently arrested on a narcotics charge.

OCTOBER 18 Reviewing the Philadelphia tryout of *Guys and Dolls*, *Variety* reports, "Here's really one for the records—a musical in which the book is apparently the standout feature." It says of the show that opened at the Shubert on October 14 that "the Frank Loesser score is likely to come into its rightful prominence when it has been reorchestrated to give greater emphasis to melody."

NOVEMBER • The handbill declares, "We, the Loft Players of Woodstock and New York have leased what was formerly the Greenwich Village Inn (5 Sheridan Square) for 10 years. We have converted this into a comfortable, informal arena theatre." "We" includes Theodore Mann and José Quintero. They name their new theatre, not the "Chicken in the Basket," as one of their colleagues is said to have

Plays and Musicals

JUNE 28 *Mike Todd's Peep Show* (278), a revue, is at the Winter Garden, where it will soon be toned down, the result of a talk between Todd and the city's Commissioner of Licenses.

AUGUST 16 The Arena Stage in Washington, D.C., mounts its first production, *She Stoops to Conquer*, in what was an old movie theatre. The company, founded by Zelda Fichandler and Edward Mangum, is performing in a 247-seat theatre-in-the-round. The audience is not racially segregated.

SEPTEMBER 25 Louis Verneuil's *Affairs of State* (610), a comedy at the Royale, set in Washington, D.C., stars Celeste Holm. **28** *New Yorker* drama critic Wolcott Gibbs's comedy *Season in the Sun* (367) is at the Cort. The cast includes Nancy Kelly, Jack Weston, and Eddie Mayehoff.

OCTOBER 12 Irving Berlin's *Call Me Madam* (644) opens at the Imperial. Ethel Merman and Russell Nype star in this musical, based on the life of ambassador and party "hostess with the 'mostess,'" Perle Mesta. Also in the cast are Paul Lukas and Pat Harrington. Songs include "It's A Lovely Day Today" and "You're Just In Love." Merman's standby in the show is Elaine Stritch. Merman is also in the 1953 film.

NOVEMBER 10 Clifford Odets's *The Country Girl* (235), with Paul Kelly as an alcoholic actor and Uta Hagen as his abused but supportive wife, opens at the Lyceum. It's a 1954 film. **14** Lilli Palmer will do anything to keep Rex Harrison, even give up witchcraft, in John Van Druten's comedy *Bell, Book and Candle* (233), at the Barrymore. The film arrives in 1958. **24** Frank Loesser's *Guys and Dolls* (1,194) opens at the Forty-sixth Street Theater. It's directed by George S. Kaufman and choreographed by Michael Kidd, with a book by Abe Burrows and Jo Swerling based on Damon Runyon's stories. In the score are "Bushel and a Peck," the title song, "If I Were a Bell," "Luck Be a Lady," "Sit Down," "Take Back Your Mink," and "Sue Me," sung by Sam

Business and Society

JULY • Off-Broadway groups are struggling. Their low budgets are not enough to pay for the installation of air-conditioning in the out-of-the-way theatres they use. • Producer Leland Hayward, explaining to investors in his previous shows why they have not been given a chance to come in on *Call Me Madam*, says that RCA is putting up all of the money because musicals these days require a very big investment, and an entertainment corporation such as RCA can make this kind of expenditure pay through the record, radio, and television rights. **19** The opening of *Mr. Roberts*, at the Coliseum in London, where Tyrone Power has the title role, reveals a cultural gap between Broadway and the West End, with several critics upset at the play's irreverence toward the military. *The Daily Herald* is appalled at the "glorifying of insubordinates and near-mutiny."

NOVEMBER 29 Cole Porter's new show *Out of this World*, opening at the Shubert in Boston, has had to delete lines that, claims the censor, "are not heard even in better class gin mills."

DECEMBER 6 *Variety* notes that "Czech

Births, Deaths, and Marriages

JUNE 2 Joanna Gleason b. **22** Jane Cowl d., in debt. Her personal effects will be auctioned off in 1952 for $1,499. When Katharine Cornell opened in *Romeo and Juliet* in the 1930s, Cowl—who held the long-run record as Juliet—declined her invitation to attend a performance, wiring Cornell: "If you were better than I it would make me sad, and if I were better than you it would still make me sad."

JULY 11 Lyricist-producer Buddy De Sylva d.

SEPTEMBER 19 Crystal Herne d.

OCTOBER 18 Playwright Wendy Wasserstein b. **23** Al Jolson d.

NOVEMBER 2 George Bernard Shaw d. **12** Julia Marlowe d.

JANUARY 25 Uta Hagen m. Herbert Berghof.

Lynn Fontanne—the show must go on, even with a broken wrist *LYNCH*

suggested, but the Circle in the Square. **3** Lynn Fontanne, on her way to the theatre in Portland, Maine, where she and her husband, Alfred Lunt, are appearing in *I Know, My Love*, falls on the steps of her hotel, breaking her wrist. She goes on anyway. **9** Without benefit of hindsight, and therefore unaware of his adjectival irony, Brooks Atkinson, in the *Times*, writes about a newcomer in *The Lady's Not for Burning*: "As a dazed but susceptible clerk, Richard Burton gives an amusingly sober performance."

DECEMBER 11 Rex Harrison and Lilli Palmer are on the cover of *Life*. **25** Louis Calhern, opening in *King Lear*, says that during rehearsals, he spoke to a cab driver who had seen Lear done by the Yiddish Art Theatre, with Joseph Schildkraut and Jacob Ben-Ami. "It'll be tough," the driver told Calhern about his production. He meant "tough" to do it in English. **25** Merry Christmas: A little over a year after it opened, Carol Channing's name appears above the title of *Gentlemen Prefer Blondes*. The producers had held off in a dispute over the extension of her contract.

JANUARY 29 "Betsy von Furstenberg: Society Girl on Broadway" is *Life*'s cover story. She debuted this month in *Second Threshold*. **29** Sidney Blackmer, still playing on the road in *Come Back, Little Sheba*, is furious that "[t]he Theatre Guild on the Air" has cast Gary Cooper opposite Shirley Booth in the February 4

Levene, as Nathan Detroit, who can't sing a note. The cast also includes Robert Alda (father of Alan Alda) as Sky Masterson, Isabel Bigley as Sarah Brown, Vivian Blaine as Miss Adelaide, with Stubby Kaye and Pat Rooney, Sr. It's on the screen in 1955, with several songs added, including "Woman in Love."

JANUARY 13 Sidney Kingsley's dramatization of Arthur Koestler's anti-Communist *Darkness at Noon* (186) opens at the Alvin. The cast features Claude Rains and Kim Hunter. Playing Glekin the Inquisitor is the actor still calling himself Walter J. (Jack) Palance. **28** *Peer Gynt* (32), produced and directed by Lee Strasberg, opens at the ANTA Playhouse, with John Garfield in the title role and Mildred Dunnock, John Randolph, Nehemiah Persoff, Sherry Britton, Sono Osato, and Karl Malden.

FEBRUARY 2 The Circle in the Square gets under way with its production of *Dark of the Moon*. **3** Tennessee Williams's *The Rose Tattoo* (300), starring Maureen Stapleton as the smoldering Serafina, with Eli Wallach, Don Murray, Phyllis Love, Martin Balsam, and 12-year-old Salvatore Mineo (later the movies' Sal Mineo), opens at

Maureen Stapleton *MSN*

actor-author George Voskovec, noted for his anti-authoritarian plays in Prague until he was expelled by the Nazis and for a short time after the war, until he eluded the Soviet secret police, has been detained at Ellis Island, N.Y., for the last six months, by order of the Department of Justice."

MARCH 20 Abe Burrows tells the House Un-American Activities Committee that he was not a Communist in the 1940s but that he did associate with Communist groups.

APRIL 4 The House Un-American Activities Committee names José Ferrer and Judy Holliday as members of Communist front groups. Holliday declares: "I am not a member of any organization listed by the Attorney General as subversive. In any instance where I lent my name in the past it was certainly without knowledge that such an organization was subversive."

MAY 22 José Ferrer, appearing before the House Un-American Activities Committee, denies ever having been a member of the Communist Party. The Committee is especially interested in any political connections he may have had to Paul Robeson, with whom he starred in an acclaimed production of *Othello*. Ferrer

30 Nancy Walker m. David Craig, her singing coach.

APRIL 15 Barbara Bel Geddes m. theatre manager Windsor Lewis. **24** Producer A. H. Woods d.

MAY 29 Fanny Brice d.

Personalities

broadcast of the play in the role that Blackmer has made famous on the stage.

FEBRUARY 28 In its review of the New Haven tryout of *The King and I*, which opened last night, *Variety* says that although it "possesses a wealth of material, it is not such a sure thing as certain other Richard Rodgers-Oscar Hammerstein, 2d, creations were at this stage of the game." The three-hour show needs cutting. "Getting to Know You," soon to become a Broadway classic, will not appear in the score until the production reaches Boston, its next stop.

Plays and Musicals

the Martin Beck. The *Herald-Tribune* calls Stapleton "one of those phenomena that come to Broadway at rare intervals—an unknown actress who wakes up famous on the day after opening." Anna Magnani, Williams's original choice for the lead role, has it in the 1955 film.

MARCH 8 *The Moon Is Blue* (924), F. Hugh Herbert's comedy about the consequences of a couple's meeting at the Empire State Building, opens at Henry Miller's Theatre. Barbara Bel Geddes and Barry Nelson are the twosome, with Donald Cook, and it's in the movie theatres in 1953. **29** "The boys have done it again," says John McLain, in the *Journal-American*, about Rodgers and Hammerstein's *The King and I* (1,246), opening at the St. James. Gertrude Lawrence is the star, with "the solid assistance of Yul Brynner," as McLain puts it. Brynner was the fourth choice to play the king, after Rex Harrison, Noel Coward, and Alfred Drake. "Getting to Know You," a song for which Rodgers had writ-

The Rose Tattoo opens at the Martin Beck PB

Business and Society

calls for the banning of the Communist Party.

Births, Deaths, and Marriages

MARCH 4 Ethel Merman appears on Tallulah Bankhead's radio program. In the scripted repartee, Merman professes to admire Bankhead's dress. A suspicious Tallulah thinks Merman's hiding something. The dialogue continues:

> **Merman:** That's more than your dress does.
> **Bankhead:** Now just a minute, Ethel. I have nothing to hide.
> **Merman:** You said it, I didn't.

25 In town with *Mr. Roberts*, Henry Fonda has to flee a Des Moines hotel fire and then helps the firemen to put it out. Just five days ago, the company, in the actor's hometown of Omaha, had to play without scenery, which was stranded on a train caught in a snowstorm. **29** With his winning of the Oscar for last year's film *Cyrano*, José Ferrer is the first actor to capture an Academy Award for a role in which he also won a Tony on Broadway.

APRIL 9 Barbara Bel Geddes is on the cover of *Time*. The caption, "For the prodigal daughter, a prodigious homecoming," refers to her return from Hollywood to star once again on Broadway, in *The Moon Is Blue*. **10** Director Alan Schneider joins the Arena Stage with a production of *The Glass Menagerie*. He will become the Company's artistic director next year. **30** Carol Channing, "exhausted," will miss two weeks of *Gentlemen Prefer Blondes*, with Bibi Osterwald stepping in as Lorelei.

MAY • Alec Guinness, whose *Hamlet* had been scheduled to reach Broadway next season, is savaged by the London critics for his portrayal of the Dane. "Poor Keats was literally killed by the critics," the actor laments, defending himself in one interview. **8** *Stalag 17* has its opening "night" at the Forty-eighth Street Theatre at 2:15 P.M. this afternoon. The play's producer, José Ferrer, is starring on Broadway, with Gloria Swanson, in a revival of *Twentieth Century*, and the early curtain is the only way that he can attend.

---

ten the music, without Hammerstein's lyrics, for *South Pacific*, only to drop it from the show, was inserted in this musical at its Boston tryout. Also in the score are "I Whistle a Happy Tune," "Hello, Young Lovers," and "Shall We Dance." The 1956 movie version stars Brynner and Deborah Kerr (Lawrence d. in 1952).

APRIL 19 *A Tree Grows in Brooklyn* (267), an Arthur Schwartz-Dorothy Fields musical based on the Betty Smith novel, opens at the Alvin. Shirley Booth and Johnny Johnston star, and songs include "Make the Man Love Me." It was a 1945 film. **29** Literary critic Edmund Wilson's political fantasy *Little Blue Light* (16), starring Martin Gabel, Arlene Francis, Burgess Meredith, Melvyn Douglas, and Peter Cookson, opens at the ANTA Playhouse. A character in the play referred to as a "pansy" sends reviewers into adjectival acrobatics, resulting in "effeminate," "peculiar," "psychopathic sissy," "unsavory swish," and "lace-fringed mannerisms" in their reviews.

MAY 8 *Stalag 17* (472), by Donald Bevan and Edmund Trzcinski, stars John Ericson and Laurence Hugo. Cast members Robert Strauss and Harvey Lembeck, in this drama of a German prisoner-of-war camp, will also appear in Billy Wilder's 1953 film. **14** Barbara Cook and Yma Sumac make their Broadway debuts at the Broadhurst in *Flahooley* (40), a musical with songs by Yip Harburg and Sammy Fain.

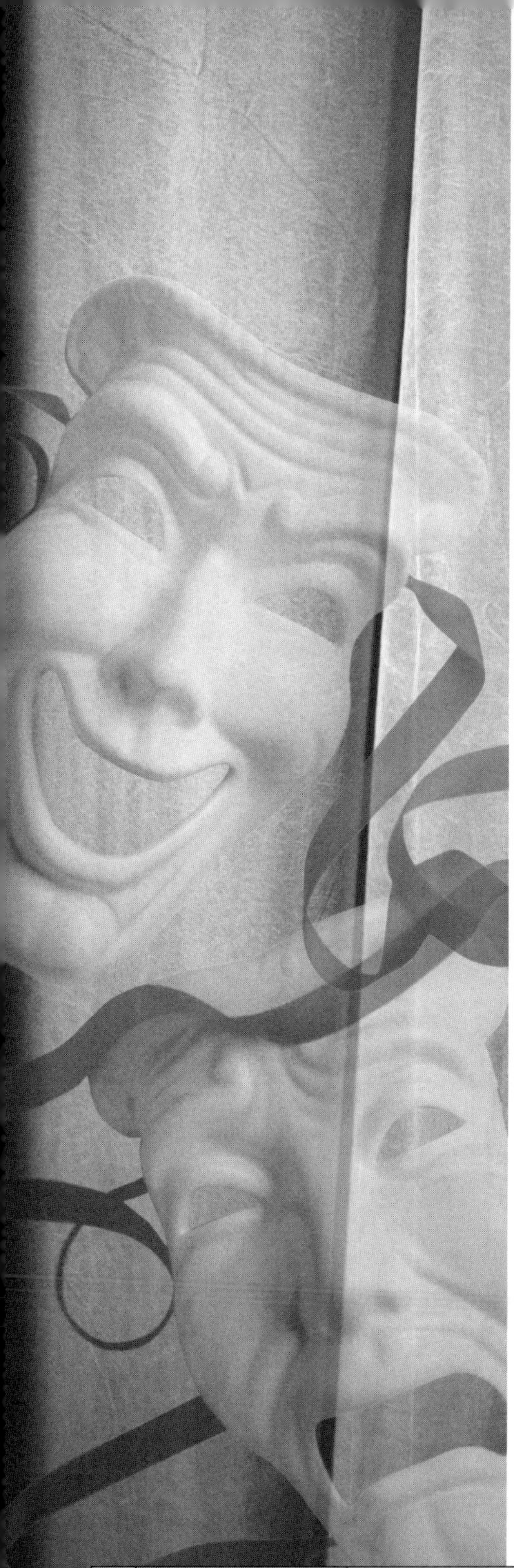

1951–52

Everyone loves Audrey Hepburn, who springs forth from *Gigi*. Hume Cronyn and Jessica Tandy are in tandem onstage, producer Leonard Sillman spotlights "new faces" galore, Geraldine Page joins the front rank of actresses, John Garfield finally gets to star in *Golden Boy*, and the new critic in town is Walter Kerr. *Variety* reports that Rodgers and Hammerstein may write a musical based on Shaw's *Pygmalion*, starring Mary Martin. Meanwhile, Elia Kazan makes a fateful decision, and the House Un-American Activities Committee may have helped to produce a real tragedy, with the deaths of Group Theatre alumni John Garfield and J. Edward Bromberg, each of whom had been tainted by testimony.

- What Jule Styne, producer of the successful revival of *Pal Joey*, gives as a gift to its composer Richard Rodgers: cufflinks shaped like a heel, evocative of the show's lead character
- Tag line in the *Herald-Tribune*'s negative review of the Yiddish theatre comedy *Bagels and Yox*: "Better Lox Next Time"
- Why critic George Jean Nathan skips his *Theatre Book of the Year* this year: "Why exercise myself and my reader's patience in the embalming of trash?"
- What George Jean Nathan is reported to have remarked about the possibility of the New York Drama Critics Circle making a revival of *Pal Joey* eligible for "Best Play": "It will make us look silly, if that's not redundant."
- Total gross for touring companies: $19,020,400, the worst in recent years
- Julie Harris's compensation from *I Am a Camera*: $1,000 a week plus 6 percent of the gross up to $1,300
- Amount that Milton Berle has invested in *Top Banana*, a show that pokes fun at him: $3,500
- Number of costume changes by Ann Sothern in *Faithfully Yours*: 8
- What Alfred Lunt tells the women in the cast of *Cosi Fan Tutti*, which he's directing at the Met: "If you beat your breast as they sometimes do in opera, I'll kill you."

Productions on Broadway: 72

Pulitzer Prize for Drama: *The Shrike* (Joseph Kramm)

New York Drama Critics Circle Awards:
Best American Play: *I Am a Camera* (John Van Druten)
Best Foreign Play: *Venus Observed* (Christopher Fry)
Best Musical: *Pal Joey* (Rodgers and Hart)

Tony Awards:
Play: *The Fourposter* (Jan de Hartog)
Actor in a Play: José Ferrer (*The Shrike*)
Actress in a Play: Julie Harris (*I Am a Camera*)
Musical: *The King & I* (Rodgers and Hammerstein)
Actress in a Musical: Gertrude Lawrence (*The King & I*)
Actor in a Musical: Phil Silvers (*Top Banana*)

June	July	August	September	October	November
Mary Martin leaves *South Pacific*	The young Barrymores are in trouble	George Abbott divorced	Ed Sullivan toasts Helen Hayes	First Cronyn–Tandy pairing	*I Am a Camera*

December	January	February	March	April	May
Olivier and Leigh on Broadway	*Pal Joey* revived	Leland Hayward shaves his head	Garfield in *Golden Boy*	Elia Kazan names names	*New Faces of 1952*

Personalities

JUNE • Mary Martin leaves the Broadway production of *South Pacific*. **11** *Life*'s cover story is "Vivian Blaine in *Guys and Dolls*." **13** Diana Barrymore, John Barrymore's daughter, is released from her role in a summer stock production of *A Streetcar Named Desire* when the producers charge her with not being in the proper physical condition to perform and behaving aberrantly. She says she has laryngitis. And her half-brother John Barrymore, Jr., scheduled to make his debut in a straw hat production of *The Hasty Heart* on July 16, has just canceled because he's "not ready." Their aunt Ethel Barrymore is reported to have reacted: "It has never

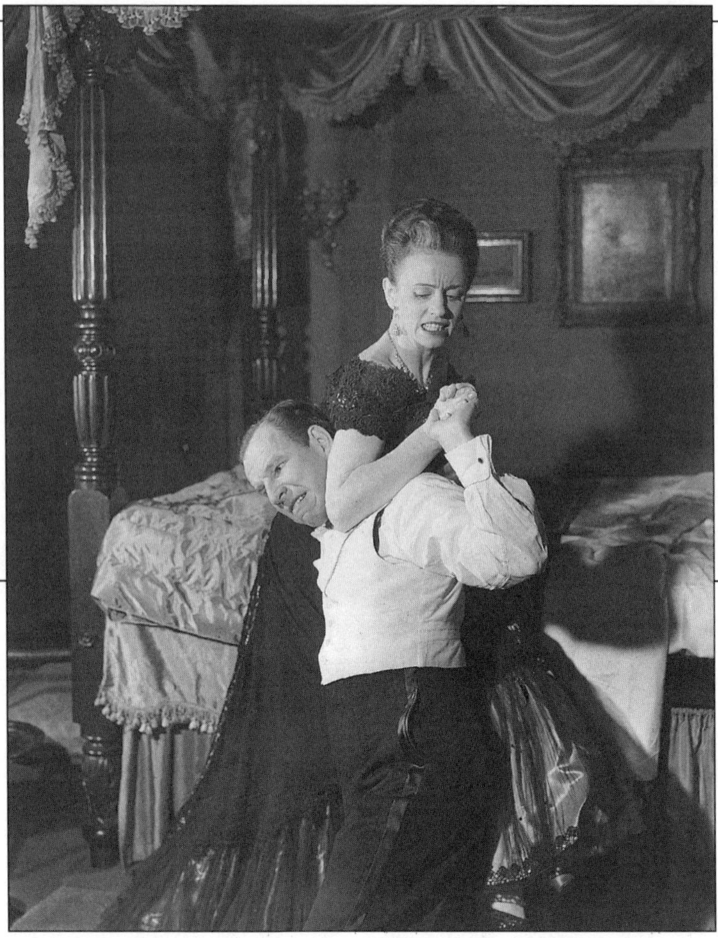

Hume Cronyn and Jessica Tandy wrestle with a problem in *The Fourposter* PF

Plays and Musicals

OCTOBER 22 For one night, at Carnegie Hall, Charles Laughton directs the first New York stage production of George Bernard Shaw's *Don Juan in Hell*, featuring Laughton and Charles Boyer, Cedric Hardwicke, and Agnes Moorehead, all appearing in evening clothes with the script in front of them. The show will tour after this very limited engagement. **24** *The Fourposter* (632), a comedy by Jan de Hartog, directed by José Ferrer at the Barrymore, pairs Hume Cronyn and Jessica Tandy on the stage for the first time. According to John Chapman, in the *Daily News*, "[P]eople were coupling the names of Tandy and Cronyn with those of Lunt and Fontanne." *Variety* says that the two "not only make 'Fourposter' a hit, but may be established as an acting team in the process."

NOVEMBER 1 Phil Silvers opens at the Winter Garden in *Top Banana* (350), a Johnny Mercer musical poking fun at the tube's current top banana: Milton Berle.

Business and Society

JUNE 26 J. Edward Bromberg, prominent in the Group Theatre, refuses to answer questions at a House Un-American Activities Committee hearing.

JULY 16 The American National Theatre and Academy (ANTA) is going through tumult. Margaret Webster and several other board members resign and Helen Hayes, president of the organization, is said to be unhappy with the way it's being run. Robert Whitehead is elected to manage its play series.

NOVEMBER • Elmer Rice resigns from the Playwrights TV Theatre, a group whose plays are given regularly on a program sponsored by the Celanese Corporation, because the company has been cooperating with the political blacklisting of actors proposed for roles in the drama.

JANUARY • Hollywood, which has been backing off from Broadway productions, is now desperate to kayo television and is again willing to spend large sums for screen rights to such shows as *Stalag 17* and *Gentlemen Prefer Blondes*.

MARCH • Hanya Holm, who choreographed

Births, Deaths, and Marriages

JUNE 27 David Warfield d.

JULY 21 Nanette Fabray and David Tebet divorce. **31** Howard Dietz m. costume designer Lucinda Ballard.

AUGUST 17 George Abbott and Mary Sinclair are divorced.

SEPTEMBER 4 Judith Ivey b.

OCTOBER 12 Leon Errol d. **28** Mady Christians d.

NOVEMBER 9 Sigmund Romberg d.

DECEMBER 6 J. Edward Bromberg d.

happened in the 300 years of the family's acting history."

JULY 25 The "mystery guest" on television's "What's My Line?" is Helen Hayes.

AUGUST 15 Julian Beck and Judith Malina, who founded the Living Theatre in 1947, stage its first performance, in their Upper West Side apartment.

SEPTEMBER 5 Reporting on an upcoming Yiddish theatre production *Borscht Capades*, *Variety* notes that in it is Joel Grey, the 19-year-old son of coproducer Mickey Katz, "mentored by Eddie Cantor, who gave the youngster a number of TV guest-shots last season." **30** Ed Sullivan features the career of Helen Hayes on his "Toast of the Town" television program.

OCTOBER 1 Bert Lahr, appearing on Broadway in *Two On the Aisle*, is on the cover of *Time*. **10** *Variety* reports that Richard Rodgers and Oscar Hammerstein are thinking of writing a musical based on Shaw's *Pygmalion*, starring Mary Martin. **17** Walter Kerr, who has been covering theatre for the Catholic magazine *Commonweal*, joins the *Herald-Tribune* as a "guest critic," beginning with his notice on Christopher Fry's *A Sleep of Prisoners*, which he terms "vigorous, dignified, and overly intellectualized." He will stay 15 years, until the paper's demise.

NOVEMBER 5 On the cover of *Life* is Ginger Rogers, "Back On Broadway" in *Love and Let Love*. In fact, the show, plagued by feuding in its tryout period, will play only 56 performances, losing about $30,000. **7** The Broadway audience is not seeing things when Phil Silvers takes his curtain call in *Top Banana* tonight. It's life imitating art. Immediately following his bows, there emerges from the wings Milton Berle, satirized in the show (in which he has invested), dressed like Silvers and taking his own bows. **14** From its pre-Broadway tryout in Philadelphia, *Variety* sends word that something special is coming up the pike in *Gigi*. It's "the performance of 22-year-old Audrey Hepburn (Scotch-Dutch girl) in the title role." She "has real talent as well as magnetic personality. Furthermore, in a wholesome and youthful way, she exudes sex." **19** On the cover of *Life* are "Three Great

---

It costars Jack Albertson, Joey Faye, and Rose Marie. **12** The premiere of Lerner and Loewe's *Paint Your Wagon* (289) at the Shubert, a musical set in a California mining camp, has been twice put off, and the tryout was elongated by seven weeks. In the score are "I Talk to the Trees" and "They Call the Wind Maria," and in the cast are James Barton and Olga San Juan. It's a film in 1969. **24** "She is an actress," *Times* critic Brooks Atkinson will say of Audrey Hepburn in *Gigi* (219), Anita Loos's play, based on Colette's stories, at the Fulton. She's "as fresh and frisky as a puppy out of a tub," says Walter Kerr in the *Herald-Tribune*. But it's Leslie Caron in Lerner and Loewe's 1958 musical version on the screen. **28** Julie Harris plays Sally Bowles in *I Am a Camera* (262), John Van Druten's adaptation of Christopher Isherwood's *Berlin Stories*, at the Empire. Harris is in the 1955 film, and it will be revived as the musical *Cabaret* in 1966, with Jill Hayworth in Harris's role. The musical, in turn, will appear as a film in 1972, starring Liza Minnelli.

DECEMBER 13 Henry Fonda opens in Paul Osborn's *Point of No Return* (364), a comedy about social climbing based on a John P. Marquand novel, at the Alvin. **20** Laurence Olivier and Vivian Leigh open at the Ziegfeld in Shakespeare's *Caesar and Cleopatra* (51). They will also be doing Shaw's *Antony and Cleopatra* (66) during this run. The top ticket price for the glamorous duo is a stiff $7.20.

JANUARY 3 The 1940 Rodgers and Hart musical *Pal Joey* (540) is revived at the Broadhurst, where it sets a new long-run record for musical revivals. In the cast are Harold Lang, Vivienne Segal, Helen Gallagher, Lionel Stander, Elaine Stritch, and Barbara Nichols. Columbia has been sitting on the film rights to the show since its first incarnation over a decade ago and will bring it to the screen in 1957 with Frank Sinatra, Rita Hayworth, and Kim Novak. **15** José Ferrer produces, directs, and stars in Joseph Kramm's *The Shrike* (161), the story of a man bent to the will of his malevolent wife. It's at the Cort, where Ferrer plays opposite Judith Evelyn. Ferrer also directs and stars in the 1955 film, with June Allyson.

Kiss Me Kate, receives a copyright for her work in that show, which she recorded in the Laban notation system. This is thought to be the first such copyright issued.

APRIL 10 Elia Kazan, testifying before the House Un-American Activities Committee, states, "I have come to the conclusion that I did wrong to withhold these names before, because secrecy serves the Communists, and it is exactly what they want. It is my obligation as a citizen to tell everything I know." He does just that, naming as former Communists several members of the Group Theatre, including Clifford Odets, J. Edward Bromberg, Morris Carnovsky, and Paula Miller, wife of Lee Strasberg. **12** In "A Statement," an ad he's taken out in *The New York Times*, Elia Kazan describes his brief membership in the Communist Party in the 1930s and urges all liberals to fight the menace that the Party represents.

MAY • Actors Equity's magazine reports that from September through March, only 13 of 692 players in Broadway shows were black—and only two of those black performers had speaking parts. The *Shrike* had the most integrated cast, with four black actors, one of whom, Leigh Whipper, had a speaking role. • A Broadway producing outfit takes over the National Theatre in

---

JANUARY • Kim Hunter m. actor Robert Emmett. **31** Producer George Broadhurst d.

MARCH 9 Barbara Cook m. actor David LeGrant

MAY 2 Christine Baranski b. **8** Playwright Beth Henley b. **21** John Garfield d.

Personalities

Ladies": Lynn Fontanne, Katharine Cornell, and Helen Hayes.

DECEMBER 17 A striking photograph of Vivian Leigh and Laurence Olivier adorns the cover of *Life*, celebrating their performances in both *Antony and Cleopatra* and *Caesar and Cleopatra*. **19** Gertrude Lawrence and Yul Brynner are both sick and will miss several performances of *The King & I*. She's more seriously ill, with pleurisy, and is hospitalized.

JANUARY 12 In a ceremony in the lobby of the Empire Theatre, Julie Harris's name is raised above the title of *I Am a Camera*, at its fiftieth performance, making her Broadway's newest star. Attending are Katharine Cornell, Helen Hayes, Gertrude Lawrence, and Dorothy Stickney. **16** Jules Irving and Herbert Blau start the Actors Workshop of San Francisco.

FEBRUARY • The already crewcut Leland Hayward, under the influence of Yul Brynner, who stars in the producer's *The King & I*, shaves his head.

MARCH • Appearing at the Circle in the Square in Garcia Lorca's *Yerma* is unknown actress Geraldine Page, playing an 80-year-old woman. She has three lines and about two minutes of stage time. **1** Harold Clurman resigns as theatre critic for *The New Republic*. **10** Brandon De Wilde is on the cover of *Life*, in costume for *Mrs. McThing*.

MAY 13 Carol Channing, at the Shubert Theatre in Boston, gives her 1000th performance as Lorelei Lee in *Gentlemen Prefer Blondes*.

Plays and Musicals

FEBRUARY 13 A duke is looking for just the right duchess in Christopher Fry's blank verse comedy *Venus Observed* (86), directed by Laurence Olivier at the Century. Rex Harrison and Lilli Palmer star. **20** Helen Hayes, Brandon De Wilde, Irwin Corey, Fred Gwynne, Jules Munshin, and Ernest Borgnine are in *Mrs. McThing* (350), a comedy-fairy tale by Mary Chase, opening at the Martin Beck. Robert Whitehead directs this production.

MARCH 12 John Garfield, who had to settle for a secondary role when Luther Adler starred in the 1937 Group Theatre production of Clifford Odets's *Golden Boy* (55), finally gets to play the lead on Broadway. Odets is directing, and also in the cast are Lee J. Cobb, Jack Klugman, Joseph Wiseman, and Arthur O'Connell.

APRIL 24 Tennessee Williams's *Summer and Smoke* (356) is revived off-Broadway at the Circle in the Square. Directed by José Quintero and starring Geraldine Page, it puts off-Broadway on the map and secures for Page a place among America's finest actresses.

MAY 16 Leonard Sillman's *New Faces of 1952* (365), opening at the Royale, will launch or boost several entertainment careers. In the cast of this revue are Eartha Kitt, singing "Monotonous," Carol Lawrence, Paul Lynde, Alice Ghostley, Ronny Graham, Robert Clary, June Carroll, and Virginia de Luce. One of the skits is by Mel Brooks.

Business and Society

Washington, D.C., which had been boycotted by Equity because of its policy of segregation, and will reopen it with nonsegregated seating. **5** The American Legion pickets the Gayety Theatre in Washington, D.C., where Uta Hagen and Luther Adler are playing in *Tovarich*. One picket sign reads "Uta Hagen Has a Record of Supporting Communist Fronts." Hagen was subpoenaed by HUAC on March 20 to testify. **19** In a letter to the House Un-American Activities Committee, playwright Lillian Hellman says that she is willing to talk about her own political activities but not those of others. She writes: "I cannot and will not cut my conscience to fit this year's fashions . . . ." Playwright Clifford Odets, testifying in person today and tomorrow, says he left the Communist Party in 1935 because the meetings "sometimes were silly." He acknowledges working with left-wing groups recently. On April 10, Elia Kazan named him as a former member of the Party. **26** Ralph Bellamy is elected president of Actors Equity.

Births, Deaths, and Marriages

1952–53

Now they say that Rex Harrison will play opposite Mary Martin in a musical version of Shaw's *Pygmalion*. Paul Newman and Joanne Woodward meet in *Picnic*. In Washington, the dark side of the decade is reflected when Jerome Robbins placates the congressional investigators of Communism by naming names, Abe Burrows is forced to grovel, and Judy Holliday plays a dumb blonde. Arthur Miller's response to this sordid drama is *The Crucible*. The Living Theatre has an early brush with the authorities over "fire regulations." And the sense of loss on Broadway is palpable, with the passing of Gertrude Lawrence.

- Cost of building the onstage swimming pool at the Imperial Theatre for *Wish You Were Here*: $28,000
- What's unusual about *Wish You Were Here*: it gives paid preview performances in lieu of out-of-town tryouts
- Phyllis Newman's one line in *Wish You Were Here*: "I don't want to be Miss Flushing—I want to be Miss Perth Amboy."
- Number of full-time members of *The New York Times* drama department: 5, including critic Brooks Atkinson
- No longer operative: Show of the Month Club, which folds
- The total weight of the scenery, lighting, drapes, etc., used in *Me and Juliet*: 19,300 pounds
- What's new in *Variety*: the beginning of regular reviews of off-Broadway shows
- Amount that real estate man William Zeckendorf has invested in Tennessee Williams's *Camino Real*: $4,600
- An RCA executive's response to a reporter asking why his company finances Broadway shows, including *Call Me Madam* and *Me and Juliet*: "It's simple, to make money."
- Profit made by Select Theatres, the Shubert company that controls the organization's theatre holdings: $644,290

Productions on Broadway: 54

Pulitzer Prize for Drama: *Picnic* (William Inge)

New York Drama Critics Circle Awards:
Best American Play: *Picnic* (William Inge)
Best Foreign Play: *The Love of Four Colonels* (Peter Ustinov)
Best Musical: *Wonderful Town* (Leonard Bernstein, Betty Comden, and Adolph Green)

Tony Awards:
Play: *The Crucible* (Arthur Miller)
Dramatic Actor: Tom Ewell (*The Seven Year Itch*)
Dramatic Actress: Shirley Booth (*Time of the Cuckoo*)
Musical: *Wonderful Town* (Leonard Bernstein, Betty Comden and, Adolph Green)
Actress in a Musical: Rosalind Russell (*Wonderful Town*)
Actor in a Musical: Thomas Mitchell (*Hazel Flagg*)

June	July	August	September	October	November
Wish You Were Here	Eric Bentley *New Republic* critic	Equity minimum pay $85/week	Gertrude Lawrence d.	Bette Davis faints onstage	*The Seven Year Itch*

December	January	February	March	April	May
George S. Kaufman TV trouble	Arthur Miller's *The Crucible*	*Picnic* and *Wonderful Town*	Shirley Booth wins third Tony	Ann Meara plays an egret	Jerome Robbins names names

Personalities

JUNE • Julie Harris will be out of *I Am a Camera* for several weeks while she films *Member of the Wedding*. Her understudy Barbara Baxley will take over as Sally Bowles. • RCA is already advertising Eddie Fisher's recording of the title song from the musical *Wish You Were Here*, which opens next month. The company has invested $20,000 in the show. **2** Responding to a report in *Life* that she "melt[s] like a bobby-soxer" over singer Johnnie Ray, Tallulah Bankhead writes in a letter to the editor that the day she does that, "*Life* may photograph me in the buff in Times Square at noon." **28** Gertrude Lawrence begins what's described as a summer vacation from the cast of *The King & I*. Celeste Holm replaces her until August 11.

JULY • Eric Bentley succeeds Harold Clurman as drama critic at *The New Republic*.

AUGUST • Maggie McNamara withdraws as a cast replacement in *The Moon Is Blue* because of exhaustion and a nervous condition. • In the ongoing speculation about a musical version of *Pygmalion*, Rex Harrison is now being paired with Mary Martin. The Theatre Guild, which would stage the production, is talking to Alan Jay Lerner and Frederick Loewe about doing the score. **16** Gertrude Lawrence misses a performance of *The King & I*. Officially, she's had an adverse reaction to an allergy shot—the actual diagnosis is jaundice from hepatitis—but, in fact, she has cancer of the liver.

SEPTEMBER • Buck and Bubbles (Ford Washington and John Sublett) are arrested in Toronto on a drug charge. Buck will draw a jail term. **6** Backstage at the St. James Theatre, where The King & I is playing, management has posted a notice about the death of Gertrude Lawrence: "This morning's event has been a very great shock. Kindly refrain from discussing it in the theatre and avoid tears or other demonstrations in the presence of performing artists." Both the matineé and the evening performances will be given today, but the show will not go on the day of her funeral. **9** Broadway's lights are dimmed

Plays and Musicals

JUNE 25 *Wish You Were Here* (598), Harold Rome's musical about romance in the Catskills, based on Arthur Kober's 1936–1937 *Having a Wonderful Time*, opens at the Imperial. The young cast includes Patricia Marand, Jack Cassidy, Sheila Bond, Florence Henderson, Tom Tryon, Larry Blyden, and Reid Shelton. Frantic rewriting will keep it going long enough to catch on, despite the bad reviews.

OCTOBER 2 Beatrice Lillie has considered, and rejected, the title "An Off Night With Hamlet Or What Isn't Under My Hat Tonight" for the revue *An Evening With Beatrice Lillie* (278), at the Booth. **15** Shirley Booth is a lonely American finding love in Venice in Arthur Laurents's *The Time of the Cuckoo* (263), at the Empire. David Lean's 1955 screen version, *Summertime*, stars Katharine Hepburn. The 1965 Richard Rodgers-Stephen Sondheim stage musical *Do I Hear a Waltz?* is also based on it. **27** Producer William De Lys's Theatre De Lys, the former Hudson Guild Playhouse, opens in Greenwich Village, with a play by John Huston, *Frankie and Johnny*, starring Pat Larson and Val Dufour. Says *Variety*: "*Frankie and Johnny* will remain part of the American folk legend, but Theatre De Lys has done 'em wrong." **29** Frederick Knott's thriller *Dial M for Murder* (552), opens at the Plymouth, with Maurice Evans starring. It will earn back its investment in less than three weeks and will become an Alfred Hitchcock film in 1954.

NOVEMBER 20 "Tom Ewell, whose woebegone face was obviously designed by the creators of Gerald McBoing-Boing," as Walter Kerr puts it, stars in *The Seven Year Itch* (1,141), opening at the Fulton. Chapman, in the *Daily News*, lauds George Axelrod's "grand and goofy comedy." Vanessa Brown is "The Girl"—the part played by Marilyn Monroe in the 1955 film, costarring Ewell.

DECEMBER 18 Patricia Neal and Kim Hunter star in a revival of *The Children's Hour* (189), at the Coronet.

Business and Society

JULY 2 *Variety*, commenting on *Wish You Were Here*, the musical that opened last week, notes an innovation in this production. The construction of the expensive onstage swimming pool—a Broadway first in itself—made brief out-of-town tryout runs impractical, so "the management substituted the unprecedented series of paid previews. . . ."

AUGUST • The New York City Fire Department closes the off-Broadway Cherry Lane Theatre and the Living Theatre's production of *Ubu the King*, supposedly because of fire law violations in the house, although it is thought that the play's rough language and homosexual theme may also be a factor. • Equity's new contract includes a week's pay for each day spent in the studio making original cast recordings. The agreement also raises the Broadway minimum for actors from $80 to $85 a week.

SEPTEMBER 24 The Senate Internal Security Committee makes public testimony given in closed session last spring. Judy Holliday seems to have affected her stage persona, pleading "stupidity" to the Committee about her ties to Communist

Births, Deaths, and Marriages

JUNE 10 Ethel Merman and Robert D. Levitt are divorced.

SEPTEMBER 6 Gertrude Lawrence d. On her deathbed, she asked that her understudy Constance Carpenter be given her role in *The King & I* and that Yul Brynner be raised to star billing. Noel Coward once told *Life* of his childhood friend that when they met, "She gave me an orange and told me a few mildly dirty stories and I loved her from then onwards."

OCTOBER 5 Janet Blair m. stage manager Nick Mayo.

NOVEMBER 30 Mandy Patinkin (Mandel Patinkin) b.

MARCH 9 Ethel Merman m. Bob Six, president of Continental Airlines. **19** Irene Bordoni d.

at 8:30 P.M. (London's West End goes dark, as well) for Gertrude Lawrence, whose funeral was held this afternoon at the Fifth Avenue Presbyterian Church. Oscar Hammerstein II delivered the eulogy, and 5,000 people who could not get in stood outside to pay their respects. Lawrence was buried in the gown she wore when dancing with Yul Brynner in *The King & I.*

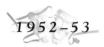

OCTOBER 19 Bette Davis, coming down with the flu, faints onstage at the opening night performance in Detroit of the revue *Two's a Crowd.* When she recovers, she insists on going on with the show, telling the audience, "You can't say I didn't fall for you."

NOVEMBER 14 Reviewing Moss Hart's *Climate of Eden*, Brooks Atkinson praises a 21-year-old newcomer, "a radiant young English actress, Rosemary Harris, who is all grace and loveliness and who can also act with perception." **16** Tallulah Bankhead appears on radio on "The Theatre Guild of the Air" in *All About Eve.* She plays Margo Channing, the character said to be partly modeled after her.

DECEMBER 21 Appearing as a panelist on the CBS TV program "This Is Show Business," the usually acerbic playwright George S. Kaufman remarks, apropos the coming Christmas holiday, "Let's make this one program on which nobody sings 'Silent Night.'" A deluge of complaints that this statement is irreligious panics the sponsor, the American Tobacco Company, which has CBS temporarily remove him from the show.

JANUARY 12 Thornton Wilder is on the cover of *Time.* **21** *Variety* reports that "sailing for Italy last week was Steve Sonheim [sic], protege of Oscar Hammerstein 2d, to put the finishing touches on a new musical for which he has written the book, music and lyrics. . . ."

FEBRUARY 21 Harold Clurman is named drama critic for *The Nation*, succeeding Joseph Wood Krutch, who has held the post since 1924. Clurman was theatre critic for *The New Republic* from 1948 to 1952.

MARCH 29 Shirley Booth wins her third Tony, for her performance in *Time of the*

JANUARY 15 Peter Ustinov's *The Love of Four Colonels* (141) opens at the Shubert. Rex Harrison and Lilli Palmer star in the comedy-fairy tale. **22** Arthur Miller's *The Crucible* (197), about witchcraft in Old Salem—and McCarthyism in today's headlines—opens at the Martin Beck. It's "a powerful play," says Atkinson in the *Times*; it's a "mechanical parable," declares Kerr in the *Herald-Tribune*. The cast includes Arthur Kennedy, Madeleine Sherwood, Walter Hampden, Beatrice Straight, E.G. Marshall, and Fred Stewart. An off-Broadway revival in 1958 runs for 571 performances. **23** Yiddish Theatre star Menasha Skulnick is on Broadway at the Cort in Sylvia Regan's comedy *The Fifth Season* (654). Skulnick is a "schlemiel"—his usual sad sack stage persona when playing on Second Avenue—whose garment manufacturing partner is making life difficult.

FEBRUARY 14 Charles Laughton's adaptation of *John Brown's Body* (65), a staged reading at the New Century Theatre, stars Raymond Massey, Judith Anderson, and Tyrone Power. Atkinson calls it a "stage performance of fire and beauty." **19** William Inge's *Picnic* (477) opens at the Music Box. Walter Kerr, while finding Kim Stanley talented, nevertheless sees too much of a female Marlon Brando and is put off by her "nervous-tic mannerisms, sing-song rhythms and lolling tongue." The cast also includes Ralph Meeker, Peggy Conklin, Arthur O'Connell, Eileen Heckart, Janice Rule, and Paul

Kim Stanley MSN

---

front groups, and telling them that she had hired someone to investigate herself because "I wanted to know what I had done." Burl Ives also testified.

NOVEMBER 12 In his second appearance before the House Un-American Activities, Abe Burrows says of his 1940s politics, "I associated with [c]ommunists and all my acts would have indicated I was one of them." When a Congressman suggests that he was naive, Burrows replies, "I'll go further than that. I'll say I was downright stupid."

DECEMBER • Touring shows are encountering a shortage of stagehands in some cities, the result of the rapid expansion of television production, which is drawing away the labor. • The Carthay Circle Theatre in Los Angeles is trying something new—linking box office sales to the 100,000-member Diners Club so that tickets can be bought by credit card.

APRIL • Negotiations between British and American Equity to ease restrictions on foreign actors in each country reach a stalemate.

MAY 5 Choreographer Jerome Robbins is one of several entertainment figures testifying at HUAC hearings in New York

---

APRIL 19 Cloris Leachman m. director George Englund. **24** Playwright-actor Eric Bogosian b.

Personalities

Cuckoo. She can put it on her mantle with the Oscar she recently won for *Come Back Little Sheba*.

APRIL 6 A review in the *New York World Telegram and Sun* of a show at the Theatre De Lys in Greenwich Village, *Which Way Home?* notes in passing that Ann Meara is "particularly effective." She plays an egret in a scene called "The Zoo." **11** The *Saturday Review* declares that young actress Kim Stanley has "added her name to an exclusive list of postwar American actresses which includes Barbara Bel Geddes, Julie Harris, Maureen Stapleton, Kim Hunter and Geraldine Page."

Shirley Booth MSN

13 Beatrice Straight, taking an eight-week leave of absence from *The Crucible* to have a baby, is replaced by Maureen Stapleton.

MAY • Ed Sullivan cancels the June 21 and June 28 appearances of Gwen Verdon, star of *Can Can*, on his television show, "The Toast of the Town," for which she was to be paid a total of $5,000. Sullivan objects to her agreeing to appear for free on Walter Winchell's show. Sullivan and Winchell have a long-standing feud. **24** Playwright Paddy Chayefsky becomes famous overnight with the telecast of *Marty*, starring Rod Steiger, on "The Goodyear Playhouse."

Plays and Musicals

Newman in a performance noted by Hollywood producers (he's also noticed by understudy Joanne Woodward, although he is now married to someone else). It's filmed in 1955. **25** Leonard Bernstein, Betty Comden, and Adolph Green, with George Abbott directing, repeat their success in *On the Town* with *Wonderful Town* (559), a musical version of the 1940 My *Sister Eileen*, at the Winter Garden. Rosalind Russell, Edie Adams, and George Gaynes star. "Ohio," which Bernstein intended as a parody of hometown sentimentality, is received in a sentimental vein by many who hear it.

MARCH 10 Leontyne Price and Cab Calloway star in a revival of *Porgy and Bess* (305), at the Ziegfeld. **19** Tennessee Williams's *Camino Real* (60), "the worst play yet written by the best playwright of his generation," according to Walter Kerr, opens at the National. Directed by Elia Kazan, its stars Eli Wallach and Jo Van Fleet.

MAY 1 Arnold Perl's dramatization of Sholem Aleichem's short stories, The *World of Sholem Aleichem* (20), opens at the Barbizon-Plaza Theatre. The cast includes Howard Da Silva, Morris Carnovsky, Phoebe Brand, Jack Gilford, and Ruby Dee. The stage manager is Ossie Davis. **7** Cole Porter's *Can-Can* (892), with a book by Abe Burrows, opens at the Shubert. But the night belongs to Gwen Verdon, who leaves the stage following her big production number in the first act, not realizing that she has literally stopped the show. Porter's "I Love Paris" is in the score, as is "C'est Magnifique." There's a film version in 1960. **28** Oscar Hammerstein II adds lyrics to the lovely tango Richard Rodgers wrote for the NBC television documentary *Victory at Sea*, creating "No Other Love," the highlight of the musical *Me and Juliet* (358), at the Majestic. This sixth Rodgers and Hammerstein show stars Isabel Bigley, Bill Hayes, Joan McCracken, and Ray Walston, with a chorine named Shirley MacLaine.

Business and Society

City. He acknowledges his Communist Party membership from 1943 to 1947 and names several other theatre figures who joined, including writers Jerome and Edward Chodorov.

Births, Deaths, and Marriages

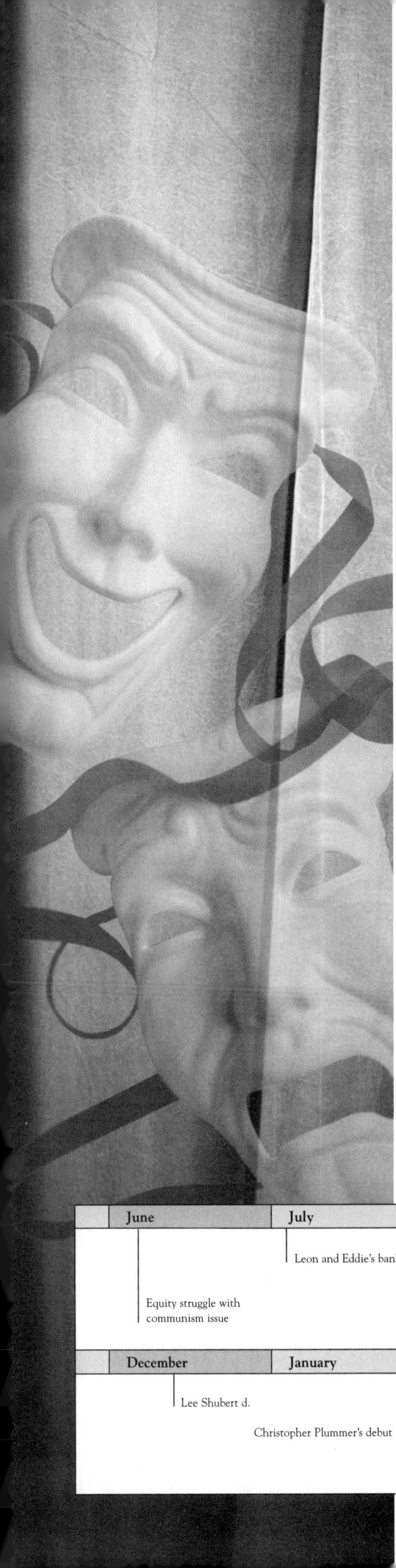

1953–54

The syndicates, limited partnerships, and corporations set up to finance shows for which producers used to supply the money themselves, have become the norm on the business side of Broadway. Off-Broadway is just now beginning to be viewed as an alternative to the Main Stem when costs become too prohibitive. Forty-two-year-old Margaret Sullavan brings off the title role in *Sabrina Fair* (played by Audrey Hepburn in the film), Stephen Sondheim is a TV sitcom writer, Rodgers and Hammerstein totally take over the tube for an evening (although they are off the boards for the first time in a long time), Billy Rose pays off his "sugar plum candy mouth," *The Pajama Game* arrives, *The Threepenny Opera* is back, and Lee Shubert and Eugene O'Neill are dead.

- Cost of staging *Ondine*, in which Audrey Hepburn stars: $102,000
- Profit from the Broadway run of *Ondine*, which closes after 156 performances when Audrey Hepburn leaves to make a movie: $40,000
- What *Ondine*'s director Alfred Lunt has to say about directing Mel Ferrer: "I learned that you cannot make a knight errant out of a horse's ass."
- Which way José Ferrer is pointed this season: forward and backward—in a repertory season at the City Center, he does both *Cyrano de Bergerac*, with his protruding nose, and *Richard III*, with a hump back
- In a bad way: Joshua Logan, who has another breakdown in the fall of 1953
- Novelists who have adapted their books for the stage this season: Herman Wouk (*The Caine Mutiny*), Calder Willingham (*End As a Man*), and Alfred Hayes (*The Girl on the Via Flamina*)
- What Tallulah Bankhead uses on the Milton Berle show for a dramatic reading: a Chinese restaurant menu
- Producers besides Lee Shubert who lived above their theatres:
  David Belasco—the Belasco
  Daniel Frohman—the Lyceum
  William Harris—the Hudson
  Billy Rose—the Ziegfeld
- Just some of the shows on Broadway this season designed by Jo Mielziner: *Guys and Dolls, Can Can, Me and Juliet, The King & I,* and *South Pacific*
- What Robert Anderson, who wrote *Tea and Sympathy*, says about his occupation: "The theatre is a place where a playwright can make a killing but not a living."

Productions on Broadway: 59

Pulitzer Prize for Drama: *Teahouse of the August Moon* (John Patrick)

New York Drama Critics Circle Awards:
Best American Play: *Teahouse of the August Moon* (John Patrick)
Best Foreign Play: *Ondine* (Jean Giraudoux)
Best Musical: *The Golden Apple* (Jerome Moross and John Latouche)

Tony Awards:
Play: *The Teahouse of the August Moon* (John Patrick)
Actor in a Play: David Wayne (*Teahouse of the August Moon*)
Actress in a Play: Audrey Hepburn (*Ondine*)
Musical: *Kismet* (Robert Wright and George Foster)
Actor in a Musical: Alfred Drake (*Kismet*)
Actress in a Musical: Dolores Gray (*Carnival in Flanders*)

June	July	August	September	October	November
Equity struggle with communism issue	Leon and Eddie's bankrupt	*Variety* reports chicanery	*Tea and Sympathy*	Sondheim scripts sitcom	Eugene O'Neill d.

December	January	February	March	April	May
Lee Shubert d.	Christopher Plummer's debut	Audrey Hepburn in *Ondine*	*The Threepenny Opera*	Mary Martin on "Person to Person"	*The Pajama Game*

Personalities

JUNE 2 John Gielgud is knighted. **15** A duet between Ethel Merman and Mary Martin is the highlight of "The Ford Fiftieth Anniversary Show," one of television's first "specials," viewed simultaneously on NBC and CBS by an audience of about 60 million. **22** Yul Brynner is back in *The King & I* after an 11-week leave.

JULY • Marlon Brando is playing in Shaw's *Arms and the Man* in summer stock in Rhode Island at $125 a week plus a percentage of the gross. His film fee is currently reported as $150,000 per picture.

Plays and Musicals

SEPTEMBER 30 Deborah Kerr and John Kerr (no relation), the son of Broadway actress June Walker, star in Robert Anderson's *Tea and Sympathy* (712), at the Barrymore. Deborah Kerr is the headmaster's wife at the boarding school John Kerr attends. His cohorts and her husband hint that he is a homosexual, but she gives herself to the boy to let him affirm his manhood. Leif Erickson costars. The homosexual theme is gone from the 1956 film, which has the same cast in the leading roles.

OCTOBER 2 Pianist-comedian Victor Borge, who has become popular on television,

David Wayne and John Forsythe in *The Teahouse of the August Moon* PB

Business and Society

JUNE 5 A group of Actors Equity members, led by Sidney Blackmer and including Thomas Mitchell and Conrad Nagel, want the union to take a stronger stand against communism. But today's Equity elections produce new members of the union's council who don't. One of them, however, Yul Brynner, almost immediately resigns, and it's reported that conservatives threatened to reveal damaging facts about his past if he doesn't quit.

JULY 31 Leon and Eddie's, the legendary theatre district eatery, declares bankruptcy.

AUGUST 19 *Variety* stirs controversy with its front-page story which claims that backers of some shows are fed up with not being consulted on production decisions and are suspicious of graft and other kinds of chicanery. Next week, Arthur Schwartz, president of the League of New York Theatres, will write a rejoinder in a full-page ad.

OCTOBER • Actors Equity adds to the various anti-Communist provisions in its constitution the rule that any "proven" Communists will be expelled. **7** In what may be its first pronouncement of a

Births, Deaths, and Marriages

JUNE 5 Roland Young and William Farnum d.

JULY 13 José Ferrer, divorced last week from Phyllis Hill, m. singer Rosemary Clooney. **17** Maude Adams d.

OCTOBER 5 Theodore Mann, a founder of the Circle in the Square, m. actress and singer Patricia Brooks.

NOVEMBER 27 Eugene O'Neill d.

DECEMBER 9 John Malkovich b. **25** Lee Shubert, known on Broadway as "Mr. Lee," d. He liked to say of Sarah Bernhardt, who toured the United States in 1906 under Shubert auspices, "English she couldn't talk; English she couldn't pronounce; but boy, could she count in English!"

AUGUST • Lionel Stander, appearing in *Pal Joey* in Chicago, is fired after a backstage altercation with company manager Joe Grossman, with whom the actor has been feuding. Grossman had complained that Stander had missed cues and was derelict in other ways. Stander says it's about his being the Equity representative in the company.

SEPTEMBER 8 Sardi's bows to royal prerogative, permitting Yul Brynner to dine despite his not conforming to the restaurant's requirement that gentlemen wear ties. **24** The *Playbill* for *Take a Giant Step*, opening at the Lyceum, states that young cast member Louis Gossett, a Brooklyn high school student, aspires to be a pharmacist. **30** According to *Variety*, the Theatre Guild wants to revive Robert Sherwood's *Reunion in Vienna*, which Lunt and Fontanne did in the 1931–32 season, pairing Marlon Brando with Audrey Hepburn.

OCTOBER 9 The cowriter of the television series "Topper," a comedy about a man and two ghosts, debuting tonight on CBS, is 23-year-old Stephen Sondheim. In one episode scripted by him, the future author of notably idiosyncratic lyrics has a character winning a contest to finish the jingle, "Everyone loves Individual Oats/. . . ." The winner is: "Everyone loves Individual Oats/ It's the cereal everyone votes—for."

NOVEMBER • Of the current shows on Broadway, eight, or one-third, bear the mark of scenic designer Jo Mielziner. He has designed 188 shows so far in his three-decade Broadway career. Among his current productions are *Guys and Dolls*, *Can Can*, *Me and Juliet*, *The King & I*, and *South Pacific*. **3** Tallulah Bankhead, appearing on television on "The Milton Berle Show," gives a dramatic reading from a Chinese restaurant menu. **10** Tallulah Bankhead is on Edward R. Murrow's "Person to Person" program, in which the subject is interviewed at home.

DECEMBER 30 The *Playbill* for *The Remarkable Mr. Pennypacker* says of director Alan Schneider: "Young Mr. Schneider is making his first appearance as a Broadway director, though he is far from

opens at the John Golden in a one-man show *Comedy In Music* (849). **15** John Patrick's *Teahouse of the August Moon* (1,027) opens at the Martin Beck. David Wayne, John Forsythe, and Paul Ford star in this comedy about the American military in postwar Japan. It becomes a film in 1956.

NOVEMBER 3 Horton Foote's *The Trip to Bountiful* (39), originally on NBC's "Television Playhouse," comes to Henry Miller's Theatre. It stars Lillian Gish, Jo Van Fleet, and also features what critic Richard Watts, Jr., in the *New York Post*, calls a "lovely performance by an attractive young actress from television named Eva Marie Saint." Geraldine Page stars in the 1985 film. **5** *The Solid Gold Cadillac* (526), a comedy by George S. Kaufman and Howard Teichmann, opens at the Belasco. It runs until the star, Josephine Hull, who plays a little old lady who manages to take over a big corporation, and who is in fact an older woman herself, is injured in a fall and has to leave the show. The last show produced by Max Gordon and the last of Kaufman's plays to be mounted on Broadway, it becomes a 1956 film, adapted for the younger Judy Holliday. **11** Margaret Sullavan stars in *Sabrina Fair* (318), Samuel Taylor's comedy about the chauffeur's daughter who captivates the two sons of her father's employer, at the National Theatre. Audrey Hepburn has the title role in the 1954 film, *Sabrina*.

Leon and Eddie's—a prominent theatre-district restaurant *BROWN*

refrain that will become familiar over the years, *Variety* warns: "High cost of Main Stem production is spurring top theatrical activity off-Broadway."

NOVEMBER 10 Leland Hayward is elected president of the League of New York Theatres.

DECEMBER • To cope with a newspaper strike in New York, the producers of

JANUARY 30 Producer John Murray Anderson d.

FEBRUARY 20 Producer-director Augustin Duncan d.

Personalities

a novice. Tagged by most of the theatrical set as one of our most promising directorial talents, he has had the rare opportunity to exhibit his abilities in many varying projects." *Cue*, the entertainment magazine, will shortly call him "the theatre's newest wonder-boy director."

JANUARY • The property settlement between producer Billy Rose and Eleanor Holm, his onetime "sugar plum candy mouth," comes to $200,000 outright and alimony of $30,000 a month. **5** Tallulah Bankhead plays Hedda Gabler on television's "The U.S. Steel Hour." **13** Christopher Plummer makes his Broadway debut in *The Starcross Story*, a short-lived production starring Eva Le Gallienne and Mary Astor. **20** Jim Bumgarner is playing a member of the court in *The Caine Mutiny Court-Martial*, opening tonight. He is not yet calling himself James Garner.

MARCH 4 Television actress Maria Riva, daughter of Marlene Dietrich, performs her first major Broadway role in *The Burning Glass*, at the Longacre, with Cedric Hardwicke and Walter Matthau. The play flops. **17** *Variety* notes, "Tony Perkins, son of the late Osgood Perkins, may take over as juvenile lead of *Tea and Sympathy* in June when John Kerr leaves for film contract." **28** For the first time, all four TV networks—NBC, CBS, ABC, and DuMont—are broadcasting the same commercially sponsored show: "The Rodgers and Hammerstein Cavalcade," a 90-minute special that is reaching the biggest entertainment audience ever. Mary Martin emcees the program, which also stars Yul Brynner, Ezio Pinza, John Raitt, Jan Clayton, Rosemary Clooney, Tony Martin, Gordon McRae, and Florence Henderson in scenes from Rodgers and Hammerstein musicals. The Trendex ratings estimate an audience of 70,000,000 for the program. **28** Three days after she won an Oscar for *Roman Holiday*, Audrey Hepburn receives a Tony for her performance in *Ondine*.

APRIL • The closing of *Me and Juliet* marks the first time in 11 years that Broadway has no show by Rodgers and Hammerstein.

Plays and Musicals

DECEMBER 1 The Phoenix Theatre opens on Second Avenue with a revival of Sidney Howard's comedy *Madam, Will You Walk?* (48), starring Hume Cronyn, playing the Devil and also codirecting, and Jessica Tandy. **3** From the music of Alexander Borodin and a play about ancient Baghdad that Otis Skinner starred in on Broadway in 1911, Robert Wright and George Forrest have fashioned the musical *Kismet* (583), at the Ziegfeld. The cast features Alfred Drake and Richard Kiley, and the score's highlights include "Stranger in Paradise" and "Baubles, Bangles and Beads." It's an MGM film in 1955. **10** Polly Bergen and Hermione Gingold make their Broadway debuts in *John Murray Anderson's Almanac* (227), the producer's final show, at the Imperial. It's also the first Main Stem outing for Richard Adler and Jerry Ross, who will shortly write the scores for *Pajama Game* and *Damn Yankees*. Also in the cast is young Harry Belafonte. **17** Franchot Tone, a psychoanalyst in a romantic tangle, needs to "shrink" himself in the Edward Chodorov comedy *Oh, Men! Oh, Women!* (382), at Henry Miller's Theatre. It's a 1957 film. **29** *In the Summer House* (55), a critically acclaimed play by Jane Bowles, primarily a writer of fiction, opens at the Playhouse. Judith Anderson and Elizabeth Ross play the clashing mother and daughter.

JANUARY 20 Henry Fonda and Lloyd Nolan star in *The Caine Mutiny Court-Martial* (405), which Herman Wouk has adapted from his own novel, at the Plymouth. Director Charles Laughton took over during rehearsals for Dick Powell, who is reported to have feuded with Fonda. The film appears later this year.

FEBRUARY 8 The homosexual theme in Ruth and Augustus Goetz's adaptation of Andre Gide's *The Immoralist* (104), opening at the Royale, sparks controversy. John Chapman of the *Daily News* is "embarrassed" by it and writes that perhaps the play should be called "From Here To Maternity." In the cast are Geraldine Page, Louis Jourdan, and James Dean.

Business and Society

Kismet use a paid promotion on television's "Tonight" show, currently hosted by Steve Allen, and producer Charles Lederer appears on Dave Garroway's "Today" program. **30** Five days after the death of Lee Shubert, federal judge John C. Knox dismisses the antitrust case filed by the Justice Department against the Shuberts on February 21, 1950.

JANUARY • J.J. Shubert and Milton Weir, one of the Shubert's attorneys and a lawyer for the League of New York Theatres, are feuding. Shubert will resign from the League.

FEBRUARY 23 Houston's Alley Theatre, with the opening of its production of *Death of a Salesman*, starring Albert Dekker, becomes a professional organization.

MARCH 7 Both the *Herald-Tribune* and the *Times* on this Sunday give prominent coverage to two upcoming off-Broadway musicals, *The Threepenny Opera* and *The Golden Apple*, a sign that off-Broadway's time is arriving. **22** The Fire Department shuts down the Circle in the Square as a fire trap with inadequate exits. Manager Theodore Mann will draw a suspended

Births, Deaths, and Marriages

30 Mary Martin is interviewed by Edward R. Murrow on his "Person to Person" television program.

MAY 24 Kaye Ballard, appearing in *The Golden Apples*, is on the cover of *Life* magazine.

18 *Ondine* (117), a play about knights and fairies by Jean Giraudoux, adapted by Maurice Valency and directed by Alfred Lunt, opens at the Forty-sixth Street Theatre. Harold Clurman, in *The Nation*, sees star Audrey Hepburn at the beginning of a great career and advises that she should "play on the stage—though I do not suggest that you give up films." Also in the cast is her husband, Mel Ferrer.

MARCH 10 *The Threepenny Opera* (95), Bertolt Brecht and Kurt Weill's mordant 1928 work that failed on Broadway in 1933, has been adapted by Marc Blitzstein, who has moved the setting from the eighteenth century to the Victorian era. It's at the Theatre De Lys. The cast is headed by Lotte Lenya (Weill's wife) as Jenny, with Scott Merrill, Jo Sullivan, Leon Lisher, Charlotte Rae, and Beatrice Arthur. "The Ballad of Mack the Knife" will become a hit in recordings by Bobby Darin and Louis Armstrong. The production, which has to vacate the theatre because it's been booked for another play, will return on September 20, 1955, and chalk up an additional 2,611 performances. **11** *The Golden Apple* (173, total), Jerome Moross and John Latouche's musical melding and updating of the *Odyssey* and the *Iliad*, opens at the Phoenix and will later move to Broadway. Priscilla Gillette, Jonathan Lucas, Steven Douglas, and Kay Ballard star, with Jerry Stiller. "Lazy Afternoon" is the most prominent song.

APRIL 7 Audiences love *Anniversary Waltz* (615), opening at the Broadhurst, even though the critics don't. McDonald Carey and Kitty Carlisle star in this Jerome Chodorov-Joseph Fields comedy about a couple whose children find out about their premarital affair.

MAY 13 *The Pajama Game* (1,063) opens at the St. James Theatre. Richard Adler and Jerry Ross have never written a book musical, Bob Fosse is debuting as a choreographer, and 25-year-old Harold Prince is coproducing his first Broadway show. John Raitt, Janis Paige, Carol Haney, and Eddie Foy, Jr. are the stars, with Peter Gennaro and Shirley MacLaine in the chorus. Songs include "Hey, There," "Steam Heat," and "Hernando's Hideway." It's a 1957 film.

sentence for the four violations. The current production at the house *The Girl on the Via Flamina* moves to the Forty-eighth Street Theatre on April 1.

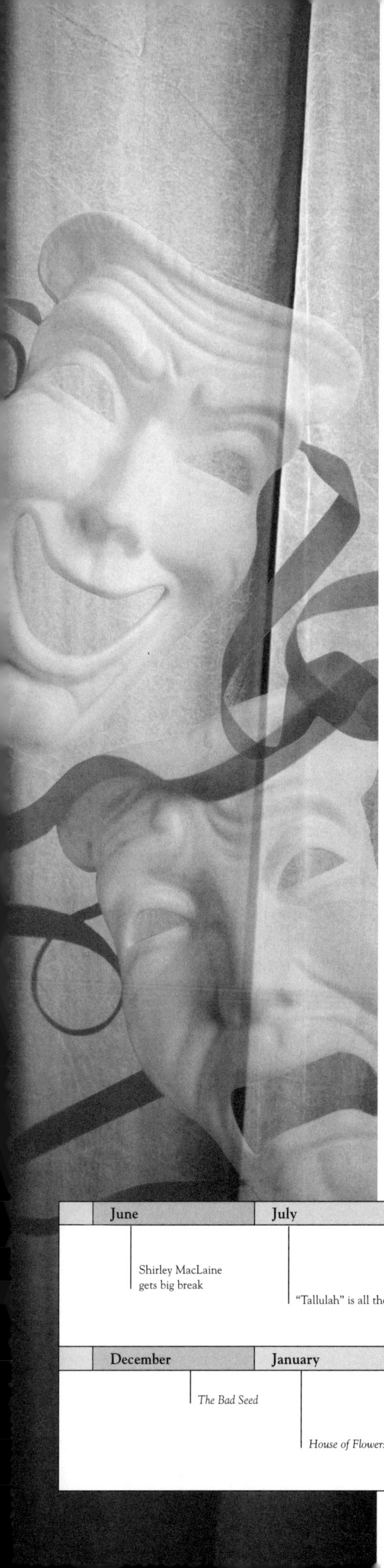

1954–55

"Mendacity" is an issue in *Cat on a Hot Tin Roof*. Off-Broadway is really being taken seriously, Joseph Papp begins to produce, and David Merrick is a success. Mary Martin flies, Patty McCormick is a hell of a child, Ray Walston is a hell of a devil, and 19-year-old Julie Andrews arrives—"Lift your skirts up higher, sister," say the photographers when the boat docks. Chorus girl Shirley MacLaine gets a big break in *The Pajama Game*, the homosexual theme in *Tea and Sympathy* continues to cause discomfort in some quarters (and will disappear in the film), and Cheryl Crawford is not amused by Betsy von Furstenberg's stage pranks. Diana Barrymore can't get her bearings, while her aunt Ethel is now a museum piece.

- Amount by which Noel Coward, his career in eclipse, is overdrawn at the bank: $60,000
- Profit made by *Peter Pan*, with Mary Martin, after its Broadway run and historic March 7 telecast on NBC, for which the producers were paid $225,000: none yet, it's still $76 in the red, absorbed by management, which pays off backers in full
- What it costs to cast Tallulah Bankhead in anything: 15 percent of the gross and 25 percent of the net
- Enemy made this year by Lillian Hellman: Harvard student John Simon, one of several people she has hired to do a literal translation of Jean Anouilh's *The Lark*; she refuses to pay because it is typed in the wrong format. As a drama critic, he will not view her plays favorably.
- First for off-Broadway: a Tony award, given to Proscenium Productions at the Cherry Lane Theatre for the "high quality" of its work
- Total amount Ethel Merman is paid for four 1-hour shows on NBC television: $100,000
- Unfounded rumor of the season: that Eddie Fisher and Debbie Reynolds will star in a 90-minute color television "special" of Rodgers and Hammerstein's *Me and Juliet*
- Number of house seats guaranteed to Ezio Pinza for each performance of *Fanny*: 4
- Tied for first place in the New York Drama Critics Circle vote for most promising actor: George Grizzard (*The Desperate Hours*) and Buddy Hackett (*Lunatics and Lovers*)
- Premium that producer Alex Cohen gives to ticket holders on his bus tour from New Haven to see *The Pajama Game*: a pair of pajamas

Productions on Broadway: 63

Pulitzer Prize for Drama: *Cat on a Hot Tin Roof* (Tennessee Williams)

New York Drama Critics Circle Awards:
Best American Play: *Cat on a Hot Tin Roof* (Tennessee Williams)
Best Foreign Play: *Witness for the Prosecution* (Agatha Christie)
Best Musical: *The Saint of Bleecker Street* (Gian-Carlo Menotti)

Tony Awards:
Play: *The Desperate Hours* (Joseph Hayes)
Actress in a Play: Nancy Kelly (*The Bad Seed*)
Actor in a Play: Alfred Lunt (*Quadrille*)
Musical: *The Pajama Game* (Richard Adler and Jerry Ross)
Actress in a Musical: Mary Martin (*Peter Pan*)
Actor in a Musical: Walter Slezak (*Fanny*)

June	July	August	September	October	November
Shirley MacLaine gets big break	"Tallulah" is all the ads say	British censor *Tea and Sympathy*	Julie Andrews's debut	Mary Martin in *Peter Pan*	Papp and Merrick produce

December	January	February	March	April	May
The Bad Seed	*House of Flowers* dissension	Frances Sternhagen's debut	*Cat on a Hot Tin Roof*	Diana Barrymore faltering	*Damn Yankees*

Personalities

JUNE 29 The *Morning Telegraph*'s critic George Freedly writes of *The Pajama Game*, in which one of the stars is dancer Carol Haney, "The night I saw the show Miss Haney was ill and her understudy Shirley MacLaine took over. It was one of the most accomplished and completely professional performances I have had the pleasure of enjoying." MacLaine will come to the attention of Hal Wallis, who signs her to a movie contract.

JULY • Newspaper ads for Tallulah Bankhead's appearance in the pre-Broadway tryout of *Dear Charles* at the Casino Theatre in Newport, Rhode Island, identify her only by her first name and beckon to potential theatregoers with her familiar "Dahling."

AUGUST 16 Gloria Vanderbilt makes her stage debut at the Pocono Playhouse in Ferenc Molnár's *The Swan*. The diamond tiara she's wearing is real, and it's hers. **24** Equity dismisses a complaint against John Barrymore, Jr. by producers Charlotte and Lewis Harmon, at the Clinton Playhouse in Connecticut. They charged him with cursing at Charlotte Harmon, who directed a recent show in which he appeared.

SEPTEMBER 29 Betsy von Furstenberg, who was fired from *Oh Man, Oh Women* by producer Cheryl Crawford because of unexcused absences, cracking up onstage, and doctoring a drink taken by costar Tony Randall in the play, writes in a letter in *Variety* that her dismissal may be attributed "to some—now well known—pranks I played on certain of my fellow actors who did not, unfortunately, share my sense of humor."

OCTOBER 21 Sylvia Miles has the first of her many off-Broadway roles in *A Stone for Danny Fisher*, which stars Zero Mostel, at the Downtown National Theatre, a former Yiddish theatre on the Lower East Side. Miles had fantasized her first opening night party at Sardi's, but it's going to be at Moskowitz and Lupowitz, where there's a seltzer bottle on every table.

NOVEMBER 4 Joseph Papirofsky, whose day

Plays and Musicals

JUNE 2 Barbara Cook is one of the stars of the City Center's revival of *Carousel* (79).

SEPTEMBER 30 Sandy Wilson's *The Boy Friend* (485), starring Julie Andrews—"at once hilarious and enormously attractive," says Richard Watts, Jr.—in her Broadway debut, is at the Royale. This affectionate look at the musicals of the 1920s features "I Could Be Happy With You." Revived twice, it will appear as a film in 1972, with Tommy Tune and Twiggy.

OCTOBER 20 "I don't know what all the fuss is about," Walter Kerr will write in the *Herald-Tribune* about *Peter Pan* (152). "I always knew Mary Martin could fly." Cyril Ritchard offers her the perfect foil as Captain Hook in this production, based on the 1905 James Barrie play, opening at the Winter Garden. The music is by Mark Charlap and Jule Styne, the lyrics by Carolyn Leigh, Betty Comden, and Adolph Green. **27** Horton Foote's *The Traveling Lady* (30), about a small Texas town, opens at the Playhouse. Richard Watts, Jr. acclaims the performance of Kim Stanley but calls the play "real and honest but not very moving." Tomorrow, Stanley receives her first star billing. **28** Geraldine Page and Darren McGavin star in *The Rainmaker* (124), by N. Richard Nash, at the Cort. It's a film in 1956 and becomes the 1963 stage musical *110 in the Shade*.

NOVEMBER 4 *Fanny* (888), David Merrick's debut as a Broadway producer, opens at the Majestic. It also has Harold Rome's music, a book by S.N. Behrman and Joshua Logan based on stories by Marcel Pagnol, and a cast that includes Ezio Pinza, Walter Slezak, and Florence Henderson. The 1960 movie drops the music.

DECEMBER 8 Maxwell Anderson's *The Bad Seed* (334) opens at the Forty-sixth Street Theatre. Patty McCormick, age nine, plays the sweet, eight-year-old child who happens to be a homicidal lunatic, the product of bad, very bad genes. She also stars in the 1956 film. **16** Agatha Christie's *Witness for the Prosecution* (645), starring Francis L. Sullivan, Gene Lyons, and Patricia Jessel, with Una O'Connor,

Business and Society

JULY • The theatres are absorbing the new New York City five percent tax on tickets purchased in advance.

AUGUST • The British censor bans performances of *Tea and Sympathy* because of its homosexual theme. And in a sign of the times, the New York *Journal-American* plays up the war record and marriage of Leif Erikson, leaving no doubt about his masculinity offstage, when it writes about his performance in the play.

OCTOBER 13 *Variety* headlines: "Off-B'way Splurge Repeats '53–'54; Volume, Quality & Coverage Boom." The Off-Broadway Theatre League, founded late last season, is setting up quarters in Times Square, where tickets for its members' productions will be available. Newspapers are beginning to print regular off-Broadway theatre listings.

NOVEMBER • Booming box offices have created a Broadway theatre shortage, which is even extending to off-Broadway. Touring companies, which did poorly last year, are also sharing in the sale of tickets.

JANUARY • David Merrick is taking the

Births, Deaths, and Marriages

JUNE 6 playwright-actor Harvey Fierstein b. **12** Producer-songwriter E. Ray Goetz d. **13** Composer-producer Arthur Schwartz m. actress Mary Grey (Mary Scott).

JULY 1 Anne Bancroft m. Martin May. **4** Viveca Lindfors m. playwright George Tabori. **24** Effie Shannon d.

AUGUST • Julie Harris divorces Jay Julien.

SEPTEMBER 20 Jerry Stiller m. Ann Meara.

OCTOBER 21 Julie Harris m. stage manager-playwright Manning Gurian.

NOVEMBER 15 Lionel Barrymore d. **26** Set designer Robert E. Jones d.

job is at CBS TV, produces an evening of scenes from Shakespeare at a church on New York's Lower East Side. His organization is the Shakespeare Workshop. It will become the New York Shakespeare Festival, and he will become Joseph Papp. **14** "Broadway's New Girl Friend a London Teenager," says the headline on the *New York Mirror's* story about the just-turned-19 Julie Andrews, who is appearing in *The Boy Friend.* She says that as soon as she got off the boat in New York, the press photographers called out, "Lift your skirts up higher, sister." **20** Sammy Davis, Jr. loses his left eye in a California auto accident.

DECEMBER • Having been quoted in the entertainment magazine *Cue* that she will be celebrating her fiftieth anniversary on the stage this spring, an embarrassed Helen Hayes corrects herself, pushing the date ahead to 1956. The First Lady of the American Theatre says that she does not keep scrapbooks.

JANUARY • Arnold Saint-Subber, producer of the dissension-racked *House of Flowers*, directed by Peter Brook, issues a statement: "I am completely happy that the differences and misunderstandings between my star, Pearl Bailey, and Peter Brook have been reconciled and clarified and are now a thing of the past." **26** Ethel Barrymore has become a museum piece, with the opening of the exhibition "Ethel Barrymore and Her Career," at the Museum of the City of New York. Her memoirs are running in *The Ladies Home Journal.*

FEBRUARY • "Lady Liza" is the latest title for the upcoming Lerner and Loewe musical based on *Pygmalion.*

MARCH • Steve Allen, host of television's late-night "Tonight" show, has begun to read on the air the just-out theatre reviews from the *Times* and *Herald-Tribune.* He also has cast members from some shows appear live after their opening night to play scenes from them. • Producer Lucille Lortel, who runs the White Barn Theatre in Westport, Connecticut, will be taking over the Theatre De Lys in Greenwich Village, it is announced. **7** As many as 70,000,000 people, about half the population of the

---

opens at Henry Miller's Theatre. It becomes Billy Wilder's 1957 film. **27** Gian-Carlo Menotti's *The Saint of Bleecker Street* (92) opens at the Broadway Theatre. It will win the Pulitzer Prize for Music and be named best musical by the New York Drama Critics Circle. It will also lose about $125,000. **29** Guy Bolton's *Anastasia* (272) opens at the Lyceum. Brooks Atkinson writes of Alan Schneider that "[t]he staging of *Anastasia* puts him in the first rank of directors." The play, starring Viveca Lindfors and Eugenie Leontovich, will become a 1956 film. **30** *House of Flowers* (165), a musical by Harold Arlen and Truman Capote about a Haitian whorehouse, opens at the Alvin, with Pearl Bailey, Juanita Hall, Diahann Carroll, in her Broadway debut, Ray Walston, Geoffrey Holder, and Alvin Ailey.

JANUARY 27 Albert Hague and Arnold B. Horwitt's *Plain and Fancy* (461), a musical about the Amish, is at the Mark Hellinger. Richard Derr and Shirl Conway star, with Barbara Cook. "It Wonders Me" is the most prominent song.

FEBRUARY 1 Frances Sternhagen makes her New York debut in Jean Anouilh's *Thieves Carnival* (152), at the Cherry Lane. **10** *The Desperate Hours* (212), which Joseph Hayes has adapted from his novel, opens at the Barrymore. Robert Montgomery directs Karl Malden, Nancy Coleman, Paul Newman, and George Grizzard, in his Broadway debut, in a story of a family held hostage by criminals in their own home. The film premieres in October. **23** Christopher Fry's *Dark Is Light Enough* (69), a drama set in Hungary in 1848, starring Tyrone Power and Katharine Cornell, is at the ANTA Playhouse. Christopher Plummer and Sydney Pollack are also in the cast. **24** Cole Porter's *Silk Stockings* (478), adapted from the film *Ninotchka*, opens at the Imperial. Don Ameche stars, with Hildegarde Neff and Gretchen Wyler. Songs include "Paris Loves Lovers." It will become a 1957 film. **28** Ben Bagley's *Shoe String Revue* (96) opens at the President Theatre, with Bea Arthur, Chita Rivera, Dody Goodman, Arte Johnson, Rhoda Kerns, Sheldon Harnick, and Charles Strouse.

---

unusual step of running national advertising for his hit show *Fanny* to pull in the out-of-town trade and is also going underground, advertising on the subway. **31** The U.S. Supreme Court, overruling a federal district court, orders the reinstatement of the Justice Department's antitrust suit against the Shuberts. It directs that the suit go to trial.

MARCH 28 "The ANTA Album" anthology of scenes from several shows, staged tonight at the Adelphi Theatre, is simultaneously broadcast over closed-circuit television to theatres in 31 other cities. Most of these venues can fill no more than half their seats, and the picture quality is poor. Tickets are priced from $2 to $10.

APRIL 15 Equity's first contract with an off-Broadway company outside of New York is with the recently founded Actors Studio Workshop, headed by Jules Irving and Herbert Blau.

MAY • Actors Equity attacks the group calling itself Aware, which has suggested that many actors are either red-tinged or agents of communism. **15** Rodgers and Hammerstein announce that they will no longer ban benefits and theatre parties from their shows, a policy they began

---

FEBRUARY 27 Trixie Friganza d.

APRIL 25 Constance Collier d.

Personalities

U.S., watch Mary Martin and Cyril Ritchard in *Peter Pan* on NBC tonight. It closed at the Winter Garden only nine days ago. The two-hour "special," which cuts into the sale of tickets to Broadway shows, trounces the video competition on this Monday night from "I Love Lucy," "Arthur Godfrey's Talent Scouts," and George Burns and Gracie Allen.

APRIL 1 Rehearsing in New Haven for the pre-Broadway tryout of a new musical called *Damn Yankees*, Gwen Verdon receives scalp lacerations when a curtain drops, hitting her in the head. **20** *The New York Times*'s Brooks Atkinson, Broadway's most influential critic, departs for two months abroad, leaving second-string reviewer Lewis Funke to cover such upcoming shows as *Damn Yankees* and *Inherit the Wind*.

MAY 28 Diana Barrymore returns to the cast of *Pajama Tops* in Boston that she left last month because of "laryngitis," since compounded by an overdose of barbiturates. "I only try to calm my nerves," she says, claiming the overdose was accidental.

Plays and Musicals

MARCH 2 "Having written a wonderful play two years ago [*Picnic*], William Inge has now written a better one. He calls it *Bus Stop* [478]," says Brooks Atkinson. Directed by Harold Clurman, it opens at the Music Box, where Kim Stanley has turned down star billing in what she regards as an ensemble production, which includes Elaine Stritch and Albert Salmi. Marilyn Monroe plays the chanteuse in next year's film. **24** Tennessee Williams's *Cat on a Hot Tin Roof* (694) opens at the Morosco. Burl Ives is Big Daddy; Barbara Bel Geddes is Maggie the Cat; and Ben Gazzara is the alcoholic Brick, with Mildred Dunnock, Pat Hingle, Madeleine Sherwood, Sonny Terry and Brownie McGhee. Smoldering passion, hetero- and homosexual, and "mendacity" underpin the plot. A few critics note what John Chapman calls the "dirty talk," some of which disappears after opening night when New York City License Commissioner Edward T. McCaffrey asks to see the script. It's a movie in 1958.

APRIL 21 *Inherit the Wind* (806), Jerome Lawrence and Robert E. Lee's drama based on the 1920s Scopes "Monkey Trial," in which the state of Tennessee challenged the teaching of evolution, opens at the National. Prosecutor William Jennings Bryan (Brady in the play) says: "I am more interested in the Rock of Ages than the ages of rocks." Paul Muni, Ed Begley, and Tony Randall star. It's a 1960 film.

MAY 5 *Damn Yankees* (1,019), by Richard Adler and Jerry Ross, opens at the Forty-sixth Street Theatre. This story of a bedeviled Washington Senators fan, who longs to have his team beat the dominant Yankees, stars Gwen Verdon and Ray Walston. Stephen Douglas and Jean Stapleton are also prominent in the cast. Among the songs are "Heart," "Whatever Lola Wants," and "Two Lost Souls." The film version is released in 1958 and the show is revived on Broadway in 1994.

Business and Society

with *Annie Get Your Gun*. Rodgers says: "The public wasn't interested in our crusade. . . . The Party system has been accepted as a normal way of going to the theatre. Furthermore, benefit audiences haven't been as cold as they used to be." **19** Members of Actors Equity and Chorus Equity vote to merge.

Births, Deaths, and Marriages

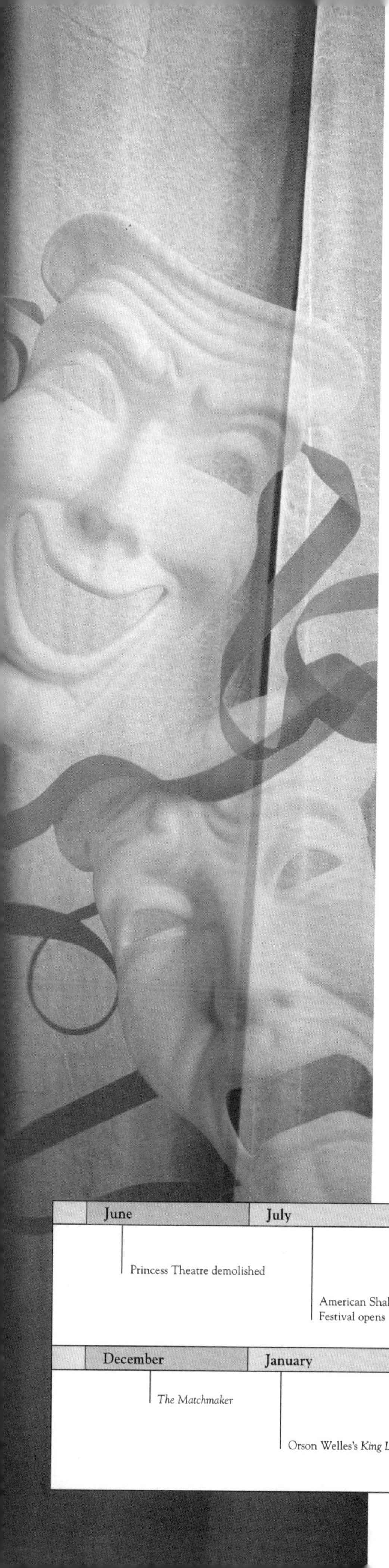

1955–56

The government tells the Shuberts: shrink. *Life* magazine's caption to go with the photo of cockney-costumed Julie Andrews, "She Sings on Broadway In Major New Musical," has to be the understatement of the year. Yet the CBS-financed *My Fair Lady*, with its hit parade songs and best-selling original cast album, does not itself set the tone for the direction of show music, for rock 'n roll is being born, and it has a future on the Broadway stage, too. Jason Robards, Jr. comes into his own in *The Iceman Cometh*, which doesn't hurt José Quintero, either. David Merrick and Kim Stanley make news, Jerry Orbach arrives off-Broadway, and the *Village Voice* invents the "Obie" Awards to acknowledge off-Broadway accomplishments. And with the opening of *Waiting for Godot*, things are really getting "absurd."

- What Boston's censor took out of *Will Success Spoil Rock Hunter?*: 3 "goddam's" and a "son of a bitch"
- Announced, for the first time: Tony Awards nominations
- Televised for the first time (locally, in New York): the Tony Awards ceremonies, on the Dumont Network
- What Michael Myerberg, producer of *Waiting for Godot*, says in ads to people thinking of seeing the play: "I respectfully suggest that those who come to the theatre for casual entertainment do not buy a ticket to this attraction."
- Conversation overheard from couple leaving the John Golden Theatre before the end of *Waiting for Godot*, according to the *New York Post*:
  Husband: "I tell you honey, it's profoundly significant. It's Death they're waiting for, I tell you."
  Wife: "I don't care. Let them wait. If I stay much longer, I'll be his first victim tonight."
- First Obie award for best actor: Jason Robards, Jr., in *The Iceman Cometh*. Julie Bovasso wins for best actress in *The Maids*.
- What Oscar Hammerstein II tells Stephen Sondheim, who is thinking of turning down an offer to write the lyrics for a new musical called *West Side Story* because he wants to compose: "I think you ought to do this."

Productions on Broadway: 56

Pulitzer Prize for Drama: *The Diary of Anne Frank* (Francis Goodrich and Albert Hackett)

New York Drama Critics Circle Awards:
Best American Play: *The Diary of Anne Frank* (Francis Goodrich and Albert Hackett)
Best Foreign Play: *Tiger at the Gates* (Jean Giraudoux)
Best Musical: *My Fair Lady* (Lerner and Loewe)

Tony Awards:
Play: *The Diary of Anne Frank* (Frances Goodrich and Albert Hackett)
Actor in a Play: Paul Muni (*Inherit the Wind*)
Actress in a Play: Julie Harris (*The Lark*)
Musical: *Damn Yankees* (Richard Adler and Jerry Ross)
Actor in a Musical: Ray Walston (*Damn Yankees*)
Actress in a Musical: Gwen Verdon (*Damn Yankees*)

June	July	August	September	October	November
Princess Theatre demolished	American Shakespeare Festival opens	Producer Margo Jones d.	Paul Muni loses eye	*The Diary of Anne Frank*	Kim Stanley leaves *Bus Stop*

December	January	February	March	April	May
The Matchmaker	Orson Welles's *King Lear*	Shubert consent decree	*My Fair Lady*	*Waiting for Godot*	*The Most Happy Fella* and *The Iceman Cometh*

Personalities

JUNE • Noel Coward opens at the Desert Inn in Las Vegas, where he plays two shows a night for a reported $30,000–$40,000 a week. He needs the money.

AUGUST 21 Among the 15,000 gathered in Central Park for an "Oklahoma Song Fest" are the governors of New York and Oklahoma, Richard Rodgers and Oscar Hammerstein II, television emcee Ed Sullivan, Eddie Fisher, and Red Buttons, all of whom are chauffeured to the stage in a surrey with a fringe on the top. The film version of the Broadway musical opens in October.

SEPTEMBER • *Threepenny Opera* cast replacement Jerry Orbach "has spent four seasons in summer stock and been a featured singer in the Chicago area," notes the program for the play. He will spend three years in this show, playing several roles, including Mack the Knife. Orbach will also play poker backstage with young Ed Asner and Jerry Stiller. • David Merrick stalks out of a meeting of the League of New York Theatres, allegedly annoyed be producer Cy Feuer's remark that Merrick's friend producer Herman Shumlin is "the rudest guy in show business." For his part, Shumlin quits the League, saying, "I do not see how I can object to this remark of Feuer's for it is common knowledge that he is the most polite and considerate man in show business." **6** Paul Muni's left eye is removed because of a tumor. He left *Inherit the Wind*, in which he has been starring, last week, replaced by an understudy. Melvyn Douglas has been engaged as a more permanent replacement. **9** Ethel Merman is the guest on Edward R. Murrow's television program "Person-to-Person."

OCTOBER • After putting up with a 20-year "chronic cough," Katharine Cornell has an operation to remove an abscess on her lung. The surgery has been precipitated by her role in *Dark Is Light Enough*, which calls for her to be dead onstage for several minutes, during which a coughing spell would be disastrous. • The new working title of Lerner and Loewe's musical based on Shaw's *Pygmalion* is "My Lady Liza,"

Plays and Musicals

JULY 12 The American Shakespeare Festival opens in Stratford, Connecticut. The first production is *Julius Caesar*, with Hurd Hatfield in the title role, and Roddy McDowall, Raymond Massey, Christopher Plummer, Jack Palance, Leora Dana, Polly Rowles, and Jerry Stiller.

SEPTEMBER 29 Arthur Miller's *A View from the Bridge* (149) opens on Broadway, at the Coronet. The cast includes Van Heflin, J. Carroll Naish, Eileen Heckart, Jack Warden, and Richard Davalos.

OCTOBER 3 *Tiger at the Gates* (217), the witty treatment of the "inevitability" of war by Jean Giraudoux, translated by Christopher Fry, is at the Plymouth. Michael Redgrave heads a cast that includes Leueen MacGrath, Morris Carnovsky, Nehemiah Persoff, and Diane Cilento as Helen of Troy. **5** *The Diary of Anne Frank* (717), a drama by Frances Goodrich and Albert Hackett, based on the manuscript left by the young Jewish girl who almost survived the Holocaust by hiding from the Nazis in a house in Amsterdam, opens at the Cort. Susan Strasberg plays Anne, and Joseph Schildkraut is her father. It's filmed in 1959. **13** George Axelrod's *Will Success Spoil Rock Hunter?* (444) opens at the Belasco. Starring in this spoof of Hollywood are Jayne Mansfield, as a Marilyn Monroe-like character, Orson Bean, Martin Gabel, as an agent who is clearly supposed to be Irving "Swifty" Lazar, Walter Matthau, and Tina Louise. Axelrod arrives at Sardi's to await the reviews accompanied by Swifty Lazar. **20** Andy Griffith stars at the Alvin in Ira Levin's comedy about a rube in the military *No Time for Sergeants* (796). It becomes a film in 1958. **26** *The Chalk Garden* (182), by Enid Bagnold, opens at the Barrymore. The cast includes Siobhan McKenna, in her Broadway debut, Fritz Weaver, Betsy von Furstenburg, Gladys Cooper, Marian Seldes, and Percy Waram. There is a 1964 British film version.

NOVEMBER 9 The Actors Studio production of Michael V. Gazzo's *Hatful of Rain* (398) opens at the Lyceum. This play

Business and Society

JUNE • The Princess Theatre on West Thirty-ninth Street, where the modern musical began, and in later years films were shown, is demolished. • Actors Equity indicates to summer stock producers that with hurricanes becoming seemingly a regular occurrence on the East Coast, theatres may no longer be allowed to classify the storms as "acts of God," justifying the nonpayment of salaries for performances canceled.

AUGUST 24 The steel beam holding up the water tower atop the Forty-eighth Street Theatre collapses this morning, sending the tank hurtling down into the empty auditorium, causing considerable damage. Demolition of the house will complete the process.

OCTOBER 14 Zero Mostel testifies before the House Un-American Activities Committee, refusing to say if he was a member of the Communist Party in the 1940s. His participation in left-wing benefits in that decade has already blacklisted him, limiting his employment in recent years. **14** The Actors Studio moves into its first permanent quarters, a converted church on West Forty-fourth Street.

Births, Deaths, and Marriages

JUNE 11 Walter Hampden d. **17** Producer John Golden d. Golden, whose productions totaled more than one hundred, once worked as a bricklayer at the building of the Garrick Theatre. **19** Julie Haydon m. critic George Jean Nathan.

JULY 24 Producer Margo Jones d. of kidney failure, caused by the inhalation of fumes from cleaning fluid. Her friend Tennessee Williams once described the founding artistic director of Theatre '47 in Dallas as "a combination of Joan of Arc and Gene Autry—and nitroglycerine."

SEPTEMBER 1 Philip Loeb commits suicide. He was active in Actors Equity and was removed from the television series "The Goldbergs" because of his left-wing politics. According to Margaret Webster, in a letter in *The New York Times* on September 16, "he died of a sickness com-

and Julie Andrews has been cast in the female lead role opposite Rex Harrison. **22** Noel Coward and Mary Martin are "Together With Music" on CBS TV tonight.

NOVEMBER • After missing many performances in *Bus Stop* because of illness and exhaustion, Kim Stanley leaves the Broadway production before the expiration of her contract. Barbara Baxley replaces her. **21** The Fulton Theatre, which opened on April 27, 1911, as the Folies-Bergere, is renamed the Helen Hayes Theatre. **28** Carol Channing is on the cover of *Life* in her costume from her new show *The Vamp*, about movie star Theda Bara, which opened November 10. This is probably the high point for the production, which will lose more than $350,000. And a drawing of Julie Harris as Joan of Arc in *The Lark* graces the cover of *Time*. **29** Performing in *The Lark*, Julie Harris splits her lip in an onstage fall, necessitating the ringing down of the curtain and a call for a doctor in the house. Temporarily patched up, she resumes her scene in the second act.

DECEMBER 1 Paul Muni, who lost an eye in an operation three months ago, returns to the Broadway production of *Inherit the Wind*, receiving an ovation from the cast as well as the audience.

JANUARY 3 Rehearsals for Lerner and Loewe's musical version of *Pygmalion* begin. Julie Andrews is learning a Cockney accent from an American phonetics professor and is struggling with the part of Eliza. Director Moss Hart will have to dismiss the rest of the company for a weekend to work just with her.

FEBRUARY 11 In an interview in *Cue*, the New York entertainment magazine, Kim Stanley says that the theatre today is being hurt by critics, who are a "bunch of fatheads." In two weeks, she will claim she was misquoted and that she really said "boneheads."

MARCH 18 On this Sunday morning, at 10:00, the cast of *My Fair Lady* assembles in Columbia's Thirtieth Street studio in Manhattan to record the original cast album. As a precaution against offending

---

about drug addiction stars Shelley Winters and Ben Gazzara. Also in the cast are Anthony Franciosa, Harry Guardino, Frank Silvera, and Henry Silva, with a film appearing in 1957. **17** *The Lark* (229), Jean Anouilh's version of the story of Joan of Arc, adapted by Lillian Hellman, opens at the Longacre. Julie Harris stars, with Christopher Plummer, Boris Karloff, Joseph Wiseman, and Theodore Bikel. There is choral music composed by Leonard Bernstein. **30** Wagnerian soprano Helen Traubel is a whorehouse madam in the Rodgers and Hammerstein musical *Pipe Dream* (246), at the Shubert. It features the Broadway debut of Judy Tyler, whose career will be cut short in two years by a fatal auto accident. Songs include "The Man I Used to Be," "All at Once You Love Her," and "Ev'rybody's Got a Home But Me," recorded by Eddie Fisher.

DECEMBER 5 Thornton Wilder's *The Matchmaker* (486), opening at the Royale, will be the source for the musical *Hello, Dolly!* Ruth Gordon is Dolly Levi this time, directed by Tyrone Guthrie, with Loring Smith as Horace Vandergelder. Robert Morse, in his Broadway debut, is Barnaby Tucker. The comedy is, itself, a reincarnation of the 1938 failure *The Merchant of Yonkers*. It's filmed in 1958.

JANUARY 12 Orson Welles, at the City Center, directs and stars in *King Lear* (21). He has "more genius than talent," says Brooks Atkinson in his *Times* review.

FEBRUARY 8 Paddy Chayefsky's *Middle of the Night* (477) opens at the American National Theatre and Academy (ANTA) Theatre. Based on the author's teleplay about an aging garment manufacturer in love with a younger woman, it stars Edward G. Robinson, back on Broadway for the first time in 25 years, and Gena Rowlands. It's on the screen in 1959.

MARCH 15 Alan Jay Lerner and Frederick Loewe's *My Fair Lady* (2,717) opens at the Mark Hellinger. The stars are Rex Harrison, who acknowledges a vocal range of "one and a half notes," as Professor Higgins, Julie Andrews as Eliza Doolittle, and Stanley Holloway as her father Alfred P. Doolittle. Also in the cast are Cathleen Nesbitt, Robert Coote, and

---

FEBRUARY • "Moritat," an instrumental of the "Mack the Knife" music from Kurt Weill and Bert Brecht's *The Threepenny Opera*, becomes the first hit recording generated by an off-Broadway show. **17** The six-year-old Justice Department antitrust suit against the Shubert organization is settled by a consent decree. The theatre empire agrees to divest itself of four of its New York houses and eight theatres out of town. It will also have to end various business practices and sever its relationship with the United Booking Office.

MARCH • Actors Equity, disturbed at the increasing number of foreign actors working on Broadway, insists that producers consult the union before engaging anyone from abroad. • Pressure from Boston's mayor and the threat of a congressional investigation push J.J. Shubert into restoring critic Elliot Norton to the press list, from which he was removed in January. The first opening he covers is *The Most Happy Fella*, which he applauds.

---

monly called 'the blacklist.'"

OCTOBER 12 Producer Arthur Hammerstein, son of the original Oscar Hammerstein and uncle of Oscar Hammerstein II, d.

NOVEMBER 9 Tom Powers d. **11** Jerry Ross, who wrote *Damn Yankees* with Richard Adler, d. at age 29. **14** Playwright Robert E. Sherwood d.

JANUARY 9 Florence Henderson m. casting director Ira Bernstein.

FEBRUARY 3 Nathan Lane (Joseph Lane) b. **13** Frances Sternhagen m. actor Tom Carlin, with whom she made her New York debut two years ago in Anouilh's *Thieves Carnival*. And Polly Bergen m. Freddie Fields of MCA. **25** Producer Alexander Cohen m. actress Hildy Parks. **26** Vaudeville star Elsie Janis d.

MARCH 8 John Emerson d. **17** Fred Allen d.

APRIL 3 Kim Stanley divorces Curt Conway. **21** Playwright Charles MacArthur, hus-

Personalities

any religious sensibilities, a line in Stanley Holloway's song "Get Me to the Church on Time" is changed from "for God's sake get me to the church on time" to "be sure and get me to the church on time." The session won't end until 3:00 Monday morning. By midweek, 100,000 copies of the LP will be on their way to record stores. **26** That cockney flower girl on the cover of *Life* is Julie Andrews. "She Sings on Broadway in Major New Musical," says the headline.

MAY 17 Noel Coward draws harsh criticism when he does not get off the boat from France when it docks in Plymouth, England.

Rex Harrison and Julie Andrews in *My Fair Lady* PF

Plays and Musicals

Reid Shelton. Among the songs: "The Rain in Spain," "I Could Have Danced All Night," "On the Street Where You Live," and "Get Me to the Church on Time." Audrey Hepburn, chosen to star in the 1964 Oscar-laden film version with Rex Harrison and Stanley Holloway, will have her voice dubbed by Marni Nixon. **22** *Mr. Wonderful* (383), a star vehicle for Sammy Davis, Jr., opens at the Broadway Theatre. This Larry Holofcener-George Weiss musical, with additional songs by Jerry Bock, features the title tune and "Too Close for Comfort" and costars Jack Carter and Chita Rivera.

APRIL 19 For John Chapman in the *Daily News*, Samuel Beckett's *Waiting for Godot* (59) is "merely a stunt, but not without its charms." The play is at the John Golden Theatre for a limited engagement. "Nothing happens, nobody comes, nobody goes—it's terrible," observes one character. *Variety* calls it a "theatrical

Business and Society

Births, Deaths, and Marriages

band of Helen Hayes, stepfather of actor James MacArthur, brother of John T. MacArthur, and publisher of *Theatre Arts*, d. His longtime collaborator Ben Hecht delivers the eulogy at the funeral.

MAY 12 Louis Calhern d.

Coward is moving to Jamaica to avoid high British income tax rates and needs to establish residency abroad. Disembarking would undermine his status.

whatsit" about "a couple of bums" with "no story and no action." But the cast, including E.G. Marshall, Bert Lahr—"the most satisfying thing I have ever done"—Kurt Kasznar, and Alvin Epstein are praised by all. Lahr professes not to understand any of his lines in this first real taste that Americans get of the theatre of the absurd.

MAY 3 *The Most Happy Fella* (676), Frank Loesser's 30-number operatic musical, based on Sidney Howard's 1924 play *They Knew What They Wanted*, is at the Imperial Theatre. Robert Weede, Jo Sullivan, and Art Lund star in this story of the California wine country. When the show hit a snag in tryouts, Loesser reached into his trunk and came up with a song that didn't make it into *Guys and Dolls*: "Standing on the Corner." "Big D" is also in the score. **8** José Quintero's revival of the 1946 Eugene O'Neill play *The Iceman Cometh* (565), opening at the Circle in the Square, off-Broadway, makes Quintero a major figure in the theatre and does the same for the young actor in the lead role. "Jason Robards, in the difficult part of Hickey," writes Richard Watts, Jr. "gives a brilliant performance." Peter Falk is also in the cast. **22** Ben Bagley's *The Littlest Revue* (32) opens at the Phoenix. The cast includes Charlotte Rae, Larry Storch, Tammy Grimes, and Joel Grey. *Variety* notes that the latter "was a cute-looking youngster with his old schnoz (he appears to have bobbed it)" and in this show "is a limber lad in everything he does."

1956–57

Any season that offers both *Auntie Mame* and *Long Day's Journey Into Night* has something for everyone. Any season is one step ahead when Maggie Smith is one of Leonard Sillman's *New Faces*. In that show, there are also words by another fresh Broadway voice—Neil Simon. Joseph Papp takes his shows into a park, where he showcases young Colleen Dewhurst, and David Merrick is interested in Gypsy Rose Lee's autobiography. Arthur Miller marries Marilyn Monroe; then he's indicted for not cooperating with HUAC. And pity the poor critic, who has to sit through everything. Walter Kerr finds the musical *Shangri-La* "rather deadly" and calls *Candide* a "great ghostly wreck." Meanwhile, in Germany, *The Diary of Anne Frank* is widely seen and pondered.

- Top ticket price for musicals: $8.05
- Top price for straight plays: $6.90
- Cost of producing a major Broadway musical: $400,000
- Cost of staging a straight play: $150,000
- Profit from the Broadway run of *Cat on a Hot Tin Roof* (closed November 17, 1956), including sale of film rights to MGM: about $470,000
- What Carol Lawrence will remember about *Shangri-La*, the musical version of *Lost Horizon*: "We were always so embarrassed by that show. You really had to work hard to mask your humiliation."
- Amount lost by *The Ziegfeld Follies*: about $350,000
- Appearing in a Mexico City production of *My Fair Lady*: aspiring opera tenor Placido Domingo
- Sardi's personnel receiving free theatre tickets from management to keep them *au courant* with Broadway: the head waiter, the night head waiter, the second-floor head waiter, and the head bartender
- Amount of capital invested in the Phoenix Theatre in its first 4 seasons: $400,000
- Amount lost by the Phoenix over four seasons: about $375,000
- What the cast of *Hatful of Rain* substitutes for the phrase "grabbing me," deleted by the Boston censor: "doing things"
- Cole Porter's American Society of Composers, Authors, and Publishers (ASCAP) royalties: $71,500
- Irving Berlin's ASCAP royalties: $102,000
- Number of original cast and film soundtrack record albums of Rodgers and Hammerstein musicals that have been sold since World War II: 3,750,000

Productions on Broadway: 62

Pulitzer Prize for Drama: *Long Day's Journey Into Night* (Eugene O'Neill)

New York Drama Critics Circle Awards:
Best American Play: *Long Day's Journey Into Night* (Eugene O'Neill)
Best Foreign Play: *The Waltz of the Torreadors* (Jean Anouilh)
Best Musical: *The Most Happy Fella* (Frank Loesser)

Tony Awards:
Play: *Long Day's Journey Into Night* (Eugene O'Neill)
Actor in a Play: Frederic March (*Long Day's Journey Into Night*)
Actress in a Play: Margaret Leighton (*Separate Tables*)
Musical: *My Fair Lady* (Lerner and Loewe)
Actor in a Musical: Rex Harrison (*My Fair Lady*)
Actress in a Musical: Judy Holliday (*Bells Are Ringing*)

June	July	August	September	October	November
Arthur Miller m. Marilyn Monroe	*My Fair Lady* film must wait	Christopher Plummer m. Tammy Grimes	Siobhan McKenna on *Life* cover	Rosalind Russell in *Auntie Mame*	*Long Day's Journey Into Night*

December	January	February	March	April	May
Candide disaster	Tallulah pounds door, breaks hand	*Visit to a Small Planet*	Amanda Plummer b.	Lunt-Fontanne's TV debut	Merrick buying Gypsy Rose Lee book

Personalities

JUNE • Elmore Torn, understudy to Alex Nichol's Brick in *Cat on a Hot Tin Roof*, is Rip Torn. When Torn takes over in Nichol's absence, it's his first Broadway role. **21** Judith Anderson is so swept up in her TV performance (live) in the play *The Circular Staircase* that she utters the word "damn" on the air. CBS will apologize tomorrow. **26** Morris Carnovsky makes his first appearance at the American Shakespeare Festival at Stratford, Connecticut, where he will play through the 1975 season. He is appearing as the Earl of Salisbury in *King John* today, but his most notable roles will be Shylock and Lear.

JULY • Alan Jay Lerner, in Hollywood to write a screenplay for the musical film *Gigi*, says of offers made for the film rights to *My Fair Lady*: "We want to wait and get a better idea of the value of the show—an idea of just how long it will run."

AUGUST 15 With Christopher Plummer unable to go on, his understudy William Shatner has the title role in *Henry V* at the Stratford, Ontario, Shakespeare Festival.

SEPTEMBER • Among the young actors receiving American Theatre Wing scholarships are James Earl Jones and Robert Prosky. **10** On the cover of *Life* is Siobhan McKenna, as she appears in *Saint Joan*.

OCTOBER • Harold Clurman is the second Broadway director since David Belasco, in 1925, to be named by France as a Chevalier of the Legion of Honor. **4** With the folding of *The Boston Post*, critic Elliot Norton will move to the Hearst-owned *Boston Daily Record*.

NOVEMBER 8 Returning to his column in the *Journal-American* after an illness, critic George Jean Nathan gives "thumbs up" to last night's opening of *Long Day's Journey Into Night* but has some reservations about the acting—an odd attitude to take by someone who did not attend the performance but rather is basing his piece on a reading of the script. **12** *Life's* cover celebrates Rosalind Russell in *Auntie Mame*, "Broadway's Red-Hot Hit." **19** In the *Playbill* for *The Girls of Summer*,

Plays and Musicals

JUNE 13 *Lost Horizon*, a bestselling novel and a beloved movie, has become a musical disaster. The final rehearsal of *Shangri-La* (21) this afternoon (opening night) should have been a warning. Part of the mountainous scenery topples, threatening to bury the cast in plastic. "Rather deadly," is Walter Kerr's assessment. "Limited Horizon" is the *Daily Mirror's* headline. The 1973 musical film will fail just as dismally. **14** Leonard Sillman's *New Faces* (220) opens at the Ethel Barrymore Theatre. In the cast are Maggie Smith and Inga Swenson, and one of the sketches is by Neil and Danny Simon. **29** Joseph Papp's free Shakespeare performances move into the 2,000-seat, concrete East River Park Amphitheater, on New York's Lower East Side, with a production of *Julius Caesar*.

AUGUST • Colleen Dewhurst is Katherine in Joseph Papp's production of *The Taming of the Shrew*, at his East River Ampitheatre space. Dewhurst's performance in it and in *The Eagle Has Two Heads*, also off-Broadway, will bring her an Obie Award.

SEPTEMBER 11 Siobhan McKenna stars in Shaw's *St. Joan* (77), at the Phoenix.

OCTOBER 4 "Playhouse 90," the peak of live drama on television, is broadcast for the first time. This CBS series, the principal director of which is John Frankenheimer, will air such plays as *The Miracle Worker* and *The Days of Wine and Roses*. **25** Terence Rattigan's *Separate Tables* (332) opens at the Music Box. Margaret Leighton and Eric Portman star in a story about loneliness among older people. The screen version will appear in 1958. **30** George Bernard Shaw's *Major Barbara* (232), opening at the Martin Beck tonight, is directed by and stars Charles Laughton, with Burgess Meredith, Cornelia Otis Skinner, Glynis Johns, and Eli Wallach. **31** Rosalind Russell commands the stage in *Auntie Mame* (639), a comedy by Jerome Lawrence and Robert E. Lee, at the Broadhurst. The plot, about her efforts to raise her nephew, is a vehicle for Russell's oddball, irrepressible, imaginative, scattered, and altogether appealing character, who will also be fea-

Business and Society

JUNE 22 Arthur Miller testifies before HUAC, acknowledging attendance at meetings of Communist front groups in the past but also refusing to name other writers who were there. **27** A Shubert executive tells a congressional committee looking into the withholding of press privileges from Boston critic Elliot Norton that he was denied free tickets because he "went out of his way to 'pour it on.'" The executive also maintains that Shubert reduced its advertising in Norton's paper for business reasons, not as punishment.

JULY 11 The New York State Court of Appeals rules that J.J. Shubert must give an accounting of his brother Lee's estate. The ruling is in response to a suit brought by two other Shubert relatives, both executors of the estate.

OCTOBER • Seven productions of *The Diary of Anne Frank* open throughout Germany. Audiences often sit stunned and silent at the final curtain. **1** Columbia Records increases the list price of original cast recording LPs from $4.98 to $5.98. Its *My Fair Lady* album has already sold almost $3,250,000 worth of records at $4.98, compared to the slightly more than

Births, Deaths, and Marriages

JUNE 2 Billy Rose m. actress Joyce Matthews. **6** Margaret Wycherly d. **18** Gretchen Wyler, now appearing in *Silk Stockings*, m. Sheppard Coleman, cellist in the pit band of *The Most Happy Fella*. **29** Arthur Miller m. Marilyn Monroe. "Bride is a film actress," says *Variety* with typical understatement. "[H]e's a playwright."

AUGUST 14 Playwright Bertolt Brecht d. **19** Christopher Plummer m. Tammy Grimes. **27** Gloria Vanderbilt m. Sidney Lumet.

SEPTEMBER 5 After divorcing Alexander Carson this morning, Carol Channing m. Charles Lowe, a TV executive who will become her manager.

OCTOBER 9 Producer-director Hassard Short d.

NOVEMBER 21 Cherry Jones b.

at the Longacre Theatre, in small print, between the act summary and the credits for the companies supplying props, is the line: "Song—*Girls of Summer*—composed by Stephen Sondheim." It's his first Broadway composition. **29** Judy Holliday, playing a switchboard operator in *The Bells Are Ringing*, actually was a switchboard operator at Orson Welles's Mercury Theatre.

DECEMBER • Rosemary Harris, back in the U.S. after several years in her native Britain, makes a decision about her career: "There are no good parts for women in the English theatre nowadays. I don't want to spend the rest of my life playing in Shakespeare." So she will remain in America to work. **6** *Happy Hunting*, opening tonight, is a sometimes unhappy show for Ethel Merman, who doesn't get along with costar Fernando Lamas. At the first rehearsal, Lamas objected to the way that Merman was delivering her lines. When she replied that she had been doing it for 25 years that way, he responded, "That doesn't mean you're right. That just means you're old." **31** Ethel Merman is on the cover of *Newsweek*.

JANUARY 12 Despite several broken ribs, Tallulah Bankhead is playing in Philadelphia in the pre-Broadway run of *Eugenia*. But even she will have to miss several performances when she breaks her hand pounding on a door onstage tonight. **14** Members of the cast of *Li'l Abner* are on the cover of *Life*. **31** Kim Stanley, who has had unkind words for critics, is on NBC's "Tonight" show, supposedly to discuss and debate the issue with the critics, but none of those invited show up this evening.

FEBRUARY 9 It's not often controversial Kim Stanley, star of *Clearing in the Woods*, who causes the commotion at the Belasco tonight. It's Onslow Stevens who has been unwilling to take direction and has deviated from the script. Joan Lorring, also in the cast, finally refused to go on with him, and he has declined to appear at the final performance tonight.

MARCH 3 In a *TV Guide* interview, television and B movie actress Anne Bancroft says, banging her fist on a table for

tured in the 1966 musical *Mame* in the person of Angela Lansbury. Bea Lillie will eventually replace Russell, who also stars in the 1958 film.

NOVEMBER 7 *Long Day's Journey Into Night* (390) opens at the Helen Hayes Theatre, violating Eugene O'Neill's wish that it not be staged until 25 years after his death. José Quintero directs Frederic March, Florence Eldridge, Bradford Dillman, Kathleen Ross, and Jason Robards, Jr., in this story of the Tyrones. *Variety* says that Robards, as the older brother, "comes through with a rousing pyrotechnical performance." And it calls the play "a monumental, overwhelming drama, terrible in its ruthlessness, searing in its self-revelation, exalting in its pity and

Frederic March

shattering in its impact." Brooks Atkinson, in the *Times*, declares that with this production, "the theatre acquires size and stature." **15** *Li'l Abner* (693), a musical based on the Al Capp comic strip, starring Peter Palmer, Edie Adams, and Stubby Kaye, opens at the St. James. "Jubilation T. Cornpone" is the highlight of the Gene de Paul-Johnny Mercer score. A film version is released in 1959. **29** At the Shubert, Judy Holliday is a wacky switchboard operator in *The Bells Are Ringing* (925). The score includes Jule Styne's "Just in Time" and "The Party's Over," with lyrics by Comden and Green, and there's Jerome Robbins and Bob Fosse's choreography, and costar Sydney Chaplin to supply Holliday's onstage—and offstage—love interest.

$1,800,000 taken in at the box office so far. **4** *The Philadelphia Inquirer* story about the Shuberts' allocating tickets to two agencies exclusively in that city, with reports of kickbacks, brings charges of monopoly against the organization and calls for another congressional antitrust investigation. Before the month is out, the Shuberts will end this practice. **24** "Yiddish Theatre Barely Alive," reports a *Variety* headline.

NOVEMBER 19 The Producers Theatre, a group whose principals include producers Robert Whitehead and Roger L. Stevens, buys *Playbill*.

FEBRUARY • The off-Broadway theatres, Circle in the Square, the Cherry Lane, and the Theatre De Lys, all in Greenwich Village, are using cooperative advertising on a single billboard and also in each other's programs. **18** Arthur Miller is indicted for contempt of Congress for refusing to answer questions posed to him by the House Un-American Activities Committee.

FEBRUARY 2 Producer Mike Todd m. actress Elizabeth Taylor. **13** Anne Bancroft and Martin May divorce.

MARCH 1 Judy Holliday divorces David Oppenheim. **4** Frank Loesser and Lynn Garland divorce. **12** Josephine Hull d. **23** Tammy Grimes, wife of Christopher Plummer, gives birth to a girl Amanda Plummer, who will also go on the stage. (Christopher's third wife, Elaine Taylor, will later say of him that he "dislikes children intensely. He likes dogs.") Amanda's middle name is Michael, after Michael Learned.

APRIL • Playwright Herb Gardner and actress Rita Gardner m. **1** Producer Jed Harris m. actress Bebe Allen. **24** Nanette Fabray m. screenwriter Ranald MacDougall. **29** Belle Baker d.

MAY 4 Shelley Winters m. Anthony Franciosa. **9** Ezio Pinza d.

Personalities

emphasis, "Someday people will know who I am." She's never recognized on the street. Recently divorced, she adds: "I'm interested in only four men: my father, my agent, my press agent and my analyst." **18** Beatrice Lillie is on the cover of *Life* on the occasion of the opening of a new edition of *The Ziegfeld Follies*, which flops.

APRIL • Diana Barrymore's autobiography *Too Much, Too Soon* is published. It's been serialized in *Look* magazine and is headed for the screen for release next year, with Dorothy Malone playing Diana and Errol Flynn as her father John Barrymore. **1** Alfred Lunt and Lynn Fontanne make

Judy Holliday in *Bells Are Ringing* PB

Plays and Musicals

DECEMBER 1 "Three of the most talented people our theater possesses—Lillian Hellman, Leonard Bernstein, Tyrone Guthrie—have joined hands to transform Voltaire's *Candide* [73] into a really spectacular disaster," says Walter Kerr. "Who is mostly responsible for the great ghostly wreck that sails like a Flying Dutchman across the fogbound stage of the Martin Beck?" Also aboard are Barbara Cook and Max Adrian. Brooks Atkinson, calling it a musical of "distinction," is in the minority. **6** Ethel Merman is in *Happy Hunting* (412), at the Majestic, with Fernando Lamas, and a Lindsay-Crouse book to go with a Matt Dubey-Harold Karr score. **18** Uta Hagen plays the title character in Bertolt Brecht's *The Good Woman of Setzuan* (24), at the Phoenix Theatre. The cast, directed by Eric Bentley, also includes Zero Mostel, Jerry Stiller, Ann Meara, Gerald Hiken, and Albert Salmi.

JANUARY 17 Ralph Richardson and Mildred

Business and Society

Births, Deaths, and Marriages

their TV debuts on NBC in *The Barretts of Wimpole Street.*

MAY • Actors Equity suspends John Barrymore, Jr. for his conduct at a summer stock theatre in 1954. He never appeared to answer charges filed against him at the time, but the matter was moot, since he had not worked on the stage until his recent stint at the Pasadena Playhouse. **13** Bert Lahr is on the cover of *Life*, on the occasion of the opening of *Hotel Paradiso.* **14** In the Chicago production of *Waiting for Godot*, opening tonight at the Studebaker Theatre, one of the tramps is played by Harvey Korman, and young Mike Nichols is getting some exposure as Lucky. **29** *Variety* reports that "David Merrick is in the process of acquiring Gypsy Rose Lee's new book *Gypsy, a Memoir,* for Broadway production as a musical."

Natwick star in Jean Anouilh's acerbic comedy *Waltz of the Torreadors* (162), opening at the Coronet. Richardson plays a retired French general, contemplating his extramarital love life. The film is released in 1962. **28** The play is abridged, the staging experimental, and *Hamlet* (2) is no gentleman when Siobhan McKenna plays him at the Theatre De Lys.

FEBRUARY 7 Cyril Ritchard is the dapper alien in Gore Vidal's comedy *Visit to a Small Planet* (388), at the Booth. He had aimed to visit the Earth during the Civil War but accidentally landed during the television-infested 1950s instead. Jerry Lewis stars in the 1960 film. **13** Joseph Fields and Peter de Vries's *The Tunnel of Love* (417), a wisecracking comedy about child-rearing in suburbia, starring Tom Ewell, opens at the Royale. It's a 1958 film.

MARCH 21 *Orpheus Descending* (68), Tennessee Williams's revision of his 1940 *Battle of Angels*, opens at the Martin Beck. Harold Clurman directs, and Maureen Stapleton and Cliff Robertson star. Brooks Atkinson, calling it Williams's "pleasentest play," couldn't have seen the production that Richard Watts, Jr., describes as "steeped in passion, hatred, frustration, bitterness and violence, and it ends in a welter of blood and death worthy of one of the Elizabethan tragedies." **31** Rodgers and Hammerstein's *Cinderella*, a 90-minute musical they have written for television, is shown on CBS. Julie Andrews stars, with Howard Lindsay, Dorothy Stickney, Ilka Chase, and Kay Ballard.

APRIL 11 Bert Lahr stars in *Hotel Paradiso* (108), a Georges Feydeau and Maurice Desvallières comedy, adapted by Peter Glenville, at Henry Miller's Theatre. It's Angela Lansbury's Broadway debut.

MAY 14 Bob Merrill's *New Girl in Town* (431), a musical version of *Anna Christie*, is at the Forty-sixth Street Theatre. Gwen Verdon, George Wallace, Cameron Prud'homme, and Thelma Ritter star, and the book and direction are by George Abbott.

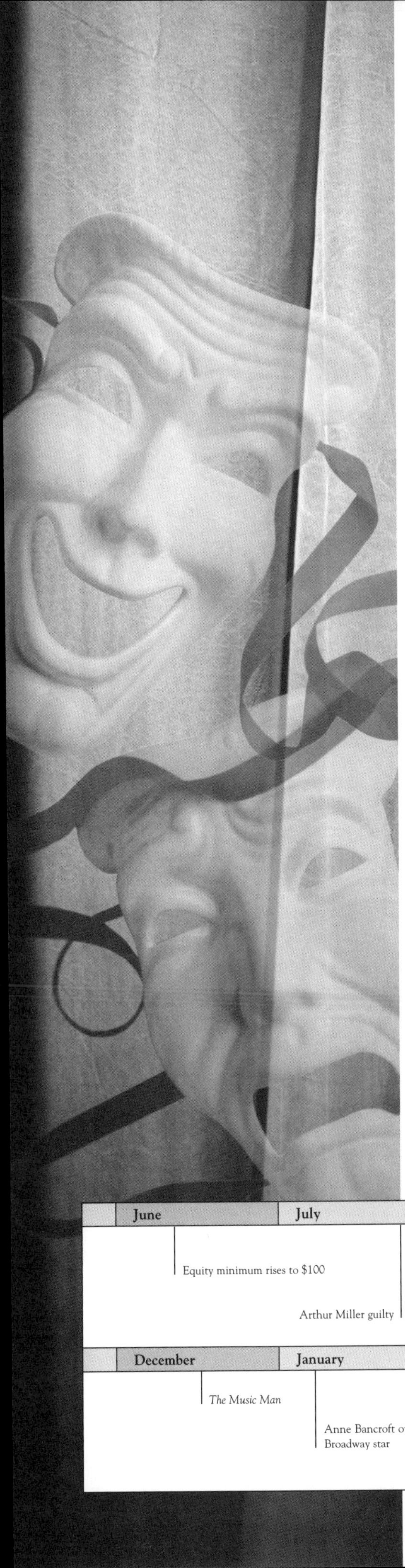

1957–58

The Equity weekly minimum for principal players on Broadway reaches $100. Morris Carnovsky and Katharine Hepburn offer a memorable *Merchant of Venice* at the American Shakespeare Festival at Stratford, Joseph Papp has Stiller and Meara, and the Lunts, like Helen Hayes, become a theatre. *Variety*, understandably, stumbles over a new player in the Broadway theatre business, calling it "Jumjamcyn." Broadway gets a look at what's making John Osborne angry, David Merrick has the magic touch, and Anne Bancroft is living out a fantasy. Rex Harrison bows out of *My Fair Lady*, Robert Preston's Professor Harold Hill may just be the most tuneful con man ever, and gee, Officer Krupke—you're in one swell show.

- Number of David Merrick productions playing on one block on Forty-fifth Street: 4—*Jamaica, Romanoff and Juliet, Look Back in Anger*, and *The Entertainer*
- Current nickname for this stretch of Forty-fifth Street: "The Merrick Parkway" (after the Merritt Parkway in nearby Connecticut)
- What the head waiter at Sardi's calls David Merrick: "Sir David"
- Why CBS turned down a chance to back *The Music Man*: the network's executives found it "corny" at an audition
- Capacity of newly renamed Lunt-Fontanne Theatre, formerly the Globe: 1,402
- What new Broadway star Anne Bancroft has played so far in B movies: Richard Widmark's girlfriend, Broderick Crawford's daughter, and Anthony Quinn's sister
- One reason why Stephen Sondheim hesitated to write the lyrics for *West Side Story*: he said he didn't know any Puerto Ricans; in fact, he didn't know any poor people at all
- Two-character plays on Broadway that preceded this season's *Two for the Seesaw*:
  The First Fifty Years (Henry Myers, 1922)
  Jealousy (Eugene Walters, 1928)
  Close Quarters (Gilbert Lennox, 1939)
  The Fourposter (Jan de Hartog, 1951)
- What producer Mike Todd liked to say on the phone to impress whomever was in the room with him: "I don't need that kind of money. You'll want me to put your mother-in-law in the chorus and I'll blow a million dollars for your lousy ten 'g's."

Productions on Broadway: 56

Pulitzer Prize for Drama: *Look Homeward Angel* (Ketti Frings)

New York Drama Critics Circle Awards:
Best American Play: *Look Homeward Angel* (Ketti Frings)
Best Foreign Play: *Look Back in Anger* (John Osborne)
Best Musical: *The Music Man* (Meredith Willson)

Tony Awards:
Play: *Sunrise at Campobello* (Dore Schary)
Actor in a Play: Ralph Bellamy (*Sunrise at Campobello*)
Actress in a Play: Helen Hayes (*Time Remembered*)
Musical: *The Music Man* (Meredith Willson)
Actor in a Musical: Robert Preston (*The Music Man*)
Actress in a Musical: a tie between Thelma Ritter (*New Girl in Town*) and Gwen Verdon (*New Girl in Town*)

June	July	August	September	October	November
Equity minimum rises to $100	Arthur Miller guilty	Merman-Lamas feud	*West Side Story*	*Look Back in Anger*	Nichols and May a "New Act"

December	January	February	March	April	May
The Music Man	Anne Bancroft overnight Broadway star	Colleen Dewhurst and George C. Scott meet	David Merrick has four hits	Cole Porter loses leg	Globe Theatre becomes the Lunt-Fontanne

Personalities

JUNE • Ethel Merman, interviewed in the *World-Telegram and Sun* about opening night audiences, complains that the one for *Happy Hunting*, in which she's now appearing, was "as dead as fish." She goes on: "All those cafe society people who come to see themselves and not see the show, jabbering about who's got who's husband, all coming in late, full of martinis, and all those dames saying 'I've got three bracelets, how many have you got?'" **7** Tennessee Williams writes to his friend Maria St. Just: "Since the failure of *Orpheus* [*Orpheus Descending*] my stock has fallen enormously." Twenty-four hours later, he will inform her: "I am supposed to leave tomorrow for the plush-lined loony-bin at Stockbridge, Massachusetts, and the start of analysis." **12** A *Variety* reviewer, who caught Carol Burnett at the Blue Angel night club, writes that she "looms like a potential in the comedy song field." The theatre gossip column in the same issue notes that "Carol Lawrence, currently appearing in *The Ziegfeld Follies*, and Larry Kert and Chita Rivera have been set for the cast of the upcoming Broadway musical, 'Gang Way.'" Right cast, wrong title—it's going to be called *West Side Story*.

AUGUST • "He has upstaged me since the play opened," says Ethel Merman about her *Happy Hunting* costar Fernando Lamas. Lamas has been stepping on her lines and wiping off her stage kiss in front of the audience. To preserve the peace, the producers replace the kiss with a hug. Then, another dispute arises when actor Gene Wesson is fired from the play. He accuses Merman of instigating his dismissal.

SEPTEMBER 1 The newspapers are reporting that Judy Holliday and her *Bells Are Ringing* costar Sydney Chaplin are in Switzerland to tell his father Charlie Chaplin that they will marry. But their romance will not survive their European trip. **29** *The New York Times* medical reporter Dr. Howard Rusk writes that Puerto Ricans are objecting to Stephen Sondheim's lyric "island of tropic diseases" in *West Side Story*, from the song "America." Rusk says that it's not true and that it hits below the belt.

Plays and Musicals

JULY 10 Morris Carnovsky's first Shylock, at the American Shakespeare Festival at Stratford, is, says John Chapman in the *Daily News*, "a creation of extraordinary depth and perception." And he calls Katharine Hepburn's Portia "a girl of intelligence, humor and iron determination—which is almost type-casting."

SEPTEMBER 26 "Tonight, tonight, it all begins tonight" for *West Side Story* (732), at the Winter Garden. Leonard Bernstein and Stephen Sondheim have written "Tonight," "Maria," "I Feel Pretty," "Somewhere," and "America," and Jerome Robbins and Peter Gennaro have choreographed this update of *Romeo and Juliet* that has evolved musically, ethnically, and geographically from the original idea of 1949 that had it as *East Side Story*. Carol Lawrence, Larry Kert, and Chita Rivera have major roles. The film version is released in 1961.

OCTOBER 1 *Look Back in Anger* (407), by John Osborne, opens at the Lyceum. "If Mr. Osborne is disgusted with England today, he is also disgusted with the pallor of British drama," writes Brooks Atkinson. The cast is headed by Alan Bates, Mary Ure, and Kenneth Haigh. The 1958 film stars Richard Burton. **8** Tyrone Guthrie directs an acclaimed production of Schiller's *Mary Stuart* (56), at the Phoenix Theatre, with Irene Worth, Eve Le Gallienne, and Max Adrian. **10** Peter Ustinov's *Romanoff & Juliet* (389), a comedy-romance with an operetta-like plot, opens at the Plymouth, where he's the star. **24** Meyer Levin and Robert Thom's adaptation of Levin's novel *Compulsion* (140) opens at the Ambassador. Starring in this dramatization of the Leopold and Loeb case are Dean Stockwell, Roddy McDowall, Howard Da Silva, Barbara Loden, and Ina Balin. It's a 1959 film. **31** Calypso comes to the Imperial in Harold Arlen and Yip Harburg's *Jamaica* (555), starring Lena Horne and Ricardo Montalban, with Adelaide Hall, Ossie Davis, Erik Rhodes, and Alvin Ailey. "Push the Button" is the most notable song. Frank Aston writes in the *World-Telegram and*

Business and Society

JUNE 11 The League of New York Theatres averts a possible Equity strike by agreeing to raise the weekly minimum for principal players from $85 to $100. The union also institutes a sliding scale for off-Broadway, with the highest minimum $75 a week for shows grossing at least $4,500.

JULY • Arthur Miller is convicted of contempt of Congress for refusing to answer questions posed by the House Un-American Activities Committee, fined $500, and given a one month suspended jail sentence. **31** According to *Variety*, the Shuberts, under the recent consent decree, have sold the St. James Theatre to the "Jumjamcyn" company. It's actually Jujamcyn, which William H. Knight, chairman of Minnesota Mining and Manufacturing, who started it, has named for his grandchildren: Judith, James, and Cynthia.

AUGUST 8 The Palace drops vaudeville for good.

SEPTEMBER 27 Today's Sunday *New York Times* will not carry the drawing of the nude couple grappling on the floor, submitted by David Merrick's office to

Births, Deaths, and Marriages

JUNE 8 Mike Nichols m. television singer Pat Scot. **27** Lee J. Cobb m. Mary Hirsch.

JULY 3 Judy Tyler, age 24, who had a major role in the Rodgers and Hammerstein show *Pipe Dream* and just finished filming *Jailhouse Rock* with Elvis Presley, is killed in an auto accident.

AUGUST • George S. Kaufman and Leueen MacGrath divorce. **11** Mary Ure m. John Osborne, and playwright David Henry Hwang b.

SEPTEMBER 24 Leo Lindemann, founder of Lindy's restaurant, d.

DECEMBER 1 Chita Rivera m. Tony Mordente who, like her, is appearing in *West Side Story*. **19** Playwright John Van Druten d. **20** Lyricist Alan Jay Lerner and Nancy

OCTOBER 31 Lena Horne, in *Jamaica,* is playing a part rewritten from the original because it was recast from male to female when Harry Belafonte had to pass it up because of illness.

NOVEMBER 4 "Ellen McRae, a newcomer to the Broadway stage, is a picture of loveliness," says *The New York Times* review of *Fair Game,* which opened last night with the actress who will become Ellen Burstyn. **13** In its "New Acts" section, *Variety* reviews the comedy team of Mike Nichols and Elaine May, calling them "hipster's hipsters." Detecting the mark of the Actors Studio in their routines, the reviewer notes that Nichols "studied with Lee Strasberg, while the femme was put through her thesping

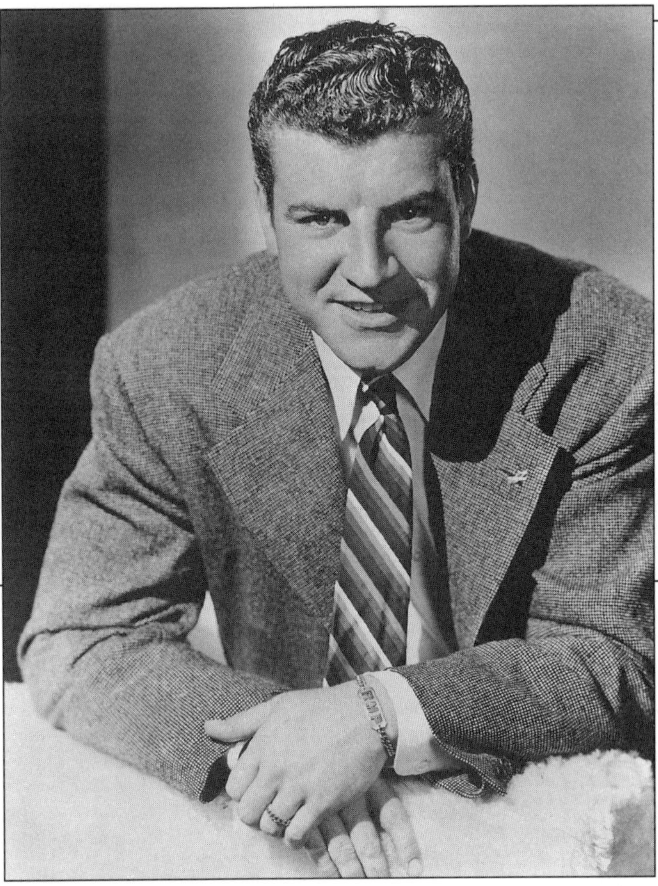

Robert Preston MSN

Sun that "its comedy may be appropriate to dusky natives of a Caribbean island, but it's not memorable." But the *Times* finds it "delightful."

NOVEMBER 12 *Time Remembered* (248), a comedy by Jean Anouilh, opens at the Morosco. Helen Hayes is the duchess who schemes to cure the prince, played by Richard Burton, of his broken heart. **14** Noel Coward's *Nude With Violin* (189), a comic rant against modern art, opens at the Belasco. The playwright also directs and stars, with a cast that includes Morris Carnovsky. **20** *The Rope Dancers* (189) opens at the Cort. Morton Wishengrad's play about an Irish-American family is directed by Peter Hall—his Broadway debut—and stars Siobhan McKenna as a wife who wields guilt like a sword and Art Carney, in his Broadway debut, as her weak husband. **28** Thomas Wolfe's *Look Homeward Angel* (564), adapted for the stage by Ketti Frings, opens at the Barrymore. George Roy Hill directs Anthony Perkins as the sensitive Eugene Gant, with Jo Van Fleet and Hugh Griffith as his parents.

DECEMBER 5 William Inge's *The Dark at the Top of the Stairs* (468) opens at the Music

accompany its ad for *Look Back in Anger*. The *Times* finds it too racy, although other papers print it.

OCTOBER • The Ford Foundation makes its first grants to the arts, including $130,000 to the Cleveland Playhouse. • Actors Equity chastises David Merrick for paying the British cast of *Look Back in Anger* a mere pittance. One of the union's executives also says that Merrick's "contest" to choose an ingenue for the female lead in *Romanoff & Juliet* was fixed.

NOVEMBER • The newly formed League of Off-Broadway Theatres opposes what it calls Actors Equity's "unilateral" pronouncements about how producers should conduct their relationships with their casts. One of the union's directives is that cast members must begin to receive medical coverage by November 17. **26** Actors Equity decides that actor Gene Wesson's complaint that Ethel Merman got him fired from *Happy Hunting* has no substance, and they censor Wesson and apologize to Merman.

JANUARY • Author Meyer Levin wins a $50,000 judgement against Kermit Bloomgarden, producer of *The Diary of Anne Frank,* and Otto Frank, Anne's father, for use of material from his drama-

Olson were recently divorced, and today he m. Micheline Muselli Pozo Di Borgo.

JANUARY 3 Composer Richard Adler (*Pajama Game, Damn Yankees*) m. Sally Ann Howes. The marriage will be over by 1966. **7** Margaret Anglin d.

FEBRUARY 5 Composer Lew Brown d. **20** Thurston Hall d.

MARCH 2 Edith Taliaferro d. **22** Producer Mike Todd is killed in a plane crash. He once said that he had turned down the opportunity to invest $10,000 for a 25 percent stake in *Oklahoma!* because the show didn't seem to be sexy enough. **24** Librettist Herbert Fields d.

APRIL 8 Critic George Jean Nathan d. He once wrote, "There are two kinds of dramatic critics: destructive and constructive. There are two kinds of guns: Krupp and pop." **22** Playwright Clare Kummer d.

Personalities

paces by the late Maria Ouspenskaya."

DECEMBER 23 Rex Harrison gives his 750th and last performance in the original Broadway production of *My Fair Lady*. Surreptitiously playing minor parts tonight are Kay Kendall, who married Harrison on June 23 of this year, and the show's director Moss Hart.

JANUARY 17 The *New York World-Telegram and Sun* reports, "Anne Bancroft, a pretty girl from the Bronx, woke up downtown today to realize an old and silly dream she had had in Christopher Columbus High School had come true: overnight she had become a Broadway star."

FEBRUARY 10 Ralph Bellamy, as Franklin D. Roosevelt in *Sunrise at Campobello*, is on the cover of *Life* magazine. **28** When the Circle in the Square revives *Children of Darkness*, the play's not the thing; it's the cast, two young and upcoming members of which meet during this production and later wed. They are Colleen Dewhurst and George C. Scott.

MARCH • It hasn't happened often on Broadway that a producer has had four simultaneous hits. Now David Merrick has *The Entertainer*, *Jamaica*, *Look Back in Anger*, and *Romanoff and Juliet*. • Producer Max Gordon requests that Actors Equity contribute to a statue of George M. Cohan in Times Square. With the memory of Cohan's vehement opposition to the union's great strike of 1919 still strong, a contribution of $250 comes back, not coincidentally the cost of a lifetime membership in Actors Equity. Oscar Hammerstein II, head of the committee building the monument, returns the check, noting his refusal "to cooperate with you in pinpricking George's ghost." **3** Sally Ann Howes, "Broadway's New 'Fair Lady'"—she's replaced Julie Andrews—is the subject of *Life*'s cover story.

APRIL 3 Cole Porter's right leg is amputated because he has developed the bone disease osteomyelitis, caused by his 1937 fall from a horse. **15** *The Boston Globe* reports that Paddy Chayefsky told

Plays and Musicals

Box. Pat Hingle, as the salesman who sells harnesses, a dead-end business in the new auto age, and Teresa Wright as his wife, star in what Brooks Atkinson calls "an uncommonly forgiving drama about the things that people do not know about each other." Eileen Heckart is also in the cast. It will reach the screen in 1960. **19** Robert Preston is "Professor" Harold Hill in *The Music Man* (1,375), "right here in River City," which comes alive at the Majestic. Meredith Willson's musical costars Barbara Cook as "Marian the Librarian." Preston, making his Broadway musical debut, sings "Seventy-six Trombones." The opening-night audience loves it, clapping in time to the beat just before the curtain falls. "Trouble," "Gary, Indiana," and "Till There Was You" are also in the score. Preston stars in the 1962 film with Shirley Jones.

JANUARY 16 *Two for the Seesaw* (750), by William Gibson, starring Ann Bancroft and Henry Fonda, opens at the Booth. *Variety* says it's "potential material for pictures" (the 1962 film stars Shirley MacLaine and Robert Mitchum) and declares that Bancroft is "an attractive, interesting looker, with a strong personality, and is a prospect for a big career." The paper adds: "Arthur Penn, a recruit from television, is an impressively resourceful and expressive stager." **28** Samuel Beckett's *Endgame* (104), directed by Alan

Anne Bancroft MSN

Business and Society

tization of her diary in their Broadway play. They had turned down his version for one by Albert and Francis Hackett. The New York State Supreme Court, however, will overturn the award.

APRIL • Ralph Bellamy has declined a third term as president of Actors Equity, and the nominating committee has proposed for the job, to be filled in June, Frederick O'Neal, the first black person ever selected for the post. • The three LPs heading the bestseller list at Goody's, the huge retailer and mail order house in New York City, are original cast albums: *The Music Man*, *West Side Story*, and *My Fair Lady*.

MAY • With the first black proposed for its presidency, an insurgent movement has been brewing in the ranks of Actors Equity, and sentiment is growing for an independent candidate to oppose Frederick O'Neal. Fearing that such a contest would have ugly racial overtones, Ralph Bellamy agrees to take a third term, and O'Neal withdraws. **24** Douglas Watt of the *New York Daily News* is one of the first critics—possibly the first—to use the term off-off-Broadway.

Births, Deaths, and Marriages

26 Playwright-producer Philip Moeller d.

MAY • Hal Linden m. chorus girl Frances Martin. **8** Stage designer Norman Bel Geddes, father of Barbara Bel Geddes, d.

Ralph Bellamy

Harvard students about New York's critics that "[w]riters suffer more from the attacks of the nine incompetents—who are usually drunk—than they would from the most violent personal onslaught." The playwright says the paper got it wrong. There are seven critics, and what he said was that "[y]ou cannot dismiss a whole city's critics as incompetent drunks."

MAY 5 The celebrity audience greeting the renamed Lunt-Fontanne Theatre on the opening night of *The Visit,* includes Katharine Cornell, Laurence Olivier, Helen Hayes, Anita Loos, Mary Martin, Beatrice Lillie, Henry Fonda, and Ginger Rogers.

Schneider, opens off-Broadway at the Cherry Lane Theatre. This play, which Richard Watts, Jr. calls "one long outpouring of almost entirely static nihilism," stars Lester Rawlins and Alvin Epstein, with P.J. Kelly and Nydia Westman as a couple who spend their entire time onstage in garbage cans. Says director Schneider: "I've tried to work in more laughs than the Paris production had."
30 Ralph Bellamy plays the young Franklin D. Roosevelt, coping with polio, in Dore Schary's *Sunrise at Campobello* (556), opening at the Cort. Mary Fickett is Eleanor Roosevelt. Making his Broadway debut is seven-year-old Richard Thomas. James Earl Jones is also in the cast. Bellamy repeats in the 1960 screen version, with Greer Garson.

FEBRUARY 12 John Osborne's *The Entertainer* (97), starring Laurence Olivier as Archie Rice, with Joan Plowright and Brenda de Banzie, opens at the Royale Theatre. The same cast stars in the 1960 film.

APRIL 3 *Say Darling* (332), with music by Jule Styne, lyrics by Betty Comden and Adolph Green, and book by Abe Burrows collaborating with Marian Bissell, opens at the ANTA Playhouse. It's about an author whose book becomes a Broadway musical. The stars are David Wayne, Jerome Cowan, Robert Morse, Horace McMahon, and pop singer Johnny Desmond, in his Broadway debut.

MAY 5 With opening night of Friedrich Duerrenmatt's *The Visit* (189), starring Alfred Lunt and Lynn Fontanne, the Globe Theatre on Forty-sixth Street is renamed the Lunt-Fontanne. The play, which the *Times* calls "devastating drama," is filmed in 1964.

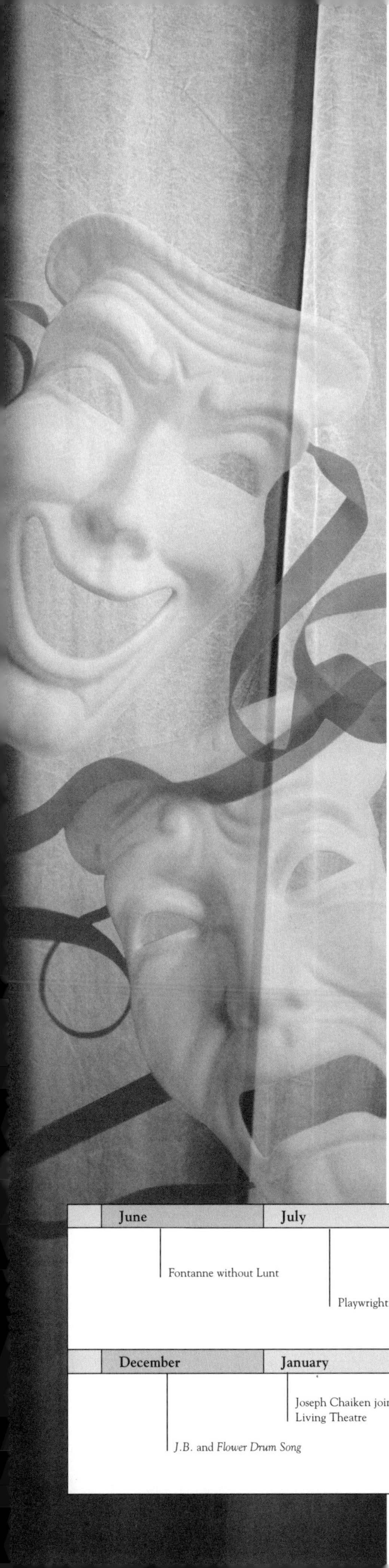

1958–59

Joseph Papp temporarily loses his day job at CBS over his radical past. Lynn Fontanne is bereft of either an "and" or a hyphen when Alfred Lunt takes ill and she goes on without him. Alan Arkin goes unnoticed. *A Touch of the Poet* brings together Helen Hayes and Kim Stanley, "the two finest actresses of their respective generations," according to Brooks Atkinson, but Stanley leaves the cast prematurely. Playwright Lorraine Hansberry and director Lloyd Richards break through on Broadway, and Bob Fosse and Gwen Verdon are in step. In Rodgers and Hammerstein's *Flower Drum Song*, Harry Truman, Truman Capote and Dewey, make for Chop Suey. And in *The World of Suzie Wong*, William Shatner consorts with a woman for whom love is an enterprise.

- A Broadway first: the total box office gross for the season tops $40 million—$40,151,300
- Cost of the best seats in the house for *Gypsy*: $9.40
- What June Havoc, sister of Gypsy Rose Lee, thinks of the show *Gypsy*: she hates it. Her mother, played on Broadway by Ethel Merman, was, says Havoc, "tiny, fragile, beguiling—and *lethal*."
- Number of jobs available on Broadway for black actors, according to Actors Equity: 24
- How many Green Stamps earned by purchases at a New York City supermarket are required for orchestra seats for *Sweet Bird of Youth*: 4 books, earned by buying $600 worth of groceries
- How *Variety* is reporting the Tony Awards, 13 years after they were inaugurated: in passing, in a gossip column (the paper features its own poll of critics on who's best)
- Where Gwen Verdon keeps her 4 Tony Awards—*Can-Can*, *Damn Yankees*, *New Girl in Town*, and *Redhead*: "in a suitcase in a closet," she says
- What they said:
  José Ferrer, interviewed by Dave Garroway on the "Today" show: "I never got a free newspaper in my life. Why do critics get free tickets?"
  George C. Scott, quoted in the *New York Post*: "I'm not a [m]ethod actor, so I try to divorce myself from any part I play. You have to do that. Otherwise, you'd be in a terrible state—unless you were playing Elwood P. Dowd and his rabbit." [in *Harvey*]
- Waiting in the wings: Hal Linden, who takes over for Sydney Chaplin in *The Bells Are Ringing* this season, will be the understudy or standby for Sydney Chaplin in *Subways Are for Sleeping*, Keith Andes in *Wildcat*, Arthur Hill and Ronny Graham in *Something More*, Robert Alda in *What Makes Sammy Run*, Alan Alda in *The Apple Tree*, and Tom Bosley in *The Education of Hyman Kaplan*

Productions on Broadway: 57

Pulitzer Prize for Drama: *J.B.* (Archibald MacLeish)

New York Drama Critics Awards:
Best Play: *A Raisin in the Sun* (Lorraine Hansberry)
Best Foreign Play: *The Visit* (Friedrich Durrenmatt)
Best Musical: *La Plume de Ma Tante* (Robert Dhery)

Tony Awards:
Play: *J.B.* (Archibald MacLeish)
Actress in a Play: Gertrude Berg (*A Majority of One*)
Actor in a Play: Jason Robards, Jr. (*The Disenchanted*)
Musical: *Redhead* (Albert Hague and Dorothy Fields)
Actress in a Musical: Gwen Verdon (*Redhead*)
Actor in a Musical: Richard Kiley (*Redhead*)

June	July	August	September	October	November
Fontanne without Lunt	Playwright Rachel Crothers d.	Arthur Miller conviction overturned	Shuberts restore free opening night tickets	*A Touch of the Poet*	Joseph Papp ordered reinstated at CBS

December	January	February	March	April	May
J.B. and *Flower Drum Song*	Joseph Chaiken joins Living Theatre	Gwen Verdon in *Redhead*, directed by Bob Fosse	*A Raisin in the Sun*	Elmer Rice quits Playwrights Company	Carol Burnett in *Once Upon A Mattress*

Personalities

JUNE 10 Meredith Willson returns to his native Mason City, Iowa—the "River City" of *The Music Man*—for its annual band festival. No one needs to be told how many trombones there are in the special band put together to honor him. **25** When Alfred Lunt is taken to the hospital with the flu, John Wyse, his understudy, goes on for him in *The Visit*. It's the first time in decades that Lynn Fontanne has played opposite anyone but her husband. **30** Hal Linden takes over the role in *Bells Are Ringing* that had been played by Sydney Chaplin. Linden's wife, Frances Martin, a chorus girl in the show, will now watch him romance Judy

Kim Stanley and Helen Hayes in *A Touch of the Poet* PF

Plays and Musicals

JUNE 10 *Ulysses in Nighttown* (206) opens off-Broadway at the Rooftop Theatre. Zero Mostel, Beatrice Arthur, and Carol O'Connor are in this play, adapted from James Joyce's *Ulysses* by Padriac Colum and directed by Burgess Meredith.

OCTOBER 2 *A Touch of the Poet* (284), by Eugene O'Neill, directed by Harold Clurman with a cast that includes Helen Hayes, Kim Stanley, Eric Portman, and Betty Field, opens at the Helen Hayes Theatre. It's about an Irish family in nineteenth century New England. Hayes and Stanley, "the two finest actresses of their respective generations," (Brooks Atkinson) play mother and daughter. **14** Can artist William Shatner find happiness with prostitute France Nuyen in Hong Kong? The question is explored in Paul Osborn's *The World of Suzie Wong* (508), at the Broadhust. It's a 1960 film. **22** *The Pleasure of His Company* (474), a comedy by Samuel Taylor and Cornelia

Business and Society

JUNE 6 Ralph Bellamy is elected to a third term as president of Actors Equity. The name of Frederick O'Neal, the black candidate who withdrew in the face of a possibly racially tinged contest against an insurgent candidate, is still on the ballot, and he draws 757 votes to Bellamy's 1,297. **19** After Joseph Papp refuses to discuss his past connection to the Communist Party with HUAC, he's fired by CBS, where he was the stage manager of the TV show "I've Got a Secret."

AUGUST 7 A U.S. Circuit Court of Appeals overturns Arthur Miller's conviction for contempt of Congress.

SEPTEMBER 3 "Arts Subsidy Goes Bigtime," *Variety* headlines, in an article describing growing contributions by foundations to such projects as the planned Lincoln Center for the Performing Arts, scheduled to rise on Manhattan's west side. **30** Under pressure from press agents and producers, the Shuberts restore most of the free opening night tickets to the press, which they had recently cut back.

NOVEMBER 12 An arbitrator orders CBS to reinstate Joseph Papp, whom they fired

Births, Deaths, and Marriages

JUNE 21 Jerry Orbach m. actress Marta Curro, whom he met in the production of *The Threepenny Opera*. As Orbach will later put it, she was the "understudy for all the whores." **29** Joel Grey m. actress Jo Wilder.

JULY 5 Playwright Rachel Crothers d.

AUGUST 1 Kim Stanley m. actor Alfred Ryder. **16** Critic Wolcott Gibbs d.

SEPTEMBER 5 Lulu Glaser d.

OCTOBER 29 Playwright Zoe Akins d.

NOVEMBER 15 Tyrone Power d.

FEBRUARY 28 Playwright Maxwell Anderson d. He once referred to theatre critics as "The Jukes Family of Journalism" [a reference to a genetically flawed family].

Holliday at every performance.

JULY 21 *Time*'s cover story celebrates Meredith Willson's *The Music Man.*

SEPTEMBER • The *New Yorker* announces that Kenneth Tynan will replace Wolcott Gibbs, who died this summer, as its theatre critic. **24** Opening at the Gate Theatre on Second Avenue is the play *Heloise*, by James Forsythe. In it and attracting no attention is 24-year-old Alan Arkin.

OCTOBER • Tallulah Bankhead, addressing the Women's National Press Club in Washington, D.C., armed with a cigarette and a glass of bourbon, identifies several figures in public life as "bastards" and then says, on the subject of the current Vice President of the United States: "Ugh, 'Tricky Dicky!' He's already gone too far. It would be horrible for the country if he went any further." **6** France Nuyen, "Broadway's Suzie Wong," is on *Life*'s cover. **8** "Comedienne looks like a sure bet for anyone's saloon," says *Variety*'s review of Dorothy Loudon, a "trim, talented young performer" who is at New York City's Blue Angel night club. **13** Columnist Leonard Lyons reports that star or no star, Anne Bancroft still had to audition for the Actors Studio last week. "She passed."

JANUARY • Joseph Chaiken joins the Living Theatre.

FEBRUARY 16 Composer Frederick "Fritz" Loewe, of Lerner and Loewe, feels ill while having dinner at the Lambs Club. "It would be just my luck," he tells his dining companion, columnist Hy Gardner, "to get a heart attack just when I'm at the peak of success in this rough business." Within a few hours, he will be having that heart attack, causing him to retire at age 60, making the upcoming *Camelot* his last show. **20** Pat Hingle is injured in a fall down an elevator shaft. **23** According to *Life*'s cover story, Gwen Verdon's "Joyous Strutting Knocks Broadway Cold." She opened on February 5 in *Redhead.* **26** Accepting a human rights award from the National Council of Christians and Jews, Richard Rodgers says that never in his career has he encountered bigotry in the arts.

Otis Skinner, who also stars in it with Cyril Ritchard, Walter Abel, Charlie Ruggles, and Dolores Hart, in her Broadway debut, opens at the Longacre. **23** *Make a Million* (308), a comedy by Norman Barasch and Carroll Moore starring Sam Levene as a television producer, is at the Playhouse. **29** The subject is sex and marriage, the stars are Claudette Colbert and Charles Boyer, and the play is Leslie Stevens's *The Marriage-Go-Round* (308). Also in the cast at the Plymouth is Julie Newmar, who is in the 1960 film with Susan Hayward and James Mason.

NOVEMBER 7 Brendan Behan's *The Quare Fellow* (126) (slang for a condemned man) opens off-Broadway, at the Circle in the Square. Liam Clancy stars in this drama of a man who is going to be hanged. **11** Robert Dhery's revue *La Plume de Ma Tante* (835) is at the Royale. Dhery has also directed and stars in the show, with music by Gerard Calvi, most notably the popular title tune.

DECEMBER 1 Gene Kelly directs and Carol Haney choreographs Rodgers and Hammerstein's *Flower Drum Song* (600), at the St. James. Set in San Francisco's Chinatown, it tells of the problems both young and old have in understanding "The Other Generation." Other songs include "You Are Beautiful," "I Enjoy Being a Girl," "Don't Marry Me," and "Grant Avenue." Miyoshi Umeki, Larry Blyden, and Pat Suzuki head the cast, with Juanita Hall and Keye Luke. It's a 1961 film. **3** Jason Robards, Jr. stars at the Coronet in the Budd Schulberg-Harvey Breit play about F. Scott Fitzgerald *The Disenchanted* (189), in which Jason Robards, Sr. is making his first Broadway appearance since 1922. Also in the cast are Rosemary Harris, George Grizzard, and Salome Jens. **11** Archibald MacLeish's *J.B.* (364) opens at the ANTA Theatre. Brooks Atkinson calls it "one of the memorable works of the century as verse, as drama and as spiritual inquiry." The cast, directed by Elia Kazan, features Christopher Plummer as the Devil, Raymond Massey as God, and Pat Hingle as the Job-like protagonist. **28** John Gielgud's one-man show *The Ages of Man* (40) opens at the Forty-sixth Street Theatre after a 13-week tour play-

---

in June for refusing to cooperate with HUAC.

DECEMBER • The last week of the month sees Broadway's box offices taking in $1 million for the first time. **11** A strike by the deliverers hits New York City newspapers.

JANUARY 10 *'Tis Pity She's a Whore*, the eighteenth-century play by John Ford, moves from the Orpheum, where it opened on December 5, to the Greenwich Village Theatre. The Orpheum management is reportedly worried that they will be harassed by the License Commissioner's office for using the "W" word in the title. In fact, the title had been changed for a few days, simply dropping the final word, but the *Times* felt that the omission made it even more suggestive and wouldn't run an ad for it that way. **29** Fire guts the Shubert Theatre in Washington, D.C., leaving the capital with the National, where the Old Vic is now playing, as its only legitimate house.

FEBRUARY • The ad copy submitted to newspapers for the stage version of *Rashomon* reads: "Was it *rape?* Was it *adultery?* Was it *lust?* Was it *love?* See *Rashomon* and judge for yourself." The *Daily News* doesn't care what it was; it

---

MARCH 6 Fred Stone d.

APRIL 12 Actor-playwright James Gleason and Emma Trentini d. Originally an opera star, Trentini moved into musical comedy in 1910. **29** Frank Loesser m. singer Jo Sullivan, who starred in his *The Most Happy Fella.*

MAY 10 Julie Andrews m. designer Tony Walton. **16** Joe Cook d.

Personalities

MARCH 7 Fledgling television comedienne Carol Burnett writes to a friend: "The Phoenix Theatre is presenting a musical comedy spoof of the old fairytale, *The Princess and the Pea* [*Once Upon a Mattress*] to open on May 12. I auditioned yesterday and got the title role! (NOT THE PEA!). And the best part—it's to be directed by George Abbott!!" (She has the role only because Abbott wanted an unknown to play it. Mary Rodgers had Nancy Walker in mind for the part when she wrote it.) Appearing in a play directed by Abbott was her goal when she came to New York in 1954, hoping to be the next Ethel Merman or Martha Raye.

Carol Burnett MSN

20 Kim Stanley leaves *A Touch of the Poet* and is replaced by Cloris Leachman. Stanley, who had missed performances due to illness, says that "I feel fine now. I'm in excellent health." She criticizes "the artistic atmosphere of the play," and *Variety* suggests that there has been tension in the cast between Stanley and Helen Hayes over Hayes's known aversion to the Actors Studio style of playing, but Hayes denies any breach. Stanley will later place the blame for her departure on Eric Portman who, she says, could not take Harold Clurman's direction and, in one scene, where he slaps her, did not learn how to pull the blow, hurting her.

APRIL • Playwright John Osborne, opposing diatribes in the London newspapers on

Plays and Musicals

ing mostly one-night stands at colleges.

FEBRUARY 5 Bob Fosse debuts as a director as well as choreographer with *Redhead* (452), the Albert Hague–Dorothy Fields musical-mystery set in a wax museum, starring Gwen Verdon and Richard Kiley. The show, which will win six Tony awards, opens at the Forty-sixth Street Theatre. During the run, the professional partnership of Fosse and Verdon will become marital as well. Songs include "Look Who's in Love" and "Just for Once." **16** Gertrude Berg, radio and television's "Molly Goldberg," forms an improbable team with the British actor Cedric Hardwicke, playing a Japanese businessman opposite her Brooklyn housewife, in *A Majority of One* (556). This Leonard Spigelgass comedy is at the Shubert.

MARCH 10 Tennessee Williams's play about an aging actress and a gigolo, *Sweet Bird of Youth* (375), with background music by Paul Bowles, opens at the Martin Beck. Elia Kazan directs Geraldine Page, Paul Newman, Sidney Blackmer, Rip Torn, Diana Hyland, and Bruce Dern. The *Times* calls Page "fabulous," says that Newman is her match, and describes the play as one of Williams's "finest dramas." Newman and Page are in the 1962 Richard Brooks film as well. **11** Lorraine Hansberry's *A Raisin in the Sun* (530), the first Broadway play by a black woman, starring Claudia McNeil and Sidney Poitier as her son, who takes money earmarked for the purchase of a house and puts it instead into a business, opens at the Barrymore. Lloyd Richards becomes the first black man to direct a Broadway show. The supporting cast includes Diana Sands, Ivan Dixon, Louis Gossett, Lonnie Elder, and Douglas Turner Ward. McNeil and Poitier repeat their roles in the 1961 film, and in 1973, the play becomes the stage musical *Raisin*.

APRIL 23 In Harold Rome's musical version of *Destry Rides Again* (473), at the Imperial, Andy Griffith has the role played by James Stewart in the 1939 film, and Dolores Gray has Marlene Dietrich's "Frenchy" role.

Business and Society

won't run ads with the words "rape" and "adultery." The *Times* will but only if it's lust, love, adultery, and rape—in that order.

MARCH 11 "Homos, Incest, Sadism [i]n Legit; Can't Get Away With That [i]n Cafés; Myron Cohen" is *Variety*'s headline on its interview with the comedian, who says that there's been a shift with night clubs. Where almost anything used to be all right in night clubs, they are now more respectable, and the theatre pushes the edge of acceptability. **18** New York City Parks Commissioner Robert Moses says that Joseph Papp's New York Shakespeare Festival must charge admission to pay for improvements and upkeep in the area where productions are staged. Papp refuses. Unions, which have kept costs to a minimum, may expect substantial compensation if the audience pays. Moses also begins a publicity campaign to undermine Papp's public image, citing his past membership in the Communist Party and suggesting that he may be financially dishonest.

APRIL • Elmer Rice, the only remaining playwright founding member of the Playwrights Company, resigns.

Births, Deaths, and Marriages

the "evil" of homosexuality in the theatre, nevertheless grants that homosexuals have too much influence in the arts. "Ever since I started working the theatrical profession," the playwright assures readers, "I have tried to attack the dominance of homosexuals in all fields."

MAY 21 David Merrick has refused opening-night tickets for *Gypsy* to *New Yorker* critic Kenneth Tynan, apparently disturbed by his review of *Destry Rides Again*. Merrick's coproducer Leland Hayward shames his partner into backing off by offering Tynan his own seats. The critic will give a "thumbs up" to *Gypsy*. **21** Ethel Merman, in *Gypsy*, vetoed Stephen Sondheim as the composer as well as lyricist because he had no experience and opted for Jule Styne instead. Merman is getting credit for her acting for the first time, and this is also the first time she has agreed to tour with a show after its Broadway run.

MAY 11 Carol Burnett stars in *Once Upon A Mattress* (460), a musical based on the fairy tale "The Princess and the Pea," at the Phoenix. It will also play in several Broadway houses. The music, by Mary Rodgers, daughter of composer Richard Rodgers, includes "Shy." **21** It's curtain up for *Gypsy* (702), with music by Jule Styne. Walter Kerr calls it "the best damn musical I've seen in years," although Atkinson, in the *Times*, says Stephen Sondheim's lyrics are "hackneyed." This story of stripper Gypsy Rose Lee (the book is by Arthur Laurents), her sister and, especially, their stage mother, is at the Broadway Theatre. Supporting Ethel Merman, who plays Rose, are Sandra Church, Lane Bradbury, Jack Klugman, and Joe Silver. Songs include "Everything's Coming Up Roses," "Together," and "If Mama Would Marry." The 1962 film stars Rosalind Russell, Natalie Wood, and Karl Malden. **25** The 1917 Jerome Kern musical *Leave It to Jane* (928) is revived off-Broadway at the Sheridan Square Playhouse.

1959–60

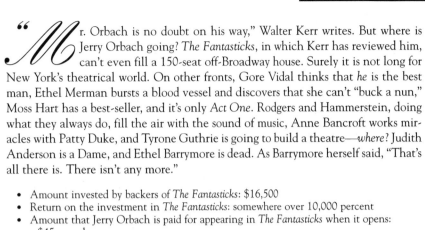

"Mr. Orbach is no doubt on his way," Walter Kerr writes. But where is Jerry Orbach going? *The Fantasticks*, in which Kerr has reviewed him, can't even fill a 150-seat off-Broadway house. Surely it is not long for New York's theatrical world. On other fronts, Gore Vidal thinks that *he* is the best man, Ethel Merman bursts a blood vessel and discovers that she can't "buck a nun," Moss Hart has a best-seller, and it's only *Act One*. Rodgers and Hammerstein, doing what they always do, fill the air with the sound of music, Anne Bancroft works miracles with Patty Duke, and Tyrone Guthrie is going to build a theatre—*where?* Judith Anderson is a Dame, and Ethel Barrymore is dead. As Barrymore herself said, "That's all there is. There isn't any more."

- Amount invested by backers of *The Fantasticks*: $16,500
- Return on the investment in *The Fantasticks*: somewhere over 10,000 percent
- Amount that Jerry Orbach is paid for appearing in *The Fantasticks* when it opens: $45 a week
- Number of weeks between Elvis Presley's release from the Army and the opening of *Bye, Bye Birdie*: 5
- Ethel Merman's reaction to Mary Martin's winning the 1960 Tony award for her performance as Maria in *The Sound of Music*, over Merman in *Gypsy*: "How do you buck a nun?"
- Question posed about by Oscar Hammerstein II to Stephen Sondheim about Richard Rodgers: "What do you think of Dick? . . . We've worked together all these years and I don't really know him."
- How being made a Dame of the British Empire will change Judith Anderson: "I find myself wearing gloves more often," says Dame Judith.
- What Noel Coward thinks about turning 60: "I certainly don't feel 60. . . . I don't think I look 60. Well, at any rate, I'm younger than Marlene Dietrich."
- Who has invested what in *The Sound of Music*:
  Mary Martin—$200,000
  Richard Rodgers and Oscar Hammerstein—$100,000
  Howard Lindsay and Russel Crouse: $80,000
  NBC—$20,000

Productions on Broadway: 57

Pulitzer Prize for Drama: *Fiorello* (book by George Abbott and Jerome Weidman; music by Jerry Bock; lyrics by Sheldon Harnick)

New York Drama Critics Circle Awards:
Best Play: *Toys in the Attic* (Lillian Hellman)
Best Foreign Play: *Five Finger Exercise* (Peter Shaffer)
Best Musical: *Fiorello* (Jerry Bock-Sheldon Harnick)

Tony Awards:
Play: *The Miracle Worker* (William Gibson)
Actress in a Play: Anne Bancroft (*The Miracle Worker*)
Actor in a Play: Melvyn Douglas (*The Best Man*)
Musical: a tie between *Fiorello!* (Sheldon Harnick and Jerry Bock) and *The Sound of Music* (Rodgers and Hammerstein)
Actress in a Musical: Mary Martin (*The Sound of Music*)
Actor in a Musical: Jackie Gleason (*Take Me Along*)

June
- Ethel Barrymore d.

July
- *The Connection*

August
- Ethel Merman bursts a blood vessel

September
- Moss Hart's book *Act One*

October
- *The Miracle Worker*

November
- *The Sound of Music*

December
- Ellis Rabb founds APA

January
- Diana Barrymore found dead

February
- *Toys in the Attic*

March
- Luther Adler denounces critic

April
- Candidate Gore Vidal

May
- *The Fantasticks*

Personalities

JUNE 30 Joseph Chaiken appears in his first Living Theatre production, Paul Goodman's *The Cave of Machpelah*.

JULY 8 Tennessee Williams writes to his friend Maria St. Just, on Diana Barrymore in a production of *A Streetcar Named Desire*, that "a couple of weeks ago, after more than the usual quota of pills and maybe a few sticks of the weed, she decided to have some scrambled eggs and somehow or other she managed to perform the neatest trick of the week, she fell ass-down, and bare-ass, into the pan of hot fat and got second-degree burns on her ass so bad that she had to go into a

Anne Bancroft stars in *The Miracle Worker* PB

Plays and Musicals

JULY 15 *The Connection* (628), Jack Gelber's play about drug addicts, accompanied by a jazz group headed by pianist Freddie Redd, opens at the Living Theatre. Directed by Judith Malina, it stars Carl Lee, Barbara Winchester, and Warren Finnerty.

OCTOBER 8 Michael Flanders and Donald Swann's two-man revue *At the Drop of a Hat* (215) is at John Golden Theatre. **19** William Gibson's *The Miracle Worker* (719), about Helen Keller, played by Patty Duke, and Annie Sullivan, the companion to the deaf and blind woman, played by Anne Bancroft, opens at the Playhouse. Bancroft and Duke win Oscars for their portrayals in the 1962 film. A television remake of the play, which itself is based on Gibson's teleplay for "Playhouse 90," will star Duke in the role of Annie Sullivan. **22** *Take Me Along*

Business and Society

JUNE 17 The New York State Court of Appeals rules that New York City Parks Commissioner Robert Moses was "arbitrary, capricious and unreasonable" in demanding that the New York Shakespeare Festival charge admission for performances in Central Park.

AUGUST 11 Lawrence Shubert Lawrence, who manages the Shubert Theatres in Philadelphia, is arrested on a charge of fraud for having offered to a broker a block of tickets that he knew he couldn't deliver.

OCTOBER 18 The National Theatre becomes the Billy Rose Theatre.

NOVEMBER 19 The Coronet Theatre, which opened in 1925 as the Forrest, becomes the Eugene O'Neill Theatre.

DECEMBER 13 The Margo Jones Theatre, founded as Theatre '47 in 1947 in Dallas, suspends operations to "reappraise" its operating and financial status.

JANUARY • Maxine Elliott's Theatre on West Thirty-ninth Street is demolished. It housed Cole Porter's first full-length

Births, Deaths, and Marriages

JUNE 18 Ethel Barrymore d. at age 79. She will be buried in Beverly Hills next to her brothers, John, who d. in 1942, and Lionel, dead since 1954. The remark that Barrymore added to the play *Sunday* in 1906, with the author's permission, became her catch phrase: "That's all there is. There isn't any more." **21** Producer Arch Selwyn d.

AUGUST • Martin Balsam m. Joyce Van Patten, a match that will last three years. **6** Clarence Derwent d. **18** Theatre Guild producer Theresa Helburn d.

SEPTEMBER 23 Jason Alexander (Jay Scott Greenspan) b. **25** Helen Broderick d.

NOVEMBER 26 Ben Gazzara m. actress Janice Rule.

hospital and whenever she sat down on the stage last night, she made a face like she had a throbbing hemorrhoid."

AUGUST • Ethel Merman bursts a blood vessel in her larynx and misses a week of *Gypsy*. • John Houseman resigns as Director of the American Shakespeare Festival over differences on artistic policy. **12** The producer at the Shubert Theatre in Cincinnati files charges with Equity after Diana Barrymore refuses to go on in *A Streetcar Named Desire*. She says she has laryngitis, but management contends it's because she has quarreled with the assistant stage manager. Her reviews have been good.

SEPTEMBER • Moss Hart's autobiography *Act One* is published and becomes one of the best-selling theatre biographies ever. **11** A bronze statue of George M. Cohan is unveiled in Times Square, opposite the Palace Theatre.

OCTOBER 1 The *New York Post* reports that "Warren Beatty, newcomer, who paid for his acting lessons at Stella Adler's school by working as a sandhog on the Lincoln Tunnel, will make his Broadway debut in the key role of Shirley Booth's son in *A Loss of Roses*." **17** John Barrymore, Jr. sails for Europe when he should be rehearsing for the October 21 opening of the road company of *Look Homeward Angel* in Wilmington, Delaware. The producer has filed charges against him with Actors Equity.

NOVEMBER • Tyrone Guthrie is visiting several U.S. cities, including San Francisco, Milwaukee, and Minneapolis, looking for a site for a new permanent repertory company. **2** Shirley Booth says that she's withdrawing from William Inge's *Loss of Roses*, now in a tryout, because of the way her part has been rewritten, pushing the younger Carol Haney and Warren Beatty into the foreground. "It's embarrassing now to be playing a third role," says Booth. **2** In costume for *Take Me Along*, Jackie Gleason sashays across the cover of *Life* magazine. **4** "*Camelot* is the new title for the Alan Jay Lerner and Frederick Loewe musical formerly called 'Jenny Kiss'd Me,'" notes *Variety*. **11** The Coronet is renamed the Eugene O'Neill Theatre. **23** Mary Martin

---

(448), Bob Merrill's musicalization of *Ah, Wilderness*, opens at the Shubert. Jackie Gleason stars, with Walter Pidgeon, Eileen Herlie, Robert Morse, Una Merkle, and Valerie Harper. The lyricists are Joseph Stein and Robert Russell, and the title tune is the most prominent one.

NOVEMBER 5 Paddy Chayefsky's *The Tenth Man* (623) opens at the Booth. The title refers to the quorum orthodox Jews need to conduct a prayer service. In the plot is a romance and an exorcism. Risa Schwartz and Donald Harron star, with Lou Jacobi, Jack Gilford, George Voskovec, and Jacob Ben-Ami. **16** "What's wrong with being sentimental?" Oscar Hammerstein II will say to the few carping critics of *The Sound of Music* (1,443), at the Lunt-Fontanne. Rodgers and Hammerstein are coproducing, with Richard Halliday and Leland Hayward, what will be their final work together. The book is by Howard Lindsay and Russel Crouse, whose original idea was to use mostly the Trapp family's music. Mary Martin stars, along with Theodore Bikel. The score includes the title song and "My Favorite Things," "Maria," "Do-Re-Mi," "Climb Every Mountain," and "Edelweiss." The 1965 film stars Julie Andrews, Christopher Plummer, and Peggy Wood. **18** Rick Besoyan's *Little Mary Sunshine* (1,143) is off-Broadway, at the Orpheum. It's a parody of the kind of operettas that Nelson Eddy and Jeanette MacDonald used to do for MGM. Star Eileen Brennan is making her New York debut. The original cast recording, on Capitol, is the first—of a whole show—for an off-Broadway musical. **23** Jerry Bock and Sheldon Harnick's *Fiorello!* (795) opens at the Broadhurst. Tom Bosley achieves stardom in his first Broadway show, about the years leading up to the election of New York City's Mayor LaGuardia and his battles with Tammany Hall. The score includes "Little Tin Box," "Politics and Poker," "Till Tomorrow," and "When Did I Fall in Love?" In the supporting cast are Howard Da Silva, Patricia Wilson, Nathaniel Fry, and Ellen Hanley.

DECEMBER 2 Jessica Tandy is at the Music Box in Peter Shaffer's *Five Finger Exercise* (337), directed by John Gielgud. The play is about a family in which husband and wife are at war with each other.

---

musical *See America First*, Jeanne Eagles in *Rain*, Lillian Hellman's *The Children's Hour*, and was once the television studio where Ed Sullivan's "The Toast of the Town" was staged. **8** The Circle in the Square moves to what was once the New Stages Theatre, on Bleecker Street in Greenwich Village.

FEBRUARY 15 The Repertory Theatre of Lincoln Center is formed.

MARCH 10 Six black theatregoers defy Georgia law and tradition, sitting in the "white" section of the Atlanta City Auditorium for a performance of *My Fair Lady*. The house manager avoids a confrontation by immediately designating the area where they are sitting a "Negro" section.

MAY • The premium brokers are allowed to charge above the price of tickets is raised from $1.25 to $1.50. **14** As a fundraiser, the Actors Studio for the first time sells tickets, priced at $50, that permit the public to view its exercise scenes. **31** Tyrone Guthrie has chosen Minneapolis for the nonprofit repertory company he will establish in the United States. He has pledged personally to stage the first three seasons of plays at the theatre, which has yet to be built.

DECEMBER 4 Rosetta Duncan d., and Rosemary Harris marries actor-director Ellis Rabb, which lasts until 1967. **14** Edna Wallace Hopper d.

JANUARY 25 The body of 38-year-old Diana Barrymore, whose biography and the film made from it, called *Too Much, Too Soon*, is found in her apartment. The doctor examining her says that she d. of "natural causes," although there are tranquilizers, sleeping pills, and empty liquor bottles nearby. **31** Adolph Green m. actress Phyllis Newman.

FEBRUARY 12 Bobby Clark d.

MARCH • Sydney Chaplin m. dancer Noelle Adam. **28** Pat Suzuki m. fashion photographer Mark Shaw.

APRIL 28 Harold Clurman, 58, m. actress Juleen Compton, 24.

MAY 4 Producer Leland Hayward m. Pamela Churchill, former wife of Randolph Churchill. **10** Maurice Schwartz d.

Personalities

is on the cover of *Life*, dressed for her wedding scene in *The Sound of Music*.

DECEMBER 24 Just as rehearsals are about to begin, George Roy Hill quits as director of Frank Loesser's *Greenwillow*. He's talked out of it, but he and Loesser will have at least one fistfight between now and opening night. In Philadelphia, at a dress rehearsal, a cow does onstage what cows often do offstage.

JANUARY • Ellis Rabb founds the Association of Producing Artists Repertory Company—the APA. The company consists of, initially, among others, Rosemary Harris (Rabb's wife), Donald Moffat, Cathleen Nesbitt, Frances Sternhagen, and playwright Tom Jones. **1** Queen Elizabeth makes Judith Anderson a Dame of the British Empire. She will be invested on July 5. When asked later how this changed her life, she will reply: "I find myself wearing gloves more often." **13** Zero Mostel suffers multiple fractures in one of his legs when hit by a bus while getting out of a cab on an icy Manhattan street. He was to appear in Garson Kanin's *The Good Soup* in a part that will now go to Jules Munshin.

MARCH 8 Frank Loesser, sensing a flop after the first act of his *Greenwillow*, leaves the Alvin to spend the rest of the opening night next door at Jilly's, Frank Sinatra's favorite New York watering hole, where he gets drunk. **17** In the process of planning a musical based on the compositions of Jerome Kern, producer Cheryl Crawford discloses that about 75 unpublished manuscripts of Kern songs have turned up. She found out about them from a singer who married Kern's widow. **29** Luther Adler, directing and starring in a touring production of Arthur Miller's *A View from the Bridge*, makes a curtain speech at the National Theatre in Washington, D.C., to denounce *Washington Star* critic Jay Carmody as "a nasty, pretentious blow-out impressed with his own importance." Carmody had described the production as "incinerated sludge."

Plays and Musicals

JANUARY 14 America has a new major playwright. Edward Albee's one-act play *Zoo Story* (582) opens at the Provincetown Playhouse. George Maharis and William Daniels star in this portrait of a deeply disaffected young man. With it is Samuel Beckett's *Krapp's Last Tape*, a one-man play starring Donald Davis.

FEBRUARY 25 Lillian Hellman's first original play in eight years, *Toys in the Attic*, (566) opens at the Hudson. Two spinster sisters fear that they will lose their brother to his new wife, touching off a tragic downward spiral of events. It's directed by Arthur Penn and stars Jason Robards, Jr., Maureen Stapleton, Ann Revere, and Irene Worth. A film version is released in 1963.

MARCH 3 Jean Genet's *The Balcony* (672), directed by José Quintero, opens at the Circle in the Square. Sylvia Myles and Salome Jens are among the employees of Nancy Marchand's bordello. "Too far out," says the *Journal-American*. A "plaster of paris play," writes Kerr in the *Herald-Tribune*. It's "the most exciting show on or off Times Square," declares George Freedly in the *Morning Telegraph*. **8** Frank Loesser's offbeat musical *Greenwillow* (95) is at the Alvin. Tony Perkins stars, along with Cecil Kellaway and Pert Kelton. **31** Will one presidential candidate reveal the homosexuality of another? That's propelling the plot in Gore Vidal's *The Best Man* (520), at the Morosco. This last play produced by the Playwrights Company stars Lee Tracy, Melvyn Douglas, and Frank Lovejoy. The film comes out in 1964.

APRIL 14 *Bye Bye Birdie* (607), Charles Strouse and Lee Adams's musical about a rock 'n roll idol, opens at the Martin Beck. Gower Champion directs his first book musical, which stars Dick Van Dyke, Chita Rivera, Paul Lynde, Kay Medford, Dick Gautier, Susan Watson, and Charles Nelson Reilly. Songs include "Put On a Happy Face," "A Lot of Livin' to Do," "Kids," and "The Telephone Hour." It's on the screen in 1963. **19** Mare Ure and Vivian Leigh engage in a

Business and Society

Births, Deaths, and Marriages

APRIL • Gore Vidal, whose play about politics *The Best Man* opened March 31, announces his candidacy for Congress in New York's 29th Congressional District.

MAY • Eighteen-year-old Barbra Streisand, a drama student from Brooklyn, is appearing in a production of *The Insect Comedy*, by Karel and Josef Čapek, at the Jan Hus Theatre in Manhattan. She plays several roles, including the second moth and second butterfly. **3** With *The Fantasticks* seemingly a failure at its opening, lyricist Tom Jones throws up in Central Park later this evening.

Jerry Orbach *MSN*

subtle joust on the issue of moral purity in Jean Giraudoux's *Duel of Angels* (51), at the Helen Hayes.

MAY 3 Who knew? *The Fantasticks*, ultimately the longest-running play in New York history, barely survives opening night at the 150-seat, off-Broadway Sullivan Street Playhouse. The reviews are lukewarm, and it will not fill the house anytime soon. The score, including "Try to Remember," is by Harvey Schmidt and Tom Jones. Starring are Jerry Orbach, Rita Gardner, and Kenneth Nelson. Walter Kerr writes that "Mr. Orbach is no doubt on his way."

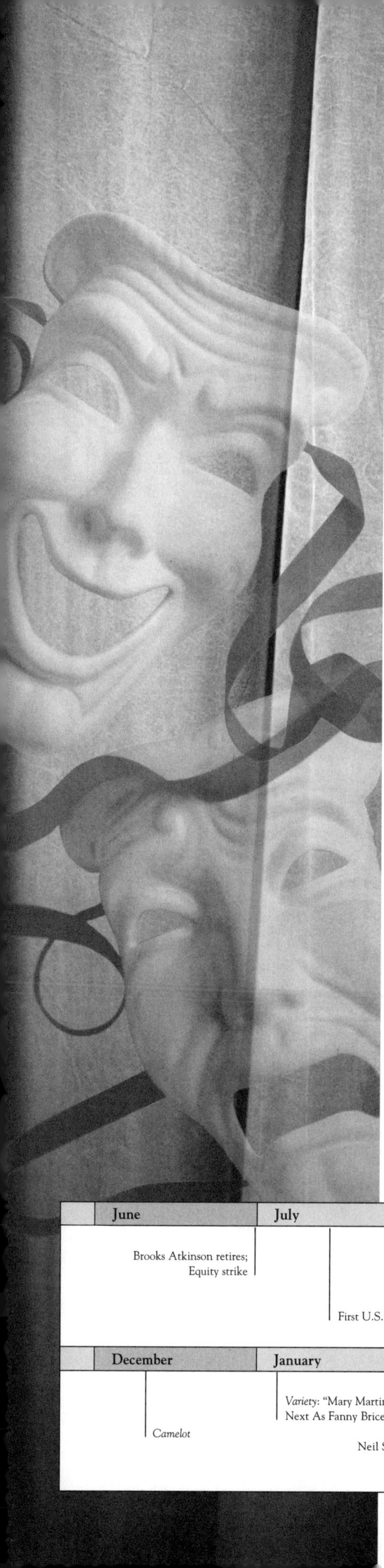

1960–61

Broadway suffers a brief strike or lockout, depending on which side is describing it. There are important productions of Jean Genet's and Edward Albee's plays, and Neil Simon is a new Broadway playwright. Brooks Atkinson gives up his job as *The New York Times* chief drama critic and has a theatre named for him. Philip Bosco gets off to a stumbling start, as does *Camelot*, which President-elect John F. Kennedy does not see, opting instead for *The Best Man*. Tennessee Williams lightens up, Jessica Tandy says Hume Cronyn is sexier than Marlon Brando, Puccini survives José Ferrer, and Brendan Behan behaves in New York, but Toronto is another matter. And Broadway pauses, turns off the lights, and contemplates the legacy of Oscar Hammerstein II.

- Number of drafts Neil Simon needs to finish his first Broadway play *Come Blow Your Horn*: 22
- Who helps *Come Blow Your Horn* become a success, despite lukewarm reviews: Noel Coward and Groucho Marx, whose endorsements are quoted in Leonard Lyons's Broadway column
- *Daily News* critic John Chapman put-down: "I see where we are going to have a play by Tennessee Williams called 'Period of Adjustment.' Whose—his?"
- Number of Secret Service agents backstage at the Morosco when President-elect John F. Kennedy arrives to see *The Best Man*: 8
- Why the new President has fewer reasons than before to say that he "owns" Broadway: City Investing Co., the real estate firm in which the Kennedys have an interest, sheds the third of the 6 Broadway theatres it once controlled
- Number of times President Eisenhower went to Washington's National Theatre in his 8 years in office: none
- Number of plays produced by Circle in the Square in its first 10 years: 20, 18 of which were directed by José Quintero
- What Tennessee Williams finds most difficult about being a playwright: "writing the piece for *The New York Times* the Sunday before my play opens"
- Winner of the first Margo Jones Award for encouraging new playwrights: Lucille Lortel, of the White Barn Playhouse in Westport, Connecticut
- How Tyrone Guthrie, establishing a repertory theatre in Minneapolis, characterizes Broadway: a "murderous, vulgar jungle"
- Number of off-Broadway professional shows: 95
- Number of Broadway theatre tickets sold to students at special rates of $1 or less: 44,407
- Number of revivals on Broadway: none, for the first time in the century

Productions on Broadway: 46

Pulitzer Prize for Drama: *All the Way Home* (Tad Mosel)

New York Drama Critics Circle Awards:
Best Play: *All the Way Home* (Tad Mosel)
Best Foreign Play: *A Taste of Honey* (Shelagh Delany)
Best Musical: *Carnival!* (Bob Merrill)

Tony Awards:
Play: *Becket* (Jean Anouilh)
Actor in a Play: Zero Mostel (*Rhinoceros*)
Actress in a Play: Joan Plowright (*A Taste of Honey*)
Musical: *Bye, Bye Birdie* (Charles Strouse and Lee Adams)
Actor in a Musical: Richard Burton (*Camelot*)
Actress in a Musical: Elizabeth Seal (*Irma La Douce*)

June	July	August	September	October	November
Brooks Atkinson retires; Equity strike	First U.S. production of a Pinter play	Oscar Hammerstein II d.	*Irma La Douce*	Moss Hart felled by heart attack	Philip Bosco's Broadway debut

December	January	February	March	April	May
Camelot	*Variety*: "Mary Martin Stars Next As Fanny Brice"	Neil Simon is a Broadway playwright	Olivier switches from King Henry to Beckett	"Rodgers and Lerner?" "Lerner and Rodgers?"	Genet's *The Blacks*

Personalities

JUNE 30 Brooks Atkinson, who turned 65 on November 28, retires as *The New York Times* daily drama critic. He will be replaced by the paper's current music critic, Howard Taubman.

JULY • Actors Equity fines John Barrymore, Jr. $5,000 for walking out of a production of *Look Homeward, Angel* last year. **4** Philip Bosco, recently with the Arena Stage in Washington, D.C., arrives in New York to audition for Joseph Papp's New York Shakespeare Festival. His car is broken into and his possessions stolen, and he makes a bad impression on Papp. It will take two more interviews and the intervention of director Alan Schneider to get Bosco hired for *Measure for Measure*. **14** Eli Wallach was to appear in the upcoming production of Ionesco's *Rhinoceros*. But producer Leo Kerz has moved up the opening, and Wallach is still filming *The Misfits*. Today, Kerz signs Ray Bolger to take Wallach's place. Not so fast, says Wallach's lawyer. And there it stands for a week until Bolger backs out. **16** Harold Pinter has his first U.S. production when the Encore Theatre in San Francisco stages *The Birthday Party*, which will open in New York in May. Until three years ago, Pinter, as an actor, was touring England under the name David Baron.

AUGUST 3 Playwright William Inge, in a letter in *Variety*, says he knew that his play *A Loss of Roses* was not up to par, giving as the reason "lack of time" to prepare it with all the changes everyone was demanding. He corrects the paper, which had reported that Inge scored the critics. "I never read them," he insists. **16** Helen Hayes is named cochairperson of the "Celebrities for Nixon-Lodge" committee. **23** From the wings of the Lunt-Fontanne, Theodore Bikel can see the mascara smear on Mary Martin's face. She's crying as she sings the title song from *The Sound of Music*. At the curtain call, she throws a kiss toward the balcony, not part of her usual routine. Lyricist Oscar Hammerstein II is dead. **31** Just before 9:00 P.M.. tonight, traffic in Times Square comes to a halt, and the entire

Plays and Musicals

SEPTEMBER 20 Brendan Behan's *The Hostage* (127), a comedy set in a Dublin whorehouse, where the I.R.A. is holding a hostage, opens at the Cort. It is said to be bawdier than the British production. Joan Littlewood directs, and the cast includes Maxwell Shaw, Alfred Lynch, and Celia Salkeld. It is revived next year at the Sheridan Square Playhouse (547). **29** *Irma La Douce* (524) opens at the Plymouth. Elizabeth Seal stars, with music by Marguerite Monnot and lyrics by David Heneker, Julian Moore, and Monty Norman. The 1963 film drops the songs but has Shirley MacLaine and Jack Lemmon.

OCTOBER 4 Nineteen-year-old Shelagh Delaney's *A Taste of Honey* (376) opens at the Lyceum. It's set in a working-class town, where a rebellious white girl sleeps with a black sailor and becomes pregnant. In the cast are Angela Lansbury, Joan Plowright, Nigel Davenport, and Billy Dee Williams. The 1961 film stars Rita Tushingham. **5** Peter Glenville's staging of Jean Anouilh's *Becket* (193) is at the St. James. Anthony Quinn is King Henry II, with Laurence Olivier playing Thomas Becket. The King's younger son is Kit Culkin, future father of McCauley Culkin. Glenville also directs the 1964 film. **8** *An Evening with Mike Nichols and Elaine May* (306), directed by Arthur Penn, opens at the Golden Theatre. **17** The new musical at the Forty-sixth Street Theatre is Sheldon Harnick and Jerry Bock's *Tenderloin* (216), with a book by George Abbott and Jerome Weidman, the same people who put together *Fiorello*. Maurice Evans plays a minister who intends to clean up a seedy part of nineteenth-century New York.

NOVEMBER 3 Meredith Willson's *The Unsinkable Molly Brown* (532), in the person of Tammy Grimes, sails into the Winter Garden. Molly is an indomitable young woman from humble beginnings who parlays luck and pluck into a position in society. The 1964 film stars Debbie Reynolds. **10** Tennessee Williams's *A Period of Adjustment* (132) is at the Helen Hayes Theatre. The playwright essays the wedding night this time

Business and Society

JUNE • The Playwrights Company, the production organization founded in 1938, is dissolved by its Board of Directors. • In response to criticism, the American Theatre Wing changes its method of nominating candidates for Tony Awards, setting up a system in which an author, two critics, a producer, and a director will make the choices. • Lawrence Shubert Lawrence is acquitted of charges that he committed fraud in the sale of tickets to brokers in Philadelphia. **2** With negotiations between Actors Equity and The New York Theatre League over the issue of a pension for players going nowhere, Equity shuts down *The Tenth Man*, and the producers close the other shows. Management claims it is a strike; lockout, says Equity. Broadway will be dark for more than a week. **9** Actors Equity and the New York League of Theatres reach an agreement ending the current strike. Theatre owners and producers agree to contribute to a pension fund. The new Broadway minimum rises to $115 a week, and the union agrees to arbitration on certain issues.

DECEMBER • Real estate developer Irving Maidman is edging the theatre district

Births, Deaths, and Marriages

JUNE 23 Mary Boland d.

AUGUST 23 Oscar Hammerstein II d.

SEPTEMBER 6 Jimmy Savo d.

DECEMBER 27 Libby Holman m painter Louis Schanker.

JANUARY 13 Blanche Ring d.

FEBRUARY 3 Producer Jed Harris and Bebe Allen are divorced. **15** Jack Whiting d.

MARCH 17 Laurence Olivier m. Joan Plowright.

APRIL 8 Robert Morse m. dancer-singer Carol D'Andre.

MAY 19 Grace George d.

Broadway theatre district is blacked out for one minute in memory of Oscar Hammerstein II. It's the first time since World War II that the lights have been turned off completely.

SEPTEMBER • Irish playwright Brendan Behan, arriving in the U.S. for the opening of his play *The Hostage*, has been preceded by his reputation. He likes to drink and has heckled his own plays from the audience. Behan, who behaves himself in New York, will appear several times on the "Tonight" television show with Jack Paar. • Dancer Gwen Verdon has foot surgery. **12** The Mansfield becomes the Brooks Atkinson Theatre, after *The New York Times* critic who just retired. **24** José Ferrer "sings" the title role in

Robert Goulet, kneeling, and Richard Burton in *Camelot* MSN

out and finds it funny. James Daley, Barbara Baxley, Rosemary Murphy, and Robert Webber have major roles, and George Roy Hill directs. The film appears in 1962. **30** Tad Mosel's *All the Way Home* (333), opening at the Belasco, is based on James Agee's *A Death in the Family*. It stars Arthur Hill and Colleen Dewhurst, with Lillian Gish and Aline MacMahon. It's filmed in 1962.

DECEMBER 3 Lerner and Loewe's *Camelot* (873) opens at the Majestic. Richard Burton is King Arthur (his understudy John Cullum, in his Broadway debut, is in the chorus), Julie Andrews is Queen Guenevere, and Robert Goulet is Sir Lancelot. Besides the title song, there's "I Wonder What the King Is Doing Tonight," "If Ever I Would Leave You," and "How to Handle a Woman." It's a 1967 film. **16** Lucille Ball comes to Broadway, at the Alvin Theatre, and digs for oil in *Wildcat* (171), with music by Cy Coleman and lyrics by Carolyn Leigh. It will take awhile before the public takes to the number that is this production's legacy: "Hey, Look Me Over." **26** *Do Re Mi* (400), opening at the St. James, is a spoof

farther west along Forty-second Street. His Maidman Playhouse, which recently opened, will soon be joined by the Jewel Box and the Showcase, on which construction has just begun, in an area that will be known as Theatre Row.

FEBRUARY • Increasingly having to compete with off-Broadway as well as television and films, many Broadway theatres are reducing ticket prices through extensive use of twofers for weekday night performances.

APRIL • Producer Leo Kerz's ads for Ionesco's *Rhinoceros* have a novel touch. They reprint entire reviews rather than brief excerpts from them. **13** Because the American Theatre Wing neglected to provide newspapers with advance notice of the Tony Award winners, announced at ceremonies last night at the Waldorf, today's papers give the winners less attention than in recent years. In the past, with prior notice, the newspapers were able to plan layouts and feature stories. Producer Alexander Cohen, disgusted with the process in which people vote even though they haven't seen all the nominated shows, says "the Tony's are phonies and always have been."

Personalities

Puccini's opera *Gianni Schicchi*, at the Brooklyn Academy of Music. *Variety* likens this turn to Olivier's dancing in *The Entertainer*: both "are wonderfully adept fakers." In fact, in the midst of the polite applause at the end of the performance, someone yells out, "Hooray for everyone but José."

OCTOBER 7 *Laurette*, the play about actress Laurette Taylor, which was to have been Judy Holliday's first straight dramatic role, closes in its Philadelphia tryout because, says the producer, she "has to undergo corrective surgery for a throat condition." In fact, she has breast cancer. **13** Jerry Orbach leaves *The Fantasticks* for the first of his several sporadic attempts to begin a film career. **14** Moss Hart, who is directing *Camelot* at its Toronto tryout, has a heart attack. Only last week, lyricist Alan Jay Lerner was felled by a bleeding ulcer, but now he will take over as director.

NOVEMBER 5 Philip Bosco makes his Broadway debut in the short-lived comedy *The Rape of the Belt* **14** Alan Jay Lerner and Frederick Loewe are on the cover of *Time* with the headline "The Rough Road to Broadway," an allusion to their trials and tribulations with the musical *Camelot*, which will open on December 3.

DECEMBER 6 President-elect John F. Kennedy attends a performance of *The Best Man*, a play that had been shown to him in its first draft by author Gore Vidal, who makes a cameo appearance onstage tonight. As a security dodge, a rumor had been started that he was going to see *Camelot*, complete with a "preview" visit by the Secret Service to divert attention from his real destination. Kennedy is seen to laugh especially hard when a candidate in the drama is told, "The people still figure that you've got so much money you won't go around stealing theirs." **21** *Variety* headlines: "Mary Martin Stars Next As Fanny Brice." The paper suggests that the show will be mounted next year or in the 1962–63 season. (*Funny Girl*, with Barbra Streisand, will, in fact,

Plays and Musicals

of the jukebox business, starring Phil Silvers and Nancy Walker, with music by Jule Styne, book by Garson Kanin, and lyrics by Betty Comden and Adolph Green. The most memorable song is "Make Someone Happy."

JANUARY 9 In Eugene Ionesco's *Rhinoceros* (256), at the Longacre, Zero Mostel turns himself into a rhinoceros in full view of the audience, without makeup or special effects. Eli Wallach, Anne Jackson, Morris Carnovsky, and Jean Stapleton costar. **24** *The American Dream* (16), starring Ben Piazza and Sudie Bond, the first of Edward Albee's plays directed by

Zero Mostel becomes a rhinoceros *PF*

Alan Schneider, opens at the York Theatre. *Time* calls it "a sort of surrealistic situation comedy," and Howard Taubman, in the *Times*, writes that "[t]he nonsense at times comes perilously close to being the gibberish it is mocking." **31** *Call Me By My Rightful Name* (127), by Michael Shurtleff, David Merrick's casting director, opens off-Broadway at the One Sheridan Square Theatre. Starring in this drama, directed by Milton Katselas, about young people and the conflicts in their lives, are Robert Duvall, Alvin Ailey, and Joan Hackett.

FEBRUARY 22 After going through 22 drafts, Neil Simon is on the boards for the first time with *Come Blow Your Horn* (677), a comedy in which a father comes

Business and Society

Births, Deaths, and Marriages

open in the 1963–64 season.)

JANUARY 10 The death of author Dashiell Hammett ends his celebrated, sometimes tortured 30-year relationship with playwright Lillian Hellman.

FEBRUARY • Writing in a Paris magazine, Eugene Ionesco complains that the Broadway production of *Rhinoceros* makes his play an attack on nonconformity, rather than the assault on totalitarianism it was meant to be. • Noel Coward, in several articles in the London *Sunday Times*, lashes out at the new generation of British playwrights, who focus on "tramps and prostitution," indulge in "vulgarity," and think that only the working class is interesting.

MARCH • Playwright Brendan Behan is hospitalized in Toronto for alcoholism after his arrest for assaulting a hotel house detective. **8** Interviewed about the leading men opposite whom she's played on the stage, Jessica Tandy tells columnist Joe Hyams about Marlon Brando: "He's what I call a pelvis actor—you know that round-back stance, slouch forward, hands on hips. He makes it look as though he's not acting, and he isn't, but he has a real dynamic personality. Hume [Hume Cronyn, her husband] has a sexier stance and more off-stage personality." **25** David Merrick's production of *Becket* closes today on Broadway and is about to go on the road. Dino de Laurentiis pays Merrick $37,500 to release Anthony Quinn from his contract so he can film *Barabbas*. On the road, Laurence Olivier switches from King to cleric, with Arthur Kennedy assuming the throne.

APRIL • Realizing that it is Lucille Ball and not *Wildcat* that is filling seats at the Alvin Theatre, the producers have her do a little "act" after the curtain rings down. She tells jokes, talks to the audience, and reprises the show's big number "Hey Look Me Over." **6** Richard Rodgers announces that he and Allen Jay Lerner will collaborate on a musical. After several false starts, however, they will abandon the project.

MAY • Writing in *Theatre Arts* under the name "George Spelvin," *Daily News* critic John Chapman takes a swipe at *Times* reviewer Howard Taubman, who has

---

to accept the individuality of his two adult sons. Lou Jacobi, Hal March, and Warren Berlinger are the stars at the Brooks Atkinson Theatre. It's "a story without a moral, a joke without a point," says *Variety*'s reviewer, who nevertheless admits that it's funny.

MARCH 1 Edward Albee's *Death of Bessie Smith* (328) opens at the York Theatre. Like *Zoo Story*, it premiered in Berlin. Rae Allen is a nurse in the hospital where the blues singer was taken after she was injured in a Memphis auto accident. **8** Judith Crist substitutes as the *Herald-Tribune* critic at the Helen Hayes Theatre tonight, while Walter Kerr is in the back of the house with his playwright wife, Jean, at the premiere of her *Mary, Mary* (1,572). Crist writes that it "shines with intelligence and sparkles with sophistication and suffers from an abundance of riches." In other words, "there are too many good lines." Barbara Bel Geddes, Barry Nelson, and Michael Rennie are the stars. It's on the screen in 1963. **29** *Under Milk Wood* (202), Dylan Thomas's depiction of a day in a Welsh village, is revived at the Circle in the Square. The cast of 10, which includes Sada Thompson, handles 63 speaking roles.

APRIL 4 Henry Denker's *A Far Country* (271) dramatizes one of Sigmund Freud's cases, at the Music Box, with Kim Stanley and Steven Hill. **13** The curtain rises without an overture at the Imperial, as "Love Makes the World Go Round" heralds the opening of Bob Merrill's *Carnival!* (719), adapted from the 1953 film *Lili*. Anna Maria Alberghetti is the star with Kaye Ballard, Jerry Orbach, and Anita Gillette, among others.

MAY 4 Jean Genet's *The Blacks* (1,408) opens at the St. Marks Playhouse. The cast includes James Earl Jones, Roscoe Browne, Louis Gossett, Cicely Tyson, Godfrey Cambridge, Raymond St. Jacques, and Charles Gordone. The *Daily News* says it's "[o]verwritten and overplayed," while the *Times* finds it "a brilliantly sardonic and lyrical tone poem." "Fascinating and disturbing," says the *Post*; "evasive," says the *Herald-Tribune*.

Personalities

complained that too many writers hold straight plays to a higher standard than musicals. Chapman writes that "Taubman himself uses a double standard invented by his predecessor, Brooks Atkinson—strict severity toward Broadway and appalling leniency toward off-Broadway."

Plays and Musicals

Business and Society

Births, Deaths, and Marriages

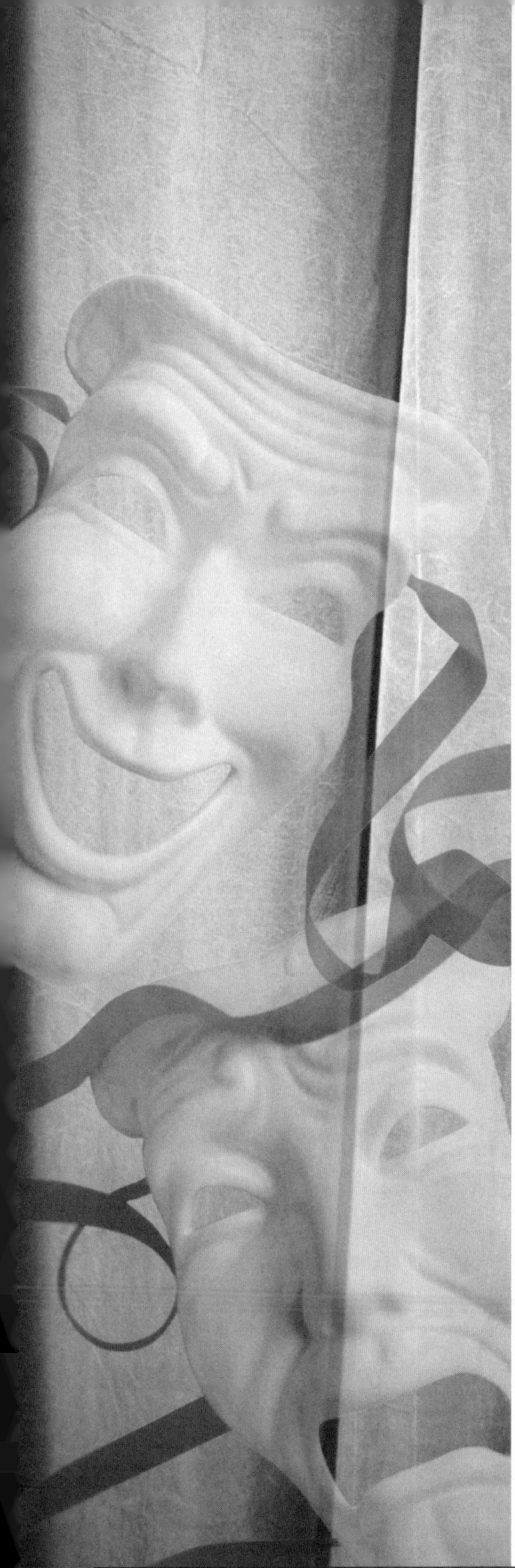

1961–62

The Sunday papers try to explain the theatre of the absurd. What does it all mean? Arthur Kopit's *Oh Dad, Poor Dad, Mamma's Hung You in the Closet and I'm Feelin' So Sad* is a "pseudoclassical tragifarce in a bastardized French tradition." The playwright says so himself. Meanwhile, in the theatre that matinée audiences can comprehend, Paul Scofield triumphs in *A Man for All Seasons*. Stephen Sondheim shows that he can write music, too, Barbra Streisand gets noticed, and Elizabeth Ashley is a star. David Merrick quotes the "critics," Robert Morse sings to a mirror, and Zero Mostel is sporting a toga. And the final curtain falls for George S. Kaufman and Moss Hart.

- Fine for sleeping on the New York City subway system, which is papered with 2,800 of David Merrick's ads for *Subways Are for Sleeping*: $10
- What Frank Fay (who dies September 25) replies to Milton Berle's challenge to a duel of wits: "I never fight with an unarmed man."
- Percentage of its new house filled by the Arena Stage in Washington, D.C.: 85 percent
- What *Times* critic Howard Taubman discovers in *I Can Get It for You Wholesale*: "The evening's find is Barbra Streisand, a girl with an oafish expression, a loud irascible voice and an arpeggiated laugh. Miss Streisand is a natural comedienne. . . . "
- What Walter Kerr discovers in the same show: "a sloe-eyed creature with folding ankles named Barbra (yes, Barbra is spelled right, and Barbra is great)."
- Barbra Streisand's understudy in *I Can Get It for You Wholesale*: Louise Lasser
- Actresses beaten out by Barbra Streisand for a role in *Another Evening with Harry Stoones*: Louise Lasser and Linda Lavin
- What Frank Loesser calls his Pulitzer Prize, which he shares with Abe Burrows for *How to Succeed in Business Without Really Trying*: his "Putziller" (an Anglo-Yiddish pun linking prize and penis)

Productions on Broadway: 50

Pulitzer Prize for Drama: *How to Succeed in Business Without Really Trying* (book by Abe Burrows, music and lyrics by Frank Loesser)

New York Drama Critics Circle Awards:
Best Play: *Night of the Iguana* (Tennessee Williams)
Best Foreign Play: *A Man for All Seasons* (Robert Bolt)
Best Musical: *How to Succeed in Business Without Really Trying* (Frank Loesser)

Tony Awards:
Play: *A Man for All Seasons* (Robert Bolt)
Actor in a Play: Paul Scofield (*A Man for All Seasons*)
Actress in a Play: Margaret Leighton (*The Night of the Iguana*)
Musical: *How to Succeed in Business Without Really Trying* (Frank Loesser)
Actor in a Musical: Robert Morse (*How to Succeed in Business Without Really Trying*)
Actress in a Musical: Anna Maria Alberghetti (*Carnival*)

June	July	August	September	October	November
Broadway blackout	Jason Robards m. Lauren Bacall	David Merrick-Anna Maria Alberghetti feud	*Purlie Victorious*	*How to Succeed in Business Without Really Trying*	*A Man for All Seasons*

December	January	February	March	April	May
Night of the Iguana	David Merrick quotes the "critics"	Albee asks: "Which Theatre Is the Absurd One?"	Barbra Streisand's Broadway debut	Sheldon Harnick m. Elaine May	*A Funny Thing Happened on the Way to the Forum*

Personalities

JUNE 7 *Variety* notes the blossoming of Carol Channing this season and suggests that "[s]he is likely to have a stunning impact if she gets a strong show."

AUGUST • Producer David Merrick and Anna Maria Alberghetti feud over her error in announcing beforehand that she would miss several performances of *Carnival* because of a hospital stay. Merrick feels that she is undercutting the box office and sends her plastic flowers to show his displeasure. He also pointedly praises her replacement, Anita Gillette. • At rehearsals for *How to Succeed in Business Without Really Trying*, composer Frank Loesser tells Rudy Vallee: "[Y]ou're singing incorrectly. You're closing on your consonants." Vallee replies, "Maybe you're right, Frank. Fortunately I've managed to squeak by with this handicap for about 33 years." On August 9, Loesser, calling Vallee a "son of a bitch" for not singing Loesser's way, takes his music and goes home. It will be three days before the composer is coaxed back.

OCTOBER 3 Playwright John Osborne sues Mary Ure for divorce, citing Robert Shaw as the other man. Osborne is involved with critic Penelope Gilliat, wife of Dr. Roger Gilliat, recently Princess Margaret's Best Man. If that's not enough, it was Penelope Gilliat who introduced Ure to Shaw. **18** A day before his Broadway debut in *A Cook for Mr. General* in a bit part 24-year-old Dustin Hoffman is late for the last run-through at the Playhouse Theatre because his motor scooter has run out of gas in Central Park. Having already come late once for a rehearsal, he messes up his clothing and tells the director he had an accident. **21** Barbra Streisand makes her off-Broadway debut at the Grammacy Arts Theatre in the revue *Another Evening with Harry Stoones*. The show, according to the director, "is really ahead of its time." Too far ahead, apparently, because it won't play another evening. **21** Ellen Stewart, a dress designer, takes possession of a 50-dollar-a-month basement space on the Lower East Side that she will turn into Café La Mama, the celebrated experimental theatre.

Plays and Musicals

SEPTEMBER 17 "Something seems to have happened and nothing has happened." It's Samuel Beckett's *Happy Days* (29), given its world premiere at the Cherry Lane Theatre. Alan Schneider directs, and the stars are Ruth White, buried in sand, and John C. Becher. **26** *From the Second City* (87), the first in a series of revues, opens at the Royale. It is here that Richard Rodgers will spot Barbara Harris and choose her for *I Picked a Daisy*, which will become *On a Clear Day*. Alan Arkin is also in the cast of tonight's show. **28** *Purlie Victorious* (261), at the Cort, a comedy by Ossie Davis, stars him, with Ruby Dee, Godfrey Cambridge, Sorrell Brooke, and Alan Alda, and is directed by Howard Da Silva. Davis has written about the kind of small Georgia town from which he came and of a black native son who thinks that the races should worship together. The 1963 film is called *Gone Are the Days*, and the play becomes the stage musical *Purlie* in 1970.

Ossie Davis MSN

OCTOBER 4 "Out of a scabrous derelict and two mentally unbalanced brothers Harold Pinter has woven a play of strangely compelling beauty and passion," the *Times*'s Howard Taubman begins his review of *The Caretaker* (165). Alan Bates, Robert Shaw, and Donald Pleasance are the cast at the Lyceum. **10** *Milk and Honey* (543), Jerry Herman's first Broadway musical, opens at the Martin

Business and Society

JUNE 13 Several Broadway shows have to cancel performances tonight because of a blackout in midtown Manhattan. Those using direct current can run. *The Sound of Music* goes on with spotlight illumination only.

JULY • In the course of arbitrating a financial dispute that My *Fair Lady* producer Herman Levin has been having with the show's composers Alan Jay Lerner and Frederick Loewe, a contract clause surfaces that shows Lerner and Loewe entitled to, among many other kinds of profits, a percentage of any ticket sales to scalpers—technically an illegal rakeoff known as "ice." **20** According to the New York *Post*, a State Department official is reported to have responded to the possibility of

Lauren Bacall MSN

Births, Deaths, and Marriages

JUNE 2 George S. Kaufman d.

JULY 4 Jason Robards m. Lauren Bacall.

AUGUST 30 Charles Coburn d.

SEPTEMBER 10 Leo Carillo d. **16** Louise Groody, who introduced the song "Tea for Two" in *No, No, Nanette* in the 1920s, d. **25** Frank Fay d. Last week, the vaudevillian, star of *Harvey* and former husband of

NOVEMBER 1 The New York City Transit Authority orders David Merrick's 2,800 advertising posters for *Subways Are For Sleeping* removed from subway cars, where they might give people the wrong idea. **24** Barbra Streisand auditions for the part of the secretary, Miss Marmelstein, in *I Can Get It For You Wholesale*. Producer David Merrick calls her "*meeskite*"—Yiddish for ugly. Streisand will be called back three more times before nailing down the role. Already hired is former elevator operator and tap dancer Elliott Gould. During rehearsals, Streisand is almost fired for being late and abrasive.

DECEMBER 28 Bette Davis, opening in *Night of the Iguana*, hates method acting, and when someone in rehearsals asked for "motivation" for removing his shoe, she told him: "For God's sake, just take the damn thing off." According to director Frank Cosaro, Davis, who drank heavily during the out-of-town tryout period and twice threatened to quit, has been making everyone in the company "feel like shit."

JANUARY 4 To publicize *Subways Are For Sleeping*, producer David Merrick has taken out ads in all the major papers with rave quotes on the show from people who have the same names as famous critics—"Brooks Atkinson," "Walter Kerr," etc. The *Times* realizes what Merrick is up to, cancels the ad, and contacts the other papers. But the first edition of the *Herald-Tribune* is already in the trucks and on its way to newsstands with the phony huzzahs.

FEBRUARY 23 The Theatre of Michigan Company, a recently founded partnership between George C. Scott and Theodore Mann, is struggling with its first venture *General Seeger*, a play by Ira Levin. William Bendix leaves the title role in the show's Detroit tryout after clashing with director Scott, who then steps into the part. There have been unconfirmed reports of fistfights between cast members, and Ann Harding, the female lead, collapsed backstage on opening night in the Motor City. **25** Edward Albee, in a *New York Times* Sunday magazine article "Which Theatre Is the Absurd One?" defends the one people are calling, among other things, absurd.

Beck. Robert Weede and Mimi Benzel star, but it is the Yiddish theatre's Molly Picon, also in her first Broadway musical, who garners much of the audience's affection. "Shalom," one of the songs, was the show's original title. **14** One of "the blue chips among musicals," the *Times* calls Frank Loesser and Abe Burrows's *How to Succeed in Business Without Really Trying* (1,417), at the Forty-sixth Street Theatre. "I Believe in You," which Robert Morse sings to himself while looking in a mirror, is the standout song. Rudy Vallee costars, and Donna McKechnie is making her Broadway debut. Morse and Vallee star in the 1967 film. It's revived in 1995. **18** *A Shot in the Dark* (389), a comedy-murder mystery, opens at the Booth. Harry Kurnitz has adapted Marcel Achard's *L'Idiote*, and Harold Clurman is the director. The stars are Julie Harris, William Shatner, and Walter Matthau, who joined the cast when Donald Cook died during the tryouts.

NOVEMBER 9 *Gideon (236)*, Paddy Chayefsky's drama of the difficult relationship between man and God, opens at the Plymouth. Frederic March is the deity, with Douglas Campbell, George Segal, and Victor Killian. The director is Tyrone Guthrie. **22** Robert Bolt's *A Man for All Seasons* (640), starring Paul Scofield, in his Broadway debut, as Sir Thomas More, whose conscience will not let him serve his king, with Leo McKern and Albert Dekker, opens at the ANTA Theatre. The 1966 film also stars Scofield. **29** A young woman in the big city looking for her first lover is picked up on a bus by Robert Redford (he won't be the one) in *Sunday in New York* (188), a comedy by Norman Krasna, at the Cort. Garson Kanin directs, and the cast includes Sondra Lee, Conrad Janis, and Pat Harrington, Sr. It becomes a 1963 film.

DECEMBER 21 *Take Her, She's Mine* (404), a comedy by Phoebe and Henry Ephron, opens at the Biltmore, making a star of Elizabeth Ashley, playing Art Carney's daughter in a Tony-winning role. It's a 1963 film. **27** A musical about homeless people, David Merrick's *Subways Are for Sleeping* (205), the work of Jule Styne, Betty Comden, Adolph Green, and choreographer Michael Kidd, is at the St.

---

subsidizing the Living Theatre's participation in an international theatre festival in Paris: "You ask me to help you get to Europe with one play about fairies, another about junkies, and a third by a Commie. Do you think I'm nuts?"

NOVEMBER • *The New York Times* accepts an ad for the Graham Greene play *The Complaisant Lover*, with the review quote calling it "an enchanting silk-smooth sex comedy about How to Succeed in Infidelity by Really Trying." But the paper's New York City radio station WQXR, dedicated to "high fidelity," will not hear of it with the word "infidelity" left in.

DECEMBER • Equity tightens its rules for the use of foreign actors.

FEBRUARY 16 Cheryl Crawford warns members of the Actors Studio that the organization is about to run out of money. An emergency fund drive will keep it afloat.

MARCH 28–31 Five performances of Paddy Chayefsky's *Gideon* are broadcast by closed-circuit television to an audience in a Rochester, New York, theatre.

MAY 26 Elia Kazan resigns from the Board of Directors of the Actors Studio. As

---

Barbara Stanwyck, was confined to a Santa Monica hospital and declared legally incompetent.

OCTOBER 1 Donald Cook d. **5** Percy Waram d. **11** Chico Marx d. **29** Guthrie McClintic d.

NOVEMBER 15 Elsie Ferguson d. **24** Ruth Chatterton d. **25** Ben Gazzara m. actress Janice Rule.

DECEMBER 20 Moss Hart d. Only six months ago, he delivered the eulogy at the funeral of his old playwriting partner George S. Kaufman. **29** Billy Rose m. actress Joyce Matthews.

FEBRUARY 18 Arthur Miller m. photographer Inge Morath. **19** James Barton d. He played Jeeter Lester in *Tobacco Road* on Broadway for over five years. **26** Chic Johnson d.

Personalities

MARCH 9 Tennessee Williams is on the cover of *Time*.

APRIL 15 Tennessee Williams complains in a letter to his friend Maria St. Just about Shelley Winters, who has replaced Bette Davis in *Night of the Iguana*: "La Winters has a fifth of Jack Daniels Tennessee sour mash whiskey in her dressing-room and nips all through the show." He also says that a few days ago, the male lead, Patrick O'Neal, threw a table at the play's director in a restaurant.

MAY • *Show* magazine notes that lyricist Stephen Sondheim will supply the music as well as the words for *A Funny Thing Happened on the Way to the Forum*. "This is not so presumptuous as it may sound," reassures the periodical, citing Sondheim's musical studies as an undergraduate and graduate work with composer Milton Babbitt. **2** Elizabeth Ashley, who won a Tony for Best Supporting Actress a few days ago, is raised to star billing in *Take Her, She's Mine*. **2** José Ferrer began having affairs almost as soon as they were married, Rosemary Clooney testifies in her divorce suit against the actor. When she confronted him about his behavior, he said he "couldn't change." She also says that he has a violent temper. **16** *Variety* corrects its erroneous report that the winner of this year's Clarence Derwent award for best performance by a male actor in a supporting role went to "Gene Williams." The winner was really a young actor named Gene Wilder. **20** Zero Mostel delivers a lecture at Harvard on comedy. He says that "the freedom of any society varies with the size of its laughter." He also reassures his audience that in the course of his talk, "unanswered questions on comic theory will remain unanswered."

Plays and Musicals

James. In the cast are Sydney Chaplin, Carol Lawrence, Orson Bean, and Phyllis Newman, costumed in a towel. Making his Broadway debut is 18-year-old dancer Michael Bennett. **28** Tennessee Williams's *Night of the Iguana* (205), in which a former cleric guides tourists in Mexico, opens at the Royale. It stars Margaret Leighton, Patrick O'Neal, and Bette Davis. At the opening tonight, Davis's appearance is greeted with a five-minute standing ovation. It becomes a John Houston film in 1964.

JANUARY 3 *Brecht on Brecht* (440), staged readings and brief scenes from the work of the German playwright, opens in Greenwich Village at the Theatre De Lys. Anne Jackson, Dane Clark, Viveca Lindfors, George Voskovec, and Michael Wagner are in the cast, as is Lotte Lenya, who also sings the songs of Brecht and her late husband Kurt Weill.

FEBRUARY 26 Arthur Kopit's *Oh Dad, Poor Dad, Mamma's Hung You in the Closet and I'm Feelin' So Sad* (454)—the playwright calls it a "pseudoclassical tragifarce in a bastardized French tradition"—opens at the Phoenix Theatre. Jerome Robbins is directing his first dramatic play, and the cast includes Jo Van Fleet, Austin Pendleton, Barbara Harris, Tony Lo Bianco, and Barry Primus.

MARCH 6 Ann Corio's *This Was Burlesque* (634) peels away the years, among other things, at the Casino East Theatre. **15** Richard Rodgers is a composer-lyricist for the only time when *No Strings* (580) opens at the Fifty-fourth Street Theatre. While the title is metaphorical, as in a love affair with no strings attached, there are also literally no strings in the orchestra. Diahann Carroll and Richard Kiley star. "The Sweetest Sounds" is the most prominent song. **17** The APA Repertory Company makes its New York debut, staging Sheridan's *School for Scandal* (21), at the off-Broadway Folksbiene Playhouse. The cast, directed by Ellis Rabb, includes Rosemary Harris, George Grizzard, and Will Geer. **21** Elliott Gould is the star of Harold Rome's *I Can*

Business and Society

codirector of the new Lincoln Center Repertory Theatre, he anticipates competing with the Actors Studio Theatre, now in the works, for stage talent. Also today, the Repertory Theatre announces that rather than wait for the completion of the Vivian Beaumont Theatre in Lincoln Center, it will rent a house so that it can mount its first productions in the coming season.

Births, Deaths, and Marriages

MARCH 8 Tom Bosley m. dancer Jean Eliot. **21** Matthew Broderick b., and Rex Harrison m. actress Rachel Roberts.

APRIL • Sheldon Harnick m. Elaine May. It will last a year. **1** Jacob Adler d. **28** Vanessa Redgrave m. director Tony Richardson.

MAY 4 Christopher Plummer m. Patricia Lewis. **9** José Ferrer and Rosemary Clooney are divorced, but the interlocutory decree will be nullified when they reconcile next year.

Get It For You Wholesale (300), opening at the Shubert. But stealing the show, as the secretary, Miss Marmelstein, is Barbra Streisand, in her Broadway debut. The cast also includes Sheree North, Bambi Linn, and Lillian Roth, returning to Broadway for the first time since 1934.

APRIL 5 Jason Robards, Jr. stars as the nonconformist, with Sandy Dennis, in Herb Gardner's *A Thousand Clowns* (428), at the Eugene O'Neill Theatre. Robards is also in the 1965 screen version.

MAY 8 There's comedy tonight at the Alvin: Stephen Sondheim's *A Funny Thing Happened on the Way to the Forum* (966). George Abbott and Jerome Robbins direct Zero Mostel, with Jack Gilford, John Carradine, Raymond Walburn, and David Burns. Burt Shevelove and Larry Gelbart wrote the book. "Comedy Tonight" is in the score. Phil Silvers, who had been considered for the lead role and who will have it in a 1972 revival, joins Mostel and Gilford in the 1966 film. Nathan Lane is in the 1996 revival.

1962–63

This is Edward Albee's season, with *Who's Afraid of Virginia Woolf?* despite some naysayers and the withholding of the Pulitzer Prize, putting him in front of the front rank of American dramatists. Actors Equity actively moves to curtail racial discrimination in the theatre. Playwright Lanford Wilson is a newcomer to the Big Apple, with no place to sleep. There are two productions of Brecht's *Man Is a Man*, opening on consecutive nights. *My Fair Lady* strikes its sets, a long newspaper strike hinders but does not seriously harm Broadway, and Irving Berlin's last musical is a dud. *Beyond the Fringe* will make you laugh out loud, very loud, Barbra Streisand begins to make records, and Judy Garland's daughter Liza debuts.

- Major playwrights with Broadway flops this season:
  - Garson Kanin, *Come on Strong*
  - Sidney Kingsley, *Night Life*
  - Tennessee Williams, *The Milk Train Doesn't Stop Here Anymore*
  - Lillian Hellman, *My Mother, My Father and Me*
- Why Nanette Fabray and choreographer Peter Gennaro have to keep their distance from each other while rehearsing Irving Berlin's *Mr. President*: they both wear hearing aids and could give each other feedback
- States that have no professional theatre because Actors Equity will not permit segregated casts or audiences: Alabama, Louisiana, Mississippi, and South Carolina
- *My Fair Lady*'s record number of performances for a musical: 2,717, over 6½ years
- *My Fair Lady*'s record (for a musical) gross receipts: $20,257,000
- Only plays running longer than *My Fair Lady*: *Tobacco Road* and *Life With Father*
- Where Edward Albee got the title for *Who's Afraid of Virginia Woolf?*: it was written on a men's room wall in a Greenwich Village bar
- Why "Here We Go Round the Mulberry Bush" and not "Who's Afraid of the Big Bad Wolf" is heard in *Who's Afraid of Virginia Woolf?*: the copyright owner of the latter wouldn't permit its use
- What the annual *Best Plays* editor calls *Who's Afraid of Virginia Woolf?*: *Long Day's Journey Into a Nightcap*
- What Ethel Merman is paid for her November engagement at the Flamingo Hotel in Las Vegas: $40,000
- What producer David Susskind calls David Merrick: "A twisted id on a sea of crocodile tears"
- What David Merrick says about David Susskind: "Mr. Susskind is head of Talent Associates. It is obvious that the talent belongs to the associates."

Productions on Broadway: 54

Pulitzer Prize for Drama: None awarded

New York Drama Critics Awards:
Best Play (the first time this category is being used): *Who's Afraid of Virginia Woolf?* (Edward Albee)

Tony Awards:
Play: *Who's Afraid of Virginia Woolf?* (Edward Albee)
Actress in a Play: Uta Hagen (*Who's Afraid of Virginia Woolf?*)
Actor in a Play: Arthur Hill (*Who's Afraid of Virginia Woolf?*)
Musical: *A Funny Thing Happened on the Way to the Forum* (Stephen Sondheim)
Actress in a Musical: Vivian Leigh (*Tovarich*)
Actor in a Musical: Zero Mostel (*A Funny Thing Happened on the Way to the Forum*)

June | **July** | **August** | **September** | **October** | **November**

- Actors studio announces production company
- Café La Mama begins
- Tennessee Williams to lay off southern belle
- *My Fair Lady* ends run
- *Who's Afraid of Virginia Woolf?*
- John Shubert d.

December | **January** | **February** | **March** | **April** | **May**

- New York newspaper strike
- *Oliver!*
- Edward Albee on cover of *Newsweek*
- Anne Bancroft in *Mother Courage*
- Liza Minnelli's debut
- Albee denied Pulitzer

Personalities

JUNE 25 Recent drama school graduate Faye Dunaway is a cast replacement in *A Man for All Seasons*. She's also been chosen for the new Lincoln Center actor training program.

JULY 5 Lanford Wilson arrives in New York, determined to become a playwright. The author, who will later immortalize this date with his play *The Fifth of July*, lacks a place to stay and sleeps in Central Park tonight.

AUGUST 1 "I don't feel inclined to write any more about the so-called [s]outhern belle," Tennessee Williams tells a reporter in a London interview.

OCTOBER 1 Barbra Streisand signs her first recording contract, with Columbia. **3** The *Playbill* for *Stop the World—I Want to get Off*, opening tonight, says, facetiously, of David Merrick that he is "[t]he theatre's most amiable producer . . . revered by both competitors and associates. Throughout his illustrious career, he has shunned the glare of publicity and neatly sidestepped the briar patch of controversy." In his latest "sidestep," the amiable Merrick, irked at the *Times*'s Howard Taubman's less than rapturous review of this musical, will quote excepts from Taubman's notice, translated into Greek, in ads for the show. **4** There is a long line at the Shubert Theatre box office the day after the opening of *Stop the World—I Want to Get Off*. This is partly because producer David Merrick has ordered that only one of the two ticket windows be used, to create the media-pleasing "long line at the box office." **13** Henry Fonda was the producer's first choice for the part of George in *Who's Afraid of Virginia Woolf?* opening tonight, but the actor's agent rejected it without ever showing him the script. Geraldine Page, who was approached to play Martha, would do it only if Lee Strasberg of the Actors Studio could attend rehearsals.

NOVEMBER • Franchot Tone, slated to costar with Colleen Dewhurst in a revival of O'Neill's *Desire Under the Elms*, at the Circle in the Square, withdraws, the third

Plays and Musicals

JUNE 18 The New York Shakespeare Festival's Delacorte Theatre in Central Park opens, with George C. Scott as Shylock in *The Merchant of Venice* (19). James Earl Jones is also in the cast.

JULY • Ellen Stewart stages her first play at Café La Mama, an adaptation of Tennessee Williams's story "One Arm." The only prop she owns is a bed.

SEPTEMBER 17 William Snyder's *The Days and Nights of Bebe Fenstermaker* (304), directed by Ulu Grossbard, opens at the Sheridan Square Playhouse. Rose Gregorio plays a young woman who comes to the big city for romance and a career and finds disaster. Also in the cast is young Robert Duvall. **18** The Living Theatre's production of Brecht's *Man Is Man* (166), about the making of a soldier, is the first of two shows, opening on consecutive nights, of English translations of the playwright's *Mann Ist Mann*. Cast in this one, directed by Julian Beck, are Joseph Chaikin and Judith Malina. **19** The New Repertory Company at the Masque Theatre presents its version of Brecht's *Mann Ist Mann, A Man's a Man* (175), translated by Eric Bentley. It stars John Heffernan and Olympia Dukakis. **29** *My Fair Lady* ends its six-and-a-half-year run on Broadway.

OCTOBER 3 *Stop the World—I Want to Get Off* (556) opens at the Shubert. Anthony Newley stars in and directs this allegory about an everyman and collaborated on the book, lyrics, and music with Leslie Bricusse. Anna Quayle costars. "What Kind of Fool Am I?" is already on the hit parade by the time the curtain rises tonight. The film version appears in 1966. **13** Edward Albee's first full-length play, *Who's Afraid of Virginia Woolf?* (664), opens at the Billy Rose Theatre. Uta Hagen, Arthur Hill, Melinda Dillon, and George Grizzard are the players. John Chapman, in the *Daily News*, says "It's three and a half hours long, four characters wide and cesspool deep." (Because of its length, a separate cast will play matinées.) The 1966 film, directed by Mike Nichols, stars Richard

Business and Society

JUNE 1 Equity members may no longer appear in any production in which the cast or audience is segregated. **11** The Actors Studio announces that it will have a production company—the Actors Studio Theatre—in operation by January and that for the first time, actors—Rip Torn and Geraldine Page—have joined the organization's Board of Directors.

AUGUST • *Equity*, the official publication of Actors Equity, carries a notice urging members to report any instance of racial discrimination in employment opportunities. The union has had a nondiscriminatory clause in its contract with the League of New York Theatres for a decade but only now enforces it.

OCTOBER 10 The Ford Foundation announces a new grant program to bolster regional theatres, committing $6.1 million to nine companies. The big winner is the Alley Theatre of Houston, which draws $2,100,000. **29** Congressman Adam Clayton Powell's House Committee on Education and Labor hears Ossie Davis testifying on discrimination in the entertainment industry. He says that although the cast of *Purlie Victorious*, which he

Births, Deaths, and Marriages

JUNE 4 Composer Jule Styne m. film actress Margaret Brown.

JULY 10 Playwright Jules Goodman d. **24** Victor Moore d.

SEPTEMBER 4 Elizabeth Ashley m. actor James Farentino.

OCTOBER 14 June Walker m. lyricist David Rogers. **26** Producer-director Harold Prince m. Judith Chaplin, daughter of producer-composer Saul Chaplin.

NOVEMBER 2 Lotte Lenya, widow of Kurt Weill, m. artist Russell Detwiller. **14** John Shubert, son of J.J. Shubert, d. Peggy Cass once described him as "the best thing the Shuberts ever produced."

time in the past two seasons he's done that during a show's rehearsals—the other two were *The Umbrella* and *When We Dead Awaken.* Dewhurst's husband, George C. Scott, replaces him.

JANUARY 9 "Washington Asks: Is Kennedy Truly [a] Theatre Buff?" headlines *Variety*. While his patronizing of the arts has been frequently noted, the President has attended the theatre in Washington only three times in almost two years in office.

FEBRUARY 4 A pensive-looking Edward Albee stares out from the cover of *Newsweek*, which characterizes him in a headline as "Odd Man In." **4** Ben Piazza replaces George Grizzard in *Who's Afraid of Virginia Woolf?* Grizzard is moving on to Minneapolis, where he will play an important role in the launching of the Tyrone Guthrie Theatre this spring.

APRIL 2 Judy Garland's daughter makes her professional New York debut in a revival of *Best Foot Forward*, at Stage 73. Her mother is not there to see Liza Minnelli, but her father Vincente Minnelli, Arthur Godfrey, Betty Comden, and Adolph Green are in the audience. *Variety* calls her "a talented lass, with a fine comic delivery, agile feet and a pleasant set of pipes." **19** Producer David Merrick, on the "Tonight" show, attacks theatre critics, especially *The New York Times*'s Howard Taubman. Later, Merrick apologizes to Taubman.

Liza Minnelli MSN

Burton, Elizabeth Taylor, George Segal, and Sandy Dennis. **20** At its Boston tryout, one critic called Irving Berlin's *Mr. President* (256) "dreadful." It bombed in Washington, and now the composer's last Broadway show opens at the St. James, where the critics are also none too pleased. But the more than $2,500,000 in advance ticket sales keeps this musical about a couple patterned after the Kennedys, starring Robert Ryan and Nanette Fabray, open for awhile. **27** The British revue opening at the John Golden Theatre is definitely *Beyond the Fringe* (673). Operating on the periphery of all things normal and straightlaced are Dudley Moore, Peter Cook, Jonathan Miller, and Alan Bennett.

NOVEMBER 17 *Little Me* (257), a Cy Coleman-Carolyn Leigh musical with a Neil Simon book, opens at the Lunt-Fontanne. It's a vehicle for star Sid Caesar, who plays seven roles. **26** Alan Schneider directs two one-act plays by Harold Pinter, *The Dumbwaiter* and *The Collection* (578), opening at the Cherry Lane. The plots are driven by murder and a phantom seduction, and among the cast members are Patricia Roe, Henderson Forsythe, and James Patterson. **27** Paul Ford and Maureen O'Sullivan play a middle-aged couple with an adult child who are about to become parents again in *Never Too Late* (1,007), a comedy by Sumner Arthur Long, a television sitcom writer, at the Playhouse. Ford and O'Sullivan are also in the 1965 film.

JANUARY 6 Bruce Prochnik is Oliver Twist and Clive Revill is Fagin in *Oliver!* (774), at the Imperial Theatre, after three years in London. Songs in Lionel Bart's musical include "As Long as He Needs Me." The film version is released in 1968. **8** The Circle in the Square revives Eugene O'Neill's *Desire Under the Elms* (384), starring George C. Scott, Colleen Dewhurst, and Rip Torn. José Quintero directs. **16** *The Milk Train Doesn't Stop Here Anymore* (69), by Tennessee Williams, arrives at the Morosco. Starring in this play about a woman looking back on life, dictating her memoirs at an Italian villa, are Mildred Dunnock, Hermione Baddley, and Paul Roebling.

wrote and in which he stars, is integrated, blacks have no role in the management of the theatre where it is playing.

DECEMBER 8 New York City's newspapers are shut down for an almost four-month strike. With a good deal of money tied up in it, the musical *Oliver!*, scheduled to open on December 27, is being heavily promoted on the radio.

FEBRUARY 25 After eleven weeks of the New York City newspaper strike, Broadway's gross is up by slightly more than $200,000, compared with the same period a year ago. Allowing for a few more shows in that period this year, the box office is running about even.

MARCH 31 The newspaper strike has been settled.

MAY 24 Today's *New York Times* page one story describing the waning theatre season as "disastrous" brings charges from the League of New York Theatres that the article is full of "half-truths." At its insistence, members of the League meet with the paper's editors to protest its allegedly anti-Broadway attitude. They claim that *Times* coverage favors off-Broadway, regional theatres and esoteric drama in general and that it also may be

Like his uncle Sam, John, who has been managing the family's theatre empire, d. on a train. As specified in his will, John Shubert's funeral is held at one of the family's theatres "on a matinée day" (displacing a performance of *Camelot*), with the scenery draped and his coffin at stage center, his widow sitting next to it. Lawrence Shubert Lawrence, John's cousin, will assume the business's managerial reins.

DECEMBER 5 Olympia Dukakis m. stage actor Louis Zorich. **15** Charles Laughton d. **26** Producer Lawrence Langner of the Theatre Guild d.

JANUARY 6 Stark Young d. **11** Five days before what would have been his 25th wedding anniversary, David Merrick is divorced from Leonore Beck, who nevertheless will continue to invest in his shows. **24** Lyricist Otto Harbach d. **26** Ole Olsen, of the comedy team of Olsen and Johnson, d. **27** Actor-director

Personalities

MAY • Richard Rodgers has four shows on the boards: a revival of *Oklahoma!* is at the City Center, where *Pal Joey* and *The King and I* will follow this season, and *No Strings* and *The Sound of Music* are on Broadway. A revival of *The Boys from Syracuse* is playing off-Broadway. • Arlene Francis is injured in an auto accident in which a passenger in the other car is killed. **6** Edward Albee's *Who's Afraid of Virginia Woolf?*, the Tony and Drama Critic's award winner for best play, is denied the Pulitzer Prize by Columbia University's advisory board. Pulitzer jurors John Mason Brown and John Gassner resign when their choice of Albee's drama is overruled. It's the sixth time since 1917 that there will be no Pulitzer Prize for Drama. **22** *Variety* is already noting tension between the artistic leaders of the Repertory Theatre of Lincoln Center Elia Kazan and Robert Whitehead and its administrative head George Woods. Kazan and Whitehead independently finance the building of the ANTA Theatre, which will temporarily house the company. • The winner of the Clarence Derwent Award this year is Gene Hackman, for his work in *Children From Their Games*. **23** Barbra Streisand, with Edie Adams and Julius Monk, appears at the White House Correspondents Dinner. Although emcee Merv Griffin warned Streisand not to delay President Kennedy on the receiving line, she nevertheless stops him and asks for his autograph. "Thanks, you're a doll," she tells him as he signs. When Griffin asks what Kennedy wrote, she replies, "Fuck you. The President." **24** Astronauts Gordon Cooper and Wally Schirra are given a heroe's welcome in New York City and an evening at a Broadway show. Although it was not their choice, David Merrick has maneuvered to have them attend his *Stop the World—I Want to Get Off*. **31** The Repertory Theatre of Lincoln Center announces that 14 young actors have been chosen from its training program to become full members of the company, including Faye Dunaway, Barbara Loden, and Barry Primus.

Plays and Musicals

FEBRUARY 4 Eli Wallach and Anne Jackson are in *The Typists* and *The Tiger* (200), two one-act plays by Murray Schisgal, opening off-Broadway at the Orpheum.

MARCH 8 Luigi Pirandello's *Six Characters in Search of an Author* (529) is revived off-Broadway at the Martinique. **11** José Quintero directs a revival of *Strange Interlude* (104), the first production of the Actors Studio Theatre Company, starring Geraldine Page and Jane Fonda, at the Hudson. Others in the cast are Franchot Tone, Ben Gazzara, Pat Hingle, and Betty Field. **13** *Enter Laughing* (419), Joseph Stein's play, said to be based on the early career of Carl Reiner, opens at Henry Miller's Theatre. One problem with it, according to *Variety*, is that "the key role of the young hero is played by a relative newcomer, Alan Arkin, who lacks sufficient experience, authority or personality projection to hold his own" with the rest of the cast, which includes Alan Mowbray, Vivian Blaine, and Sylvia Sidney. **28** Brecht's *Mother Courage and Her Children* (32), at the Martin Beck, translated by Eric Bentley, stars Anne Bancroft, with Zohra Lampert, John Randolph, Gene Wilder, and Barbara Harris.

APRIL 15 Rodgers and Hart's *The Boys From Syracuse* (500) is revived off-Broadway at Theatre Four. **23** Jerry Bock and Sheldon Harnick's *She Loves Me* (302), at the Eugene O'Neill Theatre, is Harold Prince's first directing assignment. Barbara Cook, Daniel Massey, Barbara Baxley, Jack Cassidy, and Nathaniel Fry are featured, and the title song is the most notable one.

MAY 7 The Tyrone Guthrie Theatre opens in Minneapolis with a production of *Hamlet* in Edwardian dress, starring George Grizzard, with Jessica Tandy as Gertrude. **15** The Living Theatre presents *The Brig* (177), by Kenneth Brown, a look at a day in a Marine Corps prison. The cast includes Warren Finnerty and George Bartenieff.

Business and Society

motivated by pique at producer David Merrick for his attacks on the paper's critic Howard Taubman.

Births, Deaths, and Marriages

George Bartenieff m. director Crystal Field. They will found the Theatre for the New City in 1970.

FEBRUARY 2 William Gaxton d.

MAY 6 Monty Woolley d. **25** Playwright John Osborne m. film critic Penelope Gilliat. **27** Anthony Newley m. actress Joan Collins, which will last until 1970.

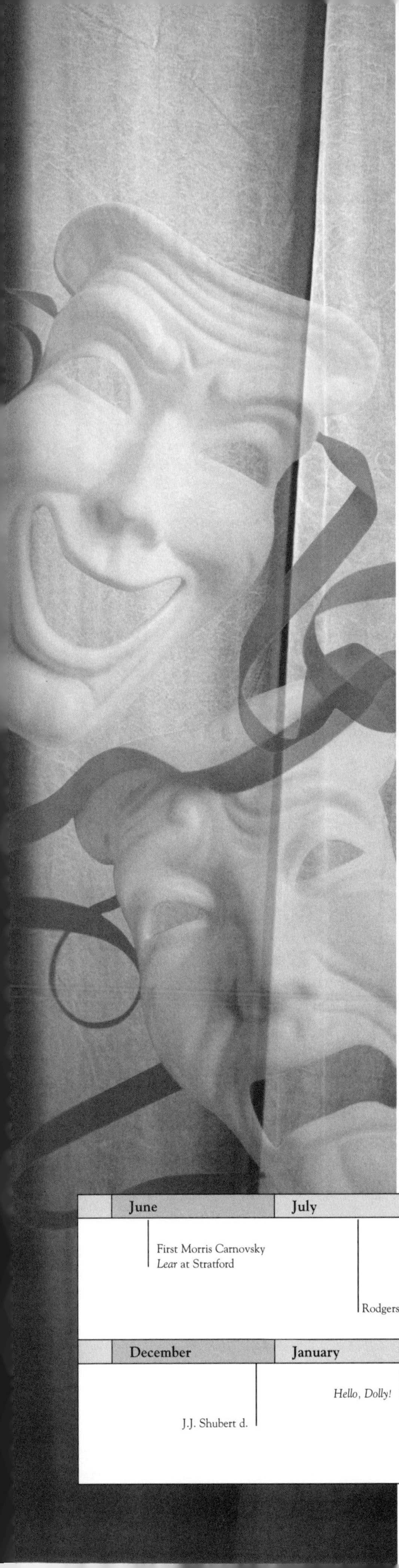

1963–64

Well, hello, Dolly. Broadway's economy wants you to feel you're right where you belong. Louis Armstrong, on a hit recording, thinks you're looking swell, too. Carol Channing, says Walter Kerr, "has gone back for another look at that advertisement labeled 'His Master's Voice,' and she has swallowed the records, the Victrola, and quite probably the dog." But Barbra Streisand also owns Broadway this season, and she says that she's "the greatest star." Tallulah Bankhead, Beatrice Lillie, and Bert Lahr take their final Broadway bows. Richard Burton does *Hamlet*, Elizabeth Ashley picks the wrong week in November to make the cover of *Life*, and the producers of *Oliver* should have booked the Ed Sullivan show for a different date. *The Deputy* causes controversy and soul-searching, and J.J. Shubert, the last of "the boys from Syracuse," is gone.

- Actresses who turned down *Hello, Dolly!*: Ethel Merman, Mary Martin, and Lucille Ball
- Number of people passing through Shubert Alley in one day: 15,000–25,000
- Advance sale for *The Subject Was Roses*: $165
- Number of songs written by Jule Styne for *Funny Girl*: 50
- Number of his songs that have made it into the show: 22
- Value of black market in Broadway show tickets ("ice"): about $10 million
- What's substituted for "Jesus H. Christ" in the Boston production of *Who's Afraid of Virginia Woolf?* to placate the censor: "Mary H. Magdalen"
- Total income of the Tyrone Guthrie Theatre at the end of its first season (January–September, 1964): $721,941.08
- Total expenses of the Tyrone Guthrie Theatre: $715,007.94
- Average attendance at the Tyrone Guthrie: 77.06 percent of capacity
- Original title of Stephen Sondheim's *Anyone Can Whistle*: *The Natives Are Restless*
- When the original cast recording of *Anyone Can Whistle* is made: the day after the ninth and final performance
- Cost of building the new, temporary ANTA Theatre in Washington Square: $540,000
- Working as a busboy at the Village Gate: Sam Shepard. He rooms with Charles Mingus, Jr., his high school classmate and son of the jazz bassist, plays drums with a group that becomes the Holy Modal Rounders, and is using amphetamines
- Another early Shepard job: "horseshit remover and hot walker" at the Santa Anita racetrack in California

Productions on Broadway: 63

Pulitzer Prize for Drama: None awarded

New York Drama Critics Circle Awards:
Best Play: *Luther* (John Osborne)
Best Musical: *Hello, Dolly!* (Jerry Herman)

Tony Awards:
Play: *Luther* (John Osborne)
Actress in a Play: Sandy Dennis (*Any Wednesday*)
Actor in a Play: Alec Guinness (*Dylan*)
Musical: *Hello, Dolly!* (Jerry Herman)
Actress in a Musical: Carol Channing (*Hello, Dolly!*)
Actor in a Musical: Bert Lahr (*Foxy*)

June
- First Morris Carnovsky *Lear* at Stratford

July
- Rodgers and Lerner split

August
- Clifford Odets d.

September
- "Mary H. Magdalen" for the Boston censor

October
- IRS seizes Living Theatre assets

November
- Broadway dark over JFK death

December
- J.J. Shubert d.

January
- *Hello, Dolly!*

February
- *The Deputy*

March
- *Funny Girl*

April
- Richard Burton's *Hamlet*

May
- Alan Jay Lerner marital drama

Personalities

JUNE • *A Girl to Remember*, the new musical starring Carol Burnett, which had been set for a November 23 opening, has been postponed because the star is pregnant. **9** Morris Carnovsky, age 64, plays *King Lear* for the first time at the American Shakespeare Festival at Stratford. **20** While Elizabeth Taylor films *Cleopatra* for $1 million, Colleen Dewhurst plays the Egyptian queen in the New York Shakespeare Festival production of *Antony and Cleopatra* in Central Park for $100 a week.

JULY • The team of Richard Rodgers and Alan Jay Lerner is breaking up without producing a show. Lerner complains that his partner wastes time and energy negotiating contracts covering all aspects of their relationship. Rodgers says that Lerner simply hasn't produced the words to go with his music. Lerner will complete their only project *I Picked a Daisy* with composer Burton Lane, calling it *On a Clear Day You Can See Forever.* **25** Producer Ray Stark, who has been looking for someone to play his mother-in-law Fanny Brice, in a new musical about her life, announces that Barbra Streisand, appearing in Las Vegas with Liberace, has been chosen for the role. Streisand was no one's first choice. Eydie Gormé and Shirley MacLaine had been considered. Fran Stark, Brice's daughter, wanted Anne Bancroft, but the actress is not up to the role's musical demands. Carol Burnett has been a strong contender, but she just isn't "Jewish enough." (Stark later says of Streisand as Brice: "Mother was a comic. She was never a nut.")

AUGUST • With a sprained ankle, Jessica Tandy plays in a wheelchair opposite her husband Hume Cronyn, who has the lead in *Death of a Salesman*, at the Tyrone Guthrie Theater in Minneapolis.

SEPTEMBER 25 According to *Variety*, Sammy Davis, Jr. says that Laurence Olivier has asked him to play Iago opposite his Othello but that Davis feels he is not yet up to the dramatic demands of the part.

OCTOBER 23 Neil Simon's lawyer, suggest-

Plays and Musicals

SEPTEMBER 25 Albert Finney, in his Broadway debut, stars in John Osborne's *Luther* (212), in which the cleric's constipation is a central theme. Tony Richardson is directing at the St. James.

OCTOBER 9 Peter Shaffer's two one-act plays at the Morosco, *The Private Ear* and *The Public Eye* (163), about shyness, love, and infidelity, star Brian Bedford, Geraldine McEwan, and Moray Watson. **17** *Jennie* (82), the new musical by Arthur Schwartz and Howard Dietz, at the Majestic, has, besides their considerable talents, Mary Martin playing a character modeled after Laurette Taylor. **23** Neil Simon's *Barefoot in the Park* (1,532), starring Elizabeth Ashley, Robert Redford, Mildred Natwick, and Kurt Kasznar, opens at the Biltmore. The *Times*'s Howard Taubman calls it a "bubbly, rib-tickling comedy," noting that "Mr. Simon evidently has no aspirations except to be diverting, and he achieves those with the dash of a highly skilled writer." Mike Nichols is directing his first Broadway show, also his first collaboration with Simon. It's filmed in 1967. **24** Harvey Schmidt and Tom Jones, who wrote *The Fantasticks*, bring a new musical *110 in the Shade* (330), based on Richard Nash's 1954 *The Rainmaker*, to the Broadhurst. It stars Robert Horton, Inga Swenson, in her Broadway debut, and Stephen Douglas, with Will Geer, Lesley Ann Warren, and Gretchen Cryer. The *Daily News* calls Swenson "a Gertrude Lawrence with a twang; a Charlotte Greenwood with curves." **30** Edward Albee's *Ballad of a Sad Cafe* (123) opens at the Martin Beck. Colleen Dewhurst, Roscoe Lee Browne, and Michael Dunn star in an evening of what *Daily News* critic John Chapman calls "magnificent theatre" and *Variety* calls "vacuous pretentiousness." **31** History professor Martin Duberman has weaved together letters, speeches, and other documents on the history of black Americans for the staged readings he calls *In White America* (493), at the Sheridan Square Playhouse.

DECEMBER 23 Michael Cacoyannis directs an acclaimed, Outer Critics Circle

Business and Society

AUGUST • Minnesota State Attorney General Walter Mondale rules that the Tyrone Guthrie Theatre in Minneapolis does not have to pay the city's real estate tax, which would have come to about $65,000 a year. At issue was whether the theatre was profit-making, as the city's mayor contends, or nonprofit, as the Guthrie's management maintains.

SEPTEMBER • *Who's Afraid of Virginia Woolf?* set for a tour of South Africa, will play in nonsegregated theatres only. For its part, the South African government focuses on dirty words, not racism, and bans the play for obscenity. **2** The Boston censor registers his concern over the nine times—his count—that the Lord's name is taken in vain in Edward Albee's *Who's Afraid of Virginia Woolf?* He's most upset with the "Jesus H. Christ" with which the performance begins. The producers respond with a bit of damnable downsizing, changing the opening line to "Mary H. Magdalen."

OCTOBER 17 The Living Theatre's assets are seized by the Internal Revenue Service. **19** The Becks lead their Living Theatre Company back into their the-

Births, Deaths, and Marriages

AUGUST 12 Carol Lawrence m. Robert Goulet. **14** Playwright Clifford Odets d.

SEPTEMBER 11 Earl Wilson reports in his syndicated column: "Geraldine Page and Rip Torn authorize me to publish that they've been secretly married 'for a considerable time.'" **13** Barbra Streisand m. Elliott Gould. When signing the application for the license, Streisand used the original spelling of her first name, "Barbara."

DECEMBER 26 Jacob J. ("J.J.") Shubert, d. in his apartment almost directly above Sardi's. The last of the three brothers who founded Broadway's most formidable theatre empire has d. 10 years and a day after his older brother Lee. (Sam d. in 1905 in a train crash.) J.J. may never have known that his son John d. more than a year ago.

ing that the odds are against his ever writing another big hit, convinces the playwright to sell the screen rights to *Barefoot in the Park,* opening tonight, and to his next play flat out, keeping no percentage. The move will shut him out of the television profits gleaned from his next play, *The Odd Couple.*

NOVEMBER • Richard Rodgers, in London, reacts to the critics' panning of a revival of *The Boys from Syracuse,* which opened at the Drury Lane on November 7, calling them "anti-American." He says his shows have always had a "bad press" here. **7** Zero Mostel, who has been dieting and has forgotten to eat today, collapses during the intermission of *A Funny Thing Happened on the Way to the Forum* and is

Carol Channing in the role that is hers for life MSN

Award–winning production of Euripides' *The Trojan Women* (600), at the Circle in the Square. The star is Mildred Dunnock.

JANUARY 1 A revised version of Tennessee Williams's *The Milk Train Doesn't Stop Here Anymore* (5), directed by Tony Richardson, at the Brooks Atkinson Theatre, is Tallulah Bankhead's Broadway swan song. **16** *Hello, Dolly!* opens at the St. James (2,844). Jerry Herman's musical, based on *The Matchmaker,* stars Carol Channing, in a role rejected by Ethel Merman, as Dolly Levi. The supporting cast includes David Burns, Eileen Brennan, and David Hartman. Walter Kerr calls it "a musical comedy dream" and writes of the star that "Miss Channing has gone back for another look at that advertisement labeled 'His Master's Voice,' and she has swallowed the records, the Victrola, and quite probably the dog. She is glorious. . . ." The title song will become a hit through a recording by Louis Armstrong. The 1969 film, much to Channing's chagrin, stars Barbra Streisand. **18** *Dylan* (273), Sidney Michael's play about poet Dylan Thomas, played by Alec Guinness, is at

atre—illegally—and give a performance of *The Brig.* Some arrests are made after the performance.

NOVEMBER 22 Broadway's theatres are dark on this Friday night, the day of President Kennedy's assassination. They will be dark again on Monday, the official national day of mourning. In between, attendance Saturday night is down. Actors will be paid for the shows missed.

DECEMBER 6 *Life's* headline, "Suddenly Ossie and Ruby are Everywhere," underlines the abrupt demand for black actors. "The civil rights upheaval has sent producers in all entertainment fields scurrying to use Negroes in their shows and movies," says the magazine. **10** New York State opens hearings into Broadway ticket scalping, kickbacks, illegal rebates on ads, and the keeping of multiple sets of books for some productions.

JANUARY • The League of New York Theatres, still smarting from *The New York Times's* denigration of the past Broadway season, issues audited figures, showing that all Broadway productions combined earned total profits of at least $336,000, including revenues from road companies and film sales. **16** Producer David Merrick, concerned with ticket scalping for *Hello, Dolly!* has refused to give tickets to brokers on consignment.

JANUARY 21 Joseph Schildkraut d. **22** Composer Marc Blitzstein's death today in Martinique is first attributed to a traffic accident, but it is later revealed that he was robbed and murdered by three sailors, whom he had apparently picked up in a bar.

MARCH • Lorraine Hansberry and Robert Nemiroff are divorced but keep it a secret because she has cancer. **1** Billy Rose m. Doris Warner, daughter of Harry M. Warner of Warner Brothers and widow of film director Charles Vidor. **15** Richard Burton m. Elizabeth Taylor. **20** Playwright Brendan Behan d., at age 41, from the complications of liver disease brought on by alcoholism.

APRIL 18 Playwright Ben Hecht d.

MAY 10 Vaudevillian Georgie Price d. **10** Carol Haney d. at age 30 from pneumonia and diabetes. The dancer-choreogra-

Personalities

unable to complete the performance. **22** Elizabeth Ashley is on the cover of *Life* magazine, billed as "Broadway's Brightest and Newest." But the publicity value for her is considerably diminished by the fact that President Kennedy is assassinated today.

DECEMBER 12 Producer Ray Stark confirms that he has bought out David Merrick's interest in the upcoming *Funny Girl* and will proceed without him.

JANUARY 26 Jason Robards, Jr. is thought to have set a record for hours onstage in a week while performing in previews and the opening performances of Arthur Miller's *After the Fall*. The actor is on for the full three-hour running time of the drama and has logged nine performances between January 20 and tonight, cumulating 27 hours. Tomorrow, he sleeps late.

FEBRUARY 6 Ordinarily, the scenes from *Oliver* on the Ed Sullivan show tonight would be worth a fortune in publicity. The only problem is that another act, also British, is stealing the limelight: the Beatles.

MARCH • Finished with Arthur Miller's *After the Fall*, Jason Robards, Jr., in an interview, calls the play "pretentious and ponderous. Boy some of the things I had to say! I couldn't wait to get out of it. Miller can defend his getting personal, but I think he said some things that were tasteless and personal in the wrong way." • Raul Julia, age 24, makes his New York debut in a Spanish-language production of Calderon's *Life is a Dream*, at the Astor Place Playhouse. **6** The Internal Revenue Service files a $99,286 tax lien against Judy Holliday. **23** Playwright Arthur Kopit resigns from the Actors Studio after an audience there for an experimental performance of his plays *Mhil'dalim* and *The Day the Whores Came Out to Play Tennis* reacts with "rudeness."

APRIL • Kim Stanley, who only recently dropped out of the cast of the upcoming Actors Studio production of Chekhov's *The Three Sisters*, has rejoined the pro-

Plays and Musicals

the Plymouth. Kate Reid plays his wife Caitlin. **23** Arthur Miller's *After the Fall* (208), a play much-criticized for what many consider an unfair depiction of Marilyn Monroe, opens at the ANTA Washington Square Theatre. This first production of the Repertory Theatre of Lincoln Center, directed by Elia Kazan, stars Jason Robards, Jr. and Barbara Loden in the "Monroe" role.

FEBRUARY 16 *Foxy* (72), the Robert Emmett Dolan-Johnny Mercer musical starring Bert Lahr, in his last show, Larry Blyden, and John Davidson, opens at the Ziegfeld. **18** Muriel Resnik's *Any Wednesday* (983), at the Music Box, is a surprise hit. Don Porter plays a businessman who cheats at everything, from parlor games to marriage. His mistress is Sandy Dennis, Rosemary Murphy is his wife, and the underling who uncovers Porter's dalliances is Gene Hackman. **26** Rolf Hochhuth's *The Deputy* (318), which questions whether Pope Pius did all he could to help save some of the Jews who perished in the Holocaust, opens at the Brooks Atkinson. Emlyn Williams plays the Pope, and Ron Leibman appears as an S.S. officer. "As a play, *The Deputy* is flawed," writes Taubman in the *Times*. "As a polemic, it is fierce and compelling." **27** Steve Lawrence plays Budd Schulberg's driven screenwriter Sammy Glick in Ervin Drake's musical *What Makes Sammy Run?* (540) at the Fifty-fourth Street Theatre. The star's many missed performances are a source of strife for this production.

MARCH 1 Athol Fugard's *The Blood Knot* (240), a two-character play about whites and blacks in South Africa, with James Earl Jones and J.D. Cannon, opens at the Cricket Theatre. **23** LeRoi Jones's one-act play *Dutchman* (366), at the Cherry Lane Theatre in Greenwich Village, stars Robert Hooks and Jennifer West. In it, a white woman tries to seduce a black man on the subway, then kills him. It becomes a 1966 film. **26** *Funny Girl* (1,348), at the Winter Garden, with a score by Jule Styne and Bob Merrill, makes Barbra Streisand the greatest star. Besides

Business and Society

FEBRUARY • Ellis Rabb's APA joins forces with the Phoenix Theatre to create the APA-Phoenix Theatre.

MARCH 6 Producer Herman Shumlin, who has been serving as acting president of the League of New York Theatres, resigns from the organization over its support for pending legislation that would give New York State greater control over the business affairs of the Broadway theatre. Harold Prince will now head the League.

APRIL 23 Producer Cheryl Crawford, noting that *Blues for Mr. Charlie* is attracting a new audience, estimates that 85 percent is black and says that the inexpensive seats have been selling out first, the reverse of what usually happens.

Births, Deaths, and Marriages

pher first became famous for the "Steam Heat" number in *The Pajama Game*.

duction just as Susan Strasberg has left it, causing speculation that the coming and going are connected. **3** Carol Channing is on the cover of *Life* in one of her Dolly costumes. **9** The opening-night party for the Richard Burton *Hamlet* at Rockefeller Center's Rainbow Room makes for strange tablemates. Seated at the main table with Burton and Elizabeth Taylor is one of Taylor's former husbands—number two—Michael Wilding, now doing publicity work as well as acting. Burton is his client. The overflow from the room is in the Rainbow Grill, where playing in a trio is pianist Dudley Moore, recently on Broadway in *Beyond the Fringe*. **24** Richard Burton as Hamlet is *Life* magazine's cover story.

MAY 6 Someone boos Richard Burton's *Hamlet* tonight at the Lunt-Fontanne. Upset at his hotel afterward when Elizabeth Taylor does not appreciate his distress, Burton kicks in the television screen. **13** Alan Jay Lerner's fourth wife, Micheline, locks him out of their 19-room, five-story town house on Manhattan's Upper East Side, touching off a court battle in which she accuses him, among other things, of becoming addicted to the mysterious "vitamin" shots he and other celebrities have been receiving from Dr. Max Jacobson—"Dr. Feelgood." Her lawyer is Roy Cohn, and his is Louis B. Nizer. **22** Barbra Streisand, "Great New Star," has made the cover of *Life*.

"People," this story of Fanny Brice has "Don't Rain On My Parade," "I'm the Greatest Star," "You Are Woman," and "Sadie, Sadie." Sydney Chaplin is Nicky Arnstein, Brice's shady gambler husband, and the cast also includes Kay Medford, Jean Stapleton, and Lainie Kazan. The 1968 film has the Fanny Brice song "My Man," which is not in the stage production.

APRIL 4 Stephen Sondheim's *Anyone Can Whistle* (9), at the Majestic, features Angela Lansbury, Lee Remick, Harry Guardino, and Gabriel Dell. It "lacks imagination and wit," says the *Times*. It also lacks luck. One cast member died in rehearsals, and a dancer fell into the orchestra pit, injuring a musician. **7** Beatrice Lillie, in her last Broadway show, stars in *High Spirits* (376), Hugh Martin and Timothy Gray's musical version of Noel Coward's 1941 *Blithe Spirit*, at the Alvin. When Lillie couldn't get along with Coward, who was directing in the tryouts, he gave way to Gower Champion. **9** *Hamlet* (137), starring Richard Burton, Alfred Drake, Hume Cronyn, and Eileen Hurlie, in street clothes on the Lunt-Fontanne's bare stage, and directed by John Gielgud, opens. John Chapman, in the *Daily News*, calls the production "cold and detached," and Walter Kerr says that Burton is "without feeling." *Time* calls Burton "more heroic than tragic." But Howard Taubman, in the *Times*, writes that it "is Shakespeare, not a self-indulgent holiday for a star." It's the longest-running *Hamlet*. **23** The Actors Studio production of James Baldwin's *Blues for Mr. Charlie* (150) opens at the ANTA. The play, about the shooting of a black southern minister by a white man, is directed by Burgess Meredith and stars Al Freeman, Jr., Rip Torn, Diana Sands, Pat Hingle, Joe Don Baker, and David Baldwin, the playwright's brother. Critics salute the play's social truths but fault its construction.

MAY 25 Twenty-four-year-old Martin Sheen has his breakthrough role in Frank Conroy's *The Subject Was Roses* (832), at the Royale Theater. This story of parents fighting for a son's love, costars Frank Albertson and Irene Daily. The film version is released in 1968. **26** The run of

Personalities

Plays and Musicals

Fade Out–Fade In (271), a Jule Styne-Betty Comden-Adolph Green musical, at the Mark Hellinger Theatre, will be interrupted by star Carol Burnett's neck and back problems. **27** Ann Jellicoe's *The Knack* (685), about a young man who would like to have his friend's romantic skills and a homely young woman who becomes a sex object, is off-Broadway, at the New Theatre, with a cast made up of Brian Bedford, Alexandra Berlin, George Segal, and Roddy Maude-Roxby, directed by Mike Nichols. Richard Lester's 1965 film stars Rita Tushingham.

Business and Society

Births, Deaths, and Marriages

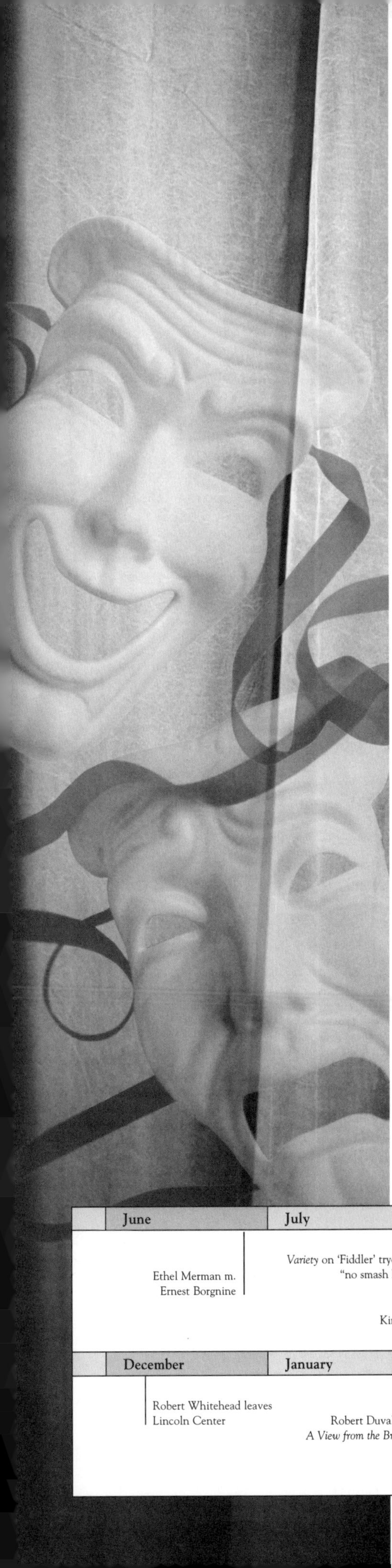

1964–65

Although not a stellar season, it does offer the Actors Studio production of *The Three Sisters*, Robert Duvall, off-Broadway, in *A View From the Bridge*, and *Fiddler on the Roof*. But it's also a season of rancor. Carol Burnett feuds with the producers of *Fade Out–Fade In* over her old injuries and her absence from their show. Robert Whitehead and Elia Kazan butt heads with the management of Lincoln Center and leave. Steve Lawrence is out too often from *What Makes Sammy Run*, and the producers call him on it. *Do I Hear a Waltz* perhaps should have been called "Do I Hear the Bell for the First Round?" Kim Stanley's mysterious problems are cutting one of the theatre's great careers short, and Edward Albee confronts his critics at a press conference. Julian Beck and Judith Malina go to jail, and Ethel Merman and Ernest Borgnine go their separate ways.

- Shows directed by Mike Nichols this season: *Barefoot in the Park*, *Luv*, *The Odd Couple*, and *The Knack*
- Newly legalized on Broadway: bars in theatres, 3 of which install them
- Derivation of term "ice," used to describe illegal premiums for choice tickets pocketed by theatre employees: from undocumented expenses charged to productions, listed as Incidental Company Expenses
- Cost of staging *Fiddler on the Roof* on Broadway: $375,000
- Who turned down the chance to write the score for *Fiddler on the Roof*: Rodgers and Hammerstein
- What Edward Albee's prospectus for potential backers of *Tiny Alice* said about a play that many people do not understand: "essentially an attack on modern institutions, modern materialism, and the illusory nature of modern life . . ."
- Subscriptions sold by the Repertory Theater of Lincoln Center: 19,000, down from last season's 47,000
- Top price of tickets at Repertory Theater of Lincoln Center: $6.50, compared to $9.90 on Broadway.
- Number of subscribers at the Arena Stage in Washington, D.C.: 15,655
- Percentage by which subscriptions for the Arena Stage are up compared to last season: 50 percent
- What Richard Rodgers says about Stephen Sondheim, his collaborator on *Do I Hear a Waltz?* whom he has known since 1942: "I watched him grow from an attractive little boy to a monster."
- Lauren Bacall's pay for *Cactus Flower*: about $5,000 a week

Productions on Broadway: 67

Pulitzer Prize for Drama: *The Subject Was Roses* (Frank D. Gilroy)

New York Drama Critics Circle Awards:
Best Play: *The Subject Was Roses* (Frank D. Gilroy)
Best Musical: *Fiddler on the Roof* (Jerry Bock and Sheldon Harnick)

Tony Awards:
Play: *The Subject Was Roses* (Frank D. Gilroy)
Actor in a Play: Walter Matthau (*The Odd Couple*)
Actress in a Play: Irene Worth (*Tiny Alice*)
Musical: *Fiddler in the Roof* (Jerry Bock and Sheldon Harnick)
Actor in a Musical: Zero Mostel (*Fiddler on the Roof*)
Actress in a Musical: Liza Minnelli (*Flora, the Red Menace*)

June	July	August	September	October	November
Ethel Merman m. Ernest Borgnine	*Variety* on 'Fiddler' tryout: "no smash hit"	Kim Stanley leaves *The Three Sisters*	*Fiddler on the Roof*	Carol Burnett out of *Fade Out–Fade In*	Ethel Merman divorces Ernest Borgnine

December	January	February	March	April	May
Robert Whitehead leaves Lincoln Center	Robert Duvall in *A View from the Bridge*	Burnett back in *Fade Out–Fade In*	Albee press conference to respond to critics	Terrence McNally's Broadway debut	'Sammy' producers fault Steve Lawrence

Personalities

JUNE 5 Judith Malina and Julian Beck are sentenced to 30 and 60 days in jail, respectively, for attempting to block IRS agents last October when they came to seize the assets of the Living Theatre. Malina and Beck also draw time for contempt for disrupting the sentencing today, to run concurrently.

JULY 29 "It seems clear this is no smash hit, no blockbuster," says *Variety*'s review of the Detroit tryout of *Fiddler on the Roof*. The music is "serviceable, rather than singable or haunting." In fact, the only thing not "ordinary" about the show is its star Zero Mostel. Only because of him, it "may have a chance for a moderate success on Broadway."

AUGUST • Elizabeth Ashley, who has been on leave from *Barefoot in the Park*, pays producer Arnold Saint-Subber $35,000 to buy her way out of the show in order to be in London with actor George Peppard, with whom she has fallen in love. Penny Fuller replaces her. **22** Kim Stanley, appearing in the acclaimed production of *The Three Sisters* that opened on June 22, continues the behavior for which she has been criticized, missing many performances because of illness. This time, her absence will lead to the end of her career in major productions. One of the most celebrated actresses of her time but apparently beset by emotional problems, she will withdraw from acting, becoming a teacher and director.

OCTOBER 17 Sammy Davis, Jr. misses the matinée preview of *Golden Boy* at the Majestic. Anxious about the musical's opening in a few days, the star later acknowledges he's on the edge of a nervous breakdown. His relationship with the original director, Fred Coe, was so bad that Davis tried to punch him. Arthur Penn has taken over the job. **17** Carol Burnett leaves the cast of *Fade Out–Fade In* to have neck and back injuries she sustained in *Once Upon a Mattress* treated. The current show will struggle along for a month with replacements and then be forced by poor ticket sales to close until Burnett can return. **19** Zero Mostel,

Plays and Musicals

JUNE 22 The critically acclaimed Actors Studio production of *The Three Sisters* (119), at the Morosco, is the first play that Lee Strasberg has directed in 13 years. He draws high praise from the critics, as does the cast of Kim Stanley, Geraldine Page, Luther Adler, Robert Loggia, Kevin McCarthy, and Barbara Baxley.

JULY • Theatre Genesis stages its first production, Malcolm Boyd's *Study in Color*, in the 74-seat parish hall of the St. Marks in the Bouwerie Church, in what will become the East Village, off-off-Broadway.

SEPTEMBER 22 *Fiddler on the Roof* (3,242) opens at the Imperial. Zero Mostel as Tevye—Danny Kaye was the first choice—becomes a superstar. Jerry Bock and Sheldon Harnick have written the title song and "Tradition," "Matchmaker, Matchmaker," "If I Were a Rich Man," and "Sunrise, Sunset." Also in the cast are Beatrice Arthur, Joanna Merlin, Austin Pendleton, Julia Mignes, Bert Convy, and Tanya Everett. Chaim Topol will have the lead role in the 1971 movie.

OCTOBER 12 The New York Shakespeare Festival production of *Othello* (224) opens at the Martinique. James Earl Jones is the Moor. **13** Friedrich Duerrenmatt's *The Physicists* (55), directed by Peter Brook, opens at the Martin Beck. Three scientists hide in a lunatic asylum to keep their knowledge from being used for destructive purposes. The stars are Robert Shaw, Hume Cronyn, Jessica Tandy, and George Voskovec. **20** *Golden Boy* (569), Clifford Odets's 1937 play about a boxer, has become a Charles Strouse–Lee Adams musical, starring Sammy Davis, Jr., at the Majestic.

NOVEMBER 1 Robert Lowell's one-act play *Beneto Cereno* (36), based on the Melville story, is at the American Place Theatre at St. Clement's Church. It's part of a grouping of plays called *The Old Glory*. In the cast are Roscoe Lee Browne and Lester Rawlins. **11** Eli Wallach, Anne Jackson, and Alan Arkin star in Murray Schisgal's *Luv* (902), at the Booth. This dark comedy is about two unhappy men and what

Business and Society

JUNE • Frederick O'Neal is the new president of Actors Equity, replacing Ralph Bellamy, who, after 12 years in the job, declined to run again. Theodore Bikel has beaten out Dorothy Gish for first vice president. **1** A new law allows New York State to more closely regulate the business practices of Broadway productions. It's a reaction to this past year's revelations of corruption in the box offices. **8** The League of New York Theatres and Actors Equity settle their differences, warding off a threatened strike. Picket lines had already gone up at a few theatres, canceling Sunday matinées of *Oliver* and *The Deputy*.

AUGUST • Martin Duberman's *In White America* is being staged by The Free Southern Theatre in Mississippi. The Student Non-Violent Coordinating Committee—SNCC—is sponsoring performances in several towns.

OCTOBER 18 The NBC television network broadcasts a production of *The Fantasticks* while the original is still running off-Broadway, the first time a play or musical has had to compete directly with a televised version of itself.

Births, Deaths, and Marriages

JUNE 27 Three decades from now, in a one-woman show, Andrea Martin will refer to Ethel Merman as "the woman who learned the language of love at the hands of Ernest Borgnine." But today, it's hugs and kisses, as Merman m. the burly movie actor.

JULY 12 Actress Geraldine Brooks, daughter of James Strook, who heads the Brooks Costume Company, the theatre's biggest, m. writer Budd Schulberg. **20** Salome Jens m. Ralph Meeker.

AUGUST 5 Anne Bancroft m. Mel Brooks. **27** Gracie Allen d.

SEPTEMBER 18 Playwright Sean O'Casey d. **28** Harpo Marx d.

OCTOBER 10 Eddie Cantor d. George Burns once said, "Maybe Eddie didn't sing so well, and he wasn't a great dancer,

"Broadway's Brightest Star," is on the cover of *Newsweek* in his Tevye costume from *Fiddler on the Roof*. **22** Critic Michael Smith writes in the *Village Voice* about a new playwright whose first works, *Cowboys* and *The Rock Garden*, are being produced at the new Theatre Genesis at the St. Marks in the Bouwerie Church in the East Village. "The playwright's name is Sam Shepard, and I know nothing about him," says Smith, "except that he has written a pair of provocative and genuinely original plays." Other critics see Shepard as an ersatz Samuel Beckett.

NOVEMBER 18 Lester Osterman and Jule Styne, producers of *Fade Out–Fade In*, which has closed because of Carol Burnett's absence, hold a press conference, at which they contend that their star aggravated her old injuries by taping a strenuous appearance on a television show and say that they are upset that she has not told them when to expect her back. They are filing charges against her with Equity. Burnett says that they are "harassing her" but acknowledges wanting to leave the show.

DECEMBER 7 Robert Whitehead resigns or is fired as codirector of the Repertory Theatre of Lincoln Center. He attacks William Schuman, the composer, who heads Lincoln Center and the board of directors of the arts complex for undercutting him. Commercially and artistically, the Repertory Company is struggling. Out of five plays so far, only *After the Fall* and the just opened *Incident at Vichy*, both by Arthur Miller, are box office successes. Elia Kazan, in sympathy with Whitehead, is withdrawing from the company, the entire membership of which has signed a letter of protest about Whitehead's departure. **30** Jason Robards, responding to charges by his former wife, Rachel Taylor, that he has defaulted on child support, accuses her of securing the terms of their 1961 separation agreement by threatening to label him an alcoholic and philanderer who committed adultery with Lauren Bacall. She will win the case, and he will have to pay. But he did marry Bacall.

JANUARY 4 On the occasion of the opening of his enigmatic play *Tiny Alice*,

happens when one of them decides to hand his wife off to the other. **18** Alan Alda is perturbed by the antics of his prostitute neighbor, played by Diana Sands, in Bill Manhoff's comedy *The Owl and the Pussycat* (421), at the ANTA Theatre. There's a 1970 screen version.

DECEMBER 3 *Incident at Vichy* (99), Arthur Miller's play that examines the issue of individual responsibility against the backdrop of the Nazi roundup of Jews in France in 1942, opens at the ANTA Theatre. The all-male cast includes Hal Holbrook, Joseph Wiseman, David Wayne, and Tony Lo Bianco. **18** Two new plays by LeRoi Jones, *The Toilet* (151), about racism and homosexuality, with abundant and graphic violence, and *The Slave*, depicting a race war in the future, open at the St. Marks Playhouse. Al Freeman, Jr. and Nan Martin are among the players. **22** Jason Robards, Jr. and Jack Dodson open in Eugene O'Neill's hotel lobby drama *Hughie* (51), at the Royale. **29** Edward Albee's *Tiny Alice* (167), starring John Gielgud and Irene Worth, opens at the Billy Rose Theatre. On the surface, it's a story about a rich woman who pays to seduce a Catholic lay brother. Above or below the surface, many critics don't get it, although Whitney Boulton says that this work makes Albee "the outstanding young playwright of our time. . . ."

JANUARY 28 Arthur Miller's *A View from the Bridge* (780), produced as a one-act play on Broadway in 1955 and now

John Gielgud *MSN*

NOVEMBER • *Fortune* magazine repeats the recent *New York Times* contention that Broadway is a financial quagmire for investors.

DECEMBER 6 The New York City License Commissioner announces that ticket brokers' books will be subject to monthly audits. There have been several arrests over the past few weeks for "ice"—the illegal premiums that box office personnel sometimes collect for premium seats—and there is now a crackdown on scalping by out-of-town brokers. **24** Martin McKnight, Minnesota Mining and Manufacturing's board chairman, confirms that he is buying the Martin Beck Theatre, giving his Jujamcyn Company a second Broadway house. It already owns the St. James.

MARCH 26 LeRoi Jones's plays *The Toilet* and *The Slave* are closed in Los Angeles because they don't have a police permit. They will obtain the permit after playing for awhile with no admission. On April 4, the *Los Angeles Times*, the only paper to carry their ads, will change its policy, declining to publish them.

APRIL 4 A Broadway benefit at the Majestic Theatre, for civil rights work in Selma, Alabama, raises $150,000. The

and most of his jokes really weren't that funny. but he did so much so fast that the audience didn't have time to notice." **15** Cole Porter d.

NOVEMBER 18 Ethel Merman divorces Ernest Borgnine.

JANUARY 12 Playwright Lorraine Hansberry d. at age 34.

MARCH 22 Composer Harry Tierney d. **25** Sarah Jessica Parker b.

MAY 15 Robert Clary, a protegé of Eddie Cantor, m. one of the singer-comedian's daughters, Natalie.

Personalities

Newsweek quotes Edward Albee: "There are two dangerous things for a writer, success and failure. I'm aware of the danger." At the Broadway debut of *Who's Afraid of Virginia Woolf?* director Franco Zefferelli, backstage afterward to congratulate Albee, had remarked to reporters that "the danger is success. Can Eduardo survive success?" **25** Herbert Blau and Jules Irving, codirectors of the Actors Workshop of San Francisco, are named to the same positions at the Repertory Theatre of Lincoln Center, replacing Robert Whitehead and Elia Kazan.

FEBRUARY 15 With Carol Burnett back in the starring role, *Fade Out–Fade In* reopens at the Mark Hellinger after a three-month hiatus and recriminations between management and its star player over her absence.

MARCH • According to Wakefield Poole, an associate choreographer on *Do I Hear a Waltz*, things got so tense in the company just before the New Haven tryout that director John Dexter, exasperated with female lead Elizabeth Allen, yelled at her, "Fuck you, you pig." **22** Edward Albee holds a press conference at the Billy Rose Theatre to discuss the controversy over his *Tiny Alice*, which opened December 29. Albee attacks critics who complain about its opaqueness, especially Walter Kerr who, says Albee, thinks that "the excellence of a play is determined by its immediate mass appeal."

MAY • Author Budd Schulberg and the producers of *What Makes Sammy Run* publicly criticize star Steve Lawrence's 21 absences from the show since Christmas. He says he's been sick, has taken some days off without pay, and criticizes their "lack of professionalism." **19** Lee Strasberg, responding to poor reviews of the Actors Studio's production of *Blues for Mr. Charlie* in London, says, "There is confusion in the play between Mr. Baldwin's dynamic anger at the racial situation and the human involvement beneath it. It is partly his fault, partly ours, if the human emotions are not sufficiently conveyed in the production."

Plays and Musicals

expanded, opens under Ulu Grossbard's direction at the Sheridan Square Playhouse. The assistant director is Dustin Hoffman, and the players include Jon Voight, Susan Anspach, in her New York debut, Richard Castellano, and in the lead role as longshoreman Eddie Carbone, Robert Duvall, who gives a searing, riveting performance.

FEBRUARY 4 The Moscow Art Theatre, last in New York 41 years ago, opens a repertory season at the City Center with Mikhail Bulgakov's adaptation of Gogol's novel *Dead Souls*.

MARCH 10 Art Carney as Felix Unger and Walter Matthau playing Oscar Madison are the original *Odd Couple* (965), Neil Simon's comedy opening at the Plymouth. The clash of the neat and the slovenly will transfer to the screen in 1968 with Jack Lemmon opposite Matthau and will reach television, starring Tony Randall and Jack Klugman, on September 24, 1970. **18** *Do I Hear a Waltz* (220), opening at the Forty-sixth Street Theatre, has music by Richard Rodgers, lyrics by Stephen Sondheim, and a book by Arthur Laurents. Walter Kerr calls it "dry," "earnest," and "thoughtful." *The Saturday Review* calls it "Dearth in Venice." It stars Elizabeth Allen, Carol Bruce, and Sergio Franchi.

APRIL 25 David Heneker's *Half A Sixpence* (512), a vehicle for Tommy Steele based on H.G. Well's novel *Kipps*, arrives at the Broadhurst. The supporting cast includes John Cleese, and one of the cast replacements for Steele will be Joel Grey. "Money to Burn" is a notable number. It's filmed in 1967. **26** It's a bumpy run for Terrence McNally in his Broadway debut when his play *And Things that Go Bump in the Night* (16) opens at the Royale.

MAY 16 *The Roar of the Greasepaint—The Smell of the Crowd* (232)opens at the Shubert. Anthony Newley stars and has again collaborated with Leslie Bricusse (*Stop the World)*, and the costar is Cyril Ritchard. "Who Can I Turn To?" is the big number.

Business and Society

talent includes: Ethel Merman, Barbra Streisand, Carol Channing, John Gielgud, Eli Wallach, Carol Burnett, Walter Matthau, Irene Worth, Art Carney, and Robert Preston.

MAY • The touring company of *Hello, Dolly!* starring Mary Martin sets a new record for grosses in an eight-performance week when it takes in $168,790 at the 4,120-seat Dallas State Fair Music Hall.

Births, Deaths, and Marriages

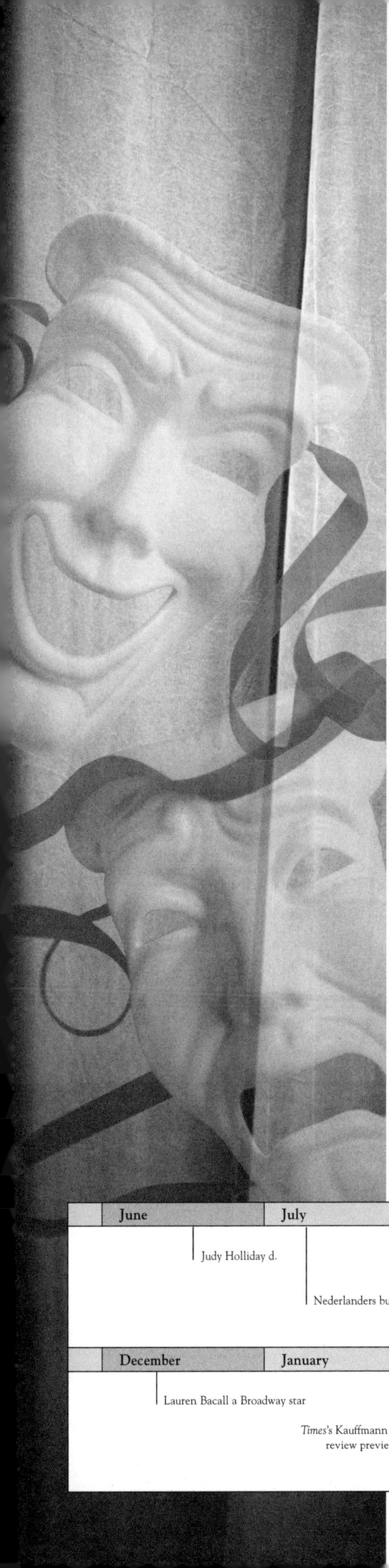

1965–66

The new critic at *The New York Times*, Stanley Kauffmann, creates controversy—and a confrontation with David Merrick—when he announces that he will review previews rather than opening nights. *Man of La Mancha* arrives without much publicity or a contract for an original cast recording. The Nederlanders become a presence on Broadway. Lauren Bacall is a new Broadway star, and Zoe Caldwell makes her Broadway debut, even if it's only for a few performances as Anne Bancroft's understudy. Carol Channing has hopes but no illusions about playing in the film of *Hello, Dolly!* Mary Martin takes the show on the road and into a war zone. Joseph Papp buys a new home for his company. And now it's Actors Equity that Edward Albee is antagonizing.

- Number of David Merrick hits on Broadway: 5—*Inadmissible Evidence, Cactus Flower, Philadelphia, Here I Come, Marat/Sade,* and *Hello, Dolly!*
- Number of words in the full title of *Marat/Sade* (*The Persecution and Assassination of Marat as Performed by the Inmates of the Asylum of Charenton Under the Direction of the Marquis de Sade*): 24
- Neil Simon's Broadway income—currently, about $20,000 a week, primarily from *Barefoot in the Park, The Odd Couple,* and the book for *Sweet Charity*
- Top sale price for Al Hirschfeld's theatre caricatures in his one-man show at the Hammer Galleries on Fifty-seventh Street: $1,000
- Top ticket price of *On a Clear Day You Can See Forever*: $11.20, Broadway's new peak
- Buy a typewriter, rewrite your name: Frederick August Kittel buys his first typewriter and changes his name, adding his middle name to his mother's maiden name to produce August Wilson
- Significant title once held by Helen Menken (d. 1966): "Mrs. Bogart"—she was Humphrey Bogart's first wife (1926–28)
- Real identity of "Norm Deploom," lyricist for one of the songs in the off-Broadway musical *The Mad Show*: Stephen Sondheim
- Number of Pulitzer Prizes for Drama awarded in the past 4 years: 1
- What it costs to stage *Mark Twain Tonight!*, Hal Holbrook's one-man show: $10,500
- Unique distinction of *The Zulu and the Zayda*: it's virtually guaranteed to appear last in any list or index of Broadway shows
- Number of professional actors on Broadway and in roadshows: 1,140
- Number of professional actors in regional theatres in the U.S. and Canada: 1,200—the first time in many years that the regional theatres have had the higher figure

Productions on Broadway: 68

Pulitzer Prize for Drama: None awarded

New York Drama Critics Circle Awards:
Best Play: *Marat/Sade* (Peter Weiss)
Best Musical: *Man of La Mancha* (Mitch Leigh and Joe Darion)

Tony Awards:
Play: *Marat/Sade* (Peter Weiss)
Actor in a Play: Hal Holbrook (*Mark Twain Tonight!*)
Actress in a Play: Rosemary Harris (*The Lion in Winter*)
Musical: *Man of La Mancha* (Mitch Leigh and Joe Darion)
Actor in a Musical: Richard Kiley (*Man of La Mancha*)
Actress in a Musical: Angela Lansbury (*Mame*)

June	July	August	September	October	November
Judy Holliday d.	Nederlanders buy Palace Theatre	Carol Channing leaves Broadway *Hello, Dolly!*	Mary Martin 'Dolly' diverted to Vietnam	*The Royal Hunt of the Sun*	*Man of La Mancha*

December	January	February	March	April	May
Lauren Bacall a Broadway star	*Times's* Kauffmann to review previews	Playwright Brian Friel's Broadway debut	*Mark Twain Tonight!*	Russel Crouse d.	Angela Lansbury in *Mame*

Personalities

JUNE 3 Columnist Sheilah Graham reports that Carol Channing is apprehensive about starring in the film of *Hello Dolly!* "I'm bracing myself for them to sign whoever happens to be the Marilyn Monroe of the moment," says the stage star, referring to the actress who beat her out for the film of *Gentlemen Prefer Blondes.* Among those already mentioned for the screen role of Dolly Levi are Lucille Ball, Doris Day, and Julie Andrews. **6** Tallulah Bankhead is the "mystery guest" on television's "What's My Line?" **19** Sydney Chaplin, playing Nick Arnstein in *Funny Girl,* leaves the show after settling with the producers for the remaining period of his contract—a buyout said to be worth $90,000. He says it's not Barbra Streisand but Ray Stark with whom he's clashed. In fact, Chaplin has been receiving notes from Streisand critiquing his performance—others in the cast have also received Streisand's report cards—and is furious. He and Streisand have each accused the other of scene-stealing as well. His permanent replacement will be Johnny Desmond.

AUGUST 4–7 At the National Playwrights Conference in Waterford, Connecticut, are several young dramatists on the verge of making their mark: John Guare, Sam Shepard, and Lanford Wilson. The Eugene O'Neill Theatre Centre that will house the increasingly important annual gathering will come to be known as "Camp Eugene." **7** Carol Channing gives her last Broadway performance in the original production of *Hello, Dolly!* Ginger Rogers will be the first of her replacements.

OCTOBER • The Stork Club closes. **10** The touring company of *Hello, Dolly!* starring Mary Martin, begins a 10-day tour of U.S. military installations in Vietnam at the Bien Hoa air base, where the audience includes General William Westmoreland and Prime Minister Nguyen Cao Ky. **22** Mary Martin is on the cover of *Life,* shown performing in *Hello, Dolly!* for American troops in Nha Trang, Vietnam.

NOVEMBER • Backstage at the Philadelphia legitimate theatre, where Gwen Verdon will open in *Sweet Charity.* **4** The Long Wharf Theatre opens in New Haven with Arthur Miller's *The Crucible.*

Plays and Musicals

JUNE 15 Jessica Tandy and Hume Cronyn open in *The Cherry Orchard,* at the Tyrone Guthrie Theatre in Minneapolis. Critic Hobe Morrison, in *Variety,* calls it "the outstanding presentation of the Chekhov classic in a lifetime of theatregoing and would be a credit to any company."

OCTOBER 8 *Generation* (300), a comedy about parents and teenagers by William Goodhart, at the Morosco, stars Henry Fonda. **13** *The Impossible Years* (670), a comedy by Bob Fisher and Arthur Marx, son of Groucho, opens at the Playhouse. Alan King stars as the psychiatrist who struggles with his own teenage daughters. **17** *On a Clear Day You Can See Forever* (273) opens at the Mark Hellinger. Alan Jay Lerner has collaborated on the score with composer Burton Lane, who stepped in when Richard Rodgers stepped out. Barbara Harris and John Collum star in this story about ESP, which reaches the screen in 1970. **26** Peter Shaffer's *The Royal Hunt of the Sun* (261), narrated by George Rose, opens at the American National Theatre and Academy (ANTA) Theatre. Christopher Plummer plays conquistador Francisco Pizarro, who gradually comes to respect the Incas of Peru, whom he has subjugated. David Carradine is the Inca king.

NOVEMBER 10 *The Zulu and the Zayda* (179), by Howard Da Silva and Felix

Christopher Plummer *MSN*

Business and Society

JUNE • President Johnson signs the legislation that creates the National Endowment for the Arts, endowed with $5 million.

JULY • The Nederlander family of Detroit buys New York's Palace Theatre and will convert it from a movie house into a

AUGUST • The producers of LeRoi Jones's *The Toilet* and *The Dutchmen,* now playing in San Francisco, run an ad in the *San Francisco Chronicle* referring to the recent rioting in the Watts neighborhood of Los Angeles, which states: "If these plays had not been 'banned' in Los Angeles, more people might have been able to see them and understand the frustration and hatred which led up to the recent rioting."

SEPTEMBER 17 New York City is hit by a 24-day newspaper strike, causing producers to scramble for other ways of promoting their shows. This strike will eventually result in the demise of the *Herald-Tribune.*

Births, Deaths, and Marriages

JUNE • Sandy Dennis m. jazz saxophonist Gerry Mulligan, at one time Judy Holliday's lover. **7** Judy Holliday d. She had once said of her "dumb blonde" stage persona, "One writer said that I started as a moron and worked my way up to an imbecile. Maybe, if I'm lucky, I can be an idiot." **23** Mary Boland d.

JULY • Colleen Dewhurst and George C. Scott divorce. **15** Director JoAnne Akalaitas m. composer Philip Glass. It lasts until 1974.

AUGUST 1 Eugene Howard d.

NOVEMBER 26 Patty Duke m. television director Harry Falk, Jr.

DECEMBER 16 Playwright Somerset Maugham d.

FEBRUARY 2 Louise Lasser m. Woody Allen.

tryout of *Inadmissible Evidence*, David Merrick, according to reports, has been sent sprawling into several trash cans. What or who knocked him off his feet is not clear. According to one cast member, the producer had quarrelled with director Anthony Page and star Nicol Williamson over the script. Later in the month, Merrick garners more publicity in Philadelphia when his *Cactus Flower* is warming up for Broadway. Young Tom Snyder, interviewing theatregoers emerging from the show for a local television station, does not recognize Merrick, who poses as a happy ticket holder. But older hands at the studio spot the ruse and cut it from the tape. **9** With the entire Northeast hit by a blackout, the opening of *The Zulu and the Zayda*, at the Cort, is postponed until tomorrow. Outside the theatre, coproducer Dore Schary says, "I never thought the Cort would go dark *before* the opening."

DECEMBER 23–25 Australian-born Zoe Caldwell, understudying Anne Bancroft in *The Devils*, makes her Broadway debut when Bancroft misses several performances. **27** Edward Albee's remark, quoted in *The New York Times* today, that the "difficult language" in his play *Tiny Alice* necessitated British actors for the principal roles will draw criticism from Actors Equity.

JANUARY • Draftee and aspiring playwright David Rabe arrives in Vietnam, where he will serve with a hospital support unit, seeing casualties but no combat. **1** Stanley Kauffmann, formerly with the *New Republic*, replaces Howard Taubman as the theatre critic of *The New York Times*. **5** *Times* theatre critic Stanley Kauffmann announces that he will review final preview performances rather than opening nights because he needs more than an hour to write. He begins today with James Kirkwood's *UBTU* ("Unhealthy To Be Unpleasant"), starring Tony Randall, Thelma Ritter and Margaret Hamilton, directed by Nancy Walker, which opened last night at the Helen Hayes Theatre. Kauffmann pans the play, the author, and director Walker, "who, as theatre people like to say, was born in a trunk. The trouble is, she has not quite got out of it." **13** With the closing of his new play

Leon, with music by Harold Rome, opens at the Cort a day late because of the blackout. Dore Schary is directing as well as coproducing this story of a Yiddish-speaking grandfather's relationship to a Zulu in South Africa. Menasha Skulnick, Lou Gossett, and Ossie Davis star, with Joe Silver and Yaphet Kotto. **11** *Hogan's Goat* (607), by William Alfred, opens at the American Place Theatre in St. Clement's Church. This highly acclaimed play about ambition and Irish-American politics in the late nineteenth century, stars Ralph Waite, Tom Ahearne, Cliff Gorman, Barnard Hughes, and, in a career-making role, Faye Dunaway, a recent drama school graduate. **15** Douglas Turner Ward's one-act plays, *Happy Ending* and *Day of Absence* (504), which satirize race relations in America, open at the St. Marks Playhouse. The casts include Ward, Esther Rolle, Frances Foster, Robert Hooks, Lonnie Elder, and Moses Gunn. **22** "The Impossible Dream" encapsulates the spirit of the Mitch Leigh-Joe Darion musical about Don Quixote, *Man of La Mancha* (2,328,), at the ANTA Theatre (it will eventually move to Broadway and the Martin Beck). Richard Kiley is the errant knight, supported by Irving Jacobson and Joan Denier, with Ray Middleton and Robert Rounseville. It's a film in 1972. **30** Nicol Williamson stars as a tormented and tormenting lawyer whose life is falling apart in John Osborne's *Inadmissible Evidence* (167), at the Belasco.

Richard Kiley *MSN*

OCTOBER 12 The Vivian Beaumont Theatre opens in Lincoln Center with *Danton's Death*.

NOVEMBER 9 Broadway and most everything else in the northeast is plunged into darkness on this Tuesday night by a blackout that hits at 5:28 P.M. and will not end until the middle of the night. *The New York Times* manages an eight-page edition, but *Variety* misses its first deadline in 60 years. Gallagher's steak house, with its auxiliary generator, is a beacon of light in the theatre district. Tomorrow's matinées will go on but with reduced attendance.

DECEMBER 31 The federal tax of 10 percent on theatre tickets is dropped.

JANUARY 1 New York City is hit by a 12-day transit strike. Broadway shows sold out in advance include *Cactus Flower*, *Hello, Dolly! Fiddler on the Roof*, and *The Odd Couple*. Actors Equity has authorized off-Broadway productions to suspend for the duration, and several do. **28** Joseph Papp's New York Shakespeare Festival buys the Astor Library, which it will convert into the Public Theatre.

FEBRUARY 2 Yale announces the appointment of Robert Brustein as Dean of its

3 Actress June Walker, mother of actor John Kerr, d. **9** Sophie Tucker d. **10** Producer Billy Rose d.

MARCH 3 Playwright Joseph Fields, son of Lew Fields and brother of Herbert and Dorothy Fields, d. **28** Helen Menken d. of a heart attack at the Lambs Club. She was Humphrey Bogart's first wife (1926–28). **30** Director Erwin Piscator d.

APRIL 3 Playwright Russel Crouse d.

Personalities

announced today, two days after it opened, Edward Albee takes out an ad in *The New York Times*, stating: "To those who have come to see 'Malcolm,' my thanks. To those who were pleased, my gratitude. To those who were disappointed, my apologies. See you next play."

FEBRUARY • Edward Albee tells a radio interviewer that the only "unhappy" experience he's had with an actor was with John Gielgud in *Tiny Alice*. Gielgud, says the playwright, was "petulant," wouldn't learn his lines, and acted like a "child." **10** Critic Stanley Kauffmann, who has been criticized for reviewing productions he saw in previews—most of his colleagues in the center aisle seats do not like it—receives tickets to the final preview performance of David Merrick's *Philadelphia, Here I Come*. Accompanying them is a note from Merrick that reads: "At your peril." **15** *Times* critic Stanley Kauffmann arrives at the Helen Hayes Theatre for the final preview of *Philadelphia, Here I Come*, by Brian Friel, only to find that producer David Merrick has canceled it, ostensibly because a generator has "failed." The marquee is dark, but as observers note, the lobby lights are burning brightly. Merrick, who is losing $2,650 from the cancellation, had been heard to say that he would "ambush" Kauffmann. The producer says that a rat got in the generator.

MARCH • David Merrick, it is said, is the "nameless" producer quoted in *Variety*, comparing *Times* critic Stanley Kauffmann to his predecessor, calling Kauffmann "Howard Taubman with a new thesaurus." Merrick has been sending columnists copies of Kauffmann's trashy novel *The Philanderers*.

APRIL • In a newspaper interview in Toronto, where he's mounting a production of Chekhov's *Ivanov*, John Gielgud, who directed Richard Burton on Broadway in *Hamlet*, says he was "horrified" by the electronically filmed version of that production. "All the little-boy vices had come back," says Gielgud of Burton, "that Shropshire Lad thing of gazing into the audience and relying on

Plays and Musicals

DECEMBER 8 Lauren Bacall becomes a Broadway star, at the Royale, in *Cactus Flower* (1,234), Abe Burrow's adaptation of a Parisian farce, his first nonmusical show. Bacall is the assistant to a dentist, played by Barry Nelson. Brenda Vaccaro plays his mistress. It reaches the screen in 1969. **27** Peter Weiss's *The Persecution and Assassination of Marat as Performed by the Inmates of the Asylum of Charenton Under the Direction of the Marquis de Sade*, a.k.a. *Marat/Sade* (145), a Royal Shakespeare Company production, opens at the Martin Beck. Peter Brook is directing a cast that includes Glenda Jackson, Ian Richardson, and Patrick Magee as de Sade. Mostly praised by critics, it still draws fire from Walter Kerr, who sees a "substitution of theatrical production for dramatic structure."

JANUARY 10 *The Mad Show* (871), an off-Broadway Mary Rodgers musical based on *Mad* magazine, is at The New Theatre. "Norm Deploom," the lyricist for one of the songs, is Stephen Sondheim. In the cast is unknown Linda Lavin. **29** Gwen Verdon is the star of *Sweet Charity* (608), adapted from Federico Fellini's 1957 film *Nights of Cabiria* at the Palace Theatre, the first time that the former vaudeville house has hosted a play or musical. The Cy Coleman-Dorothy Fields show, with book by Neil Simon and direction and choreography by Verdon's husband Bob Fosse, features "Big Spender" and "If My Friends Could See Me Now." It's on the screen in 1969.

FEBRUARY 2 A blind woman is menaced by men who think she is concealing drugs in *Wait Until Dark* (374), by Frederick Knott, directed by Arthur Penn and starring Robert Duvall and Lee Remick, at the Barrymore. The 1967 film stars Audrey Hepburn. **16** Brian Friel's *Philadelphia, Here I Come* (326), a play about a native of Ireland about to emigrate to America—will his father miss him?—opens at the Helen Hayes. The *Times*'s Stanley Kauffmann, tricked by producer David Merrick into reviewing it on opening night instead of last night at the final preview, which Merrick can-

Business and Society

School of Drama, beginning July 1. It's probably the first time that a major critic will hold such a position. **15** Actors Equity and the Society of Stage Directors and Choreographers protest *The New York Times*'s critic Stanley Kauffmann's practice of reviewing preview performances instead of opening nights. The League of New York Theatres and the Dramatists Guild have protested similarly.

MARCH • The League of Resident Theatres is formed. **29** Producer Harold Prince is experimenting with flexible ticket pricing for his campy *Superman* musical, opening tonight. Orchestra seats range from $9 to a very pricey $12—the highest on Broadway—for the most desirable locations but are pegged at only $2 in the balcony. People ordering at least a month advance were given a discount.

MAY • The New York League of Theatres and Producers for the first time jointly sponsors the Tony Awards with the American Theatre Wing.

Births, Deaths, and Marriages

personality. . . . It's sad, the waste."

MAY • On the basis of Rosemary Harris's performances this season in a revival of *You Can't Take It With You* and in *The Lion in Winter*, *Life* magazine calls its feature story on her "Broadway Finds a New First Lady." **26** A New York State Supreme Court judge orders Harold Prince (not the famous Broadway producer) of Agon Productions to refrain from soliciting funds for his projects unless he states in the prospectus that he is not *the* Harold Prince, who has brought charges against this lesser Prince.

celed, is the only critic to pan it.

MARCH 3 Rosemary Harris and Robert Preston star at the Ambassador Theatre as Henry II and his Queen, Eleanor, in James Goldman's *The Lion in Winter* (92), in roles that go to Peter O'Toole and Katharine Hepburn in the 1968 film. **8** John Arden's *Serjeant Musgrave's Dance* (135) is at the Theatre De Lys. The powerful antiwar play stars John Colicos in the title role. Young Roy Scheider is a member of the supporting cast. **23** Hal Holbrook opens at the Longacre in his one-man tour de force *Mark Twain Tonight!* (85). Holbrook has been doing the show off and on for 12 years, including off-Broadway seven years ago, but it is hitting the Main Stem for the first time tonight. **29** *It's a Bird . . . It's a Plane . . . It's Superman* (129), the Charles Strouse-Lee Adams tongue-in-cheek musical, opens at the Alvin, with Bob Holiday as the man of steel and Patricia Marand as Lois Lane.

APRIL 21 Dustin Hoffman will win an Obie for *The Journey of the Fifth Horse* (12), a play by Ronald Ribman about two failures in life, opening at the American Place Theatre in St. Clements Church.

MAY 3 John Gielgud has adapted, directs, and stars in Chekhov's *Ivanov* (47), costarring Vivian Leigh, at the Shubert. Richard Watts, Jr., in the *Post*, writes that Leigh "is especially moving in the scene when she is told brutally by her husband that she is dying." In fact, the actress herself will be dead in a year, at age 53. **24** Jerry Herman's *Mame* (1,508), a musical triumph for Angela Lansbury, thanks to Mary Martin's rejection of the role, opens at the Winter Garden. This tuneful version of *Auntie Mame* is notable for its title song and costars Beatrice Arthur. Lucille Ball stars in the 1974 movie, with Arthur and Robert Preston.

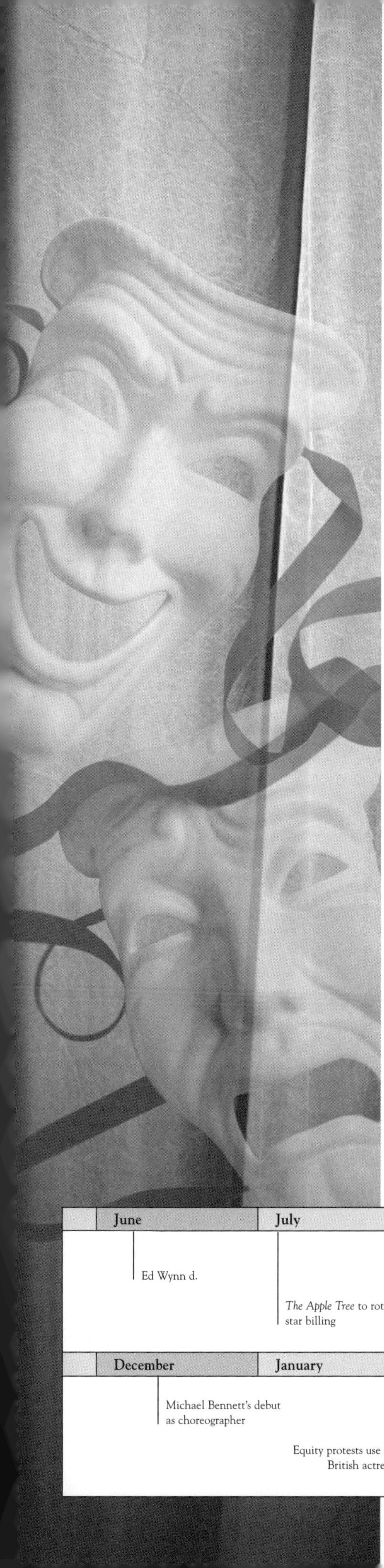

1966–67

It's holdovers that are keeping the Broadway box office healthy. Among the current long-running cash cows are *Hello, Dolly! Fiddler on the Roof*, *Funny Girl*, and *Man of La Mancha*. Off-Broadway and resident theatre managers are learning about labor-management relations, as Broadway producers did before them. Walter Kerr has the coveted job of chief critic at *The New York Times*, the Mark Taper Forum opens in Los Angeles, and one of the oddest things about *Breakfast at Tiffany's* is the idea of Edward Albee replacing Abe Burrows. The Tonys are on network TV, competing with "Bonanza." Actors Equity ratchets up its opposition to the importing of British actors to take roles that could—it contends—be played by Americans. And Harold Pinter means what he says and says what he means, but what might that be?

- Chosen Miss Ft. Worth: 19-year-old Betty Buckley, head cheerleader at Texas Christian University
- What the cast of *Breakfast at Tiffany's* calls the show when Edward Albee is brought in as a play doctor: "Who's Afraid of Holly Golightly?"
- Amount that Thornton Wilder is collecting weekly from *Hello, Dolly!* which is based on his play *The Matchmaker*: $7,000
- What Lou Jacobs's character in Woody Allen's *Don't Drink the Water* replies to his wife when she says, "Walter, be calm.": "I'm calm. Who's Walter?"
- Tallulah Bankhead's final role: "The Black Widow" on the "Batman" TV show
- Number of New York City daily newspapers at the end of this season: 3
- Number of newspapers 3 seasons ago: 7
- Capitalization of Barbara Garson's *Macbird!*: $30,000
- Biggest investor in *Macbird!*: Paul Krassner, publisher of the iconoclastic magazine *The Realist*, who put up $3,000
- What the London *Daily Mail* will say about the British production of *Macbird!*: "There has often been much ado about nothing, but not for some time has there been much ado about less."
- Number of speaking parts taken by foreign actors on Broadway out of 1,008 such parts available: 42
- Debt accumulated by the *Tulane Drama Review*: $100,000
- Out in the cold: John Steinbeck, whose play *Of Mice and Men*, often performed in the U.S.S.R., has been withdrawn there because he supports the war in Vietnam
- Amount of royalties that John Steinbeck will lose because of the withdrawal of his play: none, because the U.S.S.R. doesn't pay them
- Legal limit on premium brokers may add to the price of a theatre ticket: $1.50

Productions on Broadway: 69

Pulitzer Prize for Drama: *A Delicate Balance* (Edward Albee)

New York Drama Critics Circle Awards:
Best Play: *The Homecoming* (Harold Pinter)
Best Musical: *Cabaret* (John Kander and Fred Ebb)

Tony Awards:
Play: *The Homecoming* (Harold Pinter)
Actor in a Play: Paul Rogers (*The Homecoming*)
Actress in a Play: Beryl Reid (*The Killing of Sister George*)
Musical: *Cabaret* (John Kander and Fred Ebb)
Actor in a Musical: Robert Preston (*I Do! I Do!*)
Actress in a Musical: Barbara Harris (*The Apple Tree*)

June	July	August	September	October	November
Ed Wynn d.	*The Apple Tree* to rotate star billing	Walter Kerr named new *Times* critic	Albee's *A Delicate Balance*	Nederlanders buy Henry Miller's Theatre	*Cabaret*

December	January	February	March	April	May
Michael Bennett's debut as choreographer	Equity protests use of British actress	*Macbird!*	Tonys on network TV for first time	First Mark Taper Forum production	Pulitzer to Albee

Personalities

JUNE • Bert Lahr, signed to perform in Aristophanes' *The Birds* at the Ypsilante, Michigan, Greek Theatre, insists that the William Arrowsmith translation be purged of what the comedian calls "barnyard language." **17** Angela Lansbury, as "Mame," is on the cover of *Life*.

JULY • Star billing for the coming season's Jerry Bock-Sheldon Harnick musical *The Apple Tree* has been a sticking point, so it will be rotated between Alan Alda, Larry Blyden, and Barbara Harris.

AUGUST 31 *The New York Times* announces that Walter Kerr, the *Herald Tribune* drama critic for 15 years until that paper folded two weeks ago, will succeed Stanley Kauffmann as the *Times* drama critic. Kerr will take over next month with the opening of Edward Albee's *A Delicate Balance*.

SEPTEMBER 29 "I've always had reservations about being a full-time wife and a career girl," Elizabeth Ashley, star of *Take Her, She's Mine* and *Barefoot in the Park*, says in a *World Journal Tribune* interview. She's married actor George Peppard and, according to the paper, "The minute they were married, she retired and life has been blissful ever since." In reality, she's having a nervous breakdown, and the marriage is a disaster, especially because Peppard wants her to be a housewife rather than a working actress.

OCTOBER • The "Club Sardi," upstairs at the famous theatre district restaurant, opens. It's especially appointed for those waiting out opening-night reviews, with a television set and radio at each table.

NOVEMBER • With his musical version of *Breakfast at Tiffany's*, starring Mary Tyler Moore and Richard Chamberlain, floundering in its Boston tryout, David Merrick calls in Edward Albee to rewrite it. Abe Burrows, who adapted the book and was directing the show quits, upset with Albee's comment, published in the *Boston Globe*: "All those awful jokes will be thrown out and I hope to substitute some genuine wit." The cast begins to

Plays and Musicals

JUNE 13 Arnold Wesker's *The Kitchen* (173), about the unhappiness of people who work in a restaurant, opens at the Eighty-first Street Theatre on upper Broadway. Jack Gelber is directing a cast that includes Rip Torn, Sylvia Miles, and Mari Gorman.

SEPTEMBER 22 Edward Albee's *A Delicate Balance* (132), starring Hume Cronyn, Jessica Tandy, Marian Seldes, and Rosemary Murphy opens at the Martin Beck. Walter Kerr, in the *Times*, says it's about people who "are without occupations or preoccupations." He compares Albee unfavorably to Harold Pinter, who deals better with the theme of "hollowness."

OCTOBER 5 *The Killing of Sister George* (205), by Frank Marcus, opens at the Belasco. This British comedy about radio broadcasting and lesbians stars Beryl Reed, Eileen Atkins, and Lally Bowers. According to *Variety*, a prospective film version may cast Bette Davis with both Audrey and Katharine Hepburn. The film, starring Beryl Reid, appears in 1968. **11** The initial presentation at the Yale Drama School in the Robert Brustein era is Megan Terry's *Viet Rock*. In the cast is Gerome Ragni, later one of the creators of *Hair*. The show will open in New York at the Martinique on November 10. **16** Dustin Hoffman is the eccentric employee who brings chaos to a corporation in Henry Living's comedy *Eh?* (232) at the Circle in the Square. Alan Arkin is directing. **18** Several one-act plays set to music is rare, if not unique, on Broadway. Sheldon Harnick and Jerry Bock's *The Apple Tree* (463), originally titled "Come Back, Go Away, I Love You," opening at the Shubert, consists of *The Diary of Adam and Eve*, *The Lady or the Tiger*, and *Passionella*. Mike Nichols is directing his first musical, which stars Barbara Harris, Alan Alda, Larry Blyden, Robert Klein, and Carmen Alvarez.

NOVEMBER 5 *The Fantasticks*, with its 2,718th performance, becomes the longest-running musical in New York City history, passing *My Fair Lady*. **6** Jean-Claude

Business and Society

AUGUST • Shepard Traube, who heads the Society of Stage Directors and Choreographers, reports that his union has organized most of the directors and choreographers working off-Broadway, signing pacts with individual producers because the League of Off-Broadway Theatres refused to negotiate. Directors will make a minimum of $500 a week, choreographers $375. **12** Actors Equity and the League of Resident Theatres work out the first pact covering regional theatres. The top minimum salary for actors in these theatres, based on the average weekly gross, will be $135 a week.

SEPTEMBER • The Ziegfeld Theatre is demolished. **27** The Actors Studio Theatre, lacking funds, cancels its season. It's had just enough money to maintain an infrastructure since its last production, *The Three Sisters*, closed in October 1964.

OCTOBER • *Fiddler on the Roof* discriminates against observant Jews, charges Anna Marisse, who played the role of Tevye's eldest daughter until she was fired, she says, because she skipped performances on the High Holy Days, Rosh Hashanah and Yom Kippur. Producer Harold Prince

Births, Deaths, and Marriages

JUNE 19 Ed Wynn d.

SEPTEMBER 26 Helen Kane d.

OCTOBER 4 David Merrick divorces Jeanne Gibson. Tomorrow, miffed at his abrupt cancellation of her charge accounts at Tiffany's and Cartier, she will retaliate with a public notice in *The New York Times*: "My husband, David Merrick, having left my bed and board, I will no longer be responsible for his debts." She will also cut the sleeves off his Saville Row shirts before leaving. **13** Clifton Webb d.

NOVEMBER 15 Alan Jay Lerner m. journalist Karen Gunderson.

DECEMBER 7 Critic Ward Morehouse d. **14** Actor-director Richard Whorf d.

refer to the show as "Who's Afraid of Holly Golightly?" It will close at the Majestic on Broadway after the fourth of its 16 scheduled previews. **9** In a one-line notice in the middle of its "Legit Bits" column, *Variety* notes, about an unknown: "Bette Midler has succeeded Irene Paris as one of the villagers in the Broadway 'Fiddler.'" The column also reports that Frank Langella is now with the Lincoln Center Repertory Theatre.

DECEMBER 2 *Life*'s cover story is "Melina Mercouri: The 'Never On Sunday' Girl Comes to Broadway." She will be appearing in *Illya Darling*, opening in April. **14** Seventy-five-year-old Richard Maney, Broadway's most famous press agent, announces his retirement and in a letter

Wilkommen—it's *Cabaret* PB

van Itallie's *America Hurrah*, three one-act plays, *Interview* (directed by Joseph Chaikin), *TV*, and *Motel* (634), open at the Pocket Theatre off-Broadway. They look critically at mass production, the media, and urban life, and include in their casts Brenda Smiley and Ronnie Gilbert. **17** The author of *Don't Drink the Water* (588), at the Morosco, is cabaret performer and television writer Woody Allen. Lou Jacobi plays a caterer vacationing behind the Iron Curtain in this comedy, with Kay Medford and Anita Gillette. **20** "Willkommen." It's *Cabaret* (1,165), a John Kander-Fred Ebb musical at the Broadhurst (eventually moving to the Broadway Theatre), based on Christopher Isherwood's *Berlin Stories*, rooted in the naughty night life of Weimar Germany. Jill Haworth is Sally Bowles, a role Liza Minnelli has in the 1972 movie version. Joel Grey is the Kit Kat Klub emcee, with Jack Gilford, Lotte Lenya, and Burt Convy. One Kit Kat girl during the show's run will be Ann Reinking, former Radio City Music Hall Rockette, making her Broadway debut. The

says that she called in sick but was not home when someone from the company called her. The New York State Human Rights Commission will rule against her in January because she notified management of her planned absence not in advance but rather on the first day of the first holiday. **17** Ellen Stewart threatens to close her La Mama Experimental Theatre when Equity refuses to allow its performers to work for below scale at her cash-strapped, 74-seat house. After a month, Equity gives in. **31** Henry Miller's Theatre is sold to the Nederlander organization.

NOVEMBER • The Roundabout Theatre Company gives its first production, August Strindberg's *The Father*.

DECEMBER 16 The Society of Stage Directors and Choreographers pickets *America Hurrah* at the off-Broadway Pocket Theatre, a play that criticizes American society, because producer Stephanie Sills has not signed the minimum basic agreement, refusing to negotiate with the union. Within three days, the picket pressure will bring her into line with other producers who have signed.

FEBRUARY 9 Forty actors picket the Repertory Theatre at Lincoln Center

JANUARY 23 Set designer Lee Simonson d.

MARCH 6 Oscar Shaw d.

MAY 8 Playwright Elmer Rice d.

Personalities

in *Variety* writes: "If I've learned anything in the theatre it is that everyone stays on too long: playwrights, musical saw players, acrobats and David Merrick." **15** Michael Bennett makes his Broadway debut as a choreographer with *A Joyful Noise*, at the Mark Hellinger.

JANUARY • Barbara Garson's sharp-taloned satire on Lyndon Johnson's war in Vietnam, *Macbird!*, won't even open till next month, and it's already creating controversy. Jay Rosenblatt, who publishes *Showcard*, off-Broadway's equivalent of *Playbill*, won't publish one for this show, offended that Garson would even suggest that the Lyndon Johnson character could be connected to the assassination of President Kennedy. It's April 8 London opening will have to be held in a private club because the censor has refused it a license on the grounds that it maligns the head of a friendly state. **13** Poor reviews of the past several productions of the Repertory Theatre of Lincoln Center have apparently caused the resignation today of its codirector Herbert Blau. He says, "[T]he climate is no longer right for me to do what I came to do in the form I had in mind." **17** Carol Channing presents a 30-minute excerpt from *Hello, Dolly!* at the White House for President Johnson and other government figures.

FEBRUARY 8 "Merrick Options Tuner on Career of Mata Hari," reads the *Variety* headline, marking the opening act of what will prove to be a theatrical disaster. **16** Eli Wallach and director Alan Schneider are on a local television show in New York City trying to elicit from playwright Harold Pinter the meaning in and message of *The Homecoming*, which recently opened. "It means exactly what it says," says Pinter.

MARCH 16 Tallulah Bankhead makes her last appearance as an actress, on the "Batman" television show, playing "The Black Widow."

APRIL 21 Joel Grey's billing in *Cabaret* is raised to above the title. **30** Eric Bentley, in *The New York Times*, is sharply critical

Plays and Musicals

score includes the title song, "Tomorrow Belongs to Me," and "If You Could See Her." Grey and Liza Minnelli are in the 1972 film.

DECEMBER 5 Gower Champion directs Mary Martin and Robert Preston in Harvey Schmidt and Tom Jones's two-character musical *I Do, I Do* (584). Based on *The Fourposter*, it follows a couple through half a century of married life, on the stage of the Forty-Sixth Street Theatre.

JANUARY 5 Harold Pinter's *The Homecoming* (324), at the Music Box, is funny, murky, and dark, very dark. A son returns home to Britain with his American wife, played by Vivien Merchant, whom his brothers seduce and turn to prostitution. Peter Hall directs.

FEBRUARY 12 Peter Shaffer's one-act comedies *Black Comedy* and *White Lies* (337) open at the Barrymore. The stars are Geraldine Page, Lynn Redgrave, Michael Crawford, in his Broadway debut, Donald Madden, and Peter Bull. **22** *Macbird! (385)*, Barbara Garson's verse satire of Lyndon Johnson as Macbeth, opens at the Village Gate. The cast includes William Devane, Cleavon Little, Rue McClanahan, and Stacy Keach as the title character. **23** John Herbert's *Fortune and Men's Eyes* (382) opens at the Actors Playhouse. Its treatment of homosexuality in prisons stirs controversy. In the cast are Victor Arnold, Robert Christian, Bill Moor, Clifford Pellow, and Terry Kiser.

MARCH 7 *You're A Good Man, Charlie Brown* (1,597), opening at the Theatre 80 St. Marks in the East Village, is based not only on Charles Schultz's comic strip but also on a recording composer and lyricist Clark Gesner has already made of what will become the show's songs. Gesner also wrote the book, and the show stars Gary Burghoff, Bob Balaban, and Reva Rose. **13** Robert Anderson's *You Know I Can't Hear You When the Water's Running* (756), four playlets, opens at the Ambassador. Directed by Alan Schneider, they star

Business and Society

over the hiring of British actress Margaret Leighton for a production of *The Little Foxes*. **23** Robert Brustein announces that the Yale School of Drama plans a repertory company, beginning next season. Paul Newman has contributed $50,000 to a fund that will bring professional actors to the company to mix with students and faculty. Newman says that "[t]he students will have an academic climate but will not be fettered with the academic mentality to hamstring Mr. Brustein's efforts."

MARCH 26 The Tony Awards ceremonies are on network television for the first time.

APRIL • The American Actors Committee, a dissident faction within Actors Equity said to have as many as 300 members, is pushing for new restrictions on foreign actors. Roy Scheider is prominent in the group's leadership. On April 12, responding to this pressure, *Variety* reports that of 1,008 speaking roles accounted for this season, only 42 have been taken by foreign players, although a goodly number have been major parts. **14** By a vote of 491–2, Actors Equity members attending a special meeting vote to forbid the use of

Births, Deaths, and Marriages

of the Charles Laughton adaptation of Brecht's *Galileo,* now at the Vivian Beaumont. Neither he nor the *Times* notes that his own adaptation of the play had been rejected in favor of Laughton's by the Lincoln Center Repertory Theatre.

MAY 1 Edward Albee, despite his unhappiness at being passed over for the Pulitzer Prize in 1963 when the Board overruled the judges' choice of *Who's Afraid of Virginia Woolf?* accepts this year's award for *A Delicate Balance*. "There weren't any good plays this year except for *A Delicate Balance* and *The Homecoming*," he says, adding, "Most critics misunderstood my play." **1** The college musical *Pippin, Pippin*, opening at Carnegie-Mellon University, is by "Lawrence Stephens," who will use his real name, Steven Schwartz, when it reaches Broadway as just plain *Pippin* in five years. **7** Carol Channing, told by Twentieth Century-Fox that Barbra Streisand will play the lead in the film of *Hello Dolly*! sends Streisand yellow roses with a note: "So happy for you and Dolly, dearest Barbra. Love, Carol."

George Grizzard, Melinda Dillon, Martin Balsam, Eileen Heckart, and Joe Silver. The *World Journal Tribune* calls it "[t]he best and brightest new American play of the season."

APRIL 13 The Repertory Theatre of Lincoln Center presents Charles Laughton's adaptation of Bertolt Brecht's *Galileo* (76), with Anthony Quayle in the title role (Rod Steiger has relinquished the part because of poor health). Also in the cast, at the Vivian Beaumont Theatre, are Aline MacMahon, Estelle Parsons, Philip Bosco, George Voskovec, and Shepperd Strudwick. **14** The Mark Taper Forum stages its first production, John Whiting's *The Devils*, adapted from Aldous Huxley's *The Devils of Loudon*, starring Frank Langella, Joyce Ebert, and Ed Flanders.

foreign actors, excluding Canadians, without the union's permission.

MAY 14 The Ford Foundation announces a grant of $434,000 for the establishment of a Negro Ensemble Company, which its principles, Douglas Turner Ward, Robert Hooks, and Gerald S. Krone, have been putting together for over a year.

Photo opposite: *The Boys in the Band*—its open treatment of homosexuality is emblematic of the new frankness on the American stage. *PF*

Inhibitions and Censorship Break Down

1967–1982

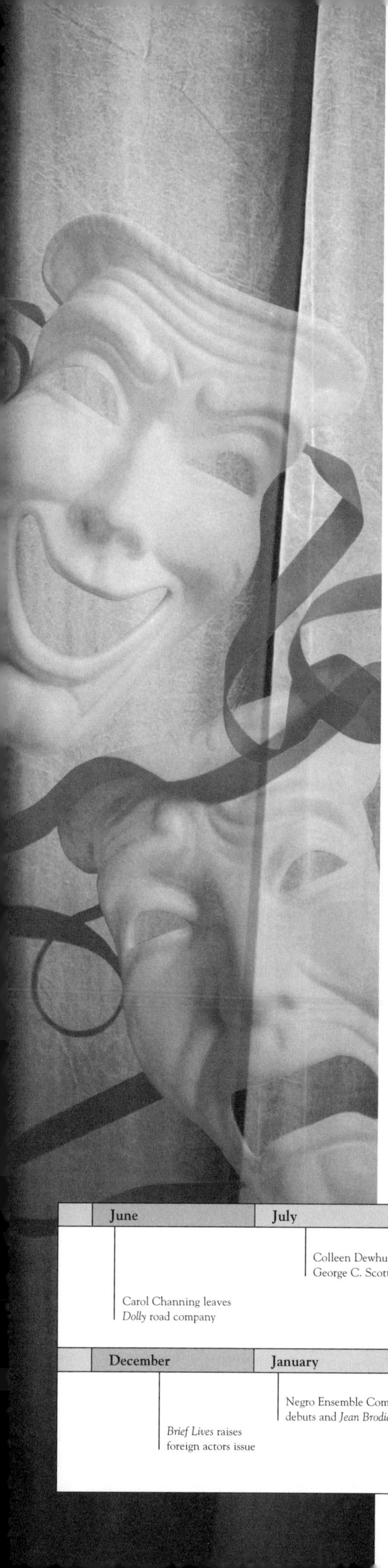

1967–68

Nudity, profanity, and homosexuality all become prominent on the legitmate stage, on and off-Broadway, with *Hair* just the most notable example of changing morés and *The Boys in the Band* the most famous instance of the closet door swinging open. But what has been accepted fairly quickly in New York will take time on the road. Meanwhile, Edward Albee and John Gielgud feud publicly. Zoe Caldwell becomes one of the theatre's leading actresses with her performance in *The Prime of Miss Jean Brodie* and marries one of its most important producers, Robert Whitehead. For David Merrick, shooting is too good for *Mata Hari*. The Negro Ensemble Company debuts. And the author of *Oh Dad, Poor Dad, Mama's Hung You in the Closet and I'm Feelin' So Sad* marries the grandaughter of the man who wrote the "Uncle Wiggly" Stories.

- The first title Mart Crowley thought of for *The Boys in the Band*: "The Birthday Party," dropped because Harold Pinter got to it first
- Why *The Boys in the Band* is significant: besides pioneering in drama about homosexuals, it helps to establish the legitimacy of the $10 top ticket price off-Broadway
- Number of original cast members of *The Boys in the Band* who will be dead of AIDS by the mid 1990s: 5 of the 9—Frederick Combs, Leonard Frey, Robert La Tourneaux, Kenneth Nelson, and Keith Prentice
- Total number of performances for Carol Channing in *Hello, Dolly!* since tryouts began in Detroit on November 18, 1963: 1,272 including 640 performances on Broadway
- Number of times since 1917 that no Pulitzer Prize for Drama was awarded, including this season: 10
- Profit earned by the Arena Stage in Washington, D.C. from the 6-week, premiere engagement of *The Great White Hope*: none—it loses $50,000
- Amount that *Great White Hope* author Howard Sackler earns from the film rights to his play: $555,000, plus a bonus clause
- Who is working with Joseph Papp in the spring of 1968: Czech playwright Vaclav Havel
- What David Merrick is said to have shouted in the auditorium of the theatre in Washington where *Mata Hari* has its disastrous premiere just before Thanksgiving: "Anyone who wants this turkey for a buck can have it."

Productions on Broadway: 73, the most since the 1950–51 season

Pulitzer Prize for Drama: None awarded

New York Drama Critics Circle Award:
Best Play: *Rosencrantz and Guildenstern Are Dead* (Tom Stoppard)
Best Musical: *Your Own Thing* (Hal Hester and Danny Apolinar)

Tony Awards:
Play: *Rosencrantz and Guildenstern Are Dead* (Tom Stoppard)
Actress in a Play: Zoe Caldwell (*The Prime of Miss Jean Brodie*)
Actor in a Play: Martin Balsam (*You Know I Can't Hear You When the Water's Running*)
Musical: *Hallelujah, Baby!* (Jule Styne, Betty Comden, and Adolph Green)
Actress in a Musical: Patricia Routledge (*Darling of the Day*) and Leslie Uggams (*Hallelujah, Baby!*)
Actor in a Musical: Robert Goulet (*The Happy Time*)

June
Carol Channing leaves *Dolly* road company

July
Colleen Dewhurst m. George C. Scott again

August
F. Murray Abraham joins *Fantasticks*

September
Clive Barnes new *Times* critic

October
Rosencrantz and Guildenstern Are Dead

November
Merrick's *Mata Hari* disaster

December
Brief Lives raises foreign actors issue

January
Negro Ensemble Company debuts and *Jean Brodie*

February
Plaza Suite

March
Tennessee Williams flop

April
The Boys in the Band and *Hair*

May
Zoe Caldwell m. Robert Whitehead

Personalities

JUNE • The yearbook of Northport High School on Long Island describes one graduate as "[m]ost musical, most dramatic, class clown, the most well-known person in school, extremely talented, outgoing, nuts, peppy, uninhibited." And it adds about Patti LuPone: "Will long be remembered." **11** With the chorus in tears at the curtain call in Houston, Carol Channing, playing her final performance in the road show of *Hello, Dolly!* tells the audience, "Don't ever say 'Goodbye, Dolly.'"

AUGUST • F. Murray Abraham joins the off-Broadway cast of *The Fantasticks*. **9** Playwright Joe Orten and his companion, writer and artist Kenneth Halliwell, are found dead in their London apartment. It appears that Halliwell killed Orten and then killed himself.

SEPTEMBER • Clive Barnes takes over from Walter Kerr as *The New York Times*'s daily drama critic, with Kerr switching to a Sundays-only slot. **10** In a letter in *The New York Times*, Edward Albee replies to John Simon's suggestion that the playwright should have rejected the Pulitzer Prize for his latest, inferior play because it was only consolation for not winning for *Who's Afraid of Virginia Woolf?*: "Mr. Simon's disapproval of my plays has been a source of comfort to me over the years and his dislike of *A Delicate Balance* gives me the courage to go on, as they say."

OCTOBER • "The honeymoon is over," reads the telegram Clive Barnes receives from David Merrick. Barnes, one month into his tenure as *The New York Times* drama critic, has panned Merrick's *Keep It in the Family*. The critic's reply: "Had no idea we were married. Did not even imagine you were that type." **16** The Post Office issues a stamp honoring Eugene O'Neill, the first time it has honored an American playwright. **29** In a letter in *The New York Times*, Tallulah Bankhead denies the recent assertion in the paper by Lillian Hellman that the members of the original cast of *The Little Foxes* were often at each others' throats.

NOVEMBER • John Simon, who reviews plays for *Commonweal* and the *Hudson Review*,

Plays and Musicals

OCTOBER 3 Harold Pinter's *The Birthday Party* (126) opens at the Booth. Directed by Alan Schneider, it has in its cast Henderson Forsythe, Ed Flanders, Alexandra Berlin, and Ruth White. It's about a "psychoneurotic rooming with a moronic couple," explains *Variety*. **9** John Bowen's allegorical treatment of religion *After the Rain* (64) is at the John Golden. Walter Kerr finds it "arch and empty," but the other critics like it. In the cast are Alec McCowen and Nancy Marchand. **10** *Scuba Duba* (704), novelist Bruce Jay Friedman's barbed comedy, in which the wife of a white liberal runs off with a black man, opens at The New Theatre. Jerry Orbach, Cleavon Little, and Jennifer Warren are in the cast. Orbach, whose character says, "I've always been afraid of Negroes; I think they all won the Golden Gloves once," will tell an interviewer that "[i]t isn't anti-liberal; it's anti-everybody. It shows that Negroes tend to stereotype us a little, too." **16** "Shouldn't we be doing something constructive?" says one lead character in Tom Stoppard's *Rosencrantz and Guildenstern Are Dead* (421), opening at the Alvin. There is something obscure in Denmark for these two, played by Brian Murray and John Wood, and it does, indeed, take them to a dead end. **24** Michael McClure's *The Beard* (100), directed by Rip Torn, with Richard Bright as Billy the Kid and Billie Dixon as Jean Harlow, opens at the off-Broadway Evergreen Theatre. With its four-letter words, nudity, and simulated oral sex, the play is very controversial. *The New York Times* will censor review quotes in a display ad, and the *New Yorker* refuses to review it. **29** Joseph Papp's production of *Hair* (65) opens at the New York Shakespeare Festival's new home in the former Astor Library. There is an admission charge—$2.50 for all seats—the first time that Papp's company has sold tickets for a production other than a benefit. By the time it reaches Broadway, it will have gone through a major revision, including the insertion of the famous nude scene. **31** *More Stately Mansions* (142), a Eugene O'Neill play that he did not want produced, opens at the Broadhurst. Ingrid

Business and Society

JUNE • David Rothenberg, press agent for and coproducer of *Fortune and Men's Eyes*, charges in the *Village Voice* and *Variety* that critics and the media in general have avoided the show because of its prominent theme of homosexuality. He describes their avoidance as "near pathological."

SEPTEMBER • *The New York Times* runs an ad for *'Tis Pity She's a Whore*, a title they would have hesitated to print in full a few years ago.

OCTOBER 4 The price of *Variety* rises from $.35 to $.50.

NOVEMBER • Depravity is not playing well in Cincinnati, where people are walking out of the road production of Harold Pinter's *The Homecoming*, winner of the New York Critics Circle and Tony Awards for best play in New York last season. **17** Renegotiating a contract rejected by its membership, Equity reaches an agreement with the League of Off-Broadway Theatres in which a bonus clause will give actors better pay for hit shows and a $70 per week minimum salary.

DECEMBER • A dispute over the value of

Births, Deaths, and Marriages

JUNE 5 Elia Kazan m. actress Barbara Loden.

JULY • Colleen Dewhurst and George C. Scott m. a second time. **8** Vivian Leigh d. She had been rehearsing for the London opening of Edward Albee's *A Delicate Balance*, in which she was to costar with Michael Redgrave. **21** Basil Rathbone d.

AUGUST 25 Paul Muni d.

SEPTEMBER 13 José Ferrer and Rosemary Clooney, having already divorced and reconciled once, divorce for good.

OCTOBER 14 David T. Nederlander, head of the Detroit theatre family, who founded the Nederlander organization in 1912, d. **21** Rosemary Harris, who this year divorced director Ellis Rabb, m. novelist

is forced out as theatre critic of New York City's educational television station, Channel 13. Simon characterizes his treatment as "unmanly" and "very cowardly," while the station describes his reviews as "misanthropic" and "harsh." **9** While two of his one-act plays, *The Trials of Brother Jero* and *The Strong Breed*, are opening off-Broadway, at the Greenwich Mews Theatre, Nigerian playwright Wole Soyinka is in a prison in his own country, accused of supporting the breakaway province of Biafra. **16** The first preview in Washington, D.C., of David Merrick's *Mata Hari* creates a legend. The scenery comes apart, making a shambles of a balcony love scene between stars Marisa Mell and Pernell Roberts. Mell's wig comes off; so do her clothes during a costume change

Zoe Caldwell in *The Prime of Miss Jean Brodie* PF

Bergman, Colleen Dewhurst, and Arthur Hill star. Whitney Boulton calls the play "unformed. . . . [I]t tends in its length more to bewilder than enchant."

NOVEMBER 12 A black cast, headed by Pearl Bailey and Cab Calloway, opens in *Hello, Dolly!* at the St. James. Carol Channing is in the audience and at the curtain comes onstage at Bailey's invitation to sing the title song with her, accompanied by the pit pianist. **21** Michael Cacoyannis is directing Euripides' *Iphigenia in Aulis* (232), at the Circle in the Square, starring Irene Papas, with Christopher Walken as Achilles.

DECEMBER 19 An acclaimed revival of *The Little Foxes* (100) moves from the Vivian Beaumont in Lincoln Center to the Barrymore Theatre. The stellar cast includes Margaret Leighton, Anne Bancroft, George C. Scott, and E.G. Marshall.

JANUARY 2 The Negro Ensemble Company presents its first production, Peter Weiss's *Song of the Lusitanian Bogey* (40), at the St. Marks Playhouse in the East Village. The cast of this drama about Portuguese colonialism in Africa includes Rosalind Cash and Moses Gunn. **13** *Your Own*

Lee Shubert's interest in the Shubert theatre empire is finally settled, with an $18 million payment going to his estate from the estate of his brother, J.J. • The New York City Board of Estimate establishes a bonus for realtors who include a theatre in the construction of new buildings. The Shubert organization, which owns 17 Broadway theatres, objects to the plan.

JANUARY • The Theatre Development Fund (TDF), financed by the National Endowment for the Arts and several private foundations, has begun operations. It will bolster quality Broadway productions that have not yet found their audience by buying large blocks of tickets and discounting them to students, teachers, and others who might not be able to afford them.

FEBRUARY • A judge rules that the Los Angeles requirement that theatrical productions secure a police permit violates free speech. At issue is a series of arrests of people associated with Michael McClure's *The Beard*, at the Warner Playhouse last month. • Ticket Reservation Systems becomes the first company to sell tickets nationally through a computerized system. Among the Broadway shows available are *I Do, I Do* and *The Prime of Miss Jean Brodie*.

John Ehle.

NOVEMBER 21 Florence Reed d.

DECEMBER 4 Bert Lahr d. **23** Vaudevillian Bee Palmer, who helped to popularize the "Shimmy," d.

JANUARY 18 Bert Wheeler d.

FEBRUARY 11 Playwright Howard Lindsay d. **28** Playwright Laurence Stallings d.

MARCH 13 Vaudevillian Gus Van, of the team of Van and Schenck, d. of injuries sustained in an auto accident. **24** Playwright Arthur Kopit, author of *Oh Dad, Poor Dad, Mama's Hung You in the Closet and I'm Feelin' So Sad*, m. Leslie Garis, granddaughter of Howard Garis, who wrote the "Uncle Wiggly" stories.

APRIL 16 Fay Bainter and Edna Ferber d.

Personalities

onstage when she is supposed to be blacked out but is not. And Mata Hari, once executed, will not stay dead. Mell feels an eyelash coming off. Her efforts to nudge it back with her arm makes the audience laugh hysterically, as the curtain, mercifully, works. David Merrick will fold the production in Washington on December 16. **20** It's a dream night for musical theatre fans at Lincoln Center, where a benefit tribute to Cole Porter—sold out since July—stars Fred Astaire, singing "Night and Day," after Ethel Merman has delivered on "Anything Goes," "I Get a Kick Out of You," and "Blow, Gabriel Blow." **22** The Montreal production of *Fortune and Men's Eyes* opens with its author John Herbert and director Mitchell Nestor locked in a closet. They felt that the city's new cultural center was not yet ready to present the work and tried stop the show. In a confrontation, the theatre's officials shoved them in the closet and locked the door.

DECEMBER • Delacorte Press, bowing to pressure from John Gielgud, says it will remove from future printings of *The Playwrights Speak* disparaging remarks about the actor made by Edward Albee, who claims that Gielgud did not give his all in preparing for his role in *Tiny Alice*. • Brendan Gill, *New Yorker* film critic since 1961, becomes its theatre reviewer, replacing John McCarten. **8** Pearl Bailey, the latest Dolly Levi in *Hello Dolly!* makes the cover of *Life*. **8** On Broadway tonight, *I Do, I Do* won't. Its current stars, Carol Lawrence and Gordon McRae, are performing selections from it at the wedding of the President's daughter Lynda Bird Johnson to Marine Captain Charles Robb.

JANUARY • The bad feeling between John Gielgud and Edward Albee over the latter's criticism of the actor in *Tiny Alice* continues. Gielgud tells a reporter that he resents the playwright's charges of "unprofessional behavior . . . especially that of being 'too slothful or frightened' to learn and perform the work assigned to me."

Plays and Musicals

Thing (933), in which Shakespeare's *Twelfth Night* is joined to Hal Hester and Danny Apolinar's rock score—with a number called "The Now Generation"—opens at the Orpheum, off-Broadway. It stars Tom Ligon, Leland Palmer, and Marian Mercer, and cast replacements will include Sandy Duncan and Raul Julia. **16** Zoe Caldwell, a second choice because Margaret Leighton was unavailable, triumphs in Jay Allen's adaptation of Muriel Spark's novel *The Prime of Miss Jean Brodie* (379), at the Helen Hayes. Wilfred Sheed, in *Life*, describes Caldwell's Jean as "beautifully overacted." Maggie Smith stars in next year's film. **17** Israel Horovitz's *The Indian Wants the Bronx* (171), at the Astor Place Theatre, stars Al Pacino, Matthew Coles, and John Cazale as the Indian whose desire to catch a bus to the Bronx gets him beaten up. It's on a double bill with the playwright's *It's Called the Sugar Plum*. **22** Opening at the Village Gate is *Jacques Brel Is Alive and Well and Living in Paris* (1,847). In the cast are Elly Stone, Shawn Elliott, Mort Shuman, and Alice Whitfield. **25** Robert Anderson conceived of *I Never Sang for My Father* (124) as a movie script, which Spencer Tracy turned down. Director John Frankenheimer said he would do it as a film with Frederic March but never did. Now, this story of a cantankerous old man and his adult children opens at the Longacre, with Hal Holbrook, Alan Webb,

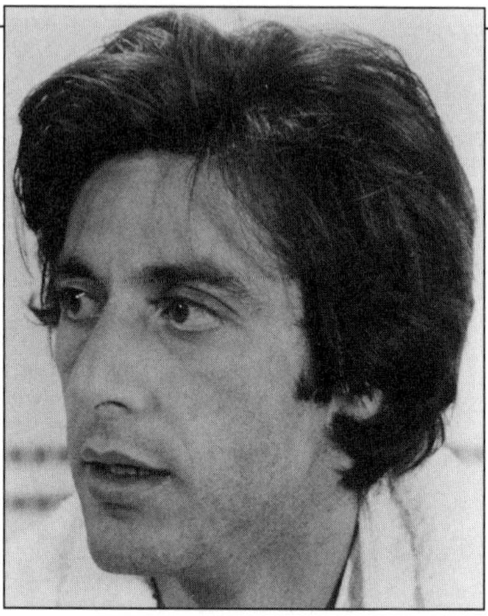

Al Pacino MSN

Business and Society

MARCH • *The New York Times* ad acceptability department deletes the line "Take her clothes off?" from an ad for the upcoming Joe Orten play *Loot*. The *Times* does, however, permit "Bury her naked? My own Mum? It is a Freudian nightmare."

APRIL • The New York City License Commission, once the municipal instrument of censorship, is put under the jurisdiction of the Markets Department, further watering down what little censorship power it still has. • The New York State Human Rights Commission criticizes Broadway for its poor record in employing black people. **5–6** Attendance is down on this Friday and Saturday night, with theatregoers fearing the spread of the urban unrest that broke out last night after the assassination of Dr. Martin Luther King. In Washington, D.C., hit especially hard by rioting, all weekend performances of *Cabaret* at the National Theatre have been canceled. **17** According to today's *Variety*, preview audiences at the Broadway production of *Hair* say that a nude scene has been added to the show that was such a big hit without it at the Public Theatre downtown. As the paper puts it, "[T]here's only one more barrier left."

Births, Deaths, and Marriages

Ferber once told George S. Kaufman and S.N. Behrman that she had a terrible nightmare: "I dreamt that I was a wallflower at an orgy!"

MAY 5 Albert Dekker d. **7** Julie Andrews divorces set designer Tony Walton. **9** Zoe Caldwell m. producer Robert Whitehead this afternoon. He's a cousin of Hume Cronyn and is the producer of *The Prime of Miss Jean Brodie*, in which she is starring. She has to be back onstage tonight.

JANUARY 4 Playwright LeRoi Jones is sentenced to two to two and a half years in prison for participating in the Newark riots last summer. He will appeal. **10** *Daily News* critic John Chapman's exit after the first act of *Staircase*, a play about gay men starring Eli Wallach and Milo O'Shea, and Chapman's panning of the drama, will draw criticism from the League of New York Theatres. Other reviewers praise it. **24** Appearing on the "Tonight" show, producer David Merrick tells Johnny Carson: "I've never seen a drama critic who wasn't a physical coward."

FEBRUARY 4 "I don't give a tuppence of crap for being a star," the Australian-born Zoe Caldwell, now starring in *The Prime of Miss Jean Brodie*, tells Rex Reed. She says that the only way she is like Jean is that "I've never been married and I'm most certainly in my prime." Asked about her love affairs, including one with Albert Finney that got her named corespondent in his wife's 1961 divorce suit, she replies, "Darling, you don't think when I'm going to all those places, playing all those roles all over the world, I was *alone*, do you?" **27** José Quintero quits as director of Tennessee Williams's *The Seven Descents of Myrtle* because of the "sadistic" meddling by David Merrick. The producer responds: "Poor José, he finally got a live author and a strong producer. Apparently it has overwhelmed him. Behind the scenes, it's just like a Tennessee Williams' play, isn't it? By the way, did Mr. Williams say what the title was today?"

MAY • John Lahr, entering the running battle between playwright Edward Albee and the critics, writes, in the *Evergreen Review,*: "Albee's strutting dignity is too often mistaken for significance. His adaptations [*The Ballad of the Sad Café* and *Malcolm*], however, illustrate that his instincts are not so much that of the artist as the entertainer." **2** *Variety* will note of Leonard Sillman's *New Faces of 1968*, opening tonight, that "[a]mong the attractive performers are Robert Klein, a comedian-singer," and "Madeleine Kahn, a singer-comedienne." **14** In her final television appearance, on the "Tonight" show, Tallulah Bankhead chats with John Lennon and Paul McCartney.

Lillian Gish, and Teresa Wright in leading roles. The 1970 film stars Melvyn Douglas, Gene Hackman, and Estelle Parsons.

FEBRUARY 1 *A Day in the Death of Joe Egg* (154), Peter Nichol's comedy about a couple with a spastic child, opens at the Brooks Atkinson. Known simply as *Joe Egg*, it stars Albert Finney and Zena Walker. The playwright himself has a child who is spastic. **4** *Golden Rainbow*, a Walter Marks musical based on the comedy *A Hole in the Head* (383), a star vehicle for Steve Lawrence and Eydie Gormé, opens at the Shubert. Among the songs is "I've Got to Be Me." **7** Arthur Miller's *The Price* (425), about tensions between two brothers, is at the Morosco. The cast consists of Arthur Kennedy, Pat Hingle, Kate Reid, and Harold Gary. **14** Neil Simon's *Plaza Suite* (1,097), three one-act plays, starring Maureen Stapleton and George C. Scott, opens at the Plymouth. Stories about a cheating suburban husband, a youthful romance resurrected, and a bride who wants to bolt are united by place: a room at the Plaza. The 1971 screen version stars Stapleton with Walter Matthau. **21** Opening at The American Place Theatre are three one-act plays *The Electronic Nigger and Others* (96, total), by black playwright Ed Bullins, his first New York productions. The three plays are *The Electronic Nigger*; *A Son, Come Home*; and *Clara's Ole Man*. On March 28, they move to the Martinique under the title *Three Plays by Ed Bullins*.

APRIL 10 Joel Grey, at the Palace, stars in *George M!* (433) as George M.Cohan, with a cast that includes the young Bernadette Peters. The score consists of the showman's best tunes. **14** Mart Crowley's *The Boys in the Band* (1,001), a breakthrough drama in its open treatment of homosexuality, opens at the Theatre Four. The setting is a birthday party, and the leads are played by Leonard Frey, Kenneth Nelson, Peter White, and Robert La Torneaux. They will be joined by Laurence Luckinbill and Cliff Gorman in the 1970 screen version. **29** It's the dawning of "the age of Aquarius" at the Biltmore Theatre, where *Hair* (1,750) opens. It has nudity—added by director Tom O'Horgan after its run at The Public Theatre—and four-, five-, and six-letter

Personalities

Plays and Musicals

words, the mildest of which is "sodomy." The score by Galt MacDermot, Gerome Ragni, and James Rado, celebrates the 60s ethic—an "American Tribal Love-Rock Musical," say the ads. It includes the title song and "Let the Sunshine In," "Aquarius," "Hare Krishna," and "Good Morning Starshine." In the cast are Rado and Ragne and, among others, Diane Keaton, Ronald Dyson, Melba Moore, and Lamont Washington. *Hair* appears as a movie in 1979.

Business and Society

Births, Deaths, and Marriages

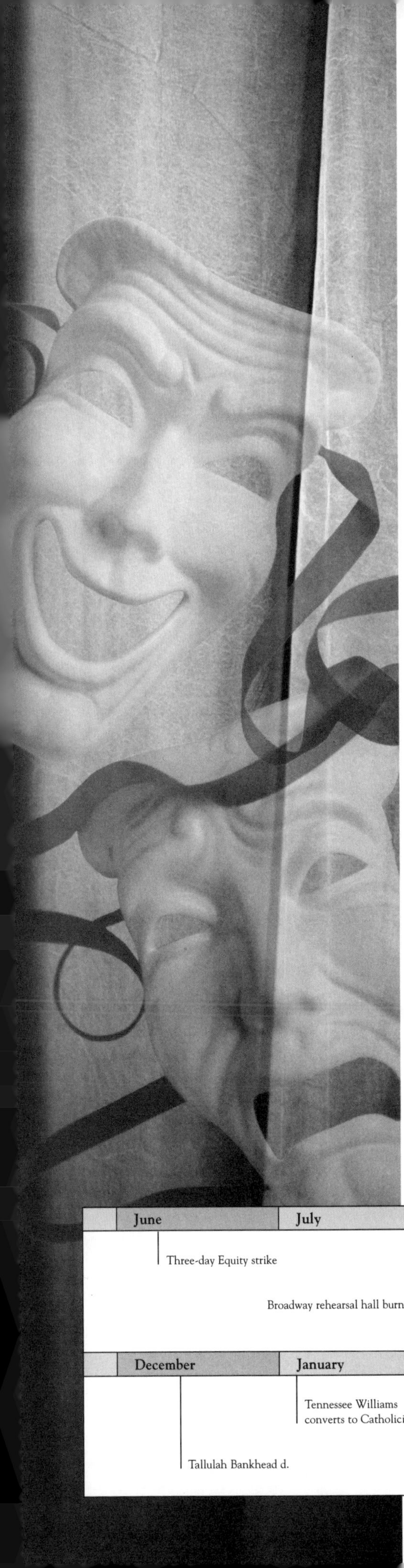

1968–69

The gestation of *The Great White Hope* at the Arena Stage before it transfers to Broadway is a harbinger of a time when regional theatres will be major suppliers of new shows for the Main Stem. Actors Equity's codification of rules about stage nudity also points to a basic change in American theatre. Julian Beck and Judith Malina's Living Theatre undermines conventional thought and behavior, even when it's just being discussed. Set designer Santo Loquasto is noticed. The new drama school at Juilliard has among its pupils Patti LuPone and Kevin Kline. And Tallulah is gone. There couldn't possibly, ever, be another like her.

- Phrases intoned in Living Theatre productions:
  "I'm not allowed to take my clothes off."
  "I'm not allowed to smoke marijuana."
  "I'm not allowed to travel without a passport."
- Jerry Orbach's salary in *Promises, Promises*: about $2,500 a week
- What Jerry Orbach made in *The Fantasticks* when it opened: $45 a week
- Overheard at the Shubert, where *Promises, Promises* opens, is a woman in the audience saying of Jerry Orbach: "With those bedroom eyes, I'm ready to take him home with me and send my husband back to his mother."
- New word in *Variety*: "gays," describing homosexuals
- Old word still in *Variety*: "homos," describing homosexuals
- Number of cigarettes smoked a day by Tallulah Bankhead: 150
- Reported to be Tallulah Bankhead's last words: "codeine . . . bourbon"
- Among Tallulah Bankhead's personal effects when she dies: several hundred unopened letters—she was a terrible correspondent
- Who's playing Clytemnestra in the Minnesota Theatre production of *The House of Atreus*, adapted from Aeschylus' *The Oresteia*: Douglas Campbell, in a bit of theatrical gender-bending
- Number of sexual acts in *Che*, closed by the courts in New York City: 23
- Percentage of the Broadway audience over the age of 35: 60 percent
- Percentage of the cost of a Broadway production that goes toward paying the production crew: 2.5 percent
- What's special about the *Playbill* for *Promises, Promises*: David Merrick has substituted cast photos for the usual biographical blurbs

Productions on Broadway: 67

Pulitzer Prize for Drama: *The Great White Hope* (Howard Sackler)

New York Drama Critics Circle Awards:
Best Play: *The Great White Hope* (Howard Sackler)
Best Musical: *1776* (Sherman Edwards)

Tony Awards:
Play: *The Great White Hope* (Howard Sackler)
Actor in a Play: James Earl Jones (*The Great White Hope*)
Actress in a Play: Julie Harris (*Forty Carats*)
Musical: *1776* (Sherman Edwards)
Actor in a Musical: Jerry Orbach (*Promises, Promises*)
Actress in a Musical: Angela Lansbury (*Dear World*)

June
Three-day Equity strike

July
Broadway rehearsal hall burns

August
Circle in the Square moves north

September
The Man in the Glass Booth

October
The Great White Hope

November
Howard Sackler clash with Arena Stage

December
Tallulah Bankhead d.

January
Tennessee Williams converts to Catholicism

February
Ceremonies in Dark Old Men, *Next*, and *Play It Again, Sam*

March
Living Theatre discussion turns chaotic

April
Clive Barnes says John Simon should "get off the pot"

May
Actors Equity policy on stage nudity

Personalities

JUNE • Clive Barnes's favorable review of *Hair* in *The New York Times* is read into the *Congressional Record* by Senator Strom Thurmond of South Carolina, who criticizes the critic for praising depravity. **3** Harold Clurman writes in *New York* magazine: "I have nothing against Broadway—it is just another foul street in our town—but it is no longer the absolute center of theatre activity in these United States." **28** Tennessee Williams's brother makes public a note from the playwright, written on a restaurant's stationery, that reads "if anything of a violent nature happens to me, ending my life abruptly, it will not be a case of suicide, as it would be made to appear." Williams hasn't been heard from in some time; he's been depressed by the failure of *The Seven Descents of Myrtle*, and New York City detectives are now searching for him. Tomorrow, he calls, saying that he's all right.

AUGUST • It sounds intriguing: a musical adapted from Bertolt Brecht's *The Exception and the Rule*—to star Zero Mostel, with music by Leonard Bernstein, lyrics by Stephen Sondheim, choreography by Jerome Robbins, and a book by John Guare. It is already scheduled for a February 18, 1969, opening at the Broadhurst, and the papers are noting it. But by October, it will be a dead issue.

SEPTEMBER 23 Classes begin in the new four-year program of the Drama Division of the Juilliard School. Among the students in the first class—called "Group I" by the school's director John Houseman—are Patti LuPone and Kevin Kline. Other graduates will include William Hurt, Christopher Reeve, and Robin Williams. **26** Julian Beck and Judith Malina of the Living Theatre are arrested in New Haven, where their company has concluded performances of *Frankenstein* and *Paradise Now* at the Yale Drama School by marching out into the street virtually undressed. Says the local police chief, "All the rest of the world may be a stage, but not the corner of York and Chapel." They will be acquitted of indecent exposure.

Plays and Musicals

JUNE 13 Boy meets pig in *Futz!* (233), a one-act comedy by Rochelle Owens, opening off-Broadway, at the Theatre De Lys. Tom O'Horgan is directing a cast that includes Sally Kirkland and John Bakos.

SEPTEMBER 18 Reneé Taylor and Joseph Bologna, husband and wife offstage, are the authors of *Lovers and Other Strangers* (70), four one-act comedies about relationships, opening at the Brooks Atkinson. The cast includes Zohra Lampert, Richard Castellano, and coauthor Taylor. **26** At the Royale and directed by Harold Pinter is *The Man in the Glass Booth* (269), writer-actor Robert Shaw's play about a Jewish survivor of the concentration camps, who insists on "confessing" to having been an Adolf Eichmann-like officer in them. Donald Pleasance plays him. Maximilian Schell stars in the 1975 film.

OCTOBER 3 Howard Sackler's *The Great White Hope* (557), which opened in December at the Arena Stage in Washington, D.C., is at the Alvin. James Earl Jones and Jane Seymour star in this drama about black boxer Jack Johnson—"Jack Jefferson" in the play. Jones will star with Jane Alexander in the 1970 film. **16** Joseph Heller's *We Bombed in New Haven* (86), an antiwar play and not, as the title might suggest, another show business drama, opens at the Ambassador. Jason Robards, Jr. and Diana Sands head the

James Earl Jones MSN

Business and Society

JUNE 17 Actors Equity begins a three-day strike. The union wants a two-and-a-half-year contract that would expire in the middle of the season, when the producers couldn't absorb a walkout, rather than four more years with the same expiration that management is pushing. Equity also wants a $200-a-week minimum, while the New York League of Theatres is offering $145. The settlement provides for a three-year pact with a June expiration and a $145 minimum with a cost-of-living clause.

JULY 11 The Variety Arts Studio on Forty-sixth Street, a major Broadway rehearsal hall, is gutted by fire.

AUGUST 1 The Circle in the Square company takes over Henry Miller's Theatre uptown in an attempt to create a beachhead on Broadway for its productions.

SEPTEMBER • The APA-Phoenix Repertory Theatre receives a severe jolt with the loss of its $250,000 grant from the National Endowment for the Arts.

OCTOBER 26 What Clive Barnes called "the most adventuresome experiment

Births, Deaths, and Marriages

JUNE 30 Legendary Broadway press agent Richard Maney d. To a fledgling producer who asked Maney what he should wear to the opening night of his first production, Maney is said to have advised: "a track suit."

SEPTEMBER 5 Sandy Duncan and Bruce Scott, both cast members of *Do Your Own Thing*, m. **18** Franchot Tone d.

OCTOBER 11 Producer George White, whose "Scandals" revues were a Broadway fixture in the 1920s, rivaling the Ziegfeld Follies, d. **18** Lee Tracy d.

DECEMBER 12 Tallulah Bankhead d. Tennessee Williams once described her as a "fantastic cross-breeding of a moth and a tiger." She said of herself: "I'm as pure as the driven slush." The always outspoken Tallulah once said of Billy Rose, with

OCTOBER • David Merrick, in his *Esquire* article "David Merrick Must Go" says that he may abandon Broadway for Hollywood. In the piece, he suggests that *The New York Times* should toss their critic Clive Barnes's "fat Limey posterior out in the street."

NOVEMBER 5 The Living Theatre's performance of *Paradise Now* on the MIT campus is disrupted by hecklers, a student who strips naked, and by small fires started in the audience. *Boston Record* critic Elliot Norton writes of the pacifist company that, confronted with opposition, they "got mad and some of them practically foamed at the mouth." He calls their play a "phony attempt to break the boundaries of conventional theatre, done as if by dirty schoolboys." **17** Playwright Howard Sackler, in a letter in *Variety*, refutes recent complaints that the Arena Stage in Washington, D.C., where his play *The Great White Hope* premiered, has been unfairly shut out of the profits from the Broadway production. Sackler says that the Fichandlers, who run the Arena Stage, knew exactly what they were getting and not getting and are now cloaking themselves in the mantle of "victimization." He says that they could have produced it on Broadway but didn't. Thomas Fichandler replies that the author had a "moral obligation" to share some of the profits with the regional house, which lost $50,000 on the production.

JANUARY 16 Tennessee Williams, an Episcopalian, converts to Roman Catholicism. The priest who performed the ceremony says that the playwright accepts all tenets of his new faith except immortality.

MARCH • The editor of *Yale/Theater*, the magazine of the Yale School of Drama, quits, charging Dean Robert Brustein with "psychological censorship." Brustein terms the charge "absurd." • In London, Nicol Williamson, starring in a production of *Hamlet*, stops in mid-act, telling the audience that he's tired from overwork and can't go on. Then he goes on. • Set designer Santo Loquasto, earning his MFA at Yale, earns his first acclaim for his work on Euripedes' *The Bacchae*, produced at the school. *Newsweek* sees

cast, which also includes Ron Leibman.

NOVEMBER 17 Herschel Bernardi stars in the John Kander-Fred Ebb musical *Zorba* (305), at the Imperial. It's the role in which Anthony Quinn made such a strong impression in the 1964 film. Costarring is Maria Karnilova. **21** *Sweet Eros* and *Witness* (78), two plays by Terrence McNally, open off-Broadway at the Grammarcy Arts Theatre. The first play is most notable for Sally Kirkland's extended nude scene. In the second, a man kidnaps and strips a woman, whom he has tied to a chair. James Coco is also in the cast.

DECEMBER 1 Burt Bacharach and Hal David's *Promises, Promises* (1,281), a musical based on the 1960 Billy Wilder film *The Apartment*, featuring "I'll Never Fall in Love Again," opens at the Shubert. Jerry Orbach, Jill O'Hara, and Edward Winter star, with Donna McKechnie. **5** Dustin Hoffman plays the title character in *Jimmy Shine* (153), Murray Schisgal's new comedy about a loser, at the Brooks Atkinson. **8** Joseph Dolan Tuotti's *Big Time Buck White* (124), a play that originated in a writing workshop in the Watts ghetto in Los Angeles, opens off-Broadway, at the Village South Theatre. The cast of this comedy with a strong racial theme is headed by Kirk Kirksey. **20** *Dames At Sea* (575), by Jim Wise, George Haimsohn, and Robin Miller, a parody of Busby Berkeley musicals such as *42nd Street*—the lead characters are "Ruby" and "Dick"—opens off-Broadway at the 188-seat Bouwerie Lane Theatre. It stars Bernadette Peters, who will be succeeded by Pia Zadora, among others. **26** Abe Burrows directs *Forty Carats* (780), Jay Allen's adaptation of a Parisian comedy, at the Morosco. Julie Harris is an older woman who has an affair with a younger man, who will also date her daughter, who prefers an older man, who happens to yearn for her mother.

JANUARY 2 *To Be Young, Gifted and Black* (380), staged readings from the works of playwright Lorraine Hansberry, opens at the Cherry Lane. The cast includes Barbara Baxley, John Beal, Rita Gardner, and Cicely Tyson. **5** Jules Feiffer's urban drama about some offbeat people, *Little Murders* (400), which flopped on

Broadway has seen in years," Theatre 69, the repertory company organized to produce serious plays at the Billy Rose Theatre, including works by Beckett and Albee, gives up after two weeks and a loss of $130,000.

NOVEMBER 6 "Hookers, Homos, Pornos Unchecked Under Civil Rights, in 'Slime Square,'" a front-page *Variety* headline intones in an old refrain.

DECEMBER 9 Ford's Theatre in Washington, D.C., announces that the Circle in the Square company will run the house, replacing the National Repertory Theatre.

JANUARY 21 Robert Montgomery is named president of the Repertory Theatre of Lincoln Center.

MARCH 2 The *New York Daily News*'s failure to review the off-Broadway play *Spitting Image*, opening tonight, appears to confirm a pattern that has become noticeable: the paper ignores shows that have homosexual subjects. It also skipped *The Boys in the Band*, *Fortune in Men's Eyes*, and *Geese*. **11** President Nixon does not reappoint Broadway producer Roger Stevens, whose term as chairperson of the National Arts Council expires today. **24** The cast of the off-Broadway play *Che!*

whom she worked, that he was "a loathsome little bully." She's buried with the lucky rabbit's foot given to her by her father.

JANUARY 2 Producer Gilbert Miller d. **19** Charles Winninger d.

MARCH 16 Critic John Mason Brown d.

MAY 1 Ella Logan d.

Personalities

his work as "catalyzing the entire production." Impressed is Joseph Papp, teaching at Yale, who will use Loquasto in David Rabe's *Sticks and Bones*. **21** Woody Allen wrote *Life*'s cover story this week: "My Secret Life with Humphrey Bogart." Allen is pictured in front of a large photo of Bogart, who has a cigarette dangling from his lips. **21** A discussion of the Living Theatre at The Theatre of Ideas, a New York City forum for prominent intellectuals, is in pandemonium, as Robert Brustein's criticism of Julian Beck and Judith Malina's company ignites disruption in the audience. The Beck supporters begin to yell, "Open the prisons."

APRIL • *Times* critic Clive Barnes tells an interviewer, who asks about critic John Simon, "If he hates the theatre so much, why doesn't he get off the pot." **3** *The Village Voice*, reviewing the off-Broadway production *Someone's Comin' Hungry*, starring Cleavon Little and Blythe Danner, says that Danner "is simply too intimately true to life, and touching, for a bunch of superlatives." *Variety* says that the newcomer "may have a future in legit." **10** Gerome Ragne and James Rado, creators of *Hair*, who also appear in it, have been dismissed from the show by producer Michael Butler, who won't even allow them into the theatre. Butler says that they have been adding bits of business with sexual innuendo that could have the musical closed down. He will also accuse them of disrupting tomorrow's rehearsal when they do show up at the theatre. The principals settle this dispute next week, at a meeting in Central Park. One of their temporary replacements, Ben Vereen, will become an understudy. **20** Warming up the television audience for the Tony Awards broadcast, producer Alexander Cohen introduces "Clive Barnes," *New York Times* drama critic. Out of the wings comes a man dressed in a gorilla suit who makes a thumbs-down gesture and departs.

Plays and Musicals

Broadway in 1967, has been rejuvenated by the Royal Shakespeare Company and opens at the Circle in the Square. In the cast: Vincent Gardenia, Linda Lavin, Elizabeth Wilson, and Fred Willard. It's a 1971 film. **8** Alec McCowen, repeating his London success, triumphs as a man who imagines himself to be the Pope, in Peter Luke's *Hadrian VII* (359), at the Helen Hayes. **12** Gus Weill's *Geese* (336), a play about gays and lesbians, with prominent nudity, opens off-Broadway, at the Players Theatre on a double bill with the author's *Parents and Children*. The controversial drama—"frank queerism," as a *Variety* headline puts it—also gives Sunday matinées in which the actors' clothing stays on.

FEBRUARY 5 *Ceremonies in Dark Old Men* (359), a Negro Ensemble Company production, written by Lonnie Elder III, opens at the St. Marks Playhouse. Douglas Turner Ward and Rosalind Cash are in this comedy-drama in which a Harlem barber becomes involved in a crime that has fatal consequences. It moves to the Pocket Theatre in April. **10** Terrence McNally's *Next* (707), at the Greenwich Mews, makes a star of James Coco. On a double bill with Elaine May's *Adaptation*, it's about a man who has been drafted. In *Adaptation*, with Gabriel Dell and Paul Dooley, life is a game show. **12** Woody Allen wrote and stars in *Play It Again, Sam* (453), as a nebbish film critic who gets romantic advice direct from Humphrey Bogart but to no avail. Tony Roberts, Diane Keaton, and Jerry Lacey as Bogie costar, at the Broadhurst. It runs for 453 performances. The same cast is in the 1972 film.

MARCH 6 The Repertory Theatre of Lincoln Center presents *In the Matter of J. Robert Oppenheimer* (64), by Heinar Kipphardt, at the Vivian Beaumont. Joseph Wiseman plays the man who helped to create the hydrogen bomb, only to have his loyalty questioned in the 1950s. **16** Sherman Edwards and Peter Stone's musical about the Declaration of Independence, *1776* (1,217), is at the Forty-sixth Street Theatre. Howard Da

Business and Society

is arrested for obscenity, consensual sodomy, and public lewdness. Hillard Elkins, producer of the upcoming *Oh, Calcutta!* reacts to the news with a denial of rumors that his show will have a fornication scene.

MAY 19 Actors Equity bans actual sex acts onstage and says that no actor will have to audition nude until first being evaluated for acting, singing, and dancing talent. Notification of required nude scenes must be made before any contract is signed. **21** *Variety*'s front-page headline is "N.Y. Legit Going Sex-Happy."

Births, Deaths, and Marriages

Silva, William Daniels, Betty Buckley, playing Martha Jefferson in her Broadway debut, and Ken Howard are in the cast. The movie appears in 1972.

MAY 1 Nicol Williamson essays *Hamlet* (50) at the Lunt-Fontanne. Barnes, in the *Times*, says this Prince is "nasal," and Martin Gottfried, in *Women's Wear Daily*, calls it "the most unintelligible performance of the role I think I have ever seen." **4** A Pulitzer Prize is in the offing for *No Place to Be Somebody* (576), the first awarded to an off-Broadway production and the first to a black playwright. Charles Gordone's drama about white domination of blacks even in the underworld opens at the Public Theatre. It stars Nathan George and Walter Jones.

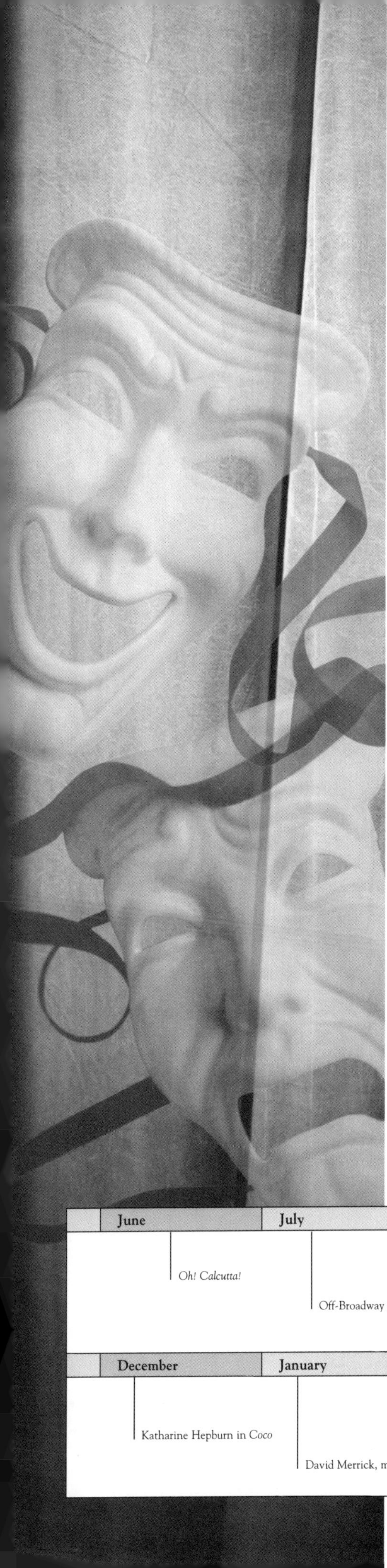

1969–70

The Boston censor is first dealing with *Hair*, while New York has moved on to *Oh! Calcutta!* which arrives the season that stripper Gypsy Rose Lee, of the old school, dies. Ethel Merman finally plays Dolly Levi, Blythe Danner is a new Broadway star, and it's *Sir* Noel Coward. Broadway observes Vietnam Moratorium Day. The New York Drama Critics Circle draws in the wagons against John Simon, Tennessee Williams has fallen on hard times, and Nicol Williamson is beginning to manifest some of the bizarre stage behavior that will become his trademark. And Anthony Newley as Napoleon, with Barbra Streisand as Josephine? Maybe the rumor mill has it backwards.

- What unemployed actor David Mamet, future author of *Glengarry Glen Ross*, is doing to pay the rent: selling real estate
- Neil Simon's weekly gross income from Broadway: about $45,000
- Sam Shepard's weekly income from his contribution to the erotic revue *Oh! Calcutta!*: $68
- Amount lost by the musical *Minnie's Boys*, about the Marx Brothers: about $750,000
- Katharine Hepburn's reaction to hearing herself "sing" on the original cast album of *Coco*: "I sound like Donald Duck."
- Cost of the costumes in *Coco*: a record $160,000
- Percentage of *Coco*'s box office going to star Katharine Hepburn: 10 percent
- What James Coco, who gets his big break in Terrence McNally's *Next*, says about taking low-paying parts off-Broadway: "It's auditioning for Broadway, and Broadway is auditioning for films."
- How the avant-garde theatre troupe Mabou Mines, which includes JoAnne Akalaitas and Philip Glass, got its name: from the Nova Scotia town where they rehearsed
- New titles: Lord Laurence Olivier and Sir Noel Coward
- The typical critic, nationally, according to a Lou Harris survey: he's a white, 45-year-old Protestant liberal who started off in journalism and accidentally ended up a critic
- Percentage of critics who have received personal threats: about 10 percent, according to the Harris survey
- Origins of Stephen Sondheim's musical *Company*: in a series of dramatic sketches that was to star Kim Stanley
- What Carol Channing doesn't sing in her London revue *Carol Channing & Her Stout-Hearted Men*: "Hello, Dolly!"
- Amount that the Nixon White House pays for the expenses—hotels, transportation, etc.—incurred by performers playing command performances: nothing
- Number of off-Broadway productions that have won Pulitzer Prizes: 1, *No Place to Be Somebody*, this season's winner

Productions on Broadway: 62

Pulitzer Prize for Drama: *No Place to Be Somebody* (Charles Gordone)

New York Drama Critics Circle Awards:
Best Play: *Borstal Boy* (Frank McMahon)
Best American Play: *The Effect of Gamma Rays on Man-in-the-Moon Marigolds* (Paul Zindel)
Best Musical: *Company* (Stephen Sondheim)

Tony Awards:
Play: *Borstal Boy* (Frank McMahon)
Actress in a Play: Tammy Grimes (*Private Lives*)
Actor in a Play: Fritz Weaver (*Child's Play*)
Musical: *Applause* (Charles Strouse and Lee Adams)
Actress in a Musical: Lauren Bacall (*Applause*)
Actor in a Musical: Cleavon Little (*Purlie*)

June	July	August	September	October	November
Oh! Calcutta!	Off-Broadway playwright wrecks set	Largest TDF grant to Kopit's *Indians*	Lindy's sold to Longchamps	Pills put Tennessee Williams in the hospital	Julie Andrews m. Blake Edwards

December	January	February	March	April	May
Katharine Hepburn in *Coco*	David Merrick, movie mogul?	Merman in *Dolly*; Noel Coward knighted	Lauren Bacall in *Applause*	Sondheim's *Company*	Billie Burke d.

Personalities

JUNE 10 A *New York Times* ad for *Life* magazine quotes from *Life*'s review of Tennessee Williams's *The Bar of a Tokyo Hotel*, saying that Williams is "played out" and "has suffered an infantile regression." The review also "predicts the demise of one of America's major playwrights." Audrey Wood, Williams's agent, and Frank D. Gilroy, head of the Dramatists League, demand but do not get an apology from the *Times* for running the ad. **16** Nicol Williamson, playing Hamlet in Boston, stops during the second act, telling the audience, "I'm played out. This is my last performance on any stage. Exit left," which he does, but he returns later.

JULY 2 According to *Variety*, Anthony Newley is said to be putting together a musical about Napoleon in which he would play opposite Barbra Streisand's Josephine. She's reported to be interested. **31** Josef Bush, who adapted *De Sade Illustrated*, which has been playing off-Broadway at the Bouwerie, wrecks the set by spreading white paint all over it, protesting the addition of a nude scene without his permission.

SEPTEMBER 15 Hume Cronyn reveals that his left eye was removed in a June operation because of a cancerous tumor.

OCTOBER • Tennessee Williams is hospitalized in St. Louis, reported to be suffering withdrawal symptoms after being taken off the six to eight sleeping pills he's been taking each night instead of the two prescribed. • The New York Drama Critics Circle votes 10 to seven to deny membership to *New York* magazine critic John Simon because of the personal nature of his vituperative reviews. **6** "A fine line exists between creative interpretation and usurpation," playwright Edward Albee tells a Drama Desk symposium. In the audience is William Ball of the American Conservatory Theatre in San Francisco, whose revival of Albee's *Tiny Alice*, now at the ANTA Theatre, has, at the playwright's insistence, been altered from the production Ball staged. **8** In a letter to the editor in *Variety*, John Herbert, author of *Fortune and Men's Eyes*, deplores the changes that director

Plays and Musicals

JUNE 17 *Oh! Calcutta!* (1,314, including Broadway run), Kenneth Tynan's revue that revels in nudity and has nothing to do with India, opens off-Broadway at the Eden Theatre. Bereft of clothes, the cast is, however, covered by the reputations of the authors of their skits, including Sam Shepard, Samuel Beckett, and John Lennon. The 1976 revival will give 5,969 performances.

OCTOBER 13 Arthur Kopit's *Indians* (96) opens at the Brooks Atkinson. Stacy Keach plays Buffalo Bill in a cast that also includes Sam Waterston, Raul Julia, and Charles Durning. The 1976 film version is called *Buffalo Bill and the Indians, or Sitting Bull's History Lesson.* **21** Blythe Danner stars at the Booth in Leonard Gershe's *Butterflies Are Free* (1,333), with Keir Dullea as the blind young man with whom Danner has an affair and Eileen Heckart as his mother. It's a film in 1972, with Heckart repeating her role and winning an Oscar.

DECEMBER 18 With a big advance sale, Katharine Hepburn, absent from Broadway for 17 years, opens as Coco Chanel in the André Previn-Alan Jay Lerner, Paramount Pictures–financed, *Coco* (332), at the Mark Hellinger. The audience hears the star, who is said to be drawing about $15,000 a week, speak seven songs and, very dramatically, say

Blythe Danner MSN

Business and Society

AUGUST • The Theatre Development Fund announces its largest grant so far, $40,000 to buy up tickets to Arthur Kopit's *Indians*. TDF will resell the tickets, mostly to students, at $2.00 each.

SEPTEMBER • Lindy's, the legendary theatre district restaurant famous for its cheesecake, where the maître d' called himself the "sturgeon-general of the United States," is taken over by the Longchamps chain. It had been owned by realtor Max Stahl since 1962. **12** The Craft Experimental Theatre in Boston has a lawyer standing by just in case when *Sweet Eros* opens there tonight, giving the Hub its first legitimate stage nudity. The audience is limited to those over 18, and the city does not interfere.

JANUARY • Stuart Ostrow, producer of *1776*, declines to make any cuts for political reasons in the musical for its upcoming full-length production at a White House command performance. Nixon speechwriter William Safire reportedly asked that some material that could be seen as antiwar be deleted. **30** California's State Supreme Court strikes down the laws used recently to censor a production of Michael McClure's sexually explicit play

Births, Deaths, and Marriages

JUNE 5 Producer Vinton Freedly d.

JULY 28 Composer-lyricist Frank Loesser d.

AUGUST 14 Claire Bloom m. Hillard Elkins, producer of *Oh! Calcutta!* It will last for five years, until he takes up with their interior decorator.

SEPTEMBER 7 Linda Lavin m. Ron Leibman.

OCTOBER 17 Trevor Nunn, the Royal Shakespeare Company's artistic director, m. Janet Suzman, an actor in the Company.

NOVEMBER 9 Sam Shepard m. actress O-Lan. In about a year, he will begin a relationship with poet and singer Patti Smith. **12** Julie Andrews m. film director Blake Edwards. **19** Vincent Sardi, founder of

Sal Mineo made in the recent Los Angeles production, taking a rape scene that had originally been offstage and putting it out front and also emphasizing a scene showing masturbation. **15** On Vietnam Moratorium Day, Harold Prince cancels *Fiddler on the Roof*, for which the cast will be paid. Although David Merrick says it's a breach of contract, Woody Allen refuses to go on in *Play It Again Sam*. (Equity has said that not performing without management's permission would be a breach of contract.) The curtain goes up on *Hair*, although proceeds are donated to the cast's choice of antiwar causes. Many off-Broadway performances are canceled. Joel Grey, performing in Dallas in *Cabaret*, is threatened when he takes out a newspaper ad explaining his absence. **21** In his syndicated column, headlined "Skinny Girl Makes Good . . . ," Earl Wilson will begin, "The New Goddess in town is Blythe Danner of the hit comedy *Butterflies Are Free*, a Philadelphia banker's daughter who's too skinny to be a slinky sexpot, and too well built to be a high fashion model . . . but just perfect to be a comedienne."

NOVEMBER 12 Under the headline "Sam Shepard: Writer on the Way Up," *The New York Times* reports that "[u]p to now the commercial theater has been blissfully unaware of Mr. Shepard." His play *Sidewinder*, which was canceled at Yale when black students objected to its portrayal of black militants, is about to open at Lincoln Center, which Shepard characterizes as a "totally bourgeois scene." Many subscribers there don't like him either and will threaten to cancel after it opens.

JANUARY • David Merrick, who owns more than 100,000 shares of stock in Twentieth Century-Fox, is reported to be part of a group that is trying to gain control of the film studio, presumably to run it better in the interests of shareholders. Merrick thinks of himself as "the Ralph Nader of Twentieth Century-Fox."

FEBRUARY 3 Noel Coward is knighted. Leaving Buckingham Palace, he remarks of the Queen: "Absolutely charming; she always is." He pauses, continuing to

---

the word "shit." When the original cast album is released, Kate says, "I sound like Donald Duck!" **28** Neil Simon's comedy *The Last of the Red Hot Lovers* (706) opens at the Eugene O'Neill Theatre. James Coco is a middle-aged married man with a sexual wanderlust, fumbling one seduction after another. Simon now has three plays on Broadway: *Plaza Suite* and *Promises, Promises* are still playing.

JANUARY 26 Gretchen Cryer and Nancy Ford's *The Last Sweet Days of Isaac* (485), two one-act musicals, opens at the Eastside Playhouse. The two works "The Elevator" and "I Want to Walk to San Francisco" feature Austin Pendleton and Frederika Weber.

FEBRUARY 17 Robert Marasco's *Child's Play* (343) opens at the Royale. Pat Hingle, Fritz Weaver, and Ken Howard star in this thriller about strange doings at a Catholic boys' school. It's filmed in 1972.

MARCH 15 Ossie Davis's 1961 play about a Southern preacher, *Purlie Victorious*, has become the Gary Geld-Peter Udell musical *Purlie* (690), opening at the Broadway Theatre. Cleavon Little is the preacher, with Melba Moore, Linda Hopkins, John Heffernan, and Sherman Hemsley. **30** Lauren Bacall stars at the Palace in *Applause* (896), a musical version of the 1950 film *All About Eve*. The music and lyrics are by Charles Strouse and Lee Adams, the book by Betty Comden and Adolph Green. **31** *Borstal Boy* (143), Frank McMahon's adaptation of playwright Brendan Behan's autobiography, is at the Lyceum. Niall Toibin plays Behan.

APRIL 7 Paul Zindel's *The Effect of Gamma Rays on Man-in-the-Moon Marigolds* (819) opens at the off-Broadway Mercer–O'Casey Theatre. Sada Thompson is the woman left by her husband to raise two teenage girls. Swoosie Kurtz is debuting in a minor role and will advance to more important parts when the play moves to a bigger theatre. Joanne Woodward is the mother in the 1972 film, directed by Paul Newman. **26** *Company* (706), Stephen Sondheim's plotless, musical meditation on urban marriage, produced by Harold Prince, with a book by George Furth and staged on Boris Aronson's Plexiglas and

---

The Beard.

FEBRUARY • A three-judge panel in New York City rules that the off-Broadway play *Che!*, which contains 23 separate onstage sex acts, is obscene. Three people associated with the production, including author Lennox Raphael, are given the choice of paying a fine or going to jail. **22** *Hair* has its first preview performance in Boston, at the Wilbur Theatre. Censor Richard Sinnott calls it "the worst collection of garbage I've ever seen on a Boston theatre stage." The desecration of the flag—added recently and dropped by the beginning of the show's regular performances—not the nudity, upsets him most. **22** *1776* is the first full-length musical performed at the White House.

MARCH 10 The stagehands local of International Association of Theatrical Stage Employees (IATSE) reaches an agreement with the New York State Human Rights Commission to open its apprenticeship program to minorities.

APRIL 9 *Hair* is banned in Boston by the state's highest court. The producers are told they can continue if they drop the nude scene, but they refuse and despite a $600,000 advance sale, close down the production and drape the theatre in black.

---

the theatre district restaurant, d.

DECEMBER 14 Blythe Danner m. producer Bruce Paltrow. And Tony Roberts, appearing in the London production of *Promises, Promises*, m. Jenny Lyons, a dancer in the show.

FEBRUARY 1 Rosie Dolly, of the Dolly Sisters, d.

APRIL 26 Gypsy Rose Lee d. **29** Ed Begley d.

MAY 14 Billie Burke d.

Personalities

reporters, "I've known her since she was a little girl."

MARCH 28 Ethel Merman takes over the starring role in the Broadway production of *Hello, Dolly!*, which Jerry Herman had composed with her in mind in the first place. It will be Merman's last Broadway show. **30** Anne Baxter, Lauren Bacall's eventual replacement in *Applause*, opening tonight, played the ingenue Eve Harrington in the movie. Baxter is thrown one night when the film's original Margo Channing shows up and watches from the wings. Penny Fuller, playing Eve, is also nervous, as she will later put it, with "Bette-fucking-Davis standing there watching me, with all those bracelets jangling."

APRIL 1 Santo Loquasto makes his first mark on the New York theatre scene with his set design for Sam Shepard's *The Unseen Hand* and *Forensic and the Navigators*. **3** "Bacall Hits Broadway with Song and Dance," announces *Life*'s cover story, celebrating Lauren Bacall's March 30 opening in *Applause*. **22** In her London debut, in a revue called *Carol Channing & Her Stout-Hearted Men*, the star does not sing "Hello, Dolly!" although it's in the overture. **26** The Broadway cast of *Hair*, three days short of the show's second anniversary, performs its music in Central Park for 10,000 people.

MAY • Charles Gordone becomes the first black playwright to win the Pulitzer Prize for Drama for *No Place to Be Somebody*. **9** Producer Kermit Bloomgarden's curtain speech attacking the war in Vietnam and President Nixon's continuation of it is read at several of his productions. There is also a moment of silence for the four young people killed at Kent State University. Lauren Bacall, who reads the speech after her performance in *Applause*, is reported to have drawn more boos than cheers for it. **17** Pearl Bailey's sudden departure for health reasons from the road show production of *Hello, Dolly!* irks producer David Merrick, who will lose hundreds of thousands of dollars' worth of bookings.

Plays and Musicals

chrome set, opens at the Alvin. Dean Jones and Elaine Stritch star, with Barbara Barrie and Donna McKechnie. Larry Kert replaces Jones a few weeks into the run because of the former's personal problems. "The Ladies Who Lunch," "Barcelona," and "Another Hundred People" are the most notable songs.

MAY 3 *Mod Donna* (56), the Susan Bingham–Myrna Lamb musical about women's liberation, directed By Joseph Papp and starring April Shawhan, opens at the Public Theatre. **4** Joe Orten's *What the Butler Saw* (224) opens at the McAlpin Rooftop Theatre off-Broadway. Laurence Luckinbill and Jan Farrand are in a story about the consequences of a married man's efforts at seduction. **6** Zoe Caldwell is *Colette* (101), adapted from Colette's writings by Elinor Jones and playing at the Ellen Stewart Theatre in the East Village. Critic John J. O'Connor finds Caldwell "quite simply mesmerizing, giving one of the virtuoistic *[sic]* flamboyant performances that prompts thoughts of legendary actresses of the past." She quits the role on August 2 because of a previous commitment. Also in the play are Mildred Dunnock and Barry Bostwick. **13** William Hanley's *Slow Dance on the Killing Ground* (36), which had a brief Broadway run five years ago, is revived off-Broadway, at the Sheridan Square Playhouse. George Voskovec, Billy Dee Williams, and Madeline Miller star. **18** *The Me Nobody Knows* (587), a best-selling compilation of the writing of ghetto schoolchildren, has become a musical by Gary Friedman and Will Holt, opening off-Broadway, at the Orpheum, with a teenaged cast of 13. It moves to the Helen Hayes in December.

Business and Society

MAY 23 *Hair* reopens in Boston after the U.S. Supreme Court upholds an injunction issued by a U.S. District Court preventing the District Attorney from prosecuting over the famous nude scene.

Births, Deaths, and Marriages

1970–71

The Public Theatre and Minneapolis's Guthrie Theatre have serious deficits. The situation is serious off-Broadway, which experiences a monthlong strike. The FBI is taking *The Trial of the Catonsville Nine* very seriously and would like to interview its author (and put him in jail). Even Neil Simon, in *The Gingerbread Lady*, is getting serious; at least that's his aim. *No, No, Nanette*, Ruby Keeler, and Danny Kaye are back. Judith Anderson always wanted to play Hamlet and, at age 72, does. Katharine Hepburn leaves *Coco* and all but takes the audience with her. *Hello, Dolly!* passes My Fair Lady and reigns supreme over musical long runs, for the moment. The new curtain time is 7:30. And who is this "Anthony Weber" (*Variety*), who has written a musical about Jesus?

- What the best seats to a Broadway musical cost on a Saturday night: you may pay $15
- How Phyllis Diller roasts David Merrick: "If I ever need a heart transplant I'd want David's heart because it's never been used."
- Ethnic background of God, according to Bruce Jay Friedman's *Steambath*: Puerto Rican
- Only cast replacement nominated for a Tony: Larry Kert, who replaced Dean Jones early on in *Company*
- Original investment in *The Boys in the Band*, closing this season: $20,000
- Profit on *The Boys in the Band*: almost $600,000
- What John Simon writes about Diana Rigg and her nude scene in *Abelard and Héloise*: "Diana Rigg is built like a brick mausoleum with insufficient flying buttresses."
- Original title for the hit thriller *Sleuth*: *Who's Afraid of Stephen Sondheim?*
- Where Harold Prince gets the idea for *Follies*: from the photo in *Life* magazine of Gloria Swanson standing in the ruins of the Roxy Theatre as it is being demolished
- How Harold Prince sees *Follies*: "a Proustian fracture of time"
- Number of acts in the two-hour-plus musical *Follies*: 1
- Number of patrons who leave their seats to go to the bathroom on opening night of *Follies*: many
- Top ticket price for *Follies*: $12
- Amount invested in *Follies*: $700,000
- Amount lost by *Follies*: $665,000
- Average cost of producing an off-Broadway play: $41,400
- What gives the new Uris Theatre a big lift: a Hydro Float Stage System, which uses hydraulics to automate the movement of sets
- Guthrie Theatre deficit: $600,000

Productions on Broadway: 47

Pulitzer Prize for Drama: *The Effect of Gamma Rays on Man-in-the-Moon Marigolds* (Paul Zindel)

New York Drama Critics Circle Awards:
Best Play: *Home* (David Storey)
Best American Play: *House of Blue Leaves* (John Guare)
Best Musical: *Follies* (Stephen Sondheim)

Tony Awards:
Play: *Sleuth*: (Anthony Shaffer)
Actress in a Play: Maureen Stapleton (*The Gingerbread Lady*)
Actor in a Play: Brian Bedford (*The School for Wives*)
Musical: *Company* (Stephen Sondheim)
Actress in a Musical: Helen Gallagher (*No, No, Nanette*)
Actor in a Musical: Hal Linden (*The Rothschilds*)

June	July	August	September	October	November
Rip Torn fired from *Steambath*	*Gamma Rays* forced out of faulty theatre	FBI watching *The Trial of the Catonsville Nine*	*Hello, Dolly!* passes *My Fair Lady*	John Simon allowed into Drama Critics Circle	Equity strikes off-Broadway

December	January	February	March	April	May
Hello, Dolly! closes	7:30 curtain and *No, No, Nanette*	John Guare's *The House of Blue Leaves*	Leland Hayward d.	Stephen Sondheim's *Follies*	*Godspell*

Personalities

JUNE • Laurence Olivier is the first actor to enter the House of Lords. **4** Rip Torn is fired from Bruce Jay Friedman's *Steambath*, which was supposed to open tonight at the off-Broadway Truck and Warehouse Theatre. Instead, another preview is given, with director Anthony Perkins filling in. Producer Ivor Balding says of Torn, who had replaced Dick Shawn in the lead role on May 26, that "he, like Mr. Shawn, was not in my opinion, serving the play. . . ."

JULY 25 *The Effect of Gamma Rays on Man-in-the-Moon Marigolds* has to suspend performances at the Mercer–O'Casey Theatre, which needs emergency repairs. The show will move to the New Theatre next month.

AUGUST • FBI agents have been noticed lurking outside the Mark Taper Forum in Los Angeles, where *The Trial of the Catonsville Nine* is premiering. Its author, the Reverend Dan Berrigan, is wanted for destroying draft board records, the subject of the play. **6** With Danille Darrieux succeeding Katharine Hepburn in *Coco*, the take at the Mark Hellinger box office drops by more than 50 percent.

SEPTEMBER 24 Seventy-two-year-old Judith Anderson begins her national tour of *Hamlet* in Santa Barbara. She's playing the prince. "Melancholy Dame" and "The Dame as Dane" were two headlines that greeted the announcement of the production last month. Reviews are tepid, at best, to which Anderson responds, "I'd rather fail at this than do inane roles on TV." Sarah Bernhardt, Eva Le Gallienne, and Siobhan McKenna have also played Hamlet.

OCTOBER 27 Testifying in court in his efforts to retain custody of his daughter, producer David Merrick states that the seven-year-old lives in her own apartment with a nurse and governess, while he and his second wife live in another in the same Park Avenue building. He wins the case. **27** The New York Drama Critics Circle reverses its vote of last year, admitting John Simon to membership.

David Merrick and Carol Channing *PF*

Plays and Musicals

JUNE 22 Athol Fugard's *Boseman and Lena* (205), starring James Earl Jones, Ruby Dee, and Zakes Mokae, opens at the Circle in the Square. Clive Barnes in the *Times* says of Dee's work that it is "one of the finest performances I have ever seen." She would like to think it could end her days as "the Negro June Allyson." **27** The Dirtiest Show in Town (509), Tom Eyen's comedy-drama that originated in April Off-Off-Broadway at the Café La Mama, opens at the Astor Place Theatre. In addition to its quota of bare flesh and simulated sex, the show, which features a young cast of unknowns, has some points to make about the disintegration of urban society. **30** Bruce Jay Friedman's new comedy, which theorizes that the midpoint between heaven and earth can be found in a *Steambath* (127), opens at the Truck and Warehouse Theatre. Anthony Perkins stars as well as directs. The Puerto Rican bath attendant, who in a higher reality turns out to be God, is played by Hector Elizondo.

SEPTEMBER 9 With its 2,718th performance at today's matinée, *Hello, Dolly!* passes *My Fair Lady* as the longest-running musical in Broadway history. The celebration will be at Sardi's after tonight's show. Dolly Levi has been played on Broadway by Carol Channing, Ginger Rogers, Martha Raye, Betty Grable, Pearl Bailey, Phyllis Diller, and,

Business and Society

JUNE • Joseph Papp's New York Shakespeare Festival is in the middle of a financial crisis.

AUGUST 7 The Pasadena Playhouse is sold at a foreclosure sale to the Bank of America.

SEPTEMBER • The Nederlander family, now the biggest operator of theatres outside of New York, where the Shubert organization still reigns, signs a lease to take over Washington, D.C.'s National Theatre, beginning in 1972. **3** A Temple University survey of 5,587 members of Actors Equity, released today, shows that most make under $2,500 a year from stage work, with only five percent earning over $10,000. **28** The closed-circuit showing of *Oh! Calcutta!* (taped September 2) at 60 to 70 locations throughout the country is a financial disappointment. There are no theatres showing it in downtown Boston. At the Orson Welles Cinema in Cambridge, where it is shown, nine employees are arrested.

OCTOBER • Several narcotics arrests plague the cast of *Hair* in Los Angeles.

Births, Deaths, and Marriages

JUNE 4 Yiddish theatre comedian Menasha Skulnick d.

JULY 7 Marjorie Rambeau d.

OCTOBER 10 Donald Pleasance m. Israeli actress Meira Shore.

DECEMBER 30 Lenore Ulric d. **31** Composer Ray Henderson d.

FEBRUARY 5 Judi Dench, of the Royal Shakespeare Company, m. fellow company member Michael Williams.

MARCH 18 Producer-agent Leland Hayward d.

MAY 1 Edith Day d. **15** Tyrone Guthrie d. **21** Dennis King d.

NOVEMBER 5 At the Broadway Association lunch to honor David Merrick as its "Man of the Year," Phyllis Diller, who has starred in the producer's *Hello, Dolly!* roasts him: "If I ever need a heart transplant I'd want David's heart because it's never been used." Ethel Merman begins the program with her version of the "Star Spangled Banner." **18** *Variety* reports in a front-page story that Edward Albee has turned down a suggestion by Richard Burton and Henry Fonda that they do an all-male, homosexual version of *Who's Afraid of Virginia Woolf?* with Warren Beatty and Jon Voight also in the cast. The playwright is said to have rejected it because it would strengthen the belief of many that *Virginia Woolf* was originally intended as a play about gays. **25** Producer Richard Barr, whom *Variety* mentioned in last week's story about Henry Fonda and Richard Burton doing a gay version of Albee's *Virginia Woolf*, says that the actors had no such idea. The paper now quotes their press agent as saying that it was proposed to them, mostly in jest, and they thought that it might be "a fun thing to do."

DECEMBER 6 Someone fires a shot into Rip Torn's Upper West Side Manhattan apartment. No one is hurt. Torn and his wife, actress Geraldine Page, are currently involved in the strike against the League of Off-Broadway Theatres.

JANUARY • John Simon wins the George Jean Nathan Award for drama criticism.

FEBRUARY 24 Noah needs more than a boat to get through *Two by Two* tonight. Danny Kaye, who stars in the musical, tore a ligament and injured his ankle in an onstage accident on February 5 and returns this evening in a green wheelchair, with one foray out of the chair on crutches. **24** Ed Flanders, who is in the cast of Reverend Daniel Berrigan's *The Trial of the Catonsville Nine*, says that he's been harassed by the FBI over his appearance in the play. Berrigan is now in prison for destroying draft board records.

MARCH 12 In the midst of a performance of *70 Girls, 70,* in Philadelphia, David Burns collapses onstage from a fatal heart attack.

---

currently, Ethel Merman.

OCTOBER 19 Jerry Bock and Sheldon Harnick score another hit with *The Rothschilds* (505), at the Lunt-Fontanne. *Variety* says it could have been called "The Boys in the Bank." Hal Linden, finally a star in a Tony-winning performance, heads a cast that also has Paul Hecht, Jill Clayburgh, and Chris Sarandon.

NOVEMBER 10 Richard Rodgers's musical *Two by Two* (352), with lyrics by Martin Charnin, opens at the Imperial. Danny Kaye is back on Broadway for the first time in almost three decades as Noah in Peter Stone's adaptation of Clifford Odets's *The Flowering Peach.* **12** Anthony Shaffer's *Sleuth* (1,222), starring Anthony Quayle and Kenneth Baxter, opens at the Music Box. The thriller, a West End hit, is about a mystery writer toying with and trapping his wife's lover. The 1972 film stars Laurence Olivier and Michael Caine. **17** John Gielgud and Ralph Richardson star in *Home* (110), by David Storey, at the Morosco. This "home" is for mental patients, five of whom are trying to make sense of it all. The director is Lindsay Anderson. John J. O'Connor, in the *Wall Street Journal*, calls it "the most extraordinary piece of theatre in years."

DECEMBER 13 *The Gingerbread Lady* (193), Neil Simon's first serious play—although the master of light comedy's alcoholic-nymphomaniac protagonist has many one-liners—opens at the Plymouth. Maureen Stapleton stars, with Betsy von Furstenberg in a supporting role. **27** The original production of *Hello, Dolly!* closes at the St. James, after a record run of 2,844 performances since it opened on January 16, 1964. Producer David Merrick jokes that comedian Flip Wilson, whose drag persona—"Geraldine"—is currently popular, once said he wanted to play Dolly Levi. Ethel Merman's last trip down the staircase tonight to the Harmonia Gardens receives a one-minute standing ovation.

JANUARY 19 The 1925 Vincent Youmans-Irving Caesar musical *No, No, Nanette* (861) is revived and becomes Broadway's

---

NOVEMBER 16 Actors Equity strikes 16 off-Broadway shows in an effort to gain something resembling parity with Broadway. The union wants a minimum of $125 a week, while the League of Off-Broadway Theatres is offering $90. The strike will last thirty-one days.

DECEMBER • *The New York Times* declines to run an ad for the show *Foreplay* depicting two naked men on a bed with the caption, "a love story." "We run ads for the homoboys," a *Times* ad department spokesperson reportedly says, "but this one [i]s too much." **16** The thirty-one day strike by Actors Equity against the League of Off-Broadway Theatres and Producers ends, with both sides agreeing to arbitration.

JANUARY • A "limited gross Broadway production agreement," developed by producers, theatre owners, and the unions, is announced. It aims to hold down costs for productions that might not otherwise be commercially viable. **2** Members of the recently formed Gay Liberation Front disrupt the final preview performance of *Stag Movie*, at the Gate Theatre, forcing its suspension tonight. The protestors say it is homophobic. **4** A 7:30 curtain, an hour earlier than the starting time that has been the custom, goes into effect for

Personalities

MAY • Jerry Orbach boasts to an interviewer about his upcoming 13th wedding anniversary, saying that "ours is one of the longest marriages we know of in show business." The run has four more years to go before the curtain comes down. **7** A court injunction halts an unauthorized concert version of *Jesus Christ Superstar*, which has been touring college campuses. Its composer, whose name is not yet a byword on Broadway, is referred to by *Variety* on May 19, in its report on the case, as "Anthony Weber." **11** A play called *Lenny*, about the late comedian-social critic Lenny Bruce, scheduled to open off-Broadway at the Village Gate, is stopped by an injunction granted at the request of the producers of the Broadway play of the same name, which will open on May 26. The production that is stopped is using material from the book *The Essential Lenny Bruce*, the rights to which are controlled by the Broadway show. The cast of the Village Gate *Lenny* is laid off. **25** Director Alan Schneider is arrested in New York City for "obstructing governmental administration." Schneider does not move quickly enough away from the scene of a construction accident when ordered to do so by a police officer, who roughs up the director, allegedly hitting him in the face. Schneider will win a $10,000 judgment against the city.

Plays and Musicals

smash hit, at the Forty-sixth Street Theatre, where it stars Helen Gallagher, Bobby Van, Jack Gilford, Patsy Kelly, and, most notably, Ruby Keeler. **20** Peter Brook directs the Royal Shakespeare Company in *A Midsummer Night's Dream* (62), at the Billy Rose Theatre, where some players make their entrances via trapeze. Alan Howard plays both Theseus and Oberon, with Sara Kestelman also doubling as Hippolyta and Titania. In the cast but not yet known to American audiences are Ben Kingsley and Patrick Stewart.

FEBRUARY 7 The Reverend Daniel Berrigan's *The Trial of the Catonsville Nine* (159) opens at the Good Shepherd-Faith Church near Lincoln Center. The cast of this antiwar drama, based on the 1968 trial of protestors against the war in Vietnam who destroyed draft records, includes Ed Flanders and Sam Waterston. **10** *The House of Blue Leaves* (337), by John Guare, opens at the Truck and Warehouse Theatre. Harold Gould stars as a zookeeper moonlighting as a singer-composer, who fantasizes about fame in the midst of a truly dysfunctional family. Anne Meara and William Atherton are also in the cast. **22** *Here Are Ladies* (67), Siobhan McKenna's one-woman show, in which she interprets the work of Irish writers, is presented by Joseph Papp at the Public Theatre. **25** Paul Zindel's *And Miss Reardon Drinks a Little* (108) is at the Morosco. The sad-funny drama of three middle-aged sisters stars Julie Harris, Estelle Parsons, and Nancy Marchand.

MARCH 2 *Man of La Mancha* comes full circle, moving downtown and off-Broadway to the Eden from the Martin Beck. The musical opened on November 22, 1965 at the ANTA Theatre in Greenwich Village. **15** Alec McCowen plays a shy professor in Christopher Hampton's *The Philanthropist* (72), at the Barrymore. Jack Kroll, in *Newsweek*, says the play "has the authentic dazzle, the sense of surprise and control, that marks the real thing, the artist." The playwright is in his early twenties. **23** An off-Broadway revival of Dale Wasserman's dramatization of Ken

Business and Society

all Broadway theatres, a policy adopted by the League of Broadway Theatres. It was last tried on an experimental basis a decade ago.

Births, Deaths, and Marriages

Kesey's *One Flew Over the Cuckoo's Nest* (1,025), at the Mercer-Hansberry Theatre, stars William Devane. Also in the cast is an unknown, Danny De Vito.

APRIL 4 Stephen Sondheim's *Follies* (522), his musical about a reunion of Ziegfeld-era performers, is at the Winter Garden. Harold Prince produces and codirects with Michael Bennett, who also choreographs the show. Alexis Smith, Gene Nelson, Dorothy Collins, and John McMartin have the leads, and songs include "Broadway Baby," "I'm Still Here," and "Could I Leave You?" **10** The Circle Repertory Company mounts its first production, David Starkwether's *A Practical Ritual to Exorcise Frustration After Five Days of Rain*, in a an Upper West Side loft. The cast includes Spalding Gray, and Lanford Wilson designed the scenery.

MAY 17 *Godspell* (2,124), Stephen Schwartz's musical, opens at the Cherry Lane, off-Broadway, and will move to the Promenade in three months. In 1976, it will be on Broadway, at the Broadhurst. As in next fall's *Jesus Christ Superstar*, Jesus is hip and up-to-date in this show, which stars Lamar Alford. **20** David Rabe's *The Basic Training of Pavlo Hummel* (363) opens at the Public Theatre. William Atherton plays a man trying to define himself through his identity as a soldier. He's killed by one of his own men. Rabe will insist that it's not an "antiwar play," as it is popularly termed, because he's trying to incite thought, not action. **26** *Lenny* (455), starring Cliff Gorman as Lenny Bruce, opens at the Brooks Atkinson. Tom O'Horgan is directing a cast that also includes Joe Silver and Erica Yohn. Dustin Hoffman stars in Bob Fosse's 1974 film.

1971–72

Grease debuts with "Look at Me, I'm Sandra Dee." The Off-Off-Broadway Alliance is formed. Joseph Papp has plans to produce on a national scale and takes a verbal whack at critic John Simon. They're singing *Two Gentlemen of Verona* at the St. James, and *Fiddler on the Roof* is the new long-run leader among musicals. Twenty-three-year-old Andrew Lloyd Webber says that *Jesus Christ Superstar* is "no more rock than Stravinsky." Critics say it's not much of anything, but the tickets and LPs are selling briskly. Walter Winchell is dead, and so is the second marriage of Colleen Dewhurst and George C Scott. David Merrick opts for a later curtain so you can enjoy your dinner, and Jerry Orbach almost eats bullets for dessert when he dines with "Crazy Joey" Gallo.

- London box office gross for *Jesus Christ Superstar*: $16.8 million
- Cost of staging a musical on the West End: a third to a half less than what it costs on Broadway
- Colleen Dewhurst's assessment of her two marriages to George C. Scott: "George and I would have made a great brother and sister."
- U.S. President in whose administration there has been the most federal funding for the arts since World War II: Richard M. Nixon
- Number of black Tony Award nominees this season: 7, the most ever
- Number of Tony Awards for Best Play won so far by Neil Simon: none, although his work already includes *Barefoot in the Park*, *The Odd Couple*, *Plaza Suite*, and *The Prisoner of Second Avenue*
- What you get free if you make dinner reservations at Sardi's through Ticketron: a carafe of wine
- What critic Walter Winchell said of his habit of giving a thumbs-up to the season's first opening: "Who am I to stone the first cast?"
- Number of profitable shows among the 19 that Harold Prince has produced since *The Pajama Game* in 1954: 10
- Why Helen Hayes has to retire: theatre dust is aggravating her asthma
- Percentage of Broadway audiences that prefer the 7:30 curtain, according to a survey conducted by the League of New York Theatres: 55.8 percent
- Number of biographies of Tallulah Bankhead published in 1972: 4

Productions on Broadway: 56

Pulitzer Prize for Drama: None awarded

New York Drama Critics Circle Awards:
Best Play: *That Championship Season* (Jason Miller)
Best Foreign Play: *The Screens* (Jean Genet)
Best Musical: *Two Gentlemen of Verona* (Galt MacDermot)

Tony Awards:
Play: *Sticks and Bones* (David Rabe)
Actor in a Play: Cliff Gorman (*Lenny*)
Actress in a Play: Sada Thompson (*Twigs*)
Musical: *Two Gentlemen of Verona* (Galt MacDermott)
Actor in a Musical: Phil Silvers (*A Funny Thing Happened on the Way to the Forum*)
Actress in a Musical: Alexis Smith (*Follies*)

June — Libby Holman commits suicide

July — *Fiddler on the Roof* overtakes *Hello, Dolly!*

August — Ann-Margaret can't be Merrick's *Sugar*

September — David Merrick holds back the curtain

October — *Jesus Christ Superstar*

November — Papp wants to direct a national theatre

December — *Two Gentlemen of Verona*

January — "Study of the New York Theatre"

February — *Grease*; Walter Winchell d.

March — Playwright Ed Bullins disrupts performance

April — Jerry Orbach dines with "Crazy Joey" Gallo

May — *That Championship Season*

Personalities

JUNE 6 Helen Hayes makes her last stage appearance in a production of *Long Day's Journey Into Night,* at Catholic University in Washington, D.C. She has to retire because of acute asthma, aggravated by theatre dust.

JULY • Julian Beck and Judith Malina, of the Living Theatre, are arrested twice in Brazil on drug charges. **1** New York *Daily News* drama critic John Chapman, who has been with the paper for 50 years, retires.

AUGUST • Ann-Margaret, David Merrick's first choice to star in the Marilyn Monroe role in the musical version of the film *Some Like It Hot,* now called *All for Sugar,* is out of the picture because of scheduling conflicts.

SEPTEMBER 13 David Merrick unilaterally breaks the New York League of Theatre's 7:30 curtain policy, replacing it with an 8:00 start for *Promises, Promises.* He says he wants the audience to enjoy a leisurely dinner. Merrick's enemy, producer Alexander Cohen, dismisses the move, suggesting it is a response to the show's sagging box office: "Twofers audiences don't eat out as a rule."

OCTOBER 15 The original cast recording of *Jesus Christ Superstar* is being made on this Sunday. It includes one new song, "Could We Start Again, Please," not present on the two-LP set that has already sold almost 3,000,000 copies. Several critics are complaining about the ad in *The New York Times* today for the show, which quotes them out of context. Producer Robert Stigwood promises to be more careful about this in the future. The show's lyricist Tim Rice, when confronted by charges that the musical is anti-Semitic, responds that "[t]he priests represent the establishment. They're establishment people, not Jewish people."

DECEMBER 7 Julie Andrews and Carol Burnett appear together in a CBS television special, "Julie and Carol at Lincoln Center." **17** Mildred Dunnock, who was to appear in a production of *A Place*

Plays and Musicals

JULY 21 With its 2,845th performance, *Fiddler on the Roof* overtakes *Hello, Dolly!* to become Broadway's longest-running musical. Celebrating the achievement, New York City Mayor John Lindsay, demonstrably old-line American, tells the audience, "If Pearl Bailey can play Dolly, I can play Tevye."

OCTOBER 12 *Jesus Christ Superstar* (720) opens at the Mark Hellinger. Composer Andrew Lloyd Webber says that "it's no more rock than Stravinsky." But it isn't Bach's *St. Matthew's Passion,* either. The *Times* calls it "less than super," and *Variety* says it's "overproduced." *Time*'s October 25 cover story dubs it "[h]eavenzappopin," likening it to the 1938 Olsen and Johnson loony revue *Hellzapoppin.* The Lloyd Webber show began life as a single hit song—the title tune—became an album, and evolved into what its director Tom O'Horgan calls a "rock opera." Stars include Jeff Fenholt and Ben Vereen. **20** Melvin Van Peeble's *Ain't Supposed to Die a Natural Death* (325), recited pieces on the state of black America accompanied by music, opens at the Barrymore. In the cast is Garrett Morris.

NOVEMBER 7 David Rabe's *Sticks and Bones* (121) opens at the Public Theatre. A Vietnam veteran, played by David Selby, returns to America to a living nightmare. His parents, "Ozzie and Harriet," offer him suicide as the only way out. When the play moves to the John Golden Theatre on March 1, Santo Loquasto will have his first Broadway set design credit. The play's total run is 366 performances. **11** Neil Simon's *The Prisoner of Second Avenue* (788), starring Peter Falk, Lee Grant, and Vincent Gardenia, opens at the Eugene O'Neill Theatre. Mike Nichols is directing this comedy about life in a big city high-rise. **14** George Furth's *Twigs* (289), directed by Michael Bennett—his first nonmusical—opens at the Broadhurst. Sada Thompson is playing four parts, three sisters and their mother.

DECEMBER 1 Joseph Papp's production of Shakespeare's *Two Gentlemen of Verona*

Business and Society

JUNE • Twofers are everywhere as the season ends and the recession deepens. Last year at this time, of the 18 shows still running on Broadway, two were giving away discount coupons. Now, 13 out of 24 productions have distributed them. The Leblang's and Golden Penn ticket brokers have merged, and McBride's, long a fixture among brokers, has gone out of business. • The Reverend Daniel Berrigan's *The Return of the Catonsville Nine,* in a return engagement at the Mark Taper Forum in Los Angeles, is reviewed in an early edition of the *Los Angeles Herald-Examiner,* a Hearst paper. The reviewer criticizes the play but admires its author. When the review mysteriously disappears from later editions, the newspaper, which has editorialized against Berrigan's antiwar activities, will not comment.

JUNE 26 The new minimum weekly salary on Broadway is $185.

SEPTEMBER • The management of Ford's Theatre in Washington, D.C. goes to court to have the Circle in the Square removed as the house's producer before the expiration of its contract. The

Births, Deaths, and Marriages

JUNE 18 Libby Holman commits suicide.

JULY 17 Nicol Williamson m. actress Jill Townsend.

OCTOBER 14 Playwright Sam Spewack d.

NOVEMBER 4 Dancer Ann Pennington d.

DECEMBER 15 John Rubinstein m. actress Judi West.

DECEMBER 18 Dorothy Loudon m. Norman Paris, her arranger.

FEBRUARY 2 Colleen Dewhurst divorces George C. Scott for the second time. "George and I would have made a great brother and sister," she will later say.

FEBRUARY 20 Walter Winchell d. The man who invented the Broadway news-

Without Doors at the Harvard University Loeb Drama Center, falls down a flight of stairs at a press conference on opening night, breaking her hip.

JANUARY 10 Joseph Papp, in a letter in *New York* magazine, attacks its theatre critic John Simon for his panning of the Public Theatre's *The Black Terror*. Papp suggests that Simon's rage stems "from the effects of a benevolent mother who undoubtedly fussed all over her precocious offspring." Concludes Papp: "[W]hy the hell doesn't he grow up?"

FEBRUARY 22 David Merrick's *Sugar*, a musical based on the film *Some Like It Hot*, opens in Philadelphia in what has become a longer than expected tryout

Joseph Papp *PF*

trek. Rumors persist that Neil Simon has been called in as a play-doctor and that Jerry Herman has been asked to beef up Jule Styne's score.

MARCH 18 Playwright Ed Bullins and a group of supporters disrupt a performance of his play *The Duplex*, at the Forum Theatre in Lincoln Center. Bullins contends that his tragedy has been gussied up with "show material" by director Gilbert Moses. Jules Irving, who heads the Repertory Theatre, says that Bullins wasn't at rehearsals, when the changes were made. The cast opposes Bullins's disruption, which ends the evening's performance.

APRIL 6 Jerry Orbach's wife, Marta Curro,

---

(613) opens at the St. James. A musical—conceived that way by director Mel Shapiro—with music and lyrics by Galt MacDermott and John Guare, it stars Raul Julia, Clifton Davis, Diana Davila, and Jonelle Allen, with Stockard Channing in her Broadway debut. **6** The new American Place Theatre, an off-Broadway 299-seat house in the Broadway theatre district, opens with two plays. Ronald Ribman's *Fingernails Blue as Flowers* (33), set at a Jamaican beach resort, stars Albert Paulsen. And Steve Tesich's *Lake of the Woods* has Hal Holbrook and Armand Assante in the story of a family taking stock of itself. **13** Jean Genet's *The Screens* (25) is given its English language premiere at the Brooklyn Academy of Music. The cast is headed by Julie Bovasso, Barry Bostwick, and Charles Bartlett.

FEBRUARY 14 *Grease* (3,388), Jim Jacobs and Warren Casey's affectionate send-up of the rock 'n' roll 1950s and early '60s, opens at the Eden Theatre. "Look at Me, I'm Sandra Dee" sets the tone for the show. Barry Bostwick and Carole Demas star, with Adrienne Barbeau and Timothy Myers. The 1978 film version will star Olivia Newton-John and John Travolta, who is in one of the touring companies of the stage production. **21** Michael Weller's *Moonchildren* (12), a moody look at young people today, opens at the Royale (12). The cast includes James Woods, Edward Herrmann, Christopher Guest, Jill Eikenberry, and Robert Prosky.

An off-Broadway revival at the Theatre De Lys (237) will be more successful.

MARCH 30 Phil Silvers stars in a revival of *A Funny Thing Happened on the Way to the Forum* (156), at the Lunt-Fontanne.

APRIL 2 Tennessee Williams's *Small Craft Warnings* (194), which portrays the downbeat scene in a California bar, opens at the Truck and Warehouse Theatre, off-Broadway. "Easily the best drama off-Broadway this season," says *Variety*. **9** The 1959 movie *Some Like It Hot* has become the Jule Styne-Bob Merrill musical *Sugar* (505), opening at the Majestic after a stormy tryout period. Tony Roberts, Robert Morse, Elaine Joyce, and Cyril Ritchard star. **19** *Don't Bother Me,*

Theatre gives as a reason the losses sustained by several productions.

NOVEMBER • Producer Joseph Papp tells reporters that he aspires to turn the New York Shakespeare Festival into a national theatre, moving productions from the Public Theatre in New York to the Kennedy Center in Washington, D.C. He sees financing coming from the government and foundation grants.

DECEMBER 4 Fire causes extensive damage at the Truck and Warehouse Theatre in the East Village, where John Guare's *The House of Blue Leaves* has been playing.

JANUARY 26 A "Study of the New York Theatre," funded by New York State and private foundations, calls for public subsidy of the theatre and more flexible ticket pricing. The report notes that ticket prices, adjusted for inflation, are about where they were in the 1920s, but the cost of producing shows has risen substantially.

FEBRUARY 7 The OOB Alliance is formed to represent the interests of off-off-Broadway Theatre. Its first act is to criticize last month's "Study of the New York Theatre," which slighted the contribution of off-off-Broadway to the arts, according to OOB. Actors Equity is com-

---

paper column referred to Broadway as the "[h]ardened [a]rtery." The onetime part-time drama critic described the typical reviewer as "a newspaperman, whose sweetheart ran away with an actor." Of his habit of giving a thumbs-up to the season's first opening, he said, "Who am I to stone the first cast?"

Personalities

is collaborating with Joseph "Crazy Joey" Gallo on the gangster's autobiography. Tonight, Jerry and Marta celebrate Gallo's birthday with him at the Copacabana. The quirky Gallo met Orbach after being delighted with the actors portrayal of a figure resembling him in the film *The Gang That Couldn't Shoot Straight*, and the two have become friends. Gallo was married at the Orbach's home on March 16. **7** Mafioso Joseph "Crazy Joey" Gallo is assassinated at Umberto's Clam House in Little Italy. "Sure, it could of been us sitting with him," says Jerry Orbach, who was with him last night. "But Joey was worth it." **12** *Variety* headlines: "Slain Gallo's Show Biz Chums Echo of Actor-Gangster Socializing in 'Dry' Era."

MAY 14 The Associated Press refuses to cover the opening of the play *Older People*, at the Public Theatre tonight, complaining that the date of the premiere has been shifted several times just to accommodate the schedule of *New York Times* critic Clive Barnes. **22** The New York Drama Critics Circle names David Rabe's *Sticks and Bones* Best Play of the season. **24** The New York Drama Critics Circle announces that they miscounted the votes for Best Play when they announced that David Rabe's *Sticks and Bones* won and that Jason Miller's *That Championship Season* actually came in first in the balloting.

Plays and Musicals

I Can't Cope (1,065), a revue about black people in America, opens at the Playhouse. Miki Grant, who wrote the words and music, is in the cast, as is Alex Bradford. **23** Tom Stoppard's one-act comedies *After Magritte*, about two dancers, and *The Real Inspector Hound* (465), which features a play-within-a-play mystery, opens at the Theatre Four to good reviews. The casts include Tom Lacy, David Rounds, Carrie Nye, and Remak Ramsay.

MAY 2 Jason Miller's *That Championship Season* (144) opens at the Public Theatre. This story of basketball players looking at their lives after the cheering stops features Charles Durning, Richard Dysart, and Paul Sorvino. It moves uptown to the Booth on September 14.

Business and Society

plaining of being similarly slighted by the report.

APRIL 12 *Variety* theatre critic Hobe Morrison, bemoaning the lack of business at the box office, even for plays with good reviews, writes: "Something is basically wrong and no one knows what it is or why. . . . Legit is in trouble, particularly Broadway legit." Still, every Broadway stage is either lit or booked.

Births, Deaths, and Marriages

1972–73

When is a Shubert not a Shubert? When he's Bernard Jacobs or Gerald Schoenfeld, the two enduring members of the triumvirate, who take over the theatre empire built by Lee and J. J. Shubert and become so identified with it that they take on, as a sort of title, the designation as "the Shuberts." Joseph Papp takes on the production duties at Lincoln Center. Noel Coward is dead. Gower Champion replaces John Gielgud in tryouts as director of the troubled but finally successful revival of *Irene*. The Uris and the Minskoff Theatres are new, big, and offer more legroom but perhaps a bit less warmth than Broadway's older houses. And for Stephen Sondheim, it's "Send in the Clowns."

- Amount of liquor that director José Quintero was consuming before quitting this season: about 1½ bottles a day
- Number of stars billed above the title in the revival of *The Women*: 4—Myrna Loy, Rhonda Fleming, Dorothy Loudon, and Alexis Smith
- Young, unknown actors appearing in various productions of *Godspell*: Gilda Radner, Jeremy Irons, Joe Mantegna, Victor Garber, and Andrea Martin
- Actor who was originally supposed to be the lead in Lanford Wilson's *Hot'l Baltimore*, in the part that went to Judd Hirsch: Christopher Lloyd
- Who is singing on the radio when *Hot'l Baltimore* begins: Arlo Guthrie
- Number of plays in which the lead character is Mary Lincoln, wife of Abraham Lincoln: 3—*The Lincoln Mask* (Eva Marie Saint), *The Last of Mrs. Lincoln* (Julie Harris), and *Look Away* (Geraldine Page)
- Missing from *Variety*: "Vaudeville," finally replaced in the summer of 1972 by the "Personal Appearances" and "Auditorium-Arena" categories
- Amount that Motown Records, which has rights to the original cast recording, has invested in *Pippin*: $135,000
- Amount that *Follies* has lost by the time it closes in Los Angeles in October of 1972: $700,000
- How much Mitzi Newhouse has contributed to Lincoln Center for its theatrical operations: $1 million
- New name of the Forum Theatre at Lincoln Center: the Mitzi Newhouse Theatre
- It's bigger on the road: road productions produce a higher gross than Broadway for the first time

Productions on Broadway: 58

Pulitzer Prize for Drama: *That Championship Season* (Jason Miller)

New York Drama Critics Circle Awards:
Best Play: *The Changing Room* (David Storey)
Best American Play: *Hot'l Baltimore* (Lanford Wilson)
Best Musical: *A Little Night Music* (Stephen Sondheim)

Tony Awards:
Play: *That Championship Season* (Jason Miller)
Actor in a Play: Alan Bates (*Butley*)
Actress in a Play: Julie Harris (*The Last of Mrs. Lincoln*)
Musical: *A Little Night Music* (Stephen Sondheim)
Actor in a Musical: Ben Vereen (*Pippin*)
Actress in a Musical: Glynis Johns (*A Little Night Music*)

June
- *Fiddler on the Roof* passes *Life with Father*

July
- Shubert organization confirms management upheaval

August
- Phil Silvers out of *Forum* with stroke

September
- Patti LuPone and Kevin Kline's New York debuts

October
- *Pippin*

November
- Theatre Hall of Fame inaugurated

December
- Neil Simon's *The Sunshine Boys*

January
- Noel Coward's last public appearance

February
- "Send in the Clowns" in *A Little Night Music*

March
- *Irene* and *Hot'l Baltimore*; Noel Coward d.

April
- Sondheim on cover of *Newsweek*

May
- Papp to produce at Lincoln Center

Personalities

JUNE 6 When an actor in his off-Broadway play *Small Craft Warnings* misses three performances, Tennessee Williams steps in, making his stage debut as a boozy character named "Doc." Williams describes the experience as "excruciating."

JULY 3 Joseph Papp is on the cover of *Newsweek*, illustrating the story "New Life in the American Theater." **3** The Acting Company, the group of Juilliard alumni directed by John Houseman, opens its first season, at the Saratoga Performing Arts Festival.

AUGUST 1 A "minor" stroke puts Phil Silvers out of the revival of *A Funny Thing Happened on the Way to the Forum*, which will close on August 12.

OCTOBER • Bob Fosse and Ann Reinking, who met during the preparation of *Pippin*, have begun a long-term relationship. Fosse's relationship with the show's composer Stephen Schwartz and lyricist Roger O. Hirson has been less cordial, and he has them banned from rehearsals.

NOVEMBER 19 The Theatre Hall of Fame is inaugurated at the new Uris Theatre. *Via Galactica* was also been scheduled to open tonight but has been delayed. Among the 120 figures enshrined in the Hall of Fame are George Abbott, Judith Anderson, Orson Welles, and Mae West. P. G. Wodehouse is in it but not Guy Bolton. **30** Arthur Miller's *The Creation of the World and Other Business* barely made it to day one. Director Harold Clurman and Barbara Harris, playing Eve, quarreled, and Harris left during rehearsals. Susan Bateson, a black actress, replaced Harris. Zoe Caldwell, wife of the show's producer Robert Whitehead, whom Miller had in mind for Eve—she had gained too much weight after giving birth recently—coaches Bateson, who says, "Aside from some racial comments [Caldwell cautioned her not to play the part 'too black'], which I excused as being made out of ignorance, she was very helpful." But with the show floundering out of town, Caldwell replaces Bateson, and Hal Holbrook, playing Lucifer, gives way to

Plays and Musicals

JUNE 17 *Fiddler on the Roof*, which has been operating at a loss for the past year, sets a new Broadway long-run record, surpassing *Life with Father*, with its 3,225th performance. *Fiddler* opened on September 22, 1964. Its sale of about 2,000,000 original cast albums is still far short of My *Fair Lady*'s 8,000,000.

SEPTEMBER 27 The City Center Acting Company opens its first New York season at the Good Shepherd-Faith Church at Lincoln Center. John Houseman is directing graduates of Juilliard's first Drama Division graduating class in a production of *School for Scandal* (12). The *New Yorker* calls Kevin Kline, playing Charles Surface, "rollicking" and "handsome" and says of Patti LuPone that she "has not yet the stage presence or dignity for Lady Teazle," although "she is appropriately merry and sly. . . ."

OCTOBER 4 *Oh Coward!* (294), a revue featuring the work of Noel Coward, is at the New Theatre, with Barbara Cason, Roderick Cook, and Jamie Ross. **17** Bob Randall's comedy *6 Rms Riv Vu* (247), about a one-nighter ignited by the quest for a New York City rental apartment, opens at the Helen Hayes Theatre. Jerry Orbach and Jane Alexander have the leads, with F. Murray Abraham. **23** Bob Fosse's treatment of a musical show that Stephen Schwartz had written in college, *Pippin* (1,944), opens at the Imperial. Ben Vereen, John Rubenstein, in his Broadway debut, Jill Clayburgh, Eric Berry, and Ann Reinking are in the cast of this story about a mythical man who settles for hearth and home when he discovers that he's just not cut out to be heroic. "No Time at All" is in the score. **31** Alan Bates stars in *Butley* (135), Simon Gray's play about a professor having a bad day—his wife and male lover are leaving him, and he's drinking. The British import, for which Bates, who draws more praise than the play, will win a Tony, is at the Morosco.

NOVEMBER 10 Eric Bentley's *Are You Now or Have You Ever Been* (19), based on the transcripts of the House Un-American

Business and Society

JUNE 30 Lawrence Shubert Lawrence, grandnephew of Lee and J. J. Shubert, is deposed as active head of the Shubert Foundation and replaced with newly elected directors Bernard Jacobs, Gerald Schoenfeld, and Irving Goldman.

JULY • The producers of *Grease* sue *Variety* for "knowingly" and "maliciously" printing incorrect box office statistics about the show. The suit will fail.

OCTOBER 26 A money crisis causes the Repertory Theater of Lincoln Center to curtail its operations. Jules Irving, its artistic director, resigns.

DECEMBER 2 The failure of *Via Galactica*, the opening attraction at the new Uris Theatre, closing tonight after 15 performances, marks the fourth big-budget musical to flop in the past two months. According to *Variety*, they represent a cumulative loss of $2.5 million. The others were *Dude*, *Ambassador*, and *Lysistrata*.

JANUARY • With desperately needed grant money probably not forthcoming, the board of directors of the Repertory Theatre of Lincoln Center decides to sus-

Births, Deaths, and Marriages

SEPTEMBER 14 George C. Scott m. actress Trish Van Devere.

SEPTEMBER 23 Staats Cotsworth m. actress Josephine Hutchinson. They met in 1932 when both were with Eve Le Gallienne's Civic Repertory Company.

OCTOBER 16 Leo G. Carroll d.

NOVEMBER 12 Rudolph Friml d.

NOVEMBER 13 Margaret Webster d.

MARCH 26 Noel Coward d.

MAY 10 Abel Green, who has been the Editor of *Variety* for four decades, d.

George Grizzard.

DECEMBER 4 *The New York Times*, in its report on Dr. Max Jacobson, "Dr. Feel Good," who has been giving injections to celebrities containing amphetamines as well as vitamins, cites Alan Jay Lerner and Tennessee Williams as recipients of the shots.

JANUARY • Gower Champion replaces John Gielgud as director of the revival of the musical *Irene*, now in tryouts. The Broadway opening night has already been pushed back three times. **14** On what will be his final visit to New York and last public appearance, Noel Coward, accompanied by Marlene Dietrich, attends a testimonial performance of the revue *Oh Coward!* The frail playwright declines to be interviewed, stating through a spokesperson, uncharacteristically, that "I haven't got anything more to say."

FEBRUARY • "I think I'm a serious writer," Neil Simon tells a *Variety* interviewer. "I don't write with the idea of making money." He protests against the focus on his wealth, even in reviews, and says he never made much more than $1 million in any single year. He complains that Barbra Streisand isn't evaluated on the basis of her income, so why should he? **7** Abe Burrows, directing a rehearsal of *No Hard Feelings*, at the Martin Beck, is hospitalized after he falls into the orchestra pit. **22** Harvey Fierstein, a young drag performer who is just beginning to write for the theatre, states in a letter to the editor of the *Village Voice*: "For the past three theatre seasons your critics have tried to compare me with Maria Callas, Selma Diamond, Tyrone Power, Lauren Bacall, Hedy Lamarr, Andy Devine, Joan Crawford, H. M. Kouttoukas, Irene Papas and finally . . . Muhammad Ali. When will they realize that I am incomparable."

MARCH 4 Tennessee Williams writes in *The New York Times*: "I have never found the subject of homosexuality a satisfactory theme for a full-length play, despite the fact that it appears as frequently as it does in my short fiction." **9** Joseph Papp's production of David Rabe's *Sticks and Bones*, scheduled for broadcast on CBS tonight, is postponed by the network

---

Activities Committee hearings of the 1940s and 1950s, opens at the Yale University Theatre in New Haven. The cast includes Stephen Joyce, Al Freeman, Jr., and Leonard Frey. **15** The Circle in the Square moves to Broadway at the Joseph E. Levine Theatre, part of the new Uris Theatre complex, with *Mourning Becomes Electra* (53), starring Colleen Dewhurst. **20** A Samuel Beckett festival gets underway, at the Forum Theatre in Lincoln Center, with *Happy Days* and *Act Without Words 1*. Featured in the casts are Hume Cronyn, Jessica Tandy, and Henderson Forsythe. **26** An unauthorized production of David Rabe's antiwar play *Sticks and Bones* opens in Moscow, directed by Polish film director Andrzei Wajda. **30** Arthur Miller's *The Creation of the World and Other Business* (20), starring Zoe Caldwell and George Grizzard, opens at the Shubert. Jack Kroll, in *Newsweek*, writes that Miller's "pastiche of the Book of Genesis deserves no comment or any attempt to unravel its stupefyingly boring muddleheadedness and I hereby order my fingers to stop typing about it." And they do; end of review.

DECEMBER 20 Neil Simon's *The Sunshine Boys* (538), directed by Alan Arkin, opens at the Broadhurst. Jack Albertson and Sam Levene are the elderly vaudevillians, modeled after Smith and Dale, estranged for over a decade and now implored by a nephew to get together for a television show. Walter Matthau and George Burns star in the 1975 screen version.

FEBRUARY 2 *Much Ado About Nothing*, the first of a projected 13 productions by the New York Shakespeare Festival on the CBS TV network, is broadcast. **13** *El Grande de Coca-Cola* (1,114), a dipsy revue at the Mercer Arts Center off-Broadway, stars its authors, Ron House, Alan Shearman, John Neville-Andrews, Diz White, and Sally Willis. **25** Stephen Sondheim's *A Little Night Music* (600), his third collaboration with producer-director Harold Prince, at the Shubert, will be remembered most for "Send in the Clowns," sung by Glynis Johns (and recorded by Judy Collins, Barbra Streisand, and Frank Sinatra). Based on Ingmar Bergman's 1955 movie *Smiles of a Summer Night*, the musical reverts to the waltz tempo that at one

---

pend operations after this season.

MARCH 6 Joseph Papp agrees to bring his New York Shakespeare Festival to Lincoln Center, replacing the Repertory Theatre of Lincoln Center. He has one major condition: new funding, with a guarantee of $1 million a year. "Without the money, no deal," he says at a press conference announcing the new affiliation. He is also bringing with him members of his own board of directors to join Lincoln Center's board.

MAY • The New York State Human Rights Appeal Board declares that the Repertory Theatre of Lincoln Center engaged in a systematic pattern of discrimination by hiring non-Asian actors to play Asian roles. **2** The League of New York Theatres, in a meeting at *The New York Times*, pressures the paper for more extensive coverage of Broadway. **30** Joseph Papp will go ahead with producing at Lincoln Center after Mitzi Newhouse, wife of publishing magnate Samuel L. Newhouse, contributes $1 million toward the operating budget—possibly the largest contribution ever solely for the operating expenses of a theatrical company. As a result, the Forum Theatre will be renamed the Mitzi Newhouse.

Personalities

until August 17. Executives fear that this grim drama of the Vietnam War will clash with the public mood, which is upbeat over the recent cease-fire in Southeast Asia. Papp calls the move "cowardly" and will cancel his contract with CBS for more New York Shakespeare Festival productions. **11** The more than three-hour, 40-song "Sondheim: A Musical Tribute," at the Shubert Theatre, celebrating the composer and lyricist, is staged on the set of *A Little Night Music*. Participants include Angela Lansbury, Nancy Walker, Alexis Smith, Hermione Gingold, Chita Rivera, Dorothy Collins, Larry Kert, Len Cariou, and Glynis Johns singing "Send in the Clowns." **18** In a letter in *The New York Times*, David Rabe attacks the unauthorized Moscow production of his *Sticks and Bones*, which the Soviets are using as propaganda against the U.S., calling it "spitting in my face." If they had kept to the spirit of the work, he says, they would have made the protagonist a soldier returning to the U.S.S.R. from Hungary in 1956 after the rebellion against Communist rule. A Soviet literary magazine will charge him with trying to distract attention from his failure to stand up to CBS for postponing the showing of his play less than two weeks ago.

APRIL 23 "Broadway's Music Man" Stephen Sondheim is on the cover of *Newsweek*.

Plays and Musicals

time was the bedrock of Broadway shows. Also starring are Len Cariou, Hermione Gingold, and Victoria Mallory. There is a film version in 1978.

MARCH 6 *The Changing Room* (191), a plotless play by David Storey set in a rugby team's locker room, with a cast that includes George Hearn and 27-year-old John Lithgow, in his Broadway debut, a Tony winner for best supporting actor, opens at the Morosco. It's "enormously vigorous," says Richard Watts, Jr. in The *Post* **13** A revival of *Irene* (604), the 1919 musical, inaugurates the Minskoff Theatre, with Debbie Reynolds, Patsy Kelly, George S. Irving, and Ruth Warrick. The advance ticket sale owes something to President Nixon's favorable review after seeing the tryout at the National Theatre. He said it would be "a big hit, perhaps not with New Yorkers, but with out-of-towners." **18** *Seesaw* (296), a Cy Coleman-Dorothy Fields musical, based on the play *Two for the Seesaw*, is at the Uris Theatre. Ken Howard, Michele Lee, and Tommy Tune star. **22** The Circle Rep's production of Lanford Wilson's *Hot'l Baltimore* (1,166) moves from off-off-Broadway to off-Broadway, at Circle in the Square. A cast that includes Mari Gorman, Judd Hirsch, and Conchata Ferrell portray the residents of the title establishment, trying to make something out of the dregs of their

Judd Hirsch MSN

Business and Society

Births, Deaths, and Marriages

lives. **27** *The River Niger* (400, total), which opened at the St. Marks Playhouse on December 5, moves uptown to the Brooks Atkinson Theatre. Joseph Walker's drama, produced by the Negro Ensemble Company, spotlights Douglas Turner Ward, who also directs this story of a Harlem family and its relationship to the struggle for civil rights.

MAY 13 Christopher Plummer opens at the Palace with a Tony-winning performance in the musical *Cyrano* (49). The music is by Michael J. Lewis, the lyrics by Anthony Burgess. Clive Barnes says that Plummer "triumphed," and the show is "altogether very good and partly excellent." Only the music in this musical is not up to par.

1973–74

A *Moon for the Misbegotten* is Broadway at its best, and Michael Bennett has an idea for a show about the gypsies who populate Broadway chorus lines. The Joseph Papp era at Lincoln Center gets off to a rocky start. Night-of-performance tickets go on sale, at a discount, in Times Square. While most Broadway shows continue to raise their curtains at 7:30, enough now start at other times to make for a staggered, easier-to-manage pedestrian traffic pattern in the theatre district. Neil Simon marries Marsha Mason, David Merrick reportedly would like Zero Mostel for *La Cage Aux Folles*, and Sylvia Miles crowns John Simon. Broadway columnist Leonard Lyons and critic Richard Watts, Jr. retire, and playwright William Inge commits suicide.

- Most unusual prop: the Kotex worn on her head by Swoosie Kurtz in *Confessions of a Female Disorder*, at the O'Neill Playwrights Conference at Waterford, Connecticut
- What actress Sylvia Miles, who has been maligned by critic John Simon, dumps on his head: steak tartar and potato salad (some reports say it is pasta)
- Number of gymnasts in Tom Stoppard's *Jumpers*: 14
- How Frances Sternhagen manages a stage career and a family of 6 children: "Yoga and dark glasses. The yoga keeps me relaxed and in good shape and the dark glasses keep me from noticing that my house is an absolute mess."
- Number of off-Broadway theatres operating at the end of the season: 15, half as many as there were a year ago
- Song written by "Broadway's newest star" (*New York Times*) in *Scapino*, Jim Dale: "Georgy Girl"
- 16-year-old inspired to become an actress by seeing Colleen Dewhurst in *Moon for the Misbegotten*: Cherry Jones
- Number of Neil Simon Plays mounted in Istanbul, Turkey, this season: 3—*The Last of the Red Hot Lovers, The Prisoner of Second Avenue*, and *Plaza Suite*
- Largest individual stockholder in Twentieth Century-Fox: Broadway producer David Merrick, with almost 9 percent of outstanding shares
- What the chorus gypsies who told Michael Bennett their stories, raw material for *A Chorus Line*, receive for their tale: $1 each
- How many of the approximately 20 gypsies who tell their stories to Bennett will appear in *A Chorus Line*: 9

Productions on Broadway: 50

Pulitzer Prize for Drama: None awarded

New York Drama Critics Circle Awards:
Best Play: *The Contractor* (David Storey)
Best American Play: *Short Eyes* (Miguel Pinero)
Best Musical: *Candide* (Leonard Bernstein and Richard Wilbur)

Tony Awards:
Play: *The River Niger* (Joseph A. Walker)
Actress in a Play: Colleen Dewhurst (*Moon for the Misbegotten*)
Actor in a Play: Michael Moriarity (*Find Your Way Home*)
Musical: *Raisin* (Judd Woldin-Robert Brittan)
Actress in a Musical: Virginia Capers (*Raisin*)
Actor in a Musical: Christopher Plummer (*Cyrano*)

June	July	August	September	October	November
All-star *Uncle Vanya*; William Inge suicide	Merrick wants Mostel for *La Cage Aux Folles*—*Variety*	Carol Channing look-alike contest	Playwright S.N. Behrman d.	Sylvia Miles dumps food on John Simon's head	David Rabe's *Boom Boom Room* flops

December	January	February	March	April	May
Moon for the Misbegotten	Birth of *A Chorus Line*	Jane Powell for Debbie Reynolds in *Irene*	Bernstein's *Candide* finally a success	Douglas Turner Ward rejects Tony	Doug Henning in *The Magic Show*

Personalities

JUNE • Carol Channing, a Democrat, turns up on President Nixon's "enemies list."

JULY 18 *Variety*, reporting that the biggest hit of the past theatre season in Paris was a comedy called *La Cage Aux Folles*, says that "David Merrick has reportedly speared it for Broadway and wants Zero Mostel as one of the queens."

AUGUST 23 One hundred transvestites, wigged, made up, and dressed like Carol Channing, attend her performance in *Lorelei*, at the Curran Theatre in San Francisco. She will judge a Carol Channing look-alike contest at a nearby hotel after the show.

SEPTEMBER • Uta Hagen's *Respect for Acting* is published and becomes a standard text.

OCTOBER 3 "Bernstein and Lerner Writing New Musical; Subber Will Produce," says the front-page *Variety* headline. *Opus One*, the tentative title—no content specified—would be their first collaboration. Saint-Subber has produced many of Neil Simon's plays. **7** Critic John Simon described actress Sylvia Miles, in *New York* magazine last week, as a "gatecrasher." Tonight, in a restaurant, she dumps a plate of food on his head. "Now you can call me a platecrasher, as well," she gloats, delivering the goods **17** David Merrick has his former wife, Jeanne Gibson, arrested for trespassing when she tries to visit their daughter, of whom Merrick has custody.

NOVEMBER 5 Peter Hall succeeds Laurence Olivier as director of the English National Theatre. **8** Joseph Papp, peeved at *Times* reviewer Clive Barnes's negative take on *Boom Boom Room*, calls him at home late tonight to berate him for it. Madeleine Kahn won the lead role in this play over Jill Clayburgh, who will later marry its author, David Rabe. Julie Newman was fired in rehearsals, as was director Julie Bovasso, with Papp taking over for her.

Plays and Musicals

JUNE 4 Mike Nichols's production of Chekhov's *Uncle Vanya* (64), a Circle in the Square presentation at the Joseph E. Levine Theatre in the Uris complex on Broadway, has an all-star cast: Lillian Gish, George C. Scott, Nicol Williamson, Julie Christie, Cathleen Nesbitt, Barnard Hughes, Conrad Bain, and Elizabeth Wilson.

OCTOBER 17 David Storey's *The Contractor* (72), in which life is reflected in wedding preparations, opens at the Chelsea Manhattan Theatre, with Reid Shelton, Lynn Ann Leveridge, and Joseph Maher. **18** *Raisin* (847), the Judd Woldin-Robert Brittan musical version of Lorraine Hansberry's 1959 *A Raisin in the Sun*, opens at the Forty-sixth Street Theatre. Virginia Capers, Joe Morton, Deborah Allen, and Ernestine Jackson star.

NOVEMBER 4 Michael Weller's *Moonchildren* (394), which opened on Broadway to good reviews but not big enough audiences almost two years ago, is revived off-Broadway, at the Theatre De Lys, with a cast of mostly young unknowns and Kenneth McMillan. **8** David Rabe's *Boom Boom Room* (37) (retitled *In The Boom Boom Room*), at the Vivian Beaumont, is Joseph Papp's first production at Lincoln Center. It's "long and tedious," says the *Daily News*. Madeleine Kahn plays a go-go dancer who survived a

Neil Simon *PF*

Business and Society

JUNE • The League of New York Theatres becomes the League of New York Theatres and Producers. **25** A discount ticket box office—ultimately called TKTS—opens in a trailer in Times Square. Unsold tickets from theatres will be available the day of the performance for half price plus a small service charge.

AUGUST 3 The off-Broadway Mercer Street Playhouse, in the Soho area downtown, collapses.

DECEMBER • The fuel shortage precipitated by the OPEC cartel is beginning to affect theatre. The Guthrie in Minneapolis has canceled an 11-week tour it had planned to begin in January. The producers of *Don't Bother Me, I Can't Cope* are changing the show's lighting to consume less electricity.

MARCH • The rules for the Tony awards specify that a revival may win if it has been sufficiently revised to be considered "new." But the rule has never been applied until now when *Candide* and *Lorelei* have been ruled eligible. The producers of other revivals, such as *Irene* and *No, No, Nanette*, complain that their productions should qualify, too. • New

Births, Deaths, and Marriages

JUNE 10 Playwright William Inge commits suicide.

JUNE 11 Frances Starr d.

AUGUST 9 Tony Perkins m. Barinthia Berenson.

SEPTEMBER 9 Playwright S.N. Behrman d.

SEPTEMBER 13 Betty Field d.

OCTOBER 5 Sidney Blackmer d.

OCTOBER 25 Neil Simon m. actress Marsha Mason, who will appear soon on Broadway in his play *The Good Doctor*.

FEBRUARY 14 Peter Cook, now appearing in the revue *Good Evening*, m. actress Judy Huxtable.

DECEMBER • The latest White House enemies list, made public through the ongoing Watergate investigations, includes the names of Paul Newman, Joanne Woodward, and Michael Butler, producer of *Hair*. • *Lorelei*, a followup to *Gentlemen Prefer Blondes*, starring Carol Channing, gets its third director. Robert Moore succeeds Betty Comden and Adolph Green, who had replaced Joe Layton. The show is in Philadelphia in the midst of its 11-month tryout trek toward Broadway. **29** The company of *Moon for the Misbegotten*, opening tonight, refers to it as "The Resurrection Play"—Jason Robards is coming off a near-fatal car crash, and director José Quintero has just given up drinking.

Colleen Dewhurst and Jason Robards, Jr. in *A Moon for the Misbegotten* PF

massively abusive childhood only to find that things are not much better as an adult. Also in the cast are Charles Durning, Robert Loggia, Warren Finnerty, and Charlotte Rae. **14** Once called *Beyond the Fridge*, the revue now known as *Good Evening* (438), with Peter Cook and Dudley Moore—previously in *Beyond the Fringe*—opens at the Plymouth. **27** Neil Simon returns to Broadway, at the Eugene O'Neill, with *The Good Doctor* (208), a series of sketches derived from Chekhov's short stories. Christopher Plummer is a kind of emcee, tying them together, and also appears in some of them. Marsha Mason, who recently married Simon, Frances Sternhagen, Rene Auberjonois, and Barnard Hughes make up the rest of the cast.

DECEMBER 3 Bette Midler opens at the Palace in a one-woman show, for which she will receive a special Tony Award. **6** Brad Dourif and Kevin Conway are at the Eastside Playhouse in Mark Medoff's *When You Comin' Back, Red Ryder?* (302), in which a thug enters the lives of patrons at a New Mexico diner. A film version appears in 1979. **29** Eugene O'Neill's *Moon for the Misbegotten* (314), staged on

York State Attorney General Louis Lefkowitz tries unsuccessfully to replace Gerald Schoenfeld, Bernard B. Jacobs, and Irving Goldman as directors of the Shubert Organization, based on charges that they have spent Shubert money carelessly, at best. Lefkowitz is running for re-election this year. **3** Broadway producers and union heads join to oppose the move by the New York State Attorney General to replace the directors of the Shubert Organization. **23** Police in Cambridge, Massachusetts, arrest two of the actors in Terrence McNally's *Sweet Eros* for "lewdness" and "fornication." Performances will continue with the actors wearing underwear.

MARCH 28 Dorothy Fields d.

APRIL 10 Patricia Collinge d.

APRIL 17 Blossom Seeley d.

APRIL 30 Agnes Moorehead d.

Personalities

JANUARY 18 Choreographer-director Michael Bennett has an idea for a show about the dancers in Broadway chorus lines. He gathers a group of dancers he knows, including Donna McKechnie, with whom he danced on television's "Hullabaloo," and has them talk about themselves in an all-night marathon session. By tomorrow, the workshop production of *A Chorus Line* will be taking shape.

APRIL • Zero Mostel, repeating an old pattern, is going off on his own in *Ulysses in Nighttown*, ad-libbing and throwing other cast members off, as they crack up. **5** Douglas Turner Ward rejects his Tony nomination for Best Supporting Actor in *The River Niger* for a role that all the reviewers described as a lead one. Turner says that the part, one of "the most powerful characters in modern drama," is "demeaned" by the nomination. The company lists all players alphabetically in its programs—there are no "stars."

MAY 19 "Jule's Friends at the Palace," a tribute to composer Jule Styne, who wrote *Bells Are Ringing*, *Gypsy*, and *Funny Girl*, features Phyllis Newman, Chita Rivera, Carol Channing, Liza Minnelli, Betty Comden and Adolph Green, Robert Morse, and Cyril Ritchard. **20** Leonard Lyons, whose "Lyons Den" column in the *New York Post* has chronicled Broadway and other show business venues for four decades, retires. **28** Richard Watts, Jr., who succeeded Percy Hammond as the theatre critic of the *Herald-Tribune* in 1936, retires as the daily drama critic of the *New York Post*. Martin Gottfried, now reviewing for *Women's Wear Daily*, will succeed him.

Plays and Musicals

Broadway in 1956–57 and off-Broadway in 1968–69, is revived on Broadway, at the Morosco. It is "stunning," says Douglas Watt in the *Daily News*, "superb," says Richard Watts in the *Post*. "[Jason] Robards gives one of the best O'Neill performances I've ever seen," writes Jack Kroll, in *Newsweek*, with Colleen Dewhurst "almost as good." Ed Flanders is also in the cast.

JANUARY 2 John Hopkins's *Find Your Way Home* (135), at the Brooks Atkinson, is a frank portrayal of a man who leaves his marriage to have an affair with another young man. Michael Moriarity and Jane Alexander star. **8** "A sexual musical" say the ads for Earl Wilson, Jr.'s *Let My People Come* (1,327), opening off-Broadway, at the Village Gate Theatre. Not coming are the critics, who haven't been invited to this mix of bare skin and bold language. Nevertheless, some review it. *Time* says it's "the least erotic show since *Oklahoma!*" At the door, naked cast members say goodnight to the audience as they leave. **27** After an 11-month tryout tour that has already recouped half the show's cost, Carol Channing opens at the Palace in *Lorelei*, the sequel to *Gentlemen Prefer Blondes* (321). Several of the numbers written for the first show by Jule Styne and Comden and Green are in this one as well, in addition to four new songs.

FEBRUARY 28 Two one-act plays by Noel Coward, *Come Into the Garden, Maude*, and *A Song at Twilight*, under the combined title *Noel Coward in Two Keys* (140), open at the Barrymore. Set in a fancy Swiss hotel, they star Hume Cronyn, Jessica Tandy, and Ann Baxter.

MARCH 6 At the Shubert, *Over Here* (348), a musical by Richard and Robert Sherman, set in the World War II period and starring the two surviving Andrews Sisters, Patty and Maxine, reflects the nostalgia of the early 1970s. Also in the cast are Ann Reinking, Treat Williams, and 20-year-old John Travolta. **10** Leonard Bernstein's *Candide* (740), which flopped on its first try in 1956, succeeds in a revival produced and directed

Business and Society

Births, Deaths, and Marriages

by Harold Prince at the Broadway Theatre, where the sets are elaborate. It stars Mark Baker, Lewis J. Stadlen, and Maureen Brennan. **10** Zero Mostel repeats his portrayal of Leopold Bloom, which he played off-Broadway in 1958, in the revival of *Ulysses in Nighttown* (69), directed by Burgess Meredith and opening at the Winter Garden. Times have changed. Molly Bloom, now played by Fionnuala Flanagan, appears nude, masturbates, and simulates sex with Danny Meehan, who plays Blaze Boyland. Stephen Dedalus is played by "Tom Lee Jones."

APRIL 22 Tom Stoppard's *Jumpers* (48) opens at the Billy Rose Theatre. Clive Barnes, in the *Times,* calls it "a stimulating evening, a thoughtful evening, and a witty evening." The playwright says that the work, cloaked in the form of a murder mystery, is about "jumping to conclusions." It stars Brian Bedford and Jill Clayburgh.

MAY 5 Terrence McNally's *Bad Habits* (273), comprising two one-act comedies, *Ravenswood* and *Dunelawn*, opens at the Booth, after a downtown run at the Astor Theatre. F. Murray Abraham heads the cast of eight in these tales of very dysfunctional people. **18** The Young Vic, at the Circle in the Square Theatre, presents *Scapino* (121), a slapstick comedy adapted from Molière, with Jim Dale in the title role. He's "Broadway's newest star," says *The New York Times.* Also in the cast is Peter Ustinov's daughter Tammy. **23** From the Public Theatre, Joseph Papp brings Miguel Pinero's *Short Eyes* (80) uptown to Lincoln Center and the Vivian Beaumont Theatre. It's a brutal drama set in a prison, where the inmates' code of conduct justifies the murder of a child molester, played by William Carden. Pinero is a former inmate himself, and the play originated with a prison drama group, several members of which are in the cast tonight.

MAY 28 *The Magic Show* (1,920) might well have been called "The Doug Henning Show" because the magician, and not Stephen Schwartz's words and music, are at the center of things at the Cort.

1974–75

Shubert marquees urge, "See a Broadway Show Today." Someone's paying attention because box offices are busy, with revenues up 24 percent over last season, and the road does well, too. The end of the season sees the beginning of a musical phenomenon: *A Chorus Line*. "I Promise You a Happy Ending," Robert Preston sings in *Mack and Mabel*, but he can't promise or produce a healthy box office for the show. Barbara Cook begins a cabaret career, Glenn Close debuts, Angela Lansbury, in a revival of *Gypsy*, and Elizabeth Ashley, in *Cat on a Hot Tin Roof*, are riding high, Ed Sullivan dies, and Flo Ziegfeld makes one last trip. The Circle Rep moves to Greenwich Village. And Katharine Cornell is gone.

- Total Broadway gross: $57,423,297, up handsomely from last year's $46,280,772
- New minimum wage on Broadway: $245 a week
- Wine that Yul Brynner insists must be stocked by hotels at which he stays while touring in the musical *Odyssey* (*Home Sweet Homer*): Chateau Gruaud Larouse '66
- Amount of spending in the U.S. generated by the Broadway theatre, according to a study by the League of New York Theatres and Producers: $168,000,000
- Working as a volunteer at the Roosevelt Hospital gift shop in New York City, where her mother is a patient: Ethel Merman, who goes largely unrecognized
- Amount of weight that Barbara Cook, who resurfaces as a cabaret star on July 11, 1974, has gained since she has been out of the limelight: about 150 pounds
- Top-priced ticket for *Equus*: $10
- Actresses who have starred on Broadway in W. Somerset Maugham's *The Constant Wife*: Ethel Barrymore (1926), Katharine Cornell (1951), and Ingrid Bergman (this season)
- Neil Simon's record to date (excluding *God's Favorite*, now playing):
  10 Broadway plays grossing an estimated $30,000,000, with a total 6,991 performances which, if played consecutively, would run for 17 years
  3, for which he wrote the books, totaling 2,146 performances

Productions on Broadway: 59

Pulitzer Prize for Drama: *Seascape* (Edward Albee)

New York Drama Critics Circle Awards:
Best Play: *Equus* (Peter Shaffer)
Best American Play: *The Taking of Miss Janie* (Ed Bullins)
Best Musical: *A Chorus Line* (Marvin Hamlisch and Edward Kleban)

Tony Awards:
Play: *Equus* (Peter Shaffer)
Actress in a Play: Ellen Burstyn (*Same Time, Next Year*)
Actor in a Play: John Kani and Winston Ntshona (*Sizwe Banzi Is Dead* and *The Island*)
Musical: *The Wiz* (Charlie Smalls)
Actress in a Musical: Angela Lansbury (*Gypsy*)
Actor in a Musical: John Collum (*Shenandoah*)

Month	Event
June	Katharine Cornell d.
July	Barbara Cook's cabaret debut
August	Cyril Ritchard collapses, and Jim Dale cracks rib
September	Angela Lansbury in *Gypsy*
October	*Equus* and *Mack and Mabel*
November	Glenn Close's debut
December	Jack Benny d.
January	*The Wiz* and *The Ritz*
February	Maggie Smith in *Private Lives*
March	Shubert's Irving Goldman indicted
April	Ingrid Bergman back on Broadway
May	*A Chorus Line* at the Public Theatre

Personalities

JUNE • Flo Ziegfeld's remains are transferred from Forest Lawn in Los Angeles to a cemetery in Valhalla, New York, to lie next to those of his second wife, Billie Burke, who died in 1970.

JULY 11 "She was nervous at the beginning of her turn, but quickly gained confidence via the approval of the SRO crowd," says *Variety* of Barbara Cook's resurrected career as a cabaret singer. Accompanied by pianist Wally Harper, she opens tonight at Brothers and Sisters, on West Forty-sixth Street.

AUGUST • In its cover story, *Esquire* calls playwright-diplomat Clare Boothe Luce the "Woman of the Century." **8** The audience at *Good Evening*, the satirical revue starring Peter Cook and Dudley Moore at the Plymouth, get two shows for the price of one tonight. Before the curtain goes up, President Nixon's resignation speech is viewed live on a large-screen television. **17** Jim Dale sustains a cracked rib during a performance of *Scapino*, at the Joseph E. Levine Theatre, taking him out of the remainder of the run—through September 1—at the theatre. He will be back in it when it reopens at the Ambassador on September 27. **25** Cyril Ritchard collapses in Los Angeles during a preview performance of *Sugar*, at the Chandler Pavillion, and is hospitalized with a heart attack.

SEPTEMBER 19 The audience at the Winter Garden for the first preview of *Gypsy*, starring Angela Lansbury, evacuates the theatre because of "technical problems." In fact, it's a bomb scare. Before the show resumes, Arthur Laurents, who wrote its book, jokes with them about Lansbury being a "bombshell."

OCTOBER 26 Rehearsals for the musical *Chicago* begin, but they will be cut short quickly by the "exhaustion" suffered by director-choreographer Bob Fosse, who will be hospitalized, putting the show on hold.

NOVEMBER 9 Starring in The New Phoenix Repertory Company's production of William Congreve's *Love for Love*

Plays and Musicals

JUNE 7 Steve Silver's *Beach Blanket Babylon* opens in San Francisco. This campy show will become America's longest-running musical revue.

SEPTEMBER 23 Sixteen years after Ethel Merman's triumph as Mama Rose in *Gypsy* (120), the spotlight is Angela Lansbury's, in a revival at the Winter Garden. Lansbury wins over everyone, despite, as *Variety* critic Hobe Morrison notes, "her visible stage fright during much of the first act." **24** Tennessee Williams's *Cat on a Hot Tin Roof* (160) is revived at the ANTA Theatre. Elizabeth Ashley is Maggie in an acclaimed performance, Keir Dullea is Brick, and Fred Gwynne plays Big Daddy. Playing Big Mamma is Kate Reid. Williams has reworked the script several times since the original Broadway production in 1956, adding profanity.

OCTOBER 6 David Merrick's musical *Mack and Mabel* (64), the story of silent film comedy director Mack Sennett and star Mabel Normand, with music and lyrics by Jerry Herman and choreography by Gower Champion, opens at the Majestic. It stars Robert Preston and Bernadette Peters, with Lisa Kirk. Preston and Peters give "two of the finest performances of the season," writes Watts in the *Post*, but despite David Merrick's television ads, it never catches on. **8** Alan Ayckbourn, enormously popular on the London stage, has a Broadway hit, *Absurd Person Singular* (592), a comedy, starring Carole Shelley, Larry Blyden, Richard Kiley, Geraldine Page, Sandy Dennis, and Tony Roberts. It's at the Music Box. **22** Linda Hopkins is Bessie Smith in *Me and Bessie* (453), at the Ambassador, which Hopkins has written with Will Holtz. **24** *Equus* (1,209), Peter Shaffer's drama about a disturbed young man who is sexually obsessed with horses, opens at the Plymouth. Peter Firth is the boy, and Anthony Hopkins stars as the psychiatrist who treats him—performances that "blaze with theatrical life," says Barnes in the *Times*. Also in the cast are Marian Seldes and Frances Sternhagen.

Business and Society

JUNE • The Winter Garden Theatre, which recently sustained water and smoke damage from a fire in a nearby restaurant, is being renovated for this fall's revival of *Gypsy*, with Angela Lansbury. • The marquee of Shubert theatres that currently have no shows urge: "See a Broadway Show Today." **2** An American Congress of Theatre, a four-day conference of a cross section of theatre groups, opens in Princeton, New Jersey. **5** *Variety*'s front-page headline is: "Theatre Is Now A National Invalid."

JULY 1 Actors Equity's new contract with the League of New York Theatres & Producers raises the minimum wage from $210 to $245 a week.

SEPTEMBER 30 *Irene*, with Debbie Reynolds, has grossed $242,867 over the past week in Chicago, topping the previous record for an eight-show week, set by Carol Channing in 1966 in *Hello, Dolly!*

OCTOBER • The Drama Desk, which had been a loosely allied, informal group of critics who sponsored monthly seminars on the theatre, splits when one group decides to incorporate it. • The Circle

Births, Deaths, and Marriages

JUNE 6 Blanche Yurka d.

JUNE 9 Katharine Cornell d. Her Broadway career spanned 40 years, from her debut in 1921 to her retirement in 1961 after the death of her husband, director Guthrie McClintic. Among the actors to whom she gave early career boosts were Orson Welles and Marlon Brando.

SEPTEMBER 6 Otto Kruger d. **15** Liza Minnelli m. Jack Haley, Jr.

OCTOBER 13 Ed Sullivan, one of the original Broadway columnists, d.

DECEMBER • Mike Nichols and Patricia Margot are divorced. **9** Alan Jay Lerner and Karen Gundersen divorce. **10** Alan Jay Lerner m. Sandra Payne. **26** Jack

at this afternoon's Saturday matinée preview performance at the Helen Hayes is Mary Ure. But by tonight's show, she will be gone, fired by Harold Prince and replaced by her understudy, an actress who had been playing the minor part of a maid and is making her Broadway debut. She is Glenn Close. Most of the critics like her, though Martin Gottfried finds her "satisfactory, if not overwhelmingly charming."

JANUARY 23 Broadway star Hal Linden becomes a television personality with the premiere of the "Barney Miller" show on ABC.

FEBRUARY 9 The Chicago *Sun-Times*, in an article on an upcoming production of Eugene O'Neill's *Beyond the Horizon*, notes that its director David Mamet "swears by Konstantin Stanislavsky. The method carried him through his years as a professional actor and later as a teacher in Vermont, when he met the nucleus of what is now the St. Nicholas Theater Company."

MARCH 2 Asked by an interviewer about the continued use of the word "Negro" in the Negro Ensemble Company, Douglas Turner Ward, the group's head, attributes it to his "stubbornness" and says, "I like 'black'—it makes a positive statement about what we are—but I loathed the posturing and attitudinizing *[sic]* that went with the total put-down of the word 'Negro.'" **10** "A Gala Tribute to Joshua Logan," at the Imperial Theatre, has Ethel Merman, José Ferrer, and the song "Minnehaha," which Logan wrote for the 1930 Princeton Triangle Club show, sung by Logan, James Stewart, and Henry Fonda. **12** *Variety* publishes a list of what Yul Brynner requires at hotels where he's staying during the tryouts for *Odyssey* (which will become *Home Sweet Homer*). They include Heineken dark beer, a king-size bed, and Chateau Gruaud Larouse '66 (a case a week, at least).

APRIL • George Rose, nominated for a Tony for his "supporting" role in *My Fat Friend*, asks to have his name withdrawn because he really has a lead role, costarring with Lynn Redgrave. **11** Ann

---

NOVEMBER 12 The Royal Shakespeare Company's production of the William Gillette-Arthur Conan Doyle *Sherlock Holmes* (421), at the Broadhurst, is played somewhat tongue-in-cheek. John Wood has the lead role. **13** Athol Fugard's *Sizwe Banzi Is Dead* (159), about a South African black man who reflects on his own identity, opens at the Edison Theatre. John Kani and Winston Ntshona make up the entire cast. It will alternate in repertory with Fugard's *The Island* (52), with the same cast.

DECEMBER 29 Murray Schisgal's farce *All Over Town* (233), set conveniently in an apartment with 12 doors, is at the Booth. Dustin Hoffman directs a cast that includes Jill Eikenberry, Barnard Hughes, and Cleavon Little.

JANUARY 5 *The Wiz* (1,672), directed by Geoffrey Holder and backed by Twentieth Century-Fox, which has the film rights and is heavily promoting it, opens at the Majestic. Stephanie Mills is Dorothy in Charlie Smalls's Afro-American musical version of the Frank Baum classic *The Wizard of Oz*, with Hinton Battle, Ted Ross, Mabel King, and Andre De Shields. "Ease on Down the Road" is the most prominent song. Diana Ross is Dorothy in the 1978 movie. **7** Based on a 1965 movie, the musical *Shenandoah* (1,050), with John Collum in the lead role, is the story of a Virginia family caught up in the Civil War. Collum, who will win a Tony, was the third choice for the part, after Robert Ryan and Jack Palance. It's at the Alvin. **20** Terrence McNally's *The Ritz* (400), originally a screenplay, opens at the Longacre. Jack Weston and Jerry Stiller have the lead roles in this story about a gay steambath in which a businessman is seeking refuge from the brother-in-law bent on killing him. Also in the cast are F. Murray Abraham and George Dzundra. **26** *Seascape* (65), Edward Albee's play about a couple whose relationship is going through a midlife crisis, opens at the Shubert. Deborah Kerr and Barry Nelson play the couple, and the strange creatures who emerge to engage them in dialogue about life are played by Frank Langella and Maureen Anderman.

Repertory Co.—the "Circle Rep"—which has been using a theatre on upper Broadway, takes over the Sheridan Square Playhouse in Greenwich Village.

NOVEMBER 18 A nonprofit company headed by producer Roger Stevens, who is also chairman of the board of the Kennedy Center, arranges to produce the shows at Washington, D.C.'s National Theatre, taking over the lease on the house held by the Nederlanders.

MARCH 13 Irving Goldman, vice president of the Shubert Organization and also the New York City Cultural Affairs Commissioner, is indicted for his involvement in a corrupt deal involving vending machines and the Transit Authority. **18** The U.S. Supreme Court says that Chattanooga, Tennessee's banning of *Hair* was unconstitutional because the officials who did it never the saw the show.

APRIL 23 Twenty-three signatures, including that of noted costume designer Theoni Aldredge, are on the letter of protest in *Variety*, responding to the decision of producer Alexander Cohen to cut from the Tony Award ceremonies the awards for best costume design and best lighting.

Benny d. He was to costar with Walter Matthau in the film version of Neil Simon's *The Sunshine Boys*, for which he will be replaced by George Burns.

JANUARY 27 Julia Sanderson d.

FEBRUARY 14 P.G. Wodehouse d.

MARCH 7 Francine Larrimore d. **16** Jacob Kalich, husband of Molly Picon and prominent director, producer, and actor in the Yiddish Theatre, d.

APRIL 14 Frederic March d.

Personalities

Meara debuts on television as a lawyer in "Kate McShane." Her nine-year-old son Benjie (Ben Stiller) thinks this is hilarious. "Gee, mom," he exclaims, "are you really going to say words like 'Objection' and 'Irrelevant'?" **17** The last time a U.S. president spent an evening at Ford's Theatre in Washington, D.C.—Abraham Lincoln, in 1865—it was his last evening. Tonight, President Ford is in the house to see James Whitmore in *Give 'em Hell, Harry*, a one-man show about Harry Truman.

Plays and Musicals

FEBRUARY 6 The revival of Noel Coward's *Private Lives* (92), at the Forty-sixth Street Theatre, is a vehicle for Maggie Smith, playing Amanda.

MARCH 10 Come to the cabaret and see *The Rocky Horror Show* (32) on Broadway, at the Belasco, where tables have replaced many of the seats, and drinks are served. Tim Curry stars in Richard O'Brien's transvestite musical from outer space. **13** *Same Time, Next Year* (1,453), Bernard Slade's two-character romantic comedy, opens at the Brooks Atkinson Theatre. Ellen Burstyn and Charles Grodin play the extramarital, once-a-year couple. Burstyn stars with Alan Alda in the 1978 film.

APRIL 7 Tony Musante is a thief, and Keir Dullea the hard-luck actor he tries to burglarize and seduce in James Kirkwood's comedy *P.S. Your Cat Is Dead* (16), at the John Golden Theatre. Also in the cast is Jennifer Warren. A 1978 revival (301) will be more successful. **14** Ingrid Bergman comes back to Broadway in W. Somerset Maugham's comedy *The Constant Wife* (32), at the Shubert, directed by John Gielgud.

MAY 4 Ed Bullins's *The Taking of Miss Janie* (42), in which a black man rapes a white woman, is at the Mitzi E. Newhouse Theatre. Gilbert Moses directs, and Kirk Kirksey is in the cast. **21** They've been selling standing room even at the preview performances, and tonight, officially, Michael Bennett's *A Chorus Line* opens at the Public Theatre. At the finale, the audience is on its feet cheering for the show that will be chosen best musical by the Drama Critics Circle even before it reaches Broadway in July, where it will make theatrical history.

Business and Society

MAY 27 The board of directors of the Shubert Foundation does not re-elect Lawrence Shubert Lawrence or Irving Goldman to its ranks.

Births, Deaths, and Marriages

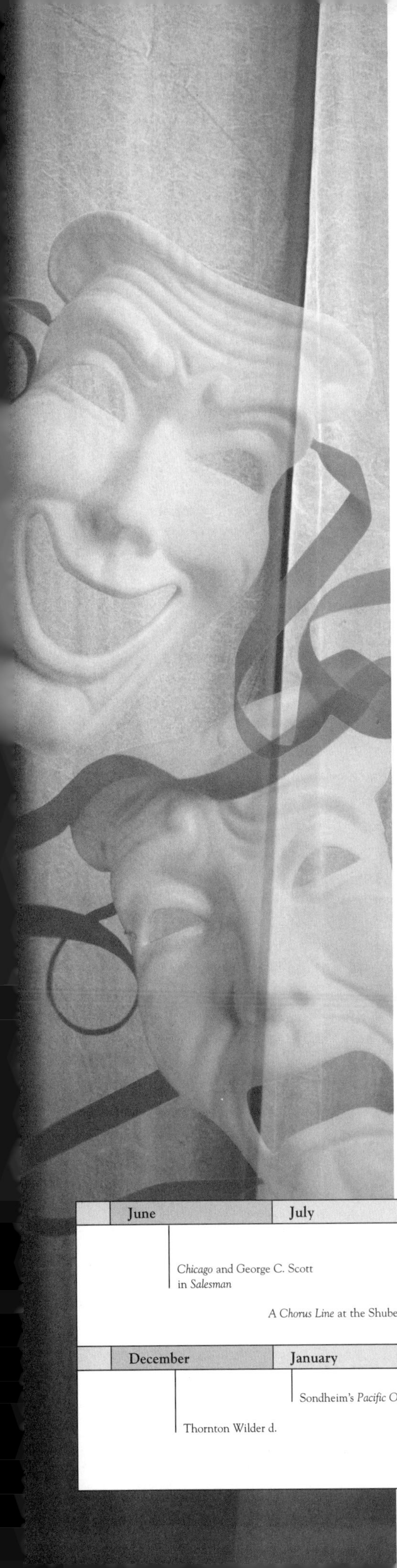

1975–76

Despite a three-week musicians' strike, this is a good season for musicals. *A Chorus Line* is a Pulitzer Prize-winning, all-time record-smashing hit on Broadway. *Chicago* opens, and Stephen Sondheim's *Pacific Overtures* is an interesting, if not commercially successful, show. George C. Scott outdoes himself as Willy Loman, John Simon goes to new extremes when he trashes Ruth Gordon, and lurking off-off-Broadway is Chicago playwright David Mamet, about to make a major impression in New York theatre. And set designer Jo Mielziner, whose name may not have been that familiar outside of theatre circles but who nevertheless did as much as anyone to make Broadway a central point in American entertainment and culture in the twentieth century, is dead.

- Broadway gross: $70,841,738, a 23 percent increase over last year
- Number of off-off-Broadway productions for newly discovered playwright David Mamet: 3—*Sexual Perversity in Chicago*, *The Duck Variations*, and *American Buffalo*
- New theatrical team: playwright David Mamet and actor Joe Mantegna
- David Mamet's résumé before he became a playwright: busboy at Second City, in Chicago, usher off-Broadway at the Theatre De Lys (later the Lucille Lortel), house manager for *The Fantasticks*, and he sold real estate in Chicago "to unsuspecting older people," as he has puts it
- At your service, for the first time: women waiting on tables at Sardi's
- Song that leads off the Tony Award ceremonies (April 18, 1976): "I Hope I Get It," from *A Chorus Line*
- Which one has the Tony?: brother and sister Robert and Patti LuPone, each nominated for a Tony, he for *A Chorus Line* and she for *The Robber Bridegroom*, do not win
- What Katharine Hepburn is being paid for appearing in *A Matter of Gravity* until it's in the black: $375 a week (plus $145 a day for expenses—she has to live)
- Acerbic critic John Simon's reaction to being called "acerbic" constantly: "Why can't I sometimes be called the barbed, biting, acidulous, peppery, sharp, tart or sardonic John Simon?"
- What Dadaist Tristan Tzara says in Tom Stoppard's *Travesties*: "My heart belongs to Dada—because Dada he treats it so well."

Productions on Broadway: 63

Pulitzer Prize for Drama: *A Chorus Line* (conceived by Michael Bennett, with a book by James Kirkwood and Nicholas Dante, music by Marvin Hamlisch, and lyrics by Edward Kleban)

New York Drama Critics Circle Awards:
Best Play: *Travesties* (Tom Stoppard)
Best American play: *Streamers* (David Rabe)
Best Musical: *Pacific Overtures* (Stephen Sondheim)

Tony Awards:
Play: *Travesties* (Tom Stoppard)
Actor in a Play: John Wood (*Travesties*)
Actress in a Play: Irene Worth (*Sweet Bird of Youth*)
Musical: *A Chorus Line* (Marvin Hamlisch and Edward Kleban)
Actor in a Musical: George Rose (*My Fair Lady*)
Actress in a Musical: Donna McKechnie (*A Chorus Line*)

June	July	August	September	October	November
Chicago and George C. Scott in *Salesman*	*A Chorus Line* at the Shubert	Liza Minnelli steps in for Gwen Verdon	Broadway musicians strike	Bob Fosse heart attack	Nederlanders buy the Alvin

December	January	February	March	April	May
Thornton Wilder d.	Sondheim's *Pacific Overtures*	Lee J. Cobb d.	Set designer Jo Mielziner d.	Arena Stage wins Tony	Nicol Williamson slaps fellow cast member

Personalities

AUGUST 8 With six days to learn the part and rehearse, Liza Minnelli steps in for Gwen Verdon in *Chicago* when Verdon is hospitalized for minor throat surgery. Minnelli will work through the middle of September. Bob Fosse's attempts to bar press coverage of the substitution to avoid comparisons between Minnelli and Verdon meets with vehement opposition from the *Times*. **21** Yul Brynner, starring in the extended pre-Broadway tour of *Odyssey* (later renamed *Home Sweet Homer*) the Eric Segal-Mitch Leigh musical, sues to be released from his contract, claiming he was only obliged to stay with it through April 15. He says the producers have threatened him with a ruinous suit if he leaves. This odyssey has been on the road since December.

OCTOBER • The American Conservatory Theatre in San Francisco produces Edward Albee's *Tiny Alice*, with revisions unauthorized by the playwright. Albee sees the play at the Geary Theatre and threatens to sue if his disclaimer is not read from the stage at each performance, but William Ball, the director, refuses, and Albee does not pursue the matter. • Director and choreographer Bob Fosse has a heart attack—an experience he will draw on for his film *All That Jazz*. His lover Ann Reinking will have to win through an audition the role in the film of a woman who is essentially based on her. Wearing a brace from the cracked vertebra she recently sustained while doing a flip in the show *Over Here*, Reinking will accompany Fosse when he leaves the hospital on December 10. **20** Joseph Papp announces that he's abandoning his project of producing five plays by new playwrights on Broadway at the Booth because it is proving financially unfeasible. The first play, Dennis J. Reardon's *The Leaf People*, opened last night and, according to critic Clive Barnes, "bombed."

NOVEMBER • Tennessee Williams publishes his memoirs, in which he discusses his homosexuality. **23** In the *New York Daily News*, Rex Reed, reviewing Jerry Orbach's performance at a recent benefit,

Plays and Musicals

JUNE 3 John Kander and Fred Ebb's *Chicago* (898), a musical version of the 1926 stage satire by Maurice Watkins, conceived by Bob Fosse, opens at the Forty-sixth Street Theatre. Gwen Verdon plays Roxie Hart, the chorus girl who kills her lover but gets off, thanks to her lawyer, played by Jerry Orbach. Chita Rivera also stars. One of the songs, "All That Jazz," will become the title of Fosse's 1979 autobiographical fantasy film, and the show is successfully revived in 1996. **26** George C. Scott as Willy Loman gives "a performance to bate your breath," says Clive Barnes in the *Times*, in the revival of Arthur Miller's *Death of a Salesman* (64), at the Circle in the Square for a limited run. Scott is also directing a cast that includes Harvey Keitel and James Farentino as his sons and Teresa Wright as his wife.

George C. Scott *MSN*

JULY 25 "One singular sensation," indeed. *A Chorus Line* (6,137) moves from Public Theatre to the Shubert. This Marvin Hamlisch-Edward Kleban musical is the brainchild of director and choreographer Michael Bennett. It's about Broadway dancers who put their inner as well as outer selves on the line to get a job. Donna McKechnie is Cassie—she marries and divorces Bennett during the show's run—with Priscilla Lopez as Morales and Pamela Blair, Kelly Bishop, Sammy Williams, and many others. The

Business and Society

AUGUST • The city of Pasadena, California, buys the famed Pasadena Playhouse.

SEPTEMBER 18 Broadway musicians, demanding a raise in their basic salary from $290 to $380 a week, go on strike, closing down nine musicals. The other unions feel that there should have been more consultations and do not respect the picket lines.

OCTOBER • Following his third indictment in less than a year on charges of corruption, Irving Goldman, who had taken a leave of absence, is suspended as president of the Shubert Foundation. **1** With the musicians' strike still on, there are now 12 musicals being kept off the boards, including three new ones that were to begin previews. **11** The musicians' strike is settled, with the union securing a new minimum of $350 a week and giving in a little on employment quotas.

NOVEMBER • The Nederlanders buy the Alvin Theatre, which opened in 1927 with Fred and Adele Astaire in *Funny Face*. They already own the Brooks Atkinson, Palace, and Uris Theatres.

Births, Deaths, and Marriages

Broadway.

JUNE 6 Larry Blyden d. in an auto accident in Morocco. He m. dancer Carol Haney in 1955, and they divorced in 1962.

DECEMBER 7 Thornton Wilder d.

JANUARY 13 Margaret Leighton d. **18** Joseph Papp m. Gail Merrifield, director of play development at the New York Shakespeare Festival. **23** Paul Robeson d.

FEBRUARY 11 Lee J. Cobb d.

MARCH 15 Jo Mielziner, who dominated Broadway set design for decades, d.

APRIL 12 Paul Ford d.

A Chorus Line—a record-breaking musical PB

calls him "a tone-deaf mediocrity" and "the night's only non-professional embarrassment" who converts two Gershwin tunes into "dirges." Orbach, appearing in *Chicago*, sues Reed for libel, asking for $6 million. He says that Reed's ire comes from a confrontation he had with Orbach's wife at Sardi's, which stemmed from Reed's criticism of Orbach's friendship with mafioso Joseph "Crazy Joey" Gallo. Orbach will lose his suit in 1978.

FEBRUARY • When director Ellis Rabb steps into the role of Tony Cavendish—modeled after John Barrymore—in the revival of *The Royal Family*, he's playing a character who is high-strung and all ego. "Don't be nervous, dear," Rabb's mother wires him, "that's just the way you've

score includes "One," "What I Did for Love," "Dance Ten, Looks Three" (the "tits and ass" number), "I Hope I Get It," "Nothing," "At the Ballet," and "The Music and the Mirror." The film version appears in 1985.

SEPTEMBER 29 *Sexual Perversity in Chicago*, David Mamet's Obie-winning play at St. Clement's Church, is New York's introduction to the playwright who will be a dominant figure on and off-Broadway for many years.

OCTOBER 7 The Acting Company's production of the Robert Waldman-Alfred Uhrey musical *The Robber Bridegroom* (15) opens at the Harkness Theatre. The young cast includes Patti LuPone and

One of their silent partners is New York Yankee owner George Steinbrenner.

DECEMBER 17 *Variety*'s headline today, "Portman Hotel Project Dead; Morosco, Hayes Theatres Okay," is premature.

MARCH • *The New York Times*, seeking to bolster its sagging Friday revenues, suggests to Broadway producers that in exchange for increased advertising for their shows, the paper will expand its theatre coverage. That coverage has been a sore spot for the producers, who have complained about the way it's dropped off.

APRIL 28 At the Majestic Theatre, prominent Broadway theatre notables join civic leaders and others for a rally to support legislation that would take the prostitutes out of the theatre district. **30** *The New York Times* begins a Friday "Weekend" section, featuring increased coverage of

Personalities

been acting all your life." **15** Richard Burton replaces Anthony Perkins, who was bought out of his contract, in *Equus*. Ticket prices rise to a top of $15 for each performance for Burton's run in the show. **16** Alan Schneider succeeds John Houseman as director of the drama division of the Juilliard School at Lincoln Center. **18** Critic John Simon drips bile over Ruth Gordon's performance tonight in Shaw's *Mrs. Warren's Profession*: "It is a generous role for womanly and impassioned actresses, and many performers have essayed it. I can think of four, however, who have not: Totie Fields, W.C. Fields, Tutankhamen's mummy, and a trained monkey. Not until now, that is; Miss Gordon's performance combines elements of all four."

APRIL 12 Upstairs, at the top of the New Amsterdam Theatre on Forty-second Street, now a tawdry movie house but once the home of *The Ziegfeld Follies*, Elizabeth Ashley is rehearsing *Legend*, a spoof of a Wild West shoot-'em-up. Downstairs, the theatre's box office is being held up for real, and two security guards are shot to death. **18** The Arena Stage in Washington, D.C. is the first regional theatre to be honored with a special Tony Award. Another first is the Langner Award for Lifetime Achievement in the Theatre—to George Abbott. The awards ceremony begins with "I

What might George Bernard Shaw have said about John Simon? *PB*

Plays and Musicals

Kevin Kline. **23** *Yentl* (224), a play by Leah Napolin and Isaac Bashevis Singer, based on his short story "Yentl, the Yeshiva Boy," opens at the Eugene O'Neill. Tovah Feldshuh stars in the role, Barbra Streisand's in the 1983 film, as an orthodox Jewish girl who wants to defy tradition and be educated like the boys. **30** John Wood stars in Tom Stoppard's *Travesties* (155), at the Barrymore, in which James Joyce and Lenin are a few of the notables passing through Zurich in 1917.

DECEMBER 7 Alan Ayckbourn's *The Norman Conquests* (76), a trilogy of three comedies about seduction in an English country house which includes *Table Manners*, *Living Together*, and *Round and Round the Garden*, opens at the Morosco. All three debut on this long Sunday at the theatre, where they will be given in rotation. The cast consists of Ken Howard, Richard Benjamin, Paula Prentiss, Estelle Parsons, Barry Nelson, and Carole Shelly. **21** *Very Good Eddie* (304), the Jerome Kern-Schuyler Green-Guy Bolton 1915 musical, is revived at the Booth, with Charles Repole in the title role. **30** A revival of the 1927 satire on the Barrymores, *The Royal Family* (232), opens at the Helen Hayes. Ellis Rabb directs Eva Le Gallienne, George Grizzard (shortly to be replaced by Rabb), Rosemary Harris, and Sam Levene.

JANUARY 4 The odyssey of *Home Sweet Homer* (1), starring Yul Brynner, which has trekked around the country in a long pre-Broadway tour, ends tonight with its opening and closing at the Palace. *Variety* says it "imposes on audience tolerance." But not for long. **11** At the Winter Garden, Stephen Sondheim's *Pacific Overtures* (193), attempting to encapsulate recent Japanese history through a Kabuki-like staging and elements of Eastern music, does not ring a big enough

Business and Society

Births, Deaths, and Marriages

Hope I Get It," from *A Chorus Line*. **21** *Variety*, reviewing Mary Martin's autobiography *My Heart Belongs To Daddy*, calls it "impossibly sweet, like caramel corn."

MAY • David Mamet quits as artistic director of the St. Nicholas Theatre in Chicago, reportedly over "artistic differences" involving the production of Julian Barry's *Sitcom*. **4** Appearing in *Who's Afraid of Virginia Woolf?* Colleen Dewhurst starts laughing hysterically—it's not in the script—when she speaks the line, "Some people feed on the calamity of others." The cast has been kidding her offstage about her attempts to stop smoking, while her part requires her to hold a cigarette almost constantly during the performance. Dewhurst takes about a minute to compose herself before returning to character. **11** Anthony Perkins is back in *Equus*, replacing Richard Burton, who replaced Perkins, who replaced Anthony Hopkins. The top ticket price of $15, jacked up for Burton, will remain. **12** Apparently exercising royal prerogative, Nicol Williamson, Henry VIII in *Rex*, slaps cast member Jim Litten at a curtain call this evening. Litten claims he said to Williamson, "It's a wrap." The stressed-out Williamson, according to his agent, heard another four-letter word that rhymes with "wrap," presumably characterizing the performance. **19** Earl Wilson's column quotes Carole Shelly, who left the cast of *The Norman Conquests*, that "[t]he show couldn't continue unless I left and I didn't want to create more ugliness." Richard Benjamin thought she was putting too much conviction into a slap she is scripted to give him every night. For her part, Estelle Parsons is not speaking to either Benjamin or Paula Prentiss, both of whom have resisted the desire of the rest of the cast to effect British accents for the play.

---

bell with Broadway audiences. The director is Harold Prince, the lyrics are by John Weidman, and the cast is Japanese.

FEBRUARY 3 Katharine Hepburn, at the Broadhurst in Enid Bagnold's *A Matter of Gravity* (79), plays an old woman reflecting on just about everything. Playing her grandson is 23-year-old Christopher Reeve, whom Hobe Morrison in *Variety* finds "presentable if not too forceful. . . ."

MARCH 2 *Bubbling Brown Sugar* (766), at the American National Theatre and Academy (ANTA) Theatre, is a revue that bubbles with the music that made Harlem famous in the 1920s and 1930s. The cast includes Joseph Attles, Vernon Washington, Lonnie McNeil, Carolyn Bird, and Barry Preston. **22** Jack Heifner's *Vanities* (1,785), at the Chelsea Westside Theatre, starring Kathy Bates, Jane Galloway, and Susan Merson, follows three high school cheerleaders as they grow up, older, and disillusioned.

APRIL 25 Nicol Williamson is Henry VIII in Richard Rodgers's *Rex* (49), at the Lunt-Fontanne, where the top price is $17.50 on weekends. Sheldon Harnick wrote the lyrics, and the cast includes Glenn Close and Penny Fuller. **28** Not counting the spirit of poet Emily Dickinson, Julie Harris has the stage to herself in *The Belle of Amherst* (116). William Luce's compilation of what Dickinson said about her life opens at the Longacre.

MAY 1 Joseph Papp revives *Threepenny Opera* (307), at the Vivian Beaumont, with Raul Julia as Mack the Knife and Caroline Kava as Polly. The cast also includes C.K. Alexander, Elizabeth Wilson, and Blair Brown. **4** Coca-Cola has poured much of its bicentennial promotional money into Leonard Bernstein and Alan Jay Lerner's *1600 Pennsylvania Avenue* (7), opening at the Mark Hellinger. But it has no fizz. Ken Howard plays several of America's presidents in this musical history of the White House.

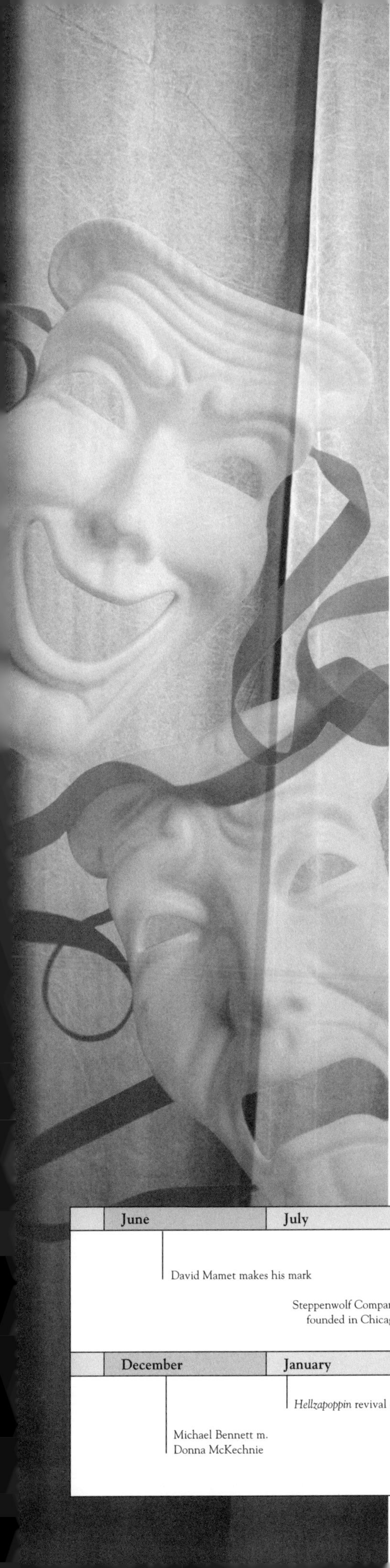

1976–77

David Mamet becomes a force to be reckoned with, on and off-Broadway. With *Guys and Dolls*, *The King & I*, and *Fiddler on the Roof* revived, Broadway begins to resemble a musicals museum. With the revival of *Oh, Calcutta!* and the Broadway opening of *Let My People Come*, the League of New York Theatres and Producers fear Broadway is beginning to resemble something else. Bob Fosse's lover Ann Reinking succeeds his former wife Gwen Verdon in *Chicago*, *Variety* complains that "moppet" Sarah Jessica Parker "chirps," producer Alexander Cohen complains that Jerry Lewis won't rehearse, and producer Robert Whitehead complains about a tardy critic and throws him out. Michael Bennett marries Donna McKechnie, briefly. And for *Annie*, there's always "Tomorrow."

- Amount of metal used by set designer Santo Loquasto to help create the junk shop in the Broadway production of *American Buffalo*: more than a ton
- Rent paid by Chicago's Steppenwolf Theatre Company, begun in a church basement: $10 a month
- Total New York State Council on the Arts grants to the theatre: $3,146,000, 11.5 percent of its total budget
- Number of Shubert theatres filled or booked mid-season: all
- Number of independent theatres filled or booked: 19 out of 20
- Number of Yiddish theatres on Second Avenue: none, for the first time
- What restaurateur Toots Shor, who dies in January, says about attending a performance of *Hamlet*: after intermission, he was the only one returning to his seat to see how it ended
- Guthrie Theatre surplus: $47, on revenues last year of $3,317,340
- Number of times in its 17-year history that the George Jean Nathan Award for Drama Criticism has been given to an academic rather than to a critic: 7, including this season
- Number of people needed to operate computerized light boards, popularized on Broadway through their use in *A Chorus Line*: 1
- Number of people needed to operate the light boards in a typical Broadway musical before the introduction of computerized lighting: 3

Productions on Broadway: 63

Pulitzer Prize for Drama: *The Shadow Box* (Michael Cristofer)

New York Drama Critics Circle Awards:
Best Play: *Otherwise Engaged* (Simon Gray)
Best American Play: *American Buffalo* (David Mamet)
Best Musical: *Annie* (Charles Strouse and Martin Charnin)

Tony Awards:
Play: *The Shadow Box* (Michael Cristofer)
Actor in a Play: Al Pacino (*The Basic Training of Pavlo Hummel*)
Actress in a Play: Julie Harris (*The Belle of Amherst*)
Musical: *Annie* (Charles Strouse and Martin Charnin)
Actor in a Musical: Barry Bostwick (*The Robber Bridegroom*)
Actress in a Musical: Dorothy Loudon (*Annie*)

June	July	August	September	October	November
David Mamet makes his mark	Steppenwolf Company founded in Chicago	Broadway producers warn about sex shows	*Oh, Calcutta!* revived	Broadway columnist Leonard Lyons d.	David Merrick's second successive flop musical

December	January	February	March	April	May
Michael Bennett m. Donna McKechnie	*Hellzapoppin* revival closes in Boston	*American Buffalo* on Broadway	*The Shadow Box*	*Annie*	*Gemini* and Martin and Merman together

Personalities

JULY 5 A headline in the *Village Voice* reads: "David Mamet: Remember That Name." **22** The Steppenwolf Theatre Company is founded in a Chicago church basement, paying $10 a month rent for the space. The Company will launch the careers of John Malkovich, Gary Sinese, Glenne Headley, and Laurie Metcalf, among others.

AUGUST 10 Kitty Carlisle Hart is appointed Chairperson of the New York State Council on the Arts.

SEPTEMBER 22 *Variety*'s review of the September 13 opening of the Boston try-out of *The Innocents* complains about one 11-year-old cast member: That "[m]oppet [Sarah Jessica] Parker mostly chirps her lines." The paper's notice of the show's October 19 Broadway opening will call her "capable" but will complain about her "unclear diction." **23** Beatrice Lillie, disabled by a series of strokes and in poor financial condition as well, is given a court-appointed conservator—her longtime companion, John Phillip Huck. **23** At the premiere of *The Oldest Living Graduate*, at the Broadhurst, producer Robert Whitehead personally walks down the aisle to where television reviewer Kevin Sanders is sitting and orders him out of the theatre for coming late.

David Mamet *PF*

Plays and Musicals

JUNE 10 Neil Simon's *California Suite* (445), about couples at war and at peace with each other and with other couples, opens at the Eugene O'Neill. Tammy Grimes, George Grizzard, Jack Weston, Leslie Easterbrook, and Barbara Barrie are in the cast. "It's *Plaza Suite* gone West," says Clive Barnes in the *Times*, but Simon's "heart is still Manhattan, very dry and on the rocks." **14** David Mamet makes his first serious mark on the New York theatre when *Duck Variations* and *Sexual Perversity in Chicago* (273) open off-Broadway, at the Cherry Lane. The two plays have already been given at St. Clement's Church uptown. **22** After five years and 2,124 performances off-Broadway, *Godspell* moves uptown, to the Broadhurst (527).

JULY 7 Ending two years at the Village Gate downtown, Earl Wilson, Jr.'s *Let My People Come* (108) has a tonier address: the Morosco. The show, which avoids an official opening, playing nothing but previews, has been disowned by its author, who doesn't like the way its being staged.

SEPTEMBER 15 *For Colored Girls Who Have Considered Suicide/When The Rainbow Is Enuf* (742), in which the author Ntozake Shange is a member of the cast, moves uptown from the Public Theatre, opening at the Booth. The cast of eight recites and dances to her poetry, the main theme of which is the poor way that women are treated by men. **24** *Oh, Calcutta!* (5,959) is revived at the Edison Theatre, where it alternates with *Me and Bessie* until December 7, after which it has the theatre to itself for several years. **25** The Houston Grand Opera brings the full-length, three-hour operatic version of *Porgy and Bess* (122) to the Uris Theatre.

OCTOBER 14 The men in *The Club* (674), Eve Merriam's satire on sexism at the downtown Circle in the Square, are played by women. Tommy Tune is directing.

DECEMBER 2 Hume Cronyn and Jessica Tandy bring their touring show *The Many Faces of Love*, staged performance-readings from many writers, to Town Hall for

Business and Society

AUGUST 31 The League of New York Theatres and Producers passes a resolution threatening future expulsion to any producer who stages a show such as *Oh, Calcutta!* or *Let My People Come*, which moved to Broadway on July 7.

SEPTEMBER • New York City Human Rights Commissioner Eleanor Holmes Norton charges that Broadway restricts opportunities for minority musicians in its pit bands.

OCTOBER 13 In a letter in *Variety*, Phil Oesterman, producer of *Let My People Come*, responds to the recent condemnation of his and similar Broadway shows by the League of Theatres and Producers. "How dare a small self-appointed vigilante clique run herd on an entire industry?" he writes. "It is unhealthy, unconscionable and un-American. It smacks of Blacklist '53."

JANUARY 2 The Broadway gross for the week ending today, $2,671,286, beats by far the old weekly record of $2,091,472. Broadway attendance for the week (a statistic that has only been compiled since last year) is 227,900.

Births, Deaths, and Marriages

SEPTEMBER 20 Producer Kermit Bloomgarden d. Among his productions was *Death of a Salesman*.

OCTOBER 7 Columnist Leonard Lyons d. **14** Edith Evans d.

NOVEMBER 28 Rosalind Russell d.

DECEMBER 4 Director-choreographer Michael Bennett m. Donna McKechnie, star of his *A Chorus Line*, a match that will last a few months. For McKechnie, the collapse of her marriage a year from now will begin a string of disasters in which her father will d., and she will have to deal with a bout of rheumatoid arthritis.

MARCH 8 Henry Hull d.

APRIL 26 Julie Harris m. writer William Carroll.

NOVEMBER • Playwright Lillian Hellman poses for print ads for Blackglama mink coats, which carry the slogan: "What becomes a legend most?"

JANUARY 18 British Equity authorizes Donna McKechnie to join the London company of *A Chorus Line* but only for a month, to fill in as Cassie until Michael Bennett can settle on a replacement for Elizabeth Seal, originally hired for the role. Bennett found Seal, who starred on Broadway in *Irma La Douce*, "miscast," and he felt that her dancing was not up to par. **20** British Equity reverses its decision to let Donna McKechnie play in the London production of *A Chorus Line*, which Michael Bennett will now have to close temporarily. **22** "It just didn't work," producer Alexander Cohen says of *Hellzapoppin*, which closes tonight in Boston, short of Broadway and, according to reports, in the hole for $1,250,000. Cohen is irked at star Jerry Lewis, in what would have been his Broadway debut, for what Cohen claims was Lewis's lack of cooperation in rehearsing the show.

FEBRUARY • Bob Fosse's lover Ann Reinking succeeds his ex-wife Gwen Verdon as Roxie Hart in *Chicago*. Fosse, asked how he feels about this, replies, "Slightly wicked." The fiftyish Verdon says of Reinking, in her mid-twenties: "Ann can kick her legs higher and keep them up longer than I can." **24** Elizabeth Ashley, opening at the Palace with Rex Harrison in *Caesar and Cleopatra*, scratches her cornea, possibly with her wig, and has to play with a patch over her eye, an injury that will put her in the hospital tomorrow.

MARCH • *The New York Times* announces that Richard Eder will succeed Clive Barnes as its daily theatre critic. **4** Ellen Stewart begins an international theatre festival at her off-off-Broadway La Mama Theatre. **22** The Brooklyn Academy of Music Company, beginning a series of revivals across the river with *The New York Idea*, is packed with talent. Members include Rosemary Harris, Ellen Burstyn, Blythe Danner, Rene Auberjonois, Margaret Hamilton, Austin Pendleton, Tovah Feldshuh, and Denholm Elliott. **23** *Variety* reports that Andrew Lloyd

---

one night only. **12** The Negro Ensemble Company presents *The Brownsville Raid* (112), Charles Fuller's look at a racially charged incident at the turn of the century. Adolph Caesar and Douglas Turner Ward are in the cast, at the Theatre De Lys. **14** George C. Scott is Foxwell J. Sly in *Sly Fox* (495), Larry Gelbart's adaptation of Ben Jonson's *Volpone*, at the Broadhurst. It was director Arthur Penn's idea to do the adaptation. Also in the cast are Jack Gilford, John Heffernan, Trish Van Devere (Scott's wife), Gretchen Wyler, Bob Dishy, and Hector Elizondo. **22** Alex Bradford, a major figure in gospel music, has written the music and lyrics for *Your Arms Too Short to Box with God* (429), based on the Book of Matthew. It opens at the Lyceum. **28** Zero Mostel returns as Tevye in a revival of *Fiddler on the Roof* (167), at the Winter Garden.

FEBRUARY 2 At the Plymouth, Simon Gray's *Otherwise Engaged* (309), a dramatic comedy, stars Tom Courtenay, in his Broadway debut. This story of a man too cool and distant for his own good is directed by Harold Pinter. **16** Directed by Ulu Grosbard, with Robert Duvall, John Savage, and Kenneth MacMillan, David Mamet's *American Buffalo* (135), which *Variety* terms "merely a situation sketch about subhumans too feeble-minded to work out a plan for a burglary," opens at the Barrymore. The play, says *Variety*, has "a higher ratio of filthy talk than any other Broadway show of offhand memory." The film is released in 1996. **17** Chekhov's *The Cherry Orchard* (62), directed by Andre Serban and translated by Jean Claude van Itallie, opens at the Vivian Beaumont. "It's a celebration of genius, like the cleaning of a great painting," writes Clive Barnes in *The New York Times*. "Irene Worth moves across the stage as if it were the living room of her heart." Also in the cast are Mary Beth Hurt, Raul Julia, George Voskovec, and Meryl Streep.

MARCH 10 James Coco eats himself into oblivion in Albert Innuarto's one-act *The Transfiguration of Benno Blimpie* (61), at the Astor Place Theatre. **30** *Mummenschanz* (1,326), a Swiss pantomime show, opens at the Bijou. **31** Michael Christofer's Pulitzer Prize- and Tony Award-winning

---

MARCH • The annual report of the Guthrie Theatre in Minneapolis says that it had a $47 surplus on revenues last year of $3,317,340.

APRIL 7 The committee administering the Tony Awards adds a new category: best revival of a play or musical. It's a response to the unhappiness created by the possibility that *Porgy and Bess*, *Threepenny Opera*, and *The Cherry Orchard* might be allowed to compete as new shows.

MAY • A group of agents, resenting Actors Equity's limitations on the commission they can charge, file an antitrust suit against the union.

Personalities

Webber and Tim Rice are going to turn their LP "Evita," which has a libretto of sorts to connect the songs, into a stage musical. The pair, whose record is selling better in Britain than in the U.S., have just appeared at The Ballroom, a New York City cabaret. **24** *Appearing Nightly*, Lily Tomlin's one-woman show, opens at the Biltmore. *The Playbill* jokingly lists opera diva Zinka Milanov as Tomlin's "standby." Milanov does not appreciate it, threatens to sue, and the jest will be dropped.

APRIL • Producer Alexander Cohen and the Minskoffs are locked in an alley fight. *Hellzapoppin*, which Cohen closed in Boston in January, was ticketed for their Broadway theatre. They take out their unhappiness with Cohen by preventing him from parking his limousines near his office in Shubert Alley, the private street which the Minskoffs own jointly with the Shubert Organization.

MAY 15 Mary Martin and Ethel Merman perform together in a one-night benefit performance at the Broadway Theatre, emceed by Cyril Ritchard. Tens of thousands of ticket orders had to be returned for the sold-out event. Critic Walter Kerr will write: "Ethel Merman is the bonfire and Mary Martin is the smoke. They go very nice together, if you're in a mood to burn up the town."

Plays and Musicals

The Shadow Box (315), set in a hospice, opens at the Morosco. Gordon Davidson directs Simon Oakland, Joyce Ebert, Laurence Luckinbill, Geraldine Fitzgerald and, in his Broadway debut, Mandy Patinkin. It's a 1980 made-for-TV movie.

APRIL 17 Eight years after the film *Bob & Carol & Ted & Alice*, Broadway gets its show about wife swapping, the Cy Coleman-Michael Stewart musical *I Love My Wife* (872). Opening at the Barrymore, it stars Lenny Baker, Ilene Graff, James Naughton, and Joanna Gleason. Among the cast replacements for Baker and Naughton are the Smothers Brothers.

Stephen Sondheim PF

18 *Side by Side by Sondheim* (384), a British revue reprising the composer-lyricist's Broadway high points—and itself the first Broadway high point for producer Cameron Mackintosh—is at the Music Box. Millicent Martin, David Kernan, Julie N. McKenzie, and Ned Sherrin make up the cast. **21** There's no doubt about the big song in *Annie* (2,377): "Tomorrow." Tonight this Charles Strouse-Martin Charnin musical, starring Andrea McArdle as Little Orphan Annie, Reid Shelton as Daddy Warbucks, and Dorothy Loudon as Agatha Hannigan, opens at the Alvin. It will be a 1982 John Huston film. **24** David Rabe's *The Basic Training of Pavlo Hummel* (107), which opened off-Broadway six years ago, is revived for a limited engagement at the

Business and Society

Births, Deaths, and Marriages

Longacre, with Al Pacino giving what Jack Kroll, in *Newsweek*, calls "a devastating performance."

MAY 2 Yul Brynner is back in the role that he owns as the King in a highly successful revival of the 1951 Rodgers and Hammerstein musical *The King & I* (696), at the Uris Theatre. Constance Towers costars. **21** *Gemini* (1,788), Albert Innaurato's play about a college student in Philadelphia in the early 1970s, coping with the possibility that he is gay, opens at the Little Theatre after an off-Broadway run at the Circle Rep. Robert Picardo plays the student, and Danny Aiello is his father. **26** The previews of *Beatlemania* (920), begun at the Winter Garden tonight, will go on and on because the producers worry that the critics won't understand the production. Retroactively, the opening date will be pegged to May 31.

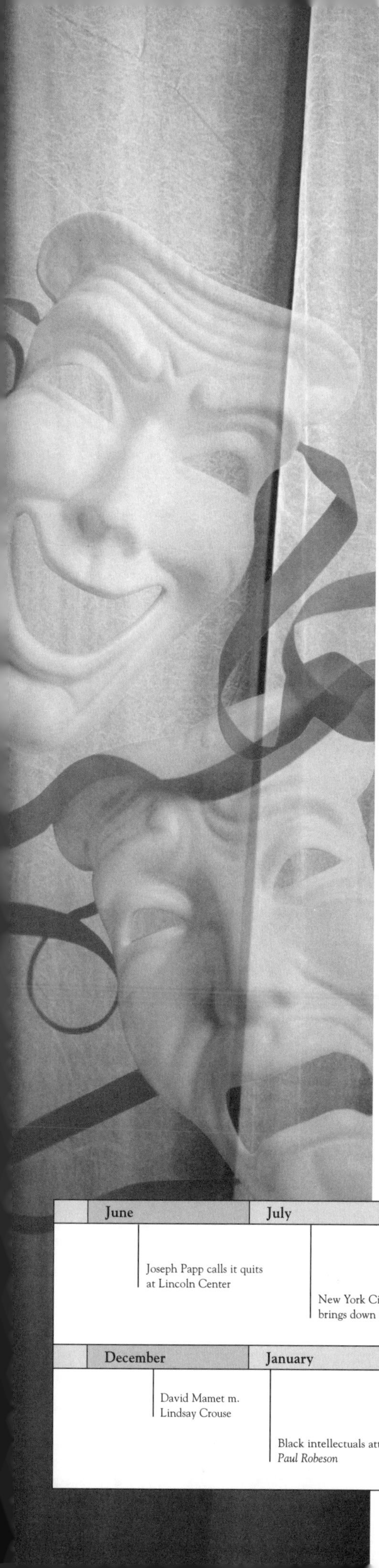

1977–78

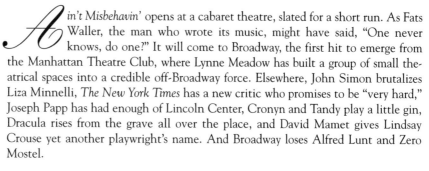

Ain't Misbehavin' opens at a cabaret theatre, slated for a short run. As Fats Waller, the man who wrote its music, might have said, "One never knows, do one?" It will come to Broadway, the first hit to emerge from the Manhattan Theatre Club, where Lynne Meadow has built a group of small theatrical spaces into a credible off-Broadway force. Elsewhere, John Simon brutalizes Liza Minnelli, *The New York Times* has a new critic who promises to be "very hard," Joseph Papp has had enough of Lincoln Center, Cronyn and Tandy play a little gin, Dracula rises from the grave all over the place, and David Mamet gives Lindsay Crouse yet another playwright's name. And Broadway loses Alfred Lunt and Zero Mostel.

- Only Broadway actress to bear the name of 3 playwrights: Lindsay Crouse Mamet—her first name is for her father Howard Lindsay, playwright Russel Crouse's literary partner. She marries David Mamet on December 21, 1977.
- Circle in the Square deficit: $600,000
- Number of times Marian Seldes will die in *Deathtrap*: over a thousand
- One of the principal investors in *Deathtrap*: Claus von Bulow
- Arguably John Wood's best line in Ira Levin's *Deathtrap*: "Nothing recedes like success."
- New top price for Broadway, established by *The Act*, with Liza Minnelli: $25
- Amount of insurance paid to the producers of *The Act* when Liza Minnelli misses 26 performances: $230,000
- Amount taken in by the Times Square discount ticket booth—TKTS—in its first 5 years: $21,000,000
- Number of cities on the *Oh, Calcutta!* tour over the past 2 seasons: 119
- Number of cities on the *Oh, Calcutta!* tour in which the producers had to go to court, mostly over censorship: 27
- Last time that Jessica Tandy—a Tony winner for *The Gin Game* this season—won a Tony: 30 years ago, for *A Streetcar Named Desire*
- Number of Broadway shows that have tryouts in Boston: 13
- Number of Pulitzer Prizes awarded for drama criticism over the years: 1, to Walter Kerr, this season
- Number of drama critics who have won Pulitzer Prizes: 2—Brooks Atkinson also won for his reporting from abroad during World War II while on leave from the *Times*'s drama desk
- Total gross for Broadway and the road: $209,543,379, an increase of 19 percent over last year
- Number of productions of *Dracula* in New York: 3—on Broadway, off-Broadway, and by the Equity Library Theatre

Productions on Broadway: 54

Pulitzer Prize for Drama: *The Gin Game* (Donald L. Coburn)

New York Drama Critics Circle Awards:
Best Play: *Da* (Hugh Leonard)
Best Musical: *Ain't Misbehavin'* (Fats Waller)

Tony Awards:
Play: *Da* (Hugh Leonard)
Actress in a Play: Jessica Tandy (*The Gin Game*)
Actor in a Play: Barnard Hughes (*Da*)
Musical: *Ain't Misbehavin'* (Fats Waller)
Actress in a Musical: Liza Minnelli (*The Act*)
Actor in a Musical: John Collum (*On the Twentieth Century*)

June	July	August	September	October	November
Joseph Papp calls it quits at Lincoln Center	New York City blackout brings down the curtains	Alfred Lunt d.	Zero Mostel d.	*The Gin Game* and *Dracula*	John Simon's slashing review of Liza Minnelli

December	January	February	March	April	May
David Mamet m. Lindsay Crouse	Black intellectuals attack *Paul Robeson*	*On the Twentieth Century* and *Deathtrap*	Bob Fosse's *Dancin'*	*The Best Little Whorehouse in Texas*	*Da* and *Ain't Misbehavin'*

Personalities

JUNE 9 Joseph Papp announces that the New York Shakespeare Festival will leave Lincoln Center, where it has been the resident production company at the Vivian Beaumont Theatre for four years. Papp has been unhappy with the artistic and financial restrictions under which he has been operating.

AUGUST 2 Mary Martin, rehearsing in Knoxville, Tennessee, for *Do You Turn Somersaults?* tears ligaments in her knee but will be back onstage tomorrow, her leg in a cast. **5** Broadway marquee lights are dimmed to honor Alfred Lunt, who died two days ago. It's only the third time this has been done. The street went dark for Gertrude Lawrence in 1952 and Oscar Hammerstein II in 1960.

SEPTEMBER • Interviewed in *Playbill*, Richard Eder, *The New York Times*'s new drama critic, says "Right now I'm the most open-minded, reasonable person in the world. My only critical rule is to be very hard." **6** Zero Mostel, scheduled to open in Arnold Wesker's *The Merchant* in Philadelphia tonight, has been in a hospital for three days, diagnosed with a virus. He will be dead in two days from a heart attack.

OCTOBER • With *The Act*, a star vehicle for Liza Minnelli, hitting some snags on its pre-Broadway route, Gower Champion is brought in to assist first time Broadway director Martin Scorsese. "Everybody around the production is being ultra careful in discussing the situation," cautions *Variety*, "for various tricky professional and psychological elements are involved." **19** The New York Drama Critics Circle protests the exclusion, a week ago, of John Simon from the opening night free-ticket list by the League of New York Theatres and Producers. Simon contends that the Shubert Organization and producer Alexander Cohen are behind the move and that the sticking point is the profanity he used when discussing *The Shadow Box* on television. (He called it "shit.")

NOVEMBER • Liza Minnelli's lip-synching of some of the lyrics in *The Act* while she

Plays and Musicals

SEPTEMBER 28 *The Passion of Dracula* (714), adapted from the Bram Stoker novel by Bob Hale and David Richmond, gets the jump on the upcoming Broadway version of the vampire tale when it premieres off-Broadway, at the Cherry Lane Theatre. Christopher Bernaw plays the Count.

OCTOBER 6 Hume Cronyn and Jessica Tandy star in D.L. Coburn's *The Gin Game* (517), directed by Mike Nichols, at the John Golden. They portray two frustrated residents of a nursing home, who engage in a not-too-friendly game of cards. The play "is extremely intelligent and immaculately performed," writes Richard Eder in the *Times*. **20** David Mamet's *A Life in the Theatre* (288), originally a teleplay, opens at the Theatre De Lys. Ellis Rabb and Peter Evans star in this story of a backstage friendship between two actors that *Variety* calls "one of the best off-Broadway productions to come along in several seasons." It will become a made-for-TV film, directed by Gregory Mosher, in 1993, starring Jack Lemmon and Matthew Broderick. **20** At the Martin Beck, Frank Langella and Edward Gorey's sets are the stars of *Dracula* (925), Hamilton Deane and John Balderston's adaptation of the Bram Stoker novel that made a name for Bela Lugosi in the 1927–28 season. Coincidentally, this is Bela Lugosi's birthday. **21** Wendy Wasserstein's *Uncommon Women and Others*

Frank Langella MSN

Business and Society

JULY 13 New York City is blacked out at 9:30 P.M., canceling the last act of most Broadway shows. The current will begin to come on, neighborhood by neighborhood, tomorrow morning. Tomorrow's attendance will be so spotty that brokers will be dumping tickets at face value.

NOVEMBER • The Los Angeles Drama Critics Circle threatens to publicly denounce any producer who quotes from their reviews out of context in ads.

JANUARY • The National Labor Relations Board files a complaint against Actors Equity, challenging its policy of charging alien actors more for their required membership than they do American citizens. The test case is Lynn Redgrave, now on Broadway in Shaw's *Saint Joan*. • Equity's new off-Broadway contract modifies the basis on which salaries are calculated, shifting the emphasis from the weekly gross to the house's capacity. **11** The price of *Variety* rises to $.85 from $.75.

FEBRUARY • A touring production of *Oh, Calcutta!* wins six of nine censorship cases in an 11-day period in three southern states.

Births, Deaths, and Marriages

JULY 22 Yiddish stage star Jacob Ben-Ami d.

AUGUST 3 Alfred Lunt d. **19** Groucho Marx d.

SEPTEMBER 1 Ethel Waters d. **8** Zero Mostel d.

NOVEMBER 30 British playwright Terence Rattigan d.

DECEMBER 18 Cyril Ritchard d. **21** Playwright David Mamet marries actress Lindsay Crouse, who was living with Robert Duvall, who starred in Mamet's *American Buffalo* in February, when she and the playwright met.

JANUARY 18 Charlotte Greenwood d.

FEBRUARY 15 Ilka Chase d.

MARCH 18 Peggy Wood d.

dances is creating a stir, although the practice has been used before. **14** Reviewing Liza Minnelli in *The Act,* in *New York* magazine, John Simon writes of her "blubber lips unable to resist the pull of gravity, and a chin trying its damnest to withdraw into the neck, apparently to avoid responsibility for what goes on above it." He has been criticized in the past for his savage attacks on the appearance of actresses. Harvey Sabinson, of the League of New York Theatres and Producers, recently likened Simon to "a sadistic guard in a Nazi camp." **25** Cyril Ritchard, narrating Stephen Sondheim's *Side by Side* in Chicago, is felled by a heart attack.

DECEMBER 8 A small fire in Liza Minnelli's Manhattan penthouse spreads to the drapes while she sleeps. Although firemen are able to put it out quickly, she has inhaled enough smoke to keep the curtain of *The Act* down tonight. **14** *Variety* reports from London that *Evita* producer Harold Prince is casting for a singer-actress to play the role of Eva Peron.

JANUARY 9 *Time* magazine drama critic Ted Kalem is criticized for his review of *A Touch of the Poet* in today's issue, in which he reuses, verbatim, part of a review that then *Time* critic Louis Kronenberger wrote about the 1958 production. **11** In a two-page ad in *Variety*, a group of black intellectuals, writers, and politicians attack the play *Paul Robeson*, headed for Broadway with James Earl Jones in the title role. They say it has reduced Robeson

John Collum and Madeline Kahn are the stars of *On the Twentieth Centruy* PB

(22), in which Swoosie Kurtz, Glenn Close, and Jill Eikenberry recall their college days, opens at the Marymount Manhattan Theatre. The critics are lukewarm toward the play but laud Kurtz's Obie-winning performance. **29** Liza Minnelli is the star of *The Act* (240), with Barry Nelson, at the Majestic. John Kander and Fred Ebb's musical, about a Hollywood star trying to resurrect her career in Las Vegas, is directed by Martin Scorsese, with some last-minute help from Gower Champion.

DECEMBER 4 Neil Simon is on familiar ground, writing in *Chapter Two* (857) about a writer-widower who finds love again, with autobiographical overtones. In the cast, at the Imperial, are Judd Hirsch, Anita Gillette, Cliff Gorman, and Anne Wedgeworth. **28** Jason Robards, Jr. and Geraldine Fitzgerald are in the revival of Eugene O'Neill's *A Touch of the Poet* (141), at the Helen Hayes.

JANUARY 5 David Mamet's *The Water Engine* (63), set in a 1930s radio studio, opens at the Public Theatre. It has, says *The New York Times*, the playwright's typical "pointillistic verbal brilliance. . . . Bit by bit . . . Mr. Mamet seems to have become our most exciting young playwright." The cast includes David Schultz and Bill Moor. Mamet is not only absent from his play's premiere but has also been out of telephone contact for several days. The play moves to the Plymouth (16) on March 6. **19** Phillip Hayes Dean's *Paul Robeson* (77), starring James Earl Jones, which has already been charged with trying to water down and domesticate a radical political figure, opens at the Lunt-Fontanne.

FEBRUARY 2 Harvey Fierstein's *International Stud* (the name of a gay bar), in which he plays Arnold, a drag queen performer, opens at La Mama ETC, off-off-Broadway, where it will run through the February 17. According to tonight's program, it's the first part of an *International Stud Trilogy*

MARCH • The Shubert Organization announces that Ticketron is creating a computerized box office system for its theatres that will be on-line late next season. **19** The producers of a show called *Sweeney Todd,* scheduled for next season, have a display ad in the Arts and Leisure section of today's Sunday *New York Times*, soliciting investment capital. They will raise over $200,000 from the $1,600 ad, about a fourth of what they need. The Securities and Exchange Commission had to approve the strategy, which was used before for Edward Albee's *Seascape*. **20** The League of New York Theatres and Producers and the United Scenic Artists—a group that the League once sued, claiming it was not a union but rather a group of independent contractors creating a monopoly for their services—reach agreement on an extraordinary 11 1/2-year contract, containing cost-of-living provisions. The design of a single set for a straight play will rate a minimum of $2,750; lighting it is worth at least $1,700.

APRIL • Michael Bennett and Actors Equity negotiate the first show contract in which the cast will share in the profits. It applies to *The Queen of the Stardust Ballroom*, which will be generated out of Bennett's workshop, similar to the way

Personalities

"from REVOLUTIONARY heroic dimensions to manageable sentimentalized size." Signers include Alvin Ailey, Maya Angelou, James Baldwin, Lonnie Elder III, Coretta Scott King, and Congressman Charles Rangel, Jr.

MARCH 14 Shelley Winters, opening at the Biltmore in the Broadway production of *The Effect of Gamma Rays on Man-in-the-Moon Marigolds*, is wearing the same nightgown worn by her friend Laurette Taylor in *The Glass Menagerie* in 1945.

APRIL • What was to have been a Broadway production of *King Lear*, starring Richard Burton and directed by Elia Kazan, is canceled by producer Alexander Cohen, who felt he needed seven performances a week to make money, while Burton was balking at more than six. It would have been the first play directed by Kazan since 1964. • David Mamet is named playwright in residence at Chicago's Goodman Theatre. He will also be associate director of the company, of which Gregory Mosher has recently been named artistic director. Last year, the company staged Mamet's *The Woods*, with Patti LuPone and Peter Weller.

Kevin Kline MSN

MAY • Jerry Orbach loses his 1975 suit for libel against columnist Rex Reed, who lambasted his performance at a benefit. **25** In a stunning typo, the *New York Daily*

Plays and Musicals

(later renamed *Torchsong Trilogy*). *The Village Voice* calls it "the BEST gay play we have seen." It will open off-Broadway, at the Players Theatre on May 22. **19** *On the Twentieth Century* (449), a Cy Coleman-Betty Comden-Adolph Green musical, based on the 1932 play *Twentieth Century*, opens at the St. James. John Collum plays producer Oscar Jaffee, and Madeleine Kahn is Lily Garland, roles played by John Barrymore and Carole Lombard in the 1934 Howard Hawks screwball comedy film. Kevin Kline and Imogene Coca are also in the cast. **26** "Trashy," says the *Daily News*; a play that "doesn't seem to know where to go," adds the *Times*. But Ira Levin's *Deathtrap* (1,809) will sell plenty of tickets at the Music Box, with a cast that includes John Wood, Marian Seldes, Victor Garber, Marian Winters, and Richard Woods. It's filmed in 1982.

MARCH 5 Carol Channing is in a revival of *Hello, Dolly!* (145) at the Lunt-Fontanne. **9** Elizabeth Swados's musical *Runaways* (80) opens at the Public Theatre, with a mostly inexperienced cast of young people in a show about troubled youth. It will move uptown to the Plymouth (267) on May 13. **27** Ann Reinking and Wayne Cilento are in Bob Fosse's *Dancin'* (1,774), at the Broadhurst, with words and music from several sources. Fosse's dance spectacular, which points the way toward Broadway shows that can play easily to foreign business travelers, without the language barrier, opens at the Broadhurst.

APRIL 17 When Carol Hall's *The Best Little Whorehouse in Texas* comes to the screen in 1982, the producers will settle for no less than Dolly Parton and Burt Reynolds. But tonight, at the Entermedia Theatre (it moves to the Forty-sixth Street Theatre on June 19 for a total 1,703 performances), the leads are Carlin Glynn and Henderson Forsythe. This MCA-Universal–backed musical is about the Chicken Ranch, where it's not plucking they're doing. **27** Lanford Wilson's *Fifth of July* (158) is at the Circle Repertory Company's Circle Theatre.

Business and Society

that *A Chorus Line* came into being.

MAY 16 The Lyceum, the oldest Broadway theatre in continuous use, is officially designated a New York City landmark, protecting its facade from unauthorized alteration.

Births, Deaths, and Marriages

News declares that José Ferrer's career includes "stag movies and television," when it meant "stage, movies and television." The actor's response: "The *News* reporter is the first to get me to admit I've done stag movies. I'm Puerto Rico's answer to Harry Reems."

William Hurt stars as disabled Vietnam veteran Kenneth Talley, whose family is at the center of this and other Wilson plays, including *Talley's Folly*. It will be revived on Broadway in 1980.

MAY 1 Barnard Hughes is the title character in *Da* (697), the Tony Award-winning play by Hugh Leonard, at the Morosco. Brian Murray plays his son in this story, set in Ireland, of a young man coming to terms with his family. In the 1996 revival, Murray plays the father. **9** *Ain't Misbehavin'* (1,604), a revue based on the music of Fats Waller, opens at the Longacre, with Nell Carter, Ken Page, Armelia McQueen, Charlaine Woodard, and Andre De Shields. It began off-broadway, at the Manhattan Theatre Club.

1978–79

Artistically, Sondheim's *Sweeney Todd* is adjudged a cut above the usual Broadway fare, but ticket sales lag. Broadway, like the movies, is beginning to put more emphasis on special effects and impressive sets. Robert Brustein is out at Yale, at the Drama School and its theatre company, replaced by Lloyd Richards, who will nurture the work of playwright August Wilson. Sam Shepard wins a Pulitzer, and Neil Simon snipes at *Times* critic Richard Eder, who panned *They're Playing Our Song.* Gerald Schoenfeld says that *A Chorus Line* has been very nice to the Shubert bottom line, "My Fair Lady" hardly characterizes Alan Jay Lerner's relationship to any of his numerous ex-wives, and Martin Charnin, replaced as director of *I Remember Mama* after clashing with Liv Ullmann, says that "there's no longer a fjord in my future."

- New top ticket price for straight plays: $20
- New price of *Variety*: an even $1.00
- Number of original cast albums *Evita* will sell: 3.5 million
- Prominent stars taking brief turns playing Lillian Hellman in the revival of *Are You Now Or Have you Ever Been?*: Liza Minnelli, Tammy Grimes, Colleen Dewhurst, Barbara Baxley, Rosemary Murphy, Frances Sternhagen, Peggy Cass, and Louise Lasser
- Last time a Broadway show had to compete directly with its film version, as with *Grease* this season: *Sleuth*, in 1972–73
- Percentage of Broadway tickets now bought with credit cards: about 25 percent
- New minimum pay for ushers: $95.70 a week
- New minimum pay for ticket takers: $145.20 a week
- Amount that José Ferrer loses from his investment in the flop *White Pelican*, in which he stars: $41,000
- Number of actresses who have played The Girl, so far, in *The Fantasticks*: 19
- What Eugene Wolsk, producer of the musical *Sarava*, calls *Times* critic Richard Eder, who after a month of previews goes ahead and reviews the show: "an unreasonable 'bleep'" and, according to *Variety*, Wolsk adds, "I hope he jumps off the roof of the *Times* building."
- Number of backers of *Sweeney Todd*: 271, possibly a record for a Broadway show
- David Mamet on his mother's relationship to his linguistic gift: "My mother said I'd be a good writer someday if I ever washed my mouth out."
- Amount lost by Michael Bennett's *Ballroom*: $2 million

Productions on Broadway: 47

Pulitzer Prize for Drama: *Buried Child* (Sam Shepard)

New York Drama Critics Circle Awards:
Best Play: *The Elephant Man* (Bernard Pomerance)
Best Musical: *Sweeney Todd* (Stephen Sondheim)

Tony Awards:
Play: *The Elephant Man* (Bernard Pomerance)
Actor in a Play: Tom Conti (*Whose Life Is It Anyway?*)
Actress in a Play: Constance Cummings (*Wings*) and Carole Shelley (*The Elephant Man*)
Musical: *Sweeney Todd* (Stephen Sondheim)
Actor in a Musical: Len Cariou (*Sweeney Todd*)
Actress in a Musical: Angela Lansbury (*Sweeney Todd*)

June	July	August	September	October	November
I'm Getting My Act Together and Taking It on the Road	Hume Cronyn held up	Only three of 36 Broadway houses are empty or unbooked	Ruth Etting d.	Raul Julia for Frank Langella in *Dracula*	Alan Jay Lerner alimony problems

December	January	February	March	April	May
Sam Shepard's *Buried Child*	Constance Cummings in Arthur Kopit's *Wings*	*They're Playing Our Song* and *On Golden Pond*	Stephen Sondheim's *Sweeney Todd*	Sam Shepard's Pulitzer a day late for *Buried Child*	Last Richard Rodgers musical flops

Personalities

JUNE 22 Yale University's new president, A. Bartlett Giametti, declines to renew the contract of the Drama School's Dean Robert Brustein, who also directs its repertory theatre. Brustein sees the action as an attempt to "deprofessionalize" the program.

JULY • Dramatist Guild president Stephen Sondheim complains to the League of New York Theatres and Producers and the American Theatre Wing about the treatment of writers on the June 4 Tony Awards telecast. They were not "allowed to stand alone on the stage, in front of millions of Americans," but instead had to share the spotlight. He says they may boycott future shows unless their grievances are addressed. **12** Hume Cronyn, his secretary, and his real estate agent are held at gunpoint in Cronyn's Pound Ridge, New York home by a man and woman posing as a prospective buyer of the house and her "architect." After handcuffing their victims, the couple begin to loot Cronyn's art collection when they hear their captive escape. They flee empty-handed.

SEPTEMBER • Joseph Papp splits with his longtime associate Bernard Gersten over whether the New York Shakespeare Festival should back Michael Bennett's *Stardust Ballroom*. Papp feels it would be inappropriately commercial.

OCTOBER 3 Raul Julia replaces Frank Langella in *Dracula*, on Broadway.

NOVEMBER 21 Alan Jay Lerner's alimony problems are dramatized in today's *New York Post* headline: "4th Ex-Wife Sues for 6th Time."

DECEMBER • The departure of Jack Lemmon from *Tribute*, on December 2, and Henry Fonda from *The First Monday in October*, on December 9, underlines Broadway's increasing dependence on movie stars, who close down otherwise successful shows, as happens here, when they have to leave for picture commitments. **24** According to an interview with director Ron Field, in the *Boston Globe*, the failure of the Broadway musical *King*

Plays and Musicals

JUNE 1 *Tribute* (212), by Bernard Slade, opens at the Brooks Atkinson. The star, Jack Lemmon, plays a Hollywood PR man with cancer, trying to come to terms with the son he has never gotten to know well. Robert Picardo plays the boy. **14** Gretchen Cryer stars in and wrote the lyrics for *I'm Getting My Act Together and Taking It on the Road* (1,165,), with music by Nancy Ford, opening at the Public Theatre. It will eventually move to the Circle in the Square. In this musical about a liberated woman, Cryer will be succeeded by Betty Buckley and Phyllis Newman, among others.

SEPTEMBER 20 *Eubie* (439), at the Ambassador, is a revue based on the music of Eubie Blake and Noble Sissle, who wrote "I'm Just Wild About Harry." The cast includes dancer Gregory Hines. At the curtain tonight, the 95-year-old Blake comes onstage for a bow. **28** *The Crucifer of Blood* (228), Paul Giovanni's version of Sherlock Holmes, is at the Helen Hayes Theatre, with Paxton Whitehead as the detective. Also in the cast is Glenn Close.

OCTOBER 3 *The First Monday in October* (79), by Jerome Lawrence and Robert E. Lee, opens at the Majestic, with Henry Fonda and Jane Alexander in the lead roles. This play about the first woman Supreme Court justice will reach the screen in 1981.

DECEMBER 5 Sam Shepard's *Buried Child* (152) opens at the Theatre De Lys, in Greenwich Village. The cast of this story about a nightmarish homecoming to a dysfunctional family includes Tom Noonan, Richard Hamilton, and Mary McDonnell. Walter Kerr calls it a "posture in search of a play." **6** Rex Harrison and Claudette Colbert, with George Rose, are in *The Kingfisher* (182), a comedy at the Biltmore about the possibilities of resurrecting a near-romance of 50 years ago. **14** *Ballroom* (116), Michael Bennett's musical based on his television production *Queen of the Stardust Ballroom*, opens at the Majestic. Billy Goldenberg wrote the music, with lyrics by Alan and Marilyn Bergman. Starring in this story of a widow, whose life now revolves around

Business and Society

JULY • New York City police are investigating the theft of $50,000 worth of tickets to *Dancin'*.

AUGUST • With only three of 36 theatres on Broadway empty or unbooked, several shows are headed for holding patterns, as the new season shapes up. • The new "I Love New York" tourism campaign focuses on Broadway as a prime attraction for out-of-towners. **9** A long New York City newspaper strike begins, which will not have the negative effect on the box office that many now fear.

SEPTEMBER 20 Actors Equity ends its practice, begun in 1964, of automatically granting Equity cards to members of other performing unions, even if they were not contracted for a legitimate stage production.

OCTOBER 11 *Variety* notes an increasing tendency for Broadway shows to stress grandiose spectacle, as in *Dracula* and *On the Twentieth Century*. Not noted by the paper is the parallel phenomenon in film, where the special effects in disaster movies and *Star Wars* have led to box office profits. **12** The Broadway produc-

Births, Deaths, and Marriages

AUGUST 5 Queenie Smith d.

SEPTEMBER 24 Ruth Etting d.

NOVEMBER 2 Producer Max Gordon d. **23** Playwright Marsha Norman m. producer Dann Byck, Jr.

JANUARY 14 Director Jerry Zaks m. actress Jill Rose.

MARCH 8 Playwright David Rabe m. actress Jill Clayburgh.

of Hearts can be attributed in part to Santo Loquasto's sets, which were "quaint" when they should have reflected an air of "decay." **28** Yale University announces the appointment of Lloyd Richards as Dean of its Drama School, beginning in July, when Robert Brustein departs for Harvard. Richards will also replace Brustein as Director of the Yale Repertory Theatre.

JANUARY • As a wave of antigay violence sweeps Key West, Florida, Tennessee Williams is knocked to the ground one evening after leaving a late-night club in the town. He jokes afterward that his assailants might have been "New York drama critics." • The League of New York Theatres and Producers restores John Simon to the list for free first-night tickets. His harsh and profane criticism of *The Shadow Box* provoked his removal last year, but he has been receiving free passes from press agents in the meanwhile, anyway.

FEBRUARY • Ina Claire, the 85-year-old Broadway star of another era, tells an interviewer: "I seldom go to the theatre now because I'm usually offended by the filthy dialogue when I do go." **19** Appearing on the "Today" show, Neil Simon, stung by *Times* critic Richard Eder's pan—"ponderous sentimentality"—of *They're Playing Our Song*, says that Eder doesn't pay attention to what he's seeing while he's at the theatre and that his paper should get rid of him.

MARCH • Alan Schneider resigns as director of the drama division of the Juilliard School over "differences" with its administration. • Martin Charnin, replaced by Cy Feuer as director of the upcoming musical *I Remember Mama*, says of its star Liv Ullmann that "Ms. Ullmann and I do not see 'I to I' *[sic]* about how musicals are made. To make a long and ugly story short, there's no longer a fjord in my future." **15** Former Broadway producer Adela Holzer is convicted of grand larceny in a swindle scheme unconnected to her theatre activities. **24** Fourteen-year-old Sarah Jessica Parker breaks a tooth in the middle of a song while performing in *Annie*. Her understudy takes over. **27** Stephen Sondheim has a mild heart attack.

going dancing, are Dorothy Loudon and Vincent Gardenia.

JANUARY 28 Arthur Kopit's *Wings* (113), which began as a radio drama and opened at the Public Theatre on June 20, moves to Broadway at the Lyceum. Constance Cummings plays a stunt flyer who has trouble communicating with people. It is well into the play before the audience learns that she has had a stroke.

FEBRUARY 11 Neil Simon wrote the book, Marvin Hamlisch the music, and Carole Bayer Singer the lyrics for *They're Playing Our Song* (1,082), at the Imperial. Hamlisch and Singer also contributed their life stories because the musical—about a composer-lyricist couple—incorporates aspects of their own personal relationship. Luci Arnaz and Robert Klein star, and cast replacements include Stockard Channing and Tony Roberts. **28** *On Golden Pond* (156), Ernest Thompson's poignant comedy about the late-in-life love between a couple married for half a century, stars Tom Aldredge and Frances Sternhagen, at the Apollo, just reclaimed from the movies on Forty-second Street. The 1981 film stars Katharine Hepburn and Henry and Jane Fonda.

MARCH 1 Stephen Sondheim's *Sweeney Todd: The Demon Barber of Fleet Street* (557), a musical based on a nineteenth century melodrama of a vengeful, throat-slitting barber and his pie-baking partner

Angela Lansbury *MSN*

tion of *Dracula* begins a two-week, $121,000 television commercial campaign. Musicals have promoted on television for some time, but straight plays are just beginning to take this route.

DECEMBER • The Nederlanders, with British partners, buy the Billy Rose Theatre, which opened as the National in 1921. It's the only Broadway house south of Forty-second Street. The theatre will be renamed the Trafalgar, and then, the Nederlander.

JANUARY 15 An arbitrator upholds the producers of *Whose Life Is It Anyway?* who insist that Tom Conti, star of the hit London production, is uniquely qualified for the lead role on Broadway and should have it under the alien actors provision of the current contract with Actors Equity. Equity disagrees.

FEBRUARY 15 There's a staff turnover at the Ethel Barrymore Theatre box office. There's also a $110,000 shortage. **18** Asian-American actors picket the Public Theatre, protesting the lack of roles for them. Joseph Papp tells them he plans a workshop that will produce dramas speaking to their ethnic experience. **20** Shubert Organization chairman Gerald Schoenfeld says that *A Chorus Line* has already cleared about $22,000,000 in

Personalities

APRIL 16 The Pulitzer Prize for Drama won by Sam Shepard for *Buried Child* is a day late. The play closed yesterday, at the Theatre De Lys. For *New York Times* columnist Russell Baker, who wins for "Commentary," it's two days late. He wrote the libretto for *Home Again, Home Again*, which closed in Toronto, a $1.25-million failure in its pre-Broadway tryout.

MAY • In an interview in *Chicago* magazine, David Mamet says, "My mother said I'd be a good writer someday if I ever washed my mouth out." **6** At the party celebrating the dedication of the Harold Clurman Theatre on Forty-second Street, director-critic Clurman is seated next to his second ex-wife, Juleen Compton. His current young companion, Joan Ungaro, is sitting nearby. But his first ex-wife, Stella Adler, wants no part of this sour musical chairs and has sent her regrets. Clurman's assessment of this situation: "I can handle Stanislavsky. I can handle criticism. I can handle the Group Theatre. But I can't handle my women."

Plays and Musicals

in crime, opens at the Uris Theatre. Len Cariou is shaving closer than close, and Angela Lansbury is at the oven in this production. The cast replacements will be George Hearn and Dorothy Loudon. It "dwarfs every other Broadway musical," says Rex Reed, and Jack Kroll, in *Newsweek*, calls it "brilliant, even sensationally so." But *Variety* notes, correctly, that theatre party and matinée audiences won't buy it. **25** *Zoot Suit* (41), by Luis Valdez, with music and lyrics by Lalo Guerrere and Daniel Valdez, about Chicano life in Los Angeles, opens at the Winter Garden. It stars Daniel Valdez and Edward James Olmos. It was originally produced and was more successful at the Mark Taper Forum. **29** Alan Ayckbourn's new play at the Brooks Atkinson is, as it says, a *Bedroom Farce* (278), but about the only thing that doesn't happen in that room is sex. It stars Michael Gough and Joan Hickson.

APRIL 17 Tom Conti stars in *Whose Life Is It Anyway?* (223) at the Trafalgar (formerly the Billy Rose). Philip Bosco is in the supporting cast of Brian Clark's play, about a man disabled in an accident, who wants the right to take his own life. Richard Dreyfuss stars in the 1981 film. **19** Bernard Pomerance's *The Elephant Man* (916) opens at the Booth Theatre on Broadway. Philip Anglim portrays the disfigured John Merrick without elaborate makeup. The cast also features Carole Shelley and Kevin Conway. Several productions of different plays about Merrick, but with the same title, are opening around the country this season. The 1980 film is not based on this play.

MAY 3 The Circle Rep presents a new play by Lanford Wilson, *Talley's Folly* (44), a prequel to his *Fifth of July*, with Judd Hirsch and Trish Hawkins, at the Circle Theatre. He's a Jewish accountant trying to woo her, a young woman from the Midwest. **31** Liv Ullmann is the star of *I Remember Mama* (108), at the Majestic, in the role played by Mady Christians in John Van Druten's play on Broadway, Irene Dunne on the screen, and Peggy Wood on television. It's Richard Rodgers's last musical, and it's a flop.

Business and Society

profits, which makes it more profitable than *My Fair Lady*, Broadway's biggest moneymaker. This is the first statement about these profits from the producers of the privately financed show.

Births, Deaths, and Marriages

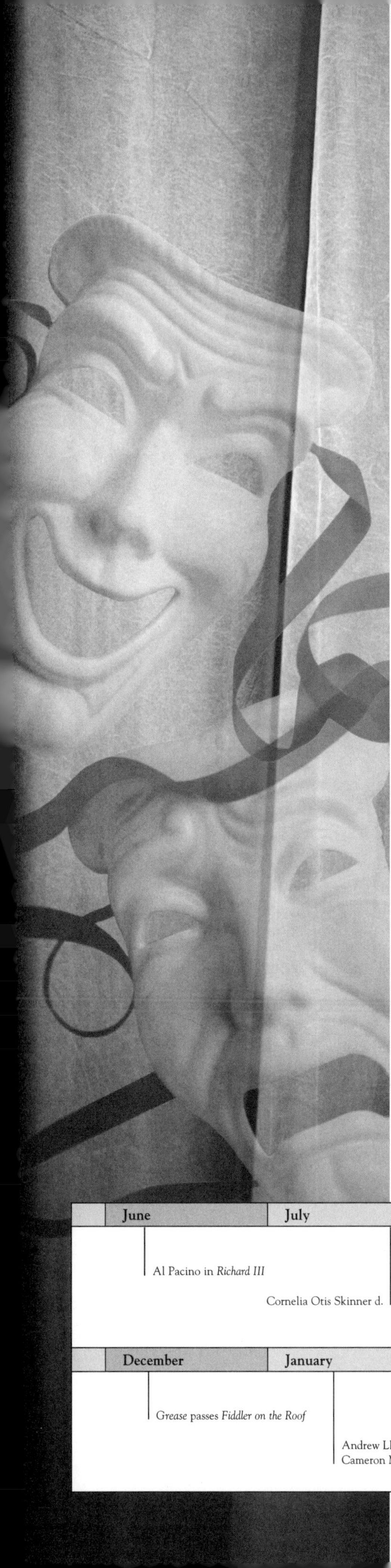

1979–80

With the opening of *Evita*, Patti LuPone is Broadway's reigning diva, and Andrew Lloyd Webber is becoming the dominant figure in the Broadway musical. Lloyd Webber's meeting with Cameron Mackintosh brings together the two men who will dictate the direction of much of Broadway's business in coming years. The Shuberts enter the world of computers and struggle with the Nederlanders over control of Washington, D.C.'s National Theatre, Lanford Wilson's compensation for an awfully bad toothache is a Pulitzer Prize, the New York City transit strike puts the skids on *Grease*, Al Pacino is the spitting image of Richard III, and Jed Harris, "Destiny's Tot," is dead.

- Number of Patti LuPone's costume changes in *Evita*: 14
- Number of wigs worn by LuPone in *Evita*: 4
- What's on "The Ethel Merman Disco Album," released by A&M Records: standards, including "There's No Business Like Show Business," "Everything's Comin' Up Roses," and "I Got Rhythm"
- What Pulitzer Prize winner Lanford Wilson will tell a workshop of younger writers: "Type 'This is the next play by last year's Pulitzer Prize winner' at the top of a page and try to write something underneath it."
- What actors in *Sweeney Todd* who move props as part of their jobs will be paid in an agreement negotiated by Actors Equity: $5 per prop
- Show that was the greatest moneymaker for Richard Rodgers, who dies December 13, 1979: it wasn't a Broadway show but rather the television program "Victory at Sea," for which he wrote the music
- What *Grease* has grossed so far on Broadway and the road combined: $70,000,000
- Number of times Richard Burton and Elizabeth Taylor have divorced each other since *Grease* opened: 2
- Number of occupants of the Oval Office since *Grease* opened: 3 (one resigned and one got there by accident)
- Average cost of staging a musical: $1,000,000
- Average cost of staging a straight play: $500,000
- What theatregoers can learn at the Longacre, where *Children of a Lesser God* opens: the American Sign Language sign for "bullshit," described by one critic as "graphically expressive"

Productions on Broadway: 56

Pulitzer Prize for Drama: *Talley's Folly* (Lanford Wilson)

New York Drama Critics Circle Awards:
Best Play: *Talley's Folly* (Lanford Wilson)
Best Foreign Play: *Betrayal* (Harold Pinter)
Best Musical: *Evita* (Andrew Lloyd Webber and Tim Rice)

Tony Awards:
Play: *Children of A Lesser God* (Mark Medoff)
Actress in a Play: Phyllis Frelich (*Children of a Lesser God*)
Actor in a Play: John Rubinstein (*Children of a Lesser God*)
Musical: *Evita* (Andrew Lloyd Webber and Tim Rice)
Actress in a Musical: Patti LuPone (*Evita*)
Actor in a Musical: Jim Dale (*Barnum*)

June	July	August	September	October	November
Al Pacino in *Richard III*	Cornelia Otis Skinner d.	Suit over *The Elephant Man*	Patti LuPone in *Evita*	Mickey Rooney revives career in *Sugar Babies*	Ann Reinking injured, Jed Harris d.

December	January	February	March	April	May
Grease passes *Fiddler on the Roof*	Andrew Lloyd Webber meets Cameron Mackintosh	*Talley's Folly*	*Children of a Lesser God*	New York City transit strike closes *Grease*	Lillian Roth d.

Personalities

JUNE 3 The Tony Awards ceremony is poignant for the surprise special award given to the ill and aged Henry Fonda, presented by daughter Jane.

AUGUST 6 Director Harold Prince, in a *People* interview, defends Patti LuPone after *Evita*'s shaky tryout has spurred rumors of her replacement. She's "a fucking gem," Prince says. "It's fun to make a star." LuPone, who says of Evita Peron, in the *New York Daily News* on August 8, "She was a whore. She became a saint." LuPone finds the role "spiritually debilitating." She also tells an interviewer: "I'm lonely. The phone never rings." LuPone

Patty LuPone in *Evita* PF

Plays and Musicals

JUNE 6 Kevin Kline and Roxanne Hart play a couple whose sexual attraction proves insufficient to keep them together in *Loose Ends* (284), Michael Weller's play, opening at the Circle in the Square. **10** Al Pacino is Shakespeare's juiciest villain in *Richard III* (33), at the Cort. *Time* says Pacino "should have sprouted a long, pointy moustache . . . so he could twirl it." *Newsweek* calls him "lowfalutin." And *Variety*, fastening on the star's "salivary yell," dubs the show "Great Expectorations."

SEPTEMBER 6 Sandy Duncan stars in a successful revival of *Peter Pan* (551), opening at the Lunt-Fontanne. George Rose plays Captain Hook. **25** "You're hopeless, I don't know what I'm going to do with you," John Houseman told Patti LuPone, class cut-up at Juilliard, when he suspended her. But tonight, she's Broadway's brightest hope as Eva Peron in *Evita* (1,567), a part that Raquel Welch, Meryl Streep, and Faye Dunaway are all said to have wanted. "Don't Cry for Me, Argentina" is

Business and Society

JUNE • The Shubert Organization computerizes the Royale Theatre box office, the cornerstone of a system that in a year and a half will link all of their houses across the country. **18** Negotiations between Equity and the off-off-Broadway theatres break down. The producers want to pay actors based on their budgets, while Equity wants gross income to be the measuring stick.

OCTOBER • The National Association of Talent Agents loses its antitrust suit against Actors Equity, filed two years ago, in which they alleged that Equity's attempt to limit their commissions was monopolistic. • The National Theatre in Washington, D.C., ends its booking ties to the Kennedy Center. **11** Broadway producers express dismay at *The New York Times*'s reversion to a policy of reviewing previews rather than opening nights. Walter Kerr, the paper's new daily critic, prefers not to race deadlines, and the *Times* also wants to be on the street with a notice when the television stations are offering their reviews. The New York Drama Critics Circle will protest when some producers honor Kerr's request for free preview tickets but do not grant them to other critics.

Births, Deaths, and Marriages

JUNE 4 Producer-director Herman Shumlin d. **6** Jack Haley d.

JULY 9 Cornelia Otis Skinner d.

SEPTEMBER 5 Guy Bolton d. Among the shows he wrote were *Sally*, *Lady Be Good*, *Girl Crazy*, and *Anything Goes*.

OCTOBER 8 Jerry Orbach m. actress Elaine Cancilla, whom he met in the national company of *Chicago*.

NOVEMBER 15 Producer-director Jed Harris d. "Destiny's tot," Noel Coward called him when Harris had four hits on Broadway in the 1927–28 season: *Broadway*, *Coquette*, *The Front Page*, and *The Royal Family*. The character Oscar Jaffe in the Hecht-MacArthur *Twentieth Century* was reportedly modeled after him. George S. Kaufman, with whom he

has ended her seven-year relationship with Kevin Kline. **13** Author Bernard Pomerance and the producers of the Broadway production of *The Elephant Man* sue the producers of the film with the same title, set to begin filming in October. Pomerance and his colleagues say they have added value to the public domain story of John Merrick and therefore have a proprietary right to the title. The moviemakers settle out of court.

SEPTEMBER • Mickey Rooney says of Philadelphia critics who panned *Sugar Babies*: "They think this is a play. It's a show. They don't know the difference." He calls one of them "Wally Patooka." • The direct mail piece soliciting subscriptions for the Ensemble Studio Theatre brags that you can attend "for less per play than it would cost to go to a movie." One of the signers is Vincent Canby, *New York Times* film critic, whose play *End of the War* was recently produced by the company. **1** Walter Kerr replaces Richard Eder as *The New York Times* daily drama critic.

OCTOBER 6 Seventy-six-year-year-old actress Dorothy Stickney, widow of Howard Lindsay, breaks her hip when she's knocked to the street in a Manhattan mugging. **28** Arnold Soboloff, playing Smee, Captain Hook's first mate in *Peter Pan* at the Lunt-Fontanne, finishes a song in Act II, exits to the wings, and then collapses with a fatal heart attack. He is 48.

NOVEMBER • Ann Reinking leaves the cast of *Dancin'* after injuring her knee backstage. The injury-prone "Flying Wallenda," as she calls herself, danced in *A Chorus Line* with a pulled groin muscle and in *Chicago* with a pulled hamstring. She is scheduled to receive a Footwear Council Award this month: "[f]or people who have done fabulous things with their feet." **30** Jessica Tandy and Hume Cronyn are on their way to the U.S.S.R. to perform in *The Gin Game*. Aeroflot, the Soviet Airline, not realizing that they are married, has seated the couple on opposite sides of the plane. But after a surfeit of togetherness, Tandy and Cronyn accept the arrangement. She will later tell a friend, "We both thought it was a good idea."

---

heard on the radio even before the curtain rises on the Andrew Lloyd Webber-Tim Rice musical, at the Broadway Theatre. Mandy Patinkin plays Ché Guevara. Madonna is in the 1996 film.

OCTOBER 8 At the Mark Hellinger, Mickey Rooney and Ann Miller star in *Sugar Babies* (1,208). The music is mostly from the pen of Jimmie McHugh and Dorothy Fields. **22** *One Mo' Time* (1,372), Vernel Bagneris's musical about black entertainer Bertha Williams, is at The Village Gate Downstairs, in Greenwich Village.

NOVEMBER 8 Bernard Slade's *A Romantic Comedy* (396) is at the Barrymore, starring Anthony Perkins and Mia Farrow as a playwright and his collaborator, who take awhile before they notice and play out the personal drama that has developed between them.

DECEMBER 2 *Bent* (240), by Martin Sherman, about homosexuals in Nazi concentration camps, opens at the Apollo. Richard Gere has the lead as a man who first says that he is a Jew, then acknowledges he is a homosexual. Gere's cast replacement will be Michael York. **8** With its 3,243rd performance, a Saturday matinée, *Grease* passes *Fiddler on the Roof* as Broadway's longest-running show. When *Fiddler* set the record, overtaking *Life With Father* on June 17, 1972, *Grease* was 128 performances into its pre-Broadway run at the Eden Theatre. **13** Samm-Art Williams, author of *Home* (82), presented by the Negro Ensemble Company at the St. Marks Playhouse, is also in the cast. A young black man refuses to fight in Vietnam and loses face as well as the wherewithal to support himself, falling into vagrancy and alcoholism.

JANUARY 5 Harold Pinter's *Betrayal* (170) opens at the Trafalgar. It stars Blythe Danner, Raul Julia, and Roy Scheider, who plays the husband in a love triangle. Peter Hall directs this play, which runs chronologically backwards. **14** *Table Settings* (264), James Lapine's satire on Jewish middle-class life in America, in which the action is occasioned by meals, opens off-Broadway, at the Playwright's Horizons, where the author is directing. The cast includes Carolyn Hurlbut and

---

NOVEMBER • Off-off-Broadway theatres have not as a group accepted Equity's demand that actors' pay be pegged to gross income, but individual houses are coming around. **7** Tonight's Broadway opening—*Devour the Snow*—is the first since *The Most Happy Fella* began its run on October 11. Four times as many theatres are dark as active now, as the emphasis shifts to fewer but more costly productions.

JANUARY 14 A fire destroys the Paper Mill Playhouse in Millburn, New Jersey. The house was converted from a 1790 mill in 1938. It will take two years to rebuild the theatre.

FEBRUARY • Actors Equity moves into its own building on West Forty-sixth Street.

MARCH • The Nederlanders and the Shubert Organization are in a struggle to control booking at the National Theatre in Washington, D.C., now that the Kennedy Center is out of the picture.

APRIL • Kennedy Center Chairperson Roger L. Stevens characterizes the suit against the Center by the National Theatre in Washington, D.C., over disputed funds related to the Center's management of booking at the National as a "double-cross." • The League of New York

---

feuded, bad-mouthed another producer by saying, "He's Jed Harris rolled into one."

DECEMBER 4 Liza Minnelli m. stage manager Mark Gero. **30** Richard Rodgers d.

JANUARY 28 Jimmy Durante d.

APRIL 10 Kay Medford d.

MAY 12 Lillian Roth d.

Personalities

DECEMBER • Fifteen cast members of *Annie* are being replaced in the two-year-old show to "refresh" it. Among the outplaced is 14-year-old Sarah Jessica Parker, told that she has outgrown the title role. *Variety* describes the sweep as "highly unorthodox on Broadway," and Equity says it will deal with it in its next contract.

JANUARY • Andrew Lloyd Webber, who has never met producer Cameron Mackintosh, invites him to lunch. "I thought he was going to be this 62-year-old wizened Scot," Lloyd Webber will recall. **9** Richard Rodgers's will, filed today, forbids his widow to allow anyone to alter or add to the lyrics of his songs. **24–25** Mary McCarthy, on Dick Cavett's TV show, calls Lillian Hellman "terribly overrated, a bad writer and dishonest writer." When asked to elaborate on "dishonest," McCarthy says that "every word she writes is a lie, including 'and' and 'the.'" In February, Hellman will sue for defamation of character, a legal action that will be pending at the playwright's death in 1984.

FEBRUARY 20 With *Talley's Folly* opening at the Brooks Atkinson, playwright Lanford Wilson is in a nearby bar. "The play was in very good shape," he will later recall, "but I wasn't." **24** The "Calendar" section of the *Los Angeles Times* has an angry letter from Neil Simon, lacing into the paper's critic Dan Sullivan, who has been lecturing Simon in print on how *I Ought To Be In Pictures*, in tryouts at the Mark Taper Forum, might be improved. "Gosh, how lucky to have Dan Sullivan as a mentor," Simon observes.

APRIL 3 Seventy-one-year-old Joshua Logan is hospitalized for injuries sustained when he falls into the orchestra pit at the Wilshire Ebell Theatre, in Los Angeles, while performing at the Writers Guild awards ceremonies. **18** Playwright Lanford Wilson, who is having root canal work done this week, wins the Pulitzer Prize.

MAY • Anna Strasberg, widow of Lee Strasberg, resigns from the Actors Studio in a dispute with artistic director Ellen

Plays and Musicals

Mark Blum. **31** Edward Albee's *The Lady from Dubuque* (12) opens at the Morosco. Irene Worth stars briefly, with Tony Musante and Frances Conroy, in a drama of a woman dying of cancer. Walter Kerr, in the *Times*, says that Albee "is still working in an ornately 'literary' style that has no conversational feel to it."

FEBRUARY 20 Lanford Wilson's *Talley's Folly* (277), a prequel to his *Fifth of July*, produced at the Circle Rep in May, moves to Broadway, at the Brooks Atkinson Theatre. Judd Hirsch and Trish Hawkins play the couple, who overcome her family's objection to his being a Jew and her fear that infertility makes her undesirable as a mate.

MARCH 30 Mark Medoff's *Children of a Lesser God* (887), directed by Gordon Davidson, in which a teacher of deaf people marries one of his pupils, opens at the Longacre Theatre. John Rubinstein is the teacher who wants his wife, played by Phyllis Frelich—who actually is deaf—to speak. Frelich is a member of the National Theatre of the Deaf.

APRIL 10 David Rounds gives a Tony Award-winning performance in Paul Osborn's domestic comedy *Mornings at Seven* (564), revived at the Lyceum. The 1939–1940 play, which originally starred Lillian Gish, now features Elizabeth

Jim Dale as P.T. Barnum *PF*

Business and Society

Theatres and Producers warns its members to stop advertising Tony nominations as if they were actual awards. **1** New York is hit by an 11-day transit strike that will prematurely end the 3,388-performance run of *Grease* on April 11.

MAY • In retaliation for the Nederlanders' attempts to block them from booking the National Theatre in Washington, D.C., the Shubert Organization denies house seats in its theatres, a common courtesy, to the rival group. **7** Both playwrights and members of Actors Equity are protesting the union's insistence that authors of off-off-Broadway showcase productions guarantee work in them for the casts if they are staged again at a future date.

Births, Deaths, and Marriages

Burstyn over what to do with money raised by a benefit in honor of her husband. Strasberg and the Studio are also clashing over ownership of 1,000 audio tapes of Lee Strasberg's coaching sessions. • Mike Nichol's pneumonia cuts short the run of *Who's Afraid of Virginia Woolf?* at the Long Wharf in New Haven. The production, running since March, also starred Elaine May, Swoosie Kurtz, and James Naughton.

Wilson, Nancy Marchand, Teresa Wright, Maureen O'Sullivan, and Gary Merrill. **30** The emphasis is on action and movement in the Cy Coleman-Michael Stewart musical *Barnum* (854), opening at the St. James. Jim Dale plays the title role, and Glenn Close plays his wife in this circus of a show. **30** Neil Simon's play about a screenwriter and his estranged daughter, *I Ought to Be in Pictures* (324), opens at the Eugene O'Neill. In the cast are Ron Leibman, who stepped in for Tony Curtis during the Los Angeles tryouts, Joyce Van Patten, and Dinah Manoff.

MAY 1 *A Day in Hollywood and a Night in the Ukraine* (588), a musical comedy in two parts, which includes a parody of the Marx Brothers, opens at the John Golden Theatre. It features Tommy Tune's choreography and the music of Frank Lazarus, who is also in the cast.

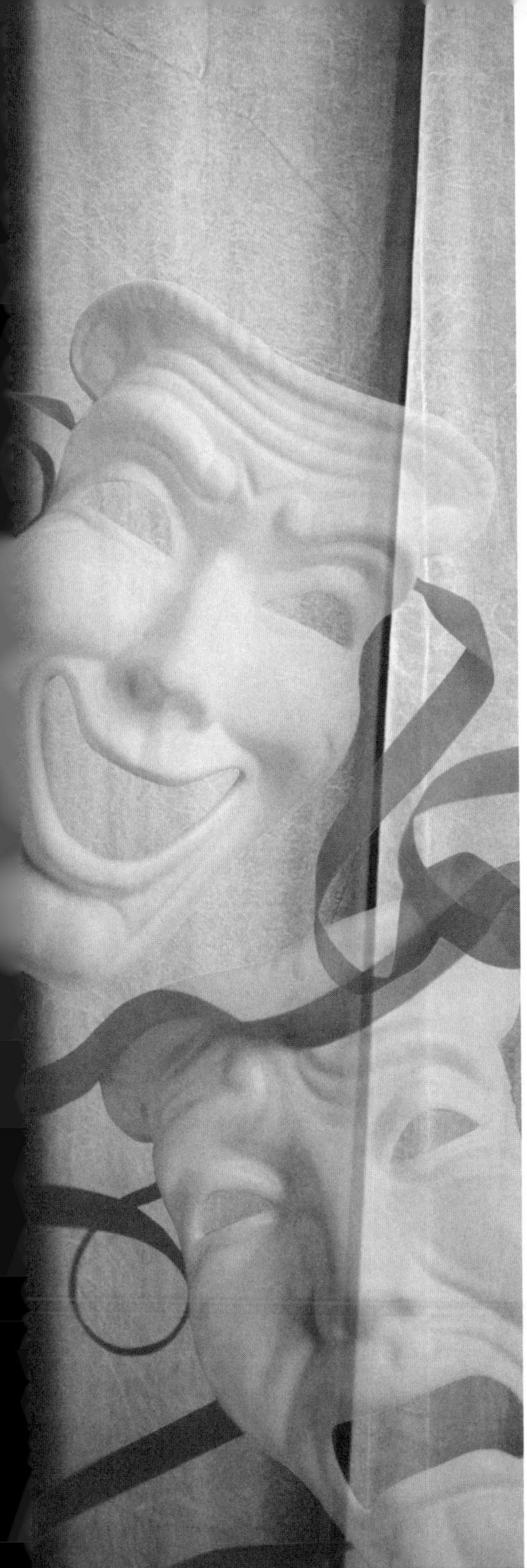

1980–81

Gower Champion goes out, dramatically, with *42nd Street.* Maureen Stapleton, costarring in a revival of *The Little Foxes*, is acting in the shadow of a very big movie star, Elizabeth Taylor, but thanks to playwright Peter Shaffer, after two hundred years in Mozart's shadow, Salieri is finally noticed in *Amadeus*. Broadway producers, so unhappy with *New York Times* critic Richard Eder, now face Frank Rich. Beth Henley makes a big splash, Sam Shepard will not wish Joseph Papp a Merry Christmas, Lauren Bacall is not Rex Reed's *Woman of the Year*, Patti LuPone complains of being stereotyped as a "blonde fascist," Mae West is dead, and George Jessel, "Toastmaster General of the United States," will speak no more.

- What Gower Champion had next on his schedule when he dies the day *42nd Street* opens: *Sayonara*, a musical
- Amount for which Elizabeth Taylor is insured in *The Little Foxes* through Lloyds of London: $27,000 per performance, with a 3-performance deductible
- Number of performances missed by Elizabeth Taylor in *The Little Foxes*: 16 of 49
- What composer Andrew Lloyd Webber says to director Trevor Nunn after playing for him a tape of songs set to T.S. Eliot's *Old Possum's Book of Practical Cats*: "Do you think there's any way in which you could turn this into a musical?"
- Percentage of Broadway audiences that are African-American: about 10 percent, according to the League of New York Theatres and Producers
- Divorced yet again: Alan Jay Lerner, from Nina Bushkin
- What James Nederlander says about the Shuberts: "I'm in business to make a profit." For them [Gerald Schoenfeld and Bernard Jacobs, who run the empire] it's all ego."
- Never reaches the starting gate: Even with a score by Jule Styne (*Funny Girl*) and a book by Herb Gardner (*A Thousand Clowns*), *One Night Stand*, a musical about a composer who kills himself, never gets to the point where critics can have a field day with the title because it closes during previews
- Number of Gilbert and Sullivan operas that have succeeded on Broadway: 1, this season's *The Pirates of Penzance*, which is also the only one of their shows to have premiered in New York (December 31, 1879) rather than in London
- Artists who have drawn the 1,000 caricatures on the wall of Sardi's, the famed Broadway theatre district restaurant: Alex Gard (first 500), Don Bevan (next 400), and Richard Baritz (the most recent 100)
- Percentage of audiences drawn from foreign tourists, according to a survey by the League of New York Theatres and Producers: 11 percent

Productions on Broadway: 67

Pulitzer Prize for Drama: *Crimes of the Heart* (Beth Henley)

New York Drama Critics Circle Awards:
Best Play: *A Lesson from Aloes* (Athol Fugard)
Best American Play; *Crimes of the Heart* (Beth Henley)

Tony Awards:
Play: *Amadeus* (Peter Shaffer)
Actor in a play: Ian McKellen (*Amadeus*)
Actress in a play: Jane Lapotaire (*Piaf*)
Musical: *42nd Street* (Harry Warren-Al Dubin)
Actor in a musical: Kevin Kline (*The Pirates of Penzance*)
Actress in a musical: Lauren Bacall (*Woman of the Year*)

June	July	August	September	October	November
Sardi's unveils 1,000th caricature	Burton back in *Camelot*	Gower Champion d. as *42nd Street* opens	Frank Rich new *Times* critic	Playwrights sue Actors Equity	Christopher Reeve and Swoosie Kurtz feuding

December	January	February	March	April	May
Amadeus and *Crimes of the Heart*	*The Pirates of Penzance*; Patti LuPone leaves *Evita*	Albee's *Lolita* "dumb, boring and gross" (*Variety*)	Lauren Bacall in *Woman of the Year*	Lauren Bacall-Rex Reed feud	Elizabeth Taylor in *The Little Foxes*

Personalities

JUNE 1 Sardi's unveils its 1,000th caricature—of American Theatre Wing president Isabelle Stevenson.

JULY 10 The Molly Picon Room is dedicated at the Second Avenue Deli in the old Yiddish theatre district. **17** Richard Burton becomes ill, with a bad reaction to medication he's taking for bursitis, during a performance of *Camelot*, and his understudy William Parry takes over.

AUGUST 25 Wanda Richert, who plays the chorus girl who makes it big in *42nd Street*, opening tonight, has also been director Gower Champion's lover. She learns of his death from producer David Merrick's curtain announcement. At the opening night party at the Waldorf, she organizes a tribute to Champion, having the dancers in the room do an impromptu performance of "One" from *A Chorus Line*.

SEPTEMBER • Patti LuPone extends her *Evita* contract after a year in the musical because she's not getting other offers. She's been stereotyped: "They think I'm blonde and much older, so unless they need a blond fascist dictator, I won't get a call." • Frank Rich is appointed chief drama critic of *The New York Times*.

OCTOBER 20 "Stars' Friend Rescues '42St.'" the *Times* headline will read tomorrow.

Gower Champion's swan song—another hit for David Merrick *PB*

Plays and Musicals

JUNE 8 *FOB* (42), David Henry Hwang's play set in a California Chinese restaurant, opens at the Public Theatre. It has a cast of six, headed by John Lone.

JULY 8 Two decades after he first played King Arthur, Richard Burton opens in a revival of *Camelot* (56), at the New York State Theatre in Lincoln Center. Christine Ebersole is Guinevere in this production. In the chorus is Davis Gaines, a future star of *Phantom of the Opera*.

AUGUST 25 At the final curtain of the opening of *42nd Street* (3,486) at the Winter Garden tonight, producer David Merrick announces that director Gower Champion died this afternoon. The musical, starring Jerry Orbach and Tammy Grimes, repeats the plot and music of the 1933 film. With a top ticket price of $30, this show breaks new ground.

OCTOBER 8 *Division Street* (21), by Steve Tesich, opens at the Ambassador. It's a wild comedy about the denizens of a Chicago apartment house, with John Lithgow and Christine Lahti.

NOVEMBER 5 Lanford Wilson's *Fifth of July* (511), a success off-Broadway, in a Circle Rep production in 1978 as *The 5th of July*, opens at the New Apollo Theatre. It stars Christopher Reeve, Swoosie Kurtz, and Amy Wright. **12** *Lunch Hour* (262), Jean Kerr's comedy about wife-swapping in the Hamptons, directed by Mike Nichols and starring Sam Waterston and Gilda Radner, opens at the Barrymore. **17** Athol Fugard's *A Lesson From Aloes* (96), directed by the playwright, is at the Playhouse. Harris Yulin, Maria Tucci, and James Earl Jones are the cast of this play about racism in South Africa.

DECEMBER 17 *Amadeus* (1,181), by Peter Shaffer, opens at the Broadhurst. Ian McKellen is Salieri and Tim Curry Mozart, with Jane Seymour as his wife.

Business and Society

JUNE 11 A Federal Court rejects the Nederlanders' challenge to the Shubert Organization plan to book the National Theatre, in Washington, D.C. The Nederlanders said that it was monopolistic, violating the Shubert's consent decree of 1956.

JULY 7 The new contract between Actors Equity and the League of New York Theatres and Producers raises the Broadway minimum to $475 a week. Later in the month, Equity members will vote down an increase in their dues, now $21, to $200 a year on a sliding scale. There's been no increase in seven years.

AUGUST 18 Actors Equity drops its executive secretary Donald Grody, a respected labor leader in the entertainment industry. The union is not happy with his managerial abilities and is now in a funds crisis.

SEPTEMBER 29 Ticket brokers refuse David Merrick's demand that they accept tickets to *42nd Street* without return privileges.

OCTOBER 27 A group of playwrights, including David Mamet, file an antitrust

Births, Deaths, and Marriages

JUNE 15 Mandy Patinkin m. actress Kathryn Grody.

JUNE 22 Luci Arnaz m. Laurence Luckinbill in an upstate New York apple orchard. Swoosie Kurtz catches the bridal bouquet.

JULY 21 Sandy Duncan, now appearing in *Peter Pan*, m. Don Correia, who's in *A Chorus Line*. **26** Kenneth Tynan d.

AUGUST 9 Elliott Nugent d. **25** Gower Champion d.

SEPTEMBER 5 Barbara Loden, winner of a Tony for *After the Fall* and wife of Elia Kazan, d. **9** Harold Clurman d. **22** Vaudeville comedian and Broadway revue star Lou Holtz d.

NOVEMBER 16 Set designer Boris Aronson d. **22** Mae West d. **27** Playwright Harold Pinter m. author Lady Antonia Fraser.

Wanda Richert is ill and can't go on, and her understudy Nancy Sinclair has quit. So Wichert's roommate, Karen Prunczik, after an emergency rehearsal, takes the part of the ingenue who becomes an overnight star.

NOVEMBER 5 Christopher Reeve and Swoosie Kurtz are starring in *Fifth of July*, opening tonight, and each thinks the other is engaged in upstaging. Kurtz, whose performance earns her a Drama Desk and Outer Critics Circle Award and a caricature of herself on the wall at Sardi's, will later say that although the play's language was tempered somewhat, she was still "able to keep a couple of fucks."

DECEMBER • Gary Sinese, a founder of the Steppenwolf Theatre Company in Chicago, is named its artistic director. **11** John Barrymore's ashes are moved from California to the Barrymore family plot in Mt. Vernon, New York. **23** Sam Shepard is feuding with Joseph Papp, who has pushed out director Robert Woodruff from the Public Theatre's production of *True West*, opening tonight. Papp accused Woodruff of "indecisiveness" and is directing himself now. "He'll never see another play of mine," Shepard says of Papp. "His judgements are out to lunch."

JANUARY 1 Patti LuPone leaves *Evita*, beginning a period of several years in which she does not land major Broadway roles. **3** Julie Harris's undisclosed illness closes the comedy *Mixed Couples* after only nine performances, at the Brooks Atkinson. Geraldine Page and Rip Torn were also in this play by James Prideaux.

FEBRUARY • Jerry Lewis agrees to an out-of-court settlement with producer Alexander Cohen over Lewis's refusal to rehearse in the 1976–1977 *Hellzapoppin*. Lewis has been in bankruptcy proceedings. **23** *Heartland*, opening at the Century Theatre, is around only briefly but not so the 20-year-old actor playing a deranged, homicidal teenager in it: Sean Penn.

MARCH • Richard Burton brings his very successful tour in *Camelot* to a close when he's hospitalized for back problems.

The *Times*'s Frank Rich reviews—favorably—a preview, rather than opening night, without informing the producers beforehand. They are not happy, but his praise tempers their anger. The 1984 film stars F. Murray Abraham and Tom Hulce. **21** Beth Henley's *Crimes of the Heart* (35), in which three sisters hold a reunion, opens at the Manhattan Theatre Club. *Variety* calls it "a zany delight that stamps its author as a new playwright of considerable talent." In the cast are Mary Beth Hurt, Mia Dillon, Lizabeth MacKay, Julie Nesbitt, Steven Burleigh, and Peter MacNicol. A screen version is released in 1986. **23** Sam Shepard's *True West* (24) opens at the Public Theatre, with Tommy Lee Jones and Peter Boyle playing brothers.

Broadway shows at the beginning of the 1980s range from *Annie* to *Oh! Calcutta!*
LYNCH

suit against Actors Equity over the union's demand that authors of off-off-Broadway showcase presentations guarantee work for the cast in future productions of the work.

NOVEMBER • David Merrick pioneers a new plateau when he pegs the top ticket price for *Forty-second Street*: $50. **23** *The New York Times*, investigating the continued problem of ticket scalping and box office rake-offs of illegal premiums on tickets, reports that random calls to many ticket agencies produced only three that would quote legitimate prices on the phone. Thirty-dollar tickets for *Evita* are going for as high as $85.

DECEMBER 18 Francis Fuller d. **21** Playwright Marc Connelly d. **28** Sam Levene d.

FEBRUARY 14 Gregory Hines m. producer Pamela Koslow. **22** Joe Smith, of the vaudeville team of Smith and Dale, d. at the age of 97. Charlie Dale d. in 1971.

MARCH 5 Lyricist E.Y. "Yip" Harburg d.

MAY 4 Playwright Paul Green d. **18** William Saroyan d. **24** George Jessel d.

Personalities

APRIL • Rex Reed, who writes for the *New York Daily News* and lives in the Dakota, the fabled Upper West Side building also home to Lauren Bacall, says of his neighbor in *Woman of the Year*: "She can hardly carry a tune." She has criticized him for being indiscreet in writing about her and other Dakota residents when their neighbor John Lennon was killed at the building in December.

MAY 7 Elizabeth Taylor receives a standing ovation when she enters Sardi's tonight after the opening of *The Little Foxes*. She's wearing a white Halston gown with plunging neckline. Halston was in the audience, as was Andy Warhol, in the first row, and super agent Swifty Lazar was in the balcony with Lee Radziwill. Liza Minnelli and Joan Fontaine were also there. **11** Andrew Lloyd Webber's *Cats* opens in London. Advance ticket sales had been slow until Elaine Paige replaced Judi Dench, who had broken an ankle. The reviews are only so-so. **15** The performance of the revival of *The Little Foxes* is canceled tonight after Elizabeth Taylor was hospitalized this evening with a torn ligament in her rib cage, caused by a coughing fit. She will miss 11 performances, for which the producers will collect $216,000 in insurance money.

Kevin Kline and Linda Ronstadt are in *The Pirates of Penzance* PB

Plays and Musicals

JANUARY 8 "The best things in life don't have to be free," writes Frank Rich in the *Times* about Gilbert and Sullivan's *The Pirates of Penzance* (772), warmly received last summer, at the Delacorte Theatre in Central Park. Starring at the Uris, on Broadway, are Linda Ronstadt, Kevin Kline, George Rose, and Estelle Parsons.

FEBRUARY 4 "Edward Albee's new play *Lolita*, currently in tryouts at Boston's Wilbur Theatre is dumb, boring and gross," opines *Variety*. The cast features Donald Sutherland, Ian Richardson, and Blanche Baker. It will flop quickly on Broadway. **5** Jane Lapotaire has the title role in Pam Gems' play *Piaf* (165), opening at the Plymouth.

MARCH 1 *Sophisticated Ladies* (767), a musical in the form of a night club show, based on the work of Duke Ellington, opens at the Lunt-Fontanne. Duke's son Mercer is conducting his orchestra, and in the cast are Gregory Hines, Judith Jamison, and Hinton Battle. **29** Lauren Bacall stars in *Woman of the Year* (770), based on the 1942 film that first paired Katharine Hepburn with Spencer Tracy. Harry Guardino costars in this John Kander-Fred Ebb musical, at the Palace.

MAY 7 Maureen Stapleton, Anthony Zerbe, and Ann Tallman are in the cast of the revival of Lillian Hellman's *The Little Foxes* (126), at the Martin Beck. But the main attraction is the Broadway debut of Elizabeth Taylor, playing the Tallulah Bankhead-Bette Davis role of Regina Giddens, "and she may just knock you out of your seat," writes Frank Rich. **18** Caryl Churchill's *Cloud 9* (440), a gender-bending, race-reversing play directed by Tommy Tune, opens at the Theatre De Lys. The cast includes Don Amendolia and Concetta Tomei. **20** William Finn's musical *March of the Falsettos* (268) opens at the Playwrights Horizons. Stephen Bogardus is in this play in which a father takes a gay lover. Songs include "Four Jews in a Room Bitching."

Business and Society

FEBRUARY • An Actors Equity referendum approves a dues increase in the form of a two percent assessment on actors who are working. • A joint New York City-New York State study proposes a detailed redevelopment plan for converting the movie houses on Forty-second Street back into legitimate theatres.

APRIL • The Nederlanders buy a 50 percent interest in the Forty-sixth Street Theatre, making it 10 houses in their mini-empire on Broadway. **9** An understudy in *Woman of the Year* is slightly injured when grazed by a piece of concrete tossed down at him while he walks in an alley next to the Palace Theatre. Similar incidents have occurred in the theatre district over the past year.

Births, Deaths, and Marriages

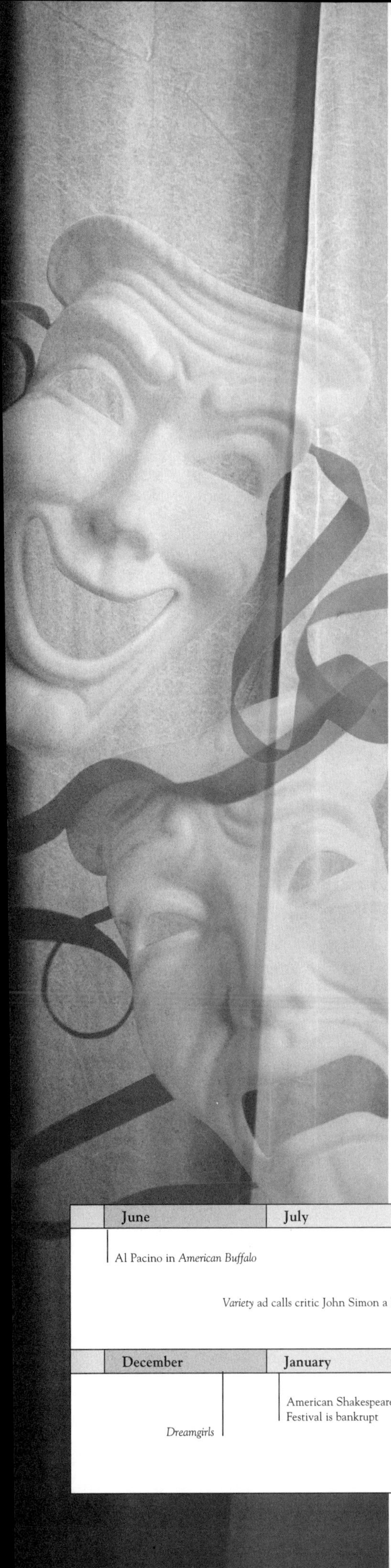

1981–82

The Adventures of Nicholas Nickleby is a phenomenon, so much so that the producers of *Crimes of the Heart*, concerned that it will overwhelm all other Tony contenders, argue that it ought to be in a separate award category. Nederlander arguments notwithstanding, the court-imposed restraints on the Shubert empire are lifted, just as several Broadway theatres disappear. Joseph Papp, who clashed with Sam Shepard last year, is now on the outs with playwright David Rabe. Lee Strasberg is dead. Show investor Claus von Bulow is accused of behaving like an angel of death. *Variety*, reviewing Matthew Broderick's debut, in *Torch Song Trilogy*, says the youngster "has a distinctive presence that augurs a bright future." And Savoyards far from Albion are sad to hear this news: with a final performance of *Pinafore*, the D'Oyly Carte Company is no more.

- Only actor to appear in 3 Pulitzer Prize-winning plays: Glenn Anders, (who dies October 26, 1981)—*Hell-Bent for Heaven, They Knew What They Wanted*, and *Strange Interlude*
- Only mother-father-daughter Tony winners: Tammy Grimes, *The Unsinkable Molly Brown* and *Private Lives*; Christopher Plummer, *Cyrano*; and Amanda Plummer, best featured actress in a play this season in *Agnes of God*
- Running time of *Nicholas Nickleby*: 8 1/2 hours
- Number of speaking parts in *Nicholas Nickleby*: 138
- Number of actors in *Nicholas Nickleby*: 42
- Number of understudies in *Nicholas Nickleby*: 3
- Number of times per week both parts of *Nicholas Nickleby* are presented on one day: 3 (Wednesday, Saturday, and Sunday)
- Length of dinner break between parts of *Nicholas Nickleby*: 55 minutes
- Long-running Broadway musicals (an increasingly evident trend) that are causing a theatre shortage: *A Chorus Line, Dancin', Ain't Misbehavin', The Best Little Whorehouse in Texas, They're Playing Our Song*, and *Annie*
- What *Deathtrap* author Ira Levin drinks to toast his play's surpassing the run of *Arsenic and Old Lace*: elderberry wine, the drink of choice in that earlier comedy-thriller
- Putting money into Broadway: Paramount Pictures, through Paramount Theatre Productions, is investing in *Agnes of God, Nine*, and other shows
- Theatres recently renamed for their owners or their owners' relatives: Virginia (formerly the ANTA, and before that, the Guild), Nederlander (the National, then the Billy Rose, then the Trafalgar), Lucille Lortel (Theatre De Lys)
- Number of Broadway theatres named for playwrights: 2—the Eugene O'Neill and the Belasco
- Number of Broadway theatres named for composers: 0

Productions on Broadway: 53

Pulitzer Prize for Drama: *A Soldier's Play* (Charles Fuller)

New York Drama Critics Circle Awards:
Best Play: *The Life and Adventures of Nicholas Nickleby* (David Edgar)
Best American Play: *A Soldier's Play* (Charles Fuller)

Tony Awards:
Best Play: *The Life and Adventures of Nicholas Nickleby* (David Edgar)
Actress in a play: Zoe Caldwell (*Medea*)
Actor in a play: Roger Rees (*Nicholas Nickleby*)
Best Musical: *Nine* (Maury Yeston)
Actor in a musical: Ben Harney (*Dreamgirls*)
Actress in a musical: Jennifer Holliday (*Dreamgirls*)

June	July	August	September	October	November
Al Pacino in *American Buffalo*	*Variety* ad calls critic John Simon a bigot	Jujamcyn doubles Broadway holdings	Court lifts restraints on Shuberts	*The Adventures of Nicholas Nickleby*	Lotte Lenya d.

December	January	February	March	April	May
Dreamgirls	American Shakespeare Festival is bankrupt	Lee Strasberg d.	Papp and 200 others arrested at theatre demolition	Nederlanders to redevelop Forty-second Street theatres	Ellen Burstyn first female president of Equity

Personalities

JUNE • Edward Albee, still smarting over the failure of *Lolita*, says as he presents an award to a children's theatre company, "I tend to confuse children's theatre and Broadway, as I did the Theatre of the Absurd and Broadway. I thought it was the same thing." **18** The off-off Broadway double bill of Laurence Holder's *When the Chickens Come Home to Roost* and *Zora Neal Thurston*, a one-woman show, opening tonight at the New Federal Theatre, contains glimmers of future stars. The first play, about Malcolm X, stars young Denzel Washington—seen in it by the equally unknown Spike Lee. In the second is Phylicia Ayers—later Phylicia Rashad.

JULY 15 "Von Bulow, B'Way Angel, Accused of Attempting to Murder His Wife" is *Variety*'s headline about Claus Von Bulow, a major investor in *Deathtrap* and *Wings*, which was about a woman who had a stroke. **29** An ad in *Variety* accuses critic John Simon's reviews of being "racist, anti-[S]emitic, misogynist, vicious, and derisive." Offered as evidence are several quotes, including excerpts from a review of *Richard III*, in which Simon wrote of an actress that she "should never be cast as anything but an itinerant gefilte fish with a nervous condition." None of the approximately 300 signers are prominent. The ad states that many signers preferred to remain anonymous.

AUGUST 13 When *Deathtrap*, with its 1,445th performance tonight, becomes Broadway's longest-running comedy-thriller, surpassing *Arsenic and Old Lace*,

The Ritz Theatre, now a Jujamcyn house LYNCH

Plays and Musicals

JUNE 3 Al Pacino stars in a revival of David Mamet's *American Buffalo* (262), at the downtown Circle in the Square. The *Daily News* says that he is "simply marvelous."

JULY 16 David Henry Hwang's *The Dance and the Railroad* (181), with music and choreography by John Lone, opens at the Public Theatre. Lone and Tzi Ma are the cast in this evocation of the life of the Chinese who worked on the Transcontinental Railroad.

SEPTEMBER • *Greater Tuna*, Jason Williams and Joe Sears's satire on the "third

Business and Society

JUNE • Actors Equity chooses labor lawyer Alan D. Eisenberg as its new executive secretary.

AUGUST • Actors Equity sells the building in which it is headquartered and leases space. Its membership balked at a dues increase soon after the union bought the property. • The Jujamcyn Theatre Corporation doubles its Broadway holdings by taking over the ANTA and Ritz Theatres. They also control the Martin Beck and the St. James. The ANTA becomes the Virginia, after Jujamcyn founder William McKnight's daughter.

SEPTEMBER 4 A federal court judge rules that the 1956 consent decree limiting the expansion of the Shubert theatre holdings be partially lifted now and that it expire completely on January 1, 1985. The Nederlanders, Shubert rivals, had argued against such a move.

OCTOBER • A Federal Court rules that the authors of *A Day in Hollywood & A Night in the Ukraine* are guilty of "unauthorized appropriation" of the image and persona of the Marx Brothers, whose heirs are entitled to monetary damages.

Births, Deaths, and Marriages

JULY 1 George Voskovec d.

AUGUST 1 Paddy Chayefsky d. **4** Melvyn Douglas d. **13** Alan Jay Lerner m. actress Liz Robertson. **18** Anita Loos d.

OCTOBER 2 John Raitt m. Rosemary Yorba Lokey. They had been engaged in 1940, but their families disapproved, and they each went on to m. others.

NOVEMBER 27 Lotte Lenya d.

JANUARY 23 Producer Leonard Sillman, who put on the *New Faces* revues from 1934 to 1968, d.

FEBRUARY 17 Lee Strasberg d.

author Ira Levin toasts the accomplishment with a glass of elderberry wine, the libation used to such good effect in *Arsenic and Old Lace*.

OCTOBER 7 The day after he opened in Boston in Bill Davis's *Mass Appeal*, Eric Roberts quits, supposedly because of "artistic disagreement" with director Geraldine Fitzgerald. Roberts was in a serious auto accident last summer.

DECEMBER • Harold Prince swears off Broadway previews and will stick to tryouts after his problems with *Merrily We Roll Along*. Working out the kinks on the Sondheim show in New York made for rumors and a bad press. Prince thinks that after it opened, audiences came with the idea that they would see a show in trouble.

FEBRUARY 14 The Actors Fund, a hundred years old, celebrates with a spectacular benefit at the Radio City Music Hall called "Night of 100 Stars." Staged by ABC, which tapes it for broadcast, the show offers up most of the Broadway galaxy, including Lauren Bacall, Carol Channing, Alfred Drake, Helen Hayes, Ethel Merman, Liza Minnelli, Jason Robards, Jr., Maureen Stapleton, and Lee Strasberg.

MARCH • Lee Remick, by "mutual consent" with the producers, withdraws from *Agnes of God*, in tryouts at Boston's Wilbur Theatre. Elizabeth Ashley will step into the role of the psychiatrist. • Eli Wallach takes over temporarily as director of the Actors Studio following the death of Lee Strasberg. **22** Demolition of the Morosco and Helen Hayes Theatres begins (the Bijou has already come down) to make way for a hotel, resulting in the formation of Save the Theatre, Inc. A demonstration led by Joseph Papp against the bulldozers brings his arrest and that of 200 others, including Richard Gere, Tammy Grimes, Estelle Parsons, Susan Sarandon, and Treat Williams.

APRIL • Katharine Hepburn, appearing in *West Side Waltz* at Boston's Shubert Theatre, stops the show in the first scene to berate as "outrageous" someone who has taken a flash picture from the audi-

---

smallest town" in Texas, opens at the Trans/Act Theatre in Austin, Texas, with the authors as the cast.

OCTOBER 4 The Royal Shakespeare Company's *The Adventures of Nicholas Nickleby* (49), a rare joint Shubert-Nederlander production, directed by Trevor Nunn, comes to the Plymouth in two parts, with a cast of 42, 138 speaking parts, a total running time of 8 1/2 hours, and a total ticket price of $100. Roger Rees has the title role. It is "one of the rare theatre experiences of our time," says the *Wall Street Journal*. **21** Christopher Durang's *Sister Mary Ignatius Explains It All to You* (947), about a nun whose pupils despise her, opens at the Playwrights Horizons. Elizabeth Franz has the title role. Clive Barnes, in the *New York Post*, writes that "Durang takes irreverence to the point of saintliness—he not only makes a profession of it, he turns it into a religion." It's on a double bill with the author's *The Actor's Nightmare*.

NOVEMBER 4 Already the winner of a Pulitzer Prize, Beth Henley's *Crimes of the Heart* (535), which played at the Manhattan Theatre Club last year, opens at the John Golden, with the original cast. **11** Ronald Harwood's *The Dresser* (200) opens at the Brooks Atkinson. Tom Courtenay, who also stars in the 1983 film, plays the title character, who has to get an aging actor, portrayed by Paul Rogers, through an evening's performance. **16** The Stephen Sondheim-George Furth musical *Merrily We Roll Along* (16), based on the Kaufman and Hart play and directed by Harold Prince, is at the Alvin. It's "a dud," says the *Daily News*; it's "a shambles," says the *Times*. Liz Callaway and Jason Alexander, in his Broadway debut, are in the cast. **20** The Negro Ensemble Company presents *A Soldier's Play*, by Charles Fuller, about a World War II training camp murder, at the Theatre Four. The cast, directed by Douglas Turner Ward, includes Denzel Washington, Adolph Caesar, and Samuel L. Jackson. The film version, *A Soldier's Story*, appears in 1984.

DECEMBER 20 *Dreamgirls* (1,522), a musical by Henry Krieger and Tom Eyen, at the Imperial, is based on the Motown

---

NOVEMBER 4 A consent agreement settles the suit brought by playwrights against Actors Equity a year ago. The writers will not be held responsible for employing actors in future productions of works that are given showcase productions, although producers of such shows will still have that liability.

JANUARY • The American Shakespeare Festival in Stratford, Connecticut, with a deficit of $2,340,000, files for bankruptcy. • Irwin Meyer and Stephen Friedman, among the producers of *Annie* and coowners of the Forty-sixth Street Theatre with the Nederlanders, draw six-month prison terms for a tax shelter scam that over the years cheated, among others, Elvis Presley. **27** *Variety* notes that ads for Broadway shows are pushing "front, mid and rear mezzanine" seats in what used to be called the "front balcony." The latter seems to have disappeared.

FEBRUARY 3 "B'way Season Looms As Worst In Years: Hit Shows Scarce, Attendance Down" is *Variety*'s gloomy headline. **27** The D'Oyly Carte Company drops its last curtain. This most famous interpreter of the works of Gilbert and Sullivan has been down at the heels for years.

MARCH 15 James Earl Jones m. actress Cecilia Hart.

APRIL 3 Composer Carol Bayer Sager m. Burt Bacharach.

Personalities

ence. Critic Kevin Kelly, in the *Boston Globe*, will criticize Hepburn's stepping out of character as a "lack of professionalism." • Richard Sinnott, the last of Boston's censors, has applied for disability payments because his nerves were jangled by the rock concerts he had to monitor. Lenny Bruce once referred to him as "Sin Not."

MAY • Ellen Burstyn is the first woman elected president of Actors Equity. **7** David Rabe disowns the production of his play *Goose and Tomtom* that opened at the Public Theatre last night. He says that producer Joseph Papp should have known that the playwright did not like it in its present state—nor do the critics—and it should never have officially opened. He and Papp, who has produced his previous plays, are now estranged.

Plays and Musicals

sound and the story of the Supremes. It stars Jennifer Holliday, Ben Harney, Sheryl Lee Ralph, and Loretta Divine.

JANUARY 15 Harvey Fierstein stars in his *Torch Song Trilogy* (117), the story of a drag performer, opening at the Actors Playhouse. Making his New York stage debut in this production is Matthew Broderick, who, says *Variety*, "has a distinctive presence that augurs a bright future." **15** The first of many editions of *Forbidden Broadway* (982) opens at Palsson's, a cabaret. This satiric review about Main Stem productions is written by Gerard Alessandri, who is also in the cast. **27** Andrew Lloyd Webber and Tim Rice's *Joseph and the Amazing Technicolor Dreamcoat*, which opened at the Entermedia Theatre, off-Broadway, transfers to the Royale (824). The cast includes Bill Hutton, David Ardeo, and Laurie Beechman, as the narrator.

FEBRUARY 3 James Earl Jones is the Moor in *Othello* (123), with Christopher Plummer as Iago, Diane Wiest as Desdemona, and Kelsey Grammer playing Cassio, at the Winter Garden. **4** *Pump Boys and Dinettes* (573), a country music revue served up by the boys who give you gas and the diner waitresses who, hopefully, don't, opens at the Princess Theatre after an off-Broadway run. Jim Wann, in the cast, wrote 12 of the show's 19 songs. **18** At the Martin Beck, Cher and director Robert Altman make their Broadway debuts in *Come Back to the 5 & Dime, Jimmy Dean, Jimmy Dean* (52), a play by Ed Graczyk, about a reunion of the actor's fan club. Also in the cast are Sandy Dennis, Kathy Bates, Karen Black, and Sudi Bond. Altman and most of the cast bring it to the screen later this year. **24** A family and its WASP culture reveals itself in a series of vignettes in *The Dining Room* (511), by A.R. Gurney, at the Playwrights Horizon. The cast includes Lois de Banzie and Remak Ramsay.

MARCH 30 *Agnes of God* (599), by John Pielmeier, opens at the Music Box. Geraldine Page, Elizabeth Ashley, and

Business and Society

MARCH 3 Jujamcyn Theatres announces that it has bought the Eugene O'Neill Theatre from Neil Simon. This gives the company five houses to the 10 controlled by the Nederlanders and 16 by the Shuberts. **3** The price of Variety rises from $1.00 to $1.25. **6** The Nederlanders have been chosen to redevelop, as legitimate houses, the New Amsterdam and Harris Theatres on Forty-second Street, which have been grind film houses for decades.

Births, Deaths, and Marriages

Amanda Plummer star in a drama set in motion by the murder of a baby in a convent. Despite some "fiery" scenes and good performances, writes Frank Rich, in the *Times*, it "falls apart—ultimately to verge on the ridiculous—because he [the author] hasn't figured out how to meld its dramatic and spiritual concerns." It's a film in 1985.

MAY 2 Robert Whitehead, who produced the acclaimed *Medea* in 1947, starring Judith Anderson, is directing for the first time, as his wife Zoe Caldwell takes the title role in a revival of the play, with Judith Anderson playing the Nurse. It's at the Cort (65). **4** *Master Harold . . . and the Boys* (344), Athol Fugard's play about a white South African boy and two of his family's black servants, opens at the Lyceum, with a cast consisting of Zakes Mokae, Danny Glover, and Lonny Price. **9** Raul Julia, the only male in the cast that includes Karen Aikers and Taina Elg, is the Fellini-like director in *Nine* (732), the Maury Yeston musical inspired by the film *8 1/2*. Tommy Tune has directed and choreographed the show, opening at the Forty-sixth Street Theatre.

Photo opposite: Andrew Lloyd Webber, composer of several mega-musicals. *PF*

The Age of the Mega-Musical

1982–1997

1982–83

When is a Broadway season like a movie theatre refreshment stand? When it offers *Good* and *Plenty*, plays that open in that order in the space of a week. Unfortunately, they do not sum up *this* season. "The legitimate theatre season of 1982–83 is depressing and, in terms of the future, ominous," writes Hobe Morrison, *Variety*'s chief theatre critic. On the whole, the crop is neither that good nor plentiful. But there's always *Cats*, "now and forever," which will run for more years than a cat has lives. And there's *Moose Murders*, exquisitely bad but fondly remembered. Elsewhere, it takes a stroke to silence David Merrick and a pill bottle cap to draw the final curtain over Tennessee Williams.

- Advance sale for *Cats*: $6,300,000, largest ever for Broadway
- Top ticket price for *Cats*: $40
- Why you should keep your eyes open at *Cats*, according to Frank Rich in *The New York Times*: "If you blink, you'll miss the plot."
- Number of *Tonys* won by *Cats*: 7
- Why seeing *Moose Murders* is a bonding experience, according to *New York Times* critic Frank Rich: "As passengers will always remember an ecstatic trans-Atlantic journey on the France, so will survivors always remember the camaraderie of their ill-starred crossing on the Titanic."
- Tommy Tune's height: 6' 6"
- Decline in Broadway attendance from last season: 24 percent, to 8,102,262
- Number of new Broadway productions that have recouped their costs by seasons end: none, for the first time
- Total amount of insurance on Elizabeth Taylor and Richard Burton for *Private Lives*: $3,250,000 (by Lloyds of London, heading a syndicate of 25 companies)
- New name chosen by Joseph Lane for his Actors Equity card (his real name is already taken): Nathan Lane, because Joseph has recently played Nathan Detroit in a dinner theatre production of *Guys and Dolls*
- First Broadway show broadcast live on pay-per-view television: *Sophisticated Ladies*
- Doing something different: the Shubert Organization, backing an off-Broadway show, *Little Shop of Horrors*
- What Mary Martin, recovering from a serious auto accident, writes in her telegram to Ethel Merman, recovering from brain surgery: "Anything I Can Do You Can Do Better"

Productions on Broadway: 49

Pulitzer Prize for Drama: *'night, Mother* (Marsha Norman)

New York Drama Critics Circle Awards:
Best Play: *Brighton Beach Memoirs* (Neil Simon)
Best Foreign Play: *Plenty* (David Hare)
Best Musical: *Little Shop of Horrors* (Alan Menken–Howard Ashman)

Tony Awards:
Play: *Torch Song Trilogy* (Harvey Fierstein)
Actor in a play: Harvey Fierstein (*Torch Song Trilogy*)
Actress in a play: Jessica Tandy (*Foxfire*)
Musical: *Cats* (Andrew Lloyd Webber)
Actor in a musical: Tommy Tune (*My One and Only*)
Actress in a musical: Natalia Makarova (*On Your Toes*)

June
Playwrights protest Tony treatment

July
Little Shop of Horrors off-Broadway

August
John Malkovich m. Glenne Headly

September
Pacino and Burstyn lead Actors Studio

October
Cats, "Now and forever"

November
Sister Mary Ignatius not welcome in St. Louis

December
Susan Sarandon and Ellen Barkin in *Extremities*

January
Peter Sellars fired from *My One and Only*
Moose Murders "despicable little thing" (Barnes)

February

March
Brighton Beach Memoirs and *'night Mother*

April
You Can't Take It With You revived

May
Miller in Beijing, Taylor and Burton on Broadway

Personalities

JUNE • On being told that her husband Rip Torn has become the father of a child by actress Amy Wright, Geraldine Page tells columnist Cindy Adams: "Of course Rip and I are still married. We've been married for years. We're staying married. What's the big fuss?" **1** *Boston Herald-American* theatre critic Elliot Norton retires after 48 years of reviewing plays. **9** The U.S. Post Office issues a stamp honoring the Barrymores in a ceremony at the Shubert Theatre. Ethel, John, and Lionel are shown in left profile, John's favorite. **9** When the *Playbills* for *Medea*, starring Zoe Caldwell, don't arrive at the Cort Theatre until intermission, the theatregoer in the sixth row, center, impatient to get the curtain up again, helps to distribute them. She's Katharine Hepburn. **23** Edward Albee, Betty Comden and Adolph Green, David Mamet, Arthur Miller, Stephen Sondheim, and other prominent writers for the stage place an open letter in a *Variety* ad, which says: "No sane person would possibly believe that authors are less important to the theatre than are actors, directors and producers. Nevertheless, from the onset of the televised Tony Awards, authors have either been totally ignored or denied their proper recognition. This situation will no longer be tolerated."

AUGUST • Tennessee Williams tells a reporter at a film festival, "If I had it all to do over again I'd only write for the movies." **20** Anne Baxter makes her Shakespearean debut, as Gertrude in *Hamlet*, on one leg, at the American Shakespeare Festival in Stratford, Connecticut. She broke her ankle backstage during previews. Christopher Walken has the lead. Says *Variety*: "Complete with blond pompadour and goatee, he's sullen, crazed and unprincely."

SEPTEMBER 5 A drunken driver in San Francisco smashes into the taxi carrying Mary Martin, her manager Ben Washer, Janet Gaynor, and her husband Paul Gregory. Washer is killed, and the others are seriously injured, including a shattered pelvis and broken ribs for Martin. **28** Al Pacino and Ellen Burstyn become

Plays and Musicals

JUNE 10 *Torch Song Trilogy* ((1,222) opens on Broadway, at The Little Theatre, after five months off-Broadway, at the Actors Playhouse. It originated, in 1981, at the off-off-Broadway Richard Allen Center. Some gays are irked by Fierstein's play for what they feel is its support for "family values."

JULY 27 First there was a throat-slitting barber on Broadway, now there's a man-eating plant downtown. *Little Shop of Horrors* (2,209) opens at the Orpheum, formerly a Yiddish theatre on Second Avenue. The Alan Menken-Howard Ashman musical, starring Lee Wilkof and Ellen Greene, is based on the 1960 Roger Corman nonmusical film. This stage musical, in turn, will be the basis for the 1986 film musical.

OCTOBER 7 "Now and forever," the tag line in ads for *Cats*, Andrew Lloyd Webber's new musical, is a good projection of its run at the Winter Garden. The $3.9 million show has an advance sale of $6.2 million, both figures unprecedented on Broadway. "Memory," the most memorable song in this show, produced by Cameron Mackintosh and based on T.S. Eliot's *Old Possum's Book of Practical Cats*, is sung by Betty Buckley, who plays Grizabella. *Cats* has sound effects, no dialogue, and plenty of special effects, including Betty Buckley literally going over the top on an old tire. **13** At the Booth, C.P. Taylor's *Good* (125), from the Royal Shakespeare Company, has Alan Howard as a university professor becoming a Nazi. **17** Sam Shepard's approved version of *True West* (762), the play that he felt was mishandled by Joseph Papp, now directed by Gary Sinese and starring Sinese and John Malkovich, opens at the Cherry Lane. **21** David Hare's *Plenty* (45), starring Kate Nelligan and Edward Herrmann, opens at the Public Theatre. In this play, the downhill course of a woman's life reflects the decline of British society. It will move uptown, to the Plymouth (95), on January 6. **21** Joe Sears and Jaston Williams bring their *Greater Tuna* (501) to the downtown Circle in the Square.

Business and Society

JUNE • New York City radio station WINS refuses to run a commercial for *Torch Song Trilogy* with the word "gay" in it. **8** A third of the terra-cotta facade of the Helen Hayes Theatre, which was supposed to be preserved as the rest of the house is demolished, collapses during the razing of the building.

JULY 27 The League of New York Theatres and Producers sues the Dramatists Guild, charging it with monopolistic practices. The League wants to negotiate with writers individually, not as a group.

SEPTEMBER • The U.S. Court of Appeals overturns the 1981 award of damages to the Marx Brothers' heirs for the "appropriation" of the comedians' personalities in *A Day in Hollywood, A Night in the Ukraine*.

OCTOBER • The Shubert Organization extends to 20 years its booking agreement with Washington's National Theatre. In return, the National receives a $1 million loan for its current renovations. **31** According to the League of New York Theatres and Producers, a minimum of 14 shows this season will be financed by movie companies.

Births, Deaths, and Marriages

JUNE 26 Elia Kazan m. writer Frances Rudge, former wife of the manager of The Rolling Stones.

JULY 1 David Merrick m. Karen Prunczik, a dancer in his *42nd Street*. He had originally characterized her as "ugly," as he once did Barbra Streisand when she was an unknown. **23** Victor Moore d.

AUGUST 2 Cathleen Nesbitt d. A prominent leading lady in her early years and a character actor later, she played Rex Harrison's mother in *My Fair Lady*, Cary Grant's mother in the film *An Affair to Remember*, and Audrey Hepburn's great-aunt in *Gigi* on Broadway. **1** John Malkovich m. Glenne Headly. They met in Chicago's Steppenwolf company. They will divorce in 1990. **12** Henry Fonda d.

co-artistic directors of the Actors Studio.

OCTOBER • David Merrick's television ads for his *42nd Street*, taking note of the new competition, ask: "Are you allergic to cats?"

NOVEMBER 20 *The New York Times* reports that as many as 70 crates of scores by George Gershwin, Richard Rodgers, and Cole Porter—some from shows in which the complete music was thought to have been lost—have been discovered in a Warner Brothers warehouse in Secaucus, New Jersey.

DECEMBER • Natalia Makarova is forced out of the revival of *On Your Toes*, at the Kennedy Center in Washington, D.C., when a pipe hits her, breaking her shoulder blade and cutting her head.

JANUARY 2 Lyricist Martin Charnin, at *Annie*'s final curtain, tells the audience there's more to Annie's story. In fact, there's more than he realizes. His efforts to bring forth *Annie 2* will turn into a mini-epic. **12** Bee Gee brother Andy Gibb is fired from *Joseph and the Technicolor Dreamcoat* by producer Zev Buffman for missing 21 of 51 performances, the latest of which is today. Gibb claims a respiratory problem but has shown no medical proof. Says Buffman: "In the theatre, missing performances is for the dead or dying." **29** The firing of director Peter Sellars and music director Craig Smith has caused the cancellation of the first preview of My *One and Only*, in Boston. It lacks "polish," says one of the producers.

FEBRUARY 2 Eve Arden, age 73, is fired from the upcoming show *Moose Murders*—according to a *New York Post* story (other sources say she quit). "It was a very difficult decision to let Eve go," says the producer in a *Post* interview, "but the show would not have survived on Broadway." It won't do terribly well without her, either. **13** Producer David Merrick is disabled by a stroke.

MARCH 5 Debbie Reynolds collapses during a performance of *Woman of the Year* and will spend several days in the hospital with what doctors term "transient global amnesia." **8** Left unattended at

---

NOVEMBER 11 Hume Cronyn and Jessica Tandy are the stars of *Foxfire* (213), coauthored by Cronyn with Susan Cooper, at the Barrymore. Costarring Keith Carradine, it's about an Appalachian Mountains family and their ties to the land.

DECEMBER 22 Susan Sarandon, Ellen Barkin, James Russo, and Deborah Hedwall are in *Extremities* (325), a play by William Mastrosimone about the consequences of an attempted rape. It's at the Cheryl Crawford Theatre. **29** Caryl Churchill's *Top Girls* (129) opens at the Public Theatre. Gwen Taylor stars in the story of a woman who rises in the business world.

FEBRUARY 22 "Things can hardly get worse than this," *Variety* comments, optimistically. "This" is *Moose Murders* (1), an instant legend in its own very brief time, at the Eugene O'Neill, and Broadway's new touchstone for how bad is "bad." A "despicable little thing," critiques Clive Barnes in the *Post*. Eve Arden escaped during rehearsals from this dramatic sinkhole. The rest of the cast will be excused after tonight. **24** *Quartermaine's Terms* (375), Simon Gray's play about frustrated British academics, has a cast that includes Remak Ramsay and Kelsey Grammer. It opens at the Playhouse. Jack Kroll, in *Newsweek*, sees it as a "metaphor for a Britain atrophying with spiritual noodledom."

MARCH 6 Natalia Makarova stars in a revival of the 1936 Rodgers and Hart show *On Your Toes* (505), opening at the Virginia Theatre. George Abbott is the director **27** Neil Simon's autobiographical *Brighton Beach Memoirs* (1,530) is at the Alvin, which will be renamed for the playwright during the show's run. Matthew Broderick stars, with Joyce Van Patten and Elizabeth Franz, in the story of two families trying to make a go of it in Depression-era Brooklyn. **31** Kathy Bates is the daughter who announces her impending suicide, and Anne Pitoniak plays her mother in Marsha Norman's *'night Mother* (380), at the John Golden. It's "a shattering evening," says Rich, in the *Times*; "a sort of situation tragedy, a sit-trag as it were," says Barnes, disagreeing, in the *Post*. *Variety* thinks "the defiantly non-box office subject makes it a

---

NOVEMBER • The Archbishop of St. Louis condemns a production of Christopher Durang's *Sister Mary Ignatius Explains It All to You* as "a vile diatribe against all things Catholic." A hotel theatre where it was due to play has withdrawn the space, but a local college has stepped in, offering its theatre. **3** The New York Drama Critics Circle votes down a proposal to admit broadcast media critics to its ranks. **5** *Sophisticated Ladies* becomes the first Broadway show broadcast live on pay-per-view television. It's a special performance, with much of the cast made up from the touring company. Members of the Broadway company are not happy with the pay for this day's work.

FEBRUARY 11 A 20-inch snowfall cancels only one Broadway show, *Merlin*, in previews, when a horse and panther needed for Doug Henning's magic are stuck in New Jersey.

MARCH 28 An editor at the *Daily News* admits that it refused a request from the producers of *On Your Toes* for feature story coverage because the show took a full-page ad in the *Times*, which didn't like the show, and quoted from the *News*'s review, which was positive. News gossip columnist Liz Smith says she's been told not to mention *On Your Toes*.

JANUARY 15 Shepperd Strudwick d.

FEBRUARY 12 Eubie Blake d. at age 100. **25** Tennessee Williams d. in the "Sunset Suite" of the Elysse Hotel, in Manhattan. He is thought to have choked to death on the cap from a pill bottle.

APRIL 23 Selena Royle d.

MAY 12 David Merrick divorces Karen Prunczik.

Personalities

the Rusk Institute, where he's recovering from a stroke, David Merrick escapes into the rain in his wheelchair. The police find him six blocks away, in a noodle factory. He has become the object of a custody battle between one of his of his former wives, Etan Aronson, and his intended-ex-wife-to-be, Karen Prunczik. **13** Network television cameras are omnipresent in Boston for the opening of *Private Lives*, at the Shubert, starring the not so private Elizabeth Taylor and Richard Burton. Selling tickets is no problem, but good reviews are another matter. Kevin Kelly, in the *Boston Globe*, says that the twice-former Mrs. Burton sounds like "Minnie Mouse" and that both seem to be plodding through the play on "snowshoes."

MAY 7 Arthur Miller is in Beijing, directing the first Chinese production of *Death of a Salesman*. Five days ago, while he was away, a fire caused extensive damage to his home in Connecticut. **18** John Malkovich wins the Clarence Derwent Award for most promising actor of the season. **24** Jacqueline Fierstein, school librarian and mother of playwright Harvey Fierstein, is interviewed in the *Village Voice* on her experience of seeing *Torch Song Trilogy*. "A true mother never knows her own child," she says. "I couldn't believe my child had that talent. He was a poor speller."

My One and Only features the music of George Gershwin *PB*

Plays and Musicals

doubtful prospect for an extended Broadway run."

APRIL 4 *You Can't Take It With You* (312), the Kaufman and Hart play from 1936, is revived at the Plymouth, with a cast headed by Jason Robards, Jr., Colleen Dewhurst, James Coco, and Elizabeth Wilson. **24** Lonette McKee is the first black woman to play Julie in a Broadway production of *Show Boat* (73), when the Houston Grand Opera Company brings the Kern-Hammerstein musical to the Uris Theatre.

MAY 1 *My One and Only* (767), originally intended by Tommy Tune to be a revival of the 1927 Gershwin musical *Funny Face*, has gone through turmoil and transformation in tryouts to emerge as a new musical with a different story when it opens at the St. James tonight. But it still has toe-tapping Gershwin music and stars Tune, Twiggy, Charles "Honi" Coles, and Roscoe Lee Browne. **8** After all the hoopla, Elizabeth Taylor and Richard Burton open at the Lunt-Fontanne in Noel Coward's *Private Lives* (63) to not-very-good reviews but an initially strong box office. By the end of June, it will be on twofers. **26** Sam Shepard's *Fool For Love* (1,000) opens at the Circle Rep. Ed Harris and Kathy Baker are lovers and half-brother and -sister in this Obie-winning play. Cast replacements include Ellen Barkin and Bruce Willis. It's a 1985 film.

Business and Society

APRIL 29 The Dramatists Guild, which is being sued for monopolistic practices by the League of New York Theatres and Producers, countersues the League on the same grounds.

Births, Deaths, and Marriages

1983–84

What if they gave a Broadway season and no shows came? It's so quiet on Broadway in the autumn you can hear the leaves fall (and there are very few trees on the Rialto). But this season's high points are high enough. Dustin Hoffman in *Death of a Salesman* has guaranteed it. In David Mamet's *Glengarry Glen Ross*, the dirtiest four-letter word is "sell." "Ticket prices, it's generally agreed, cannot go much higher than the current $45 top for musicals and $40 for straight plays," reports *Variety*. Lynn Fontanne is dead. And it doesn't seem possible, but the voice of Ethel Merman has been stilled forever.

- Number of LPs of the original cast recording of *La Cage aux Folles* sold in the first month: 130,000
- Productions about show business personalities that flop this year: *Chaplin*, *Marilyn*, and *Tallulah*
- Harvey Fierstein's income from:
  Torch Song Trilogy: about $8,000 a week
  La Cage aux Folles: about $9,000 a week
- Number of times Chita Rivera has been nominated for a Tony before finally winning this season for *The Rink*: 6—in *West Side Story*, *Bye, Bye Birdie*, *Bajour*, *Chicago*, *Bring Back Birdie*, and *Merlin*
- What's new: soliciting investment capital for new shows through inserts in *Playbill*
- What Cole Porter said about Ethel Merman: "When you write lyrics for Ethel Merman they'd better be good because everyone's going to hear them."
- Number of costumes Theoni Aldridge has designed for Broadway shows in her career: 1,000
- Largest number of subscribers among nonprofit resident theatres: 41,000, at the Old Globe in San Diego
- Number of new subscribers the Old Globe has gained in the past 18 months through telemarketing: 28,000
- Number of Pulitzer Prizes won by plays staged in the John Golden Theatre in the past 6 years: 3—*The Gin Game*, *'night Mother*, and *Glengarry Glen Ross*

Productions on Broadway: 36, a new low

Pulitzer Prize for Drama: *Glengarry Glen Ross* (David Mamet)

New York Drama Critics Circle Awards:
Best Play: *The Real Thing* (Tom Stoppard)
Best American Play: *Glengarry Glen Ross* (David Mamet)
Best Musical: *Sunday in the Park with George* (Stephen Sondheim)

Tony Awards:
Play: *The Real Thing* (Tom Stoppard)
Actress in a play: Glenn Close (*The Real Thing*)
Actor in a play: Jeremy Irons (*The Real Thing*)
Musical: *La Cage aux Folles* (Jerry Herman-Harvey Fierstein)
Actress in a musical: Chita Rivera (*The Rink*)
Actor in a musical: George Hearn (*La Cage aux Folles*)

Month	Event
June	The Alvin Theatre renamed the Neil Simon Theatre
July	Lynn Fontanne d.
August	*La Cage aux Folles*
September	*A Chorus Line* passes *Grease*
October	Neil Simon and Marsha Mason divorce
November	George Abbott m. a woman half his age
December	*Noises Off* and *The Tap Dance Kid*
January	Jeremy Irons's Broadway debut
February	Ethel Merman is gone
March	*Glengarry Glen Ross* and *Death of a Salesman*
April	*Jerry's Girls* a disaster area
May	*Sunday in the Park with George*

Personalities

JUNE 11 *New York Post* critic Clive Barnes attacks the *Times*'s Walter Kerr's panning of *Fool for Love* with some harsh asides about *Mary, Mary*, the hit play by Kerr's wife Jean. **20** Director Ellis Rabb takes over for James Coco in *You Can't Take It With You* when the latter hurts his leg in an onstage accident. **20** In an interview with Harvey Fierstein by *Screw* editor Al Goldstein in the *New York Native*, a gay newspaper, Goldstein suggests that the success of the playwright's *Torch Song Trilogy* and the upcoming *La Cage aux Folles*, for which he wrote the book, could get Fierstein co-opted by the establishment, tempting him "to suddenly become the corporate cross-dresser." Fierstein replies: "I definitely see by next year a Harvey cosmetics for men, and Harvey dresses for construction workers." **29** The Alvin Theatre is renamed the Neil Simon Theatre.

JULY • The Little Theatre is renamed the Helen Hayes Theatre. It's the second house named for her—the first was demolished.

AUGUST 10 Watergate burglar G. Gordon Liddy, who read for the part of Willy Loman's brother in the Lincoln Center Production of *Death of a Salesman*, is rejected. "It had to do with ability and talent," a spokesperson for producer Robert Whitehead says. "It had nothing

La Cage aux Folles—"naughty but nice" PB

Plays and Musicals

AUGUST 21 Broadway has long drawn on the talents of gay writers, composers and performers, and now for the first time, there is a musical with gay protagonists. *La Cage aux Folles* (1,761), opens at the Palace. It's "naughty but nice," says the *Daily News*, pointing to a source of the show's success. Gene Barry and George Hearn star, with score by Jerry Herman and book by Harvey Fierstein. The film appeared in 1978.

SEPTEMBER 29 With its 3,389th performance, *A Chorus Line* passes *Grease* as Broadway's longest-running show.

OCTOBER 16 The 1968 musical *Zorba* (362) is revived at the Broadhurst, with Anthony Quinn and Lila Kedrova, who played the same roles in the 1964 film *Zorba the Greek*, on which the musical is based. Michael Cacoyannis, who directed the film, is also directing this production.

NOVEMBER 22 *Painting Churches* (206), by Tina Howe, in which an artist confronts a family crisis, opens at the Lambs Theatre. In the cast are Elizabeth McGovern, Marian Seldes, and George N. Martin. McGovern's standby is Frances McDormand.

DECEMBER 11 *Noises Off* (553), by Michael Frain, in which a repertory company tours with a sex farce called "Nothing On," is at the Brooks Atkinson. It stars Dorothy Loudon, Brian Murray, and Victor Garber. **15** Wendy Wasserstein's revised version of *Isn't It Romantic* (733), which debuted in 1981 at the Phoenix, opens at the Playwrights Horizon. In it, two women, played by Christine Rose and Lisa Banes, deal with careers and romance in the big city. Betty Comden is making her dramatic debut as a Jewish mother. **21** *The Tap Dance Kid* (669), with a score by Henry Krieger and Robert Lorick, opens at the Broadhurst. Hinton Battle stars as the uncle of a young boy who must deal with his father's opposition to a show business career for

Business and Society

JUNE • Structural flaws have put off the Nederlanders' plans to reopen the New Amsterdam Theatre, which they've been renovating. **1** The New York City Department of Consumer Affairs issues specifications for theatre seating locations designated "front" or "rear" mezzanine. "We are trying to make sure that people aren't surprised to find they have tickets in the upper right-hand corner of heaven," says a Department spokesperson.

AUGUST • Actors Equity, recognizing the increasing tendency of performers to work in a variety of media, eases its restrictions on granting Equity cards to those in other fields.

SEPTEMBER • Broadway has almost hit a dead calm, with only three new shows scheduled before November.

FEBRUARY 19 "These days, theatre is a special interest, occupying a ghetto on the cultural landscape," writes *New York Times* critic Frank Rich. "Of all the ills that plague the American theatre right now," he says, "none is more disturbing than the widespread perception that American plays simply don't matter any more."

Births, Deaths, and Marriages

JULY 15 Eddie Foy, Jr. d.

JULY 29 Raymond Massey d. **30** Howard Dietz, who wrote lyrics for Broadway musicals such as *The Band Wagon*, with Arthur Schwartz's music, d. Dietz wrote the lyrics for "Dancing in the Dark," "You and the Night and the Music," and "That's Entertainment." **30** Richard Burton, now starring on Broadway with his second and third wife Elizabeth Taylor, m. Sally Hay. Lynn Fontanne d.

AUGUST 6 Mary Beth Hurt m. director-screenwriter Paul Schrader. **17** Lyricist Ira Gershwin d. **30** David Merrick remarries his third wife, Etan Aronson.

OCTOBER • Marsha Mason and Neil Simon divorce. **10** Ralph Richardson d.

NOVEMBER 22 George Abbott, age 96, m.

to do with politics."

SEPTEMBER 13 Yul Brynner is playing the title role in *The King and I*, at the Pantages Theatre in Los Angeles, for the 4,000th time. **16** Cicely Tyson is fired from the lead role in the revival of *The Corn Is Green*, now at the Lunt-Fontanne. She missed the September 8 performance when she accompanied husband Miles Davis, the jazz trumpeter, on a trip without telling the producers in advance. They say that she also has not been willing to take direction in the play that opened August 22 and will close in two days. **30** James Earl Jones, playing in *Master Harold . . . and the Boys* in Toronto, suffers a detached retina and will be replaced in the cast by Zakes Mokae.

OCTOBER 21 Ben Kingsley, starring in *Edmund Keane*, is asleep in his dressing room this afternoon at the Brooks Atkinson, while two robbers hold up the box office at gunpoint, stealing $5,000. **8** James Hayden, costarring with Al Pacino in the current revival of *American Buffalo*, is discovered dead in his Manhattan apartment, along with drug paraphernalia.

DECEMBER • Etan Aronson, who has been caring for her ex-husband David Merrick, and former New York City Mayor Robert Wagner are appointed conservators for the producer, who has been disabled by a stroke. • *Noises Off* might as well be financed by Worker's Compensation. The pratfalls and other acrobatics required of the cast will take its toll. Dorothy Loudon, for example, will break her hand, chip her knuckles, and suffer crushed toes.

FEBRUARY 25 Despite breaking her arm in an offstage accident, Carol Channing continues her performance tonight in a preview, in Palm Beach, of *Jerry's Girls*, a revue based on the music of Jerry Herman. **26** A bitter Estelle Parsons, who starred with Jack Lemmon in Ernest Thompson's *A Sense of Humor*, which folded short of Broadway at San Francisco's Curran Theatre, attacks the author of the play—and of *On Golden Pond*—for his absence from rehearsals. "I expect him to learn something from me as an actor," she says. "The theatre is collaborative."

---

his son. Alfonso Ribeiro plays the boy. **27** C.P. Taylor's *And a Nightingale Sang. . .* (177), a play about a British family in wartime, opens at the Mitzi Newhouse Theatre in Lincoln Center. Joan Allen will receive the Clarence Derwent Award for the season's most promising female actress.

JANUARY 5 Tom Stoppard's comedy *The Real Thing* (566), directed by Mike Nichols and starring Jeremy Irons and Glenn Close, is at the Plymouth. Irons makes his Broadway debut as a witty playwright who marries an actress played by Close. Christine Baranski and Kenneth Welch are also in this play. **19** *Ian McKellen Acting Shakespeare* (37) is just that, plus the actor's comments and parodies of other actors. He's at the Ritz.

FEBRUARY 9 Chita Rivera and Liza Minnelli are mother and daughter in the John Kander-Fred Ebb musical *The Rink* (129) at the Martin Beck. The book is by Terrence McNally.

MARCH 25 David Mamet's *Glengarry Glen Ross* (378) opens at the John Golden. A list of sales prospects is pilfered, the occasion for a look into the despair and degradation of high-pressure real estate sales. "In the jagged riffs of coarse, monosyllabic words, we hear and feel both the exhilaration and sweaty desperation of the huckster's calling," writes Frank Rich, in the *Times*. "Sell" is only one of the four-letter words salting the dialogue, as in "What the fuck. What bus did *you* get off of? We're here to fucking *sell*." The cast includes Robert Prosky and Joe Mantegna. The film version is released in 1992. **29** Dustin Hoffman is Willy Loman in a revival of Arthur Miller's *Death of a Salesman* (158), at the Broadhurst. Kate Reid is his wife, and John Malkovich is his son Biff. Hoffman is "truly remarkable," says the *Wall Street Journal*; he's "brave and uncompromising," reports *Newsweek*. Clive Barnes, in the *New York Post*, calls this production, directed by Michael Rudman, "definitive" and says that Hoffman gives "a performance of genius."

APRIL 19 *Shirley MacLaine on Broadway* (47) opens at the Gershwin.

MARCH • For the first time, Joseph Papp's New York Shakespeare Festival is coproducing a show when it moves its musical version of *The Human Comedy* from the Public Theatre to Broadway. Its partner is the Shubert Organization. • Producer Alexander Cohen is soliciting money for *Play Memory* through inserts in the *Playbill* for *Carmen*, at the Vivian Beaumont—the first time capital has been raised this way.

MAY • Vincent Sardi, Jr. sells Sardi's to Show Biz Restaurants, Inc. Sardi remains as a consultant. **20** David Rabe's *Hurly Burly* sets what is thought to be a new off-Broadway record for ticket sales on the first day the box office opens. It sells 800 tickets at the Promenade Theatre in six hours on this Sunday for a total of $23,000. By August, it will be on Broadway at the Barrymore.

Joy Valderrama, 52.

JANUARY 13 Critic Brooks Atkinson d. He had an epiphany in old age: "I'm becoming very vain about my humility."

FEBRUARY 15 Ethel Merman d. George Abbott said of her: "If everybody were as talented and conscientious as Ethel, all shows would be hits and the theatre would be undiluted pleasure."

MARCH 22 Andrew Lloyd Webber m. Sarah Brightman, who was in the London production of *Cats*. He's just divorced his first wife, also named Sarah.

APRIL 10 Ray Middleton d.

MAY 3 Director Alan Schneider, known for his productions of the work of Beckett and Albee, d. from injuries he sustained when hit by a motorcycle in London while walking to a rehearsal.

Personalities

MARCH 19 Tennessee Williams's estate sues to block the renaming of the Playhouse after the late playwright. Claiming that the motive is commercial exploitation of his name, the estate secures an injunction preventing it.

APRIL 2 Carol Channing, who has already broken her arm during the tour of *Jerry's Girls*, is singing in the show at the Orlando Performing Arts Center when a storm puts out the lights. Using their one working spotlight, she, Leslie Uggams, and Andrea McArdle gather around the piano (the orchestra can't see its music) and continue singing. **9** The newspaper ads for tonight's performance of *The Rink* give no indication that costar Liza Minnelli is in Hollywood for the Oscars, to be replaced for the evening on Broadway by Leonora Nemitz. The producers knew about her Oscar appearance well in advance. **25** *Variety* reports that David Merrick is making an estimated $500,000 a week from his total ownership of the three current productions of *42nd Street*—a record for weekly profits.

MAY 3 The rarely ill Carol Channing is in a New Haven hospital with laryngitis, canceling performances of *Jerry's Girls*. This follows her broken arm on the tour and the storm-caused blackout in Florida. **7** Avant-garde actor-director Joseph Chaiken suffers a stroke during heart surgery. **9** *Variety* reports that film director Blake Edwards will "meet with Henry Mancini and Leslie Bricusse to prepare for the Broadway bow of their musicalized *Victor/Victoria* starring Julie Andrews and Robert Preston." **10** An emergency appendectomy knocks Andrea McArdle out of *Jerry's Girls*, now in Toledo. So far this year, the production has seen Carol Channing's broken arm, her hospitalization with laryngitis, and a blackout during a Florida performance.

Plays and Musicals

MAY 2 Stephen Sondheim brings a George Seurat painting to musical life and, with a book by James Lapine, meditates on the creative process in the Pulitzer Prize-winning *Sunday in the Park with George* (604), starring Mandy Patinkin and Bernadette Peters. It opens at the Booth. **27** Beth Henley's *The Miss Firecracker Contest* (131) opens at the Manhattan Theatre Club. "A wonderful actress named Holly Hunter opens the evening by bouncing quite literally about," reports *The New York Times*. Hunter is also in the 1989 film. **31** The Circle Rep hosts the Steppenwolf Company's production of Lanford Wilson's *Balm in Gilead* (253). Directed by John Malkovich and set in a Broadway coffee shop, this "stunning" performance (Frank Rich) stars Terry Kinney, Tanya Berezin, Gary Sinese, and Glenne Headly.

Bernadette Peters and Mandy Patinkin in *Sunday in the Park with George* PF

Business and Society

Births, Deaths, and Marriages

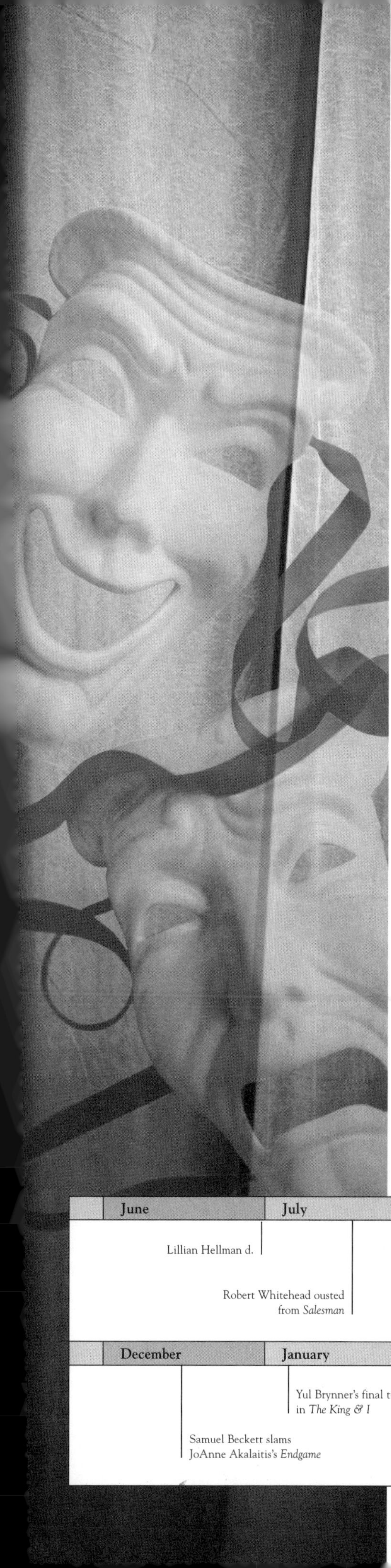

1984–85

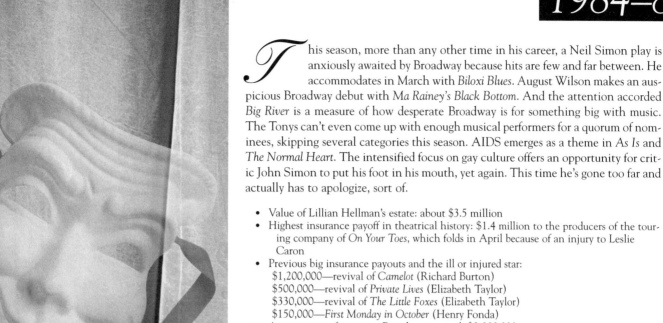

This season, more than any other time in his career, a Neil Simon play is anxiously awaited by Broadway because hits are few and far between. He accommodates in March with *Biloxi Blues*. August Wilson makes an auspicious Broadway debut with *Ma Rainey's Black Bottom*. And the attention accorded *Big River* is a measure of how desperate Broadway is for something big with music. The Tonys can't even come up with enough musical performers for a quorum of nominees, skipping several categories this season. AIDS emerges as a theme in *As Is* and *The Normal Heart*. The intensified focus on gay culture offers an opportunity for critic John Simon to put his foot in his mouth, yet again. This time he's gone too far and actually has to apologize, sort of.

- Value of Lillian Hellman's estate: about $3.5 million
- Highest insurance payoff in theatrical history: $1.4 million to the producers of the touring company of *On Your Toes*, which folds in April because of an injury to Leslie Caron
- Previous big insurance payouts and the ill or injured star:
  $1,200,000—revival of *Camelot* (Richard Burton)
  $500,000—revival of *Private Lives* (Elizabeth Taylor)
  $330,000—revival of *The Little Foxes* (Elizabeth Taylor)
  $150,000—*First Monday in October* (Henry Fonda)
- Average cost of staging a Broadway musical: $3,000,000
- Cost of a straight play: $750,000–$1,500,000
- Number of Broadway shows since 1945 that appeared first on the screen: 64—46 musicals and 18 straight plays
- Number of members of Actors Equity: 30,000—double what it was a decade ago
- New weekly minimum for Broadway musicians: $650
- New top minimum for actors in off-Broadway shows (sliding scale): $225 a week
- Words used in *Hurly Burly* to describe women: "bitches," "broads," and "ghouls"
- How to revive a corpse: give it a London tryout, which the producers of *Corpse*, first staged 2 years ago at the American Stage Festival, are now doing
- Transitions and transformations: *Coming of Age in Soho*, by Albert Innaurato, is that rare straight play, possibly the first, in which the protagonist changes gender as it's rewritten during previews

Productions on Broadway: 31, another new low

Pulitzer Prize for Drama: *Sunday in the Park with George* (Stephen Sondheim-James Lapine)

New York Drama Critics Circle Award:
Best Play: *Ma Rainey's Black Bottom* (August Wilson)

Tony Awards:
Play: *Biloxi Blues* (Neil Simon)
Actress in a play: Stockard Channing (*Joe Egg*)
Actor in a play: Derek Jacobi (*Much Ado About Nothing*)
Musical: *Big River* (Roger Miller)
Actress in a musical: none
Actor in a musical: none

June
- Lillian Hellman d.

July
- Robert Whitehead ousted from *Salesman*

August
- David Rabe's *Hurly Burly*

September
- Boston Mayor backs pickets of *Sister Mary Ignatius*

October
- *Ma Rainey* is August Wilson's Broadway debut

November
- Lloyd Webber says his work won't play South Africa

December
- Samuel Beckett slams JoAnne Akalaitis's *Endgame*

January
- Yul Brynner's final turn in *The King & I*

February
- Bernadette Peters is a monkey's namesake

March
- Neil Simon's *Biloxi Blues*

April
- *The Normal Heart* and *Big River*

May
- Tony committee shuts out musical performers

Personalities

JUNE 5 Peter Sellars, only four years out of Harvard, is appointed artistic director of the Kennedy Center. Roger Stevens, the Center's chairman, is asked if Sellars's avant-garde propensities could be a problem. "We'll find out, won't we," he replies. Sellars, who staged the opera *Don Giovanni* with the Don eating a Big Mac in the banquet scene, hopes to establish an American National Theatre. **24** Walter Kerr, in *The New York Times*, declares that "Hollywood and the New York Stage are no longer separate, sealed-off entities." Where Broadway was once the place to begin and end a career, with the lucrative movies the meat of the sandwich, now there has arisen "a sort of film-stage ensemble," consisting of stars such as Glenn Close, William Hurt, Dustin Hoffman, Raul Julia, and Christopher Walken, who are bicoastal, moving between cameras and live audiences.

JULY • The planned musical version of *Victor/Victoria* has been shelved because, it is reported, Blake Edwards has mononucleosis. • Producer Robert Whitehead, partners with Arthur Miller and Dustin Hoffman in the current production of *Death of a Salesman*, is forced out, primarily by Miller. Miller and Hoffman want to decrease Whitehead's royalty share—the play recouped in Chicago and is now pure profit—since most of the producer's work is done. They are also unhappy that Whitehead was in Australia in April and May, directing his wife Zoe Caldwell in *Medea*.

AUGUST 21 Stephen Sondheim enters New York Hospital for several weeks, where he will spend part of the time in the cardiac intensive care unit.

SEPTEMBER 14 The *New York Post* reports that Sarah Brightman, a cast member of *Cats*, who is now Mrs. Andrew Lloyd Webber, has adjusted to her new lifestyle. She says, according to the *Post*, that "she loves wearing diamond rings because they distract from her bitten fingernails."

OCTOBER 31 "Sondheimania Grips *N.Y. Times*," claims a *Variety* headline over an

Plays and Musicals

AUGUST 7 David Rabe's *Hurly Burly* (343)—originally titled "Spinoff"—moves to the Barrymore from off-Broadway, with a cast that includes William Hurt, Harvey Keitel, Sigourney Weaver, Christopher Walken, Judith Ivey, Cynthia Nixon, and Jerry Stiller. It's about men trying to find themselves against a backdrop of show business.

OCTOBER 11 *Ma Rainey's Black Bottom* (275), opening at the Cort, "reveals in August Wilson a new writer of talent and power," *Variety* will report. The setting is a recording session, and the protagonist is one of the great blues singer's musicians. "This play is a searing inside account of what white racism does to its victims," says Frank Rich, in the *Times*, "and it floats on the same authentic artistry as the blues music it celebrates." Theresa Merrit is Ma Rainey, and the musician is Charles Dutton. **24** A new entertainment personality opens a one-woman show, at the Lyceum: *Whoopi Goldberg* (148), directed by Mike Nichols. "Long may she whoop," writes Douglas Watt, in the *Daily News*.

NOVEMBER 1 Larry Shue's comedy *The Foreigner* (686), about an Englishman vacationing in Georgia, is at the Astor Place Theatre. The author is in the cast.

JANUARY 7 Yul Brynner returns to Broadway for the last time in *The King & I* (191). The revival is at the Broadway Theatre. **21** *Tracers* (186), a play conceived of by John Di Fusco and written by several Vietnam War veterans, some of whom are in the cast, opens at the Public Theatre.

FEBRUARY 6 *Tom and Viv* (37), Michael Hasting's look at T.S. Eliot's first, disastrous marriage, is at the Public Theatre, with Edward Herrmann and Julie Covington in the title roles.

MARCH • The American National Theatre gets under way at the Kennedy Center with a production of *King Henry IV, Part 1*, starring John McMartin, John Heard, and Patti LuPone. The critics

Business and Society

AUGUST • The Minetta Lane Theatre opens in a former tin can factory in Greenwich village. It was built by M-Square, one of several companies now assembling groups of off-Broadway theatres in the Shubert-Nederlander-Jujamcyn manner. M-Square is owned by Marvin Meit and Mitchell Maxwell.

SEPTEMBER • Movie producer Jerry Weintraub buys out the interest of Joseph Nederlander in the Mark Hellinger, Forty-sixth Street, Neil Simon, Lunt-Fontanne, New Amsterdam, and Nederlander theatres for about $4 million. He intends to produce shows with James Nederlander.

OCTOBER • Lloyds of London pays what is reported to be the biggest insurance claim ever in the theatre—$1.4 million to the producers of *On Your Toes*, which was touring last spring, when it was closed down by Leslie Caron's torn hip muscle. • The Kennedy Center, which lost $1,878,000 in the fiscal year that just ended, is excused by Congress from paying $33,000,000 in interest on loans taken for the Center's construction. **8** The new top minimum salary on off-Broadway's sliding scale is $225 a week.

Births, Deaths, and Marriages

JUNE 20 Estelle Winwood d.

JUNE 21 Lyricist Tom Jones (*The Fantasticks*) m. choreographer Janet Watson. **30** Playwright Lillian Hellman d.

AUGUST 5 Richard Burton d.

SEPTEMBER 4 Broadway and Hollywood composer Arthur Schwartz d. With his partner Howard Dietz, who d. last year, he wrote "That's Entertainment," "Dancing in the Dark," and "You and the Night and the Music."

DECEMBER 8 Luther Adler d. He was married to actress Sylvia Sydney from 1938 to 1947.

FEBRUARY 21 Ina Claire d.

article that says the *Times* acts as a publicity machine for the composer-lyricist, just as it has begun to do for new playwright August Wilson.

NOVEMBER • Andrew Lloyd Webber forbids the production of any of his work in South Africa because of apartheid.

DECEMBER 13 The production of Samuel Beckett's *Endgame*, directed by JoAnne Akalaitis, with its Philip Glass music and subway tunnel set, goes on at Harvard's Loeb Drama Center tonight but only with Beckett's disclaimer inserted in the program. He calls it a "parody" and says that "[a]nybody who cares for the work couldn't fail to be disgusted by this." **13** The New York State Court of Appeals upholds the injunction preventing the renaming of Playhouse Theatre for Tennessee Williams against the wishes of his heirs.

JANUARY • David Merrick resumes control of his financial affairs. • The day after leaving *Noises Off*, in which she suffered a variety of injuries, Dorothy Loudon breaks her toe—at home. **23** The Post Office issues a stamp honoring Jerome Kern.

FEBRUARY 24 Bernadette Peters leaves the cast of *Sunday in the Park with George*. As a going away present for their colleague, who is known for her love of animals, the other members of the company endow a monkey at the Bronx Zoo with her name. Bernadette, the monkey, was born on October 9.

MARCH • Critic John Simon, in *New York* magazine, refers to the play *The Octet Bridge Club* as "faggot nonsense." *Daily News* gossip columnist Liz Smith also reports this month that many people overheard Simon remark after a play, "Homosexuals in the theatre! My God, I can't wait until AIDS gets all of them." Simon later says that may not be exactly what he said, but whatever he did say, he's sorry he said it. • The Dramatists Guild suspends the four creators of the musical *Grind*, now in tryouts in Baltimore, for agreeing to a contract that falls below the Guild's standards. Larry Fitzhugh, Ellen Grossman, Fay Kanin, and

trash it. **27** A revival of Peter Nichols's *A Day in the Death of Joe Egg* (102), which opened off-Broadway on January 6, transfers to the Longacre. It stars Jim Dale and Stockard Channing. **28** In a season sparse with successful shows, Broadway has what it needed, yet another Neil Simon hit: *Biloxi Blues* (524), at the Neil Simon Theatre, starring Matthew Broderick as Eugene Jerome, the character he played in *Brighton Beach Memoirs* (still running on Broadway). Now it's World War II, and Eugene is undergoing Army basic training. Frank Rich, although pleased with much of the play, writes, in the *Times*, that one of the play's lines applies to Simon's recent Hollywood and Broadway work: "Once you start compromising your thoughts, you're a candidate for mediocrity."

Matthew Broderick MSN

APRIL 10 *Hannah Senesh* (161), about a Jewish partisan fighter in Hungary during World War II, based on her writings, opens off-Broadway, at the Cherry Lane. David Shechter has written it with the collaboration of Lori Wilner, who stars with John Fistos. Shechter and Elizabeth Swados have written the accompanying music. **16** *Grind* (79), a musical about an interracial romance at a burlesque house, opens at the Mark Hellinger. The Larry Grossman–Ellen Fitzhugh show stars Ben Vereen, Leilani Jones, Timothy Nolen, and Stubby Kaye. The book is by Fay Kanin. **18** It's magic, carny-style, at the Westside Arts Theatre, where *Penn and Teller* (666) opens. Could the number

29 The Old Globe Theatre in San Diego has its second arson fire in six years. This one does $500,000 worth of damage.

NOVEMBER • The New York City Department of Consumer Affairs issues a summons to the producers of *Alone Together* for deceptive advertising. In their ads, they quote Frank Rich of the *Times* on how "it's the kind of play we hardly see on Broadway anymore." But he also wrote that it was "quite awful."

JANUARY 23 "More U.S. Shows Trying London First," says the *Variety* headline. It costs less to debut a show on the West End, and success there lends a production a certain cache.

FEBRUARY • The committee that administers the Tony awards is expanded from 13 to 20 members with the addition of representatives of several unions, including Equity. • The Dramatists Guild and the League of New York Theatres and Producers, which had been suing each other for violating the antitrust laws, reach an agreement that will reduce royalty payments early in a show's run to allow a quicker payoff to investors but give authors more money up front and guarantee them a minimum of $1,000 for the entire run.

MARCH 21 Michael Redgrave d.

MAY 17 Abe Burrows d.

Personalities

Harold Prince (whose writing work on the show is uncredited) are off the rolls.

APRIL • An arbitrator rules that Cicely Tyson was unfairly dismissed from *The Corn Is Green* in 1983 and awards her $600,000. **7** After 1,929 performances, Jerry Orbach leaves the cast of *42nd Street.* **18** Anna Strasberg, the widow of Lee Strasberg, and the Actors Studio settle a two-year battle for control of some 1,000 audio tapes of her husband's sessions at the famous school. Strasberg will retain ownership, with the organization receiving copies for educational use. People other than Strasberg heard on the tapes will retain the publication rights to their portions of the recordings. **29** The Lincoln Center Theatre announces the appointment of Gregory Mosher, formerly of Chicago's Goodman Theatre, as its new artistic director.

MAY 11 *Angelo's Wedding* is taken off the boards at the Circle Rep after a fight breaks out between the playwright Julie Bovasso, winner of five Obies, and the stage manager, who is trying to evict her from the house. Unhappy with the cast of Scott Glenn, Cliff Gorman, and Mari Gorman and with Marshall Mason's directing, she mounted the stage during a preview and told the audience to go home. She says of Mason: "Who does he think he is, commissar of the theatre?"

Plays and Musicals

of performances they give be merely a coincidence? **21** Larry Kramer's *The Normal Heart* (294), a play about AIDS, opens at the Public Theatre. It has a cast headed by Brad Davis, eventually replaced by Joel Grey. *Times* critic Frank Rich finds much of the play "powerful" but criticizes its "pamphleteering tone," which occasionally becomes "hysterical." He says the Public Theatre's production "does not always pump up the writing's flaccid passages." **25** Roger Miller's musical *Big River: The Adventures of Huckleberry Finn* (1,005), which will garner seven Tony Awards, opens at the Eugene O'Neill. Daniel Jenkins is Huck, Ron Richardson is Jim, and also in the cast are John Goodman, Rene Auberjonois, Reathel Bean, and Bob Gunton.

MAY 1 *As Is* (285), an early drama about AIDS, which opened downtown at the Circle Rep on March 10, moves to the Lyceum. The author is William Hoffman, and Jonathan Hogan plays a man who has the disease. The plot centers on his relationship with his former lover. It is the first play under the new Improved Production Contract, reducing weekly royalties to give shows a better chance to recoup their investment. **7** Steppenwolf Theatre presents Lyle Kessler's *Orphans* (285), about the consequences of a kidnapping, at the Westside Arts Theatre. Kevin Anderson, Terry Kinney, and John Mahoney are in this three-character play directed by Gary Sinese. **8** *Doubles* (277), a comedy by David Wiltse about tennis among the middle-aging, stars John Cullum, Tony Roberts, Ron Leibman, and Austin Pendleton. It's at the Ritz. **16** *The Marriage of Bette and Boo* (86), Christopher Durang's comedy about a substantially less than happy match, opens at the Public Theatre. Durang narrates, with a cast that includes Joan Allen, Olympia Dukakis, and Mercedes Ruehl.

Business and Society

APRIL 22 Accompanying its review of *The Normal Heart* is *The New York Times*'s denial of a charge made in the play that the paper "suppressed" early news about AIDS, citing its article of July 3, 1981, as one of the first about the disease.

MAY 2 The lack of good musicals causes the committee administering the Tonys to drop the best actor and actress in a musical and best choreographer category for this year.

Births, Deaths, and Marriages

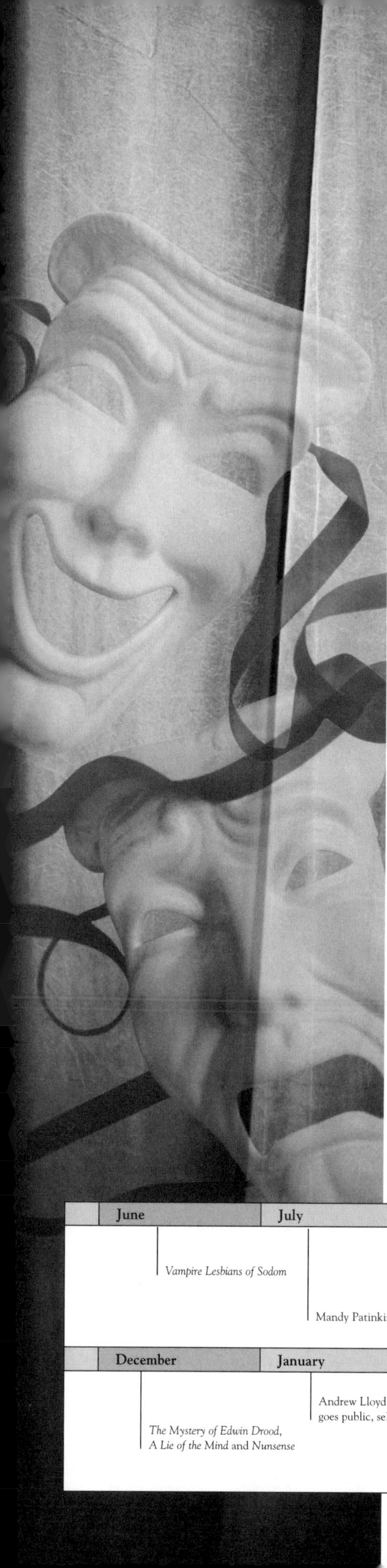

1985–86

It's the same old song, with many musical revivals and revues. Broadway is reaching its nadir, with attendance at 6,527,498, down for the fifth season in a row, and the box office gross down again to its lowest point in six years, despite an average ticket price that has doubled in that period to about $33. At the Imperial, you paid for the ticket to *The Mystery of Edwin Drood*, so you pick the ending. *Variety* reviews the London premiere of *Les Miserables*, calling it too diffuse and opera-like, which "suggests mixed word of mouth and public acceptance problems." A closing notice posted for *The Fantasticks*, a show with more legs than a centipede, brings a surge of ticket orders. And America loses Orson Welles and Yul Brynner on the same day.

- Gone national: the League of New York Theatres and Producers, which has become the League of American Theatres and Producers
- How David Mamet characterizes critics Frank Rich of the *Times* and John Simon of *New York* magazine: "the syphilis and gonorrhea of the theatre"
- How much Gerald Schoenfeld and Bernard B. Jacobs are paid to be "Shuberts": $840,000 a year each, plus bonuses
- How Shubert Organization president Gerald Schoenfeld characterizes the landmarking of Broadway theatres: "a tragedy and a farce at the same time"
- Amount lost by *Sunday in the Park with George*: more than $500,000
- Name of one of the conference rooms at the new Marriott Marquis Hotel in Times Square, which houses the Marquis Theatre: the Brecht Room
- Number of cans of hairspray used each week in *Beehive*, the tribute to sixties singers, at the Village Gate: 15
- Number of wigs in *Beehive*: 35
- Percentage of nonprofit theatres in the U.S. with a deficit: more than 50 percent
- Work weeks for Equity members offered by the (nonprofit) League of Resident Theatres: 56,750
- Work weeks for Equity members available on Broadway and in its touring companies: 53,823—the first time it is less than work available in resident theatres
- Where you can look down at the stars: in front of the Second Avenue Deli, in the old Yiddish Theatre district, which starts a Hollywood Boulevard-type "walk of fame," with stars imbedded in the sidewalk honoring Yiddish Theatre luminaries such as Maurice Schwartz, Boris Tomashevsky, Paul Muni, and Molly Picon

Productions on Broadway: 33

Pulitzer Prize for Drama: None awarded

New York Drama Critics Circle Awards:
Best Play: *A Lie of the Mind* (Sam Shepard)
Best Foreign Play: *Benefactors* (Michael Frayne)

Tony Awards:
Play: *I'm Not Rappaport* (Herb Gardner)
Actor in a play: Judd Hirsch (*I'm Not Rappaport*)
Actress in a play: Lily Tomlin (*The Search for Intelligent Life in the Universe*)
Musical: *The Mystery of Edwin Drood* (Rupert Holmes)
Actor in a musical: George Rose (*The Mystery of Edwin Drood*)
Actress in a musical: Bernadette Peters (*Song and Dance*)

June	July	August	September	October	November
Vampire Lesbians of Sodom	Mandy Patinkin film career fizzles	Broadway theatres landmarked	Patti LuPone with Royal Shakespeare Company	Yul Brynner and Orson Welles d.	*I'm Not Rappaport*

December	January	February	March	April	May
The Mystery of Edwin Drood, *A Lie of the Mind* and *Nunsense*	Andrew Lloyd Webber goes public, selling stock	IRS after Alan Jay Lerner	Vaclav Havel at the Public Theatre	Chita Rivera breaks a leg	Closing notice for *The Fantasticks*

Personalities

JUNE • Ellen Stewart of La Mama Experimental Theatre receives a MacArthur Foundation "genius" grant. • Colleen Dewhurst succeeds Ellen Burstyn as president of Actors Equity. **3** Producer Alexander Cohen resigns from the League of American Theatres and Producers. He gives no reason, but at the rehearsal for last night's Tony Awards broadcast, a show which usually has a theme, Cohen, according to *The New York Times*, "made an obscene suggestion in regard to Mr. [Frank] Rich [the *Times*'s theatre critic] as a proposal for this year's theme." During the show, off camera, Cohen attacked New York Governor Mario Cuomo, not present to receive a special award, because Cuomo "hasn't been to the theatre in 25 years and he didn't want to break his record." **30** The revival of *The King & I*, with a $75 top for its (and Yul Brynner's) final Broadway performance, sets a new one-week record in its last week, drawing $605,546 at the box office.

JULY • The Second Avenue Deli, in the old Yiddish Theatre district, embeds 30 five-pointed stars in the sidewalk in front of its door, each bearing the name of two Yiddish actors, including Maurice Schwartz, Boris Tomashevsky, Paul Muni, and Molly Picon. Deli owner Abe Lebewohl says that "one neighbor thought they were employees who died." **24** Mandy Patinkin, trying to create a career in Hollywood as well as on Broadway, is fired by director Mike Nichols after one day of filming on *Heartburn* and replaced by Jack Nicholson. Patinkin is seen weeping in a restaurant this evening, and the incident will throw him into a personal and creative crisis.

AUGUST 8 Three secondary players in *Biloxi Blues* are replaced for cutting up onstage. Star Matthew Broderick has also been criticized by management for fooling around—"longrun-itis," is the diagnosis—and is absent from tonight's performance.

SEPTEMBER • Patti LuPone is the first

Plays and Musicals

JUNE 19 Depravity goes to camp in Charles Busch's charming *Vampire Lesbians of Sodom* (2,024), opening on a double bill with his *Sleeping Beauty, Or Coma*, off-Broadway, at the Provincetown Playhouse. Busch himself plays several parts, including that of the Virgin Sacrifice.

JULY 2 In the cast are no household names—Don Correia, Peter Slusker, Mary D'Arcy, and Faye Grant—but everyone knows *Singin' in the Rain* (367), the 1952 film that has become a musical at the Gershwin, with Santo Loquasto's sets and the Broadway debut of Twyla Tharp's choreography.

SEPTEMBER 18 Andrew Lloyd Webber's music, interpreted by Bernadette Peters and Christopher d'Amboise, is in *Song and Dance* (474), at the Royale. **26** Lily Tomlin's one-woman show *The Search For Intelligent Signs of Life in the Universe* (398) is at the Plymouth. **29** Eugene O'Neill's *The Iceman Cometh* (55), directed by José Quintero, is revived at the Lunt-Fontanne, with Jason Robards, Jr. as Hickey. It's "magnificent," says Linda Winer, in *USA Today*.

OCTOBER 9 *Tango Argentino* (198), a surprisingly popular music and dance revue, opens at the Mark Hellinger. **28** Wallace Shawn's *Aunt Dan and Lemon* (191) is at the Public Theatre, with Shawn and Linda Hunt in the cast.

Harold Prince *PF*

Business and Society

JUNE 5 Harold Prince resigns from the League of American Theatres and Producers, protesting its lack of concern over the rising price of tickets and the labor costs of mounting a show.

JULY • The nonprofit Lincoln Center Theater, directed by Gregory Mosher, with Bernard Gersten as executive producer, takes over the Vivian Beaumont and Mitzi Newhouse Theatres.

AUGUST • The New York City Landmarks Preservation Commission designates for its protection the Neil Simon, Ambassador, and Virginia Theatres.

NOVEMBER 10 The first day of advance ticket sales for the December 5 opening of Sam Shepard's *Lie of the Mind*, with a stellar cast, sets a new one-day mark for off-Broadway of $41,210.

JANUARY 21 Shares of Andrew Lloyd Webber's Really Useful Group go on sale on the London stock exchange.

Births, Deaths, and Marriages

AUGUST 24 Playwright Morrie Ryskind d. **28** Ruth Gordon d. Someone once described her as "a small but manageable forest fire."

SEPTEMBER 14 Julian Beck d.

OCTOBER 10 Yul Brynner and Orson Welles d. President Franklin D. Roosevelt once told Welles: "You and I are the two best actors in America." **19** Liz Callaway m. actor Dan Foster.

NOVEMBER 1 Phil Silvers d.

DECEMBER 27 Audrey Wood, agent for many playwrights, including Tennessee Williams, William Inge, and Arthur Kopit, d. Her father was the first manager of the Palace Theatre.

American to play a principal role with the Royal Shakespeare Company when she opens as Fantine in *Les Miserables* in London. It will help her win an Olivier Award.

NOVEMBER 11 "True West," says the headline on the cover of *Newsweek* over a photo of Sam Shepard in sunglasses.

DECEMBER 8 Patti LuPone receives a Laurence Olivier Award in Britain for her roles in *The Cradle Will Rock* and *Les Miserables*. **18** It's coming. "Mackintosh Plans 'Miserables' West End Hit, For B'way in 1987," headlines today's *Variety*.

JANUARY 7 Director Mike Nichols is hospitalized with chest pains, delaying the pre-Broadway development of *Social Security*, scheduled for this spring at the Barrymore. **22** Michael Bennett, it is announced, has withdrawn as director of the new musical *Chess* because of "angina." Trevor Nunn replaces him. A coproducer characterizes as "nonsense" the rumor that Bennett was unhappy with star Elaine Paige.

FEBRUARY 18 The U.S. government files a $1.4 million suit against Alan Jay Lerner for back taxes and penalties. **23** Of the 82 performances given so far by Sam Shepard's *A Lie of the Mind*, Harvey Keitel has missed 21.

MARCH • Ben Stiller, playing Swoosie Kurtz's son in John Guare's *The House of Blue Leaves*, at the Mitzi Newhouse Theatre, gives her a present appropriate to her part, "Bananas Saughnessy": a big yellow bananaphone. **20** Martin Sheen has the lead in the London production of the AIDS drama *The Normal Heart*, to be followed by Tom Hulce.

APRIL 7 Chita Rivera breaks her leg in an auto accident, forcing her out of *Jerry's Girls*.

MAY 12 President Reagan presents Helen Hayes with the Medal of Freedom.

Variety finds it "stupifyingly dull . . . another whatsit with no plot, flabby writing, no scene structure, arbitrary and unmotivated characterizations and extraneous graphic sex. In short, zero dramatic craftsmanship."

NOVEMBER 11 *The Golden Land* (277), a revue recalling the golden days of the Yiddish theatre, is at the Second Avenue Theatre. **19** Opening at the Booth, *I'm Not Rappaport* (890), by Herb Gardner, will win a Tony despite a pan from *The New York Times*. Judd Hirsch and Cleavon Little are the white man and black man who come to terms with aging. Hal Linden and Ossie Davis will be their cast replacements. It "often seems didactive and repetitive," writes Rich, in the *Times*. "This proves there's life after Frank Rich," says the author about the play's success.

DECEMBER 2 Played at the Delacorte Theatre in Central Park for free last summer, *The Mystery of Edwin Drood* (608), adapted by Rupert Holmes from the Dickens novel, opens on Broadway tonight, at the Imperial. Cast members include George Rose, Betty Buckley, Donna Murphy, and George N. Martin. The ending for this mystery that Dickens never finished is chosen each night by the audience. **5** Sam Shepard is directing his own play *A Lie of the Mind* (186), at the Promenade, in which violence is one of the elements binding two families together. It stars Harvey Keitel, Amanda Plummer, Geraldine Page, and Aidan Quinn. Salome Jens is among the cast replacements. **12** What would Sister Mary Ignatius make of *Nunsense* (3,672)? The musical, which poses the problem of what to do with dead nuns, is off-Broadway, at the Cherry Lane, where its composer Dan Gogginis is directing, and Semina De Laurentis is playing Sister Mary Amnesia. The ticket-taker is dressed as a monk, and in the appreciative audiences will be many nuns and priests. **18** The long-touring *Jerry's Girls* (139), a revue based on the music of Jerry Herman, opens at the St. James, with Leslie Uggams, Dorothy Loudon, and Chita Rivera. **22** Michael Frayn's *Benefactors* (217), in which everything seems to be crumbling in an architect's

---

FEBRUARY • An investigation by the New York State Attorney General into the salaries of Shubert Foundation heads Gerald Schoenfeld and Bernard B. Jacobs—they work for a charitable trust, which the state regulates—concludes that they are "uniquely qualified" and that their $840,000 per year each, plus bonuses, is justified.

MARCH 21 The League of New York Theatres and Producers informs media editors that it intends "to institute a single opening night for review purposes, with no media attendance at preview performances. . . ." After hearing what editors think of this, the League next month will declare it a "dead issue." **26** Michael J. Lazar, of the Cambridge Investment Group, which is redeveloping five Forty-second Street theatres with the Nederlanders, is indicted on several charges of fraud, complicating the already slow redevelopment.

APRIL 19 The Pasadena Playhouse, known as the "Pasadena Poorhouse" since it was closed by the IRS in 1966, reopens. Twelve miles from Hollywood, which valued it highly when talkies came in during the late 1920s, it opened as a community playhouse in 1917.

JANUARY 27 Lilli Palmer d.

FEBRUARY 16 Howard Da Silva d.

APRIL 14 Playwright Jean Genet d. **23** Composer Harold Arlen d.

MAY 18 John W. Bubbles, of the vaudeville dance team of Buck and Bubbles, d. He invented rhythm tap dancing and played Sportin' Life in the original production of *Porgy and Bess*.

Personalities

Plays and Musicals

life, opens at the Brooks Atkinson. The cast includes Sam Waterston, Glenn Close, Mary Beth Hurt, and Simon Jones.

JANUARY 19 Eric Bogosian begins to make his mark in his series of monologues *Drinking in America* (94), at the American Place Theatre.

MARCH 9 Kevin Kline has a run in *Hamlet* (70), at Joseph Papp's Public Theatre. Kline is "mesmeric," says the *Times*'s Frank Rich. **11** Larry Gallagher's *Beehive* (600), a tribute to the female singers of the sixties, opens at the Village Gate Upstairs. **25** Vaclav Havel, a writer who has been persecuted in his native Czechoslovakia, is the author of *Largo Desolato* (40), a play about a writer with similar experiences. The writer is played by Josef Sommer, at the Public Theatre. Sally Kirkland, Diane Venora, and Joseph Wiseman are also in this production.

APRIL 17 Mike Nichols is directing Andrew Bergman's comedy *Social Security* (385), in which a suburban couple are visiting their sophisticated Manhattan relatives, and an aging mother, played by Olympia Dukakis, is causing a commotion. The cast also includes Ron Silver, Marlo Thomas, Joanna Gleason, and Kenneth Welsh. It's at the Barrymore. **27** *Sweet Charity* is revived at the Minskoff (368), with Debbie Allen in the title role. **29** Swoosie Kurtz gives a Tony and Obie Award-winning performance as Bananas Saughnessy—she cooks Brillo burgers—in a 398-performance revival, at the Vivian Beaumont, of John Guare's 1971 play *The House of Blue Leaves* (398), which has moved upstairs from the Mitzi Newhouse Theatre, where it opened in March.

MAY • A closing notice is posted for *The Fantasticks* for June 8 and then taken down after two weeks when the publicity brings a surge of ticket orders at the box office. So far, it has repaid backers 9,642 percent.

Business and Society

Births, Deaths, and Marriages

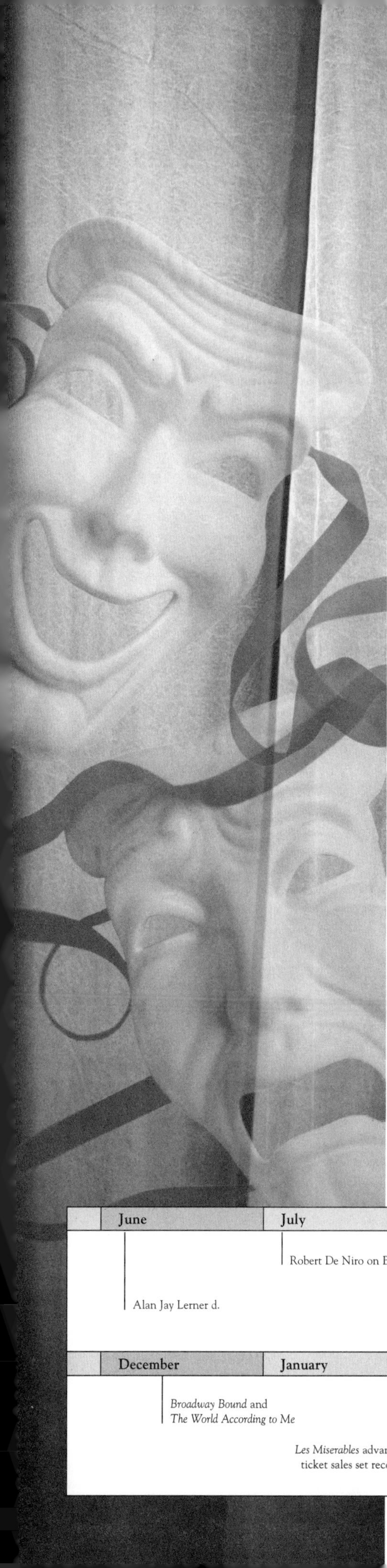

1986–87

Broadway's financial health, such as it is, can be substantially summed up in 17 words: Andrew Lloyd Webber, Trevor Nunn, Cameron Mackintosh, *Cats*, *Les Miserables*, *Starlight Express*, and *Me and My Girl*—none of which bears the label "Made in the U.S.A." The most commercially successful of the homegrown product comes from Neil Simon and television and night club comic Jackie Mason. August Wilson continues to establish himself in the forefront of American playwrights, winning his first Pulitzer Prize for *Fences*. But, ominously, just when the theatre needs more talent and vigor, Joseph Papp is diagnosed with cancer and Michael Bennett with AIDS.

- Number of times lyricist Alan Jay Lerner (who died on June 14, 1986) was married: 8
- First composer-lyricist with 3 1,500-performance shows: Jerry Herman (*Hello, Dolly!*, *Mame*, and *La Cage aux Folles*)
- Attendance on Broadway: 6,968,277, first increase in 5 seasons
- Top ticket price for *Dreamgirls* in Tokyo: $93
- Title of Brazilian production of *Born Yesterday*: *Miss Banana*
- Amount taken in by the Broadway Theatre box office on the first day of ticket sales for *Les Miserables*: $447,275
- Amount cleared at the Winter Garden on the first day *Cats* tickets were sold: $206,230
- Amount by which top price of *Les Miserables* tickets exceeds those for *Cats* when it opened: $7.50—$47.50 to $40
- Theatre and film people who have received early exposure at La Mama: Sam Shepard, Lanford Wilson, Bette Midler, F. Murray Abraham, Elizabeth Swados, Harvey Fierstein, Robert De Niro, Nick Nolte, and Harvey Keitel
- How Ellen Stewart signals the beginning of a performance at La Mama: she rings a cow bell
- Amount invested by MCA (which has the recording rights) in *Starlight Express*: $5 million
- Amount invested in New York production of *Les Miserables* by Mutual Benefit Life Insurance Company: $1,125,000
- Cost of staging the 1970 off-Broadway production of *The Effect of Gamma Rays on Man-in-the-Moon Marigolds*: $40,000
- What it would cost to stage the same production today: $300,000

Productions on Broadway: 40

Pulitzer Prize for Drama: *Fences* (August Wilson)

New York Drama Critics Circle Awards:
Best Play: *Fences* (August Wilson)
Best Foreign Play: *Les Liaisons Dangereuses* (Christopher Hampton)
Best Musical: *Les Miserables* (Alain Boublil and Claude-Michel Schonberg)

Tony Awards:
Play: *Fences* (August Wilson)
Actor in a play: James Earl Jones (*Fences*)
Actress in a play: Linda Lavin (*Broadway Bound*)
Musical: *Les Miserables* (Alain Boublil and Claude-Michel Schonberg)
Actor in a musical: Robert Lindsay (*Me and My Girl*)
Actress in a musical: Maryann Plunkett (*Me and My Girl*)

June	July	August	September	October	November
Alan Jay Lerner d.	Robert De Niro on Broadway	*For Me and My Girl*	*Variety* slams show by Gretchen Cryer and Nancy Ford	Cheryl Crawford d.	Tina Howe's *Coastal Disturbances*, with Annette Bening

December	January	February	March	April	May
Broadway Bound and *The World According to Me*	*Les Miserables* advance ticket sales set record	Broadway shows discount balcony seats	*Les Miserables* opens on Broadway	*Driving Miss Daisy*	Michael Bennett has AIDS, and Charles Ludlam d. from it

Personalities

JUNE 26 The Hyde Park Festival Theatre in Hyde Park, New York, gives a rare revival performance of *Sex*, the Mae West play of the 1920s that earned her 10 days in the workhouse. Playing the role taken by West in the drama, that of a "professional woman," is Margot Kidder. One of the few surviving summer barn theatres, it will burn down in April.

JULY • Marshall Mason resigns as artistic director of the Circle Rep Company and is succeeded by Tanya Berezin.

AUGUST • David Rabe's *Goose And Tom Tom* receives a workshop production at Lincoln Center. In the cast: Madonna and Sean Penn. **21** The talk about the musical *Rags* centers on whether the fragile opera star Teresa Stratas can sing every night. It's a moot point because the downbeat musical about immigrant Jews in America, a Charles Strouse-Stephen Schwartz show, won't make it past four performances, at the Mark Hellinger. Martin Heinfling, of Sergio Valente Jeans, had $2 million invested in it.

SEPTEMBER 3 *Variety*, reviewing *Eleanor (Don't Frighten the Horses!)*, by Gretchen Cryer and Nancy Ford, at the Williamstown Theatre Festival in Massachusetts, declares: "It may be the most misconceived, misdirected, and mis-acted new musical ever to see the light of day."

DECEMBER • Gary Sinese steps down as Steppenwolf's artistic director. • Ann Reinking goes to the hospital with mouth blisters when a stagehand, sterilizing a bottle from which she drinks in a revival of *Sweet Charity*, carelessly leaves some ammonia in it. **14** Carol Channing breaks her arm when she trips over a vacuum cleaner cord during the run of *Legends*, in Miami Beach, in which she stars with Mary Martin. Channing has been unhappy with Martin's problems remembering her lines. During the show's run, Martin will be prompted via a radio earpiece.

MARCH • Nancy Walker, absent from Broadway for a decade, won't be back this season, despite the two years of work that

Plays and Musicals

JUNE 4 *Swimming to Cambodia* (39), a series of Spaulding Gray monologues, is at the Mitzi Newhouse Theatre and on the screen in 1987.

JULY 16 Robert De Niro plays a drug pusher who is afraid that his son might follow in his father's footsteps, in Reinaldo Povod's *Cuba and His Teddy Bear* (53), transferring from the Public Theatre to the uptown Longacre for a limited engagement. De Niro will play no more than six performances a week. Producer Joseph Papp has scaled down balcony seats to $10, and they are selling out. There are no free tickets for the press or for Tony voters (the play won't be around long enough to benefit from a Tony next spring anyway).

AUGUST 10 Broadway has a much-needed musical hit, the British import *Me and My Girl* (1,420), a revival of a 1937 show. It's the first legitimate stage production in the new Marquis Theatre in Times Square, the former site of the Morosco and Helen Hayes Theatres. The show, with a score by Noel Gay, Arthur Rose, and Douglas Furber, stars Robert Lindsay, in his Broadway debut, and features "The Lambeth Walk."

OCTOBER 19 Simon Gray's *The Common Pursuit* (353), a British import about college friends publishing a magazine, opens at the Promenade. In the cast are Kristoffer Tabori, Judy Geeson, and Nathan Lane.

NOVEMBER 19 Tina Howe's *Coastal Disturbances* (45) opens at the Second Stage. Starring in this play about romantic entanglements at the beach, in her New York debut, is Annette Bening, of the American Conservatory Theatre in San Francisco. On March 4, it moves to the Circle in the Square (102).

DECEMBER 4 *Broadway Bound* (756), the third of Neil Simon's autobiographical plays which include *Brighton Beach Memoirs* and *Biloxi Blues*, opens at the Broadhurst. Linda Lavin plays Eugene Jerome's mother. The cast also includes

Business and Society

JULY • The Tony Awards nominating committee expands its membership to put greater emphasis on the creative side of the business, adding, among others, Alfred Drake, Garson Kanin, and José Ferrer. **30** The producers of *The Little Prince*, which folded in 1982, are awarded $1 million in damages in the New York State Supreme Court from the Nederlander Organization, which posted its own closing notice at the Alvin (now the Neil Simon) Theatre. The Nederlanders behaved unreasonably, the jury decides.

SEPTEMBER 21 *Cuba and His Teddy Bear*, closing today, is thought to have inspired the new Tony Award rule taking effect October 1, excluding from consideration any show that does not offer free tickets to Tony voters.

DECEMBER • There have been only two new American plays on Broadway so far this season. One, *Cuba and His Teddy Bear*, featured a movie star, Robert De Niro, and the other, Neil Simon's *Broadway Bound*, opens this month. **11** The bankruptcy of Chargit, which sells tickets over the phone to credit card purchasers, creates cash flow problems on

Births, Deaths, and Marriages

JUNE 14 Lyricist Alan Jay Lerner d. Frederick Loewe, in a tribute to his partner, says: "I was always amazed how good we were and how simple it was." **30** Margalo Gillmore d.

AUGUST 19 Hermione Baddley d.

OCTOBER 7 Producer Cheryl Crawford d.

NOVEMBER 16 Siobhan McKenna d.

JANUARY 15 Ray Bolger d.

FEBRUARY 17 Verree Teasdale d. She had an extensive Broadway career in the '20s and '30s before making pictures and was married to Adolphe Menjou. **25** James Coco d.

has gone into *Back on the Town*, a revue designed as a vehicle for her. Walker has opted for television work. **10** *The New York Times* reports that the crates of unpublished manuscripts by Jerome Kern, George Gershwin, Victor Herbert, Richard Rodgers, and others, discovered in a warehouse in 1982, are even richer than first thought. Copyright complications have kept them in a vault until now. Conductor and musicologist John McGlinn is likening them to the treasures of King Tut's tomb. Included are 70 lost Gershwin tunes, music from *Show Boat* that did not get into the original show, and the original manuscripts for songs such as "Ol' Man River." **25** With its 1,500th performance, *La Cage aux Folles* makes Jerry Herman the only com-

A scene from August Wilson's Pulitzer Prize- and Tony Award-winning *Fences* PF

John Randolph, Phyllis Newman, and Jason Alexander. Frank Rich, in the *Times*, calls it Simon's "most accomplished writing to date" but still finds it lacking in humor and emotion. **22** Jackie Mason opens at the Brooks Atkinson in the first of a series of shows featuring his monologues. This one is *Jackie Mason's The World According to Me* (367).

MARCH 12 It's here, at the Broadway Theatre, and none too soon for an ailing Rialto. *Les Miserables*, the international blockbuster musical by Alain Boublil and Claude-Michel Schonberg, based on the Victor Hugo novel, with English lyrics by Herbert Kretzmer, is produced by Cameron Mackintosh and directed by Trevor Nunn and John Caird. Colm Wilkinson is Jean Valjean, Terrence Mann is Javert, and Randy Graff is Fantine. Frank Rich, in the *Times*, lauds its "electrifying showmanship," but reviews are beside the point. The ticket lines tell the tale. **15** Andrew Lloyd Webber's *Starlight Express* (761), the little engine that could on roller skates, rolls into the Gershwin Theatre. *Variety* asks, "[C]an Lloyd Webber's reputation, hollow spectacle and marketing hype turn

Broadway for the Nederlanders. About $400,000 worth of tickets for shows in its theatres have been sold through that company.

JANUARY 12 Tickets for *Les Miserables* go on sale at the box office of the Broadway Theatre, where previews begin February 28. In the first week, the show takes in $1,721,098, a new record. Today, alone, the gross is $447,275, also a record.

FEBRUARY • Several Broadway shows are cutting the price of balcony seats to generate business.

MARCH • According to *Variety*, one out of every three tickets sold to the 22 shows on Broadway is for one of four British musical productions: *Cats*, *Les Miserables*, *Starlight Express*, or *Me and My Girl*. Andrew Lloyd Webber or director Trevor Nunn are connected to all but *Me and My Girl*. • Ticketron, which handles phone credit card orders for the Jujamcyn Theatres, will do the same for the Nederlanders, replacing the bankrupt Chargit.

MARCH 3 Danny Kaye d. **5** Producer Alfred de Liagre, Jr. d. His shows ranged from *Voice of the Turtle* to *Deathtrap*. **21** Robert Preston d. **28** Charles Ludlam, artistic director of The Ridiculous Theatre Company, d. of AIDS.

MAY 24 Hermione Gingold d.

Personalities

poser-lyricist to have had three shows run that long on Broadway. The others were *Hello, Dolly!* and *Mame*.

APRIL 1 Joseph Papp is diagnosed with prostate cancer.

MAY 18 A court affidavit in a lawsuit reveals that Michael Bennett is suffering from an unidentified "life-threatening disease," which is AIDS. **27** Britain's Conservative Party announces that Andrew Lloyd Webber has written political theme music for Prime Minister Margaret Thatcher's re-election campaign.

Plays and Musicals

this milk train into a box office winner?" Somewhere in John Napier's high-tech set is Andrea McArdle. **26** August Wilson's Pulitzer Prize-winning *Fences* (526) opens at the Forty-sixth Street Theatre. It stars James Earl Jones and Mary Alice, both of whom win Tonys. "I'm going to build me a fence around what belongs to me," Jones says in this drama about a black family in the late 1950s. The Theater Development Fund (TDF) accounts for much of the advance and will sell 10,000 tickets to union members, teachers, and other groups in the opening weeks.

APRIL 15 *Barbara Cook: A Concert for the Theatre* (13) opens at the Ambassador. **15** Morgan Freeman, Dana Ivey, and Ray Gill are the cast of Alfred Uhry's one-act *Driving Miss Daisy* (1,195), which looks at the relationship between a southern white woman and her black chauffeur over 25 years. This "little gem" (*Time*), "a miniature with a power far beyond its apparent size" (*Daily News*), is at Playwrights Horizons. Freeman, Jessica Tandy, and Dan Aykroyd star in the 1989 film. **28** The Royal Shakespeare Company's production of Christopher Hampton's *Les Liaisons Dangereuses* (148) is at the Music Box. Alan Rickman and Lindsay Duncan star in this tale of decadence among eighteenth-century aristocrats. The 1988 film is *Dangerous Liaisons*.

MAY 28 Eric Bogosian's *Talk Radio* (210), in which he plays a voluble talk show host who brings out the worst listeners and the worst in them, is at the Public Theatre. He also stars in the 1988 film. With this play, says the *Times*, Bogosian "takes a long leap from performance artist to playwright."

Business and Society

Births, Deaths, and Marriages

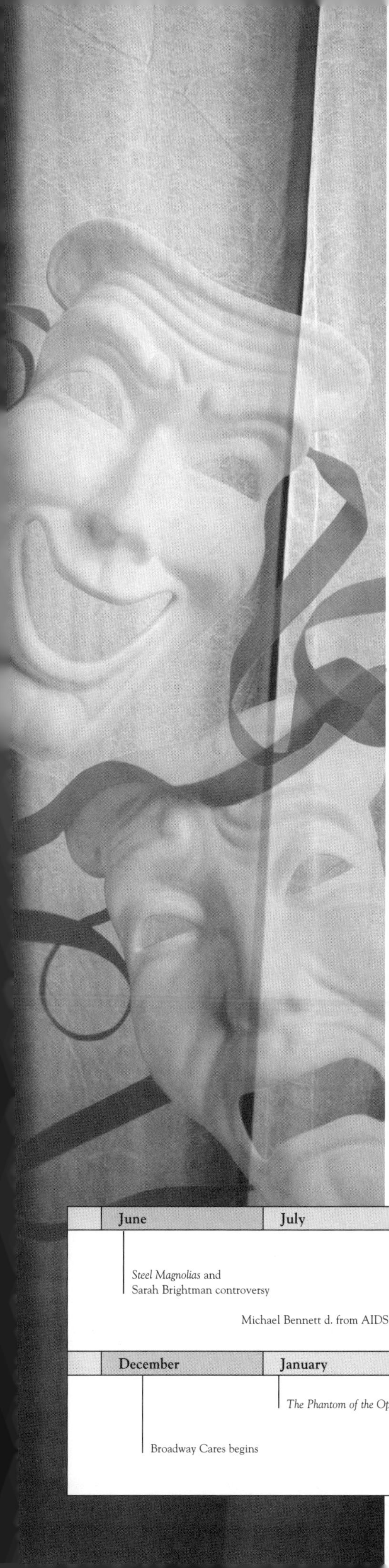

1987–88

Who is that masked man? It's Michael Crawford in *The Phantom of the Opera*, another Andrew Lloyd Webber spectacle, come to save the Broadway box office. *Macbeth*, the theatre's traditional jinx play, lives up to its reputation. Birnam Wood not only seems like a doubtful arrival in Dunsinane, its chances of even clearing Baltimore look dicey. *Carrie* is a mishap of a musical, and *Chess* is a bad move. Tony and Tina know exactly how much the "guests" have given them at their wedding. Rocco Landesman becomes an important player on Broadway. Broadway Cares is launched, and Broadway loses Michael Bennett, Bob Fosse, and Geraldine Page.

- Amount of dry ice it takes to produce the fog at each performance of *The Phantom of the Opera*: 400 pounds
- Number of stagehands on *The Phantom of the Opera*: 40
- Launched: *Theatre Week* magazine
- "MacJinx": *Macbeth*, the play that theatre people traditionally believe is jinxed, goes through multiple Macduffs, 3 directors, 2 set designers, and 2 lighting designers in tryouts, during which star Christopher Plummer suffers multiple injuries
- Amount that Jujamcyn Theatres has sunk in the disastrous musical *Carrie*: $1 million
- How David Mamet views Hollywood, the theme of *Speed the Plow*: "a sinkhole of slime and depravity"
- How far into his *New York Times* review of David Mamet's *Speed The Plow* critic Frank Rich can get before mentioning Madonna: six paragraphs.
- Cumulative net profit on the Broadway production of *Les Miserables* by the end of the season: $6,000,000
- Total weekly gross for 3 current U.S. productions of *Cats*: $2,000,000
- It's not just the Brits dominating Broadway: 9 or 10 U.S. shows are running on the West End at any given time
- Top ticket price for West End musicals: about $35, $15 cheaper than Broadway
- The Mark Taper Forum's surplus in its twentieth season: $600,000
- Top salary for actors at the Mark Taper Forum: $600 a week
- Salary of Mark Taper Forum Artistic Director Gordon Davidson: about $100,000 a year
- Number of Broadway productions originating at the Yale Repertory Theatre: 3—*Fences*, *Joe Turner's Come and Gone*, and *A Walk in the Woods*
- What 100-year-old George Abbott is doing in Cleveland when his centenary is celebrated: working 6 hours a day rehearsing a revival of *Broadway*
- How producers of *Burn This* announce the imminent departure of John Malkovich from the cast: they quote from the play's dialogue—"People, I'm outta here."

Productions on Broadway: 31, tying the all-time low set in 1984–85

Pulitzer Prize for Drama: *Driving Miss Daisy* (Alfred Uhry)

New York Drama Critics Circle Awards:
Best Play: *Joe Turner's Come and Gone* (August Wilson)
Best Foreign Play: *The Road to Mecca* (Athol Fugard)
Best Musical: *Into the Woods* (Stephen Sondheim and James Lapine)

Tony Awards:
Play: M. *Butterfly* (David Henry Hwang)
Actor in a Play: Ron Silver (*Speed the Plow*)
Actress in a Play: Joan Allen (*Burn This*)
Musical: *The Phantom of the Opera* (Andrew Lloyd Webber)
Actor in a Musical: Michael Crawford (*The Phantom of the Opera*)
Actress in a Musical: Joanna Gleason (*Into the Woods*)

June	July	August	September	October	November
Steel Magnolias and Sarah Brightman controversy	Michael Bennett d. from AIDS	*Theater Week* begins publication	Rocco Landesman heads Jujamcyn	Patti LuPone in *Anything Goes*	Joseph Papp to do all of Shakespeare

December	January	February	March	April	May
Broadway Cares begins	*The Phantom of the Opera*	*Tony n' Tina's Wedding*	M. *Butterfly*	Frank Cosaro to direct Actors Studio	Madonna and *Carrie* come to Broadway

Personalities

JULY 20 Kevin Marcum, playing a minor role in *Les Miserables* but also understudying lead Colm Wilkinson and slated to replace the star when he leaves in November, is found dead in his apartment of "acute cocaine intoxication."

AUGUST 6 Matthew Broderick suffers a broken leg and his girlfriend, actress Jennifer Grey, is slightly injured in an auto accident in Ireland in which two women in the other car are killed. Broderick, who is driving, will be fined.

OCTOBER • The Actors Studio announces that it will skip this fall semester. Director Ellen Burstyn is busy with other work, there are complaints that the organization is adrift, and rumors have it that Paul Newman, President of the Board of Directors and a major contributor, is very unhappy with the Studio's leadership—which he denies. **19** Interviewed on the occasion of the opening of *Anything Goes*, in which she stars, Patti LuPone says that she is still being stereotyped based on her role as Eva Peron in *Evita*. One television executive who called her for a role said that she would have to dye her hair to darken it. Informed that she was a brunette, he insisted that she was really a blond. When she auditioned for the role of Reno Sweeney in *Anything Goes*, LuPone held a photo of Ethel Merman in front of her face (Merman was the original Sweeney). When Madonna opens in a nearby theatre, LuPone hangs a sign in her dressing room: "Only one Sicilian diva at a time allowed."

NOVEMBER • Joseph Papp announces that the Public Theatre will stage all 36 of Shakespeare's plays over a projected six years. He estimates the cost at $33 million.

JANUARY • Buckingham Palace announces that Prince Edward will become a production assistant at Andrew Lloyd Webber's Really Useful Company next month. **11** Norman Keane, who coproduced the long-running revival of *Oh, Calcutta!* kills his wife, actress Gwyda DonHowe (she's apparently been having an affair) and then kills himself. **18** Andrew Lloyd

Plays and Musicals

JUNE 19 *Steel Magnolias* (1,126), by Robert Harling, transfers from the WPA Theatre to the Lucille Lortel. The cast of this "amiable evening of sweet sympathies and smalltown chatter," according to the *Times*, includes Kate Wilkinson and Rosemary Prinz. It's a 1989 film.

OCTOBER 13 Terrence McNally's *Frankie and Johnny in the Clair de Lune* is at the Manhattan Theatre Club (533). A middle-aged cook and waitress spend the night together, and she's the one who doesn't want to get involved. Kathy Bates and Kenneth Welsh star onstage, with Michelle Pfeiffer and Al Pacino in the 1991 film. **13** Peter Brook's adaptation of Jean-Claude's *Mahabharata* (25), itself an adaptation of an ancient Sanskrit poem, played in three parts, opens at the Brooklyn Academy of Music. **14** Lanford Wilson's *Burn This* (437), which has played at the Mark Taper Forum and off-Broadway at the Circle Rep, opens at the Plymouth. The cast of this play about a bully and the dancer who finds him appealing consists of John Malkovich, Joan Allen, Jonathan Hogan, and Lou Liberatore. **19** Cole Porter's 1934 *Anything Goes* (804) is revived at the Vivian Beaumont. Patti LuPone, taking Ethel Merman's role of Reno Sweeney, is "the top," says Frank Rich in the *Times*. She has "lips so insinuatingly protruded they could make the Pledge of Allegiance sound lewd." Several

John Malkovich *MSN*

Business and Society

JUNE 10 Despite a personal plea from Harold Prince, Actors Equity denies permission to producer Cameron Mackintosh to bring over Sarah Brightman from the London production of *The Phantom of the Opera* to play on Broadway. They've okayed Michael Crawford because he is an international star. **30** Equity reverses it earlier position and will allow Sarah Brightman to play in *The Phantom of the Opera* but for a limit of six months. British Equity also makes some concessions on other issues.

AUGUST 17 *Theater Week* begins publication.

SEPTEMBER 1 Rocco Landesman becomes president of the Jujamcyn Theatres, and Jack Viertel its creative director. The company, already giving an annual $50,000 award to a resident theatre, is trying to forge closer ties to these institutions to develop more sources for Broadway productions. **27** A century after its founding, members of The Players club vote to admit women.

OCTOBER 19 Although the stock market plunges today, *Anything Goes* takes in $67,800 at the box office, sparked by

Births, Deaths, and Marriages

JUNE 13 Geraldine Page d. She was appearing on Broadway in a revival of Noel Coward's *Blithe Spirit*. **22** Fred Astaire d.

JULY 2 Michael Bennett d. from AIDS.

SEPTEMBER 23 Bob Fosse d. on a Washington, D.C., street while walking with his former wife Gwen Verdon. He had been directing a revival of *Sweet Charity* at the National Theatre, where he instructed the cast to "dance like you're going to percussion heaven." Fosse left $25,000 for a gang of friends, including Dustin Hoffman, Ben Vereen, and Roy Scheider so that they can "have dinner on me."

OCTOBER 3 Playwright Jean Anouilh d. **9** Playwright Clare Boothe Luce d.

Webber, "Magician of the Musical," is on the cover of *Time*, celebrating the opening of *The Phantom of the Opera* on Broadway. **26** Cameron Mackintosh's opening-night party for *The Phantom of the Opera* is for 1,100, at the Beacon Theatre, where the buffet is stocked with leek chiffonade en barquette.

FEBRUARY • Christopher Plummer's production of *Macbeth*, due at the St. James in April, is undergoing turmoil in tryouts. The latest involves a change of directors. **9** The opening-night party for Caryl Churchill's *Serious Money*, a satire of Wall Street, is held at the Commodity Exchange, with many traders accepting invitations and enjoying it. Churchill, who is not present, is puzzled and uncomfortable with this.

MARCH • Rehearsals in a Boston hotel for the troubled production of *Macbeth* are being drowned out by the noise of a delicatessen under construction next door. Stage manager Amy Pell characterizes the scene as "like something out of *Noises Off*." • Jim Dale, appearing in *Me and My Girl*, is taking the first week of the month off for a vacation. But his name is still appearing in ads in *The New York Times* for the show, read by unsuspecting ticket buyers. **2** "Is there a doctor in the house?" *Variety* asks in its review of the Stratford-on-Avon tryout of the musical *Carrie*. Barbara Cook, who has been playing the mother of the teleknetic title character, has quit and is replaced by Betty Buckley.

APRIL • The publication of Elia Kazan's memoirs, *Elia Kazan: A Life*, revives the controversy over his naming names to the House Un-American Activities Committee in 1952. • New York newspaper columnist Jimmy Breslin comes under fire for telling an interviewer that Lanford Wilson's *Burn This* is "a fag play." **7** Frank Cosaro is named artistic director of the Actors Studio. He has been directing at the New York City Opera and directed *Hatful of Rain* in 1955 and the 1961 production of *Night of the Iguana*.

MAY 9 Bowing to pressure, the *Playbill* for *The Phantom of the Opera*, at the Majestic, finally credits Gaston Leroux, on whose 1910 novel the play is based, with being the show's "inspiration."

Porter tunes have been added to the original score.

NOVEMBER 5 *Into the Woods* (765), Stephen Sondheim's look at fairy tales—if you live happily ever after, how happy is happy, and how much after?—with a book by James Lapine, who also directs the musical, opens at the Martin Beck. In the cast are Joanna Gleason and Bernadette Peters. **15** "Great actor meets great role" is *Variety* on Derek Jacobi, who is playing math genius Alan Turing, persecuted for his homosexuality in Hugh Whitmore's *Breaking The Code* (161), at the Neil Simon Theatre.

DECEMBER 1 *Penn & Teller* (130), Penn Jillette and Ray Teller, bring their fun and magic to Broadway at the Ritz Theatre. **2** John Krizanc's *Tamara* (1,036), a play about the poet Gabriel d' Annunzio, in which the audience moves around to various movie-like sets to view the action, opens at the Park Avenue Armory, where a champagne buffet from Le Cirque comes with the play. Frederick Rolf stars.

JANUARY 12 The opening of *A Midsummer Night's Dream* (81), at the Public Theatre, with F. Murray Abraham and Elizabeth McGovern, begins Joseph Papp's planned six-year production cycle of all of Shakespeare's plays. **26** The lyrics are by Charles Hart, but it's Andrew Lloyd Webber's *The Phantom of the Opera*—"hocum *cordon bleu*," *Variety* calls it—opening at the Majestic Theatre with $16 million in advance ticket sales. The next available orchestra seats are at Thanksgiving. Michael Crawford is wearing a mask, and Sarah Brightman plays Christine (except for Thursday evenings and Saturday matinées when Rebecca Luker takes over). Songs include "The Music of the Night" and "All I Ask of You." And there's the chandelier. **28** *Sarafina* (597), an antiapartheid South African musical by Mbongeni Ngema and Hugh Masekela, transfers to the Cort on Broadway from Lincoln Center, where it's been since October. It's played by a company of young South African singers.

FEBRUARY 6 *Tony n' Tina's Wedding*, improvisational theatre emulating working class nuptials, opens at the

---

good reviews. Broadway revenues, in general, hold up well.

NOVEMBER • Actors Equity raises more than $50,000 in what is planned as the first annual Equity Fights AIDS Week. **23** The Majestic box office begins to sell tickets for *The Phantom of the Opera*. From 7:00 A.M. to midnight, the take is $920,272, beating the old one-day record of $447,000 set in eight hours by *Les Miserables*, where the top price was $47.50, compared to *The Phantom*'s $50.

DECEMBER • The New York City Landmarks Preservation Commission adds the Music Box, Longacre, Majestic, Lunt-Fontanne, Eugene O'Neill, and Plymouth Theatres to its protection, making 28 theatres in all. • The Nederlander Theatre on Forty-first Street, mostly empty in recent years, is leased to a religious group. **10** The Biltmore Theatre, one of the few Broadway houses not owned by a big chain, is hit by an arson fire. It's been on the block, and only recently, the Landmarks Preservation Commission designated its interior for protection. **16** Broadway Cares, an ongoing program to fight the threat of AIDS, is launched.

JANUARY 5 The Shubert Organization is sued by theatre party agents, who charge

---

FEBRUARY 14 Composer Frederick Loewe d.

APRIL 29 Director Mike Nichols m. broadcaster Diane Sawyer.

MAY 5 George Rose is killed by his adopted son and several other men while vacationing in the Dominican Republic. He had been taking a break from the tour of *The Mystery of Edwin Drood*.

Personalities

Leroux, uncredited, had been the real phantom in the house.

Plays and Musicals

Washington Square Methodist Church. An "invitation" costs $55, which includes the reception at Carmelita's, a nearby restaurant.

MARCH 20 David Henry Hwang's *M. Butterfly* (777) opens at the Eugene O'Neill Theatre. A French diplomat is tricked into revealing state secrets to his lover of 20 years, who he does not realize is a man. John Lithgow plays the diplomat, and B.D. Wong plays his lover. The 1993 film stars Jeremy Irons and John Lone. **27** August Wilson's *Joe Turner's Come and Gone* (105), another of his periodic evocations of the African-American community in Pittsburgh, this time in 1911, opens at the Barrymore. In the cast are Angela Bassett and Delroy Lindo. The Turner in the title—from a W.C. Handy song—was a southern planter, not the famous blues singer.

APRIL 28 Athol Fugard's *The Road to Mecca* (172), at the Promenade, is a three-character play, with a cast of the author, Amy Irving, and Yvonne Bryceland. In it, an aging artist is in conflict with a minister. **28** *Chess* (68), a cold war musical, opening at the Imperial, was written by Benny Andersson, Bjorn Ulvaens, and Tim Rice. The cast includes Judy Kuhn, David Carroll, and Harry Goz.

MAY 3 Madonna is the very big star, in her Broadway debut, and the play is David Mamet's satire on Hollywood *Speed-the-Plow* (278), also starring Joe Mantegna and Ron Silver. Frank Rich, in the *Times*, praises Madonna's "intelligent, scrupulously disciplined comic acting" and calls the play "a brilliant black comedy." The Lincoln Center Theatre is presenting it on Broadway, at the Royale. **12** "When was the last time you saw a Broadway song and dance about the slaughter of a pig?" asks the *Times*'s Frank Rich. *Carrie* (5) is at the Virginia Theatre. *Variety* notes that "[t]he costuming of the girls suggests their high school offers a minor in prostitution." Howard Kissel, in the *Daily News*, says it's "so disgusting it makes *Chess* look adorable."

Business and Society

that it violates the antitrust laws by holding back the good seats for its own group sales outlets. **19** The cast of *Me and My Girl* complains to Equity about unsafe and unsanitary conditions backstage at the Marquis Theatre, which is less than a year old—it's cold enough to see your breath, and it stinks, literally.

MARCH 21 *The New York Times* reports that real estate development in the theatre district is pricing rehearsal spaces out of the market. The City Planning Commission now requires five percent of newly developed space to be reserved for such use.

Births, Deaths, and Marriages

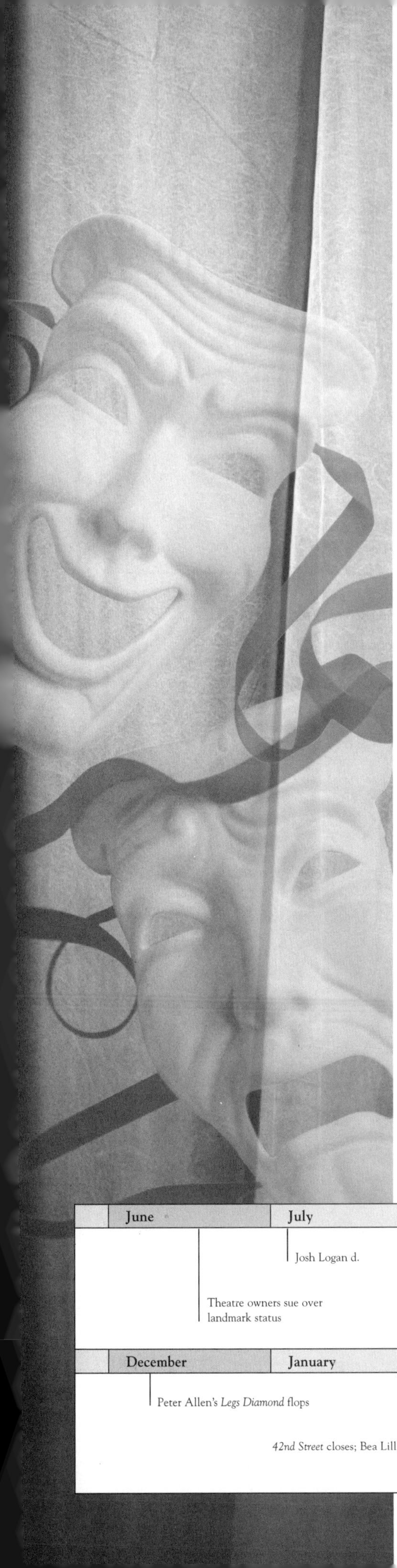

1988–89

Baby boomers find their bard in Wendy Wasserstein and *The Heidi Chronicles*, Rocco Landesman criticizes Lincoln Center for its "commercialism," and Eugene O' Neill is turning into a no-sell on Broadway. *Jerome Robbins' Broadway*, yet another show where words are irrelevant, steps all over the musical competition, Peter Allen's *Legs Diamond* has plenty of previews but neither staying power nor sparkle, and Andrew Lloyd Webber's *The Phantom of the Opera* has a ghost, Ken Hill's production, based on the same source. Lloyd Webber is also having trouble selling his 17-room *pied-à-terre* in the Trump Tower. Madonna takes the box office with her when she leaves *Speed-the-Plow*. And just how much ziti can the cast of *Tony n' Tina's Wedding* eat?

- Rehearsal time for *Jerome Robbins' Broadway*: an extended 22 weeks
- Amount of time that *Legs Diamond* spends in previews: 2 months
- Peter Allen's standby in *Legs Diamond*: Larry Kert, who starred in *West Side Story*
- Nederlander loss on *Legs Diamond*: at least $5 million
- What happens to the Mark Hellinger Theatre when *Legs Diamond* folds: the theatre, where "Get Me to the Church on Time" in *My Fair Lady* once rang out, becomes a church
- Size of the rent increase demanded from the Minskoff Rehearsal Studios by Tishman Realty, forcing the closing of the space: 250 percent
- Heard for the first time in 6 decades: the complete score of *Show Boat*, in John McGlinn's recording, featuring Teresa Stratas, Frederica Van Stade, and Jerry Hadley
- The odds against a playwright having more than one hit play on Broadway in a career, according to playwright Peter Stone, who has examined the records of the past 40 years: 10 to 1
- Weekly cost of renting the catering space for *Tony n' Tina's Wedding*: $1,385
- Maximum number of guests at *Tony n' Tina's Wedding*: 150 (ticket includes reception)
- What *Tony n' Tina's Wedding* "guests" have been eating at the reception at Carmelita's restaurant: baked ziti and rum cake
- What the Mark Taper Forum charges for selected performances: Name your price—it's whatever you can afford
- What playwright David Mamet says to actors who need amplification in a 1,000-seat house: "You should get off the stage and go home."
- Net weekly profit from the four U.S. companies of *Les Miserables*: $600,000

Productions on Broadway: 29, the lowest ever

Pulitzer Prize for Drama: *The Heidi Chronicles* (Wendy Wasserstein)

New York Drama Critics Circle Awards:
Best Play: *The Heidi Chronicles* (Wendy Wasserstein)
Best Foreign Play: *Aristocrats* (Brian Friel)

Tony Awards:
Play: *The Heidi Chronicles* (Wendy Wasserstein)
Actress in a play: Pauline Collins (*Shirley Valentine*)
Actor in a play: Philip Bosco (*Lend Me a Tenor*)
Musical: *Jerome Robbins' Broadway*
Actress in a musical: Ruth Brown (*Black and Blue*)
Actor in a musical: Jason Alexander (*Jerome Robbins' Broadway*)

June
- Theatre owners sue over landmark status

July
- Josh Logan d.

August
- "Blind pools" allowed for play investing

September
- Madonna leaves *Speed-the Plow*

October
- A.R. Gurney's *The Cocktail Hour*

November
- *The Heidi Chronicles*

December
- Peter Allen's *Legs Diamond* flops

January
- *42nd Street* closes; Bea Lillie d.

February
- *Jerome Robbins' Broadway*

March
- Roger Moore won't do musical comedy

April
- Papp and Dewhurst demand firing of John Simon

May
- Andrew Lloyd Webber troubled by *Phantom's* phantom

Personalities

JUNE • Colleen Dewhurst wins a second three-year term as president of Actors Equity. **7** The Jujamcyn Theatres, along with three independent producers, establish the American Playwrights Project to commission new plays for Broadway. The first $20,000 stipends, plus expenses—the money is not tied to royalties—goes to Christopher Durang, David Rabe, Marsha Norman, David Henry Hwang, Terrence McNally, and Wendy Wasserstein. **23** With the closing of revivals of *Ah, Wilderness* and *Long Day's Journey Into Night*, which had been playing in repertory, there have now been five consecutive unprofitable productions of O'Neill plays on Broadway. None have made money since *Anna Christie*, starring Liv Ullmann, in the 1976–77 season. Subsequent flops include *A Moon for the Misbegotten*, starring Kate Nelligan, *Strange Interlude*, with Glenda Jackson, *The Iceman Cometh*, with Jason Robards, Jr., and *Long Day's Journey Into Night*, starring Jack Lemmon.

AUGUST • The reception for *Tony n' Tina's Wedding* has been shifted to Vinnie's, in Greenwich Village, where New York State champagne is quaffed with the baked ziti, a dish the cast is getting tired of eating every night.

SEPTEMBER • The cast turnover in *Speed-the-Plow*, with Felicity Huffman replacing Madonna, plows under the box office gross, which drops as much as 75 percent. **13** Andrew Lloyd Webber puts up for sale his 17-room duplex at Manhattan's Trump Tower. "Andrew wants something a bit smaller and quieter, a little more low key," says his spokesperson. But the market has turned, and there are no takers.

OCTOBER 11 At a Hollywood symposium on nontraditional casting on stage and screen, sponsored by the California Theatre Council, James Earl Jones plays Big Daddy in a scene from *Cat on a Hot Tin Roof*.

NOVEMBER • Maggie Smith's broken shoulder, suffered in a bicycle accident, will postpone *Lettice & Lovage*, scheduled for Broadway in April. **30** Tonight's episode

Plays and Musicals

JUNE 14 Eugene O'Neill's *Long Day's Journey Into Night* (28), with José Quintero directing, is revived, at the Neil Simon Theatre. Jason Robards, Jr. is James Tyrone, and Colleen Dewhurst is Mary Tyrone. It's playing in repertory with *Ah, Wilderness*. Frank Rich, in the *Times*, calls it "rewarding, if imperfect" and says Dewhurst plays Mary as "a killer, forever twisting the knife in old familial wounds."

JULY 7 Jon Robin Baitz's *The Film Society* (31) opens at the Second Stage Theatre, off-off-Broadway. Nathan Lane gives another well-received performance as a white South African teacher who manages to keep his moral compass in the midst of apartheid.

OCTOBER 20 *The Cocktail Hour* (351), a play by A.R. Gurney, opens at the Promenade. Nancy Marchand is a woman whose son, played by Bruce Davison, has written a play about his family. The drama originated at the Old Globe in San Diego.

NOVEMBER 6 They've sent in the clowns, at the Mitzi Newhouse Theatre in Lincoln Center. Robin Williams and Steve Martin star, for a limited run, in Samuel Beckett's *Waiting for Godot* (25), with F. Murray Abraham and Bill Irwin, directed by Mike Nichols. With this cast, says *Variety*, "it would do business on the Galapagos." Sylviane Gold, in the *Wall Street Journal*, says it's "neither a great 'Godot' nor an all-star mess" but is "surprisingly, demoralizingly average." **17** The dinner party host has attempted suicide, but the guests will keep it under wraps in Neil Simon's *Rumors* (531), at the Broadhurst. It stars Christine Baranski, Ron Leibman, Joyce Van Patten, Jessica Walter, Andre Gregory, Ken Howard, and Lisa Banes.

DECEMBER 26 Peter Allen's musical *Legs Diamond* (64), with Allen in the title role, is a major flop at the Mark Hellinger, although about 90,000 people did see it in nine weeks of previews.

JANUARY 5 Richard Greenberg's comedy *Eastern Standard* moves from the

Business and Society

JUNE 20 The Jujamcyn, Nederlander, and Shubert groups sue New York City, seeking to overturn the landmark status of Broadway theatres.

AUGUST • A New York State law permits producers to assemble show financing through "blind pools," without disclosing to investors which productions funds raised for groups of shows will finance.

SEPTEMBER • A federal court judge dismisses the suit brought against the Shubert Organization by theatre party agents over the issue of the Shuberts' withholding the best seats for its own group sales.

DECEMBER 11 In a *New York Times* article, Rocco Landesman, Jujamcyn Theatres head, attacks Gregory Mosher and Bernard Gersten of the Lincoln Center Theatre for using their nonprofit base to launch commercial attractions such as *Speed-the-Plow*, starring Madonna, and *Waiting for Godot*, with Robin Williams and Steve Martin, which compete unfairly with Broadway.

JANUARY • With the death of Richard Barr, Cy Feuer becomes president of the League

Births, Deaths, and Marriages

JUNE 22 Playwright Rose Franken d.

JULY 12 Director Joshua Logan d.

AUGUST 1 Florence Eldridge d.

OCTOBER 9 Playwright Edward Chodorov d. He was blacklisted in the fifties after choreographer Jerome Robbins told the House Un-American Activities Committee that Chodorov had been a Communist. **31** John Houseman d., the day after the fiftieth anniversary of the Mercury Theatre of the Air production of *War of the Worlds*.

DECEMBER 12 Patti LuPone m. cameraman Matt Johnson on the stage of the Vivian Beaumont Theatre, where she is performing in *Anything Goes*.

of "Tattinger" on NBC will be titled "Barrymore's," with a cast that includes Elaine Stritch, Blythe Danner, Jerry Stiller, Mary Beth Hurt, with cameos by George Abbott and Garson Kanin.

JANUARY 31 If producing plays on Broadway is a gamble, Rick Steiner is the man for the job. The coproducer of *Into the Woods* and *Big River* wins $50,000 in seven-card stud at the Caesars Palace Super Bowl of Poker in Las Vegas.

FEBRUARY 27 Mandy Patinkin, who has never given a concert, begins a series of them, at the Public Theatre. He calls it "a terrifying jaunt into an unknown world."

MARCH 13 "Live and let die" is what Roger Moore does to his incipient stage musical career. A month before the London opening of Andrew Lloyd Webber's *Aspects of Love*, the former James Bond, set to star, says, "I now do not think the musical stage is for me" and leaves the cast.

APRIL 3 With his regular editor at *New York* magazine on vacation, critic John Simon reviews the Public Theatre's production of Shakespeare's *The Winter's Tale*. Simon says black actress Alfre Woodard, miscast, evokes Butterfly McQueen. He also says that Mandy Patinkin, a Jewish actor, resembles "a caricature in the notorious Nazi publication *Der Sturmer*." (Simon once wrote: "The one show that could run forever on

Christine Lahti, one of the actresses who will play Dr. Heidi Holland in *The Heidi Chronicles* *PF*

Manhattan Theatre Club to Broadway at the John Golden Theatre (92). Kevin Conroy and Ann Meara star in a story of Manhattan go-getters, out for success, who stop to help a bag lady along the way. **26** Linda Hopkins, Ruth Brown, and teenage dancer Savion Glover are part of the cast of *Black and Blue* (824), a revue at the Minskoff featuring mostly African-American music.

FEBRUARY 16 Willy Russell's one-character play *Shirley Valentine* (324), starring Pauline Collins as the housewife who goes to Greece, opens at the Booth. She also stars in the 1989 film with Tom Conti. **16** Wall Street sharks headed for a hostile takeover are the subject of Jerry Sterner's *Other People's Money* (990), starring Kevin Conway and Mercedes Ruehl, off-Broadway, at the Minetta Lane Theatre. Danny DeVito is in the 1991 film. **26** *Jerome Robbins' Broadway* (634), put together by the choreographer, summarizes his career. The cast at the Imperial features Jason Alexander. It has an advance of about $10 million and tomorrow will set a new one-day record at the box office of $535,000.

Most unusual ticketholder at *Jerome Robbins' Broadway*: Michael McClean, who will pick up his ticket during a burglary in the borough of Staten Island. (Not only is he foolish enough to attend the show with a stolen ticket, he and his partner have also been breaking into and robbing the homes of Mafia bigwigs in the tonier part of the borough.)

of American Theatres and Producers.

FEBRUARY • The Nederlander organization rents the Mark Hellinger Theatre, where "Get Me to the Church on Time" was once heard in *My Fair Lady*, to the Times Square Church. Says James Nederlander, "There's *[sic]* no shows being produced. We have to keep the theatres filled." • *Cats*, with net profits approaching $50 million, has gone deeper into the black than *A Chorus Line*, becoming the most profitable Broadway show ever.

MARCH • *The New York Times* directs its staff not to participate in choosing Tony or New York Drama Critics Circle Award winners or in any other activity that might represent a conflict of interest with, or "dilute," their reviewing and reporting on plays and the theatre. **1** With construction finished on the new office building next door to the Broadway Theatre, *Les Miserables* can now play Wednesday matinées.

MAY • The Nederlanders are rumored to be negotiating with City Cinemas to turn the Lunt-Fontanne Theatre into a multiplex cinema.

JANUARY 8 Producer Richard Barr, head of the League of American Theatres and Producers since 1967, d. He produced *Who's Afraid of Virginia Woolf?*, *The Boys in the Band*, and *Sweeney Todd*. **20** Beatrice Lillie d. In its obituary, *The New York Times* will report: "One spring day, while she was serving tea to friends in her East End Avenue apartment in New York, a pigeon flew in the window and sat on the arm of a chair. Some of Miss Lillie's guests were startled, but she merely looked at the bird and asked, 'any messages?'" Her longtime companion and court-appointed conservator, John Phillip Huck, 30 years her junior, will d. tomorrow of a heart attack.

FEBRUARY 19 Kate Nelligan m. pianist Robert Reale.

MARCH 12 Maurice Evans d.

MAY 14 Judith Ivey m. producer Tim Braine.

Personalities

Broadway would be a vulgar musical about Jewish Negroes.") Joseph Papp and Equity president Colleen Dewhurst demand that he be fired. Simon says of Dewhurst: "I'm afraid actors are not generally known for their intellects." **5** A full-page ad in *Variety* announces the national tour, beginning in November, of *Grover's Corners*, by Tom Jones and Harvey Schmidt, a new musical based on *Our Town*, starring Mary Martin. But Martin's illness will cancel it.

MAY • Which "Phantom" is merely a phantom? Georgia orders the company selling tickets to Ken Hill's production of *The Phantom of the Opera*—billed as "The Original London Stage Musical"—at the Fox Theatre in Atlanta, to warn patrons that it's not the more famous Andrew Lloyd Webber show. Hill's production, which Webber saw before writing his version, uses public domain opera music.

Plays and Musicals

MARCH 2 What do you do with two Otellos? Ken Ludwig's comedy *Lend Me a Tenor* (481), at the Royale, has the answer. Victor Garber, Philip Bosco, and Tovah Feldshuh are in the cast. Frank Rich, in the *Times*, thinks it's "all things farcical except hilarious" but likes it. The *Daily News* calls it the "most outrageous and funny romp to land on Broadway since *Noises Off*." **9** Wendy Wasserstein's Pulitzer Prize–winning *The Heidi Chronicles* (621) moves from the Playwrights Horizon to Broadway, and the Plymouth Theatre. Joan Allen plays Heidi, who, with her baby boomer friends, assesses what has happened to their ideals and relationships over two decades. Boyd Gaines is also in the cast. Sarah Jessica Parker was in it off-Broadway.

APRIL 25 Brian Friel's *Aristocrats* (186), a family drama set in Ireland, produced by the Manhattan Theatre Club, opens at Theatre Four. John Pankow is in the cast.

Business and Society

Births, Deaths, and Marriages

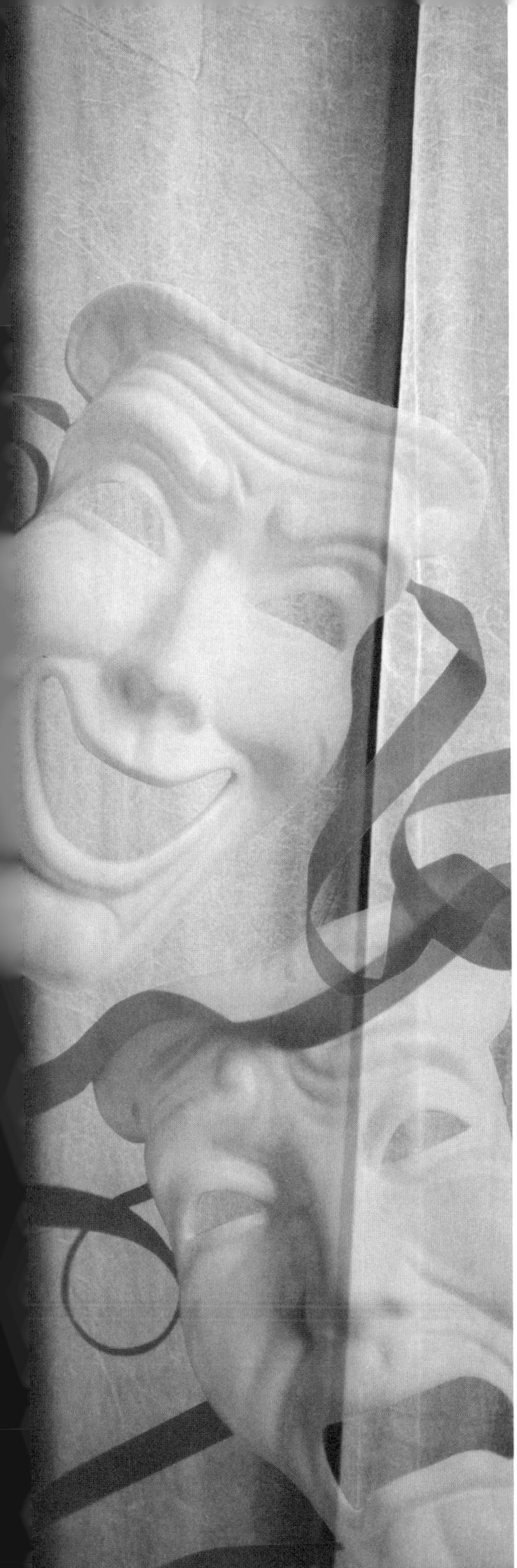

1989–90

Any season in which Neil Simon (*Jake's Women*) and Andrew Lloyd Webber (*Aspects of Love*) each have a flop sends a tremor through all box offices. *Annie 2* is the butt of jokes, but if it's a dog at the moment, there's always tomorrow. Garth Drabinsky's Livent becomes a force to be reckoned with, Walter Kerr and Richard Rodgers have theatres named for them, August Wilson's *The Piano Lesson* makes him a two-time winner, *Gypsy* becomes a three-time winner, and *A Chorus Line* comes to the end of the line.

- Only actress to play Mama Rose in *Gypsy* on Broadway who did not win a Tony for it: Ethel Merman
- Number of Al Hirschfeld drawings so far in a 65-year career: 13,000–14,000
- Ratio of hits to flops for straight plays on Broadway in the 1980s: 33 of 137 plays, or 1:4.15. Of the 33, 4 are by Neil Simon
- Weekly operating cost of *The Phantom of the Opera*: $405,000
- Number of original cast albums of *A Chorus Line* sold during its Broadway run: more than 1,250,000
- Split of the $50 million profit from *A Chorus Line* between the New York Shakespeare Festival and Michael Bennett: 75–25
- Only actor to originate roles in 4 Arthur Miller plays: Arthur Kennedy (who dies January 1990)—*All My Sons*, *Death of a Salesman*, *The Crucible*, and *The Price*
- Number of 5-play subscriptions sold by Jujamcyn: a disappointing 1,500
- First off-Broadway play turned into an Oscar-winning (Best Picture) film: *Driving Miss Daisy*
- Number of Broadway theatres named for critics: 2—Brooks Atkinson and, as of this season, Walter Kerr
- Playwrights with at least 2 Pulitzer Prizes: Eugene O'Neill (4), Robert E. Sherwood (3), and with 2 each, Thornton Wilder, George S. Kaufman, Tennessee Williams, Edward Albee, and now, August Wilson
- Number of Broadway productions that open this season between late December and late March: 1, a revival of *Miss Margarida's Way*, and it flops
- Increasingly successful: national tours of off-Broadway plays (*Driving Miss Daisy*, with Julie Harris and Brock Peters, makes more than $1.2 million in profit)
- Why the musical *City of Angels* is unusual for these days: it was written for Broadway and not adapted from another medium
- Total profit returned so far by *Nunsense*, now in its fifth season: $1 million
- Weekly profit from *Tony n' Tina's Wedding*: about $10,000

Productions on Broadway: 35

Pulitzer Prize for Drama: *The Piano Lesson* (August Wilson)

New York Drama Critics Awards:
Best Play: *The Piano Lesson* (August Wilson)
Best Foreign Play: *Privates on Parade* (Peter Nichols)
Best Musical: *City of Angels* (Cy Coleman-David Zippel)

Tony Awards:
Play: *The Grapes of Wrath* (Frank Galati, adaptation of John Steinbeck novel)
Actress in a Play: Maggie Smith (*Lettice & Lovage*)
Actor in a Play: Robert Morse (*Tru*)
Musical: *City of Angels* (Cy Coleman-David Zippel)
Actress in a Musical: Tyne Daly (*Gypsy*)
Actor in a Musical: James Naughton (*City of Angels*)

June
Martin Charnin announces *Annie 2: Miss Hannigan's Revenge*

July
Laurence Olivier d.

August
Stephen Sondheim appointed at Oxford

September
Andrew Lloyd Webber in Hollywood; Irving Berlin d.

October
David Hare-Frank Rich feud

November
Gypsy, with Tyne Daly, and *Grand Hotel: The Musical*

December
City of Angels

January
Jujamcyn subscription plan

February
Eric Bogosian's *Sex, Drugs, Rock & Roll*

March
Prelude to a Kiss and Kathleen Turner as Maggie the Cat

April
Aspects of Love opens, *A Chorus Line* closes

May
Robert Brustein attacks Lloyd Richards

Personalities

JUNE • Rex Harrison is knighted. **7** In the works is *Nick and Nora*, a musical based on *The Thin Man*. Arthur Laurents is writing the book and directing, with a score by Charles Strouse and Richard Maltby, Jr. "While it is always risky business to handicap legit shows," says *Variety* about this one, gestating now for five years, "the team behind *Nick and Nora* instills confidence that the show will bear the stamp of quality." **13** *Annie* lyricist Martin Charnin announces *Annie 2: Miss Hannigan's Revenge*, a "continuation of the story." He says it's Broadway bound.

JULY 9 Eileen Brennan breaks her leg when she falls into the orchestra pit at the Starlight Theatre in Kansas City. She was rehearsing the role of Miss Hannigan in *Annie*, which opens tomorrow.

AUGUST • Stephen Sondheim is appointed the first visiting professor of drama and musical theatre at Oxford University, his year-long tenure to begin in January. The chair was endowed by producer Cameron Mackintosh to the tune of $2.85 million.

SEPTEMBER • Andrew Lloyd Webber is in Hollywood, "really excited by the prospect of working in film," aiming to bring *Cats*, *The Phantom of the Opera*, and *Aspects of Love* to the screen. He says that his "first consideration is not about money, but about finding the right home for the right project." • The opening of *The Phantom of the Opera* at the Pantages Theatre in Toronto is the beginning of a string of successes for producer Garth Drabinsky's Live Entertainment Co. ("Livent"). The former CEO of Cineplex-Odeon is spearheading the city's development as a leading venue for big-budget musicals. Also active and influential on this scene is producer David Mirvish. **23** Broadway marquees are dimmed to honor the memory of Irving Berlin, who died yesterday.

OCTOBER 26 *Times* critic Frank Rich's panning of David Hare's *The Secret Rapture* (12), at the Barrymore, enrages the playwright, who writes to Rich, calling him "dishonest" and "irresponsible" in the way he exercises his institutional power.

Plays and Musicals

JUNE 6 Terrence McNally's *The Lisbon Traviata* (128), about obsessive gay opera fans and a romance that ends explosively, is at the Manhattan Theatre Club. "Nathan Lane brings a piquant buoyancy to a juicy role," writes Laurie Winer, in the *Wall Street Journal*.

AUGUST 22 A.R. Gurney's *Love Letters*, in which a different cast each week reads letters written over 50 years between two people, is off-Broadway, at the Promenade (64), and will move to the Edison (96) on October 31. It opens with John Rubenstein and Stockard Channing. Jason Robards, Jr., Cliff Robertson, Colleen Dewhurst, and Swoosie Kurtz are among others who will perform. **22** Peter Nichol's *Privates on Parade* (64), at the Roundabout, is about a British military entertainment troupe in late 1940s Malaya, which includes a female impersonator. Jim Dale and Donna Murphy are in the cast.

NOVEMBER 12 Tommy Tune directs and choreographs *Grand Hotel: The Musical* (1,018), at the Martin Beck, based on the early thirties play and film. The score is by Robert Wright, George Forrest, and Maury Yeston. But the emphasis is on staging and spectacle. The stars are David Carroll and Liliane Montevecchi. **15** *A Few Good Men* (497), a military courtroom drama by Aaron Sorkin, with a cast headed by Tom Hulce, opens at the Music Box. It's already been sold to Hollywood, which will bring it to the screen in 1992. **16** Tyne Daly is Mama Rose in the revival of *Gypsy* (476, plus 105 in a return engagement in 1991 at the Marquis), at the St. James. Christa Moore plays Louise. A rave from the *Times*'s Frank Rich (it's his favorite musical)—"goose bump-raising torrents of laughter and tears"—is enough to produce long lines at the box office tomorrow, where the take will be $335,275. Clive Barnes, though, says "the show looks second-hand and dry-cleaned," and the *Wall Street Journal* calls it "a disappointment."

DECEMBER 14 Robert Morse plays Truman

Business and Society

AUGUST • The Dramatists Guild, unable to agree with nonprofit theatres on a standard contract, declares unilaterally that a minimum royalty of five percent of the gross is in effect. Resident theatres saying that conditions vary throughout the country, making such a pact impractical, ignore it. • The new pact between Actors Equity and the League of American Theatres and Producers raises minimum pay on Broadway for actors to $813.75 a week.

OCTOBER • *Jerome Robbins' Broadway* raises the roof on Broadway ticket prices with a new $60 top.

DECEMBER 7 The New York State Supreme Court upholds landmark status for 22 Broadway theatres.

JANUARY • The Jujamcyn Theatres begins an unsuccessful attempt to sell tickets to Broadway shows by subscription, a practice that has been tried a number of times but only worked for the Theatre Guild. In the plan, $204 buys *Gypsy*, *Grand Hotel*, *City of Angels*, *Cat on a Hot Tin Roof*, and *The Piano Lesson*.

Births, Deaths, and Marriages

JULY 11 Laurence Olivier d.

AUGUST 31 Claire Luce d.

SEPTEMBER 22 Irving Berlin d. at age 101. The opera composer Puccini once said to an interviewer: "Your best composer is Berlin, isn't he?"

DECEMBER 22 Samuel Beckett d.

JANUARY 5 Arthur Kennedy d. He was the only actor to originate roles in four Arthur Miller plays: *All My Sons*, *Death of a Salesman*, *The Crucible*, and *The Price*.

APRIL 27 Playwright Bella Spewack d. Her husband and coauthor Samuel d. in 1971.

NOVEMBER • *Newsweek* critic Jack Kroll, who has voiced support for playwright David Hare's attack on *Times* critic Frank Rich—and criticized his colleague in a private conversation with Hare—is temporarily removed from the theatre beat by his magazine. *Variety*'s headline on the contretemps: "Ruffled Hare Airs Rich Bitch."

DECEMBER 13 Julie Andrews, who played Carnegie Hall with Carol Burnett in 1962 and did a television special with her in 1971, appears yet another time with Burnett on ABC in "Julie & Carol: Together Again."

JANUARY 4 A woman watching *Steel Magnolias* at the Lucille Lortel Theatre in Greenwich Village is shot in the knee when a pistol is dropped and goes off. The weapon's owner is not found, and the show goes on after a 45-minute break. **6** *Legs Diamond* choreographer Michael Shawn wins a $175,000 settlement out of court from the Nederlanders and other producers of the show over his claim that he was fired when he tested positive for AIDS. **17** In his opening monologue on the "Tonight" show, Johnny Carson says he looked at his investment portfolio and found that "I put all my money into AT&T, Bloomingdales, and *Annie 2*." The musical has died in Washington, D.C. The producers, with leftover scenery, would like to revive the original *Annie*, but neither star Dorothy Loudon nor the Nederlanders, whose Marquis Theatre on Broadway *Annie 2* was heading for, will bite.

MARCH 5 Jujamcyn Theatres renames the Ritz the Walter Kerr Theatre, after the *Herald-Tribune* and *Times* critic. At the celebrity-studded ceremony, Colleen Dewhurst draws laughs by giving a dramatic reading of the honoree's pan of her performance in the 1964 *Antony and Cleopatra*. **8** *Jake's Women*, opening at the Old Globe in San Diego, will be dead in a month, only the second Neil Simon play to fold short of Broadway. The other was *Actors and Actresses*, in 1983. **27** The Nederlanders rename the Forty-sixth Street Theatre the Richard Rodgers Theatre. The composer's *Do I Hear a Waltz?* played here. *Damn Yankees* and

---

Capote in Jay Allen's play *Tru* (295), adapted from the author's works, at the Booth. **11** *City of Angels* (878), the Cy Coleman-David Zippel musical, with book by Larry Gelbart, is at the Virginia Theatre after no tryouts but nine weeks of rehearsals and three and a half weeks of previews. Striking special effects and sets by Robin Wagner highlight the parallel plots involving the life of a Hollywood producer and the *film noir* he's producing. Randy Graff, James Naughton, and Rene Auberjonois are in the cast. **19** Dustin Hoffman is Shylock in *The Merchant of Venice* (81), at the Forty-sixth Street Theatre. Peter Hall directs, and Geraldine James is Portia. Hoffman's performance "is a character actor's polished gem rather than a tragedian's stab at the jugular," Frank Rich writes in the *Times*, approving of the star's approach.

FEBRUARY 9 Eric Bogosian's one-man show *Sex, Drugs, Rock & Roll* (103) opens at the Orpheum.

MARCH 14 Alec Baldwin and Mary-Louise Parker star in the Craig Lucas fantasy *Prelude to a Kiss*, which speculates on one thing that could happen when you kiss the bride, at the Circle Rep (33). It transfers to Broadway, at the Helen Hayes (440), on May 1, after a rave review from the *Times*, with Timothy Hutton replacing Baldwin, who has other business in Hollywood. Baldwin and Meg Ryan are in the 1992 film. **21** Kathleen Turner is Maggie—she's "triumphant," says Clive Barnes in the *Post*—in the revival of Tennessee Williams's *Cat on a Hot Tin Roof* (149), at the Eugene O'Neill. Charles Durning also draws praise as Big Daddy. **22** The Steppenwolf Company's production of *The Grapes of Wrath* (188), adapted by Frank Galati, opens at the Cort. Gary Sinese and Terry Kinney star. A white woman breast-feeding a black man is a notable touch toward the end of the play. The *Times*'s Frank rich calls it "an epic achievement" but also notes with irony that to see this play about the "Oakies," "audiences must step around homeless people to get to the theatre." **25** Maggie Smith is a tourist guide with an overactive imagination in Peter Shaffer's *Lettice & Lovage* (284), costarring Margaret Tyzack, at the Barrymore.

FEBRUARY 28 Variety reports: "Broadway looks more like the Sahara desert than a theatrical capital this winter, with just one new show, the flop revival of *Miss Margarida's Way*, between the December 19 opening of *Merchant of Venice* and March 21 bow of *Cat On A Hot Tin Roof*."

APRIL • Cameron Mackintosh tells theatre party agents that for *Miss Saigon*, they will not get the standard 10 percent commission but rather a sliding scale, from five to 10 percent, with only the slow-moving locations bringing top dollar. They respond with a threatened boycott. **2** Equity, in a meeting with Jerome Robbins and the Shubert Organization's Bernard Jacobs, complains that there is only one black performer in *Jerome Robbins' Broadway*. Similar complaints have been made about *The Phantom of the Opera* and *Les Miserables*. **18** The New York State Redevelopment Corporation takes title to the Victory and Liberty Theatres on Forty-second Street through a condemnation order to speed up their renovation.

MAY 24 Representatives of New Musicals, an organization started to nurture productions from workshop to major opening, meets with *New York Times* editors to ask that the paper not review their workshop performances. The *Times* refuses and

Personalities

How to Succeed in Business Without Really Trying were also staged at the theatre.

APRIL • Maggie Smith, appearing in *Lettice & Lovage* at the Barrymore, complains to the Shubert Organization that while onstage, she can hear the gospel music coming from the Longacre next door, which is playing *Truly Blessed.* **8** The West End is in an uproar, and Producer Cameron Mackintosh is furious. His Broadway-bound musical *Miss Saigon* has been passed over for an Olivier Award in favor of *Return to the Forbidden Planet.*

MAY • David Carroll, sick with AIDS, has to leave the cast of the musical *Grand Hotel.* **17** At the opening of *Annie 2* at the Goodspeed Opera House in Connecticut, Chelsea has replaced Beau in the part of the dog Sandy because, lyricist Martin Charnin says, Beau "was not energized enough." Lauren Gaffney is the new Annie. **21** Robert Brustein, reviewing *The Piano Lesson* in *The New Republic,* attacks Lloyd Richards, Brustein's successor as Dean of the Yale Drama School, for devoting too much of the school's resources to nurturing the career of playwright August Wilson.

Plays and Musicals

APRIL 8 Now Andrew Lloyd Webber as well as Neil Simon has a flop this season. *Aspects of Love* (377), with lyrics by Don Black and Charles Hart, is at the Broadhurst, where it has an $11 million advance to keep it open for a while. The *Times's* Frank Rich, no Lloyd Webber fan, says the composer's mistake was to try to write about people rather than "cats, roller-skating trains and falling chandeliers." **16** Four days after winning the Pulitzer Prize, August Wilson's *The Piano Lesson* (329) opens at the Walter Kerr Theatre. Charles S. Dutton and S. Apatha Merckerson play brother and sister in 1930s Pittsburgh, struggling over whether to sell a family heirloom. Lloyd Richards is directing. The show is being offered to the 13,000 subscribers of the off-Broadway Manhattan Theatre Club as one of the plays in their subscription. **28** *A Chorus Line*, the longest-running show in Broadway history, gives its 6,137th and final performance. The original 1975 cast is onstage at the end for a six-minute standing ovation, as a large image of Michael Bennett is unfurled. When it opened, the *Playbill* read: "An Audition, Time: Now." Lately, it's read: "Time: 1975."

August Wilson PF

MAY 20 *Forever Plaid* (1,811), Stuart Ross's send-up and songfest of 1950s music, opens at Steve McGraw's cabaret, where the cast consists of Stan Chandler, David Engle, Jason Graae, and Guy Stroman.

Business and Society

reviews *The Kiss of the Spiderwoman* in its workshop incarnation.

Births, Deaths, and Marriages

1990–91

The voice of an era is silenced with the death of Mary Martin. Box office receipts are down for the first time in five years, by more than five percent, and attendance has dropped nine percent compared to last season. Japanese investment capital, becoming a major factor on Broadway, helps launch *The Will Rogers Follies*. Cameron Mackintosh battles Equity over the cast of *Miss Saigon*. The Broadway Alliance, an attempt to drop production costs and ticket prices at certain theatres, starts slowly. David Merrick produces much publicity but little business for *Oh, Kay!* Nicol Williamson dramatically makes a point, and *Shogun* shoots blanks but still almost manages to kill its star.

- Street price of *Miss Saigon* tickets: as much as $275 each
- First actor to win 3 Tony Awards in the featured performer category: Hinton Battle, who wins for *Miss Saigon* and previously took Tonys for *Sophisticated Ladies* and *The Tap Dance Kid*
- Number of people using taxis each night in the Broadway theatre district, according to the League of American Theatres and Producers: about 20,000
- What David Hampton, who inspired John Guare to write *Six Degrees of Separation* when he claimed that he was Sidney Poitier's son, says he's doing these days: trying to become an actor
- Amount lost by *La Bete*: over $2 million, possibly the most ever for a straight play
- Actor who does the voice of Flo Ziegfeld in *The Will Rogers Follies*: Gregory Peck
- Amount lost by *Shogun*: about $7 million
- Only Broadway musical this season with a song praising dildos: *Shogun*
- Song Philip Casnoff is singing at a press preview of the musical *Shogun* when he's knocked unconscious by falling scenery: "Death Walk"
- Musical that mega-flop *Shogun* was booked in place of at the Marquis Theatre: *Annie 2*, which flopped out of town
- Cost of one set for a Broadway play: more than $50,000
- Weekly operating cost of an off-Broadway musical: $60,000
- Home away from home: *After the Fall* and *The Crucible* are being produced in London, where Arthur Miller is now more popular than in America
- Subject of Al Hirschfeld's first caricature published in a newspaper: Sacha Guitry
- Most "Ninas" in a Hirschfeld caricature: by his recollection, the 40 in the one he did of Whoopi Goldberg in 1984

Productions on Broadway: 28, a new low

Pulitzer Prize for Drama: *Lost in Yonkers* (Neil Simon)

New York Drama Critics Circle Awards:
Best Play: *Six Degrees of Separation* (John Guare)
Best Foreign Play: *Our Country's Good* (Timberlake Wertenbaker)
Best Musical: *Will Rogers Follies* (Cy Coleman-Betty Comden-Adolph Green)

Tony Awards:
Play: *Lost in Yonkers* (Neil Simon)
Actress in a play: Mercedes Ruehl (*Lost in Yonkers*)
Actor in a play: Nigel Hawthorne (*Shadowlands*)
Musical: *The Will Rogers Follies* (Cy Coleman-Betty Comden-Adolph Green)
Actress in a musical: Lea Salonga (*Miss Saigon*)
Actor in a musical: Jonathan Pryce (*Miss Saigon*)

June	July	August	September	October	November
Broadway Alliance and *Six Degrees of Separation*	*New York Times* attacks Equity	Equity says "no," then "yes" on Jonathan Pryce	He's back: David Merrick	Director Lloyd Richards calls for profit sharing	Mary Martin d.

December	January	February	March	April	May
Ron Silver withdraws from *La Bete*	Arbiter puts Lea Salonga in *Miss Saigon*	Neil Simon's *Lost in Yonkers*	Andre Bishop succeeds Gregory Mosher at Lincoln Center	*Miss Saigon* opens	*The Will Rogers Follies*

Personalities

SEPTEMBER 13 In a rare public appearance since his 1983 stroke, David Merrick attends a dress rehearsal of *Oh, Kay!* When he sees a journalist who criticized him in *Vanity Fair*, he points to the door and shouts "Out!" several times until she leaves. **15** Jerry Zaks, described by Jujamcyn Theatres head Rocco Landesman as "the most sought-after director now working," leaves the Lincoln Center Theater to become director-in-residence for Jujamcyn. He's directed *Six Degrees of Separation* and *Lend Me a Tenor* and wanted to do Stephen Sondheim's *Assassins*, but the Lincoln Center's Gregory Mosher didn't.

OCTOBER 21 Lloyd Richards, a coproducer as well as director of August Wilson's *The Piano Lesson*, has convinced his colleagues to share future profits from the play—profitable, as of today—with the cast.

NOVEMBER 2 Sardi's, closed in July because the owners couldn't pay their bills, is back in the hands of Vincent Sardi, Jr. and reopens today. **5** Producer David Merrick, enraged at Frank Rich's negative review in *The New York Times* of *Oh, Kay!* and Alex Witchel's panning of the musical in her column in the paper, takes an ad in the *Times* alluding to the couple's personal relationship. The ad has a heart, with the words: "At last people are holding hands in the theatre again." The *Times* withdraws it after the first edition. **13** Philip Casnoff, singing the song "Death Walk" in a press preview of *Shogun: The Musical*, is knocked unconscious by a large screen that falls on him. A doctor in the house rushes to his aid, and the show is over for the evening. In two days, he will be back for opening night. **15** In a TV appearance, self-help author Dr. Miriam Stoppard, wife of playwright Tom Stoppard, criticizes "women who betray other women." Her playwright husband is said to be carrying on a relationship with actress Felicity Kendall.

DECEMBER • A.R. Gurney resigns from the Dramatists Guild because of its boycott of nonresident theatres, which have

Plays and Musicals

JUNE 14 He's Sidney Poitier's son, the man says. John Guare's *Six Degrees of Separation*, with Jerry Zaks directing, opens at the Mitzi E. Newhouse Theatre (185), in Lincoln Center. "Extraordinary high comedy," Frank Rich says in the *Times*. The cast includes Stockard Channing, Kelly Bishop, and Robin Morse, daughter of Robert Morse. On November 8, it moves upstairs to the bigger Vivian Beaumont Theatre (496). The film arrives in 1993. **28** The musical *Falsettoland* (215), a sequel to *March of the Falsettos*, is at the Playwrights Horizon and will later move to the Lucille Lortel. AIDS looms large in this show by William Finn and James Lapine, directed by Lapine, with a cast that includes Stephen Bogardus.

OCTOBER 16 In *The Sum of Us* (335), off-Broadway, at the Cherry Lane, Tony Goldwyn is the gay son whose father, played by Richard Venture, is trying to come to terms with him. The play, set in Australia, is by David Stevens. **18** *Once on This Island* (469), a Stephen Flaherty-Lynn Ahrens musical steeped in Caribbean fairy tales, opens at the Booth, a transfer from the Playwrights Horizon. It stars an actress-singer named La Chanze, Jerry Dixon, and Kecia Lewis-Evans.

NOVEMBER 1 The revival of the 1926 Gershwin show *Oh, Kay!* (77), David Merrick's first musical in a decade, opens at the Richard Rodgers Theatre. The revised book has shifted the scene from Long Island to Harlem, and the all-black cast features Angela Teek. It's "chintzy" and "innocuous," says Frank Rich, in the *Times*; it's "surprisingly terrific," says Clive Barnes in the *Post*. **4** Paul Hipp plays the title role in *Buddy: The Buddy Holly Story* (225), featuring the music of the rock 'n' roll legend, opening at the Shubert. **11** William Nicholson's play *Shadowlands* (169)—originally his screenplay for a 1985 British film starring Joss Ackland and Claire Bloom—about the romance between C.S. Lewis and American poet Joy Davidman, is at the Brooks Atkinson. It stars Nigel Hawthorne and Jane Alexander. The 1993

Business and Society

JUNE • The League of American Theatres and Producers and Broadway unions reach agreement on a plan, called The Broadway Alliance, to cut the cost of producing shows at several of Broadway's underused houses: the Walter Kerr, Belasco, Lyceum, and Nederlander Theatres. The unions make concessions, with profit sharing as compensation. Ticket prices will also be kept low. **29** The National Endowment for the Arts, under pressure from conservatives, rejects grant proposals from four performance artists because of the sexual content of their work.

JULY • New Musicals, an organization created less than a year ago to nurture along works from showcase to Broadway, is already faltering and will flounder after *Kiss of the Spider Woman*, hurt by bad reviews, does not draw as expected. Jujamcyn Theatres and Capital Cities/ABC are among the investors.

AUGUST 7 Equity bars the use of British actor Jonathan Pryce in the Broadway production of *Miss Saigon* because, potentially, he would be taking the place of an American actor and would be a

Births, Deaths, and Marriages

JUNE 2 Rex Harrison and Jack Gilford d. **7** Barbara Baxley d. **19** Marian Seldes m. writer Garson Kanin. She appeared in his play *A Gift of Time* in 1962.

AUGUST 29 Sandy, the beige terrier mix who played "Sandy" in *Annie*, is dead at age 16. An abused puppy, bought from the Connecticut Humane Society for $8 on the day he was to have been killed as an unclaimed animal, he missed only 14 of the show's 2,377 performances and only then to make a special appearance in Las Vegas with Liberace and the musical's original star, Andrea McArdle.

OCTOBER 10 Producer Irene Mayer Selznick, whose shows included *A Streetcar Named Desire* and *Bell, Book, and Candle*, d.

refused to accept the guild's standardized contract. Gurney's play *The Snow Ball* is being produced at the Old Globe, in San Diego. • Andrew Lloyd Webber takes his production company, the Really Useful Group, private. **28** Ron Silver withdraws from *La Bete*, now in a Boston tryout. Although all agree to "irreconcilable interpretive differences" as a reason, it's said that he just couldn't handle the verse in this verse drama, including a 20-page monologue. Tom McGowan, his understudy, takes over.

FEBRUARY • The tour of *Lettice & Lovage*, set to star Vanessa Redgrave, is canceled when investors are scared off by the actress's remarks that sound like support for Iraq's Saddam Hussein.

Mercedes Ruehl *MSN*

MARCH • Gregory Mosher, artistic director of the Lincoln Center Theatre, resigns and is succeeded by Andre Bishop.

APRIL 30 Davis Gaines dons the mask to play the lead in the first of his 1,937 performances in *The Phantom of the Opera.*

MAY 2 Actor Evan Handler has good reason to find the title of the play *I Hate Hamlet* appropriate. Nicol Williamson yells at Handler during tonight's performance: "[P]ut some life into it" and makes his point, sharply, with his foil. Handler responds by making an unscheduled stage exit—and he will not be back. **21** David Merrick's estranged wife Etan charges in their divorce case that their film stars Anthony Hopkins and Debra Winger. **20** James Clavell's bestselling novel *Shogun* (72) becomes an unsuccessful musical, at the Marquis Theatre. The Paul Chihara-John Priver show, with elaborate costumes and sets, stars Philip Casnoff. "Pillowing" is the only song in a Broadway musical this season in praise of dildos: "It never tires of women like a lazy, jaded man."

JANUARY 27 Stephen Sondheim's musical *Assassins* (25), directed by Jerry Zaks, with a book by Jerome Weidman, is at Playwrights Horizon. Victor Garber is in this show, in which a number of assassins interact across time and space.

FEBRUARY 10 Andrew Lloyd Webber, a coproducer of *La Bete* (25), obviously thought that a play in the style of Molière, in rhymed couplets, starring the unknown Tom McGowan, could make it on Broadway, at the Eugene O'Neill, at this time. It can't. **21** Neil Simon's *Lost in Yonkers* (780), a comedy in which some of the laughs stick in the throat, opens at the Richard Rodgers Theatre. Mercedes Ruehl, Irene Worth, and Kevin Spacey are the principals in this story of a dictatorial grandmother presiding over a family whose imperfections are endearing and disturbing. It's on the screen in 1993. **28** The Broadway Alliance's first attempt to bring theatregoers back to Broadway's periphery houses with moderately budgeted, low-price ticket productions is Steve Tesich's *The Speed of Darkness* (36), at the Belasco. This play about Vietnam veterans, starring Len Cariou, won't do it.

APRIL 2 David Merrick won't say die on *Oh, Kay!* which closed at the Richard Rodgers on January 8. He's recast the lead, with Rae Dawn Chong, poured several hundred thousand dollars into the show in hopes of a Tony nomination, and has reopened with previews at the Lunt-Fontanne. It will close again, still in previews, on April 14. **11** *Miss Saigon*, with a plot inspired by *Madam Butterfly*, and an advance sale approaching $40 million, opens at the Broadway Theatre. Jonathan Pryce, Lea Salonga, Hinton Battle, and Liz Callaway are in the cast of this Claude-Michel Schonberg-Alain Boublil-Richard Maltby, Jr. musical. With Caucasian playing a Eurasian when actors of Asian extraction are available. Producer Cameron Mackintosh says no Pryce, no Broadway production. **16** Equity reverses its stand of August 7, permitting Jonathan Pryce to play on Broadway in *Miss Saigon* because he's an international star uniquely qualified for it. Cameron Mackintosh still threatens cancellation unless he gets more concessions. **22** Asian-Americans in the arts take a full-page ad in *Variety* protesting the casting of Jonathan Pryce in *Miss Saigon.*

SEPTEMBER 17 Cameron Mackintosh, satisfied that Equity has acknowledged his control over casting, agrees to go ahead with bringing *Miss Saigon* to Broadway. He's also agreed to make an effort to cast Asian-Americans in it. **18** New York City creates the Forty-second Street Entertainment Corporation to reenergize the flagging redevelopment of the one-time heart of the theatre district. The board of directors includes Chita Rivera and Terrence McNally.

OCTOBER • The Dramatists Guild threatens resident theatres with a boycott unless they agree to the group's standardized contract.

When Irene Mayer Selznick quarrelled with Elia Kazan, director of *A Streetcar Named Desire,* she shouted at him: "I've survived Louis B. Mayer and I've survived David O. Selznick. It's no use. You better lay off." He laid off.

NOVEMBER 4 Mary Martin d. A *New York Times* editorial wistfully says: "[W]hat we wouldn't give to have a tape of Mary Martin and Ethel Merman, one of the few performers who played in the same league, sitting on tall stools 37 years ago for a TV spectacular and showing the audience what show biz was all about." One of her grandsons once introduced her to his friend as "Peter Pan." **5** Herbert Berghof d.

MAY 26 Playwright Tom Eyen d.

Personalities

second marriage was never consummated. But the 79-year-old's live-in-lover Natalie Lloyd says that "sexually, he is very, very good for a man his age."

Plays and Musicals

Cameron Mackintosh producing, its creators are essentially the *Les Miserables* team. Production designer John Napier's helicopter is a dramatic touch. Reviews are mixed, with the *Times* calling it "gripping entertainment," while *Variety*'s reviewer "can't recall another musical in which so many lyrics had to rhyme with ass, in which so many breasts and backsides were grabbed." **14** The Steppenwolf Theatre Company moves into its new $8.2 million, 500-seat house, south of Chicago's Loop. The inaugural production at this first theatre built for itself by a Windy City troupe is Ronald Harwood's *Another Time*, starring Albert Finney. **25** *The Secret Garden* (706), a Lucy Simon-Marsha Norman musical about an orphan, her uncle, and a ghost-ridden house, opens at the St. James. Susan Schulman is directing, with a cast that includes Rebecca Luker, Mandy Patinkin, and Daisy Eagan. The production is physically resplendent. **29** Convicts transported to Australia in the eighteenth century stage a play in Timberlake Wertenbaker's *Our Country's Good* (48), at the Nederlander Theatre. The cast, including Cherry Jones, Tracey Ellis, and Adam LeFevre, switch roles during the play, the second produced under terms of the Broadway Alliance.

MAY 1 *The Will Rogers Follies* (963), a Cy Coleman-Betty Comden-Adolph Green musical, opens at the Palace, where it will receive 11 Tony nominations and win for Best Musical, the same accolade it gets from the New York Drama Critics Circle. Keith Carradine is the humorist, and direction and choreography is by Tommy Tune.

Business and Society

DECEMBER • Joseph Papp lays off 30 workers at the Public Theatre, a consequence of his refusal to take $750,000 in Endowment for the Arts grant money that has political strings attached. • The New York City Human Rights Commission holds hearings into discrimination in theatre and film casting. Among those testifying are Tony Randall and playwright David Henry Hwang.

JANUARY 7 Lea Salonga, a Filipino, has a featured role in *Miss Saigon* on Broadway, as she did in London, thanks to an arbiter's ruling. Asian-American actors protest that the role can just as easily been given to an Asian-American.

APRIL • Jujamcyn Theatres forms a partnership with TV Asahi, a Japanese broadcasting company that will partly finance some of the shows at Jujamcyn houses.

Births, Deaths, and Marriages

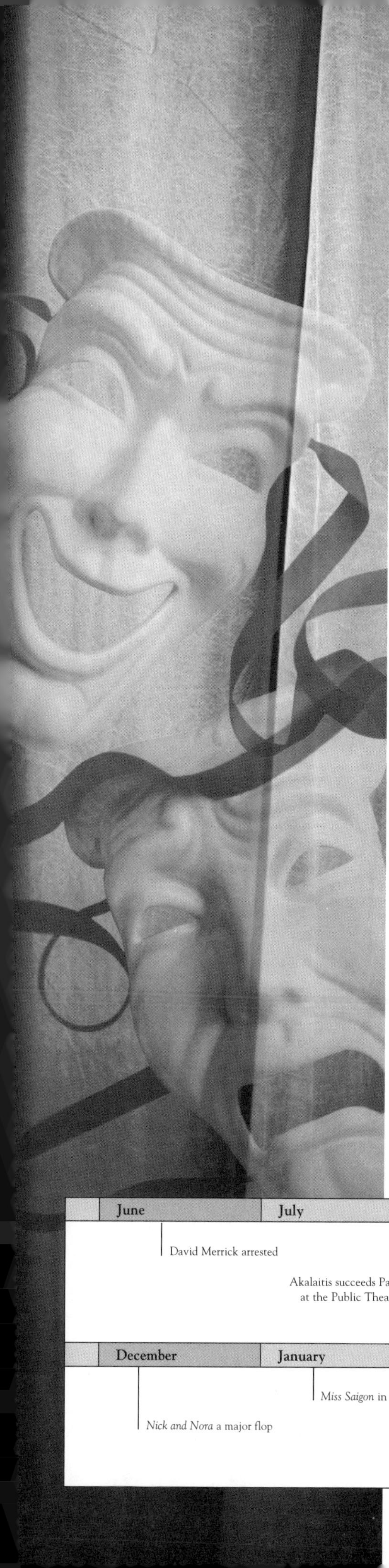

1991–92

Brian Friel's *Dancing at Lughnasa*, Terrence McNally's *Lips Together, Teeth Apart*, and George Gershwin's *Crazy for You* all appear by mid February. But the developing trend that has major openings crowd the tail end of the season, right before the Tonys, rather than in the fall, is manifested in the late-season debuts of Herb Gardner's *Conversations with My Father*, the Alec Baldwin-Jessica Lange glamour cast in *A Streetcar Named Desire*, August Wilson's *Two Trains Running*, *Guys and Dolls* with Nathan Lane, *Jelly's Last Jam*, and *Falsettos*—all within four weeks. The much-heralded *Nick and Nora*, on the other hand, opens in December. *Variety*'s verdict: "Asta ain't the only dog onstage." Death's toll is especially heavy this season. Among those gone are Eva Le Gallienne, Colleen Dewhurst, Joseph Papp, Judith Anderson, Nancy Walker, José Ferrer, and Molly Picon.

- Percentage of this season's Broadway productions opening from March through May: more than 50 percent
- Number of times Tony Randall and Jack Klugman have played in Neil Simon's *The Odd Couple* on Broadway: just once, in June, at a benefit for Randall's National Actors Company
- Back on Broadway: more neon lights as the new office buildings in Times Square begin to open
- New fine for producers neglecting to identify preview performances in display ads for shows: $300–$500
- Amount spent per week publicizing *Miss Saigon*: $22,000
- How *Miss Saigon* profits are divided between producer Cameron Mackintosh and investors: 60–40
- What *Variety* calls producer Cameron Mackintosh: "Mack the Marketer"
- Number of preview performances given by *Nick and Nora*: 71
- Number of regular performances for *Nick and Nora*: 9
- Who tipped off the Manhattan District Attorney that there was as much as $300,000 missing from *Catskills on Broadway* receipts: comedian Freddie Roman, who finds the discrepancy between the size of the audiences and the money in the box office not at all amusing
- Percentage of money spent on all theatre tickets bought in U.S. and Canada that goes into the box offices of *Les Miserables* and the *The Phantom of the Opera*: more than 50 percent
- Only country where *Les Miserables* has played and is not a smash hit: France, where it originated

Productions on Broadway: 36

Pulitzer Prize for Drama: *The Kentucky Cycle* (Robert Schenkkan)

New York Drama Critics Circle Awards:
Best Play: *Dancing at Lughnasa* (Brian Friel)
Best American Play: *Two Trains Running* (August Wilson)

Tony Awards:
Play: *Dancing at Lughnasa* (Brian Friel)
Actor in a play: Judd Hirsch (*Conversations with My Father*)
Actress in a play: Glenn Close (*Death and the Maiden*)
Musical: *Crazy for You* (George and Ira Gershwin)
Actor in a musical: Gregory Hines (*Jelly's Last Jam*)
Actress in a musical: Faith Prince (*Guys and Dolls*)

June	July	August	September	October	November
David Merrick arrested	Akalaitis succeeds Papp at the Public Theatre	Colleen Dewhurst d	Julie Bovasso d.	Brian Friel's *Dancing at Lughnasa*	Joseph Papp d.

December	January	February	March	April	May
Nick and Nora a major flop	*Miss Saigon* in the black	*Crazy for You*	Sandy Dennis and Nancy Walker d.; John Simon m.	*Guys and Dolls* and *Jelly's Last Jam*	Sondheim rejects National Medal of Arts

Personalities

JUNE • Ron Silver is elected president of Actors Equity. • Zelda Fichandler, who cofounded the Arena Stage in Washington, D.C., in 1950, leaves to become Artistic Director of the Acting Company in New York. She also has headed the graduate acting program at NYU since 1984. Douglas Wager is new Artistic Director of the Arena Stage. **2** Hinton Battle, who collects his Tony Award tonight for his work in *Miss Saigon*, is refused admission to the dinner at the Marriott Marquis Hotel after the ceremony because he never received a ticket. **12** David Merrick is arrested at JFK airport when he attempts to fly to London carrying $145,000 in undeclared cash and traveler's checks. Just a few days ago, his pistol was confiscated at the same airport before a London flight. **21** Nicol Williamson, in a curtain speech at *I Hate Hamlet*, where he's playing John Barrymore, criticizes the Tony nominating process that did not acknowledge his show. Alluding to Irving Berlin's "There's No Business Like Show Business," Williamson adds: "[E]verything about it is appalling."

JULY 1 Carol Channing, asked in a *Theater Week* interview if she got any satisfaction from the failure of the film *Hello, Dolly!* in which Barbra Streisand, rather than she, played the title role, replies: "Oh, yes. You know the set from 'The Harmonia

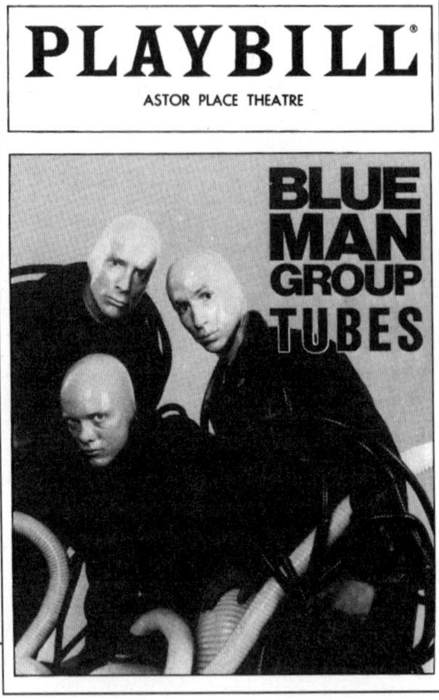

"Mummenschanz on acid," according to *Variety* *PB*

Plays and Musicals

JUNE 25 Terrence McNally's *Lips Together, Teeth Apart* (250), about two married couples on Fire Island on the Fourth of July, opens at the Manhattan Theatre Club at the City Center. In the cast are Swoosie Kurtz, Nathan Lane, Anthony Heald, and Christine Baranski. It moves to the Lucille Lortel in January.

OCTOBER 13 The 499-seat off-Broadway Variety Arts Theatre opens on the edge of the East Village with the musical *Return to the Forbidden Planet*, written by Bob Carton and loosely based on a 1950s science fiction film. It features that era's rock 'n' roll. **24** Brian Friel's *Dancing at Lughnasa* (421), a Tony, Drama Critics Circle, and Olivier Award winner, opens at the Plymouth. Set in 1930s Ireland, it's about the Mundy family, in which the five sisters are unmarried and unhappy. Gerard McSorely plays the son who grows up and remembers it all, narrating in place of the playwright. It "does exactly what theatre was born to do," writes Frank Rich, in the *Times*, "carrying both its characters and audience aloft." **31** *The Ride Down Mount Morgan*, the first of Arthur Miller's plays to debut outside the U.S., is at the Wyndham Theatre in London. It stars Tom Conti as a man with two wives.

NOVEMBER 17 *Tubes*, the Blue Man Group's performance art, opens at the Astor Place Theatre. *Variety* calls it "Mummenschanz on acid."

DECEMBER 5 Freddie Roman's *Catskills on Broadway* (452) brings borscht belt humor to the Lunt-Fontanne Theatre, with the author, Marilyn Michaels, Mal Z. Lawrence, and Dick Capri. "Truth in advertising," one reviewer calls it. **8** "Asta ain't the only dog onstage," *Variety* says about *Nick and Nora* (9), a musical based on *The Thin Man*, by Charles Strouse and Richard Maltby, Jr., with a book by Arthur Laurents, at the Marquis. Its cast includes Barry Bostwick, Joanna Gleason, Christine Baranski, Remak Ramsay, and Chris Sarandon. It

Business and Society

JUNE • The off-Broadway Roundabout Theatre takes over the Criterion-Stage-Right Theatre in the Broadway Theatre district.

JULY • Actors Equity charges the producers of *The Will Rogers Follies* with discrimination for their lack of casting of minorities.

AUGUST • The Shubert Organization, which controlled seven Chicago theatres before the decline of road tours, sells the last of them, the Shubert, to the Nederlanders. • Polygram buys 30 percent of Andrew Lloyd Webber's Really Useful Group.

OCTOBER • The Broadway Alliance plan is revised to allow for more leeway in ticket pricing and money raised through investors after the first two plays under its previous guidelines flopped last season.

NOVEMBER 20 New York City's Commissioner of Consumer Affairs, Mark Green, informs the League of American Theatres and Producers that preview performances must be identified in ads. His directive is occasioned by the nine weeks of previews, largely at full price, given for the musical *Nick and Nora*.

Births, Deaths, and Marriages

JUNE 3 Eva Le Gallienne d. Rosemary Harris said of her: "If you listen to Miss Le G you can hear 15 shades of meaning in 15 syllables." Le Gallienne said, "I would rather play Ibsen than eat—and that's often just what it amounts to." **5** Larry Kert d. of AIDS. **14** Peggy Ashcroft d.

JULY 5 Mildred Dunnock d. **10** Gerome Ragne d. The coauthor of *Hair* was 48.

AUGUST 22 Colleen Dewhurst d.

SEPTEMBER 14 Julie Bovasso d. She won three Obies, and her Tempo Playhouse, which she opened in New York in the 1950s, was a beachhead of the Theatre of the Absurd.

OCTOBER • David Mamet, formerly m. to Lindsay Crouse, m. actress Rebecca Pidgeon. **12** Aline MacMahon d. **31** Joseph Papp d.

Gardens' is still there. They were doing "The Love Boat" on top of it. Every time I'm there I do a dance of death on it." **26** JoAnne Akalaitis succeeds Joseph Papp as artistic director of the New York Shakespeare Festival.

AUGUST 23 Broadway's lights dim for two minutes at 8:00 P.M. for Colleen Dewhurst.

OCTOBER • Jessica Lange, in *Vanity Fair*, describes her romance with Sam Shepard. She says that she would kill him if he were unfaithful. She also says that during her relationship with Bob Fosse, they often went to Forty-second Street sex shows.

NOVEMBER 1 Broadway's lights dim to honor Joseph Papp, who died yesterday.

gave 71 preview performances. **10** Tony Randall's National Actors Theatre debuts at the Belasco with a limited-run revival of Arthur Miller's *The Crucible* (32). The stars are Martin Sheen, Martha Scott, and Michael York. **19** Patrick Stewart is a notable success in his dramatic staged reading of Dickens's *A Christmas Carol* (14), at the Eugene O'Neill Theatre.

JANUARY 31 Jon Robin Baitz's *The Substance of Fire* (205), a drama about publishing, moves to the Mitzi Newhouse Theatre, Lincoln Center's off-Broadway house, after 140 performances at Playwrights Horizon. The cast includes Sarah Jessica Parker, Ron Rifkin, and Maria Tucci.

FEBRUARY 19 *Crazy for You* (1,622), a ren-

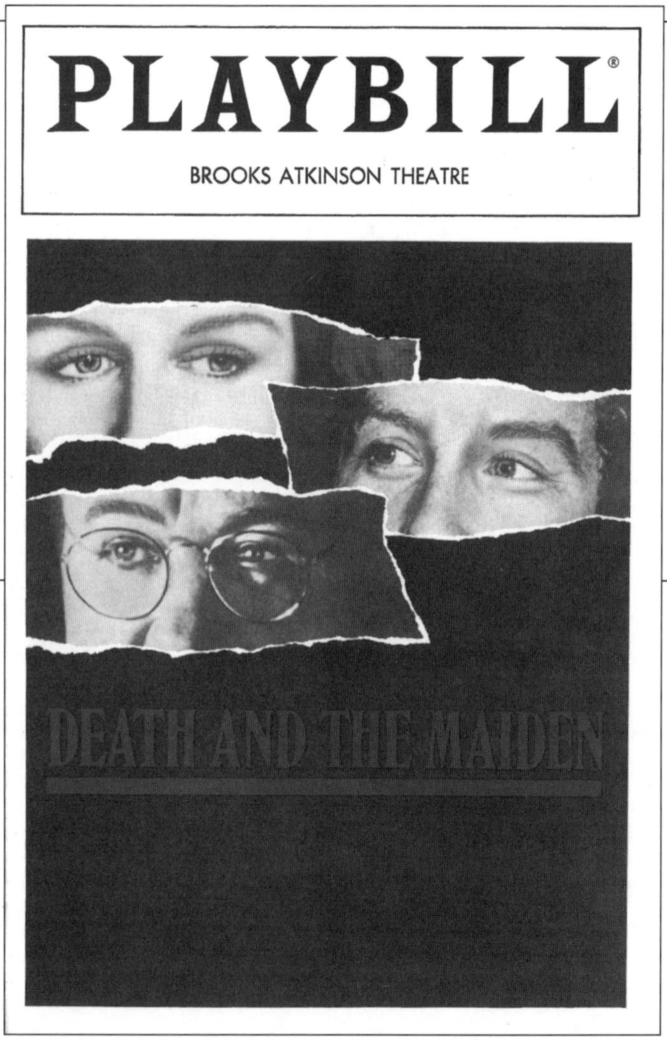

The 'eyes' of *Death and the Maiden* belong to Glenn Close, Richard Dreyfuss and Gene Hackman PB

DECEMBER 4 New York City's Consumer Affairs Commissioner backtracks from his directive of a month ago, no longer requiring theatres to mention in classified as well as display ads that a show is still in previews. The justification is that this would add to the expense of the advertisement. **6** The Nederlander organization is selling the Mark Hellinger Theatre, where *My Fair Lady* played, to the Times Square Church, it is announced.

JANUARY • Broadway theatre unions go on record opposing Shubert efforts to turn the Longacre Theatre over to New York City for use as a courthouse. The unions are worried about losing more jobs. **1** The Broadway theatre district is now patrolled by a private, uniformed security force in addition to the police. **12** *Miss Saigon* goes into the black, recovering its $10.9 million capital investment in 39 weeks, compared to the 60 weeks it took *The Phantom of the Opera*, with an $8 million investment, to do it.

FEBRUARY 2 Ticketmaster begins discounting day-of-performance seats with a flexible discount schedule, which will force the TKTS booth in Times Square to adopt the same policy on February 24. TKTS has been selling only at a 50 percent discount.

NOVEMBER 14 Director Tony Richardson d. of AIDS. **29** Ralph Bellamy d.

JANUARY 3 Judith Anderson d. **26** José Ferrer d. "There was never a better Cyrano in the world," says Helen Hayes. "You know you're in the right racket if you love the drudgery that goes with it," said Ferrer.

FEBRUARY 9 Andrew Lloyd Webber, who recently divorced Sarah Brightman, m. Madeleine Gurdon.

MARCH 2 Sandy Dennis d. She won Tonys for her work in *A Thousand Clowns* and *Any Wednesday*. **12** Critic John Simon m. singer and teacher Patricia Hoag. "She was last seen as the stripper in *Gypsy*," says the groom. "I can't stand this man, and the things he says about women are appalling," the bride remembers thinking when she met Simon. Philip Bosco is one of the guests. **25** Nancy Walker d. A generation has grown up knowing her not as the Broadway musical star but rather as the person on television commercials who called Bounty Towels "the quicker-

Personalities

The funeral was at the Public Theatre this afternoon. Meryl Streep, Elizabeth Swados, Martin Sheen, and Raul Julia delivered eulogies. Mandy Patinkin, according to *The New York Times*, sang "a song in Yiddish, 'Yossel, Yossel'. . . . , [Papp's original first name] which began softly and ended with sobbing emotion as he sang out, stamped his feet, clapped and held up his hands. As he left the stage he ran to the coffin, knelt and kissed the white Star of David on the black cloth draped over it." **6** Edward Albee tells an interviewer that "we should forget about Broadway—leave it to the Shubert Organization and the other real estate groups, leave it to the advertising department of *The New York Times*. . . . "

JANUARY • British composer Malcolm Williamson, told that Andrew Lloyd Webber, not he, has been asked to compose music for the fortieth anniversary of the Queen's coronation, says of his rival that the "difference between good music and Andrew Lloyd Webber's is the difference between Michelangelo and a cement mixer."

FEBRUARY 27 Producer Kim Poster files for Equity arbitration in a dispute with Tommy Tune. He's committed himself to a new musical called *Busker Alley* but told Poster last August that she had not raised the amount of capital specified in his contract. She says he wants out on a technicality because he can make more money—$60,000–70,000 a week—touring in *Bye, Bye Birdie*.

MARCH • If Andrew Lloyd Webber's *The Phantom of the Opera* ever makes it to the screen, it won't be directed by Joel Schumacher, who has given up for a second time in a struggle for artistic control with the composer. **11** David Carroll, who has AIDS, collapses and dies while recording the cast album for *Grand Hotel*.

APRIL 15 At a London art auction, Andrew Lloyd Webber buys Canaletto's "Old Horse Guards" for $17.7 million. **23** The Public Theatre is renamed the Joseph Papp Public Theatre. **29** David Hampton,

Plays and Musicals

ovated version of Gershwin's 1930 *Girl Crazy*, with 13 Gershwin tunes added to the score, opens at the Shubert. Director Michael Okrent and choreographer Susan Stroman are together for the first time as a team. The *Times*'s Frank Rich writes that in the future, this may be seen as the date when "Broadway finally rose up to grab the musical back from the British." Heading the cast are Harry Groener and Jodi Benson.

MARCH 17 At the Brooks Atkinson, Glenn Close, Richard Dreyfuss, and Gene Hackman have produced a big advance ticket sale, but Ariel Dorfman's play about the aftermath of political torture, *Death and the Maiden* (159), directed by Mike Nichols, gets mixed reviews. Frank Rich, in the *Times*, calls it the "first escapist entertainment about political torture." **24** Alan Alda is the unhappy writer in Neil Simon's 26th play *Jake's Women* (245), opening to a mixed critical reaction at the Neil Simon Theatre. Brenda Vaccaro, Tracy Pollan, Joyce Van Patten, and Kate Burton are also in the cast. **29** Judd Hirsch gives a Tony-winning performance in Herb Gardner's *Conversations with My Father* (402), at the Royale. Hirsch is the unsuccessful man who resents his son's achievements. Tony Shalhoub, David Marguiles, and Marilyn Sokol are also in the cast. It's "pungent, deep-felt and very powerful," says Clive Barnes in The *New York Post*.

APRIL • Robert Schenkkan's *The Kentucky Cycle* is a surprise Pulitzer Prize winner. It debuted in Seattle and is now at the Mark Taper Forum in Los Angeles, another indication of the increasing importance of regional theatre. **8** Clarke Peters's revue *Five Guys Named Moe* (445), based on the music of rhythm and blues artist Louis Jordan, opens at the Eugene O'Neill. The show, produced by Cameron Mackintosh, stars Jerry Dixon. **12** Alec Baldwin, Jessica Lange, and Amy Madigan are the stars in the revival of Tennessee Williams's *A Streetcar Named Desire* (137), directed by Gregory Mosher, at the Barrymore. It's mostly thumbs-down from the critics. **13** August Wilson's *Two*

Business and Society

APRIL • Broadway Cares and Equity Fights AIDS have merged.

MAY • The Circle in the Square is the first company fined for not properly identifying a preview performance in a display ad—for *Salome* and *Chinese Coffee*, starring Al Pacino. • The U.S. Supreme Court upholds the landmarking of Broadway theatres.

Births, Deaths, and Marriages

picker-upper." **27** Leueen MacGrath d. One of the actress-playwright's five husbands was George S. Kaufman.

APRIL 5 Molly Picon d. at age 94. Told once that Picon was known as the "Helen Hayes of the Yiddish Theatre," Hayes said she was going to call herself the "Shiksa Molly Picon."

whose claim that he was Sidney Poitier's son inspired John Guare's *Six Degrees of Separation*, loses his $100 million suit in New York State Supreme Court against Guare and the show's producers, who Hampton claimed had exploited his life without his consent.

MAY 8 Stephen Sondheim, in a letter to the National Endowment for the Arts, rejects its National Medal of Arts because, recently, the organization "has become a victim of its own and other's political infighting and is rapidly being transformed into a conduit and a symbol of censorship and repression rather than encouragement and support." **8** In a letter to the editor of *The New York Times*, the cast of *Shimada*, including Ellen Burstyn and Estelle Parsons, complains about the paper's review, which said that the play, about Japanese business, was anti-Japanese.

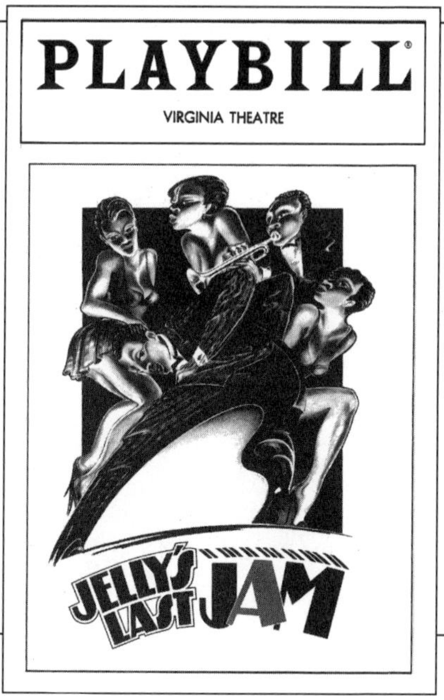

"Jelly Roll" Morton—the man and his music

PB

Trains Running (160), directed by Lloyd Richards, opens at the Walter Kerr. This latest play in Wilson's ongoing look at the African-American community in Pittsburgh is set in a restaurant in 1969 and stars Larry Fishburne, Roscoe Lee Browne, and Cynthia Martells. The only negative reaction is from Clive Barnes, in the *Post*, who says it has "less immediacy and more padding than the cycle's earlier plays." **14** Nathan Lane plays Nathan Detroit in a revival of Frank Loesser's *Guys and Dolls* (1,144), opening to critical acclaim, at the Martin Beck. Faith Prince and Peter Gallagher also star in this Tony winner, with direction by Jerry Zaks and set design by Tony Walton.

APRIL 26 *Jelly's Last Jam* (569), a musical based on the life and music of Jelly Roll Morton, is at the Virginia Theatre. George C. Wolfe's show stars Savion Glover as the younger Morton and Gregory Hines as the adult composer-musician. Ruben Santiago-Hudson is also in the cast. **29** *Falsettos* (487), by William Finn, with a book by James Lapine, opens at the John Golden. It combines Finn's off-Broadway shows about gays, *March of the Falsettos* and *Falsettoland*, with a cast that includes Michael Rupert and Stephen Bogardus. *Variety* says that Finn "is sure to be compared with Sondheim, and the comparison is apt."

MAY 12 Anna Deveare Smith's *Fires in the Mirror* (109), a one-woman examination of urban conflict between blacks and Jews, opens at the Public Theatre.

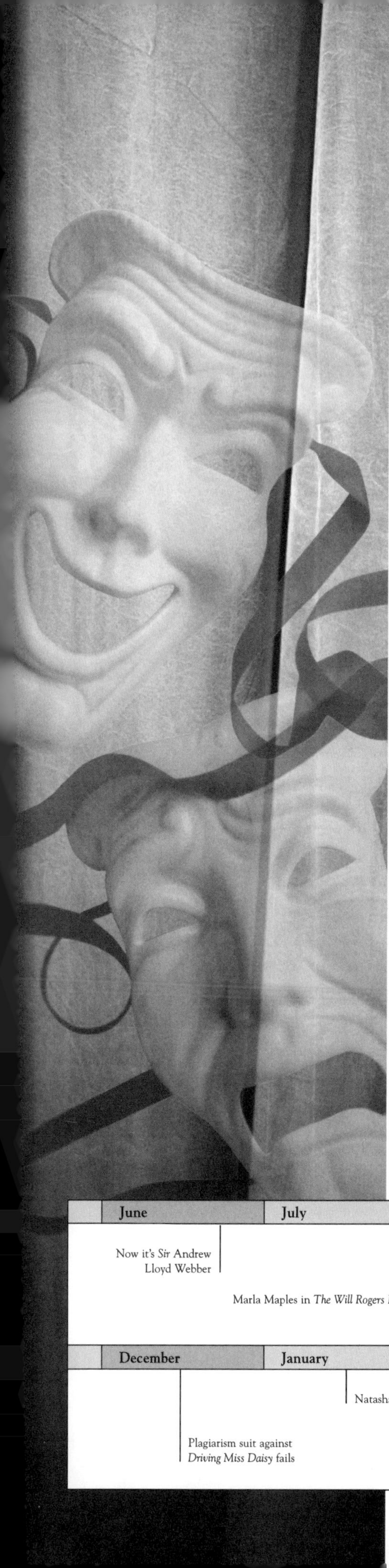

1992–93

Helen Hayes is dead. Tony Kushner's *Angels in America* opens after a buildup that critic Linda Winer calls "probably the longest foreplay in Broadway history." The recession, receding for the rest of the country, remains for resident theatres, with corporate contributions off, government grants down, and operating deficits on the rise in many houses. Fran and Barry Weissler, producers of *Falsettos*, are trying to sell it as a "family" show, dogs come and go in *Annie Warbucks*, and Patti LuPone snares her second major role in an Andrew Lloyd Webber show, *Sunset Boulevard*, set to open in London with Broadway next, or so she's been told. Glenn Close will open it in Los Angeles. And now that he's Sir Andrew Lloyd Webber, will it be "the music of the knight?"

- Number of condoms used to protect body mikes from sweat in the first decade of *Cats*'s run at the Winter Garden: 33,280
- Amount of yak's hair used so far for wigs in *Cats*: 1,870 pounds
- First decade's gross at the Winter Garden for *Cats*: $254 million ($1.4 billion worldwide)
- Among those who have recorded "Memory" from *Cats*: Shirley Bassey, Sarah Brightman, Michael Crawford, Howard Keel, Liberace, Julian Lloyd Webber, Johnny Mathis, Elaine Paige, and Barbra Streisand. Also Barry Manilow, Pavarotti-Domingo-Carreras, and the Coldstream Guards
- Ticket sales for *Angels in America* on April 12, the day before it wins the Pulitzer Prize: $24,115
- Ticket sales for *Angels in America* on April 14: $61,265
- Number of nonprofit theatres producing on Broadway: 4—National Actors Company, Roundabout Theatre Company, Circle in the Square, and the Lincoln Center Theatre
- Annual budget of Ellen Stewart's La Mama Experimental Theatre Club: $950,000
- Average ticket price at La Mama: $12
- Circle in the Square deficit: $1.5 million
- How *Variety* begins its review of the off-Broadway musical *Anna Karenina*: "All hit musicals are like one another; each flop flops in its own way."
- *Variety*'s lead on its review of *Ain't Broadway Grand*, a musical about producer Mike Todd: "No, it ain't."

Productions on Broadway: 34

Pulitzer Prize for Drama: *Angels in America: Millennium Approaches* (Tony Kushner)

New York Drama Critics Circle Awards:
Best Play: *Angels in America: Millennium Approaches* (Tony Kushner)
Best Foreign Play: *Someone Who'll Watch Over Me* (Frank McGuinness)
Best Musical: *Kiss of the Spider Woman* (John Kander-Fred Ebb, book by Terrence McNally)

Tony Awards:
Play: *Angels in America: Millennium Approaches* (Tony Kushner)
Actor in a play: Ron Leibman (*Angels in America: Millennium Approaches*)
Actress in a play: Madeleine Kahn (*The Sisters Rosensweig*)
Musical: *Kiss of the Spider Woman* (John Kander-Fred Ebb, book by Terrence McNally)
Actor in a musical: Brent Carver (*Kiss of the Spider Woman*)
Actress in a musical: none

June | July | August | September | October | November

Now it's *Sir* Andrew Lloyd Webber
Marla Maples in *The Will Rogers Follies*
Les Miserables passes *Oklahoma!*
Morris Carnovsky and Anthony Perkins d.
Wendy Wasserstein's *The Sisters Rosensweig*
The Negro Ensemble Company raises enough to continue

December | January | February | March | April | May

Plagiarism suit against *Driving Miss Daisy* fails
Natasha Richardson in *Anna Christie*
Lillian Gish d.
JoAnne Akalaitas replaced at Public Theatre
Blacks protest *Show Boat*
Angels in America: Millennium Approaches

Personalities

JUNE 10 "Sondheim—A Celebration at Carnegie Hall" is a musical tribute to the lyricist and composer, featuring Jerry Hadley, Madeleine Kahn, Dorothy Loudon, Patti LuPone, Liza Minnelli, Victor Garber, Bernadette Peters, Glenn Close, Betty Buckley, and Mandy Patinkin. **21** On the Queen's official birthday, Andrew Lloyd Webber is made a knight of the realm. "This is extremely embarrassing," says Sir Andrew. "I've been sent up rotten by all my friends."

AUGUST • Marla Maples, Donald Trump's close friend, is making her Main Stem debut as a cast replacement in *The Will Rogers Follies*. • *Falsettos*, in which the experiences of a gay man is a key plot element, is being promoted in print ads with emphasis on the play's family appeal and with quotes from religious figures endorsing it. Coproducer Barry Weissler tells *Variety*: "I want folks to feel its safe to come to see this, that a nun has said it's okay, a rabbi says its okay. Next week I have three Koreans. It's universal."

Patti LuPone MSN

SEPTEMBER • John Lahr, son of Bert Lahr, becomes the *New Yorker*'s drama critic. **2** *Annie 2*, reborn as *Annie Warbucks* and on the road, gets another canine cast change. Chelsea, who had replaced Beau in the part of Sandy, "didn't want to be in show biz anymore," says lyricist Martin Charnin. It's the big break for Cindy,

Plays and Musicals

JUNE 24 To help raise money for the Circle in the Square, Al Pacino is appearing in a limited run of two plays, Ira Lewis's *Chinese Coffee* (25), opening today, and Oscar Wilde's *Salome* (34), opening on June 28, in which the star will go way up and over the top as King Herod.

AUGUST 24 *Les Miserables* gives its 2,213th performance, passing *Oklahoma!*'s run.

OCTOBER 20 Larry Kramer's *The Destiny of Me* (175), a continuation of the AIDS drama he began in his play *The Normal Heart*, is at the Lucille Lortel Theatre. The Circle Repertory Company production stars Jonathan Hadary. Piper Laurie is also in the cast. **22** Wendy Wasserstein's *The Sisters Rosensweig* (149) opens at the Mitzi E. Newhouse Theatre. Jane Alexander, Madeleine Kahn, Robert Klein, and Frances McDormand are in this comedy about the lives and loves of sisters. It will move to Broadway and the Barrymore (85) on March 18. It's a "generous group portrait," says Rich, in the *Times*; it's "mean-spirited," says Jeremy Gerard, in *Variety*. **25** *Oleanna* (513), a two-character David Mamet play about a professor accused by his student of sexual harassment, opens at the Orpheum. Rebecca Pidgeon (the new Mrs. Mamet) and William H. Macy are the cast, and the more than $200,000 advance sale is exceptionally healthy for an off-Broadway production. **27** John Leguizamo's *Spic-O-Rama* (86), at the Westside Theatre, is the second major one-man show by the author and star of *Mambo Mouth*. In this one, he's a child looking at his family, which he characterizes as "monsters, freaks, and weirdos."

NOVEMBER • Tony Kushner's *Angels in America*—both parts—opens at the Mark Taper Forum in Los Angeles. **23** Frank McGuiness's play about hostages held in Beirut, *Someone Who'll Watch Over Me* (232), opens at the Booth. The three-member cast consists of Alec McCowen, Stephen Rea, and James McDaniel. John Simon, in *New York* magazine, says: "[Y]ou don't want to miss a line, a facial expression, a single silent beat."

Business and Society

JULY • The Negro Ensemble Company announces that its $250,000 deficit will probably force it to fold by year's end. Government funding, which had been providing $600,000 a year has dropped to $300,000. Two years ago, the Company lost its theatre on Fifty-fourth Street. **15** The first annual "Broadway on Broadway," excerpts from current shows performed for free by cast members in Times Square, is staged. The occasion is the Democratic Convention, being held at nearby Madison Square Garden.

SEPTEMBER • New York State buys the New Amsterdam Theatre on Forty-second Street, once home to *The Ziegfeld Follies*, from the Nederlanders and will go ahead with renovating it under the Forty-second Street Development Project.

OCTOBER • Ticketmaster's computer system now enables purchasers to know their exact location, not just the section where they will sit.

NOVEMBER • The Negro Ensemble Company has raised enough from small contributors to keep it going and will not have to close, as had been forecast last

Births, Deaths, and Marriages

JUNE 3 Robert Morley d.

JULY 25 Alfred Drake d.

SEPTEMBER 1 Morris Carnovsky d. **12** Anthony Perkins d. of AIDS.

OCTOBER 16 Shirley Booth d.

DECEMBER 9 Vincent Gardenia d. **21** Stella Adler d. **29** Onetime musical comedy star Vivienne Segal d.

FEBRUARY 27 Lillian Gish d. She was 99.

MARCH 17 Helen Hayes d.

Chelsea's understudy. **21** "We have yet to discover whether the role of Norma Desmond—immortalized on the screen by Gloria Swanson—will go to Meryl Streep or Patti LuPone in Andrew Lloyd Webber's musical version of *Sunset Boulevard*," *Variety* gossips.

DECEMBER • Playwright Henry Denker's plagiarism suit against Alfred Uhry, author of *Driving Miss Daisy*, is dismissed. Denker's play *Horowitz and Mrs. Washington* flopped after seven performances on Broadway in 1980. It was about a black woman hired to take care of a white Manhattan man and the friendship that gradually grows between them.

JANUARY 5 Today's open casting call for

Ron Liebman in the first part of *Angels in America* PF

JANUARY 14 Eugene O'Neill's *Anna Christie* (54) is revived by the Roundabout Company at the Criterion Center Stage Right, with Natasha Richardson, in her Broadway debut, as Anna, and Rip Torn, Liam Neeson, and Anne Meara. "Thrilling," says Frank Rich, in the *Times*, of this production, directed by David Leveaux. He calls Richardson "astounding."

FEBRUARY 25 *Fool Moon* (1,098), a display of comic performance art, starring Bill Irwin and David Shiner, is a surprise hit at the Richard Rodgers Theatre.

MARCH 6 *Jeffrey* (365), Paul Rudnick's look at AIDS and what it has done to the gay world, starring John Michael Higgins, opens off-Broadway, at the Minetta Lane. John Simon describes it as "a prime specimen of a rising new genre, the AIDS comedy."

APRIL 1 *Putting It All Together* (59), Stephen Sondheim and Julia McKenzie's revue based on the composer's work, is at the Manhattan Theatre Club at the City

summer.

DECEMBER • Jujamcyn Theatres wins out over the Shuberts, who are also vying to bring *Angels in America* to Broadway. The Shubert Organization was so confident of snaring it that they were already offering Jujamcyn a chance to invest in "their" show. JoAnne Akalaitas also wanted it for the Public Theatre.

JANUARY 6 The film industry boycott of New York City almost two years ago has had a negative effect on the city's theatre, which has lost acting and production talent to the west coast, according to an independent study.

MARCH 1 Readjustments in Equity's health insurance plan will leave several thousand unemployed actors without coverage. The union's health fund is nearly depleted. **13** A severe snowstorm curtails Broadway attendance, with many theatres offering refunds or exchanges to those who can't make it.

Personalities

the lead role in *Annie Warbucks*, says *The New York Times*, "recalls the running of the bulls at Pamplona."

FEBRUARY • *Annie Warbucks*, the successor to *Annie 2*, the sequel to *Annie*, is still breathing but barely. Its April booking at the Neil Simon Theatre on Broadway has fallen through, with the producers $1 million short of what they need to stage it. Lyricist Martin Charnin says he still believes in "Tomorrow." • With Patti LuPone set to star, tickets go on sale in London for the summer opening of Andrew Lloyd Webber's *Sunset Boulevard*, with the highest top ever, $46. **26** Andrew Lloyd Webber receives a star in the Hollywood Walk of Fame.

MARCH 18 JoAnne Akalaitas is replaced as artistic director of the Public Theatre by George C. Wolfe, who is now busy directing *Angels in America*.

APRIL • Andrew Lloyd Webber announces that Glenn Close will play Norma Desmond in the Los Angeles production of *Sunset Boulevard* next season. • Responding to protests by black artists, producer Garth Drabinsky says that director Harold Prince will be especially sensitive to the depiction of blacks in the upcoming revival of *Show Boat*, set to open the new Performing Arts Center in York, near Toronto, this fall.

MAY • Joan Peyser's *The Memory of All That: The Life of George Gershwin* asserts that the composer sired an illegitimate son, Alan, the result of Gershwin's affair with chorus girl Mollie Charlston. When other Gershwin biographers question her claim, she says that there's a "cover-up." **17** At a folk concert at the Ninety-second Street YMHA in New York City, Paul Robeson, Jr. follows a recording of his father singing "Ol' Man River" with an attack on the song and *Show Boat*, the musical from which it comes. The show's revival is drawing protests from other prominent blacks.

Plays and Musicals

Center. Julie Andrews, Christopher Durang, Stephen Collins, Michael Rupert, and Rachel York constitute the cast. The presence of Andrews in her first New York show in decades has sold out the house. **22** *The Who's Tommy* (899), a revival of the Pete Townshend rock opera, at the St. James, stars Michael Cerveris as the title character. **23** Willy Russell's musical *Blood Brothers* (839), about class conflict and twins separated at birth, from the author of *Shirley Valentine* and *Educating Rita*, opens at the Music Box. John Simon calls it "anemic," and Clive Barnes writes, in the *Post*, that "it's heavy-handed, heavy-footed, with not too much up top and precious little in between." **26** Lynn Redgrave is in her own one woman-show, *Shakespeare for My Father* (272), at the Helen Hayes. In it, she recounts moments with her famous family and remembers stage luminaries she's known.

MAY 3 *Kiss of the Spider Woman* (906), a John Kander-Fred Ebb musical, with book by Terrence McNally, based on the Manuel Puig novel, opens at the Broadhurst. Harold Prince is directing a cast that includes Brent Carver and Anthony Carville, as the two prisoners, and Chita Rivera. *New York Newsday* says it's "flashy trash and shamelessly lobotomizes the politics of the prison drama. But it's the only new show with a wild heart and a fresh eye. . . ." The film appeared in 1985. **4** The first half of Tony Kushner's play about being gay, *Angels in America: Millennium Approaches* (367), stars Ron Leibman as Roy Cohn, Joe Mantello, Marcia Gay Harden, Stephen Spinella, and Kathleen Chalfant, most of whom play more than one role in both genders. It will lose about $660,000 in its Broadway engagement at the 945-seat Walter Kerr Theatre. John Lahr, in the *New Yorker*, calls this production a good accounting of "Kushner's gorgeous work."

Business and Society

Births, Deaths, and Marriages

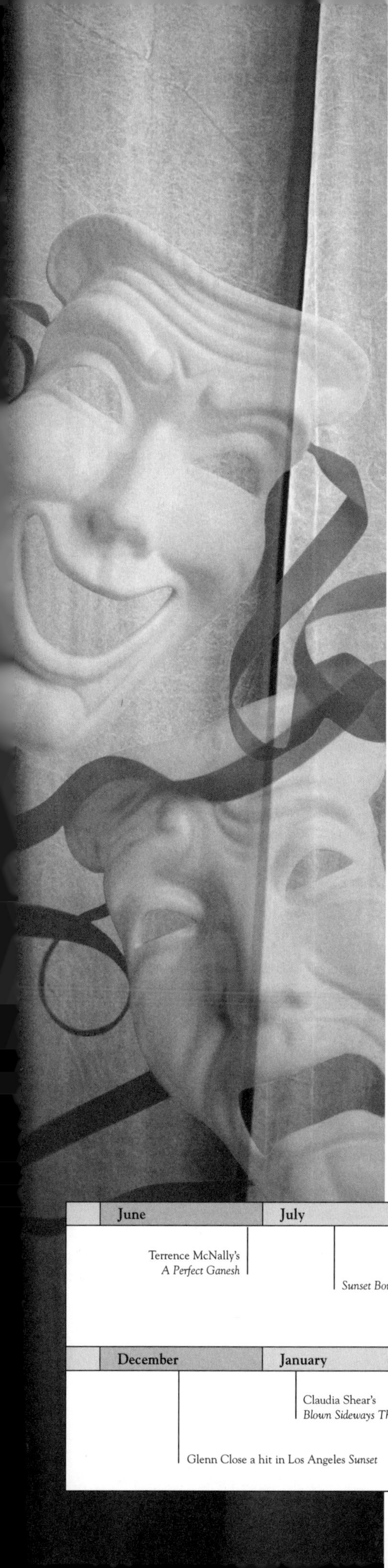

1993–94

Despite the rumors about her replacement, which are getting too close for comfort, Patti LuPone insists that Andrew Lloyd Webber is committed to her as Norma Desmond in *Sunset Boulevard* when it comes to Broadway. Frank Rich steps down as chief drama critic at *The New York Times*, causing the voodoo dolls to go back in the closets in producers' offices all over Broadway. Edward Albee is back with *Three Tall Women*, an acclaimed play; Disney's *Beauty and the Beast*, disparaged by the critics and slighted by the Tonys, is selling tickets as fast as they can be printed; and "Tomorrow" is finally here for *Annie Warbucks*, which opens a successful run in New York, albeit off-Broadway.

- Going over the top: the Broadway and road gross combined—$1,043,741,612, exceeding $1 billion for the first time
- Advance sale for *Sunset Boulevard* on Broadway: $37 million
- What Patti LuPone says about her relationship to *Sunset Boulevard*: "I am pivotal to the success or failure of this show. Andrew [Lloyd Webber] actually told me that."
- What Patti LuPone does when told that Glenn Close will take *Sunset Boulevard* to Broadway: "I had batting practice in my dressing room. Things went flying into the street."
- Amount of money pumped into the New York City economy by Broadway: $2.3 billion
- Number of off-Broadway houses: (100–500 seats): 32
- Number of off-off-Broadway theatres in New York City: about 250
- Name of the racehorse owned jointly by Andrew Lloyd Webber and producers Cameron Mackintosh and Robert Stigwood: "Frank Rich," a gelding, named for *The New York Times* theatre critic
- Cost of a full-page color ad in the Arts and Leisure section of the Sunday *New York Times* (the paper is new to hue): $60,700
- What Stella Adler says to *Passion* star Donna Murphy when the young actress presents a scene for her teacher wearing red patent leather boots with platform heels and a high-cut leotard: "Whores! Why do you all look like whores?"
- What it costs the Disney Company to bring *Beauty and the Beast* to Broadway: $11.9 million, a capital record
- Number of Tonys won by *Beauty and the Beast*: just 1, for costumes
- Reaction of ticket buyers to *Beauty and the Beast*'s "Tony-impairment": ticket sales set a new record the day after the awards are given out
- Who, according to *People*, will star in *Evita*, the movie, Andrew Lloyd Webber's phantom film, percolating now for several years: Michelle Pfeiffer

Productions on Broadway: 37

Pulitzer Prize for Drama: *Three Tall Women* (Edward Albee)

New York Drama Critics Circle Awards:
Best Play: *Three Tall Women* (Edward Albee)

Tony Awards:
Best Play: *Angels in America: Perestroika* (Tony Kushner)
Actor in a play: Stephen Spinella (*Angels in America*)
Actress in a play: Diana Rigg (*Medea*)
Musical: *Passion* (Stephen Sondheim)
Actor in a musical: Boyd Gaines (*She Loves Me*)
Actress in a musical: Donna Murphy (*Passion*)

June	July	August	September	October	November
Terrence McNally's *A Perfect Ganesh*	*Sunset Boulevard* opens in London	Lloyd Webber denies unhappiness with Patti LuPone	Frank Rich steps down as *Times* critic	Lloyd Webber again denies rumors on Patti LuPone	Pulitzer winner *The Kentucky Cycle* flops big

December	January	February	March	April	May
Glenn Close a hit in Los Angeles *Sunset*	Claudia Shear's *Blown Sideways Through Life*	Lloyd Webber says it's Close, not LuPone, on Broadway	*Damn Yankees* and *Carousel* revived	Disney's *Beauty and the Beast*	Stephen Sondheim's *Passion* revived; *Grease* revived

Personalities

JUNE 5 Stephen Spinelli, nominated for a Tony for his role in *Angels in America*, in which he appears naked onstage with what appear to be lesions associated with AIDS, says in a *New York Times* interview that he has mixed feelings about telling those who ask that he does not have the disease. A gay man, he "doesn't like to see the community divided up between people who are positive and negative. . . ."

AUGUST • Andrew Lloyd Webber is irritated by what he sees as the misdirected marketing of the new Barbra Streisand album, which features "With One Look" from *Sunset Boulevard*. "If I had done the song with Sarah Brightman, we would have been on radio, on television shows plugging it away," he ruefully tells a reporter. In the future, says Sir Andrew, "I'll always do it with artists who are under my control." **12** Playwright Israel Horovitz, artistic director of the Gloucester Stage Company, denies charges by several women that he sexually harassed them. **23** *Variety* reports that sources within Andrew Lloyd Webber's Really Useful Group are casting doubt on Patti LuPone's staying with *Sunset Boulevard* when it comes to Broadway. "It's totally untrue," says a spokesperson of the rumor. Sir Andrew is "very pleased" with LuPone, who just recorded the original cast album. **24** An arbitrator rules that Tommy Tune did not breach his contract with producer Kim Poster when he continued touring in *Bye, Bye Birdie* in 1991 rather than fulfill his agreement to star in the musical *Busker Alley*.

SEPTEMBER • Gregory Mosher, former artistic director of the Lincoln Center Theatre, says that the theatre is through in America and may not even be missed. "Certainly, no one seems to miss vaudeville," he says. "Or grand opera. Or the Hula-Hoop." **30** *The New York Times* announces that its controversial chief theatre critic Frank Rich, who has held that job since 1980, will leave the post to become a columnist for the paper.

OCTOBER • "We are very happy with Patti and look forward to seeing her play the

Plays and Musicals

JUNE 27 Terrence McNally's *A Perfect Ganesh* (124), at the Manhattan Theatre Club at the City Center, concerns a benign Indian elephant God and the Americans who discover it. The cast features Zoe Caldwell, Frances Sternhagen, Fisher Stevens, and Dominic Cuskern.

JULY 12 Andrew Lloyd Webber's *Sunset Boulevard*, starring Patti LuPone, opens in London, where her contract says that she will play the lead in the Broadway production as well. In the audience is Billy Wilder, who directed the 1950 film. One dark cloud is Frank Rich's review in *The New York Times*. He finds LuPone "miscast and unmoving as Norma Desmond."

AUGUST • The curtain finally goes up, off-Broadway, at the Variety Arts Theatre, on *Annie Warbucks* (200), the successor to the notoriously unsuccessful *Annie 2*, which was supposed to be the sequel to *Annie*. Notable in the cast is Donna McKechnie.

NOVEMBER 14 *The Kentucky Cycle* (34), Robert Schenkkan's Pulitzer Prize-winning play about generations of families in the mountains of Kentucky, starring Stacy Keach, opens at the Royale. It's shown in two parts, runs a total of more than six hours, and will lose over $2 million. **22** Neil Simon's *Laughter on the 23rd Floor* (218), directed by Jerry Zaks, with a cast that includes Nathan Lane, opens at the Richard Rodgers Theatre. It's based on Simon's experiences as a television writer for comedian Sid Caesar in the 1950s. **23** *Angels in America, Part II: Perestroika* (216), the second half of Tony Kushner's play about being gay, opens at the Walter Kerr, where it plays in repertory with the first part, *Millennium*. John Simon writes that it's finally opening after so much revision because "Frank Rich, an 'Angels' enthusiast, is quitting his post as chief drama critic of the *Times*, and his successor is said to be only a luke warm *[sic] Angelist*: hence the need to catch Rich before he leaves." Rich obliges, calling it "a true millennial work of art."

JANUARY 7 *Blown Sideways Through Life*

Business and Society

JUNE 4 The National Endowment for the Arts agrees to give grants to the four artists, including performance artist Karen Finley, who were denied the awards in 1990 in the midst of controversy over tax dollars subsidizing "obscene" art. The four agree to drop their lawsuit.

JULY • The Nederlanders, along with Stewart F. Lane, with whom they jointly own the Palace Theatre, buy the Biltmore Theatre. **14** The second annual Broadway on Broadway, a free concert in Times Square of show excerpts with original casts, draws a crowd of 40,000. This year's event is billed as part of Broadway's Centennial, commemorating the opening of the American Theatre on Forty-second Street in 1893.

SEPTEMBER 30 Lacking evidence, the Manhattan District Attorney closes the investigation into the 1991 disappearance of several thousand dollars from the Lunt-Fontanne box office while *Catskills on Broadway* was playing.

DECEMBER 28 An arbitrator rules that producers may insist that an actor agree to appear in a pay-per-view broadcast of a show, as they can insist on participation

Births, Deaths, and Marriages

OCTOBER 6 Choreographer Agnes DeMille, who characterized herself as a "storyteller," d. Her shows included *Oklahoma!*, *Carousel*, and *Paint Your Wagon*. **25** Vincent Price d. **26** Composer Harold Rome d.

NOVEMBER 7 Adelaide Hall d. **25** Claudia McNeil d.

JANUARY 23 Set designer Oliver Smith d. Among the shows whose "look" was his work were *On the Town*, *Brigadoon*, *Auntie Mame*, *West Side Story*, *The Sound of Music*, *Hello, Dolly! Plaza Suite*, and *The Odd Couple*.

MARCH 28 Playwright Eugene Ionesco d.

APRIL 26 Producer Arnold Saint-Subber d. He began as the coproducer of *Kiss Me Kate* and produced several early Neil

role of Norma on Broadway," says a spokesperson for Andrew Lloyd Webber, responding to rumors that LuPone might not make it to the Main Stem in the show. LuPone, "shellshocked" at the talk that she might be dumped, says that she has received personal reassurances from Webber, who would pay a price—"and $1 million wouldn't cover it"—should she be replaced. She also says of the composer's intense anxiety about critical reaction to his shows: "Andrew is an extremely—and this is a euphemism—sensitive man." **26** *The New York Times* names David Richards its new chief theatre critic to replace Frank Rich.

DECEMBER • The critical acclaim that greets Glenn Close's performance in the Los Angeles production of *Sunset Boulevard* fuels the rumors that she and not Patti LuPone will play Norma Desmond on Broadway. **9** The revival of *My Fair Lady*, at the Vivian Beaumont, heralds a possible star in the making. David Richards, in the *Times*, is enchanted by a "beguiling" Melissa Errico. She is "irrepressible, gawky, and altogether endearing," he writes.

JANUARY • Composer Jonathan Larson wins a $45,000 Richard Rodgers Studio Production Award, which will finance a workshop production of his musical *Rent* in October. Stephen Sondheim, chairman of the jury that made the award, has become Larson's mentor.

Claudia Shear works her way through life *PB*

(262), Claudia Shear's one-woman show about the 64 jobs she's held—including bordello receptionist—opens at the Cherry Lane.

FEBRUARY 9 *Encores*, a highly successful series of concert versions of past Broadway musicals, gets underway at the City Center with *Fiorello*. Starring in the revival of the 1959 Bock-Harnick show is director Jerry Zaks as the legendary New York City mayor, with Faith Prince, Philip Bosco, Liz Callaway, Donna McKechnie and a walk-on by a ringer, former Mayor Ed Koch. **13** "Albee Is Back," *Time* will headline its review—"stunning"—of Edward Albee's *Three Tall Women*, opening off-Broadway, at the 125-seat Vineyard Theatre (29). (It will move to upper Broadway and the Promenade (65) on April 5.) The play looks back at the life of an older woman played by three actresses at different ages. Marian Seldes, Jordan Baker, Myra Carter, and Michael Rhodes star. Michael Feingold, in *The Village Voice*, says it's so good that critics should shelve their usual reservations and instead "sponsor parades" for it. **27** *Stomp*, a percussion performance in which everyday objects are used as instruments, opens at the Orpheum. The cast includes Luke Cresswell, who created the work with Steve McNicolas.

MARCH 3 *Damn Yankees* (510), the Richard Adler–Jerry Ross musical, is revived at the Marquis Theatre. This hit stars Victor Garber, eventually replaced by Jerry Lewis, as Mr. Applegate and Bebe Neuwirth as Lola. **24** *Carousel* (337), directed by Nicholas Hytner, is revived at the Vivian Beaumont. This production, which emphasizes the dark and passionate side of the Rodgers and Hammerstein musical, stars Sally Murphy, Michael Hayden, Audra McDonald, Shirley Verrett, and Fisher Stevens. "The good news," writes Howard Kissel, in the *Daily News*, noting audience reaction, is that "the sobs are audible." He calls the staging "astonishing."

APRIL 7 Diana Rigg stars in Euripdes' *Medea* (83), at the Longacre. **17** Anna Deveare

in a recording of it.

FEBRUARY • The Disney Company pays $29 million for the New Amsterdam Theatre on Forty-second Street and will renovate the former home of *The Ziegfeld Follies*. • One of the worst winters ever in New York City has put the chill on Broadway box offices. Fifteen snowstorms and near-zero temperatures cut day-of-performance sales at the discount TKTS booth by as much as 25 percent.

MARCH 31 The Actors Studio announces that it will combine with the New School for Social Research to offer a masters program in the theatre arts. This is the first time that the Actors Studio has taught nonprofessionals.

APRIL 7 The Tony Administration Committee approves the division of the Best Revival category into Best Revived Play and Best Musical. There are a total of 17 revivals on Broadway this season. **19** The day after *Beauty and the Beast* opened to thumbs-down reviews, the thumbs at the Palace box office are busy counting money, $603,494 to be precise, a new one-day record for ticket sales.

Simon plays, including *The Odd Couple* and *Plaza Suite*.

MAY 5 Choreographer-director Joe Layton d. Shows he choreographed include *Once Upon a Mattress* and *The Sound of Music*. He directed as well as choreographed *No Strings* and *George M!*, winning Tonys for each.

Personalities

FEBRUARY 3 Andrew Lloyd Webber announces that Betty Buckley will succeed Patti LuPone in the London production of *Sunset Boulevard.* Questioned about whether LuPone is still headed for Broadway in the show, he says he's sticking to "announced policy." **17** Andrew Lloyd Webber announces that Glenn Close and not Patti LuPone will star in *Sunset Boulevard* when it comes to Broadway. Critical reaction to each of their performances—particularly the American critics who panned LuPone in the London production—have swayed his backers and him. LuPone's reaction, according to her agent, when gossip columnist Liz Smith scooped the official announcement three days ago: "She got hysterical." LuPone is making $25,000 a week in the role, and this is a breach of her contract.

APRIL 12 Edward Albee wins the Pulitzer Prize for Drama for *Three Tall Women*. It's his third Pulitzer, tying him with Robert Sherwood and leaving both one behind Eugene O'Neill.

MAY • Heard on Nathan Lane's answering machine: "Hi, there. I can't come to the phone right now. As you probably know, I didn't get nominated for a Tony, so I've decided to give up show business and devote my life to the Lord." **9** A *New Yorker* parody of David Mamet's writing style, by Frank Cammuso and Hart Seely, offers excerpts from an L.L. Bean–type catalog as Mamet might have written it. A pair of pants are hawked: "You think chinos are queer? Let me tell you something. Everybody's queer. So what? You cheat on your wife? Live with it. You own a pair of bell-bottoms? Deal with it. At least these chinos have a fly that stays up, and you're not paying a hundred dollars for some piece of puke-colored polyester." **16** Representatives of Patti LuPone and Andrew Lloyd Webber announce that they have reached a financial settlement from his breach of her contract that promised her the starring role in the Broadway production of *Sunset Boulevard.* No terms are announced, but the amount is said to be $1 million.

Plays and Musicals

Smith is in her own one-woman show *Twilight: Los Angeles, 1992* (72), at the Cort. She's based it on her interviews with people involved in the recent Los Angeles riots sparked by the arrest and beating of Rodney King. **18** *Beauty and the Beast*, the Disney Company's $12 million, critic-proof musical, based partly on their 1991 animated cartoon feature, opens at the Palace. Terrence Mann, Susan Egan, Tom Bosley, Wendy Oliver, and Burke Moses are prominent in the cast. Special effects include a spectacular levitation in the last scene. It's "vapid, shallow and, yes, cartoonish," says *Time*, echoing much of the critical reaction. **27** J.B. Priestly's *An Inspector Calls* (454) is revived, with an elaborate set, at the Royale. Rosemary Harris, Philip Bosco, and Kenneth Cranham star.

MAY 9 Stephen Sondheim's *Passion* (280), starring Donna Murphy as Fosca, a woman driven by obsessive love, opens at the Plymouth. John Lahr, in the *New Yorker*, hears only "surface sophistication" in the music but calls Murphy "stunning." **11** A Tommy Tune revival of the 1972 *Grease* opens at the Eugene O'Neill Theatre. The casting of Rosie O'Donnell sets a pattern for this show, which will regularly bring in star replacements such as Brooke Shields and Joe Piscopo, who have made reputations elsewhere than on Broadway.

Business and Society

Births, Deaths, and Marriages

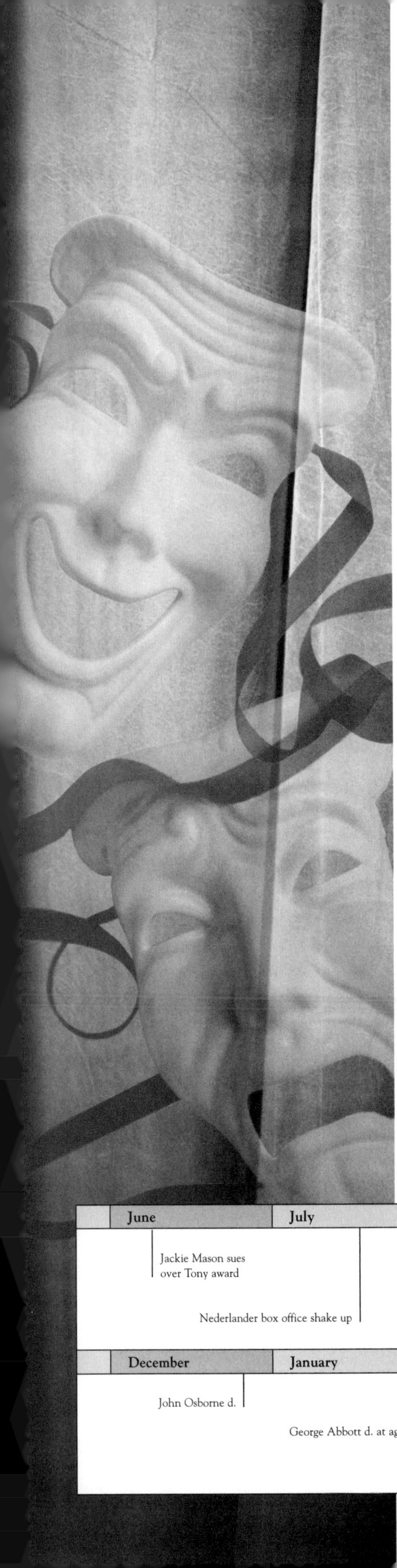

1994–95

George Abbott—"Mr. Abbott"—dies, at age 107. Neil Simon's *London Suite*, opening off-Broadway, points to the changes that high costs and high-budget extravaganzas have wrought on the Main Stem. After all the hoopla, Glenn Close opens in *Sunset Boulevard*, Cherry Jones becomes a major star in *The Heiress*, and Nathan Lane turns in another fine performance, this time in *Love! Valor! Compassion!* Jerry Lewis finally makes his Broadway debut as the devil, in *Damn Yankees*; Matthew Broderick has the Robert Morse role in *How to Succeed . . .*; and the Garth Drabinsky-Harold Prince *Show Boat* docks at the Gershwin.

- Broadway attendance: over 9 million for the first time in 13 years
- What Glenn Close is earning in *Sunset Boulevard*: $30,000 a week, plus 10 percent of the gross over $600,000
- What people are saying about Nathan Lane, according to him: "Hey, wasn't he that rat thing in *The Lion King*?"
- Broadway's biggest theatre: the Gershwin, which seats 1,924, where the revival of *Show Boat* opens
- Size of the 1927 *Show Boat* Company: 96
- Size of the 1994 revival company: 68
- Top ticket price for Flo Ziegfeld's *Show Boat*: $5.50
- Top price for Garth Drabinsky's revival: $75
- Weekly gross for *Show Boat*: as much as $900,000
- Weekly cost of running *Show Boat*: more than $600,000
- Projected cost of mounting Neil Simon's *London Suite* at a Broadway house: $1.5 million
- Cost of producing it off-Broadway: $600,000
- Number of unionized actors in New York Theatre: 100,000
- Number of actors who work in any week: 800
- Number who will make more than $35,000 this year: about 1,200
- Combined number of Broadway and off-Broadway productions that have been running for at least 7 years: 5 (*Cats*, *The Fantasticks*, *Les Miserables*, *The Phantom of the Opera*, and *Tony n' Tina's Wedding*)
- Number of Public Theatre subscribers: 6,000, compared to 3,200 in 1992–93
- TV rating for the June 1995 show on which the Tony Awards for this season are given out: 7.7
- Ratings for the Oscars show: 30.3

Productions on Broadway: 29

Pulitzer Prize for Drama: *The Young Man from Atlanta* (Horton Foote)

New York Drama Critics Circle Awards:
Best Play: *Arcadia* (Tom Stoppard)
Best American Play: *Love! Valor! Compassion!* (Terrence McNally)

Tony Awards:
Play: *Love! Valor! Compassion!* (Terrence McNally)
Actress in a play: Cherry Jones (*The Heiress*)
Actor in a play: Ralph Fiennes (*Hamlet*)
Musical: *Sunset Boulevard* (Andrew Lloyd Webber)
Actress in a musical: Glenn Close (*Sunset Boulevard*)
Actor in a musical: Matthew Broderick (*How to Succeed in Business Without Really Trying*)

June | **July** | **August** | **September** | **October** | **November**

- Jackie Mason sues over Tony award
- Nederlander box office shake up
- Faye Dunaway sues Andrew Lloyd Webber
- Jessica Tandy d.
- *Show Boat* revival
- Glenn Close stars in *Sunset Boulevard*

December | **January** | **February** | **March** | **April** | **May**

- John Osborne d.
- George Abbott d. at age 107
- *A Tuna Christmas*
- *The Heiress* and *How to Succeed in Business . . .*
- Neil Simon opens *London Suite* off-Broadway
- Andrew Lloyd Webber buys $30 million painting

Personalities

JUNE 7 Jackie Mason returns the special Tony Award he received in 1987 in protest against not being nominated for an award this year for *Jackie Mason: Politically Incorrect*, his one-man show. In August, Mason will unsuccessfully sue the five organizations that choose the nominees for $25 million. **22** Faye Dunaway, who was to replace Glenn Close on July 12 in the Los Angeles production of *Sunset Boulevard*, is informed that composer Andrew Lloyd Webber has dismissed her and is closing the show. Webber maintains that her singing isn't up to par. Dunaway calls it "yet another capricious act by a capricious man." **27** Vanessa Williams replaces Chita Rivera in *Kiss of the Spider Woman*. Her acclaimed performance will raise flagging attendance from 70 percent of the house to standing room by August. Many of the new ticket buyers are black, attracted by the African-American Williams. **29** David Mamet's *The Cryptogram* debuts in London. Producer Fran Gero is incensed that the playwright has ignored the occasion. "Not only did he not attend his world premiere," says Gero, "but he hasn't even bothered to send a note to the actors. To be ignored like this is the worst of all insults."

AUGUST • Composer Ray Repp loses his suit against Andrew Lloyd Webber, in which Repp claimed that *The Phantom of*

Glenn Close MSN

Plays and Musicals

OCTOBER 2 Harold Prince's elaborate revival of the 1927 *Show Boat*, with the racism theme highlighted, opens at the Gershwin Theatre. Lonette McKee is Julie, with Rebecca Luker as Magnolia, Mark Jacoby as Gaylord Ravenal, Michel Bell as Joe, Elaine Stritch as Parthy, and John McMartin as Cap'n Andy. For the most part, the word "nigger" has been retained, although the opening lyrics reflect Oscar Hammerstein II's own revision, making it "Colored folks work on the Mississippi." The critics are fulsome in their praise.

NOVEMBER 1 Nathan Lane, John Glover (as twins), Stephen Bogardus, and Stephen Spinella are in Terrence McNally's *Love! Valor! Compassion!* (248, total), opening off-Broadway at the Manhattan Theatre Club and moving to the Walter Kerr, with Joe Mantello directing, on February 14. In it, eight middle-aged gay men look at their lives during weekends in the country. It's a comedy, although shadowing everything is AIDS. **17** Glenn Close stars in *Sunset Boulevard*, Andrew Lloyd Webber's musical version of the Billy Wilder film, opening at the Minskoff. Close "looks like a demon in a Kabuki play," says Vincent Canby, in *The New York Times*, who also describes her powerful performance as "Dracula-like." "As if We Never Said Goodbye" is prominent in the score. Alan Campbell is the writer who takes a wrong turn into her life, and George Hearn plays Max, her manservant. **21** Vanessa Redgrave is Vita Sackville-West, and Eileen Atkins is Virginia Woolf in *Vita and Virginia* (129), at the Union Square Theatre. In what the *Times* calls "a literary tea-for-two," Atkins has adapted their correspondence, and Zoe Caldwell directs. Atkins has played Woolf before, in *A Room of One's Own*.

DECEMBER 12 Tony Kushner's *Slavs* (64)—called by the author "a coda" to *Angels in America*—at the New York Theatre Workshop, covers, among other things, philosophy, love, despair, and mutant children in the Soviet Union. In the cast are Marisa Tomei, Mary Schultz, Joseph

Business and Society

JUNE • The top ticket price for *Grease* goes to $67.50.

JULY • The Nederlander Organization shifts several of its box office treasurers to different theatres, said to be an aftershock of the disappearance of a large sum from the Lunt-Fontanne several years ago when *Catskills on Broadway* was playing.

OCTOBER 2 The opening of *Show Boat* on Broadway does not bring the protests of racism that greeted the show in Toronto. On television commercials, James Earl Jones does the voice-over. **19** Neil Simon announces that his next play, *London Suite*, will open off-Broadway. It costs $1.5 million to mount a straight play on Broadway but less than $600,000 off-Broadway.

NOVEMBER 18 The day after it opens, *Sunset Boulevard* breaks the one-day record for ticket sales only recently set by *Beauty and the Beast*. A total of $1,491,110 enter the Minskoff coffers today.

JANUARY 6 At a meeting, off-Broadway producers reject the idea of Tony Awards

Births, Deaths, and Marriages

SEPTEMBER 11 Jessica Tandy d. In an eerie coincidence, Hume Cronyn, her husband and frequent stage partner, tonight receives an Emmy Award for his performance in a TV drama, "To Dance With the White Dog," as a man mourning his recently deceased wife. Tandy had been nominated for her role in the same program but did not win. **12** Tom Ewell d. **20** Composer Jule Styne d. His compositions include "Diamonds Are a Girl's Best Friend," "The Party's Over," and "People."

OCTOBER 24 Raul Julia d. **25** Mildred Natwick d.

DECEMBER 24 Julie Haydon and playwright John Osborne d.

JANUARY 31 Producer-director-playwright-actor George Abbott, after a career spanning more than eight decades and 120

the Opera contains music plagiarized from his 1978 song "Till You." Lloyd Webber's counter-suit, claiming that Repp copied from him, will also fail. **23** Josephine Abady, recently fired by the Cleveland Play House, is appointed co-artistic director, along with Ted Mann, of the financially troubled Circle in the Square. **25** Faye Dunaway sues Andrew Lloyd Webber for $6 million, claiming that her June dismissal from the Los Angeles production of *Sunset Boulevard* was merely the pretext to close a show that was not making money.

NOVEMBER • Andrew Lloyd Webber tells critic Martin Gottfried that he's worried about the younger generation, who are writing musicals in a "sob style" with the emphasis on being "politically correct." • Elaine Paige steps in for Betty Buckley in the London production of *Sunset Boulevard* when Buckley has an emergency appendectomy. **1** In his dialogue in *Love! Valor! Compassion!* Nathan Lane says of *A Funny Thing Happened on the Way to the Forum*, a show in which he will soon be starring, that "the only thing that happens is nothing and it's not funny. . . ." **27** Arthur Miller is appointed a professor of contemporary literature at Oxford University.

DECEMBER 16 Following yesterday's surprise resignation of David Richards, who has been *The New York Times* theatre critic for only a year, the paper names Vincent Canby to succeed him. The former *Times* film critic has recently served as its Sunday drama reviewer. **31** Victor Garber, bowing out as Mr. Applegate in *Damn Yankees*, is tricked by a cast member at the curtain into doing his famous imitation of Glenn Close as Norma Desmond in *Sunset Boulevard*. He's dumbfounded when he turns to stage left and sees coming out of the wings Glenn Close herself, imitating him imitating her. When he recovers from the joke, they sing "Auld Lang Syne" together.

FEBRUARY • Austin Pendleton becomes Artistic Director of the struggling Circle Repertory Company. **1** Broadway's lights are dimmed for a minute at 8:00 P.M. in memory of George Abbott.

Wiseman, and Gerald Hiken. **15** The little town of Tuna, Texas, is on the boards again in *A Tuna Christmas* (20), Joe Sears and Jaston Williams's 22-character, two-man show, at the Booth for a limited holiday engagement.

FEBRUARY 16 "Encores! Great American Musicals in Concert" stages *Call Me Madam* at the City Center. Melissa Errico steals the show from co-star Tyne Daly.

MARCH 2 *Smokey Joe's Cafe*, a feast of Jerry Lieber and Mike Stoller's rock 'n' roll hits from the fifties and sixties, from B.J. Crosby's rendition of "Hound Dog" to "Stand By Me," directed by Jerry Zaks, opens at the Virginia Theatre. **9** Cherry Jones and Philip Bosco star in the roles played by Wendy Hiller and Basil Rathbone in the original 1947 production of *The Heiress* (340), opening at the Cort. Bosco has just appeared in *An Inspector Calls*, also a revival of a 1947 production. Ruth and Augustus Goetz's adaptation of Henry James's *Washington Square*, highly successful with critics and at the box office, costars Frances Sternhagen and Jon Tenny. The 1949 film starred Olivia de Havilland, Ralph Richardson, and Montgomery Clift. **23** A revival of the 1961 Frank Loesser musical *How to Succeed in Business Without Really Trying* (548)—"as fast, funny and glitzy as it ever was," says the *Times*—which cost $310,000 ($1.5 million current dollars) to mount then but now needs well over $5 million, is at the Richard Rodgers Theatre. Matthew Broderick stars. **26** Rob Becker's one-man show about men and women, *Defending the Caveman (671)*, opens at the Helen Hayes after turning into a surprise hit in Chicago last fall. It will become the longest-running one-person, nonmusical show in Broadway history. **30** Tom Stoppard's *Arcadia (204)* opens at the Vivian Beaumont, directed by Trevor Nunn. Victor Garber stars as an academic trying to solve a mystery, while in parallel action occurring more than a century earlier, another mystery is being scrutinized. Gradually, the parallel worlds converge, meet, and meld.

APRIL 6 *Having Our Say* (308), a two-character play based on Sarah Delany's

---

for their productions. The need to supply two free tickets to each of the 600-plus voters for the awards is a consideration.

FEBRUARY 14 Terrence McNally's *Love! Valor! Compassion!*, now at the Walter Kerr, will become the first profitable show operating under the Broadway Alliance cost-cutting system instituted in 1990. It skips the Wednesday matinée, giving two shows on Sunday. "We felt it wasn't a Wednesday matinée play," says a spokesperson.

MARCH 29 *Daily Variety* reports that the box office figures reported to *Variety* for *Sunset Boulevard* for the first week of star Glenn Close's vacation, March 7 to 12, were $155,000 over the actual receipts—she's scheduled to leave the show in July. The figures came from the Really Useful Group, composer Andrew Lloyd Webber's production company. It is presumably in the company's interest to demonstrate that the show can get along without Close. **30** Andrew Lloyd Webber describes the inflating of box office numbers for *Sunset Boulevard* as "idiotic."

APRIL 9 Several members of the International Alliance of Theatrical Stage Employees (IATSE) hand out leaflets reading: "Neil Simon Leaves

---

productions on and off-Broadway, d. at age 107. He always wanted to be called "George" but was invariably addressed as "Mr. Abbott."

FEBRUARY 2 Donald Pleasance d. **9** David Wayne, one of the first actors to be awarded a Tony (he won for his portrayal of a leprechaun in *Finian's Rainbow*), d.

MARCH 20 Playwright Sidney Kingsley d. **29** Katherine Squire d.

APRIL 6 Ron Richardson, who won a Tony for his portrayal of Jim in *Big River* in 1985, d. of AIDS. **14** Burl Ives and director Gilbert Moses d.

MAY 7 Producer Ernest Martin d.

Personalities

MARCH 12 Jerry Lewis takes over the role of the Devil in *Damn Yankees*. **31** Glenn Close writes to Andrew Lloyd Weber that she is "furious and insulted" by the inflation of *Sunset Boulevard*'s box office figures while she was on vacation. "I made it a hit," she reminds the composer-producer and denounces his belief—expressed in a letter posted backstage at the Minskoff Theatre—that the show is a hit independent of who stars in it.

MAY 17 Andrew Lloyd Webber announces that he was the mystery bidder who purchased a Picasso "Blue Period" painting at auction last week for $29.2 million.

Plays and Musicals

book about herself and her sister, opens at the Booth. Emily Mann's adaptation of the book stars Gloria Foster and Mary Alice in what Vincent Canby, of the *Times*, calls "the most provocative and entertaining family play to reach Broadway in a long time." **9** Neil Simon's *London Suite (169)*, four one-act comedies that Vincent Canby, in the *Times*, rates as medium-level Simon, opens off-Broadway, at the Union Square Theatre. The cast includes Carole Shelly, Kate Burton, Jeffrey Jones, and Paxton Whitehead. **13** David Mamet's *The Cryptogram (62)*, starring Ed Begley, Jr., Felicity Huffman, and Shelton Dane, opens at the Westside Theatre Upstairs. A father leaves his wife and son, illuminating the underpinnings of American family life. **27** Sean Mathias's *Indiscretions* (220), a revival of Jean Cocteau's 1938 farce *Les Parents Terribles*, about a middle class-family in which passion and self-absorption run amuck, opens at the Barrymore. *The New York Times* calls it a "bewitching theatrical experience." Kathleen Turner stars and, says the *Times*, "When she opens up and lets fly with that sexy, near-baritone delivery, she threatens the stability of the house like no one since Tallulah Bankhead."

MAY 2 Ralph Fiennes opens at the Belasco in the Almeida Theatre Company of London's acclaimed production of *Hamlet* (121).

Business and Society

Broadway to Avoid Union Labor. He Makes Millions But Will Not Pay for Stagehand Benefits." The show is mounted by three stagehands. **14** The committee administering the Tony Awards changes the rules, allowing any show nominated in any category to win an award. Previously, there had to be at least two nominees in a category for an award to be made. That would have shut out *Sunset Boulevard* this season in the best score and best book categories, where it has no competition.

Births, Deaths, and Marriages

1995–96

Older women may still find it hard in Hollywood, but on Broadway this season, they triumph. Julie Andrews, Carol Burnett, and Zoe Caldwell are in their 60s, and Carol Channing and Uta Hagen are in their 70s. *Victor/Victoria* is victorious at the box office, if not with the critics, and certainly not enough with the Tony judges, according to Julie Andrews. George C. Scott, in *Inherit the Wind*, takes ill and then takes off when charged with sexual harassment. Edward Albee's comeback continues with a revival of *A Delicate Balance*. But the season's greatest drama is the sudden death of 35-year-old composer Jonathan Larson, just before his musical *Rent* opens and sweeps the major awards.

- First posthumous Pulitzer Prize for Drama: this season, to Jonathan Larson, for *Rent*
- Number of children performing on Broadway: with the opening of *The King & I* and *Big*, there are 43
- Number of the original 36 cast members of *Cats* still in the show: 2
- Total number of performances of Andrew Lloyd Webber's *The Phantom of the Opera* given, worldwide, since it opened in London 9 years ago: about 27,000
- Worldwide gross for *Phantom*: $1.5 billion
- Cost of modifying theatres to accommodate the half-ton dropping chandelier for *Phantom*: $50,000 to $100,000
- Amount lost by *Indiscretions*, held over from last season and a success with the critics: about $1 million
- Current terms of the Broadway Alliance: shows produced under it must spend no more than $750,000 on production and charge a top price of no more than $45 for tickets
- Actresses besides Zoe Caldwell who won Tony Awards for Broadway productions of *Medea*: Judith Anderson and Diana Rigg
- Number of theatres outside of New York controlled by the Shuberts: 3—the National in Washington, D.C., the Forrest in Philadelphia, and the Shubert in Los Angeles
- How Rosemary Harris and George Grizzard, appearing in *A Delicate Balance* (their 8th show together) as man and wife, have been related before on the stage: mother and son (*The Seagull*) and brother and sister (*Twelfth Night*)
- Number of subscribers to Tony Randall's National Actor's Theatre in 1991, its first season: about 28,000
- Number of subscribers this season: 12,000–15,000

Productions on Broadway: 38

Pulitzer Prize for Drama: *Rent* (Jonathan Larson)

New York Drama Critics Circle Awards:
Best Play: *Seven Guitars* (August Wilson)
Best Foreign Play: *Molly Sweeney* (Brian Friel)
Best Musical: *Rent* (Jonathan Larson)

Tony Awards:
Play: *Master Class* (Terrence McNally)
Actress in a Play: Zoe Caldwell (*Master Class*)
Actor in a Play: George Grizzard (*A Delicate Balance*)
Musical: *Rent* (Jonathan Larson)
Actress in a Musical: Donna Murphy (*The King & I*)
Actor in a Musical: Nathan Lane (*A Funny Thing Happened on the Way to the Forum*)

June | July | August | September | October | November

Terrence McNally speech cut off at Tonys
Betty Buckley in *Sunset Boulevard*
Jed Bernstein heads League of American Theatres
Tempest hot at box office
Moon Over Buffalo, *Mrs. Klein*, and *Victor/Victoria*
Zoe Caldwell in *Master Class*

December | January | February | March | April | May

New Victory Theatre opens on Forty-second Street
Rent composer Jonathan Larson d.
Rent opens off-Broadway
August Wilson's *Seven Guitars*
Nathan Lane in *Forum*
Julie Andrews "declines" Tony

Personalities

JUNE 4 Terrence McNally's speech is cut off the air when time runs out at the televised Tony Awards ceremonies.

JULY • Betty Buckley replaces Glenn Close in *Sunset Boulevard. Variety* says that Patti LuPone was the "Sicilian" Norma Desmond, and Glenn Close gave the part a "Kabuki" spin. But Buckley is the "Broadway" version.

OCTOBER 3 After breaking his foot for the second time in two years two nights ago, Tommy Tune is reduced to singing and acting his part in *Busker Alley*, at its tryout at the Tampa Bay Performing Arts Center, while two others dance for him. It won't work, and the show's November 16 New York opening—with poor tryout reviews hanging over it anyway—will be called off. The $3.5 million insurance on Tommy Tune will not cover the production's $6 million tab. **13** The U.S. Postal Service issues a stamp honoring Tennessee Williams.

NOVEMBER 14 "Last Weeks to See Matthew Broderick" say the ads for *How to Succeed in Business Without Really Trying.* In fact, the star is away this week, infuriating some ticket buyers, who find out after the fact. **16** Plans to move the revival of *Company* to a Broadway theatre fall through. Its composer Stephen Sondheim, denounces as a mere "money man" producer John Hart, who balked at the move when director Scott Ellis won't replace Boyd Gaines, who has laryngitis, with Michael Rupert.

JANUARY 13 Julie Andrews's understudy in *Victor/Victoria* Anne Runolfsson had other plans than to be in bed with Michael Nouri on this Saturday, but her beeper alerted her to the star's inability to complete her performance because of the flu, and in the middle of Act II, it's Runolfsson rather than Andrews whom Nouri finds under the sheets. During Andrews's absence in the next week, attendance will drop by almost 40 percent, with a loss of $220,000 at the box office.

FEBRUARY 21 It is the oysters that Zoe

Plays and Musicals

AUGUST 24 Nicky Silver's *The Food Chain* (332) opens at the Westside Upstairs Theatre. Patrick Fabian, Hope Davis, Phyllis Newman, and Tom McGowan, in a body suit, playing 400-pound Otto, are among the neurotics who are mostly talking to themselves in this dark comedy about alienated Manhattanites.

OCTOBER 1 Carol Burnett, back on Broadway three decades after *Fade Out–Fade In*, stars in Ken Ludwig's comedy *Moon Over Buffalo* (308), with Philip Bosco, at the Martin Beck. *The New York Times* celebrates her "game goofiness," saying that Burnett and Bosco, as a bargain basement Lunt and Fontanne, shine, but the *Times* calls the play "unfinished." **5** Stephen Sondheim's 1970 *Company* (68) is revived at the Roundabout Theatre. Boyd Gaines stars, singing a new song, "Marry Me a Little." Critical reaction is mixed. **12** *Patti LuPone on Broadway* (46), the diva's one-woman show, is at the Walter Kerr. **19** Carol Channing returns with another revival of *Hello, Dolly!* (118) at the Lunt-Fontanne, 31 years after she first played Dolly Levi. **24** Uta Hagen plays child psychologist Melanie Klein in Nicholas Wright's *Mrs. Klein* (280), opening at the Lucille Lortel. Laila Robins and Amy Wright costar with the 76-year-old Hagen who, says the *Times*, turns "a pedestrian text into a theatrical bonfire." **25** *Victor/Victoria* (738), starring Julie Andrews and directed by her husband Blake Edwards, who helmed the film version 13 years ago, opens at the Marquis Theatre. Andrews has not been on Broadway since *Camelot*, in 1960. Tony Roberts and Michael Nouri costar, and the score, featuring "Le Jazz Hot," is by Henry Mancini and Leslie Bricusse, with additional music by Frank Wildhorn. **27** *Bring in 'Da Noise, Bring in 'Da Funk*, a show with tap dancing at its heart, by Reg E. Gaines, Savion Glover, and George C. Wolfe, opens at the Public Theatre. By April, it will be uptown at the Ambassador.

Business and Society

JUNE 30 Unable to pay the rent for its Sheridan Square basement theatre in Greenwich Village and $100,000 in debt, the Ridiculous Theatre Company leaves the home it has occupied since 1977.

JULY • The Theatre League begins to use an advertising logo—"Destination Broadway"—to promote New York's stage offerings like a product. It also offers packaged tours that guarantee good seats for at least one Broadway show.

AUGUST 1 The League of American Theatres and Producers names advertising executive Jed Bernstein its new director. Past directors have had backgrounds in entertainment. **16** Fire destroys $750,000 worth of sets for this fall's

Births, Deaths, and Marriages

SEPTEMBER 1 Benay Venuata d.

OCTOBER 25 Viveca Lindfors d. **31** Rosalind Cash d.

NOVEMBER 17 Playwright Charles Gordone, who became the first African-American to win the Pulitzer Prize for Drama with his *No Place to Be Somebody*, d.

DECEMBER 9 Vivian Blaine d. **31** Director Michael Okrent m. choreographer Susan

"Big" also describes the investment required to stage a Broadway musical. PB

Caldwell ate at Sardi's after today's Wednesday matinée that knock her out of *Master Class* tonight, 20 minutes after the curtain has gone up. She collapses onstage and has to be carried off and taken to a hospital. By May, she will be saying, "I'm *so* bored with oyster jokes." **26** *Variety* reports a near-fistfight between former friends, producer Emanuel Azenberg and the Shuberts' Gerald Schoenfeld. Azenberg is upset over the Shuberts' unwillingness to confront the unions over rising labor costs. **28** Julie Andrews is missing from *Victor/Victoria* again, this time because of the removal of her gall bladder, which will keep her out for two weeks.

MARCH • Back in *How to Succeed in Business Without Really Trying* after being away on a leave, Matthew Broderick finds a familiar face onstage—it's his new costar, Sarah Jessica Parker, with whom he's been living offstage for the past four years. **6** Director Trevor Nunn is named to head Britain's National Theatre. **27** By dint of a $1 million investment, David Merrick has his name in the credits as coproducer of *State Fair*, opening tonight. He is back on Broadway for the first time since the unsuccessful *Oh, Kay!* in 1990. By the count of the 84-year-old Merrick, who has been disabled by a stroke for 13 years, it's his 88th show.

MAY 2 George C. Scott misses tonight's performance of *Inherit the Wind*. He has not been feeling well, and the accusations by his former assistant Julie Wright that he sexually harassed her, have not made him feel better. He issues a statement denying her charges. **3** George C. Scott flies to California for medical treatment, leaving behind Julie Wright's $3 million lawsuit and the production of *Inherit the Wind*, in which Tony Randall takes over his role but can't save the show. **8** The *New York Post* headlines: "Mary Poppins Hoppin' Mad." Julie Andrews, the recipient yesterday of the only Tony Award nomination accorded the musical *Victor/Victoria*, makes a curtain speech at today's matinée, saying that she's declining the honor as a matter of "conscience" and will "stand instead with the egregiously overlooked cast." **21** David Merrick sues, unsuccessfully, to stop the Tony

NOVEMBER 1 At the Broadhurst, Patrick Stewart, of "Star Trek" and the Royal Shakespeare Company, is Prospero in *The Tempest* (71), the first time since 1972 that The Public Theatre has mounted Shakespeare on Broadway. **5** Terrence McNally's *Master Class*, starring Zoe Caldwell as Maria Callas (a central figure in McNally's *The Lisbon Traviata*), opens at the John Golden, a rare straight play opening in a Broadway house. Audra McDonald plays one of her pupils. Caldwell's husband Robert Whitehead has coproduced this hit that will make back its $600,000 cost in less than three weeks. **20** David Hare's *Racing Demon* (48), opening at the Vivian Beaumont, is a piercing look at the Anglican Church in Britain. It stars Josef Sommer, Cathleen Chalifant, George N. Martin, and Brian Murray.

JANUARY 7 *Molly Sweeny (145)*, by Brian Friel, opens at the Roundabout. In this work that will win the Lucille Lortel Award for best off-Broadway play, Catherine Byrne plays a woman who regains her sight after several decades of blindness. Jason Robards, Jr. and Alfred Molina costar. **11** Frank Langella stars, with Gail Strikland and Angela Bettis, in August Strindberg's *The Father* (54), a Roundabout production at the Criterion Center Stage Right. *Variety* calls Langella's performance "hair-raising."

FEBRUARY 13 With echoes of *La Bohème*, *Rent*, "the most sensational musical in maybe a decade" (*Variety*), with a rock score, about New York City's East Village, opens at the New York Theatre Workshop on a bittersweet evening in which the critic's applause goes unheard by 35-year-old playwright Jonathan Larson, who died on January 25 of an aneurysm. It stars Adam Pascal and Daphne Rubin-Vega.

MARCH 28 August Wilson's *Seven Guitars* (187), directed by Lloyd Richards, is at the Walter Kerr. The *Times*'s Vincent Canby calls it "the highlight of what now seems to be a brand-new theater season." It's set in Pittsburgh in the 1940s. Ken Davis is bluesman Floyd Barton, whose funeral is the launching point for the flashback narrative. The cast also

Broadway revival of *Hello, Dolly!* with Carol Channing.

NOVEMBER 13 Andrew Lloyd Webber's Really Useful Company inaugurates its World Wide Web site—"Andrew Lloyd Website," *The New York Times* dubs it. Tee shirts are for sale at www.reallyuseful.com.

DECEMBER • The makeover of Forty-second Street goes into high gear with the opening of the New Victory Theatre, with its facade evocative of a much older Broadway. **8** For the third time, a performance of *Sunset Boulevard* has to be canceled for mechanical reasons. Tonight, it's the sprinkler system, which has put the Minskoff orchestra pit under four inches of water.

JANUARY 6 *Northeast Local*, at the Mitzi Newhouse Theatre in Lincoln Center, closes three performances before the end of its run when fire destroys much of its scenery and props. **8** With New York City at the tail end of a blizzard that has covered the Big Apple with 20 inches of snow, only one Broadway show opens on this Monday night: *Grease*, which sells standing room.

MARCH • When the month begins, 16 of Broadway's 32 theatres are empty. But by

Stroman. In lieu of a honeymoon, they go to work tomorrow on rehearsals for the upcoming musical *Big*.

JANUARY 24 Jonathan Larson, a 35-year-old songwriter who has just attended the final dress rehearsal of his musical *Rent* and only two hours ago gave an interview to *The New York Times* about what will be his Pulitzer Prize- and Tony Award-winning triumph, d. of an aneurysm.

MARCH 9 George Burns d.

Personalities

Awards because *State Fair* has been excluded in the competition for best score.

Lou Diamond Phillips, before the haircut *MSN*

Plays and Musicals

includes Reuben Santiago-Hudson, Viola Davis, Rosalyn Coleman, and Roger Robinson.

APRIL 11 Lou Diamond Phillips opens in *The King & I*, at the Neil Simon Theatre. Donna Murphy is Anna in this revival of the Rodgers and Hammerstein classic, which has a 53-member company and some dialogue added from the 1956 film. **18** "Brazenly retro," says *The New York Times*, lauding the revival of Stephen Sondheim's *A Funny Thing Happened on the Way to the Forum*, opening at the St. James. It may not be all Nathan Lane, but the evening is certainly built around the magnetic star. **21** Edward Albee's 1966 *A Delicate Balance* (186) is revived and very well-received by the critics (a better fate than befell the original, although it went on to win a Pulitzer), at the Plymouth, with a cast that features Rosemary Harris, George Grizzard, Elaine Stritch, and Mary Beth Hurt. **29** *Rent* moves to Broadway, at the Nederlander. **30** A revival of Sam Shepard's *Buried Child (77)*—the producers contend there are enough changes to qualify it for a Tony for new plays—opens at the Brooks Atkinson, bringing Shepard to Broadway for the first time. The Steppenwolf Theatre Company, under the direction of Gary Sinese, includes Lois Smith, James Gammon, and Jim True in this drama of a family made miserable.

MAY 1 Oscar Wilde's *An Ideal Husband (308)* is revived at the Barrymore. Peter Hall directs his own company, which includes Anna Carteret and Martin Shaw, in the biting comedy about money and power.

MAY 15 Caryl Churchill's *The Skriker* opens at the Public Theatre. Jayne Atkinson is starring as a fairy-demon in a story about a young woman who kills her baby. The *Times*'s Ben Brantley calls it "astonishing."

Business and Society

the end of April, only four houses will be dark, as the season comes on with a rush at the end.

MAY 9 The League of American Theatres and Producers and the American Theatre Wing start a Tony Awards website on the internet.

Births, Deaths, and Marriages

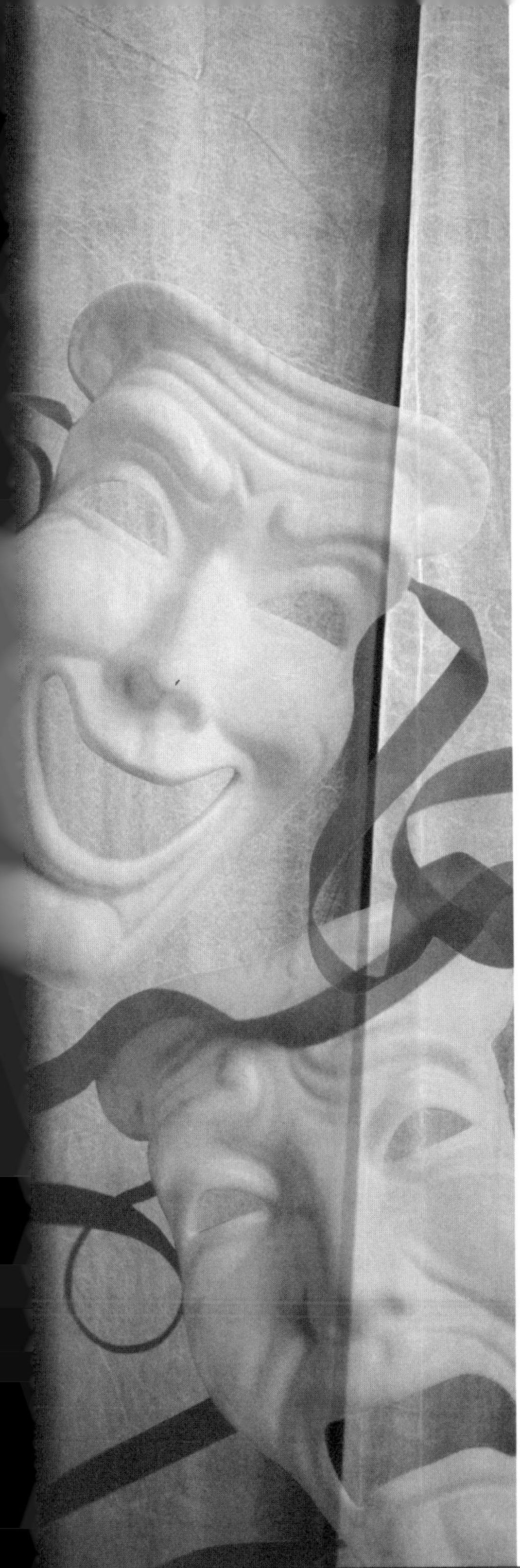

1996–97

Bawdy Forty-second Street, once the heart of the theatre district, becomes a family thoroughfare, with Disney's renovations of the New Amsterdam and Livent's combination of the old Apollo and Lyric theatres into one large, sparkling new house. Andrew Lloyd Webber joins a very exclusive peer group when he becomes Lord Lloyd Webber, but with the closing of *Sunset Boulevard* shy of the break-even point and the lackluster Washington tryout of *Whistle Down the Wind*, the British hit-maker is not having a vintage season. Producers are beginning to use focus groups, and the Dodgers production company has a winner in *Titanic*.

- How much of a lift Elaine Paige gives *Sunset Boulevard*: 6 inches worth, the amount by which the famous stairs need to be raised to make sure that the short actress can be seen over the banister
- What the *Victor/Victoria Playbill* says about Liza Minnelli during her one-month substitution for Julie Andrews: not a thing
- Number of performances given by Davis Gaines in *The Phantom of the Opera*: 1,937, including more than 2 years on Broadway
- Number of actresses who played Christine opposite Davis Gaines in the more than 5 years he has been the Phantom: 12
- Number of Andrew Lloyd Webber's wives present at the 10th anniversary celebration of *The Phantom of the Opera* in London: all 3—his current spouse, Madeleine, and former wives Sarah Brightman and Sarah Norris
- Cost, per week, of running *Miss Saigon*: $400,000
- Cost, per week, of running *Sunset Boulevard*, which closes short of its break-even point: $730,000
- Why the Circle Rep finally went under, according to one of its founders, Tanya Berezin: "We never really had a talent on the business side that equaled that of the artistic talent."
- Cost of a two-page ad in the fall preview Sunday *New York Times* Arts & Leisure section: about $135,000. Number of pages of theatre ads in that section: 21
- Tag line on ads for *Rent*, aimed at the youth market and placed in the New York City subways: "Don't You Hate the Word 'Musical?'"
- What dealing with Bernard B. Jacobs of the Shubert Organization was like, according to agent Sam Cohn: like "the worst migraine you ever had in your life." What Jacobs said about Cohn, upon hearing of this remark: "I don't like Sam."
- Broadway's divas, according to *Theatre Week* magazine: Angela Lansbury, Patti LuPone, Bernadette Peters, and Chita Rivera
- Only Broadway house that never goes dark: the Gaiety, the male burlesque theatre next to the Lunt-Fontanne

Pulitzer Prize for Drama: None awarded

New York Drama Critics Circle Awards:
Best Play: *How I Learned to Drive* (Paula Vogel)
Best Foreign Play: *Skylight* (David Hare)
Best Musical: *Violet* (Jean Tesori and Brian Crawley)

Tony Awards:
Play: *Last Night of Ballyhoo* (Alfred Uhry)
Actor in a play: Christopher Plummer (*Barrymore*)
Actress in a play: Janet McTeer (*A Doll's House*)
Musical: *Titanic* (Maury Yeston)
Actor in a musical: James Naughton (*Chicago*)
Actress in a musical: Bebe Neuwirth (*Chicago*)

June	July	August	September	October	November
Ben Brantley new *Times* critic	*The Fantasticks'* 15,000th performance	Circle in the Square bankrupt	Mosher heads Circle in the Square	Purge at *Les Miserables*	*Chicago* revived

December	January	February	March	April	May
Andrew Lloyd Webber out of ideas	August Wilson and Robert Brustein clash	No "Tomorrow" for *Annie* star	Whoopi Goldberg replaces Nathan Lane	Twenty-one musicals on Broadway	Renovated New Amsterdam reopens

Personalities

JUNE 2 Nathan Lane opens the Tony Awards ceremonies costumed as Julie Andrews, as she appears in *Victor/Victoria*. He says of the star, who criticized the Tonys for shortchanging her show and is not present: "Did you really think she would show up? That would be like the Pope showing up for Madonna's shower." And, surprise, it is Donna Murphy, not Andrews, who wins for Best Actress in a Musical. **11** Savion Glover, star of *Bring in Da' Noise, Bring in Da' Funk*, is sentenced to community service for a December arrest for "disorderly conduct." The original charge was driving while impaired and possessing marijuana. **12** *The New York Times* names Ben Brantley as its new chief drama critic.

JULY 25 Patti LuPone replaces Zoe Caldwell in *Master Class*. She speeds up the play by as much as a half hour.

SEPTEMBER • Elaine Paige replaces Betty Buckley in *Sunset Boulevard*. The main set's elaborate staircase has been raised six inches to accommodate the shorter Paige. • Nathan Lane, off for a week from *A Funny Thing Happened on the Way to the Forum*, now knows how much he's worth, as box office receipts plunge by a precipitous $350,000 in his absence.

OCTOBER 9 At the 10th anniversary celebration for *The Phantom of the Opera*, at Her Majesty's Theatre in London, Andrew Lloyd Webber appears onstage for the first time with Sarah Brightman, his second ex-wife, with whom he wrote "Music of the Night." In the audience are his first ex-wife, Sarah Norris, and his current spouse Madeleine. **27** Twelve members of the Broadway cast of *Les Miserables* are told that the show is being recast for its 10th anniversary, in March, and that their employment will end in January. Codirector John Caird says that the aim is to deal with "long-run-itis." Equity executive secretary Alan Eisenberg calls it "very distressing."

NOVEMBER • Dramaturge Lynn M. Thompson sues the estate of Jonathan Larson for 16 percent of the revenues from *Rent*, con-

Plays and Musicals

JULY 24 *The Fantasticks* gives its 15,000th performance at the Sullivan Street Playhouse, in Greenwich Village. **29** The Gate Theatre of Dublin begins the first complete cycle of the 19 plays of Samuel Beckett ever staged in the United States, at Lincoln Center. Barry McGovern will appear in three of them.

AUGUST 22 "Bravo," says *The New York Times* about Al Pacino in the Circle in the Square's revival of Eugene O'Neill's *Hughie* (56), the playwright's under-an-hour work set in a hotel lobby.

SEPTEMBER 17 David Mamet's *Edmond* is revived at the Atlantic Theatre, off-Broadway, in a limited engagement. David Rasche gives a performance that the *Times*'s Ben Brantley calls "a major, one-of-a-kind and seriously comic interpretation that gives new credence to a much maligned play." **19** David Hare's *Skylight* opens at the Royale. Michael Gambon, once "The Singing Detective" on television, stars in his Broadway debut with Lia Williams in a play about a man who tries, unsuccessfully, to rekindle an old romance.

NOVEMBER 14 "Hello, suckers!" It's the revival of the Kander and Ebb musical *Chicago*, at the Richard Rodgers. The reviews are very favorable—"pulse-racing," says Brantley, in the *Times*—for this show, starring Ann Reinking as Roxie Hart (she also choreographed, "in the style" of Bob Fosse), Bebe Neuwirth, Joel Grey, and James Naughton. It will win six Tonys. **18** "Frank Langella inhabits the tux-and-sherry world of Noel Coward as naturally as a cocktail pianist dons tails," says *Variety* about the revival of *Present Laughter*, directed by Scott Elliott, with nudity, at the Walter Kerr. The *New Yorker* is out this morning, before the opening, with John Lahr's negative review—an accident, he and the publication insist.

DECEMBER 5 David Copperfield brings his *Dreams and Nightmares* magic spectacle to the Martin Beck for a limited run. He's averaging 15 shows a week, which helps

Business and Society

JUNE • Ticketmaster now accepts fax orders for theatre tickets. **2** There is widespread unhappiness with the broadcast of the 50th annual Tony Awards, which shortens acceptance remarks and uses pre-taped highlights of the announcement of 13 of the 21 awards. One Actors Equity official describes it as "hateful." The ratings are also poor. **6** *The New York Times* reveals that the Shubert Organization's Gerald Schoenfeld and Bernard B. Jacobs have received hundreds of thousands of dollars in consultant fees from their own employees' pension and welfare funds.

AUGUST 23 The Circle in the Square declares bankruptcy and Theodore Mann, its cofounder and co-artistic director, resigns. Ironically, its production of O'Neill's *Hughie*, starring Al Pacino, opened last night to good reviews and a healthy box office.

SEPTEMBER 4 Gregory Mosher is named to head the Circle in the Square. He says that he no longer believes what he said after leaving the Lincoln Center Theatre several years ago: that the American theatre is "dying." **17** Michael Sovern, for-

Births, Deaths, and Marriages

JUNE 10 Jo Van Fleet d.

AUGUST 27 Bernard B. Jacobs, of the Shubert Organization, d.

OCTOBER 9 Walter Kerr, drama critic for the *New York Herald-Tribune* and *The New York Times*, d. His reply to David Merrick's claim that Kerr's playwright wife Jean influenced his reviews by nudging him on opening night was this: "She likes me, that crazy girl. Surely, somewhere, sometime, someone must have liked you well enough, Mr. Merrick, to give you a dig with an elbow. No? Ah, well." **23** Theatrical caricaturist Al Hirschfeld m. theatre historian Louise Kerz.

JANUARY 5 Composer Burton Lane d.

tending that her reshaping of his work makes her coauthor. **7** Equity head Ron Silver threatens not to sign the recent contract negotiated with producers until the *Les Miserables* firings are clarified. The union is under pressure because its executive secretary, Alan Eisenberg, has apparently known about the cast moves for some time without saying anything. Yesterday, several hundred actors demonstrated outside Equity headquarters.

DECEMBER 2 Andrew Lloyd Webber, addressing the National Press Club in Washington, and noting that he's written more musicals than Rodgers and Hammerstein, says, "This is the first time I can truthfully say that I don't have an idea for a show at all." **12** New York State fines the two hospitals that treated *Rent* composer Jonathan Larson just before his death, in January, for not being thorough and aggressive enough. He died of an undiagnosed aneurysm.

JANUARY 26 The *New York Post* reports that *Victor/Victoria* costar Tony Roberts is calling in sick because Liza Minnelli, substituting for vacationing star Julie Andrews, has been muffing her lines, with "I'm a second-rate hoofer" coming out as "I'm a second-rate hooker." All concerned deny the rift, maintaining that Roberts has the flu. **27** Playwright August Wilson and critic Robert Brustein debate the issue of race in the American theatre at New York's Town Hall. Wilson argues for a separate black theatre, saying that African-Americans need to "champion our own values, our own culture," and attacks nontraditional casting, defended by Brustein.

FEBRUARY • Andrew Lloyd Webber threatens to leave Britain if the Labour Party wins the next election. • Matthew Broderick, recovering from surgery, appears in Horton Foote's *The Death of Papa*, at the Playmakers Repertory in Chapel Hill, North Carolina, on crutches and wearing a knee brace. **2** Liza Minnelli finishes her monthlong run as a fill-in for Julie Andrews in *Victor/Victoria* by missing her third performance this week, with a throat condition. **10** Andrew Lloyd Webber cancels the June 15 Broadway opening of *Whistle Down the*

Broadway go over the $12 million mark in weekly ticket sales for the first time. **19** Sarah Jessica Parker stars in the revival of the Mary Rodgers musical *Once Upon a Mattress*, at the Broadhurst.

JANUARY 29 Rob Becker's *Defending the Caveman*, which closed on January 4 after Becker's 545th performance—a record for a one-person, nonmusical show—reopens at the Booth, with Michael Chiklis discoursing on men and women.

FEBRUARY 20 Pam Gems's Olivier Award-winning *Stanley*, about painter Stanley Spencer, is the first production at the Circle in the Square under new director Gregory Mosher. Antony Sher and Deborah Findlay star, with John Caird directing. **27** *The Last Night of Ballyhoo*, by Alfred Uhry, author of *Driving Miss Daisy*, opens at the Helen Hayes Theatre. The cast of this drama about a Jewish family in Atlanta in 1939 includes Dana Ivey, Jessica Hecht, and Paul Rudd. The reviews are mixed, with *Newsday*'s Linda Winer finding the show too "self-satisfied."

MARCH 12 Recast and recostumed, *Les Miserables* celebrates its 10th anniversary on Broadway. **16** Paula Vogel's play about a pedophile, *How I Learned to Drive*, opens off-Broadway, at the Vineyard Theatre. This winner of the New York Drama Critics Circle Award for best American play stars David Morse and Mary-Louise Parker. **25** Christopher Plummer stars in *Barrymore*, at the Music Box. As John Barrymore in William Luce's play, says *The New York Times*, Plummer "confirms his reputation as the finest classical actor of North America." **27** Horton Foote's *The Young Man from Atlanta* (85), a Pulitzer Prize winner two years ago, opens at the Longacre. Rip Torn and Shirley Knight star in this drama about a couple in the 1950s coping with domestic disasters.

APRIL 2 Ibsen's *A Doll's House* is revived in a limited engagement, at the Belasco. Janet McTeer is acclaimed for her work in this "new version" by Frank McGuiness. Owen Teel costars. **8** With the beginning of previews for *The Life*, there are 21 musicals on Broadway, the most in sever-

---

mer president of Columbia University, becomes president of the Shubert Foundation, and Philip J. Smith, executive vice president of the Shubert Organization, which runs the company's theatres, moves up to president. Both jobs were held by Bernard B. Jacobs, who died last month.

OCTOBER 7 The 28-year-old Circle Repertory Company, which owes the IRS $700,000, folds.

DECEMBER • Seeking a younger audience and moving away from subscriptions, The Circle in the Square announces a new policy in which members who pay a yearly fee of $37.50 will pay only $10 for each ticket. The ticket price for nonmembers is $45. • Broadway's Christmas week gross of $13.9 million, inflated by David Copperfield's playing as many as three shows a day of his *Dreams and Nightmares*, sets a record. • *The Players Guide*, an annual begun in 1944 that contained photos of and information about New York actors, folds, its function now taken over by promotional videos and websites.

JANUARY 6 After an almost 10-year run, *Theater Week* magazine ceases publication.

FEBRUARY • Livent's Garth Drabinsky is the first producer to add a building maintenance surcharge to ticket prices—for

---

FEBRUARY 2 Sanford Meisner, original member of the Group Theatre and acting teacher, d.

Personalities

Wind, which faltered in its Washington tryout that closed yesterday. **19** ABC acknowledges that Barbara Walters, who interviewed Andrew Lloyd Webber in December on "20/20," had invested $100,000 in his *Sunset Boulevard*, a fact she did not disclose. **24** A month before the opening of the revival of *Annie*, its producers fire 12-year-old Joanna Pacitti, who won the lead role in a competition chronicled on network television.

MARCH 6 Whoopi Goldberg replaces Nathan Lane in *A Funny Thing Happened on the Way to the Forum*. **18** A sprained ankle will keep Ann Reinking out of *Chicago* until April 13.

Andrew Lloyd Webber *MSN*

APRIL 11 Seventy-seven-year-old Tony Randall, artistic director of the National Actors Theatre, becomes a father for the first time.

MAY 21 The $5.8 million realized from the auction of Andrew Lloyd Webber's wine collection is a new wine auction record. Lloyd Webber hopes the wines have found "good loving homes."

Plays and Musicals

al decades. Five musicals will open in the week before the April 30 deadline for Tony nominees. **13** Kate Nelligan stars in Wendy Wasserstein's *An American Daughter*, at the Cort. Lynn Thigpen, Hal Holbrook, and Penny Fuller costar. The reviews are mixed for this drama about the nomination of a candidate for Surgeon-General. **23** *Titanic*, which literally had trouble sinking during a preview, opens at the Lunt-Fontanne, sailing toward this year's Tony for best musical. John Cunningham plays the captain, with music and lyrics by Maury Yeston. The reviews are mixed. **24** *Steel Pier (76)*, John Kander and Fred Ebb's musical about marathon dancing in Atlantic City in the 1930s, opens at the Richard Rodgers Theatre. Karen Ziemba stars in the show. **27** Good reviews greet Cy Coleman and Ira Gasman's *The Life*, a musical about prostitution in Times Square in the 1980s, opening at the Barrymore. Pamela Isaacs, Kevin Ramsey, and Lillias White star. The score has already appeared on a recording featuring Liza Minnelli. **8** This is the moment, at the Plymouth, for *Jekyll and Hyde*, Frank Wildhorn and Leslie Bricusse's musical, with Robert Cuccioli as the two-faced doctor-degenerate. Linda Eder costars. **29** *Candide*, "Harold Prince's sour, exhaustingly overstaged production of the Leonard Bernstein musical," according to Ben Brantley, opens at the Gershwin. The cast includes Harolyn Blackwell, Andrea Martin, and Jim Dale. **30** Brian Bedford delivers what the *Times* calls "the comic performance of the season" in Dion Boucicault's *London Assurance*, at the Roundabout.

MAY 18 The Disney-renovated New Amsterdam Theatre, for years a Forty-second Street movie house but once home of *The Ziegfeld Follies*, reopens with a limited run of the musical *King David*.

Business and Society

next season's *Ragtime*. • *Cats* is sued for $6 million by a theatregoer who claims that one of the cast member's interaction with the audience—a feature of the show—was overdone on her person a year ago.

MARCH 15 The Theatre Development Fund, which runs the TKTS discount booth in Times Square, removes Jed Bernstein as one of its directors. TDF is feuding with the League of American Theatres and Producers, headed by Bernstein, which intends to open its own discount operation.

APRIL 15 Continental Airlines becomes Broadway's "official airline" and its first full-season corporate sponsor.

Births, Deaths, and Marriages

Bibliography

Variety and *The New York Times* were indispensable to this project, as was the annual *Best Plays* series, begun by Burns Mantle in the 1920s and continued to this day by Applause Books. Also helpful were the annual *Theatre World* series, begun by Daniel Blum, the *New York Dramatic Mirror*, the *New York Herald-Tribune*, the *Performing Arts Bulletin*, and *Theater Week*.

———. *Who Was Who in the Theatre, 1912–1976: A Biographical Dictionary of Actors, Actresses, Directors, Playwrights, and Producers of the English-Speaking Theatre*. 4 vols. Detroit: Gale Research Co., 1972.

Atkinson, Brooks. *Broadway*. New York: Macmillan, 1970.

Avery, Lawrence, ed. *Dramatist in America: Letters of Maxwell Anderson, 1912–1958*. Chapel Hill, NC: The University of North Carolina Press, 1977.

Bentley, Joanne. *Hallie Flanagan: A Life in the American Theatre*. New York: Alfred A. Knopf, 1988.

Bergreen, Laurence. *As Thousands Cheer: The Life of Irving Berlin*. New York: Viking, 1990.

Blum, Daniel. *A Pictorial History of the American Theatre, 1860–1970*. 3rd rev. ed. New York: Crown, 1969.

Boardman, Gerald. *American Musical Theatre: A Chronicle*. New York: Oxford University Press, 1978.

———. *The Oxford Companion to American Theatre*. 2nd ed. New York: Oxford University Press, 1992.

———. *American Theatre: A Chronicle of Comedy and Drama, 1869–1914*. New York: Oxford University Press, 1994.

———. *American Theatre: A Chronicle of Comedy and Drama, 1914–1930*. New York: Oxford University Press, 1995.

Bakish, David. *Jimmy Durante: His Show Business Career*. Jefferson, NC: McFarland & Co., 1995.

Bradshaw, Jon. *Dreams That Money Can Buy: The Tragic Life of Libby Holman*. New York: William Morrow and Company, Inc., 1985.

Brown, Jared. *The Fabulous Lunts: A Biography of Alfred Lunt and Lynn Fontanne*. New York: Atheneum, 1986.

Bryan, George B., comp. *Stage Deaths: A Biographical Guide to International Theatrical Obituaries, 1850–1990*. 2 vols. New York: Greenwood Press, 1991.

———. *Ethel Merman: A Bio-Bibliography*. Westport, CT: Greenwood Press, 1992.

Bryer, Jackson R., ed. *The Playwright's Art: Conversations With Contemporary American Dramatists*. New Brunswick, NJ: Rutgers University Press, 1995.

Buehrer, Beverly B. *Cary Grant: A Bio-Bibliography*. Westport, CT: Greenwood Press, 1990.

Carrier, Jeffrey L. *Tallulah Bankhead: A Bio-Bibliograpy*. Westport, CT: Greenwood Press, 1991.

Clements, Cynthia, and Sandra Webber. *George Burns and Gracie Allen: A Bio-Bibliography*. Westport, CT: Greenwood Press, 1996.

Churchill, Allen. *The Great White Way: A Recreation of Broadway's Golden Era of Theatrical Entertainment*. New York: E.P. Dutton & Co., Inc., 1962.

———. *The Theatrical 20s*. New York: McGraw-Hill, 1975.

Cole, Stephen. *Noel Coward: A Bio-Bibliography*. Westport, CT: Greenwood Press, 1993.

Courtney, Marguerite. *Laurette*. New York: Rinehart & Company, 1955.

Davis, Allen F. *Actors and American Culture, 1880–1920*. Philadelphia: Temple University Press, 1984.

Davis, Lee. *Bolton and Wodehouse and Kern: The Men Who Made Musical Comedy*. New York: James H. Heineman, Inc., 1993.

Durham, Weldon B., ed. *American Theatre Companies, 1888–1930*. New York: Greenwood Press, 1987.

———. ed. *American Theatre Companies, 1931–1986*. New York: Greenwood Press, 1989.

Ewen, David. *The New Complete Book of the American Musical Theater*. New York: Holt, Rinehart and Winston, 1970.

Fordin, Hugh. *Getting to Know Him: A Biography of Oscar Hammerstein II*. New York: Random House, 1977.

Gabler, Neal. *Winchell: Gossip, Power and the Culture of Celebrity*. New York: Knopf, 1994.

Ganzl, Kurt. *Ganzl's Book of the Broadway Musical: 75 Favorite Shows From H.M.S. Pinafore to Sunset Boulevard*. New York: Schirmer Books, 1995.

Gelb, Arthur, and Barbara Gelb. *Eugene O'Neill*. New York: Harper, 1962.

Gilbert, Douglas. *American Vaudeville: Its Life and Times*. New York: Whittlesy House, 1940.

Gildzen, Alex, and Dimitris Karageorgiou. *Joseph Chaiken: A Bio-Bibliography*. Westport, CT: Greenwood Press, 1992.

Gill, Brendan. *Tallulah*. New York: Holt, Rinehart & Winston, 1972.

Goldman, Herbert G. *Jolson: The Legend Comes to Life*. New York: Oxford University Press, 1988.

Gottfried, Martin. *A Theater Divided: The Postwar American Stage*. Boston: Little Brown and Company, 1967.

———. *Jed Harris: The Curse of Genius*. Boston: Little, Brown and Company, 1984.

———. *All His Jazz: The Life and Death of Bob Fosse*. New York: Bantam Books, 1990.

Green, Stanley. *Broadway Musicals of the '30s*. New York: Da Capo, 1971.

———. *Encyclopedia of the Musical Theatre*. New York: Da Capo, 1980.

———. *Broadway Musicals: Show by Show*. Milwaukee: Hal Leonard Books, 1985.

Grossman, Barbara W. *Funny Woman: The Life and Times of Fanny Brice*. Bloomington, IN: Indiana University Press, 1991.

Guernsey, Otis L., Jr. *Curtain Times: The New York Theatre: 1965–1987*. New York: Applause Theatre Books, 1987.

Hay, Peter. *Broadway Anecdotes*. New York: Oxford University Press, 1989.

Hayman, Ronald. *John Gielgud*. London: Heinemann, 1971.

Higham, Charles. *Ziegfeld*. Chicago: Henry Regnery, 1972.

Hirsch, Foster. *Harold Prince and the American Musical Theatre*. Cambridge, England: Cambridge University Press, 1989.

Horn, Barbara Lee. *Colleen Dewhurst: A Bio-Bibliography*. Westport, CT: Greenwood Press, 1993.

———. *David Merrick: A Bio-Bibliography*. Westport, CT: Greenwood Press, 1992.

Houseman, John, and Jack Landau. *The American Shakespeare Festival: The Birth of a Theatre*. New York: Simon & Schuster, 1959.

Hughes, Glenn. *A History of the American Theatre: 1700–1950*. New York: Samuel French, 1951.

Jablonski, Edward, and Lawrence D. Stewart. *The Gershwin Years*. Garden City, NY: Doubleday & Co., 1958.

Kimball, Robert, and Alfred Simon. *The Gershwins*. New York: Athenuem, 1973.

Kimball, Robert, ed. *Cole*. New York: Delta, 1992.

Kinne, Wisner P. *George Pierce Baker and the American Theatre*. Cambridge, MA: Harvard University Press, 1954.

Kissel, Howard. *David Merrick: The Abominable Showman*. New York: Applause Books, 1993.

Koseluk, Gregory. *Eddie Cantor: A Life in Show Business*. Jefferson, NC: McFarland & Co., 1995.

Lees, Gene. *Inventing Champagne: The Worlds of Lerner and Loewe*. New York: St. Martin's Press, 1990.

Le Gallienne, Eva. *With A Quiet Heart: An Autobiography*. New York: Viking, 1953.

Little, Stuart W. *Off-Broadway: The Prophetic Theatre*. New York: Coward, McCann & Geoghegan, 1972.

Loesser, Susan. *A Most Remarkable Fella: Frank Loesser and the Guys and Dolls in His Life—A Portrait by His Daughter*. New York: Donald I. Fine, Inc., 1993.

Loney, Glenn. *Twentieth Century Theatre*, Volume I. New York: Facts on File Publications, 1983.

Longley, Marjorie, with Louis Siverstein and Samuel A. Tower. *America's Taste: The Cultural Events of a Century Reported by Contemporary Observers in the Pages of the New York Times*. New York: Simon & Shuster, 1959.

McArthur, Benjamin. *Actors and American Culture, 1880–1920*. Philadelphia: Temple University Press, 1984.

McGill, Raymond D., ed. *Notable Names in the American Theatre*. Clifton, NJ: James T. White & Co., 1976.

McGovern, Dennis, and Deborah Grace Winer. *Sing Out, Louise: 150 Stars of the Musical Theatre Remember 50 Years on Broadway*. New York: Schirmer Books, 1993.

Maney, Richard. Fanfare: The Confessions of a Press Agent. New York: Harper, 1957.

Meredith, Scott. *George S. Kaufman and His Friends*. Garden City, NY: Doubleday and Company, 1974.

Morehouse, Ward. *Mattineé Tomorrow: Fifty Years of Our Theatre*. New York: Whittlesey House, 1949.

Morley, Sheridan. *The Great Stage Stars: Distinguished Theatrical Careers of the Past and Present*. New York: Facts On File Publications, 1986.

Morris, Lloyd. *Curtain Time: The Story of the American Theatre*. New York: Random House, 1953.

Murphy, Donn B., and Stephen Moore. *Helen Hayes: A Bio-Bibliography*. Westport, CT: Greenwood Press, 1993.

Nadel, Norman. *A Pictorial History of the Theatre Guild*. New York: Crown, 1969.

Newman, Phyllis. *Just In Time: Notes From My Life*. New York: Simon & Schuster, 1988.

Nolan, Frederick. *Lorenz Hart: A Poet on Broadway*. New York: Oxford University Press, 1994.

Norden, Martin F. *John Barrymore: A Bio-Bibliography*. Westport, CT: Greenwood Press, 1995.

Payn, Graham and Sheridan Morely, eds. *The Noel Coward Diaries*. Boston: Little, Brown and Company, 1982.

Peters, Margot. *The House of Barrymore*. New York: Simon & Schuster, 1990.

Poggi, Jack. *Theatre in America: The Impact of Economic Forces, 1870–1967*. Ithaca, NY: 1968.

Riese, Randall. *Her Name Is Barbra: An Intimate Portrait of the Real Barbra Streisand*. New York: Birch Lane Press, 1993.

Rivadue, Barry. *Mary Martin: A Bio-Bibliography*. Westport, CT: Greenwood Press, 1991.

Robinson, Alice M., Vera Mowry Roberts, and Milly S. Barranger. *Notable Women in the American Theatre: A Biographical Dictionary*. New York: Greenwood Press, 1989.

Rollyson, Carl. *Lillian Hellman: Her Legend and Her Legacy*. New York: St. Martin's Press, 1988.

St. Just, Maria. *Five O'Clock Angel: Letters of Tennessee Williams to Maria St. Just, 1948–1982*. New York: Alfred A. Knopf, 1990.

Sanjek, Russell and David Sanjek. *American Popular Music Business in the 20th Century*. New York: Oxford University Press, 1991.

Schanke, Robert A. *Eva Le Gallienne: A Bio-Bibliography*. New York: Greenwood Press, 1989.

———. *Shattered Applause: The Lives of Eva Le Gallienne*. Carbondale, IL: Southern Illinois University Press, 1992.

Schwartz, Charles. *Gershwin: His Life and Music*. Indianapolis: Bobbs-Merrill Company, Inc., 1973

Sheward, David. *It's a Hit: The Back Stage Book of Longest-Running Broadway Shows, 1884 to the Present*. New York: Back Stage Books, 1994.

Slide, Anthony. *The Vaudevillians: A Dictionary of Vaudeville Performers*. Westport, CT: Arlington House, 1981.

———. *Selected Vaudeville Criticism*. Metuchen, NJ: The Scarecrow Press, 1988.

———. *The Encyclopedia of Vaudeville*. Westport, CT: Greenwood Press, 1994.

Smith, Wendy. *Real Life: The Group Theatre and America, 1931–1940*. New York: Alfred A. Knopf, 1990.

Snyder, Robert W. *The Voice of the City: Vaudeville and Popular Culture in New York*. New York: Oxford University Press, 1989.

Spoto, Donald. *The Kindness of Strangers: The Life of Tennessee Williams*. Boston: Little, Brown and Company, 1985.

Stagg, Jerry. *The Brothers Shubert*. New York: Random House, 1968.

Stevenson, Isabelle, ed. *The Tony Award: A Complete Listing With a History of the American Theatre Wing*. New York: Crown, 1980.

Taraborrelli, J. Randy. *Laughing Till It Hurts: The Complete Life and Career of Carol Burnett*. New York: William Morrow and Company, Inc., 1988.

Taylor, Deems. *Some Enchanted Evenings: The Story of Rodgers and Hammerstein*. New York: Harper and Brothers, 1953.

Thomas, Bob. *I Got Rhythm: The Ethel Merman Story*. New York: G. P. Putnam's Sons, 1985.

Timberlake, Craig. *The Bishop of Broadway: The Life and Work of David Belasco*. New York: Library Publishers, 1954.

Van Hoogstraten, Nicholas. *Lost Broadway Theatres*. New York: Princeton Architectural Press, 1991.

Wertheim, Frank, ed. *Will Rogers at the Ziegfeld Follies*. Norman, OK: University of Oklahoma Press, 1992.

Willett, John. *The Theatre of Erwin Piscator: Half a Century of Politics in the Theatre*. London: Eyre Methuen, 1978.

Zadan, Craig. *Sondheim & Co*. New York: Macmillan, 1974.

Ziegfeld, Richard and Paulette Ziegfeld. *The Ziegfeld Touch: The Life and Times of Florenz Ziegfeld, Jr.*. New York: Harry N. Abrams, Inc., 1993.

Ziegler, Joseph Wesley. *Regional Theatre: The Revolutionary Stage*. New York: Da Capo, 1977.

Index

Aaron, Alfred E., 16
Aarons, Alexander, 8, 85, 109, 157
Abady, Josephine, 419
Abbey Theatre, 17, 116
Abbott, George,7, 13, 18–19, 41, 64, 80–81, 86, 109, 118, 125, 127, 135, 138,–39, 148, 172, 174–75, 180, 182, 197–98, 204, 225, 236, 239, 246, 255, 312, 330–31, 369, 371–73, 387, 393, 417–19
Abbott, Judith, 172
Abbott and Costello, 137, 138, 164
Abel, Walter, 76, 116, 190, 235
Abelard and Héloise, 301
Abe Lincoln in Illinois, 130, 133, 134
Abide with Me, 120
Abie's Irish Rose, 53, 56–7, 59, 73, 85, 86
Abraham, F. Murray, 286, 312, 321, 325, 356–57, 383, 389, 392
Abraham's Bosom, 79
Absurd Person Singular, 324
Achard, Marcel, 253
Ackland, Joss, 400–401
Ackroyd, Dan, 386
Act, The, 339–41
Actors and Actresses, 397
Actors Equity, 17, 18, 23, 24, 29, 32, 39, 41, 42, 43, 46, 47, 50, 54, 61, 63, 88, 90–2, 107–8, 111–13, 115–17, 120–21, 124, 129–31, 139, 142–43, 147, 148, 150, 155, 157, 165, 178–79, 182, 199–200, 213–14, 216, 217, 225, 228, 229, 230, 233, 234, 241, 246, 253, 257–58, 268, 273–74, 278–80, 286, 292, 294, 299
Actors Fidelity League, 92, 124
Actors Fund of America, 6, 125
Actors Society of America, 9
Actors Studio, 177, 179, 182, 187, 216, 229, 235, 236, 241, 253, 258, 264–65, 268, 278
Adam, Noelle, 241
Adams, Edie, 204, 223, 260
Adams, Lee, 242, 245 268, 275, 297, 299
Adams, Maude, 5, 10, 13, 27, 29, 134, 206
Adamson, Harold, 182
Adaptation, 294
Adding Machine, The, 60, 173
Ade, George, 11, 12, 15
Adelphi Theatre, 167
Adler, Jacob, 4, 254
Adler, Luther, 12, 112, 118, 125, 130–31, 134, 167, 174, 200, 242, 268, 376
Adler, Richard, 54, 208–9, 211, 214, 215, 217, 229, 415
Adler, Stella, 11, 59, 111, 115–16, 118, 125, 139, 156, 187, 241, 410, 413
Admiral Had a Wife, The, 147, 148
Adonis, 7
Adrienne Lecouvreur, 6
Adrian, Max, 224, 228
Adventures of Nicholas Nickleby, The, 359, 361
Affairs of State, 192
Affair to Remember, An, 368
Africana, 86
After Magritte, 310
After the Fall, 264, 269, 356, 399
After the Rain, 286
Agee, James, 247
Ages of Man, The, 235
Agnes of God, 359, 361–63
Ah, Wilderness!, 113, 392
Ahearne, Tom 273
Ahrens, Lynn, 400
Aiello, Danny, 337
Aiken, George L., 4
Aikers, Karen, 363
Ailey, Alvin, 213, 228, 248, 342
Ain't Broadway Grand? 409
Ain't Misbehavin', 339, 343, 359
Ain't Supposed to Die a Natural Death, 308
Akalaitas, JoAnne, 130 272, 297 375, 377, 403, 405, 409, 411–12
Akins, Zoe, 115, 117, 234
Albee, Albert, 352, 355, 358, 360
Albee, Edward F., 8, 13, 24, 38, 41, 45, 58, 248–49, 253, 257–60, 262, 267, 269–70, 273–74, 277–78, 281, 286, 288–89, 298, 303 323, 325, 328, 303, 328, 341, 368, 395, 406, 413, 415–16 421, 424
Alberghetti, Anna Maria, 249, 251, 252
Albert, Eddie, 125, 127, 135, 171, 188
Albertson, Frank, 125, 265
Albertson, Jack, 156, 313, 199
Alda, Alan, 233, 252, 269, 278, 326, 406
Alda, Robert, 191–93, 233
Alderman, Myrl, 134, 135
Aldredge, Theoni, 325
Aldredge, Tom, 347
Aldridge, Theoni, 371
Alessandri, Gerald, 362
Alexander, C.K., 331
Alexander, Jane, 138, 312, 320, 346, 400–401, 410
Alexander, Jason, 240, 361, 384–85, 391, 393
Alexander, Rod, 189
Alford, Lamar, 305
Alfred, William, 273
Alice, Mary, 386, 419–20
Alice Sit-By-the-Fire, 174
Alive and Kicking, 189
Al Jolsen Theatre, 55, 156
All About Eve, 191, 203
Allegro, 177–79
Allen, Bebe, 223, 246
Allen, Deborah, 318, 382
Allen, Elizabeth, 270
Allen, Fred, 8, 92, 217

Allen, Gracie, 57, 60, 75, 80, 83, 110, 213–14, 268
Allen, Jay, 288, 293, 396–97
Allen, Joan, 373, 378, 387–88, 394
Allen, Jonelle, 308–9
Allen, Peter, 391–92
Allen, Rae, 249
Allen, Steve, 207–8, 213
Allen, Vera, 174
Allen, Viola, 7, 9, 179
Allen, Woody, 272, 277, 279, 294, 299
Alley Theatre, 177
All for Sugar, See Sugar
All God's Chillun Got Wings, 61, 63, 64, 65
Allgood, Sara, 17, 87
All In Fun, 144
All My Sons, 173, 176, 178, 395
All Over Town, 325
All That Jazz, 328
All the Way Home, 245, 247
Allworth, Frank, 120
Allyson, June, 141–42, 145, 148, 199
Alone Together, 377
Altman, Robert, 362
Alvarado, Don, 109
Alvarez, Carmen, 278
Alvin Theatre, 87, 158, 328–29. *See also* Neil Simon Theatre
Amadeus, 355–57
Ambassador, 312
Ambassador Theatre, 52, 156, 164, 380
Ameche, Don, 213
Amendolia, Don, 358
America Hurrah, 279
Americana, 108
American Blues, 136
American Buffalo, 327, 333, 335, 340, 359–60, 373
American Daughter, An, 428
American Dream, The, 248
American Federation of Actors, 138–39
American Mercury, The, 64
American National Theatre and Academy. *See* ANTA
American Negro Theatre, 142, 144, 166
American Play Company, 108
American Repertory Theatre, 173
American Shakespeare Festival, 216, 222, 241, 361
American Society of Composers, Authors, and Publishers (ASCAP), 221
American Theater, 8
American Theatre Wing, The, 149, 150, 155, 156, 166, 222, 246, 247
American Tragedy, 79
American Way, The, 136
Ames, Robert, 60
Amphytrion 38, 130
Amy, Frank, 156
Anastasia, 213
And a Nightingale Sang..., 373
Anderman, Maureen, 325
Anders, Glenn, 7, 55, 64, 69, 359
Anderson, Gwen, 156
Anderson, John Murray, 7, 207
Anderson, Judith, 10, 61, 80, 117, 124–25, 134, 136, 148–49, 158, 171, 177, 178, 179, 203, 208, 222, 239, 242, 301–2, 312, 363, 403, 405, 421
Anderson, Kevin, 378
Anderson, Lindsay, 303
Anderson, Maxwell, 7, 68, 91, 107, 110, 113–14, 120, 122–23, 125, 130, 134, 139, 156, 163, 166, 172, 175, 182–83, 188, 212, 234
Anderson, Robert, 205–6, 280, 288
Andersson, Benny, 390
Andes, Keith, 233
And Miss Reardon Drinks a Little, 304
Andrews, Ann, 87
Andrews, Julie, 121, 211–13, 217, 218, 225, 230, 235, 241, 247, 272, 288, 298, 308, 374, 397, 411–12, 421–23, 425–26
Andrews, Maxine, 320
Andrews, Patty, 320
Andreyev, Leonid, 55
And Things that Go Bump in the Night, 270
An Evening With Beatrice Lillie, 202
Angel in the Wings, 177
Angelo's Wedding, 378
Angels in America, Part II: Perestroika, 413–14
Angels in America: Millennium Approaches, 409–12, *411*
Angel Street, 149
Anglim, Philip, 348
Anglin, Margaret, 92, 150, 229
Always You, 45
Anna and the King of Siam, 189
Anna Christie, 53–55, 225, 392, 409, 411
Anna Karenina, 409
Anna Lucasta, 166, 172, 176
Ann Christie, 166
Anne of the Thousand Days, 181–83
Annie, 333, 336, 352, 359, 361, 369, 428
Annie Get Your Gun, 169, 171–73, 213–4
Annie 2: Miss Hannigan's Revenge, 395–98, 399. *See also Annie Warbucks*
Annie Warbucks, 409–12, 413–14
Anniversary Waltz, 209
Ann-Margaret, 307–8
Another Evening with Harry Stoones, 251, 252
Another Part of the Forrest, 175
Another Time, 402
Anouilh, Jean, 16, 211, 213, 217, 221, 225, 229, 245, 246, 388
Anspach, Susan, 270
ANTA, 176, 180, 198. *See also* Virginia Theatre
Antigone, 171
Antony and Cleopatra, 15, 130, 262, 177, 199–200, 397
Anouilh, Jean, 171
Anyone Can Whistle, 261, 265
Anything Goes, 115, 117, 350, 387–89, 392
Any Wednesday, 261, 264, 405
APA Repertory Company, 254
Apolinar, Danny, 285, 288
Apollo Theatre, The, 51
Appearing Nightly, 336
Applause, 297, 299, 300
Apple of His Eye, 172
Apple Tree, The, 233, 277, 278
Arcadia, 417, 419
Archer, William, 52
archy and mehitabel, 58
Arden, Eve, 17, 148, 369
Arden, John, 275
Ardeo, David, 362
Ardrey, Robert, 172
Are You a Crook?, 18
Are You Now or Have You Ever Been, 312–13, 345
Aristocrats, 394
Arkin, Alan, 235, 252, 260, 268, 278, 313
Arkinson, Brooks, 173
Arlen, Harold, 12, 108, 166, 171, 213, 228, 381
Arlen, Michael, 74
Arliss, George, 5, 11–2, 16, 51, 131, 171
Armed Forces, 165
Arms, Frances, 81
Arms and the Man, 8, 206
Armstrong, Louis, 209, 263
Armstrong, Robert, 70
Army Emergency Relief Fund, 156, 161, 163
Army Special Services, 165
Arnaz, Desi, 138–39
Arnaz, Luci, 347, 356
Arnold, Edward, 63
Arnold, Victor, 280
Arnstein, Carrie 40
Arnstein, Nicky, 17, 39, 40, 41, 46, 49, 70, 86
Aronson, Boris, 299, 356
Aronson, Etan, 369–70, 372–73
Around the World in 80 Days, 172, 174
Arrowsmith, William, 278
Arsenic and Old Lace, 141, 143–44, 156, 359–61
Arthur, Beatrice, 76, 137, 178, 189, 209, 213, 234, 268, 275

Arthur, Jean, 169, 171, 190, 192
Artists and Models, 61–2
Asch, Sholem, 59
Ashcroft, Peggy, 14, 125, 182, 404
Ashley, Elizabeth, 137–38, 253, 254, 258, 262, 264, 268, 278, 323–24, 330, 335, 361–63
Ashman, Howard, 367–68
Ashton, Herbert, Jr., 91
As Is, 375, 378
Asner, Ed, 216
Aspects of Love, 393, 395–96, 398
Assante, Armand, 309
Assassins, 400–401
Associated Actors and Artists of America, 130
Association of Producing Artists Repertory Company (APA), 242
Astaire, Adele, 37, 69, 87, 109, 328–29
Astaire, Fred, 35, 37, 45, 69, 85, 87, 109, 111, 288, 328–29, 388
As The Girls Go, 182, 188
As Thousands Cheer, 112
Aston, Frank, 228
Astor, Mary, 62, 123–24
As You Like It, 189
Atherton, William, 304–5
Atkins, Eileen, 278, 418
Atkinson, Brooks, 8, 74, 79–80, 86, 109, 113, 116–17, 124–25, 132, 133, 134, 135, 136, 137, 139, 142, 143, 144, 147–48, 158, 170, 174, 175, 178, 179, 180, 182–83, 189–90, 191, 193, 199, 201, 203, 213–14, 217, 223, 224, 225, 228, 230, 234, 235, 237, 246, 250, 339, 373, 395
Atkinson, Jayne, 424
At the Drop of a Hat, 240
Attles, Joseph, 331
Atwill, Lionel, 7, 51, 58, 172
Auberjonois, Rene, 319, 335, 378, 397
Augustus, Thomas, 4
Auntie Mame, 221, 222, 223, 414
Authors League Fund, 125
Authors League of America, 54–55, 74, 91
Awake and Sing, 118, 135, 173
Away We Go, 155, 158, 159
Awful Truth, The, 58
Axelrod, George, 202
Ayckbourn, Alan, 324, 330, 348
Azenberg, Emannuel, 423

Bab, 50
Babbitt, Milton, 254
Babes in Arms, 123, 126
Babes in Toyland, 12
Bacall, Lauren, 252, 267, 269, 274, 297, 299, 300, 355, 358, 361
Bacharach, Burt, 293, 361
Back on the Town, 384–85
Back Stage Club, 68
Back to Methuselah, 53, 56
Bacon, Frank, 40, 47, 54
Baddley, Hermione, 13, 259, 384
Bad Habits, 321
Bad Seed, The, 211–12
Bagels and Yox, 197
Bagley, Ben, 213, 219
Bagneris, Vernel, 351
Bagnold, Enid, 216, 331
Bailey, Pearl, 171–72, 213, 287, 288, 300, 302
Bain, Conrad, 318
Bainter, Fay, 8, 33, 42, 76, 90, 114, 124, 177, 287
Baitz, Jon Robin, 392, 405
Bajour 371
Baker, Belle, 8, 30, 38, 82, 138, 223
Baker, Blanche, 358
Baker, George Pierce, 5, 13, 24, 28, 42, 58, 117
Baker, Joe Don, 265
Baker, Jordan, 415
Baker, Josephine, 52
Baker, William H., Jr., 162
Baker, Kathy, 370
Baker, Lenny, 336
Baker, Mark, 320–21
Baker, Russell, 348
Bakos, John, 292
Balaban, Bob, 280
Balanchine, George, 126–27, 132, 134–35, 142, 182
Balcony, The, 242
Balderston, John, 86, 340
Balding, Ivor, 302
Baldwin, Alec, 397, 403, 406
Baldwin, David, 265
Baldwin, James, 265, 342
Balieff, Nikita, 55
Balin, Ina, 228
Ball, Lucille, 247, 249, 261, 272
Ball, William, 328
Ballad of a Sad Cafe, 262
Ballard, Kaye, 209, 225, 249
Ballard, Lucinda, 198
Ballroom, 345–47
Balm in Gilead, 374
Balsam, Martin, 45, 179, 193–94, 240, 281, 285
Bancroft, Anne, 212, 223, 227, 230, 235, 239, 240, 260, 262, 268, 273, 287
Band Wagon, The, 372
Banes, Lisa, 372, 392
Banjo Eyes, 118, 149
Bankhead, Tallulah, 11, 35, 38, 43, 44, 45, 52, 53, 55, 59, 91–2, 80, 112–14, 117–18, 129–30, 133–36, 141–43, 145, 148–50, 157, 164, 167–68, 171, 181, 182, 183, 184, 189, 191, 195, 202–3, 205, 207–8, 211–12, 223, 235, 263, 272, 277, 280, 286, 289, 291, 292, 307
Banks, Leslie, 188
Bannister, Harry C., 80
Bara, Theda, 32, 217
Baranski, Christine, 199, 373, 392, 404–5
Barasch, Norman, 235
Barbara Cook: A Concert for the Theatre, 386
Barbeau, Adrienne, 309
Barefoot in the Park, 262, 263, 267, 268, 271
Baritz, Richard, 355
Barkin, Ellen, 367, 369–70
Barnes, Clive, 81, 286, 292, 293, 294, 295, 321, 324, 328, 334–35, 361, 369, 372–73, 396–97, 400, 406–7, 412
Barnes, Howard, 157, 174, 189, 191
Barnum, 349, 353
Bar of a Tokyo Hotel, The, 298
Barr, Richard, 303, 392–93
Barretts of Wimpole Street, The, 113, 166, 189–90
Barrie, Barbara, 300, 334
Barrie, J.M. 42, 174
Barrie, James, 10, 13
Barry, Gene, 157, 372
Barry, Julian, 331
Barry, Philip, 9, 13, 58, 60, 87, 91, 118, 133, 157, 168, 188
Barry, Tom, 90
Barrymore, 425, 427
Barrymore, Barry, 357
Barrymore, Diana, 52, 198–99, 211, 214, 224, 240, 241
Barrymore, Ethel, 3, 6, 8, 11–12, 18, 35, 45, 47, 52, 54, 57, 62, 81, 91, 111–13, 121, 134, 142, 151, 155, 164, 213, 240, 323, 368
Barrymore, John, 3, 5–6, 12, 15–6, 30, 31, 34, 37, 38, 41, 42, 43, 46, 47, 50, 59, 62–3, 52, 57, 71, 123–24, 134, 137, 139–42, 147, 149, 151, 224, 329–30, 368
Barrymore, John, Jr. 198–99, 212, 225, 241, 246
Barrymore, Lionel, 3, 6, 11, 34, 38, 42, 47, 212, 368
Barrymore, Maurice, 3, 12
Barrymore Theatre, 124, 158, 159
Bart, Jean, 81
Bart, Lionel, 259
Bartels, Louis John, 65
Bartenieff, George, 260
Bartlett, Charles, 309
Barto, Dewey, 15, 56
Barton, James, 8, 126, 136, 138, 141, 174, 199, 253
Basic Training of Pavlo Hummel, The, 305, 333, 336–37
Basquette, Lina, 74
Basset, Angela, 390

Bassey, Shirley, 409
Bates, Alan, 113, 228, 252, 311–12
Bates, Blanche, 11, 13, 15, 17, 149
Bates, Kathy, 331, 362, 369–70, 388
Bateson, Susan, 312–13
Bathsheba, 175
Battle, Hinton, 325, 358, 372–73, 399, 401–2, 404
Battle of Angels, 144–45, 225
Battles, John, 178
Baum, Frank, 11
Baxley, Barbara, 68, 192, 202, 217, 247, 260, 268, 293, 345, 400
Baxter, Anne, 300, 320, 368
Baxter, Kenneth, 303
Bayes, Nora, 6, 14, 15, 17, 23, 34, 31, 34, 36, 41, 45, 49, 52, 58–9, 77, 87, 163
Beach Blanket Babylon, 324
Beal, John, 113, 293
Bean, Orson, 216, 254
Bean, Reathel, 378
Beard, The, 286, 287, 299
Beatlemania, 337
Beatty, Roberta, 70
Beatty, Warren, 241, 303
Beau Brummell, 7, 62
Beautiful People, The, 145
Beauty and the Beast, 413, 415–16, 418
Becher, John C., 252
Beck, John, 380
Beck, Julian, 69, 182, 199, 258, 268, 292, 294, 308
Beck, Leonore, 132, 259
Beck, Martin, 15, 18, 23, 41, 42, 163, 168
Becker, Rob, 419, 427
Becket, 245, 246, 249
Beckett, Samuel, 13, 218, 230, 242, 252, 298, 375, 377, 392, 396, 426
Bedford, Brian, 117, 262, 266, 301, 321, 428
Bedroom Farce, 348
Beechman, Laurie, 362
Beehive, 379, 382
Beery, Noah, 168
Beggar on Horseback, 61, 65
Beggar's Holiday, 173, 175
Beggar's Opera, 175
Begley, Ed, 11, 299, 176, 214
Begley, Ed, Jr, 420
Behan, Brendan, 235, 246, 247, 249, 263
Behrman, Samuel Nathaniel, 8, 13, 109, 124, 134, 136, 157, 188, 317–18
Belafonte, Harry, 137, 163, 208, 229
Belasco, David, 4, 6, 8, 11, 12–13, 14, 15, 17, 27, 36, 41, 43, 47, 55, 60, 62, 69, 71, 80, 82, 205, 222
Belasco Theatre, 16, 139, 166, 400
Belcher, Marjorie, 178
Bel Geddes, Barbara, 8, 58, 141, 145, 163, 170, 193, 194, 195, 204, 214, 230, 249
Bel Geddes, Norman, 8, 120–21, 136, 230
Bell, Book and Candle, 192, 400
Bell, Marion, 176
Bell, Michel, 418
Bellamy, Ralph, 12, 86, 159, 171, 182, 184, 188, 200, 227, 230, 231, 234, 268, 405
Belle, Lulu, 79
Belle, Monte, 86
Belle of Amherst, The, 331, 333
Bell for Adano, A, 167, 170
Bells Are Ringing, The, 221, 223, 228, 233, 234, 320
Ben-Ami, Jacob, 8, 24, 45, 49, 51, 138, 193, 241, 340
Benchley, Robert, 7, 24, 52, 53, 61, 63, 81, 171
Bendix, William, 138, 253
Benefactors, 379, 381–82
Beneto Cereno, 268
Benevente, Jacinto, 80
Ben Hur, 10
Bening, Annette, 383–84
Benjamin, Richard, 330–31
Bennett, Alan, 259
Bennett, Barbara, 5, 164
Bennett, Constance, 5
Bennett, Joan, 5
Bennett, Michael, 157, 254, 280, 305, 308, 317, 320, 326, 327, 328, 329, 333, 334, 335, 341–42, 345, 346, 347, 381, 383, 386, 387–88, 395, 398
Bennett, Richard, 5, 13, 18, 54, 55, 59, 69, 74, 120, 166
Benny, Jack, 8, 53, 61, 65, 71, 107, 323, 324, 325
Benson, Jodi, 405–6
Bent, 351
Bentham, Josephine, 156
Bentley, Eric, 201–2, 224, 258, 260, 280, 312–13
Benzel, Mimi, 253
Berenson, Barinthia, 318
Beresford, Harry, 58
Berezin, Tanya, 374, 384, 425
Berg, Gertrude, 233, 236
Bergen, Polly, 148–49, 208, 217
Berghof, Herbert, 15, 150, 191–92, 401
Bergman, Alan 346–47
Bergman, Andrew, 382
Bergman, Ingrid, 173, 175, 176, 287, 323, 326
Bergman, Marilyn, 346–47
Berkeley, Busby, 86
Berle, Milton, 14, 57, 59, 67, 69, 107, 108, 111, 112, 138, 139, 149, 159, 169, 170, 180, 185, 197, 198, 199, 205, 251
Berlin, Alexandra, 266, 286
Berlin, Irving, 7, 13–14, 16, 17, 23, 25, 27, 30, 33, 38, 39, 40, 43, 44, 53, 54, 58, 63, 69, 73, 74, 76, 79, 82, 86, 111, 112, 114, 124, 140, 142, 156, 157, 158, 163, 171, 172, 173, 175, 188, 192, 221, 257, 259, 395–96
Berlinger, Warren, 249
Berlin Stories, 199
Bernardi, Herschel, 62, 293
Bernaw, Christopher, 340
Bernays, Edward, 18
Bernhardt, Sarah, 3, 6, 13, 18, 19, 59, 302
Bernie, Ben, 53, 57
Bernstein, Ira, 217
Bernstein, Jed, 421, 428
Bernstein, Leonard, 167, 201, 204, 217, 224, 228, 292, 317, 320–21, 331
Berrigan, Rev. Daniel, 302, 303, 304, 308
Berry, Eric, 312
Besoyan, Rick, 241
Besser, Joe, 149
Best Foot Forward, 148, 259
Best Little Whorehouse in Texas, The, 339, 342, 359
Best Man, The, 239, 242, 245, 248
Best Years of Our Lives, The, 173, 175
Betrayal, 349, 351–52
Betsy, 82
Bettger, Lyle, 150
Bettis, Angela, 423
Between the Devil, 131
Bevan, Donald, 195, 355
Beverly Hills, 137
Beyond the Fridge, 319. *See also* Good Evening
Beyond the Fringe, 259, 265, 319
Beyond the Horizon, 325
Bickel, Frederick, 51
Bickford, Charles, 82
Big, 422–23
Big Boy, 71
Bigley, Isabel, 192–93, 204
Big River, 375, 378, 393, 419
Big Time Buck White, 293
Bikel, Theodore, 217, 241, 246, 268
Billingsley, Sherman, 115
Bill of Divorcement, A, 55
Billy Rose Theatre, 240, 347. *See also* National Theatre; Nederlander Theatre; Trafalger Theatre
Biloxi Blues, 375, 377, 380, 384–85
Biltmore Theatre, 158, 389, 414
Binford, Lloyd T., 135
Bing, Rudolph, 187
Bingham, Susan, 300
Biography, 109, 110
Bird, Carolyn, 331
Bird in Hand, 92
Bird of Paradise, The, 17
Birds, The, 278
Birthday Party, The, 246, 286
Bishop, Andre, 399, 401

Bishop, Kelly, 328–29, 400
Bissell, Marian, 231
Black, Don, 398
Black, Karen, 362
Black and Blue, 391, 393
Blackbirds of 1928, 88
Black Comedy, 280
Black Crook, The, 5
Blackmer, Sidney, 9, 55, 108, 112, 156, 164, 187, 189–90, 193–94, 206, 236, 318
Blackouts of 1942, 156
Blacks, The, 249
Black Terror, The, 309
Blackwell, Harolyn, 428
Blaine, Vivian, 62, 166, 192–93, 198, 260, 422
Blair, Betsy, 142, 145, 148
Blair, Janet, 202
Blair, Mary, 56, 63
Blair, Pamela, 328–29
Blake, Eubie, 52, 54, 346
Blandick, Clara, 64
Blau, Herbert, 200, 270, 280
Bledsoe, Jules, 10, 87, 88, 89, 162
Blithe Spirit, 147, 148, 265, 388
Blitzstein, Marc, 12, 130, 144, 174, 209, 263
Blondell, Joan, 178, 180
Blood Brothers, 412
Blood Knot, The, 264
Bloom, Claire, 298, 400–401
Bloomer Girl, 166, 167, 188
Bloomgarden, Kermit, 182, 229, 300, 334
Blossom Time, 54, 155
Blown Sideways Through Life, 413–14, *415*
Blue Light, Little, 195
Blue Monday, 58
Blues for Mr. Charlie, 264, 265, 270
Blum, Mark, 351–52
Blyden, Larry, 202, 235, 264, 278, 324, 328
Blythe, Ann, 145
Bob & Carol & Ted & Alice, 336
Bock, Jerry, 90, 218, 239, 241, 246, 260, 267, 268, 278, 303
Bogardus, Stephen, 358, 400, 407, 418
Bogart, Humphrey, 56, 71, 74, 76, 115, 117
Bogosian, Eric, 203, 382, 386, 395, 397
Boland, Mary, 7, 74, 120, 150, 246, 272
Boles, John, 62
Boleslavski, Richard, 7, 124
Bolger, Ray, 12, 109, 118, 149, 156, 161, 162, 163, 181–82, 246, 384
Bologna, Joseph, 292
Bolt, Robert, 251, 253
Bolton, Guy, 6, 7, 26, 29, 34, 36, 37, 38, 41, 44, 51, 81, 117, 164, 213, 312, 330, 350
Bombo, 55
Bon Voyage, 115, 116–17
Bond, Frederica, 79
Bond, Sheila, 202
Bond, Sudi, 248, 362
Bondi, Beulah, 91
Bonstelle, Jesse, 5, 90, 108
Boom Boom Room, 317, 318
Boone, Richard, 178–79
Booth, Edwin, 3, 5, 6, 7, 8
Booth, John Wilkes, 5
Booth, Shirley, 14, 71, 118, 123, 124, 136, 143, 145, 156, 159, 162, 182, 187, 189, 193, 194, 195, 201, 202, 203, *204*, 241, 410
Boothe, Clare, 11, 12, 62, 109, 112, 117, 120, 125, 134, 138, 149, 158, 324, 388, 396
Booth Theatre, 18, 124, 162, 183
Bordoni, Irene, 9, 92, 140, 202
Boretz, Alan, 127
Borge, Victor, 206–7
Borgnine, Ernest, 200, 268, 269
Born Yesterday, 169, 171
Borodin, Alexander, 208
Borstal Boy, 297, 299
Bosco, Philip, 246, 248, 281, 348, 391, 394, 405, 415–16, 419, 422
Bosdavi, Count Anthony de, 91, 92
Boseman and Lena, 302
Bosley, Tom, 86, 233, 241, 254, 416
Bostwick, Barry, 300, 309, 333, 404–5
Both Your Houses, 107, 110
Boublil, Alain, 383, 385, 401–2
Boucicault, Dion, 428
Bought and Paid For, 16
Boulton, Agnes, 88
Boulton, Whitney, 269, 287
Bovasso, Julie, 215, 309, 318, 378, 403–4
Bowen, John, 286
Bowers, Lally, 278
Bowery Theatre, 3
Bowles Paul, 236
Bowles, Jane, 208
Boyd, Malcolm, 268
Boyd, William, 68
Boyer, Charles, 198, 235
Boy Friend, The, 212–13
Boyle, Peter, 357
Boys from Syracuse, The, 134, 135, 174, 260, 263
Boys in the Band, The, 285, 289, 301, 393
Bracken, Eddie, 138
Bradbury, Lane, 237
Bradford, Alex, 309–10, 335
Bradley, June, 62
Brady, Alice, 25, 41
Brady, William, 5, 27, 188
Braham, Horace, 91
Braine, Tim, 393
Braithwaite, Lillian, 74
Brand, Phoebe, 14, 112, 118, 131, 148, 204
Brando, Marlon, 62, 137, 161, 164, 165, 166, 167, 172, 174, 178, 179, 180, 182, 206–7, 249, 324
Brandon, Mary, 58, 116
Brantley, Ben, 424, 425–26, 428
Breakfast at Tiffany's, 277, 278
Breaking the Code, 389
Brecht, Bertolt, 10, 110, 209, 217, 222, 224, 281, 292
Brecht on Brecht, 254
Breit, Harvey, 235
Brennan, Eileen, 241, 263, 396
Brennan, Maureen, 320–21
Brent, George, 108, 116
Breslin, Jimmy, 389
Brian, Donald, 13, 14, 24
Brice, Fanny, 8, 15–16, 17, 27, 28, 29, 32, 36, 39, 40, 41, 46, 49, 50, 53, 54, 58, 61, 62, 63, 65, 69, 70, 71, 73, 74, 80, 86, 87, 89, 90, 91, 111, 114, 119, 121, 121, 134, 150, 189, 191, 193
Bricusse, Leslie, 258, 270, 422, 428
Brig, The, 260, 263
Brigadoon, 173, 176, 178, 414
Bright, Richard, 286
Bright Boy, 164
Brightman, Sarah, 373, 376, 387–89, 405, 409, 414, 425–26
Brighton Beach Memoirs, 367, 369, 384–85
Bring Back Birdie, 371
Bring in 'Da Noise, Bring in 'Da Funk, 422, 426
Brittan, Robert, 317–18
Britton, Pamela, 161, 176
Britton, Sherry, 193
Brixton Burglary, 11
Broadhurst, George, 13, 16, 24, 50, 199
Broadhurst Theatre, 35, 36
Broadway, 80
Broadway Alliance, The, 400, 404, 421
Broadway Association, 108
Broadway Bound, 383–84
Broadway Cares, 389
Broadway Coquette, 79, 350
Broadway Theatre, 156, 163
Broderick, Helen, 8, 240
Broderick, Matthew, 254, 340, 359, 362, 369, *377*, 380, 388, 417, 419, 422–23, 427
Brokaw, George, 62
Bromberg, J. Edward, 110, 112, 197, 198, 199
Brook, Peter, 68, 213, 268, 274, 304, 388
Brooke, Sorrell, 252
Brooks, David, 170, 176
Brooks, Geraldine, 268

Brooks, Lawrence, 166
Brooks, Mel, 200, 268
Brooks, Patricia, 206
Brooks, Richard, 236
Brooks Atkinson Theatre, 247
Brother Rat, 125
Brothers, 91
Broun, Heywood, 7, 36, 42, 45, 51, 54, 55, 68, 74, 112, 117, 133, 135, 139,
Brown, Anne, 120, 149
Brown, Blair, 331
Brown, John Mason, 11, 13, 109, 118, 130, 134, 135, 139, 148–49, 182, 293
Brown, Kenneth, 260
Brown, Lew, 8, 80, 86, 91, 117, 229
Brown, Margaret, 258
Brown, Ruth, 391, 393
Brown, Vanessa, 202
Browne, Porter Emerson, 15
Browne, Roscoe Lee, 249, 262, 268, 370, 406–7
Brownsville Raid, The, 335
Bruce, Carol, 140, 171, 270
Bruce, Lenny, 304
Brustein, Robert, 81, 273, 280, 293, 294, 345, 346, 347, 395, 398, 425, 427
Bryan, William Jennings, 214
Bryceland, Yvonne, 390
Brynner, Yul, 28, 148, 171, 191, 194–95, 200, 202, 206, 207, 208, 323, 325, 328, 330, 337, 373, 375–76, 379–80
Bryon, Arthur, 131
Bubbles, John W., 11, 90, 120, 202, 381. *See also* Buck and Bubbles
Bubbling Brown Sugar, 331
Buchanan, Jack, 64, 131
Buck and Bubbles, 11, 189, 202
Buckley, Betty, 178, 277, 295, 346, 368, 381, 389, 410, 416, 421–22, 426
Bucks County Playhouse, 137, 138, 156
Buddy: The Buddy Holly Story, 400
Bulgakov, Mikhail, 270
Bull, Peter, 280
Bullins, Ed, 116, 289, 307, 309, 323, 326
Bumgarner, Jim, 208
Bunk of 1926, 80
Burgess, Anthony, 315
Burghoff, Gary, 280
Buried Child, 345–46, 348, 424
Burke, Billie, 7, 14, 19, 25, 26, 28, 57, 58, 119. 137, 140, 299, 324
Burke, Maurice, 168
Burleigh, Steven, 357
Burnett, Carol, 109, 228, 236, 237, 262, 266, 268, 269, 270, 308, 397, 421–22
Burning Glass, The, 208
Burns, David, 255, 263, 303
Burns, George, 9, 57, 60, 75, 80, 83, 110, 213–4, 268, 324–25, 423
Burn This, 387–88
Burrows, Abe, 16, 191, 192, 193, 201, 203–4, 231, 251, 253, 274, 278, 293, 313, 377
Burstyn, Ellen, 109, 229, 323, 326, 335, 352–53, 359, 362, 367, 368, 369, 380, 388, 407
Burton, Kate, 406, 420
Burton, Richard, 74, 183, 191, 193, 228, 229, 245, 247, 259, 263, 265, 274, 303, 330–31, 342, 349, 355, 356, 357, 367, 370, 372, 375–76
Busch, Charles, 380
Bush, Josef, 298
Bushkin, Nina, 355
Busker Alley, 406, 414, 422
Bus Stop, 214, 217
Butler, Michael, 294, 319
Butler, Pierce, 3
Butley, 311, 312
Butter and Egg Man, The, 76
Butterflies Are Free, 298, 299
Buttons, Red, 148, 163, 216
Byck, Dann, Jr., 346
Bye, Bye Birdie, 239, 242, 245, 371, 406, 414
By Jupiter, 156, 162
Byrne, Catherine, 423

Cabaret, 199, 277, 279, 280, 288, 299
Cabin in the Sky, 142
Cacoyannis, Michael, 262, 287, 372
Cactus Flower, 267, 271, 273, 274
Caesar, Adolph, 335, 361
Caesar, Irving, 9, 64, 74, 83
Caesar, Sid, 259
Caesar and Cleopatra, 199–200, 335
Café La Mama, 252
Cagney, James, 75, 80, 180
Cahill, Marie, 74
Cahn, Sammy, 178
Caine, Michael, 303
Caine Mutiny Court-Martial, The, 208
Caird, John, 385, 426–27
Caldwell, Zoe, 112, 273, 285, 288, 289, 300, 312–13, 359, 363, 368, 376, 414, 418, 421–23, 426
Calhern, Louis, 76, 80, 109, 142, 170, 193, 218
California Suite, 334
Callaway, Liz, 361, 380, 401–2, 415
Calling All Stars, 117
Call Me By My Rightful Name, 248
Call Me Madam, 191–92, 201, 419
Call Me Mister, 172, 174
Calloway, Cab, 204, 287
Calvert, Louis, 58
Calvi, Gerard, 235
Cambridge, Godfrey, 249, 252
Camelot, 235, 241, 245, 247, 248, 355, 356, 357, 375, 422
Camille, 8
Camino Real, 201, 204
Cammuso, Frank, 416
Campbell, Alan, 418
Campbell, Douglas, 253, 291
Campbell, Mrs. Patrick, 5, 11, 25, 139
Canby, Vincent, 351, 418, 419, 420, 423–24
Can-Can, 204, 205, 207, 233
Cancilla, Elaine, 350
Candida, 12, 70, 113
Candide, 221, 224, 317–18, 320–21, 428
Cannon, J.D., 264
Cannon, Maureen, 168
Cantor, Eddie, 8, 25, 28, 31, 32, 35, 36, 40, 43, 44, 45, 47, 49, 50, 52, 56, 60, 61, 62, 63, 64, 69, 86, 88, 91, 107, 149–50, 170–71, 268
Čapek, Josef, 59, 242
Čapek, Karel, 57, 58, 59, 242
Capers, Virginia, 317–18
Capote, Truman, 213
Capri, Dick, 404
Caprice, 124
Captain Jinks of the Horse Marines, 11
Captive, The, 79, 80, 82
Carden, William, 321
Caretaker, The, 252
Carey, MacDonald, 144, 209
Carey, William, 52
Carillo, Leo, 6, 25, 33, 36, 74, 252
Cariou, Len, 138, 313–14, 345, 348, 401
Carlin, Tom, 217
Carlisle, Kitty, 28, 173, 174–75, 209, 334
Carmen, 163
Carmen Jones, 163, 172
Carmody, Jay, 242
Carney, Art, 229, 253, 270
Carnival!, 245, 249, 252
Carnival in Flanders, 205
Carnovsky, Morris, 10, 59, 88, 92, 110, 112, 118, 131, 143, 148, 199, 204, 216, 222, 228, 229, 248, 262, 410
Carol Channing & Her Stout-Hearted Men, 297, 300
Caron, Leslie, 199, 375–76
Carousel, 51, 165, 168, 169, 170, 212, 413–15
Carpenter, Constance, 86, 202
Carr, Alexander, 18, 36
Carradine, David, 272
Carradine, John, 183, 255
Carradine, Keith, 369, 402
Carrie, 387, 389–90
Carroll, David, 390, 396, 398, 406

Carroll, Diahann, 120, 213, 254
Carroll, Earl, 8, 32, 34, 61, 62, 68, 73, 76, 80, 83, 90, 112, 123, 124, 178, 184
Carroll, June, 200
Carroll, Leo G., 8, 74, 113, 149, 167, 170, 312
Carroll, Madeleine, 182
Carroll, Marie, 56
Carroll, Paul Vincent, 129, 131, 133, 135
Carroll, William, 334
Carson, Alexander, 222
Carson, Johnny, 397
Carter, Jack, 218
Carter, Mrs. Leslie, 4, 9, 80, 131
Carter, Myra, 415
Carter, Nell, 182, 343
Carteret, Anna, 424
Carthay Circle Theatre, 203
Carton, Bob, 404
Carus, Emma, 6, 80, 86
Carver, Brent, 409, 412
Carville, Anthony, 412
Caryl, Ivan, 16, 25
Casey, John, 55, 109
Casey, Warren, 309
Cash, Rosalind, 135, 287, 294, 422
Casino Theatre, 75
Casnoff, Philip, 399, 400, 401
Cason, Barbara, 312
Cass, Peggy, 188, 258, 345
Cassidy, Jack, 202, 260
Castellano, Richard, 270, 292
Castle, Irene, 17
Castle, Vernon, 15, 17
Cat and the Canary, The, 56
Catherine Was Great, 165
Catlett, Walter, 51, 69, 76
Cat on a Hot Tin Roof, 211, 214, 221, 222, 323–24, 392, 397
Cats, 358, 367–68, 373, 376, 383, 385, 393, 396, 409, 417, 421
Catskills on Broadway, 403–4, 414, 418
Caulfield, Joan, 158
Cave Man, The, 17
Cave of Machpelah, The, 240
Cavett, Dick, 352
Cawthorn, Joseph, 24, 75
Cazale, John, 288
Century Theatre, 168
Ceremonies in Dark Old Men, 294
Cerf, Bennett, 174–75
Cerveris, Michael, 412
Chaiken, Joseph, 120, 235, 240, 258, 279, 374
Chalfant, Kathleen, 412, 423
Chalk Garden, The, 216
Chamberlain, Richard, 278
Champion, Gower, 54, 178, 242, 265, 280, 311, 313, 324, 340–41, 355, 356
Chandler, Stan, 398
Changing Room, The, 311, 314
Channing, Carol, 51, 141, 144, 148, 158, 181, 183, 187–88, *189*, 191, 193, 195, 200, 217, 222, 252, 261, 263, 265, 270, 272, 280, 281, 285, 286, 287, 297, 302, 317, 318, 319, 320, 324, 342, 361, 373–74, 384, 404–5, 421, 422, 423
Channing, Margo, 300
Channing, Stockard, 163, 308–9, 347, 375, 377, 396, 400
Chaperone, 15
Chaplin, 371
Chaplin, Charlie, 75, 162, 228
Chaplin, Judith,258
Chaplin, Saul, 258
Chaplin, Sydney, 75, 223, 228, 233, 234, 241, 254, 265, 272
Chapman, John, 139, 162, 167, 198, 208, 214, 218, 228, 245, 249, 250, 258, 262, 265, 289, 308
Chapman, William, 3
Chapter Two, 341
Charig, Phil, 164
Charlap, Mark, 212
Charley's Aunt, 142
Charlot's Revue, 63, 64
Charnin, Martin, 303, 333, 336, 345, 347, 369, 395–96, 398, 410, 411, 412
Chase, Ilka, 80, 125, 149, 225, 340
Chase, Mary, 165, 167, 200
Chatterton, Ruth, 8, 24, 68, 108, 116, 253
Chauve-Souris, 55
Chayefsky, Paddy, 59, 204, 217, 230, 241, 253, 360
Che!, 291, 293, 299
Cher, 362
Cherry Lane Theatre, 68, 202
Cherry Orchard, The, 59, 272, 335
Chess, 381, 387, 390
Chicago, 81, 82, 327, 328, 329, 333, 335, 350–51, 371, 425–26, 428
Chicken Every Sunday, 164
Chihara, Paul, 401
Chiklis, Michael, 427
Children's Hour, The, 202
Children From Their Games, 260
Children of a Lesser God, 349, 352
Children of Darkness, 230
Children of Pleasure, 75
Children's Hour, The, 115, 116, 241
Child's Play, 297, 299
Chin Chin, 25, 27
Chinese Coffee, 406, 410
Chinese Honeymoon, A, 11
Chodorov, Edward, 19, 203–4, 208, 392
Chodorov, Jerome, 19, 143, 149, 203–4, 209
Chong, Rae Dawn, 401
Chorus Line, A, 317, 320, 323, 326, 327, 328, 329, 335, 341–42, 345, 347–48, 351, 356, 359, 371–72, 393, 395, 398
Chorus People's Alliance, 18
Christian, Robert, 280
Christians, Mady, 10, 145, 148, 166, 198
Christie, Audrey, 112, 125, 163
Christie, Julie, 318
Christmas Carol, A, 405
Christofer, Michael, 335–36
Chu Chin Chow, 86
Church, Sandra, 237
Churchill, Caryl, 134, 358, 369, 389, 424
Churchill, Pamela, 241
Cilento, Diane, 216
Cilento, Wayne, 342
Cinderella, 13, 225
Circle in the Square, 425–26
Circle Repertory Company, 144, 324–25, 427
Circular Staircase, The, 222
City, The, 15
City Center Theatre, 163
City of Angels, 395, 397
Civic Repertory Theatre, 79, 80
Civilization, 18
Clair de Lune, 52
Claire, Dorothy, 176
Claire, Helen, 134
Claire, Ina, 8, 58, 91, 107, 109, 110, 133, 135, 376
Clancy, Liam, 235
Clarence Derwent Award, The, 168
Clark, Bobby, 7, 17, 69, 81, 121, 137, 138, 156, 163, 182, 188, 241
Clark, Dane, 254
Clark, Philip, 348
Clary, Robert, 200, 269
Clash By Night, 148, 149
Claudia, 144
Clayburgh, Jill, 303, 312, 318, 321, 346
Clayton, Jan, 168, 171, 172, 208
Clayton, Lou, 61, 79, 82
Clearing in the Woods, 223
Cleese, John, 270
Clements, Colin, 158
Cleveland Play House, 129, 130
Clift, Montgomery, 120, 139, 157, 164, 169, *170*, 182, 419
Climate of Eden, 203
Clipper, The, 62
Clooney, Rosemary, 206, 208, 254, 286

Close, Glenn, 176, 323, 324, 325, 331, 340–41, 346, 353, 371, 373, 376, 381–82, 403, 405, 406, 409–10, 412, 413, 416, 417, *418*, 419, 420, 422
Close Quarters, 125, 227
Cloud, 358
Club, The, 334
Club Durant, 63
Clurman, Harold, 11, 53, 71, 88, 111, 114, 118, 131, 156, 172, 180, 200, 202–3, 209, 214, 222, 225, 234, 236, 241, 253, 292, 312–13, 356
Coastal Disturbances, 383–84
Cobb, Lee J., 17, 118, 125, 131, 139, 163, 181, 182, *183*, 184, 188–89, 200, 228, 327–28
Cobra, 61
Coburn, Charles, 47, 109, 252
Coburn, Donald L., 339
Coca, Imogene, 114, 342
Cocktail Hour, The, 391, 392
Cocktail Party, The, 187, 189
Coco, 297, 298, 301, 302
Coco, James, 91, 293, 294, 297, 299, 335, 370, 372, 384
Cocoanuts, The, 73, 76
Cody, Lew, 62
Coe, Fred, 268
Cohan, George M., 6, 7, 11, 12, 13, 14, 16, 18, 24, 52, 55, 59, 113, 127, 129, 130, 155, 156, 163, 230, 241
Cohen, Alexander, 211, 217, 247, 294, 308, 325, 333, 335–36, 340, 342, 357, 373, 380
Cohen, Myron, 236
Cohn, Harry, 159
Colbert, Claudette, 12, 235, 346
Cole, David, 190
Coleman, Cy, 247, 259, 274, 314, 336, 342, 353, 395, 397, 399, 402, 428
Coleman, Nancy, 213
Coleman, Rosalyn, 423–24
Coleman, Sheppard, 222
Coleman, Warren, 120, 188
Coles, Charles "Honi", 188, 370
Coles, Matthew, 288
Colette, 300
Colicos, John, 275
Collection, The, 259
College Widow, The, 12
Collier, Constance, 6, 108, 142
Collinge, Patricia, 8, 135, 319
Collins, Dorothy, 305, 314
Collins, Jean, 162, 260
Collins, Pauline, 391, 393
Collins, Stephen, 411–12
Colman, Ronald, 51
Colouris, George, 135, 145
Colton, John, 59, 77
Colum, Padriac, 234
Comden, Betty, 24, 201, 204, 138, 149, 167, 212, 223, 231, 248, 253, 259, 266, 285, 299, 319–20, 342, 368, 372, 399, 402
Come Back, Little Sheba, 187, 189–90, 193–94, 203–4
Come Back to the 5 & Dime, Jimmy Dean, Jimmy Dean, 362
Come Blow Your Horn, 245, 248
Comedienne, The, 82
Comedy in Music, 206–7
Comedy of Errors, 135
Come Into the Garden, Maude, 320
Come on Strong, 257
Coming of Age in Soho, 375
Command Decision, 177, 178
Common Pursuit, The, 384
Commonweal, 286
Company, 297, 299, 301, 422
Complaisant Lover, The, 253
Compton, Betty, 91
Compton, Juleen, 241
Compulsion, 228
Condon, Norman, 175–76
Confessions of a Female Disorder, 317
Congreve, William, 324–25
Conklin, Peggy, 117, 126, 190, 203–4
Connecticut Yankee, A, 86, 163
Connection, The, 240
Connelly, Madeleine, 120
Connelly, Marc, 8, 54, 56, 59, 61, 65, 113, 116, 120, 357
Connolly, Walter, 139
Conroy, Frances, 352
Conroy, Frank, 81, 135, 265
Conroy, Kevin, 392, 393
Constant Wife, The, 81, 323, 326
Consul, The, 187, 189–90
Conti, Tom, 345, 347–48, 393, 404
Contractor, The, 317
Conversation Piece, 116
Conversations with My Father, 403, 406
Convy, Bert, 268, 279
Conway, Curt, 217
Conway, Kevin, 149, 319, 348, 393
Conway, Shirl, 213
Cook for Mr. General, A, 252
Cook, Barbara, 86, 147, 161, 191, 195, 199, 212–13, 224, 230, 260, 323–24, 389
Cook, Donald, 11, 182, 194, 253
Cook, Joe, 7, 235
Cook, Peter, 259, 318–19, 324
Cook, Roderick, 312
Cooke, Elisha, Jr., 113
Cookson, Peter, 178, 195
Cooper, Gary, 193–94
Cooper, Gladys, 125, 216
Cooper, Susan, 369
Coote, Robert, 217
Copland, Aaron, 53
Copperfield, David, 426–27
Coquette, 86, 174
Corbin, John, 58, 59, 110
Corey, Irwin, 200
Corey, Wendell, 171
Corio, Ann, 254
Corman, Roger, 368
Cornell, Katharine, 8, 52, 53, 54, 55, 70, 74, 109, 110, 111, 113, 117, 121, 125, 133, 134, 136, 138, 139, 145, 149, 157, 166, 171, 177, 180, 192, 199–200, 213, 216, 231, 323–24
Corn Is Green, The, 141, 142, 151, 155, 373, 379
Coronet Theatre, 240
Corpse, 375
Correia, Don, 356, 380
Cort Theatre, 17, 156, 167
Cosaro, Frank, 253, 387, 389
Cosi Fan Tutti, 197
Costello, Dolores, 58
Cotsworth, Staats, 312
Cotten, Joseph, 136
Count of Monte Cristo, The, 7, 16–17
Country Girl, The, 191–92
Courage, 90
Courtenay, Tom, 335, 361
Cousin Kate, 12
Covington, Julie, 376
Cowan, Jerome, 110, 231
Coward, Noel, 10, 73, 74, 79, 92, 107, 109, 110, 115, 116, 119, 121, 125, 126–27, 142, 147, 148, 149–50, 161, 162, 165, 167, 182, 194–95, 202, 211, 216, 217, 218, 219, 229, 239, 245, 249, 265, 299, 311, 312, 313, 320, 326, 350–51, 370, 388, 426
Cowboys, 269
Cowl, Jane, 7, 12, 13, 17, 57, 60, 62, 82, 87, 133, 135, 150, 192
Coy, Edward H., 74, 90
Cradle Snatchers, 74
Cradle Will Rock, The, 129, 130, 381
Craig, Helen, 142
Craig's Wife, 73, 76
Cranham, Kenneth, 416
Craven, Frank, 5, 16, 131–32, 170
Craven, John, 132
Crawford, Broderick, 8, 131, 227
Crawford, Cheryl, 11, 127, 149, 174, 178, 181, 211–12, 242, 253, 264, 383–84
Crawford, Michael, 149, 280, 387, 388, 389, 409
Crawley, Brian, 425
Crazy for You, 403, 405–6
Creation of the World and Other Business, The, 312–13
Cresswell, Luke, 415
Crews, Laura Hope, 6, 25, 82, 156
Crimes of the Heart, 355, 357, 359, 361

Crist, Judith, 249
Cristofer, Michael, 335–36
Critic, The, 172
Cromwell, John, 26, 76
Cronyn, Hume, 16, 115, 116, 125, 155, 156, 197, 198, 208, 249, 262, 265, 268, 272, 278, 298, 313, 320, 334, 345–46, 339, 340, 351, 369, 418
Crooked Square, The, 61
Crosby, Bing, 170–71
Crothers, Rachel, 6, 13, 52, 65, 92, 108, 109, 129, 130, 137, 139–40, 149, 174, 234
Crouse, Lindsay, 339, 340, 404
Crouse, Russel, 8, 115, 117, 124, 125, 138, 169, 171, 224, 239, 241, 273
Crowley, Mart, 289
Crucible, The, 201, 203–4, 272, 395, 399, 405
Crucifer of Blood, The, 346
Cryer, Gretchen, 121, 262, 299, 346, 383–84
Cryptogram, The, 418, 420
Cuba and His Teddy Bear, 384
Cuccioli, Robert, 428
Culkin, Kit, 246
Cullum, John, 247, 272, 323, 325, 339, 378, 342
Cummingham, John, 428
Cummings, Constance, 15, 92, 345, 347
Cummings, Robert, 114
Curro, Marta, 234, 309–10
Curry, Tim, 326, 356–57
Curtis, Tony, 137, 353
Cushing, Tom, 55
Cuskern, Dominic, 414
Cyrano, 61, 63, 173, 195, 315, 317, 359
Cyrano de Bergerac, 63, 173, 174, 205

Da, 339
Dahomey, 12
Dailey, Dan, 126
Daily, Irene, 265
Dale, Alan, 4, 24, 87
Dale, Charlie, 357
Dale, Jim, 120, 317, 321, 323–24, 349, 353, 377, 389, 396, 428
Dale, Margaret, 74
Daley, James, 247
Dall, John, 167
Dalton, Dorothy, 62
Daly, Arnold, 12, 13
Daly, Augustin, 5, 77
Daly, Tyne, 395–96, 419
Daly's Theatre, 6
Damaged Goods, 18
Dames At Sea, 293
Damn Yankees, 208, 211, 214, 215, 217, 233, 413, 415, 417, 419–20
Dana, Leora, 183, 189, 216
Dance and the Railroad, The, 360
Dance Me A Song, 189
Dancin', 339, 342, 346, 351
Dancing at Lughnasa, 403–4
Dancing Mothers, 68
D'Andre, Carol, 246
Dandridge, Dorothy, 163
Dane, Shelton, 420
Danger, 55
Daniels, Mark, 163
Daniels, William, 242, 295
Danner, Blythe, 155, 294, 298, 299, 335, 351–52, 393
Danton's Death, 273
D'Arcy, Mary, 380
Darin, Bobby, 209
Darion, Joe, 271, 273
Dark at the Top of the Stairs, The, 178, 229
Dark Hours, The, 109
Dark is Light Enough, 213, 216
Darkness at Noon, 191, 193
Dark of the Moon, 168, 191, 193–94
Dark Victory, 118
Darling of the Day, 285
Darling of the Gods, 11
Darling, Jean, 170
Darrieux, Danille, 302
Dash, Sue, 163
Da Silva, Howard, 15, 130, 131, 158, 204, 228, 241, 252, 272, 295, 381
Dauphin, Claude, 175, 189
Davalos, Richard, 216
Davenport, Harry, 55
Davenport, Nigel, 246
David Harum, 11
David, Hal, 293
Davidson, Gordon, 109, 335–36, 352, 387
Davidson, John, 264
Davila, Diana, 308–9
Davis, Bette, 191, 201, 203–4, 253, 254
Davis, Bill, 361
Davis, Brad, 378
Davis, Clifton, 308–9
Davis, Donald, 242
Davis, Edgar B., 80
Davis, Frank J., 80
Davis, Hope, 422
Davis, Ken, 423–24
Davis, Miles, 373
Davis, Ossie, 164, 169, 172, 182, 190, 228, 252, 258, 273, 299, 381
Davis, Owen, 57, 60, 63
Davis, Sammy, Jr., 213, 166, 218, 262, 268
Davis, Viola, 423–24
Davison, Bruce, 392
Dawn, Hazel, 16, 54, 55
Day, Doris, 91, 272
Day, Edith, 9, 60, 302
Day in Holywood and a Night in the Ukraine, A, 353, 360, 368
Day in the Death of Joe Egg, A, 289, 377
Day of Absence, 273
Days and Nights of Bebe Fenstermaker, The, 258
Days of Wine and Roses, The, 222
Day the Whores Came Out to Play Tennis, The, 264
Days Without End, 114
Deacon and the Lady, 16
Dead End, 119
Dead Souls, 270
Dean, Hamilton, 86
Dean, James, 208
Dean, Phillip Hayes, 341
Deane, Hamilton, 340
Dear Charles, 212
Dearest Enemy, 75
Dear Ruth, 167
Death and the Maiden, 403, 405, 406
Death in the Family, A, 247
Death of a Salesman, 181–84, 188, 190, 208, 262, 327–28, 334, 370, 371, 372, 373, 375–76, 395
Death of Bessie Smith, 249
Death of Papa, The, 427
Deathtrap, 339, 342, 359, 360, 361, 385
de Banzie, Brenda, 231
de Banzie, Lois, 362
Deburau, 51
Dee, Ruby, 68, 169, 172, 182, 204, 252, 302
Deep Are the Roots, 169, 170, 172
Defending the Caveman, 419, 427
Defour, Val, 202
de Hartog, Jan, 197–98, 227
de Havilland, Olivia, 419
Dekker, Albert, 88, 117, 125, 208, 253, 288
Delaney, Shelagh, 245, 246
de Laurentiis, Dino, 249
De Laurentis, Semina, 381
Delbridge, Alice, 86
de Liagre, Alfred, 385
Delicate Balance, A, 277, 278, 281, 286, 421, 424
Dell, Gabriel, 265, 294
Delmar, Ethel, 58
de Luce, Virgina, 200
De Lys, William, 202
Demas, Carole, 309
DeMille, Agnes, 12, 124, 158, 162, 166, 168, 176, 178, 182, 414
DeMille, Cecil B., 12, 14
Demi-Virgin, The, 53, 54, 55
Dempsey, Jack, 54
Dench, Judi, 302, 358
Denier, Joan, 273
De Niro, Robert, 383–84
Denker, Henry, 249
Dennis, Sandy, 124, 255, 259, 261, 264, 272, 324, 262, 403, 405
de Paul, Gene, 223
Deputy, The, 264

Dern, Bruce, 236
Derr, Richard, 213
Derwent, Clarence, 7, 166, 171–72, 188, 240
Desert Song, The, 81
De Shields, Andre, 325, 343
Design For Living, 109
Desire Under the Elms, 68, 69, 74, 88, 258, 259
Deslys, Gaby, 7, 16, 17
Desmond, Johnny, 231, 272
Desperate Hours, The, 211, 213
Destiny of Me, The, 410
Destry Rides Again, 236, 237
Desvallières, Maurice, 225
Detective Story, 182, 184
Detroit Civic Theatre, 90
Detwiller, Russell, 258
Deval, Jacques, 83
Devall, Robert, 335, 340
Devane, William, 280, 305
Devils, The, 273, 281
DeVito, Danny, 305, 393
Devour the Snow, 351
de Vries, Peter, 225
Dewey, Thomas, 174–75
Dewhurst, Colleen, 68, 173, 174–75, 221, 222, 230, 247, 258, 259, 262, 272, 286, 287, 307–8, 313, 317, *319*, 320, 331, 345, 370, 380, 391, 392, 393, 394, 396–97, 403, 405
De Wilde, Brandon, 188–89, 200
Dexter, John, 270
Dhery, Robert, 233, 235
Dial M for Murder, 202
Diamond, Jack "Legs", 63, 67, 68
Diamond, Zelda, 171
Diamond Lil, 184
Diary of Anne Frank, The, 215, 216, 221, 222, 229
Die Fledermaus, 157
Dietrich, Marlene, 161, 164, 180, 239, 313
Dietz, Howard, 9, 92, 180, 198, 262, 372, 376
Di Fusco, John, 376
Digges, Dudley, 6, 51, 60, 123, 127, 131, 132, 142, 148, 164, 174, 178–79
Diller, Phyllis, 301, 302, 3033
Dillingham, Charles, 5, 15, 25, 55, 63, 80, 82, 112, 116
Dillman, Bradford, 223
Dillon, Melinda, 258, 281
Dillon, Mia, 357
Dingle, Charles, 135
Dining Room, The, 362
Dinner at Eight, 108–9
Dirtiest Show in Town, The, 302
Disenchanted, The, 233, 235
Dishy, Bob, 335
Disraeli, 16
Divine, Loretta, 361–62
Division Street, 356
Dixey, Henry E., 7
Dixon, Billie, 286
Dixon, Ivan, 236
Dixon, Jean, 142
Dixon, Jerry, 400, 406
Dockstadter, Lew, 4, 14
Doctor's Dilemma, The, 149
Dodson, Jack, 269
Dodsworth, 114
Dog Beneath the Skin, The, 178
Do I Hear a Waltz, 270
Dolan, Robert Emmett, 264
Doll's House, A, 129, 131, 425, 427–28
Dolly, Jennie, 6, 16, 8, 148
Dolly, Rosie, 6, 16, 8, 299
Dolly Varden, 11
Domingo, Placido, 221
Donahue, Jack, 75, 88
Donaldson, Walter, 86, 91
Don Giovanni, 376
Don Juan in Hell, 198
Donlevy, Brian, 68, 83
Donnelly, Dorothy, 54, 69
Don't Bother Me, I Can't Cope, 309–10, 318
Don't Drink the Water, 277, 279
Dooley, Paul, 294
Do Re Mi, 247
Dorfman, Ariel, 406
Doubles, 378
Doughgirls, The, 155, 158
Douglas, Kirk, 158, 184
Douglas, Melvyn, 11, 116, 195, 216, 239, 242, 360
Douglas, Paul, 171
Douglas, Stephen, 209, 214, 262
Dourif, Brad, 319
Dowling, Eddie, 131, 138, 168
Downes, Olin, 120, 189
D'Oyly Carte Company, 359, 361
Do You Turn Somersaults? 340
Drabinsky, Garth, 395–96, 412, 417, 427–28
Dracula, 85, 86, 339, 345, 346, 347
Drag, The, 82
Drake, Alfred, 23, 24, 126, 141, 148, 158, 175, 183, 187–88, 194–95, 205, 208, 265, 361, 384, 410
Drake, Ervin, 264
Dramatic Workshop, 139
Dramatists Guild, 73, 74, 112, 122, 124, 130, 142, 167, 274,
Dream Girl, 171
Dreamgirls, 359, 361–62, 383
Dreams and Nightmares, 426–27
Dresser, The, 361
Dresser, Louise 25, 29, 41, 47
Dressler, Marie, 5, 17, 47, 75, 116, 158
Drew, John, 4, 5, 14, 27, 47, 86
Dreyfuss, Richard, 348, 405, 406
Dr. Faustus, 125
Drifting, 56
Drinking in America, 382
Drinkwater, John, 92
Driving Miss Daisy, 383, 386, 387, 395, 409, 411, 427
DuBarry Was a Lady, 137, 139, 158
Duberman, Martin, 262, 268
Dubey, Matt, 224
Dubin, Al, 75, 355
Duck Variations, The, 327, 334
Dude, 312
Duel of Angels, 242
Duerrenmatt, Friedrich, 231, 268
Dukakis, Olympia, 258, 259, 378, 382
Duke, Patty, 240, 272
Duke, Vernon, 142, 149
Dulcy, 54
Dullea, Keir, 298 324, 326
Dumbwaiter, The, 259
Dumont, Margaret, 76
Dunaway, Faye, 258, 260, 273, 350–51, 417, 418, 419
Duncan, Augustin, 5, 207
Duncan, Lindsay, 386
Duncan, Rosetta, 11, 68, 241
Duncan, Sandy, 288, 292, 350, 356
Duncan, Todd, 120, 142, 149, 188
Duncan, William Carey, 63
Duncan Sisters, the, 51, 68, 70
Dunelawn, 321
Dunn, James, 142
Dunn, Michael, 262
Dunne, Eithne, 174
Dunne, Irene, 145, 166
Dunning, Philip, 80
Dunnock, Mildred, 10, 175, 182, 183, 184, 193, 214, 259, 263, 300, 309, 404
Duplex, The, 309
Dupree, Minnie, 58
Durang, Christopher, 182, 361, 378, 392, 411–12
Durante, Jimmy, 8, 61, 63, 79, 82, 111, 114, 119, 123, 124, 351
Durning, Charles, 298, 310, 318–19, 397
Durrenmatt, Friedrich, 233
Duryea, Dan, 135
Duse, Eleanora, 8, 62
d'Usseau, Arnaud, 159, 170
Dutchman, The, 264, 272
Dutton, Charles S., 376, 398
Duvall, Robert, 248, 258, 270, 274
Dylan, 261, 263
Dynamo, 91
Dysart, Richard, 310
Dyson, Ronald, 290
Dzundra, George, 325

Eagan, Daisy, 402
Eagels, Jeanne, 8, 27, 57, 59, 71, 74, 80, 81, 83, 85, 86, 87, 88, 90, 91, 134, 241
Eagle Has Two Heads, The, 222

Eames, Clare, 9, 81
Earl Carroll's Vanities, 62, 68, 108, 174, 331
Earl Carroll Theatre, 62
Easiest Way, The, 15
Easterbrook, Leslie, 334
Eaton, Mary, 63, 64, 182
Ebb, Fred, 277, 279, 293, 328, 341, 358, 373, 409, 412, 428
Ebersole, Christine, 356
Ebert, Joyce, 281, 335–36
Ebsen, Buddy, 171
Eddy, Nelson, 68, 90
Eder, Linda, 428
Eder, Richard, 335, 340, 345, 347, 351, 355
Edgar, David, 359
Edmond, 426
Edmund Keane, 373
Education of Hyman Kaplan, The, 233
Edward, My Son, 182–83
Edwards, Blake, 374, 376, 422
Edwards, Cliff "Ukelele Ike", 69, 75, 180
Edwards, Gus, 6, 25, 63, 110, 170–71
Edwards, Julie, 298
Edwards, Sherman, 291, 294
Effect of Gamma Rays on Man-in-the-Moon Marigolds, The, 297, 299, 301–2, 342, 383
Egan, Susan, 416
Eh?, 278
Eikenberry, Jill, 309, 325, 340–41
Eisenberg, Alan, 360, 426
El Capitan Theatre, 156
El Fey Club, 67, 68
El Grande De Coca-Cola, 313
Elder, Lonnie, 236, 273, 294, 342
Eldridge, Florence, 11, 56, 59, 81, 131, 157, 175, 178, 182, 223, 392
Eleanor (Don't Frighten the Horses!) 384
Electronic Nigger and Others, The, 289
Elephant Man, The, 345, 348, 349, 351
Elg, Taina, 363
Eliot, Jean, 254
Eliot, T.S., 187, 189
Elizondo, Hector, 302, 335
Elkins, Hillard, 294, 298
Ellen, Vera, 142, 156
Ellington, Duke, 175, 358
Ellington, Mercer, 358
Elliott, Denholm, 335
Elliott, Maxine, 5, 15, 139
Elliott, Scott, 426
Elliott, Shawn, 288
Ellis, Evelyn, 86
Ellis, Mary, 68
Ellis, Scott, 422
Ellis, Tracey, 402
Elser, Frank B., 116
Eltinge, Julian, 6, 12, 143
Eltinge Theatre, 17
Emerson, John, 5, 62, 80, 91, 217
Emery, Gilbert, 54, 63
Emmett, Robert, 199
Emperor Jones, 51
Empire Theatre, 83
Enchantment, 110
Encores, 415
Endgame, 230, 375, 377
End of the War, 351
Enemy, The, 76
Engle, David, 398
Englund, George, 203
Enter Laughing, 260
Entertainer, The, 227, 230, 231
Ephron, Phoebe and Henry, 159, 253
Epstein, Alvin, 219, 231
Equity. *See* Actors Equity
Equity Library Theatre, The, 161, 164
Equity Players, 58
Equus, 323–24, 330–31
Ericson, John, 195
Erikson, Leif, 140, 156, 212
Erlanger, Abraham L., 4, 9, 11, 13, 17, 28, 37, 39, 42, 55, 119
Errol, Leon, 6, 16, 17, 18, 24, 28, 33, 45, 49, 51, 59, 77, 198
Etting, Ruth, 14, 56, 58, 86, 91, 129, 131, 134, 135, 345–46
Eubie, 346
Eugene O'Neill Theatre, 240, 389
Eugenia, 223
Evangeline, 52
Evans, Edith, 7, 117, 334
Evans, Maurice, 11, 124, 125–26, 134, 148–49, 165, 176, 202, 246, 393
Evans, Peter, 340
Evans, Wilbur, 168
Evelyn, Judith, 149, 199
Eve of St. Mark, The, 156
Evening with Mike Nichols and Elaine May, An, 246
Everett, Tanya, 268
Evers, Herbert, 156
Everybody's Magazine, 52
Evita, 345, 349, 350, 351, 355, 356, 357, 388, 413
Ewell, Tom, 15, 135, 172, 179, 182, 201–2, 225, 418
Exception and the Rule, The, 292
Excess Baggage, 87
Experimental Theatre, 145
Expressing Willie, 65
Extremities, 367, 369
Eyen, Tom, 148, 302, 361–62, 401

Fabian, Patrick, 422
Fabray, Nanette, 147, 148, 178, 181, 187–88, 198, 223, 257, 259
Fade Out-Fade In, 266, 268, 269, 270, 422
Fain, Sammy, 195
Fair Game, 229
Fairbanks, Douglas, Sr., 6–7, 15, 51, 139
Faithfully Yours, 197
Falk, Peter, 219, 308
Falsettoland, 400, 407
Falsettos, 403, 407, 409–10
Family Portrait, 171
Fancy Free, 167
Fanny, 80, 211, 212, 213
Fantasticks, The, 239, 242, 248, 262, 268, 278, 286, 291, 345, 376, 379, 382, 417, 425–26
Far Country, A, 249
Farentino, James, 258, 328
Farmer, Frances, 131, 139, 140, 156
Farmer Takes a Wife, The, 116
Farnum, Dustin, 5, 6
Farnum, William, 5, 6, 12, 206
Farrand, Jan, 300
Farrow, Mia, 351
Farther Off from Heaven, 178
Fashion, 3
Father, The, 17, 279, 423
Faversham, William, 5, 9, 13, 139
Fawcett, George, 4, 13, 138
Fay, Frank, 10, 54, 71, 90, 92, 112–13, 168, 169, 170–71, 178, 183, 251, 252
Faye, Joey, 199
Federal Theatre Project, 119, 129, 130, 131, 133, 134, 138
Fedora, 12
Feiffer, Jules, 293
Feingold, Michael, 415
Feldshuh, Tovah, 330, 335, 394
Fences, 383, 385, 386, 387
Fenholt, Jeff, 308
Ferber, Edna, 7, 82, 87, 108, 124, 142, 287
Ferguson, Elsie, 7, 253
Ferrell, Conchata, 314
Ferrer, José, 17, 61, 119, 120, 125, 133, 134, 135, 139, 142, 148, 161, 163, 171, 173, 174, 176, 182, 184, 191, 193, 194, 195, 197–98, 205, 209, 233, 247, 254, 286, 325, 342–43, 384, 403, 405
Ferrer, Mel, 205, 209
Feuer, Cy, 16, 216, 347, 392–93
Few Good Men, A, 396
Feydeau, Georges, 225
Fichandler, Thomas, 171, 293
Fichandler, Zelda, 68, 192, 404
Fickett, Mary, 231
Fiddler on the Roof, 188–89, 267, 268, 269, 273, 278, 299, 307–8, 311–12, 333, 335, 349, 351
Field, Betty, 144, 149, 171, 192, 234, 260, 318
Field, Crystal, 260
Field, Ron, 346–37
Field, Sylvia, 76, 87

Field, Virginia, 158, 182
Fields, Benny, 55, 121, 123
Fields, Dorothy, 5, 13, 88, 168, 195, 233, 236, 274, 314, 319, 351
Fields, Freddie, 217
Fields, Herbert, 5, 10, 75, 229
Fields, Joseph, 5, 9, 25, 27, 28, 143, 149, 158, 209, 225, 273
Fields, Lew, 3, 5, 9, 15, 27, 44, 46, 74, 75, 148
Fields, W.C., 6, 25, 28, 32, 36, 40, 46, 47, 50, 54, 58, 61, 62, 120, 143, 175
Fiennes, Ralph, 417, 420
Fierstein, Harvey, 212, 313, 341–42, 362, 367–68, 370, 371–72, 383
Fierstein, Jacqueline, 370
Fifth Column, 139, 140
Fifth of July, 258, 342–43, 348, 352, 356–57
Fifth Season, The, 203
Fifty Miles From Boston, 14
50 Million Frenchmen, 120
Fighting Hope, The, 15
Film Society, The, 392
Find Your Way Home, 317, 320
Findlay, Deborah, 427
Fingernails Blue as Flowers, 309
Finian's Rainbow, 173, 175–76, 179, 419
Finklehoffe, Fred, 125, 156
Finley, Karen, 414
Finn, William, 358, 400, 407
Finnegans Wake, 155, 159
Finnerty, Warren, 240, 260, 318–19
Finney, Albert, 122, 262, 289, 402
Fiorello!, 239, 241, 246, 415
Firebrand, The, 68
Firefly, The, 17
Fires in the Mirror, 407
Fires of Youth, 86
First Fifty Years, The, 227
First Monday in October, The, 346, 375
Firth, Peter, 324
Fishburne, Larry, 406–7
Fisher, Bob, 272
Fisher, Eddie, 202, 211, 216, 217
Fiske, Harrison Grey, 4, 7, 12, 13, 25, 156
Fiske, Minnie Maddern, 5, 7, 12, 13, 15, 25, 134
Fistos, John, 377
Fitch, Clyde, 5, 7, 11, 12, 15
Fitzgerald, Barry, 116, 135
Fitzgerald, Geraldine, 335–36, 341, 361
Fitzhugh, Ellen, 377
Fitzhugh, Larry, 377–78
Five Finger Exercise, 239, 241
Five Guys Named Moe, 406
Flagg, Hazel, 201
Flag Is Born, A, 174
Flaherty, Stephen, 400
Flahooley, 195
Flanagan, Fionnuala, 321
Flanagan, Hallie, 119, 122, 134
Flanders, Ed, 281, 286, 303–4, 319–20
Flanders, Michael, 240
Fleming, Rhonda, 311
Flight to the West, 144
Flippen, Jay C., 68
Flora, the Red Menace, 267
Florodora, 11
Flower Drum Song, 235
Flowering Peach, The, 303
Flynn, Errol, 224
FOB, 356
Foch, Nina, 176
Follies, 301, 305, 307, 311
Follies of 1907, The, 14
Follies of 1908, 14
Follies of 1909, 15
Follies of 1910, 15–16
Follow the Girls, 164, 171
Follow Thru, 91
Fonda, Henry, 12, 111, 114, 116, 139, 177, *180*, 188–89, 195, 199, 208, 230, 231, 258, 272, 303, 325, 346, 350, 368, 375
Fonda, Jane, 260, 350
Fontanne, Lynn, 7, 13, 16, 44, 54, 56, 68, 85, 88, 108, 109, 120, 130, 133, 134, 139, 149, 157, 161, 163, 169, 171, 188, *193*, 371–72, 199–200, 207, 224, 231, 234. *See also* Lunt-Fontanne
Food Chain, The, 422
Fool, The, 58
Fool For Love, 370
Foolish Notion, 168, 171
Fool Moon, 411
Fool There Was, A, 15
Foote, Horton, 207, 212, 417, 427
Forbes, Ralph, 68, 108
Forbidden Broadway, 362
For Colored Girls Who Have Considered Suicide/When The Rainbow Is Enuf, 334
Ford, Helen, 75
Ford, John, 235
Ford, Nancy, 299, 346, 383–84
Ford, Paul, 11, 207, 259
Foreigner, The, 376
Forensic and the Navigators, 300
Foreplay, 303
Forever Plaid, 398
Forrest Theatre, 167
Forrest, George, 166, 208, 396
Forrest, Sam, 81
Forsythe, Henderson, 259, 286, 313, 342
Forsythe, James, 235
Forsythe, John, 206, 207
Fortune and Men's Eyes, 280, 286, 288, 298
Fortune Hunter, The, 15
Forty Carats, 291, 293
Forty-eighth Street Theatre, 81, 167, 216
Forty-five Minutes from Broadway, 13
Forty-fourth Street Theatre, 157, 163, 168
42nd Street, 355–57, 368–69, 374, 378, 391
Forty-sixth Street Theatre, 86, 168, 397–98
Forum Theatre, 313
Fosse, Bob, 86, 174, 189, 209, 223, 236, 274, 312, 324, 327–28, 333, 335, 339, 342, 387–88, 405
Foster, Claiborne, 91
Foster, Dan, 380
Foster, Frances, 273
Foster, George, 205
Foster, Gloria, 419–20
Fourposter, The, 197–98, 227, 280
Four Saints in Three Acts, 111, 114
Foxfire, 367, 369
Foxy, 261, 264
Foy, Eddie, 4, 12, 25, 16, 87
Foy, Eddie, Jr. 15, 170, 209, 372
Franchi, Sergio, 270
Franciosa, Anthony, 217, 223
Francis, Arlene, 125, 156, 158, 172, 195, 260
Frank, Manuel, 166
Frank, Otto, 229
Franken, Rose, 10, 144, 392
Frankenheimer, John, 222
Frankie and Johnny, 202
Frankie and Johnny in the Clair de Lune, 388
Franklin, Irene, 6, 148
Franklin, Lidija, 176
Franz, Elizabeth, 361, 369
Frawley, Louise, 80
Frawley, William, 80, 109
Frayne, Michael, 372, 379, 381–82
Frazee, H.H., 6, 64
Frederick, Pauline, 55
Freedly, George, 164, 170, 212, 242
Freedly, Vinton, 85, 109, 115, 117, 298
Freeman, Al, 265, 269, 312–13
Freeman, Morgan, 386
Frelich, Phyllis, 349, 352
Frey, Leonard, 289, 312–13
Friars Club, 14, 51, 114, 139
Friderici, Blanche, 54
Fried, Walter, 182
Friedman, Bruce Jay, 286, 301–2
Friedman, Gary, 300
Friedman, Stephen, 361
Friel, Brian, 91, 274, 394, 403–4, 421, 423
Friml, Rudolph, 6, 17, 68, 88, 312
Frings, Ketti, 227, 229
Frink, Carol, 90, 108
Frohman, Charles, 4, 7, 8, 23, 25, 28, 35, 58
Frohman, Daniel, 4, 6, 143, 205

From Rags to Riches, 12
From the Second City, 252
Froman, Jane, 157
Front Page, The, 79, 90, 350–51
Fruscello, Constance, 117
Fry, Christopher, 191, 197, 199–200, 213, 216
Fry, Nathaniel, 241, 260
Fugard, Athol, 264, 325, 355–56, 363, 387, 390
Fuller, Charles, 335, 359, 361
Fuller, Frances, 113
Fuller, Francis, 357
Fuller, Penny, 268, 300, 331, 428
Fulton of Oak Falls, 127
Fulton Theatre, 17, 164, 217
Fumed Oak, 164
Funke, Lewis, 214
Funny Face, 87, 88, 328–29, 370
Funny Girl, 248, 261, 264, 272, 320
Funny Thing Happened on the Way to the Forum, A, 254, 255, 257, 263, 307, 309, 312, 419, 421, 424, 426, 528
Furber, Douglas, 384
Furth, George, 299, 308, 361
Futz!, 292
Fyles, Franklyn, 8

Gabel, Martin, 131, 172, 195, 216
Gaffney, Lauren, 398
Gahagan, Helen, 11
Gaiety, the, 150
Gaines, Boyd, 394, 413, 422
Gaines, David, 356, 401, 425
Gaines, Reg E., 422
Gaines, Richard, 149
Galati, Frank, 395, 397
Gale, Zona, 51
Galileo, 178, 281
Gallagher, Ed, 5, 17, 54, 58, 75
Gallagher, Helen, 176, 199, 301, 303–4
Gallagher, Larry, 382
Gallagher, Peter, 407
Gallo, Joseph "Crazy Joey", 309–10, 328–29
Galloway, Jane, 331
Galsworthy, John, 5, 109
Gambon, Michael, 426
Gammon, James, 424
Garber, Victor, 183, 311, 342, 372, 394, 401, 410, 415, 419
Gard, Alex, 355
Gardella, Tess, 87
Gardenia, Vincent, 55, 294, 308, 346–47, 410
Gardner, Herb, 223, 379, 381, 403, 406
Gardner, Hy, 235
Gardner, Rita, 223, 242, 293
Garfield, John (Jules), 18, 114, 118, 125, 126, 130, 177–78, 193, 197, 199–200
Garland, Judy, 157, 158, 172, 259
Garland, Lynn, 223
Garrett, Betty, 166, 172
Garrick Gaieties, The, 71
Garrick Theatre, 216
Garroway, Dave, 207–8, 233
Garson, Barbara, 277, 280
Garson, Greer, 165, 231
Gary, Harold, 289
Gasman, Ira, 428
Gaul, George, 58
Gaunt, Percy, 8
Gautier, Dick, 242
Gaxton, William, 8, 86, 113, 117, 134, 150, 260
Gay, John, 175
Gay, Noel, 384
Gay Divorce, 109, 111
Gaynes, George, 204
Gaynor, Janet, 368
Gazzara, Ben, 214, 217, 240, 253, 260
Gazzo, Michael V., 216
Gear, Luella, 10, 109
Geer, Will, 11, 130, 141, 254, 262
Geese, 294
Geeson, Judy, 384
Gelbart, Larry, 255, 335
Gelber, Jack, 240, 278
Geld, Gary, 299
Gemini, 333, 337
Gems, Pam, 358, 427
General Seeger, 253
Generation, 272
Genet, Jean, 16, 242, 249, 307, 309, 381
Genn, Leo, 175
Gennaro, Peter, 209, 228, 257
Gentleman From Mississippi, A, 15
Gentlemen Prefer Blondes, 80, 187, 188, 189, 193, 195, 198, 200
George, Gladys, 116, 120
George, Grace, 6, 246
George, Nathan, 295
George Jean Nathan Award for Drama Criticism, 333
George M!, 289, 415
George Washington Slept Here, 142, 143
George White's Scandals, 54, 55, 58, 62, 80, 117, 138
Georgie, Leyla, 68
Gerard, Jeremy, 410
Gere, Richard, 351, 361
Gero, Fran, 418
Gero, Mark, 351
Gershe, Leonard, 298
Gershwin, George, 10, 23, 27, 54, 58, 67, 68, 69, 74, 79, 81, 86, 87, 88, 107, 108, 109, 113, 120, 129, 130, 163, 174–75, 369–70, 385, 403
Gershwin, Ira, 9, 69, 80, 81, 87, 88, 109, 113, 120, 144, 372, 403
Gershwin, Morris, 67
Gersten, Bernard, 346, 380, 392
Gesner, Clark, 280
Gest, Morris, 6, 15, 60, 138, 149
Get-Rich-Quick Wallingford, 16
Getting Gertie's Garters, 54
Ghostley, Alice, 200
Ghosts, 121
Gibb, Andy, 369
Gibbs, Walcott, 11, 163, 192, 234, 235
Gibson, Jeanne, 278
Gibson, William, 24, 230, 239, 240
Gideon, 253
Gielgud, John, 12, 71, 87, 123, 124, 134, 142, 178, 179, 180, 206, 235, 241, 265, 269, 270, 274, 275, 288, 301, 311, 313, 326
Gift of Time, A, 400
Gigi, 197, 199, 368
Gilbert, John, 86, 91
Gilbert, Ronnie, 279
Gilford, Jack, 14, 204, 241, 255, 279, 303–4, 335, 400
Gill, Brendan, 24, 288
Gill, Ray, 386
Gill, William, 7
Gillette, Anita, 249, 252, 279, 341
Gillette, Priscilla, 209
Gillette, William, 4, 5, 10, 123, 124–25
Gilliat, Penelope, 252, 260
Gillmore, Frank, 91, 113, 130, 157
Gillmore, Margalo, 10, 55, 82, 83, 88, 125, 384
Gilmore, Virginia, 167
Gilpin, Charles, 6, 51
Gilroy, Frank, 74, 267, 298
Gin Game, The, 339–40, 351, 371
Gingerbread Lady, The, 301, 303
Gingold, Hermione, 208, 313–14, 385
Giovanni, Paul, 346
Giraudoux, Jean, 6, 130, 163, 183, 205, 209, 215, 215, 242
Girl Crazy, 350
Girl Friend, The, 77
Girl I Left Behind Me, The, 8
Girl in Pink Tights, The, 5
Girl of the Golden West, The, 13
Girl on the Via Flamina, 208
Girls of Summer, The, 222
Girl to Remember, A, 262
Gish, Dorothy, 268
Gish, Lillian, 10, 17, 115, 116, 124, 130, 207, 247, 289, 318, 352–53, 409–10
Give 'em Hell, Harry, 326
Glad of It, 12
Glad to Be Alive, 189
Glaser, Lulu, 5, 11, 234
Glaspell, Susan, 6, 182
Glass, Philip, 272, 297, 377

Glass Menagerie, The, 163, 165, 167, 168, 170, 182, 195
Glazer, Benjamin, 139
Gleason, Jackie, 161, 239, 241
Gleason, James, 7, 70, 76, 235
Gleason, Joanna, 192, 336, 382, 387, 389, 404–5
Glengarry Glen Ross, 371, 373
Glenn, Scott, 378
Glenville, Peter, 225, 246
Globe Theatre, 15, 74
Glover, Danny, 363
Glover, John, 418
Glover, Savion, 393, 407, 422, 426
Glynn, Carlin, 342
Goddard, Paulette, 82, 164, 188
Godfrey, Arthur, 259
God of Vengeance, 59, 68
Godspell, 301, 305, 311, 334
Goetz, Augustus, 178, 208, 419
Goetz, E. Ray, 92, 212
Goetz, Ruth, 178, 208, 419
Goetzel, Anselm, 52
Gogginis, Dan, 381
Gold, Sylviane, 392
Goldberg, Rube, 92
Goldberg, Whoopi, 399, 425, 428
Golden, John, 5, 59, 63, 81, 92, 121, 139, 150, 164, 166, 216
Golden Apple, The, 205, 208–9
Goldenberg, Billy, 346–47
Golden Boy, 129, 130–31, 197, 200, 268
Golden Land, The, 381
Golden Rainbow, 289
Goldman, Edward, 149
Goldman, Irving, 312, 318–19, 323, 325–26, 328
Goldman, James, 275
Goldsmith, Clifford, 132
Goldwyn, Tony, 400
Good, 368
Good and Plenty, 367
Good Bad Woman, A, 68
Good Boy, 90
Goodbye, My Fancy, 182
Goodbye Again, 109
Good Evening, 318, 319, 324
Goodhart, William, 272
Good Little Devil, A, 17
Goodman, Dody, 188, 213
Goodman, John, 378
Goodman, Jules, 6, 258
Goodman, Paul, 240
Goodman, William O., 74
Goodman Theatre Company, The, 74
Good News, 85, 86
Goodrich, Frances, 216, 215
Good Soup, The, 242
Goodwin, Nat, 4, 18
Good Woman of Setzuan, The, 224
Goose and Tomtom, 362, 384
Gordon, Arthur, 58
Gordon, Leon, 63
Gordon, Max, 8, 230, 346
Gordon, Ruth, 9, 82, 129, 131, 155, 156, 163, 175, 217, 327, 330, 380
Gordon, Waxey, 69
Gordone, Charles, 249, 295, 297, 300, 422
Gorey, Edward, 340
Gorman, Cliff, 273, 305, 307, 341, 378
Gorman, Mari, 278, 314, 378
Gormé, Eydie, 262, 289
Gorney, Jay, 108
Gossett, Louis, 122, 207, 236, 249, 273
Gottfried, Martin, 295, 320, 324–25, 419
Gottschalf, Ferdinand, 60
Gough, Michael, 348
Gould, Elliott, 253, 254, 262
Gould, Harold, 304
Goulet, Robert, 112, 247, 262, 285
Governor's Son, The, 11
Gow, James, 159, 170
Goz, Harry, 390
Grable, Betty, 139, 302
Graczyk, Ed, 362
Graff, Ilene, 336
Graff, Randy, 385, 397
Graham, Martha, 174
Graham, Ronny, 200, 233
Graham, Sheilah, 272
Grammer, Kelsey, 362, 369
Grand Army Man, A, 14
Grand Hotel, 395–96, 398, 406
Grant, Cary, 163
Grant, Faye, 380
Grant, Lee, 164, 184, 308
Grant, Miki, 309–10
Grapes of Wrath, The, 395, 397
Gray, Dolores, 205, 236
Gray, Simon, 312, 333, 335, 369, 384
Gray, Spalding, 305
Gray, Timothy, 265
Grayson, Betty, 157
Grease, 307, 309, 312, 345, 349, 351–52, 371–72, 413, 418, 423
Great Adventure, The, 18
Greater Tuna, 360–61, 368
Great God Brown, The, 76
Great Strike of 1919, 47
Great Waltz, The, 115, 116
Great White Hope, The, 285, 291, 292, 293
Green, Abel, 11, 150, 312
Green, Adolph, 138, 148, 167, 201, 204, 212, 223, 231, 241, 248, 253, 259, 266, 284, 299, 319–20, 342, 368, 399, 402
Green, Anita, 74
Green, Mark, 404
Green, Paul, 8, 79, 82, 124, 145, 357
Green Bay Tree, The, 113
Greenberg, Richard, 392–93
Greene, Ellen, 368
Greene, Graham, 253
Greene, Luther, 174
Green Goddess, The, 51
Green Grow the Lilacs, 156, 159
Green Hat, The, 74
Green Pastures, 139
Greenstreet, Sidney, 113, 139, 130
Greenwich Village Theatre, 77
Greenwillow, 242
Greenwood, Charlotte, 8, 17, 58, 340
Gregorio, Rose, 258
Gregory, Andre, 392
Gregory, Paul, 368
Grey, Clifford, 83
Grey, Jennifer, 388
Grey, Joel, 199, 219, 234, 270, 279, 280, 289, 299, 378, 426
Grey, Lita, 75
Grieg, Edward, 166
Griffin, Merv, 260
Griffith, Andy, 216, 236
Griffith, Hugh, 229
Grimes, Tammy, 113, 219, 222, 223, 246, 297, 334, 345, 356, 359, 361
Grind, 377–78
Grizzard, George, 87, 211, 213, 235, 254, 258, 259, 260, 281, 312–13, 330, 334, 421, 424
Grodin, Charles, 326
Grody, Kathryn, 356
Groener, Harry, 405–6
Groody, Louise, 9, 75, 83, 252
Grossbard, Ulu, 258, 270, 335
Grossman, Ellen, 377–78
Grossman, Joe, 207
Grossman, Larry, 377
Group Theatre, 8, 88, 112, 114, 124, 125, 127, 130, 136
Grover's Corners, 394
Guardino, Harry, 217, 265, 358
Guardsman, The, 67, 68
Guare, John, 132, 272, 292, 301, 304, 308–9, 381–82, 399–400
Guerrere, Lalo, 348
Guest, Christopher, 309
Guild Theatre, 86, 88
Guinan, Texas, 68, 112
Guinness, Alec, 189, 195, 261, 263
Gundersen, Karen, 324
Gunn, Moses, 273, 287
Gunton, Bob, 378
Gurdon, Madeleine, 405
Gurian, Manning, 212
Gurney, A.R., 362, 391–92, 396, 400–401
Guthrie, Tyrone, 11, 217, 224, 228, 241, 245, 253, 302
Guys and Dolls, 191–93, 198, 205, 207, 219, 333, 367, 403, 407
Gwenn, Edmund, 158, 159

Gwynne, Fred, 200, 324
Gypsy, 59, 91, 92, 233, 237, 239, 241, 320, 323–24, 395–96, 405

Haas, Dolly, 157, 170
Hackett, Albert, 215, 216, 230
Hackett, Buddy, 174, 211
Hackett, Francis, 230
Hackett, James H., 3
Hackett, Joan, 248
Hackett, Walter, 24
Hackman, Gene, 260, 264, 405, 406
Hadary, Jonathan, 410
Hadley, Jerry, 391, 410
Hadrian VII, 294
Hagan, James, S., 110
Hagen, Jean, 175
Hagen, Uta, 129, 130, 132, 134, 139, 148, 161, 163, 182, 187–88, 191–92, 200, 224, 257, 258, 421–22
Hague, Albert, 213, 233, 236
Haigh, Kenneth, 228
Haimsohn, George, 293
Haines, William Wister, 178
Hair, 286, 288, 289, 292, 294, 299, 300, 302, 319, 325
Hairy Ape, The, 56, 57, 88
Hale, Bob, 340
Hale, Ruth, 112
Haley, Jack, 10, 71, 91, 167, 180, 350
Half a Sixpence, 270
Hall, Adelaide, 16, 88, 228, 414
Hall, Bettina, 13, 117
Hall, Brattle, 156
Hall, Carol, 342
Hall, Juanita, 171, 184–85, 188–89, 213, 235
Hall, Peter, 229, 280, 318, 351–52, 397, 424
Hall, Thurston, 6, 229
Hallelujah, Baby!, 285
Halliday, John, 6, 68, 139, 178
Halliday, Richard, 139, 241
Halliday, Robert, 8, 82, 90
Halliwell, Kenneth, 286
Halperin, Nan, 62
Hamilton, Hale, 16
Hamilton, Margaret, 273, 335
Hamilton, Patrick, 149
Hamilton, Richard, 346
Hamlet, 5, 11, 18, 51, 57, 59, 63, 71, 76, 124, 130, 133, 134, 176, 188, 195, 225, 260, 265, 293, 295, 301–2, 368, 382, 417, 420
Hamlisch, Marvin, 166, 323, 327, 328, 329, 347
Hammerstein, Arthur, 5, 41, 47, 62, 217
Hammerstein, Oscar, 3, 5, 9, 16, 18, 169, 177, 178, 179, 181, 188, 189, 190, 197, 199, 205, 208, 211, 213–4, 217
Hammerstein, Oscar, II, 9, 31, 35, 36, 42, 43, 44, 45, 60, 63, 68, 75, 81, 82, 87, 90, 91, 108, 113, 116, 136, 156, 159, 163, 171, 174, 179, 181–82, *184*, 185, 187, 194, 202, 203, 204, 215, 216, 217, 230, 239, 241, 246, 247, 340. *See also* Rodgers and Hammerstein
Hammerstein Theatre, 90
Hammett, Dashiell, 249
Hammond, Percy, 5, 15, 64, 83, 86, 110, 117, 119, 122, 320
Hampden, Walter, 6, 15, 61, 63, 203, 216
Hampton, Christopher, 304, 383, 386
Hampton, David, 399, 406–7
Handler, Evan, 401
Haney, Carol, 209, 212, 235, 241, 263, 328
Hanley, Ellen, 241
Hanley, William, 300
Hannah Senesh, 377
Hansberry, Lorraine, 233, 236, 263, 269, 293
Happy Birthday, 169, 173, 174, 179–80
Happy Days, 252
Happy Days and Act Without Words, 313
Happy Ending, 273
Happy Hunting, 223, 224, 228, 229
Happy Time, The, 285
Harbach, Otto, 5, 16, 29, 38, 42, 47, 50, 60, 68, 73, 75, 82, 113, 259
Harburg, E.Y."Yip", 10, 108, 142, 166, 176, 195, 228, 357
Harden, Marcia Gay, 412
Harding, Ann, 63, 80, 82, 86, 253
Harding, Warren G., 51
Harding Theatrical League, the, 51
Hardwicke, Cedric, 131, 171, 198, 208, 236
Hare, David, 178, 367–68, 395–97, 423, 425–26
Harem, The, 69, 70, 71
Harling, Robert, 388
Harmon, Charlotte, 212
Harmon, Lewis, 212
Harned, Virginia, 9, 11
Harney, Ben, 359, 361–62
Harnick, Sheldon, 62, 213, 239, 241, 246, 254, 260, 267, 268, 278, 303, 331
Harold Clurman Theatre, 348
Harper, Valerie, 241
Harper, Wally, 324
Harriet, 158, 163
Harrigan, William, 77, 180
Harrington, Pat, 142, 192, 253
Harris, Barbara, 252, 254, 260, 272, 277, 278, 312–13
Harris, Ed, 370
Harris, Elmer, 142
Harris, Jed, 74, 79, 91, 11, 113, 118, 131, 134, 149, 174, 188, 223, 246, 349–50
Harris, Julie, 74, 165, 168, 174–75, 188–89, 197, 199–200, 202, 204, 212, 215, 217, 253, 291, 293, 304, 311, 331, 333–34, 357, 395
Harris, Katherine, 16, 37
Harris, Rosemary, 203, 223, 235, 241, 242, 254, 271, 275, 286, 330, 3335, 416, 421, 424
Harris, Sam, 5, 12, 42, 47, 50, 63, 81, 109, 114, 127, 135, 148
Harris, William, 205
Harrison, Rex, 14, 157, 181–83, 189, 192–95, 200, 201, 202, 203, 217, 218, 221, 230, 254, 335, 346, 396, 400
Harris Theatres, 362
Harron, Donald, 241
Hart, Cecilia, 361
Hart, Charles, 389, 398
Hart, Dolores, 235
Hart, John, 422
Hart, Lorenz, 9, 31, 46, 71, 134, 155, 156, 161, 163, 197, 199. *See also* Rodgers and Hart
Hart, Moss, 12, 112, 116, 120, 123, 125, 130, 138, 141, 144, 145, 163, 173, 174–75, 179, 182, 188–89, 203, 217, 230, 241, 248, 253
Hart, Richard, 168
Hart, Roxanne, 350
Hart, William S., 10, 13
Hartman, David, 263
Hartman, Grace, 177
Hartman, Paul, 177
Harvey, 165, 167, 168, 170–71, 178, 233, 252
Harwood, Ronald, 361, 402
Hasting, Michael, 376
Hasty Heart, The, 198–99
Hatfield, Hurd, 216
Hatful of Rain, 216, 221, 389
Hatton, Fanny and Frederic, 29, 33, 36, 38
Havel, Vaclav, 285, 379, 382
Having A Wonderful Time, 126, 202
Having Our Say, 419–20
Havoc, June, 32, 59, 92, 143, 164, 166, 179
Hawkins, Trish, 348, 352
Hawks, Howard, 188
Hawley, Joyce, 73, 76, 80, 83
Haworth, Jill, 279
Hawthorne, Nigel, 399–401
Hay, Mary, 75
Hay, Sally, 372
Hayden, James, 373
Hayden, Michael, 415
Haydon, Julie, 15, 131, 138, 168, 216, 418
Hayes, Alfred, 205
Hayes, Bill, 204
Hayes, Helen, 11, 15, 35, 36, 42, 44, 50, 56, 68, 89, 90, 108, 113, 119, 125, 129, 133, 134, 138, 139, 149, 158, 163, 171, 173, 174, 176, 180, 188, 190, 197, 198, 199, 200, 213, 218, 227, 229, 231, 234, 236, 246, 307–8, 361, 381, 405–6, 409–10
Hayes, Joseph, 211

Hayes, Margaret, 156
Hays, Mary, 63
Hayward, Dubose, 107
Hayward, Leland, 11, 108, 124, 190, 192, 197, 200, 207, 237, 241, 301–2
Hayward, Susan, 235
Hayworth, Jill, 199
Hayworth, Rita, 199
Headly, Glenne, 334, 367–68, 374
Heald, Anthony, 404
Heard, John, 376–77
Hearn, George, 116, 314, 347–48, 371–72, 418
Heart of Maryland, The, 9
Heartbreak House, 51, 132
Heartburn, 380
Heartland, 357
Hearts of Oak, 6
Heatherton, Ray, 126
Hebrew Actors Union, 10
Hecht, Ben, 8, 90, 107, 109, 149, 174, 218, 263
Hecht, Jessica, 427
Hecht, Paul, 303
Heckart, Eileen, 41, 163, 203–4, 216, 230, 281, 298
Hedda Gabler, 8
Hedwall, Deborah, 369
Heffernan, John, 258, 299, 335
Heflin, Van, 136, 216
Heggen, Thomas, 177, 180
Heggie, O.P., 6, 30, 113, 121
Heidi Chronicles, The, 391, 394
Heifner, Jack, 331
Heinfling, Martin, 384
Heiress, The, 177–79, 417, 419
Helbrun, Theresa, 7, 122, 125–26, 140, 144, 162, 240
Held, Anna, 5, 9, 17, 19, 40
Helen Hayes Theatre, 217, 361, 368, 372
Hell-Bent for Heaven, 61, 64, 65, 359
Heller, Joseph, 292
Hellinger, Mark, 69, 121, 178–79
Hellman, Lillian, 13, 74, 115, 116–17, 135, 141, 145, 148, 161, 163, 164, 167, 175, 200, 211, 217, 224, 239, 241, 242, 249, 257, 286, 335, 352, 358, 375–76
Hello Dolly!, 135, 217, 261, 263, 270, 271, 272, 273, 277, 280, 285, 286, 287, 288, 300, 301, 302, 303, 307–8, 324, 342, 383, 385–86, 404–5, 414, 422–23
Hell's Bells, 71
Hellzapoppin, 133, 134, 143, 174, 333, 335–36, 357
Heloise, 235
Hemsley, Sherman, 299
Henderson, Florence, 161, 202, 208, 212, 217
Henderson, Ray, 9, 80, 86, 91, 302
Heneker, David, 246, 270
Henken, Helen, 11
Henley, Beth, 199, 355, 357, 361, 374
Henning, Doug, 317, 321, 369
Henreid, Paul, 144
Henry V, 222
Henry VIII, 174
Henry Miller's Theatre, 38, 156, 158, 163, 167
Hepburn, Audrey, 197, 199, 205, 207, 208, 209, 218
Hepburn, Katharine, 15, 127, 133, 136, 140, 150–51, 155, 157, 158, 171, 189, 202, 228, 297, 298, 301–2, 327, 331, 358, 361–62, 368
Herbert, Evelyn, 90
Herbert, F. Hugh, 158, 194
Herbert, John, 280, 288, 298
Herbert, Victor, 4, 12, 13, 15, 16, 18, 32, 33, 37, 58, 63, 170, 385
Her Cardboard Lover, 83, 86, 87, 88, 91
Here Are Ladies, 304
Here Come the Clowns, 133
Herlie, Eileen, 241
Herman, Jerry, 112, 252, 261, 263, 275, 300, 309, 324, 371, 373, 381, 383, 385–86
Her Master's Voice, 113
Herne, Crystal, 7, 65, 76, 192
Herne, James A., 3, 6, 8, 11
Hero, The, 54
Herrmann, Edward, 309, 368, 376
Hershey, John, 167
Hester, Hal, 285, 288
Heston, Charleston, 174
He Who Gets Slapped, 55, 59
Hewitt, Alan, 144, 148
Heyward, Dorothy, 135
Heyward, Dubose, 7, 108, 135
Hickson, Joan, 348
Higgins, John Michael, 411
High Button Shoes, 178
Higher and Higher, 140
High Spirits, 265
High Tor, 123, 125
Hiken, Gerald, 81, 224, 418–19
Hill, Arthur, 58, 233, 247, 257, 258, 287
Hill, George Roy, 229, 242, 247
Hill, Ken, 391
Hill, Phyllis, 182
Hill, Ruby, 171
Hill, Steven, 249
Hiller, Wendy, 17, 178, 419
Hilliard, Robert., 4, 13, 15, 86
Hines, Elizabeth, 59
Hines, Gregory, 171, 346, 357–58, 403, 407
Hingle, Pat, 68, 174, 214, 230, 235, 260, 265, 289, 299
Hipp, Paul, 400
Hipper's Holiday, 116
Hippodrome, The, 12
Hirsch, Judd, 117, 311, *314*, 341, 348, 352, 379, 381, 403, 406
Hirsch, Louis, 6, 38, 41, 50, 63
Hirsch, Mary, 228
Hirschfeld, Al, 12, 157, 169, 170, 271, 395, 399, 426
Hirschfeld, Nina, 157
Hirson, Roger O., 312
His Girl Friday, 90
Hitchcock, Alfred, 149, 202
Hitchcock, Pat, 149
Hitchcock, Raymond, 5, 11
Hit the Deck!, 83
Hobart, George V., 5, 75
Hochhuth, Rolf, 264
Hoey, Evelyn, 120
Hoffa, Portland, 92
Hoffman, Dustin, 130, 183–84, 252, 270, 275, 278, 293, 305, 325, 371, 373, 376, 388, 397
Hoffman, William, 378
Hogan, Jonathan, 378, 388
Hogan's Goat, 273
Holbrook, Hal, 68, 269, 271, 275, 288, 309, 312–13, 428
Hold On to Your Hats, 142, 144, 157
Holder, Geoffrey, 213, 325
Holder, Laurence, 360
Hole in the Head, A, 289
Holiday, 91
Holiday, Bob, 275
Holland, George, 117
Holland, Joseph, 131, 132
Holliday, Jennifer, 359, 361–62
Holliday, Judy, 58, 138, 168, 169, 171, 179, 188–89, 191, 193–94, 201–2, 207, 221, 223, 228, 235, 248, 264, 272
Holloway, Stanley, 217, 218
Holloway, Sterling, 71
Holm, Celeste, 41, 138, 155, 158, 166, 192, 202
Holm, Eleanor, 139, 208
Holm, Hanya, 198–99
Holm, John Cecil, 118
Holman, Libby, 12, 67, 68, 71, 92, 107, 108, 109, 131, 133, 135, 175, 246, 307–8
Holmes, Rupert, 379, 381
Holofcener, Larry, 218
Holt, Will, 300
Holtz, Lou, 8, 54, 73, 114, 356
Holtz, Will, 324
Holzer, Adela, 347
Home, 301, 303, 351
Home Again, 26
Home Again, Home Again, 348
Home Sweet Homer, 330. *See also Odyssey*
Homecoming, The, 277, 280, 286
Homeier, Skip, 155, 159
Homolka, Oscar, 166
Honeymoon Express, The, 17
Honeymoon Lane, 80
Hooks, Robert, 264, 273, 281
Hope, Bob, 113, 124

Hopkins, Anthony, 324, 331, 400–401
Hopkins, Arthur, 6, 86, 115, 189
Hopkins, John, 320
Hopkins, Linda, 299, 324, 393
Hopkins, Miriam, 54, 62, 87, 112, 144
Hopper, De Wolfe, 4, 7, 8, 18, 120–21
Hopper, Edna Wallace, 5, 241
Hopper, Hedda, 54
Hopwood, Avery, 6, 15, 29, 44, 49, 50, 55, 70, 90
Horne, Lena, 36, 228, 229
Horovitz, Israel, 288
Horowitz and Mrs. Washington, 411
Horton, Edward Everett, 167
Horton, Robert, 262
Horwin, Jerry, 139
Horwitt, Arbold B., 213
Hoschna, Karl, 6, 16, 17
Hostage, The, 246, 247
Hotel Paradiso, 225
Hot'l Baltimore, 311, 314
Houdini, Harry, 5, 28, 31, 33, 80
House, Ron, 313
Houseman, John, 11, 112, 121, 123, 125, 130, 145, 159, 175, 241, 292, 312, 330, 350–51, 392
House of Blue Leaves, The, 301, 304, 309, 381–82
House of Connelly, The, 8
House of Flowers, 211, 213
House Un-American Activities Committee, 134, 216, 221, 222, 223, 228, 234, 235
Hovick, Rose, 59, 92
Howard, Alan, 304, 368
Howard, Bronson, 5, 7
Howard, Cordelia, 4
Howard, Esther, 76
Howard, Eugene, 6, 17, 19, 26, 76, 80, 272
Howard, Ken, 295, 299, 314, 330–31, 392
Howard, Leslie, 8, 74, 115, 117, 123, 124, 162
Howard, Sidney, 8, 9, 13, 54, 67, 69, 76, 81, 82, 114, 134, 138, 171, 208, 219
Howard, Willie, 7, 19, 26, 54, 90, 138, 183
Howe, Tina, 131, 372, 383–84
Howes, Sally Ann, 229, 230
How I Learned to Drive, 425, 427
How to Succeed in Business Without Really Trying, 251, 252, 253, 417, 419, 422–23
Hoyt, Charles, 8
Hubert's Museum, 74
Huck, John Phillip, 334
Huckleberry Finn, 189
Hudson Guild Playhouse. *See* Theatre De Lys
Hudson Theatre, 12
Huffman, Felicity, 392, 420
Hughes, Barnard, 273, 318–19, 325, 339, 343
Hughes, Hatcher, 6, 61, 64, 65, 170
Hughes, Langston, 91, 120, 175–76
Hughie, 269, 426
Hugo, Laurence, 195
Hulce, Tom,357, 381, 396
Hull, Henry, 8, 56, 59, 77, 114, 141, 334
Hull, Josephine, 7, 125, 144, 167, 207, 223
Human Comedy, The, 373
Humphreys, Cecil, 158
Humphries, Doris, 108
Huneker, James Gibbons, 4, 51
Hunt, Martita, 181, 183
Hunter, Glenn, 9, 59, 171
Hunter, Holly, 374
Hunter, Kim, 58, 179–80, 193, 199, 202, 204
Hurlbut, Carolyn, 351–52
Hurlbut, William J., 15, 18
Hurlie, Eileen, 265
Hurly Burly, 10, 373, 375–76
Hurt, Mary Beth, 182, 335, 357, 372, 381–82, 393, 424
Hurt, William, 292, 342–43, 376
Hussey, Ruth, 171
Huston, John, 7, 149, 202
Huston, Walter, 7, 68, 114, 133, 134, 139, 180, 189
Hutchinson, Josephine, 312
Hutton, Betty, 141, 142, 145, 172
Hutton, Bill, 362
Hutton, Timothy, 397
Huxtable, Judy, 318
Hwang, David Henry, 228, 356, 360, 387, 390, 392, 402
Hyams, Joe, 249
Hyde, Weldon, 92
Hyland, Diana, 236
Hyman, Earle, 166
Hytner, Nicholas, 415
Hyward, Dubose, 142

I Am a Camera, 197, 199–200, 202
I Am Different, 134
Ian McKellen Acting Shakespeare, 373
Ibsen, Hendrik, 3, 8, 13, 52, 121
I Can Get It For You Wholesale, 253, 255, 251
Icebound, 57, 60
Iceman Cometh, The, 114, 173, 174, 175, 176, 180, 215, 219, 392
Ideal Husband, An, 424
Idiot's Delight, 119, 121, 122, 123, 125, 135, 142
I Do! I Do!, 277, 280, 288
I'd Rather Be Right, 130
I Hate Hamlet, 401, 404
I Know, My Love, 188, 193
Illington, Margaret, 6, 113
I'll Say She Is, 65
Illya Darling, 279
I Love My Wife, 336
Ilse, Marvenga, 69–70
I Married An Angel, 129
I'm Getting My Act Together and Taking It on the Road, 345–46
Immoralist, The, 208
I'm Not Rappaport, 379, 381
Imperial Theatre, 55, 63, 131, 162, 166
Importance of Being Earnest, The, 9
Impossible Years, The, 272
In Abraham's Bosom, 79, 82
Inadmissible Evidence, 271, 273
Incident at Vichy, 269
Indian Wants the Bronx, The, 288
Indians, 298
Indiscretions, 420, 421
I Never Sang for My Father, 288
Inge, William, 18, 178, 187, 189, 201, 203–4, 214, 229, 241, 246, 317, 318, 380
Ingomar, 7
Ingram, Rex, 142, 171, 176
Inherit the Wind, 214, 215, 216, 217, 421, 423
Innaurato, Albert, 184, 375
Inness, Jean, 86
Innocents, The, 190, 334
Insect Comedy, The, 242
Inside U.S.A. 180
Inspector Calls, An, 416, 419
In the Boom Boom Room, 318
In the Matter of J. Robert Oppenheimer, 294
In the Summer House, 208
International Alliance of Theatrical Stage Employees, 138
International Stud Trilogy. *See* *Torch Song Trilogy*
In Time to Come, 149
In White America, 262, 268
Into the Woods, 387, 389, 393
Ionesco, Eugene, 246, 247, 248, 249, 414
I Ought To Be In Pictures, 352–53
Iphigenia in Aulis, 287
I Picked a Daisy, 252, 262
I Remember Mama, 165, 166, 167, 169, 345, 347–48
Irene, 311, 313–14, 318, 324
Irma La Douce, 245, 246, 335
Irons, Jeremy, 311, 371, 373, 390
Iroquois Theatre, 12
Irving, Amy, 390
Irving, George S., 314
Irving, Henry, 7, 9
Irving, Jules, 200, 270, 309, 312, 323

Irwin, Bill, 392, 411
Irwin, May, 4, 75, 134
Irwin, Will, 171
Isaacs, Pamela, 428
Isherwood, Christopher, 199, 279
Isn't It Romantic, 372
Is Zat So, 70
It Can't Happen Here, 123, 124, 134
It's a Bird...It's a Plane...It's Superman, 274, 275
It's a Gift, 168
It's Called the Sugar Plum, 288
Ivanov, 275
Ives, Burl, 135, 156, 202, 214, 419
Ivey, Dana, 386, 427
Ivey, Judith, 198, 376, 393

Jack and Jill, 60
Jack and the Bean Stalk, 179
Jackie Mason's The World According to Me, 385
Jackie Mason: Politically Incorrect, 418
Jackson, Anne, 80, 179, 248, 254, 260, 268
Jackson, Eddie, 79, 82
Jackson, Ernestine, 318
Jackson, Glenda, 274, 392
Jackson, Samuel L., 361
Jacobi, Derek, 134, 375, 389
Jacobi, Lou, 241, 249, 277, 279
Jacobowsky and the Colonel, 161
Jacobs, Bernard B., 311, 312, 318–19, 379, 381, 397, 425, 426, 427
Jacobs, Jim, 309
Jacobson, Dorothy Blanchard, 91
Jacobson, Irving, 273
Jacoby, Mark, 418
Jacques Brel Is Alive and Well and Living in Paris, 288
Jaffe, Jack, 156
Jaffe, Sam, 59, 142, 143, 170
Jaffee, Oscar, 342
Jake's Women, 395, 397, 406
Jamaica, 227, 228, 229, 230
James, Geraldine, 397
Jamison, Judith, 358
Jane Eyre, 127
Janie, 156
Janis, Conrad, 253
Janis, Elsie, 7, 24, 80, 124, 217
Jazz Singer, The, 73, 74, 76, 86
J.B., 233, 235
Jealousy, 227
Jeanmaire, Zizi, 5
Jeanne Doré, 19
Jeb, 172
Jeffer, Robinson, 178–79
Jefferson, Joseph, 3, 5, 6, 12
Jeffrey, 411
Jeffreys, Ann, 175–76
Jekyll and Hyde, 428
Jellicoe, Ann, 266
Jelly's Last Jam, 403, 405, 407
Jenkins, Allen, 90
Jenkins, Daniel, 378
Jennie, 262
Jens, Salome, 235, 242, 268, 381
Jerome Robbins' Broadway, 391, 393, 396, 397
Jerome, Helen, 127
Jerry, 19
Jerry's Girls, 371, 373–74, 381
Jessel, George, 10, 15, 24, 25, 35, 36, 44, 50, 63, 73, 74, 76, 80, 111, 113, 115, 170–71, 355, 357
Jessel, Patricia, 212–13
Jesus Christ Superstar, 304–5, 307–8
Jewish Theatrical Alliance,63
Jezebel, 112
Jillette, Penn, 389
Jilts, The, 58
Jimmie, 51
Jimmy Shine, 293
Joan of Lorraine, 173, 175
Job, Thomas, 150
Joe Egg, 375
Joe Turner's Come and Gone, 387, 390
Johann, Zita, 90, 112
Johanson, Bland, 74
John Brown's Body, 203
John Bull's Other Island, 177
John Loves Mary, 176
John Murray Anderson's Almanac, 208
Johnny Belinda, 142, 143, 155, 158
Johnny Johnson, 124, 125
Johns, Brooke, 60
Johns, Glynis, 222, 311, 313–14
Johnson, Arte, 213
Johnson, Chic, 8, 133, 134, 149–50, 253
Johnson, Edward, 189–90
Johnson, James P., 63
Johnson, Moffat, 59
Johnson, Raymond Edward, 158
Johnson, Van, 119, 138, 141, 143
Johnston, Johnny, 195
Jolson, Al, 7, 14, 16, 17, 27, 30, 35, 37, 38, 41, 43, 44, 49, 50, 51, 53, 54, 55, 58, 62, 69, 71, 80, 85, 86, 90, 107, 108, 113, 141, 142, 143, 144, 150, 157, 191–92
Jolson's Fifty-ninth Street Theatre, 164
Jonay, Roberta, 178
Jones, Cherry, 222, 317, 402, 417, 419
Jones, Dean, 300, 301
Jones, Elinor, 300
Jones, James Earl, 222, 231, 249, 258, 264, 268, 291, 292, 302, 341–42, 356, 361–62, 373, 383, 386, 392, 418
Jones, Jeffrey, 420
Jones, John Price, 86
Jones, Leilani, 377
Jones, LeRoi, 116, 264, 269, 272, 289
Jones, Margo, 19, 165, 166, 175, 177, 190, 216
Jones, Robert E., 7, 212
Jones, Simon, 381–82
Jones, Stephen, 62
Jones, Tom, 87, 242, 262, 376, 394
Jones, Tommy Lee, 357
Jones, Walter, 295
Jordan, Louis, 406
Jory, Victor, 86, 174
Joseph and the Amazing Technicolor Dreamcoat, 362, 369
Joseph Papp Public Theatre, 406
Jourdan, Louis, 208
Journey of the Fifth Horse, The, 275
Joyce, Elaine, 309
Joyce, James, 159, 234, 330
Joyce, Peggy Hopkins, 55, 92
Joyce, Stanley, 55
Joyce, Stephen, 312–13
Joyful Noise, A, 280
Jubilee, 120
Jujamcyn Theatres, 360, 362, 392, 396–97, 392, 402, 411
Julia, Raul, 139, 264, 288, 298, 308–9, 331, 335, 345–46, 351–52, 363, 376, 406, 418
Julien, Jay, 174–75, 212
Julius Caesar, 131, 132, 216, 222
Jumbo, 119
Jumpers, 317, 321
Junior Miss, 147, 149, 156
Juno and the Paycock, 77

Kaaren, Suzanne, 156
Kahn, Gus, 91
Kahn, Madeleine, 289, 318, 342, 409–10
Kalem, Ted, 341
Kalich, Bertha, 5, 12, 135, 138
Kalich, Jacob, 157, 325
Kalmar, Bert, 7, 178
Kander, John, 81, 277, 279, 293, 328, 341, 358, 373, 409, 412, 428
Kane, Helen, 12, 90, 109, 278
Kani, John, 323, 325
Kanin, Fay, 17, 182, 377–78
Kanin, Garson, 17, 155, 156, 161, 163, 171, 188–89, 242, 248, 253, 257, 384, 393, 400
Karloff, Boris, 141, 143, 144, 156, 190, 217
Karlweiss, Oscar, 157
Karnilova, Maria, 293
Karr, Harold, 224
Kasznar, Kurt, 219, 262
Katselas, Milton, 248

Kauffmann, Stanley, 273, 274, 278
Kaufman, George S., 7, 33, 35, 36, 41, 54, 56, 59, 61, 65, 73, 74, 76, 86, 87, 90, 91, 108, 109, 112, 113, 116, 123, 124, 125, 130, 131, 132, 138, 141, 143, 163, 167, 183, 192–93, 201, 203, 207, 228, 252, 253, 350–51, 395, 406
Kaufman and Hart, 136, 141, 142
Kaye, Danny, 17, 137, 138, 139, 141, 144, 147, 148, 268, 301, 303, 385
Kaye, Stubby, 192–93, 223, 377
Kazan, Elia, 15, 109, 111, 112, 115, 118, 125, 157, 170, 172, 176, 177, 178, 179, 180, 181, 183, 197, 199–200, 204, 235, 236, 253, 260, 264, 269, 286, 342, 356, 368, 389, 401
Kazan, Lainie, 265
Keach, Stacy, 280, 298, 414
Keane, George, 176
Keane, Norman, 388
Keaton, Buster, 15, 25
Keaton, Diane, 290, 294
Kedrova, Lila, 372
Keel, Howard, 161, 170, 172, 409
Keeler, Ruby, 57, 90, 143, 301, 303–4
Keep 'Em Laughing, 150
Keep It in the Family, 286
Keitel, Harvey, 328, 376, 381, 383
Keith, B.F., 7, 8, 11, 13, 18, 19
Keith, Ian, 58
Keith, Robert, 77
Kellaway, Cecil, 242
Kelly, Gene, 135, 138, 141, 143, 148, 157, 235
Kelly, George, 64, 65, 73, 76
Kelly, Gregory, 76
Kelly, Kevin, 361–62, 370
Kelly, Nancy, 192, 211
Kelly, P.J., 231
Kelly, Patsy, 15, 164, 303–4, 314
Kelly, Paul, 177–78, 192
Kelly, Robert, 59, 91
Kelton, Pert, 242, 76
Kemble, Fannie, 3
Kempy, 56
Kendall, Kay, 230
Kenne, Laura, 5
Kennedy, Arthur, 19, 176, 183–84, 203, 249, 289, 395–96
Kennedy, Madge, 24, 62
Kent, William, 88, 91
Kentucky Cycle, The, 403, 406, 413–14
Kern, Jerome, 7, 12, 16, 17, 23, 24, 26, 29, 34, 35, 36, 37, 38, 41, 51, 75, 81, 87, 108, 113, 130, 157, 169, 171, 188–89, 237, 242, 330, 377, 385
Kernan, David, 336
Kerns, Rhoda, 213
Kerr, Deborah, 182–83, 194–95, 206, 325
Kerr, Jean, 62, 188, 249, 356, 372
Kerr, John, 12, 206, 208
Kerr, Walter, 18, 73, 162, 188, 197, 199, 202, 203, 204, 212, 221, 222, 224, 237, 242, 249, 251, 263, 265, 270, 274, 278, 286, 336, 339, 346, 350, 351, 352, 372, 376, 395, 418–19, 426
Kert, Larry, 116–17, 228, 300, 301, 314, 391, 404
Kerz, Leo, 246, 247
Kerz, Louise, 426
Kesey, Ken, 304–5
Kesselring, Joseph, 144
Kessler, Lyle, 378
Kestelman, Sara, 304
Key Largo, 139
Kid Boots, 63, 64
Kidd, Michael, 44, 179, 192–93, 253
Kidder, Margot, 384
Kiley, Richard, 55, 164, 208, 233, 236, 254, 271, 273, 324
Killian, Victor, 253
Killing of Sister George, The, 277, 278
King, Alan, 272
King, Charles, 83
King, Dennis, 10, 68, 75, 88, 132, 164, 302
King, Edith, 55
King, Mabel, 325
King & I, The, 191, 194–95, 197, 200, 202, 205, 206, 207, 260, 333, 337, 373, 375–76, 380, 421, 424
King David, 428
Kingfisher, The, 346
King Henry IV, Part I, 376–77
King John, 222
King Lear, 143, 193, 217, 262, 342
King of Hearts, 346–47
Kingsley, Ben, 304, 373
Kingsley, George, 193
Kingsley, Sidney, 13, 111, 112, 114, 138, 155, 158, 184, 191, 257, 419
Kinney, Terry, 374, 378, 397
Kipphardt, Heinar, 294
Kirk, Lisa, 178, 183, 324
Kirkland, Alexander, 112, 156
Kirkland, Jack, 114, 131
Kirkland, Patricia, 175
Kirkland, Sally, 292, 293, 382
Kirksey, Kirk, 293, 326
Kirkwood, James, 58, 273, 326
Kiser, Terry, 280
Kismet, 17, 188, 205, 207–8
Kiss and Tell, 158
Kissel, Howard, 390, 415
Kiss Me Kate, 181, 183, 198–99, 414
Kiss of the Spider Woman, 400, 397–98, 409, 412, 418
Kiss the Boys Goodbye, 134
Kiss Them for Me, 168
Kitchen, The, 278
Kitt, Eartha, 166, 200
Klaw, Marc, 4, 9, 13, 17, 28, 37, 39, 42, 124
Kleban, Edward, 323, 327, 328, 329
Klein, Charles, 12, 13, 18
Klein, Robert, 278, 289, 347, 410
Kline, Kevin, 178, 292, 311–12, 329–30, 342, 350–51, 355, 358, 82
Klugman, Jack, 200, 237, 403
Knack, The, 266, 267
Knickerbocker Holiday, 133, 134
Knickerbocker Theatre, 75
Knight, June, 133, 135
Knight, Shirley, 427
Knott, Frederick, 202, 274
Knox, Alexander, 158
Kober, Arthur, 74, 126, 202
Koch, Howard, 149
Kopit, Arthur, 125, 254, 264, 287, 298, 347, 380
Korman, Harvey, 225
Koslow, Pamela, 357
Kotto, Yaphet, 273
Kramer, Larry, 378, 410
Kramm Joseph, 197, 199
Krapp's Last Tape, 242
Krasna, Norman, 176, 253
Krassner, Paul, 277
Kretzmer, Herbert, 385
Krieger, Henry, 361–62, 372–73
Krizanc, John, 389
Kroll, Jack, 336, 347–48, 369, 397
Krone, Gerald S., 281
Kronenberger, Louis, 168, 171
Kruger, Otto, 7, 44, 56, 63, 87, 150, 324
Krutch, Joseph Wood, 203
Kuhn, Judy, 390
Kummer, Clare, 5, 33, 36, 51, 55, 113, 229
Kurnitz, Harry, 253
Kurrz, Frank, 166
Kurtz, Swoosie, 166, 299, 317, 340–41, 353, 355, 356, 357, 381–82, 396, 404
Kushner, Tony, 409–10, 412, 413, 418–19

La Belle Paree, 16
La Bete, 399, 401
La Bohéme, 423
La Cage Aux Folles, 317–18, 371, 372, 383, 385–86
Lacey, Jerry, 294
La Chanze, 400
Lackerman, Abe, 91, 112
Lacy, Tom, 310
Ladder, The, 79, 80
Ladies of the Evening, 68
Lady Be Good, 67, 69, 86, 350
Lady from Dubuque, The, 352
Lady in the Dark, 141, 143, 144, 145, 149, 150, 170

Lady Says Yes, A, 168
Lady's Not for Burning, The, 191, 193
Lady Windermere's Fan, 174
Lahr, Bert, 9, 60, 61, 91, 107, 125, 137, 139, 148, 199, 219, 225, 261, 264, 278, 287, 289
Lahr, John, 410, 412, 416, 426
Lahti, Christine, 356, 393
Lake of the Woods, 309
La Mama Experimental Theatre, 187, 279
Lamas, Fernando, 223, 224, 228
La Marr, Bubbles, 164
Lamb, Myrna, 300
Lamp at Midnight, The, 179
Lampert, Zohra, 260, 292
Landesman, Rocco, 387–88, 391–92, 400
Lane, Burton, 17, 142, 176, 262, 272, 426
Lane, Nathan, 217, 255, 367, 384, 392, 396, 403–4, 407, 414, 416, 417, 418, 419, 421, 424, 425–26, 428
Lang, Harold, 199
Lange, Jessica, 403, 405–6
Lange, Sven, 51
Langella, Frank, 279, 281, 325, 340, 345–46, 423, 426
Langley, Noel, 182
Langner, Lawrence, 7, 144, 162, 259
Langtry, Lillie, 4, 6, 31, 32, 91
Lansbury, Angela, 74, 223, 225, 246, 265, 271, 275, 278, 291, 314, 323–24, 345, 347, 348, 425
Lapine, James, 183, 351–52, 375, 387, 400
La Plume de Ma Tante, 233, 235
Lapotaire, Jane, 355, 358
Lardner, Ring, 112
Largo Desolato, 382
Larimore, Earle, 82, 83, 109, 114
Lark, The, 211, 215, 217
Larrimore, Francine, 52, 81, 82, 92, 325
Larson, Jonathan, 421, 423, 426–27
Larson, Pat, 202
Lasser, Louise, 251, 272, 345
Last Night of Ballyhoo, The, 425, 427
Last of Mrs. Lincoln, The, 311
Last of the Red Hot Lovers, The, 299
Last Sweet Days of Isaac, The, 299
Lastfogel, Abe, 81
La Torneaux, Robert, 289
Latouche, John, 142, 149, 205, 209
Lauder, Harry, 5, 189
Laugh Parade, The, 109
Laughter on the 23rd Floor, 414
Laughton, Charles, 10, 119, 178, 198, 203, 208, 222, 259, 281
Laurents, Arthur, 40, 202, 237, 270, 396
Laurette, 248
Laurie, Piper, 410
Lavin, Linda, 251, 274, 294, 298, 384–85
Lawlor, Mary, 86
Lawrence, Carol, 200, 221, 228, 254, 262, 288
Lawrence, Gertrude, 10, 61, 64, 81, 118, 125, 130, 131, 133, 134, 137, 140, 141, 142, 144, 145, 147, 149, 150, 156, 163, 166, 167, 169, 170, 171, 179, 194–95, 197, 200, 201, 202, 203, 340
Lawrence, Jerome, 214, 222, 346
Lawrence, Lawrence Shubert, 240, 246, 326
Lawrence, Mal Z., 404
Lawrence, Steve, 264, 270, 289
Layton, Joe, 319, 415
Lazar, Irving "Swifty", 216, 358
Lazarus, Frank, 353
Leachman, Cloris, 189, 203, 236
Leaf People, The, 328
League of American Theatres and Producers, The, 422, 428
League of New York Theatres, 121, 139, 150, 178, 182, 216, 228, 258, 259, 263, 264, 268, 274, 289
League of Off-Broadway Theatres, 229, 278, 286
League of Resident Theatres, 274, 278
Lean, David, 202
Learned, Michael, 223
Leave It to Jane, 12, 237
Leave It To Me!, 134–35
Lebewohl, Abe, 380
Leblang Theatre Ticket Agency, 166
Lederer, Charles, 207–8
Lederer, Francis, 131, 138
Lee, Canada, 135, 145, 174
Lee, Carl, 240
Lee, Gypsy Rose, 123, 130, 137, 156, 221, 225, 233, 237, 299
Lee, Michelle, 314
Lee, Robert E., 214, 222, 346
Lee, Sondra, 253
Lee, Spike, 360
LeFevre, Adam, 402
Le Gallienne, Eva, 10, 19, 23, 24, 29, 52, 54, 63, 79, 80, 113, 121, 129, 130, 135, 150, 174, 208, 228, 302, 330, 403–4
Legend, 330
Legends, 384
LeGrant, David, 199
Legs Diamond, 391–92, 397
Leguizamo, John, 410
Lehman, Benjamin, 125, 134
Leibman, Ron, 131, 264, 293, 298, 353, 378, 392, 409, 411, 412
Leigh, Carolyn, 212, 247, 259
Leigh, Mitch, 271, 273
Leigh, Vivian, 18, 141, 142, 197, 199–200, 242, 257, 275, 286
Leighton, Margaret, 55, 172, 221, 222, 251, 254, 280, 287, 288, 328
Leinsdorf, Erich, 139
LeMarie, Rufus, 74
Lembeck, Harvey, 195
Lemmon, Jack, 180, 246, 340, 346, 373, 392
Lend An Ear, 181, 183
Lend Me a Tenor, 391, 394, 400
Lenihan, Winifred, 64
Lennon, John, 298
Lennox, Gilbert, 227
Lenny, 304–5, 307
Lenya, Lotte, 11, 125, 209, 254, 258, 279, 359–60
Leon and Eddie's, 206, 207
Leon, Felix, 273
Leonard, Hugh, 339
Leonard, Sheldon, 126
Leontovich, Eugenie, 109, 213
Lerner and Loewe, 215, 216, 217, 221, 241, 247, 248, 252
Lerner, Alan Jay, 40, 173, 176, 189, 199, 202, 222, 228, 248, 249, 262, 265, 272, 278, 298, 324, 331, 345–46, 355, 360, 379, 381, 383–84. *See also* Lerner and Loewe
Lerner, Robert, 172
Leroux, Gaston, 389–90
Les Liaisons Dangereuses, 383, 386
Les Mains Sales, 182–83
Les Miserables, 379, 380, 381, 383, 385, 387, 388, 389, 391, 393, 397, 401–2, 403, 409–10, 417, 425–27
Les Parents Terribles, 420
Lesson from Aloes, A, 355–56
Lester, Richard, 266
Let My People Come, 320, 333–34
Let's Face It!, 148
Let Them Eat Cake, 113
Lettice & Lovage, 392
Lettice & Lovage, 395, 397–98, 401
Let Us Be Gay, 92
Leveaux, David, 411
Levene, Sam, 108, 118, 127, 138, 182, 192–93, 235, 313, 330, 357
Leveridge, Lynn Ann, 318
Levin, Herman, 252
Levin, Ira, 216, 253, 339, 342, 359, 360, 361
Levin, Meyer, 228, 229
Levitt, Robert D., 149
Lewis, Ira, 410
Lewis, Jerry, 225, 333, 335, 357, 415, 417, 420
Lewis, Michael J., 315
Lewis, Patricia, 254
Lewis, Robert, 112, 125, 131, 178

Lewis, Sinclair, 74, 114, 123, 124, 134, 174–75

Lewis, Ted, 54

Lewis-Evans, Kecia, 400

Liberace, 409

Liberatore, Lou, 388

L'Idiote, 253

Lieber, Jerry, 419

Lieberson, Goddard, 172

Liebling, A.J., 139

Lie of the Mind, A, 379, 380, 381

Life, The, 427–28

Life and Adventures of Nicholas Nickeby, The, 359

Life Begins at 8:40, 118

Life in the Theatre, A, 340

Life is a Dream, 264

Life with Father, 137, 138, 141, 162, 165, 166, 177–78, 257, 311–12, 351

Lightnin', 54

Lights of New York, The, 90

Light Up the Sky, 182

Ligon, Tom, 288

Li'l Abner, 223

Liliom, 52, 168

Lillie, Beatrice, 8, 61, 63, 64, 107, 127, 142, 147, 150, 167, 180, 202, 223, 224, 231, 265, 334, 393

Lily of the Valley, 149

Lincoln Center Theatre, 380

Lincoln Mask, The, 311

Lindemann, Clara, 54

Lindemann, Leo, 54, 228

Linden, Hal, 230, 233, 234, 301, 303, 325, 381

Lindfors, Viveca, 51, 212–13, 254, 422

Lindo, Delroy, 390

Lindsay, Howard, 7, 86, 113, 115, 117, 124, 138–39, 165, 166, 169, 171, 224, 225, 239, 241, 287,

Lindsay, Robert, 383–84

Lindy's, 53, 54

Linn, Bambi, 158, 168, 189, 255

Lion and the Mouse, The, 13

Lion in Winter, The, 271, 275

Lion King, The, 417

Lips Together, Teeth Apart, 403–4

Lisbon Traviata, The, 396, 423

Lisher, Leon, 209

Lithgow, John, 170, 314, 356, 390

Litten, Jim, 331

Little, Cleavon, 280, 286, 294, 297, 299, 325, 381

Little Devil, The, 80

Littlefield, Emma, 162

Little Foxes, The, 133, 135, 142, 143, 175, 280, 286, 287, 355, 358, 375

Little Jesse James, 62

Little Johnny Jones, 12

Little Mary Sunshine, 241

Little Me, 259

Little Minister, The, 10

Little Murders, 293

Little Nelly Kelly, 59

Little Night Music, A, 311, 313, 314

Little Prince, The, 384

Little Shop of Horrors, 367–68

Little Show, The, 92

Littlest Revue, The, 219

Little Theatre, 92. *See* Helen Hayes Theatre

Littlewood, Joan, 246

Livent, 395–96

Living Theatre, 235, 262, 268

Living Together, 330

Living, Henry, 278

Lloyd, Christopher, 311

Lloyd, Harold, 167

Lloyd Webber, Andrew, 177, 179, 307–8, 335–36, 349–52, 355, 358, 362, 367–68, 373, 375, 377, 379–80, 383, 385–86, 387–89, 391–94, 395–96, 398, 400–401, 405–6, 409–12, 413–16, 417–20, 421, 423, 425–27, 428

Lloyd Webber, Julian, 409

Lo Bianco, Tony, 254, 269

Locke, Katherine, 126, 139

Lockridge, Richard, 113, 135

Loden, Barbara, 228, 260, 264, 286, 356

Loeb, Philip, 71, 117, 127, 136, 142, 170, 216

Loesser, Frank, 16, 182, 191, 192, 193, 219, 221, 223, 235, 242, 251, 252, 253, 298, 407

Loewe, Frederick, 11, 173, 176, 199, 202, 235, 384. *See also* Lerner and Loewe

Loew, Marcus, 86

Loew's State Theatre, 54

Loftus, Cissie, 6, 71, 74, 162

Logan, Ella, 18, 149, 156, 165, 168, 173, 175–76, 293

Logan, Joshua, 15, 115, 118, 132, 134, 142, 143, 149, 174, 177, 180, 184–85, 187, 190, 205, 325, 352, 391–92

Loggia, Robert, 268, 318–19

Lolita, 355, 358, 360

Lombardo, Guy, 110

London Assurance, 428

London Suite, 417, 420

Lone, John, 356, 360, 390

Lonergan, Lenore, 167

Long, Avon, 149

Long, Sumner Arthur, 259

Longacre Square, 12. *See also* Times Square

Longacre Theatre, 18, 131, 389

Long Day's Journey Into Night, 147, 148, 221, 222, 223, 307, 392

Long Goodbye, The, 140

Long Wharf Theatre, 272

Look Away, 311

Look Back in Anger, 227, 228, 229, 230

Look Homeward Angel, 227, 229, 241, 246

Loos, Anita, 8, 62, 80, 174, 188–89, 199, 231, 360

Loose Ends, 350

Loot, 288

Lopez, Priscilla, 328–29

Lopez, Vincent, 57

Loquasto, Santo, 293, 300, 333, 346–47, 380

Lorca, Garcia, 200

Lord, Pauline, 55, 69

Lorelei, 188, 318, 319, 320

Lorick, Robert, 372–73

Lorraine, Lillian, 15–16, 17, 40, 44, 19, 110

Lorring, Joan, 223

Lortel, Lucille, 213, 245

Loss of Roses, A, 241, 246

Lost Horizon, 221

Lost in the Stars, 188

Lost in Yonkers, 399, 401

Loudon, Dorothy, 112, 235, 308, 311, 333, 336, 346, 347, 348, 372–73, 377, 381, 397, 410

Louise, Tina, 216

Louis the 14th, 77

Louisiana Purchase, 140

Love, Phyllis, 193–94

Love and Let Love, 199

Love for Love, 324–25

Love in a Village, 3

Love Letters, 396

Love Life, 181

Love of Four Colonels, The, 201, 203

Lovejoy, Frank, 242

Lovers and Other Strangers, 292

Love! Valor! Compassion! 417, 418, 419

Lowe, Charles, 222

Lowell, Robert, 268

Lowenfels, Walter, 109

Loy, Myrna, 311

Lucas, Craig, 397

Lucas, Jonathan, 209

Luce, Clare Boothe. *See* Boothe, Clare

Luce, Henry, 117, 120–21

Lucille Lortel Theatre, 359

Luckinbill, Laurence, 300, 335, 336, 356

Lucky, 82

Lucky Sam McCarver, 76

Lucrece, 109, 110

Ludlam, Charles, 157, 383, 385

Ludwig, Ken, 394, 422

Luft, Lorna, 172

Lugosi, Bela, 85, 86, 112, 340

Lukas, Paul, 145, 192

Luke, Keye, 235

Luke, Peter, 294

Luker, Rebecca, 389, 402, 418

Lulu Belle, 73, 77

Lumet, Sidney, 136, 222

Lunatics and Lovers, 211

Lunch Hour, 356

Lunchtime Follies, 155, 156
Lund, Art, 219
Lunt, Alfred, 8, 31, 32, 37, 43, 44, 56, 60, 67, 68, 81, 85, 88, 107, 108, 109, 121, 122, 130, 132, 134, 135, 137, 139, 149, 157, 163, 169, 171, 174, 187–88, 193, 197, 205, 207, 209, 211, 224, 231, 234, 339–40
Lunt-Fontanne, 60, 67, 107, 132, 135, 137
Lunt-Fontanne Theatre, 33, 227, 231, 389
LuPone, Patti, 183, 286, 292, 311–12, 327, 329–30, 342, 349–51, 350, 355, 356, 357, 376–77, 379, 380, 381, 387, 388, 389, 392, 409, *410*, 410, 411, 412, 413, 414, 415, 416, 422, 425–26
LuPone, Robert, 327
Lute Song, 171
Luther, 261, 262
Luv, 267, 268
Lyceum Theatre, 12, 342, 400
Lyceum School of Acting, 7
Lynch, Alfred, 246
Lynde, Paul, 200, 242
Lyon, Ben, 88
Lyon, Peter, 192
Lyons, Gene, 212–13
Lyons, Jenny, 299
Lyons, Leonard, 13, 114, 135, 235, 245, 320, 333–34
Lyric Theatre, 12, 425
Lysistrata, 312
Lytell, Bert, 91, 148

MacArthur, Charles, 9, 77, 90, 107, 108, 109, 188, 217
MacArthur, James, 218
MacArthur, John T., 218
MacArthur, Mary, 174, 188
Macbeth, 4, 119, 148–49, 387, 389
Macbird!, 277, 280
MacDermot, Galt, 290, 307, 309
MacDonald, Jeanette, 68, 90
MacDougall, Ranald, 223
Macgowan, Kenneth, 62
MacGrath, Leueen, 24, 183, 216, 228, 406
Machinal, 90
Mack, Cecil, 63
Mack, Charles, 112–13
Mack, Willard, 80
Mack and Mabel, 323–24
Mackay, Ellin, 73, 75
MacKay, Lizabeth, 357
Mack the Knife, 217
MacKellar, Helen, 63
Mackintosh, Cameron, 175, 336, 349, 352, 368, 383, 385, 388, 389, 396, 397, 398, 399, 400, 401, 402, 403, 406, 413
MacLaine, Shirley, 204, 209, 211–12, 230, 246, 262
MacLeish, Archibald, 233, 235
MacMahon, Aline, 247, 281, 404
MacMillan, Kenneth, 335
MacMurray, Fred, 113
MacNicol, Peter, 357
MacRae, Gordon, 159, 168, 208, 288
Macready, William, 4
Macy, William H., 410
Madam, Will You Walk? 208
Madame Butterfly, 11
Madame Sherry, 16
Madden, Donald, 280
Maddern, Minnie. *See* Fiske, Minnie Maddern
Madigan, Amy, 406
Madonna, 350–51, 384, 387, 388, 390, 391, 392
Mad Show, The, 274
Madwoman of Chaillot, The, 181, 183
Magee, Patrick, 274
Magic Show, The, 317, 321
Magnani, Anna, 193–94
Mahabharata, 388
Maharis, George, 242
Maher, Joseph, 318
Mahoney, John, 378
Mahoney, Will, 82
Maidman, Irving, 246
Maids, The, 215
Main, Marjorie, 125
Majestic Theatre, 11, 83, 158, 168, 389
Major Barbara, 222
Majority of One, A, 233, 236
Makarova, Natalia, 367, 369
Make a Million, 235
Make It Snappy, 56
Malden, Karl, 18, 131, 139, 144, 172, 179–80, 182, 193, 213, 237
Male Animal, The, 137, 139
Malina, Judith, 80, 137, 182, 199, 240, 258, 268, 292, 294, 308
Malina, Luba, 170
Malkovich, John, 206, 334, 367–68, 370, 373–74, 387, 388
Mallory, Victoria, 313–14
Malone, Dorothy, 224
Maltby, Richard, Jr., 131, 396, 401, 404
Malvaloca, 58
Mamba's Daughters, 135, 136
Mambo Mouth, 410
Mame, 271, 275, 383, 385–86
Mamet, David, 297, 325, 327, 329, 331, 333, 334, 335, 356–57, 339, 340, 341, 342, 345, 348, 360, 368, 371, 373, 379, 387, 390, 391, 404, 410, 416, 418, 420, 426
Mamoulian, Rouben, 88, 158, 162, 168, 172, 188
Managers Protective Association, 62
Man and Superman, 177
Mancini, Henry, 422
Maney, Richard, 8, 143, 148, 279, 292
Mangum, Edward, 192
Manhoff, Bill, 269
Man for All Seasons, A, 251, 253, 258
Man From Home, The, 14–15
Manilow, Barry, 409
Man in the Glass Booth, The, 292
Man Is Man, 258
Mann, Iris, 190
Mann, Ted, 419
Mann, Terrence, 385, 416
Mann, Theodore, 63, 192, 206, 253, 426
Manners, J. Hartley, 17, 56, 63, 82, 91, 116
Manoff, Dinah, 353
Man of La Mancha, 271, 273, 304
Man's a Man, A, 258
Mansfield, Jayne, 216
Mansfield, Richard, 4, 7, 8, 11, 12, 13, 14, 134
Mansfield Theatre, 166, 247
Mantegna, Joe, 311, 327, 373, 390, 412, 418
Mantle, Burns, 5, 56, 67, 76, 118, 136, 141, 161, 162, 175–76, 179
Man Who Came to Dinner, The, 137, 138, 143
Man Who Had All the Luck, The, 167
Many Faces of Love, The, 334
Maples, Marla, 409, 410
Ma Rainey's Black Bottom, 375–76
Marand, Patricia, 202, 275
Marasco, Robert, 299
Marat/Sade, 271, 274
March, Frederic, 10, 51, 81, 130–31, 156, 157, 167, 170, 173, 175–76, 178, 181–82, 221, 223, 253, 325
March, Hal, 249
Marchand, Nancy, 242, 286, 304, 352–53, 392
March of the Falsettos, 358, 400, 407
Marco Millions, 88
Marcum, Kevin, 388
Marcus, Frank, 278
Margaret Fleming, 8
Margin for Error, 138
Margo, 171, 120
Margo Jones Theatre, 240
Margot, Patricia, 324
Marguiles, David, 406
Margules, Annette, 63
Marilyn, 371
Marinoff, Fania, 54
Marion, George, 55
Marisse, Anna, 278
Mark Hellinger Theatre, 183, 391, 405
Marks, Walter, 289
Mark Twain Tonight!, 271, 275
Marlowe, Julia, 5, 7, 12, 15, 192

Marquand, John P., 167
Marquis, Don, 58, 109
Marriage Is a Private Affair, 162
Marriage-Go-Round, The, 235
Marriage of Bette and Boo, The, 378
Marsh, Howard, 69, 87
Marshall, E.G., 15, 157, 182, 203, 219, 287
Martells, Cynthia, 406–7
Martin, Andrea, 268, 311, 428
Martin, Ernest, 419
Martin, Frances, 230, 234
Martin, George N., 372, 381, 423
Martin, Hugh, 180, 265
Martin, Mary, 19, 124, 133, 134–35, 136, 139, 161, 162, 163, 164, 166, 171, 181, 184–85, 187, 189, 197–99, 201–2, 205–6, 208–9, 211, 213–4, 217, 231, 239, 241, 246, 248, 261, 262, 270, 272, 275, 280, 333, 336, 340, 367–68, 384, 394, 399, 401
Martin, Millicent, 336
Martin, Nan, 269
Martin, Steve, 392
Martin, Tony, 208
Martin Beck Theatre, 68, 91, 157
Marty, 204
Marx, Arthur, 272
Marx, Chico, 8, 253
Marx, Groucho, 8, 245, 340
Marx, Harpo, 7, 53, 138, 147, 268
Marx Brothers, 5, 17, 24, 26, 65, 73, 74, 76, 90, 114, 127, 360, 368. *See also under separate names*
Mary, Mary, 249, 372
Mary Jane McKane, 63
Mary of Scotland, 113, 114
Mary Stuart, 228
Maschke, Bud, Jr., 109, 120
Masekela, Hugh, 389
Mason, Jackie, 383, 385, 417–18
Mason, James, 175–76, 235
Mason, John, 13, 14
Mason, Marsha, 317–19, 371–72
Mason, Marshall, 378, 384
Masque of Kings, The, 127
Mass Appeal, 361
Massey, Daniel, 260
Massey, Ilona, 159
Massey, Raymond, 9, 133, 134, 161, 164, 171, 179, 203, 216, 235, 372
Master Class, 421–23, 426
Master Harold...and the Boys, 363, 373
Mastosimone, William, 369
Mata Hari, 285, 287
Matchmaker, The, 135, 217, 263, 277
Mathias, Sean, 420
Mathis, Johnny, 409
Matter of Gravity, A, 327, 331
Matthau, Walter, 137, 208, 216, 253, 267, 270, 324–25
Matthews, Brander 65
Matthews, Inez, 163, 188
Matthews, Joyce, 149, 222, 253
Mature, Victor, 144
Maude-Roxby, Roddy, 266
Maugham, W. Somerset, 5, 81, 272, 323, 326
Maxine Elliott's Theatre, 86, 240
Maxwell, Elsa, 117
Maxwell, Mitchell, 376
May, Elaine, 229, 254, 294, 353
May, Martin, 212, 223
Mayehoff, Eddie, 192
Mayer, Edwin Justus, 68
Mayfield, Julian, 188
M. Butterfly, 387, 390
McArdle, Andrea, 336, 374, 385–86, 400
McCarten, John, 288
McCarthy, Joseph, 64, 82
McCarthy, Kevin, 144, 182, 268
McCarthy, Mary, 352
McClanahan, Rue, 280
McClintic, Guthrie, 18, 53, 54, 117, 124, 139, 159, 253, 324
McClure, Michael, 286, 287, 298
McComas, Carroll, 51, 63
McCormack, Patty, 211–12
McCormick, Myron, 148, 184–85
McCormick, Patty, 170
McCowen, Alec, 69, 286, 294, 304, 410
McCraken, Joan, 204
McCullers, Carson, 187–89
McCullough, Paul, 17, 69, 81, 121
McDaniel, James, 410
McDonald, Audra, 415, 423
McDonnell, Mary, 346
McDormand, Frances, 372, 410
McDowall, Roddy, 216, 228
McEwan, Geraldine, 262
McGavin, Darren, 212
McGhee, Brownie, 214
McGlinn, John, 385, 391
McGovern, Barry, 426
McGovern, Elizabeth, 372, 389
McGowan, John, 87
McGowen, Tom, 401, 422
McGuiness, Frank, 409, 410, 427
McGuire, Dorothy, 141, 144
McHugh, Jimmy, 75, 88, 182, 351
McKechnie, Donna, 141, 142, 253, 293, 300, 320, 327–29, 333, 334, 335, 414, 415
McKee, Lonette, 370, 418
McKellan, Ian, 133, 135, 355, 356
McKenna, Siobhan, 56, 174, 216, 222, 225, 229, 302, 304, 384
McKenzie, Julia, 411–12
McKenzie, Julie N., 336
McKern, Leo, 253
McKnight, Martin, 269
McLain, John, 194–95
McLellan, C.M.S., 12, 16
McLerie, Allyn Ann, 188
McMahon, Aline, 156
McMahon, Frank, 297, 299
McMahon, Horace, 231
McMartin, John, 305, 376–77, 418
McMillan, Kenneth, 318
McNally, Terrence, 139, 270, 293, 294, 297, 319, 321, 325, 388, 392, 396, 401, 403–4, 409, 412, 413–14, 417, 418, 419, 421–23
McNamara, Maggie, 202
McNeil, Claudia, 236, 414
McNeil, Lonnie, 331
McNicolas, Steve, 415
McQueen, Armelia, 343
McQueen, Butterfly, 139, 393–94
McSorely, Gerard, 404
McTeer, Janet, 425, 427–28
Meadow, Lynne, 175, 339
Me and Bessie, 324, 334
Me and Juliet, 201, 204, 205, 207–8, 211
Me and My Girl, 383, 384, 385, 389, 390
Meara, Anne, 164, 201, 204, 212, 224, 304, 325–26, 392, 393, 411
Measure for Measure, 246
Me Nobody Knows, The, 300
Mecca Temple Theatre, 163
Medcraft, Russell, 74
Medea, 177, 178, 179, 359, 363, 368, 413, 415, 421
Medford, Kay, 242, 265, 279, 351
Medoff, Mark, 319, 349, 352
Meehan, Danny, 321
Meehan, John, Jr., 157
Meek, Donald, 54, 175
Meeker, Ralph, 203–4, 268
Megrue, Roi Cooper, 6, 24, 28, 81
Meighan, Thomas, 12, 87
Meisner, Sanford, 71, 118, 125, 427
Meit, Marvin, 376
Melby, John, 167
Mell, Marisa, 287
Member of the Wedding, The, 187–89, 202
Memory of All That: The Life of George Gershwin, The, 412
Memory, 116
Men in White, 111, 112, 114
Menjou, Adolphe, 384
Menken, Alan, 367–68
Menken, Helen, 56, 58, 76, 80, 90, 108, 113, 117, 273

Menotti, Gian-Carlo, 176, 187, 189–90, 211, 213
Mercer, Johnny, 171, 198–99, 223, 264
Mercer, Marian, 288
Merchant, The, 340
Merchant, Vivien, 280
Merchant of Venice, The, 57, 60, 258, 397
Merchant of Yonkers, The, 135, 217
Merckerson, S. Apatha, 398
Mercouri, Melina, 279
Mercury Theatre, 129, 131
Meredith, Burgess, 15, 110, 113, 120, 121, 125, 130, 134, 149, 150, 163, 164, 170, 174, 188, 195, 222, 234, 265, 321
Merivale, Philip, 7, 63, 82, 125, 172
Merkle, Una, 241
Merlin, 369, 371
Merlin, Joanna, 268
Merman, Ethel, 14, 92, 107, 115, 117, 123, 124, 137, 139, 141, 142, 148, 149, 158, 165, 166, 169, 172, 189, 191–92, 195, 202, 206, 211, 216, 223, 224, 228, 229, 233, 236, 237, 239, 241, 257, 261, 263, 268, 269, 270, 288, 300, 302–3, 323–25, 333, 336, 349, 361, 367, 371, 373, 388–89, 395, 401
Merriam, Eve, 334
Merrick, David, 17, 86, 131–32, 137, 158, 164, 187–88, 211–13, 216, 221, 225, 227, 228, 229, 230, 237, 248, 249, 251, 252, 253, 257, 258, 259, 260, 263, 264, 271, 273, 274, 278, 280, 285, 286, 287, 288, 289, 291, 293, 299, 300, 301–3, 307, 308, 309, 317–18, 324, 356–58, 367, 368, 369, 370, 372, 373, 374, 377, 399, 400, 401, 402, 403–4, 423–24, 426
Merrick, Lynn, 171
Merrifield, Gail, 328
Merrill, Bob, 225, 241, 245, 249, 264, 309
Merrill, Gary, 156, 171, 352–53
Merrill, Scott, 209
Merrily We Roll Along, 116, 361
Merrit, Theresa, 376
Merry Widow, The, 11, 14
Merson, Susan, 331
Merton of the Movies, 59
Metaxa, George, 121
Metcalf, Laurie, 334
Mexican Hayride, 161, 163, 166
Meyer, Irwin, 361
Mhil'dalim, 264
Michael, Sidney, 263
Michaels, Marilyn, 404
Middle East Diary, 167
Middle of the Night, 217
Middlemass, Robert, 76
Middleton, George, 36, 44
Middleton, Ray, 190, 273, 373
Midler, Bette, 279, 319, 383
Midnight Frolic, 25, 31, 32, 45
Midsummer Night's Dream, A, 12, 304, 389
Mielziner, Jo, 11, 120, 161, 187, 205, 207, 327–28
Mignes, Julia, 268
Mikado, The, 150
Mike Todd's Peep Show, 192
Milanov, Zinka, 336
Miles, Emily, 54
Miles, Sylvia, 108, 212, 278, 317–18
Milk and Honey, 252
Milk Train Doesn't Stop Here Anymore, The, 257, 259, 263
Miller, Ann, 138, 351
Miller, Arthur, 28, 123, 125, 165, 167, 173, 176, 178, 181, 183, 188–89, 201, 203, 216, 221, 222, 223, 228, 234, 242, 253, 264, 269, 272, 289, 312–13, 328, 367–70, 373, 376, 395–96, 399, 404–5, 419
Miller, Gilbert, 4, 7, 88, 293
Miller, Henry, 4, 7, 9, 38, 45, 75
Miller, Jason, 307, 310, 311
Miller, Jonathan, 259
Miller, Madeline, 300
Miller, Marilyn, 10, 23, 24, 26, 38, 40, 41, 44, 47, 49, 51, 53, 54, 56, 57, 58, 61, 63, 75, 82, 88, 109, 112, 116, 121, 163, 189
Miller, Paula, 113, 125, 199
Miller, Robin, 293
Miller, Roger, 375, 378
Mills, Florence, 9, 52, 86, 87
Mills, Stephanie, 325
Mineo, Sal, 193–94, 299
Minetta Lane Theatre, 376
Mingus, Charles, Jr., 261
Minnelli, Liza, 169, 172, 199, 259, 267, 320, 324, 327–28, 339–41, 345, 351, 361, 373–74, 410, 425, 427–28
Minnelli, Vincente, 172, 259
Minnie's Boys, 297
Minskoffs, 336
Minsky brothers, the, 69
Miracle Worker, The, 222, 239, 240
Miranda, Carmen, 137, 138, 149, 155, 156
Mirvish, David, 396
Misleading Lady, The, 18–19
Miss Banana, 383
Miss Firecracker Contest, The, 374
Miss Liberty, 188
Miss Lulu Bett, 51
Miss Margarida's Way, 395, 397
Miss Saigon, 397–98, 399, 400, 401, 402, 403, 404, 405, 425
Mister Roberts, 177, 180, 182, 191–92, 195
Mitchell, Cameron, 183–84
Mitchell, Grant, 24, 36, 62
Mitchell, Norman, 74
Mitchell, Thomas 41, 42, 77, 190, 201, 206
Mitchell, William, 3
Mitchum, Robert, 230
Mitzi Newhouse Theatre, 311, 313, 380
Mixed Couple, 357
Mod Donna, 300
Modjeska, Helena, 3, 6, 11, 15
Moeller, Philip, 6, 88, 230
Moffat, Donald, 242
Mokae, Zakes, 302, 363, 373
Molina, Alfred, 423
Molly Picon Theatre, 156
Molly Sweeney, 421, 423
Molnár, Ferenc, 52, 63, 168, 212
Monk, Julius, 260
Monnot, Marguerite, 246
Monroe, Marilyn, 188, 202, 214, 221, 222
Montalban, Ricardo, 228
Monterey, Carlotta, 56, 88
Montevecchi, Liliane, 396
Montgomery, David, 11, 13, 15, 25, 33
Montgomery, Robert, 213, 293
Moonchildren, 309, 318
Moon for the Misbegotten, 176, 317, 319–20, 392
Moon Is Blue, The, 194–95, 202
Moon Is Down, The, 150
Moon Over Buffalo, 421–22
Moor, Bill, 280, 341
Moor, Gar, 182
Moore, Carroll, 235
Moore, Christa, 396
Moore, Constance, 156
Moore, Dudley, 259, 265, 319, 324
Moore, Grace, 63, 69
Moore, Jill Esmond, 92
Moore, Julian, 246
Moore, Mary Tyler, 278
Moore, Melba, 290, 299
Moore, Robert, 319
Moore, Roger, 391, 393
Moore, Victor, 5, 13, 81, 87, 91, 113, 117, 134, 137, 140, 150, 162, 258, 368
Moorehead, Agnes, 198, 319
Moose Murders, 367, 369
Moran, George, 113, 188
Morath, Inge, 253
Mordente, Tony, 228
Morehouse, Ward, 10, 164, 168, 168, 170, 278
More Stately Mansions, 286
Morgan, Frank, 88
Morgan, Helen, 11, 51, 69, 82, 87, 89, 109, 115, 116, 119, 120, 140, 147, 148, 163
Moriarity, Michael, 317, 320
Morison, Patricia, 183
Morley, Robert, 14, 134, 182, 410
Mornings at Seven, 352–53
Morosco, Oliver, 5, 51, 76, 169, 170

Morosco Theatre, 161, 163, 361
Moross, Jerome, 205, 209
Morris, Garrett, 308
Morris, Howard, 174, 188
Morris, William, 5, 63, 11, 13, 15, 63, 108
Morrison, Hobe, 272, 367
Morse, David, 427
Morse, Robert, 217, 231, 241, 246, 251, 253, 309, 320, 395, 396, 397
Morse, Robin, 400
Morton, Jelly Roll, 407
Morton, Joe, 318
Moscow Art Theatre, 57, 59, 60
Mosel, Tad, 245, 247
Moses, Burke, 416
Moses, Gilbert, 156, 309, 326, 419
Moses, Robert, 236, 240
Mosher, Gregory, 183, 342, 378, 380, 392, 406, 414, 425, 426, 427
Moss, Paul, 156, 162, 166
Mostel, Zero, 24, 147, 150, 156, 157, 175, 212, 216, 224, 234, 242, 245, 248, 254, 255, 257, 263, 267, 268, 292, 317–18, 320–21, 335, 339–40
Most Happy Fella, The, 69, 217, 219, 221, 222, 235, 351
Motel, 279
Mother Courage and Her Children, 260
Mountain Man, The, 55
Mourning Becomes Electra, 313
Mowatt, Anna Cora, 3
Mowbray, Alan, 260
Mr. and Mrs. North, 141
Mr. Preedy and the Countess, 16
Mr. President, 257, 259
Mr. Wonderful, 218
Mrs. Klein, 421–22
Mrs. McThing, 200
Mrs. Minniver, 165
Mrs. Warren's Profession, 24, 330
Much Ado About Nothing, 313, 375
Mulatto, 120
Mummenschanz, 335
Mundy, Meg, 184
Muni, Paul, 81, 90, 139, 174, 214, 215, 216, 217, 286, 379–80
Munshin, Jules, 172, 200, 242
Murder at the Vanities, 112
Murphy, Alice, 188
Murphy, Donna, 381, 396, 413, 416, 421, 423–24, 426
Murphy, Rosemary, 247, 264, 278, 345
Murphy, Sally, 415
Murray, Brian, 286, 343, 372, 423
Murray, Don, 193–94
Murray, J. Harold, 82
Murray, John, 127
Murray, Ken, 82, 156
Murray, Wynn, 126, 135
Murrow, Edward R., 216
Musante, Tony, 326, 352
Music Box Revue, The, 53, 63, 69, 70
Music Box Revue of 1921, 54
Music Box Revue of 1922, 58
Music Box Theatre, 54, 74, 82, 389
Music Corporation of America, 80
Music Man, The, 227, 230, 234, 235
Music Master, The, 12
Muson, Ona, 91
My Dear Children, 137, 139, 140
Myerberg, Michael, 215
Myers, Henry, 227
Myers, Timothy, 309
My Fair Lady, 67, 215, 217, 221, 222, 230, 241, 252, 257, 258, 278, 301–2, 312, 327, 347–48, 368, 405
My Heart's in the Highlands, 136
Myles, Sylvia, 242
My Mother, My Father and Me, 257
My One and Only, 367, 369, 370
My Sister Eileen, 141, 143, 204
Mystery of Edwin Drood, The, 379, 381

Nadzo, Guido, 132
Nagel, Conrad, 163, 171, 206
Naish, J. Carroll, 216
Napier, John, 164, 385–86, 401–2
Napolin, Leah, 330
Nash, N. Richard, 212
Nash, Ogden, 162
Nash, Richard, 262
Nathan, George Jean, 6, 36, 50, 62, 108–9, 130, 155, 158, 161, 163, 164, 168, 197, 216, 222, 229
Nathan the Wise, 150
Nation, The, 203, 209
National Anthem, The, 56
National Endowment for the Arts, 272
National Recovery Act, 112
National Theatre, 54, 157, 158, 182, 240, 302. *See also* Billy Rose Theatre
Native Son, 143, 144, 145, 258
Natwick, Mildred, 13, 14, 148, 174, 225, 262, 418
Naughton, James, 336, 353, 395, 397, 425–26
Naughty Marietta, 16
Nazimova, Alla, 6, 25, 121, 170
Neal, Patricia, 175–76, 202
Nederlander, David T., 286
Nederlander, James, 55, 163, 355
Nederlander Theater, 359, 392, 397–98, 400. *See also* Billy Rose Theatre
Nederlanders, 272, 362
Ned McCobb's Daughter, 81
Neeson, Liam, 411
Neff, Hildegarde, 213
Negro Ensemble Company, 281, 409–10
Neighborhood Playhouse, 26, 81
Neil Simon Theatre, 87, 328–29, 371–72, 380
Nelligan, Kate, 368, 392–93, 428
Nelson, Barry, 163, 182, 194, 249, 274, 325, 330, 341
Nelson, Gene, 305
Nelson, Kenneth, 242, 289
Nemiroff, Robert, 263
Nemitz, Leonora, 374
Nervous Wreck, The, 63
Nesbit, Evelyn, 13, 76
Nesbitt, Cathleen, 7, 17, 189, 217, 242, 318, 368
Nesbitt, Julie, 357
Nestor, Mitchell, 288
Nethersole, Olga, 10–11
Neuwirth, Bebe, 415, 425–26
Never Too Late, 259
Neville-Andrews, John, 313
New Amsterdam Theatre, 12, 91, 124, 125, 362, 372, 425, 428
New Century Theatre, 164
Newell, Michael, 179
New Faces of 1952, 200
New Faces of 1968, 289
New Faces, 111, 114, 221, 222, 360
New Girl in Town, 225, 227, 233
Newhouse, Mitzi, 311
Newley, Anthony, 258, 260, 270, 298
Newman, Julie, 318
Newman, Paul 201, 203–4, 213, 236, 280, 319, 388
Newman, Phyllis, 201, 241, 254, 320, 346, 384–85, 422
Newmar, Julie, 235
New Moon, 90
New School for Social Research, 164, 167
New Stages Theatre, 177
New Theatre, The, 15
Newton-John, Olivia, 309
New Victory Theatre, 421, 423
New York Drama Critics Award, 121, 129, 133, 138, 141, 147, 163, 169, 173, 177, 191, 197, 201, 205, 211, 215, 239, 221, 227, 233, 245, 251, 257, 261, 267, 271, 277, 285, 291, 297, 301, 307, 311, 317, 323, 327, 333, 339, 345, 349, 355, 359, 367, 375, 379, 383, 387, 391, 395, 399, 403, 409, 413, 417, 421, 425, 427
New York Idea, The, 335
New York League of Theatres, 292
New York Shakespeare Festival, 236, 240, 258

New York Theatre Critics Circle Awards, 187
New York Theatre League, The, 246
Next, 294, 297
Ney, Richard, 165
Ngema, Mbongeni, 389
Nice People, 52
Nichol, Alex, 222
Nicholas Brothers, 126
Nichols, Anne, 53, 56
Nichols, Barbara, 199
Nichols, Dudley, 87
Nichols, Lewis, 158
Nichols, Mike, 225, 228, 229, 258, 262, 266, 267, 278, 308, 318, 324, 340, 353, 356, 373, 376, 380, 381, 382, 392, 406
Nichols, Peter, 289, 377, 395–96
Nicholson, Jack, 380
Nicholson, Kenyon, 112
Nicholson, William, 400–1
Nick and Nora, 396, 403, 404, 405
Niesen, Gertrude, 164
Nigger, The, 15
'night, Mother, 367, 369–70, 371
Night and Day, 163
Night Hawk, The, 79
Night Life, 257
Night of the Iguana, 251, 253, 254, 389
Night They Raided Minsky's, The, 69
Nights at Folies Bergères, 139
Nillson, Carlotta, 13
Nine, 359, 363
Nixon, Cynthia, 376
Nixon, Marni, 218
No, No, Nanette, 64, 73, 74, 252, 301, 303–4, 318
Nobel Prize, 119, 120, 126
No Exit, 173, 175
No For an Answer, 144
No Hard Feelings, 313
Noises Off, 371, 372, 373, 377
Nolan, Doris, 158
Nolan, Lloyd, 110, 208
Nolen, Timothy, 377
Nolte, Nick, 383
Noonan, Tom, 346
No Place to Be Somebody, 295, 297, 300, 422
Nora Bayes Theatre, 62
Normal Heart, The, 375, 378, 381, 410
Norman Conquests, The, 330–31
Norman, Marsha, 178, 346, 367, 369–70, 392, 402
Norman, Monty, 246
Normand, Mabel, 324
Norris, Sarah, 425–26
North, Sheree, 255
Northeast Local, 423
Norton, Elliot, 12, 217, 222, 293, 368
Norworth, Jack, 14, 17
No Strings, 254, 260, 415
No Time for Comedy, 133, 136, 138
No Time for Sergeants, 216
Nouri, Michael, 422
Novak, Kim, 199
Ntshona, Winston, 323, 325
Nude With Violin, 229
Nugent, Elliott, 10, 56, 139, 161, 163, 356
Nugent, John Charles, 56
Nunn, Taylor, 355
Nunn, Trevor, 139, 298, 361, 381, 383, 385, 419, 423
Nunsense, 379, 381, 395
Nuyen, France, 234, 235
Nye, Carrie, 310
Nye, Louis, 188
Nype, Russell, 192

Oakland, Simon, 335–36
Obie Awards, 215
O'Brien, Edmond, 163, 178
O'Brien, Richard, 326
O'Brien-Moore, Erin, 91, 136
O'Casey, Sean, 7, 77, 87, 115, 116, 268
Ochs, Adolph, 74, 89, 90
O'Connell, Arthur, 200, 203–4
O'Connor, Carol, 234
O'Connor, John J., 300
O'Connor, Una, 17, 212–13
Octet Bridge Club, The, 377
Odd Couple, The, 263, 267, 270, 271, 273, 403, 414–15
O'Dea, Dennis, 174
Odets, Clifford, 112, 115, 118, 120, 124, 129, 130–31, 135, 139, 157, 192, 199–200, 262, 268, 303
O'Donnell, Rosie, 416
Odyssey, 323, 325, 328. *See also Home Sweet Homer*
Oedipus Rex, 172
Oesterman, Phil, 334
Of Mice and Men, 129, 131, 277
Of Thee I Sing, 113, 161
Off-Broadway Theatre League, 188
Oh, Kay!, 81, 399–401, 423
O'Hara, Jill, 293
O'Hara, John, 143
Oh! Calcutta!, 297, 298, 294, 302, 333–34, 339–40, 388
Oh Coward! 312–13
Oh Dad, Poor Dad, Mamma's Hung You in the Closet and I'm Feelin' So Sad, 254
Oh Man, Oh Women, 208, 212
O'Horgan, Tom, 76, 289, 292, 305, 308
Oklahoma!, 155, 156, 157, 158, 159, 161, 162, 165, 168, 170, 173, 174, 177, 179–80, 229, 260, 409–10, 414
Okrent, Michael, 405–6, 422–23
Oleanna, 410
Old Dutch, 15
Older People, 310
Oldest Living Graduate, The, 334
Old Globe Theatre, The, 377
Old Heidelberg, 12
Old Maid, The, 115, 117
Old Soak, The, 58
Old Town, The, 15
Oliver, Edna May, 60, 74, 87, 156
Oliver!, 259, 264
Olivier, Laurence, 14, 113, 136, 138, 141, 142, 172, 197, 199–200, 231, 246, 249, 262, 302–3, 318, 395–96
Olmos, Edward James, 348
Olsen, Ole, 8, 63, 133, 134, 149–50, 187, 190, 259
Olson, Nancy, 189, 229
Olympia Theatre, 9
O Mistress Mine, 171
On a Clear Day You Can See Forever, 252, 262, 271, 272
On Borrowed Time, 131, 132
Once on This Island, 400
Once Upon a Mattress, 237, 268, 415, 427
Ondine, 205, 208–9
O'Neal, Frederick, 230, 234, 268
O'Neal, Patrick, 254
One Flew Over the Cuckoo's Nest, 305
110 in the Shade, 212, 262
O'Neill, Eugene, 3, 7, 13, 14, 15, 16–17, 23, 24, 31, 32, 33, 35, 36, 37, 41, 42, 43, 45, 46, 50, 51, 53, 54, 55, 56, 63, 64, 65, 68, 69, 74, 76, 87, 91, 111, 113, 114, 118, 119, 120, 124, 126, 145, 147, 148, 162, 173, 174, 175, 176, 177, 180, 192, 205–6, 219, 221, 223, 234, 258, 259, 269, 286, 319–20, 325, 341, 391–92, 395, 411, 416
O'Neill, James, 7, 16–17, 41, 50
O'Neill, Oona, 162
One Mo' Time, 351
One Night Stand, 355
One Sunday Afternoon, 110
One Touch of Venus, 161, 162, 164, 166
On Golden Pond, 345, 347, 373
On the Town, 167, 204, 414
On the Twentieth Century, 109, 339, 342, 346, 350–51
On Your Toes, 367, 369, 375–76
Oppenheim, David, 179, 223
Orange Blossom, 58
Orbach, Jerry, 121, 216, 234, 239, 242, 248, 249, 286, 291, 293, 304, 307, 309–10, 312, 328–29, 342, 350, 356, 378
Orphans, 378
Orpheum Theatre, 7, 15, 62, 85

Orpheus Descending, 225, 228
Orten, Joe, 286, 288, 300
Osato, Sono, 170, 193
Osborn, Paul, 131, 167, 199, 234, 352–53
Osborne, John, 227, 228, 231, 236, 252, 260, 261, 262, 273, 417–18
Oscar Wilde, 134
O'Shea, Michael, 170
O'Shea, Milo, 289
Osterman, Lester, 269
Osterwald, Bibi, 195
Ostrow, Stuart, 298
O'Sullivan, Maureen, 259, 352–53
Othello, 3, 161, 162, 166, 193–94, 268, 362
Other People's Money, 393
Otherwise Engaged, 333, 335
Our American Cousin, 5
Our Country's Good, 399, 402
Our Town, 129, 131, 134, 170, 173, 394
Ouspenskaya, Maria, 114, 230
Out of the Frying Pan, 145
Out of this World, 192
Outward Bound, 135
Over Here, 320, 328
Over 21, 163
Owens, Rochelle, 292
Owl and the Pussycat, The, 269
Oy, Is Dus a Leben!, 156

Paar, Jack, 247
Pacific Overtures, 327, 330–31
Pacino, Al, 139, 288, 333, 336–37, 349–50, 359–60, 367, 368, 369, 373, 388, 406, 410, 426
Pacitti, Joanna, 428
Page, Anthony, 273
Page, Geraldine, 68, 197, 200, 204, 207–8, 212, 236, 258, 260, 262, 268, 280, 303, 311, 324, 357, 362–63, 368, 381, 387–88
Page, Ken, 343
Paige, Elaine, 358, 381, 409, 419, 425–26
Paige, Janis, 209
Paige, Shirley, 162
Painting Churches, 372
Paint Your Wagon, 199, 414
Pajama Game, The, 205, 208–9, 211–12, 264
Pajama Tops, 214
Palace Theatre, 18, 58, 87, 92
Palance, Jack, 193, 216
Pal Joey, 141, 143, 162, 197, 199, 207, 260
Palmer, Bee, 54, 287
Palmer, Leland, 288
Palmer, Lilli, 19, 157, 192–93, 200, 203, 381
Palmer, Peter, 223
Paltrow, Bruce, 299
Panama Hattie, 141, 142, 145, 158
Pankow, John, 394
Pantages, Alexander, 5, 121
Papas, Irene, 287
Paper Mill Playhouse, 351
Papp, Joseph, 54, 211, 212, 213, 221, 222, 234, 236, 273, 285, 286, 294, 300, 302, 304, 307–8, 309, 311, 312, 313, 314, 318, 321, 328, 331, 339–40, 346–47, 355, 357, 359, 361–62, 368, 373, 382, 383–84, 386, 387, 388, 389, 391, 393–94, 402, 403, 404, 405
Paradise Now, 293
Parado, Alan, 81
Pardon My English, 109, 110
Pardon Our French, 190
Parents and Children, 294
Paris, 92
Paris, Irene, 279
Paris Bound, 87
Parisian Romance, A, 13
Parker, Dorothy, 8, 61, 62, 133, 163
Parker, Mary-Louise, 397, 427
Parker, Sarah Jessica, 269, 333–34, 347, 352, 394, 405, 423, 427
Parks, Hildy, 217
Parks, Larry, 166
Parkway Theatre, 158
Parlor Match, The, 9
Parry, William, 356
Parsons, Estelle, 86, 281, 304, 330–31, 358, 361, 373, 407
Pasadena Playhouse, 302, 328, 381
Pascal, Adam, 423
Pascal, Milton, 164
Passing Show of 1912, 17
Passing Show of 1915, 26
Passing Show of 1921, 54
Passion, 413, 416
Passion of Dracula, The, 340
Pastor, Tony, 3, 6, 15
Patinkin, Mandy, 202, 335–36, 350–51, 356, *374*, 379–80, 393, 402, 406, 410
Patrick, John, 205, 207
Patriots, The, 87, 155, 158
Patterson, James, 259
Patti, Adelina, 183
Patti LuPone on Broadway, 422
Paul Robeson, 339, 341–42
Paulsen, Albert, 309
Paul Whiteman Orchestra, 63
Payne, Sandra, 324
Peace on Earth, 114
Peardon, Patricia, 149
Pearl, Jack, 109–10
Peck, Gregory, 178, 399
Peer Gynt, 193
Peg o' My Heart, 17, 19, 26
Pellow, Clifford, 280
Pemberton, Brock, 7, 170–71, 176, 178, 189
Pendleton, Austin, 139, 254, 268, 299, 335, 378, 419
Penn, Arthur, 230, 242, 246, 268, 274, 335
Penn, Leonard, 120
Penn, Sean, 357, 384
Penn & Teller, 377–78, 389
Pennington, Ann, 8, 18, 24, 40, 44, 54, 55, 60, 308
Peppard, George, 268, 278
Perelman, Sidney Joseph "S.J.", 12, 162
Perfect Fool, The, 55
Perfect Ganesh, A, 413, 414
Period of Adjustment, A, 246
Perkins, Anthony, 8, 109, 130, 208, 229, 242, 302, 318, 330–31, 351, 409–10
Perkins, Osgood, 8, 90, 109, 130, 131
Perl, Arnold, 204
Perry, Albert, 51
Perry, Antoinette, 7, 14, 15, 80, 121, 137, 140, 173, 174, 176
Perry, Margaret, 7, 121, 174
Persoff, Nehemiah, 193, 216
Personal Appearance, 116
Peter Pan, 13, 190, 192, 211, 212, 213, 214, 350–51, 356
Peters, Bernadette, 179, 289, 293, 324, *374*, 375, 377, 379, 389, 410, *425*
Peters, Brock, 395
Peters, Clarke, 406
Peters, Rollo, 60
Peters, Susan, 189–90
Peter Weston, 61
Petrified Forest, The, 115, 117
Peyser, Joan, 412
Pfeiffer, Michelle, 388, 413
Phantom of the Opera, The, 356, 387, 388, 389, 390, 391, 394, 395, 396, 397, 401, 403, 405–6, 417, 418, 419, 421, 425–26
Philadelphia, Here I Come, 271, 274
Philadelphia Stage Door Canteen, 156
Philadelphia Story, The, 133, 136
Philanthropist, The, 304
Philips, Lou Diamond, 424
Philips, Mary, 77, 88, 110, 116
Phillips, Margaret, 182
Phoenix Theatre, 221
Physicists, The, 268
Piaf, 358
Piano Lesson, The, 395, 398, 400
Piazza, Ben, 248, 259
Picardo, Robert, 337, 346
Pickford, Jack, 56, 58
Pickford, Mary, 14, 17, 51
Picnic, 201, 203–4
Picon, Molly, 10, 156, 253, 325, 379–80, 403
Pidgeon, Rebecca, 404, 410
Pidgeon, Walter, 150, 241
Pielmeier, John, 362–63
Pinafore, 359
Pinchot, Rosamond, 131

Pinero, Miguel, 317, 321
Pink Lady, The, 16
Pins and Needles, 129, 131
Pinter, Harold, 246, 252, 259, 277, 278, 280, 286, 292, 335, 349, 351–52, 356
Pinza, Ezio, 184–85, 187, 190, 208, 211–12, 223
Pi-Pa-Ki, 171
Pipe Dream, 217, 228
Pippin, 281, 311–12
Pirandello, Luigi, 5, 58, 124, 260
Pirate, The, 157, 163
Pirate of Penzance, The, 355, 358
Piscator, Erwin, 8, 137, 139, 167, 273
Piscopo, Joe, 416
Pitoniak, Anne, 369–70
Place Without Doors, A, 308–9
Plain and Fancy, 213
Plantation Revue, 76
Platt, Jean, 155, 158
Platt, Louise, 149
Playboy of the Western World, The, 17, 174
Playhouse Theatre, 164, 168
Play It Again, Sam, 294, 299
Playwrights Company, 62, 130, 133, 134, 139, 149, 236, 246
Plaza Suite, 289, 334, 414–15
Pleasance, Donald, 252, 292, 302, 419
Pleasure Man, 90
Pleasure of His Company, The, 234
Plenty, 367–68
Plough and the Stars, The, 87, 116
Plowright, Joan, 231, 245, 246
Plummer, Amanda, 223, 359, 362–63, 381
Plummer, Christopher, 205, 208, 213, 216, 217, 222, 223, 235, 241, 254, 272, 315, 317, 319, 359, 362, 387, 389, 425, 427
Plunkett, Maryann, 383
Plymouth Theatre, 124, 157, 183, 389
P.M., 165, 168
Point of No Return, 199
Poitier, Sidney, 236
Pollack, Sydney, 213
Pollen, Tracy, 406
Pollock, Channing, 6, 58, 76, 174–75
Pomerance, Bernard, 345, 348, 351
Poppy, 61, 62
Porgy and Bess, 119, 120, 149, 204, 334–35, 381
Porter, Cole, 8, 27, 28, 30, 86, 109, 116–17, 119, 120, 123, 124, 129, 130, 131, 133, 134, 135, 139, 142, 148, 158, 163, 164, 181, 183–84, 192, 204, 213, 221, 230, 240, 269, 288, 369, 371, 388–89
Porter, Don, 264
Porter, Elsie, 56
Portman, Eric, 222, 234, 236
Portuguese Gal, 120
Poster, Kim, 406, 414
Potash and Permutter, 18
Potter, Paul M., 9
Povah, Phyllis, 60, 125, 131
Povod, Reinaldo, 384
Powell, Dick, 208
Powell, Eleanor, 91
Powell, Jane, 317
Powell, William, 180
Power, Tyrone, 5, 59, 192, 203, 213, 234
Powers, Tom, 8, 63, 217
Practical Ritual to Exorcise Frustration After Five Days of Rain, A, 305
Pratt, David, 87
Praying Curve, 79
Prelude to a Kiss, 395, 397
Preminger, Otto, 135, 138, 149, 163
Prentiss, Paula, 330–31
Present Laughter, 426
Presley, Elvis, 228, 239, 361
Preston, Barry, 331
Preston, Robert, 227, 230, 270, 275, 277, 280, 323–24, 374, 385
Pretty Little Parlor, 164
Previn, André, 298
Price, Georgie, 58, 80, 116, 263
Price, Harold, 428
Price, Leontyne, 204
Price, Lonny, 363
Price, The, 289, 395
Price, Vincent, 16, 127, 149, 414
Prideaux, James, 357
Priestly, J.B., 131, 416
Prime of Miss Jean Brodie, The, 285, 288, 289
Primus, Barry, 254, 260
Prince, Faith, 403, 407, 415
Prince, Harold, 87, 209, 258, 260, 264, 274, 278, 299, 301, 305, 307, 313–14, 320–21, 324–25, 330–31, 341, 350–51, 361, 377–78, 380, 388, 412, 417–18,
Prince, William, 156, 176
Princess and the Pea, The, 236
Princess Theatre, 23, 26, 216
Prinz, Rosemary, 388
Prisoner of Second Avenue, The, 308
Private Ear, The, 262
Private Lives, 181–83, 191, 297, 323, 326, 359, 367, 370, 375
Privates on Parade, 395–96
Priver, John, 401
Prochnik, Bruce, 259
Proctor, Frederick F., 4
Prodigal Daughter, The, 8
Producers Theatre, 223
Producing Managers Association, 62
Professional Children's School, 57
Promises, Promises, 291, 293, 308
Proof Through the Night, 158
Prosky, Robert, 222, 309, 373
Proud Prince, The, 12
Provincetown Players, 31, 32, 37, 41, 62
Provincetown Playhouse, 63, 142
Provincetown Theatre, 82
Prude, Walter, 162
Prud'homme, Cameron, 225
Prunczik, Karen, 356–57, 368, 369, 370
Pryce, Jonathan, 399, 400, 401, 402
Pryor, Roger, 82
P.S. Your Cat Is Dead, 326
Public Eye, The, 262
Public Theatre, The. *See* Joseph Papp Public Theatre
Puck, Eva, 77
Pulaski, Jack, 136
Pulitizer Prize for Drama, 5, 35, 38, 40, 43, 49, 57, 60, 61, 64, 65, 67, 73, 79, 82, 85, 89, 51, 53, 55, 107, 111, 114, 121, 122, 129, 133, 137, 138, 139, 140, 141, 145, 169, 177, 181, 187, 197, 201, 205, 211, 215, 221, 227, 233, 239, 245, 251, 267, 277, 291, 297, 301, 307, 311, 323, 327, 333, 339, 345, 348, 349, 355, 359, 361, 367,371, 374, 375, 383, 387, 391, 395, 399, 406, 409, 413, 416, 417, 421–22, 424, 427
Pump Boys and Dinettes, 362
Punch and July Theatre, 25
Punch for Judy, A, 58
Purcell, Charles, 52, 75
Purge, 425
Purlie Victorious, 252, 258, 299
Purlie, 252, 297, 299
Putting It All Together, 411–12
Pygmalion, 19, 23, 25, 81, 171, 197, 199, 201–2, 213, 216, 217

Quadrille, 211
Quare Fellow, The, 235
Quartermaine's Terms, 369
Quayle, Anna, 258
Quayle, Anthony, 281, 303
Queen of the Stardust Ballroom, The, 346–47, 341–42
Queen's Husband, The, 90
Quinn, Aidan, 381
Quinn, Anthony, 227, 246, 249, 372
Quintero, José, 68, 147, 192, 200, 219, 223, 242, 245, 259, 260, 289, 311, 319, 392

Rabb, Ellis, 241, 242, 254, 264, 329–30, 340, 372
Rabe, David, 139, 273, 294, 305, 307–8, 310, 313–14, 318, 336, 346, 359, 362, 373, 375–76, 384, 392
Racing Demon, 423
Racket, The, 87

Radio City Music Hall, 109
Radner, Gilda, 311, 356
Rado, James, 290, 294
Radziwill, Lee, 358
Rae, Charlotte, 209, 219, 318–19
Raft, George, 67, 68
Ragni, Gerome, 278, 290, 294
Rain, 57, 59, 63, 71, 80, 166, 241
Rainmaker, The, 212, 262
Rains, Claude, 191, 193
Raisin, 236, 317–18
Raisin in the Sun, A, 233, 236
Raitt, John, 32, 161, 168, 208–9, 360
Ralph, Sheryl Lee, 361–62
Rambeau, Marjorie, 7, 32, 36, 302
Ramblers, The, 81
Ramsay, Remak, 310, 362, 369, 404–5
Ramsey, Kevin, 428
Rand, Sally, 111
Randall, Addison, 164
Randall, Bob, 312
Randall, Tony, 45, 164, 174, 212, 214, 273, 402, 403, 421, 423, 428
Randolph, Clemence, 59
Randolph, John, 193, 260, 384–85
Rape of the Belt, The, 248
Raphael, Lennox, 299
Rasche, David, 426
Rascoe, Burton, 162, 163
Rashad, Phylicia, 360
Rashomon, 235
Rathbone, Basil, 8, 63, 80, 82, 113, 117, 177, 178, 179, 286, 419
Rattigan, Terence, 16, 171, 177, 179, 222, 340
Rave, David, 327
Ravenal, Gaylord, 418
Ravenswood, 321
Rawlins, Lester, 231, 268
Ray, Kathryn, 80
Ray, Nicholas, 175
Raye, Martha, 142, 236, 302
Rea, Stephen, 410
Reagan, Ronald, 381
Reale, Robert, 393
Real Inspector Hound, The, 310
Real Thing, The, 371, 373
Reardon, Dennis J., 328
Red, Hot and Blue, 123, 124
Redd, Freddie, 240
Redford, Robert, 253, 262
Red Gloves, 182–83
Redgrave, Lynn, 157, 280, 325, 340, 412
Redgrave, Michael, 14, 216, 377
Redgrave, Vanessa, 124, 254, 401, 418
Redhead, 233, 235, 236
Redman, Joyce, 182–83
Red Mill, The, 13, 170
Red Petticoat, The, 17
Red Shoes, The, 188
Reed, Beryl, 278
Reed, Florence, 6, 77, 80, 90, 148, 287
Reed, Mark, 126
Reed, Rex, 289, 328–29, 342, 347–48, 355, 358
Rees, Roger, 359, 361
Reeve, Christopher, 292, 331, 355, 356, 357
Regan, Sylvia, 203
Rehan, Ada, 4, 5
Reid, Beryl, 277
Reid, Kate, 264, 289, 324, 373
Reilly, Charles Nelson, 242
Reiner, Carl, 174, 180, 260
Reinhardt, Gottfried, 157
Reinhardt, Max, 125, 163
Reinking, Ann, 188, 279, 312, 320, 328, 333, 335, 342, 349, 351, 426, 428
Reitell, Elizabeth, 148
Remarkable Mr. Pennypacker, The, 207–8
Remick, Lee, 265, 274, 361
Rennie, Michael, 249
Rent, 421, 423–24, 425, 426, 427
Repertory Theatre of Lincoln Center, 241, 269, 280, 293, 312
Repole, Charles, 330
Repp, Ray, 418–19
Resnik, Muriel, 264
Respectful Prostitute, The, 183–84
Return of Peter Grimm, The, 17
Return of the Catonsville Nine, The, 308
Return to the Forbidden Planet, 398, 404
Reuben, Paul, 17
Reunion in Vienna, 207
Revere, Ann, 117, 182, 242
Revill, Clive, 259
Revue of Revues, The, 16
Revuers, The, 138
Rex, 331
Reynolds, Debbie, 45, 211, 246, 314, 317, 324, 369
Rhinoceros, 245, 246, 247, 248, 249
Rhodes, Erik, 109, 228
Rhodes, Harrison, 15
Rhodes, Michael, 415
Ribeiro, Alfonso, 372–73
Ribman, Ronald, 275, 309
Rice, E.E., 7
Rice, Elmer, 8, 24, 60, 91, 110, 115, 117, 121, 130, 134, 144, 149, 171, 175–76, 198, 236, 279
Rice, Tim, 166, 308, 335–36, 349, 350, 351, 362, 390
Rich, Frank, 355, 356, 357, 358, 362–63, 367, 369, 372, 373, 374, 376, 377, 378, 379, 380, 381, 382, 384–85, 387, 388, 389, 390, 392, 394, 395, 396, 397, 398, 400, 404, 405, 406, 410–11, 413–14
Richard Rodgers Theatre, 397–98
Richard II, 125
Richard III, 205, 350, 360
Richards, David, 415, 419
Richards, Donald, 176
Richards, Lloyd, 236, 345, 347, 395, 398, 399–400, 406–7, 423–24
Richardson, Howard, 168
Richardson, Ian, 274, 358
Richardson, Natasha, 409, 411
Richardson, Ralph, 11, 224, 303, 372, 419
Richardson, Ron, 378, 419
Richardson, Tony, 254, 262, 263, 405
Richert, Wanda, 356–57
Richman, Arthur, 58
Richman, Harry, 70
Richmond, David, 340
Rickman, Alan, 386
Ride Down Mount Morgan, The, 404
Ridiculous Theatre Company, 422
Rifkin, Ron, 405
Rigg, Diana, 134, 301, 413, 415, 421
Riggs, Lynn, 156
Riggs, Sidney, 70
Riley, Lawrence, 116
Ring, Blanche, 5, 17, 246
Ring, Frances, 16
Rink, The, 371, 373–74
Rio Rita, 82
Rip Van Winkle, 5
Ritchard, Cyril, 10, 212, 213, 214, 225, 235, 270, 309, 320, 323–24, 336, 340–41
Ritt, Martin, 131, 144, 178
Rittenhouse, Florence, 63
Ritter, Thelma, 225, 227, 273
Ritz, The, 323, 325, 397
Riva, Maria, 208
Rivals, The, 8, 150
River Niger, The, 315, 317, 320
Rivera, Chita, 107, 109, 213, 218, 228, 242, 314, 320, 328, 371, 373, 379, 381, 401, 412, 418, 425
Road to Mecca, The, 387, 390
Road to Rome, The, 82
Roar of the Greasepaint-The Smell of the Crowd, The, 270
Robards, Jason, Jr., 58, 164, 177, 179, 215, 219, 223, 233, 235, 242, 252, 255, 264, 269, 292, 319, 320, 341, 361, 370, 392, 396, 423
Robards, Jason, Sr., 8, 235
Robber Bridegroom, The, 327, 329–30, 333
Robbin, Leo, 83
Robbins, Jerome, 167, 178, 180, 191, 201, 203–4, 223, 228, 254, 255, 292, 392, 397
Roberta, 113, 157
Roberts, Eric, 361
Roberts, Joan, 158

Roberts, Pernell, 287
Roberts, Rachel, 254
Roberts, Tony, 294, 299, 309, 324, 347, 378, 422, 427
Robertson, Cliff, 225, 396
Robertson, Liz, 360
Robeson, Paul, 10, 51, 52, 61, 63, 65, 82, 90, 156, 161, 162, 163, 166, 169, 188–89, 193–94, 328
Robeson, Paul, Jr., 412
Robin, Laila, 422
Robin, Leo, 188
Robinson, Bill "Bojangles", 6, 73, 88, 90, 144, 156, 163, 187–88
Robinson, Charles, 112
Robinson, Edward G., 60, 85, 87, 217
Robinson, Jay, 189
Robinson, Joseph S., 124–25
Robinson, Roger, 423–24
Rockefeller Foundation, 166
Rock Garden, The, 269
Rocky Horror Show, The, 326
Rodgers, Mary, 236, 237, 274, 427
Rodgers, Richard, 31, 38, 43, 46, 71, 11, 134, 148, 155, 159, 162, 169, 171, 174, 177, 178, 179, 181, *184*, 185, 187, 188, 189, 190, 194, 197, 199, 202, 204, 205, 208, 211, 213–14, 216, 235, 237, 239, 249, 252, 254, 260, 262, 263, 267, 270, 272, 303, 331, 345, 348, 349, 351–52, 369, 385, 395. *See also* Rodgers and Hammerstein; Rodgers and Hart
Rodgers and Hammerstein, 52, 155, 166, 168, 217, 221, 225, 228, 235, 239, 241, 267
Rodgers and Hart, 43, 44, 46, 67, 71, 123, 126, 130, 132, 135, 138, 143, 155, 156, 163
Roe, Patricia, 259
Roebling, Paul, 259
Rogers, David, 258
Rogers, Ginger, 16, 199, 231, 272, 302
Rogers, Paul, 277, 361
Rogers, Richard, 169
Rogers, Will, 13, 17, 31, 32, 35, 36, 39, 40, 43, 53, 54, 58, 61, 108, 119, 120
Rolf, Frederick, 389
Rolfe, Mary, 156
Rolle, Esther, 273
Rollo's Wild Oat, 51
Roly Poly, 17
Roman, Freddie, 403–4
Romanoff and Juliet, 227, 228, 229, 230
Romantic Comedy, A, 351
Romberg, Sigmund, 7, 19, 28, 30, 32, 35, 36, 54, 69, 88, 90, 168, 198
Rome, Harold, 14, 131, 172, 202, 212, 236, 254, 273, 414
Romeo and Juliet, 12, 57, 60, 62, 87, 113, 117, 151, 192, 228
Ronstadt, Linda, 358
Room of One's Own, A, 418
Room Service, 127
Rooney, Mickey, 349, 351
Rooney, Pat, 8, 185, 193
Roosevelt, Eleanor, 132, 149, 163
Rope Dancers, The, 229
Rosalie, 88
Rosalinda, 155, 157
Rose, Arthur, 384
Rose, Billy, 10, 68, 91, 119, 134, 139, 149, 166, 205, 208, 222, 253, 263, 273
Rose, Christine, 372
Rose, George, 272, 325, 327, 346, 350, 358, 381
Rose, Reva, 280
Rose Girl, The, 52
Rose Maid, The, 17
Rose Marie, 199
Rose-Marie, 68, 73
Rose of the Rancho, 13
Rose Tattoo, The, 191, 193, *194*
Rosen, Samuel, 117
Rosenblatt, Jay, 280
Rosencrantz and Guildenstern Are Dead, 285, 286
Ross, Anthony, 168
Ross, Diana, 325
Ross, Elizabeth, 208
Ross, Jamie, 312
Ross, Jerry, 208, 209, 211, 214, 215, 217, 415
Ross, Kathleen, 223
Ross, Stuart, 398
Ross, Ted, 325
Roth, Lillian, 16, 57, 62, 109, 141, 149, 255, 349, 351
Rothenberg, David, 286
Rothschilds, The, 301, 303
Rothstein, Arnold, 53, 68, 69, 89, 91
Round and Round the Garden, 330
Rounds, David, 310, 352
Rounseville, Robert, 273
Routledge, Patricia, 285
Rowlands, Gena, 217
Rowles, Polly, 216
Royal Family, The, 79, 187, 142, 174–75, 330, 350
Royal Hunt of the Sun, The, 272
Royale Theatre, 80
Royle, Edwin Milton, 13
Royle, Selena, 12, 114, 150
Rubinstein, John, 175, 308, 349, 312, 352, 396
Rubin-Vega, Daphne, 423
Rudd, Paul, 427
Rudge, Frances, 368
Rudman, Michael, 373
Rudnick, Paul, 411
Ruehl, Mercedes, 378, 393, 399, *401*
Rufus LeMarie's Affairs, 83
Rugged Path, The, 170–71
Ruggles, Charlie, 235
Rule, Janice, 203, 240, 253
Rumors, 392
Runaways, 342
Runnin' Wild, 61, 63
Runolfsson, Anne, 422
Runyon, Damon, 7, 54, 108, 175
Rupert, Michael, 407, 412, 422
R.U.R. (Rossum's Universal Robots), 57, 58
Russell, Jane, 188
Russell, Lillian, 4, 6, 58
Russell, Robert, 241
Russell, Rosalind, 17, 76, 201, 204, 222, 222, 237, 334
Russell, Willy, 393, 412
Russo, James, 369
Rutherford, Dr. Charles, 55
Ryan, Meg, 397
Ryan, Robert, 259
Ryder, Alfred, 234
Ryerson, Florence, 158
Ryskind, Morrie, 9, 76, 86, 109, 113, 140, 380

Sabinson, Harvey, 341
Sabrina Fair, 205, 207
Sabrina, 207
Sackler, Howard, 285, 291, 292, 293
Sackville-West, Vita, 418
Sadie, 165, 166
Sag Harbor, 11
Sager, Carol Bayer, 361
Sailor, Beware!, 112
Saint, Eva Marie, 207, 311
Saint Joan, 64, 121, 222, 340
Saint of Bleecker Street, The, 211, 213
Saint-Subber, Arnold, 213, 268, 414
Saks, Gene, 189
Salkeld, Celia, 246
Sally, 51, 54, 59, 350
Salmi, Albert, 214, 224
Salome, 406, 410
Salonga, Lea, 399, 401, 402
Salvation Nell, 15
Same Time, Next Year, 323, 326
Samson and Delilah, 51
Samuels, Arthur, 62
Sanborn, Marjorie, 179
Sanderson, Julia, 7, 17, 24, 325
Sands, Diana, 236, 265, 269, 292
Sands, Ralph, 159
Sandy, 400
San Juan, Olga, 199
Santiage-Hudson, Reuben, 407, 424
Sapho, 10–11
Sarafina, 389
Sarandon, Chris, 303, 404–5
Sarandon, Susan, 361, 367, 369
Saratoga, 5
Sarava, 345
Sardi, Vincent, Jr., 373
Sardi, Vincent, 298
Sardi's, 52, 53, 155, 216, 221, 227, 278

Sardou, 12
Sarnoff, Dorothy, 157
Saroyan, William, 15, 136, 137, 138, 140, 145, 147, 148, 357
Sartre, Jean-Paul, 173, 175, 181, 182, 183
Saturday Night, 80
Saturday's Children, 82
Savage, John, 335
Save Me the Waltz, 132
Savo, Jimmy, 9, 135, 174, 246
Saxon, Don, 175–76
Saxon, Luther, 163
Say Darling, 231
Sayonara, 355
Scandals, 79, 122, 174
Scandals of 1924, 67, 68
Scapino, 317, 321, 324
Scarsi, Nick, 87
Schaffer, Anthony, 303
Schanker, Louis, 246
Schary, Dore, 227, 231, 273
Scheider, Roy, 275, 280, 351, 388
Schenck, Joe, 8
Schenkkan, Robert, 403, 406, 414
Schildkraut, Joseph, 9, 52, 56, 59, 68, 138, 150, 193, 216, 263
Schildkraut, Rudolf, 59, 62, 138
Schisgal, Murray, 80, 260, 268, 293, 325
Schmidt, Harvey, 242, 262, 280, 394
Schneider, Alan, 137, 165, 166, 195, 207–8, 213, 231, 246, 248, 252, 259, 280, 286, 304, 330, 347, 373
Schoenfeld, Gerald, 311–12, 318–19, 345, 347–48, 379, 381, 423, 426
Schonberg, Claude-Michel, 383, 385, 401–2
School for Scandal, 6, 254, 312
School for Wives, 301
Schrader, Paul, 372
Schreuer, Carl, 163
Schroeder, Mildred, 125, 139
Schubert, J.J., 56
Schulberg, Budd, 235, 268
Schulman, Susan, 402
Schultz, Charles, 280
Schultz, David, 341
Schultz, Mary, 418–19
Schumacher, Joel, 406
Schuman, William, 269
Schumlin, Herman, 188
Schwartz, Arthur, 11, 92, 180, 195, 206, 212, 262, 372, 376
Schwartz, Maurice, 108, 241, 379–80
Schwartz, Risa, 241
Schwartz, Stephen, 305, 312, 321, 384,
Schwartz, Steven, 281
Scofield, Paul, 55, 251, 253
Scorsese, Martin, 340–41
Scot, Pat, 228
Scott, Bruce, 292
Scott, George C., 183–84, 230, 233, 253, 258, 259, 272, 286, 287, 289, 307–8, 312, 318, 327, 328, 335, 421, 423, 86
Scott, Martha, 132, 405
Scott, Mary, 212
Screens, The, 307, 309
Scuba Duba, 286
Seagull, The, 132, 421
Seal, Elizabeth, 245, 246, 335
Search for Intelligent Life in the Universe, The, 379
Searching Wind, The, 161, 164
Sears, Joe, 360–61, 368, 419
Seascape, 323, 325, 341
Season in the Sun, 192
Second Man, The, 83
Second Threshold, 193
Secret Garden, The, 402
Secret Rapture, The, 396
See America First, 241
Seeley, Blossom, 8, 17, 31, 32, 33, 41, 50, 55, 62, 121, 123, 319
Seely, Hart, 416
Seesaw, 314
Segal, George, 253, 259, 266
Segal, Vivienne, 9, 28, 38, 82, 88, 132, 143, 199, 410
Selby, David, 308
Seldes, Marian, 90, 178–79, 216, 278, 324, 339, 340, 341, 342, 372, 400, 415
Sellars, Peter, 367, 369, 376
Selnick, Irene Mayer, 177–78
Selwyn, Arch, 6, 116, 163, 240
Selwyn, Edgar, 5, 6, 25, 50, 68, 163
Selwyn, Rae 24
Selznick, Irene Mayer, 400–1
Semple, Ellen, 58
Sennett, Mack, 113, 178, 324
Sense of Humor, A, 373
Sentinel, the, 59
Separate Rooms, 139
Separate Tables, 221, 222
Serban, Andre, 162, 335
Serena Blandish, 92
Serious Money, 389
Serjeant Musgrave's Dance, 275
Servoss, Mary, 91
Seven Days, 15
Seven Descents of Myrtle, The, 289, 292
Seven Guitars, 421, 423–24
Seven Keys to Baldpate, 18
1776, 291, 294, 298, 299
Seventh Heaven, 58, 63
70 Girls, 70, 303
Seven Year Itch, The, 201–2
Sex, 77, 79, 83
Sex, Drugs, Rock & Roll, 397
Sexual Perversity in Chicago, 327, 329, 334
Seymour, Jane, 110, 170, 292, 356–57
Shadow and Substance, 129, 131
Shadow Box, The, 333, 340, 347
Shadowlands, 399–401
Shadow of the Glen, 164
Shaffer, Anthony, 301
Shaffer, Peter, 76, 239, 241, 262, 272, 280, 323–24, 355–57, 397
Shakespeare for My Father, 412
Shalhoub, Tony, 406
Shame Woman, The, 63
Shange, Ntozake, 334
Shanghai Gesture, The, 77, 80
Shangri-La, 221, 222
Shannon, Effie, 5, 51, 212
Shapiro, Dan, 164
Shapiro, Mel, 308–9
Sharpe, Albert, 176
Shatner, William, 222, 234, 253
Shaw, George Bernard, 4, 8, 23, 24, 25, 26, 27, 36, 51, 12, 13, 19, 53, 56, 58, 64, 70, 132, 177, 192, 198–99, 206, 216, 222, 328
Shaw, Irwin, 180
Shaw, Mark, 241
Shaw, Martin, 424
Shaw, Maxwell, 246
Shaw, Oscar, 7, 69, 81, 279
Shaw, Robert, 252, 268, 292
Shawhan, April, 300
Shawn, Dick, 302
Shawn, Michael, 397
Shean, Al, 5, 17, 54, 58, 188
Shear, Claudia, 413–14, *415*
Shearer, Moira, 188
Shearman, Alan, 313
Shechter, David, 377
She Done Him Wrong, 88
Sheed, Wilfred, 288
Sheen, Martin, 142, 265, 381, 405–6
Sheldon, Edward, 7, 13, 15, 77, 172
Shelley, Carole, 324, 330–31, 345, 348, 420
She Loves Me, 260, 413
She Loves Me Not, 113
Shelton, Reid, 202, 218, 318, 336
Shenandoah, 7, 323, 325
Shepard, Sam, 163, 261, 269, 272, 297, 298, 299, 300, 345–46, 348, 355, 357, 359, 368, 370, 379–81, 383, 405, 424
Sher, Antony, 427
Shepley, Ruth, 24, 44
Sherlock Holmes, 10, 325
Sherman, Martin, 351
Sherman, Richard, 320
Sherman, Robert, 320
Sherrin, Ned, 336
Sherwood, Madeleine, 203, 214
Sherwood, Robert E., 9, 58, 82, 90, 116, 117, 120, 130, 133, 134, 137, 139, 140, 141, 142, 144, 145, 149, 166, 170–71, 174, 188, 207, 217, 395, 416
Shevelove, Burt, 255

Shields, Brooke, 416
Shimada, 407
Shiner, David, 411
Shirley MacLaine on Broadway, 373
Shirley Valentine, 391, 393
Shoe String Revue, 213
Shogun, 399–400
Shor, Toots, 333
Shore, Dinah, 191
Shore, Meira, 302
Short, Hassard, 6, 222
Short Eyes, 317, 321
Shot in the Dark, A, 253
Show, 254
Show Boat, 35, 38, 82, 85, 86, 87, 88, 89, 90, 108, 116, 169, 171, 370, 385, 391, 409, 412, 417–18
Showcard, 280
Show-Off, The, 64, 65
Show Time, 156
Shrike, The, 197, 199
Shriner, Herb, 180
Shubert, Franz, 54–55
Shubert, J.J., 6, 11, 23, 25, 31, 33, 39, 41, 42, 54, 168, 170, 179, 208, 217, 222, 262, 287, 311–12
Shubert, John, 258
Shubert, Lawrence, 167
Shubert, Lee, 5, 11, 15, 59, 79, 138, 150, 158, 167, 169, 170, 174, 179, 205–6, 208, 222, 287, 311–12
Shubert, Sam, 5, 11, 12
Shubert Alley, 187
Shubert Theatres, 18, 131, 156, 162, 166, 168, 183, 235, 392
Shuberts, the, 11, 12–13, 17, 18, 26, 27, 29, 35, 36, 38, 44, 47, 49, 50, 53, 54, 55, 58, 60, 61, 62, 109, 134, 135, 137, 138, 139, 156, 217, 222, 223, 228, 234, 287, 404. *See also under separate names*
Shue, Larry, 376
Shuffle Along, 51, 54
Shulberg, Budd, 270
Shuman, Mort, 288
Shumlin, Herman, 10, 135, 178, 216, 264, 350
Shurtleff, Michael, 248
Side by Side, 336
Sidewinder, 299
Sidney, Sylvia, 134, 260
Siegel, Al, 54
Silk Stockings, 213, 222
Sillman, Leonard, 14, 114, 143–44, 197, 200, 221, 222, 289, 360
Sills, Stephanie, 279
Silva, Henry, 217
Silver, Joe, 237, 273, 281, 305
Silver, Nicky, 422
Silver, Ron, 174, 382, 387, 390, 399, 401, 404, 427
Silver, Steve, 324
Silver Cord, The, 82
Silvera, Frank, 217
Silverman, Sid, 189
Silverman, Sime, 5, 17, 112, 189–90
Silvers, Phil, 16, 178, 197–99, 248, 255, 307, 309, 311–12, 380
Simmons, Georgia, 168
Simms, Hilda, 166
Simon, Danny, 222
Simon, John, 69, 211, 286, 294, 298, 301–3, 307, 309, 317–18, 327, 330, 339–41, 359–60, 375, 377, 379, 391, 393–94, 403, 405, 410–12
Simon, Lucy, 402
Simon, Neil, 86, 221, 222, 245, 248, 259, 262, 270, 271, 274, 289, 297, 299, 301, 303, 307–9, 311, 313, 317–19, 318, 323–25, 334, 345, 347, 352–53, 367, 369, 371–72, 375, 377, 383–85, 392, 395, 397–98, 399, 401, 403, 406, 414, 417–20
Simonson, Lee, 7, 279
Sinatra, Frank, 199
Sinclair, Arthur, 17, 87, 116
Sinclair, Mary, 172, 198
Sinese, Gary, 334, 357, 368, 374, 378, 384, 397, 424
Singer, Carole Bayer, 347
Singer, Isaac Bashevis, 330
Singin' in the Rain, 380
Sissle, Noble, 52, 54, 346
Sister Mary Ignatius Explains It All to You, 361, 367, 369
Sister Mary Ignatius, 375
Sisters Rosensweig, The, 409–10
Sitcom, 331
Six Characters in Search of an Author, 58, 260
Six-Cylinder Love, 54
Six Degrees of Separation, 399–400
1600 Pennsylvania Avenue, 331
6 Rms Riv Vu, 312
Sizwe Banzi Is Dead 323, 325
Skinner, Cornelia Otis, 11, 148, 149, 164, 174, 222, 234, 349–50
Skinner, Otis, 4, 5, 9, 17, 149
Skin of Our Teeth, The, 155, 157, 159, 173
Skipworth, Alison, 63
Skriker, The, 424
Skulnick, Menasha, 10, 203, 273, 302
Skydrift, 171
Skylight, 425–26
Skyscraper, 171
Slade, Bernard, 326, 351, 346
Slave, The, 269
Slavs, 418–19
Sleeping Beauty Or Coma, 380
Sleep of Prisoners, A, 199
Sleuth, 301, 303, 345
Slezak, Walter, 109, 145, 157, 211–12
Slow Dance on the Killing Ground, 300
Slusker, Peter, 380
Sly Fox, 335
Small Craft Warnings, 309, 312
Smalls, Charlie, 323, 325
Smarty, 87
Smiley, Brenda, 279
Smith, Al, 81
Smith, Alexis, 305, 307, 311, 314
Smith, Anna Deveare, 407, 415–16
Smith, Ben 91
Smith, C. Aubrey, 5, 81, 182
Smith, Chase, 189
Smith, Craig, 369
Smith, Edgar, 4, 132
Smith, Harry B., 4, 25, 14, 121
Smith, Joe, 7, 357
Smith, Harry B. 25
Smith, Kate, 40, 76, 79, 80
Smith, Kent, 190
Smith, Liz, 369, 377
Smith, Lois, 424
Smith, Loring, 217
Smith, Maggie, 221, 222, 323, 326, 392, 395, 397–98
Smith, Michael, 269
Smith, Muriel, 163
Smith, Oliver, 37, 414
Smith, Philip J., 426–27
Smith, Queenie, 11, 44, 346
Smith, William J., 142, 148
Smith, Winchell, 15, 28, 32, 40, 41, 55
Smokey Joe's Cafe, 419
Smothers Brothers, 336
Snow Ball, The, 400–401
Snyder, Martin "Moe the Gimp", 58, 131, 134, 135
Snyder, Tom, 273
Snyder, William, 258
Soboloff, Arnold, 351
Social Security, 381–82
Society of Stage Directors and Choreographers, 274, 278, 279
So I Hear a Waltz?, 202
Sokol, Marilyn, 406
Sokoloff, Vladimir, 183
Sokolsky, George, 156
Soldier's Play, A, 359, 361
Solid Gold Cadillac, The, 207
Solitaire, 149
Somebody Loves Me, 55
Someone's Comin' Hungry, 294
Someone Who'll Watch Over Me, 409, 410
Something For the Boys, 158, 162
Something More, 233
Sommer, Josef, 382, 423
Sondheim, Stephen, 116, 202, 203, 205, 207, 215, 223, 227, 228, 237, 239, 254, 255, 257, 261, 265, 267, 270, 271, 274, 292, 297, 299, 301, 305, 311, 313–14, 327, 330–31, 336, 345–48, 361, 368, 371, 374, 375–76, 387, 389, 395–96,

400–401, 403, 407, 411–12, 413, 416, 422, 424,
Song and Dance, 379
Song at Twilight, A, 320
Song of the Lusitanian Bogey, 287
Song Revue, 15
Songs of Norway, 166
Song Writer, The, 75
Sons O' Fun, 149
Sophisticated Ladies, 358, 367, 369, 399
Sorkin, Aaron, 396
Sorvino, Paul, 310
Sothart, Herbert, 68
Sothern, Ann, 197
Sothern, E.H., 4, 11, 12, 15, 112
Sothern, Georgia, 156
Sound of Hunting, A, 179
Sound of Music, The, 239, 241, 242, 246, 252, 260, 414–15
South Pacific, 172, 181, 184–85, 187–88, 190, 194–95, 197–98, 205, 207
Southerners, The, 12
Sovern, Michael, 426–27
Sovey, Raymond, 113
Soyinka, Wole, 287
Spacey, Kevin, 401
Speed of Darkness, The, 401
Speed-the-Plow, 387, 390, 391, 392
Spencer, John, 138, 139
Spewack, Bella, 10, 164, 183, 396
Spewack, Sam, 10, 164, 183, 308, 396
Spice of 1922, 58
Spier, William, 179
Spigelgass, Leonard, 236
Spinella, Stephen, 412, 413–14, 418
Spitting Image, 293
Spring in Brazil, 170
Spring Thaw, 132
Springtime for Henry, 138
Squall, The, 79, 81
Squaw Man, The, 13
Squire, Katherine, 109, 419
Stadlen, Lewis J., 320–21
Stage Door, 124
Stage Door Canteen, 147, 150, 169, 171
Stage Relief Fund, 112
Stag Movie, 303
Staircase, 289
Stalag 17, 191, 195, 198
Stallings, Laurence, 8, 68, 287
Stander, Lionel, 199, 207
Stanislavsky, Constantin, 57, 60
Stanley, 427
Stanley, Kim, 68, 164, 203, 204, 212, 214, 217, 223 , 234, 236, 249, 264, 268
Stanwyck, Barbara, 68, 87, 90, 92, 253
Stapleton, Jean, 59, 214, 248, 265
Stapleton, Maureen, 74, 173, 174, 184, 188, 191, 193, 204, 225, 242, 289, 301, 303, 355, 358, 361
Star and Garter, 156, 157
Star-Cross Story, The, 208
Stardust Ballroom, 346
Stark, Ray, 262, 264, 272
Starkwether, David, 305
Starlight Express, 383, 385–86
Star Maker, The, 170–71
Starr, Frances, 7, 13, 15, 318
Star Wagon, The, 130
State Fair, 423–24
State of the Union, 169, 171
Stavis, Barrie, 179
St. Denis, Ruth 27, 29, 41
Steambath, 301–2
Steele, Tommy, 270
Steel Magnolias, 387–88, 397
Steel Pier, 428
Steiger, Rod, 137, 159, 204, 281
Stein, Gertrude, 114
Stein, Joseph, 241, 260
Steinbeck, John, 129, 131, 277
Steiner, Rick, 393
Steppenwolf Company, 333–34
Sterling, Richard, 65
Sterner, Jerry, 393
Sternhagen, Frances, 211, 213, 217, 242, 317, 319, 324, 345, 347, 414, 419
Stevens, David, 400
Stevens, Fisher, 414–15
Stevens, Leslie, 235
Stevens, Onslow, 223
Stevens, Roger L., 15, 223, 293, 325, 351–52, 376
Stevens, Ruby, 68, 85
Stevens, Warren, 184
Stevenson, Isabelle, 356
Stevenson, Richard, 63
Stewart, Ellen, 187, 190, 252, 258, 279, 335, 380, 383, 409
Stewart, Fred, 203
Stewart, James, 167, 178, 325
Stewart, Johnny, 189
Stewart, Michael, 336, 353
Stewart, Patrick, 142, 304, 405, 423
St. Helena, 124
Stickney, Dorothy, 11, 86, 89, 90, 139, 165, 166, 180, 200, 225, 351
Sticks and Bones, 294, 307–8, 310, 313–14
Stigwood, Robert, 308, 413
Stiller, Ben, 381
Stiller, Jerry, 86, 209, 212, 216, 224, 325, 376, 393
St. Jacques, Raymond, 249
St. James Theatre, 81, 157, 158, 161, 168
St. Louis Woman, 171, 172
Stockwell, Dean, 228
Stoker, Bram, 86
Stokes, Leslie and Sewell, 134
Stoller, Mike, 419
Stomp, 415
Stone, Carol, 168
Stone, Elly, 288
Stone, Ezra, 132, 156, 158
Stone, Fred, 5, 11, 13, 15, 19, 25, 37, 46, 50, 51, 90, 235
Stone, Lewis, 19
Stone, Peter, 294, 303, 391
Stone for Danny Fisher, A, 212
Stop! Look! Listen!, 27, 29
Stoppard, Mary, 400
Stoppard, Tom, 130, 285, 286, 310, 317, 321, 327, 330, 371, 373, 400, 417, 419
Stop the World-I Want to Get Off, 258, 260
Storch, Larry, 219
Storey, David, 301, 303, 311, 314, 317–18
Storm Operation, 166
Stoska, Polyna, 175–76
Stothart, Herbert, 45, 51, 60, 63
Stowe, Harriet Beecher, 158
Straight, Beatrice, 40, 203, 204
Strange, Michael, 52
Strange Fruit, 171
Strange Interlude, 85, 87, 88, 109, 125–26, 260, 359, 392
Strasberg, Anna, 352–53, 378
Strasberg, Lee, 11, 71, 88, 112, 113, 124–25, 139, 187, 193, 229, 258, 268, 270, 359–61
Strasberg, Susan, 216, 265
Stratas, Teresa, 384, 391
Strauss, Robert, 195
Straw Hat Revue, The, 138
Streamers, 327
Streep, Meryl, 335, 350–51, 406, 411
Streetcar Named Desire, A, 116, 177–80, 182, 188, 198–99, 240, 241, 339, 400, 403, 406
Street Scene, 89, 91, 175–76
Streets of Paris, The, 138
Streisand, Barbra, 149, 242, 248, 251, 252, 253, 255, 258, 260, 262, 263, 264, 265, 270, 272, 281, 298, 404–5, 409, 414
Strickland, Gail, 423
Strike Up the Board, 86
Strindberg, August, 17, 279, 423
Strip for Action, 157
Stritch, Elaine, 68, 137, 192, 199, 214, 300, 393, 418, 424
Stritch, Kim, 164
Stroman, Guy, 398
Stroman, Susan, 405–6, 422–23
Strong, Austin, 17, 41, 58
Strong Breed, The, 287
Strouse, Charles, 90, 213, 242, 245, 268, 275, 297, 299, 333, 336, 384, 396, 404–5
Strudwick, Shepperd, 14, 110, 281
Strunsky, Leonore, 80
Student Prince, The, 69

Studio Theatre, 142–43
Study in Color, 268
Stuyvesant Theatre, 14, 16
Styne, Jule, 13, 178, 188, 197, 212, 223, 231, 237, 248, 253, 258, 261, 264, 266, 269, 285, 309, 320, 355, 418
Subject Was Roses, The, 261, 265, 267
Sublett, John. *See* Bubbles, John W.; Buck and Bubbles
Substance of Fire, The, 405
Subways Are for Sleeping, 233, 253, 251
Sugar, 308–9, 324
Sugar Babies, 349, 351
Sullavan, Margaret, 124, 161, 163, 205, 207
Sullivan, Brian, 175–76
Sullivan, Dan, 352
Sullivan, Ed, 11, 107, 108, 180, 197, 199, 204, 216, 323–24
Sullivan, Francis L., 212–13
Sullivan, Jo, 209, 219, 235
Sullivan, Lee, 176
Sultan of Sulu, 11
Sumac, Yma, 195
Summer and Smoke, 182, 200
Summertime, 202
Sum of Us, The, 400
Sun, 164, 168
Sun-Up, 60
Sunday, 12, 73, 75, 240
Sunday in New York, 253
Sunday in the Park with George, 371, 375, 377, 379
Sunrise at Campobello, 227, 230, 231
Sunset Boulevard, 409–12, 413–14, 416, 417–20, 421–23, 425–26, 428
Sunshine Boys, The, 311, 313, 324–25
Sunshine Girl, The, 17
Susan and God, 129, 130, 131, 163
Susskind, David, 257
Sutherland, Donald, 358
Suzman, Janet, 298
Suzuki, Pat, 235, 241
Swados, Elizabeth, 342, 377, 383, 406
Swan, The, 63, 212
Swann, Donald, 240
Swanson, Gloria, 195, 411
Sweeney Todd, 67, 341, 345, 347–48, 349, 393
Sweet Bird of Youth, 233, 236, 327
Sweet Charity, 271, 272, 274, 382, 384, 388
Sweet Eros, 293, 298, 319
Sweethearts, 18
Sweet Nell of Old Drury, 60
Swenson, Inga, 222, 262
Swerling, Jo, 192
Swimming to Cambodia, 384
Swingin' the Dream, 139
Swords, 54
Sydney, Basil, 58, 76
Sydney, Sylvia, 376

Tabbert, William, 184–85
Taber, Richard, 70
Table Manners, 330
Table Settings, 351–52
Tabori, George, 212
Tabori, Kristoffer, 384
Take a Giant Step, 207
Take Her, She's Mine, 253, 254
Take Me Along, 113, 239, 240, 241
Taking of Miss Janie, The, 323, 326
Taliaferro, Edith, 8, 229
Taliaferro, Mabel, 8
Talk Radio, 386
Talley's Folly, 342–43, 348, 349, 352
Tallman, 358
Talluh, 371
Talmadge, Norma, 111, 113
Tamara, 113, 134, 389
Taming of the Shrew, The, 120, 183, 189, 222
Tandy, Jessica, 15, 131, 135, 155, 156, 179–80, 187–88, 197, 198, 208, 241, 249, 260, 262, 268, 272, 278, 313, 320, 334, 339–40, 351, 367, 369, 386, 417–18
Tanguay, Eva, 6, 25, 45, 81, 15, 176
Tap Dance Kid, The, 371–73, 399
Tarkington, Booth, 5, 14, 38, 44, 172
Tarnish, 63
Taste of Honey, A, 245, 246
Taubman, Howard, 246, 248, 249, 250, 251, 252, 258, 259, 260, 262, 264, 265, 273
Taylor, C.P., 373
Taylor, Don, 163
Taylor, Elaine, 223
Taylor, Elizabeth, 223, 259, 262, 263, 265, 349, 355, 358, 367, 370, 372, 375
Taylor, Gwen, 369
Taylor, Laurette, 7, 12, 17, 19, 26, 33, 43, 46, 56, 60, 63, 79, 82, 91, 110, 116, 118, 135, 165, 167, 168, 170, 175, 248
Taylor, Rachel, 269
Taylor, Renée, 292
Taylor, Samuel, 207, 234
Tea and Sympathy, 205–6, 208, 211, 212
Teahouse of the August Moon, 205, 206, 207
Tearle, Conway, 45, 108
Teasdale, Veree, 13, 81, 384
Tebet, David, 198
Teek, Angela, 400
Teel, Owen, 427–28
Teichmann, Howard, 207
Telephone and the Medium, The, 176
Tell Me More, 67
Teller, Ray, 389
Tempest, The, 421, 423
Templeton, Fay, 5, 10, 13, 74, 113, 138
Ten Best Plays, 67
Tenderloin, 246
Ten Little Indians, 165, 166
Tenny, Jon, 419
Tenth Man, The, 241, 246
Terris, Norma, 87
Terry, Ellen, 3, 7, 90
Terry, Ethelind, 82
Terry, Megan, 278
Terry, Sonny, 214
Tesich, Steve, 309, 356, 401
Tesori, Jean, 425
Tevye's Daughters, 188–89
Thank You, 55
That Championship Season, 307, 310, 311
Thaw, Harry K., 13
Theatre Arts, 62, 180, 218, 249
Theatre De Lys, 202. *See also* Lucille Lortel Theatre
Theatre Development Fund (TDF), 287, 428
Theatre '47, 166, 177–78, 216
Theatre Guild, 39, 42, 49, 51, 55, 56, 57, 58, 71, 73, 74, 81, 108, 113, 122, 124, 125, 127, 129, 140, 141, 144, 145, 150, 156, 159, 161, 162
Theatre Hall of Fame, 311–12
Theatre League, The, 422
Theatre Syndicate, 9, 10, 11, 18
Theatre Union, 113–14
The Good Doctor, 318–19
The Island, 323, 325
The Late George Apley, 167
Then There Were None, 166
There Shall Be No Night, 139, 140, 141, 145, 149
They, Too Arise, 125
They Knew What They Wanted, 67, 68, 69, 74, 219, 359
They're Playing Our Song, 345, 347, 359
Thieves, 80
Thieves Carnival, 213, 217
Thigpen, Lynn, 428
Thin Man, The, 396, 404–5
This Is The Army, 155, 156, 157, 161
This Was Burlesque, 254?
Thom, Robert, 228
Thomas, A. E. 33
Thomas, Augustus, 14, 38, 116
Thomas, Dylan, 249
Thomas, Marlo, 382
Thomas, Richard, 231
Thompson, Ernest, 347, 373
Thompson, Lynn M., 426–27
Thompson, Sada, 249, 299, 307–8
Thomson, Virgil, 114, 124
Thousand Clowns, A, 255, 405
Three Little Businessmen, 62
Three Men on a Horse, 118, 124
Three Musketeers, The, 88
Three of Us, The, 13
Three Sisters, The, 80, 157, 159, 264, 268
Three Stooges, 138

Three Tall Women, 413, 415–16
Three's a Family, 159
Threepenny Opera, The, 110, 205, 208–9, 216, 217, 234, 331, 335
Thurber, James, 137, 139
Thwarp, Twyla, 380
Tierney, Harry, 7, 64, 82, 269
Tierney-Joseph, 64
Tiger at the Gates, 215, 216
Tiger, The, 260
Till the Day I Die, 118
Time and the Conways, 131
Time of the Cuckoo, 201–4
Time of Your Life, The, 137, 138, 140, 148, 172
Time Remembered, 227, 229
Times Square, 8, 9, 12, 165, 167
Times Square Theatre, 76, 80, 90
Times Syndicate, 12–13
Tinney, Frank, 6, 18, 65, 68, 142
Tiny Alice, 267, 269, 270, 273, 274, 288, 328
Tip Top, 46, 51
'Tis Pity She's a Whore, 235, 286
Titanic, 425, 428
Tobacco Road, 111, 114, 115, 126, 136, 138, 141, 143, 145, 187, 253, 257
To Be Young, Gifted and Black, 293
Tobias, George, 68, 125
Todd, Mike, 14, 155, 156, 163, 170–71, 178, 180, 182, 188, 192, 223, 227, 229, 409
Together With Music, 217
Toibin, Niall, 299
Toilet, The, 269, 272
Tolstoy, Alexei, 60
Tom and Viv, 376
Tomashevsky, Boris, 5, 62, 135, 138, 379–80
Tomashevsky's Broadway Theatre, 62
Tomei, Concetta, 358
Tomei, Marisa, 418–19
Tomlin, Lily, 336, 379
Tomorrow the World, 155, 159, 162
Tone, Franchot, 13, 92, 139, 208, 258, 260, 292
Tonight at 8:30, 126, 142
Tony Award, 7, 173, 177, 187, 191, 197, 201, 205, 211, 215, 221, 227, 233, 239, 245, 246, 247, 257, 267, 271, 274, 277, 280, 285, 291, 294, 301, 307, 311, 317, 327, 333, 339, 349, 355, 359, 367, 375, 379, 383, 387, 395, 399, 403, 409, 413, 417, 421, 425
Tony n' Tina's Wedding, 387, 389–90, 391–92, 395, 417
Too Many Girls, 138
Top Banana, 197–99
Top Girls, 369
Topsy and Eva, 68, 70
Torch Song Trilogy, 341–42, 359, 362, 367–68, 370, 371–72
Torn, Rip, 222, 236, 258, 259, 262, 265, 278, 286, 302–3, 357, 368, 411, 427
Tortilla Flat, 131
Toscanini, Arturo, 115
To See Ourselves, 118
To the Ladies, 56
Touch and Go, 188
Touch of the Poet, A, 234, 236, 341
Tovarich, 200, 257
Townsend, Jill, 308
Townshend, Pete, 412
Toys in the Attic, 239, 242
Tracers, 376
Tracy, Lee, 10, 65, 80, 90, 242, 292
Tracy, Spencer, 157, 170–71, 358
Trafalgar Theatre. *See* Billy Rose Theatre; Nederlander Theatre
Transfiguration of Benno Blimpie, The, 335
Traube, Shepard, 278
Traubel, Helen, 217
Traveling Lady, The, 212
Traveling Salesman, The, 14
Travers, Henry, 88, 125
Travesties, 327, 330
Travolta, John, 309, 320
Treacher, Arthur, 142, 159
Treadwell, Sophie, 90
Tree, Dorothy, 91
Tree Grows in Brooklyn, A, 195
Trentini, Emma, 16, 17, 74, 235
Trial of Mary Dugan, The, 86
Trial of the Catonsville Nine, The, 301–4
Trials of Brother Jero, The, 287
Tribute, 346
Trilby, 9
Trio, 165, 167
Trip to Bountiful, The, 207
Trip to Chinatown, A, 8
Trojan Women, The, 145, 263
Trowbridge, Charles, 76
Truckline Café, 172
True, Jim, 424
True West, 357, 368
Truex, Ernest, 7, 17, 29, 54, 142
Truly Blessed, 398
Tryon, Tom, 202
Trzcinski, Edmund, 195
Tsar Fyodor Ivanovitch, 60
Tsk, Tsk, Tsk Paree. *See Pardon Our French*
Tubes, 404
Tucci, Maria, 148, 356, 405
Tucker, Sophie, 7, 11, 13, 15, 16, 18, 24, 27, 30, 36, 38, 45, 50, 54, 68, 69, 71, 76, 89, 90, 91, 112, 116, 121, 134, 135, 138, 139, 273
Tulane Drama Review, 277
Tully, Richard W., 6, 13, 166
Tuna Christmas, A, 417, 419
Tune, Tommy, 135, 212, 314, 334, 353, 358, 363, 367, 370, 396, 402, 406, 414, 416, 422
Tunnel of Love, The, 225
Tuotti, Joseph Dolan, 293
Turner, Kathleen, 395, 397, 420
Turner, Lana, 162
Turney, Catherine, 139
Twelfth Night, 148, 161, 164, 421
Twentieth Century, 109, 195
Twiggy, 212, 370
Twigs, 307–8
Twilight: Los Angeles, 1992, 415–16
Two by Two, 303
Two for the Seesaw, 227, 230
Two Gentlemen of Verona, 307–9
Two Mrs. Carrolls, The, 162
Two On the Aisle, 199
Two's a Crowd, 203
Two Trains Running, 403, 406–7
Tyler, George C., 5, 172
Tyler, Judy, 217, 228
Tynan, Brandon, 62
Tynan, Kenneth, 81, 235, 237, 298, 356
Typists, The, 260
Tyson, Cicely, 249, 293, 373, 378
Tyzack, Margaret, 397
Tzara, Tristan, 327
Tzi Ma, 360

UBTU, 273
Ubu the King, 202
Udell, Peter, 299
Uggams, Leslie, 285, 374, 381
Uhry, Alfred, 329–30, 386, 387, 411, 425, 427
Ullmann, Liv, 345, 347–48, 392
Ulric, Lenore, 8, 36, 41, 55, 70, 71, 73, 77, 108, 112, 120, 139, 302
Ulvaens, Bjorn, 390
Ulysses in Nighttown, 234, 320–21
Umbrella, The, 259
Umeki, Miyoshi, 235
Uncle Harry, 150
Uncle Tom's Cabin, 4, 70
Uncle Vanya, 92
Uncommon Women and Others, 340–41
Under the Bamboo Tree, 56
Unequal Match, The, 6
Under Milk Wood, 249
Union Square Theatre, 8
United Booking Office, 15, 18, 24, 28, 32, 36, 37, 38, 217
United Scenic Artists, 130–31
United States Amusement Company, 13
United Theatre Relief, 109
Unseen Hand, The, 300
Unsinkable Molly Brown, The, 246, 359
Up in Central Park, 168

Up in the Park, 167
Up the Ladder, 56
Urban, Joseph, 5, 25, 27, 28, 33, 46, 50, 112
Ure, Mary, 228, 242, 252, 324–25
Uris Theatre, 301, 312
U.S.O., 157, 165, 163, 168
Ustinov, Peter, 201, 203, 228
Ustinov, Tammy, 321

Vaccaro, Brenda, 274, 406
Vagabond King, The, 75
Vajda, Ernest, 70
Valderrama, Joy, 372–73
Valdez, Daniel, 348
Valdez, Luis, 348
Vale, Martin, 162
Valency, Maurice, 183, 209
Vallee, Rudy, 114, 121–22, 142, 151, 252, 253
Vamp, The, 217
Vampire Lesbians of Sodom, 379–80
Van, Bobby, 303–4
Van, Gus, 287
Van and Schenck, 8
van Cleve, Edith L., 142
Van Devere, Trish, 312, 335
Van Druten, John, 149, 163, 166, 197, 199, 228, 348
Van Dyke, Dick, 242
Van Fleet, Jo, 204, 207, 229, 254, 426
Van Patten, "Dickie", 157
Van Patten, Joyce, 240, 353, 369, 392, 406
Van Peeble, Melvin, 308
Van Stade, Frederica, 391
Van Vechten, Carl, 136
Vance, Nina, 177, 179
Vance, Vivian, 124, 148
Vanderbilt, Gloria, 212, 222
Vanities of 1923, 62. *See also Earl Carroll's Vanities*
Varesi, Gilda 50
Vargas, Alberto 44
Veiller, Bayard, 5, 17, 162, 86
Veiller, Marguerite Vale, 162
Velez, Lupe, 131
Venora, Diane, 382
Venture, Richard, 400
Venuata, Benay, 16, 156, 422
Venus Observed, 197, 200
Verdon, Gwen, 189, 204, 214, 215, 225, 227, 233, 235, 236, 247, 272, 274, 327–28, 333, 335, 388
Vereen, Ben, 175, 294, 308, 311–12, 377, 388
Verneuil, Louis, 192
Verrett, Shirley, 415
Very Good Eddie, 330
Via Galactica, 312
Vickery, James, 174
Victor/Victoria, 421–23, 425–27, 374, 376
Victoria Regina, 87, 119, 127, 129
Victory Belles, 164
Vidal, Gore, 74, 225, 242, 248
Viertel, Jack, 388
Viet Rock, 278
View from the Bridge, A, 216, 242, 269
Violet, 425
Virginia Theatre, 359–60, 380
Virginian, The, 12
Virgin Man, 79
Visit to a Small Planet, 225
Visit, The, 231, 233, 234
Vita and Virginia, 418
Vivian Beaumont Theatre, 380
Vogel, Paula, 425, 427
Voice of the Turtle, The, 161, 163, 385
Voight, Jon, 270, 303
Vollmer, Lula, 60, 63
Volstead Act, 52
von Bulow, Claus, 339, 359–60
von Furstenberg, Betsy, 193, 211–12, 216, 303
von Stroheim, Erich, 156
Vortex, The, 74
Voskevec, George, 13, 192–93, 241, 254, 268, 281, 300, 335, 360

Wager, Douglas, 404
Wagner, Michael, 254
Wagner, Robert, 373
Wagner, Robin, 397
Wait Until Dark, 274
Waite, Ralph, 273
Waiting for Godot, 218, 225, 392
Waiting for Lefty, 117, 118, 125, 135
Wajda, Andrzei, 313
Walburn, Raymond, 255
Waldman, Robert, 329–30
Waldron, Charles, 5, 172
Wales Theatrical Padlock Bill, 81
Walk in the Woods, A, 387
Walken, Christopher, 157, 287, 368, 376
Walker, Jimmy, 74, 91
Walker, Joseph A., 315, 317
Walker, June, 12, 54, 63, 80, 206, 258, 273
Walker, Nancy, 15, 56, 147, 148, 167, 177, 180, 181–82, 188, 193, 236, 273, 314, 384–85, 403, 405–6
Walker, Zena, 289
Wall Street Girl, The, 17
Wallace, Edna, 8
Wallace, George, 225
Wallace, Marie, 68
Wallace, Regina, 65
Wallace, William, 135
Wallach, Eli, 28, 164, 171, 174, 179, 181, 193–94, 204, 222, 246, 248, 260, 268, 270, 280, 289, 361
Wallack's Theatre, 6
Waller, Fats, 339, 343
Wallis, Hal, 163, 212
Walston, Ray, 37, 204, 211, 213–14, 215
Walter Kerr Theatre, 397, 400
Walter, Eugene, 14, 15, 45, 51, 227
Walter, Jessica, 392
Walters, Barbara, 428
Walton, Tony, 116, 235, 288, 407
Waltz of the Torreadors, The, 221, 225
Wanger, Walter, 47
Wann, Jim, 362
Waram, Percy, 6, 135, 175–76, 180, 216, 253
Ward, Aida, 88
Ward, Douglas Turner, 236, 273, 281, 294, 315, 317, 320, 325, 335, 361
Warden, Jack, 216
Warfield, David, 5, 10, 11, 12, 17, 27, 54, 57, 60, 89, 134, 137, 198
Warner, H.B., 60
Warner, Sam, 74
Warner Brothers Theatre. *See* Mark Hellinger Theatre
War of the Worlds, The, 133, 135, 392
Warren, Harry, 355
Warren, Jennifer, 286, 326
Warren, Lesley Ann, 262
Warrens of Virginia, The, 14
Warrick, Ruth, 314
Washington Square, 419
Washington Square Players, 26, 33, 34, 37, 38
Washington, Buck, 90
Washington, Denzel, 360–61
Washington, Ford. *See* Buck and Bubbles
Washington, Lamont, 290
Washington, Vernon, 331
Wasserstein, Wendy, 192, 340–41, 372, 391–92, 394, 409–10, 428
Watch on the Rhine, 141, 145, 148
Water Engine, The, 341
Waters, Ethel, 11, 76, 86, 90, 112, 133, 135, 136, 142, 148, 188–89, 340
Waterston, Sam, 298, 304, 356, 381–82
Watch Your Step, 23, 25
Watkins, Maurice, 328
Watkins, Maurine, 82
Watson, Janet, 376
Watson, Lucile, 12, 15, 24, 60, 126, 140, 145
Watson, Moray, 262
Watson, Susan, 242
Watt, Douglas, 230
Watter, George M., 86
Watts, Richard, Jr., 88, 131, 132, 138, 157, 174, 189, 207, 212, 219, 225, 231, 275, 320
Wayne, David, 19, 182, 205, 206, 207, 231, 269, 419
We Bombed in New Haven, 292
Weaver, Fritz, 75, 216, 297, 299
Weaver, Sigourney, 376

Webb, Alan, 288
Webb, Clifton, 7, 30, 75, 92, 112, 148, 149, 278
Weber, Anthony, 301
Weber, Frederika, 299
Weber, Joe, 3, 5, 9, 25, 27, 28, 74, 75, 148, 149
Weber, Laura, 63
Weber and Fields's Music Hall, 9, 17, 158
Webber, Robert, 247
Webster, Lucille, 76
Webster, Margaret, 12, 124, 125, 132, 145, 148–49, 174, 189, 198, 216, 312
Wedgeworth, Anne, 341
Weede, Robert, 219, 253
Weidman, Charles, 108
Weidman, Jerome, 239, 246
Weidman, John, 330–31
Weill, Gus, 294
Weill, Kurt, 11, 75, 91, 110, 119, 120, 124, 134, 144, 162, 163, 174, 175–76, 187–90, 209, 217, 254
Weintraub, Jerry, 376
Weir, Milton, 208
Weisenfreund, Muni, 81
Weiss, George, 218
Weiss, Peter, 271, 274, 287
Weissler, Barry, 409–10
Weissler, Fran, 409
Welch, Elizabeth, 63, 88
Welch, Kenneth, 373
Welch, Raquel 350–51
Weller, Michael, 309, 318, 350
Weller, Peter, 342
Welles, H.G., 135
Welles, Orson, 24, 111, 113, 115, 117, 119, 125, 130, 131, 132, 133, 135, 143, 145, 172, 173, 174, 217, 223, 312, 324, 379–80
Welsh, Kenneth, 382, 388
Werfel, Franz, 161
Wertenbaker, Timberlake, 399
Wesker, Arnold, 278, 340
Wesselhoeft, Eleanor, 77
Wesson, Gene, 228, 229
West, Jennifer, 264
West, Judi, 308
West, Mae, 8, 17, 70, 77, 79, 82, 83, 88, 90, 165, 184, 312, 355–56
Westphal, Frank 36, 50
West Side Story, 215, 227, 228, 230, 371, 391, 414
West Side Waltz, 361–62
Westley, Helen, 5, 41, 42, 51, 58, 60, 156
Westman, Nydia, 231
Weston, Jack, 192, 325, 334
What a Life, 132
What Makes Sammy Run?, 233, 264, 270
What Price Glory, 67, 68
What the Butler Saw, 300
Wheeler, Bert, 24, 28, 63, 80, 82, 287
Wheeler, Betty, 24, 28, 63, 80
Whelan, Arleen, 158
When Ladies Meet, 108
When the Chickens Come Home to Roost, 360
When We Dead Awaken, 259
When You Comin' Back, Red Ryder? 319
Where's Charley? 181–82
Whipper, Leigh, 199–200
Whirl of Society, The, 17
Whirl of the World, The, 19
Whistle Down the Wind, 425, 427–28
White, Diz, 313
White, Frances, 33, 51
White, George, 7, 16, 28, 36, 41, 43, 44, 54, 62, 67, 68, 74, 79, 108, 122, 173, 174, 292
White, Lillias, 428
White, Peter, 289
White, Ruth, 252, 286
White, Sammy, 77
White, Stanford, 13
White Cargo, 63
Whitehead, Paxton, 346, 420
Whitehead, Robert, 28, 198, 200, 223, 260, 269, 288, 312–13, 333–34, 363, 372–73, 375, 376, 423
Whitehouse, Frances, 18
White Lies, 280
Whitemen, Paul, 57
Whiteoaks, 134
White Pelican, 345
White Rats, the, 11, 29, 31, 32, 33, 36, 38, 45, 47
White Steed, The, 133, 135
Whitfield, Alice, 288
Whiting, Jack, 11, 91, 246
Whiting, John, 281
Whitmore, Hugh, 389
Whitmore, Nina 45
Whitmore, James, 174, 326
Whitney, Jock, 119, 125
Whittaker, James 44
Whitty, May, 23, 145
Whole Town's Talking, The, 62
Whoopee, 63
Whoopi Goldberg, 376
Whorf, Richard, 13, 278
Who's Afraid of Virginia Woolf?, 257, 258, 259, 260, 261, 262, 270, 281, 303, 331, 353, 393
Whose Life Is It Anyway? 345, 347–48
Who's Tommy, The, 412
Why Marry?, 35, 38, 40
Widmark, Richard, 158, 227
Wiesenfreund, Muni, 90
Wiest, Diane, 362
Wilbur, Richard, 317
Wildcat, 233, 247, 249
Wilde, Cornel, 131
Wilde, Oscar, 4, 9, 11, 174, 410, 424
Wilder, Billy, 195, 414
Wilder, Gene, 254, 260
Wilder, Jo, 234
Wilder, Thornton, 9, 109, 110, 117, 129, 131, 134, 135, 155, 157, 159, 203, 217, 277, 327–28, 395
Wildflower, 60
Wildhorn, Frank, 422, 428
Wilding, Michael, 265
Wilkinson, Colm, 385, 388
Wilkinson, Kate, 388
Wilkof, Lee, 368
Will Rogers Follies, The, 399, 402, 404, 409–10
Willard, Fred, 294
Willard, Jess 28
Willard, John, 55–56
William Morris agency, 32, 86
William, Warren, 92
Williams, Bert, 5, 12, 15–16, 17, 24, 28, 32, 36, 44, 55, 56
Williams, Billy Dee, 246, 300
Williams, Emlyn, 13, 141, 142, 264
Williams, Herschel, 156
Williams, Hope, 91
Williams, Jaston, 360, 368, 419
Williams, Jesse Lynch, 5, 35, 38, 40
Williams, Lia, 426
Williams, Michael, 302
Williams, Rhys, 158, 164
Williams, Robert B., 56
Williams, Robin, 292, 392
Williams, Samm-Art, 351
Williams, Sammy, 328–29
Williams, Sybil, 183
Williams, Tennessee, 16, 116, 133, 134, 136, 137, 140, 141, 144, 145, 161, 162–63, 165, 167, 168, 169, 170, 177, 178, *179*, 180, 181–82, 184, 191, 193–94, 200, 201, 204, 211, 214, 216, 225, 228, 236, 240, 245, 246, 251, 254, 257, 258, 259, 263, 289, 292, 293, 298, 309, 312–13, 324, 328–29, 347, 367–68, 374, 380, 395, 397, 406, 422
Williams, Treat, 320, 361
Williams, Vanessa, 418
Williamson, Malcolm, 406
Williamson, Nicol, 134, 273, 293, 295, 298, 308, 318, 327, 331, 399, 401, 404
Willingham, Calder, 205
Willis, Bruce, 370
Willis, Sally, 313
Willow and I, The, 158
Willson, Meredith, 133, 227, 230, 234, 235, 246
Will Success Spoil Rock Hunter?, 215, 216
Wilner, Lori, 377
Wilson, Adelaide 47
Wilson, August, 166, 271, 345, 375–77, 383, 386, 387, 390, 395, 398, 400, 403, 406–7, 421, 423–24, 425, 427
Wilson, Earl, 167, 262, 299, 320, 331, 334
Wilson, Edmund, 195
Wilson, Elizabeth, 294, 318, 331, 352–53, 370
Wilson, Francis, 4, 47, 121
Wilson, Frank, 86
Wilson, Harry L., 14
Wilson, Imogene, 65, 68
Wilson, Lanford, 124, 258, 272, 305, 311, 314, 342–43, 348, 349, 352, 356, 374, 383, 388

Wilson, Marie, 156
Wilson, Patricia, 241
Wilson, Sandy, 212
Wiltse, David, 378
Winchell, Walter, 9, 15, 38, 50, 67, 68, 69, 81, 87, 90, 114, 117, 121, 134, 155, 167, 307–9
Winchester, Barbara, 240
Windham, Donald, 169, 170
Windsor Theatre, 158
Wine, Women and Song, 156
Winer, Laurie, 396
Winer, Linda, 409, 427
Winged Victory, 163
Winger, Debra, 400–401
Wingfield, Amanda, 167
Wingless Victory, The, 125
Wings, 345, 347, 360
Wings Over Europe, 170
Winninger, Charles, 7, 17, 45, 75, 87, 89, 293
Winslow Boy, The, 177, 179
Winter Garden Theatre, 16, 159, 164
Winter, Edward, 293
Winter, William, 3, 36, 135
Winters, Lawrence, 172
Winters, Marian, 342
Winters, Shelley, 155, 157, 161, 217, 223, 254, 342
Winterset, 120, 122
Winter's Tale, The, 393–94
Winwood, Estelle, 6, 37, 38, 166, 183, 376
Wisdom Tooth, The, 77
Wise, Jim, 293
Wiseman, Joseph, 184, 200, 217, 269, 294, 382, 418–19
Wishengrad, Morton, 229
Wish You Were Here, 126, 201–2
Wisteria Trees, 190
Witchel, Alex, 400
Witching Hour, The, 14
With a Song in My Heart, 157
Withee, Mabel, 52
Witherspoon, Cora, 81
Within the Gates, 115, 116
Within the Law, 17
Without Love, 150–51, 155, 158
Witness, 293
Witness for the Prosecution, 211–13
Wiz, The, 323, 325
Wizard of Oz, The, 11
Wodehouse, Pelham Grenville "P.G.", 6, 34, 36, 37, 38, 42, 81, 83, 88, 117, 141, 142, 312, 325
Woldin, Judd, 317–18
Wolfe, George C., 407, 412, 422
Wolfe, Thomas, 229
Wolfit, Donald, 11
Wolheim, Louis, 56, 68
Wolsk, Eugene, 345
Woman of the Year, 355, 358, 369
Women, The, 125, 131, 311
Wonderful Town, 143, 201, 204
Wong, B.D., 390
Wood, Audrey, 12, 132, 167, 178, 298, 380
Wood, Birnam, 387
Wood, John, 286, 325, 327, 330, 339, 342
Wood, Natalie, 237
Wood, Peggy, 8, 15, 25, 36, 148, 167, 241, 340
Woodard, Alfre, 393–94
Woodard, Charlaine, 343
Woodruff, Robert, 357
Woods, A.H., 55, 88, 193
Woods, Albert Herman, 5
Woods, George, 260
Woods, James, 309
Woods, Richard, 342
Woods, The, 342
Woodward, Joanne, 201, 203–4, 319
Woollcott, Alexander, 7, 23, 25, 26, 29, 46, 50, 55, 58, 68, 74, 87, 109, 125, 132, 138, 157
Woollcott, William, 135
Woolley, Monty, 7, 86, 138, 260
Woolsey, Robert, 28, 82
World, 68, 71, 87
World According to Me, The, 383
World of Sholem Aleichem, 204
World of Suzie Wong, The, 234
World We Live In, The, 59
Worth, Irene, 32, 161, 162, 172, 189, 228, 242, 267, 269, 270, 327, 335, 352, 401
Wouk, Herman, 205
Wright, Amy, 356, 368, 422
Wright, Haidee, 87
Wright, Julie, 423
Wright, Nicholas, 422
Wright, Richard, 145
Wright, Robert, 166, 205, 208, 396
Wright, Teresa, 40, 230, 289, 328, 352–53
Wycherly, Margaret, 6, 33, 59, 60, 114, 222
Wyler, Gretchen, 182, 213, 222, 335
Wyngate, Valerie, 83
Wynn, Ed, 7, 16, 18, 24, 28, 32, 41, 46, 47, 55, 107, 109, 133, 136, 278
Wyse, John, 234

Yale School of Drama, 168, 280
Yankee Circus, A, 12
Years Ago, 173, 175
Yentl, 330
Yerma, 200
Yes, My Darling Daughter, 126
Yeston, Maury, 359, 396, 425, 428
Yiddish Art Theatre, 41, 148
Yip, Yip, Yaphank!, 39, 40, 142
Yohn, Erica, 305
Yorba, Rosemary, 360
Yordan, Philip, 166
York, Michael, 351, 405
York, Rachel, 411–12
Yoshe Kalb, 108
You and I, 58, 60
You Can't Take It With You, 123, 125, 275, 367, 370, 372
You'd be Surprised, 46
You Know I Can't Hear You When the Water's Running, 280, 285
Youmans, Vincent, 10, 60, 63, 64, 74, 83, 110, 169, 171, 172
Young, Mary, 68
Young, Rida Johnson, 5, 16, 36, 76
Young, Roland, 7, 33, 51, 65, 113, 139, 206
Young, Stark, 6, 74, 132, 163, 259
Young, William, 10
Young Man from Atlanta, The, 417, 427
You Never Can Tell, 177
You Never Know, 131
Your Arms Too Short to Box with God, 335
You're A Good Man, Charlie Brown, 280
Your Own Thing, 285, 287–88
You Touched Me, 169, 170
Yr. Obedient Husband, 130–31
Yulin, Harris, 356
Yurka, Blanche, 7, 58, 59, 324

Zadora, Pia, 293
Zaks, Jerry, 175, 346, 400–1, 407, 414–15, 419
Zefferelli, Franco, 270
Zell, Marguerite 36
Zerbe, Anthony, 358
Ziegfeld, Florenz "Flo", 5, 9, 13, 14, 15–16, 17, 19, 25, 31, 32, 33, 37, 38, 40, 43, 44, 45, 47, 49, 50, 51, 52, 56, 57, 58, 60, 62, 63, 68, 80, 81, 82, 87, 88, 90, 91, 107, 108, 110, 140, 323–24, 417
Ziegfeld Follies, The, 3, 12, 16, 17, 18, 23, 27, 31, 35, 36, 38, 39–40, 45, 47, 50, 54, 57, 58, 62, 63, 65, 68, 74, 82, 86, 88, 114, 117, 121, 122, 155, 159, 174, 221, 224, 228, 410, 415, 428
Ziegfeld Theatre, 82, 166, 278
Ziemba, Karen, 428
Zimbalist, Efrem, Jr. 174
Zindel, Paul, 297, 299, 301, 304
Zippel, David, 395, 397
Zoo Story, 242, 249
Zoot Suit, 348
Zora Neal Thurston, 360
Zorba, 293, 372
Zorich, Louis, 259
Zorina, Vera, 132, 134–35, 140, 172
Zulu and the Zayda, The, 271, 272, 273